S0-BRS-254

PROPERTY OF
DPL
DETROIT PUBLIC LIBRARY

Encyclopedia *of* African~American Culture *and* History

Editorial Board

second edition

THE BLACK EXPERIENCE IN THE AMERICAS

ENCYCLOPEDIA *of* AFRICAN~AMERICAN CULTURE *and* HISTORY

published in association with

THE SCHOMBURG CENTER FOR RESEARCH IN BLACK CULTURE

COLIN A. PALMER
Editor in Chief

VOLUME 1 *A-B*

MACMILLAN REFERENCE USA
An imprint of Thomson Gale, a part of The Thomson Corporation

Detroit • New York • San Francisco • San Diego • New Haven, Conn. • Waterville, Maine • London • Munich

Encyclopedia of African-American Culture and History, Second Edition

Colin A. Palmer, Editor in Chief

For more information, contact
Macmillan Reference USA
An imprint of Thomson Gale
27500 Drake Rd.
Farmington, Hills, MI 48331-3535
Or you can visit our Internet site at
http://www.gale.com

LIBRARY OF CONGRESS CATALOGING-IN-PUBLICATION DATA

Encyclopedia of African-American culture and history : the Black experience in the Americas / Colin A. Palmer, editor in chief.— 2nd ed.
p. cm.
Includes bibliographical references and index.
ISBN 0-02-865816-7 (set hardcover : alk. paper) —
ISBN 0-02-865817-5 (v. 1) — ISBN 0-02-865818-3 (v. 2) —
ISBN 0-02-865819-1 (v. 3) — ISBN 0-02-865820-5 (v. 4) —
ISBN 0-02-865821-3 (v. 5) — ISBN 0-02-865822-1 (v. 6)
1. African Americans—Encyclopedias. 2. African Americans—History—Encyclopedias. 3. Blacks—America—Encyclopedias. 4. Blacks—America—History—Encyclopedias. I. Palmer, Colin A., 1942-

E185.E54 2005
973'.0496073'003—dc22 2005013029

This title is also available as an e-book.
ISBN 0-02-866071-4

Contact your Thomson Gale representative for ordering information.

Printed in the United States of America
10 9 8 7 6 5 4 3 2 1

Editorial *and* Production Staff

Contents

Preface to the First Edition

The history of African Americans, beginning in 1619 with the arrival of the first slaves from Africa, is to a great extent the history of the United States. Yet, until the second half of the twentieth century too few historians made African-American culture and history their area of expertise. Because of this long neglect of a vital part of the nation's history, important knowledge about almost 15 percent of America's current population has gone unexamined or remained accessible only to a small group of scholars.

In 1989 the Center for American Culture Studies at Columbia University approached Macmillan Publishing Company with the proposal to remedy this lack of accurate, easily available information by preparing an encyclopedia that would present the lives and significance of African Americans in the broadest way possible. The result is this 1.8-million-word set covering all aspects of the African-American experience.

The Editorial Board began its work by establishing several criteria for inclusion of biographical entries in the Encyclopedia and the amount of space given to each. Perhaps the most significant was the decision that only African Americans should warrant biographies. Therefore, one will not find entries on such figures as Franklin Delano Roosevelt, Carl Van Vechten, Joel Spingarn, Harriet Beecher Stowe, or even Abraham Lincoln, even though each of these played an imporant role in the lives of black Americans. It was the Board's opinion that it was far more important to reserve space for information about a wide range of African Americans and to preserve a record of achievement not covered elsewhere.

Also not to be found here are entries on Africans, for example, Nelson Mandela and Wole Soyinka, even though they have exerted a great influence in North America. We did include several articles on Africa, specifically an entry on the regions from which most slaves were taken and a general anthropological overview of the continent ["Africa: An Introduction" in the front matter of this second edition]. Also included are articles on influential West Indians and overview entries on Canada and Mexico. Among the many editorial issues requiring attention was that which led to the decision to use the terms "African American" and "black" interchangeably; "Negro" and "colored" are used only when the historical context demands their use.

About two-thirds of the 2,200 entries are biographies that range from the beginning of the seventeenth to the end of the twentieth century, from jazz greats such as Louis Armstrong to William Grant Still, composer of the opera *Troubled Island*; from the Nobel Prize–winning author Toni Morrison to Jupiter Hammon, an eighteenth-century slave and poet; from Michael Jordan to the baseball player Monte Irvin; from W. E. B. Du Bois and Martin Luther King Jr. to Congressman Ron Dellums; and from George Washington Carver to Norbert Rillieux, inventor of the vacuum-chamber evaporation process used to produce sugar.

The remaining entries deal not with people but with events, historical eras, legal cases, areas of cultural achievement (music, architecture, the visual arts), professions, sports, and places. The Encyclopedia also includes entries for all fifty states as well as separate articles for cities with a special significance for black Americans, past or present.

One of the features that will make this Encyclopedia stand out from other reference works is the inclusion of a number of large essays by well-known scholars that examine the importance and legacy of such events as the Civil War and the various civil rights movements or discuss the role of religion in the lives of African Americans. Beyond information, these entries provide an intellectual interpretation and synthesis that will help readers to see historical events and creative accomplishments in a larger perspective. Examples are the entry on "Literature" by Arnold Rampersad and John S. Wright's article on "Intellectual Life."

We have taken the word "culture" to mean all expressions by which people define themselves and not just Art with a capital *a*. Thus the reader will find entries on "Black English Vernacular," on "Comic Strips," and on "Hair and Beauty Culture." Indeed, the reader is encouraged to review the entire list of article titles that begins on page xi [now on page xxxvii] to form an idea of the vast scope of this Encyclopedia.

Another important feature and exciting part of the Encyclopedia is the large number of illustrations—more than one thousand—that enrich these volumes. Much time and effort was spent in obtaining historical photographs from state historical societies, pictures of representative art works, and images from private photograph collections. The Photographs and Prints Division of the Schomburg Center for Research in Black Culture was the single largest source for historical images. The Moorland-Spingarn Research Center at Howard University provided many others. From the collections of the Library of Congress and the National Archives we obtained illustrations for the Civil War and civil rights eras, while commercial repositories provided up-to-date photos of athletes, politicians, and entertainers. These illustrations have never before been brought together in one publication.

The extensive Appendix in Volume 5 [now in Volume 6] provides statistical information for many subjects. Among others are tables of African-American population by state and over time, lists of awards, economic data, degrees earned in education, and sports championships. This information provides rich supplemental background for many entries in the body of the Encyclopedia.

The entries have been arranged alphabetically. In addition, a system of cross-references makes it easy to find one's way through the Encyclopedia. For example, in the entry titled "Elaine, Arkansas, Race Riot of 1919," references to the "Red Summer," "World War I," and the "National Association for the Advancement of Colored People" are set in small capital letters, indicating that there are separate entries for these terms. By reading these additional articles, one becomes aware of the political climate during which the riot took place.

The *Encyclopedia of African-American Culture and History* does not claim to be a complete record of the history of African Americans. It will take many more years of intensive scholarship to unearth all the riches in forgotten or neglected archives. We will consider ourselves successful in our work if the material presented here inspires future students of history to complete the task.

A work of this magnitude calls for appropriate words of thanks to those who supported its development over several years. We offer collective thanks to the many who made this work possible. At the same time, we would like to single out one person and dedicate this work to the historian John Hope Franklin, who turned eighty as we neared completion of the Encyclopedia. His has been a remarkable life, as he has been and remains a remarkable human being. It is impossible to count the number of people who have been touched and inspired by him, and we consider ourselves fortunate to be among them. This work is dedicated to John Hope Franklin because his scholarship provided so much of what we know about African-American history and because his teaching—at North Carolina Central University, Howard University, Brooklyn College, the University of Chicago, Duke University, or as an expert witness before the U.S. Supreme Court—made us understand the importance of doing what we do with our lives.

JACK SALZMAN (1996)
DAVID LIONEL SMITH (1996)
CORNEL WEST (1996)

Preface to the Second Edition

This second edition of the *Encyclopedia of African-American Culture and History* (EAACH-2) is a revision of the 1996 Encyclopedia and its 2001 supplement. The nearly 1,300 alphabetically-arranged articles in this edition, whether new, revised, updated, or reprinted from the earlier publications, are signed by experts in the field and are accompanied by a selected bibliography. In addition to essays, EAACH-2 includes an appendix of statistical data and primary source documents, a thematic outline of contents, and a comprehensive index. Cross-references are provided at the ends of articles to inform readers of related topics. Blind entries direct readers from alternate names of topics to the name used in this set. The text is embellished with nearly 450 photographs and illustrations as well as occasional sidebars that highlight notable tangents.

The second edition's editorial board evaluated the 2,500 articles from the first edition and supplement and decided which to keep, which to update, and which not to include in the new edition. Some first edition essays and many biographies were excluded from EAACH-2 to make room for more thematic essays and to enable coverage of the African-American experience beyond the United States and throughout the western hemisphere. The encyclopedia still offers a strong list of commonly-studied U.S. personages—including Muhammad Ali, Toni Morrison, and Colin Powell—and is complemented by pieces on important Caribbean and Latin American figures such as Machado de Assis, Pelé, Portia Simpson-Miller, and Eric Williams.

ARTICLES REPRINTED FROM THE FIRST EDITION AND SUPPLEMENT. Approximately one-third of the 1.6 million words in the new edition were reprinted with no changes or with minor changes only. Articles on individuals such as Richard Allen, W. E. B. Du Bois, Booker T. Washington, and Ida B. Wells-Barnett and topics such as the Black Arts Movement, Emancipation in the United States, and the Harlem Renaissance appear essentially unchanged. The editorial staff attempted to contact each author of the 800 carry-over articles, whether they were selected to be updated or reprinted "as is." Authors were invited to update or revise their material as they saw fit, including refreshing their bibliographies with new citations. As a result of these efforts, approximately 400 reprinted articles include such updates. Articles reprinted from the first edition or the supplement with few or no changes have *1996* or *2001* following the original author's byline. If the bibliography was updated for this edition, *Updated bibliography* appears below the byline.

ARTICLES UPDATED FOR THE SECOND EDITION. Approximately one-third of EAACH-2's word count is revised or otherwise updated. Articles on such topics as art, education, literature, music, politics, and religion were expanded to provide coverage of the western hemisphere and update U.S. coverage. Articles such as Reparations, Affirmative Action, and Muslims in the Americas now reflect current affairs and more recent scholarship. Articles revised by the original author are noted with *Updated by author 2005* in the byline. When the original authors could not be located or were unable to update their material, the publishers updated as necessary and *Updated by publisher 2005* appears in the byline. If a different writer provided an update to an article from the first edition, the article will have two bylines, the original author's name followed by "(1996)" and the second edition author's name followed by "(2005)."

NEW ARTICLES IN THE SECOND EDITION. The editorial board identified and selected almost 400 new topics for this edition. These new articles represent one-third of the 1.6 million words in EAACH-2, which now includes longer thematic articles, such as African Diaspora, Anti-colonial Movements, Economic Condition, and Military Experience. New articles for the second edition have *2005* as part of their bylines. This information is included in the List of Articles and the Directory of Contributors, both included in the front matter of this first volume. Wherever possible, the publishers have provided current affiliation information for authors of first edition articles reprinted in this edition.

Acknowledgments

We would like to thank Colin Palmer and the editorial board for their tireless dedication to recruiting talented and knowledgeable scholars to write and update articles. Not including the hundreds of contributors who worked only on the first edition and its supplement, almost 500 authors worked to implement the editorial board's revision of an already stellar reference source, and we thank them for their scholarship and cooperation.

As it did for the first edition, the Schomburg Center for Research in Black Culture again provided assistance and enriched the product by providing access to its extensive collection of texts and images. Many thanks are due to Howard Dodson, director of the Schomburg Center, Mary Yearwood, curator of the Photographs and Prints division, and to the staff who generously assisted in many ways.

Foreword

This second edition of the *Encyclopedia of African-American Culture and History* (EAACH) is being published in association with the Schomburg Center for Research in Black Culture of the New York Public Library. A product of the most recent scholarship on the African American and African Diasporan Experience, EAACH is a comprehensive compendium of knowledge on the historical and cultural development of people of African descent in the Americas at the beginning of the twenty-first century. It differs from the first edition in that it includes a broad array of subjects on the black experience in Latin America and the Caribbean as well as the United States and Canada. Broader treatment of institutions, organizations, and events have been added to counterbalance the heavily biographical focus of the first edition.

A century ago an encyclopedia such as this was unthinkable, much less imaginable. The reigning unwisdom in the United States at the time was that people of African descent had no history or culture. A foundation on which the myths of black racial inferiority and white supremacy were based, this notion that black people were history- and culture-less beings provided the ideological justification for the European colonization of Africa and the establishment and enforcement of systems of racial segregation in the United States during the nineteenth century. Systems of colonization and segregation based on race survived in Africa and the southern United States, respectively, well into the twentieth century. This predominant view transcended geographical, class, regional and even racial boundaries. Newspapers, journals, and magazines promoted it, churches and religious bodies subscribed to it, legal systems were invented to enforce it, and colleges and universities taught it and produced the "scholarship" to affirm its truth. It was not a regional, southern belief. It was national (and indeed international). European colonial powers who were flexing their triumphal colonizing muscles like their Euro-American counterparts in the United States were convinced of the truth of their mythology. Their dominance of African people (and people of color in general) proved, for them at least, that their white supremacist mythology was true.

Fledgling efforts to rescue and reconstruct the history and cultural heritage of people of African descent had been made throughout the nineteenth century. Black newspapers founded to defend "the race" from these racist assaults, challenged the reigning unwisdom throughout the century. Black churches and black ministers challenged the Christian myth that attributed the presumed inferiority of black folk to the Biblical curse on Ham. Nineteenth century black historians including William Wells Brown and

George Washington Williams, wrote histories of black folk that disproved the myth of black racial inferiority; all to little or no avail. The overwhelming preponderance of the testimony if not evidenced through the end of the nineteenth century came down on the side of the reigning unwisdom. And so it reigned.

By the first decades of the twentieth century, vindicationist collectors and scholars had started gathering evidence and creating new works of scholarship whose purpose was to destroy the myth of black racial inferiority and document the place of people of African descent in the making of human history, civilization and culture.

A number of bibliophiles and collectors of the late nineteenth and early twentieth centuries assumed leadership roles in amassing collections of documents, images, artworks, books, and memorabilia to support the new research and scholarship. Daniel Alexander Payne Murray started his career at the Library of Congress in 1871 and over a period of fifty-two years devoted most of his time to collecting Afro-Americana. His planned, *"Murray's Historical and Biographical Encyclopedia of the Colored Race throughout the World,"* a six-volume compendium never came to fruition, but the Africana collections he assembled at the Library of Congress were among the strongest in the United States at the turn of the twentieth century. Other distinguished collectors of this period included Jesse Moorland whose collection became one of the foundations on which Howard University's Moorland-Spingarn Collection was built, and Henry Proctor Slaughter whose collection was eventually purchased by Atlanta University, Wendell Dabney, William Carl Bolivar, and Robert Mara Adger (Sinnette, 76–87).

Foremost among these vindicationist collectors, however, was Arturo Alfonso Schomburg, a Puerto Rican of African descent who began his collecting adventures toward the end of the nineteenth century and continued until his death in 1938. By 1926 he had amassed a collection of over 10,000 items—all containing evidence of the place and role of people of African descent worldwide in the making of human history, culture, and civilization. The foundation on which today's Schomburg Center is based, the 10,000-item collection has grown to more than 10 million sources of evidence on the historical and cultural legacies of African peoples around the globe. It is arguably the most comprehensive research library in the world devoted exclusively to documenting the global black experience. It was the emergence of collections such as these that inspired and supported the work of researchers and scholars who sought to rescue and reconstruct the true history of black people.

In the meantime, African American scholars took the lead in creating the new twentieth century scholarship on the African American and African experience. W.E.B. Du Bois and Carter G. Woodson, both Ph.D. graduates of Harvard University's History Department were among the foremost creators and exponents of this new scholarship during the first half of the twentieth century. Du Bois, working from his base at Atlanta University, produced both historical and sociological studies of Africans and African Americans. His *Souls of Black Folk* remains a classic work in African American Studies. Woodson, frequently called the father of black history (in the United States), founded the Association for the Study of Negro Life and History, the *Journal of Negro History*, the *Bulletin of Negro History,* and Associated Publishers. Beginning in 1916, and continuing until his death in 1950, Woodson used these tools to organize and conduct research on the black experience, publish research findings, disseminate the new knowledge to public audiences and promote the study of the black experience.

It should not be surprising that these same two twentieth century scholars of the African American experience, W. E. B. Du Bois and Carter G. Woodson, would follow Daniel Murray's lead and attempt to publish encyclopedias of the black experience. Each was possessed of encyclopedic knowledge of the subject and each was committed to making the available knowledge accessible to the public. Each was committed to, on the basis of authoritative information and scholarship, setting the record straight and challenging the "reigning wisdom" with unimpeachable facts and truths. Du Bois first proposed to publish an encyclopedia in 1909. Woodson proposed such a work in 1921. Du Bois's efforts eventually produced a preparatory volume. An enlarged 216-page volume appeared under the auspices of the Phelps Stokes Fund in 1945. Principally a list of subjects to be included in such a work with the sources to support each entry, Du Bois's preparatory volume demonstrated the scope of such a project and the potential such a compendium had for enhancing public knowledge and appreciation of the African American historical and cultural experience. Funding for such an effort was not forthcoming, however.

The Woodson proposal never materialized in any form during his lifetime. Like Du Bois, Woodson was unable to raise the funding from traditional foundations and other philanthropic sources to give material form to his ideas. The Association for the Study of Negro Life and History, which Woodson had founded in 1915 published a multi-volume *International Library of Negro Life and History* in 1967, which had largely been inspired by Woodson's encyclopedia idea. Organized thematically, the volumes treated specific subjects in African American history and culture but did not conform to the alphabetical ordering by entry title that has become the norm for encyclopedias.

Meanwhile, Du Bois's later efforts to revise his *Encyclopedia Africana* idea under the sponsorship of President Kwame Nkrumah and the independent republic of Ghana was not completed prior to his death in 1963. While scholars in Ghana continue to work on it, it is more an aspiration rather than a reality. Henry Louis Gates and Anthony Appiah's one-volume *Encyclopedia Africana*, which was published in 1999, three years after the publication of the first edition of the *Encyclopedia of African-American Culture and History*, was inspired by the Du Bois project.

At the beginning of the twentieth century, an encyclopedia such as this was, indeed, unimaginable and unthinkable. At the beginning of the twenty-first century, the state of knowledge and scholarship on the African American and African Diasporan experience is such that it insists that the *Encyclopedia of African-American Culture and History* be published. Over the last century and especially the last four decades, interest in things African American has increased exponentially. So has the quantity and quality of books, articles, essays, artworks, and audiovisual materials on the black experience. The emergence of African American Studies programs and other formal degree-granting programs that encouraged research and scholarship on the black experiences contributed significantly to the proliferation of these new works. Publishing houses and scholarly journals in traditional disciplines have also found African American subject matter economically and intellectually profitable enterprises. As a result, the quantity and quality of knowledge on the black experience requires an encyclopedia format to simply introduce the public to the vast array of information currently available on this, diverse and increasingly complex field of human endeavor and intellectual interest. The pace at which new knowledge is being produced in this field is part of the reason why the *Encyclopedia of African-American Culture and History* demands a second edition a mere ten years since it was first published. Changes in the way the field of African American Studies has evolved also demand such updating.

As new intellectual paradigms have raised questions about the experience, so has the nature of the scholarship changed. Biographical compendiums of great men and women are being complemented or replaced by broader social history inquiries. The lives and struggles of ordinary people are being given equal weight with those of leaders and heroes. Studies exploring the economic, intellectual and cultural history of black people are complementing the traditional political histories. The relationships between the African American experience in the United States and the African, Caribbean and Latin American experiences of people of African descent are also being explored in new and exciting ways. The roles of blacks in major events in mainstream American history are being complemented by approaches to African American history that are defined by the major events and movements in African American and African Diasporan history. Scholars writing entries for this edition of the *Encyclopedia of African-American Culture and History* reflect these new trends in African American history writing.

Approaches to the teaching of African American culture have also been changing. Traditional approaches focused largely on arts and entertainment and emphasized the biographies of great black artists. The area of African American cultural studies has expanded to include the products of day-to-day living and human interaction and creativity. Family and community life, religious practices, the diverse genres of African-based musics, dances, literatures and visual arts throughout the Americas are all part of the African American cultural pallet and are explored in this encyclopedia. In addition, totally new entries reflecting these emerging trends in scholarship are also included.

This second edition of the *Encyclopedia of African-American Culture and History* is a comprehensive survey of knowledge on the African American experience (in the hemispheric sense of the term), which has been updated based on the scholarship produced over the last decade or so. Organized alphabetically by entry, it is easy to use and written in a language that makes complex concepts and ideas accessible to a general reading audience.

The scholarship produced on the black experience over the last century has long since laid to rest, intellectually, the myth of black racial inferiority. The reigning unwisdom has been exposed for what it is—white supremacist mythology masquerading as scholarship. Scholars, especially those of the last four decades, have therefore turned their attention to the more complex problem of documenting and interpreting the remarkable processes of human development and social, political and cultural change that have characterized the African American experience in the Americas over the last five hundred years. This second edition of the *Encyclopedia of African-American Culture and History* is designed to introduce the public to this new knowledge.

HOWARD DODSON (2005)

Director, Schomburg Center for Research in Black Culture, New York Public Library

Introduction

According to the written historical record, the first person of African descent arrived in the Americas in 1494 as a member of Christopher Columbus's entourage in his second voyage. He was apparently a free man. In 1501, confronted with a declining indigenous population and with the Spanish colonists unwilling to perform their own labor, Governor Nicolas de Ovando of Hispaniola requested the monarchs, Ferdinand and Isabella, to introduce African slaves. The first human cargo disembarked on the island in 1502, inaugurating almost four centuries of African slavery in the Americas. In time, the institution spread to the colonies established by the Portuguese, the English, the French, the Dutch, and the Danes in the hemisphere. Estimates vary, but by the time the human commerce ended in the nineteenth century, some ten to thirteen million Africans had been transported to the Americas as slaves. This number, it should be noted, does not include the millions who were the progeny of these Africans and who were born into slavery.

This encyclopedia addresses the experiences of these Africans and their descendants in the societies of the Americas. It identifies some of the major issues and problems that have informed their lives since the sixteenth century. The entries highlight the significant events in their trajectory over time as well as the outstanding men and women who have made enduring contributions to the history and culture of their people. In addition, the encyclopedia's range includes entries on the cultures of these African descended peoples in the Americas and their roles in shaping the contours of the societies in which they live and their animating intellectual currents.

Although African Americans receive disproportionate attention in the volumes, this is in large measure a function of the extant scholarship. Most of the entries are country specific but others, particularly those that are thematic, are comparative in their focus. The distinctiveness of the encyclopedia resides in its hemispheric and comparative emphases and in its attempt to strike a balance between biographical entries and those that are thematic. The original manuscripts that are included in volume 6 capture the voices of prominent personages and important moments in the history of these African peoples in the Americas. Numerous photographs and illustrations enrich the appeal of the entries.

It is a matter of considerable satisfaction that an encyclopedia of this intellectual breadth and depth could have been compiled. A pioneering venture, the appearance of the collection demonstrates the vibrancy of scholarship on the peoples of African descent and its increasing importance in the curriculum of schools, colleges, and universities in the hemisphere. Still, it should be recognized that the study of blacks in the diaspora is still in its infancy. The methodologies of this emerging multidisciplinary field are constantly being refined, new areas of enquiry identified, and fresh questions asked.

The African peoples who were enslaved in the Americas were denied access to literacy. Masters of the land, the European slave owners wanted Africans for their brawn, not their intellect. An expanding body of pseudo-scientific literature, particularly in the late eighteenth and nineteenth centuries, promoted the doctrine of white supremacy and the biological inferiority of African peoples. This ideology was more vociferously and aggressively articulated in the United States of America than elsewhere in the Americas, but it was invoked everywhere. Not only was the personhood of blacks assaulted, but their heritage was systematically denigrated. Africa and her peoples were deemed not to have a history or cultures deserving of serious study. The debasement of Africa and Africans had no national boundaries.

Throughout the Americas, the peoples of African descent had the burden of affirming their humanity and challenging negative definitions of themselves by others. In the early nineteenth century, free blacks in the United States undertook the task of studying and celebrating their African heritage, underscoring the achievements of African civilizations and emphasizing the role of Egypt in the construction and development of Western civilization. These African-American writers opposed slavery and castigated whites for their mistreatment of African peoples. Recognizing that history could play a powerful role in the psychological liberation of a people, they urged their readers to recover, study, and write about their past.

In time, a number of black writers responded to this admonition. Hosea Easton, James W. Pennington, William Nell, George Washington Williams, among others, all wrote histories of African Americans during the nineteenth century, laying the foundations of the historiography of a people. These pioneering writers were essentially self-taught and would be succeeded by such university trained scholars as W. E. B. Du Bois and Carter G. Woodson. In 1896, Du Bois published the *Suppression of the African Slave Trade to the United States of America 1638–1870*, the first of his many books in a long and distinguished career. Popularly known as the father of black history, Woodson published *The Education of the Negro Prior to 1861* in 1915. These men did not stand alone, to be sure. Benjamin Brawley, for example, published his *Short History of the American Negro* in 1913.

African Americans were far more successful than their brethren elsewhere in the Americas in pioneering and shaping scholarship about themselves. In March 1897, a group of African Americans led by the Episcopal priest and scholar Alexander Crummell, founded the American Negro Academy in Washington, D.C., to promote scholarship on the peoples of African descent. Possessing a higher literacy rate and more abundant resources than others of African descent in the Americas, African Americans established schools, colleges, and universities and set their curricula, sometimes with the assistance of white philanthropists. On the other hand, the European colonies in the Caribbean had no control over the curriculum of their schools and were fed a steady Eurocentric educational diet that glorified the achievements of the mother country. Students of the elementary schools in the Anglophone Caribbean sang "Rule Britannia, Britannia rules the waves, Britons never never shall be slaves," a supreme irony since the singers were the descendants of slaves. The black populations in Latin America fared hardly better as they were marginalized in their native lands.

Carter G. Woodson's founding of the Association for the Study of Negro Life and History in 1915 gave an inestimable boost to the study of the history of the peoples of African descent. A year later, he launched the *Journal of Negro History*, and it would become the principal vehicle for the publication of historical scholarship on blacks. It has since been renamed the *Journal of African American History*. In order to underscore the importance of black history, Woodson founded Negro History Week in 1926, which evolved into Negro History Month.

The history of African descended peoples and their cultures did not become serious and sustained areas of scholarly enquiry until substantial changes had taken place in the racial ethos and power relations of the societies of the Americas. In the case of the United States of America, an increasingly pugnacious African-American community began to demand their civil rights, forcing the larger society to effect reforms and to keep faith with the nation's founding principles. Beginning in the late 1960s, university students and others demanded that the study of Africa and the peoples of African descent be included in the curriculum. Responding to these demands, many universities hastily created Black Studies programs and began to hire black professors. Reflecting the pernicious racist assumptions of the larger society, white administrators at these institutions doubted the intellectual integrity of such programs and the subjects of their study, funded them inadequately, hired ill prepared black instructors, and accorded little respect even to those who were academically distinguished. This should not have been a surprising development since white administrators and academics were not immune to the racist virus that had infected the society for so long and so intensely. The Black Studies movement, however, had the salutary effect of stimulating research on black history and on the contemporary black condition and many outstanding works of scholarship appeared and continue to appear.

These intellectual currents were not confined to the United States. The achievement of self government and the end of colonial rule in some of the Anglophone Caribbean islands in the 1960s allowed the leaders of these societies to rethink and reimagine the nature and emphases of their educational systems. Black heads of government such as Eric Williams of Trinidad and Tobago and Michael Manley of Jamaica presided over the expansion of educational opportunities for their citizenry and the introduction of a curriculum that responded to their people's circumstances and needs. Eric Williams, a former professor, emphasized in his book *Education in the British West Indies* that the role of the educational system "should be that of a midwife to the emerging social order." Similar reforms have not yet been embraced in any systematic fashion in Latin American societies.

The uneven nature of curricula reform notwithstanding, scholarship on the peoples of African descent has made remarkable advances since the 1960s, a fact that is reflected in the generally high quality of the published works and the range of the issues they address. Some of these scholars, especially those based in the United States, have embraced a conceptual framework characterized as Afrocentric. Molefi Asante is the principal advocate of such a theoretical strategy, which he defines in his book *The Afrocentric Idea* as "placing African ideals at the center of any analysis that involves African culture and behavior." This approach has its critics but there can be no doubt that the Eurocentric conceptual paradigm that was prevailing had to be challenged. Increasingly, scholars are situating their studies in an African diasporic framework, emphasizing a shared heritage and the interrelationships among the peoples of African descent regardless of their societal location. The recently founded Association for the Study of the Worldwide African Diaspora (ASWAD) gives organizational expression to this imperative.

Conceptually, this encyclopedia reflects a diasporic approach to the study of the peoples of African descent in the Americas. As such, it stands at the forefront of contemporary scholarship. Hemispheric wide in scope, it situates the peoples of African descent at the center of their history and culture. In spite of the enormous difficulties that the peoples of African descent have confronted historically, they have never been vanquished. They are, for the most part, depicted in these volumes as actors in their own lives, beating against the barriers, sometimes successfully. Their lives, struggles, and accomplishments in spite of considerable oppression constitute an important part of a universal human quest for justice and self-affirmation.

COLIN A. PALMER (2005)

Africa: An Introduction

This essay deals with the African background of African Americans as a means of understanding the ecological aspects of the continent from which the ancestors of this population came, and the history and nature of the major biological, linguistic, and sociocultural processes that produced those Africans. Although many of these processes were continent-wide, specific attention is paid to West and Central Africa, the regions that contributed most of the ancestors of Africans in the Americas.

African Americans may have more reasons than other people to ponder the symbolism in the very shape of Africa—a question mark. After pondering the question of their connection to Africa for several centuries, as did Countee Cullen in his classic poem "Heritage" (1925), most African Americans now fully affirm their link with what Cullen described as a land of:

Copper sun or scarlet sea,
Jungle star or jungle track,
Strong bronzed men, or regal black
Women from whose loins I sprang
When the birds of Eden sang? (Cullen, 1947)

Today, African Americans point with pride to their many Pan-African links, especially with black South Africans, whose political emancipation they view as ending the long, bitter years of alien domination of the continent. Many proudly wear articles associated with Ghana's "kente-cloth complex" (the royal colors of kings and queens).

Almost as soon as African Americans had mastered elements of European culture, they fought against the notion that "the superior white man must bear the burden of civilizing colonial peoples of the world, if necessary against the will of those peoples" (Drake and Cayton, 1970, p. 47). They especially resented and resisted the assertion that "The very existence of social order [in America] is believed to depend upon 'keep[ing] the Negro in his place'" (Drake and Cayton, 1970, p. 756). African Americans were determined to disprove the implications of the belief that "it would be a matter of a thousand years before Africans could develop high forms of civilization or become dangerous to the white race" (Beale, 1956, p. 44). The issue for African Americans was not to become "dangerous to the white race," but to liberate themselves and Africa from the control of those who questioned their very humanity. African Americans were determined to disprove the common belief that Africa had no history.

African Americans were among the first persons of African origin to insist that the brilliance of the Egyptian past is only one episode in the history of a continent that gave the world so much. Furthermore, while most of the ancestors of African Americans came from the Atlantic coasts of the continent, their cultural background undoubtedly shared many aspects of a widespread and ancient civilization. More than most continents, Africa has always been a veritable museum where kaleidoscopic cultural patterns from various epochs and their syntheses have coexisted. To avoid confusion, it is best to describe many aspects of Africa in the past tense—as part of history, since the African background often resonates as a heritage in the lives of its now far-flung peoples.

The Geography of Africa

A realm of abundant sunshine, Africa bisects the equator; 80 percent of its land mass falls between the tropics of Cancer and Capricorn. The continent's 11.7 million square miles makes it more than three times the size of the United States, including Alaska. Its northern part borders the Mediterranean. To its east lie the Red Sea and the Indian Ocean; South Africa is surrounded by a confluence of the Indian and the Atlantic oceans. The Atlantic borders all of the western coasts of Africa. Madagascar, the largest of the continent's islands, lies to the southeast, surrounded by the Indian Ocean, and the other African islands—São Tomé, Príncipe, Bioko, Cape Verde, and the Canaries—are westward in the Atlantic Ocean.

Some geologists believe that Africa was the geo-morphological core of an ancient supercontinent known as Gondwanaland. Around 200 million years ago, this enormous land mass, averaging about 2,500 feet above sea level, fractured, leaving Africa as a high plateau of ancient Precambrian rocks sloping toward the north, while the other pieces drifted away to form South America, the Indian Subcontinent, Australia, and Antarctica. Although this giant fracture created very few mountain ranges and water basins within Africa, it did create a system of spectacular trenches known as the Great Rift Valley in eastern Africa. Starting in Anatolia of northern Turkey, the rift goes south for a distance of some six thousand miles, through what are now the Jordan Valley and the Dead Sea; through the Gulf of Aqaba and the length of the Red Sea; bisecting the Ethiopian Massif and continuing down into East Africa, where it divides into two branches in which are found lakes Kivu, Edward, Rudolf (Turkana), Albert, Victoria (the source of the Nile River and the second largest of the world's freshwater lakes), Malawi, and Tanganyika, whose bottom is several thousand feet below sea level; and finally ending at the mouth of the Zambezi River.

The majestic glacier-tipped Kilimanjaro, 19,340 feet above sea level and the highest mountain in Africa, was formed, like the other mountain ranges, by tectonic forces after the ancient faulting. The Atlas range in the northwest rises to some 13,000 feet, the Tibesti Massifs in the Sahara are over 13,000 feet, and the Cameroon Highlands in the west are comparable in height. In East Africa there are the Ethiopian Highlands with Mount Ras Dashan (15,158 feet), and further south are the great extinct volcanoes of Mounts Elgon, Kenya, and Ruwenzori (the Mountains of the Moon), which average about 17,000 feet high. The Drakensberg Mountains in southeast Africa rise to more than 11,000 feet.

Large inland basins, which are drained by the continent's spectacular rivers, often extend from the base of these mountain ranges. Characteristically, most African rivers are navigable for great distances across the continent's interior plateau until they plunge over impassable rapids or cataracts as they approach an extraordinarily narrow and relatively straight coastal plain. The advantage here is that the points at which these rivers leave the plateau can be the sites for hydroelectric dams. The disadvantage is that the rivers enter the ocean through deltas and shifting sandbars rather than through estuaries, thereby depriving the African continent of a large number of bays and gulfs that provide natural harbors in other parts of the world.

For example, the Zambezi drops some 343 feet over the spectacular Victoria Falls—more than twice the height of Niagara—before it heads for the sea. The Nile, along whose banks early civilizations bloomed, flows northward out of Central Africa and drops over several cataracts before joining the Mediterranean. The Niger River rises in the Liberian Highlands and goes east and then south, picking up such tributaries as the Benue and Cross rivers before emptying into the Atlantic. The great Congo River with its huge tributaries, the Kasai and the Ubangi, drains thousands of square miles before tumbling over falls to flow into the Atlantic. Many of Africa's smaller river systems, such as the Limpopo, Orange, Senegal, Vaal, and Voltas, exhibit the same pattern. Without outlets to the sea, such internal drainage systems as Lake Chad in the north and the Okavango Swamp in the south end up in shallow, brackish lakes or salt marshes.

Africa has basically seven climatic and vegetation zones. There is a central equatorial zone, and, radiating both north and south, replicating subtropical savanna zones, low-altitude desertlike zones, and Mediterranean zones. All of these are influenced by the contour of the land, and by monsoons and coastal currents. Africa's humid equatorial zone, though often referred to as "jungle," is smaller than those found either in South America or in parts of Asia. It covers Central Africa, strips along the Guinea coast, and parts of Gabon, Cameroon, and northern Congo. Here the temperatures range between 90°F during the day and 70°F during the nights. Rainfall is highest following the equinox (March and September), with an annual amount of about 50 to 70 inches. In some coastal areas where moisture-laden winds ascend steep slopes, the total can rise to more than 200 inches. The East African Highlands, situated on the equator, have lower temperatures and rainfall than the lowlands. In the lowlands there are tropical rain forests characterized by liana and dense vegetation, as well as species of valuable palm trees, mahogany, ebony, teak, sapele, niangon, and kolas. The vegetation in the East African Highlands includes deciduous forests and evergreens.

The subtropical savanna ecological zones, which lie both north and south of the equatorial zone, occupy the largest area on the continent and differ only by altitude and proximity to the oceans. The fairly large northern ecological zone, which is also incidentally lower and wider, covers parts of Nigeria, the Sudan, and Chad. The temperatures can range up to 100° F, especially from March to May, just before the rains, but are usually between 70 and 50 degrees; temperatures in December and January are lower, especially during the harmattan, a dry, dusty wind that blows from the Sahara southward. Temperatures are lower in the southern subtropical zone because of the higher elevation and decreased width. The annual rainfall in both zones is 30 to 60 inches. Both subtropical zones are marked by the preponderant vegetation cover of the continent—grass—and within grasslands are found scattered trees of species such as the baobab and (where rainfall permits) acacia. At particularly high elevations such as the Cameroon Highlands, or the highlands and rolling plateaus of Kenya (Mounts Kilimanjaro and Ruwenzori have permanent ice fields), the upland grasslands are replaced by forests, such as the High Veldt of Transvaal, or by steep mountain slopes. Taken as a whole, this region is the one that supports many of the continent's herbivores, and pastoral activities play an important role in the economies of the indigenous peoples.

Low, dry, hot ecological zones are found both north and south as one moves further away from the equator. The Sahel in West Africa gradually shades into the Sahara, the desert of the Horn, and the Kalahari and Namid deserts are found in the south. The temperatures in the desert areas are quite variable, with great changes in daily temperature, except near the coasts. And while annual precipitation in the northern desert ranges from only 4 inches downward to zero, the popular image of the African deserts as barren rock and sand dunes bereft of vegetation is incorrect. The deserts actually support scrub and, on the margins, even grass for pasturage. The Sahara, in particular, is dotted with oases that support intensive agriculture, and in the east there is the fertile Nile Valley. The Namid Desert, which borders the Atlantic coast of southwestern Africa, is more desolate, receiving less than 10 inches of rain annually; but the Kalahari, inland from the Namid, is really only a semidesert, receiving as much as 15 inches per year. The Kalahari comes to quick life with the first sprinkling of rain, and often has stands of grasses and inland pans of water.

Mediterranean subtropical ecological zones are the next latitudinal regions. Characteristic of these are winter rains (from 25 to 32 inches) and summer droughts. The winters are mild, between 50°F and 60°F, and the summers around 70° F. The variable rainfalls and temperatures in these zones permit the growth of forests and brush.

The climate of Madagascar, Africa's largest island, ranges from tropical to largely subtropical. Its coastal lowlands are wet, hot, and covered with tropical forests, while the Central Highlands are drier, fairly cool, and covered with grass and interspersed woodlands. Bioko (the former Fernando Po) and São Tomé possess equatorial ecologies; the Cape Verde Islands share the ecology of the Sahel and are often plagued by droughts.

The distribution of African soils reflects the belts of temperature and especially rainfall. Approximately 36 percent of Africa, especially the equatorial zone of the Democratic Republic of the Congo and the Guinea coast, may be characterized as humid, 22 percent semiarid, 26 percent arid, and 16 percent desert. This means that nearly two-thirds of Africa has a moisture deficiency during all or part of the year. The amount of water available is a function of regional and seasonal swings; it ranges from excess water, due to persistent rainfall and high humidity, to too little rainfall and high evaporation. The result is that if the soil is suddenly exposed to the elements by either humans or nature, there is severe erosion and a loss of the fertility so necessary for crop cultivation. Nevertheless, most if not all African soils are good for short periods, provided that they have a long fallow period. The soils in humid and semiarid areas, while initially rich in humus content, lose their fertility and become lateritic if cultivated continuously. The soils of the arid lands are relatively rich in inorganic minerals but low in humus content, and need additional water in order to be usable. Typically, seasonal variation in moisture distribution sets limits on the types and amounts of crops grown. Several parts of Africa have suffered from droughts and "hungry periods" due to shortages of food.

Mineral, Plant, and Animal Resources.

Africa is immensely rich in minerals, in flora, and in fauna. The continent has about two-thirds of the world's phosphorites, some 45 percent of the world's bauxite, 20 percent of its copper, 16 percent of its uranium, and substantial reserves of iron ore, manganese, chromium, cobalt, platinum, and titanium. The food crops of Africa include coffee, ensete (a banana-like fruit), varieties of yams and rice, millets, sorghums, varieties of oil palms, the kola nut, and melons, all of which are believed to be indigenous to the continent; wheat, barley, and oats, of Middle Eastern origin; varieties of bananas and plantains, thought to be of Southeast Asian origin; and maize, manioc, peanuts, tomatoes, varieties of potatoes, and some tubers and cocoa beans—all cultigens that arrived in Africa as a result of the post-Columbus great plant migration. Cotton is common in the northern savanna belt, and species of trees produced bark used for making cloth. In addition, the hardwoods and lianas of the tropical forests have been utilized by human beings for shelter and for many useful products over generations.

The domestic animals of the continent include varieties of cattle, sheep, goats, horses, donkeys, camels, pigs, dogs, chickens, ducks, and the semidomesticated guinea fowl. Africa is famous for its wide variety of animals representing thousands of species of mammals, reptiles, amphibians, fish, birds, and insects. Huge herds of a variety of antelopes, giraffes, and zebras roam the savannas, providing the prey for cheetahs, leopards, and lions. Herds of elephants still roam parts of eastern and southern Africa, having been largely eliminated in the north and west. The hippopotamus still lives in tropical rivers; varieties of water birds, such as the flamingo, are among the enormous range of African birds. Many of the animals in Africa, such as the rhinoceros, are now under stress for survival as a result of excessive hunting and the growth of the human populations.

Africa and the Origin of Human Beings

A growing number of paleontologists and human geneticists now believe that the origins of the billions of human beings on earth can be traced to a woman who lived in Africa some 200,000 years ago and left an unmistakable signature on the DNA of all *Homo sapiens.* This was the most important stage in a process that started some four million years ago, when the genus *Homo* emerged from the *Australopithecus,* giving rise to *Homo erectus, Homo neanderthalensis,* and other varieties of *Homo.* Then, some 250,000 to 100,000 years ago, modern humans—with lighter skeletons, "their more capacious brains, and their softer brows" and possibly "with language"—radiated out from "their African homeland and overwhelmed or supplanted the many more primitive humans who were then living in Asia and Europe" (Angier, 1991, C1). That such a theory is gaining ground is all the more remarkable since in the past, the prejudice against all things African was pronounced. Charles Darwin suggested that in view of the abundance of animal life there, especially that of the primates, it would be wise to look to Africa as the possible cradle of humankind, but this was rejected by his contemporaries, who were convinced of white supremacy.

Biologists now believe that as human beings moved about within and outside the African continent, they retained the ability to interbreed, but their geno-phenotypes (often referred to as geographical "races") emerged as adaptations to different ecological zones. No one knows what the earliest *Homo sapiens* in Africa looked like, but the so-called Negro-appearing people became the dominant physical type in sub-Saharan Africa (pockets of these Negroid people also lived in the oases of the Sahara). The Negroes in the Nile Valley tend to be taller and darker; eastward, in the Horn of Africa, the people appear to be a mixture of Negroids and the so-called Caucasoids. Caucasoid populations live in northern Africa and in the northern parts of the Sahara and the Nile Valley. A short variety of Negroids, popularly known as Pygmies (Twa), live scattered among their taller neighbors in the central regions, and in southern Africa live another fairly short population, yellowish in skin color and possessing wiry hair, known as the Khoisan. Also in southern Africa and parts of eastern Central Africa are found Caucasoid and Caucasoid-like populations of European and Indian provenance; Malayo-Polynesian populations are settled in Madagascar.

Challenges to Human Life

The human populations in Africa have had to cope with a variety of insect-borne and other diseases that flourish in the tropics, and in a few cases they have adapted geno-phenotypically to these. Yellow fever and malaria, carried by mosquitoes, have been widespread, and some populations, especially in West Africa, have acquired a certain immunity to sicklemia (sickle-cell anemia), caused by malaria. Trypanosomiasis, or sleeping sickness, whose vector or carrier is the tsetse fly, is found primarily in humid forested or savanna areas and is dangerous to both human beings and animals, especially cattle and horses. Schistosomiasis, by far the most widespread of African diseases, is caused by parasites of the genus *Schistosoma,* which live in running water and enter the human body through the skin after a complex life cycle that includes the snail as an intermediate host. Also associated with river valleys is onchocerciasis, or river blindness, which is carried by a species of fly, *Simulium damnosum.* In addition to these, there are varieties of diseases caused by nematodes such as guinea worms, liver flukes, and tapeworms.

HIV/AIDS is the most recent virulent disease to have appeared. In contrast to many other parts of the world, where it is often associated with homosexuality and intravenous drug use, in Africa HIV/AIDS is often associated with heterosexual activities. While no cure has been found for HIV/AIDS, such diseases as schistosomiasis, malaria, yellow fever, and trypanosomiasis are less morbid than in the past, and yaws and leprosy have been largely eliminated from African populations. A new source of concern is the appearance of a rare but virulent disease called Ebola. Africans are increasingly concerned about identifying and dealing with new diseases.

African Languages

Africa's 750 to 800 different languages not only represent the largest group of languages found on any continent but are spoken by populations differing in physical types and cultures. The debate about the classification, nature, and number of African languages continues, due to the lack of agreement among scholars as to criteria used to determine genetic relationships and differences between languages and their dialects. One major consensus, however, is that all African languages fall into four major families. The languages of the largest family, the Niger-Kordofanian, are spoken in western, central, eastern, and southern Africa. The Bantu languages—one of six subgroups of the Benue-Congo languages—are believed to have recently spread over most of central and southern Africa, since they are closely related to each other. Swahili, spoken in many parts of East Africa, is an Arabized Bantu language. In southern Africa and in parts of Tanganyika are found a small but important group of languages belonging to the Khoisan family. This family is believed to be the source of the "clicks" found in the Bantu languages.

The Nilo-Saharan languages are not only the second largest group of African languages, but members are found widely separated in the Nile Valley and in the Niger Basin of West Africa. Also widely distributed are members of the Afro-Asiatic family, which include Semitic languages such as Arabic and Hebrew spoken outside of Africa, as well as Berber, Hausa, and ancient Egyptian, in addition to such Cushitic languages as Amharic, found in Ethiopia. Malayo-Polynesian languages are found in Madagascar; Germanic and Latin languages were brought into Africa by the incoming Europeans.

Peoples and Cultures of Africa

Africa was the site not only of important steps in the evolution of the human species, but of a parallel development: the evolution of culture, a distinctive human characteristic. Some of the earliest traces of human cultural activities—such as stone assemblages—subsequently spread, and the evolution of these artifacts both within the African continent and outside of it, with frequent interchange, attests to the processes by which African cultures subsequently developed. Initially, all African populations lived by foraging, but by 13,000 years before the present there is evidence that the Mesolithic (Middle Stone Age) population, which lived in the valley of the Nile around Khartoum, included harvested wild cereals in its diet. By 6,000 years ago, the peoples in the Nile Valley shared the practice of crop cultivation and animal domestication with those in other parts of the Fertile Crescent, which extended eastward to the Tigris and Euphrates river valleys. Within the limits of ecological constraints, these food-production techniques involving plants and animals specific to Africa spread to various parts of the continent, replacing but not totally eliminating earlier foraging patterns. The same generalization can be made about the invention and spread of Iron Age technologies and other traits important to early African peoples (Wai Andah, 1981, p. 592; Posnansky, 1981, pp. 533–534).

Partly as a result of the interchange of indigenous cultural elements within Africa and the addition of those from exogenous regions, it has never been unusual to find Africans with differing physical types, speaking different languages, and having different sociocultural systems living contemporaneously in the same or neighboring ecological niches. For example, in Central Africa, foraging populations such as the Batwa (Bantu-speaking Pygmies) have lived in contact with the pastoral Hima and agricultural Hutu (both of which are also Bantu speakers). And while these groups borrowed sociocultural traits from each other, they did not necessarily change their ways of life. In other cases, groups in contact changed their physical types, languages, and sociocultural traits, such as their economic, political, and religious systems. In this way, Africa often presented a veritable museum where the surviving evidence of important stages in the evolution of humans and culture could be witnessed. It is partly because of the interdigitation of African peoples that the classification of their societies has proved difficult—made more so by the cultural, ethnic, and biological chauvinism of Africans themselves and of foreigners who used notions about the level of cultural attainment of Africans as rationalizations for conquest, colonization, and exploitation.

Regional variations of Paleolithic, Mesolithic, and Neolithic cultural assemblages appeared in all parts of Africa, a function of both indigenous development and external influences. From the Neolithic period onward, the cultural assemblages in the Nile Valley had a brilliant florescence as a result of this mingling of indigenous development and external contacts. And while until recently—for racist, historical, and political reasons and because of various strictures peculiar to particular academic disciplines—Egyptian civilization was viewed strictly in terms of its relationship to Asia and the Mediterranean, that view is now changing. One well-known scholar remarked that "if the history of early Africa is unthinkable without Egypt, so too is the history of early Egypt inexplicable without Africa. Ancient Egypt was essentially an African civilization" (Davidson, 1991, p. 49; see also Diop, 1974). Nevertheless, it is also true that during certain epochs many parts of Africa were firmly linked to external civilizations, and that at other times some external areas were viewed as African. How these links were seen was very much a function of military and political power relations of the world in a given period.

Many early scholars and even contemporary ones have been so impressed by the remarkable similarities of the sociocultural institutions throughout Africa that some have speculated incessantly about whether the migrating "children of the sun" from Egypt diffused such traits as divine kingship, dual monarchies, and matriliny to all parts of the continent, and in some cases to outside areas. One may even postulate the existence of a widespread early "Ur-African" culture, or proto-African cultural elements that constituted a foundation upon which elaborate cultural complexes or centers in such areas as Egypt, the Upper Nile, the Niger, the Democratic Republic of the Congo, and the Zambezi were constructed. What follows is a description of African sociocultural institutions, especially those of the western and central regions, which most nearly resemble those of the millions of Africans who were transported to the western hemisphere during the terrible transatlantic slave trade.

Economic Organization

Most Africans, including the ancestors of those who came to the Americas, were slash-and-burn horticulturists or agriculturists who used irrigation techniques where warranted. Wheat, barley, and oats were commonly produced in the Nile Valley and North Africa by plow agriculture with irrigation. In other savanna regions, in East, Central, and South Africa and the western Sudan, cereals such as millets, sorghums, and—to a limited extent—varieties of rice and legumes were cultivated by means of the hoe. Root crops, such as yams and other tubers, and varieties of rice and bananas were widely cultivated in the more tropical regions of West Africa and the Democratic Republic of the Congo. Cotton was widely cultivated in the drier regions, and bark for bark-cloth processing was produced in such forested regions as Ashanti.

And while pastoralism based on the herding of cattle, sheep, goats, camels, donkeys, and horses was an important food-producing strategy, it was feasible primarily in the savanna areas that were free from the tsetse fly. Nevertheless, few of the so-called classic pastoralist societies, such as the Masai, the Nuer, the Dinka, the Kabbabish Arabs, and the Somali, lived primarily by the products of their herds. Most of them, including the cattle-keeping people of East, Central, and southern Africa and the Fulani of West Africa, lived in symbiotic relations with their cultivator neighbors. Especially in West Africa, many cattle herders often became sedentary cultivators when disease or droughts decimated their herds. This was not so difficult for them, since they moved in transhumance cycles among horticulturists between the forest zones and the desert, as pasturage and rainfall permitted. (Islamic practices appear to have limited the rearing of pigs, even in those areas where climatic factors made this possible.) In many parts of southern and East Africa, there were populations with mixed economies of horticulturists and pastoralists, though in many cases animals were the most valued products.

A minuscule number of African societies, such as the Batwa of the Democratic Republic of the Congo, the Hadtsa and Sandawe of East Africa, and the Kung-San of southern Africa, retained an early adaptation to hunting and general foraging activities, but these economic strategies largely gave way to fishing, pastoralism, and horticulture. Hunting remained only an ancillary economic pursuit among all Africans, including the Mande, Akan, Mossi, Bakongo, and Baluba peoples of West and Central Africa. Fishing, too, declined as a major economic activity, except among a few riverine and coastal populations such as the Ebrie people of coastal West Africa and the Bozo people of the inland Niger River area.

A marked division of labor based on gender existed among all African food producers. Among the cultivators in most West and Central African societies, males were primarily responsible for the heavy work of clearing and preparing the land and growing specific crops. Women generally did most of the actual cultivation, harvesting, and processing of food. In addition, they often cultivated certain crops that were viewed as "women's" crops. Families who needed additional food for ceremonial or fiscal reasons obtained labor from voluntary organizations of youths and adults, whom they paid or entertained. In the more complex Mande, Bakongo, and Fon societies, free persons and war captives who had become serfs and slaves were obliged to produce foodstuffs for their masters. In certain parts of the Sudan and the Sahel, horticulturists kept animals when conditions permitted, or traded vegetable products for animal products from neighboring pastoralist populations or foragers who hunted wild animals. The pastoralists, such as the Fulani of West Africa and the Kabbabish Arabs of the eastern Sudan, moved their herds in transhumance cycles between the tsetse-infected forest zones and the drier savannas. Males did most of the herding, leaving women to milk animals and to process and trade milk products. Hunting, whether among cultivators, pastoralists, or foragers, was the occupation of males, while women among all of these groups gathered wild products for food. Both males and females kept chickens, ducks, and small domestic animals.

Crafts, Manufactured Products, and Systems of Exchange

Almost all African cultivators used iron implements produced by male blacksmiths whose wives often made pots. These persons were often the only specialists in small-scale subsistence societies. Nevertheless, even these small-scale societies often produced surplus goods and interacted economically with the larger African societies, where specialization gave rise to other smiths who worked such metals as tin, copper, silver, and gold, procured either by mining or by placer washing. This was especially prevalent in West Africa, the Nile Valley, and the Zimbabwe region in southeastern Africa. Weavers, carpenters, glassmakers, and other specialists—especially in North Africa, the Nile Valley, Ethiopia, and West Africa—produced surpluses for high-status persons or for trade in local periodic markets and with long-distance caravaners who supplied complex economies. Many producers of craft goods—for example, smiths, weavers, potters, and leather workers in the western Sudan—were organized into endogamous castelike guilds that posted members along trade routes. And while most of the guilds were egalitarian, others gave unequal access to their economic assets.

Barter persisted in small African communities that were largely self-sufficient, but also continued to play an economic role in some of the larger communities. Silent trade involving barter for gold and other products—such as occurred, for instance, between the ancient Malians and Phoenicians—persisted for a long time in many parts of Africa where vast differences in language and culture made face-to-face trade hazardous. Also employed were various types of currencies that ran the gamut from iron implements, lengths of cloth, beads, necklaces, bracelets, anklets, and waist bands to cowrie shells, gold dust, and slaves. In the Niger River areas, merchant guilds took goods on consignment, and used credit to procure goods for sale.

The notion of profit was well developed in various parts of North, East, and West Africa, except where inhibited by Islam. Also in parts of West Africa, destitute persons could pawn themselves or dependents for money. Those pawns who were unredeemed were often married, if female, by the creditors, or became serfs or slaves if male. The urban, or palace- and temple-based, complex economies in Egypt, the western Sudan, and East Africa were often the transit points for international products leaving from or arriving in many African ports of trade. Many West Africans were involved in the economic complex of the Niger River described below.

Lying between the desert and the forest regions of West Africa was a veritable *sahil* (an Arabic word for *shore*), part of a well-known ecosystem that facilitated the rise of a complex sociocultural system serving as a transit point for persons and products coming from north, south, and east. This region had among its characteristics a large floodplain suitable for cereal agriculture and livestock rearing, numerous waterways that provided easy transportation for natural resources and manufactured products, and an extensive savanna rich in minerals and in faunal and floral resources. Here arose the core states or empires of Ghana, Mali, and Songhay, whose influence radiated throughout West and Central Africa.

As an example of the complexity, Leo Africanus, the sixteenth-century Spanish-born traveler and author, described Jenne, one of the most important cities of the Mali empire, as a "place exceedingly aboundeth with barlie, rice, cattel, fishes, and cotton: and their cotton they sell unto the merchants of Barbarie, for cloth of Eirope, for brazen vessels, for armor and other such commodities. Their coine is of gold without any stampe or inscription at all" (Leo Africanus, 1956, p. 468). A number of traditions hold that the gold used to mint the first English coin, the guinea, came from Jenne (Jennie or Guinea). A local scholar, al-Sadi, writing about 1655, described Jenne as,

> large, flourishing and prosperous; it is rich, blessed and favoured by the Almighty.... There one meets the salt merchants from the mines of Teghazza and merchants carrying gold from the mines of Bitou.... The area around Jenne is fer-

> tile and well populated; with numerous markets held there on all the days of the week. It is certain that it contains 7077 villages very near to one another. (Al-Sadi. 1987, p. 97)

These reports from West Africa could easily be replicated from other parts of the continent with complex economies such as the Democratic Republic of the Congo, Zimbabwe, the Swahili coast, and Mogadishu in East Africa, North Africa—which at one time served as the granary of Rome—and, of course, Egypt and the Sudan.

Social Organization

There was a basic notion that the complementary relationship, or what is now being called *complementarity,* between females and males lay at the center of the social organization of most African societies. Again, with very few exceptions, the people in African societies always emphasized the "extended family": that is, a group of married and unmarried males, females, and children, living in common or contiguous habitations, normally under the directorship of men. In most cases these men were descended from a common ancestor or ancestress, and the adults tended to interact most frequently with persons of their own gender except for purposes of reproduction. This is contrasted to the so-called nuclear family, where males and females maintained close relations for economic purposes as well as for reproduction and the rearing of children. A common domestic cycle was for a woman (rarely a man) to leave her natal family on marriage, join the extended family of a spouse, and return to her own natal family before death or, in spirit, after death.

The overwhelming majority of African societies emphasized corporate descent groups that were patrilineal: Both females and males traced their descent in the male line to a known apical ancestor, and children belonged to the husband's lineage. The size of the lineages varied in different societies, with subsidiary branches made up of descendants of subordinate known ancestors. In contrast were a small number of matrilineal societies such as the Akan in the Côte d'Ivoire and Ghana, the Lele in the Democratic Republic of the Congo, and the Tonga in eastern Central Africa, where descent was traced to apical female ancestors and children belonged to the lineages of mothers. Where, as among the Akan, both men and women tended to marry others in neighboring areas, they could remain in their natal villages and visit spouses nearby; or either males or females could join the villages of their spouses. In Central Africa the men of matrilineages tended to join the villages of their wives, or in some cases men could remain at home and have the husbands of daughters or sisters join them. In a very few societies, such as the Yako of contemporary Nigeria, people recognized both lines, making for what is called "double descent."

Despite the emphasis on either patriliny among the Mande, Mossi, Yoruba, and Igbo or matriliny among the Akan of Ghana and Lele of the Democratic Republic of the Congo, people usually recognized the lineage of their other parent, and sought help and refuge from these relatives when the need arose. Sometimes relationships between such relatives were so close that they risked jeopardizing the rule of corporate lineage affiliation. So important were kin relations in African societies that with few exceptions, the siblings of fathers and mothers (among the Yoruba, for example) were glossed by the same term—that is, *father* and *mother,* with terminological distinction based on relative age. It followed then that most of the children of uncles and aunts were considered brothers and sisters, instead of cousins, and the children of these as sons and daughters instead of nephews and nieces.

In societies where parental siblings were distinguished from parents, there were terms that were glossed as *aunt* and *uncle* and, of course, the children of these were glossed as *cousins.* A variation on this theme occurred when the siblings of only one set of parents, as among the Tuareg, were equated, thereby making their children "brothers" and "sisters," while the children of unequated siblings were "cousins." In some cases, these "cousins" were eligible as spouses while the children of other parental siblings were not, and in such situations the normal incest rule against marriage with relatives was strongly invoked. Noted exceptions to this rule pertained in ancient divine Egyptian families, especially among the pharaohs, where brother-sister marriages were preferred so as not to dilute their divinity.

With very few exceptions, the families in African societies exchanged or transferred valuables upon the marriage of their children, whether (as among the Lobi) young people chose their own spouses or (as among the Kikuyu) spouses were chosen for them. In what has been called *restricted exchange,* families exchanged women among one another (one can say men or grooms were exchanged, but Africans would not agree with that formulation) over an extended period of time. More common was a Hebraic-like *bride service* in which men provided labor for the families of their future spouses. Most common were marriages involving the gift of valuables by the family of the groom to the family of the bride. Referred to variously as *bride price, bride wealth,* and *progeny price,* these valuables, usually provided by sections of the corporate lineage, legitimized marriages and especially the parentage of the children. Significantly, matrilineal societies such as the Ashanti of Ghana and the Tonga of Zambia made comparably little use of the bride price even though, as in Ashanti and Baule, ritual drinks confirmed the marriage.

What the bride price or progeny price entailed was the responsibility of a family to provide additional brides if the one involved was deemed infertile, a practice known as the *sororate* (marriage of sisters). Women often divorced men who were judged infertile, or if husbands died young, women married their husbands' brothers, another Hebraic-like practice known as the *levirate.* Like African men, African women deemed it proper to bear children, either for their own lineages, if matrilineal, or for their husbands' lineages, if patrilineal. There were almost no cases of marriages in Africa whereby a woman's family transferred valuables to the family of a potential husband. In almost all African societies, however, women took valuable goods with them, often household items, when they joined their husbands.

The practice of having plural wives, or *polygyny,* was the ideal marital state for most African men, but actually most marriages were monogamous, that is, a man had only one wife. Nevertheless, most men hoped to become polygynous because, they insisted, polygyny guaranteed progeny. Within the household, however, polygyny was not always viewed as a blessing because there was the recognition that care was necessary to avoid conflict among co-wives. Husbands had to provide wives with separate dwellings and were cautioned to treat them as equitably as possible. In successful polygynous marriages, senior wives often actively sought additional wives for their husbands, not only to ease their own domestic chores, but to increase their own prestige and that of the husband. Apropos to this, in a number of African societies, including such West African cultures as the Fon, Mossi, and Yoruba (all patrilineal societies), women who were able to pay a bride price were able to procure other women as their own "wives," but not for sexual purposes. Such "wives" performed domestic or commercial duties for their "female husbands," but any children born to them by men were either transferred to the female husband's patrilineage or could be given to the patrilineages of the female husband's patrilineage.

The existence of polygynous marriages and extended families influenced the structure of family life in most African societies. The men of such extended families, whether matrilineal or patrilineal (but especially the latter), tended to bond together, interacting with each other both economically and socially. The wives of men in extended families followed the same pattern, allowing, of course, for conflicts between co-wives. Domestically, however, individual women tended to form a unit with their own children, which sought its interest against the domestic units of co-wives, or of the wives of other men in the extended family. Thus, while the authority of husbands and fathers over their wives and children was fully acknowledged—domestically and, especially, publicly—women were very much in charge of their own hearth and family. Moreover, as African women aged, their status and roles also changed. From timid and prudent brides new to the family of their spouse, they increasingly asserted themselves as they became mothers and senior and respected female relatives in their own households and own lineages. Later, they continued to gain respect as confidants of aging husbands, and finally as the often stern mothers-in-law whose duty it was to watch over the morals of incoming brides.

Since most African women shared many attributes of their domestic units and of their lineages, those women of royal descent and wives of important men often exercised a great deal of power within their domestic units and political systems. They not only had slaves and "wives" but were not above threatening the power of the ruler. From Mali there is an anecdote about a serious dispute between the ruling king and his wife, the daughter of his maternal uncle. She was "his partner in rule according to the custom of the Sudan, and her name was mentioned with his from the throne." Much to the chagrin of his subjects, the ruler suddenly imprisoned his queen and took a commoner as wife. The queen did not reveal the source of the conflict, but sought to shame her husband by placing dust on her head as a mark of humiliation and standing beside the council chamber. The king summoned a servant, who told the court that the queen had sent her to the king's cousin with a message expressing support for the cousin if he were to replace the sovereign, and promising, "I and all the army are at your service." The courtiers agreed that such treachery deserved death, but the queen escaped by seeking sanctuary in a mosque (Levtzion and Hopkins, 1981, pp. 294–295).

Africans generally desired children as necessary links in the chain of human life. Throughout the continent there were elaborate naming ceremonies, carried to great lengths by the Wolof, Akan, and Mande groups. In addition to training children at home, most African societies—particularly the ancient Egyptians, the Nuba in the Sudan, and the Somali, Kikuyu, Nyakyusa, Zulu, Bakongo, and Mossi—placed their pubescent children in special schools. There, in addition to undergoing ritual circumcision for boys and clitoridectomy for girls, the young were often enrolled in age-sets and age-grades where they were taught the facts of life, certain social graces, economic activities, political responsibilities, and religious beliefs. Among the Mende of what is now Sierra Leone, the age-set/age-grade systems, called *Poro* for boys and *Sande* for girls, provided the basis for their economic, military, social, political, and religious life. Chaka of the Zulu, the Masai, and many martial societies used these units as part of their military establishment. Here friendships and values were formed for life, and prepared people to take their future place in society. In some complex cultures, such as the Baganda, requirements of the political system were also taught. In ancient Egypt, the Sudan, and Ethiopia and in Islamic societies, where literacy was important for bureaucracies and for the priesthood, boys and sometimes girls went to special schools (*madrassa*).

Political Organization

African societies differed in scale and had a wide range of mechanisms for preserving order. While such acephalous groups as the Igbo, the Nuer, and the Kikuyu have attracted attention with their ability to preserve order without complex political structures, there is a wide consensus that Africans developed what one scholar claimed to be "relatively large-scale political societies" that could be studied. It was also suggested that "of all the areas inhabited by nonliterate peoples, Africa exhibits the greatest incidence of complex governmental structures. Not even the kingdoms of Peru and Mexico could mobilize resources and concentrate power more effectively than could some of these African monarchies" (Herskovits, 1948, p. 332; Skinner, 1963, p. 134).

Those simple African foraging societies, such as the San and the Batwa, that used kinship, name, and clientelistic ties within their own groups to maintain internal order utilized the same mechanisms to live in peace with their more powerful neighbors. And while many of the pastoral societies, such as the Kipsigis and the Masai, were especially bellicose, they had to protect themselves and their herds, and they used kinship solidarity for such purposes. The Somali used what was called *dia-paying* groups of kinsmen to pay for damages and seek revenge. The pastoral Fulani and Tuareg of West Africa utilized powerful individuals, sometimes known as *sheiks,* to maintain order. The Nuer and Dinka of the Nilotic Sudan also had recourse to ritual specialists such as *leopard-skin chiefs* and *prophets,* who restored peace (Evans-Pritchard, 1940, pp. 209, 134; Herskovits, 1948, p. 32).

Some of the small-scale African horticultural groups organized in village communities, such as the Alur, Lugbara, Tiv, Igbo, Kpelle, and Tallensi, used such institutions as shrines, rain medicines, and medicine men for maintaining peace (Southall, 1956, pp. 181–196; Middleton and Tait, 1958, pp. 131, 224; Fortes, 1945, p. 53). Some of these societies used marriage alliances, common ritual paraphernalia, and myths that they had requested governors from larger and imperialistic African societies in order to live in peace and security. These myths also provided legitimacy for dominant or domineering groups.

The institution of the divine king, who ruled with the legitimacy of heaven and with the support of royal ancestors, appears throughout Africa. Examples include the pharaohs in Egypt; the Ethiopia *negus,* who had the title "King of Kings and Lion of the Tribe of Judah"; the *reth* of the Shilluk in the Sudan; the *kabaka* of the Baganda; the king of the Bakongo; the kings of the Ashanti; the Alafin of Oyo among the Yoruba; the *mais* of the Kanuri; and the Mogho Naba of the Mossi in western Sudan. Often complementing these rulers were royal women who, as in Egypt, the Sudan, and Angola, ruled in their own right but were also royal consorts, queen mothers, queen sisters, or princesses. The Candaces and the Cleopatras of the Sudan and Egypt are well known; their counterparts, such as Queen Nzinga of Angola and Amina of the Hausa, are less renowned. Both male and female rulers often had shrines, groups of priests, and religious paraphernalia that helped legitimize their rule.

These rulers had elaborate courts or temple complexes, as in the Nile Valley, from which they ruled over provinces, districts, and villages. Quite common was the tendency of rulers to relocate their capitals when they assumed power, and in the case of the Egyptians and Sudanese they were not above erasing the names of predecessors on the stelae about the kingdom. It was also common for monarchs to use royal relatives to rule outlying provinces and districts. But neither was it uncommon to see these personages replaced by administrative officials when the state became more secure. Many were the mechanisms used by African rulers to take censuses and to obtain the revenue to support their thrones and their states. Children were counted during puberty rites; priests reported the number of protective devices given to peasants to save animals from disease; spies reported the riches of subordinate rulers. In this manner, bureaucrats knew the amount of taxes to expect. These taxes included custom receipts from traders and manufacturers, products from fields cultivated for the state, and part of the temple tithes and presents destined for local deities and for the rulers themselves. Rulers received wives not only for their bedchambers but to be used as pawns in dynastic marriages or to cultivate fields.

Scholars have been impressed by what is considered to be an African court tradition that was remarkably similar throughout the continent. With respect to West Africa, some of the early court traditions of Ghana, Mali, and

Songhay still persist among the Mossi and Ashanti. The Malian king held court in a domed pavilion in which stood ten horses covered with gold-embroidered materials; behind him stood ten pages holding shields and swords decorated with gold, and on his right were the sons of vassal kings wearing splendid garments, with their hair plaited with gold. Before him sat the governor of the city and his ministers, and guarding the pavilion were pedigreed guard dogs that wore gold and silver collars studded with balls of the same metals. When the beating of a drum announced that the king would receive his visitors, those who professed the king's religion (that is, all except the Muslims) approached him, fell on their knees in greeting, and sprinkled dust on their heads. Visitors reported the Malians to be "the humblest of people before their king and the most submissive towards him. They swear by his name, saying: Mansa Sulayman ki (the king has spoken)" (Levtzion and Hopkins, 1981, p. 291). The revenue of this king included all gold nuggets found in the country; he received one golden dinar on every load of salt that entered the kingdom, and two dinars when this amount was exported.

African communities and polities used a range of devices to maintain peace internally and to wage war against outsiders. Small village communities, such as those in Ebo land, used ridicule, various types of ordeals, expulsion, and belief in the efficacy of supernatural entities, often disguised as masked figures, to sanction evildoers. The acceptance of the decision of moot courts in larger societies was often enough to restore social harmony, in the absence of bodies that could enforce the law. State-level societies permitted the use of many informal legal devices at local levels, but all insisted upon judicial review at higher levels, with the monarch sitting as judge. Women often had parallel quasi-judicial and judicial institutions. The death penalty was often meted out for heinous crimes, such as rape, murder, and treason. The legal philosophy in most African societies was based on concern for what "reasonable persons" would do if provoked or would expect as punishment for crimes.

Of course, African judges were not infallible, and the complaints of those who believed that they were treated unjustly have come down to us. The legal codes of dwellers in the Nile Valley are well known, and ethnographers have furnished details of legal decisions in other societies. In addition, one reporter from fourteenth-century Mali cited the "lack of oppression," and "the security embracing the whole country, so that neither traveller there nor dweller has anything to fear from thief or usurper." We are told that the ancient Malians "do not interfere with the wealth of any white man who dies among them, even though it be quintar [coins] upon quintar. They simply leave it in the hands of a trustworthy white man until the one to whom it is due takes it." Persons suspected of wrongdoing were subject to the poison ordeal. The innocent was applauded and the guilty punished (Levtzion and Hopkins, 1981, p. 217).

The smaller African polities had no standing armies and waged war only when the men had completely taken in the harvest. In contrast, an aggressive ruler such as Shaka of the Zulus used his society's age-set/age-grade system to build a standing army as a vehicle for conquest. Ancient rulers in Egypt and the Sudan used standing armies not only to unify the valley of the Nile, but to wage war against the ancient Libyans and Assyrians. Hannibal took his elephants across France and the Alps to wage war on Rome, and in revenge the Romans destroyed Carthage in what is now Tunisia. Then when Arab armies conquered Egypt and their converts waged war in the western Sudan, they found that the king of Ghana could put an army of 200,000 soldiers in the field, including 40,000 archers and cavalry. West African soldiers served in the Muslim armies that conquered Spain and governed it until the Reconquista ended their rule.

Religion

Beliefs in the supernatural are often the oldest aspects of human cultures. Therefore, it is not surprising that certain African beliefs were continent-wide. And while God and other deities were ready references to most Africans, the conduct and fate of human beings appeared to remain the center of their religious concerns. In this context it is not surprising that for one critic, religion is a language that "allows humans to insert themselves into intimate relationships with the universe" (Mudimbe, 1991, p. 9). Myths featuring a creator-god, who lived in the sky and was often personified as the sun, the earth, the moon, and all things that ever lived and will live, were almost universal throughout Africa. The Re/Osiris/Isis/Horus mythic complex of the Nile shares many features with Amma among the Dogon, Mangala among the Mande, Oludarame/Olorum (who came down to earth in an ark) among the Yoruba, Winnam/Naba Zid Winde among the Mossi, and Nyame among the Akan—all creator-gods associated with the sky and the sun. In the larger state societies, important rulers such as the pharaohs and Yoruba/Nago kings such as Sango were deified. Also participating in aspects of the divine were deities responsible for death, dealing such diseases as smallpox. Other tutelary deities included the serpent and religious referents in bori, mammy water, orisha, vodun, and other possession cults through which spirits and humans expressed their will.

The Mande creation story tells how Mangala, the creator, made "the egg of the world" in which were pairs of seeds and pairs of twins, prototypes of future people. One male twin, Pembe, desiring to dominate creation, erupted from the egg, tearing away a piece of his placenta as he plunged through empty space. That piece of placenta became the dry, barren, and polluted earth, but Pembe could not fructify it, and so he returned to the sky for seeds. Meanwhile, Mangala, who had created the sun, sacrificed another male twin, Faro, to account for Pembe's sin. Mangala cut Faro's body into sixty pieces and scattered them through space until they fell to earth, becoming vegetation, symbols of resurrection. Faro was restored to heaven in human form, and Mangala, using part of his placenta, created an ark in which he sent eight ancestral pairs of human beings, plants, and animals down to earth. These human ancestors, like Faro himself, had a common vital force (soul) and complementary male and female spiritual forces. Emerging from the ark, the ancestors watched for the first time the rising of the sun (Dieterlen, 1957, pp. 124–138).

As the Mande myth indicates, human beings possessed elements of the divine, such as souls, the "breath of life," and "shadows," whose fates and needs could be divined and propitiated when deemed necessary. Belief that one's fate or destiny could be known and influenced was found in the cult of Fa among the Yoruba/Nago and the notion of *chi* (personality characteristics) in Igbo country. There was often the need for people to protect themselves against evildoers (sorcerers), who were believed capable of bringing harm and even death by magical means. There were priests who also knew how to acquire the power to heal—aided, of course, by the more powerful ancestors.

Ancestor veneration was an important feature in most African religions. The ancestors provided a chain across generations, often warning their descendants through dreams or divination that the illnesses, misfortunes, and infertility being experienced were punishments for sins that had to be propitiated. By insisting upon moral rectitude among their descendants, and insisting that only sacrifices to them would bring human happiness, African ancestors could be said to have attempted to cheat death by remaining in the lives of the living. Among the West African Igbo the ancestors were represented as masked figures who came from the land of the dead to preside at court cases of living people. Here, as in many other societies throughout Africa, people believed in forms of reincarnation in which ancestors were reborn. With their emphasis on living human beings, Africans attached less significance to the notion of the land of the dead, or of heaven and hell.

Those external religions that came into Africa—such as early Christianity in ancient Egypt, North Africa, and Ethiopia—usually adapted to local conditions. Monophysite Christianity in Egypt, Ethiopia, and the Sudan successfully resisted pressure from Rome and Byzantium and indeed attempted to impose its doctrines on external Christians. Evangelical and militant Islam failed to dislodge Egyptian Coptic Christianity, but eliminated the churches in North Africa and eventually those in the Sudan. Through the *jihad* (holy war) and peaceful merchants, Islam gained many adherents in North, West, and East Africa, but not in central or southern regions. Islam, too, adapted to the realities of Africa, and its many practices and beliefs were modified throughout the continent. A number of African rulers in the Sudan used the jihad to enlarge their realm and to challenge local traditional beliefs. In some cases, rulers did not adopt Islam since they needed the legitimacy of traditional religion, but they permitted nonruling royals to do so. In East Africa, Islam added another dimension to the Swahili culture, which was an early synthesis of African and Arab cultures.

Sciences and Arts

Ancient Africans probably made the first tools used by human beings, the so-called *eoliths* or *dawn stones,* and these were progressively modified as Africans and their neighbors entered the Copper Age, the Bronze Age, and finally the Iron Age. Along with inventing tools for food production and implements for warfare, early populations in the various river valleys learned about seed selection, and developed complex forms of irrigation that depended upon the invention and use of mathematics for measuring fields and astronomical tables that charted the course of heavenly bodies. Mathematics was important to the architecture used in the building of pyramids, palaces, and cities in the Sudan and Egypt. Some of these inventions remained valid for thousands of years, and undoubtedly diffused and adapted themselves to local cultural traditions throughout Africa and beyond. Mud brick pyramids among the pastoral Nuer people of the Upper Nile come to mind, and the elaboration of an imposing acropolis in Zimbabwe, based on the cattle kraal, is another example of that type of development. Pastoral and agricultural peoples throughout the continent, such as the Fulani and Dogon, had calendars based on the movements of such configurations of stars as the Pleiades cluster to know when to begin transhumance cycles in search of pastures, and when to plant certain crops. No doubt, the need of evolving states for correct data stimulated the evolution of symbolic writing systems that led to the development of hieroglyphic and its more common version, hieratic. These systems recorded the deeds of royalty on temples and pyramids, as well as hymns of praise to them and to gods in several books of the dead. The need to embalm the dead led inexorably to the knowledge of anatomy and medicines, and the practice of autopsies to determine the causes of death influenced religious beliefs.

The relationship between these aspects of African cultures can be seen in a description of ancient Ghana. The king's town was said to be a complex of domed buildings, groves, and thickets in which he lived surrounded by priests of the traditional cult, who cared for royal graves decorated with statues. Only the king and his heir could wear sewn clothes (the others dressed in flowing robes), and the monarch wore strands of necklaces and bracelets. He also wore a high cap decorated with gold and wrapped in a turban of fine cotton.

What has been glossed as "art"—in the form of jewelry, statues, carvings, or masks—was well developed, whether used for funerary or other religious purposes, for secular functions, or for both. There is evidence that prehistoric Africans and their descendants transformed their natural bodily characteristics (for example, by creating hairstyles) and used various forms of painting and decoration, as if to move beyond the realm of the "natural" to the domain of the "cultural." The so-called African rock art, consisting of engravings on rocky surfaces both outside and within caves found in the Saharan region of North Africa, the Libyan desert, the Nile Valley, the Sudan, West and Central Africa, and East and South Africa, dates to the sixth millennium BCE, and may be related to comparable examples in Spain and southern France. Whether in the Tassili region of the Sahara or in Botswana and Namibia, the art depicts the activities of everyday life, grooming and decorating the body, walking, running, dancing, hunting, feasting, fighting, and worshiping.

Much of African art is symbolic, with those aspects of the body involving fertility or power highlighted, whereas other parts of the body are not highlighted. Even in areas with elaborate naturalistic statues, such as Egypt, Ethiopia, the Sudan, and Nigeria, symbolic forms are often included. Egyptian art, with its mixture of anthropomorphic and zoomorphic characteristics, is well known; less well known are the terra-cotta Nok art figures from northern Nigeria, dating from 900 BCE or earlier, which may have been the prototype for the naturalistic bronze portrait heads of kings and queens of Benin and of the early Portuguese travelers in the region. The art and architectural complex of ancient Zimbabwe suggests not only a heroic period, but also provided an artistic pattern for building work, implements, and decoration throughout southern Africa. The stelae of Egypt, Aksum, and the Sudan provided dynastic histories in artistic form, and recorded totemic relations between humans and the natural and supernatural worlds. Articles used by crafts producers, such as whorls and spindles, were themselves often carved; domestic articles such as calabashes, water bags, pots, and spoons and other utensils were often decorated. Women obtained pot covers on which were carved symbols representing unacceptable behavior; they used these to cover dishes of food, which they brought to their husbands to signal displeasure of their spouses' conduct.

The word—language itself—was the basis of elaborate oral traditions in African societies. Incantations, oaths, warnings, edicts, epics, and praises affected the lives of African peoples. Used for didactic reasons in theater, legends, myths, poetry (especially among the Swahili), riddles, parables, and proverbs were common. Fourteenth-century travelers in the Niger area recorded the presence of "poets" exhorting the monarch to rule well: "This bambi [throne] on which you are sitting was sat upon by such-and-such a king, and his good deeds were so-and-so; so you do good deeds which will be remembered after you." The traveler was specifically informed that this practice "was already old before Islam, and they had continued this to this day" (Levtzion and Hopkins, 1981, p. 296).

Africans possessed an impressive number of musical genres, musical instruments, songs, and dances for secular as well as religious purposes. The simple musical bow of the foragers evolved into such chordophones (stringed instruments) as the four-stringed fiddle of the Congos, the chora in Mali, and, of course, the harp in the Nile Valley. The idiophones ranged from simple sticks, rattles, and large varieties of bells to veritable xylophone orchestras among the Chopi in the Congo/Zimbabwe region to the West African region. The membranophones, or varieties of drums, such as the "hourglass," pot, gourd, and frame drums, often formed part of orchestras with the xylophones, or were used to send messages. Adding to this musical mélange were aerophones, consisting of trumpets, horns, flutes, whistles, and the like. These instruments were often used together in intricate musical rhythms.

African songs ranged from lullabies, children's didactic songs, initiation chants, love melodies, and work songs to praise songs, religious chants, and funeral dirges. Here again, the songs were either performed by themselves or accompanied by musical instruments. Many melodies emphasized "call and response"—that is, one person sang and the chorus responded—but Africans often utilized two-, three-, or four-part harmonies. In most cases, however, songs were sung as people danced. The type of dances varied within societies and across regional or cultural areas. Again, dances also varied with the social function involved, from dances of welcome to the stately and slow dances of royalty. And while most African dances were collective, soloists often broke ranks to highlight individual skills, then rejoining the group's intricate choreography. Finally, music and masked dancers often contributed to theatrical festivals and communal rituals.

Given the reasons for which Africans were uprooted and transported to the Americas, not all aspects of their cultures were either encouraged or permitted to survive. What is surprising, however, is just how much of this traditional background was reinterpreted and/or syncretized with elements of other cultural systems to act as guides for the behavior of African Americans over the centuries. What is also surprising is the way aspects of the African background often remained quiescent and unrecognized, only to emerge when necessary for survival. Lastly, many contemporary African Americans are going to Africa and seeking forms of culture that they are bringing back to America, and implanting as part of a continuum between the past and the present. This is often quite successful, since for human beings of every time and place, whatever happened before they were born—regardless of how long ago—becomes part of their cultural background to be used as a guide to action.

The cataclysmic changes that occurred during and after World War II are still transforming the various people and cultures of Africa, creating new political systems, changing the names of old societies and often reinventing past political systems. While initially Africans outside of Africa, commonly known as "Africans in the diaspora," played a dominant role in what was know as the Pan-African movement, they have yielded sway to Africans living in Africa, many of whom have studied outside of Africa.

Today, almost all the traditional societies of Africa are independent, and new nation states are struggling to survive. The results have been conflict and increasing transformation of African customs. This is exemplified in the struggles for peace and reconciliation that occurred after the ethic genocide in Rwanda and Burundi. The years of conflict and resulting ethic migrations in the former Zaire, now the Democratic Republic of the Congo, have led to political and social upheaval resulting in the fluctuation of names and political realties. The constant renaming of African societies often creates problems for persons attempting to understand the peoples and cultures of this exciting continent. Also to be noted is that although increasingly affected by the outside world, African institutions are being transformed and in some cases are attempting to reinvent older institutions and political organizations. Surprisingly, one of the more dynamic regions of change in Africa has been South Africa, a region long believed to be the "new homeland" of European settlers. This area is becoming the center of hope for millennial change directed by Africans in the interests of all Africa and other parts of the world.

Also of importance is the emergence of African leaders in the global system. Among these is Kofi Annan, who became secretary-general of the United Nations in 1997. In the United States such persons of African descent as Colin Powell and Condoleezza Rice have served as secretary of state. Perhaps most significant of all is that there are now in the United States more persons who were born in Africa and migrated the United States than the millions of Africans who were enslaved and became part of American society. The history of these new American immigrants will no doubt greatly influence the nature of the future United States and the world.

Bibliography

Al-Sadi. *African Civilizations, Precolonial Cities, and States in Tropical Africa: An Archaeological Perspective.* Translated by Graham Connah. New York and Cambridge, UK: Cambridge University Press, 1987.

Angier, Natalie. "New Debate Over Humankind's Ancestress: Biologists Insist All Human Lineages Track Back to a Woman in Africa 200,000 Years Ago." *New York Times* (October 1, 1991): C1.

Beale, Howard K. *Theodore Roosevelt and the Rise of America to World Power.* Baltimore, Md.: Johns Hopkins University Press, 1956.

Cullen, Countee. *On These I Stand: An Anthology of the Best Poems of Countee Cullen.* New York: Harper, 1947.

Davidson, Basil. *African Civilization Revisited: From Antiquity to Modern Times.* Trenton, N.J.: Africa World Press, 1991.

Dieterlen, Germaine. "The Mande Creation Myth." *Africa* 17, no. 2 (1957): 124–138.

Diop, Cheikh Anta. *The African Origin of Civilization: Myth or Reality.* Translated by Mercer Cook. New York: L. Hill, 1974.

Drake, St. Clair, and Horace R. Cayton. *Black Metropolis: A Study of Negro Life in a Northern City,* rev. ed. New York: Harcourt, 1970.

Evans-Pritchard, E. E. *The Nuer: A Description of the Modes of Livelihood and Political Institutions of a Nilotic People.* Oxford: Clarendon, 1940.

Evans-Pritchard, E. E. *The Azande: History and Political Institutions.* Oxford: Clarendon, 1971.

Fortes, Meyer. *The Dynamics of Clanship Among the Tallensi.* London: Oxford University Press, 1945.

Herskovits, Melville J. *Man and His Works: The Science of Cultural Anthropology.* New York: Knopf, 1948.

Leo Africanus. *Description de l'Afrique.* Vol. 2. Translated by A. Épaulard, Th. Monod, H. Lhote, and R. Mauny. Paris: Adrien-Maisonneuve, 1956.

Levtzion, N., and J. F. P. Hopkins, eds. *Corpus of Early Arabic Sources for West African History.* Translated by J. F. P. Hopkins. New York and Cambridge, UK: Cambridge University Press, 1981.

Middleton, John, and David Tait, eds. *Tribes Without Rulers: Studies in African Segmentary Systems.* London: Routledge, 1958.

Mokhtar, G., and Joseph K. Zerba, eds. *General History of Africa.* Vols. 1 and 2. London: Heinemann, 1981.

Mudimbe, V. Y. *Parables and Fables: Exegesis, Textuality, and Politics in Central Africa.* Madison: University of Wisconsin Press, 1991.

Posnansky, M. "Introduction to the Later Prehistory of Sub-Saharan Africa." In *General History of Africa*, vol. 1., edited by G. Mokhtar and Joseph K. Zerba. London: Heinemann, 1981.

Skinner, Elliott P. *The Mossi of the Upper Volta: The Political Development of a Sudanese People.* Stanford, Calif.: Stanford University Press, 1964.

Southall, Aidan W. *Alur Society: A Study in Processes and Types of Domination.* Cambridge, UK: W. Heffer, 1956.

Wai Andah, B. "West Africa before the Seventh Century." In *General History of Africa*, vol. 2, edited by G. Mokhtar and Joseph K. Zerba. London: Heinemann, 1981.

ELLIOTT P. SKINNER
Updated by author 2005

List of Articles

Articles included in the second edition of the Encyclopedia are listed below in alphabetic order. First appearance in the set is indicated by "First edition" (1996), "Supplement" (2001), or "Second edition" (2005). Changes made for 2005 are noted thereafter. If a significant update was provided by someone other than the publisher or the original author, that person's name appears in the "updated by" line.

G

H

M

O

P

T

U

V

W

Directory of Contributors

Authors are listed below in alphabetic order followed by their affiliations and the article(s) they contributed. Articles reprinted from the first edition (1996) or from the supplement (2001) are indicated by dates in parentheses. The year 2005 indicates a new article or significant update written for the second edition. Current affiliations are offered whenever possible.

Martha Abreu
Universidade Federal Fluminense, Niterói, Rio de Janeiro, Brazil
History Department
CARNEIRO, EDISON (2005)
DAS NEVES, EDUARDO (2005)

Patricia Acerbi
University of Maryland
Department of History
REBOUÇAS, ANDRÉ (2005)

Marian Aguiar
Carnegie Mellon University
English Department
NATIONAL FEDERATION OF AFRO-AMERICAN WOMEN (1996)
THIRD WORLD WOMEN'S ALLIANCE (1996)

Siraj Ahmed
Columbia University
ALEXANDER, SADIE TANNER MOSSELL (1996)
BURKE, YVONNE BRATHWAITE (1996)
CARNEY, WILLIAM H. (1996)
COLEMAN, BESSIE (1996)
FARD, WALLACE D. (1996)
MOTLEY, CONSTANCE BAKER (1996)
MURRAY, PAULI (1996)
NORTH CAROLINA MUTUAL LIFE INSURANCE COMPANY (1996)
ROBESON, ESLANDA (1996)
SPAULDING, CHARLES CLINTON (1996)
WALKER, A'LELIA (1996)

Funso Aiyejina
The University of the West Indies at St. Augustine, Trinidad
Department of Liberal Arts
LOVELACE, EARL (2005)

Philip N. Alexander
Massachusetts Institute of Technology
Program in Writing and Humanistic Studies
CALLOWAY, NATHANIEL (1996)
PATENTS AND INVENTIONS (1996)
TROPICAL DISEASES (1996)

Omar H. Ali
New York, New York
COLORED FARMERS ALLIANCE (2001)
MFUME, KWEISI (2005)

Nicole N. Aljoe
University of Utah
Department of English
HART SISTERS OF ANTIGUA (2005)
PRINCE, MARY (2005)
SEACOLE, MARY (2005)
SLAVE NARRATIVES OF THE CARIBBEAN AND LATIN AMERICA (2005)

Anita L. Allen
University of Pennsylvania
School of Law
AFFIRMATIVE ACTION (2005)

Zita Allen
New York, New York
ALLEN, DEBBIE (1996)
HOLDER, GEOFFREY (1996)

Mike Alleyne
Middle Tennessee State University
Department of Recording Industry
DANCEHALL (2005)

Derek M. Alphran
University of the District of Columbia
David A. Clarke School of Law
JACKSON, MAYNARD HOLBROOK, JR. (2005)

Carmelo Álvarez
Chicago, Illinois
PENTECOSTALISM IN LATIN AMERICA AND THE CARIBBEAN (2005)

Jervis Anderson
Deceased
RANDOLPH, ASA PHILIP (1996)

William L. Andrews
University of North Carolina at Chapel Hill
Department of English
AUTOBIOGRAPHY, U.S. (1996)
SLAVE NARRATIVES (1996)

Stephen W. Angell
Earlham School of Religion
Quaker Studies
PROTESTANTISM IN THE AMERICAS (2005)
TURNER, HENRY MCNEAL (1996)

René Antrop-González
University of Wisconsin–Milwaukee
Department of Curriculum and Instruction
ALBIZU CAMPOS, PEDRO (2005)

Eric Arnesen
University of Illinois at Chicago
Departments of African-American Studies and History
LABOR AND LABOR UNIONS (1996)

A. James Arnold
University of Virginia
Department of French
CÉSAIRE, AIMÉ (2005)

Melvin S. Arrington Jr.
University of Mississippi
Department of Modern Languages
DE JESUS, CAROLINA MARIA (2005)

Elizabeth Fortson Arroyo
Carleton College
EVERS, MEDGAR (1996)
JAMES, DANIEL "CHAPPIE" (1996)
PORT ROYAL EXPERIMENT (1996)
SMALLS, ROBERT (1996)

Arthur R. Ashe Jr.
Deceased
AMERICAN TENNIS ASSOCIATION (1996)
GIBSON, ALTHEA (1996)
TENNIS (1996)

Allan D. Austin
Springfield College
MUSLIMS IN THE AMERICAS (2005)
WEBB, FRANK J. (1996)

Michael Awkward
Emory University
Department of English
WALKER, ALICE (1996)

Christine Ayorinde
Oxford, England
LUPERÓN, GREGORIO (2005)
YORUBA RELIGION AND CULTURE IN THE AMERICAS (2005)

R. Reid Badger
University of Alabama
EUROPE, JAMES REESE (1996)

Hans A. Baer
University of Arkansas
SPIRITUAL CHURCH MOVEMENT (1996)

Jane Sung-ee Bai
Columbia University
HOPKINS, PAULINE ELIZABETH (1996)

William J. Baker
University of Maine
Department of History
ABDUL-JABBAR, KAREEM (1996)
BASKETBALL (1996)
OWENS, JESSE (1996)

Lewis V. Baldwin
Vanderbilt University
Religious Studies Department
AFRICAN UNION METHODISM (1996)

Tomiko C. Ballantyne-Nisbett
Princeton University
Department of History
FRANCISCO, SLINGER "THE MIGHTY SPARROW" (2005)

Gretchen G. Bank
Perkins Eastman Architects
ARCHITECTURE (1996)

James A. Banks
University of Washington
Center for Multicultural Education
BLACK STUDIES (1996)

Manley Elliott Banks II
Virginia Commonwealth University
L. Douglas Wilder School of Government and Public Affairs
BARRY, MARION (2005)
WILDER, LAWRENCE DOUGLAS (2005)

Cameron Bardrick
Columbia University
YERBY, FRANK (1996)

William Barlow
Howard University
RADIO (1996)

Robert K. Barney
University of Western Ontario
School of Kinesiology, International Centre for Olympic Studies
OLYMPIANS (2005)

V. Eudine Barriteau
The University of the West Indies at Cave Hill, Barbados
Centre for Gender and Development Studies
CHARLES, EUGENIA (2005)

John Baugh
Stanford University
School of Education
LABOV, WILLIAM (2005)

Dalea M. Bean
The University of the West Indies at Mona, Jamaica
Department of History and Archaeology
BURKE, RUDOLPH AUGUSTUS (2005)
NETHERSOLE, NOEL NEWTON (2005)

Herman Beavers
University of Pennsylvania
Department of English
WIDEMAN, JOHN EDGAR (1996)

Monique Bedasse-Samuda
University of Miami
REGGAE AESTHETICS (2005)

Silvio A. Bedini
Smithsonian Institution
Historian Emeritus
BANNEKER, BENJAMIN (1996)

Robert A. Bellinger
Suffolk University
Department of History
HASTIE, WILLIAM HENRY (1996)

Neal Benezra
San Francisco Museum of Modern Art
PURYEAR, MARTIN (1996)

Sholomo Ben Levy
Beth Elohim Hebrew Congregation
Saint Albans, New York
JUDAISM (1996)

Dionne Bennett
Loyola Marymount University
African American Studies Department
DOCUMENTARY FILM (2005)
URBAN CINEMA (2005)

Ira Berger
Brooklyn, New York
APOLLO THEATER (1996)

Edward A. Berlin
Miller Place, New York
JOPLIN, SCOTT (1996)
RAGTIME (1996)

Ira Berlin
Miller Place, New York
FREE BLACKS, 1619–1860 (1996)

Lee Bernstein
State University of New York at New Paltz
Department of History
CRIMINAL JUSTICE SYSTEM (2005)

Esme Bhan
Annapolis, Maryland
HOWARD UNIVERSITY (1996)

Andrew Bienen
Columbia University
JOHN HENRY (1996)

Kenneth M. Bilby
Smithsonian Institution
Department of Anthropology
OBEAH (2005)

Rodger C. Birt
San Francisco State University
Humanities Department
VANDERZEE, JAMES (1996)

Allison Blakely
Boston University
History Department and African American Studies
GRAVENBERCH, ADOLF FREDERIK (2005)
HUISWOUD, OTTO (2005)
RIER, CARL P. (2005)

Michael L. Blakey
College of William and Mary
Department of Anthropology
AFRICAN BURIAL GROUND PROJECT (2005)

David W. Blight
Yale University
Department of History
EMANCIPATION IN THE UNITED STATES (1996)

Sean Bloch
Las Cruces, New Mexico
CHRISTOPHE, HENRI (2005)
DESSALINES, JEAN-JACQUES (2005)
DUVALIER, FRANÇOIS (2005)
ESTIMÉ, DUMARSAIS (2005)

Lawrence D. Bobo
Stanford University
Department of Sociology
SOCIOLOGY (2005)

Peter Bodo
Southern Connecticut State University
Department of Economics and Finance
ASHE, ARTHUR (1996)

Anthony Bogues
Brown University
Africana Studies Department
MARLEY, BOB (2005)
REGGAE (2005)

Machel Bogues
London, England
REGGAE (2005)

O. Nigel Bolland
Colgate University
Department of Sociology & Anthropology
PRICE, GEORGE (2005)

William Boone
Temple University
Doctoral candidate, Africana Studies
HIP-HOP (2005)

Grissel Bordoni-Seijo
Columbia University
SANTERÍA (1996)

Joseph Boskin
Boston University
Department of History, Emeritus
REPRESENTATIONS OF BLACKNESS IN THE UNITED STATES (2005)

Joshua Botkin
University of Michigan
ABBOTT, ROBERT SENGSTACKE (1996)
CHICAGO DEFENDER (1996)

Keisha Bowman
University of Wisconsin–Madison
Department of English
POETRY, U.S. (2005)

Horace Clarence Boyer
Amherst, Massachusetts
CLEVELAND, JAMES (1996)
DORSEY, THOMAS A. (1996)
GOSPEL MUSIC (1996)
JACKSON, MAHALIA (1996)

James Bradley
Brooklyn, New York
DINKINS, DAVID (1996)
HARRIS, PATRICIA ROBERTS (1996)
O'LEARY, HAZEL ROLLINS (1996)

Carol Brennan
Freelance writer
Detroit, Michigan
TYSON, MIKE (2005)

Bridget Brereton
The University of the West Indies at St. Augustine, Trinidad
Department of History
AMELIORATION (2005)
BELMANNA RIOTS (2005)
GOVEIA, ELSA V. (2005)

Isolde Brielmaier
Vassar College
Department of Art
PHOTOGRAPHY, DIASPORIC (2005)

Alejandra Bronfman
University of British Columbia
Department of History
PARTIDO INDEPENDIENTE DE COLOR (2005)

LeRonn Brooks
Graduate Center, City University of New York
LIGON, GLENN (2005)
MARSHALL, KERRY JAMES (2005)

Debi Broome
Columbia University
HARRIS, BARBARA CLEMENTINE (1996)
HOLINESS MOVEMENT (1996)
JACKSON, LUTHER PORTER (1996)

VARICK, JAMES (1996)
WILLIAMS, PETER, JR. (1996)

AGGREY BROWN
The University of the West Indies at Mona, Jamaica
Dean, Faculty of Humanities and Education
MEDIA AND IDENTITY IN THE CARIBBEAN (2005)

ALEXANDRA K. BROWN
Florida Atlantic University
Department of History
MALÊ REBELLION (2005)
TAILOR'S REVOLT (2005)

ANTHONY BROWN
University of California, Berkeley
Department of Music
BLAKEY, ART (BUHAINA, ABDULLAH IBN) (1996)
NEWTON, JAMES (1996)
ROACH, MAX (1996)

ERNEST BROWN
Williams College
Department of Music
SUN RA (BLOUNT, HERMAN "SONNY") (1996)

JACQUELINE BROWN
Wilberforce University
WILBERFORCE UNIVERSITY (1996)

KAREN MCCARTHY BROWN
Drew University
Theological School
VOODOO (1996)

RAE LINDA BROWN
University of California, Irvine
Department of Music
BONDS, MARGARET (1996)

ELIZABETH BROWN-GUILLORY
University of Houston
Department of English
BAMBARA, TONI CADE (1996)
CHILDRESS, ALICE (1996)

DICKSON D. BRUCE JR.
University of California, Irvine
Department of History
DIALECT POETRY (1996)
DUNBAR, PAUL LAURENCE (1996)
GRIMKÉ, ANGELINA WELD (1996)
GRIMKÉ, ARCHIBALD HENRY (1996)
GRIMKÉ, CHARLOTTE L. FORTEN (1996)

MATTHEW BUCKLEY
Rutgers University
Department of English
LITERARY MAGAZINES (1996)
MCDANIEL, HATTIE (1996)

MICHAEL A. BUCKNOR
The University of the West Indies at Mona, Jamaica
Department of Literatures in English
CLARKE, AUSTIN (2005)

ROBERT MAXWELL BUDDAN
The University of the West Indies at Mona, Jamaica
Department of Government
HILL, KEN (2005)
LEON, ROSE (2005)
SHEARER, HUGH (2005)
WEST INDIES DEMOCRATIC LABOUR PARTY (2005)
WEST INDIES FEDERAL LABOUR PARTY (2005)

KATHY WHITE BULLOCK
Berea College
Department of Music
CAESAR, SHIRLEY (1996)

A'LELIA PERRY BUNDLES
Alexandria, Virginia
WALKER, MADAM C. J. (1996)

AMY J. BUONO
University of California, Santa Barbara
Department of History
LISBOA, ANTÔNIO FRANCISCO (2005)

THORALD M. BURNHAM
York University
Department of History
CHAMOISEAU, PATRICK (2005)
MAKANDAL, FRANÇOIS (2005)
TOUSSAINT-LOUVERTURE (2005)

NSENGA K. BURTON
University of North Carolina at Charlotte
Department of Communications
POPULAR CULTURE (2005)

KIM D. BUTLER
Rutgers University
Department of Africana Studies
AFRICAN DIASPORA (2005)
BLACK PRESS IN BRAZIL (2005)
FRENTE NEGRA BRASILEIRA (2005)

KEITH E. BYERMAN
Indiana State University
Department of English
JONES, GAYL (1996)

ALEXANDER X. BYRD
Rice University
Department of History
GEORGE, DAVID (2005)

MICHAEL BYRD
Boston, Massachusetts
MEDICAL ASSOCIATIONS (1996)

HEATHER CAINES
Carmanville School Complex
CHILDREN'S LITERATURE (1996)

CARL C. CAMPBELL
The University of the West Indies at Mona, Jamaica
Department of History and Archaeology
EDUCATION IN THE CARIBBEAN (2005)
SHERLOCK, PHILIP (2005)
UNIVERSITY OF THE WEST INDIES (2005)

MARY SCHMIDT CAMPBELL
New York University
Tisch School of Arts
BEARDEN, ROMARE (1996)

CHARLES V. CARNEGIE
Bates College
Department of Anthropology
BAHÁ'Í COMMUNITIES IN THE CARIBBEAN (2005)

ANDRÉ M. CARRINGTON
New York University
AUTOBIOGRAPHY, U.S. (2005)
LESBIANS (2005)

SELWYN H. H. CARRINGTON
Howard University
Department of History
MANNING, PATRICK (2005)
ROBINSON, A. N. R. (2005)
WILLIAMS, ERIC (2005)

CLAYBORNE CARSON
Stanford University
Department of History
BLACK PANTHER PARTY FOR SELF-DEFENSE (1996)
KING, MARTIN LUTHER, JR. (1996)
STUDENT NONVIOLENT COORDINATING COMMITTEE (SNCC) (1996)

Emmett D. Carson
The Minneapolis Foundation
PHILANTHROPY AND FOUNDATIONS (2005)

Dan T. Carter
University of South Carolina
Department of History
SCOTTSBORO CASE (1996)

Judith Casselberry
Yale University
Department of African American Studies
TAYLOR, KOKO (2005)

Richard-Duane S. Chambers
Massachusetts Institute of Technology
ASTRONAUTS (2005)

Camille Z. Charles
University of Pennsylvania
Department of Sociology
SOCIAL PSYCHOLOGY, PSYCHOLOGISTS, AND RACE (2005)

Barbara Chase-Riboud
Paris, France
BAKER, JOSEPHINE (1996)

Amy Chazkel
Queens College, City University of New York
Department of History
TIA CIATA (2005)

R. Johnny Cheltenham
Barbados Privy Council
ADAMS, GRANTLEY (2005)

Barry Chevannes
The University of the West Indies at Mona, Jamaica
Department of Sociology, Psychology and Social Work
RASTAFARIANISM (2005)

Yvonne P. Chireau
Princeton University
FOLK RELIGION (1996)

Robert Chrisman
University of Nebraska at Omaha
Department of Black Studies
BLAXPLOITATION FILMS (1996)
LEE, SPIKE (1996)

Barbara T. Christian
Deceased
ANGELOU, MAYA (1996)
JORDAN, JUNE (1996)

George Elliott Clarke
University of Toronto
Department of English
CANADIAN WRITERS IN ENGLISH (2005)

William S. Cole
Stamford, Connecticut
COLTRANE, JOHN (1996)
DAVIS, MILES (1996)
PARKER, CHARLIE (1996)

Lisa Gail Collins
Vassar College
Art Department and Africana Studies Program
SAAR, ALISON (2005)

James H. Cone
Union Theological Seminary
Systematic Theology
LIBERATION THEOLOGY (2005)
MALCOLM X (2005)
THEOLOGY, BLACK (2005)

Michael A. Cooke
University of West Alabama
Department of History
MISSISSIPPI FREEDOM DEMOCRATIC PARTY (1996)

Bridget R. Cooks
Santa Clara University
Department of Art and Art History
MUSEUMS (2005)

Wayne F. Cooper
Springvale, Maine
MCKAY, CLAUDE (1996)

David L. Covin
California State University Sacramento
Ethnic Studies Department
MOVIMENTO NEGRO UNIFICADO (2005)

Edward L. Cox
Rice University
Department of History
BLAIZE, HERBERT (2005)
GAIRY, ERIC (2005)

Michael Craton
University of Waterloo
History Department
MAROON SOCIETIES IN THE CARIBBEAN (2005)

Thomas Cripps
Morgan State University
FILM IN THE UNITED STATES (1996)

George P. Cunningham
Brooklyn College, City University of New York
Department of Africana Studies
JOHNSON, JAMES WELDON (1996)
NEW NEGRO (1996)

Linda Dahl
Freelance writer
Brewster, New York
JAZZ SINGERS (2005)

David D. Daniels III
McCormick Theological Seminary
PENTECOSTALISM IN NORTH AMERICA (1996)

Dekker Dare
New York, New York
BRATHWAITE, EDWARD KAMAU (1996)
KILLENS, JOHN OLIVER (1996)
SANCHEZ, SONIA (2005)

William A. Darity Jr.
University of North Carolina at Chapel Hill
Department of Economics
ECONOMIC CONDITION, U.S. (2005)
HARRIS, ABRAM LINCOLN, JR. (2005)
REPARATIONS (2005)

J. Michael Dash
New York University
Department of Africana Studies
GLISSANT, EDOUARD (2005)
LITERATURE OF HAITI (2005)

Jannette L. Dates
Howard University
The John H. Johnson School of Communications
COSBY, BILL (1996)

Jerry Dávila
University of North Carolina at Charlotte
Department of History
RACE AND EDUCATION IN BRAZIL (2005)

Darién J. Davis
Middlebury College
Department of History
FILM IN LATIN AMERICA AND THE CARIBBEAN (2005)
REVOLTA DA CHIBATA (2005)

Thadious M. Davis
Vanderbilt University
English Department
LARSEN, NELLA (1996)

Jean D'Costa
Hamilton College
Department of English
MAIS, ROGER (2005)
WILLIAMS, FRANCIS (2005)

Charles E. DeBose
California State University Hayward
Department of English
BAILEY, BERYL LOFTMAN (2005)

Jeffrey Louis Decker
University of California, Los Angeles
Department of English
MADHUBUTI, HAKI R. (LEE, DON L.) (1996)

Thomas F. DeFrantz
Massachusetts Institute of Technology
Music and Theater Arts Section
AILEY, ALVIN (2005)
BALLET (2005)
BREAKDANCING (2005)
DANCE THEATER OF HARLEM (1996)
DOVE, ULYSSES (1996)
JAMISON, JUDITH (2005)
MITCHELL, ARTHUR (2005)

James de Jongh
City College of New York of the City University of New York
English Department
FISHER, RUDOLPH (1996)
WALCOTT, DEREK ALTON (2005)

Dominique-René de Lerma
Lawrence University
Conservatory of Music
ANDERSON, MARIAN (1996)
NORMAN, JESSYE (1996)
OPERA (1996)
PRICE, MARY VIOLET LEONTYNE (1996)

Fernando Delgado
Minnesota State University, Mankato
College of Graduate Studies and Research
SOCCER (2005)

Jane M. DeLuca
Brooklyn, New York
SICKLE-CELL DISEASE (1996)

Gina Dent
University of California, Santa Cruz
Feminist Studies, History of Consciousness, and Legal Studies
DOVE, RITA (1996)
KINCAID, JAMAICA (1996)

T. J. Desch-Obi
Baruch College, City University of New York
Department of History
CAPOEIRA (2005)

Scott DeVeaux
University of Virginia
Department of Music
HANCOCK, HERBIE (1996)
MODERN JAZZ QUARTET (1996)
MONK, THELONIOUS SPHERE (1996)

Amina Dickerson
National Museum of African Art
MUSEUMS (1996)

Dennis C. Dickerson
Vanderbilt University
History Department
AFRICAN METHODIST EPISCOPAL CHURCH (1996)
MAYS, BENJAMIN E. (1996)

Kenya Dilday
New York, New York
BROWN, CLAUDE (1996)
ROLLE, ESTHER (1996)
SCOTT, HAZEL (1996)
WINFREY, OPRAH (1996)

Quinton H. Dixie
Union Theological Seminary
NOBLE DREW ALI (1996)
PAN-AFRICAN ORTHODOX CHURCH (THE SHRINE OF THE BLACK MADONNA) (1996)

Bill Dixon
Bennington College
COLEMAN, ORNETTE (1996)

Paul B. Dixon
Purdue University
Department of Foreign Languages and Literatures
MACHADO DE ASSIS, JOAQUIM MARIA (2005)

Jualynne Dodson
Schomburg Center for Research in Black Culture
New York Public Library
COPPIN, FANNY JACKSON (1996)

Max Dorsinville
McGill University
Department of English
CANADIAN WRITERS IN FRENCH (2005)

Richard Dozier
Florida A&M University
School of Architecture
ARCHITECTURE (1996)

David C. Driskell
University of Maryland
Center for the Study of the African Diaspora
TANNER, HENRY OSSAWA (1996)

Gwendolyn DuBois Shaw
Harvard University
Department of History of Art and Architecture
WALKER, KARA (2005)

James Alexander Dun
Princeton University
History Department
HAITIAN REVOLUTION, AMERICAN REACTION TO THE (2005)

Garrett Albert Duncan
Washington University in St. Louis
African and African American Studies Program
EDUCATION IN THE UNITED STATES (2005)
IDENTITY AND RACE IN THE UNITED STATES (2005)
OGBU, JOHN (2005)
SCIENCE (2005)

Stefanie Dunning
Miami University of Ohio
Department of English
LITERATURE OF THE UNITED STATES (2005)

Jill Dupont
University of North Texas
Department of History
JOHNSON, EARVIN "MAGIC" (2005)

Margaret L. Dwight–Barrett
North Carolina Agricultural and Technical State University
Department of History
WELLS-BARNETT, IDA B. (1996)

Mervyn Dymally
California State Assembly
POLITICS IN THE UNITED STATES (1996)

Michael Eric Dyson
University of Pennsylvania
Department of Religious Studies
JACKSON, JESSE (1996)

Doris Dziwas
Berlin, Germany
HAMMON, BRITON (1996)
MARRANT, JOHN (1996)

Gerald L. Early
Washington University in St. Louis
Department of Arts & Sciences
ALI, MUHAMMAD (1996)
BOXING (1996)
CULLEN, COUNTEE (1996)
LOUIS, JOE (1996)

George E. Eaton
York University
School of Analytic Studies and Information Technology
BUSTAMANTE, ALEXANDER (2005)

Brent Edwards
Rensselaer Polytechnic Institute
GRIGGS, SUTTON ELBERT (1996)

Lillie Johnson Edwards
Drew University
Department of History
EPISCOPALIANS (1996)

Peter Eisenstadt
Albany, New York
RHYTHM AND BLUES (1996)

Dena J. Epstein
Chicago, Illinois
FOLK MUSIC (1996)
SPIRITUALS (1996)

Alana J. Erickson
Columbia University
BRIMMER, ANDREW FELTON (1996)
COUNCIL ON AFRICAN AFFAIRS (1996)
LEAGUE OF REVOLUTIONARY BLACK WORKERS (1996)
NASH, WILLIAM BEVERLY (1996)
RAPIER, JAMES THOMAS (1996)
RED SUMMER (1996)
TURNER, BENJAMIN STERLING (1996)
UNITED STATES COMMISSION ON CIVIL RIGHTS (1996)
WASHINGTON, MARGARET MURRAY (1996)

Lise Esdaile
Graduate Center, City University of New York
Department of English
SORORITIES, U.S. (2005)

Demetrius L. Eudell
Wesleyan University
History and African American Studies
WYNTER, SYLVIA (2005)

Shelly Eversley
Baruch College, City University of New York
Department of English
LITERARY CRITICISM, U.S. (2005)

Geneviève Fabre
Université de la Sorbonne Nouvelle, Paris
American Studies
FESTIVALS, U.S. (1996)

Michel Fabre
Université de la Sorbonne Nouvelle, Paris
Research Center in African American Studies
BRADLEY, DAVID (1996)
DIXON, MELVIN (1996)
DUNBAR-NELSON, ALICE (1996)
PINCHBACK, P. B. S. (1996)
WRIGHT, RICHARD (1996)

Crystal N. Feimster
Boston College
Department of History
PAINTER, NELL IRVIN (2005)

Tamara L. Felton
Richmond, Virginia
SAAR, BETYE IRENE (1996)

Gerard Fergerson
New York University
Robert F. Wagner Graduate School of Public Service
RACE, SCIENTIFIC THEORIES OF (1996)

Ada Ferrer
New York University
Department of History
BANDERA, QUINTÍN (2005)
MONCADA, GUILLERMO (2005)

Henry J. Ferry
Howard University
Department of Divinity
GRIMKÉ, FRANCIS JAMES (1996)

Ângela Figueiredo
Salvador, Brazil
HAIR AND BEAUTY CULTURE IN BRAZIL (2005)

Paul Finkelman
University of Tulsa
College of Law
BLACK CODES (1996)
BROWN V. BOARD OF EDUCATION OF TOPEKA, KANSAS (1996)
DRED SCOTT V. SANDFORD (1996)
PLESSY V. FERGUSON (1996)
SLAVERY AND THE CONSTITUTION (1996)

Tom Finkelpearl
New York, New York
HAMMONS, DAVID (1996)

Roy E. Finkenbine
University of Detroit Mercy
Department of History
ATTUCKS, CRISPUS (1996)
CHRISTIANA REVOLT OF 1851 (1996)
NAMES CONTROVERSY (1996)
NELL, WILLIAM COOPER (1996)
PAYNE, DANIEL ALEXANDER (1996)

Dawn-Elissa Fischer
University of Florida
LITERACY EDUCATION (2005)

Leroy Fitts
Baltimore, Maryland
BAPTISTS (1996)
CAREY, LOTT (1996)
NATIONAL BAPTIST CONVENTION, U.S.A., INC. (1996)

Michael W. Fitzgerald
Saint Olaf College
Department of History
BUREAU OF REFUGEES, FREEDMEN, AND ABANDONED LANDS (1996)
FIFTEENTH AMENDMENT (1996)
GRANDFATHER CLAUSE (1996)
THIRTEENTH AMENDMENT (1996)

UNION LEAGUE OF AMERICA (1996)

SUZANNE FLANDREAU
Columbia College Chicago
Center for Black Music Research
MUSIC COLLECTIONS, BLACK (2005)

NICOLE R. FLEETWOOD
University of California, Davis
American Studies Program
NEW MEDIA AND DIGITAL CULTURE (2005)

MARVIN E. FLETCHER
Ohio University
Department of History
DAVIS, BENJAMIN O., JR. (1996)

WALTER EARL FLUKER
Morehouse College
Department of Philosophy & Religion
THURMAN, HOWARD (1996)

BARBARA CLARE FOLEY
Rutgers University
Department of English
FEDERAL WRITERS' PROJECT (1996)

ELIZABETH V. FOLEY
Columbia University
GOSSETT, LOUIS, JR. (1996)
PARKS, SUZAN-LORI (1996)
VAN PEEBLES, MELVIN (1996)

ROBERT ELLIOT FOX
Southern Illinois University
Department of English
DELANY, SAMUEL R. (1996)

DONETTE A. FRANCIS
Binghamton University, State University of New York
Department of English
CARIBBEAN/NORTH AMERICAN WRITERS (CONTEMPORARY) (2005)

WIGMOORE WASHINGTON ADOLPHUS FRANCIS
The University of the West Indies at Mona, Jamaica
Department of History and Archaeology
SCHOLES, THEOPHILUS (2005)

JIMMIE LEWIS FRANKLIN
Vanderbilt University
Department of History
COPPIN, LEVI JENKINS (1996)

JOHN HOPE FRANKLIN
Duke University
Department of History
LYNCH, JOHN ROY (1996)
WILLIAMS, GEORGE WASHINGTON (1996)

ADRIAN FRASER
Kingstown, St. Vincent and the Grenadines
MCINTOSH, GEORGE (2005)
MULZAC, HUGH (2005)

CARY FRASER
Pennsylvania State University
Africana Research Center, African-American Studies
CHAGUARAMAS (2005)
HOYTE, DESMOND (2005)

C. GERALD FRASER
New York, New York
BUNCHE, RALPH (1996)

GERTRUDE J. FRASER
New York, New York
MIDWIFERY (1996)

RHONDA FREDERICK
Boston College
English Department
CAREW, JAN (2005)
COLÓN MAN (2005)

HARRIS FRIEDBERG
Wesleyan University
Department of English
JACKSON, JANET (2005)
JACKSON, MICHAEL (2005)
JACKSON FAMILY (2005)

TAMI J. FRIEDMAN
Brock University
Department of History
FORTUNE, T. THOMAS (1996)
GUARDIAN, THE (1996)
HOPE, JOHN (1996)
MESSENGER, THE (1996)
TROTTER, JAMES MONROE (1996)
TROTTER, WILLIAM MONROE (1996)
VOTING RIGHTS ACT OF 1965 (1996)
YOUNG, WHITNEY M., JR. (1996)

WALTER FRIEDMAN
Columbia University
FOURTEENTH AMENDMENT (1996)
INSURANCE COMPANIES (1996)
LIBERATOR, THE (1996)
SANTERÍA (2005)

SABRINA FUCHS
Montclair State University
BRAWLEY, EDWARD MCKNIGHT (1996)
CRAFT, ELLEN AND WILLIAM (1996)
EDELMAN, MARIAN WRIGHT (1996)
FREEMAN, MORGAN (1996)
FULLER, CHARLES (1996)
GLOVER, DANNY (1996)
JONES, JAMES EARL (1996)
LAWRENCE, MARGARET (1996)
PROCTOR, HENRY HUGH (1996)
TYSON, CICELY (1996)

TIMOTHY E. FULOP
King College
Department of Religion and Department of History
ABYSSINIAN BAPTIST CHURCH (1996)
COKER, DANIEL (1996)
PRIMITIVE BAPTISTS (1996)

MICHAEL WADE FUQUAY
Columbia University
Department of History
GRANDMASTER FLASH (SADDLER, JOSEPH) (2001)

JÚNIA FERREIRA FURTADO
Universidade Federal de Minas Gerais
CHICA DA SILVA (2005)

NANCY GAGNIER
Columbia University
JAMES, C. L. R. (1996)

JANE GAINES
Duke University
Department of Literature
MICHEAUX, OSCAR (1996)

VANESSA NORTHINGTON GAMBLE
Tuskegee University
National Center for Bioethics in Research
HOSPITALS IN THE UNITED STATES, BLACK (1996)
NATIONAL HOSPITAL ASSOCIATION (1996)

PHYL GARLAND
New York, New York
JOURNALISM (2005)

REEBEE GAROFALO
University of Massachusetts Boston
College of Public and Community Services
RECORDING INDUSTRY (2005)

David J. Garrow
Emory University
School of Law
KING, MARTIN LUTHER, JR. (1996)
SOUTHERN CHRISTIAN LEADERSHIP CONFERENCE (SCLC) (1996)

Willard B. Gatewood
University of Arkansas
Department of History (Emeritus)
SKIN COLOR (1996)

Kyra D. Gaunt
New York University
Department of Music
SUPREMES, THE (1996)
TEMPTATIONS, THE (1996)
WONDER, STEVIE (MORRIS, STEVLAND) (1996)

John Gennari
University of Vermont
Department of English
JAZZ IN AFRICAN-AMERICAN CULTURE (2005)

Carol V. R. George
Baldwinsville, New York
CONGRESS OF RACIAL EQUALITY (CORE) (1996)
RUSTIN, BAYARD (1996)

Rawle Gibbons
The University of the West Indies at St. Augustine, Trinidad
Center for Creative and Festival Arts
HILL, ERROL (2005)
ORISHA (2005)

Jonathan Gill
Manhattan School of Music
ASSOCIATION FOR THE ADVANCEMENT OF CREATIVE MUSICIANS (1996)
DE PASSE, SUZANNE (1996)
DIDDLEY, BO (MCDANIEL, OTHA ELIAS) (1996)
GILLESPIE, DIZZY (1996)
GORDY, BERRY (1996)
JEFFERSON, BLIND LEMON (1996)
JONES, QUINCY (1996)
LAST POETS (1996)
LEADBELLY (LEDBETTER, HUDSON WILLIAM) (1996)
MUSICAL INSTRUMENTS (1996)
NUMBERS GAMES (1996)
PRIDE, CHARLEY FRANK (1996)
RHYTHM AND BLUES (1996)
SAVOY BALLROOM (1996)
SCOTT, JAMES SYLVESTER (1996)
WALROND, ERIC DERWENT (1996)
ZYDECO (1996)

Carolina Giraldo
Rutgers University
Institute for Health
MORTALITY AND MORBIDITY IN LATIN AMERICA AND THE CARIBBEAN (2005)

Eddie S. Glaude Jr.
Princeton University
Program in African-American Studies and Department of Religion
NATIONALISM IN THE UNITED STATES IN THE NINETEENTH CENTURY (2005)

Piero Gleijeses
Johns Hopkins University
School of Advanced International Studies
DREKE, VÍCTOR (2005)
RISQUET, JORGE (2005)

Jacqueline Goggin
Boston, Massachusetts
ASSOCIATED PUBLISHERS (1996)
ASSOCIATION FOR THE STUDY OF AFRICAN AMERICAN LIFE AND HISTORY (1996)
BLACK HISTORY MONTH/NEGRO HISTORY WEEK (1996)
JOURNAL OF AFRICAN AMERICAN HISTORY, THE (1996)
WOODSON, CARTER G. (1996)

Leonard Goines
New York, New York
JAZZ: OVERVIEW (2005)

Neil Goldstein
Columbia University
SHUTTLESWORTH, FRED L. (1996)

Flávio Gomes
Universidade Federal do Rio de Janeiro
Department of History
NASCIMENTO, ABDIAS DO (2005)
PALMARES (2005)
TRINDADE, SOLANO (2005)

Michael A. Gomez
New York University
Department of History
MIGRATION IN THE AFRICAN DIASPORA (2005)
SLAVE RELIGIONS (2005)

Jennifer A. González
University of California, Santa Cruz
History of Art and Visual Culture Department
WILSON, FRED (2005)

Paul Goodman
Deceased
WALKER, DAVID (1996)

Lewis R. Gordon
Temple University
Department of Philosophy
FANON, FRANTZ (2005)

Dave St. A. Gosse
The University of the West Indies at Mona, Jamaica
Department of History and Archaeology
ALLAN, HAROLD (2005)
JAMAICA LABOUR PARTY (2005)
LIGHBOURNE, ROBERT (2005)

Sandra Y. Govan
University of North Carolina at Charlotte
Department of English
BUTLER, OCTAVIA (1996)

Dale Torston Graden
University of Idaho
Latin American Studies Program
DA SILVA, BENEDITA (2005)

Jessica L. Graham
Cornell University
FREEDOM RIDES (2001)

Maryemma Graham
University of Kansas
English Department
WALKER, MARGARET (1996)

Richard Graham
University of Texas at Austin
Retired
REBOUÇAS, ANTÔNIO PEREIRA (2005)

Joanne Grant
New York, New York
BAKER, ELLA J. (1996)

Norma L. Grant
The University of the West Indies at Mona, Jamaica
Department of Educational Studies
CHILDREN'S LITERATURE (2005)

Dorith Grant-Wisdom
University of Maryland
Department of Government and Politics
INTERNATIONAL RELATIONS OF THE ANGLOPHONE CARIBBEAN (2005)

Obika Gray
University of Wisconsin–Eau Claire
Department of Political Science
PATTERSON, PERCIVAL JAMES "P. J." (2005)
SANGSTER, DONALD (2005)
URBAN POVERTY IN THE CARIBBEAN (2005)

John Graziano
Flushing, New York
BLAKE, EUBIE (1996)

James N. Green
Brown University
Department of History
MADAME SATÃ (DOS SANTOS, JOÃO FRANCISCO) (2005)

Lisa Green
University of Texas at Austin
Department of Linguistics
ENGLISH, AFRICAN-AMERICAN (2005)

Veronica Marie Gregg
Hunter College, City University of New York
Department of Africana and Puerto Rican/Latino Studies
BRODBER, ERNA (2005)

Farah Jasmine Griffin
Columbia University
Department of English and Comparative Literature
BURNETT, CHARLES (1996)
DASH, JULIE (1996)

Betty Kaplan Gubert
Schomburg Center for Research in Black Culture
New York Public Library, retired
ART COLLECTIONS (2005)
HUTSON, JEAN BLACKWELL (2005)
RINGGOLD, FAITH (2005)

Ed Guerrero
New York University
Department of Cinema Studies
POITIER, SIDNEY (1996)

Norris White Gunby Jr.
Elon University
Business Administration Department
HOSPITALS IN THE UNITED STATES, BLACK (2005)
MORTALITY AND MORBIDITY IN THE UNITED STATES (2005)

Grey Gundaker
College of William and Mary
American Studies Program
GARDENS AND YARD ART (2005)

L. Ray Gunn
University of Utah
Department of History
LYNCHING (1996)

E. Leo Gunter
Kingston, Jamaica
CAMPBELL, CLIFFORD CLARENCE (2005)
GLASSPOLE, FLORIZEL (2005)

Frank A. Guridy
University of Texas at Austin
History Department
APONTE, JOSÉ ANTONIO (2005)
CLUB ATENAS (2005)
MACEO, ANTONIO (2005)

Adam Gussow
University of Mississippi
Department of English and Program in Southern Studies
BLUES IN AFRICAN-AMERICAN CULTURE (2005)

Gwendolyn Midlo Hall
Southern University System
SLAVE CODES (2005)

Robert L. Hall
Northeastern University
Department of African American Studies
AMISTAD MUTINY (1996)

Dona Cooper Hamilton
Lehman College, City University of New York
GREAT DEPRESSION AND THE NEW DEAL (1996)

D. Antoinette Handy
Deceased
WILLIAMS, MARY LOU (1996)

Richard C. Hanes
Eugene, Oregon
LOWNDES COUNTY FREEDOM ORGANIZATION (2001)

Rachel E. Harding
Iliff School of Theology
Veterans of Hope Project
CANDOMBLÉ (2005)

Karen Bennett Harmon
Smithsonian Institution
JET (1996)
ROSS, DIANA (1996)

F. Zeal Harris
Los Angeles, California
SMITH, ANNA DEAVERE (2001)

Michael D. Harris
University of North Carolina at Chapel Hill
Department of Art
STOUT, RENEÉ (2005)

Robert L. Harris Jr.
Cornell University
Africana Studies and Research Center
HISTORIANS AND HISTORIOGRAPHY, AFRICAN-AMERICAN (2005)

Wesley L. Harris
Massachusetts Institute of Technology
Department of Aeronautics and Astronautics
ASTRONAUTS (2005)

William J. Harris
Pennsylvania State University
Department of History
REED, ISHMAEL (1996)

Melissa V. Harris-Lacewell
University of Chicago
Department of Political Science
POLITICAL IDEOLOGIES (2005)

Daphne D. Harrison
University of Maryland, Baltimore County
BLUESWOMEN OF THE 1920S AND 1930S (2005)
RAINEY, MA (1996)
SMITH, BESSIE (1996)

Faye V. Harrison
University of Florida
Department of Anthropology
ANTHROPOLOGY AND ANTHROPOLOGISTS (2005)

Robert C. Hayden
University of Massachusetts Boston
College of Public and Community Service
DREW, CHARLES RICHARD (1996)

Michael F. Hembree
Johnson County Community College
Department of History
AFRICAN CIVILIZATION SOCIETY (AFCS) (1996)
ANTEBELLUM CONVENTION MOVEMENT (1996)
BROWN, HENRY "BOX" (1996)
CHRISTIAN RECORDER (1996)
FREDERICK DOUGLASS' PAPER (1996)
FREEDOM'S JOURNAL (1996)
HENSON, JOSIAH (1996)
LANGSTON, JOHN MERCER (1996)
QUARLES, BENJAMIN (1996)
REMOND, CHARLES LENOX (1996)
SMITH, JAMES MCCUNE (1996)
WRIGHT, THEODORE SEDGWICK (1996)

Carol E. Henderson
University of Delaware
Department of English
WHITEHEAD, COLSON (2005)

David Henderson
New York, New York
BERRY, CHUCK (1996)
HENDRIX, JIMI (1996)
PRINCE (NELSON, PRINCE ROGERS) (1996)

Mae G. Henderson
University of North Carolina at Chapel Hill
Department of English
THURMAN, WALLACE (1996)

Marc Adam Hertzman
University of Wisconsin–Madison
Department of History
MUSIC, RELIGION, AND PERCEPTIONS OF CRIME IN EARLY TWENTIETH-CENTURY RIO DE JANEIRO (2005)

Gad Heuman
University of Warwick
Department of History and Center for Caribbean Studies
MORANT BAY REBELLION (2005)

Constance Valis Hill
Hampshire College
Humanities, Arts, and Cultural Studies
BUBBLES, JOHN (1996)
HINES, GREGORY (2005)
ROBINSON, BILL "BOJANGLES" (1996)
TAP DANCE (1996)

Errol G. Hill
Deceased
ALDRIDGE, IRA (1996)

Robert A. Hill
University of California, Los Angeles
Department of History
AFRICAN BLOOD BROTHERHOOD (1996)
BRIGGS, CYRIL (1996)
GARVEY, MARCUS (1996)
UNIVERSAL NEGRO IMPROVEMENT ASSOCIATION (1996)

Charles Hobson
New York, New York
TELEVISION (1996)

Martha E. Hodes
New York University
Department of History
PRINCE, LUCY TERRY (1996)

Graham Russell Hodges
Colgate University
Department of History
AFRICAN FREE SCHOOL (1996)
RUGGLES, DAVID (1996)
RUSSWURM, JOHN BROWN (1996)

Juanita Marie Holland
University of Maryland
Department of Art History
BANNISTER, EDWARD MITCHELL (1996)

Timothy W. Holley
North Carolina Central University
Music Building
NEGRO STRING QUARTET (1996)

Joseph E. Holloway
California State University Northridge
Department of Pan African Studies
AFRICANISMS (1996)
NAMES AND NAMING, AFRICAN (1996)

Dwight N. Hopkins
Oakland, California
CONE, JAMES H. (1996)

Gerald Horne
University of North Carolina at Chapel Hill
Communication Studies
BRADLEY, TOM (1996)
NATIONAL NEGRO CONGRESS (1996)

Jessica Hornik-Evans
Freelance writer
Alplaus, New York
MATHEMATICIANS (2005)
MAYORS (2005)

Helen R. Houston
Tennessee State University
Department of English
COCHRAN, JOHNNIE L., JR. (2005)
PHYLON (2001)

Philip A. Howard
University of Houston
Department of History
ALMEIDA BOSQUE, JUAN (2005)

Sharon M. Howard
Schomburg Center for Research in Black Culture
New York Public Library
HARLEM WRITERS GUILD (1996)

James Sterling Hoyte
Harvard University
Faculty of Arts and Sciences
ENVIRONMENTAL RACISM (2005)

T. K. Hunter
Columbia University
Department of History
LAW AND LIBERTY IN ENGLAND AND AMERICA (2005)

Laennec Hurbon
French National Center for Scientific Research—Paris
Université de Quisqueya (Port-au-Prince, Haiti)
HAITIAN REVOLUTION (2005)

Marshall Hyatt
New York, New York
HARLEM, NEW YORK (1996)
LEWIS, JOHN (1996)
MOSES, ROBERT PARRIS (1996)
POOR PEOPLE'S CAMPAIGN (1996)

M. Thomas Inge
Randolph-Macon College
Department of English
COMIC STRIPS (2005)

Qadri Ismail
University of Minnesota
Department of English Language and Literature
FEELINGS, THOMAS (1996)
LUCY FOSTER, AUTHERINE (1996)
MOODY, ANNE (1996)

Irene V. Jackson
Port Chester, New York
THARPE, "SISTER" ROSETTA (1996)

C. M. Jacobs
Harrison College, Barbados, and The University of the West Indies at Cave Hill, Barbados
Department of History
ALLEYNE, GEORGE (2005)
BARROW, ERROL (2005)
BARROW, NITA (2005)
BISHOP, MAURICE (2005)
WALCOTT, FRANK (2005)
WEST INDIES FEDERATION (2005)

Margaret D. Jacobs
New Mexico State University
BETHUNE-COOKMAN COLLEGE (1996)

Portia P. James
Smithsonian Institution
Anacostia Museum
INVENTORS AND INVENTIONS (1996)

Kenneth Robert Janken
University of North Carolina at Chapel Hill
African and Afro-American Studies
LOGAN, RAYFORD W. (1996)

Kenneth John
Barrister, Kingstown, St. Vincent and the Grenadines
JOSHUA, EBENEZER (2005)

Robert L. Johns
Pennsylvania State University
CLARKE, LEWIS G. (2001)
CLEAGE, ALBERT B., JR. (2001)
CROCKETT, GEORGE WILLIAM, JR. (2001)
EASTON, HOSEA (2001)
FLAKE, FLOYD H. (2001)
FREEMAN, ELIZABETH (MUM BETT, MUMBET) (2001)
LAFAYETTE PLAYERS (2001)
MITCHELL, PARREN J. (2001)
NORTH STAR (2001)
WILSON, FLIP (2001)

Audreye E. Johnson
University of North Carolina at Chapel Hill
School of Social Work
SOCIAL WORK (1996)

Michele A. Johnson
York University
Department of History
DOMESTIC WORKERS (2005)

Ollie A. Johnson III
Wayne State University
Department of Africana Studies
POLITICS AND POLITICIANS IN LATIN AMERICA (2005)

James H. Jones
Houston, Texas
TUSKEGEE SYPHILIS EXPERIMENT (1996)

Aleric J. Josephs
The University of the West Indies at Mona, Jamaica
Department of History and Archaeology
BURKE, LILLY MAE (2005)
DALTON-JAMES, EDITH (2005)
LONGBRIDGE-BUSTAMANTE, GLADYS (2005)
MORRIS KNIBB, MARY (2005)

Barbara P. Josiah
John Jay College of Criminal Justice, City University of New York
Department of History
BROWN, ANDREW BENJAMIN (2005)
BURNHAM, FORBES (2005)
CRITCHLOW, HUBERT NATHANIEL (2005)
DENBOW, CLAUDE H. A. (2005)
GASKIN, WINIFRED (2005)
MOODY, HAROLD ARUNDEL (2005)
PEOPLE'S NATIONAL CONGRESS (2005)
PHILLIPS-GAY, JANE (2005)

Eileen Julien
University of Indiana
Comparative Literature Department
NÉGRITUDE (2005)

Mitch Kachun
Western Michigan University
Department of History
ATTUCKS, CRISPUS (1996)

Robin D. G. Kelley
Columbia University
Department of Anthropology
COMMUNIST PARTY OF THE UNITED STATES (1996)

Randall Kennedy
Harvard University
Law School
MARSHALL, THURGOOD (1996)

Nathan Kernan
New York, New York
BASQUIAT, JEAN-MICHEL (1996)

Virginia Kerns
College of William and Mary
Department of Anthropology
BLACK CARIBS (2005)

Jeffrey R. Kerr-Ritchie
University of North Carolina at Greensboro
History Department
ANTI-COLONIAL MOVEMENTS (2005)

Cheryl L. Keyes
University of California, Los Angeles
Department of Ethnomusicology
RAP (2005)

Robina Khalid
Graduate Center, City University of New York
MUTUAL AID SOCIETIES (2005)

Elizabeth Kiddy
Albright College
Latin American Studies Department
CARNIVAL IN BRAZIL AND THE CARIBBEAN (2005)

Jo H. Kim
Columbia University
JOHNSON, CHARLES SPURGEON (1996)

Nicole R. King
Philadelphia, Pennsylvania
LORDE, AUDRE (1996)

Leslie King-Hammond
Maryland Institute College of Art
Art History
PAINTING AND SCULPTURE (2005)

Kenneth Kinnamon
University of Arkansas
Department of English
GAINES, ERNEST J. (1996)

Jeffrey L. Klein
Columbia University
BIBB, HENRY WALTON (1996)

Bud Kliment
Columbia University
FITZGERALD, ELLA (1996)
FRANKLIN, ARETHA (1996)
HOLIDAY, BILLIE (1996)
MCRAE, CARMEN (1996)
REDDING, OTIS (1996)
SMITH, MAMIE (1996)
VAUGHAN, SARAH (1996)

Franklin W. Knight
Johns Hopkins University
Department of History
HEARNE, JOHN (CAULWELL, EDGAR) (2005)
SLAVERY (2005)

Karen Kossie-Chernyshev
Texas Southern University
Department of History
CHRISTIAN DENOMINATIONS, INDEPENDENT (2005)

Barbara Krauthamer
New York University
History Department
BLACK-INDIAN RELATIONS (2005)

Mikael D. Kriz
St. Louis University
Pius XII Library
ARCHITECTURE (2005)

Vera M. Kutzinski
Vanderbilt University
Center for the Americas
HARRIS, WILSON (2005)

Othal Hawthorne Lakey
Atlanta, Georgia
CHRISTIAN METHODIST EPISCOPAL CHURCH (1996)

José Antonio Lammoglia
Temple University
DIVINATION AND SPIRIT POSSESSION IN THE AMERICAS (2005)

Jane Landers
Vanderbilt University
Department of History
GRACIA REAL DE SANTA TERESA DE MOSE (2005)

Alycee Jeannette Lane
California State University Northridge
Department of Pan African Studies
LESBIANS (1996)

Ann J. Lane
University of Virginia
Department of History
BROWNSVILLE, TEXAS, INCIDENT (1996)

Saadia Nicoe Lawton
University of Wisconsin–Madison
Department of Art History
JONES, PHILIP MALLORY (2005)

Jill Lectka
Waterville, Maine
WOODS, TIGER (1996)

Bénédicte Ledent
University of Liège
Department of English
PHILLIPS, CARYL (2005)

Chana Kai Lee
University of Georgia
Department of History
CLARK, SEPTIMA (1996)
HAMER, FANNIE LOU (TOWNSEND, FANNIE LOU) (1996)

Theresa Leininger-Miller
University of Cincinnati
School of Art
DOUGLAS, AARON (1996)
FULLER, META VAUX WARRICK (1996)
SAVAGE, AUGUSTA (1996)

Steven J. Leslie
Columbia University
BRAWLEY, BENJAMIN GRIFFITH (1996)
BROOKE, EDWARD W. (1996)
COOK, MERCER (1996)
DEPRIEST, OSCAR STANTON (1996)
DIGGS, CHARLES, JR. (1996)
FARMER, JAMES (1996)
MEREDITH, JAMES H. (1996)
REDDING, JAY SAUNDERS (1996)
WILLIAMS, HOSEA LORENZO (1996)

Daniel Letwin
University of North Carolina at Chapel Hill
NATIONAL NEGRO LABOR COUNCIL (1996)

David Levering Lewis
New York University
Department of History
HARLEM RENAISSANCE (1996)

Petra E. Lewis
Brooklyn, New York
NEGRO ELECTIONS DAY (1996)

Samella Lewis
Museum of African American Art, Los Angeles
BARTHÉ, RICHMOND (1996)

C. Eric Lincoln
Deceased
NATION OF ISLAM (1996)

Arturo Lindsay
Spelman College
Department of Art History
CONGOS OF PANAMA (2005)
SANTERÍA AESTHETICS (2005)

Daniel C. Littlefield
University of South Carolina
Department of History
SLAVE TRADE (2005)

Leon F. Litwack
University of California, Berkeley
Department of History
FRANKLIN, JOHN HOPE (1996)
JIM CROW (1996)

Michael A. Lord
Williamsburg, Virginia
BALTIMORE AFRO-AMERICAN (1996)
JOHNSON, MORDECAI WYATT (1996)

Paul E. Lovejoy
York University
Department of History
ARCHIVAL COLLECTIONS (2005)

Joseph E. Lowndes
University of Oregon
Department of Political Science
CAIN, RICHARD HARVEY (1996)
GREEN, AL (1996)
PARSONS, LUCY (1996)
TYSON, CICELY (1996)

Wahneema Lubiano
Duke University
John Hope Franklin Center, African American Studies
MORRISON, TONI (1996)

Learie B. Luke
South Carolina State University
Department of Social Sciences
BIGGART, JAMES (2005)
CONSTANTINE, LEARIE (2005)
JAMES, A. P. T. (2005)

RALPH E. LUKER
Antioch College
SOCIAL GOSPEL (1996)

CHRISTINE A. LUNARDINI
Saint Michael Academy, New York
BROWN, RONALD H. (1996)
CLARK, KENNETH BANCROFT (1996)
CONYERS, JOHN (1996)
DAVIS, ANGELA (1996)
DU BOIS, SHIRLEY GRAHAM (1996)
HIGHLANDER CITIZENSHIP SCHOOL (1996)
JORDAN, BARBARA (1996)
ROOSEVELT'S BLACK CABINET (1996)
SPELMAN COLLEGE (1996)
YOUNG, ANDREW (1996)

PAUL DAVID LUONGO
Philadelphia, Pennsylvania
ALEXANDER, RAYMOND PACE (1996)

JANE LUSAKA
Washington, D.C.
DELANEY, JOSEPH (1996)
WASHINGTON, DENZEL (1996)

LOIS LYLES
San Francisco State University
Department of English
EVERS, CHARLES (1996)

DAVID R. MAGINNES
Chevy Chase, Maryland
BURNS, ANTHONY (1996)

JACQUI MALONE
New York, New York
THEATRICAL DANCE (1996)

LAWRENCE HALEEM MAMIYA
Vassar College
Department of Religion
FARRAKHAN, LOUIS (2005)
ISLAM (2005)
MUHAMMAD, ELIJAH (1996)
NATION OF ISLAM (2005)

KENNETH R. MANNING
Massachusetts Institute of Technology
Writing and Humanistic Studies
COBB, W. MONTAGUE (1996)
FOLK MEDICINE (1996)
JUST, ERNEST (1996)
MATHEMATICIANS (1996)
SCIENCE (1996)

WENDI N. MANUEL-SCOTT
George Mason University
Department of History
FARM WORKER PROGRAM (2005)

EDWARD MARGOLIES
College of Staten Island, City University of New York
Department of English and Department of American Studies
EQUIANO, OLAUDAH (1996)
HIMES, CHESTER (1996)

JONATHAN MARKS
University of North Carolina at Charlotte
Department of Sociology and Anthropology
RACE, SCIENTIFIC THEORIES OF (2005)

ROBERTO MÁRQUEZ
Mount Holyoke College
Latin American Studies
GUILLÉN, NICOLÁS (2005)

LOUIS MARRIOTT
Michael Manley Foundation
MANLEY, MICHAEL (2005)

REGINALD MARTIN
Memphis State University
NEAL, LARRY (1996)

SANDY DWAYNE MARTIN
University of Georgia
Department of Religion
AFRICAN METHODIST EPISCOPAL ZION CHURCH (1996)
MISSIONARY MOVEMENTS (1996)

TONY MARTIN
Wellesley College
Department of Africana Studies
NEGRO WORLD (2005)

WALDO E. MARTIN JR.
University of California, Berkeley
Department of History
DOUGLASS, FREDERICK (1996)
KARENGA, MAULANA (2005)

DELLITA MARTIN-OGUNSOLA
University of Alabama at Birmingham
Department of Foreign Languages and Literatures
FOLKLORE: LATIN AMERICAN AND CARIBBEAN CULTURE HEROES AND CHARACTERS (2005)

PAULA J. MASSOOD
Brooklyn College, City University of New York
Department of Film
FILM IN THE UNITED STATES, CONTEMPORARY (2005)
FILMMAKERS, LOS ANGELES SCHOOL OF (2005)

SARAH-JANE (SAJE) MATHIEU
Princeton University
Department of History
CANADA, BLACKS IN (2005)

PORTIA K. MAULTSBY
Indiana University
Department of Folklore and Ethnomusicology
MUSIC IN THE UNITED STATES (2005)

LOUISE P. MAXWELL
Columbia University
ALLEN, MACON BOLLING (1996)
AMERICAN MORAL REFORM SOCIETY (1996)
DURHAM MANIFESTO (1996)
FREEDMAN'S BANK (1996)
GULLAH (1996)
HANCOCK, GORDON BLAINE (1996)
HOOKS, BENJAMIN L. (1996)
KEITH, DAMON JEROME (1996)
KING, CORETTA SCOTT (1996)
TUBMAN, HARRIET (1996)
WATERS, MAXINE MOORE (1996)
WHIPPER, WILLIAM (1996)

BARBARA MCCASKILL
University of Georgia
Department of English
POWERS, HARRIET (2005)

JILLEAN MCCOMMONS
Freelance writer
Westland, Michigan
QUERINO, MANUEL (2005)

DEBORAH MCDOWELL
University of Virginia
Department of English
WEST, DOROTHY (1996)

ERIK S. MCDUFFIE
University of Illinois at Urbana-Champaign
African American Studies & Research Program and Gender and Women's Studies
COMMUNIST PARTY OF THE UNITED STATES (2005)

Doris Evans McGinty
Washington, D.C.
FISK JUBILEE SINGERS (1996)
NATIONAL ASSOCIATION OF NEGRO MUSICIANS (1996)

Susan McIntosh
Columbia University
DAVIS, OSSIE (1996)
DEE, RUBY (1996)
FOXX, REDD (1996)
GLOVER, DANNY (1996)
GOLDBERG, WHOOPI (1996)
HOLLY, JAMES T. (1996)
KITT, EARTHA MAE (1996)
MURPHY, EDDIE (1996)
STEPIN FETCHIT (PERRY, LINCOLN) (1996)

Nellie Y. McKay
University of Wisconsin–Madison
Department of Afro-American Studies
HURSTON, ZORA NEALE (1996)

James B. McKee
Michigan State University
Department of Sociology (retired)
SOCIOLOGY (1996)

Genette McLaurin
New York Public Library
SCOTT-HERON, GIL (1996)

Melton A. McLaurin
University of North Carolina at Wilmington
CELIA (1996)

Linda O. McMurry
North Carolina State University
Department of History
CARVER, GEORGE WASHINGTON (1996)
WORK, MONROE NATHAN (1996)

Genna Rae McNeil
University of North Carolina at Chapel Hill
Department of History
HOUSTON, CHARLES HAMILTON (1996)

Lydia McNeill
Columbia University
BARBADOES, JAMES G. (1996)
CAIN, RICHARD HARVEY (1996)
DICKSON, MOSES (1996)
FREEDMEN'S HOSPITAL (1996)
HAMILTON, WILLIAM (1996)
HANCOCK, GORDON BLAINE (1996)
HOOD, JAMES WALKER (1996)
LAWRENCE, MARGARET (1996)
MARTIN, JOHN SELLA (1996)
MOORE, RICHARD BENJAMIN (1996)
NASH, DIANE (1996)
NAYLOR, GLORIA (1996)
WALKER, WYATT TEE (1996)

Derek Lee McPhatter
New York University
FRATERNITIES, U.S. (2005)

Eddie S. Meadows
San Diego State University
Department of Music
ECKSTINE, BILLY (1996)
MARSALIS, WYNTON (1996)
MINGUS, CHARLES (1996)

Edna Greene Medford
Howard University
Department of History
AFRICAN BURIAL GROUND PROJECT (2005)
CIVIL WAR, U.S. (2005)

Brian Meeks
The University of the West Indies at Mona, Jamaica
Department of Government
NEW JEWEL MOVEMENT (2005)

D. H. Melhem
Manhattan, New York
BROOKS, GWENDOLYN (2005)

Michael Meyers
New York Civil Rights Coalition
WILKINS, ROY (1996)

Reginald D. Miles
Howard University
The John H. Johnson School of Communications
COMMUNITY RADIO (2005)

Albert G. Miller
Oberlin College
Religion Department
NATIONAL BLACK EVANGELICAL ASSOCIATION (1996)

Allison X. Miller
Columbia University
CARNEY, WILLIAM H. (1996)
JACKSON, LILLIE MAE CARROLL (1996)
LATIMER, LEWIS HOWARD (1996)

Ivor L. Miller
Graduate Center, City University of New York
Institute for Research on the African Diaspora in the Americans and the Caribbean (IRADAC)
ABAKUÁ (2005)

James A. Miller
George Washington University
Department of English
ATTAWAY, WILLIAM (1996)
BLACK WORLD/NEGRO DIGEST (1996)
GREGORY, DICK (1996)

Jeanne-Marie A. Miller
Howard University
BULLINS, ED (1996)

Monica L. Miller
Barnard College, Columbia University
Department of English
BLACK DANDY, THE (2005)

Michael Mitchell
Arizona State University
Department of Political Science
RACIAL DEMOCRACY IN BRAZIL (2005)

Patricia Mohammed
The University of the West Indies at St. Augustine, Trinidad
Centre for Gender and Development Studies
KING, IRIS (2005)
MANLEY, EDNA (2005)

Brian L. Moore
Colgate University
Department of Africana and Latin American Studies and Department of History
HEADLEY, GEORGE (2005)

Lisa Marie Moore
Columbia University
TUSKEGEE UNIVERSITY (1996)

Robin Moore
Temple University
The Esther Boyer College of Music
AFROCUBANISMO (2005)

Zachary R. Morgan
William Paterson University
Department of History and Latin American Studies Program
RIOTS AND POPULAR PROTESTS (2005)

MERVYN MORRIS
The University of the West Indies at Mona, Jamaica
Department of Literatures in English
BENNETT, LOUISE (2005)
DUB POETRY (2005)

RANDALL S. MORRIS
Director, Cavin Morris Gallery
ART IN HAITI (2005)

WILSON J. MOSES
Pennsylvania State University
Department of History
CRUMMELL, ALEXANDER (1996)
PAN-AFRICANISM (1996)

WILLIAM J. MOSES
Pennsylvania State University
Department of History
TOUSSAINT, PIERRE (1996)

ALFRED A. MOSS JR.
University of Maryland
Department of History
AMERICAN NEGRO ACADEMY (ANA) (1996)

LUIZ MOTT
Universidade Federal da Bahia
Anthropology Department
EGIPCÍACA, ROSA (2005)

LYDIE MOUDILENO
University of Pennsylvania
Department of Romance Languages
CONDÉ, MARYSE (2005)

JAMES E. MUMFORD
University of Indiana
Department of Afro-American Studies
BELAFONTE, HARRY (1996)
HORNE, LENA (1996)
LINCOLN, ABBEY (1996)
MATHIS, JOHNNY (MATHIAS, JOHN ROYCE) (1996)
WATERS, ETHEL (1996)

H. ADLAI MURDOCH
University of Illinois at Urbana-Champaign
Department of French
LITERATURE OF MARTINIQUE AND GUADELOUPE (2005)

GREGORY J. MURPHY
Palo Alto, California
HAMPTON INSTITUTE (1996)

DEREK CONRAD MURRAY
University of California, Berkeley
Department of History of Art
ART IN THE UNITED STATES, CONTEMPORARY (2005)

NASSER MUSTAPHA
The University of the West Indies at St. Augustine, Trinidad
Department of Behavioural Sciences
ISLAM IN THE CARIBBEAN (2005)

ELIZABETH MUTHER
Bowdoin College
OPPORTUNITY: JOURNAL OF NEGRO LIFE (1996)
OWEN, CHANDLER (1996)

PREMILLA NADASEN
Queens College, City University of New York
Department of History
ALEXANDER, SADIE TANNER MOSSELL (1996)
BLACK ACADEMY OF ARTS AND LETTERS (1996)
BLACK WOMEN'S CLUB MOVEMENT (1996)
BRAWLEY, EDWARD MCKNIGHT (1996)
BURROUGHS, NANNIE HELEN (1996)
CIVIL RIGHTS CONGRESS (1996)
CONGRESS OF NATIONAL BLACK CHURCHES, INC. (1996)
COOPER, ANNA J. (1996)
NATIONAL ASSOCIATION OF COLORED WOMEN (1996)
NATIONAL WELFARE RIGHTS ORGANIZATION (1996)
PARKS, ROSA (1996)
PATTERSON, WILLIAM (1996)
REVOLUTIONARY ACTION MOVEMENT (1996)
ROBINSON, JO ANN GIBSON (1996)
RUDOLPH, WILMA (1996)
SISTERS OF THE HOLY FAMILY (1996)
WILLIAMS, ROBERT FRANKLIN (1996)

SUPRIYA NAIR
Tulane University
Department of English
LAMMING, GEORGE (2005)

GARY B. NASH
University of California, Los Angeles
National Center for History in the Schools
ALLEN, RICHARD (1996)
JONES, ABSALOM (1996)

JIM NAUGHTON
Washington, D.C.
JORDAN, MICHAEL (1996)

ALONDRA NELSON
Yale University
Department of African American Studies and Department of Sociology
DIGITAL CULTURE (2005)

REX M. NETTLEFORD
The University of the West Indies at Mona, Jamaica
Vice Chancellor Emeritus
MANLEY, NORMAN (2005)

RENEE NEWMAN
Cambridge, Massachusetts
BLACKBURN, ROBERT (1996)
WEEMS, CARRIE MAE (1996)

RICHARD NEWMAN
Harvard University
W. E. B. Du Bois Institute for African and African American Research, retired
AFRICAN ORTHODOX CHURCH (1996)
GATES, HENRY LOUIS, JR. (2001)
GRACE, SWEET DADDY (1996)
GRAY, WILLIAM H., III (1996)
LINCOLN THEATRE (1996)
SCHOMBURG, ARTHUR (1996)
WALKER, AIDA OVERTON (1996)
WEST, CORNEL (2001)

CHARLES H. NICHOLS
Brown University
Department of English
BONTEMPS, ARNA (1996)

ALBERT NICKERSON
Staten Island, New York
ANTI-APARTHEID MOVEMENT (1996)

LINDA NIEMAN
University of Texas Health Science Center at Houston
Medical School
DOUGLAS, AARON (1996)
MURALISTS (1996)

Mansur M. Nuruddin
Brooklyn, New York
AL-AMIN, JAMIL ABDULLAH (BROWN, H. "RAP") (1996)
CHAVIS, BENJAMIN FRANKLIN, JR. (1996)
DU SABLE, JEAN BAPTISTE POINTE (1996)
KAWAIDA (1996)

Levi A. Nwachuku
Lincoln University
Department of History
LINCOLN UNIVERSITY (1996)
SEALE, BOBBY (1996)

Marie-José N'Zengou-Tayo
The University of the West Indies at Mona, Jamaica
Department of Modern Languages and Literatures
DANTICAT, EDWIDGE (2005)

Robert G. O'Meally
Columbia University
Department of English and Comparative Literature
ELLISON, RALPH (1996)

Michael O'Neal
Freelance writer
Moscow, Idaho
LITERARY MAGAZINES (2005)
SIMPSON, O. J. (2005)
WINFREY, OPRAH (2005)

Andrew Jackson O'Shaughnessy
Thomas Jefferson Foundation, Inc.
International Center for Jefferson Studies, Monticello
DECLARATION OF INDEPENDENCE (2005)
NETTLEFORD, REX (2005)

Rachel Sarah O'Toole
Villanova University
History Department
SAN MARTÍN DE PORRAS (2005)

Naomi Pabst
Yale University
Department of African American Studies
CRITICAL MIXED-RACE STUDIES (2005)

Gustavo Pacheco
Universidade Federal do Rio de Janeiro
LACED–Museu Nacional, Associação Cultural Caburé
JONGO (2005)

Bruce Paddington
The University of the West Indies at St. Augustine, Trinidad
Department of Educational Research and Development
FILMMAKERS IN THE CARIBBEAN (2005)
PECK, RAOUL (2005)

Nell Irvin Painter
Princeton University
Department of History
DELANY, MARTIN R. (1996)
HUDSON, HOSEA (1996)

Michael Paller
Columbia University
Department of Drama and Theatre Arts
AMERICAN NEGRO THEATRE (1996)
FOXX, REDD (1996)
FULLER, CHARLES (1996)
GIOVANNI, NIKKI (1996)
JACKSON, JIMMY LEE (1996)
JOHNSON, NOBLE AND GEORGE (1996)
MACKEY, WILLIAM WELLINGTON (1996)
NEGRO SANHEDRIN (1996)
SULLIVAN, LEON HOWARD (1996)
VOTING RIGHTS ACT OF 1965 (1996)

Melina Ann Pappademos
University of Connecticut
Department of History
GÓMEZ, JUAN GUALBERTO (2005)

Robert L. Paquette
Hamilton College
History Department
MANZANO, JUAN FRANCISCO (2005)

Louis J. Parascandola
Long Island University, Brooklyn Campus
Department of English
CORTEZ, JAYNE (2005)
SHANGE, NTOZAKE (2005)

Lizabeth Paravisini-Gebert
Vassar College
Department of Hispanic Studies
HEALING AND THE ARTS IN AFRO-CARIBBEAN CULTURES (2005)
WOMEN WRITERS OF THE CARIBBEAN (2005)

Freddie Parker
North Carolina Central University
Department of History
RUNAWAY SLAVES IN THE UNITED STATES (2005)

Kevin Parker
Medgar Evers College, City University of New York
GARVEY, AMY ASHWOOD (1996)
LATIMER, LEWIS HOWARD (1996)

LaRose T. Parris
City University of New York
English Department
FOLKLORE: U.S. FOLK HEROES AND CHARACTERS (2005)
PELÉ (NASCIMENTO, EDSON ARANTES DO) (2005)
SPORTS (2005)

Mary Pattillo-McCoy
Northwestern University
Department of Sociology and Department of African-American Studies
BLACK MIDDLE CLASS (2001)

Carleen Payne-Jackson
The University of the West Indies at Cave Hill, Barbados
Clarence Fitzroy Bryant College
BRADSHAW, ROBERT (2005)
SOUTHWELL, PAUL (2005)

Willie J. Pearson Jr.
Georgia Institute of Technology
School of History, Technology and Society
MORTALITY AND MORBIDITY IN THE UNITED STATES (1996)

D. Rita Pemberton
The University of the West Indies at St. Augustine, Trinidad
Department of History
AUGIER, ROY (2005)
CARIBBEAN COMMISSION (2005)

Imani Perry
Rutgers University School of Law–Camden
CRITICAL RACE THEORY (2005)
TENNIS (2005)
WILLIAMS, PATRICIA JOYCE (2005)

Jeffrey B. Perry
Westwood, New Jersey
HARRISON, HUBERT HENRY (2005)

Lewis Perry
Saint Louis University
Department of History
ABOLITION (2005)

James Peterson
Pennsylvania State University, Abington
English Department
HIP-HOP (2005)
MUSIC IN LATIN AMERICA (2005)

Paula F. Pfeffer
Loyola University Chicago
Department of History
BROTHERHOOD OF SLEEPING CAR PORTERS (1996)

Ineke Phaf-Rheinberger
Berlin, Germany
LITERATURE OF SURINAME (2005)
LITERATURE OF THE NETHERLANDS ANTILLES (2005)
WINTI IN SURINAME (2005)

Anthony De Vere Phillips
The University of the West Indies at Cave Hill, Barbados
Department of History
BARBADOS LABOUR PARTY (2005)

Glenn O. Phillips
Morgan State University
Department of History and Geography
NURSING IN THE CARIBBEAN (2005)
SOBERS, GARFIELD (2005)

Lily Phillips
Columbia University
HANSBERRY, LORRAINE (1996)
NAYLOR, GLORIA (1996)

Dianne M. Pinderhughes
University of Illinois at Urbana-Champaign
Department of Political Science
WASHINGTON, HAROLD (1996)

Walter Pinto
Rio de Janeiro, Brazil
DOS PRAZERES, HEITOR (2005)

Thomas Pitoniak
Columbia University
JACK AND JILL OF AMERICA (1996)

Anthony M. Platt
California State University Sacramento
Department of Social Work
FRAZIER, EDWARD FRANKLIN (1996)

Nicole Plummer
The University of the West Indies at Mona, Jamaica
Department of History and Archaeology
BLAKE, VIVIAN (2005)
REVIVALISM (2005)

Fritz G. Polite
University of Central Florida
Institute for Diversity in Sport
WILLIAMS, VENUS AND SERENA (2005)

Horace Porter
University of Iowa
African American World Studies
BALDWIN, JAMES (1996)

Marcela Poveda
Steinhardt School of Education, New York University
Department of Music and Performing Arts Professions
MUSIC IN LATIN AMERICA (2005)

Richard J. Powell
Duke University
Department of Art and Art History
PRINTMAKING (1996)

Heitorzinho dos Prazeres
Rio de Janeiro, Brazil
DOS PRAZERES, HEITOR (2005)

Quandra Prettyman
Barnard College, Columbia University
Department of English
BRAITHWAITE, WILLIAM STANLEY (1996)
CARY, MARY ANN SHADD (1996)
FOOD AND CUISINE, U.S. (2005)
HAMMON, JUPITER (1996)
HORTON, GEORGE MOSES (1996)
TERRELL, MARY ELIZA CHURCH (1996)
WARD, SAMUEL RINGGOLD (1996)

Richard Price
College of William and Mary
Department of Anthropology
RUNAWAY SLAVES IN LATIN AMERICA AND THE CARIBBEAN (2005)

Sally Price
College of William and Mary
Department of Anthropology
MAROON ARTS (2005)

George Priestley
Queens College, City University of New York
Department of Latin American and Latino Studies and Department of Political Science
PANAMA CANAL (2005)
WESTERMAN, GEORGE (2005)

Frank "Trey" Proctor III
Whitman College
Department of History
COARTACIÓN (2005)

Marc E. Prou
University of Massachusetts Boston
Africana Studies Department
HAITIAN CREOLE LANGUAGE (2005)

Jean Muteba Rahier
Florida International University
Department of Sociology and Anthropology
REPRESENTATIONS OF BLACKNESS IN LATIN AMERICA AND THE CARIBBEAN (2005)

Arnold Rampersad
Stanford University
School of Humanities and Sciences
DU BOIS, W. E. B. (1996)
HUGHES, LANGSTON (1996)
LITERATURE OF THE UNITED STATES (1996)
ROBESON, PAUL (1996)

Guthrie P. Ramsey Jr.
University of Pennsylvania
Department of Music
HAMPTON, LIONEL LEO (1996)

Valena Randolph
Wilberforce University
WILBERFORCE UNIVERSITY (1996)

Karen E. Reardon
Columbia University
MITCHELL, ARTHUR WERGS (1996)

Rhoda E. Reddock
The University of the West Indies at St. Augustine, Trinidad
Centre for Gender and Development Studies
FRANÇOIS, ELMA (2005)
JEFFERS, AUDREY (2005)

Charlene Regester
University of North Carolina at Chapel Hill
Department of African and African-American Studies
MICHEAUX, OSCAR (1996)

Robert Reid-Pharr
Graduate Center, City University of New York
Department of English
BIOGRAPHY, U.S. (2005)
GAY MEN (1996)

Matthew Restall
Pennsylvania State University
History Department
GARRIDO, JUAN (2005)
SAN LORENZO DE LOS NEGROS (2005)

Terry Rey
Florida International University
Department of Religious Studies
CATHOLICISM IN THE AMERICAS (2005)
ROMAINE-LA-PROPHÉTESSE (2005)

Jesse Rhines
New York, New York
DAVIS, SAMMY, JR. (1996)

Nelson Rhodes
Freelance writer
Chicago, Illinois
COOKE, HOWARD (2005)
SIMPSON-MILLER, PORTIA (2005)

Micheline Rice-Maximin
Swarthmore College
Department of Modern Languages and Literatures
CONDÉ, MARYSE (2005)

Wilbur C. Rich
Wellesley College
Department of Political Science
YOUNG, COLEMAN (1996)

Sandra L. Richards
Northwestern University
School of Communication, Performance Studies
DRAMA (1996)

Bonham C. Richardson
Virginia Polytechnic Institute and State University
Department of Geography
DEMOGRAPHY (2005)
NATURAL RESOURCES OF THE CARIBBEAN (2005)

Marilyn Richardson
Watertown, Massachusetts
LEWIS, EDMONIA (1996)

Steven A. Riess
Northeastern Illinois University
Department of History
BASEBALL (1996)
JOHNSON, JACK (1996)
PATTERSON, FLOYD (1996)
ROBINSON, SUGAR RAY (1996)

Thomas L. Riis
University of Colorado
American Music Research Center
MUSICAL THEATER (2005)

Kim Robbins
Columbia University
REMOND, SARAH PARKER (1996)

John W. Roberts
Ohio State University
Department of African American and African Studies
FOLKLORE: OVERVIEW (1996)

Samuel Roberts
Columbia University
Mailman School of Public Health, Department of Sociomedical Sciences
NURSING IN THE UNITED STATES (2005)

Gemma Robinson
University of Newcastle upon Tyne
School of English Literature, Language, and Linguistics
CARTER, MARTIN (2005)

Greg Robinson
New York, New York
ANGLO-AFRICAN, THE (1996)
ATLANTA RIOT OF 1906 (1996)
BARNETT, MARGUERITE ROSS (1996)
BLACKWELL, UNITA (1996)
BOND, JULIAN (1996)
BUTTS, CALVIN (1996)
CAYTON, HORACE (1996)
CHAMBERLAIN, WILT (1996)
CLARKE, JOHN HENRIK (2001)
CLAY, WILLIAM LACY (1996)
CORNISH, SAMUEL E. (1996)
COX, OLIVER CROMWELL (1996)
CROUCH, STANLEY (2001)
CRUSE, HAROLD (1996)
DAVIS, ALLISON (1996)
DILLARD UNIVERSITY (2001)
DOMINGO, W. A. (1996)
DU SABLE, JEAN BAPTISTE POINTE (1996)
EBONY (1996)
ELDERS, JOYCELYN (1996)
FRAZIER, JOE (1996)
GOMES, PETER JOHN (2001)
HARLEM GLOBETROTTERS (1996)
HIGGINBOTHAM, A. LEON, JR. (2001)
HILL-THOMAS HEARINGS (1996)
JACKSON, JOSEPH HARRISON (1996)
JOHN HENRY (1996)
MAYORS (1996)
MILLION MAN MARCH (2001)
MITCHELL, CLARENCE, JR. (1996)
MOTON, ROBERT RUSSA (1996)
MYERS, ISAAC (1996)
NAACP LEGAL DEFENSE AND EDUCATIONAL FUND (1996)
NIAGARA MOVEMENT (1996)
NORTON, ELEANOR HOLMES (1996)
PENNINGTON, JAMES W. C. (1996)
POOR, SALEM (1996)
RENAISSANCE BIG FIVE (HARLEM RENS) (1996)
RIGGS, MARLON (1996)
ROWAN, CARL T. (1996)
SHABAZZ, BETTY (2001)
SHARPTON, AL (1996)
SMITH, VENTURE (1996)
SPINGARN MEDAL (1996)
TURNER, LORENZO DOW (1996)
TWILIGHT, ALEXANDER (1996)
UNITED NEGRO COLLEGE FUND (1996)
WALCOTT, JERSEY JOE (1996)
WATTS, J. C. (2001)
YERGAN, MAX (1996)

Jontyle Theresa Robinson
Atlanta, Georgia
MOTLEY, ARCHIBALD JOHN, JR. (1996)

Marcia C. Robinson
Syracuse University
Department of Religion
RELIGION (2005)

Pearl T. Robinson
Tufts University
Department of Political Science
TRANSAFRICA FORUM (1996)

Don Robotham
Graduate Center, City University of New York
Department of Anthropology
PEOPLE'S NATIONAL PARTY (2005)

Justin Rogers-Cooper
Astoria, New York
FRATERNAL ORDERS (2005)
GAY MEN (2005)

W. Donn Rogosin
Schenectady, New York
BASEBALL (1996)

Noliwe Rooks
Princeton University
Program in African American Studies
WOMEN'S MAGAZINES (2005)

Joel N. Rosen
Oxford, Mississippi
MOUND BAYOU, MISSISSIPPI (1996)

Leah Reade Rosenberg
University of Florida
Department of English
MARSON, UNA (2005)

Marlon B. Ross
University of Virginia
Department of English
MASCULINITY (2005)

Rob Ruck
Pittsburgh, Pennsylvania
GIBSON, JOSH (1996)
PAIGE, SATCHEL (1996)

Frederik L. Rusch
John Jay College of Criminal Justice, City University of New York
TOOMER, JEAN (1996)

Thaddeus Russell
Barnard College, Columbia University
Department of History
BOND, HORACE MANN (1996)
BROWN, WILLIE (1996)
CAMBRIDGE, GODFREY MACARTHUR (1996)
COTTON CLUB (1996)
DELLUMS, RON (1996)
FORD, JAMES W. (1996)
HAYWOOD, HARRY (1996)
HENSON, MATTHEW A. (1996)
JONES, CLAUDIA (1996)
KECKLEY, ELIZABETH (1996)
KING, DON (1996)
KITT, EARTHA MAE (1996)
KNIGHT, GLADYS (1996)
LEONARD, SUGAR RAY (1996)
LOWERY, JOSEPH E. (1996)
MAYS, WILLIE (1996)
MICHAUX, ELDER (1996)
MOSELEY-BRAUN, CAROL (1996)
NEGRO AMERICAN LABOR COUNCIL (1996)
NORTHRUP, SOLOMON (1996)
RANGEL, CHARLES BERNARD (1996)
REPUBLIC OF NEW AFRICA (1996)
SALEM, PETER (1996)
SIMPSON, O. J. (1996)
SINGLETON, BENJAMIN "PAP" (1996)
STILL, WILLIAM (1996)
STOKES, CARL BURTON (1996)
WALKER, GEORGE WILLIAM (1996)

Selwyn Ryan
The University of the West Indies at St. Augustine, Trinidad
Sir Arthur Lewis Institute of Social and Economic Studies
FEBRUARY REVOLT (2005)
WOODFORD SQUARE (2005)

Layn Saint-Louis
Silver Spring, Maryland
BLYDEN, EDWARD WILMOT (1996)

Maurice St. Pierre
Morgan State University
Department of Sociology and Anthropology
BENN, BRINDLEY (2005)
CARTER, JOHN (2005)
CHASE, ASHTON (2005)
KING, SYDNEY (KWAYANA, EUSI) (2005)
RODNEY, WALTER (2005)

Jack Salzman
Columbia University
American Culture Studies
BROWN, ROSCOE, JR. (1996)

Linda Salzman
Columbia University
ALEXANDER, CLIFFORD L., JR. (1996)
CHARLES, EZZARD (1996)

Carlos Sandroni
Federal University of Pernambuco
Center for Ethnomusicology
SAMBA (2005)

Rosita M. Sands
Columbia College Chicago
Center for Black Music Research
ODETTA (GORDON, ODETTA HOLMES FELIOUS) (1996)
SIMONE, NINA (WAYMON, EUNICE KATHLEEN) (1996)

Pedro L. San Miguel
University of Puerto Rico
Department of History
ANTI-HAITIANISM (2005)

David Sartorius
Whittier College
Department of History
NEGROS BRUJOS (2005)

D. Gail Saunders
Bahamas National Archives
PINDLING, LYNDEN OSCAR (2005)

Vasanti Saxena
Columbia University
CARROLL, DIAHANN (1996)

Peter Schilling
Wagner College
Information Technology Department
HALL, PRINCE (1996)
JORDAN, VERNON E., JR. (1996)
MAYFIELD, JULIAN (1996)
METCALFE, RALPH (1996)
WILSON, HARRIET E. ADAMS (1996)

Christopher Schmidt-Nowara
Fordham University
Department of History
EMANCIPATION IN LATIN AMERICA AND THE CARIBBEAN (2005)

Monica Schuler
Wayne State University
Department of History
BEDWARD, ALEXANDER (2005)
MYAL (2005)

Anna Beatrice Scott
University of California, Riverside
Department of Dance History and Theory
PERFORMANCE ART (2005)

Benjamin K. Scott
Columbia University
FLIPPER, HENRY O. (1996)
LIELE, GEORGE (1996)

Deirdre A. Scott
Cooper-Hewitt, National Design Museum, Smithsonian Institution
SIMPSON, LORNA (1996)

Michael D. Scott
Oakland, California
BASIE, WILLIAM JAMES "COUNT" (1996)
CALLOWAY, CAB (1996)
GAYE, MARVIN (GAY, MARVIN PENTZ) (1996)

Otey M. Scruggs
Syracuse University
Department of History and Department of African-American Studies
GARNET, HENRY HIGHLAND (1996)

Ann Sears
Wheaton College
BURLEIGH, HARRY T. (1996)

Milton C. Sernett
Maxwell School of Syracuse University
Dept of African American Studies
RELIGION (1996)

Helen M. Shannon
New Jersey State Museum
WOODRUFF, HALE (1996)

Sandra G. Shannon
Howard University
Department of English
WILSON, AUGUST (2005)

Verene A. Shepherd
The University of the West Indies at Mona, Jamaica
Department of History and Archaeology
NANNY OF THE MAROONS (2005)
SHARPE, SAMUEL (2005)

John C. Shields
Normal, Illinois
WHEATLEY, PHILLIS (1996)

Ann Allen Shockley
Fisk University Library
Department of Special Collections
FISK UNIVERSITY (1996)

Evan A. Shore
Columbia University
BOND, JULIAN (1996)
FORTEN, JAMES (1996)
NORTON, ELEANOR HOLMES (1996)

Jack Sidnell
University of Toronto
Department of Anthropology
CREOLE LANGUAGES OF THE AMERICAS (2005)

Eduardo Silva
Centro de Estudos Históricos, Brasil
DOM OBÁ II D'ÁFRICA (2005)

Linda Crocker Simmons
Washington, D.C.
JOHNSON, JOSHUA (1996)

Lowery Stokes Sims
The Studio Museum in Harlem
LAM, WIFREDO (2005)

Merrill Singer
Hispanic Health Council
Center for Community Health Research
AIDS IN THE AMERICAS (2005)

Amritjit Singh
Bryant University
CLEAVER, ELDRIDGE (1996)
LESTER, JULIUS (1996)
MCMILLAN, TERRY (1996)

Kelvin Singh
The University of the West Indies at St. Augustine, Trinidad
Department of History
BUTLER, URIAH (2005)
MOYNE COMMISSION (2005)

Nikhil Pal Singh
University of Washington
Department of History
CIVIL RIGHTS MOVEMENT, U.S. (2005)

Harvard Sitkoff
University of New Hampshire
History Department
WEAVER, ROBERT CLIFTON (1996)

Rene Skelton
Perth Amboy, New Jersey
KERNER REPORT (1996)

Joseph T. Skerrett Jr.
University of Massachusetts Amherst
Department of English
MARSHALL, PAULE (2005)

Elliott P. Skinner
Columbia University
Anthropology Department, Emeritus
Former U.S. Ambassador to Upper Volta
AFRICA: AN INTRODUCTION (FRONT MATTER) (2005)

Robert W. Slenes
Universidade Estadual de Campinas
Departamento de História, Instituto de Filosofia e Ciências Humanas
CENTRAL AFRICAN RELIGIONS AND CULTURE IN THE AMERICAS (2005)

Jean Small
St. Catherine, Jamaica
CARIBBEAN THEATER, ANGLOPHONE (2005)

David Lionel Smith
Williams College
Department of English
BARAKA, AMIRI (JONES, LEROI) (1996)
BLACK ARTS MOVEMENT (1996)
BROWN, STERLING ALLEN (1996)
COMEDIANS (2005)
COMIC BOOKS (2005)
LITERARY CRITICISM, U.S. (1996)
OBAC WRITERS' WORKSHOP (1996)

Faith Smith
Brandeis University
Department of African & Afro-American Studies
LITERATURE OF THE ENGLISH-SPEAKING CARIBBEAN (2005)

Frederick H. Smith
College of William and Mary
Department of Anthropology
ARCHAEOLOGY AND ARCHAEOLOGISTS (2005)

Jessie Carney Smith
Fisk University
John Hope and Aurelia E. Franklin Library
COLLINS, CARDISS (2001)
HOUSTON, WHITNEY (2001)
MCHENRY, DONALD F. (2001)
SIMMONS, RUTH J. (2001)
SMITH, BARBARA ("B. SMITH") (2001)
WILSON, WILLIAM JULIUS (2001)

LORRIE N. SMITH
Saint Michael's College
Department of English
TROUPE, QUINCY (2005)

THEOPHUS H. SMITH
Emory University
Department of Religion
SPIRITUALITY (1996)

THOMAS G. SMITH
Nichols College
History Department
FOOTBALL (1996)

RAYMOND W. SMOCK
U.S. House of Representatives
WASHINGTON, BOOKER T. (1996)

JEAN E. SNYDER
Edinboro University of Pennsylvania
Music Department
BURLEIGH, HARRY T. (2005)

WERNER SOLLORS
Harvard University
Department of English
JOHNSON, CHARLES RICHARD (1996)
PASSING (1996)

SALLY SOMMER
New York, New York
DUNHAM, KATHERINE (1996)
SOCIAL DANCE (1996)
TAP DANCE (1996)

JAMES M. SORELLE
Baylor University
Department of History
AARON, HANK (2005)
ATLANTA COMPROMISE (1996)
BROWN FELLOWSHIP SOCIETY (2005)

RENÉE SOULODRE-LA FRANCE
King's University College at the University of Western Ontario
Department of History
PALENQUE SAN BASILIO (2005)

DANIEL SOYER
Fordham University
Department of History
BRUCE, BLANCHE KELSO (1996)
DICKSON, MOSES (1996)
FOREMAN, GEORGE (1996)
INSTITUTE OF THE BLACK WORLD (1996)
PROFESSIONAL ORGANIZATIONS (1996)

DEVYN M. SPENCE
University of North Carolina at Chapel Hill
Department of History
MONTEJO, ESTEBAN (2005)

ROBYN C. SPENCER
Pennsylvania State University
Department of African and African American Studies
AL-AMIN, JAMIL ABDULLAH (BROWN, H. "RAP") (1996)
CHANEY, JAMES EARL (1996)
FREEDOM SUMMER (1996)
HAIR AND BEAUTY CULTURE IN THE UNITED STATES (2005)
INNIS, ROY (2005)
JACKSON, GEORGE LESTER (1996)
KAWAIDA (1996)
KWANZA (1996)
MCKISSICK, FLOYD B. (1996)
NASH, DIANE (1996)
NEWTON, HUEY P. (1996)
SHAKUR, ASSATA (CHESIMARD, JOANNE DEBORAH BRYON) (2005)
TILL, EMMETT (2005)
WILLIAMS, HOSEA LORENZO (1996)

DIANE M. SPIVEY
Culinary Historian
Miami, Florida
FOOD AND CUISINE, LATIN AMERICAN AND CARIBBEAN (2005)

CASSANDRA A. STANCIL
Virginia Beach, Virginia
DOZENS, THE (1996)

MAREN STANGE
Cooper Union for the Advancement of Science and Art
DECARAVA, ROY (1996)

ROBERT W. STEPHENS
Ohio Valley University
CHARLES, RAY (ROBINSON, RAY CHARLES) (1996)
COLE, NAT "KING" (1996)
JAMES, ETTA (1996)

JOHN C. STONER
Binghamton University, State University of New York
Department of History
BROADSIDE PRESS (1996)
HUNTON, WILLIAM ALPHAEUS, JR. (1996)
MOREHOUSE COLLEGE (1996)
OPERATION PUSH (PEOPLE UNITED TO SERVE HUMANITY) (1996)
POWELL, COLIN (2005)
WILLIAMS, BILLY DEE (DECEMBER, WILLIAM) (2005)

WILLIE STRONG
University of South Carolina
School of Music
NEGRO NATIONAL ANTHEM (1996)

JEAN STUBBS
London Metropolitan University
Caribbean Studies Centre
GRAJALES CUELLO, MARIANA (2005)

JAMES H. SWEET
University of Wisconsin–Madison
Department of History
AFROCENTRISM (2005)
ANASTÁCIA (2005)
BARBOSA GOMES, JOAQUIM BENEDITO (2005)

DURAHN TAYLOR
Columbia University
Department of Continuing Education
BRUCE, JOHN EDWARD (1996)
CONGRESSIONAL BLACK CAUCUS (1996)
HATCHER, RICHARD GORDON (1996)
LAMPKIN, DAISY (1996)
MITCHELL, ARTHUR WERGS (1996)
NATIONAL AFRO-AMERICAN LEAGUE/AFRO-AMERICAN COUNCIL (1996)
SULLIVAN, LOUIS (1996)
SUTTON, PERCY ELLIS (1996)

QUINTARD TAYLOR
University of Washington
Department of History
BLACK TOWNS (1996)

ULA Y. TAYLOR
University of California, Berkeley
African American Studies
GARVEY, AMY JACQUES (1996)

JEROME TEELUCKSINGH
The University of the West Indies at St. Augustine, Trinidad
PADMORE, GEORGE (2005)
SOLOMON, PATRICK (2005)
WILLIAMS, HENRY SYLVESTER (2005)

JEANNE THEOHARIS
Brooklyn College, City University of New York
Department of Political Science
BEVEL, JAMES (1996)
BLACK MANIFESTO (1996)
GARY CONVENTION (1996)

DARIUS L. THIEME
Nashville, Tennessee
HAYES, ISAAC (2001)

DANIEL THOM
Long Beach, California
HOOKER, JOHN LEE (1996)
KING, B. B. (1996)
LITTLE RICHARD (PENNIMAN, RICHARD) (1996)
MUDDY WATERS (MORGANFIELD, MCKINLEY) (1996)

LAMONT D. THOMAS
University of Bridgeport
School of Arts & Sciences
CUFFE, PAUL (1996)

SASHA THOMAS
Columbia University
BAGNALL, ROBERT (1996)
HOLLAND, JEROME HEARTWELL (1996)
HOPE, JOHN (1996)
NABRIT, JAMES MADISON (1996)
NATIONAL BANKERS ASSOCIATION (1996)
SCOTT, EMMETT J. (1996)
TANNER, BENJAMIN TUCKER (1996)
VARICK, JAMES (1996)

GORDON THOMPSON
City University of New York
CHESNUTT, CHARLES W. (1996)
TOLSON, MELVIN B. (1996)

KRISTA A. THOMPSON
Northwestern University
Department of Art History
ART IN THE ANGLOPHONE CARIBBEAN (2005)
HUIE, ALBERT (2005)

J. MILLS THORNTON III
University of Michigan
Department of History
MONTGOMERY, ALA., BUS BOYCOTT (1996)
MONTGOMERY IMPROVEMENT ASSOCIATION (1996)
NIXON, EDGAR DANIEL (1996)

JOHN THORNTON
Boston University
African American Studies
ETHNIC ORIGINS (2005)

DANIEL B. THORP
Virginia Polytechnic Institute and State University
Department of History
MORAVIAN CHURCH (1996)

ROBERT L. TIGNOR
Princeton University
Department of History
LEWIS, ARTHUR (2005)

SALAMISHAH MARGARET TILLET
Harvard University
History of American Civilization Department
FEMINIST THEORY AND CRITICISM (2005)

JEFF TODD TITON
Brown University
Department of Music
BLUES, THE (2005)
FRANKLIN, C. L. (1996)

ROBERT C. TOLL
Oakland, California
MINSTRELS/MINSTRELSY (1996)
WILLIAMS, BERT (1996)

CHRISTINE TOMASSINI
Freelance writer
Livonia, Michigan
BERRY, HALLE (2005)
CARIBBEAN COMMUNITY AND COMMON MARKET (CARICOM) (2005)
LABOR AND LABOR UNIONS (2005)
NATIONAL ASSOCIATION FOR THE ADVANCEMENT OF COLORED PEOPLE (NAACP) (2005)
RADIO (2005)
RAINBOW/PUSH COALITION (2005)
RHYTHM AND BLUES (2005)
RICE, CONDOLEEZZA (2005)
SIMMONS, RUSSELL (2005)
SMITH, WILL (2005)
TELEVISION (2005)

LOUISE TOPPIN
East Carolina University
School of Music
BATTLE, KATHLEEN (2005)

KIMBERLY C. TORRES
University of Pennsylvania
Department of Sociology
SOCIAL PSYCHOLOGY, PSYCHOLOGISTS, AND RACE (2005)

MICHAEL F. TOUSSAINT
The University of the West Indies at St. Augustine, Trinidad
Department of History
CHAMBERS, GEORGE (2005)
PEOPLES NATIONAL MOVEMENT (2005)

JOE W. TROTTER JR.
Carnegie Mellon University
Department of History
MIGRATION/POPULATION, U.S. (1996)

BRUCE TUCKER
Highland Park, New Jersey
BROWN, JAMES (1996)

RENEE TURSI
College of Charleston
Department of English
GUARDIAN, THE (1996)
MESSENGER, THE (1996)

JULES TYGIEL
San Francisco State University
Department of History
ROBINSON, JACKIE (1996)

BRENDESHA TYNES
University of Illinois at Urbana-Champaign
African American Studies & Research Program and Department of Educational Psychology
EDUCATIONAL PSYCHOLOGY AND PSYCHOLOGISTS (2005)

GINA ULYSSE
Wesleyan University
Anthropology Department
WOMEN TRADERS OF THE CARIBBEAN (2005)

FRANK UNTERMYER
Roosevelt University
DRAKE, ST. CLAIR (1996)

WILLIAM L. VAN DEBURG
University of Wisconsin–Madison
Department of Afro-American Studies
BLACK POWER MOVEMENT (2005)
CARMICHAEL, STOKELY (2005)

Nancy E. van Deusen
Western Washington University
History Department
JESÚS, ÚRSULA DE (2005)

Julia Van Haaften
New York Public Library
Digital Library Program
PARKS, GORDON (1996)
SLEET, MONETA J., JR. (1996)

Colleen A. Vasconcellos
Atlanta, Georgia
DEMERARA REVOLT (2005)

Linnette Vassell
Women's Resource and Outreach Centre, Kingston, Jamaica
BAILEY, AMY (2005)

Diana L. Vélez
University of Iowa
Department of Spanish and Portuguese
SANTOS-FEBRES, MAYRA (2005)

John Michael Vlach
George Washington University
American Studies and Anthropology Departments
ARCHITECTURE, VERNACULAR (1996)
CEMETERIES AND BURIALS (2005)
FOLK ARTS AND CRAFTS (2005)

Maude Southwell Wahlman
University of Missouri–Kansas City
Department of Art and Art History
TEXTILES, DIASPORIC (2005)

Keith Wailoo
Rutgers University
Department of History
MORTALITY AND MORBIDITY IN LATIN AMERICA AND THE CARIBBEAN (2005)

Alexis Walker
Oregon State University
Department of Human Development and Family Science
CHAVIS, BENJAMIN FRANKLIN, JR. (1996)
DODSON, OWEN (1996)
HALEY, ALEX (1996)
REDDING, JAY SAUNDERS (1996)

Clarence E. Walker
University of California, Davis
Department of History
CARDOZO, FRANCIS L. (1996)
REVELS, HIRAM RHOADES (1996)
THOMAS, CLARENCE (1996)

Juliet E. K. Walker
University of Texas at Austin
Department of History
ENTREPRENEURS AND ENTREPRENEURSHIP (1996)

Randolph Meade Walker
Lemoyne-Owen College
ABERNATHY, RALPH DAVID (1996)

Cheryl A. Wall
Rutgers University–New Brunswick/Piscataway
English Department
FAUSET, JESSIE REDMON (1996)

Karen Smyley Wallace
Howard University
Department of Modern Languages and Literatures
LITERATURE OF FRENCH GUIANA (2005)

Wendy S. Walters
Rhode Island School of Design
Department of Liberal Arts
EXPERIMENTAL THEATER (2005)
PIPER, ADRIAN (2005)

Hanes Walton Jr.
University of Michigan
Department of Political Science
POLITICS IN THE UNITED STATES (2005)

Keith Q. Warner
George Mason University
Department of Modern and Classical Languages
CALYPSO (2005)
FILMMAKERS IN THE CARIBBEAN (2005)
PECK, RAOUL (2005)

Maureen Warner-Lewis
Kingston, Jamaica
KENNEDY, IMOGENE QUEENIE (2005)
KUMINA (2005)

Margaret Washington
Cornell University
Department of History
TRUTH, SOJOURNER (1996)

Irma Watkins-Owens
Fordham University
Department of African and African American Studies
JAMAICA PROGRESSIVE LEAGUE (2005)

Denton L. Watson
College at Old Westbury, State University of New York
Department of American Studies
NATIONAL ASSOCIATION FOR THE ADVANCEMENT OF COLORED PEOPLE (NAACP) (1996)
WHITE, WALTER FRANCIS (1996)

Jill M. Watts
California State University San Marcos
College of Arts & Sciences, Department of History
FATHER DIVINE (1996)

Robert Weisbrot
Colby College
History Department
CIVIL RIGHTS MOVEMENT, U.S. (1996)

Judith Weisenfeld
Vassar College
Department of Religion
BATES, DAISY (1996)
BETHUNE, MARY MCLEOD (1996)
BROWN, CHARLOTTE HAWKINS (1996)
CHISHOLM, SHIRLEY (1996)
CHRISTIANITY IN FILM (2005)
HARPER, FRANCES ELLEN WATKINS (1996)
HEIGHT, DOROTHY (1996)
HOPE, LUGENIA BURNS (1996)
HUNTER-GAULT, CHARLAYNE (1996)
LAVEAU, MARIE (1996)
MOORE, AUDLEY "QUEEN MOTHER" (1996)
NATIONAL COUNCIL OF NEGRO WOMEN (1996)
NATIONAL LEAGUE FOR THE PROTECTION OF COLORED WOMEN (1996)
OBLATE SISTERS OF PROVIDENCE (1996)
WILLIAMS, FANNIE BARRIER (1996)
WOMAN'S ERA (1996)

Nancy J. Weiss
Princeton University
Department of History
NATIONAL URBAN LEAGUE (1996)

Yvonne Welbon
Independent filmmaker
Chicago, Illinois
PALCY, EUZHAN (2005)

Ellen Harkins Wheat
Indianola, Washington
LAWRENCE, JACOB (1996)

Krista Whetstone
Columbia University
BAILEY, PEARL (1996)

Norman E. Whitten Jr.
University of Illinois at Urbana-Champaign
Department of Anthropology
DIASPORIC CULTURES IN THE AMERICAS (2005)

David K. Wiggins
George Mason University
School of Recreation, Health, and Tourism
MOORE, ARCHIE (2005)

Pamela Wilkinson
Columbia University
DANDRIDGE, DOROTHY (1996)
KENNEDY, ADRIENNE (1996)
LABELLE, PATTI (HOLT, PATRICIA LOUISE) (1996)
MABLEY, JACKIE "MOMS" (1996)

Carla Williams
Oakland, California
WILLIS, DEBORAH (2005)

Chad Williams
Princeton University
Department of History
MILITARY EXPERIENCE, AFRICAN-AMERICAN (2005)

Christolyn A. Williams
Westchester Community College of the State University of New York
BIRD, V. C. (2005)
HECTOR, TIM (2005)

Claudette Williams
The University of the West Indies at Mona, Jamaica
Department of Modern Languages and Literature
MOREJÓN, NANCY (2005)

Dessima M. Williams
Brandeis University
Department of Sociology
POLITICS: WOMEN AND POLITICS IN LATIN AMERICA AND THE CARIBBEAN (2005)

John A. Williams
Teaneck, New Jersey
PRYOR, RICHARD (1996)
SCHUYLER, GEORGE S. (1996)

Martin Williams
Deceased
ARMSTRONG, LOUIS (1996)
ELLINGTON, EDWARD KENNEDY "DUKE" (1996)

Patrick G. Williams
University of Arkansas
Department of History
SWEATT V. PAINTER (1996)

Erica Williams Connell
The University of the West Indies at St. Augustine, Trinidad
Eric Williams Memorial Collection
MCBURNIE, BERYL (2005)
TESHEA, ISABEL (2005)

Deborah Willis
New York University
Tisch School of the Arts
PHOTOGRAPHY, U.S. (2005)

Gayraud S. Wilmore
Atlanta, Georgia
PRESBYTERIANS (1996)

Swithin Wilmot
The University of the West Indies at Mona, Jamaica
Department of History and Archaeology
BOGLE, PAUL (2005)
FREE VILLAGES (2005)
GORDON, GEORGE WILLIAM (2005)
JORDON, EDWARD (2005)

Clint C. Wilson II
Howard University
The John H. Johnson School of Communications
CRISIS, THE (1996)
PITTSBURGH COURIER (1996)

Francille Rusan Wilson
University of Maryland
Department of African American Studies
WESLEY, CHARLES HARRIS (1996)

Robin Marie Wilson
University of Michigan
School of Music
DANCE, DIASPORIC (2005)

Raymond Winbush
Morgan State University
Institute for Urban Research
FRANKS, GARY (2001)
HILLIARD, EARL FREDERICK (2001)
MCKINNEY, CYNTHIA ANN (2001)
MEEK, CARRIE (2001)
RAINES, FRANKLIN D. (2001)

Julie Winch
University of Massachusetts Boston
Department of History
MANUMISSION SOCIETIES (1996)
PURVIS, ROBERT (1996)

Peter H. Wood
Duke University
Department of History
GABRIEL PROSSER CONSPIRACY (1996)
NAT TURNER'S REBELLION (1996)
STONO REBELLION (1996)

James P. Woodard
University of Maryland
Department of History
GAMA, LUIZ (2005)

Drexel G. Woodson
University of Arizona
Bureau of Applied Research in Anthropology
ARISTIDE, JEAN-BERTRAND (2005)

John S. Wright
University of Minnesota
Department of Afro-American and African Studies
INTELLECTUAL LIFE (1996)
LOCKE, ALAIN LEROY (1996)

Lucius R. Wyatt
Prairie View A&M University
Department of Music and Drama
STILL, WILLIAM GRANT (1996)

Donald Yacovone
Arlington, Massachusetts
UNDERGROUND RAILROAD (1996)

Richard Yarborough
University of California, Los Angeles
Ralph J. Bunch Center for African American Studies
BROWN, WILLIAM WELLS (1996)

Jean Fagan Yellin
Pace University
English Department
JACOBS, HARRIET ANN (2005)

Nancy Yousef
Baruch College, City University of New York
Department of English
BLACKWELL, UNITA (1996)
BURROUGHS, MARGARET TAYLOR (1996)
KWANZA (1996)
LEONARD, SUGAR RAY (1996)
REVOLUTIONARY ACTION MOVEMENT (1996)

Michael Yudell
Drexel University
School of Public Health, Department of Community Health and Prevention
RACE AND SCIENCE (2005)

Jeanne Zeidler
Hampton University Museum
CATLETT, ELIZABETH (1996)

Rachel Zellars
Cornell University
BLACK ENTERTAINMENT TELEVISION (BET) (2001)
COMBS, SEAN (2001)
GLOVER, SAVION (2001)
HEMPHILL, ESSEX (2001)
L. L. COOL J (SMITH, JAMES TODD) (2001)
QUEEN LATIFAH (OWENS, DANA ELAINE) (2001)
RUN-D.M.C. (2001)
SINGLETON, JOHN (2001)
SMITH, BARBARA (2001)

Aaron, Hank

February 5, 1934

Baseball player Henry Louis "Hank" Aaron grew up in relative poverty in Mobile, Alabama. The third of eight children born to Herbert and Estella Aaron, he developed an early love for baseball, playing whenever possible on vacant lots and, later, at municipally owned, though racially restricted, diamonds in his neighborhood. He played semipro ball for the Mobile Black Bears before signing a contract in 1952 with the Indianapolis Clowns of the American Negro League. Aaron quickly attracted the attention of major league scouts, and in May 1952 he signed with the Boston Braves of the National League. The Braves sent him to their Northern League farm club in Eau Claire, Wisconsin, where he won Rookie of the Year honors. In 1953 Aaron and two other black ball players were selected to integrate the South Atlantic League by playing for the Braves' Class A farm team in Jacksonville, Florida. In 1954 he was elevated to the Braves' major league club, which had moved to Milwaukee the previous year. Aaron rapidly became one of the mainstays for the Braves, both in Milwaukee and, from 1966 to 1974, in Atlanta, leading the Milwaukee club to World Series appearances in 1957 and 1958 and a world championship in 1957, and Atlanta to the National League championship series in 1969. In 1957 he was named the National League's most valuable player. In 1975, after twenty-one seasons with the Braves, Aaron was traded to the American League's Milwaukee Brewers, where he completed his playing career in 1976.

The most celebrated highlight of Aaron's major league career came on April 8, 1974, when he eclipsed the career home run record of Babe Ruth by connecting off the Los Angeles Dodgers' Al Downing at Fulton County Stadium in Atlanta. The home run, his 715th in the major leagues, climaxed a very difficult period in Aaron's life as he confronted various forms of abuse, including racial insults and death threats, from those who did not want an African American to surpass Ruth's mark. "It should have been the happiest time of my life, the best year," Aaron said. "But it was the worst year. It was hell. So many bad things happened. . . . Things I'm still trying to get over, and maybe never will. Things I know I'll never forget" (Capuzzo, 1992, p. 83).

Aaron's lifetime record of 3,771 base hits ranks behind only those of Pete Rose and Ty Cobb, and he is the all-time leader in home runs (755), runs batted in (2,297), extra-base hits (1,477), and total bases (6,856). His 2,174 runs scored tie him for third place (with Ruth) behind

Rickey Henderson and Cobb. These credentials, established over a 23-year career, easily earned "Hammerin' Hank" induction into the Major League Baseball Hall of Fame at Cooperstown, New York, in his first year of eligibility, 1982. In 1997 his hometown of Mobile honored Aaron by naming its new baseball stadium, home to the Southern League's AA franchise BayBears, in his honor.

Following his retirement as a player, Aaron returned to the Braves' organization as director of player development and later was promoted to a senior vice presidency. In this capacity, he has been one of the most outspoken critics of Major League Baseball's sparse record of bringing minorities into executive leadership positions both on and off the playing field. In addition, he is a vice president of Turner Broadcasting Company and maintains a number of business and charitable interests in the Atlanta area.

See also Baseball

Bibliography

Aaron, Hank, with Lonnie Wheeler. *I Had a Hammer: The Hank Aaron Story*. New York: HarperCollins, 1991.

Capuzzo, Mike. "A Prisoner of Memory." *Sports Illustrated* (December 7, 1992): 80–92.

Tygiel, Jules. *Baseball's Great Experiment: Jackie Robinson and His Legacy*. New York: Oxford University Press, 1983.

JAMES M. SORELLE (1996)
Updated by author 2005

Abakuá

Abakuá, a mutual aid society for men based on religion, was established by Africans in Regla, Havana, in the 1830s. It represents one of the least known yet most powerful examples of West African cultural influence in the Americas. The Abakuá society is derived principally from the male "leopard societies" of the Àbàkpà (Qua Ejagham), Efut, and Èfik peoples of the Cross River Basin (Old Calabar, now called Calabar), in southeastern Nigeria, and southwestern Cameroon. These societies are called Ngbè and Ékpè, after the Ejagham and Èfik terms for leopard.

A variety of distinct ethnic groups from southeastern Nigeria and western Cameroon were brought to the Caribbean region as slaves. Because the port many departed from was called Old Calabar, and because the language of many others (from the Niger delta) was Kalabari, many of them became known as "Calabarí," (and later in Cuba, "Carabalí," reversing the "l" and "r"), in the same way that various Yorùbá subgroups became known collectively as "Lukumí" and various Bantu groups became known as "Congo."

As Africans were brought to Cuba during the slave trade, the Spanish government divided them ethnically by encouraging those in urban areas to form *cabildos*, or "nation-groups." These *cabildos* became important centers for the conservation of African languages and cultural practices. Carabalí peoples formed several *cabildos* in the eighteenth century, and titled members of the leopard societies were among them.

Cuban Abakuá have never sought repatriation to the African continent, as did the original Rastafarians of Jamaica. Instead, because Abakuá *fundamentos* (sacred objects) were established by Africans in northwestern Cuba, this region is the center of the society's activities. The consecration of land that accompanied the creation of the first *fundamento* by Calabari immigrants definitively established Abakuá in Cuban soil.

Because their primary allegiance is to Ékue, their central *fundamento*, Abakuá consider their society to exist as a separate state within the nation, with their own language and laws. Although each group is distinct, with a pattern of independent settlement closely resembling the social organization of precolonial Southeastern Nigeria, all Abakuá groups share a common mythology and organizing structure. Following the *tratado* (origin myth) of each group, they are identified with Cross River ethnic groups—Efí (Èfik), Efó (Efut), and Orú (Oron). These groups are relatively independent, yet they are answerable to an informal council of elders (recognized for their mastery of Abakuá lore) who convene in times of crisis.

Language

Many key Abakuá terms are slightly transformed Èfik terms still used in the Calabar region. For example, the word *íreme* (spirit dancer) derives from *ídem* (body), while *ékue* (sacred drum) derives from *ékpè* (leopard). Used to evoke ancestral and other divine forces, Abakuá words are believed to motivate inanimate forces into action.

The Abakuá language has influenced Cuban popular speech: *chébere* (or chévere), used popularly to mean "valiant, wonderful, excellent," derives from "Ma' chébere," a title of the Abakuá dignitary Mokóngo. The Abakuá terms *asére* (greetings), *ekóbio* (ritual brother), and *monína* (ritual brother) are used as standard greetings among urban Cuban males.

National and Popular Culture

Partially inspired by the Harlem Renaissance and "Bohemian" Paris of the 1920s and 1930s, the intellectual and artistic movement called Afrocubanismo emerged in Havana during this same period. Seeking to define a national culture, the movement drew inspiration from local black and mulatto working-class cultures. Because the Abakuá were anticolonial, endemic to Cuba, highly organized, exclusively male, secret, and uniquely costumed, they became an important symbol for the Afrocubanistas.

At the forefront of this movement were Fernando Ortiz (1881–1969), who in 1923 founded the Sociedad de Folklore Cubano; Nicolás Guillén (1902–1989), who published his first book of poetry, *Motivos de son,* in 1930; Alejo Carpentier (1904–1980), who published his first novel, *¡Ecue-Yamba-O!,* using an Abakuá theme, in 1933; and Lydia Cabrera (1900–1991), who published *Contes Nègres de Cuba,* in 1936. The composer Ernesto Lecuona (1895–1963) used Abakuá themes in his 1930 composition "Danza de los náñigos [Abakuá]", and the singer Rita Montaner performed Félix Caignet's (1892–1926) composition "Carabalí" in Paris in the late 1920s.

Cuba's renowned painter Wifredo Lam (1902–1982) returned from an apprenticeship with Pablo Picasso in France to live in Cuba from 1941 to 1952, where Alejo Carpentier and Lydia Cabrera encouraged his exploration of African-derived themes. A 1943 painting (untitled) depicts an Abakuá *íreme* with conical headgear and playing a drum. The conical Abakuá mask appears repeatedly in Lam's later work in abstracted forms. In 1947 he painted "Cuarto Fambá," his imaginary recreation of the Abakuá initiation room, which of course he never saw.

Many important musicians of Cuban popular music have been Abakuá members. Because the rumba percussion ensembles were marginalized and rarely recorded before the 1950s, many early composers and compositions remain obscure. Ignacio Piñeiro (1888–1969), a member of the Abakuá group Efóri Nkomón, founded the *son* group Septeto Nacional in 1927. Piñeiro was known as "the poet of the *son*" because his over 400 compositions helped create the global *son* craze of the 1930s. Chano Pozo (1915–1948), a member of the group Muñánga Efó, composed the classic "Blen, blen, blen" in 1940. His later compositions and performances with jazz great Dizzy Gillespie in the late 1940s helped create the bebop genre and are celebrated as a foundation to Latin jazz. Pozo and Gillespie collaborated on compositions in Afro-Cuban jazz (or Latin jazz), including "Manteca" and "Afro-Cuban Suite," performed in 1947 with the Gillespie Band, integrating Abakuá ceremonial music and chants with jazz harmonies. In "Afro-Cuban Suite," Pozo chants "Jeyey baribá benkamá," a ritual phrase in homage to the celestial bodies. Dizzy performed these compositions into the mid-1980s as standards, fusing Abakuá rhythms to popular music in the United States.

The enduring legacy of the Pozo-Gillespie collaboration is felt in numerous ways. In the late 1940s, conga and bongo drums became symbols for the emerging beatnik movement, and the conga drum is now a standard instrument in the United States. Musical tributes to Chano Pozo began in 1949, the year after his death, and continue in the twenty-first century. Irakere, an important jazz group in Cuba in the 1970s and 1980s, also used Abakuá themes.

See also Africanisms; Afrocubanismo

Bibliography

Brown, David H. *The Light Inside: Abakuá Society Arts.* Washington, D.C.: Smithsonian Institution Press, 2003.

Cabrera, Lydia. *La Sociedad Secreta Abakuá: narrada por viejos adeptos.* Havana: Ediciones C. R., 1959.

Cabrera, Lydia. *Anaforuana: Ritual y símbolos de la iniciación en la sociedad secreta Abakuá.* Madrid: Ediciones Madrid, 1975.

Cabrera, Lydia. *La Lengua Sagrada de los Ñañigos.* Miami: Colección del Chicherekú en el exilio, 1988.

Matibag, Eugenio. *Afro-Cuban Religious Experience: Cultural Reflections in Narrative.* Gainesville: University Press of Florida, 1996.

Miller, Ivor. "A Secret Society Goes Public: The Relationship Between Abakuá and Cuban Popular Culture." *African Studies Review* 43, no. 1 (April, 2000.): 161–188.

Ortiz, Fernando. *La "tragedia" de los ñáñigos.* Havana: Colección Raíces, 1950. Reprint, 1993.

Ortiz, Fernando. *Los bailes y el teatro de los negros en el folklore de Cuba.* Havana: Letras Cubanas, 1951. Reprint, 1981.

Thompson, Robert Farris. *Flash of the Spirit: African and Afro-American Art and Philosophy.* New York: Vintage, 1983.

Sound Recordings

Dizzy Gillespie/Max Roach in Paris. BMG Music CD 09026-68213-2, 1995. Includes "Afro-Cuban Suite."

Irakere: Selección de exitos 1973–1978 (Live). Areito, 1978. Includes "Iya" and "Aguanille Bonko."

IVOR L. MILLER (2005)

Abbott, Robert Sengstacke

November 28, 1868
February 22, 1940

The editor and publisher Robert S. Abbott was born in the town of Frederica on Saint Simon's Island, Georgia, to former slaves Thomas and Flora (Butler) Abbott. He developed an interest in African-American rights at a young age, and after learning the trade of printer at the Hampton Institute between 1892 and 1896 earned an LL.B. from Chicago's Kent College of Law in 1898. Abbott practiced law for a few years but soon gave up the profession, for reasons that are unclear, and began a career in journalism.

On May 6, 1905, he founded the *Chicago Defender,* a weekly newspaper that, over the next three and a half decades, evolved into the most widely circulated African-American weekly ever published. As its title suggests, the paper was conceived as a weapon against all manifestations of racism, including segregation, discrimination, and disfranchisement.

The *Defender* gave voice to a black point of view at a time when white newspapers and other sources would not, and Abbott was responsible for setting its provocative, aggressive tone. Among the paper's most controversial positions were its opposition to the formation of a segregated Colored Officers Training Camp in Fort Des Moines, Iowa, in 1917; its condemnation in 1919 of Marcus Garvey's Universal Negro Improvement Association (UNIA); and its efforts to assist in the defeat of U.S. Supreme Court nominee John J. Parker in 1930. The *Defender* frequently reported on violence against blacks, police brutality, and the struggles of black workers, and the paper received national attention in 1915 for its antilynching slogan, "If you must die, take at least one with you."

In addition to exerting community leadership through the newspaper, Abbott was active in numerous civic and art organizations in Chicago. He was a member of the Chicago Commission of Race Relations, which in 1922 published the well-known study *The Negro in Chicago.* In 1932 Abbott contracted tuberculosis; he died in Chicago of Bright's disease on February 29, 1940. His newspaper continues to be published. Its archives, in addition to housing complete files of the *Defender,* contain the Robert S. Abbott Papers.

See also *Chicago Defender*; Lynching; Universal Negro Improvement Association

Bibliography

"Robert S. Abbott." *Contemporary Black Biography.* Detroit, Mich.: Gale, 2001.

Obituary. *Current Biography* (March 1940): 2.

Obituary. *New York Times,* March 1, 1940, p. 21.

Saunders, Doris E. "Robert Sengstacke Abbott." In *Dictionary of American Negro Biography,* edited by Rayford W. Logan and Michael Winston. New York: Norton, 1982, p. 1.

Yenser, Thomas, ed. *Who's Who in Colored America 1941–1944.* New York, 1944.

JOSHUA BOTKIN (1996)
Updated bibliography

Abdul-Jabbar, Kareem

April 16, 1947

Basketball player Kareem Abdul-Jabbar was born Lewis Ferdinand Alcindor, the only child of Ferdinand Lewis and Cora Alcindor, in the Harlem district of New York City. His father took a degree in musicology from the Juilliard School of Music on the GI bill but worked most of his life as a prison corrections officer and as a policeman for the New York Transit Authority. In 1950 the family moved to the Dyckman Street projects, city-owned middle-class housing in the Inwood section of Manhattan. Surrounded by books and jazz in his home, young Alcindor attended a parochial elementary school, Saint Jude's, and in 1961 he enrolled at another Roman Catholic school in Manhattan, Power Memorial Academy.

Alcindor began playing basketball competitively at age nine. Standing six feet, eight inches tall at fourteen years of age, he proceeded to lead Power Memorial High School to two New York City interscholastic basketball championships and to two national crowns; he made All-City and All-American three times each. Widely recruited by colleges, in 1965 he chose the University of California at Los Angeles (UCLA), whose basketball program thrived under coach John Wooden. Freshmen were then ineligible for varsity competition, but in all three of his varsity years Alcindor led the Bruins to National Collegiate Athletic Association (NCAA) championships. By now he was more than seven feet tall, making it virtually impossible for opponents to block his trademark shot, the skyhook. But another of his tactics proved to be more controversial. After his sophomore season, his awesome dunk shot (jamming the ball in the basket) provoked NCAA officials to establish a rule against dunking. The "Alcindor Rule" lasted for just ten years.

During his three varsity seasons, Alcindor scored 2,325 points, averaged 26.4 points per game, and achieved the rare distinction of making first-team All-American for all three years. Yet as a collegian he is probably best remembered for a single game he played in 1968, one of the most famous games in the history of college basketball. In the Houston Astrodome, a live audience of more than fifty thousand and a television audience of millions watched Elvin Hayes and the unbeaten Houston Cougars challenge Alcindor and unbeaten UCLA. Suffering double vision from an eye bruised in an earlier game, Alcindor still performed well, but Hayes's thirty-nine points led the Cougars to a two-point victory. Later, in the NCAA semifinals, UCLA with a healthy Alcindor demolished Houston, 101–69.

Never a mere athlete, Alcindor emerged in 1968 as a person of political and religious principles. In high school in the early 1960s, his racial consciousness had been raised by the civil rights movement, Birmingham church bombings, Harlem riots, and a racially insensitive coach. He wore his hair Afro-style, participated in the verbal and visible "revolt of the black athlete" led by California sociology professor Harry Edwards, and in 1968 effectively boycotted the Mexico City Olympics by refusing to compete for an assured place on the United States Olympic basketball team. For some time he had been studying Islam, and in 1968 he dispensed with his Catholic religion to become a Muslim. His Muslim mentor gave him a new name, Kareem Abdul-Jabbar, "generous and powerful servant of Allah"; three years later he legally changed his name.

In 1969 Abdul-Jabbar launched his professional career with the Milwaukee Bucks, winning the Rookie of the Year award. In 1971, following the acquisition of veteran Oscar Robertson, the Bucks seized the National Basketball Association (NBA) championship. For six seasons with the Bucks, Abdul-Jabbar averaged more than thirty points per game and won three Most Valuable Player (MVP) trophies. Yet he was never really happy at Milwaukee, whose culture and climate were vastly different from anything he had ever known. Marriage and a child provided little solace. Burrowing deeper into his Islamic faith, in 1972 he studied Arabic at a Harvard summer school and bought a house for the extended family of his Muslim teacher, Hamaas. Tragedy struck in January 1973, when rival Muslims massacred several members of that family; two years later, Hamaas and several comrades were sent to prison for their illegal activities in opposition to a public showing of a film that negatively portrayed Muhammad.

In that same year, 1975, Abdul-Jabbar went to the Los Angeles Lakers in a six-player exchange. Within his first five years with the Lakers, he won three MVP awards. After a frustrating first year, he led the Lakers to the NBA playoffs thirteen consecutive times and (teamed with Earvin "Magic" Johnson in the golden Laker decade of the 1980s) to three NBA championships. For a man seemingly always in search of inward peace, however, sad moments continued to intrude upon Abdul-Jabbar's personal life. In 1983 fire destroyed an expensive California home and an irreplaceable collection of jazz recordings; in 1987 Abdul-Jabbar lost $9 million in bad business deals. All the while two sons and two daughters bounced back and forth from their mother, Habiba, to their father in an on-and-off marriage.

After thirty-three years of competitive basketball, Abdul-Jabbar retired in 1989 at the age of forty-two. His numerous NBA records included the most seasons, games, and minutes played; the most field goals attempted, the most made, and the most points scored; and the most personal fouls and blocked shots. In a total of 1,560 NBA outings, he averaged 24.6 points per game. Into retirement he carried six MVP awards, six championship rings, and memories from nineteen NBA All-Star games.

After his retirement Abdul-Jabbar turned his attention to African-American history and the plight of minorities. He authored or coauthored numerous books on the subject, including *A Season on the Reservation: My Sojourn with the White Mountain Apaches.*

See also Basketball

Bibliography

Abdul-Jabbar, Kareem, with Peter Knobler. *Giant Steps: The Autobiography of Kareem Abdul-Jabbar.* New York: Bantam Books, 1983.

Abdul-Jabbar, Kareem, with Mignon McCarthy. *Kareem.* New York: Random House, 1990.

Abdul-Jabbar, Kareem, with Stephen Singular. *A Season on the Reservation: My Sojourn with the White Mountain Apaches.* New York: Morrow, 2000.

Smith, Gary. "Now, More than Ever, a Winner." *Sports Illustrated* (December 23–30, 1985): 78–94.

WILLIAM J. BAKER (1996)
Updated by publisher 2005

Abernathy, Ralph David

March 11, 1926
April 17, 1990

Born in Linden, Alabama, clergyman and civil rights leader Ralph Abernathy was initially called only "David" among family members; later, through the inspiration a teacher gave one of his sisters, the appellation "Ralph" was added. In his formative years, Abernathy was deeply influenced by his hardworking father, William L. Abernathy, who was a Baptist deacon and a farmer who owned five hundred acres of choice real estate. The son's admiration for his father was a major factor in his work in public life. After serving in the U.S. Army during World War II, Abernathy seized the opportunity offered by the GI Bill and earned a B.S. degree in 1950 from Alabama State College (now Alabama State University). In 1951 he earned an M.A. in sociology from Atlanta University.

In 1948 Abernathy was ordained a Baptist minister and went on to serve as pastor of the congregations at the Eastern Star Baptist Church in Demopolis, Alabama, in 1950 to 1951, then at the First Baptist Church in Montgomery, Alabama, from 1951 to 1961 and the West Hunter Street Baptist Church in Atlanta from 1961 to 1990.

While a student at Alabama State, Abernathy had two experiences that would prepare him for his later role as a civil rights leader: He was urged to contribute to the freedom struggle of African Americans by such professors as J. E. Pierce and Emma Payne Howard; and, as president of the student council, he led two campus protests for improved cafeteria services and dormitory conditions. Because of his dignified protests, Abernathy won the respect of the institution's administration. As a result, in 1951 he returned to his alma mater to become dean of men.

While pastor of First Baptist, Abernathy became a close friend of the courageous pastor of the Dexter Avenue Baptist Church, Vernon Johns. Johns, as an older, seasoned pulpiteer, displayed extraordinary boldness in his personal defiance of Montgomery's oppressive Jim Crow climate. When Johns's ties with Dexter were severed, Abernathy developed an even closer friendship with his successor, Martin Luther King Jr. The two young pastors' families became intertwined in a fast friendship that prompted alternating dinners between the two households. At these social meetings numerous conversations were held that frequently centered around civil rights.

In 1955 the two friends' ideas were propelled into action by the arrest of Rosa Parks, a black seamstress. After a long day of toil, Parks refused to yield her seat on a public bus for a white passenger who boarded after her. This refusal by Parks was in violation of the city's segregationist laws. Her action was not the first of its kind by African Americans in Montgomery. However, when Parks was arrested, her quiet, admirable demeanor coupled with her service as secretary of the local NAACP branch helped to stir the black community to protest.

King and Abernathy became leaders of what came to be known as the Montgomery Improvement Association (MIA). Through meetings in churches, the two men spearheaded a mass boycott of Montgomery's buses. While King served as head of the MIA, Abernathy functioned as program chief. Nonviolence was the method with which the protest was implemented. Despite having been a soldier, Abernathy, like King, was convinced that nonviolence was the only acceptable means of dissent. Both had read and accepted the philosophies of Henry David Thoreau and Mahatma Gandhi. The boycott persisted for more than a year. Despite the inordinate length of the struggle, the black community was consolidated in its refusal to ride segregated buses. Finally, in June 1956 a federal court upheld an injunction against the bus company's Jim Crow policy.

This successful boycott inspired the two young clergymen to expand their efforts to win civil rights for American's black citizens. As a result, in January 1957 the Southern Christian Leadership Conference (SCLC) was born in Atlanta. King was elected president of the new organization, and Abernathy became its secretary-treasurer. While he attended this meeting, Abernathy's home and church were bombed in Montgomery. Although it was a close call, Abernathy's family was spared any physical harm.

King moved to Atlanta in 1960 and a year later persuaded Abernathy to follow him and take on the pastorate of West Hunter Street Baptist Church. In the years that followed, the two men, under the auspices of SCLC, led nonviolent protests in cities such as Birmingham and Selma, Alabama; Albany, Georgia; Greensboro, North Carolina; and St. Augustine, Florida. As a consequence, both were arrested many times and experienced violence and threats of violence. In 1965 Abernathy became vice president at large of SCLC. When King was assassinated in Memphis, Tennessee, in 1968, Abernathy was unanimously elected his successor. Soon after, Abernathy launched King's planned Poor People's Campaign. He led other protests until he resigned as head of SCLC in 1977.

After Abernathy assumed the leadership of SCLC, many compared him to King. Unfortunately, he was often perceived as lacking the charisma and poise of his friend. Some even accused Abernathy of being cross or crude in his leadership style. Perhaps the best historical defense of Abernathy's reputation came from himself in the publishing of his autobiography, *And the Walls Came Tumbling Down* (1989). However, its content and literary style were unappreciated by many because of the book's revelations about King's extramarital affairs. Critics accused Abernathy of betraying his long-deceased friend.

Abernathy died in 1990.

See also Civil Rights Movement, U.S.; Jim Crow; King, Martin Luther, Jr.; Montgomery Improvement Association; Montgomery, Ala., Bus Boycott; Parks, Rosa; Southern Christian Leadership Conference (SCLC)

Bibliography

Abernathy, Danzaleigh. *Partners To History: Martin Luther King Jr., Ralph David Abernathy, and the Civil Rights Movement.* Los Angeles: General Publishing, 1998.

Abernathy, Ralph David. *And the Walls Came Tumbling Down: An Autobiography.* New York: Harper, 1989.

Branch, Taylor. *Parting the Waters: America in the King Years, 1954–1963.* New York: Simon and Schuster, 1988.

RANDOLPH MEADE WALKER (1996)
Updated by publisher 2005

ABOLITION

Scholars often distinguish "abolitionism" from "antislavery," with the latter designating all movements aiming to curtail slavery, no matter how slowly or cautiously, and "abolitionism" reserved for the most immoderate opposition. This distinction echoes the usage of radical abolitionists, who described their goal as "immediate abolition" and disparaged other reformers' gradualism. The gradualists, for their part, labeled the radicals "ultraists," a term some "immediatists" embraced despite its intended derogatory connotations. As this war of labels suggests, controversies over methods and goals were recurrent in the history of organized opposition to slavery. In addition, rifts between black abolitionists and white abolitionists in the United States have led some scholars to speak of two abolitionisms.

If they cling to the radicals' narrow definitions, scholars may get a skewed perspective on the movement's progress: Immediatism emerged only in the early 1830s and was submerged in broad-scale political movements in the 1840s and 1850s. To stress sectarian disagreements is to obscure the success of slavery's foes in winning allies and eliminating a mammoth institution during a remarkably brief period of history.

In a series of sardonic letters, "To Our Old Masters," published in Canada West (now Ontario) in 1851, Henry Walton Bibb, an ex-slave speaking for all the "self-emancipated"—those who had escaped from the American South's peculiar institution—placed abolitionism in a broader context. Improving the opportunities that freedom provided for the study of history, Bibb had learned "that ever since mankind formed themselves into communities, slavery, in various modifications, has had an existency." The master class's own ancestors had experienced subjugation in eras when Romans and Normans invaded England. History proved other lessons, too: "the individuals held in bondage never submitted to their yoke with cheerfulness," and in slavery's entire history no moral argument had ever been "adduced in its favor; it has invariably been the strong against the weak." Modern masters were crueler than any before, in Bibb's view, but they also were broadly despised: "you elicit the contempt of the whole civilized world." Inevitably, they would have to "adopt one of the many proposed schemes which the benevolent have put forth for our emancipation," or they would reap the whirlwind. Bibb may have been wrong about past justifications for bondage, but his sense that slavery had lost legitimacy and was approaching its termination turned out to be accurate.

The economic historian Robert William Fogel points out, for example, "how rapidly, by historical standards, the institution of slavery gave way before the abolitionist onslaught." A small group of English reformers formed a society to abolish the slave trade in 1787; by 1807 they had won that fight, by 1833 the slave system in the British Empire was toppled, and slavery was abolished in its last stronghold, Brazil, in 1888. "And so, within the span of little more than a century, a system that had stood above criticism for three thousand years was outlawed everywhere in the Western world" (Fogel, 1989, pp. 204–205). In the United States, where slavery was a deeply entrenched institution and antislavery coalitions looked comparatively weak, the period required to outlaw slavery was even shorter. Thus, discussion of abolitionist factionalism must be balanced by recognition of its triumph.

Early English and American Endeavors

In England, the Quakers, a small sect with little political influence, took most of the early steps against slavery. Alliances with other dissenting sects broadened support for antislavery in a political system increasingly responsive to popular agitation. When antislavery gained the support of

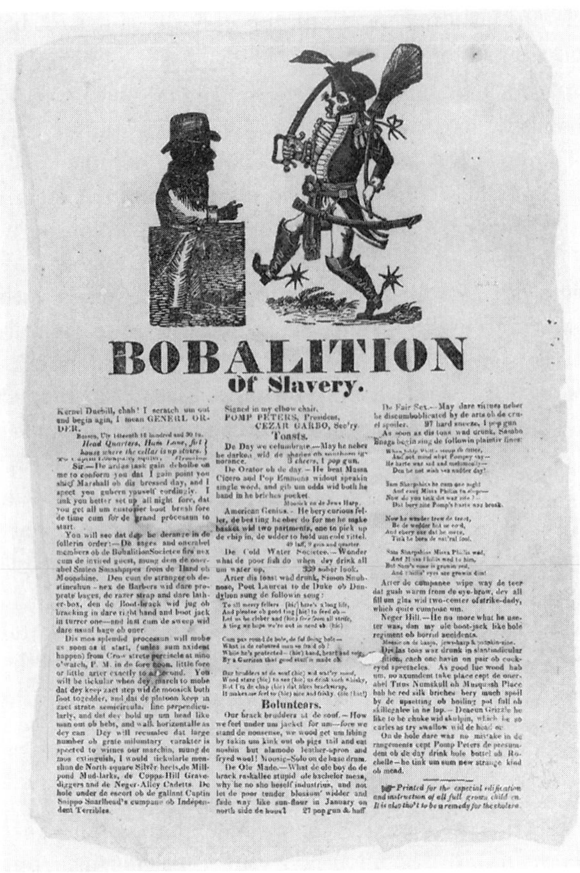

BOBALITION

Of Slavery.

Toasts.

Bolunteers.

Broadside marking the "bobalition" of slavery. *A series of broadsides marked the anniversary celebrations of the abolition of the slave trade in the United States, where the importation of new slaves was formally prohibited beginning in 1808. Created in the form of reports and letters parodying black dialect and stereotypes, these broadsides appeared in Boston between 1819 and 1832.* THE LIBRARY OF CONGRESS

William Wilberforce, Granville Sharp, and other Anglican evangelicals, it acquired respectable voices in Parliament. While advancing the view that slavery was obsolete and immoral, English leaders ensured that no fundamental threat to property rights was associated with abolition.

Slave owners retained their human property during a six-year transitional "apprenticeship," and they received compensation for their losses. Having abolished its own immoral institution, England assumed responsibility for campaigns against the slave trade on the high seas, in the Islamic world, and in India. These campaigns had the effect of spreading British imperial influence and promoting British views of civilization.

As British antislavery approached its great triumphs, it began to send speakers, books and pamphlets, and some financial support to its American counterpart. Some Americans viewed British encouragement of American antislavery efforts as unwelcome meddling that endangered American independence and welfare. Both black and white abolitionists venerated names like Wilberforce and applauded the British example, but there was little resemblance between slavery in the two economies and political systems. American antislavery was compelled to address issues affecting a growing black population, a prosperous domestic economic institution, and sectional animosities in a federal political system for which England's experience offered little precedent. On the other hand, there was no existing English equivalent to the network of organizations among northern free blacks, who sought to embolden white reformers to pursue the cause of abolition more aggressively and to combat racial discrimination wherever it occurred.

As they had in England, Quakers took early leadership in American antislavery activities; they were joined, sometimes, by liberal and evangelical movements to whom old institutions no longer seemed sacred and unchanging. Unlike England, the United States experienced a revolution that supplemented religious reform motivations with strong new reasons for opposing traditional inequalities. Slavery not only violated the law of God, but in an age of liberation and enlightenment, it contradicted the rights of man. Neither religious nor secular arguments necessarily obliged whites to combat racial prejudice or extend humanitarian aid to free blacks. Though black abolitionists would often accuse whites of coldhearted bigotry, it may still be the case that the American Revolution "doomed" slavery.

In the 1780s abolitionist societies were formed in most states (including the upper South). A national abolitionist "convention" met annually from 1794 to 1806 and periodically thereafter. In the decades after the revolution, northern states abolished slavery, often after organized antislavery campaigns. In 1808 Congress, which had previously prohibited slavery in the Northwest Territory, ended the foreign slave trade. This was assumed to be a blow to North American slavery (though some slave owners supported the measure, and later experience showed that the slave population grew rapidly without imports). Appeals to the great principles of republican government seemed ready to transform American society.

Those who believed in an optimistic scenario of revolutionary liberation underestimated the ways in which persistent white hostility to blacks would impede antislavery activity. They also overlooked obstacles imposed by the Constitution. Most abolitionists accepted the prevailing consensus that the federal government lacked any constitutional power over slavery in the states. While antislavery coalitions prevailed in states like New York and Pennsyl-

Anthony Burns, fugitive slave, 1855. Wood engraving featuring a portrait of Burns. Copyrighting works such as this print under the name of the subject was a common abolitionist practice. THE LIBRARY OF CONGRESS

vania, residents of a northern state had no way of influencing legislatures in South Carolina or Tennessee. When controversies over slavery arose in the U.S. Congress, as in debates over fugitive slave acts from 1793 to 1817, proslavery forces won repeated victories. With the elimination of slavery in northern states, abolition societies lost membership and purpose.

The Colonizationist New Departure

Only a change of direction, one that attracted support among southern slaveholders as well as black and white Northerners, revitalized antislavery commitments in the 1820s. Some southerners had long entertained hopes of deporting freed slaves (a solution to racial problems somewhat analogous to Indian removal). If ex-slaves could be relocated in the West, perhaps, or Africa or Central America, slaveholders might be less reluctant to free them, nonslaveholding whites might be less anxious about competition for work, and northern and southern townspeople might show less fear of the social consequences of emancipation. Some northern reformers believed that American society would never accept blacks as equals. Appealing simultaneously to those who hated or feared free blacks and those who deplored or regretted American racism, removal schemes raised hopes of forging an irresistible coalition that might, once and for all, end slavery.

The premier organization advancing these schemes was the American Colonization Society (ACS), founded in 1816, which rapidly won the approval of prominent leaders of church and government in both the North and South. It sent only a few thousand blacks to its colony Liberia before 1830, however, and it failed to get federal funding for its efforts. Enthusiasm for the movement began to subside (although the ACS survived into the twentieth century) as doubts of its practicality grew. Modern scholars frequently dismiss its efforts as futile and its objectives as racist—both irrefutable charges. Less often pointed out are that slavery's most implacable champions hated the ACS; that with its decline, hopes for a national antislavery movement virtually disappeared; and that its predictions of enduring racism and misery for free blacks were realistic. If it included in its numbers such slaveholders as Henry Clay, it also included many northerners who would hold fast to abolitionist purposes for decades to come. It attracted the support of some northern blacks, including John B. Russwurm, a Bowdoin College graduate who spent much of his life in Liberia, and free southern blacks, such as those who appealed to Baltimore's white community in 1826 for help in leaving a republic where their inequality was "irremediable." Not only did they seek for themselves rights and respect that America seemed permanently to withhold, but they also upheld an antislavery vision: "Our absence will accelerate the liberation of such of our brethren as are in bondage."

Black support for colonization was undeniable. It was also extremely limited, while rejection of such schemes by prominent black abolitionists intensified during the 1820s. As early as 1817 a Philadelphia meeting had protested against the ACS's characterizations of blacks as a "dangerous and useless" class; linking manumission to colonization, the meeting continued, would only strengthen slavery. Even such black leaders as James Forten, who privately favored emigration and believed African Americans would "never become a people until they come out from amongst the white people," joined in the protest. By 1829 militant documents, such as David Walker's Appeal, denounced "the Colonizing Plan" as evidence of the pervasive racism that caused "Our Wretchedness."

The Immediatist New Direction

Anticolonizationist societies were launched in free black communities throughout the North, and several efforts were made to establish national newspapers to coordinate the movement. (Russwurm edited one before his conversion to colonizationism.) It was clear, however, that blacks could never sink the ACS without enlisting white allies. This meant, in practice, that blacks would have to speak in a less militant voice than Walker and other leaders might have preferred: They could not stress the virulence of racism or doubt the responsiveness of whites to conciliatory tactics. They could not advocate violent resistance to slavery or discrimination. They might also have to accept subsidiary roles in a coalition movement led by whites. These risks seemed tolerable, however, in light of the emergence in the early 1830s of a new, radical, and interracial antislavery movement that defined itself in opposition to the ACS. What for whites was a bold new departure was for blacks an episode in prudent compromise and coalition building.

Black abolitionists discovered a white champion in William Lloyd Garrison. James Forten and other blacks emboldened him to reject colonizationism and embrace the idea of human equality. Black readers enabled him in 1831 to launch his Boston-based newspaper, the *Liberator,* and they made up the great majority of subscribers to this weekly organ of immediate abolitionism throughout its early years. David Walker was one of several blacks who named children after Garrison; others gave him financial support or protected him as he walked home at night. Many viewed the *Liberator* as their voice in American public life. Maria Stewart was one of many blacks who contributed articles condemning slavery, prejudice, and colonizationism. Garrison adopted a style of denunciation thrilling to his friends and infuriating to those whom he opposed: "I will be as harsh as truth, and as uncompromising as justice. . . .I will not equivocate—I will not excuse—I will not retreat a single inch—AND I WILL BE HEARD," proclaimed his first issue. He took up the view of the ACS that blacks had urged in the previous decade and gave it powerful and influential expression. In its first year the *Liberator* published ten times as many articles denouncing the ACS as explaining immediate abolition. Garrison's *Thoughts on African Colonization* (1832), a withering critique of racist and proslavery quotations from colonization leaders, was widely distributed and persuaded many young reformers to change loyalties and follow a new course.

The attack on the ACS was a means of redefining antislavery strategy that appealed to a new generation of reformers in the early 1830s. Besides Garrison, the most influential of these was Theodore Dwight Weld, a restless and charismatic leader from upstate New York who had traveled extensively and worked for causes ranging from religious revivals to educational reform. As a student at Cincinnati's Lane Seminary in the early 1830s, he worked with blacks in the student body and local community, precipitating a crisis by forcing discussion of slavery and racial prejudice. He had no peer at a style of earnest, emotional antislavery lecturing, facing down mobs and winning converts to the cause, that he taught to other abolitionist speakers. Though Garrison and Weld were (in a not fully acknowledged sense) rivals, the former's uncompromising editorial stance and the latter's confrontational lecture style joined in shaping an exciting new era for abolitionism. Other important abolitionist leaders included the brothers Lewis and Arthur Tappan, merchants in New York City, well connected with prominent evangelical reform movements, who furnished a sober counterpoint to Weld's and Garrison's romantic outbursts. John Greenleaf Whittier, early in a career that led to great fame as a poet, was a valued new convert.

Despite condemnation by Andrew Jackson and other public figures, anticolonizationism spread with remarkable velocity. In 1832 eleven persons formed the New England Anti-Slavery Society, "the first society of this kind created on this side of the Atlantic," as the South Carolina political leader James Henry Hammond later recalled. Though slaveholders initially mocked this news, by 1837 Massachusetts had 145 societies, and New York and Ohio, where the Tappans and Weld held influence, had 274 and 213, respectively. In December 1833 sixty-three men (three of them black) formed the American Anti-Slavery Society (AASS). Earlier that year, interracial female antislavery societies were formed in Boston and Philadelphia, and in 1837 the first "national" (northern) women's antislavery convention took place. By 1838 the AASS claimed 1,350 affiliated societies, with membership approaching a quarter million. Important new voices, including those of ex-southerners James G. Birney and Angelina and Sarah Moore Grimké, added to the excitement of the mid-1830s.

The positive meaning of the immediatist, anticolonizationist doctrines that stirred up so much commotion was never a simple matter to establish. For decades scholars have argued over which of two strategies—political coercion or nonviolent persuasion—was more consistent with the immediatist commitment of the early 1830s. The truth is that immediatism had more than two potential meanings, as it blended rather unrealistic expectations of religious transformation with cautious recognition of obstacles to reform. On the one hand, some abolitionists wished to persuade slaveholders to let their slaves go free, or they hoped, at least, to encourage antislavery majorities to form in southern states. Conceding the lack of federal authority to interfere with state institutions, founders of

Redeemed in Virginia
By Catherine S. Lawrence. Baptized in Brooklyn, at Plymouth Church, by Henry Ward Beecher, May, 1863. Fannie Virginia Casseopia Lawrence, a Redeemed SLAVE CHILD, 5 years of age.
Entered according to Act of Congress, in the year 1863, by C. S. Lawrence, in the Clerk's Office of the district Court of the United States, for the Southern District of New-York.
Photograph by Renowden, 65 Fulton Av. Brooklyn.

Propaganda portrait of Fannie Virginia Casseopia Lawrence. *Fannie Lawrence, five years old in this photograph, was redeemed from slavery, or freed through the payment of a fee, in Virginia by Catherine S. Lawrence.* PHOTOGRAPHS AND PRINTS DIVISION, SCHOMBURG CENTER FOR RESEARCH IN BLACK CULTURE, THE NEW YORK PUBLIC LIBRARY, ASTOR, LENOX AND TILDEN FOUNDATIONS.

the AASS were obliged to adopt a conciliatory stance toward the South. In particular, they denied any intention to use coercion; slavery must end by "moral suasion." On the other hand, the harsh, categorical denunciations of slavery that distinguished the new movement from the ACS were hardly conciliatory. In letters of instruction and training sessions for antislavery lecturers, Weld (who injured his own voice and retired from the field) insisted that they should not get bogged down in political or economic issues: "the business of abolitionists is with the heart of the nation, rather than with its purse strings." Slavery was, he taught, "a moral question," and the conviction to drive home was simply that "slavery is a sin." Once convinced of that, clergymen and other opinion leaders would exert pressure on slaveholders to give up their sin. Repentant slaveholders would soon be impelled to change their lives. If they did not, morally awakened democratic majorities had to compel them.

Schism and Variation

By decade's end it was obvious that slavery was not going to succumb to northern condemnation, no matter how conciliatory or intemperate. Disagreements among abolitionists, subdued during years of enthusiasm, took on new seriousness. The AASS split in two at its 1840 convention when the Tappans and other prominent reformers walked out after a woman, Abby Kelley, was elected to a committee. They protested that under Garrison's leadership the movement was too defiant of social conventions, thus offending the clergy and other respectable leaders of society, and too enthusiastic about new radical causes, especially a new form of nonviolent anarchism called "nonresistance." The departing abolitionists believed the cause could gain popular support by shunning "extraneous," controversial positions. Many on this side were moving toward more active participation in politics. For Garrison's loyal cadres in the AASS, including such radical pacifists as Henry C. Wright, abolitionist commitments led toward broad condemnation of coercive behavior and institutions. The AASS survived as a separate organization, open to all who chose to join, while in the *Liberator* and in speeches and writings, Garrisonians gave increasing attention to nonviolence, utopian communities, women's rights, and other enthusiasms of the 1840s. (They showed less sympathy with working-class reforms.) They remained adamant in opposing political ventures, some out of anarchistic convictions, others out of dismayed assessment of the receptiveness of American politicians to antislavery principles.

Many black abolitionists continued to admire Garrison, but they, too, often criticized the lengths to which he carried the logic of moral suasion. Some agreed with the charge that he depleted antislavery energy by his romantic penchant for adopting new causes. But he, at least, was unwilling to compromise the principle of equality in order to appease northern majorities. Although blacks tended to favor political action, they appreciated Garrison's scorn when political abolitionism bowed to necessity by accepting slavery where it existed in the South and segregation as it worsened in the North. They complained repeatedly that all factions of white abolitionists relegated blacks to subsidiary roles, at best, in their organizations. Such inability to accept blacks in visible leadership positions showed that white abolitionists had not really understood the links between bigotry and slavery. It was difficult, moreover, to interest whites in combating Jim Crow in northern streetcars with the zeal aroused by movements to keep slavery (and African Americans) out of the territories. After the schism of 1840 black abolitionists met more frequently in their own organizations, held their own conventions, and supported their own newspapers, such as Samuel E. Cornish's *Colored American* and *Frederick Douglass's Paper.*

In a powerful 1843 address to slaves, Henry Highland Garnet urged, "Resistance! Resistance! Resistance!" His controversial text was suppressed until 1848, but in the following years, similar militancy among other black leaders became increasingly noticeable. Talk of moral suasion gave way to insistence on the universal right of revolution. If whites did not concede to blacks the right to self-defense, some leaders asked, and if blacks never showed their willingness to fight, then how could southern slavery and northern injustice ever be ended? Blacks (with limited white support) engaged in civil disobedience against segregated schools and streetcars, and they used all available means to assist fugitives from slavery. But such militancy coincided with renewed interest in emigration, either to Canada, where tens of thousands of blacks, many of them fugitives, lived in constant rebuke to conditions in the northern and southern United States, or perhaps to Liberia (despite continuing black denunciation of the ACS), or Haiti, favored by Garnet as late as 1861. Douglass, James McCune Smith, and other black leaders deplored any possible abandonment of the cause of civil rights for free blacks and emancipation of the slaves.

After the war with Mexico from 1846 to 1848, a series of political events and court decisions—particularly events and decisions returning fugitives to bondage—struck abolitionists as calamities. Not only were some black leaders resigned to emigration, but many white Garrisonians denounced the political system dominated by proslavery leaders. Theodore Parker, Thomas Wentworth Higginson, and some others began to contemplate acts of violent resistance to proslavery legislation. Wendell Phillips advocated disunion: the northern states must sunder connections with southern sinfulness. At one public meeting in 1854, Garrison denounced the Fugitive Slave Act and burned the Constitution as "a covenant with Death and an agreement with Hell." Southern extremists portrayed Garrisonians as men and women of enormous influence in the North. They had no such influence, but in taking positions of uncompromising moral purity, these skilled agitators created an atmosphere of escalating moral concern. While eschewing politics, they guaranteed that southern political victories brought the fate of slavery closer and closer to the center of national political debate.

Political abolitionists, meanwhile, tried various courses of action. Some, including many blacks, voted for the Whigs; others experimented with third parties. During a period of confusing political realignment, skilled publicists such as the journalist Horace Greeley and clergyman Henry Ward Beecher used newspapers, lecture platforms, and other popular institutions to disseminate selected elements of the abolitionist message—that the slave power jeopardized the liberty and prosperity of all workers and farmers—across the North and much of the West. In this endeavor they gained the cooperation of antislavery politicians, who were usually reluctant to confront racial prejudice or clarify the meanings of equality. An antislavery majority probably could not have been assembled without ambiguous appeals to expediency and prejudice as well as to principle. It is important to note, nevertheless, that as political abolitionism augmented its small shares of the electorate (the Liberty Party garnered about 6,000 votes in the 1840 presidential election and 60,000 in 1844, and the Free Soil party polled about 290,000 in 1848), the clarity of its attacks on slavery blurred. Both Weld and Garrison had counseled abolitionists to stick to the moral high ground, to denounce the iniquity of slavery and racism. Antislavery opinion grew in the North and West, however, as slavery was seen as threatening to the economic welfare of whites. More often than not, antislavery public opinion of the kind that sustained the Republican Party's slim majority in 1860 was saturated by racial prejudice. It would have been content to tolerate slavery where it already existed, if proslavery politicians had not repeatedly fueled northern fears and resentments and if escalating violence, sometimes subsidized and carried out by abolitionists, had not made a final confrontation seem inevitable.

The Triumph of Antislavery

Abolitionism existed in a tense love-hate relation with Abraham Lincoln and the Republicans in the 1860s. Abolitionists took credit for preparing the ground for the new party's success, but some sought to oust Lincoln in 1864. If anything, Garrisonians were more willing than other factions to excuse the Republicans' slow advance toward the goal of abolishing slavery, a goal promoted by all abolitionists throughout the war. Abolitionists did what they could to pressure the Union army to mobilize black soldiers and treat them fairly once in uniform. Black abolitionists worked at recruitment, and some, including Martin R. Delaney, as well as whites such as Thomas Wentworth Higginson, served as officers. Pacifistic abolitionists volunteered for medical duties in hospitals and on the battlefield. Before slavery was abolished, abolitionist men and women went south to work among freedmen in

Celebration of the abolition of slavery in the District of Columbia, April 19, 1866. *After Emancipation, many northern blacks began traveling south in search of friends and family who had been sold during slavery. Others moved back to the South to teach or to establish churches. F. Dielman's wood engraving was printed in* Harper's Weekly *on May 12, 1866.* PHOTOGRAPHS AND PRINTS DIVISION, SCHOMBURG CENTER FOR RESEARCH IN BLACK CULTURE, THE NEW YORK PUBLIC LIBRARY, ASTOR, LENOX AND TILDEN FOUNDATIONS.

areas occupied by Union armies, thus setting a pattern for educational and related endeavors during Reconstruction and afterward.

At the end of the Civil War, and with enactment of the Thirteenth Amendment, abolitionists were jubilant. The *Liberator* ceased publication, and the AASS disbanded. But abolitionists, especially younger ones who had entered the movement in the 1850s, continued to promote education for African Americans and condemn violations of their civil rights long after the war. As the century approached its end, such endeavors increasingly seemed futile, and many victories of Civil War and Reconstruction days were overturned. At the same time, ironically, some northerners lauded abolitionists as an example of a principled minority who had led the nation to higher moral conceptions and practices.

Some of this glorification can be discounted as an expression of sectional pride and Republican partisanship. It was offset, for many decades, by scholarly condemnation of abolitionists as fanatics responsible, along with southern fire-eaters, for disrupting the Union. Nevertheless, the merging of abolitionist principles, espoused by a zealous minority, with the concerns and interests of a majority of citizens, led to the destruction of slavery, for so long an accepted social institution, and this triumph has gained a prominent place in the history of American democracy. Abolitionists tested the openness of democratic politics to reform, and they agitated successfully for the extension of the nation's founding principles to groups that had formerly been left out. Their triumph has served as an inspiring model for subsequent movements, on both the left and right, from woman's suffrage before 1920, to civil rights from the 1940s through the 1960s, to both gay rights and antiabortion activism in the early twenty-first century.

See also Douglass, Frederick; Emancipation; Forten, James; Frederick Douglass' Paper; Free Blacks 1619–1860; *Liberator, The*; Manumission Societies; Slave Codes; Slavery; Thirteenth Amendment

Bibliography

Blackburn, Robin. *The Overthrow of Colonial Slavery, 1776–1848.* London: Verso, 1988.

Davis, David Brion. *The Problem of Slavery in the Age of Revolution, 1770–1823.* Ithaca, N.Y.: Cornell University Press, 1975.

Dillon, Merton L. *Slavery Attacked: Southern Slaves and Their Allies, 1619–1865.* Baton Rouge: Louisiana State University Press, 1990.

Fogel, Robert William. *Without Consent or Contract: The Rise and Fall of American Slavery.* New York: Norton, 1989.

Goodman, Paul. *Of One Blood: Abolitionism and the Origins of Racial Equality.* Berkeley: University of California Press, 1998.

Jeffrey, Julie Roy. *The Great Silent Army of Abolitionism: Ordinary Women in the Antislavery Movement.* Chapel Hill: University of North Carolina Press, 1998.

McKivigan, John R., and Stanley Harrold, eds. *Antislavery Violence: Sectional, Racial, and Cultural Conflict in Antebellum America.* Knoxville: University of Tennessee Press, 1999.

Newman, Richard. *The Transformation of American Abolitionism: Fighting Slavery in the Early Republic.* Chapel Hill: University of North Carolina Press, 2002.

Pease, Jane H., and William H. Pease. *They Who Would Be Free: Blacks' Search for Freedom, 1830–1861.* Urbana: University of Illinois Press, 1974.

Perry, Lewis. *Radical Abolitionism: Anarchy and the Government of God in Antislavery Thought.* Knoxville: University of Tennessee Press, 1995.

Rael, Patrick. *Black Identity and Black Protest in the Antebellum North.* Chapel Hill: University of North Carolina Press, 2002.

Ripley, C. Peter, et al., eds. *The Black Abolitionist Papers.* 5 vols. Chapel Hill: University of North Carolina Press, 1985–1992.

Stewart, James Brewer. *Holy Warriors: The Abolitionists and American Slavery.* New York: Hill and Wang, 1997.

Stauffer, John. *The Black Hearts of Men: Radical Abolitionists and the Transformation of Race.* Cambridge, Mass.: Harvard University Press, 2002.

Yellin, Jean Fagan, and John C. Van Horne, eds. *The Abolitionist Sisterhood: Women's Political Culture in Antebellum America.* Ithaca, N.Y.: Cornell University Press, 1994.

LEWIS PERRY (1996)
Updated by author 2005

Abyssinian Baptist Church

The Abyssinian Baptist Church in New York City, one of the oldest African-American Baptist churches in the northern states, was founded in 1808 when a white-led church, the First Baptist Church, restricted black worshippers to a segregated area of the sanctuary. In response, The Reverend Thomas Paul, a black minister from Boston, and eighteen black Baptists left and founded their own congregation on Anthony Street (now Worth Street). The name of the church allegedly derives from a group of seamen and merchants from Ethiopia (then known as Abyssinia) who helped found the new church. Abyssinia was a historically Christian African country. The church soon moved to larger quarters on Waverly Place in Greenwich Village. By 1840 the church's membership numbered more than four hundred, and it was the largest African-American Baptist congregation outside the South.

After the Civil War, the church's membership grew slowly, reaching about one thousand by the turn of the century. Since New York's black population had moved uptown, the Reverend Robert D. Wynn repeatedly urged that the church be relocated in the rising African-American center of Harlem. But in 1902, under the leadership of the Reverend Charles S. Morris, the church moved into a new building on West 40th Street.

In 1908, the hundredth anniversary of the church, a dynamic leader, the Reverend Adam Clayton Powell Sr. (1865–1953), was installed as pastor. Powell campaigned successfully to raise money for a church building in Harlem, and in 1923 the new building opened at 132 West 138th Street. The new church cost $350,000 to build and had lush carpets, a recreational center, and an imported marble pulpit.

Despite the cost, the Abyssinian Baptist Church was considered the "church of the people." Its membership, which grew to fourteen thousand by 1937 (the year the Reverend Powell Sr. retired), reflected the social and economic composition of the surrounding black community. Most of the church's members were poor or lower middle class, and there were few professionals among them.

Once settled in Harlem, the church immediately became active in social programs. Powell continued the antiprostitution efforts he had begun on 40th Street, and in 1926 he founded a senior citizens' home at 732 St. Nicholas Avenue, which was named in his honor. Under the leadership of his son, the Reverend Adam Clayton Powell Jr. (1908–1972), the church opened a federal credit union and the Friendly Society, a benevolent organization.

Church activities increased with the coming of the Great Depression. In 1930 a soup kitchen opened, followed by a day nursery, an employment bureau, and, most significantly, an adult education school, which had some two thousand students by 1935. After succeeding his father as pastor in 1937, the younger Powell led boycotts and picket lines aimed at obtaining jobs for blacks in Harlem. Even after he became a New York City councilman in 1941, and then a U.S. congressman in 1945, Powell retained his pulpit at the Abyssinian Baptist Church, where he was renowned for his oratory.

After the death of Adam Clayton Powell Jr. in 1972, the church selected the Reverend Samuel Dewitt Proctor (1921–1997), a former president of both North Carolina A&T College and Virginia Union University in Richmond, to become its next pastor. Proctor continued the social activism for which the church was known. Under his leadership, the church created the Abyssinian Housing Development Fund Company, which provides housing to needy families in Harlem. Proctor also invited the New York Philharmonic to give annual concerts in the church.

In 1990 the Reverend Calvin Butts, who had been the executive minister under Proctor, assumed the pastorate of the church. Butts expanded the church's role in housing development, child care, and adult education through the Abyssinian Development Corporation. A powerful but often controversial leader, Butts has carried out highly publicized campaigns against alcoholism and against alcohol and tobacco companies that target black and Latino consumers for their products. In 1993 Butts began a heated campaign to boycott rap songs with lyrics that denigrate black men and women. Though the membership of the church has dropped over the years to about five thousand, the Abyssinian Baptist Church is still one of the largest and most powerful black churches in America.

See also Baptists; Butts, Calvin; Protestantism in the Americas; Religion

Bibliography

Gore, Bob. *We've Come This Far: The Abyssinian Baptist Church, A Photographic Journal.* New York: Stewart, Tabori, & Chang, 2001.

Powell, Adam Clayton, Sr. *Upon This Rock.* New York: Abyssinian Baptist Church, 1949.

TIMOTHY E. FULOP (1996)
Updated by publisher 2005

ADAMS, GRANTLEY

April 28, 1898
November 28, 1971

Grantley Herbert Adams was born in Barbados to Fitzherbert and Rosa Adams. Grantley was one of seven children and received his primary education at St. Giles Boys' School, where his father was head teacher. Thereafter, he was educated at Harrison College and won the prestigious Barbados Scholarship in Classics in 1918. After winning the scholarship, Grantley served for a year on the staff of his alma mater. That scholarship enabled him to receive his tertiary education and professional training at St. Catherine College at Oxford University and at the Honourable Society of Gray's Inn, London.

In 1925 Adams returned to Barbados and was called to the bar. It did not take him too long to establish his reputation as a formidable advocate and build up a reasonably thriving practice. He combined the practice of law with journalism as lead writer of the *Agricultural Reporter,* a daily newspaper owned and supported by the ruling class of merchants and planters.

In 1934 Adams won a seat in the Barbados House of Assembly, which he held until 1958 when he retired to contest the federal elections and serve in the federal parliament.

The conditions in Barbados at the time of his birth and up to the riots of 1937 and beyond need to be accurately described if Adams's contribution is to be fully appreciated and properly assessed.

The majority of Barbadians was black and had neither the right to vote nor any strength in relation to the elite. So severely restricted was the franchise that in 1932 only 4,807 persons were on the electoral register. According to Adams himself, "Power in the colony rests in the hands of a narrow, bigoted, selfish and grasping plutocracy." Color discrimination was "greatly practised" and it was a rare sight to see men of color holding positions in the civil service, the professions, or the church. Wages for all categories of workers were low and rarely exceeded one shilling, or twenty-four cents a day. Unemployment was high and living conditions were deplorable. Those who lived in the slums around Bridgetown were said to be existing under "horrible animal conditions." The society was semi-feudal in character, highly stratified with little or no social mobility. Sugar, the mainstay of the economy, employed upwards of one quarter of the working population on a seasonal basis.

Generally speaking, these conditions were similar elsewhere in the English-speaking Caribbean, and by 1935 a wave of violent dissatisfaction broke out across the region, starting in St. Kitts. From July 26 to July 31, 1937 Barbados experienced "riotous disorders." Shop windows in Bridgetown were smashed and businesses were robbed and vandalized. In addition, police patrols were stoned and cars were overturned. A state of emergency was declared, and armed police and volunteers shot and killed some fourteen persons and injured forty-seven. In the rural parishes, potato fields were raided and shops broken into.

A local commission of inquiry, which came to be known as the Disturbances or Deane Commission, was es-

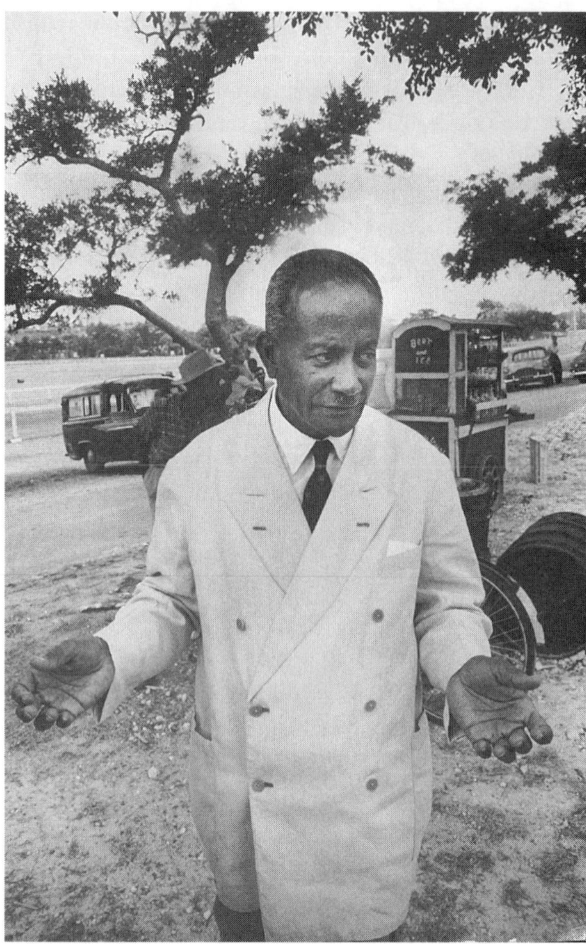

Sir Grantley Adams (1898–1971). *Known as the "Father of Barbadian Democracy," Adams was the first premier of Barbados and the prime minister of the short-lived West Indies Federation.* TIME LIFE PICTURES/GETTY IMAGES

tablished one month after the riots. It found that although there was an event that triggered the riots, the underlying cause was "the large accumulation of explosive material" on the island. Put differently, the fundamental cause of the riots was "economic" and arose from what Adams in his testimony before the commission referred to as "the deteriorating social economic conditions" in the country.

Resulting from the testimony given to the Disturbances Commission and its recommendations, and from the expectation that a high-powered commission would be established by the British Government in relation to events across the English-speaking Caribbean, there was an upsurge of energy and expectations that needed be mobilized and channeled. The establishment of a political party was an urgent necessity. Adams and his supporters saw this clearly and by March 1938 a committee was formed that founded the Barbados Labour Party. An interim executive was put in place, and Adams was named vice president in *absentia*. By mid-April 1938 the name was changed to the Barbados Progressive League, but by 1945 it was again called the Barbados Labour Party.

Within a year of its launch there was a struggle within the newly formed party over ideology, tactics, and leadership. Adams triumphed in this struggle, and in the ensuing special general meeting Adams became the first president-general of the Barbados Progressive League.

As early as 1940 the Barbados Progressive League campaigned in the general election as an organized party, and Adams and his colleagues laid out a comprehensive and enlightened program which informed policy initiatives in Barbados for at least a generation. The program called for a living wage for all workers. It emphasized, too, a modern medical service, well-planned slum clearance, and housing schemes for the whole island. It committed the league to compulsory education, the establishment of free technical schools, and the provision of meals for schoolchildren. The program stressed the importance of old-age pension at age sixty-five and unemployment insurance for workers. Adult suffrage, the creation of new industries, and the conduct of an economic survey and census to provide accurate information on employment were at the heart of the program.

The Progressive League was to contest each and every succeeding election until it was renamed the Barbados Labour Party, and from then on the party, which was the party in office in 2005, has been a major political institution in Barbados and is the oldest party in the English-speaking Caribbean.

Although the idea of a federation of the English-speaking Caribbean was discussed for many years, it was not until the Montego Bay Conference held in Jamaica in 1947 that the concept was given practical definition and significant momentum. The conference was organized by Labour leaders in the region, and Adams's proposals called for a strong central federal government. They were accepted, and he was thereafter seen as the "architect" of the federation, although it was not formally established until 1958, with its capital in Trinidad.

Following the federal elections in March 1958, Adams assumed the office of Prime Minister of the first West Indies Federation, which comprised the countries of Jamaica, Trinidad and Tobago, Barbados, St. Kitts, Nevis and Anguilla, Antigua and Barbuda, Montserrat, Grenada, St. Lucia, and St. Vincent.

Many factors contributed to the dissolution of the federation on May 31, 1962. To begin with, the federal constitution was colonial in character, with considerable discretionary powers given to the governor general. Further, Her Majesty's government was granted reserve powers to legislate in matters relating to defense, external affairs, and the finances of the federation.

On the question of the powers of the federal government, there was a sharp division of opinion between the two biggest territories participating in the federation, Jamaica and Trinidad and Tobago. Dr. Eric Willams, Premier of Trinidad, favored a strong central government. He argued that "only powerful and centrally directed coordination and interdependence can create the foundations of a nation." Jamaica on the other hand wanted the powers of the federal government, already weak, to be further restricted.

There was doubtful support for the federation in Jamaica, and the matter was tested in a referendum on September 19, 1961, following which Jamaica, and soon thereafter, Trinidad and Tobago withdrew from the federation.

Adams returned home, and by 1964 he was active in Barbadian politics. In 1966 he led the Barbados Labour Party in the general election and he was again elected to the House of Assembly, where he served as opposition leader. In October 1970 he was forced to retire from the House of Assembly for the second and final time. His long tenure in politics and his disappointment over the collapse of the federation had taken a toll upon his health.

After Adams's death in 1971, he was accorded a state funeral and is buried in the churchyard of the Cathedral of St. Michael and All Angels in Bridgetown. Buried there, too, are his wife, Grace, and their only son J. M. G. "Tom" Adams, who followed his father in law and politics and was the second prime minister of Barbados (1976 to 1985).

Adams held many positions of public trust and responsibility, and he achieved many firsts in his lifetime. He was the first president-general of the Barbados Progressive League. He was also the first chairman of the Barbados Labour Party. He was the first premier of Barbados and the first and only prime minister of the ill-fated West Indies Federation. His most enduring contribution rests on the large role he played in wresting power from the old ruling elite of merchants and planters in Barbados and locating it in the hands of the masses. His campaign and that of his party to win adult suffrage—one man, one woman, one vote—in September 1950 moved the black masses of Barbadians from the periphery of national politics to the center of the political process. This, combined with the transformation he realized in improving the living standards of Barbadians, in providing them with economic opportunities and in laying the infrastructure for a modern country, earned him the sobriquet of "Father of Barbadian Democracy and of the Social Revolution." He was knighted by Queen Elizabeth II in 1957 for his contribution to Barbados and the West Indies through public service. He has, too, been admiringly referred to by the masses as "Moses." Of equal importance was his strategy of incorporating the old ruling class into the national development effort by accommodation rather than confrontation. It has been followed by successive leaders and governments and helps to account for the stability and cohesion in the Barbadian society.

See also Barbados Labour Party; West Indies Federation

Bibliography

Beckles, W.A., comp. *The Barbados Disturbances 1937, Reproduction of the Evidence and Report of the Deane Commission.* Bridgetown: Advocate Co. Ltd., 1937.

Cheltenham, Richard L. "Constitutional and Political Development in Barbados: 1946–66." Ph.D. diss., University of Manchester, England, 1970.

Hoyos, F. A. *Builders of Barbados.* London & Basingstoke: Macmillan Education Ltd., 1972.

Hoyos, F. A. *Grantley Adams and the Social Revolution.* London & Basingstoke: Macmillan Education Ltd., 1974.

Lewis, G. K. *The Growth of the Modern West Indies.* New York & London: Modern Reader Paperbacks, 1969.

Mark, Francis. *History of Barbados Workers' Union.* Bridgetown: Advocate Commercial Printery, 1966.

Mordecai, J. *The West Indies, the Federal Negotiations Epilogue by W. Arthur Lewis.* London: Allen & Unwin, 1968.

Worrell, D., ed. *The Economy of Barbados 1946–1980.* Bridgetown: Central Bank of Barbados, 1982.

R. "JOHNNY" CHELTENHAM (2005)

Affirmative Action

Affirmative action is an act, policy, plan, or program designed to remedy the negative effects of wrongful discrimination. "Affirmative action" can remedy the perceived injustice of discrimination on the basis of a person's race, national origin, ethnicity, language, sex, religion, disability, sexual orientation, or affiliation. As a civil rights policy affecting African Americans, "affirmative action" most often denotes race-conscious and result-oriented efforts undertaken by private entities and government officials to correct the unequal distribution of economic opportunity and education that many attribute to slavery, segregation, poverty, and racism.

What counts as affirmative action varies from one field to the next. Affirmative action in employment has generally meant seeking to hire a racially mixed and balanced workforce that includes a representative number of

Americans of African, Latin, Asian-Pacific, or native ancestry, using the distribution of minority groups in the national or local population to gauge adequate representation. Self-described "equal opportunity/affirmative action" employers may voluntarily seek to hire African Americans, sometimes with explicit numerical goals and timetables in mind. For example, an employer whose workforce is two percent African American begins to hire additional blacks aiming at a workforce that will eventually include ten percent African Americans, three percent of whom will occupy management positions within three years.

Employers may base affirmative-action programs on the assumption that they can achieve racially balanced workforces through race-conscious hiring and promotion preferences. Preferential employment strategies involve affirmative action on behalf of a racial minority group when a person's minority race results in employment for which race is not otherwise a significant qualification. A person's race may sometimes be a bona fide job-related qualification (Fullinwider, 1980). For instance, undercover police work in black neighborhoods may require black police officers; realistic filmmaking about African-American history may require black actors. In such instances, preferring black workers is not affirmative action.

Not all racial preferences involve affirmative action, and not all affirmative action involves racial preferences. For example, to attract more African-American job applicants, an employer with a mainly white workforce begins to advertise job openings in the city's neighborhood newspapers, including newspapers circulated in black neighborhoods. This change in practice is potentially effective affirmative action, but it is not preferential treatment in the sense of according blacks employment advantages over whites or other groups (Greenawalt, 1983). However, if the same employer committed itself to hiring blacks over similarly qualified or better qualified whites, or by exempting blacks from the adverse impact of seniority rules, one could describe the employer as according blacks preferential treatment as an affirmative-action measure.

Affirmative action in public and private education has focused on such race-conscious programs as "desegregation," "integration," "diversity," and "multiculturalism." Whether voluntarily or pursuant to court orders, to achieve desegregation in public primary and secondary schools formerly subject to state-imposed racial segregation, school officials have expressly mandated numerical goals, ratios, and quotas for faculty hiring and pupil enrollment. At some schools, voluntary affirmative action has meant allocating financial resources to recruiting and retaining minority students with special scholarships, curricula, and social programs. At others, it has also meant admissions procedures that de-emphasize standardized test scores and other traditional qualifications. Some colleges and universities have adopted legally controversial minority admissions quotas or diversity criteria aimed at enrolling a representative percentage of nonwhite students each year. In many schools the ideal of a diverse, multicultural student body is thought to require affirmative action to employ teachers and to enroll and retain students of varied racial and ethnic backgrounds.

Beyond employment and education, the distribution of public or private benefits on the basis of race for the remedial purpose of redressing group discrimination fits the definition of affirmative action. Hence, minority "set-aside" requirements that reserve a percentage of public contracts for minority businesses qualify as affirmative action. The concept also reaches special effort made by public and private scientific, humanistic, and arts organizations to disburse a share of their grants, awards, and prizes to members of once-neglected minority groups. The concept even reaches redistricting to aggregate minority voters into district to remedy a history of inadequate political representation.

Viewing affirmative action goals as quotas is often designed to suggest "that they, like yesterday's quotas, serve an immoral end" (Ezorsky, 1991). Indeed, the affirmative action practiced in employment, education, and other fields has excited intense moral and legal debate. The debate centers on the charges that race-conscious remedies designed to redress invidious discrimination against some groups amount to wrongful "reverse discrimination" against others (Steele, 1990). Opponents of affirmative action raise particular concern about any form of affirmative action that involves numerical mandates, especially goals and quotas. Although the word *goals* often connotes flexible guidelines for group inclusion and *quotas* often connote rigid limits with discriminatory intent, both entail optimal percentages or numbers of persons belonging to specific groups targeted to serve in specific capacities (Fullinwider, 1980). The strongest proponents of affirmative action argue that numerical mandates, whether termed "goals" or "quotas," are just and effective remedies for persistent discrimination (Bowen and Bok, 1998; Johnson, 1992).

History

The idea that special effort is needed to remedy discrimination on the basis of race is as old as President Abraham Lincoln's Emancipation Proclamation and the Thirteenth Amendment to the Constitution ending slavery. However, affirmative action as a distinct race-relations policy did not come about until the crest of the civil rights movement of the 1960s (Anderson, 2004). The term "affirmative action" quietly made its debut in American law in 1935, the year Congress passed the Wagner Act, expressly requiring "affirmative action" of employers guilty of discrimination against workers on the basis of union membership.

In June 1941 President Franklin D. Roosevelt issued Executive Order 8802, a precursor of affirmative-action policies in the arena of race relations, which called for "special measures" and "certain action" to end "discrimination in the employment of workers in the defense industries or government [occurring] because of race, creed, color, or national origin." Roosevelt's historic move was intended to boost the wartime economy and reduce severe black unemployment, as urged by A. Philip Randolph and other leaders. Executive Order 8802 was not consistently enforced, but in some states sudden black competition for traditionally white jobs prompted hostility and violence against blacks.

Internal White House discussions of employment policy during the presidency of Dwight D. Eisenhower included consideration of mandatory affirmative action. On March 8, 1961, President John F. Kennedy issued Executive Order 10925 establishing a President's Committee on Equal Employment Opportunity to expand and strengthen efforts to promote full equality of employment opportunity across racial lines. Order 10925 also required that all government contractors agree not to "discriminate against any employee or applicant for employment because of race, creed, color, or national origin" and to "take affirmative action to ensure that applicants are employed, and that employees are treated during employment, without regard to their race, creed, color, or national origin."

The monumental Civil Rights Act of 1964 outlawed the most blatant forms of racial discrimination in employment, education, housing, public accommodations, and voting. The 1964 act desegregated restaurants, cinemas, retail stores, hotels, transportation, and beaches. Building on *Brown v. Board of Education* (1954), the historic Supreme Court decision that ended legal racial segregation of public primary and secondary schools and pronounced that school desegregation should occur "with all deliberate speed," the act blocked federal aid to segregated schools. The act banned unequal application of the requirements of voter registration. The Voting Rights Act of 1965 went even further in protecting the franchise, restricting literacy tests and authorizing federal election supervision in the states. Title VII of the 1964 act banned discrimination by employers of twenty-five or more, labor unions, and employment agencies, and created the Equal Employment Opportunity Commission (EEOC). Title VII empowered the federal courts to order "affirmative action as may be appropriate" to remedy past workplace discrimination.

Finally, on September 28, 1965, in the wake of the Civil Rights Act of 1964, President Lyndon B. Johnson's Executive Order 11246 launched affirmative action as the centerpiece of national employment policy and race relations. Aimed at "the full realization of equal employment opportunity," Executive Order 11246, like Kennedy's earlier order, required that firms conducting business with the federal government and these firms' suppliers "take affirmative action to ensure that applicants are employed, and that employees are treated during employment, without regard to their race, creed, color, or national origin." Order 11246 was amended by Executive Order 11375 and implemented by Labor Department Revised Order No. 4, requiring that government contractors in "good faith" set "goals" and "timetables" for employing previously "underutilized" minority group members available and qualified for hire. The Labor Department's Office of Federal Contract Compliance, awarded responsibility for implementing Order 11246 and its amendments, developed regulations defining a program of "affirmative action" as "a set of specific and result-oriented procedures" undertaken with "every good faith effort" to bring about "equal employment opportunity." Vice President Hubert Humphrey coordinated the Johnson administration's civil rights and affirmative action policies. On August 20, 1965, at a White House conference on equal employment opportunity, Humphrey had revealed a broad understanding of the economic plight of blacks. Humphrey said America had "neglected the Negro too long" and that "government, business and labor must open more jobs to Negroes [and] must go out and affirmatively seek those persons who are qualified and begin to train those who are not."

In 1967 the Department of Health, Education, and Welfare (HEW) began requiring colleges and universities receiving federal funds to establish affirmative-action goals for employing female and minority faculty members. In 1972 HEW issued guidelines for higher education requiring both nondiscrimination and efforts to recruit, employ, and promote members of formerly excluded groups "even if that exclusion cannot be traced to particular discriminatory actions on the part of the employer." The HEW guidelines also indicated that colleges and universities were not expected to lower their standards or employ less qualified job candidates. The HEW guidelines distinguished affirmative-action "goals," which its directives required as an indicator of probable compliance, from "quotas," which its directives expressly prohibited. Critics of HEW have argued that a firm distinction is untenable since "a positive 'goal' for one group must be a negative 'quota' for another" (Goldman, 1977). Numerous efforts to distinguish goals from quotas have left some analysts unpersuaded: although the purpose of goals may be inclusion and quotas exclusion, "getting people in, where the shape of the 'in' is fixed, will be possible only by keeping others out" (Fullinwider, 1980).

By the early 1970s affirmative action in employment became a full-fledged national policy. The EEOC had taken the stand that an obligation of result-oriented affirmative action extended to all employers within its jurisdiction, not just federal contractors or educational institutions receiving federal funds. Political support for the federal government's affirmative action initiatives was initially strong and broad based. Some maintained that affirmative action utilizing numerical goals and timetables was a necessary complement to the 1964 civil rights statutes. A century after the formal abolition of slavery, African Americans as a group remained substantially poorer, less well educated, and politically less powerful than whites as a group. Legally enforced segregation had intensified black inequality.

The leadership of the NAACP, the Congress on Racial Equality, the NAACP Legal and Educational Defense Fund, and the National Urban League quickly endorsed affirmative action. Diverse sectors of the economy promptly responded to Washington's affirmative action programs. For example, in 1966 the city of New York, the Roman Catholic Church in Michigan, and the Texas-based retailer Neiman Marcus were among the organizations announcing voluntary plans requiring that their suppliers and other contractors to take affirmative steps toward hiring African Americans.

The political popularity of affirmative action during the Johnson administration subsequently yielded to controversy. An erosion of political support in Congress and the White House for higher education affirmative-action programs was evident as early as 1972, seemingly prompted by opposition from faculty members and administrators fearing the demise of traditional standards of scholarly merit. In 1975 U.S. Attorney General Edward H. Levi publicly stated that affirmative action constitutes "quotas" and is "not good government." After 1976, both during and after the one-term presidency of the pro-affirmative action Democrat Jimmy Carter, disagreements over the legality, morality, and efficacy of affirmative action strained African-Americans' relationships with labor unions, the Republican Party, and white liberal Democrats, including Jewish liberals who supported the civil rights movement but who were suspicious of government-backed racial quotas that historically had been used to exclude Jews.

Ronald Reagan and George H. W. Bush campaigned for the presidency on opposition to affirmative-action "quotas." President Reagan spoke out against affirmative-action's numerical goals and quotas, and this opposition became one of the cornerstones of his public policy agenda on issues affecting African Americans. High-profile conservatives defended the ideal of a colorblind society and characterized blacks as overly dependent upon welfare, affirmative action, and other government programs promulgated chiefly by liberal democrats. *Time* and *Newsweek* magazines, as well as other mainstream media, lavished more publicity on affirmative-action controversies than any other topic related to blacks, including unemployment, health, hunger, and homelessness (Daniel and Allen, 1988). The NAACP and the National Urban League maintained their support for affirmative action and the civil rights laws. Consistent with the Reagan agenda, however, the federal government lessened its enforcement of federal contracts compliance programs in the 1980s, and a number of Supreme Court cases curbed affirmative action in employment and other key fields.

In the 1990s some were prepared to attribute significant gains for blacks to affirmative action, including an increase in black employment and promotion at major corporations, in heavy industry, in police and fire departments, and in higher education (Ezorsky, 1991). Yet persistent critics converted "affirmative action" into a virtual pejorative, along with "preferential treatment," "reverse discrimination," and "quotas." Symbolic of the era, Democrat Bill Clinton, a supporter of affirmative-action policies, after election to the presidency in 1992 abruptly withdrew the nomination of Lani Guinier to the Justice Department after her critics labeled her affirmative-action policies as outside the mainstream.

In June 1995 the Supreme Court ruled that all race-based programs would be subject to "strict scrutiny" and must be narrowly tailored to suit specific goals. The following month, President Clinton, responding to congressional pressure to roll back minority preferences, proposed a new initiative on affirmative action that would "mend it, not end it." Despite continued support from Clinton, support for affirmative action nationwide continued to erode. In July 1995, following a lengthy campaign by California governor Pete Wilson, the trustees of the University of California voted to end minority preferences in state college admissions. The following year, a coalition led by Wilson and African-American businessman Ward Connerly introduced Proposition 209, which barred affirmative action programs under the guise of promoting equal rights for all racial groups.

The state of California successfully passed Proposition 209 in November 1996, thereby prohibiting the state from discriminating, or granting "preferential treatment," on the basis of race, sex, color, ethnicity, or national origin in the fields of employment, education, or contracting. Similarly, in 1998 the voters of Washington State adopted the ballot initiative known as I-200. Essentially ending the state's use of affirmative action, Initiative 200 expressly prevented any government entity from making hiring, promotion, and contracting decisions based on racial criteria and gender.

The enactment of Proposition 209 by California voters (and the U.S. Supreme Court's subsequent dismissal of legal challenges to it) paved the way for similar measures in other states. Although in 1997 Houston's voters defeated a challenge to the city's affirmative-action program, the vote was suspended after a court fight. Despite the efforts of influential educators such as Nathan Glazer and Derek Bok to defend the social impact of minority preferences, by the late 1990s the future of affirmative action was more than ever in doubt.

Although such initiatives may point to public support of anti–affirmative action policies, there is evidence that public sentiment may be changing. In 2003 the Racial Privacy Initiative, also known as Proposition 54, was placed on the California ballot. Overwhelmingly rejected by California voters, Proposition 54 would have prohibited state and local governments from classifying and collecting data on the basis of one's race or ethnicity.

Affirmative action debates are not unique to the United States (Sowell, 2004). Tending to focus on ensuring equal opportunity, many countries outside the United States have adopted a version of affirmative action described as "positive action" (Appelt and Jarosch, 2000)—for example, targeted advertising campaigns in Europe encourage ethnic minority candidates to join the police force. Other countries like South Africa and Canada have passed Employment Equity Acts requiring certain employers to draw up an Equity Plan outlining the company's commitment to equity (i.e., promotion of diversity, development and training of designated group, preferential treatment and numerical goals to ensure equitable representation). India has implemented a system that targets discrimination based on caste status by reserving certain positions in university and government to historically disadvantaged people known as the "untouchables," while New Zealand offers preferential access to university courses and scholarships to individuals of Maori or other Polynesian descent. While use of affirmative action had previously been questioned by the European legal community, a 1997 European Court of Justice determined that appointing women to public-sector jobs where they are underrepresented was a legal form of "positive action" provided that rigid quotas were not involved.

Moral and Policy Debates

Reflecting ties to the civil rights movement, the stated goals of affirmative action range from the forward-looking goal of improving society by remedying distributive inequities to the backward-looking goal of righting historic wrongs (Curry and West, 1996; Ezorsky, 1991; McGary, 1977–78). Affirmative action on behalf of African Americans often was, and often is, defended by scholars as compensation or reparation owed to blacks by whites or a white-dominated society (Boxhill, 1984; Thomson, 1977). In particular, it is argued that after two centuries of legally enforced slavery, racial segregation, and racism, African Americans now deserve the jobs, education, and other benefits made possible through affirmative action. Beyond compensatory or reparative justice, goals ascribed to affirmative action include promoting economic opportunity for minority groups and individuals; eradicating racial subordination; neutralizing the competitive advantages many whites enjoy in education, business, and employment; educating a cadre of minority professionals for service in underserved minority communities; creating minority role models, intellectuals, artists, and civic leaders; and, finally, acknowledging society's cultural diversity (Goldberg, 1994; Ezorsky, 1991; Boxhill, 1984; Greenawalt, 1983).

African Americans widely support affirmative action policies. To be sure, some African-American neoconservatives, such as Glen Loury, Thomas Sowell, and Clarence Thomas, have rejected affirmative action on the grounds that it is incompatible with a "colorblind" civil rights policy. Other African Americans sometimes have also criticized affirmative action, often on pragmatic grounds (Carter, 1991; Steele, 1990; Wilson, 1987). They have joined those who argue that preferential treatment in education and employment mainly benefits middle-class blacks, leaving the problem of profound rural and urban black poverty untouched (Goldman, 1979; Cohen, 1980). Critics say affirmative action reinforces pervasive negative stereotypes of blacks as inferior to whites (Jencks, 1983). African Americans have noted this and have argued that racial preferences are demeaning or dispiriting to minorities, that they compromise African-Americans' self-esteem or self-respect (Sowell, 1976). Some reject affirmative action because it has proven to be socially divisive, having bred resentment among white Americans (Nagel, 1977).

As an antidote to simmering white resentments, William J. Wilson (1987) has proposed promoting race-neutral "universal policies" aimed at the health and employment problems of the poor rather than merely promoting affirmative action for racial minorities. The search for factors beyond race and racism to explain persistent

U.S. Supreme Court Associate Justice Clarence Thomas, 2003. *Thomas was nominated to the Supreme Court by George H. W. Bush and joined the court in October 1991. Like some other African-American neoconservatives, he has rejected affirmative action on the grounds that it is incompatible with a "colorblind" civil rights policy.*

black inequality in the post-civil-rights era has led some politically conservative opponents of affirmative action to advance the argument that minority economic inequality stems from a pervasive breakdown in work, family, and community values in minority communities.

Supporters of affirmative action offer pertinent replies to all of these arguments (Ezorsky, 1991). To the contention that affirmative action does not help the poorest blacks, a reply has been that affirmative action nonetheless enhances the lives of some deserving blacks. To the argument that affirmative action lowers esteem for blacks and blacks' self-esteem, a reply is that blacks are held in very low esteem already and are vulnerable to low self-esteem because of their inferior education and employment. To the argument that affirmative action is racially divisive and breeds resentment, a reply is that blacks should not be deprived of the benefits of affirmative action simply because of white resentment unless that resentment can be shown to stem from genuine racial injustice. Finally, to the "fingerpointing" argument that blacks' problems result from lapses of individual responsibility, one reply is that communities of poverty, drugs, and violence result from decades of private and public decision making concerning legal, economic, and social policy.

Gertrude Ezorsky (1991), who supports affirmative action, has noted a libertarian argument against affirmative action: employers should be free to choose their own workers as a basic moral freedom, comparable to the freedom to choose one's own spouse. The more common libertarian argument asserts that social and economics benefits should be distributed solely in accordance with colorblind principles of entitlement, merit, and personal characteristics. In liberal academic and intellectual circles, opponents of affirmative action have questioned the coherence of the idea that blacks as a group are entitled to, merit, or deserve affirmative action as compensation or reparations for past wrongdoing (Sher, 1977). Corrective justice, some philosophers say, is both causal and relational. That is, when an injury occurs, the person who caused that injury must personally pay his or her victim. Yet affirmative action makes white males pay for societal injuries to women and minorities that they did not cause (Paul, 1991). The ex-slaves wronged by slavery are dead, as are the people who wronged them. It is therefore illogical, the argument continues, to hold all current whites responsible for the evils of slavery that were perpetrated by the remote ancestors of some whites on the remote ancestors of some blacks (Sher, 1977). In sum, set-asides and other preferential programs that fall under the rubric of affirmative action "reward an ill-defined class of victims, indiscriminately favor some in that class and leave others totally uncompensated, benefit groups whose members were never the victims of state imposed discrimination, and most importantly, do not concentrate recompense on those whose rights were most flagrantly violated, namely, the black slaves, now long dead" (Simon, 1977).

Against the commonly asserted argument that African Americans who stand to benefit by affirmative action were never in bondage to whites and may have led lives free of egregious discrimination, some philosophers defend affirmative action as a moral right of persons belonging to groups that have been uniquely harmed in the past by public law and that are disproportionately poor or otherwise disadvantaged today. Admitting that white citizens are not personally at fault for slavery and may not harbor racist sentiments, these advocates of affirmative action observe that white citizens benefit from the system of racial privilege and institutional racism that continued to pervade American institutions after blacks' emancipation from slavery and segregation (Thomson, 1977). Whites have a competitive advantage over blacks that society may fairly seek to erase through affirmative action.

Legal Dimensions

Frequently challenged in the courts of scholarly and public opinion, affirmative action also has been litigated frequently in the nation's federal courts. The question of the legality of racial quotas and other affirmative-action measures has no simple answer. From 1969 to 1993 alone, the Supreme Court decided more than twenty major cases relating to the legality of diverse race-conscious remedies. In the same period at least five cases considered the legality of affirmative action on behalf of women. While a number of these twenty-five cases validated one or another form of affirmative action, several important cases related to education, employment, minority business opportunity, and voting rejected it as a legal strategy.

Paramount in affirmative-action cases are the implications of Title VII of the Civil Rights Act of 1964 and other civil rights statutes enacted by Congress. Equally important when plaintiffs contest affirmative action by governmental entities are the principles of equal protection embodied in the Fifth and Fourteenth Amendments of the Constitution. The U.S. Supreme Court has established that the Constitution prohibits discrimination on the basis of race by state and federal government as a denial of equal protection of law. The Court's equal-protection jurisprudence presumes that racial classifications are potentially invidious, giving rise to the need for "strict scrutiny" when challenged. Defined as a stringent, virtually impassable standard of judicial review, strict scrutiny requires government to justify its law or conduct by appealing to a compelling governmental interest. The constitutional conundrum posed by affirmative action is whether the provisions of the Constitution that presumptively ban state and federal government discrimination on the basis of race and entail the need for strict scrutiny review nonetheless permit the use of the race-conscious remedies to redress racial discrimination. Whether framed by constitutional or statutory questions, affirmative-action cases commonly involve procedural complexities relating to assigning the burdens of proving or disproving that the absence of minorities or women in an institution is the result of intentional or other unlawful discrimination.

Endorsing Race-Conscious Remedies

The Supreme Court unanimously endorsed quotas and other race-conscious numerical requirements to achieve school desegregation in *United States v. Montgomery County Board of Education* (1969) and *Swann v. Charlotte-Mecklenburg Board of Education* (1971). In a different context the Court again endorsed race-conscious remedies in *United Jewish Organizations v. Carey* (1977). Over Fourteenth Amendment and other constitutional objections, the Court upheld a New York redistricting plan that explicitly attempted to increase the voting strength of "nonwhite" voters—blacks and Puerto Ricans—seemingly at the expense of a community of Hasidic Jews, viewed as whites under the plan. Four justices agreed that the use of race as a factor in districting and apportionment is constitutionally permissible; that express findings of past discrimination were not required to justify race-conscious policies; and that racial quotas in electoral districting were not by definition unconstitutional. Chief Justice Warren Burger dissented from the judgment of the Court, stressing his discomfort with putting the "imprimatur of the State on the concept that race is a proper consideration in the electoral process."

Seniority Limits on Workplace Preferences

In 1977 the Court established a limitation on affirmative action that it would reiterate in subsequent cases. *International Brotherhood of Teamsters v. United States* (1977) held that a disparate impact on minorities alone does not make a seniority system illegal under Title VII. Justice Thurgood Marshall, partly dissented from the majority, joined by Justice William Brennan. The Court's lone African-American justice, Marshall cited Federal Court of Appeals opinions, EEOC decisions, scholarly materials, and legislative history to attest to the broadness of the remedial goal of Title VII. Marshall admitted that Congress had expressed reservations about orders of retroactive seniority in a nonremedial context or based solely upon a showing of a policy's disparate impact on minorities without any evidence of discriminatory intent. But Marshall argued that Congress did not clearly intend to preserve seniority systems that perpetuate the effects of discrimination. Seven years after the teamsters case, *Firefighters Local Union No. 1784 v. Stotts* (1984) overturned a district court's injunction prohibiting the city of Memphis from following its seniority system's "last hired, first fired" policy during layoffs. In *Wygant v. Jackson Board of Education* (1986), Justice Marshall again dissented from a ruling elevating seniority rules over affirmative-action principles. Here the Court invalidated the provision of a collective-bargaining agreement between a school board and the local teachers' union that would have preserved minority representations in teaching staff in the event of layoffs. Justice Powell applied strict scrutiny to the contested provision, arguing for the Court that strict scrutiny applies to any racial classification, even when the classification "operates against a group that historically has not been subject to discrimination." Justices Sandra Day O'Connor and

Justice Byron White concurred in the use of strict scrutiny review to assess the impact of affirmative action on whites.

School Admissions: No Strict Quotas Allowed

Two cases involving affirmative action in law and medical school admissions evidence the Court's judgment of limited constitutional tolerance for affirmative-action plans involving numerical quotas: *Defunis v. Oregaard* (1977) and *Regents of the University of California v. Bakke* (1978). In *Defunis,* a law school applicant challenged the race-conscious admissions policies of the state-supported University of Washington Law School as a violation of his right to equal protection under the Fourteenth Amendment. The school had established a separate admissions process for minorities and a fifteen to twenty percent admissions goal for applicants who described their dominant ethnic origin as black, Chicano, American Indian, or Filipino. The *Defunis* case was not decided on its merits; the Court declared the case moot after Defunis matriculated in law school while the suit was pending. However, in a dissenting opinion, Justice William O. Douglas criticized conventional law school admissions criteria and stressed that schools can and should broaden their inquiries beyond test scores and grades. Douglas opined that race could be a factor in admissions, consistent with the constitutional requirement of race neutral evaluation, so long as all persons are judged "on an individual basis, rather than according to racial classifications."

Decided fully on the merits, the highly publicized *Bakke* case struck down the special admissions program of the public Medical School of the University of California at Davis. The program featured a sixteen percent quota for "blacks, Chicanos, Asians, and American Indians." The purpose of the program was to increase minority representation in the medical field, to compensate minorities for past societal discrimination, to increase medical care in underserved communities, and to diversify the student body. Allen Bakke, a twice-rejected white applicant to the medical school, challenged its admissions program both under Title VI of the Civil Rights Act of 1964 and under the Equal Protection Clause of the Fourteenth Amendment.

The court issued a long and complex series of opinions to resolve Bakke's case. In the final analysis, the case declared minority admissions quotas unlawful at schools receiving federal dollars, but upheld the use of race as a factor in selecting a diverse student body. Five members of the Court affirmed the illegality of the Davis program and directed Bakke to be admitted to the school. Justice Powell affirmed the illegality of the school's admissions program but voted with Justices Brennan, White, Marshall, and Blackmun to approve the use of race as a factor in higher education admissions. Justice Stevens and three others thought it unnecessary to decide the constitutional issues raised by the case, finding that the admissions policy was invalid under Title VI. They ascertained that the plain language of the statute prohibiting discrimination was sufficient justification for nullifying the program.

The dissenting opinion of Justices Brennan, White, Marshall, and Blackmun cautioned that the nation's "colorblind" values were purely aspirational. They argued that a reading of the history and purpose of Title VI did not rule out race-conscious remedies. Taking up the constitutional issues, these justices rejected strict scrutiny review in favor of a lower, "intermediate" level of scrutiny. They reasoned that intermediate scrutiny permits racial classification "substantially related to an important government objective" and concluded that the university's purpose of counteracting an actual or potential disparate racial impact stemming from discrimination was sufficiently important to justify race-conscious admissions. Justice Marshall also separately wrote a dissenting opinion expressing his sense of irony at the Court's reluctance to uphold race-conscious remedies: "[It] is unnecessary in 20th century

Justice Thurgood Marshall

"It is because of a legacy of unequal treatment that we now must permit the institutions of this society to give consideration to race in making decisions about who will hold the positions of influence, affluence, and prestige in America. For far too long, the doors to those positions have been shut to Negroes. If we are ever to become a fully integrated society, one in which the color of a person's skin will not determine the opportunities available to him or her, we must be willing to take steps to open those doors. I do not believe that anyone can truly look into America's past and still find that a remedy for the effects of that past is impermissible."

DISSENTING OPINION IN *UNIVERSITY OF CALIFORNIA BOARD OF REGENTS V. BAKKE,* 438 U.S. 265 (1978).

America to have individual Negroes demonstrate that they have been victims of racial discrimination; the racism of our society has been so pervasive that none, regardless of wealth or position, has managed to escape its impact."

In 1982 the Supreme Court again took up the subject of affirmative action in professional school admissions in *Mississippi University for Women v. Hogan*. The nursing school of the university denied full admission to male students (admitted only as auditors) on the grounds that the education of women was "educational affirmative action" intended to mitigate the adverse effects of discrimination on women. A man denied admission brought suit under the Equal Protection Clause. A five-justice majority that included Justices Marshall and O'Connor invalidated the single-sex policy on his behalf. Justice O'Connor wrote for the Court, applying the intermediate scrutiny standard of review. This same standard is the one the Court normally applies to gender classification cases brought under the Fourteenth Amendment's Equal Protection Clause. It is also the standard that Justice Marshall defended as appropriate for affirmative-action cases involving remedial racial classifications. The Court required that Mississippi advance an "exceedingly persuasive justification" for its gender distinction in nursing education that included a claim that the distinction was substantially related to an important government goal. Finding no such relationship or justification, the Court disparaged the ideal of a single-sex learning environment in nursing as a "self-fulfilling prophecy" based on the stereotype that nursing is "women's work." Dissenting Justices Powell, Blackmun, and Rehnquist, and Chief Justice Burger denied that the case raised a serious question of gender discrimination. Powell stressed that no woman had complained about the school and that coed nursing education was available elsewhere in the state. Although the majority limited its holding to the nursing school, the dissenters raised concerns about the implication of the case for traditional same-sex higher education in the United States. It appears that affirmative action for women may not be used as a rationale for excluding men from women's traditional provinces.

In its first ruling on affirmative action in higher education admissions since *Regents of the University of California v. Bakke*, the Supreme Court in two landmark decisions involving the University of Michigan's affirmative-action policies ruled that race could be used in university admission decisions for a specific purpose (Stohr, 2004). In *Grutter v. Bollinger* (2003), a rejected white applicant challenged the University of Michigan Law School's admission policies. Upon an investigation revealing that African Americans and ethnic minorities who had lower overall admissions scores were admitted, the petitioner brought suit, arguing that she had been a victim of illegal discrimination. In a five-to-four decision, the Court upheld the law school's policy, declaring that race could be one of many factors considered by colleges when selecting their students because it furthers "a compelling interest in obtaining the educational benefits that flow from a diverse student body." The Supreme Court, however, in *Gratz v. Bollinger* (2003) ruled six to three that the more formulaic approach of the University of Michigan's undergraduate admissions program, which uses a point system that rates students and awards additional points to minorities, had to be modified because it violated equal protection provisions of the Constitution. The undergraduate program, unlike the law school's, did not provide the "individualized consideration" of applicants deemed necessary in previous Supreme Court decisions, nor was its use of race "narrowly tailored" to achieve the university's diversity goals.

Barbara Grutter (l), of Plymouth, Michigan, and Jennifer Gratz of Oceanside, California. *Two of the plaintiffs in the University of Michigan affirmative action cases, Grutter and Gratz leave a news conference held by Ward Connerly at the University on July 8, 2003. Connerly, chair of the American Civil Rights Association, had introduced California Proposition 209, which barred affirmative action programs in higher education.* AP/WIDE WORLD PHOTOS

While the political and legal debate continues, the impact of affirmative action programs is significant. In an empirical analysis of academic, employment, and personal data collected from more than 45,000 students of all races who attended academically selective universities from the 1970s to the early 1990s, the aggregate statistics support the argument for the use of affirmative action in college and university admissions (Bowen and Bok, 1998). Upon examination, the study determined that candidates assist-

President George W. Bush's Remarks on the University of Michigan Affirmative Action Case, January 15, 2003

The Supreme Court will soon hear arguments in a case about admission policies and student diversity in public universities. I strongly support diversity of all kinds, including racial diversity in higher education. But the method used by the University of Michigan to achieve this important goal is fundamentally flawed.

At their core, the Michigan policies amount to a quota system that unfairly rewards or penalizes perspective students, based solely on their race. So, tomorrow my administration will file a brief with the court arguing that the University of Michigan's admissions policies, which award students a significant number of extra points based solely on their race, and establishes numerical targets for incoming minority students, are unconstitutional.

Our Constitution makes it clear that people of all races must be treated equally under the law. Yet we know that our society has not fully achieved that ideal. Racial prejudice is a reality in America. It hurts many of our citizens. As a nation, as a government, as individuals, we must be vigilant in responding to prejudice wherever we find it. Yet, as we work to address the wrong of racial prejudice, we must not use means that create another wrong, and thus perpetuate our divisions.

America is a diverse country, racially, economically, and ethnically. And our institutions of higher education should reflect our diversity. A college education should teach respect and understanding and goodwill. And these values are strengthened when students live and learn with people from many backgrounds. Yet quota systems that use race to include or exclude people from higher education and the opportunities it offers are divisive, unfair and impossible to square with the Constitution.

In the programs under review by the Supreme Court, the University of Michigan has established an admissions process based on race. At the undergraduate level, African American students and some Hispanic students and Native American students receive 20 points out of a maximum of 150, not because of any academic achievement or life experience, but solely because they are African American, Hispanic or Native American.

To put this in perspective, a perfect SAT score is worth only 12 points in the Michigan system. Students who accumulate 100 points are generally admitted, so those 20 points awarded solely based on race are often the decisive factor.

At the law school, some minority students are admitted to meet percentage targets while other applicants with higher grades and better scores are passed over. This means that students are being selected or rejected based primarily on the color of their skin. The motivation for such an admissions policy may be very good, but its result is discrimination and that discrimination is wrong....

Schools should seek diversity by considering a broad range of factors in admissions, including a student's potential and life experiences....

America's long experience with the segregation we have put behind us and the racial discrimination we still struggle to overcome requires a special effort to make real the promise of equal opportunity for all. My administration will continue to actively promote diversity and opportunity in every way that the law permits.

ed in admission stayed in school, graduated, and did very well academically. Further assessments of salary information, workforce participation, family structure, and leisure activities revealed that graduates of selective colleges, especially black matriculants even more than their white counterparts, tended to do extremely well after graduation.

Title VII Permits Voluntary Quotas

In a significant decision, the Supreme Court reconciled Title VII of the Civil Rights Act of 1964 with voluntary affirmative-action programs in *United Steel Workers v. Weber* (1979). By a vote of five to two (two justices did not participate in the decision), the Court in *Weber* upheld an employer's affirmative-action plan that temporarily required a minimum of fifty percent African-American composition in a skill-training program established to increase African-American representation in skilled positions. The lower courts had ruled that any racial preferences violated Title VII, even if they were established in the context of an affirmative-action plan. Importantly, the Court held that Title VII's ban on all racial discrimination did not apply to affirmative-action plans. Dissenting Justices Burger and Rehnquist disagreed, arguing in separate opinions that the plain language of Title VII and its legislative history banned voluntary racial preferences, even those employed as affirmative-action remedies. *Newsweek* magazine reported the *Weber* decision as a "Victory for Quotas." Eleanor Holmes Norton, the African-American head of the EEOC, declared that "employers and unions no longer need fear that conscientious efforts to open job opportunities will be subjected to legal challenge." Senator Orrin Hatch responded differently, asserting that the purpose of the Civil Rights Act had not been to "guarantee any racial group a fixed proportion of the positions and perquisites available in American society" and that the "American dream" of true liberty was "in real danger."

In *Johnson v. Transportation Department* (1987) the Court held (six to three) that Title VII permits affirmative consideration of employees' gender when awarding promotions. In *Johnson* the Court upheld the promotion of Diane Joyce, made according to the Transportation Agency of Santa Clara County's voluntarily adopted affirmative-action plan. Permitting the use of sex, minority status, and disability as factors for promotional consideration, the plan survived a challenge under Title VII by a man passed over for a road dispatcher position. In another case, *Local No. 93, International Association of Firefighters v. Cleveland* (1986), the Court held that parties to a consent decree may agree to relief that might not be within a court's ordering authority under Title VII. An African-American and Latino firefighters' organization, the Vanguards, had filed a complaint against the city of Cleveland for intentional discrimination in "hiring, assignment, and promotion." Since the city had previously been unsuccessful in defending other discrimination suits, it sought to settle with the Vanguards. Local 93 (the union) intervened, not bringing any claims for or against either party but voicing strenuous opposition to a settlement including any race-conscious action. When a consent decree that provided for the action was agreed upon and entered, the union filed its unsuccessful formal complaint that the decree exceeded a court's authority under Title VII.

Title VII permits affirmative action that includes numerical goals, and may permit courts to order it. In *Local 28 of the Sheet Metal Workers' International Association v. EEOC* (1986), the Supreme Court upheld a court-ordered membership plan for a trade union found guilty of racial discrimination by violating Title VII. The plan included a membership goal of twenty-nine percent African American and Latino. The Court was again willing to permit a numerically based affirmative-action remedy in *United States v. Paradise* (1987). In this case the Court validated a temporary affirmative-action plan ordered by a lower court that required a one-for-one promotion ratio of whites to qualified blacks in the Alabama Department of Public Safety. The department had been found guilty of discrimination in 1972, but had failed to adopt promotion procedures that did not have a disparate impact on blacks. Justice William Brennan argued that the affirmative-action order was a narrowly tailored means to achieve a compelling government purpose, so it therefore met the requirements of strict scrutiny imposed by the Equal Protection Clause of the Fourteenth Amendment.

Noncongressional Business Set-Asides

A year after the *Weber* case, in *Fullilove v. Klutznick* (1980), the Court upheld a provision of the congressional Public Works Employment Act, which mandated that ten percent of $4 billion in federal funds allocated for local public construction projects go to "minority business enterprises," statutorily defined as at least fifty percent owned by citizens who are "Negroes, Spanish-speaking, Oriental, Indians, Eskimos, and Aleuts." The provision had been challenged under equal protection principles. Chief Justice Burger delivered the judgment of the Court, joined by Justices White and Powell. Justice Marshall, concurring in the judgment in *Fullilove* and joined in his opinion by Justices Brennan and Blackmun, argued that "Congress reasonably determined that race-conscious means were necessary to break down the barriers confronting participation by minority enterprises in federally funded public works projects." *Fullilove* survived challenge in the Court at a time when critics of federal support for minority business enterprises argued that, in addition to raising questions of fairness raised by all affirmative action, the disbursal of funds under the 1977 Public Works Employment Act by the Commerce Department's Economic Development Administration was subject to abuse (Ross, 1979). The Government Accounting Office uncovered hundreds of instances of federal dollars being awarded both to minority brokers serving as go-betweens for nonminority firms and government administrators and to nonminority firms feigning minority ownership with the help of minority "fronts" installed as phony partners or owners.

Richmond v. J. A. Croson Co. (1989) successfully attacked an affirmative-action plan reserving specific numerical percentages of a public benefit for minorities. The invalidated "minority set-aside" plan required prime contractors with the city of Richmond to "subcontract at least 30 percent of the dollar amount of the contract to one or more Minority Business Enterprises." The plan was challenged under 42 U.S.C. §1983, a civil rights statute, by a nonminority firm that lost a contracting opportunity because of noncompliance with the program. The justices widely disagreed about the outcome and the reasoning of the case. Justice O'Connor delivered the opinion of the Court with respect to three of its parts, joined by Chief Justice Rehnquist and Justices Stevens, White, and Kennedy; Justices Stevens and Kennedy filed separate partial concurrences; Justice Scalia filed a concurring opinion; Justice Marshall dissented, joined in his opinion by Justices Brennan and Blackmun; finally, Justice Blackmun filed a dissenting opinion, joined by Justice Brennan. A major task for the majority was to explain how they could invalidate the set-aside in *Croson* when the Court had previously validated a similar set-aside in *Fullilove*. Justice O'Connor distinguished the *Fullilove* case on the ground that its set-aside had been created by Congress and involved an exercise of federal congressional power, whereas the set-aside in *Croson* was a creature of municipal government. Justice Thurgood Marshall dissented from the judgment in *Croson*, warning that the Court's ruling threatened all affirmative action plans not specifically enacted by Congress—virtually all plans.

Metro Broadcasting, Inc. v. FCC (1990) upheld two race-conscious Federal Communications Commission programs designed to enhance program diversity. The race-conscious set-asides were challenged under equal protection principles by a nonminority broadcasting company that had lost its bid to acquire a broadcasting license to a minority-owned company. The Court argued that programming diversity, a goal both the FCC and Congress linked to ownership diversity, was derived from the public's First Amendment interest in hearing a wide spectrum of ideas and viewpoints. The interest was a sufficiently important one to justify race-conscious allocation policies. Justice O'Connor and three other justices dissented from what they considered excessive deference to Congress and a refusal to apply strict scrutiny to an instance of race-conscious thinking grounded in racial stereotypes.

Future Directions

Decided by the slimmest majority and largely on unusual First Amendment grounds, *Metro Broadcasting* leaves standing the basis for Justice Marshall's concerns about the future of all affirmative action. So, too, does *Shaw v. Reno* (1993). This case held that white voters stated a legitimate Fourteenth Amendment equal protection claim against North Carolina for creating a voter redistricting plan described as "so irrational on its face that it c[ould] be understood only as an effort to segregate voters" on the basis of race. Justices White, Souter, and Stevens dissented. In an attempt to comply with the Voting Rights Act, North Carolina had created a redistricting plan with two irregularly shaped "majority-minority" (majority black and Native American) districts. In reversing the lower court, the Court invoked the ideal of a "colorblind" society and warned of the dangers of "political apartheid." Nonetheless, the constitutionality of the districts was subsequently upheld by a federal judicial panel.

The ideal of a colorblind society continues to vex proponents of race-conscious remedies to discrimination. The greatest consistency in the evolving law of affirmative action is that, at any given time, its precise contour mirrors the mix of perspectives represented on the Court concerning the deepest purposes and meaning of the 1964 Civil Rights Act and the Fourteenth Amendment of the Constitution. The Supreme Court has upheld key affirmative-action measures in the past, and may again in the future. A series of rulings in the spring and summer of 1995 narrowed the allowable scope of affirmative action beyond the university. Notably, in the case of *Adarand Constructors v. Peña* (1995) the Court ruled, five to four, that the federal government's affirmative-action programs must be able to meet the same strict standards for constitutional review as had previously been applied by the Court to state and local programs. *Grutter v. Bollinger* (2003), the University of Michigan law school admissions case, proves that affirmative action can be constitutional, but the debate over affirmative action continues.

See also Civil Rights Movement, U.S.; Marshall, Thurgood

Bibliography

Anderson, Terry, H. *The Pursuit of Fairness: A History of Affirmative Action.* New York: Oxford University Press, 2004.

Appelt, Erna, and Monika Jarosch. *Combatting Racial Discrimination: Affirmative Action as a Model for Europe.* Oxford: Berg, 2000.

Belz, Herman. *Affirmative Action from Kennedy to Reagan: Redefining American Equality.* Washington, D.C.: Washington Legal Foundation, 1984.

Berry, Mary Francis, and John W. Blassingame. *Long Memory: The Black Experience in America.* New York: Oxford University Press, 1982.

Bowen, William G., and Derek Bok. *The Shape of the River.* Princeton, N.J.: Princeton University Press, 1998.

Boxhill, Bernard. *Blacks and Social Justice*. Totowa, N.J.: Rowman and Littlefield, 1984.

Capaldi, Nicholas. *Out of Order: Affirmative Action and the Crisis of Doctrinaire Liberalism*. Buffalo, N.Y.: Prometheus Books, 1985.

Cashman, Dean Dennis. *African Americans and the Quest for Civil Rights, 1900–1990*. New York: New York University Press, 1990.

Curry, George E., and Cornell West, eds. *The Affirmative Action Debate*. Reading, Mass.: Addison-Wesley, 1996.

Daniel, Jack, and Anita Allen. "Newsmagazines and the Black Agenda." In *Discrimination and Discourse*, edited by Geneva Smitherman-Donaldson and Teun A. van Dijk, pp. 23–45. Detroit, Mich.: Wayne State University Press, 1988.

Eastland, Terry, and William Bennett. *Counting by Race: Equality from the Founding Fathers to Bakke and Weber*. New York: Basic Books, 1979.

Ezorsky, Gertrude. *Racism and Justice: The Case for Affirmative Action*. Ithaca, N.Y.: Cornell University Press, 1991.

Finch, Minnie. *The NAACP: Its Fight for Justice*. Metuchen, N.J.: Scarecrow Press, 1981.

Fullinwider, Robert K. *The Reverse Discrimination Controversy: A Moral and Legal Analysis*. Totowa, N.J.: Rowman and Allanheld, 1980.

Goldman, Alan. *Justice and Reverse Discrimination*. Princeton, N.J.: Princeton University Press, 1979.

Green, Kathanne. *Affirmative Action and Principles of Justice*. New York: Greenwood Press, 1989.

Greenawalt, Kent. *Discrimination and Reverse Discrimination*. New York: Knopf, 1983.

Gross, Barry. *Discrimination in Reverse: Is Turn-about Fair Play?* New York: New York University Press, 1978.

Horne, Gerald. *Reversing Discrimination: The Case for Affirmative Action*. New York International Publishers, 1992.

Guinier, Lani. *Tyranny of the Majority: Fundamental Fairness in Representative Democracy*. New York: Martin Kessler Books, 1995.

Johnson, Alex M. "Defending the Use of Quotas in Affirmative Action: Attacking Racism in the Nineties." *University of Illinois Law Review* (1992): 1043–1073.

Kull, Andrew. *The Color-Blind Constitution*. Cambridge, Mass.: Harvard University Press, 1992.

Livingston, John C. *Fair Game? Inequality and Affirmative Action*. San Francisco: W. H. Freeman, 1979.

Loury, Glenn. "Why Should We Care About Group Inequality?" *Social Philosophy and Policy* 5 (1988): 249–271.

McGary, Howard, Jr., "Justice and Reparations." *Philosophical Forum* 9 (1977–78): 250–263.

Mosley, Albert G. "Affirmative Action and the Urban Underclass." In *The Underclass Question*, edited by Bill Lawson, pp. 140–151. Philadelphia, Pa.: Temple University Press, 1992.

Neiman, Donald G. *Promises to Keep: African Americans and the Constitutional Order, 1776 to the Present*. New York: Oxford University Press, 1991.

Newton, Lisa. "Reverse Discrimination as Unjustified." *Ethics* 83 (1973): 1–4.

Rosenfeld, Michel. *Affirmative Action: A Philosophical and Constitutional Inquiry*. New Haven, Conn.: Yale University Press, 1996.

Rossum, Ralph A. *Reverse Discrimination: The Constitutional Debate*. New York: M. Dekker, 1980.

Schwartz, Bernard. *Behind Bakke: Affirmative Action and the Supreme Court*. New York: Oxford University Press, 1988.

Sowell, Thomas. *Affirmative Action around the World: An Empirical Study*. New Haven, Conn.: Yale University Press, 2004.

Steele, Shelby. "A Negative Vote on Affirmative Action." *New York Times Magazine*, May 13, 1990.

Steele, Shelby. *The Content of Our Character: A New Vision of Race in America*. New York: St. Martin's Press, 1990.

Stohr, Greg. *A Black and White Case: How Affirmative Action Survived Its Greatest Legal Challenge*. New York: Bloomberg Press, 2004.

"A Stricter Standard for Affirmative Action." *New York Times* (July 21, 1995).

Thomson, Judith J. "Preferential Hiring." In *Equality and Preferential Treatment*, edited by Marshall Cohen, Thomas Nagel, and Thomas Scanlon, pp. 19–39. Princeton, N.J.: Princeton University Press, 1977.

Wilson, William Julius. *The Truly Disadvantaged*. Chicago: University of Chicago Press, 1987.

ANITA L. ALLEN (1996)
Updated by author 2005

African Blood Brotherhood

The African Blood Brotherhood (ABB) was the first black organization in the twentieth-century United States to advance the concept of armed black self-defense on behalf of African-American rights. It was founded in September 1919 by the West Indian radical Cyril Valentine Briggs.

A semisecret, highly centralized propaganda organization, the ABB was a product of the upsurge of militant racial consciousness enshrined in the New Negro movement that arose following America's 1917 entry into World War I. Formally entitled the African Blood Brotherhood for African Liberation and Redemption, it was organized specifically in response to the convulsions spawned by the race riots that swept various cities in the United States during the summer of 1919 and caused it to become known as the Red Summer.

Formation of the brotherhood was announced in the October 1919 issue of Briggs's magazine *Crusader*, which became the official organ of the ABB. With Briggs as its executive head, the group was governed by a supreme executive council that included Theo Burrell (secretary), Otto E. Huiswoud (national organizer), Richard B. Moore (educational director), Ben E. Burrell (director of historical research), Grace P. Campbell (director of consumers' cooperatives), W. A. Domingo (director of publicity and propaganda), and William H. Jones (physical director).

Combining revolutionary Bolshevik principles with fraternal and benevolent features, the ABB warned in its recruiting propaganda that "Those only need apply who are willing to go to the limit!" (Hill, 1987, vol. 2/2, p. 27). From its inception, the brotherhood was aligned with the nascent Communist Party USA (CPUSA). Along with fellow West Indians Otto Huiswoud (from Suriname) and Arthur Hendricks (from Guyana), Briggs was among the party's charter members at the time of its founding.

As the first black auxiliary of the CPUSA, the brotherhood served as a vehicle for Communist recruitment efforts in black communities. It also was the mechanism through which the party attempted to exert ideological influence on other black organizations, most notably against Marcus Garvey's leadership of the Universal Negro Improvement Association (UNIA).

Although it derived symbolic inspiration from the "blood brotherhood ceremony performed by many tribes in Black Africa" (Hill, 1987, vol. 5/3, pp. 6, 32), the ABB was modeled on the Irish Republican Brotherhood, which dated back to 1858 and the founding of the Irish Fenian movement. The group's ritual was said to resemble that of a fraternal order, with the regular trappings of degrees, passwords, signs, initiation ceremony, and a brotherhood oath. Organizationally, it comprised a series of posts, such as the Menelik Post in New York, directed by individual post commanders.

Membership in the brotherhood was by enlistment, making it difficult to reconstruct even an approximate number of members. It is doubtful, however, that membership ever consisted of more than a few hundred. Commentators such as W. A. Domingo and Claude McKay, who were adherents of the brotherhood, even asserted that the ABB was never more than a paper organization.

The only public demonstration the ABB is known to have mounted occurred in August 1921, during the second annual international convention of Garvey's UNIA in Harlem, at which the ABB attempted unsuccessfully to lobby convention delegates outside Liberty Hall in support of the link proposed by the ABB with UNIA. Prior to this, in June 1921, the group was catapulted into national attention, if only briefly, by a race riot in Tulsa, Oklahoma; the media linked the resistance raised by the Tulsa African-American community with ABB organizers. The ABB was also involved in the All Race Conference of Negroes, better known as the Negro Sanhedrin, which met in Chicago in February 1924, with Briggs as secretary.

Self-described as a workers' organization, the ABB claimed to be "an organization working—openly where possible, secretly where necessary—for the rights and legitimate aspirations of the Negro workers against exploitation on the part of either white or black capitalists." In terms of its political program, one of ABB's distinguishing ideological features was its attempt to marry the principle of racial self-determination to the goal of revolutionary class consciousness. As stated in its program, the ABB sought "a liberated race" while working to achieve "cooperation with other darker races and with class-conscious white workers."

Liquidated in 1924 to 1925 by decision of the CPUSA (following the latter's shift from an underground organization to an aboveground movement), the ABB was replaced by a succession of front organizations subsequently set up by the party, most notably the American Negro Labor Congress and the League of Struggle for Negro Rights.

See also Black Power Movement; Communist Party of the United States; Huiswoud, Otto; Red Summer; Universal Negro Improvement Association

Bibliography

Foner, Philip S., and James S. Allen, eds. *American Communism and Black Americans: A Documentary History, 1919–1929.* Philadelphia: Temple University Press, 1986.

Hill, Robert A., ed. *The Crusader* (1918–1922), 3 vols. New York: Garland, 1987.

Kuykendall, Ronald A. "African Blood Brotherhood: Independent Marxism During the Harlem Renaissance." *Western Journal of Black Studies* 26 (Spring 2002): 16.

ROBERT A. HILL (1996)
Updated bibliography

African Burial Ground Project

In the summer of 1991, during preparation for a federal office building in lower Manhattan, archaeologists unearthed an eighteenth-century cemetery that had been appropriated for use by Africans and African-descended people in colonial New York. The five- to six-acre site—the oldest and largest colonial cemetery ever excavated in North America—is estimated to have been the final resting place of between 10,000 and 20,000 people before its closing in the 1790s. Although researchers have not uncovered recorded evidence of the burial ground's existence before 1712, the presence of a free black community in the vicini-

African Americans preparing to bury a casket, c. 18th century. *Illustration by the artist Charles Lilly, 1994, depicting an interment at the lower Manhattan site now known as the African Burial Ground Memorial in New York City.* ART AND ARTIFACTS DIVISION, SCHOMBURG CENTER FOR RESEARCH IN BLACK CULTURE, THE NEW YORK PUBLIC LIBRARY, ASTOR, LENOX AND TILDEN FOUNDATIONS.

ty as early as the 1640s suggests earlier origins. The excavated portion—less than one city block long and located today just north of City Hall—is bounded by Duane, Reade, and Elk Streets and Broadway. The cemetery had survived for more than 200 years after its closing because of the topography of the original site. During the colonial period the African Burial Ground was located outside the palisades in a low-lying area near the "Collect," also called Fresh Water Pond. As the city expanded at the end of the eighteenth century, between sixteen and twenty-eight feet of fill was used to grade the area. That soil fill protected the graves from destruction as roadways and buildings were constructed.

The rediscovery of the cemetery generated a great deal of interest within the African-American community, especially in New York City, where residents demanded proper memorialization and study. Their activism led to the burial ground's designation as a National Historic Landmark in 1993, and to the General Services Administration (the federal agency responsible for construction on the site) funding a multidisciplinary study of both the disinterred remains and the society in which New York Africans lived and labored during the colonial era. The research team, drawn from across the nation, conducted its work under the auspices of Howard University in Washington, D.C.

For nearly a dozen years, scholars in biological anthropology, history, and archaeology examined the 419 sets of skeletal remains, studied thousands of artifacts, and combed through thousands of documentary sources as they sought to reconstruct the lives of persons interred in

African Burial Ground Memorial Site, Lower Broadway, New York City, 2003. *New York City officials, including Mayor Michael Bloomberg (far right), stand behind four coffins containing the remains of free and enslaved African Americans, some 300 years after they were first laid to rest. The eighteenth-century burial ground is estimated to contain as many as 20,000 graves.* AFP/GETTY IMAGES

the African Burial Ground, most of whom were enslaved. Researchers pursued a diasporic approach that drew on the expertise of specialists in Africa and the Caribbean, as well as those familiar with the experiences of African peoples in colonial America. This methodology reflected recognition of the relevance of origins and the significance of experiences New York Africans may have had before they arrived in the colonial city.

The African Burial Ground Project was also distinguished by the extent to which it involved the public, especially New York's African-American community. The project considered that community to be its "ethical client," and the study was conducted with the community's permission and input. The public was most directly engaged through the efforts of the project's Office of Public Education and Information, which conducted workshops and sponsored tours of significant African-American sites around the city. A reading room with literature on the African presence in New York was also established.

The African Burial Ground not only offered researchers the opportunity to study the African presence in colonial New York, but also to investigate the broad dimensions of the African-American experience. The site provides a unique vantage point from which to study ethnic origins, physical stressors, and assimilation, as well as cultural continuities and resistance. Heretofore, slavery in a northern, urban setting had been considered mild and devoid of the odious features that characterized the institution in a southern, plantation setting. The physical remains suggested otherwise, however. They revealed high infant mortality, significantly elevated death rates among women of the fifteen to twenty-five age range, and a life expectancy that was much shorter than that enjoyed by European Americans. Anthropologists observed numerous fractures, spinal and limb joint degeneration, enlarged muscle attachments, and other musculoskeletal stress markers, apparently as a result of strenuous physical labor. Nearly half of those disinterred from the site were children, and they were found to have suffered from a variety of ailments, including nutritional deficiencies, dental pathologies, and developmental defects such as slowed, disrupted, or stunted growth.

Historical study has confirmed the often arduous and diverse labor experiences of New York Africans and documented the ways in which ethnic origins and experiences—as well as the nature of slavery within colonial New York—may have shaped black social institutions. However, both archaeological and documentary evidence—including beads fashioned into a belt that encircled the waist of a woman, a silver earring that appears to have been strung around the neck of a child, the discovery of crystals, and references to "shake-down" dancing—suggest the rich culture of New York's African population.

The disinterred remains were reinterred on October 4, 2003, following a two-day journey of four representative sets of remains from Howard University to the cities of Baltimore, Wilmington, Philadelphia, and Newark, and then finally to the memorial site in New York. There, they were met by hundreds of African Americans who had gathered to honor the men, women, and children who had built the colonial city and left a legacy of dignity and humanity in the face of oppression.

The anthropological, archaeological, and historical research serves as a reminder that the African presence in America was national, and that the institution of slavery, although differing from one region to another, shared characteristics that sought to dehumanize and debase the enslaved. But in their refusal to think of themselves as someone's property, New York Africans asserted their humanity in myriad ways, especially in the manner in which they commended loved ones to a final resting place.

See also Africanisms; Archaeology and Archaeologists; Cemeteries and Burials; Historians and Historiography

Bibliography

Blakey, Michael L., and Lesley Rankin-Hill, eds. "The New York African Burial Ground Skeletal Biology Final Report." United States General Services Administration, Northeast and Caribbean Region, 2004.

Howson, Jean, Warren Perry, et al. "The New York African Burial Ground Archaeology Draft Report." United States General Services Administration, Northeast and Caribbean Region, 2004.

Medford, Edna Greene, ed. "The New York African Burial Ground History Final Report." United States General Services Administration, Northeast and Caribbean Region, 2004.

United States General Services Administration. "African Burial Ground: Return to the Past in Order to Build the Future." Available from http://www.africanburialground.com/ABG_Main.htm

EDNA GREENE MEDFORD (2005)
MICHAEL L. BLAKEY (2005)

African Civilization Society (AfCS)

The African Civilization Society was a Christian missionary and black-emigration organization. After it was founded in September 1858, the society was led by Henry Highland Garnet (1815–1882), a well-known Presbyterian clergyman. From the beginning, the AfCS had close ties with the New York State Colonization Society, and several of the Colonization Society's leaders sat on the eighteen-member AfCS board of directors. Both societies had their offices in Bible House in New York City, and both shared an interest in settling free blacks in Africa, although the white-sponsored colonization movement had been vigorously opposed by northern free blacks ever since its founding in 1817.

The AfCS constitution advocated the "civilization and evangelization of Africa, and the descendants of African ancestors in any portion of the earth, wherever dispersed." Under Garnet's leadership, the AfCS focused this broad directive on establishing a colonial settlement in Yoruba, a region of West Africa. Garnet envisioned the Yoruban settlement as a base from which to extend the supposed benefits of Western civilization—particularly commerce and Christianity—to the entire African continent. The Yoruban settlement also had an antislavery objective. AfCS leaders believed that by encouraging native Africans to grow cotton, they might undermine the profitability of American slavery and the slave trade.

The AfCS generated much interest and gained a substantial following, particularly through the endorsement of Henry M. Wilson, Elymas P. Rogers, and several other noted African-American clergymen. But the society's close association with leaders of the New York State Colonization Society made it suspect in the minds of many black leaders. Frederick Douglass (1818–1895), James McCune Smith (1813–1865), and J. W. C. Pennington (1807–1870) led the anti-emigrationist attack and criticized Garnet personally for his involvement in the African emigration movement.

The society's financial resources never matched its ambitious program. One of the AfCS directors, Theodore Bourne (1821–1910), traveled to England early in 1860 to build interest and gain financial backing for the Yoruban settlement. Even with the support of an English AfCS affiliate, the African Aid Society, Bourne encountered insurmountable difficulties. Martin R. Delany (1812–1885), the organizer of the Niger Valley Exploring Party, was also in Britain promoting his own African settlement proposal. Competition between the two programs created doubt and confusion and dampened enthusiasm among British reformers. Later in 1860, Elymas P. Rogers led an AfCS-sponsored expedition to West Africa to survey possible locations for the Yoruban settlement. The mission was cut short by Rogers's death from malaria shortly after his arrival in Liberia. Garnet traveled to England in August 1861 in a final, futile effort to revive flagging interest in African settlement.

In the early 1860s the AfCS began distancing itself from the controversial subject of African emigration, focusing more on home missions. The Civil War opened up new opportunities for missionary activity among former slaves in the South. Under the guidance of a new president, the Presbyterian clergyman George W. Levere, the AfCS directed its attention to freedmen's education. From 1863 through 1867, the AfCS sponsored several freedmen's schools in the Washington, D.C., area and parts of the South.

See also Garnet, Henry Highland; Missionary Movements

Bibliography

Bell, Howard H. *Search for a Place: Black Separatism and Africa, 1860.* Ann Arbor: University of Michigan Press, 1971.

Miller, Floyd J. *Search for a Black Nationality*. New York, 1982.

MICHAEL F. HEMBREE (1996)

AFRICAN DIASPORA

The *African diaspora* is a term that refers to the dispersal of African peoples to form a distinct, transnational community. It is most often used to refer to Africans and their descendants living outside the continent, but diasporas have formed within Africa as well. At its simplest, the word *diaspora* is defined as a dispersion of a people from their original homeland. The term derives from the Greek verb *diaspeirein* meaning "to scatter" (Tölöyan, p. 9), and it is expressed in English in other words with the *spr* root, such as "spore," "disperse," and "sperm." Until relatively recently, the term was most closely associated with the dispersion of Jewish peoples, although there are also extensive bodies of literature about the Armenian, Greek, and African diasporas. The term *African diaspora* was first adopted by scholars in the mid-twentieth century, but the concept of a global community of African descendants may be traced back much further.

It can be argued that all of humanity may be considered part of the African diaspora, based on the archaeological evidence that humankind originated in East Africa, subsequently migrating to other regions of the world. However, the use of *diaspora* as an interpretive concept requires greater specificity about what types of migrations are diasporas. As the field of diaspora studies developed in the late twentieth century, scholars began to identify certain features that distinguish diasporas from other types of migrations.

First, diaspora refers to a dispersion of people from a homeland to multiple destinations. This reflects the scattering implicit in the word itself, and it creates conditions under which different segments of the diaspora can create relationships among themselves.

Second, diasporas are connected in some form to an actual or imagined homeland. Each segment of the diaspora shares a common bond with the homeland, the place from which they all originated. This makes diasporas different from nomadic groups without a fixed homeland. The reason that some homelands exist only in the imagination is that the process of diasporization—the departure of large segments of the population—is often the result of traumatic political or economic situations that sometimes destroy the homeland.

Third, diasporas have self-awareness of the group's identity. Diasporic communities are consciously part of an ethno-national group—a "nation" of people defined by a collective ethnic, or group, identity. This shared identity binds the dispersed peoples not only to the homeland, but to each other. Especially in the cases of diasporas for whom the homeland no longer exists, or those who have been separated from the homeland for many generations, this identity has been pivotal to their existence and survival as a cultural unit. Further, the internal networks between the various segments of a diaspora are a unique feature that differentiates them from other types of migrations.

A fourth distinguishing feature of diaspora is its existence over two or more generations. A group meeting all of the above criteria, but able to return within a single generation, may be more appropriately described as temporary exiles. (Gérard Chaliand and Jean-Pierre Rageau also included the criterion of time in their definition of diaspora.)

There are many migrations that may be classified as diasporas in African history, beginning with the spread of early humans from eastern Africa to populate the rest of the world. From around 3000 BCE, Bantu-speaking peoples moved from the region that is now modern Nigeria and Cameroon to other parts of the African continent and to the Indian Ocean. From the fifth century BCE onward, as societies and commerce became more complex, African

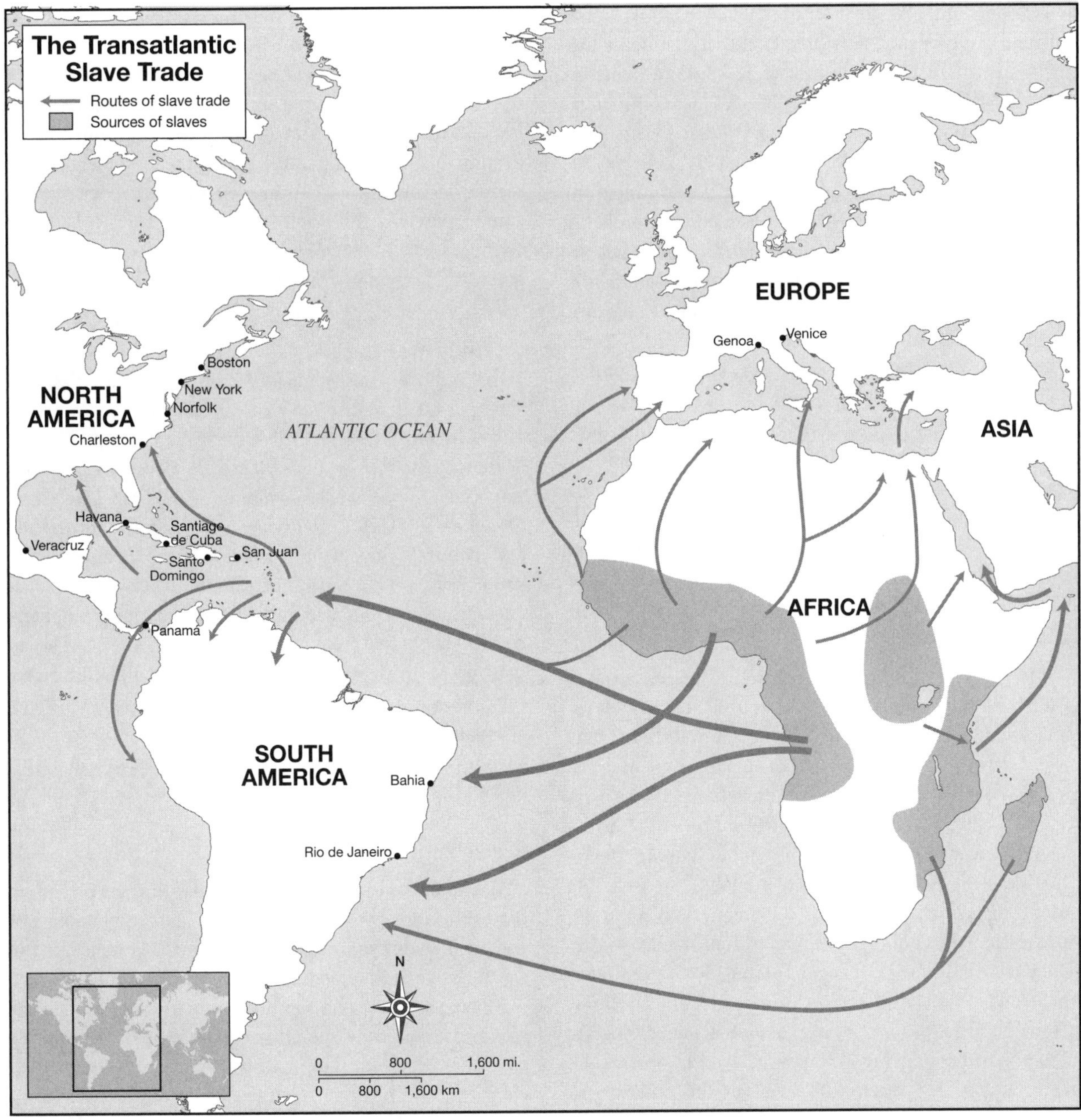

The transatlantic slave trade, tracing the movement of African peoples to the Americas and other parts of the world. *During a period of nearly four centuries, from 1502 until slavery was finally abolished in the western hemisphere in 1888, about ten million Africans were taken from their homeland to become forced laborers in the Americas. More than 90 percent of these slaves were taken to Central and South America and the Caribbean.* MAP BY XNR PRODUCTIONS. THE GALE GROUP.

traders, merchants, slaves, soldiers, and others began circulating around parts of the Middle East, Europe, and Asia. This movement led to a significant African presence in Europe during the height of the Greco-Roman empires, and to the establishment of North African empires that extended northwards into modern Spain and Portugal (the Moors).

The modern African diaspora arose from three great historical traumas and their aftermaths: the Atlantic slave trade, the Indian Ocean slave trade, and European colonization on the African continent. The Atlantic slave trade was directly responsible for removing upwards of ten million people from the continent over four centuries, destroying whole nations in the process and enslaving the descendants of the original captives. The violent nature of both the dispersal and subsequent captivity created a distinct Afro-Atlantic diaspora history and culture (which is the focus of this encyclopedia). A much older commercial network trading in slaves across the Indian Ocean dates back to the first or second century CE. This trade was responsible for African relocations within the continent, to India, Pakistan, Iraq, Iran, Turkey, Yemen, and probably as far as China. European military and commercial involvement in Africa culminated in colonization in the nineteenth and twentieth centuries, and subsequent migrations of Africans between the continent and colonial capitals led to the creation of many diasporic communities in Europe. While each of these branches of the modern African diaspora has unique characteristics, the entire diaspora has at times been mobilized around such issues as African independence, the struggle against apartheid, or the politics of race, particularly in world capitals where members of all branches reside. Since lived experience and scholarship tends to revolve around communities of shared history, "the" African diaspora is a universe comprised of many constellations.

The African diaspora in the Americas is concentrated in the Caribbean and Brazil, where colonial economies relied on enslaved Africans to produce such export commodities as sugar, tobacco, and coffee. However, Africans and their descendants were integral to all aspects of American life, thought, and culture throughout the entire hemisphere. Africans participated in the conquest of the Americas, and they fought in the trenches to win its independence. They contributed to American architecture, technological innovation, the arts, and more, yet the societies arising on the pillars of slavery were predicated on inequality and exploitation. Thus, after the abolition of slavery, a host of Africans and their descendants migrated to pursue better living and economic conditions, resulting in additional scattering throughout the Americas as well as to Europe and continental Africa.

The literature on the African diaspora dates back to before the term entered the academic canon. As with all scholarship, it reflects contemporary concerns at the time each work was written. In the nineteenth century, international matters, such as relations with Haiti, missionary work and repatriation to Africa, and the implications of African colonization deeply concerned African Americans in the United States. Moreover, the continued racial exploitation and escalating violence around the turn of the twentieth century contributed to a sense of racial solidarity among all African peoples. Yet in the Americas, declaring such kinship with Africans was still a delicate matter. Because the full rights of citizenship were denied to most blacks in the Americas on the pretense that Africans were genetically inferior, there was both a distancing and an embrace of continental connections at this time. The work of George Washington Williams (1849–1891) in the 1880s took on the myth of Africa's limited contributions to civilization and knowledge, anticipating much subsequent research documenting the transformative influence of African peoples and philosophy throughout the world, as well as the extent to which global cultures are, to varying degrees, themselves of African origin.

The partitioning and colonization of Africa, followed by World War I, marked the beginning of a new era of global political consciousness within the African diaspora. This period gave rise to political endeavors such as the Pan-African Congresses, diaspora organizations such as Marcus Garvey's Universal Negro Improvement Association (UNIA), periodicals such as the *African Times and Orient Review* and the *Journal of Negro History*, and artistic and cultural movements including the Harlem Renaissance and *Négritude*. The scholarship of the early twentieth century documented and analyzed the multiple interconnections that constituted the changing African diaspora, as evidenced in the work of W. E. B. DuBois, Arthur Alfonso Schomburg, Anna Julia Cooper, and others. These scholars, along with significant contributions from such figures as C. L. R. James and Eric Williams in Trinidad and Tobago, simultaneously addressed the politics behind not only the contemporary diaspora, but its very foundations.

Also in the early twentieth century, the new discipline of anthropology was beginning to challenge the tenets of genetic inequality through culture study. Though much of the early work grappled with the "Negro problem"—the implications of having significant citizens of African descent particularly in the emerging nations of the Americas—the resulting comparative ethnographies helped chart the cultural terrain of the African diaspora. The anthropologists Melville Herskovits and Roger Bastide greatly influenced this early generation of culture scholars, and pioneers such as the writer Zora Neale Hurston and the dancers Katherine Dunham and Pearl Primus innovated methods of interpreting the new research through the arts.

Despite the extent of early scholarship, scholars did not begin to characterize their work as "diaspora" until the mid-twentieth century. The term had particular resonance in the United States during an era of black nationalism and increasing disillusionment about the failure of the nation to fulfill its commitment to its black citizens. The first widely cited use of the term was a paper and panel on "The African Abroad, or the African Diaspora," presented at a meeting of the International Congress of African Historians in 1965. An emerging field of African diaspora studies took root in newly created black studies programs, and other academic disciplines began to consider the African experience. The First African Diaspora Studies Institute convened an international group of scholars at Howard University in 1979, followed by a host of conferences, research projects, and academic programs, not only at American universities but around the world.

Today, scholarship on the African diaspora focuses on the ways in which individuals and communities experience the diaspora, as well as the social processes that create and sustain diaspora communities. Recent research has allowed for focus on the many diasporas contained within the larger diaspora, such as dispersals from individual nations or regions. An example of this would be the Caribbean diaspora, with communities throughout Europe, the United States, and Latin America. As a component of black studies, it affords scholars an analytical tool to examine how transnational communities form, operate, and interact within the global African experience. It also allows for better understanding of specific branches of the diaspora through comparison with other branches of the African diaspora and with other diasporas as well.

See also Afrocentrism; Black Studies; Slave Trade

Bibliography

Butler, Kim D. "Defining Diaspora, Refining a Discourse." *Diaspora* 10, no. 2 (2001): 189–219.

Chaliand, Gérard, and Jean-Pierre Rageau. *The Penguin Atlas of Diasporas.* New York: Penguin, 1995.

Harris, Joseph E. *Global Dimensions of the African Diaspora*, 2nd ed. Washington, D.C.: Howard University Press, 1993.

Harris, Joseph E., Alusine Jalloh, and Stephen E. Maizlish, eds. *The African Diaspora.* College Station: Texas A & M University Press, 1996.

Jayasura, Shihan de S., and Richard Pankhurst, eds. *The African Diaspora in the Indian Ocean.* Trenton, N.J.: Africa New World Press, 2003.

Okpewho, Isidore, Carole Boyce Davies, and Ali A. Mazrui, eds. *The African Diaspora: African Origins and New World Identities.* Bloomington: Indiana University Press, 1999.

Tölöyan, Khachig. "Rethinking Diaspora(s): Stateless Power in the Transnational Moment." *Diaspora* 5, no. 1 (1996): 3–36.

Walker, Sheila, ed. *African Roots/American Cultures: Africa in the Creation of the Americas.* Lanham, Md.: Rowman and Littlefield, 2001.

KIM D. BUTLER (2005)

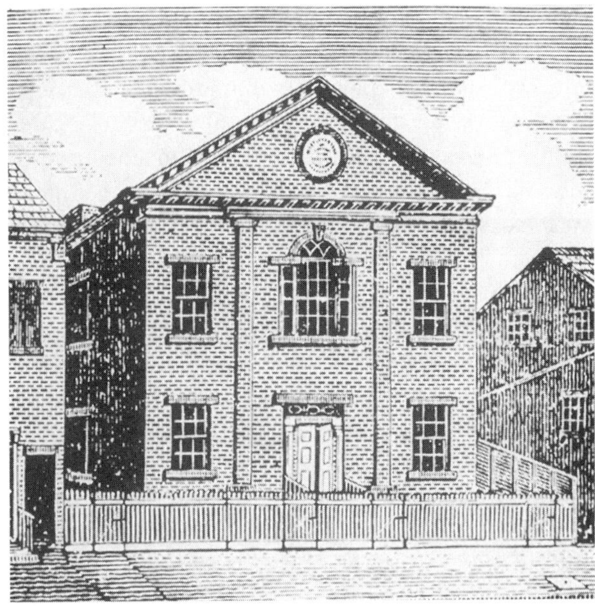

African Free School No. 2, New York City. *The New York African Free Schools were sponsored by the New York Manumission Society, which was educating 500 pupils annually by 1820. This depiction is from an 1830 engraving of a drawing made by P. Reason, a 13-year-old student at the school.* PHOTOGRAPHS AND PRINTS DIVISION SCHOMBURG CENTER FOR RESEARCH IN BLACK CULTURE, THE NEW YORK PUBLIC LIBRARY, ASTOR, LENOX AND TILDEN FOUNDATIONS. REPRODUCED BY PERMISSION.

African Free School

The African Free School opened in a private home on Cliff Street in New York City in 1787 with forty-seven students. It was supported by the New York Manumission Society, a joint effort of Anglicans and Quakers. Over the next fifty years the school was the primary vehicle for black education in New York City. Descended from the Trinity Church School for blacks, first headed by Elias Neau and maintained until 1778, the African Free School had served over 2,300 students by 1814. In 1809 it was the largest single school in the city, with 141 pupils. Like other charitable schools, it received city assistance beginning in 1796.

In 1813 a state law provided that the African Free School would receive both city and county school funds. Four more such schools had been opened by 1827. The first nonprivate building for the African Free School was at William and Duane streets. Later, schools opened at Mulberry and Grand streets (these were turned into an all-female school in 1831, with additional buildings at Sixth Avenue and Nineteenth Street, at 161 Duane Street, and at 108 Columbia Street). The Free School taught a basic curriculum of reading, writing, and arithmetic, augmented with poetry, drawing, and public speaking. Navigation skills were emphasized, an indication of the importance of seafaring for black employment. Teachers gave special lessons on Haiti. As scrapbooks of award-winning assignments show, the students performed admirably. School rules were strict. Students were required to attend church and read the scripture, and were continually warned about the minor sins of lying, dishonesty, profanity, and "cruelty to beasts." School commenced at 9 a.m. and again at 2 p.m., with penalties for lateness. The school used the Lancastrian system of education, employing student monitors to assist in instruction. Despite the racism its graduates encountered, the African Free School was the training ground of a generation of talented African Americans. Among its most illustrious graduates were James McCune Smith, Ira Aldridge, Peter Williams Jr., James Varick, Charles Lewis Reason, Alexander Crummell, and Thomas Sydney.

After a period of declining enrollments, Samuel Eli Cornish, editor of *Freedom's Journal*, spearheaded efforts to double the student body by 1830. Four new schools opened in 1832. The Free School survived, despite bitterness among African Americans toward the procolonization stance of the longtime head of the school, Charles Andrews. It also faced competition, since other members of the black community had opened private schools as early as 1812.

The Free Schools did not go above the lower grades. Efforts by Peter Williams Jr. and David Ruggles between 1831 and 1837 failed to establish permanent, black-maintained high schools. African-American students were thus forced to continue to patronize the Free Schools, without much hope for advancement. In 1834 the Free Schools were transferred to the control of the New York State Public School Society, the major local conduit for state funds. In reality, the schools had already ceased to be philanthropic institutions and had become public schools.

See also Education in the United States; Manumission Societies

Bibliography

Andrews, Charles. *The History of the New-York African Free-Schools, from Their Establishment in 1787 to the Present Time; Embracing a Period of More than Forty Years.* New York: M. Day, 1830.

Barnett, Enid Vivian. "Educational Activities by and in Behalf of the Negroes in New York, 1800–1830." *Negro History Bulletin* 4 (1951): 102ff.

Curry, Leonard P. *The Free Black in Urban America, 1800–1850: The Shadow of the Dream.* Chicago: University of Chicago Press, 1981.

GRAHAM RUSSELL HODGES (1996)

AFRICANISMS

An Africanism is any cultural (material or nonmaterial) or linguistic property of African origin surviving in the Americas or in the African diaspora. The study of Africanisms in the Americas has sparked much debate over the survival of African culture in North America.

AVENUES OF TRANSMISSION

The transatlantic slave trade was the main avenue for the transmission of African culture to the Americas, establishing a permanent link between Africa and North America as Africans sold into slavery transplanted their culture to North America. Africanisms survived in North America by a process of cultural transference, cultural synthesis, and cultural transformations. Africans, unlike European immigrants, were deprived of their freedom to transport their kinship structures, courts, guilds, cult groups, market, and military. However, Africans made substantial contributions in agriculture, aesthetics, dance, folklore, food culture, and language.

African cultural retentions were found at various levels of the plantation work force. Some of the earliest groups to have a major impact on American culture were the first Africans—Mandes and Wolofs from Senegambia—arriving in colonial South Carolina. Between 1650 and 1700, the dominant group of Africans imported to South Carolina were Senegambian in origin, and they were the first Africans to have elements from their language and culture retained within the developing language and culture of America. David Dalby has identified early linguistic retention among this group and traced many Americanisms to Wolof, including *bogus, boogie-woogie, bug* (insect), *dig* (to understand), *guy, honky, jam, jamboree, jitter(bug), jive, John, juke(box), fuzz* (police), *hippie, mumbo-jumbo, OK, phony, rooty-toot(y),* and *rap,* to name just a few.

African culture also survived in the form of folklore. Brer Rabbit, Brer Wolf, Brer Bear, and Sis' Nanny Goat were part of the heritage the Wolof shared with other West African peoples such as the Hausa, Fula (Fulani), and Mandinka. The Hare (Rabbit) stories are also found in parts of Nigeria, Angola, and East Africa. Other animal fables that remained popular in North America include the Tortoise stories found among the Yoruba, Igbo, and Edo-Bini peoples of Nigeria, and the Spider *(Anansi)* tales, found throughout much of West Africa, including Ghana, Liberia, and Sierra Leone. The latter have reappeared in the United States in the form of Aunt Nancy stories, which found their way into American culture through Joel Chandler Harris's Uncle Remus stories, as well as through more authentic African-American sources.

Many slaves, including Mande house servants in South Carolina, served as intermediaries in the acculturation of both the planters and the field slaves. The house servant incorporated African cultural patterns into the culinary, religious, and folkloric patterns of the planters. At the same time, the slaves learned European cultural standards. So while house servants drew their European heritage from the planters, planters drew their African heritage from their black servants.

Reciprocal Acculturation and Isolation

The acculturation process was mutual as well as reciprocal: Africans assimilated white culture and planters adopted some aspects of African customs and practices, including African methods of rice cultivation, African cuisine (which had a profound impact on what became southern cooking), open grazing of cattle, and the use of herbal medicines to cure diseases. For example, Africans are credited with bringing folk treatments for smallpox to America, as well as antidotes for snakebites and other poisons. Through the root doctor, Africans brought new health practices to the plantations. The African house servants also learned new domestic skills, including the art of quilting, from their mistresses. They took a European quilting technique and Africanized it by combining an appliqué style, reflecting a pattern and form which is still found today in the Akan and Fon textile industries of West Africa.

In South Carolina and Louisiana, the field slaves were mainly Angolan and Congolese, and they brought a homogeneous, identifiable culture. They often possessed good metallurgical and woodworking skills, and had a particular skill in ironworking, making the wrought-iron balconies in New Orleans and Charleston. But as field workers, the Angolans were kept away from the developing mainstream of white American culture. This isolation worked to the Angolans' advantage in that it allowed them to escape acculturation and maintain their cultural homogeneity.

Angolan contributions to South Carolina and Louisiana include not only wrought-iron balconies but also wood carvings, basketry, weaving, baked clay figurines, and pottery. Cosmograms, grave designs and decorations, funeral practices, and the wake are also Bantu in origin. Bantu musical contributions include banjos, drums, diddley bows, mouthbows, the washtub bass, jugs, gongs, bells, rattles, ideophones, and the *lokoimni,* a five-stringed harp.

After 1780 the Angolans had a substantial presence in South Carolina and other areas of the southeastern United States, including Alabama and Louisiana. In areas such as the Sea Islands of South Carolina, the Angolans were predominantly field hands or were used in capacities that required little or no contact with Euro-Americans, so they were not confronted with the same problems of acculturation as were West African domestic servants and artisans. Living in relative isolation from other groups, they were able to maintain a strong sense of unity and to retain a cultural vitality that laid the foundation for the development of African-American culture.

Culinary Culture

Much of Mande culture was transmitted to white Americans by way of the "big house." African cooks introduced deep-fat frying, a cooking technique that originated in Africa. Most southern stews (gumbos) and nut stews are African in origin. Gumbo *(kingombo),* a soup made of okra pods, shrimp, and powdered sassafras leaves, was known to most southerners by the 1780s. Other southern favorites are jambalaya *(bantu tshimbolebole)* and callaloo, a thick soup similar to gumbo.

Another African dish that was recreated by the descendants of Africans in North America is *fufu,* a traditional African meal eaten from Senegambia to Angola. In South Carolina, it is called "turn meal and flour." Cornbread was mentioned by slavers as one of the African foods provided for their African cargo. From this *fufu* mixture, slaves made hoecake in the fields. Later hoecake evolved into pancakes and hot-water cornbread. As early as 1739 American naturalist Marc Catesby noted that slaves made a mush from cornmeal called pone bread. He also noted that slaves used Indian corn hominy and made grits (similar to the African dish *eba.*) Other African dishes that became part of southern cuisine are hop-n-johns (rice and black-eyed peas cooked together) and jollof rice (red rice).

Some important crops brought directly from Africa during the transatlantic slave trade were gathered for Africans on board slave ships, including okra, tania, black-eyed peas, and kidney beans. Other crops introduced into North America from Africa are coffee, peanuts, millet, sorghum, guinea melon, watermelon, yams, and sesame seeds.

Soul food goes back to the days when plantation owners gave slaves discarded animal parts, such as hog maw (stomach), hog jowl, pigs' feet, and ham hocks. To these, African Americans added African cooking methods and a group of African foods that included collard greens, dandelion greens (first recorded in 1887), poke greens, turnip greens, and black-eyed peas (first brought to Jamaica from Africa in 1674 and to North America by 1738).

Agriculture and Livestock

The first rice seeds were imported to South Carolina directly from Madagascar in 1685. Africans supplied the labor and the technical expertise, and Africans off the coast of Senegal trained Europeans in its cultivation. The methods of rice cultivation used in West Africa and South Carolina were identical.

Africa also contributed to American cattle raising. Fulanis accustomed to cattle raising in the Futa Jallon in Senegambia oversaw the rapid expansion of the British-American cattle herds in the middle of the eighteenth century. They were responsible for introducing open grazing patterns, now practiced throughout the American cattle industry. This practice is used worldwide in cattle culture today. Open grazing made practical use of an abundance of land and a limited labor force.

Longhorn and shorthorn cattle were common across much of western Africa, particularly in the River Gambia area. Many Africans entering South Carolina after 1670 were experienced in tending large herds. Eighteenth-century descriptions of West African animal husbandry bear a striking resemblance to what appeared in Carolina and later in the American dairy and cattle industries. The harvesting of cattle and cattle drives to centers of distribution were also adaptations of African innovations, and Africans introduced the first artificial insemination and the use of cow's milk for human consumption in the British colonies.

The historian Peter Wood has argued that the word *cowboy* originated from this early relationship between cattle and Africans in the colonial period, when African labor and skills were closely associated with cattle raising. Africans stationed at cow pens with herding responsibilities were referred to as cowboys, just as Africans who worked in the "big house" were known as houseboys.

Africanisms

Much of the early language associated with cowboy culture had a strong African flavor. The word *bronco* (probably of Efik/Ibibio and Spanish origins) was used centuries ago to denote Spanish and African slaves who worked with cattle and horses. The word *buckra* (a poor white man) is derived from *mbakara,* the Efik/Ibibio word for "white man." *Buckra* described a class of whites who worked as broncobusters—bucking and breaking horses, perhaps because planters used *buckras* as broncobusters when slaves were too valuable to risk injuring. A related term of cowboy culture is *buckaroo,* another Efik/Ibibio word also derived from *mbakara.* Another African word that found its way into popular cowboy songs is *dogie,* which grew out of the Kimbundu words *kidogo,* "a little something," and *dodo,* "small."

Africanisms are not exclusive to African-American culture, but contributed to an emerging American culture. One area that has been largely ignored in the debate over African cultural survival in the United States is the survival of African culture among white Americans. Many Africanisms have entered southern culture as a whole, including the banjo, the elaborate etiquette of the South with respect for elders, its use of terms of endearment and kinship in speaking to neighbors, and its general emphasis on politeness. White southerners have adopted African speech patterns and have retained Africanisms from baton twirling and cheerleading to such expressions and words as *bodacious, bozo, cooter* (turtle), *goober* (peanut), *hullabaloo, hully-gully, jazz, moola* (money), *pamper, Polly Wolly-Doodle, wow, uh-huh, unh-unh, daddy, buddy,* and *tote,* to list a few.

These are only some of the ways in which African culture contributed to what was to become American culture. Americans share a dual cultural experience—one side European and the other African.

See also Dance; English, African-American; Folk Arts and Crafts; Folklore; Folk Religion; Food and Cuisine; Gullah

Bibliography

Dalby, David. "The African Element in Black English." In *Rappin' and Stylin' Out,* edited by Thomas Kochman. Urbana: University of Illinois Press, 1972.

Gamble, David P. *The Wolof of Senegambia, Together with Notes on the Lebu and the Serer.* London: International African Institute, 1957.

Holloway, Joseph E. *Africanisms in America Culture.* Urbana: University of Illinois Press, 1990.

Holloway, Joseph E., and Winifred K. Vass. *The African Heritage of American English.* Urbana: University of Illinois Press, 1993.

Joyner, Charles. *Down by the Riverside: A South Carolina Slave Community.* Urbana: University of Illinois Press, 1984.

Levine, Lawrence. *Black Culture and Black Consciousness: Afro-American Folk Thought from Slavery to Freedom.* Oxford, UK: Oxford University Press, 1977.

Vass, Winifred K. *The Bantu Speaking Heritage of the United States.* Los Angeles: University of California, Center for Afro-American Studies, 1979.

Wood, Peter H. *Black Majority: Negroes in Colonial South Carolina from 1670 through the Stono Rebellion.* New York: Knopf, 1974.

JOSEPH E. HOLLOWAY (1996)

African Methodist Episcopal Church

Richard Allen (1760–1831), the founder of the African Methodist Episcopal (AME) Church, was born a slave in Philadelphia, Pennsylvania, on February 14, 1760. The slaveholder Benjamin Chew sold Allen, his parents, and his three siblings to Stokley Sturgis of Kent County, Delaware, around 1768. Methodist Church circuit riders frequently preached in the area, and Allen responded to their evangelism—perhaps also to their antislavery reputation—and joined the Wesleyan movement. His piety deepened because Sturgis permitted him to attend Methodist services regularly and to hold religious gatherings in the slave owner's own home. Sturgis also allowed Allen and his brother to buy their freedom, a task that was accomplished in 1783. For three years, Allen traveled through the Middle Atlantic states as an itinerant Methodist preacher, finally settling in Philadelphia to preach to blacks at the St. George Methodist Episcopal Church.

The founding of the Free African Society of Philadelphia in 1787, and a racial altercation, caused him to leave St. George, which in turn led to the building of Philadelphia's Bethel African Methodist Episcopal Church (often known as the Mother Bethel Church) in 1794. In 1807, efforts by several pastors at St. George to control the congregation moved Allen to gain judicial recognition of Bethel's independence. A final attempt in 1815 by a St. George pastor to assert authority at Bethel Church induced Daniel Coker (1780–1846), the leader of Baltimore's black Methodists, to preach a sermon the following year commending Allen for his successful stand. Not long after, Allen drew Coker and other blacks from Baltimore, Salem, New Jersey, and Attleborough, Pennsylvania, to meet with his Philadelphia followers to form the AME Church.

At the AME's 1816 conference in Philadelphia, Coker was elected bishop, but he declined the offer, perhaps because of his light skin color. Allen was then chosen bishop, and under his leadership the denomination rapidly expanded. African Methodism spread north to New York and New England; south through Maryland, the District of Columbia, and (for a time) South Carolina; and west to the Ohio Valley and the old Northwest Territory. During the antebellum period, the denomination included congregations in the slave states of Kentucky, Missouri, and Louisiana. Missionaries such as William Paul Quinn (1788–1873), an AME bishop after 1844, founded scores of congregations in the Midwest in the 1830s and 1840s. Along the Pacific Coast, the AME church spread from Sacramento and San Francisco in the early 1850s to other locations in California and adjoining territories. AME loyalists also had success in Canada and made some inroads into Haiti. In 1864, thirty-three years after Allen's death, the AME Church had a membership of 50,000 in 1,600 congregations.

During the antebellum period, while the AME Church was largely restricted to the northern states, numerous clergy and congregations gave direct aid to the abolition movement. Morris Brown, who became the second bishop of the church after Allen's death, had been implicated in Denmark Vesey's abortive slave insurrection in South Carolina in 1822. Vesey himself was an AME preacher who, according to white authorities, planned the slave revolt during AME church services. The abolitionist stances of Allen, Quinn, and Brown were reaffirmed at the 1840 Pittsburgh Annual Conference. Stating that "slavery pollutes the character of the church of God, and makes the Bible a sealed book to thousands of immortal beings," the delegates resolved that their denomination should use its "influence and energies" to destroy black bondage.

Daniel A. Payne (1811–1893), who became a bishop in 1852, greatly influenced the development of the AME church. Freeborn in Charleston, South Carolina, Payne was a schoolteacher in his early adult years, until a South Carolina state law forbade the education of blacks and forced him to close his school. In 1835 he moved north and matriculated at Gettysburg Theological Seminary in Pennsylvania. After his ordination into the AME ministry in 1843, Payne pastored in Baltimore and crusaded for an educated clergy. He later served the denomination as historiographer. In 1863 Payne convinced reluctant AME leaders to commit to a daring venture in higher education by founding Wilberforce University, the first black college started by African Americans. Wilberforce was only the first of several colleges founded by the AME. Others include Allen University (1880) in South Carolina, Morris Brown College (1881) in Georgia, Paul Quinn College (1881) in Texas, and Kittrell College (1886) in North Carolina.

The period of the Civil War and Reconstruction proved pivotal to AME Church development. Recruitment of black soldiers occurred on the premises of AME congre-

Sketch of Rev. Deaton Dorrell, 1852. Dorrell was pastor of the AME Church in New Bedford, Massachusetts. PHOTOGRAPHS AND PRINTS DIVISION, SCHOMBURG CENTER FOR RESEARCH IN BLACK CULTURE, THE NEW YORK PUBLIC LIBRARY, ASTOR, LENOX AND TILDEN FOUNDATIONS.

gations such as Israel Church in Washington, D.C. Four AME ministers—Henry M. Turner, William H. Hunter, David Stevens, and Garland H. White—served with ten other black chaplains in the Union Army. Additional AME clergy, including some who would become bishops, also fought on the Union side.

As northern victories liberated Confederate strongholds in Virginia and North Carolina, the Baltimore Annual Conference dispatched AME preachers in 1864 to those states to attract blacks into African Methodism. In 1865, Bishop Daniel A. Payne sailed from New York City to his hometown, Charleston, South Carolina, to establish the AME mission in the South. The rapid acquisition of members and congregations from Virginia to Texas swelled the denomination in 1880 to 387,566 persons in 2,051 churches.

The development of the AME Church in Alabama is illustrative of the denomination's expansion in the postbellum South. Mobile had the first AME congregation as early as 1820, though it was short-lived. The denomination revived when two AME ministers preached in the state in 1864. Formal organization of an Alabama Annual Conference occurred in Selma in 1868, a year after missionaries arrived from Georgia; it started with 6 churches, 31 missions, and 5,617 members. Preachers such as Winfield Henri Mixon played a large role in spearheading AME Church growth. Born a slave near Selma in 1859, Mixon began a long career in 1882 as a pastor and presiding elder, serving until his death in 1932. As a presiding elder, he reported that between 1892 and 1895 he launched fourteen new congregations. When he started his ministry, the state comprised three annual conferences: the Alabama, the Central Alabama, and the North Alabama. As a result of his efforts and those of other church founders, Mixon mapped out three additional jurisdictions, including the East, South, and West Alabama annual conferences. In 1890 there were 247 AME congregations in the state, with 30,781 total members. Mixon helped to increase these numbers to 525 congregations and 42,658 members in 1916.

These evangelistic efforts paralleled the unprecedented political involvement of the AME clergy in Reconstruction state governments and in the U.S. Congress. Approximately fifty-three AME ministers served as officeholders in the legislatures of South Carolina, Florida, Alabama, Georgia, and other states. Henry McNeal Turner (1834–1915), a Republican, was elected to the Georgia state legislature in 1868, only to be ousted that same year by triumphant Democrats. Richard H. Cain (1825–1887), then pastor of Emmanuel Church in Charleston, served in the South Carolina state senate from 1868 through 1870, and then in the U.S. House of Representatives from 1873 through 1875. Turner and Cain became AME bishops in 1880.

Bishop Payne was unhappy about the ascent of Turner and Cain to the AME episcopacy. He and other northern-based bishops were wary of the new generation of denominational leaders whose followers came from the South. Many of these new leaders, among them Turner and Cain, had experiences in elective offices that Payne believed caused an unfortunate politicization of denominational affairs. In the late nineteenth century, regional backgrounds of ministers determined regional alliances and formed the bases of power within the AME Church.

There was also increasing political involvement of AME clergy in the northern branch of the denomination. Ezekiel Gillespie, a lay founder of the St. Mark Church in Milwaukee, for example, initiated a state supreme court case that won suffrage for Wisconsin blacks in 1866. Benjamin W. Arnett, who became a bishop in 1888, won an

The bishops of the African Methodist Episcopal (AME) Church, 1876. *The post–Civil War engraving depicts Richard Allen, the founder of the AME Church, surrounded by later church bishops. Vignettes in the corners depict the church's educational and missionary endeavors.* GETTY IMAGES

election in 1886 to the Ohio legislature, where he became a friend of the future president William McKinley. He successfully pushed a repeal of Ohio's discriminatory Black Laws.

In the late nineteenth century, the denomination expanded outside of the United States. In 1884 the British Methodist Episcopal (BME) Church, in existence since 1856, united with the AME Church. Thereafter, BME congregations throughout Canada, Bermuda, and South America were part of the AME fold. In 1891, Bishop Turner, who was an influential African emigrationist, established annual conferences in West Africa, Sierra Leone, and Liberia. Five years later, Turner formally received the Ethiopian Church of South Africa into the denomination. This church was established in 1892, when dissident Africans led by M. M. Mokone withdrew from the white-dominated Wesleyan Methodist Church after experiencing the same kind of racial discrimination that had brought the AME Church into existence in the United States. Turner invited an Ethiopian delegation to the United States, where they accepted membership. (In 1900, Bishop Levi J. Coppin became the first resident bishop in South Africa.)

Bishop Turner's missionary interests were not confined to Africa. Between 1896 and 1908 he presided as bishop of Georgia, and he mobilized support and manpower from this jurisdiction for expansion into Cuba and Mexico. He commissioned presiding elders from Georgia to establish congregations among black Latinos in both countries, and several successful AME missions were instituted.

Whenever AME advocates for overseas expansion combined this perspective with black nationalism, ideological fissures surfaced in denominational affairs. Turner's espousal of emigration drew vehement opposition from Benjamin T. Tanner (1835–1923). Tanner—who in 1868 became editor of the *Christian Recorder,* a weekly founded in 1852—started the *AME Church Review* in 1884, and he edited it until his election to the episcopacy in 1888. Concerning Turner's back-to-Africa efforts, Tanner asserted that those who wished to escape the fight for racial equality in the United States counseled "cowardice." He felt that blacks should remain in the United States to secure their full constitutional privileges. However, while Tanner opposed black emigration to Africa, he and other AME leaders did not fully disagree with all of Turner's nationalist views. Tanner, for example, authored *Is the Negro Cursed?* (1869) and *The Color of Solomon, What?* (1895), both of which challenged racist interpretations of scripture and argued that persons of color figured prominently in Biblical history. In 1893, Benjamin Arnett, who served as bishop with Turner and Tanner, told the World's Parliament of Religions (in his speech "Christianity and the Negro") that St. Luke was black and so were other important figures in the early church.

Between 1890 and 1916 the AME Church grew from 494,777 members in 2,481 congregations to 548,355 members in 6,636 congregations. In 1926 the denomination included 545,814 members in 6,708 congregations. There was significant numerical strength in Georgia, where 74,149 members worshipped in 1,173 congregations. Florida had 45,541 members in 694 churches. There was some decline in AME strength by 1936, however, when the church reported 4,578 congregations and 493,357 members.

While the AME Church in the South was growing, so was the church in the industrial North. The massive black migration from southern rural communities to industrial centers in the North, South, and West during the two World Wars caused major growth in AME churches in New York, Philadelphia, Chicago, St. Louis, Atlanta, Birmingham, Los Angeles, and other major cities. In these settings, clergy fashioned a version of the Social Gospel that required their involvement with numerous issues in housing, social welfare, unionization, and politics. In the 1920s the Reverend Harrison G. Payne, pastor of Park Place Church in Homestead, a mill town near Pittsburgh, initiated an effort to supply housing to blacks newly arrived from the South; during World War II, investigators with the federal Fair Employment Practices Committee found cooperative AME pastors in numerous cities. Many AME pastors worked with labor unions. Dwight V. Kyle of the Avery Chapel Church in Memphis, Tennessee, for example, sided with the efforts of the Congress of Industrial Organizations (CIO) to unionize black and white mass-production workers in a dangerous antiunion setting.

The burgeoning civil rights movement of the late 1940s and early 1950s found substantive support within the AME clergy. J. A. Delaine, a pastor and school principal in Clarendon County, South Carolina, and Oliver Brown, the pastor of St. Mark Church in Topeka, Kansas, filed suits against public school segregation. Their efforts culminated in the landmark *Brown v. Board of Education of Topeka, Kansas* (1954) decision in which the U.S. Supreme Court nullified the "separate but equal" doctrine. Threats against Delaine pushed him out of South Carolina to New York City. Activist AME clergy moved the denomination at the 1960 general conference to establish a social action department; Frederick C. James, a South Carolina pastor and future bishop, became its first director.

When Bishop Richard Allen authorized Jarena Lee in 1819 to function as an exhorter in the AME Church, he opened the door to women in the ministry. For nearly 150 years, unordained female evangelists played important roles as preachers, pastors, and founders of congregations. During the nineteenth and early twentieth centuries, Amanda Berry Smith, Sarah Hughes, and Lucy Thurman preached in AME pulpits. Smith, for example, evangelized widely in the United States and then preached abroad in the British Isles, India, and West Africa. Like many, Millie Wolfe, a woman preacher in Waycross, Georgia, focused her efforts on the denomination's Women's Home and Foreign Missionary Society. She published a book of sermons that included "Scriptural Authority for Women's Work in the Christian Church." Female evangelists in the Rocky Mountain states in the early 1900s became crucial to AME Church expansion in Colorado, New Mexico, Arizona, Wyoming, and Montana. They established congregations and frequently supplied pulpits throughout this large region. While the gifted preaching of Martha Jayne Keys, Mary Watson Stewart, and others sustained the visibility of female ministers in the first half of the twentieth century, it was not until 1960 that the denomination allowed the full ordination of women. (An earlier attempt by Henry M. Turner to ordain women in 1885 had been promptly overturned by a church conference.)

Ecumenical efforts among African-American Christians also drew upon AME church leadership. In 1933, Bishop Reverdy C. Ransom (1861–1959) called together black denominational leaders to establish the Fraternal Council of Negro Churches. Similarly, in 1978 Bishop John Hurst Adams spearheaded the founding of the Congress of National Black Churches. Subsequently, Bishop Philip R. Cousin became president of the National Council of Churches in 1983, while Bishop Vinton R. Anderson became president of the World Council of Churches in 1991.

The Black Theology movement, which lasted from the late 1960s into the 1980s, drew AME participation through AME-trained theologians Cecil W. Cone (author of *The Identity Crisis in Black Theology* [1975]) and James H. Cone (author of *Black Theology and Black Power*

Juliann Jane Tillman, preacher of the African Methodist Episcopal (AME) Church, 1844. *Though the AME Church did not ordain women as ministers until the mid-twentieth century, female preachers played an important role from the earliest years of the denomination.* THE LIBRARY OF CONGRESS

[1969]). Jacqueline Grant, another theologian out of the AME tradition, pioneered the development of feminist theology. Her ideas were explored in *White Women's Christ and Black Women's Jesus* (1989).

Throughout its history, the AME Church has embraced congregations that crossed lines of class, culture, and geography. Several elements of Wesleyan worship remain in AME services, regardless of location and demography. A standard order of worship, mainly consisting of hymn singing, remains a staple of AME worship. Baptismal practices and the communion service make the AME Church virtually indistinguishable from white Methodist congregations. However, other practices rooted in African-American tradition—such as extemporaneous praying, singing of spirituals and gospels, and shouting—were observed depending on the cultural makeup of the congregation.

Since its formal founding in 1816, the AME Church's quadrennial General Conference has remained the supreme authority in denominational governance. Annual conferences, over which active bishops preside, cover particular geographical areas. During these yearly jurisdictional meetings, ministers receive their pastoral appointments. Within the annual conferences, districts have been established; these are superintended by presiding elders. The AME episcopacy, from Richard Allen's election and consecration in 1816 to the present, has been a lifetime position. General officers who administer such programs as publishing, pensions, Christian education, and evangelism serve for four years, but they can stand for re-election. Bishops and general officers are chosen at the general conference by elected ministerial and lay delegates. By 1993 the denomination had grown to 2,000,000 members in 7,000 congregations in the United States and thirty other countries in the Americas, Africa, and Europe. The AME Church has no central headquarters, although its publishing house is located in Nashville, Tennessee. At the turn of the twenty-first century, twenty-one active bishops and nine general officers made up the AME Church leadership. In 2005, the AME Church listed 2,500,000 adherents in the United States and 300,000 in other countries.

See also African Methodist Episcopal Zion Church; African Union Methodism; Allen, Richard; Black Codes; *Brown v. Board of Education of Topeka, Kansas*; Cain, Richard Harvey; Congress of National Black Churches, Inc.; Payne, Daniel Alexander; Social Gospel; Turner, Henry McNeal

Bibliography

Dickerson, Dennis C. *A Liberated Past: Explorations in A.M.E. Church History.* Nashville, Tenn.: A.M.E. Church Sunday School Union, 2003.

Gregg, Howard D. *History of the African Methodist Episcopal Church.* Nashville, Tenn.: AME Church, 1980.

Payne, Daniel A. *History of the African Methodist Episcopal Church.* Nashville, Tenn.: AME Church Sunday School Union, 1891. Reprint, 1998.

Walker, Clarence E. *Rock in a Weary Land: The African Methodist Episcopal Church during the Civil War and Reconstruction.* Baton Rouge: Louisiana State University Press, 1982.

Wright, Richard R., Jr. *The Bishops of the African Methodist Episcopal Church.* Nashville, Tenn.: AME Church Sunday School Union, 1963.

DENNIS C. DICKERSON (1996)
Updated by publisher 2005

African Methodist Episcopal Zion Church

The African Methodist Episcopal Zion Church (AMEZ) was organized in the early 1820s, but its roots go back to the late eighteenth century. A few black congregations in the New York City area in the 1790s sought greater freedom of worship and some measure of autonomy from white-controlled congregations in the predominantly white Methodist Episcopal denomination. With approximately 5,000 members by 1860, the AMEZ Church by the 1990s had a membership in excess of 1.3 million, with 3,000 clergy, 2,900 congregations, and 100,000 members overseas, principally in Africa and the Caribbean. By 1900 the group also had shifted most of its operations from New York to North Carolina and had become a truly national denomination.

The AMEZ has organized agencies and divisions devoted to such matters as youth, Christian education, domestic and overseas missions, and social concerns. Its highest organizational authority is the General Conference, which includes representatives from both clergy and laity. Two other main operational bodies are the Connectional Council, composed of the thirteen bishops as well as other significant ecclesiastical officers, and the Board of Bishops. The denomination has a publishing house located in Charlotte, North Carolina, where it publishes, among other works, the church newspaper, the *Star of Zion*. It supports four colleges: Livingstone College in Salisbury, North Carolina; Clinton Junior College in Rock Hill, South Carolina; Lomax-Hannon Junior College in Greenville, Alabama; and AME Zion Community College in Monrovia, Liberia.

Like the other black denominations, associations, and conventions founded prior to the Civil War, the AMEZ Church was formed primarily for the sake of greater autonomy in church participation and leadership, and to evangelize and serve in other ways the needs of African Americans in the late 1700s and the 1800s. The evangelical American Christianity that came to its earliest fruition during the Great Awakening (1730–1750) and the Second Great Awakening (1790–1825) had a profound impact upon the membership of the Christian churches in the United States. Evangelicalism was most clearly manifested during the Second Great Awakening in groups such as the Methodists, revivalist elements in the Church of England (Protestant Episcopal church), the Baptists, and some Presbyterian and Congregational churches.

Compared with their nonevangelical counterparts, white evangelicals were more receptive to black membership in their societies and churches and even sometimes open to various roles of black leadership. Thus, by the Revolutionary era, evangelicalism was a racially mixed phenomenon, with whites and blacks acting as missionaries, teachers, and preachers, although the preponderance of these activities were still intraracial. By the 1780s and 1790s, evangelical blacks were members of a movement and of churches in which they exercised a considerable degree of freedom of religion, relative to the treatment of blacks in nonevangelical churches.

The Revolutionary age brought with it intense rhetoric about the equality of all men and their inalienable rights. Not surprisingly, therefore, when a number of white-controlled (though not always predominantly white) congregations began to curb religious freedom, to introduce new strictures of racial segregation and discrimination, and to refuse to modify policies and practices of caste, many African Americans, especially those with leadership talents, rebelled.

With these rebellious leaders—Peter Spencer in Wilmington, Delaware; Richard Allen in Philadelphia; and William Miller in New York City—lie the origins of the independent black Methodist congregations. In the first quarter of the nineteenth century, they joined forces to form three separate black denominations: the Union Church of Africans, in Delaware, in 1813; the African Methodist Episcopal Church (AME Church), based in Philadelphia, in 1816; and the Zion group, based in New York City, in the 1820–1824 period. For the AMEZ, the focal point seems to have been the John Street Methodist Episcopal Church in New York.

By 1793 the John Street congregation's membership was about 40 percent black. Yet blacks were blocked from the higher orders of the ministry and faced discrimination at the Holy Communion table as well as in seating. In 1796 Peter Williams and William Miller helped start a separate black Methodist congregation. They founded the African Chapel in a shop owned by Miller. By 1800 the group gathered around these two men constructed a church building, and in 1801 their congregation was incorporated. These Methodists emphasized their desire to be free of white domination by restricting trustee membership to those of African descent.

Like their forerunners in the Union Church of Africans and the African Methodist Episcopal denomination, these black Methodists were struggling to establish and maintain a significant degree of autonomy in the midst of clear, overt white opposition to their efforts. By ensuring that control of their church was in the hands of African

Americans, these Methodists were guaranteeing that they would not again be relegated to the status of second-class membership in their own church, as they had been in John Street and other Methodist Episcopal congregations. With the assistance of a white preacher, John McClaskey, nine men incorporated the African Chapel church in 1801: Francis Jacobs, Peter Williams, David Bias, George E. Moore, George Collins, George White, Thomas Sipkins, Thomas Cook, and William Brown. The church was incorporated as the African Methodist Episcopal Church of the City of New York.

From 1816 to 1824 this small group of black Methodists moved more decisively toward the establishment of a separate denomination. In 1816 the Zion Church (formerly the African Chapel) joined with the Asbury Church to petition the Methodist Episcopal Conference of New York to establish a separate circuit for African Methodists. In 1820 the beginnings of a split in the white parent body, the Methodist Episcopal Church, had ramifications for African Methodists. William Stillwell, a white minister who had been appointed pastor of the Zion Church, withdrew from the larger body in an attempt to introduce more democratic procedures.

This move of Stillwell's occasioned further reflection on the part of the African Methodists concerning their own organizational relationship with the Methodist Episcopal Church. In August 1820 the African Methodists became a separate black conference within the larger denomination; by October they had established a discipline (a set of church policies, beliefs, and rules) for the two congregations, Zion and Asbury. A pivotal move took place on June 21, 1821, when the African Methodists held their first annual conference and rejected affiliation with the AME Church, also deciding against reaffiliation with the white-controlled Methodist Episcopal Church. Many scholars date the origins of the AMEZ denomination from this year. It was not until 1824, however, that the African Methodists in New York made it clear they were not under any supervision of the Methodist Episcopal denomination.

The new denomination registered slow but steady growth from 1821 to the advent of the Civil War. At the 1821 conference (their first annual meeting), the Zionites had six churches with fewer than 1,500 members: Zion Church (763) and Asbury Church (150) of New York City, and congregations from Long Island, New York (155); New Haven, Connecticut (24); Easton, Pennsylvania (18); and Philadelphia (Wesleyan Church, with 300). In 1822 the group selected James Varick, the pastor of Zion Church, as its first superintendent. He served until 1828, when he was replaced by Christopher Rush, who had migrated north from eastern North Carolina. Throughout the nineteenth century there was intense controversy, friction, debate, and rivalry between the Zion denomination and the AME denomination—much of it fueled by the fact that both, prior to the New York–based group's addition of "Zion" to its title in 1848, termed themselves the African Methodist Episcopal Church.

"Mother Zion," AME Zion Church in Harlem, New York. *A street view of the church, taken from "Harlem, Mecca of the New Negro," the March 1925 issue of* Survey Graphic, *highlights its prominent double doors with gothic arches, as well as adjacent row apartments.* MANUSCRIPTS, ARCHIVES AND RARE BOOKS DIVISION, SCHOMBURG CENTER FOR RESEARCH IN BLACK CULTURE, THE NEW YORK PUBLIC LIBRARY, ASTOR, LENOX AND TILDEN FOUNDATIONS.

Given their competition for new members and the alliances of black Methodist congregations, this similarity in names caused confusion and charges of misrepresentation. There was also a lively debate as to which was actually the first organized group. Each extended the date of its founding back into the eighteenth century to coincide with the rise of the oldest congregation of the connection. Concomitantly, each tended to overlook or downplay the origins of the first congregation of the rival group. The Zion group, moreover, was beset by schism in the 1850s arising from controversy surrounding the status of one of its bishops.

With the coming of the Civil War, the AMEZ, like other independent black denominations and conventions, embarked upon a new era of opportunity and growth. Whereas the Zionites had only a few more than 1,400 members and 22 ministers in 1821, by 1860 they had grown to 4,600 members with 105 ministers. But this slow growth in membership was outdistanced considerably by the phenomenal rise during and following the Civil War. By 1884 the AMEZ registered 300,000 members; by 1896, the number had increased to 350,000.

Both the AMEZ and the AME experienced rather small growth during the pre–Civil War years because both were mainly confined to the northern portion of the country, especially the Northeast. Understandably, independent black organizations, religious or secular, mainly comprising free persons committed to an antislavery stance, were not welcomed in the slaveholding South. In addition, most African-American Methodists in New York, Pennsylvania, and elsewhere elected for a number of reasons to remain with the predominantly white Methodist Episcopal denomination. Much of the black Methodist Episcopal constituency had a degree of autonomy as largely black congregations with black ministers, while maintaining the advantages of continued association with a white organization. With the coming of the Civil War, however, and the emancipation of previously enslaved blacks, the doors for inclusion in northern-based, independent black denominations and conventions were opened much wider.

A substantial number of black southern Christians did remain with the white-controlled Methodist Episcopal Church–South, and the Methodist Episcopal Church (North) gained a considerable number of congregations, ministers, and members from their ranks. The vast majority of black Christians, however, flocked to the independent black ecclesiastical groups that followed Union troops into the old Confederacy. The black Baptist churches secured the most members, followed by the AME. But the AMEZ captured a significant and substantial segment of southern black Christians for its connection.

The Zion denomination has encountered a number of significant challenges. One of the main reasons for its debut was the evangelization and religious training of people of African descent. A number of organizations connected with the denomination were formed over the years to deal with these goals. The denomination not only expanded in the South following the Civil War but entered the Midwest, the Far West, Canada, and the Caribbean. Nova Scotia and the Caribbean areas figured prominently in the AMEZ's outreach efforts during the postbellum years. During the 1870s and 1880s the AMEZ, like its AME and black Baptist counterparts, joined in the efforts to missionize Africa. Andrew Cartwright, the first Zion missionary in Africa, and Bishop John Bryan Small, who later was the first to have episcopal jurisdiction in Africa, were forerunners in the African mission program. The AMEZ Church, like other black Christian groups, pursued the missionizing of Africa for reasons that connected evangelical interests with practical concerns for the well-being of African people.

Sketch of Christopher Rush (1777–1873). *Rush, who succeeded James Varick as general superintendent (bishop) of the AME Zion Church, was the first historian of the denomination and was responsible for much of its antebellum growth. The sketch is from Carter G. Woodson's* History of the Negro Church, *c. 1921.* GENERAL RESEARCH AND REFERENCE DIVISION, SCHOMBURG CENTER FOR RESEARCH IN BLACK CULTURE, THE NEW YORK PUBLIC LIBRARY, ASTOR, LENOX AND TILDEN FOUNDATIONS.

The AMEZ has always been intimately involved in efforts to achieve greater citizenship rights for African Americans. Outstanding nineteenth-century AMEZ members such as Sojourner Truth, Harriet Tubman, Jermain Loguen, Catherine Harris, and Frederick Douglass fought to abolish slavery, gain equal rights and justice for black citizens, and expand the freedom of American women. Jermain Loguen's classic address "I Will Not Live a Slave" testifies to the precarious position of many people of color who had escaped bondage in the South and border states, and points out the connections between free people of the North and their enslaved brothers and sisters.

An issue of internal concern in the Zion denomination was the debate over the role and meaning of the terms "superintendent" and "bishop." Zion, like the predominantly white Methodist Protestant Church, envisioned itself originally as a more democratic institution than the mother Methodist Episcopal Church. It selected the name "superintendent" for its episcopal overseers and mandated their election every four years rather than for life, as was the case in the Methodist Episcopal and African Methodist Episcopal Churches. When their AME rivals cast doubts on the episcopal validity of Zion's superintendents, the AMEZ changed its title to bishop and passed a rule stipulating that each was elected for life. This last rule was later modified to require retirement at a certain age. Bishop James Walker Hood was instrumental during the 1800s in defending the validity of Zion's episcopacy and undergirding the "high church" tradition of episcopacy within the Zion church.

The Zion church has been at the forefront within American Methodism in advancing democracy within its membership by expanding representation in its highest councils to laypersons. It also supported the ordination of women to the office of elder, the church's highest ministerial office except for bishop. In 1898 Bishop Charles Calvin Pettey ordained Mary Julia Small, a bishop's wife, as the first woman elder in the Zion church, or any major American Methodist denomination. Julia Foote, an author, evangelist, and supporter of the Holiness Movement, was ordained an elder by Bishop Hood. Although Bishops Pettey and Hood stood by their controversial actions, not until the 1980s and 1990s were a significant number of women ordained to the eldership. At the start of the twenty-first century, none of the major black Methodist groups, including the AMEZ, has appointed a female bishop, unlike the United Methodist Church, which has appointed both black and white women to the episcopacy.

Another area of concern to Zionites has been ecumenism, especially within the family of black Methodist churches. The first serious and hopeful efforts at black Methodist unity came during the Civil War, in 1864, when the AME and the AMEZ nearly agreed upon a document cementing the union of the two churches. The measure failed because conferences within the AME Church, where the matter was submitted for ratification, rejected the proposal. Other discussions since then have included dialogues with the AME, the Christian Methodist Episcopal Church (CME), and the Methodist Episcopal denominations. The CME and the AMEZ were close to union at one point during the 1980s, but progress stalled. It appeared that independent black denominations are torn between racial solidarity on one hand and transracial unity on the other—between the ideal of union across racial lines and the reality of continued racial prejudice and discrimination, even in ecclesiastical circles.

The AMEZ Church, like most other black denominations, however, has been involved in ecumenical efforts at cooperation, such as the Federal Council of Churches (later the National Council of Churches) and the World Council of Churches. It has participated with other black Methodists, as well as other Christians, in interfaith efforts to advance the civil, political, and economic progress of African Americans. Its membership in the National Fraternal Council of Negro Churches, founded in 1933, serves as an example of Zion's work in this regard.

There have been other major figures in AMEZ history. Bishop Joseph J. Clinton commissioned James Hood and other missionaries for work in the South during and following the Civil War; his efforts greatly facilitated the geographical and numerical expansion of Zion's ranks. Rev. Joseph C. Price, popularly esteemed as an orator, was one of the founders and the first president of Livingstone College. Mary Jane Talbert Jones, Meriah G. Harris, and Annie Walker Blackwell were early leaders in the Woman's Home and Foreign Missionary Society, established in 1880.

The historical and theological significance of the AMEZ Church rests in the claims that black people, when their humanity was greatly compromised in the eyes of many whites, were capable of managing and directing enterprises without the governance and supervision of whites, and the theological position that the Christian faith condemns racial discrimination as sin and heresy.

See also African Methodist Episcopal Church; Allen, Richard; Truth, Sojourner; Tubman, Harriet

Bibliography

Baldwin, Lewis V. *"Invisible" Strands in African Methodism: A History of the African Union Methodist Protestant and Union American Methodist Episcopal Churches, 1805–1980.* Metuchen, N.J.: Scarecrow Press, 1983.

Bradley, David Henry, Sr. *A History of A. M. E. Zion Church.* 2 vols. Nashville, Tenn.: Parthenon Press, 1956, 1971.

Hood, James Walker. *One Hundred Years of the African Methodist Episcopal Zion Church.* New York: A. M. E. Zion Book Concern, 1895.

Johnson, Dorothy Sharpe, and Williams, Lula Goolsby. *Pioneering Women of the African Methodist Episcopal Zion Church.* Charlotte, N.C.: A. M. E. Zion Publishing House, 1996.

McClain, William B. *Black People in the Methodist Church: Whither Thou Goest?* Cambridge, Mass.: Shenkman Publishing Co., 1984.

Richardson, Harry V. *Dark Salvation: The Story of Methodism as It Developed Among Blacks in America.* Garden City, N.Y.: Anchor Press, 1976.

Walls, William J. *The African Methodist Episcopal Zion Church: Reality of the Black Church.* Charlotte, N.C.: A. M. E. Zion Publishing House, 1974.

SANDY DWAYNE MARTIN (1996)

African Orthodox Church

The African Orthodox Church (AOC) was founded September 2, 1921, by George Alexander McGuire, an Antiguan follower of Marcus Garvey who had been ordained a priest in the Protestant Episcopal Church. The purpose of the new denomination was originally to create a kind of state church for the Universal Negro Improvement Association and to further black nationalist religious symbolism, but when the AOC did not become an official part of the Garvey movement, it concentrated on defending the validity of its claims to apostolic succession through orders from the West Syrian Jacobite Church of Antioch.

The AOC has never grown beyond a few thousand members in the United States, and they are concentrated primarily along the East Coast. Its clergy and members have been largely West Indian, although it occasionally appeals to dissident Roman Catholics and a few traditional Protestants. The church's liturgy is formal and high, a combination of Anglican and Roman rites with some Orthodox influences and usages. The AOC spread to Africa, where its membership numbers in the millions and where it exists uniquely as an independent church with legitimate ties to historic Christianity as well as involvement in African cultural nationalism.

In the United States, the AOC has been a channel of "valid though irregular" ordinations and consecrations among so-called Old Catholic bodies. McGuire was canonized in 1983, but the church did not participate in or benefit from the post–civil rights movement surge of black nationalism. In California, a communitarian group formerly gathered around the widow of jazz musician John Coltrane has affiliated with the AOC and appears to give the denomination its best hope for active continuity.

See also Garvey, Marcus; Universal Negro Improvement Association

Bibliography

Newman, Richard. "The Origins of the African Orthodox Church." In *The Negro Churchman* (1923–1931). Millwood, N.Y.: Kraus Reprint, 1977, pp. iii-xxiv.

Platt, Warren C. "The African Orthodox Church: An Analysis of Its First Decade." *Church History* 58, no. 4 (December 1989): 474–488.

RICHARD NEWMAN (1996)

African Union Methodism

African Union Methodism is the common name shared by those churches stemming from the movement founded by the Maryland ex-slave Peter Spencer in Wilmington, Delaware, in 1805. In its contemporary usage, it refers to the African Union Methodist Protestant (AUMP) Church and the Union American Methodist Episcopal (UAME) Church, the only two remaining bodies with roots in the Spencer tradition.

In June 1805 Spencer and William Anderson led some forty African Americans out of the predominantly white Asbury Methodist Episcopal Church in Wilmington. Racial discrimination and the desire for black religious independence figured prominently in the secession. The dissenters immediately formed Ezion Methodist Episcopal Church, designed to function as a black "mission church" under the auspices of Asbury Church and the Methodist Episcopal Conference. A second secession occurred in 1813, mainly because of the arbitrary exercise of power against blacks by white elders and disputes over seating arrangements. On September 18, 1813, Spencer took the lead in organizing the Union Church of Africans, also known variously as the Union Church of African Members, the African Union Church, the African Union Methodist Church, and the Union Methodist Connexion.

The new denomination remained essentially Methodist in its articles of religion, general rules, discipline, and multiple conference system. However, the episcopacy, the itineracy, and the strong connectional system of the Methodists were rejected in favor of a more democratic style involving lay elders, elder ministers, deacons, licensed preachers, local congregational autonomy, and the stationed pastorate.

Beginning in the 1850s, a series of schisms interfered with the growth and development of the Spencer churches. In 1855 to 1856 conflict in the Union Church of Africans over the authority of elder ministers resulted in the formation of a rival body known as the Union American Methodist Episcopal Church. In 1866 the remaining congregations in the Union Church of Africans merged with the First Colored Methodist Protestant Church of Baltimore, Maryland, resulting in the African Union First Colored Methodist Protestant Church, also called the African Union Methodist Protestant Church. A serious rift occurred in the UAME Church in 1935 when three candidates ran unsuccessfully for the episcopacy. This schism culminated in the organization of the rival Reformed Union American Methodist Episcopal Church, a body that no longer exists.

From their founding, the AUMP and UAME churches have remained regional due to insufficient resources, poor missionary outreach, the lack of strong connectional systems, numerous schisms, and a dearth of vigorous, educated leadership. In 1990 both the AUMP and the UAME churches reported fewer than ten thousand members located in congregations in Delaware, Maryland, Pennsylvania, New Jersey, New York, Connecticut, Rhode Island, and Washington, D.C. Since the late 1970s the UAME Church has also struggled to build congregations in parts of the West Indies.

Both the AUMP and the UAME churches remain significantly smaller and less socially active than the larger national branches of black Methodism, such as the African Methodist Episcopal (AME) Church, the African Methodist Episcopal Zion (AMEZ) Church, and the Christian Methodist Episcopal (CME) Church.

See also African Methodist Episcopal Church; African Methodist Episcopal Zion Church; Christian Methodist Episcopal Church

Bibliography

Baldwin, Lewis V. *"Invisible" Strands in African Methodism: A History of the African Union Methodist Protestant and Union American Methodist Episcopal Churches, 1805–1980.* Philadelphia: American Theological Library Association, 1983.

Baldwin, Lewis V. *The Mark of a Man: Peter Spencer and the African Union Methodist Tradition.* Lanhan, Md.: University Press of America, 1987.

Russell, Daniel J. *History of the African Union Methodist Protestant Church.* Philadelphia: Union Star, 1920.

LEWIS V. BALDWIN (1996)

Molefi Kete Asante. *Dr. Asante, credited with establishing the first doctoral program in African-American Studies, coined the term afrocentrism in 1976, defining it as a worldview that consciously places Africa, rather than Europe, at the center of scholarly focus.* COURTESY OF MOLEFI KETE ASANTE

AFROCENTRISM

Afrocentrism has a long and often misunderstood history. Though usually associated with the intellectual lineage that runs from Cheikh Anta Diop (1923–1986) to Molefi Asante (1942–), the ideology actually has a pedigree that dates back to some of the most distinguished African-American intellectuals of the nineteenth century, including David Walker, Henry Highland Garnet, Martin Delany, Alexander Crummell, and Edward Wilmot Blyden. The actual term *Afrocentric* apparently was coined by W. E. B. Du Bois only in the early 1960s. Du Bois wrote that his proposed *Encyclopedia Africana* would be "unashamedly Afro-centric" in focus. Asante resurrected the term in his 1980 work, *Afrocentricity*, injecting new energy into an old approach to the study of Africans and their descendants. By the late 1980s, the term *Afrocentric* was used to describe a range of thinkers, from mainstream historians like Sterling Stuckey to more controversial scholars like Leonard Jeffries.

While the term *Afrocentric* has been applied to both credible and dubious attempts at scholarly analysis, at its broadest, it is simply an attempt to place Africa, instead of Europe, at the center of scholarly analysis of peoples of African descent. In his 1987 book, *The Afrocentric Idea*, Molefi Asante defines *Afrocentricity* as "the placing of African ideals at the center of any analysis that involves African culture and behavior" (p. 6). It should be emphasized that this perspective is not an explicit argument for African superiority in culture and history, although some scholars have used it to that end. Rather, it is a conceptual tool for seeing the history of African-descended peoples through their own lens, and not through the lens of Europe or the West. As a mode of analysis, Afrocentrism has remained remarkably durable over the past two hundred years; however, scholars have often reached radically different conclusions in their utilization of this analytical tool.

Black Nationalism, Afrocentrism, and the Academy

A crucial prerequisite to an Afrocentric perspective is the recognition of Africa as a common "homeland" to all peoples of African descent. The earliest expressions of this sentiment emerged out of late eighteenth-century African-American communities, where figures like Prince Hall and Paul Cuffe initiated movements to return to Africa and create settlements there. In 1787 Hall, the most prominent free black in Boston, petitioned the General Court of Massachusetts to aid African Americans "to return to Africa, our native country." For black people born in America, as well as for various African societies, the notion of a singular African homeland represented the reality of shared historical trajectories in the diaspora. By defining themselves as "Africans," rather than as "Americans," "Yorubas," or "Kongos," these early Afrocentrists played a crucial role in conceptualizing a shared history of African-descended peoples, regardless of natal background.

Because of the connections between emigration and racist slave-holding interests, many African Americans rejected emigration schemes of the early nineteenth century; however, new initiatives in the 1850s once again drew attention to the shared history of peoples of African descent. In 1858 Henry Highland Garnet called for the construction of "a great center for Negro nationality" in Africa or the Americas. One year later, in 1859, Martin Delany traveled to West Africa in the hopes of realizing his vision of "Africa for the African race and black men to rule them." Similar expressions could be found in the ideas of Henry McNeal Turner, and much later, Marcus Garvey. These "back-to-Africa" movements faded after the 1920s, but by this time the idea of Africa as the common homeland of African-descended peoples was well established.

Concurrent with emerging ideas about a singular "Africa" were new interpretations of African history and culture. Challenging racist characterizations of Africa as a dark continent lacking science and history, a number of nineteenth-century black intellectuals pointed to the achievements of Egypt and Ethiopia as evidence of Africa's rich and glorious past. In *Appeal* (1829), David Walker highlighted "the arts and sciences—wise legislators—the pyramids and other magnificent buildings . . . by the sons of Africa . . . among whom learning originated, and was carried thence into Greece." Similar emphasis on Egypt, and especially the ancient Christian tradition of Ethiopia, can be found in the works of Frederick Douglass, James C. Pennington, and Henry Highland Garnet.

While Egypt eventually emerged as central in the debates over Afrocentrism in the mid-twentieth century (see below), these earlier imperatives were aimed at recovery and redemption of the African past. As such, Egypt represented a convenient and easily accessible entry point to deeper explorations of Africa's complex history. Nowhere is this clearer than in the evolution of Edward Wilmot Blyden. In his early writings, Blyden adopted the position of a linear connection between Egyptians and African Americans, and he repeated the argument that Egypt spawned Greek "civilization." Though he never completely abandoned this teleology, by the time of his death in 1912, Blyden had devoted himself to the study of West African languages, cultures, and histories. As a result, he moved away from static interpretations of a homogenous Africa toward interpretations that recognized the diversity of the continent, still emphasizing the strong cultural and historical connections between various peoples, becoming the first to emphasize the importance of an "African personality."

If Blyden was a pioneer in seriously considering the depth and diversity of West Africa, others quickly followed. Hubert Henry Harrison, a socialist and Garveyite who emigrated from the Virgin Islands to New York in 1900, was renowned for his knowledge of Africa, applying a sophisticated Afrocentric analysis to the history of African-descended peoples. In *When Africa Awakes* (1920), Harrison implored African Americans to:

> go to Africa, live among the natives and LEARN WHAT THEY HAVE TO TEACH US (for they have much to teach us). . . . Let us begin by studying the scientific works of the African explorers and stop reading and believing the silly slush which ignorant missionaries put into our heads about the alleged degradation of our people in Africa. Let us learn to know Africa and Africans

> so well that every educated Negro will be able at a glance to put his hand on the map of Africa and tell where to find Jolofs, Ekoisi, Mandingoes, Yorubas, Bechuanas or Basutos and can tell something of their marriage customs, their property laws, their agriculture and system of worship. For not until we can do this will it be seemly for us to pretend to be anxious about their political welfare. (Harrison, 1920, pp. 34–35)

Here, Harrison clearly evokes the depth and diversity of Africa. Moreover, he appeals to African Americans to learn about "our people," not from Europeans, but through the eyes of Africans themselves.

The idea that African-American culture was essentially African soon gained currency in the mainstream academic world. Carter G. Woodson's *The African Background Outlined* (1936) demonstrated African survivals in religion, folklore, art, and music in African-American communities. Perhaps the most enduring contribution to modern-day Afrocentrism is Melville Herskovits's *The Myth of the Negro Past* (1941). Herskovits emphasized West African cultural survivals in the Americas, particularly in South America and the Caribbean. Though he has been criticized in recent years for applying his argument for cultural survivals too broadly and for homogenizing West Africa, Herskovits's research influenced the works of many Afrocentric scholars, including Roger Bastide, Robert Farris Thompson, St. Clair Drake, and Sterling Stuckey. Among these, Stuckey makes the most eloquent and forceful argument for African survivals in the United States. In *Slave Culture* (1987), Stuckey argued that the organizing sociocultural principle of African-American communities is the African-derived "ring shout," a religious ritual performed in a circle of dancing, with singing participants moving in a counterclockwise motion that culminates in spirit possession. Stuckey traced elements of this religious ritual from West and West Central Africa, to North American slave communities, and finally to contemporary African-American culture. The approach of Herskovits, Stuckey, and more recently Michael Gomez, Paul Lovejoy, and John Thornton, has not gone unchallenged. Anthropologists and historians such as Sidney Mintz, Richard Price, Ira Berlin, and Philip Morgan have criticized the emphasis on African survivals, claiming that the agency and creativity of the enslaved were more important than the African past. Thus, they challenge the Afrocentric mode of analysis and the centrality of Africa to the African-American past.

Molefi Kete Asante

"Afrocentricity is a frame of reference wherein phenomena are viewed from the perspective of the African person. The Afrocentric approach seeks in every situation the appropriate centrality of the African person."

"THE AFROCENTRIC IDEA IN EDUCATION." *JOURNAL OF NEGRO EDUCATION* (SPRING 1991)

Egyptocentrism and Populist Afrocentrism

Since the 1950s, another stream of Afrocentric thought has emerged that builds on earlier attempts to trace a direct lineage between ancient Egyptians, sub-Saharan Africans, and Africans in the diaspora. This stream of thought has tended to dominate popular and even some scholarly understandings of Afrocentrism ever since. The "grandfather" of this school of Afrocentrism, the intellectual forefather of Molefi Asante, Leonard Jeffries, and Martin Bernal, was Senegalese scholar Cheikh Anta Diop. In his *The African Origin of Civilization*, first published in French in 1955, Diop argued that Africa was the cradle of humanity and civilization. Not only did the letters and sciences emerge in Egypt; black Egyptians spawned the greatest of human social attributes, distinguishing themselves from the "ferocity" of Eurasians in their "gentle, idealistic, peaceful nature, endowed with a spirit of justice and gaiety" (Diop, 1974, pp. 111–112). Climate played a prominent role in Diop's formulations: Egypt's warm, favorable climate, as opposed to Eurasia's cold and forbidding climate, went far in explaining the benevolence of the African personality. Diop also repeated the assertion that ancient Greece drew all of the important elements of its civilization from Egypt and Africa, a claim that was made even more forcefully in American George James's *Stolen Legacy* (1954).

Elements of Diop's arguments can be found in nearly all of the populist and Egyptocentric scholarship of the late twentieth century. In fact, very little in the recent scholarship goes beyond Diop's central claims, other than the application of the term *Afrocentric* to this particular mode of inquiry. In 1980 Molefi Asante reintroduced the term *Afrocentric* to the scholarly world in his book *Afrocentricity: The Theory of Social Change.* In this book and his *Kemet, Afrocentricity, and Knowledge* (1990), Asante set out to define what he claimed was an entirely new discipline of academic inquiry. Despite these claims of originality, much of what Asante argued was drawn from scholars going back to the 1800s, and more particularly from Diop. According to Asante's theory of Afrocentricity, humanity developed and was perfected in Africa, therefore endowing Africans with a head start on other humans. Egypt, or Kemet, was the first great civilization, forming the foundation for all of the great African cultures that would follow it. Moreover, Egyptians passed on to other African peoples "an African orientation to the cosmos" that resulted in common spiritual values. The arts, letters, and sciences of Egypt were stolen by ancient Greece, and ultimately transferred to all of Europe. Europeans then conspired to hide Egypt's greatness from Africans, convincing them that Europe was the source of all civilization. The lineage of intellectual greatness and African personality was passed down to all peoples of African descent, including those in the diaspora, and it is their obligation to reclaim the glories of this common African past.

Notwithstanding the lack of originality in Asante's major works, his charisma and energy injected new life into the Egyptocentric stream of Afrocentrism. As chair of the Department of African American Studies at Temple University in Philadelphia from 1984 to 1996, Asante developed a graduate curriculum that produced dozens of Ph.D.s. He has spoken at numerous public events and at more than a hundred different colleges and universities. Asante has lobbied for curriculum changes in America's public schools, particularly around the issue of African-American speech and language, or *Ebonics*. Asante also has been a prolific writer, publishing dozens of books and articles. *Afrocentricity* has been widely read by mainstream scholars, as well as the broader public. While many have criticized the teleology and hagiography that characterize much of Asante's approach to Afrocentrism, there is little doubt that the energy and attention he has brought to the Afrocentric paradigm have made an immense contribution to scholarship, forcing scholars of all stripes to be more serious in their considerations of the African past. In this way, his contributions far surpass those of his intellectual predecessors in the nineteenth century, and even Diop.

Perhaps the most controversial contribution to this new stream of Afrocentric scholarship relates to the question of Egypt's influence on ancient Greece. The idea of the "stolen" Egyptian legacy received serious consideration from the scholarly community with the publication of Martin Bernal's *Black Athena* (1987–1991). Indeed, Bernal's book became a lightning rod for controversies surrounding Afrocentrism, dominating much of the debate. Bernal, a white professor at Cornell University, made arguments that were strikingly similar to those made by earlier African-American intellectuals, such as Marcus Garvey, Cheikh Anta Diop, and others. In short, Bernal argued that the Greeks were indebted to Egyptian influences in the building of Western civilization. However, Bernal went one step further when he argued that portions of the ancient Greek population were actually derived from Egyptians who colonized the region. He shows that until the late eighteenth century, even European scholars acknowledged the influence of the Egyptians on Greece. Only with the emergence of pseudoscientific racism was this "Ancient Model" replaced by the "Aryan Model" that views ancient Greece as almost entirely "white" and European.

What separated Bernal from scholars who preceded him was his expertise in ancient history and languages, as well as the rigorous methodology he employed in researching his book. Evocative and dramatic in its rendering, *Black Athena* has been criticized by some classicists as being too imaginative in its use of archaeological and linguistic evidence. Nevertheless, other scholars of ancient Greece find Bernal's arguments provocative and compelling.

Unfortunately, some of Bernal's critics refused to engage his research on its merits, preferring instead to resort to broadside assaults. Foremost among these critics was Mary Lefkowitz. Her *Not Out of Africa* (1996) bears on its dust cover a bust of Socrates wearing a Malcolm X baseball cap. Its contents are no less subtle. Rather than trying to understand the historical imperatives that inspire claims of Socrates' or Cleopatra's blackness, Lefkowitz smugly refutes all claims that the ancient world was anything other than "Aryan." In her high-handed attempt to dismiss the evidentiary basis for Egyptian and African claims to the ancient world, she unwittingly feeds into the very marginalization and exclusion that initiated these inquiries in the first place.

Take, for example, her claim that the Egyptian "stolen legacy" theory "robs the ancient Greeks and their modern descendants of a heritage that rightly belongs to them" (Lefkowitz, 1996, p. 126). Here, she tacitly excludes Africans and their descendants from what most would consider the *human* heritage of Greek achievement. In yet another passage, Lefkowitz writes:

> Any attempt to question the authenticity of ancient Greek civilization is of direct concern even to people who ordinarily have little interest in the remote past. Since the founding of this country, ancient Greece has been intimately connected with the ideals of American democracy. Rightly

or wrongly, since much of the credit belongs to the Romans, we like to think that we have carried on some of the Greeks' proudest traditions: democratic government, and freedom of speech, learning, and discussion (Lefkowitz, 1996, p. 6).

Again, Lefkowitz belies her own racialized assumptions. Not only does she fail to recognize that for most of the country's history African Americans have been excluded from the "ideals of American democracy," she implicitly reinscribes this exclusion in her use of the word *we*, a *we* that, given her overall argument, can only be interpreted as "we *white* Americans." Thus, democracy remains a peculiarly "white" historical legacy. Unfortunately, Lefkowitz fails to recognize that it was precisely this exclusion that first prompted Afrocentric inquiries as early as the nineteenth century. And, erroneous as some Afrocentric conclusions might be, reactionary tracts like hers only confirm the deepest suspicions of those who claim a stolen legacy. As Wilson Moses noted in his fine examination of the history of Afrocentrism, *Afrotopia* (1998), "the appearance of Lefkowitz's book has been heralded with jubilation by paranoid black nationalists and Egyptocentrists. What better proof [of the stolen legacy] could they have desired than such a volume?" (p. 8).

The deepest irony of Lefkowitz's attack on Afrocentrism is that it unwittingly replicates some of the very same essentialist, separatist racism that can be found on the furthest fringes of Afrocentrism. Building on Diop's ideas about climatology, Leonard Jeffries, one-time chair of the Black Studies Department at the City College of New York, has argued that white "Ice People" are biologically inferior to black "Sun People." In Jeffries's views, white people's lack of melanin and their underdeveloped genes are products of the ice age, resulting in cold, callous, and selfish people. Meanwhile, the abundance of melanin in African-descended peoples results in creativity, communalism, and a love of humanity. Jeffries is not alone in this biological essentialism. Psychologist Frances Cress Welsing replicates Jeffries's arguments regarding the benefits of high levels of melanin in black people. Yet in her book, *The Isis Papers* (1991), she goes one step further when she argues that white males, obsessed with their lack of melanin, engage in a series of self-negating behaviors aimed at manufacturing more melanin. As an example, she argues that homosexuality is "a symbolic attempt to incorporate into the white male body more male substance. . . . [Thus] the self-debasing white male may fantasize that he can produce a product of color, albeit that the product of color is fecal matter. This fantasy is significant for white males, because the males who can produce skin color are viewed as the real men" (p. 47). Though easy to reject, some have assumed that the ideas of people like Jeffries and Welsing are synonymous with Afrocentrism, writ large. At the risk of sounding like an apologist for such extremism, it bears repeating that Afrocentrism is not a set of fixed ideas; rather, it is a method of inquiry that centers Africa and African-descended peoples in their own cultures and histories. How that method is applied can result in radically different sets of conclusions.

Ultimately, Afrocentrism defies many of the simplistic assumptions that have been applied to it. As an approach to the study of African and African-descended peoples, it has a long and distinguished lineage. Indeed, scholars continue to utilize the Afrocentric "survivals" paradigm in their analysis of African contributions to the Americas. The best of these studies go well beyond the homogenous Africa of Egyptian teleology to note the specific ethnic and even family histories of Africans in their journeys through the diaspora. Yet most of the scholarly mainstream still insists on labeling Afrocentrism an essentially anti-intellectual, methodologically flawed endeavor. While there is little doubt that there is a vast gulf between those who romanticize the African past and those who study Africans and their descendants on their own terms, there is also little doubt that the imperatives driving these approaches are common ones—an attempt to raise questions that emanate out of the black experience, centering African-descended peoples in their own temporal and historical realities.

See also Anthropology and Anthropologists; Black Arts Movement; Black Power Movement; Blyden, Edward Wilmot; Civil Rights Movement, U.S.; Garnet, Henry Highland; Garvey, Marcus; Turner, Henry McNeal

Bibliography

Asante, Molefi K. *Afrocentricity: The Theory of Social Change.* Buffalo, N.Y.: Amulefe, 1980.

Asante, Molefi K. *The Afrocentric Idea.* Philadelphia: Temple University Press, 1987. Rev. ed., 1998.

Asante, Molefi K. *Kemet, Afrocentricity, and Knowledge.* Trenton, N.J.: Africa World Press, 1990.

Bastide, Roger. *African Civilisations in the New World.* Translated by Peter Green. New York: Harper, 1971.

Berlin, Ira. *Many Thousands Gone: The First Two Centuries of Slavery in North America.* Cambridge, Mass.: Balknap, 1998.

Bernal, Martin. *Black Athena: The Afroasiatic Roots of Classical Civilization.* 2 vols. New Brunswick, N.J.: Rutgers University Press, 1987–1991.

Diop, Cheikh Anta. *The African Origin of Civilization: Myth or Reality.* Translated by Mercer Cook. New York: Lawrence Hill, 1974.

Diop, Cheikh Anta. *Civilization or Barbarism: An Authentic Anthropology.* Translated by Yaa-Lengi Meema Ngemi. New York: Lawrence Hill, 1991.

Drake, St. Clair. *Black Folk Here and There: An Essay in History and Anthropology.* 2 vols. Los Angeles: UCLA Afro-American Studies Center, 1987–1990.

Gomez, Michael A. *Exchanging Our Country Marks: The Transformation of African Identities in the Colonial and Antebellum South.* Chapel Hill: University of North Carolina Press, 1998.

Harrison, Hubert Henry. *When Africa Awakes: The "Inside Story" of the Stirrings and Strivings of the New Negro in the Western World.* New York: Porro, 1920.

Herskovits, Melville J. *The Myth of the Negro Past.* New York: Harper, 1941.

Howe, Stephen. *Afrocentrism: Mythical Pasts and Imagined Homes.* London: Verso, 1998.

James, George G. M. *Stolen Legacy.* New York: Philosophical Library, 1954.

Lefkowitz, Mary. *Not Out of Africa: How Afrocentrism Became an Excuse to Teach Myth as History.* New York: Basic Books, 1996.

Lovejoy, Paul E. "The African Diaspora: Revisionist Interpretations of Ethnicity, Culture, and Religion Under Slavery." *Studies in the World History of Slavery, Abolition, and Emancipation* 2 (1997): 1–23.

Mintz, Sidney, and Richard Price. *The Birth of African-American Culture: An Anthropological Perspective.* Boston: Beacon Press, 1992.

Morgan, Philip D. *Slave Counterpoint: Black Culture in the Eighteenth-Century Chesapeake and Lowcountry.* Chapel Hill: University of North Carolina Press, 1998.

Moses, Wilson Jeremiah. *Afrotopia: The Roots of African American Popular History.* Cambridge, UK: Cambridge University Press, 1998.

Stuckey, Sterling. *Slave Culture: Nationalist Theory and the Foundations of Black Culture.* New York: Oxford University Press, 1987.

Thompson, Robert Farris. *Flash of the Spirit: African and Afro-American Art and Philosophy.* New York: Random House, 1983.

Thornton, John K. *Africa and Africans in the Making of the Atlantic World, 1400–1680,* 2d ed. Cambridge, UK: Cambridge University Press, 1998.

Welsing, Frances Cress. *The Isis Papers: The Keys to the Colors.* Chicago: Third World Press, 1991.

Woodson, Carter G. *The African Background Outlined, or, Handbook for the Study of the Negro.* Washington, D.C.: Association for the Study of Negro Life and History, 1936.

JAMES H. SWEET (2005)

Afrocubanismo

Afrocubanismo was the name given to an influential artistic movement of the late 1920s and 1930s in Cuba, similar in many respects to the Harlem Renaissance. It was characterized by an explosion of interest in Afro-Cuban themes in music, novels, painting, ballet, and other forms of expression that had no precedent in the Caribbean prior to that time. These were the first decades in which the culture of the black working class came to be accepted as a legitimate form of national expression by Cuban society as a whole. Afrocubanismo influenced virtually all types of art, both elite and popular, including the poetry of Emilio Ballagas, José Tallet, and Nicolás Guillén; the paintings of Eduardo Abela, Jaime Valls, and Wilfredo Lam; the novels of Alejo Carpentier; the musical theater of Ernesto Lecuona, Jaime Prats, and Gonzalo Roig; the symphonic compositions of Alejandro García Caturla, Amadeo Roldán, and Gilberto Valdés; and the phenomenal popularity of Cuban *son* music and commercial dance bands.

Afrocubanismo art was created and promoted by various groups. Formally trained (and primarily white) middle-class artists created representations of black culture that had a tremendous impact on national consciousness, especially through the medium of popular song. Cuba's black middle classes contributed significantly to the popularization of such repertoire as well, though primarily as interpreters. Working-class Afrocubans supported the movement more directly by forming carnival bands, popularizing new musical genres from within their own communities, performing for tourists, and by infusing commercial arts of various kinds with influences from cultural traditions (e.g., linguistic, musical, choreographic) of African origin.

While progressive in many respects, the movement was characterized by fundamental contradictions. Most exponents of Afrocubanismo tended to be middle-class Euro-Cubans who drew inspiration from black working-class culture but created highly stylized representations of it, depictions that at times bordered on being racist. Afrocubanismo art underscores the unease with which much of the middle class viewed African-influenced culture, as well as the racially divided nature of Cuban society at that time. Examples of Afrocubanismo recordings include those of pianist and singer Ignacio Villa (1911–1950), better known as Bola de Nieve. Villa, himself a middle-class black performer with classical training, became one of the most popular performers of songs by white composers such as Eliseo Grenet (1893–1950) that straddled the line between ridicule and celebration of Afro-Cuban heritage. The same sort of ambivalence is found in other works. Nevertheless, some middle-class black artists took part in the Afrocubanismo movement and promoted decidedly positive images of blackness, using their art as a means of addressing issues of racism and racial oppression. Examples include the paintings of Alberto Peña ("Peñita") (1894–1938) and sculptures of Teodoro Ramos Blanco (1902–1972). Clearly, the movement had different meanings for particular artists and their audiences.

Various international influences contributed to the development of Afrocubanismo. The 1920s saw fundamental changes in the commercial music of nearly all Western countries. Its most obvious manifestation involved concession to blue-collar and non-Western aesthetics on an unprecedented scale. This was the era of the tango, the jazz craze, bohemian Paris, the primitivists, the fauvists, *Naive Kunst*, and a host of related movements drawing inspiration from non-European traditions. From the perspective of the present day, the 1920s can be seen as a crucial first step in the gradual democratization of national cultures globally, paralleled by the emergence of musical genres such as calypso and samba and presaging negritude and black nationalism in other parts of the hemisphere.

Afrocubanismo art represented a reaction against foreign influences as well, primarily from the United States. Artwork with Afro-Cuban themes might be considered a counter-discourse of sorts in the face of European and North American assertions of inherent racial and cultural superiority. Economic upheaval in the 1920s made issues of sovereignty especially important. Underemployment and poverty became severe following the U.S. stock-market crash of 1929. This in turn threatened the political stability of the administration of Cuba's president Gerardo Machado (1871–1939), culminating in outright civil war in 1933. Machado had allied himself closely with the United States; resentment towards him was fueled by the widespread perception that the United States had contributed to Cuba's economic instability and that it could not keep from meddling in the country's domestic affairs. During the rebellion against Machado, and for a short time after its resolution, the country's intellectual elite attempted to more actively promote uniquely Cuban culture. The sudden prominence of African-influenced expression within Cuba owe much to these events.

Contrary to what might be expected, most spokespersons of the black middle class reacted negatively to Afrocubanismo art. They took exception with the tendency of the movement to stereotype blacks as a whole and to depict them in a demeaning fashion. After having struggled for decades to overcome discrimination, characterizations in poetry and song that too often described them as drunken, lascivious, or worse inspired outrage. Many objected to the very term "Afro-Cuban," pointing out that the common distinction of the period between "Cuban"—implicitly a white category— and "Afro-Cuban" implied that blacks had an identity distinct from that of other citizens. They did not view the new vogue of blackness as an attempt to redress the marginal status of Afro-Cuban culture historically, but rather as a means of further exoticizing and excluding them. To many, therefore, the emphasis on African-derived culture tended to factionalize the population.

The movement went into decline toward the end of the 1930s, primarily because Cuban society was not yet ready to fully embrace African-influenced arts. Mainstream Cuban audiences had come to accept representations of blackness in national culture, but only from a certain perspective, using particular stereotypes, and limited to well-defined aesthetic conventions. Listening to a white vocalist in blackface sing slave laments, or to a black middle-class artist read a humorous poem about the African god Babalú-Ayé could be tolerated, even enjoyed. But when working-class blacks themselves became increasingly involved in commercial entertainment and more openly infused their compositions with influences from African-derived religions, when street drummers began to predominate as entertainers in cabarets, when scholars and folklorists arranged to have Yoruban *batá* drums performed on the concert stage, most middle-class listeners were horrified. Developments of this sort forced the intelligentsia to confront the fact that Afrocubanismo art had little in common with the actual expression of the black working class.

Perhaps the most defining characteristic of the Afrocubanismo movement was its ambivalence towards African-influenced expression. Imagery of African deities, of slaves during the colonial period, of drumming practices, and all other perceived Africanisms served as simultaneous sources of pride and embarrassment to the nation. They were powerful local icons to rally behind and markers of degeneracy—reminders of a cultural legacy that most considered shameful. An ongoing antagonism characterized the 1920s and 1930s, antagonism between an emergent racially and culturally based nationalism incorporating mulatto imagery and a widespread belief in the inherent superiority of whites over those of black or mixed ancestry. For the most part, the depictions of black culture from the period represent a fantasy of sorts, a middle-class projection that transformed the reality of the nation into a more Europeanized form. Despite these shortcomings, however, Afrocubanismo constitutes a relatively progressive moment in Cuba's history, and an important harbinger of change. The music, dance, literature, and visual art that it generated continue to influence present-day artists and have served as the conceptual foundation of modern Cuban culture ever since.

See also Africanisms; Guillen, Nicolás; Harlem Renaissance; Lam, Wilfredo; Music in Latin America; Representations of Blackness in Latin America and the Caribbean

Bibliography

Arredondo, Alberto. *El negro en Cuba.* Havana: Editorial Alfa, 1939.

Ballagas, Emilio. *Antología de la poesía negra hispanoamericana.* Madrid: M. Aguilar, 1935.

Cairo Ballester, Ana. *El Grupo Minorista y su tiempo.* Havana: Editorial de Ciencias Sociales, 1978.

de la Fuente, Alejandro. "Anídotos de Wall Street: Raza y Racismo en las Relaciones entre Cuba y Estados Unidos." In *Culturas encontradas: Cuba y los Estados Unidos*, edited by Rafael Hernández and John H. Coatsworth, pp. 243–262. Havana: Centro Juan Marinello; and Cambridge, Mass.: David Rockefeller Center for Latin American Studies, 2001.

Kutzinski, Vera M. *Sugars Secrets: Race and the Erotics of Cuban Nationalism.* Charlottesville: University Press of Virginia, 1993.

Moore, Robin. *Nationalizing Blackness: Afrocubanismo and Artistic Revolution in Havana, 1920–1940.* Pittsburgh: The University of Pittsburgh Press, 1997.

Seoane Gallo, José. *Eduardo Abela cerca del cerco.* Havana: Editorial Letras Cubanas, 1986.

Villa, Ignacio. *El inigualable Bola de Nieve.* EGREM compact disc, #CD 0011. Canada: EGREM, 1994.

ROBIN MOORE (2005)

AIDS IN THE AMERICAS

AIDS is one of the most devastating diseases in human history. The global count of people living with HIV/AIDS reached forty million by the end of 2004; millions more had already succumbed to the disease. Although HIV/AIDS is worldwide in its spread, it is not equally divided among the populations of the world.

The Distribution of AIDS in the Americas

One way of understanding the impact of the disease on populations of African descent in the Americas is by looking at the worldwide number of people living with HIV/AIDS disease along a continuum. At one end of the continuum is sub-Saharan Africa, which remains the region hardest hit by the disease, with approximately 25.5 million people now living with HIV/AIDS infection and an adult (ages 15–49) prevalence rate of 7.4 percent. Near the opposite end of the continuum falls North America, with about a million people living with HIV/AIDS and an adult prevalence rate of 0.6 percent, which is not significantly above that of Oceania, the region of the world with the lowest prevalence rate. Between these two epidemiological regions lie the island nations of the Caribbean, with under half a million cases and a prevalence rate of 2.3 percent. After sub-Saharan Africa, the Caribbean is now the second most intensely impacted region of the world. HIV/AIDS prevalence has grown rapidly in the Caribbean since the mid-1990s. Consequently, there were more cases of HIV reported in the Caribbean between 1995 and 1998 than from the early 1980s until 1995 (World Health Organization, 1998). AIDS has emerged as the leading cause of death in the English-speaking, African-American sector of the region among people fifteen to forty-four years of age.

These figures only give a broad sense of the extent and impact of the epidemic in the far-flung African-American populations of the New World. In Haiti, prevalence has surpassed 6 percent, the highest of any country outside of sub-Saharan Africa. Because of AIDS, life expectancy at birth in Caribbean countries like Haiti and Trinidad with majority African-American populations is projected by the year 2010 to be nine to ten years shorter than it would have been without the disease.

Other islands in the Caribbean with large populations of African descent have also developed significant AIDS epidemics. The Centers for Disease Control and Prevention (CDC) ranks the U.S. Virgin Islands, for example, fourth in the United States in AIDS incidence. Among women in the Virgin Islands, the AIDS-case rate of approximately 30 per 100,000 population is nearly three times the U.S. national rate (with 27 percent of AIDS cases and 47 percent of combined HIV/AIDS cases among women). By late 2000, there were over four hundred AIDS cases in the Virgin Islands; 54 percent of those with the disease had already died (Nelson, Todman, and Singer, 2005).

Based on frozen tissue samples, the oldest confirmed case of AIDS in the Americas was a fifteen-year-old African-American male from St. Louis who was hospitalized in 1968 with an aggressive form of Kaposi's sarcoma. Twenty years later, his stored serum specimens tested positive for HIV-antibodies (Gerry, et al., 1988). Today, the AIDS case rate (for all ages) per 100,000 population in the United States is 6.1 among white non-Hispanics compared to 58.2 among African Americans. HIV/AIDS is more prevalent among African Americans, and significantly so, than any other racial/ethnic population in the country, a pattern that holds across age and gender subgroups.

Among men, for example, the AIDS case rate is over eight times greater among African Americans than among non-Hispanic whites (Centers for Disease Control and Prevention, 2003). Among women, the difference is even greater. In terms of actual number of cases, almost twice as many African Americans have contracted HIV/AIDS than non-Hispanics whites. Importantly, while the number of deaths among whites living with HIV/AIDS steadily fell from 1999 to 2003, among African Americans a clear trend has not emerged, with the number of deaths due to AIDS going up and down from year to year. Overall, however, while African Americans comprise about 12.3 percent of the U.S. population, from 1999 to 2003 they accounted for over 50 percent of the people who died of AIDS during those five years. By the end of 2003, almost 200,000 African Americans had died of AIDS. In other words, while compared to some other parts of the world the HIV/AIDS prevalence is low in the United States, HIV-related morbidity and mortality are notably concentrated in the African-American sector of the population. Moreover, in 2002 African Americans who died from HIV/AIDS had over ten times as many age-adjusted years of potential life lost before age seventy-five years as whites (Office of Minority Health, 2005).

AIDS also has reached significant levels among Brazilians of African descent. The first reported case of AIDS in Brazil was diagnosed in 1983. During the 1990s Brazil emerged as the epicenter of HIV/AIDS in South America with just under sixty percent of all AIDS cases in Latin America and the Caribbean combined. Cumulative AIDS cases passed a quarter of a million in 2003, with an adult prevalence rate for HIV/AIDS of 0.7 percent. Infection is not generally dispersed in the population but rather is concentrated among those who are twenty to thirty-five years of age and belong to at least one of four groups: men who have sex with men, sexually transmitted disease patients, commercial sex workers, and injection drug users. The latter two groups, in particular, tend to be poor, and they disproportionately comprise darker skinned Brazilians. Although the proportion of HIV/AIDS cases among women is rising—especially among those who have male sex partners who engage in high-risk behaviors—rates of infection are significantly higher among men (U.S. Agency for International Development, 2004).

BlackAIDS.org

According to the BLACKAIDS.org website, the Black AIDS Institute is the "first black HIV/AIDS policy center dedicated to reducing HIV/AIDS health disparities by mobilizing black institutions and individuals." The group's motto is "Our People, Our Problem, Our Solution."

The AIDS epidemic has had a disproportionate impact on black communities. As early as 1983, African Americans, who represented over 13 percent of the population, accounted for more than a quarter of reported AIDS cases. Now, African Americans account for greater than 50 percent of all new HIV infections in the United States. BlackAIDS.org is making an effort to reduce this trend.

The site focuses on global coordination and is a sort of alternative news center. Policymakers and other influential people who shape the general consciousness are interviewed. Every week new stories are featured and columnists' perspectives are offered, all centering around this topic. The goal is to educate people and to investigate stories that the mainstream media might have a tendency to overlook. Also of interest is a section devoted to arts addressing HIV. BlackAIDS.org is an excellent tool for anyone serious about learning more on this epidemic and its effect on African Americans.

AIDS as a Syndemic: The Political Economy of Suffering

AIDS does not exist in isolation from other diseases or from a social and political economic environment that shapes the general health, access to food and shelter, and availability of medical treatment. To help frame this critical biosocial, perspective medical anthropologists introduced the concept of "syndemic" in the mid-1990s (Baer, Singer, and Susser, 2003; Singer and Clair, 2003). While biomedical understanding and practice, traditionally, have been characterized by the tendency to isolate, study, and treat diseases as if they were distinct entities that existed separate from other diseases and independent of the social contexts in which they emerge, a syndemic model focuses on trying to understand social and biological interconnections as they are shaped and influenced by inequalities within society. At its simplest level, the term *syndemic* refers to two or more epidemics (i.e., notable increases in the rate of specific diseases in a population), interacting synergistically with each other inside human bodies and contributing, as a result of their interaction, to excess burden of disease in a population. The term *syndemic* refers not only to the temporal or locational co-occurrence of two or more diseases or health problems, however, but also to the health consequences of the biological interactions among copresent diseases, such as between HIV and tuberculosis. HIV-positive individuals infected with TB are a hundred times more likely to develop an active disease than those who are HIV-negative, and TB is disproportionately prevalent among African Americans. In Jamaica this interrelationship of diseases has been found increasingly among children, with TB severity being greatest among children who are co-infected with HIV (Geoghagen, et al., 2004). Similarly, research has shown both that individuals co-infected with hepatitis (HCV) and HIV have higher HCV viral loads than those infected with only HCV alone and that African Americans have significantly higher HCV loads among co-infected individuals than do whites, suggesting important interrelations between copresent diseases and the differential consequence of co-infection across race/ethnicity (Matthews-Greer, et al., 2001).

Beyond the notion of disease clustering in a social location or population and the biological processes of interaction among diseases, the term *syndemic* also points to the determinant importance of social conditions in disease interactions and consequences. As Farmer (1999, pp. 51–52) has emphasized, "the most well demonstrated cofactors [for HIV] are social inequalities, which structure not only the contours of the AIDS pandemic but also the nature of outcomes once an individual is sick with complications of HIV infection." Living in poverty, for example, increases the likelihood of exposure to a range of diseases, including HIV. Also, poverty and discrimination place the poor at a disadvantage in terms of access to diagnosis and treatment for HIV, as well as ability to adhere to treatment plans because of structurally imposed residential instability and the frequency of disruptive economic and social crises in poor families. Haiti is by far the most impoverished country in the Americas, and it is not coincidental that it is the country in this hemisphere that has been hardest hit by AIDS thus far.

In multiethnic New World countries, racism is another critical social condition that appears to contribute to higher levels of HIV risk and infection among peoples of African descent. In Brazil, for example, while race-based oppression is denied officially and at the popular level, studies show that "the structures of racism are present in everyday experience" (Goldstein, 2003, p. 105). Consequently, writing of internalized racism in Brazil, Neusa Santos Souza (1983), notes that dark-skinned Brazilians commonly feel inferior and ugly because of all of the subtle reminders to which they are subjected each day that whiteness equals beauty. Internalized racism, no less than open color-based discrimination, is linked with heightened levels of HIV risk and infection (Baer, Singer, and Susser, 2003). Ultimately, such social factors as poverty, racism, sexism, and marginalization may be of far greater importance in HIV morbidity and mortality among people of African descent than the nature of the human immunodeficiency virus. Overall, populations of African descent in the Americas encounter HIV/AIDS not as a single life-threatening disease but as part of a set of interacting diseases and toxic social conditions with a resulting significant toll on their health and well-being.

AIDS Stigma: AIDS and Accusation

Goffman (1963) first defined *stigma* as the negative image that a social collectivity creates of a person or group based on some physical, behavioral, or social attribute that is perceived to diverge from established group norms. More recently, Link and Phelan (2001, p. 365) offered a definition of *stigma* in terms of "status loss and discrimination that lead to unequal outcomes" and argue that "stigmatization is entirely contingent on access to social, economic, and political power that allows the identification of differentness, the construction of stereotypes, the separation of labeled persons into distinct categories, and the full execution of disapproval, rejection, exclusion, and discrimination." Notably, this definition emphasizes the centrality of political economy in the emergence and distribution of stigma. Health-related stigma, in short, tends to reinforce other axes of social inequality.

AIDS stigma has had a significant impact on HIV-infected individuals of African heritage. At the national level AIDS stigma has been tied to efforts to blame AIDS on people of African origin, especially Africans and Haitians (Farmer, 1992). Such accusation is unsubstantiated by any research, as AIDS is a disease capable of infecting all humans and is impervious to ethnic or national boundaries. Stigma has also been significant at the individual level. A study among HIV/AIDS infected Haitian-American women, for example, found that they perceived five areas of AIDS-stigmatization in their lives: rejection by the dominant society, self-doubt, diminished self-esteem, stress in intimate relationships, and rejection by other Haitians within their community (Santana and Dancy, 2000). Comparative research on African-American women in the southern United States who were in treatment for either HIV or breast cancer found that reported levels of hope were significantly lower for those with HIV,

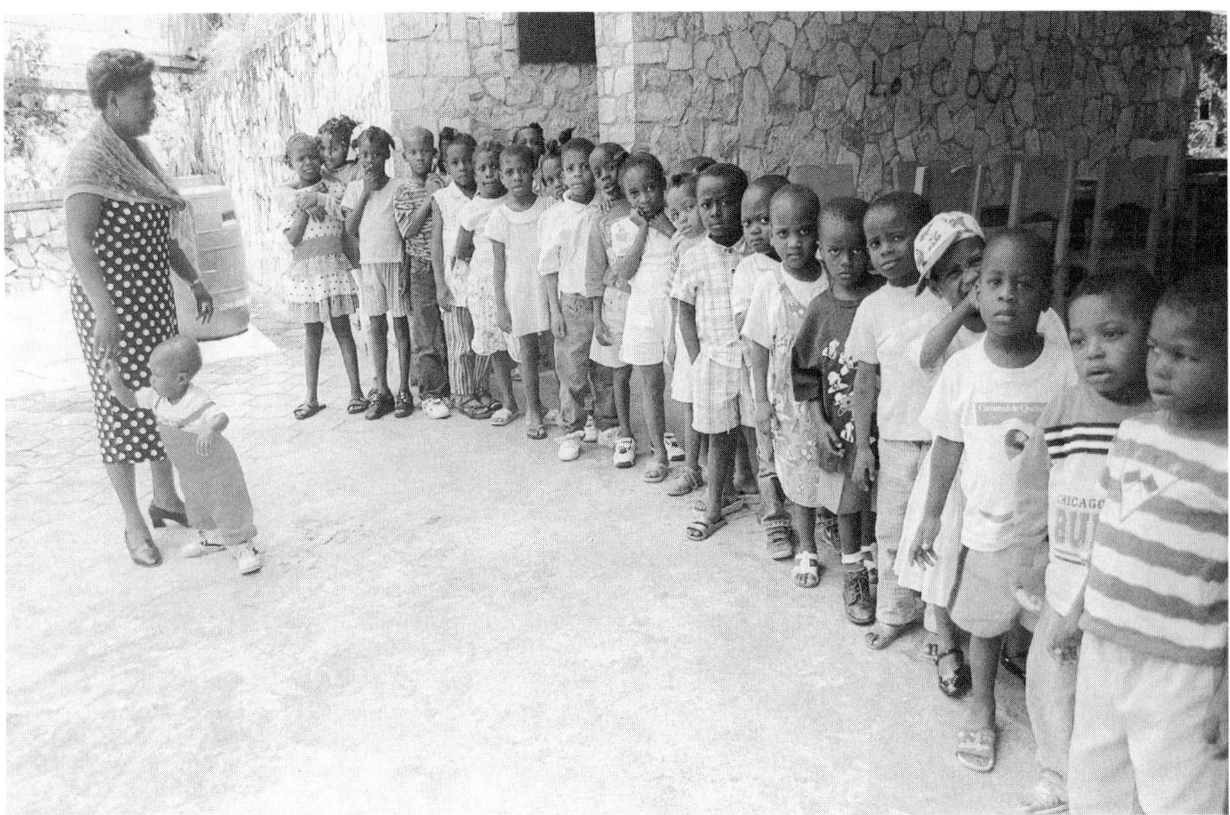

Haitian children, orphaned after losing their parents to AIDS, line up outside their classroom at the Rainbow House shelter in Boutillier, 1999. *In Haiti, the disease afflicts more than six percent of the total population, the highest rate of any country outside of Africa.* THONY BELIZAIRE/AFP/GETTY IMAGES

as were their assessed coping skills, affirming the damage done by AIDS stigma (Phillips and Sowell, 2000).

Various researchers have asserted that AIDS-related stigma functions as a barrier to HIV-infected individuals voluntarily seeking counseling and testing. Research in rural Haiti, however, suggests that the introduction of high-quality HIV care can lead to a significant reduction in stigma and to increased rates of HIV testing (Castro and Farmer, 2005). Rather than stigma, these researchers argue, it is logistic and economic barriers that primarily determine who will access available HIV services. This finding further affirms the importance of understanding AIDS stigma in terms of the prevailing structures of social and economic inequality.

Conspiracy Theories: AIDS and Defensive Accusation

The flip side of AIDS stigma and blame is found in popular ideas about AIDS as a government conspiracy to exterminate people of color. A telephone survey of five hundred African Americans, for example, found that a significant proportion, especially men, held AIDS conspiracy beliefs (Bogart and Thorburn, 2005). Similar findings have been reached in door-to-door surveys with African-American populations (Klonoff and Landrine, 1999). Notably, those who embraced this perspective are much more likely to have negative attitudes about condom use and inconsistent condom use patterns, suggesting that belief in conspiracy theories is a barrier to AIDS prevention. Such attitudes are believed to have their origin in a defensive response to a long history of racial discrimination in health care as well as in medical research, including the infamous Tuskegee syphilis study of 1932 to 1972.

Coping with AIDS: The Range of National Responses

National responses to AIDS have varied considerably. Some predominant black nations, like the Bahamas, have demonstrated considerable success in responding to the epidemic. In 1994 the Bahamas recorded just over seven hundred new cases of HIV infection; by 1999, by contrast, the annual number of new cases was about half this level. The mortality rate for AIDS also fell by about half during this period as well (Baer, Singer, and Susser, 2003). Brazil, after an initial hesitation, has also demonstrated an effective response to AIDS. In the early 1990s Parker (1994, p. 28) noted that the "history of the epidemic in Brazil has been marked by the relative failure of government authorities to develop cohesive policies and programs." Consequently, the World Bank predicted that by the year 2000 there would be 1.2 million people infected with HIV in Brazil. Instead, a significant change in governmental response, including guaranteeing AIDS care, the manufacture and broad distribution of AIDS medicines, and the emergence of an aggressive community-based response to the epidemic, resulted in only about half as many infections as had been expected by the turn of the twenty-first century.

In the United States, in 1998 the CDC released findings on the distribution of HIV/AIDS that revealed significantly disproportionate rates of infection among African Americans. In response, the Congressional Black Caucus requested the Secretary of the Department of Health and Human Services to declare the HIV/AIDS epidemic in the African-American community a "public health emergency." Instead, the government announced a comprehensive new initiative to improve the nation's effort to prevent the spread of AIDS in African-American and Latino communities and to enhance the level of care provided to people of color living with the disease. While new levels of funding were made available to state and city departments of public health and community-based organizations to implement AIDS prevention in communities of color, the epidemic has continued to have far greater impact among people of African descent than among the rest of the U.S. population. Even more drastic is the case of Haiti, which, because of continued political and economic crises, has not been able to sustain an effective national AIDS prevention program, resulting in a continued out-of-control AIDS epidemic.

Future of a Health Crisis

The AIDS epidemic has exacted an enormous toll on populations of African descent throughout the Americas, especially among people of childbearing age and the young. While the predominant mode of viral transmission has been through sexual contact, especially heterosexual contact, rates of infection have also been high among men who have sex with men, and, in some areas, injection and noninjection drug users. National responses have varied, and while the AIDS epidemic has not been effectively controlled in any country, coordinated government/community responses have been able to slow the rate of new infections in some countries or with some at-risk populations. Research on mathematical modeling of the epidemic in English-speaking Caribbean nations suggests that if the incidence of HIV cases is not reduced, it will lead to negative growth (i.e., falling gross domestic product rates) in future years (Nicolls, et al., 1998). Such a drop will lower the ability of countries to respond to the epidemic, further accelerating the negative health and social effects of HIV/AIDS in a potentially disastrous downward spiral. Relatively successful responses to the epidemic, as seen in the cases of the Bahamas or Brazil, or even Haiti on a limited scale, suggest alternative, less dismal futures for the epidemic.

See also Mortality and Morbidity

Bibliography

Baer, Hans, Merrill Singer, and Ida Susser. *Medical Anthropology and the World System.* Westport, Conn.: Praeger, 2003.

Bogart, L., and S. Thorburn. "Are HIV/AIDS Conspiracy Beliefs a Barrier to HIV Prevention Among African Americans?" *Journal of Acquired Immune Deficiency Disease* 38, no. 2 (2005): 213–218.

Castro, Arachu, and Paul Farmer. "Understanding and Addressing AIDS-Related Stigma: From Anthropological Theory to Clinical Practice in Haiti." *American Journal of Public Health* 9, no. 1 (2005): 53–59.

Farmer, Paul. *AIDS and Accusation: Haiti and the Geography of Blame.* Berkeley: University of California Press, 1992.

Farmer, Paul. *Infections and Inequalities: The Modern Plagues.* Berkeley: University of California Press, 1999.

Garry, R., M. Witte, A. Gottlieb, M. Elvin-Lewis, M. Gottlieb, C. Witte, S. Alexander, W. Cole, and W. Drake. "Documentation of an AIDS Virus Infection in the United States in 1968." *Journal of the American Medical Association* 260, no. 14 (1988): 2085–2087.

Geoghagen, M., J. Farr, I. Hambleton, R. Pierre, and C. Christie. "Tuberculosis and HIV Co-infections in Jamaican Children." *Journal of West Indian Medicine* 53, no. 5 (2004): 339–345.

Goffman, Irving. *Stigma.* Englewood Cliffs, N.J.: Prentice Hall, 1963.

Goldstein, Donna. *Laughter Out of Place: Race, Class, Violence and Sexuality in a Rio Shantytown.* Berkeley: University of California Press, 2003.

Klonoff, E., and H. Landrine. "Do Blacks Believe That HIV/AIDS Is a Government Conspiracy Against Them?" *Preventive Medicine* 28, no. 5 (1999): 451–457.

Link, B., and J. Phelan. "Conceptualizing Stigma." *Annual Review of Sociology* 27 (2001): 363–385.

Matthews-Greer, Janice, Gloria Caldito, Sharon Adley, Regina Willis, Angela Mire, Richard Jamison, Kenny McRae, John King, and Wun-ling Chang. "Comparison of Hepatitis C Viral Loads in Patients with or without Human Immunodeficiency Virus." *Clinical Diagnosis and Laboratory Immunology* 8, no. 4 (2001): 690–694.

Nelson, Agatha, Patricia Todman, and Merrill Singer. "The Risks of Paradise: Project RARE and the Fight against AIDS in the U.S. Virgin Islands." In *Communities Assessing Their AIDS Epidemics: Results of the Rapid Assessment of HIV/AIDS in U.S. Cities,* edited by Ben Bowser, Ernest Quimbey, and Merrill Singer. Lanham, Md.: Lexington Books, 2005.

Nicholls, Sheldon, Roger McLean, Karl Theodore, Ralph Henry, and Camara Bilali. *Modeling the Macroeconomic Impact of HIV/AIDS on the English Speaking Caribbean: The Case of Trinidad and Tobago and Jamaica.* St. Augustine, Trinidad and Tobago: University of the West Indies, 1998.

Office of Minority Health. *Health Disparities Experienced by Black or African Americans—United States. Morbidity and Mortality Weekly Report* 54, no. 1 (2005): 1–3.

Phillips, K., and R. Sowell. "Hope and Coping in HIV-Infected African-American Women of Reproductive Age." *Journal of the National Black Nurses Association* 11, no. 2 (2000): 18–24.

Santana, M., and B. Dancy. "The Stigma of Being Named 'AIDS Carriers' on Haitian-American Women." *Health Care for Women Internationally* 21, no. 3 (2000): 161–171.

Singer, Merrill, and Scott Clair. "Syndemics and Public Health: Reconceptualizing Disease in Bio-Social Context." *Medical Anthropology Quarterly* 17, no. 4 (2003): 423–441.

Souza, Neusa Santos. *To Become Black or the Vicissitudes of Identity in Upwardly Mobile Black Brazilian.* Rio de Janeiro, Brazil: Graal, 1983.

U.S. Agency for International Development. *Country Profile: HIV/AIDS, Brazil.* Washington, D.C.: USAID, 2004.

World Health Organization. *Database on Violence among Women.* Geneva, Switzerland: WHO, 1998.

MERRILL SINGER (2005)

Ailey, Alvin

January 5, 1931
December 1, 1989

Born in Rogers, Texas, the only child of working-class parents who separated when he was two, dancer and choreographer Alvin Ailey moved to Los Angeles with his mother in 1942. Shy from his itinerant Texas life, Ailey reluctantly turned to dance when a high-school classmate introduced him to Lester Horton's Hollywood studio in 1949. He poured himself into study and developed a weighty, smoldering performance style that suited his athletic body. Ailey moved to New York in 1954 to dance with partner Carmen DeLavallade in the Broadway production of *House of Flowers.* Performing success and study with leading modern dance and ballet teachers Martha Graham, Doris Humphrey, Charles Weidman, and Karel Shook led Ailey to found his own dance theater company in 1958. The Alvin Ailey American Dance Theater (AAADT) began as a repertory company of seven dancers devoted to both modern dance classics and new works created by Ailey and other young artists. The critically successful first concerts in 1958 and 1960 marked the beginning of a new era of dance performance devoted to African-American themes. *Blues Suite* (1958), set in and around a barrelhouse, depicts the desperation and joys of life on the edge of poverty in the South. Highly theatrical and immediately accessible, the dance contains sections of early twentieth-century social dances, Horton dance technique, Jack Cole–inspired jazz dance, and ballet partnering. Early performances of *Revelations* (1960) established Ailey's company as the foremost dance interpreter of African-American experience. The dance quickly became the company's signature ballet, eclipsing previous concert attempts at dancing to sacred black music. Set to a series of spirituals and gospel selections arranged by Brother John Sellers, *Revelations* depicts a spectrum of black religious worship, including richly sculpted group prayer ("I've Been Buked"), a ceremony of ritual baptism ("Wade in the Water"), a moment of introverted, private communion ("I Wanna Be Ready"), a duet of trust and support for a minister and devotee ("Fix Me, Jesus"), and a final, celebratory gospel exclamation, "Rocka My Soul in the Bosom of Abraham."

Several Ailey dances established precedents for American dance. *Feast of Ashes* (1962), created for the Harkness Ballet, is acknowledged as the first successful pointe ballet choreographed by a modern dancer. In 1966 Ailey contributed dances for the New York Metropolitan Opera's inaugural production at Lincoln Center, Samuel Barber's *Antony and Cleopatra.* In 1970 he created *The River* for the American Ballet Theatre. Set to an original score commissioned from Duke Ellington, this ballet convincingly fused theatrical jazz dancing and ballet technique. In 1971 Ailey created the staging for Leonard Bernstein's rock-influenced *Mass,* which opened the newly built Kennedy Center in Washington, D.C.

Major distinctions and honors followed Ailey throughout his choreographic career, which spanned the creation of more than fifty dances for his own company, the American Ballet Theater, the Joffrey Ballet, the Paris Opera Ballet, the London Festival Ballet, and the Royal Danish Ballet. Among his many awards were honorary doctorates in fine arts from Princeton University, Bard College, Adelphi University, and Cedar Crest College; a United Nations Peace Medal, and an NAACP Spingarn Medal, in 1976. In 1988 he was celebrated by the president of the United States for a lifetime of achievement in the arts at the Kennedy Center Honors.

Company and Repertory

In its earliest years the AAADT spent much time on the road, touring and bringing dance to a large audience of

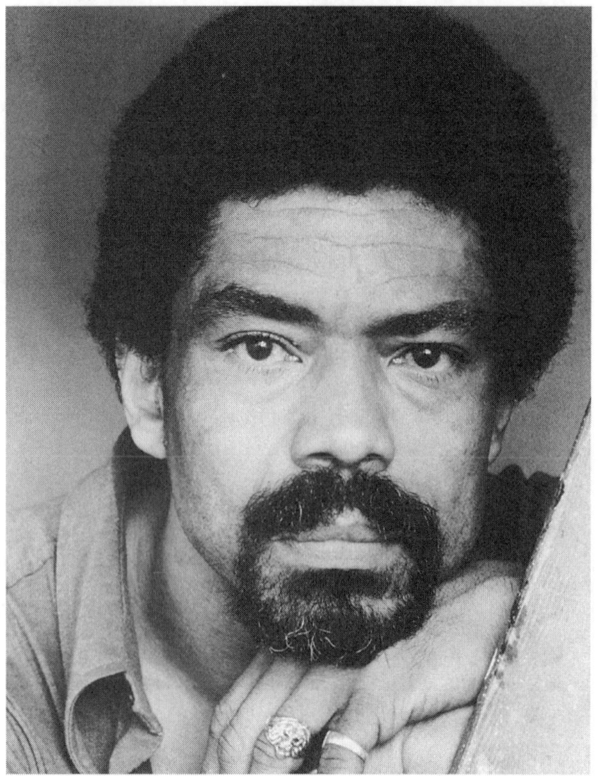

Alvin Ailey (1931–1989). *A pioneer in modern dance, Ailey founded the racially integrated and popular modern dance troupe, the Alvin Ailey Dance Theatre.* © BETTMANN/CORBIS. REPRODUCED BY PERMISSION.

people who had never heard of concert performance. This largely African-American audience provided the wellspring of support essential to the Ailey enterprise. The AAADT established its vast international reputation through a series of tours begun in 1962 by a five-month engagement in Southeast Asia and Australia. Sponsored by the International Exchange Program under the Kennedy administration, this tour established a pattern of performance in foreign countries that continued with a trip to Rio de Janeiro (1963); a European tour including London, Hamburg, and Paris (1964); an engagement at the World Festival of Negro Arts in Dakar, Senegal (1966); a sixteen-week European tour, including the Holland Festival in Amsterdam (1967); a visit to Israel (August 1967); a U.S. State Department–sponsored nine-nation tour of Africa (1967); and a performance at the Edinburgh Festival in Scotland (1968). In 1970 the AAADT became the first American modern dance company to perform in the post-war Soviet Union. The company retained peerless stature as a touring ambassador of goodwill beginning in the 1970s; high points included a prize-winning performance at the International Dance Festival in Paris (1970); a second Far East tour (1977); a Brazil tour (1978); and several command performances for heads of state and royalty. By 2004 the AAADT had been seen by some nineteen million people worldwide.

Active in the pursuit of dance history, the varied repertory of the AAADT has, in the words of Ailey in an American Broadcast Company television program, *Americans All*, sustained an "impulse to preserve modern dance to know where it's been in order to know where it's going, and to encourage the participation of the audience" in that process (1974). The eclectic repertory was provided by choreographers working in a variety of dance modes, including ballet, jazz dance, Graham modern, Horton, and Dunham technique. Important pieces danced by the company included Donald McKayle's *Rainbow 'Round My Shoulder* (1959), Talley Beatty's *The Road of the Phoebe Snow* (1959), Anna Sokolow's *Rooms* (1965), Louis Johnson's *Lament* (1965), Geoffrey Holder's *Prodigal Prince* (1967), Ulysses Dove's *Vespers* (1986), Judith Jamison's *Forgotten Time* (1989), Donald Byrd's *Dance at the Gym* (1991), Jawolle Willa Jo Zollar's *Shelter* (1992), Ronald K. Brown's *Grace* (1999), and Alonzo King's *Following the Subtle Current Upstream* (2000), as well as dances by venerable American choreographers Ted Shawn, Pearl Primus, Katherine Dunham, Joyce Trisler, and Lester Horton. In 1976 the AAADT celebrated composer Duke Ellington with a festival featuring fifteen new ballets set to his music, a project that highlighted Ellington's musical achievement.

Company Members

Ailey encouraged his dancers to present individualized and highly emotional performances, a strategy that created the first series of star personalities in American modern dance. Judith Jamison's electrifying performance of *Cry* presented a coherent relationship between the dancing body and the experience of living as a black woman in America. Created in 1971 as a birthday present for Ailey's mother, Lula Cooper, *Cry* has been successfully assumed by several dancers, most notably Donna Wood, Renee Robinson, Sara Yarborough, and Nasha Thomas. In 1972 Ailey created the elegiac solo *Love Songs* for dancer Dudley Williams, revived in 1993 by dancer Michael Joy. Dancer Gary DeLoatch, a longtime principal with the company, brought an eloquent intensity to his roles, especially as the pusher in Talley Beatty's *The Stack-Up* (1983) and as Charlie Parker in Ailey's *For "Bird"—With Love* (1984). Innumerable significant dance personalities have passed through the AAADT, including Marilyn Banks, Hope Clarke, Carmen DeLavallade, George Faison, Miguel Godreau, Dana Hash, Linda Kent, Dwight Rhoden, Desmond Richardson, Kelvin Rotardier, Elizabeth Roxas, Matthew

Rushing, Clive Thompson, James Truitte, Andre Tyson, and Sylvia Waters.

School and Outreach

In 1969 Ailey founded the Alvin Ailey American Dance Center to educate dance students in the history and art of ballet and modern dance. Courses were offered in dance technique and history, music for dancers, dance composition, and theatrical design. In 1974 the Alvin Ailey Repertory Ensemble, a professional performance ensemble, was formed under the direction of Sylvia Waters as a bridge between study and membership in professional dance companies. In 1984 the Alvin Ailey Student Performance Group was created under the direction of Kelvin Rotardier. The Student Performance Group offered lecture-demonstrations to communities traditionally underserved by the arts. In 1989 Dance Foundation Inc., the umbrella organizations for the AAADT and the Ailey School, initiated the Ailey Camps program, an outreach program designed to "enhance the self-esteem, creative expression, and critical thinking skills of inner-city youth through dance," according to a Dance Theater Foundation press release in 1989. Success of the initial venture in Kansas City, Missouri, led to similar programs begun in New York City (1990) and Baltimore, Maryland (1992).

Ailey created the AAADT to feature the talents of his African-American colleagues, although the company was never exclusively black. Ailey integrated his company to counter the "reverse chauvinism in being an all-black anything." He told the *New York Times,* "I am trying to show the world that we are all human beings and that color is not important. What is important is the quality of our work (1988)." In the last interview conducted before his death, he commented that the essence of the Ailey enterprise was that "the dancers be fed, kept alive, interested" in the work. "We're trying to create a whole spectrum of experience for the dancer as well as the audience," he said, dramatically understating the realities of his achievements.

Ailey stopped dancing in 1965 and slowed his choreographic assignments in the 1970s to attend to the administrative and fund-raising operations associated with his ever expanding company. Upon Ailey's death, Judith Jamison was appointed artistic director of the company, to work closely with rehearsal director and longtime company member Masazumi Chaya. The AAADT finally emerged from financial difficulties in 1992, when *Dance Magazine* proclaimed it "recession-proof" because of powerful development efforts on the part of the Dance Foundation Inc.'s board of directors. Jamison has led the troupe to great fiscal and artistic strength, with her own choreography featured in the newest repertory. In 2005, the Alvin Ailey Dance Center opened in Manhattan as the nation's largest facility devoted to dance.

Although Ailey gave numerous interviews throughout his career, he was decidedly private about his personal life. He described himself as "a bachelor and a loner" to writer John Gruen (1972) and hardly ever allowed outsiders into his most private thoughts. In 1980 Ailey was briefly hospitalized for stress-related conditions. His death followed a long, solitary struggle that had taken him out of the limelight for some time. Ailey's legacy to the dance world was to foster a freedom of choice—from ballet, modern, and social dance performance—to best express humanity in movement terms suited to the theatrical moment.

See also Ballet; Dove, Ulysses; Dunham, Katherine; Ellington, Edward Kennedy "Duke"; Holder, Geoffrey; Jamison, Judith; Parker, Charlie; Spingarn Medal; Spirituals

Bibliography

DeFrantz, Thomas F. *Dancing Revelations: Alvin Ailey's Embodiment of African American Culture.* New York: Oxford University Press, 2004.

Emery, Lynne Fauley. *Black Dance in the United States from 1619 to 1970.* Palo Alto, Calif.: National Press Books, 1972.

Goodman, Saul. "Brief Biographies: Alvin Ailey." *Dance Magazine* (December 1958): 70.

Gruen, John. "Interview with Alvin Ailey." Transcript of interview, collection of New York Public Library, 1972.

Kisselgoff, Anna. "Alvin Ailey: Dancing the Dream." *New York Times* (December 4, 1988): H2.

Latham, Jacqueline Quinn. "A Biographical Study of the Lives and Contributions of Two Selected Contemporary Black Male Dance Artists:Arthur Mitchell and Alvin Ailey." Ph.D. diss., Texas Women's University, 1973.

Long, Richard. *The Black Tradition in American Dance.* New York: Rizzoli, 1989.

Mazo, Joseph H., and Susan Cook. *The Alvin Ailey American Dance Theater.* New York: Morrow, 1978.

Moore, William. "Alvin Ailey (1931–1989)." *Ballet Review* 17, no. 4 (1990): 12–17.

THOMAS F. DEFRANTZ (1996)
Updated by author 2005

Al-Amin, Jamil Abdullah

October 4, 1943

Writer and activist Jamil Abdullah Al-Amin, formerly known as H. Rap Brown, was born Hubert Gerold Brown in Baton Rouge, Louisiana. He became involved in the civil rights movement while a student at Southern High School. Brown attended Southern University in Baton Rouge, but in 1962 he left school and devoted his time to the civil rights movement. He spent summers in Washington, D.C., with his older brother, Ed, and became a member of the Nonviolent Action Group (NAG). In 1964 Brown was elected chairman of NAG. Simultaneously, he became involved with the Student Nonviolent Coordinating Committee (SNCC).

In May 1966 Brown was appointed director of the SNCC voter registration drive in Alabama. He increased his involvement with SNCC, and in June 1967 he became Stokely Carmichael's successor as national chairman of SNCC, where he continued its militant stance. In 1968 Brown also served as minister of justice for the Black Panther Party during a brief working alliance between the two black power organizations.

As urban rebellions expressing black discontent spread across the United States, Brown's militant advocacy of black power made him a popular public speaker; his advocacy of black self-defense and condemnations of American racism—perhaps most memorably in his oft-quoted aphorism that "violence is as American as cherry pie"—made him a symbol of resistance and black pride within the Black Power movement. His rhetorical and vituperative talents—the source of his adopted name, "Rap"—were displayed in his one book, *Die Nigger Die!* (1969), a semiautobiographical account of his experiences with white racism. Brown embraced the term "nigger" as an embodiment of black resistance against racism.

Brown was consistently harassed by the police and was targeted by the FBI's Counter Intelligence Program (COINTELPRO) because his speeches supposedly triggered volatile situations and violent outbreaks. On July 24, 1967, he was accused of "counseling to arson" in Cambridge, Maryland, because a city school that had been set on fire twice before was burned a third time after one of his speeches.

On August 19, 1967, Brown was arrested for transporting weapons across state lines while under indictment, although he had never been formally notified that he was under indictment. In May 1968 Brown resigned as SNCC chairman. Later that year he was found guilty of the federal weapons charges and sentenced to five years in prison. He was released on bond to stand trial on the Cambridge, Maryland, charges. Brown never appeared at the Maryland trial; two of his friends had recently been killed in a suspicious automobile explosion, and his defense attorney claimed that Brown would be endangered if he appeared. Brown went into hiding, and in 1970 he was placed on the FBI's Ten Most Wanted List. He was apprehended in 1972 but was released four years later.

Brown converted to Islam while in prison and took the name Jamil ("beautiful") Abdullah ("servant of Allah") Al-Amin ("the trustworthy"). Upon his release from jail, he moved to Atlanta, Georgia. In the 1990s Al-Amin continued to reside in Atlanta as the proprietor of a grocery called the Community Store and as the imam (leader) of the Community Mosque. He was the spiritual leader of hundreds of Muslim families in Atlanta and in thirty other cities, including Chicago, New York, and Detroit. Al-Amin practiced a strict Sunni interpretation of the Qur'an, with his followers maintaining a spiritual distance from the larger society.

In September, 1999, Al-Amin was indicted on charges of theft and impersonating an officer. When he failed to appear for his pre-trial hearing, a warrant was issued for his arrest. The following March, Al-Amin was charged with the shooting death of the sheriff's deputy who had come to deliver his arrest warrant, and for seriously wounding another deputy on that same occasion. Two years later, a jury sentenced him to life in prison without parole, rejecting a request for execution.

See also Black Panther Party for Self-Defense; Black Power Movement; Carmichael, Stokely; Civil Rights Movement, U.S.; Student Nonviolent Coordinating Committee (SNCC)

Bibliography

Haskins, James. *Profiles in Black Power.* New York: Doubleday, 1972.

Van Deburg, William. *A New Day in Babylon: The Black Power Movement and American Culture, 1965–1975.* Chicago: University of Chicago Press, 1992.

MANSUR M. NURUDDIN (1996)
ROBYN SPENCER (1996)
Updated by publisher 2005

Albizu Campos, Pedro

1891
April 21, 1965

According to popular historical accounts (i.e., Ribes Tobar, 1971), Puerto Rican labor leader and nationalist

Pedro Albizu Campos was born on September 12, 1891 in Barrio Mochuelo Abajo, located in Ponce, Puerto Rico. However, in archival documents housed at Harvard University, Albizu Campos lists his date of birth as June 29, 1893. His parents were Alejandro Albizu Romero, who was from the Basque country in Spain, and Juliana Campos, a Creole. As a dark-skinned Afro–Puerto Rican, Albizu Campos felt much discrimination from North Americans and other Puerto Ricans across the color gradient who internalized racism. He once stated: "For us, race has nothing to do with biology. Nor dusky skin, nor frizzy hair, nor dark eyes. Race is a continuity of characteristic virtues and institutions. We are distinguished by our culture, our courage, our Chivalry, our Catholic sense of civilization" (quoted in Ribes Tobar, p. 17).

Albizu Campos was regarded as an intellectually gifted and brilliant student. His formative years through high school were spent in Ponce, Puerto Rico, where he attended Ponce High School from 1909 to 1912. As a result of his high academic achievement, the high school's principal, Charles Terry, recommended he receive an Aurora Lodge of Ponce scholarship. In turn, he was admitted to the University of Vermont, where he began a formal course of study in agriculture from 1912 to 1913. Because of his continued academic achievement, he was awarded a second academic scholarship to transfer to Harvard University to complete his undergraduate education from 1913 to 1916. He also studied law and military science (ROTC) from 1913 to 1916 at the same institution. His studies were briefly interrupted because of World War I, during which he served as a second lieutenant in the segregated U.S. Army. Most biographical accounts report that the discrimination he felt as an Afro–Puerto Rican soldier led to his eventual philosophical/political transformation to nationalist thought and its eventual application within a Puerto Rican context. In 1921, Albizu Campos returned to Harvard to complete his law degree.

Albizu Campos was heavily influenced by Irish and Indian nationalist thought. On the Irish side, Father Ryan of Boston, Massachusetts, conversed often with the future leader of Puerto Rican nationalism while at Harvard. Furthermore, both were influenced by Irish Republican Army (IRA) leader Eamon de Valera, who gave a speech at Harvard in 1919 seeking support for Irish independence. Finally, as founder of the Irish Socialist Party, James Connolly shaped Albizu Campos's thinking around challenging and dismantling "home rule" (i.e., colonial governors). On the Indian side, Rabindranath Tagore, a Hindu poet and supporter of Indian independence, also shaped the young Puerto Rican student's beliefs about nationalism and decolonization.

In sum, Albizu Campos was able to weave his passion for anticolonial politics in the various leadership positions he held while a student at Harvard. These included such organizations as the Cosmopolitan Club, the League to Enforce Peace, and the International Polity Club, among others. Moreover, he was conversant in Spanish, English, German, Latin, Portuguese, and French.

Upon his return to Puerto Rico in 1921 at the age of thirty, Albizu Campos began to represent the rights of sugar workers. He began to give public speeches denouncing U.S. imperialism and its colonial relationship to the island. As a result, he was arrested, tried, and convicted of "seditious conspiracy to overthrow the United States government" under the Smith Act of 1940, also known as the "Gag Law." This law (still in effect) declared it unlawful to encourage, teach, or belong to any group advocating the forceful overthrow of any government in the United States. The evidence produced against Albizu Campos by the U.S. government included Federal Bureau of Investigation (FBI) tape recordings of his speeches, which are housed at the U.S. Library of Congress. Consequently, he was sentenced to ten years to the federal prison in Atlanta, Georgia. In 1947 he returned to Puerto Rico and subsequently helped lead and organize resistance movements against U.S. imperialism in the Puerto Rican municipalities of Adjuntas, Jayuya, Mayagüez, and Utuado. These protests were suppressed by the Puerto Rico National Guard with bombs and armed troops. In 1951 Albizu Campos was jailed again and sentenced to eighty years in prison.

While Albizu Campos served this sentence, his health began to deteriorate as a result of radiation exposure while incarcerated. Because of his deteriorating health and pleas by empathetic political leaders, Governor Luis Muñoz Marín (a former ally of Albizu Campos who later became the intellectual author of Puerto Rico's current colonial status) pardoned him in 1953. However, this pardon was revoked one year later by Muñoz Marín when Lolita Lebrón, Rafael Cancel Miranda, Andrés Figueroa, and Irving Flores opened fire in the U.S. House of Representatives and pronounced, "Long live a free Puerto Rico!" In 1964 Muñoz Marín again pardoned Albizu Campos, who died the following year on April 21, 1965. The memory of Albizu Campos lives through the Puerto Rican Nationalist Party and in such Puerto Rican communities as Chicago, Illinois, and other urban centers in the diaspora. Additionally, several public schools in Puerto Rico and Havana, Cuba, are named in his honor.

See also Anti-Colonial Movements; Labor and Labor Unions; Nationalism in the United States in the Nineteenth Century

Bibliography

Albizu Campos, Pedro. *República de Puerto Rico.* Montevideo, Uruguay: Siglo Ilustrado, 1972.

Albizu Campos, Pedro. *Writings of Pedro Albizu Campos.* New York: Gordon Press, 1993.

Corretjer, Juan Antonio. *Albizu Campos.* Montevideo, Uruguay: Siglo Ilustrado, 1969.

Ribes Tobar, Federico. *Albizu Campos: El Revolucionario.* New York: Plus Ultra Educational, 1971.

Rivera Correa, R. R. *The Shadow of Don Pedro.* New York: Vantage Press, 1970.

RENÉ ANTROP-GONZÁLEZ (2005)

Aldridge, Ira

July 24, 1809
August 7, 1867

Born a free black in New York City, Ira Aldridge traveled to London at the age of seventeen to pursue a theatrical career. When he died fifty years later, he was known throughout Britain, Europe, and Russia as the greatest actor of his time.

Aldridge attended the African Free School in New York and possibly performed with the African Theatre of lower Manhattan before he left for England as a steward to the actor James Wallack. His first London stage appearance took place in 1825 at the Coburg Theatre, primarily a house for melodrama, where in a six-week season he performed five leading parts, including the title role of Oroonoko in Thomas Southerne's play and Gambia in *The Slave,* a musical drama by Thomas Norton.

Ira Aldridge as Othello, c. 1860s. *Aldridge, who was educated at the African Free School in New York City, traveled abroad at the age of seventeen to pursue a career as an actor. By the middle of the nineteenth century, Aldridge was widely regarded as one of the greatest actors of his day.* PHOTOGRAPHS AND PRINTS DIVISION, SCHOMBURG CENTER FOR RESEARCH IN BLACK CULTURE, THE NEW YORK PUBLIC LIBRARY, ASTOR, LENOX AND TILDEN FOUNDATIONS.

Six years of touring followed in the English provinces, in Scotland, and Ireland. The title role in Shakespeare's *Othello* and Zanga the Moor in Edward Young's *The Revenge* were added to his repertoire. Aldridge also excelled as Mungo, the comic slave in Isaac Bickerstaffe's musical farce *The Padlock,* which was often billed as an afterpiece to Othello. In consequence, Aldridge was later compared to the great eighteenth-century English actor David Garrick, who was equally renowned in both tragedy and comedy.

Having exhausted the number of acceptable black characters in dramatic literature, Aldridge began to perform traditionally white roles such as Macbeth, Shylock, Rob Roy from Walter Scott's novel, and Bertram in the Rev. R. C. Maturin's *Bertram, or, The Castle of Aldobrand.* He received high praise in the provincial press, being referred to as "an actor of genius" and "the perfection of acting." By this point he was only twenty-four, and he set his heart on performing at a major London theater. His opportunity came in 1833, when the leading English actor Edmund Kean collapsed while playing Othello at the Covent Garden theater. Despite resentment from several London papers, Aldridge accepted the role, which he played to public, though not critical, acclaim.

After further provincial traveling, Aldridge at forty-five began touring in Europe, concentrating on performing Shakespeare. To his repertory of *Othello, Macbeth,* and *The Merchant of Venice* he had added *King Lear, Hamlet, Richard III,* and Aaron the Moor in an edited version of *Titus Andronicus.* He played in bilingual productions, speaking English himself while the rest of the cast spoke their native language. These tours were largely successful and brought him considerable fame; many honors were conferred on him by ruling houses. "If he were Hamlet as he is Othello, then the Negro Ira Aldridge would [be] the greatest of all actors," wrote a German critic. The Moscow correspondent for the French publication *Le Nord* praised Aldridge's "simple, natural and dignified declamation . . . a hero of tragedy speaking and walking like a common mortal."

Aldridge was invited to perform Othello in 1858 at the Lyceum Theatre in London, and in 1865 at the Haymarket, winning a favorable press on both occasions. He was thinking of returning to the United States when he died in 1867 of lung trouble while on tour; he was buried in Lódz, Poland.

Aldridge was twice married and raised four children, three of whom were professional musicians. In addition, his daughter Amanda taught voice production and diction.

Bibliography

Marshall, Herbert, and Mildred Stock. *Ira Aldridge: The Negro Tragedian.* Carbondale and Edwardsville: Southern Illinois University Press, 1958. Reprint, Carbondale: Southern Illinois University Press, 1968; Washington, D.C.: Howard University Press, 1993.

ERROL G. HILL (1996)

Alexander, Clifford L., Jr.

September 3, 1933

Clifford Alexander, Jr., a lawyer, was born in New York City. His parents, Clifford L., Sr., and Edith Alexander, strongly influenced his decision to pursue a political career. Alexander graduated from Harvard University in 1955, where he was the first black president of the student council. In 1958 he received a degree from Yale Law School, and then worked as an assistant district attorney for New York County for two years. In 1961 he became the executive director of the Manhattanville-Hamilton Grange Neighborhood Conservation Project, where he worked to get landlords to meet housing code standards. He then became the Program and Executive Director of Harlem Youth Opportunities Unlimited (HARYOU) Inc. (1962–1963), an antipoverty program that attempted to improve the public schools and delinquency problems in Harlem.

In 1963 President John F. Kennedy asked Alexander to serve as foreign affairs officer of the National Security Council. In 1964 President Lyndon B. Johnson appointed him deputy special assistant to the president, associate special counsel, and deputy special counsel to the president. Johnson sought his advice on civil rights issues, and in 1967 he made Alexander chairman of the Equal Employment Opportunities Commission (EEOC), an agency that focused on uncovering evidence of discrimination. Alexander left the EEOC when the Nixon administration took office in 1969 and accepted a partnership in the law firm of Arnold and Porter in Washington, D.C., where he remained until 1975, when he briefly joined the firm of Verner, Lipfert, Bernhard, McPherson & Alexander.

From 1971 to 1974 Alexander was host and coproducer of the television show *Cliff Alexander: Black on White;* in addition, he held part-time teaching positions at Georgetown Law School and at Howard University. In 1974 he ran for mayor of Washington, D.C., but he lost to Walter Washington. In 1977 President Jimmy Carter named him Secretary of the Army, a position he held until January 1981. Later that same year Alexander established Alexander & Associates, a corporate consulting firm in Washington, D.C., which provides advice on workforce inclusiveness for corporate directors and executives. Alexander has received numerous honors and awards, including the Department of the Army's Outstanding Civilian Service Medal and the Department of Defense Distinguished Public Service award, the highest such award given to a civilian.

Alexander is on the board of directors of several national corporations and is also on the board of governors of the American Stock Exchange.

See also Civil Rights Movement, U.S.; Politics in the United States

Bibliography

Elliot, Jeffery M. *Black Voices in American Politics.* San Diego, Calif.: Harcourt, 1986.

Mortiz, Charles, ed. *Current Biography.* New York: W. H. Wilson, 1977.

LINDA SALZMAN (1996)
Updated by publisher 2005

Alexander, Raymond Pace

October 13, 1898
November 23, 1974

The lawyer, politician, and judge Raymond Pace Alexander was born to parents of humble means and worked his way through high school as a paper boy and through college as a Pullman porter. In 1917 he graduated from Philadelphia's Central High School, where he became the first African American to deliver the commencement address. He received his B.A. from the University of Pennsylvania in 1920 and his law degree from Harvard Law School in 1923. That same year he returned to Philadelphia, established a private law practice, and married Sadie Tanner Mossell, who held a Ph.D. in economics and later graduated from the University of Pennsylvania Law School.

Alexander quickly earned a reputation as a talented and accomplished trial lawyer and worked through the legal system to overcome racism. Although he is credited with ending discrimination in many Philadelphia hotels and restaurants, two of his most famous early successes were the Berwyn Schools (1923) and the Aldine Theater (1925) desegregation cases; the latter ended discrimination in Philadelphia movie theaters.

In 1935 his law practice had become so profitable that he was able to buy land and construct a building to house his law firm in the heart of the almost exclusively white Center City of Philadelphia. Alexander served two years as president of the largely African-American National Bar Association (1933–1935) and was a cofounder of the *National Bar Journal* (1925). He gained national recognition in 1951 when he replaced Thurgood Marshall as one of the National Association for the Advancement of Colored People (NAACP) counsels in the Trenton Six trial, defending two of the six black men wrongly accused of murdering a white shop owner and his wife in Trenton, New Jersey. Alexander also prosecuted the Girard College desegregation case on behalf of the city of Philadelphia from 1953 to 1958. Although the desegregation ruling Alexander obtained was confirmed by the U.S. Supreme Court, it was rendered moot by a technical decision of the Philadelphia Orphans Court.

Alexander also had a career in politics. In the 1930s he made many attempts to secure a local judgeship but was thwarted by the racism of the local political parties. During the 1940s he sought various types of appointments at the federal level, but the appointment of William H. Hastie to the U.S. Circuit Court of Appeals effectively closed the doors to a similar appointment for Alexander. He was named honorary consul to the republic of Haiti in 1938 and in 1951 was nominated by President Truman (but not confirmed) for the ambassadorship to Ethiopia. Alexander made a successful foray into elective politics in 1951, when he was elected to the city council as a member of the Democratic reform platform, a position to which he was reelected in 1955.

In 1958 he was appointed by Pennsylvania Governor George Leader to the Common Pleas Court of Philadelphia, becoming the first African American to hold a position on that court. He entered semiretirement as a presiding judge of the Common Pleas Court in 1970 and died of a heart attack while working late in his office in 1974.

See also Hastie, William Henry; Marshall, Thurgood; National Association for the Advancement of Colored People (NAACP)

Bibliography

The Alexander Papers Collection, University of Pennsylvania Archives, Philadelphia.

PAUL DAVID LUONGO (1996)

Alexander, Sadie Tanner Mossell

January 2, 1898
November 1, 1989

Sadie T. M. Alexander was a pioneer among African-American women in law and education and a committed civil rights activist. She was born Sadie Tanner Mossell in Philadelphia, to an accomplished family: Bishop Benjamin Tucker Tanner, among the most prominent of nineteenth-century black clergymen, was her grandfather, and the painter Henry Ossawa Tanner was her uncle. Educated in Philadelphia and in Washington, D.C., she graduated from the M Street High School (now Dunbar High School) in Washington. She entered the University of Pennsylvania's School of Education in 1915, receiving a B.S. in education with honors in 1918. (That year, she helped found the Gamma Chapter of the Delta Theta Sorority.) She earned an M.A. (1919) and a Ph.D. in economics (1921) from the University of Pennsylvania and was one of the first two African-American women to earn a Ph.D. in the United States and the first African American to receive a doctorate in economics.

Sadie Tanner Mossell Alexander, flanked by two of the other guest speakers appearing at a civil rights conference in Philadephia, 1948. *Alexander, an attorney, economist, and civil rights activist, served on the presidential commission that produced the report* To Secure These Rights *(1948), which called for an immediate end to all forms of segregation. The report contributed directly to the integration of the armed forces the following year.* © BETTMANN/CORBIS

From 1921 to 1923 Alexander was an assistant actuary for the North Carolina Mutual Life Insurance Company, a black-owned company in Durham, North Carolina. On November 29, 1923, she married Raymond Pace Alexander, a graduate of Harvard Law School, who thereafter worked with his wife in numerous Philadelphia-area civil rights cases. Sadie Alexander continued to be a trailblazer for African-American women in the fields of law and education: She entered the University of Pennsylvania Law School in 1924 (where her father, Aaron Albert Mossell, had graduated in 1888, becoming the first African American to graduate from the law school), worked on the law review, and was admitted to the Pennsylvania bar after graduating in 1927. During the late 1920s and 1930s she served as the assistant city solicitor of Philadelphia and as a partner in her husband's law firm. In November 1943 Alexander became the first woman to be elected secretary (or to hold any office) in the National Bar Association, a position she held until 1947.

In addition to her personal achievements and triumphs in overcoming racial barriers, for over half a century Sadie Alexander was at the forefront of the movement for civil rights for African Americans. In the 1920s and 1930s she and her husband successfully challenged discrimination in public accommodations in Pennsylvania. She also worked to integrate the University of Pennsylvania and the U.S. Armed Forces. On December 5, 1946, President Harry S. Truman appointed her to the President's Commission on Civil Rights. She helped prepare its report, "To Secure These Rights" (1948), which was influential in the formulation of civil rights policy in the years that followed. Alexander worked with her husband until 1959, when he was appointed judge in the Philadelphia Court of Common Pleas and she began her own law practice. In 1976 she joined the law firm of Atkinson, Myers, Archie & Wallace as counsel, advising the firm on a part-time basis in estate and family law. Alzheimer's disease forced her retirement in 1982. She died in Philadelphia seven years later.

See also Civil Rights Movement, U.S.

Bibliography

Dannett, Sylvia G. L. *Profiles of Negro Womanhood*, vol. 3: *20th Century*. Yonkers, N.Y.: Educational Heritage, 1966.

Malveaux, Julianne. "Missed Opportunity: Sadie Tanner Mossell Alexander and the Economic Profession." *American Economic Review* 81, no. 2 (March 1991): 307–310.

SIRAJ AHMED (1996)
PREMILLA NADASEN (1996)

ALI, MUHAMMAD

JANUARY 17, 1942

Boxer Muhammad Ali was born Cassius Marcellus Clay, Jr., in Louisville, Kentucky. He began boxing at the age of twelve under the tutelage of Joe Martin, a Louisville policeman. Having little interest in school and little affinity for intellectual endeavors, young Clay devoted himself wholeheartedly to boxing. He showed great promise early on and soon developed into one of the most impressive amateurs in the country. He became the National Amateur Athletic Union (AAU) champion in 1959 and 1960 and also won a gold medal in the light-heavyweight division at the 1960 Olympics in Rome. As a result of his boyish good looks and his outgoing personality—his poetry recitations, his good-natured bragging, and his undeniable abilities—Clay because famous after the Olympics. Shortly after returning from Rome, he turned professional and was managed by a consortium of white Louisville businessmen. Carefully nurtured by veteran trainer Angelo Dundee, he accumulated a string of victories against relatively mediocre opponents and achieved a national following with his constant patter, his poetry, and his boyish an-

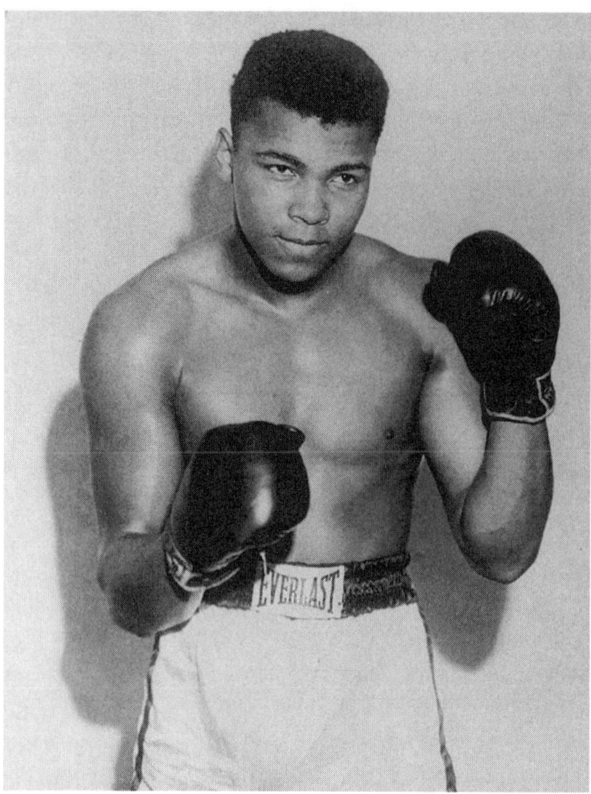

Muhammad Ali, 1962. *Olympic gold medal winner Cassius Clay, pictured at a Madison Square Garden studio, shocked the world when he defeated Sonny Liston for the heavyweight title in 1964. That same year, Clay announced that he was a member of the Nation of Islam and was changing his name to Muhammad Ali.* AP/WIDE WORLD PHOTOS. REPRODUCED BY PERMISSION.

tics. At six feet three inches and a fighting weight of around two hundred pounds, he astonished sportswriters with his blazing hand and foot speed, his unorthodox style of keeping his hands low, and his ability to avoid punches by moving his head back. No heavyweight in history possessed Clay's grace or speed.

On February 25, 1964, Clay fought as the underdog for the heavyweight title against Sonny Liston. Liston, an ex-convict, was thought by many to be virtually invincible because of his devastating one-round victories against former champion Floyd Patterson. An air of both the theater of the absurd and of ominousness surrounded the bout in Miami. Publicly, Clay taunted and comically berated Liston. He called him "the Bear," harassed him at his home, and almost turned the weigh-in ceremony into a shambles as he seemingly tried to attack Liston and appeared on the verge of being utterly out of control. Privately, however, Clay was seen with Malcolm X and members of the Nation of Islam (NOI). Rumors started that he had joined the militant, mysterious sect. Soon after, it was discovered that he had been secretly visiting NOI mosques for nearly three years and that he had indeed become a friend of Malcolm X, who sat ringside at the Liston fight.

Clay beat Liston fairly easily in seven rounds, shocking the world by becoming heavyweight champion. Immediately after the fight, he announced that he was a member of the NOI and that his name was no longer Cassius Clay but Muhammad Ali. The response from the white press, white America, and the boxing establishment generally was swift and intensely hostile. The NOI was seen, largely through the rhetoric of Malcolm X, its most stylish spokesman, as an antiwhite hate group. (When Malcolm X broke with the NOI shortly after the Liston fight, Ali remained loyal to Elijah Muhammad and ended his friendship with Malcolm X.) Following his public conversion to Islam, Ali was publicly pilloried. Most publications and sports journalists refused to call him by his new name. Former champion Floyd Patterson nearly went on a personal and national crusade against the NOI in his fight against Ali on November 22, 1965, but Patterson later became one of the few fighters to defend Ali publicly during his years of exile. Indeed, not since the reign of Jack Johnson was the white public and a segment of the black population so enraged by the opinions and life of a black athlete.

After winning his rematch with Liston in Lewiston, Maine, on May 25, 1965, in a bizarre fight that ended with Liston apparently being knocked out in the first round, Ali spent most of the next year fighting abroad, primarily because of his unpopularity in the United States. Among his most important matches during this period were a fifteen-round decision over George Chuvalo in Toronto, a sixth-round knockout of Henry Cooper in London, and a fifteen-round decision over Ernest Terrell in Houston. While Ali was abroad, American officials changed his draft status from 1-Y (unfit for army services because of his low score on army intelligence tests) to 1-A (qualified for induction). Many saw this change as a direct response to the negative public opinion concerning Ali's political views and the mounting war in Vietnam. Ali refused to serve in the army on the grounds that it was a violation of his religious beliefs. (Elijah Muhammad, leader of the NOI, had served time in prison during World War II for refusing to serve in the armed services.) In 1967 Ali was convicted in federal court of violation of the Selective Service Act, sentenced to five years in prison, and immediately stripped of both his boxing title and his boxing license. For the next three and one-half years, Ali, free on bond while appealing his case (which he eventually won on appeal to the U.S. Supreme Court), was prohibited from boxing. Still, he had inspired black athletes to become more militant and more politically committed. Medal-winning track stars John

Carlos and Tommie Smith gave a clenched-fist salute during the playing of the National Anthem at the Olympic Games in Mexico City in 1968, and Harry Edwards became one of the more outspoken leaders of a new cadre of young black athletes who saw Ali as a hero.

By 1970, with public opinion decidedly against the Vietnam War and a growing black influence in several southern state governments, Ali was given a license to fight in Georgia. He returned to the ring on October 26 to knock out Jerry Quarry in the third round. Although he was still a brilliant fighter, the nearly four-year layoff had diminished some of Ali's abilities. He took far more punishment in the ring during the years of his return than he had taken before. This was to have dire consequences for him as he grew older.

In the early 1970s Ali fought several of his most memorable matches. On March 8, 1971, he faced the undefeated Philadelphian Joe Frazier in New York City. Frazier had become champion during Ali's exile. The fifteen-round fight, which Frazier won in a close decision, was so fierce that both boxers were hospitalized after it. Many have speculated that this fight initiated Ali's neurological deterioration. In July of that year Ali won the North American Boxing Federation (NABF) heavyweight title by knocking out Jimmy Ellis in twelve rounds. His next major boxing challenge came in March 1973, when Ken Norton captured the NABF title from Ali in a twelve-round decision. Ali regained the title six months later with a twelve-round decision over Norton. In January of the following year, Ali and Frazier staged their first rematch. This nontitle bout at Madison Square Garden ended with Ali victorious after twelve hard-fought rounds. Ali finally regained the world heavyweight title in Kinshasa, Zaire, on October 30, 1974, when he knocked out a seemingly indestructible George Foreman in eight rounds. To counter Foreman's awesome punching power, Ali used what he called his "rope-a-dope" strategy, by which he leaned back against the ropes and covered his head, allowing Foreman to punch himself out. The next year, Ali and Frazier faced off one last time in what Ali dubbed "the Thrilla in Manila." Both boxers received tremendous punishment during this bludgeoning ordeal. Ali prevailed, however, when Frazier's trainer refused to let the boxer come out for the fifteenth round.

During the 1970s Ali was lionized. No longer seen as a race demon, he virtually became a national icon. He appeared in movies—including *The Greatest* (1977), based on his autobiography of the same name (1975). Like Jackie Robinson and Joe Louis before him, Ali played himself in the film, and he also appeared in television programs and in commercials. He was one of the most photographed and interviewed men in the world. Indeed, Ali even beat Superman in the ring in a special issue of the comic devoted to him. Part of Ali's newfound popularity was a result of a shift in attitude by the white public and white sportswriters, but part of it was also a reflection of Ali's tempered approach to politics. Ali became a great deal less doctrinaire in the political aspects of his Islamic beliefs and he eventually embraced Wallace D. Muhammad's more ecumenical form of Islam when the NOI factionalized after the death of Elijah Muhammad in 1975. Finally, as befitting a major celebrity, Ali had one of the largest entourages of any sports personality in history, resembling that of a head of state.

> *Muhammad Ali*
>
> "Keep asking me, no matter how long
>
> On the war in Viet Nam, I sing this song
>
> I ain't got no quarrel with them Viet Cong."

On February 15, 1978, Ali again lost the title. His opponent this time was Leon Spinks, an ex-Marine and native of a north St. Louis housing project. Spinks had fought in only eight professional bouts before he met Ali. Ali, however, became the first heavyweight in history to regain the title for a third time when he defeated Spinks on September 15 of the same year.

In 1979 Ali was aged and weary; his legs were shot, his reflexes had slowed, and his appetite for competition was waning as a result of the good life that he was enjoying. He retired from the ring at that time, only to do what so many other great champions have so unwisely done, namely, return to battle. His return to the ring included a savage ten-round beating on October 2, 1980, at the hands of Larry Holmes, a former sparring partner who had become champion after Ali's retirement. His next fight was a ten-round decision lost to Trevor Berbick on December 11 of the following year. After the Berbick fight, Ali retired for good. His professional record stands at fifty-six wins, thirty-seven by knockout, and five losses. He was elected to the Boxing Hall of Fame in 1987.

During Ali's later years, his speech became noticeably more slurred, and after his retirement he became more aged: moving slowly, speaking with such a thick tongue that he was almost incomprehensible, and suffering from attacks of palsy. There is some question as to whether he has Parkinson's disease or a Parkinson's-like deterioration of the neurological system. Many believe that the deterioration of his neurological system is directly connected to the punishment he took in the ring. By the early 1990s, although his mind was still sound, Ali gave the appearance of being a good deal older and more infirm than he actually was. He found it difficult to write or talk, and he often walked slowly. Despite this, he lived a full life, traveled constantly, and seemed to be at peace with himself. During the late 1990s he became the object of renewed public interest. In 1996, in tribute to his travels for peace, Ali was chosen to light the Olympic torch in Atlanta. The same year, he was featured in *When We Were Kings,* a documentary movie about his 1974 defeat of George Foreman in Kinshasa.

Ali's personal life was turbulent. He was married four times and had several children as well as numerous affairs, especially during his heyday as a fighter. His oldest daughter, Maryum, is a rap artist, following in her father's footsteps as a poet—Ali made a poetry recording for Columbia Records in 1963 called *The Greatest.* Maryum recorded a popular rap dedicated to her father.

In 2001 *Ali,* a critically acclaimed movie starring Will Smith, was made about his life. Ali has received countless honors and in 2003 participated in the opening ceremonies of the Special Olympics World Summer games.

It would be difficult to overestimate Ali's impact on boxing and on the United States as both a cultural and political figure. He became one of the most recognized men in the world, an enduring, if not always appropriate, stylistic influence on young boxers, and a man who showed the world that it was possible for a black to speak his mind publicly and live to tell the tale.

See also Boxing; Foreman, George; Frazier, Joe; Louis, Joe; Malcolm X; Muhammad, Elijah; Nation of Islam; Patterson, Floyd; Robinson, Jackie

Bibliography

Ali, Muhammad, with Hana Ali. *The Soul of a Butterfly: Reflections on Life's Journey.* New York: Simon and Schuster, 2004.

Dennis, Felix. *Muhammad Ali: The Glory Years.* New York: Miramax, 2003.

Hauser, Thomas. *Muhammad Ali: His Life and Time.* New York: Simon and Schuster, 1991.

Mailer, Norman. *The Fight.* New York: Little, Brown, 1975.

McCallum, John D. *The World Heavyweight Boxing Championship: A History.* Radnor, Pa.: Chilton, 1974.

Olsen, Jack. *Black Is Best: The Riddle of Cassius Clay.* New York: Putnam, 1967.

Plimpton, George. *Shadow Box.* New York: Putnam, 1977.

Roberts, Randy. *Papa Jack: Jack Johnson and the Era of White Hopes.* New York: Free Press, 1983.

Sheen, Wilfred. *Muhammad Ali.* New York: Crowell, 1975.

Torres, Jose. *Sting Like a Bee: The Muhammad Ali Story.* New York: Abelard-Schuman, 1971.

GERALD L. EARLY (1996)
Updated by publisher 2005

Allan, Harold

March 15, 1895
February 18, 1953

Sir Harold Allan was born in Spring Bank, Portland, Jamaica. He was educated at Calabar Elementary School and Mico Teacher's College, as well as being privately tutored. He later became assistant headmaster at Calabar and headmaster at Titchfield Upper School. He entered the Jamaican legislature in 1935, representing the parish constituency of eastern Portland as an independent legislator. In 1938 he was one of the three commissioners appointed by the secretary of the state for the colonies, Malcolm McDonald, to investigate the disturbances at the Frome Sugar Estate following labor riots all over Jamaica. In late 1938, he pleaded Jamaica's deplorable socioeconomic conditions to the Colonial Office in London and was successful in establishing the Unemployment Scheme and the West Kingston Rehabilitation Center, as well as factories to produce cornmeal and condensers.

Allan played a critical role in the formation of a new constitution in 1944, since as an independent member of the legislature he was the bridge between the two main political parties (the Jamaica Labour Party and the People's National Party). Allan's impressive ability as a legislator led Jamaica's chief minister, Alexander Bustamante, to appoint him minister of finance and general purposes after the first general elections, in 1944. Allan was the first Jamaican to preside over the country's budget and initiate financial discussions in the Legislative Council, as this was the traditional task of the colonial secretary.

In 1947 Allan led the international trade talks on behalf of the West Indian delegation in Geneva. He defended preferential tariffs, trade within the British Commonwealth, and an increase in the export of West Indian goods. Later, in 1947, he was appointed British West Indian advisor to the British delegation at the Havana Conference on Trade and Employment. He also created numerous administrative departments in Jamaica, such as the Land Authority and the Central Housing Authority. He also introduced the concept of the Non-Residents' Business Law, which led to a revision of Jamaica's immigration laws. In 1948, in recognition of his service, Allan was knighted by King George VI of Great Britain.

In 1951, at the annual Festival of Britain (where colonial members were usually invited as delegates), Allan used the opportunity to lobby James Griffiths, the secretary of state for the colonies. Allan noted that Great Britain undermined the export of Jamaican cigars by not signing the General Agreement on Trade and Tariffs (GATT). He also lobbied for a more liberal immigration policy to aid West Indian migrants and for fewer restrictions on work visas.

Allan remained an independent candidate until his premature death at the age of fifty-eight. At the time of his death he was the chair of a committee drafting a self-governing constitution, and it was expected that he would become the first minister of finance under a revised constitution in 1953. Allan, a trained teacher, left an indelible mark as a civic leader and politician. He was a legislator between 1935 and 1953; a privy counselor from 1942 to 1945; the leader of the House of Representatives in 1945; an organizer, founder, and secretary of the Association of Local Government; and he organized Jamaica's All-Island Championships in football and cricket.

See also Bustamante, Alexander; Jamaica Labour Party; People's National Party

Bibliography

Eaton, George E. *Alexander Bustamante and Modern Jamaica.* Kingston, Jamaica: Kingston Publishers, 1975.

DAVE GOSSE (2005)

ALLEN, DEBBIE

JANUARY 16, 1950

Dancer and television producer Debbie Allen was born in Houston, Texas, where her father, Andrew Allen, was a dentist and her mother, Vivian Ayers Allen, was a Pulitzer Prize–nominated writer. Her sister, Phylicia Rashad, became well known for her role as Claire Huxtable on the television series *The Cosby Show.*

As a child Allen tried to take ballet classes at the Houston Foundation for Ballet, but she was rejected for reasons her mother thought were discriminatory. Allen began learning dance by studying privately with a former dancer from the Ballet Russes and later by moving with her family to Mexico City, where she danced with the Ballet Nacional de Mexico. Allen reauditioned for the Houston Foundation for Ballet in 1964, and this time was admitted on a full scholarship and became the company's first black dancer.

After high school Allen hoped to attend North Carolina School of Arts, but when she was rejected she decided to pursue a B.A. at Howard University (1971) with a concentration in classical Greek literature, speech, and theater. During her college years, she continued to dance with students at the university and with choreographer Michael Malone's dance troupe. After graduating in 1971 Allen relocated to New York City, where she would develop her talents as a dancer, actress, and singer in her appearances on Broadway and eventually in television shows and movies.

Allen's Broadway experience began in 1971 when she became a member of the chorus in *Purlie,* the musical version of Ossie Davis's *Purlie Victorious.* The following year, when chorus member George Faison left the show to form the Universal Dance Experience, Allen became his principal dancer and assistant. By 1973 she had returned to Broadway, and for two years she played the role of Beneatha Younger in *Raisin,* a musical adaptation of Lorraine Hansberry's *A Raisin in the Sun.*

Allen began receiving critical attention in 1980, when she appeared in the role of Anita in a Broadway revival of *West Side Story,* which earned her a Tony Award nomination and a Drama Desk Award. The next year she made her movie debut in the film version of E. L. Doctorow's novel *Ragtime,* and then appeared in the hit movie *Fame,* with a small part as the dance teacher Lydia Grant. When the movie was turned into a television series of the same name, Allen returned as Lydia Grant and developed the role, which brought her recognition by international audiences. She remained on the show until it went off the air in 1987, serving as a choreographer, and eventually as a director and producer.

During the 1980s Allen also acted in the television movie *Women of San Quentin* (1983), appeared in Richard Pryor's movie *Jo Jo Dancer, Your Life Is Calling* (1985), and played Charity in a Broadway revival of *Sweet Charity* (1986). In 1988 she became director of *A Different World* and helped turn it into a top twenty television hit. The next year she hosted her first television special on ABC, *The Debbie Allen Show,* and later that year she directed the television musical *Polly,* which was followed in 1990 by *Polly: One More Time.* During the 1990–1991 season Allen directed episodes of NBC's *Fresh Prince of Bel-Air* and *Quantum Leap.* She was a choreographer for the Academy Awards show from 1991 to 1994, and in 1992 she produced and directed the television movie *Stompin' at the Savoy.*

Allen remained active throughout the late 1990s. In 1997 she realized a decades-long dream by producing Steven Spielberg's epic *Amistad*. The following year, she directed the musical *Brothers of the Knight* at the Kennedy Center in Washington, D.C.

Allen has long been involved with children and in 2001 opened the Debbie Allen Dance Academy to help combat shrinking arts programs in the schools.

See also Television; Theatrical Dance

Bibliography

Burden, Martin. "'Fame' Comes to Debbie Allen." *New York Post,* August 18, 1982.

"Debbie Allen: On Power, Pain, Passion, and Prime Time." *Ebony* (March 1991): 24–32.

Dunning, Jennifer. "Debbie Allen Chips Away at the Glass Ceiling." *New York Times,* March 29, 1992.

Gallo, Hank. "Performing Powerhouse: Debbie Allen May Be Small but Then So Is Dynamite." *Daily News,* March 2, 1989.

Hine, Darlene Clark, ed. *Black Women in America: An Historical Encyclopedia.* Brooklyn, N.Y.: Carlson, 1993, pp. 20–21.

ZITA ALLEN (1996)
Updated by publisher 2005

Allen, Macon Bolling

1816
October 15, 1894

The lawyer A. Macon Bolling was born in Indiana. Little is known about Bolling's early life, but by the 1840s he had established himself as a businessman in Portland, Maine. In January 1844 Bolling had his name changed to Macon Bolling Allen by an act of the legislature in Massachusetts, where he was presumably a resident. With the assistance of white abolitionists, Allen first tried to gain admittance to the Maine bar in 1844 but was rejected on the grounds that he was not a United States citizen. However, the following year he passed the requisite exam and was admitted to the bar, becoming the first licensed African-American attorney in the United States.

Discouraged by the small black population in Maine, Allen chose to practice law in Boston. He was admitted to the Suffolk County bar on May 3, 1845, the first African American to become a member of the bar in Massachusetts. Although Allen opposed slavery, he clashed with New England abolitionists in 1846 when he refused to sign a pledge not to support the government in its war effort in Mexico. In 1847 Allen was appointed justice of the peace by Massachusetts Governor George N. Briggs. He was the first African American, after Wentworth Cheswill, of New Hampshire, to hold a judicial post. Allen's appointment was renewed in 1854, and he continued to practice law in Massachusetts until the advent of Reconstruction. In the late 1860s, Allen moved to Charleston, South Carolina, to practice law and enter politics.

In 1868 Allen joined William J. Whipper and Robert Brown Elliot in establishing Whipper, Elliot, and Allen, the country's first black law firm. Like his colleagues, who were both members of the South Carolina legislature (Elliot also served in the U.S. Congress), Allen sought political office. His 1872 race for South Carolina secretary of state, however, was unsuccessful.

In February 1873 Allen was elected to fill out the term of the deceased George Lee, an African American elected to the judgeship of the Inferior Court of South Carolina in 1872. Allen was subsequently elected to the probate court, on which he served from 1876 to 1878. At the end of his term, Allen returned to his law practice in Charleston; little is known about his career after the late 1870s. Allen died in Washington, D.C.

See also Abolition; Whipper, William

Bibliography

Brown, Charles Sumner. "The Genesis of the Negro Lawyer in New England." *The Negro History Bulletin* (April 1959): 147–152.

Smith, J. Clay, Jr. *Emancipation: The Making of the Black Lawyer, 1844–1944.* Philadelphia: University of Pennsylvania Press, 1993.

LOUISE P. MAXWELL (1996)

Allen, Richard

February 14, 1760
March 26, 1831

As a reformer and institution builder in the post-Revolutionary period in the United States, Richard Allen was matched in achievements by few of his white contemporaries. At age twenty, only a few months after buying his freedom in Kent County, Delaware, Allen was preaching to mostly white audiences and converting many of his hearers to Methodism. At twenty-seven, he was a cofounder of the Free African Society of Philadelphia, probably the first autonomous organization of free blacks in the United States. Before he was thirty-five, he had become the minister of what would be Philadelphia's largest black congregation—Bethel African Methodist Episcopal Church. Over a long lifetime, he founded, presided over, or served as officer in a large number of other organizations designed to improve the condition of life and expand the sphere of liberty for African Americans. Although he received no formal education, he became an accomplished writer, penning and publishing sermons, tracts, addresses, and remonstrances; compiling a hymnal for black Methodists; and drafting articles of organization and governance for various organizations.

Enslaved at birth in the family of the prominent Philadelphia lawyer and officeholder Benjamin Chew, Allen was sold with his family to Stokely Sturgis, a small farmer near Dover, Delaware, in about 1768. It was here, in 1777, that Allen experienced a religious conversion, shortly after most of his family had been sold away from Dover at the hands of the itinerant Methodist Freeborn Garretson. Three years later he and his brother contracted with their master to purchase their freedom.

For a short time, Allen drove a wagon carrying salt for the Revolutionary army. He also supported himself as a woodchopper, brickyard laborer, and shoemaker as he carried out a six-year religious sojourn as an itinerant Methodist preacher. In something akin to a biblical journey into the wilderness, Allen tested his mettle and proved his faith, traveling by foot over thousands of miles, from North Carolina to New York, and preaching the word to black and white audiences in dozens of villages, crossroads, and forest clearings. During this period of his life, it seems, Allen developed the essential attributes that would serve him the rest of his career: resilience, toughness, cosmopolitanism, an ability to confront rapidly changing circumstances, and skill in dealing with a wide variety of people and temperaments.

Allen's itinerant preaching brought him to the attention of white Methodist leaders, who in 1786 called him to Philadelphia to preach to black members of the Methodist congregation that worshiped at Saint George's Methodist Church, a rude, dirt-floored building in the German part of the city. Allen would spend the rest of his life there.

In Philadelphia, Allen's career was marked by his founding of Mother Bethel, the black Methodist church that opened its doors in 1794, and by the subsequent creation, in 1816, of the independent African Methodist Episcopal Church (AME Church). Soon after his arrival in 1786, he began pressing for an independent black church. His fervent Methodism brought him into contention with

The Reverend Richard Allen (1760–1831). *The founder and first bishop of the African Methodist Episcopal (AME) Church, Allen was also active in a host of other organizations dedicated to improving the lives of African Americans.* NEW YORK PUBLIC LIBRARY PICTURE COLLECTION

other emerging black leaders who wished for a nondenominational, or "union," church, and thus within a few years two black churches took form. Both were guided by the idea that African Americans needed "to worship God under our own vine and fig tree," as Allen put it in his autobiographical memoir. This was, in essence, a desire to stand apart from white society, avoiding both the paternalistic benevolence of its racially liberal members and the animosity of its racially intolerant members. Allen's Bethel church, after opening its doors in a converted blacksmith's shop in 1794, grew into a congregation of more than five hundred members by 1800.

Bethel's rise to the status of Philadelphia's largest black church was accomplished amid a twenty-year struggle with white Methodist leaders. White Methodists were determined to make the popular Allen knuckle under to their authority, and this ran directly counter to Allen's determination to lead a church in which black Methodists, while subscribing to the general doctrines of Methodism, were free to pursue their churchly affairs autonomously. The struggle even involved the ownership of the church building itself. The attempts of white Methodists to rein in Allen and his black parishioners reached a climax in

1815 and was resolved when the Pennsylvania Supreme Court ruled on January 1, 1816, that Bethel was legally an independent church. Just a few months later, African-American ministers from across the mid-Atlantic region gathered in Philadelphia to confederate their congregations into the African Methodist Episcopal Church, which was to spread across the United States and abroad in the nineteenth and twentieth centuries.

Allen's epic twenty-year battle with white Methodist authorities represents a vital phase of the African-American struggle in the North to get out from under the controlling hand of white religionists. The AME Church, with Allen as its first bishop, quickly became the most important of the autonomous institutions created by black Americans that allowed former slaves to forge an Afro-Christianity that spoke in the language and answered the needs of a growing number of northern—and, later, southern—blacks. For decades the AME Church helped to heal the disabling scars of slavery and facilitated the adjustment of black southern migrants to life as citizens in the North. Allen's success at Bethel had much to do with the warmth, simplicity, and evangelical fervor of Methodism, which resonated with a special vibrancy among the manumitted and fugitive southern slaves reaching Philadelphia in the early nineteenth century.

Between the founding of Bethel in 1794 and the organization of the AME Church, Allen founded schools for black youths and mutual aid societies that would allow black Philadelphians to quash the idea that they were dependent upon white charity. A successful businessman and a considerable property owner, Allen also wrote pamphlets and sermons attacking the slave trade, slavery, and white racism. The most notable of them, coauthored with Absalom Jones in 1794, was "A Narrative of the Proceedings of the Black People, During the Late Awful Calamity in Philadelphia, in the Year 1793." In this pamphlet, Allen and Jones defended the work of black citizens who aided the sick and dying during the horrendous yellow fever epidemic of 1793, but they went on to condemn the oppression of African Americans, both enslaved and free. In the first quarter of the nineteenth century, almost every African-American institution formed in Philadelphia included Allen's name and benefited from his energy and vision.

In the later years of his life, Allen was drawn to the idea of colonization—to Africa, Haiti, and Canada—as an answer to the needs of African Americans who, as freedpersons, faced discrimination and exploitation. His son, John Allen, was one of the leaders of the Haitian immigrants in 1824. The capstone of Allen's career came six years later, when he presided over the first meeting of the National Negro Convention movement—an umbrella organization that launched a coordinated reform movement among black Americans and provided an institutional structure for black abolitionism. When death came to Allen shortly thereafter, his funeral was attended by a vast concourse of black and white Philadelphians.

See also African Methodist Episcopal Church

Bibliography

George, Carol V. R. *Segregated Sabbaths: Richard Allen and the Rise of Independent Black Churches.* New York: Oxford University Press, 1972.

Wesley, Charles H. *Richard Allen, Apostle of Freedom.* 2d ed. Washington, D.C.: Associated Publishers, 1969.

GARY B. NASH (1996)

Alleyne, George

October 7, 1932

On December 15, 2003, representatives of the University of the West Indies met at the university's Cave Hill Campus in Barbados to witness the formal installation of the first Barbadian to become chancellor of the University of the West Indies, and the first chancellor of that school to be installed at a campus other than the original Mona Campus of the university in Jamaica. In an impressive and emotional ceremony, Sir George Alleyne also became the first chancellor to have received his university education at the institution.

George Allenmore Oganen Alleyne was born at Saint Philip, Barbados. The son of a schoolteacher, in 1943 his early academic promise was rewarded with a Primary First Grade Scholarship to Harrison College. He graduated from Harrison College in 1950 with the Barbados Scholarship in the Classics. Ignoring conventional wisdom, which led Island scholars to study at universities in the United Kingdom, Alleyne entered the fledgling University College of the West Indies.

Alleyne was among the earliest students who enrolled for medical training at what was then a two-year-old single-campus university at Mona, Jamaica. Medicine was one of the university's earliest faculties. Public health had been one of the major concerns of those responsible for establishing the university, so public and community health received special emphasis.

Alleyne excelled in these areas. He was the outstanding student in the class of 1957 and was awarded, among other prizes, the University Gold Medal. The school of medicine recruited him to conduct research and train new students.

Alleyne's research into such health problems as malnutrition in children established him as an internationally respected expert in the field, especially during the time when he was a member of the Tropical Metabolism Research Unit. During his career, he published more than one hundred scientific papers. In 1976, he was one of the coauthors of the *Protein Energy Malnutrition,* which remains a standard text on the subject.

His research extended to renal function and disease. When the British Medical Research Council relinquished the Tropical Metabolism Unit, which was then fully integrated into the Faculty of Medicine, Alleyne was appointed professor within that department. He led a research team that published some forty papers in international journals, mostly on renal biochemistry.

His work began to receive favorable notice in both the region and the hemisphere. He was made a Fellow of the Royal College of Physicians in 1973 and in 1975 he was admitted to the American College of Physicians. He first became a member of the Advisory Committee on Medical Research of the Pan American Health Organization (PAHO), then its chairman, and later director of medical research. In 1995, Alleyne became director of the Pan American Sanitary Bureau and later director of PAHO itself. He was the first representative of the Anglophone Caribbean to be elected to such a position and his re-election, by acclamation in 1998, was without precedent, as directors of PAHO are generally chosen by the formal process of nomination, campaigning, and voting.

In 1990, he was made Knight Bachelor by Queen Elizabeth II for his contribution to medicine. Honorary doctorates and similar honors have been conferred on him by universities throughout the Americas, as well as from the University of the West Indies. In 2001, Alleyne received the Order of the Caribbean Community. In 2002 the Pan American Health Organization published a selection of his speeches.

After retiring as director of PAHO in February 2003, he was appointed United Nations Special Envoy for HIV/AIDS for the Caribbean Region. In July, he was appointed by the Caribbean Community (CARICOM) to head a new commission to examine health issues, including HIV/AIDS, confronting the region. In October, he was appointed chancellor of the University of the West Indies, bringing to the position a gift for oratory and a lifetime of commitment to regional and hemispheric development. The medical challenges the Caribbean faced had changed significantly since he entered the University of the West Indies as a medical student. Whereas in the 1950s the major public health problem was malnutrition, it is now such diseases as diabetes, hypertension, and HIV/AIDS.

See also Caribbean Community and Common Market (CARICOM); University of the West Indies

Bibliography

Alleyne, G. A. O., et al. *Protein Energy Malnutrition.* London: Edward Arnold, 1977.

Alleyne, George, Sir, and Karen Sealey. *Whither Caribbean Health.* Saint Michael, Barbados: West Indian Commission Secretariat, 1992.

Alleyne, Sir George. *A Quest for Equity/En busca de la equidad: Selected Speeches of George Alleyne, 1995–2002.* Washington, D.C.: Pan American Health Organization, 2002.

Augier, F. R., ed. *The University of the West Indies Fortieth Anniversary Lectures.* 1990.

The Face of Man: The Eric Williams Memorial Lectures, 2 vols. Port of Spain, Trinidad: Central Bank of Trinidad and Tobago, 1994.

Health, Economic Growth, and Poverty Reduction: Report of Working Group 1 of the Commission on Macroeconomics and Health. Geneva: World Health Organization, 2002.

C. M. JACOBS (2005)

Almeida Bosque, Juan

February 17, 1927

The Cuban revolutionary leader Juan Almeida Bosque was born into poverty in Havana. He had to drop out of school after completing only the fourth grade in order to find a job so he could help his parents take care of his brothers and sisters. Even while working as a bricklayer in the early 1950s, Almeida continued to give some of what he described as "a miserable salary" to his parents. Although he worked daily, his salary was never enough to prevent him from enduring hunger and misery. Almeida's economic condition was undoubtedly a result of his ethnicity. As a mulatto, Almeida confronted a racist system that generally denied Cubans of African descent the opportunity to obtain the skills and experience required by labor organizations to hold the title of master bricklayer.

Almeida's political and economic career began after Fulgencio Batista overthrew the Cuban government of President Carlos Prío Socarrás in March 1952. After the coup occurred, Almeida went to the University of Havana

Major Juan Almeida Bosque, commander of the Cuban army. *Almeida (r.) is shown with Cuban dictator Fidel Castro at the Theresa Hotel in New York City, September 22, 1960. The two were in New York for Castro's address to the General Assembly of the United Nations.* GETTY IMAGES

with a friend, Armando Mestre, to protest Batista's actions. One of the principal leaders of the protest was a young lawyer by the name of Fidel Castro Ruz. Almeida and Castro immediately became friends for life. Almeida was inspired to become politically active by discussions with Castro on how to create a revolution against the man responsible for compromising Cuba's political development since the mid-1930s and by Castro's call for unity between young Cubans and those in other sectors of society who had not been collaborators of Batista in the past. It appears that their friendship grew out of mutual respect. According to Castro, Almeida could be trusted because he was a "man of the people."

After joining the Orthodox Party, Almeida helped Castro and others organize the resistance against Batista in the province of Matanzas, though their effort was unsuccessful. Their failure led them to conclude that they themselves had to overthrow the Batista government. Establishing clandestine groups that trained without communicating with each other, Almeida, Castro, and other conspirators, including Abel Santamaria, met in July 1953 in Santiago de Cuba in order to attack the Moncada army barracks, hoping to seize a large cache of weapons and to encourage the Cuban nation to rise up against Batista. The attack failed miserably, and Castro, Almeida, and other *moncadistas* fled into the nearby Sierra Maestra Mountains to avoid capture. Nevertheless, on August 1, 1953, both Almeida and Castro were caught. In October, Almeida was tried and sentenced to ten years in prison on the Isle of Pines. In prison for a total of eighteen months, he and the other *moncadistas* were released in May 1955 after Batista issued an amnesty decree.

By February 1956, Almeida had joined Castro and other opponents of the Batista regime in Mexico, where they began training for an invasion to force Batista out of power, planned for the fall of 1956. On November 25, 1956, Almeida, now holding the rank of captain, and with twenty-two men under his command, boarded the yacht

Granma along with Castro and sixty other rebels and sailed for Cuba.

Juan Almeida demonstrated exceptional courage, heroism, and leadership during the revolution. On December 5, 1956, he saved the life of Ernesto Che Guevara, one of the masterminds of the revolution, and others at the Battle of Alegria de Pio. Between the spring of 1957 and the fall of 1958, Almeida commanded the rebel army of the Third Front. He became responsible for engaging and weakening Batista's troops in the territory that stretched from Santiago de Cuba to Guantanamo. In October 1958, Castro ordered Almeida's army to take Santiago de Cuba. The assault on the city proved to be the first step of the final rebel offensive that encouraged Batista to capitulate by the end of 1958.

Because of his loyalty to Castro, as well as his military prowess, Juan Almeida Bosque has been appointed to numerous high-ranking positions within both the Revolutionary government and the Communist Party. Promoted to the rank of major as Batista left the country, Castro appointed Almeida to head the Cuban Air Force in June 1959, following the dismissal of Diaz Lanz for insubordination.

According to some writers of Afro-Cuban history, Fidel Castro cynically used Juan Almeida in the early 1960s as a symbol of the revolutionary government's committed endeavors to address and end racism and racial discrimination and segregation in Cuban society. These writers point to Castro's 1960 visit to New York City, where he addressed members of the United Nations, as proof. After Castro moved the Cuban delegation to a hotel located in Harlem, he urgently sent for Almeida, who was living in Santiago de Cuba. Upon his arrival, Castro proceeded to parade Almeida through the streets of black Harlem. Almeida even dined with leaders of black America. Some have claimed that Almeida's token presence in New York allowed Castro to strategically employ race as a fundamental element in Cuba's foreign policy as a way of enhancing Castro's status among members of the Non-Aligned Movement centered in Africa and Asia, as well as among leaders of the African-American community of the United States.

Nevertheless, it appears that within Cuba Almeida has never been regarded as a token figure. In 1961 he became a member of the Integrated Revolutionary Organizations, a body that preceded the formation of a new Communist Party. He also served as the president of JUCEI, or the Board of Coordination and Inspection, for the province of Las Villas. This government agency sought to convey the interests and power of workers and peasants at the local level. In 1966 he graduated from the Superior Academy for Officers of the Revolutionary Armed Forces. Since 1965 Almeida has continuously served on the Politburo of the Communist Party, and in 1998 the Cuban state awarded him the honorary title of "Hero of the Republic of Cuba." Since 1993 he has served as president of the National Association of Combatants of the Cuban Revolution, and he represents the Cuban government and nation before foreign dignitaries at home and abroad as vice president of the Cuban Council of State. Almeida has also become one of the most popular musicians and poets in Cuba; he has written over three hundred songs and sixty or more poems.

See also International Relations of the Anglophone Caribbean; Politics and Politicians in the Caribbean

Bibliography

Franqui, Carlos. *Diario de la revolución Cubana.* Barcelona, Spain: R. Torres, 1976. Translated as *Diary of the Cuban Revolution.* New York: Viking, 1980.

Matthews, Herbert L. *Revolution in Cuba: An Essay in Understanding.* New York: Scribner, 1975.

Moore, Carlos. *Castro, the Blacks, and Africa.* Los Angeles: University of California Press, 1988.

PHILIP A. HOWARD (2005)

AMELIORATION

In the history of the former British territories in the Caribbean, the term *Amelioration* (literally, "making better") refers to the efforts of the Imperial government to improve the situation of the enslaved people in its colonies during the decade between 1823 and the abolition of slavery by Parliament in 1834. The relative failure of this London-driven program of reform pushed both the British antislavery movement and the British government and Parliament to abandon "gradualism" and opt for outright abolition of slavery by 1834.

The abolition of the British slave trade in 1807 did not produce the improvements in the slaves' situation that the antislavery movement expected. In 1823 the Society for the Mitigation and Gradual Abolition of Slavery Throughout the British Dominions was established. As its title suggests, gradualism was dominant in the British antislavery movement until 1830. Its parliamentary leader, Thomas F. Buxton (1786–1845), decided to move resolutions in the House of Commons in May 1823 calling for immediate amelioration of the slaves' situation and eventual emancipation. The Tory leader in the House of Commons, George Canning (1770–1827), countered with resolutions of his own, reflecting a previously agreed-upon compromise between the antislavery lobby and the West India Interest, which represented the absentee slave-owners in London (many of whom were members of Parliament). These resolutions committed the House to emancipation "at the earliest period that shall be compatible with the well-being of the slaves themselves, with the safety of the colonies, and with a fair and equitable consideration of the interests of private property." They also envisaged "a progressive improvement in the character of the slave population, such as may prepare them for equal rights and privileges, as enjoyed by others of His Majesty's subjects" (Green, 1972, p. 102).

But how was a program to improve the slaves' lives and "character" to be implemented without abolishing the basic elements of chattel slavery? Any such program looking toward emancipation, even in the distant future, would certainly be resisted furiously by the planters and their organs, the elected Assemblies. The British government did not want to "coerce" them by enacting laws in Parliament and imposing them on the colonists; this, it was felt, was how the mainland American colonies had been lost fifty years before. So the Amelioration reforms would be imposed by direct legislation only on the "Crown Colonies," which had no elected Assemblies; the other colonies would be "persuaded" to enact similar laws themselves. This refusal to use the power of Parliament, as well as the strong resistance of the planters, ensured that the Amelioration program would have only limited success over the next ten years.

The main points of the program were circulated to the Caribbean governors in mid-1823. Slaves were to be given Christian instruction, and Sunday markets were to be abolished to encourage religious worship on that day. Marriages were to be encouraged, and slave families were not to be broken up by sale. Slave evidence, under certain conditions, was to be admitted in the courts. Enslaved persons were to be allowed to purchase their freedom, even against their owners' wishes. The informally recognized right of slaves to own property was to be backed by law. And corporal punishment, the core of plantation discipline, was to be limited: the flogging of women was to be absolutely prohibited, that of men restricted, and the whip was no longer to be carried (and used) by the drivers (gang foremen) as an instrument to coerce labor in the field. These were the major planks of the Amelioration policy. To the antislavery lobby, they were designed to prepare the slaves for freedom; to the government, their aim was to remove the most objectionable features of slavery and thus stave off emancipation for the foreseeable future.

To the planters in the colonies, these policies were wholly unacceptable. West Indian Assemblies responded with fury to the proposals: such reforms would undermine owners' control over their property, overturn plantation discipline, and incite slave rebellion. The uprising in Demerara (modern Guyana) in August 1823 seemed to vindicate their arguments. But London persisted. Despite strong objections from the planters of Trinidad, one of the Crown Colonies, an Order in Council—a law coming directly from the British government—was issued in March 1824 embodying all the main elements of the 1823 program. It was first to apply only to Trinidad—the "model colony" chosen because its Spanish legal heritage was believed to be especially favorable to the slaves—and was then to be extended to the other Crown Colonies; the colonies with Assemblies were expected to enact laws similar to the Trinidad Order.

The Order in Council became law in June 1824, with a protector of slaves appointed to implement its measures despite planter opposition. Yet even in the model Crown Colony, Amelioration achieved little by way of significant improvements in the slaves' lives. Only a handful of slaves were ever certified as competent to give evidence in court; very few slave marriages were legalized; manumissions did increase after 1824 but were made very difficult by the ridiculously high prices demanded by the owners. Solitary confinement, the stocks, and the treadmill were all used to punish women instead of flogging. Sunday work, prohibited by the order, generally continued, as did Sunday markets. Very few owners were ever prosecuted for breaches of the order, and it was extremely risky for a slave to make a complaint. The order had no teeth; and in the face of planter opposition and official indifference, Amelioration achieved little even in Trinidad, where all its main elements were enacted in law from mid-1824.

The colonies with their own Assemblies were able to resist the policy even more successfully, though eventually they were obliged, grudgingly, to comply with London's "persuasion" up to a point. Most limited the flogging of men, some removed the whip from the field, but few exempted women from corporal punishment—it was said to be impossible to "discipline" the women without flogging and, by the 1820s, the field gangs on West Indian plantations were predominantly female. Some colonies admitted slave evidence but (as in Trinidad) made it almost impossible to "qualify." Overall, the progress of Amelioration in the colonies with Assemblies—the majority of them—was difficult.

The Colonial Office in London worked hard to "persuade" and to bully the Assemblies, especially the two leading antislavery civil servants at the time, James Stephen (1789-1859) and Henry Taylor (1800–1886). Cases of ill treatment of slaves were reviewed and adjudicated with great care; voluminous papers were published for Parliament and disseminated in the antislavery press; many colonial laws were vetoed because they did not comply with the Trinidad Order; and the colonies were warned that direct parliamentary legislation would be inevitable if they did not pass the necessary laws themselves.

The years 1830 and 1831 were a watershed for the antislavery movement. Impatience at the slow progress and limited achievements of Amelioration was a major factor in the movement calling for immediate emancipation and more radical modes of agitation. But ministers persisted; in August 1831 the colonial secretary assured the colonists that he would not abandon "that course of progressive improvement, which has had for its avowed object, the ultimate extinction of Slavery (Green, 1976, p. 112)." The last serious effort to implement Amelioration was the ambitious Order in Council of November 1831, which applied to all the Crown Colonies. This elaborate law (no fewer than 121 clauses) strengthened the previous orders and introduced new and tougher regulations to protect the slaves' rights and guarantee better standards of food, clothing, housing, and hours of work. It also made it possible to bring criminal prosecutions against owners charged with breaches of the order. This "121-pronged scourge" (to quote a Trinidad newspaper) was greeted with fury, both in the Crown Colonies, where it became law early in 1832, and in the colonies with Assemblies, to which it was recommended as a model for legislation. Jamaica, and all the Leeward Islands, flatly refused to enact any similar law.

An impasse, therefore, seemed to have arrived by early 1832; Amelioration was clearly a failure. The great Christmas Rebellion of 1831 in Jamaica, and the terrible reprisals that followed, convinced even conservative legislators and ministers in London that the costs and risks of withholding emancipation and persisting with Amelioration were simply too high. Once the Reform Act became law and the Commons was reformed—and purged of most of its "West Indian" members—emancipation was politically possible. The passage of the Slavery Abolition Act of Emancipation in August 1833, to become law on August 1, 1834, marked the end of Amelioration.

If the main purpose of Amelioration was to secure some improvements in the slaves' lives while staving off immediate emancipation, it can be judged a short-term, and limited, success. A few improvements in material living conditions were probably achieved; punishments were reduced, especially in Trinidad, where flogging of women was more or less stopped; and the rate of manumissions accelerated. Emancipation was postponed for a decade. If its purpose was to prepare the enslaved people for freedom, however, it was clearly a failure, or, rather, hopelessly misconceived. In the long run, planter obduracy and ministerial timidity doomed what was probably always a misguided attempt to tinker with chattel slavery while preserving its essential elements. Its failure made legislative emancipation inevitable.

See also Abolition; Emancipation in Latin America and the Caribbean; Slavery

Bibliography

Brereton, Bridget. *A History of Modern Trinidad, 1783–1962.* London: Heinemann Education, 1989.

Green, William A. *British Slave Emancipation The Sugar Colonies and the Great Experiment 1830–1865.* Oxford: Clarendon Press, 1976.

Ward, J. R. *British West Indian Slavery, 1750-1834 The Process of Amelioration.* Oxford: Clarendon Press, 1988.

BRIDGET BRERETON (2005)

American Moral Reform Society

The American Moral Reform Society (AMRS) was organized in 1836 by a group of elite black leaders in Philadelphia to promote morality among both white and black Americans through the influence of temperance, education, economy, and universal liberty.

The AMRS grew directly out of the National Convention Movement (NCM), which first met in Philadelphia in 1830, and it embraced many of the movement's programs for reform. At the fifth annual NCM convention in 1835, the delegates adopted a proposal, devised by the black abolitionist attorney William Whipper, for the formation of the AMRS. Black Philadelphians dominated the proceedings and comprised the majority of the officers chosen to the society. Among those appointed were Bishop Morris Brown of the African Methodist Episcopal Church, and James Forten Sr., who served as the first president of the AMRS. Although plans were made for an NCM convention to meet in New York the following year, it was never held, and the AMRS replaced the convention movement until the AMRS disbanded.

Even at the society's first convention on August 8, 1836, there was factionalism among the leaders from Philadelphia as well as an intercity rivalry between the delegates from that city and those from New York. Opponents of the AMRS accused its leaders of being too visionary and unrealistic. Two AMRS policies proved particularly divisive: the AMRS commitment to morally reforming the entire American population, regardless of race, and Whipper's insistence on banning the use of such terms as *colored* and *African.* The society's critics argued that terms of racial identification were not objectionable and asserted that the AMRS should limit its sphere of action to free blacks.

Following the first annual meeting of the AMRS in 1837, a clear split took place among northern black leaders over these issues, with Whipper, Forten, and Robert Purvis emerging as the primary supporters of the AMRS. Whipper, the chief promoter of the AMRS, redoubled his promotional efforts and helped the AMRS establish its own journal, the *National Reformer,* which failed after only one year. Opponents of the AMRS, meanwhile, became more unified and more insistent in their calls for the revival of the National Convention Movement.

In an attempt to broaden its base of support, the AMRS admitted its first female delegates to the 1839 convention, but its Garrisonian anticlericalism and the revival of the National Convention Movement worked against the AMRS. It ceased to be an effective organization after its sixth convention in 1841.

See also Abolition; Forten, James; Purvis, Robert; Whipper, William

Bibliography

Bell, Howard H. "The American Moral Reform Society." *Journal of Negro Education* 27 (Winter 1958): 34–40.

Winch, Julie. *Philadelphia's Black Elite: Activism, Accommodation, and the Struggle for Autonomy, 1787–1848.* Philadelphia: Temple University Press, 1988.

LOUISE P. MAXWELL (1996)

American Negro Academy (ANA)

The American Negro Academy (ANA), founded on March 5, 1897, in Washington, D.C., was the first national African-American learned society. Although American blacks had established numerous local literary and scholarly societies from the late 1820s on, the goals and membership of the American Negro Academy made it a distinct and original endeavor. The academy's constitution defined it as "an organization of authors, scholars, artists, and those distinguished in other walks of life, men of African descent, for the promotion of Letters, Science, and Art" (Moss, 1981, p. 1). The decision to exclude women was based on the belief that "literary . . . and social matters do not mix."

Although the chief concerns of the ANA's founders were to strengthen the intellectual life of their racial community, improve the quality of black leadership, and ensure that henceforth arguments advanced by "cultured despisers" of their race were refuted, it was equally significant that the organization was established at a time when European Americans were creating hundreds of learned, professional, and ethnic historical societies. The academy's birth was an expression of this general movement among educated members of the American middle class.

From its establishment until its demise in 1928, the academy claimed as members some of the most important male leaders in the African-American community. Alexander Crummell, its first president, was an Episcopal clergyman who held an A.B. from Queen's College, Cambridge University. Other founders included Francis J. Grimké, a Presbyterian clergyman trained at Lincoln University and Princeton Theological Seminary; W. E. B. Du Bois, professor of economics and history at Atlanta University and later a founder of the National Association for the Advancement of Colored People (NAACP); William H. Crogman, professor of classics at Clark University in Atlanta; William S. Scarborough, a scholarly classicist who was on the faculty of Wilberforce University; and John W. Cromwell, a lawyer, politician, and former editor of the *People's Advocate,* a black newspaper published in Washington, D.C., from 1878 to 1884. Throughout its existence, the academy continued to attract a number of the most intellectually creative black men in the United States. Some of those associated with the organization who achieved their greatest prominence after the turn of the century were John Hope, president of Morehouse College and later of Atlanta University; Alain Locke, writer, critic, and key figure in the Harlem Renaissance; Carter G. Woodson, historian; and James Weldon Johnson, poet, writer, and civil rights leader.

Relatively speaking, only a handful of educated black men were ever members of the academy. There were several reasons for this: The ANA was a selective organization, to which entrance was controlled by the membership; its activities and goals appealed mainly to a small group of black men who sought to function as intellectuals and who believed that the results of their efforts were crucial to the development and defense of their racial group; it experienced continuous difficulties in realizing its goals; and it never enjoyed the support of Booker T. Washington, the powerful principal of Tuskegee Institute, who for over half the organization's life was the dominant figure in the African-American community. Washington was invited to become a founding member of the ANA and to attend the inaugural meeting in 1897, but he declined, pleading a busy schedule and prior commitments. The real reason for his absence and lack of involvement was his recognition that the major founders and early leaders of the academy—especially Crummell—were sharply critical of his educational theories, particularly his stress on industrial training as the best education for the majority of his race, and of his willingness to compromise with prominent white racists in both the South and the North.

Between 1897 and 1924, the ANA published twenty-two "Occasional Papers" on subjects related to the culture, history, religion, civil and social rights, and social institutions of African Americans. The process of choosing who would be invited to present papers at academy meetings and selecting which of the talks delivered would be printed as Occasional Papers was managed by the executive committee, a body composed of the president, first vice president, corresponding secretary, recording secretary, and treasurer. Although the quality of the papers varied, all of them illuminate the many ways in which, during the first quarter of the twentieth century, an important segment of the small community of educated American blacks attempted intellectually to defend their people, justify their own existence, and challenge ideas, habits, attitudes, and legal proscriptions that seemed to be locking their race permanently into an "inferior caste" (Moss, 1981, p. 2).

Throughout its existence, the ANA was preoccupied with survival. As a result, its officers and members were forced to put as much energy into keeping the organization alive as they did into conducting its programs. And yet the society survived for thirty-one years, functioning as a setting in which members and friends shared their intellectual and scholarly work with each other and engaged in critical reflection on it. Through annual meetings, Occasional Papers, exhibits, and the public interest they generated, the ANA was able to initiate dialogues in both the black and white communities that were important contributions to a growing discussion in the United States, Africa, and Europe about race and the relationship between blacks and whites; to introduce the concerns and opinions of educated blacks into quarters where previously they had been ignored or gone unnoticed; and to encourage the growing pride among African Americans in their culture and history.

The American Negro Academy was both a sustainer and a perpetuator of the black protest tradition in an age of accommodation and proscription. By functioning as a source of affirmation and encouragement for an important segment of the black intelligentsia and as a setting in which they could seek to understand the meaning of the African-American experience, it was a model for other and sometimes more successful black organizations founded after 1897 that engaged in similar work or attempted to realize goals that the ANA found unattainable. Perhaps most important, for its active members, the academy's various programs and activities and the interactions they promoted formed a dynamic process in which participants began to free themselves from the entanglements and confusions of ideas and theories that made them feel insecure about their own worth, ashamed of the history and condition of blacks, and doubtful of their race's future possibilities. By strengthening and adding to the intellectual autonomy and insight of its members, the academy helped to prepare them for more informed, honest dialogue with each other, with blacks in the United States and other parts of the world, and, when they would listen, with whites.

See also Crummell, Alexander; Du Bois, W. E. B.; Grimké, Francis James; Harlem Renaissance; Hope, John; Johnson, James Weldon; Locke, Alain Leroy; Washington, Booker T.; Woodson, Carter G.

Bibliography

Meier, August. *Negro Thought in America, 1880–1915.* Ann Arbor: University of Michigan Press, 1968.

Moss, Alfred A., Jr. *The American Negro Academy: Voice of the Talented Tenth.* Baton Rouge: Louisiana State University Press, 1981.

ALFRED A. MOSS JR. (1996)

American Negro Theatre

The American Negro Theatre (ANT) was founded in the Harlem section of New York City in 1940 by Abram Hill, a writer, and Frederick O'Neal, an actor. Their goal was to establish a community-based theater to provide opportunities for black theater artists, much as the Negro Units of the Federal Theatre Project had done before they were discontinued by Congress in 1939.

The theater was incorporated as a cooperative, and all members shared in expenses and profits, reflecting the theater's policy of emphasizing an ensemble style of acting rather than individual stars. Some officers were paid part-time salaries for their work through a Rockefeller Foundation grant, but most workers donated their time. Those who also performed outside the company paid 2 percent of their earnings to help keep ANT solvent. In 1942 Hill and O'Neal established the ANT Studio Theatre (the first black theater institution sanctioned by the New York State Board of Education) to train a new generation of black theater artists.

From 1940 through 1949, ANT produced nineteen plays, twelve of which were new. ANT's biggest success was *Anna Lucasta* (1944), but the production also sowed the seeds of the company's eventual failure. Based on a play by Philip Yordan about a Polish-American family, Hill and director Harry Gribble Wagstaff adapted it for a black cast. After a five-week run at ANT's theater in the 135th Street branch of the New York Public Library, it moved to Broadway, where it played for two years, becoming the longest-running black drama in Broadway history. A national tour and a film followed, but ANT received no royalties from these, and only a small one from the Broadway production. In addition, the fact that only a few actors from the Harlem production were used on Broadway caused discord within the company, some of whose members became more interested in performing on Broadway than in Harlem. *Anna Lucasta* brought many critics to Harlem to see subsequent ANT productions, but their critical judgments were based on Broadway standards. The ANT seemed to change its standards as well, straying further and further from its original mission as a community-based theater. After 1945 it produced plays by theater playwrights only, such as Sean O'Casey's *Juno and the Paycock* (1945–1946), George Kaufman and Moss Hart's *You Can't Take It With You* (1945–1946), and John Synge's *Riders to the Sea* (1948–1949). Although ANT transferred three more plays to Broadway, they were not financially successful. With growing financial problems in the late 1940s, the ANT lacked the finances to mount complete productions. They turned, instead, to producing inexpensive variety shows and by 1949 had ceased production entirely.

A number of prominent black actors and writers began their careers in American Negro Theatre productions or in the Studio school. They include Ruby Dee, Lofton Mitchell, Alice Childress, Earl Hyman, Sidney Poitier, and Harry Belafonte.

See also Childress, Alice; Drama

Bibliography

Durham, Weldon, ed. *American Theatre Companies, 1931–1986.* New York: Greenwood Press, 1989.

Hill, Errol G., and James V. Hatch. *A History of African American Theatre.* Cambridge, UK: Cambridge University Press, 2003.

Walker, Ethel Pitts. "The American Negro Theatre." In *The Theater of Black Americans,* edited by Errol Hill. Englewood Cliffs, N.J.: Prentice-Hall, 1980.

MICHAEL PALLER (1996)
Updated bibliography

American Tennis Association

The American Tennis Association (ATA) is the oldest continuously operated noncollegiate black sports organization in the United States—although it was not the first organization to offer opportunities for black tennis players. Sometime in the late nineteenth century (the date is uncertain), the Monumental Tennis Club, now called the Baltimore Tennis Club, had been formed to give blacks a venue in which to complete. Then in the spring of 1916 the ATA was formed by prominent African Americans in Washington, D.C., and Baltimore to provide encouragement, information, and tournaments for black tennis players. The attendees at the organizational meeting were Henry Freeman, John F. N. Wilkinson, Talley Holmes, H. Stanton McCard, William H. Wright, B. M. Rhetta, and Ralph Cook. Cook's brother, Charles, was one of the first coaches at Howard University.

The ATA listed four goals that are still followed today: to develop the sport among blacks, to spur the formation of clubs and the building of courts, to encourage and develop junior players, and to foster the formation of local associations. The ATA's first national championships, hosted by the Monumental Tennis Club, were held at Druid Hill Park in Baltimore in August 1917; twenty-three clubs sent thirty-nine entrants for the men's singles, won by Talley Holmes. Women's singles were added the following year, when Lucy Diggs Slowe became the first titleholder and the first black female national champion in any sport.

In the 1920s and 1930s the ATA concentrated on enlarging its summer tournament schedule to provide competitive opportunities for its members. Black college stars at white universities came out of the ATA-inspired programs: Henry Graham at Michigan, Richard Hudlin at the University of Chicago, Reginald Weir at the City College of New York, and Douglas Turner at the University of Illinois. In 1929 the ATA and the sport's white governing body, the United States Tennis Association (USTA), had a confrontation over the rejection of two players, Reginald Weir and Gerald Norman, from the USTA Junior Indoors tournament. The USTA had an unwritten rule that blacks could not participate in tournaments, and when Weir and Norman were barred, the NAACP made a formal complaint to the USTA. While the NAACP had rarely taken a stand on discrimination in sports during the period, it played a role in the USTA dispute because tennis was a middle-class sport with an avid following in the NAACP's professional constituency.

Black women's tennis during the 1920s and 1930s was not dominated by a single player. In the first twenty years of the ATA's existence, however, there were only five different female winners: Lucy Slowe, M. Rae, Isadore Channels, Lulu Ballard, and Ora Washington. Channels and Washington dominated the tournaments, with Channels winning four ATA national titles (1922, 1923, 1924, 1926) and Washington winning a record eight (each year from 1929 to 1935 and 1937). Washington was unorthodox in her approach to the game; she held the racquet high up on the handle, hardly ever took a full swing, and had unsurpassed foot speed. She maintained her championship standing until 1936, when Lulu Ballard defeated her. Into the 1940s and 1950s other outstanding players included singles champion Flora Lomax (titleholder in 1938, 1939, 1941, and 1942) and the team of Margaret and Roumania Peters, who won the ATA women's doubles crown a record fourteen times (each year from 1938 to 1941 and from 1944 to 1953).

The depression of the 1930s posed many advantages and many challenges for tennis players. The decade saw an expansion of tennis facilities under President Franklin D. Roosevelt's Works Project Administration (WPA), including the addition of park courts in black neighborhoods. However, the economic hardships of the 1930s left many people without the resources to spend time playing or watching tennis.

One stronghold of tennis activity during the period was in black colleges, which always had a close relationship with the ATA. Many ATA members were college professors or administrators, and tennis was the most popular participant sport among black female professionals. One early ATA member was R. Walter Johnson, who played football at Lincoln University. He directed the organization's junior development program, which began in the early 1940s and produced tennis champion Althea Gibson. Cleveland Abbott, Tuskegee University's famed athletic director, was an ATA president. In 1937 the ATA arranged an exhibition tour by its best players at eight high schools and twenty-one colleges.

When racial integration of professional sports began between 1946 and 1950, the ATA adjusted quickly, since acceptance into USTA events was slow for blacks. The ATA and the USTA had an arrangement beginning in 1951 whereby the ATA nominated the black players to compete in the USTA nationals. Sixteen-year-old Arthur Ashe was a nominated player in 1959. The ATA provided indispensable competition for the best black players until the early 1970s, when all racial restrictions were lifted. Blacks nurtured through ATA events captured nearly seventy USTA national junior and senior titles.

The ATA, headquartered in Silver Spring, Maryland, continues to sponsor training programs for young players and to conduct regional championships. Its National Championships remains a highlight of the African-American summer sports schedule.

See also Tennis

Bibliography

Ashe, Arthur. *A Hard Road to Glory: A History of the African-American Athlete, 1919–1945.* New York: Warner Books, 1988.

ARTHUR R. ASHE JR. (1996)
Updated by publisher 2005

AMISTAD MUTINY

The *Amistad* mutiny was a rebellion of African captives that occurred off the northern coast of Cuba in July 1839. The mutineers had been seized in Africa, herded onto a Portuguese slave ship along with hundreds of others, and then transported illegally from the African island of Lombokor to Cuba (then a Spanish colony). Upon reaching Havana, the Africans were smuggled ashore under cover of night, in violation of an 1817 treaty between England and Spain that prohibited the slave trade. Fifty-three captives—forty-nine adult males, three girls, and a boy—were sold to two Spaniards, José Ruiz and Pedro Montes; they were then shipped along the Cuban coast to Puerto Príncipe aboard the Spanish schooner *La Amistad.*

On July 1–2, 1839, just a few days after the *Amistad* set sail, the captured Africans rose up in revolt. Led by Sengbe Pieh (or Joseph Cinqué), they freed themselves from their irons and launched an armed assault against their captors, killing the ship's captain and cook. Several

Death of Capt. Ferrer, the Captain of the Amistad, July, 1839.
Don Jose Ruiz and Don Pedro Montez, of the Island of Cuba, having purchased fifty-three slaves at Havana, recently imported from Africa, put them on board the Amistad, Capt. Ferrer, in order to transport them to Principe, another port on the Island of Cuba. After being out from Havana about four days, the African captives on board, in order to obtain their freedom, and return to Africa, armed themselves with cane knives, and rose upon the Captain and crew of the vessel. Capt. Ferrer and the cook of the vessel were killed; two of the crew escaped; Ruiz and Montez were made prisoners.

The death of Captain Ferrer aboard the slave ship* Amistad, *July 1839. *As slaveowners Don Ruiz and Don Pedro Montez look on in horror, captives aboard the* Amistad *kill the ship's captain.* CORBIS

crew members disappeared, and one African was killed in the fray. The mutineers spared Ruiz and Montes, ordering them to sail the ship back to Africa. The Spaniards, however, maintained a meandering northerly course that, by late August, brought the ship to New York state waters.

On August 25, the Africans, desperate from hunger and thirst, anchored the now-bedraggled *Amistad* off the coast of Long Island in New York to search for provisions. But they had been spotted by the crew of the USS *Washington;* after a show of resistance, they surrendered to the ship's commanders and were towed to New London, Connecticut. They were shortly afterward taken to New Haven, where they languished in jail while awaiting a hearing on their case. So began an ordeal for the "Mendians" (many of the Africans had come from Mende) that lasted for more than two years.

The *Amistad* case attracted widespread attention along the Atlantic seaboard, and even on an international scale. Ruiz and Montes insisted that the Africans had already been slaves in Cuba at the time of purchase and were therefore legal property; as such, they could be tried on charges of piracy and murder. Cuban and Spanish authorities demanded the return of the ship and its surviving human "cargo"—thirty-nine adults and the four children. But abolitionists mobilized in defense of the mutineers, hoping to prove that they had been unlawfully enslaved and should therefore be set free. Some antislavery advocates sought to use the case to demonstrate that the principle of natural rights applied to black people.

The *Amistad* Committee, composed of such prominent abolitionists as Lewis Tappan, Joshua Leavitt, and Simeon Jocelyn, launched a vigorous campaign to raise funds for the defense. They also succeeded in generating substantial public sympathy for the defendants, even among many who did not oppose the institution of slavery itself. Activists located two African-born seamen, James Covey and Charles Pratt, who were able to communicate with the prisoners, including the undisputed leader, Cinqué. The Africans were sketched by artists and displayed on speaking tours; models of them were made and sent along to sites where they could not personally appear. They were also taught English and instructed in Christianity. Throughout the prolonged period of litigation that followed their arrest, the case was hotly debated in the press.

Thousands of onlookers converged on Hartford, Connecticut, when the U.S. Circuit Court convened in September 1839. The court refused to release the captives and remanded the case to the U.S. District Court. It was not until January 1840 that a ruling was issued. Judge Andrew T. Judson determined that the Africans had indeed been illegally kidnapped and sold, and that they had legitimately rebelled to win back their freedom. At the same time, he upheld the institution of slavery by ordering the return to Cuba of Antonio, who actually had been a slave of the slain *Amistad* captain. Judson also ordered the return of the mutineers to Africa.

The U.S. government, under the administration of President Martin Van Buren, had been expecting a verdict that would uphold its own position: that the Africans should be returned to Spain under Pinckney's Treaty of 1795. A naval vessel, the USS *Grampus,* was anchored in New London harbor, waiting to spirit the Africans out of the country and back to Cuba before the abolitionist forces could appeal the ruling. But now it was the government that filed an appeal. After Judson's decision was upheld in May 1840, the *Amistad* case was sent to the U.S. Supreme Court.

A majority of the Court were southerners who had been slave owners at one time, including Chief Justice Roger B. Taney. The *Amistad* Committee was able to secure the services of John Quincy Adams, former president of the United States, who argued the case before the Court. In March 1841, the Court delivered its opinion, affirming the original ruling by an eight-to-one margin. The *Amistad* mutineers were free. Antonio, at risk of being sent back to Cuba, was transported secretly to Canada via the Underground Railroad, while the *Amistad* Committee set about raising private funds to return the remaining Africans to their homeland.

On November 27, 1841, thirty-five Africans (the others had died while imprisoned in Connecticut), along with the translator James Covey and five white missionaries, left New York for Sierra Leone. Traveling with protection from the British, they reached Africa in mid-January 1842. Little is known of Cinqué after his repatriation—according to some accounts, he died some time around 1879—but he remains one of the leading symbols of resistance to the Atlantic slave trade. Although the Spanish government demanded reparations, their effort was hampered by sectional divisions within the U.S. Congress and was eventually abandoned with the coming of the U.S. Civil War.

See also Slave Trade; Slavery; Slavery and the Constitution

Bibliography

Amistad. Directed by Steven Spielberg. DreamWorks Pictures, 1997.

Barber, John Warner. *A History of the* Amistad *Captives.* New Haven, Conn.: Barber, 1840. Reprint, New York: Arno Press, 1969.

Cable, Mary. *Black Odyssey: The Case of the Slave Ship* Amistad. New York: Viking, 1971.

Jones, Howard. *Mutiny on the* Amistad: *The Saga of a Slave Revolt and Its Impact on American Abolition, Law, and Diplomacy.* New York: Oxford University Press, 1987.

McClendon, R. Earl. "The Amistad Claims: Inconsistencies of Policy." *Political Science Quarterly* 48 (1933): 386-412.

Osagie, Iyunolu Folayan. *The* Amistad *Revolt: Memory, Slavery, and the Politics of Identity in the United States and Sierra Leone.* Athens: University of Georgia Press, 2000.

ROBERT L. HALL (1996)
Updated bibliography

Anastácia

c. 1740s
UNKNOWN

There are numerous variations of Anastácia's life story, but the most detailed goes as follows: On April 9, 1740, the slave ship *Madalena* arrived in Bahia from Angola with 112 slaves on board. Among these newly arrived Africans was a woman named Delminda. Some years after her arrival, Delminda's master raped her, and upon discovering that she was pregnant, sold her away to the town of Pompeu in Minas Gerais. Delminda's daughter, Anastácia, was born with blue eyes and was widely recognized as beautiful. As Anastácia grew up, her master's son made numerous sexual overtures toward her, even offering her money to sleep with him.

After steadfastly refusing the boy's advances and fighting him off on several occasions, Anastácia was outfitted with an iron collar and a leather mask in order to make her acquiescent. This mask and iron collar were a common form of punishment in Brazil, particularly for runaway slaves. The mask was also utilized to prevent slaves from eating dirt, a common response to nutritional deficiency. Anastácia was tortured and raped, and the mask was removed only when it was time for her to eat. Suffering great pain and infection from the iron collar digging into her flesh, Anastácia maintained a quiet dignity throughout her ordeals. Eventually she was carried to Rio de Janeiro, where she died in agony on an uncertain date, still wearing the mask. Supposedly, she was buried in Igreja do Rosário in Rio de Janeiro, but her remains disappeared when the church was destroyed by fire.

In his ethnographic study of devotion to Anastácia, John Burdick has shown that veneration of a masked, collared female slave dates back until at least the 1940s, especially in Minas Gerais. The legend of Anastácia, which apparently was passed down through oral history in the years following her death, was exposed to a broader Brazilian audience beginning in the early 1970s. In 1968, the Museum of the Negro, an annex of the Igreja do Rosário in Rio de Janeiro, opened an exposition commemorating the eightieth anniversary of abolition. In order to illustrate methods of slave torture, an etching by the French traveler and artist Jacques Arago was included in the exposition. The exposition received little notice until 1971, when the remains of Princess Isabel, the "great liberator" of Brazil's slaves, were brought from Portugal. Before being taken to Petrópolis for burial, Isabel's coffin was put on display at the Museum of the Negro. Thousands arrived at the museum to pay their respects. Upon seeing the Arago etching, people immediately associated it with the Anastácia of oral tradition. Ironically, Arago's original drawing was intended to depict a young man punished for running away from his enslavement. Arago's intentions aside, Brazilians were inspired by what they interpreted as a visual representation of the mythical Anastácia.

The oral tradition was quickly transcribed and published by a vanity press. The Brazilian media also eagerly consumed her story. As newspapers, radio, and television presented versions of Anastácia's life history, spiritual devotion to her spread throughout the country. By the mid-1980s, Anastácia claimed thousands of adherents who publicly recited her miracles. In 1984 her supporters circumvented official channels and appealed directly to the pope for Anastácia's canonization. Alarmed by Anastácia's growing popularity, Brazilian cardinal Dom Eugênio hired a historian to research whether Anastácia ever truly existed. After two years of research, the Church's historian determined that there was no evidence to support the existence of Anastácia. As a result of this ruling, Cardinal Dom Eugênio ruled that all objects related to the devotion of Anastácia must be removed from the Igreja do Rosário. Thus, the cardinal squashed any hopes that Anastácia would be accepted into church orthodoxy.

Despite the church's denial of Anastácia's historical existence, her adherents, especially black women, continue to maintain their devotion to her. The majority of these women believe that Anastácia was not of mixed ancestry but rather was a beautiful African woman. As a symbol of black phenotypical beauty, resistance to white and male power, and ultimate forgiveness, Anastácia represents a node of historical familiarity and temporal strength for Brazil's black women. By the mid-1990s there were four pilgrimage sites in Rio de Janeiro that attracted hundreds of people daily. Moreover, images and icons of Anastácia are widely available, thereby facilitating individual devotion. Some estimates claim that she has as many as twenty-eight million adherents.

See also Slavery

Bibliography

Burdick, John. *Blessed Anastácia: Women, Race, and Popular Christianity in Brazil.* New York: Routledge, 1998.

Handler, Jerome S., and Michael L. Tuite, Jr. "The Atlantic Slave Trade and Slave Life in the Americas: A Visual Record." Available from <http://hitchcock.itc.virginia.edu/Slavery/details.php?filename=NW0191>.

Oliveira, Eduardo de, ed. "Escravo Anastácia." In *Quem é quem na negritude brasileira, biografias*, vol. 1. São Paulo: Congresso Nacional Afro-Brasileiro, 1998, pp. 102–103.

JAMES H. SWEET (2005)

Anderson, Marian

February 17, 1897
May 19, 1993

Opera and concert singer Marian Anderson, a contralto of international repute, may be best remembered as the first African American to sing at the Metropolitan Opera Company. She grew up in Philadelphia, where her family members were active as musicians at the Union Baptist Church. An interest in singing was stimulated by her participation in the church choirs, and she began local solo performances by the age of ten, singing professionally while still in high school. Initial venues, in addition to her church, included the Philadelphia Choral Society, New York's Martin-Smith School of Music, the National Association of Negro Musicians (which in 1921 awarded her its first scholarship), the NAACP, the National Baptist Convention, schools, and various regional organizations.

Anderson's formal recital debut, at Town Hall in New York in 1922, was not a success, obligating further study. In 1925 she won a vocal competition that granted her a successful performance with the New York Philharmonic at Lewisohn Stadium, but the major appearances that followed were initially in Scandinavia. Her Parisian debut, in 1935, was attended by Sol Hurok, who then became her manager. That summer she won the notice of a distinguished audience at a private recital in Salzburg, Austria; in December she presented a Town Hall recital, this one well received.

Anderson's international acclaim encouraged Howard University in 1939 to seek a recital for her in Washington, D.C. When she was denied access for racial reasons to Constitution Hall by the Daughters of the American Revolution, the public protest approached that of a scandal. Eleanor Roosevelt resigned her DAR membership, and criticism came from opera singer Lawrence Tibbett, New York Mayor Fiorello La Guardia, conductor Leopold Stokowski, and other major figures. Secretary of the Interior Harold Ickes granted Anderson use of the Lincoln Memorial for an Easter Sunday concert as an alternative. Seventy-five thousand people heard her program, which began in subtle irony with "My Country 'Tis of Thee" and ended with "Nobody Knows the Trouble I've Seen." The location for this performance was not forgotten nearly a quarter of a century later by the Rev. Dr. Martin Luther King, Jr., who arranged for her to sing there again during the 1963 March on Washington.

Anderson's tour schedule intensified, and Metropolitan Opera manager Rudolph Bing determined that she would appear as Ulrica in Verdi's *Un Ballo in Maschera.*

She sang the role eight times, starting on January 7, 1955, although she was no longer in her prime. (In 1958 RCA Victor issued a recording of highlights from the opera with Dimitri Mitropoulos conducting and Anderson in the role of Ulrica.) She retired from the stage at Carnegie Hall on Easter Day 1965, after presenting fifty-one farewell concerts across the country. Her repertory was centered on sacred arias by J. S. Bach and Handel, spirituals (especially Harry Burleigh's "Deep River"), lieder (Schubert's "Ave Maria" was a favorite), and some opera arias—notably "O Mio Fernando" from Donizetti's *La Favorita,* in which she demonstrated that, given the chance, she could have excelled in bel canto roles. When granted the Bok Award in 1940, Anderson established a scholarship fund for vocalists whose awards have been granted to McHenry Boatwright, Grace Bumbry, Gloria Davy, Reri Grist, Bonia Hyman, Louise Parker, Rawn Spearman, Camellia Williams, and others.

Her primary voice teacher was Giuseppe Boghetti, although she worked in London with Amanda Aldridge, a daughter of the actor Ira Aldridge. Early in her career she was accompanied by minstrel pianist William King, then by Kosti Vehanen from Finland, and later by Franz Rupp of Germany. Anderson was appointed in 1958 to the U.S. delegation to the United Nations, where she spoke on behalf of the independence of African nations. Although she denied playing an overt role in the civil rights movement, Anderson's dignity and artistry brought about social change and opened the door for the many concert singers who followed her. In tribute on her seventy-fifth birthday in Carnegie Hall, Leontyne Price paid her respects succinctly: "Dear Marian Anderson, because of you, I am."

See also Aldridge, Ira; Burleigh, Harry; National Association of Negro Musicians

Bibliography

Anderson, Marian. *My Lord, What a Morning: An Autobiography.* New York: Viking Press, 1956.

Newman, Shirlee Petkin. *Marian Anderson, Lady from Philadelphia.* Philadelphia: Westminster Press, 1965.

Sims, Janet L. *Marian Anderson: An Annotated Bibliography and Discography.* Westport, Conn.: Greenwood Press, 1981.

DOMINIQUE-RENÉ DE LERMA (1996)

Angelou, Maya

April 4, 1928

Born Marguerite Annie Johnson on April 4, 1928, to Vivian Baxter and Bailey Johnson in St. Louis, Missouri, writer Maya Angelou was raised in Stamps, Arkansas, by her grandmother, Anne Henderson. She related her experience of growing up in her popular autobiography *I Know Why the Caged Bird Sings* (1970), a title taken from the poetry of Paul Laurence Dunbar. It was nominated for a National Book Award. Like many African-American autobiographers, Angelou saw herself not only as an individual but as a representative of black people.

What *Caged Bird* contributed to the tradition of African-American autobiography was its emphasis on the effects of growing up black and female in the South. Angelou writes of the rape of the protagonist by her mother's boyfriend. Until the late twentieth century, intragroup rape and incest were taboo subjects in African-American literature; *Caged Bird* helped to break that silence. Her second biography, *Gather Together in My Name* (1974), a title taken from the Bible, focuses on the vulnerable Angelou's entry into the harsh urban world of Los Angeles, while her third autobiography, *Singin' & Swingin' & Gettin' Merry Like Christmas* (1976), relates the experience of her first marriage and of raising her son while pursuing her singing, dancing, and acting career.

The fourth autobiography, *The Heart of a Woman* (1981), a title taken from a poem by Harlem Renaissance poet Georgia Douglas Johnson, presents a mature Angelou who works with the Rev. Dr. Martin Luther King, Jr., and Malcolm X. Active in the civil rights movement, she served as northern coordinator for the Southern Christian Leadership Conference in 1959–1960. In her fifth autobiography, *All God's Children Need Traveling Shoes* (1986), Angelou goes to Ghana, where she experiences the complexity of being an African American in Africa. She also wrote a volume of inspirational essays, *Wouldn't Take Nothing for My Journey Now* (1993). Her sixth book in her autobiography series, *A Song Flung Up to Heaven* (2003), tells the story of Angelou's return from Africa to the United States. In this book Angelou describes the civil rights movement in the United States and recounts poignant stories about the assassinations of Malcolm X and Dr. Martin Luther King, Jr. Angelou turned this book into a series of four CDs in which she chants, sings, and vocalizes the stories of her life. In 2003 Angelou won a Grammy Award for Best Spoken Word Album for *A Song Flung Up to Heaven.*

Angelou has also published many volumes of poetry: *Just Give Me a Cool Drink of Water 'fore I Diiie* (1971), which was nominated for a Pulitzer Prize; *Oh Pray My Wings Are Gonna Fit Me Well* (1975); *And Still I Rise* (1978); *Shaker Why Don't You Sing?* (1983); *Now Sheba Sings the Song* (1987); and *I Shall Not Be Moved* (1990). As these titles indicate, Angelou's poetry is deeply rooted in the African-American oral tradition and is uplifting in tone. Angelou says, "All my work is meant to say 'You may encounter many defeats but you must not be defeated.'"

A versatile writer, Angelou has written for television: the PBS ten-part series *Black, Blues, Blacks* (1968); a teleplay of *Caged Bird;* and for the screen, *Georgia Georgia* (1971) and *Sister, Sister* (1979). As well as being a prolific writer, Angelou has been a successful actress and received a Tony nomination for best supporting actress in the TV miniseries *Roots.* In 1998 she directed her first film, *Down in the Delta.* Angelou says of her creative diversity, "I believe all things are possible for a human being and I don't think there's anything in the world I can't do." On January 20, 1993, at the request of President Bill Clinton, Angelou concluded the president's inauguration by reading a poem composed for the occasion, "On the Pulse of Morning," which celebrated a new era of national unity.

See also Civil Rights Movement, U.S.; Dunbar, Paul Laurence; Harlem Renaissance; King, Martin Luther, Jr.; Malcolm X; Southern Christian Leadership Conference (SCLC)

Bibliography

Cudjoe, Selwyn R. "Maya Angelou and the Autobiographical Statement." In *Black Women Writers (1950–1980),* edited by Mari Evans. New York: Anchor, 1984.

Maya Angelou, interview in Claudia Tate, ed. *Black Women Writers at Work.* New York: Continuum, 1983.

BARBARA T. CHRISTIAN (1996)
Updated by publisher 2005

Anglo-African, The

The *Weekly Anglo-African* newspaper and the *Anglo-African* magazine were perhaps the most influential African-American journals of the late 1850s and the Civil War era. They were unique in that they served as forums for debate rather than simply reflecting the views of the publisher. They were owned by the journalist Thomas Hamilton (1823–1865), the son of New York City community leader William Hamilton. He and his brother Robert were the editors.

The *Weekly Anglo-African,* whose first issue was dated July 23, 1859, was a four-page weekly, with seven columns of large type to a page. It cost four cents per copy, with a yearly subscription price of two dollars. Its motto was "Man must be free; if not through the law, then above the law." Unlike most black newspapers of the time, which published only a few issues before folding, the paper was an almost immediate success. It came to be respected for its sophisticated analysis of issues such as violent resistance to slavery, the ramifications of the *Dred Scott* Decision, and John Brown's Raid.

The *Anglo-African* magazine, a thirty-two-page monthly with a yearly subscription price of one dollar, began on January 1, 1859. It was one of the first illustrated African-American publications. Its prospectus proclaimed that the magazine was devoted to the cause of literature, science, statistics, and the advancement of the cause of freedom. Among its other features were biographies of outstanding figures such as actor Ira Aldridge, evaluations of the abolitionist cause, comic prose, and fiction.

Many leading black writers and abolitionists, including Martin R. Delany, Frances Ellen Watkins Harper, J. W. C. Pennington, and James Theodore Holly, were frequent contributors to the journals. Other luminaries, such as Frederick Douglass, William Cooper Nell, Mary Ann Shadd Cary, Daniel Payne, and John Mercer Langston, wrote occasional pieces. The *Anglo-African* magazine, and later the *Weekly Anglo-African,* serialized Delaney's novel *Blake: or, The Huts of America,* one of the first African-American novels (it was not printed in book form until 1970). Hamilton also was a book publisher. His list included such books as Robert Campbell's *A Pilgrimage to My Motherland: An Account of a Journey among the Egbas and Yorubas of Central Africa, 1859–1860* (1861) and William Wells Brown's *The Black Man: His Antecedents, His Genius, and His Achievements* (1863).

By early 1860, despite their critical success, the Hamiltons developed severe financial problems. The *Anglo-African* magazine ceased publication, and they sold the *Weekly Anglo-African* to James Redpath, a prominent white abolitionist and emigrationist. By fall 1861 they had regained control, with Robert Hamilton handling the business affairs. The radical abolitionist Henry Highland Garnet, named "Editor of the Southern Department," reported on events in Washington. During the Civil War, the paper covered war news and carried messages from black soldiers. Hamilton became a fervent supporter of the Republican Party, although he remained critical of northern discrimination. On March 29, 1862, he warned that northern prejudice was a "strong impediment" to black advancement. Hamilton and Garnet called for citizenship and proper education for freedmen. On September 9, 1865, in one of the paper's last issues, Hamilton praised and defended northern black teachers who went south, claiming such work was blacks' chief responsibility and greatest service. The newspaper folded in December 1865.

See also Hamilton, William

Bibliography

Bullock, Penelope. *The Afro-American Periodical Press, 1838–1909.* Baton Rouge: Louisiana State University Press, 1981.

Hutton, Frankie. *The Early Black Press in America, 1827–1860.* Westport, Conn.: Greenwood, 1993.

Penn, Irving Garland. *The Afro American Press and Its Editors* (1891). Salem, N.H., 1988.

GREG ROBINSON (1996)

Antebellum Convention Movement

The antebellum convention movement consisted of a series of national, regional, and state conventions held by blacks in North America on an irregular basis from 1830 to 1861. The movement began in the 1830s and revealed the growing consensus among northern free blacks on the importance of moral reform. Six annual conventions, held from 1830 to 1835, were the first attempts by African Americans to address their concerns on a national level. Samuel E. Cornish (1795–1858), editor of *Freedom's Journal,* and others had called for a national gathering on several occasions, but it was the threatened enforcement of the Ohio black laws in 1829 and the revival of the African colonization movement that provoked the first national convention.

Several state laws restricted black civil rights in Ohio, including a requirement that all blacks register and post a $500 security bond or leave the state. When Cincinnati officials called for rigorous enforcement of this provision in 1829 and the city experienced an antiblack riot the following year, blacks in Ohio and other northern states feared a new wave of legal and extralegal racial oppression. Northern free blacks were also alarmed by the rapid growth of the American Colonization Society and its state auxiliaries in the late 1820s. The white-sponsored society, founded in 1816, sought to colonize free black Americans in Africa and vigorously lobbied federal and state governments for financial support.

In response to the Ohio crisis and colonizationist activities, forty blacks from nine states, including Virginia, Maryland, and Delaware, met at Philadelphia in September 1830. Fearful of local white hostility to the assembly, the delegates held the first five days of sessions in secret. The delegates focused on Canadian emigration as a possible solution to the tandem threat posed by state black laws and forced resettlement in Africa. At the 1831 convention, after the crisis in Ohio had abated and the need to organize a black exodus to Canada seemed less urgent, moral reform emerged as the predominant issue. White abolitionists who attended the conventions encouraged the delegates to direct their attention to moral reform. William Lloyd Garrison, Arthur Tappan, and Simeon S. Jocelyn addressed the 1831 convention. Following their recommendations, the convention accepted a proposal for a manual-labor school in New Haven. The national conventions recognized temperance as a principal component of moral reform, and at the 1833 convention, a committee on temperance recommended the establishment of a national auxiliary—the Coloured American Temperance Society.

From the beginning, the convention movement was marred by personal and intercity rivalries. New York and Philadelphia delegates quarreled over procedural questions as well as issues of substance. Much time at the conventions was given over to formulating admission policies, certifying delegates, and appointing committees. These procedural disagreements revealed not just an intercity rivalry but, more profoundly, the problem of national leadership. Many who attended the conventions had questionable credentials, representing themselves and little else.

The conventions of the 1830s were reserved, even circumspect, in their official pronouncements. To protest the injustice of slavery and racial prejudice, the 1831 convention recommended "a day of fasting and prayer." The following year the convention agreed to establish provisional state committees, but cautiously added "where the same may be safely done." The 1834 convention condemned public demonstrations by blacks as "vain expenditures" of time and resources, serving only to incite racial prejudice.

Philadelphia delegates had the resources, organization, and leadership to dominate the 1830s convention movement (five of the six conventions were held in that city), and their interest in moral reform eventually prevailed. Led by William Whipper (1804–1876), the Philadelphia delegation turned the 1835 convention into a founding meeting of the American Moral Reform Society, an interracial organization committed to the principles of moral reform.

The antebellum convention movement underwent a profound transition in the 1840s, expanding to include numerous state and regional gatherings. Several conventions focused on single issues, such as temperance, Christian missions, and emigration. The national convention sites—including Buffalo (1843), Troy, N.Y. (1847), Cleveland (1848), and Rochester, N.Y. (1853)—marked the geographical shift away from the Atlantic coastal cities. A new generation of black leaders, many of them former slaves, came forward to claim positions of leadership in the convention movement. Frederick Douglass (1818–1895), Henry Highland Garnet (1815–1882), James McCune Smith (1813–1865), and others sought to imbue the movement with a more practical outlook and a militant, independent spirit. Racial progress through moral reform, the staple of the conventions of the previous decade, was subsumed by the call for more forceful tactics and political action.

Not all black leaders welcomed a renewal of the convention movement. Those who held to strict integrationist principles counseled against convening separate black assemblies or establishing racially separate organizations. Others considered it wasteful of time and scarce resources to revisit the well-worn, intractable issues debated at past conventions. But most blacks favored continuing the convention process. The disagreements, often intense, centered mainly on form, agenda, and leadership.

David Ruggles's (1810–1849) revival of the national convention movement at New Haven in 1840 and New York City in 1841 attracted only a few delegates. Poor organization, vague objectives, and editorial opposition from the *Colored American* contributed to the dismal outcome. Henry Highland Garnet had more success in promoting the 1843 national convention in Buffalo. This convention set a new tenor for the movement with Garnet's controversial call for slave insurrection (disapproved by a narrow majority of the assembly) and the heated discussion of a resolution endorsing the Liberty Party. The 1847 and 1848 national conventions (in Troy and Cleveland, respectively) highlighted the theme of black independence. James McCune Smith and Frederick Douglass addressed the delegates on the symbolic and practical need for self-reliance and independent black initiatives. These insightful speeches on independence and racial identity affirmed their reputation as two of the leading black intellectuals of the antebellum period.

Just as in the 1830s, these later national conventions served primarily as a forum for competing ideas and leadership. The delegates approved plans for a national black press, an industrial-arts college, and other proposals of a practical nature. But without adequate resources, none of these objectives could be achieved. The conventions also sought continuity through the establishment of a permanent national organization. In the early 1840s, Ruggles anticipated the need for a national body with the short-lived American Reform Board of Disfranchised Commissioners. By the 1850s, however, even racial assimilationists like Douglass and Smith had come to accept the idea of a separate black national organization. Douglass promoted this as part of an ambitious agenda for the 1853 national convention in Rochester.

The Rochester convention marked the high point of the antebellum convention movement. Over 160 representatives from ten northern states attended. The convention established the National Council of the Colored People, a major advance in black organization, even if it suffered from a contentious leadership and lack of popular support. The council faded quietly after the 1855 convention at Philadelphia—the last national convocation before the Civil War. The Philadelphia convention was lackluster and unproductive in comparison with the previous meeting in Rochester. Dominated by the seventy-member Pennsylvania delegation, the convention deferred substantial issues and engaged in a lively debate on procedural questions, particularly the propriety of seating a woman delegate, Mary Ann Shadd Cary (1823–1893).

Several conventions in the 1850s reflected the growing pessimism among African Americans. As hopes faded for racial progress in the United States, a black emigration movement gained increasing support. The North American Convention (1851) reflected the growth and growing influence of black communities in Canada West (modern Ontario). Canadian and American delegates meeting in Toronto considered the recent enactment of the Fugitive Slave Act of 1850 and its ramifications. They recognized that the law threatened all African Americans, not just former slaves, with arbitrary arrest and enslavement. The convention highlighted the advantages of Canadian and Jamaican emigration, and urged blacks living in the United States to come under the fair and equitable rule of British law. At the national emigration conventions of 1854 and 1856 in Cleveland, delegates weighed proposals for settlement in Haiti, Central America, and Africa. The interest in emigration continued well into the early 1860s.

In shaping a more practical agenda, blacks brought the convention movement to the state level in the 1840s and 1850s. The state meetings were better suited to address specific civil rights issues, and much of the struggle against racial discrimination involved state laws and municipal ordinances. The black vote, where permitted, weighed more heavily in state and local elections. State conventions thus made protection and expansion of black voting rights their primary concern. New York blacks held the first state convention at Albany in 1840 to launch a petition campaign against a property requirement that severely limited their franchise. Blacks in Pennsylvania, Michigan, New Jersey, and Connecticut followed with a similar agenda at state conventions during the 1840s.

Emerging black communities in the western states—Ohio, Indiana, Illinois, and California—also challenged voting rights restrictions and proscriptive black laws at state conventions in the 1850s. California blacks focused on restrictions against black testimony in court as well as the suffrage issue. Maryland blacks held the only convention permitted in a slave state before the Civil War. The 1852 Maryland convention, closely scrutinized by the Baltimore press, discussed colonization, the enslavement of free blacks, and the petitioning of the state legislature on civil rights issues. The convention's careful deliberations and guarded resolutions reflected the delegates' anxiety over the white response to their gathering.

Despite the energetic and determined efforts made by the many state and national conventions, blacks achieved few of their avowed goals. But, in the process, the conventions provided a sounding board for new ideas, strategies, and tactics. Many blacks established their credibility and their leadership through participation in these conventions, and the convention movement ultimately enhanced the sense of racial unity, identity, and purpose among black communities across the North American continent.

See also Cornish, Samuel E.; Douglass, Frederick; Garnet, Henry Highland; Politics; Ruggles, David; Smith, James McCune; Whipper, William

Bibliography

Bell, Howard H., ed. *Minutes of the Proceedings of the National Negro Conventions, 1830–1864.* New York: Arno, 1969.

Foner, Philip S., and George E. Walker, eds. *Proceedings of the Black State Conventions, 1830–1865.* 2 vols. Philadelphia: Temple University Press, 1979–1980.

MICHAEL F. HEMBREE (1996)

Anthropology and Anthropologists

Anthropology is a social science that devotes itself to the holistic study of humankind in its variation and commonality across time and space. It encompasses four major subdisciplines: (1) cultural/social anthropology, also called ethnology, which focuses largely on contemporary cultures and societies, representing its findings in ethnography; (2) archaeology, which examines the evolutionary and historical past by excavating artifacts and other material remains; 3) anthropological linguistics, which studies the development, structure, and sociocultural dynamics of languages; and 4) physical or biological anthropology, the study of human biology as it has evolved over time and adapted to diverse biocultural environments. The anthropology of African Americans brings together concepts, perspectives, and methodological tools from all the discipline's subfields into a specialization that concentrates on African descendants in the Americas.

Although the United States has been a setting in which African-American studies has developed extensive institutional support, scholarly projects of this sort have not been restricted to the United States nor to academic settings. There are parallel yet interconnected African-American anthropologies in the Caribbean and Latin America. While each national project has had its own approach, there have been shared themes that unify these complementary bodies of knowledge into a cohesive inquiry. The field has developed, in part, from the efforts of scholars who have belonged to networks connecting them to their counterparts in other parts of the world. Ideas have been exchanged and cross-fertilized within these transnational circuits that have not been confined to university-based and formally trained researchers. Also, individuals trained in other professions have made their mark on the field. The father of U.S. anthropology, Franz Boas, began his career in physical geography. The physician, diplomat, and politician Jean Price-Mars founded Haiti's *Institut d'Ethnologie,* and the father of Afro-Cuban studies, Fernando Ortiz, initially worked as a lawyer.

The major themes within the various African-American anthropologies are: (1) nature versus nurture in explaining racial differences; (2) folklore; (3) African survivals versus New World or "Creole" cultural rebirth; (4) diasporic religions; (5) social organization; (6) forms of difference and inequality (e.g., race, class, ethnicity, and gender) and their implications for identity, social action, and political mobilization; and (7) the political economy of poverty, social mobility, and development. Anthropologists have brought historical depth, cross-cultural perspective, and geographical breadth to these concerns.

Debating the Biology and Biologization of Race

In the U.S. context, anthropology emerged as a profession in the middle of the nineteenth century. It played a leading role in the development of scientific racism, which gave a veneer of legitimacy to the idea that African Americans were inferior and unworthy of full citizenship and equal rights. Race crossing was seen as a danger to white purity and national progress. Antimiscegenation laws promoted boundary maintenance and population control. While these devices did not prevent intimate interracial contact, they stigmatized it. This distinctly American approach contrasted with the way that interracial unions and mixedness were dealt with in other parts of the hemisphere. Intermediate categories between black and white existed, and national ideologies espousing the virtues of *mestizaje* (mixedness) prevailed. The implicit goal of these nations, however, was whitening. Whereas in the United States biologized thinking assumed that races were mutually exclusive and permanent, the version of Social Darwinism that took hold in Latin America and the Caribbean allowed for the racial mobility of the few individuals with sufficient money and cultural prestige to offset the stigma of blackness. Despite racial harmony myths, governments encouraged the immigration of Europeans and implemented other policies to reduce the population of blacks and mulattos, who were concentrated in the lowest sectors of the socioeconomic structure.

In his 1854 speech "The Claims of the Negro Ethnologically Considered," Frederick Douglass initiated the nature versus nurture debate in U.S. public culture. In another part of the New World, Anténor Firmin, a Haitian statesman and member of the Paris Anthropology Society, refuted the validity of Arthur de Gobineau's 1853–1855 treatise, *Essay on the Inequality of Human Races,* with a counterargument entitled *The Equality of the Human Races.* This 1885 publication offered an alternative to biological determinism. Firmin's accomplishment inspired Jean Price-Mars, who established an ethnological school in the early twentieth century, to document the cultural roots of Haitian national identity. W. E. B. Du Bois's *Health and Physique of the Negro American* (1906) reported the results of anthropometric research that demonstrated the effects of environment on physique and health. In 1932 Carolyn Bond Day published *A Study of Some Negro-White Families in the United States.* She combined anthropometry and ethnography to demonstrate the normalcy of middle- and upper-middle-class African-American families in Atlanta, who because of their admixture were misrepresented as degenerate threats to the nation. In the 1920s Melville Herskovits conducted a study in Harlem, West Virginia, and the historically black Howard University in Washington, D.C. He concluded that African Americans were a new racial amalgam of tri-racial origins. Due to segregation, they had developed a distinctive physical type marked by relatively low variability. His observations at Howard convinced him that intelligence was not correlated with the amount of "white blood." W. Montague Cobb, a professor of anatomy and medicine at Howard (1930s–1980s), established a laboratory and skeletal collection with which he refuted biodeterminism and promoted socially responsible research on health.

Today critical biological anthropologists are examining racism's effects on health and learning, underscoring that genetic endowment never operates independently of social environments. Recent bio-archaeological investigations document the stresses that Africans and African descendants faced at work and in other domains of their lives. Manifested in diet, disease, childbirth, accidents, and violence, the abuses of both slavery and freedom had effects on bodies, revealed by skeletal and DNA remains. The excavation of burial grounds uncovers evidence on religious practices as well as clues about the regions of African origins.

Folklore

From the late nineteenth century through the first half of the twentieth century, black folklore was an important focus of anthropological interest. Franz Boas was an advocate for collecting myths, legends, tales, songs, conundrums, jokes, and games as evidence for studying continuities and discontinuities with the past. He assumed that African Americans would eventually assimilate into Euroamerican culture and that the mass migration of southern blacks to northern cities would accelerate the loss of folk traditions. Hence, it was urgent to collect folk narratives while they remained elements of black popular life and cultural specificity. African Americans recruited and trained to collect folkloric materials included Arthur Huff Faucet and Zora Neale Hurston. Faucet studied blacks in Nova Scotia, Canada, emphasizing cultural hybridity and diversity among various African diasporic communities rather than diffusion from Africa. Hurston's research in the U.S. South and the Caribbean was published in *Mules and Men* (1935), *Tell My Horse* (1938), and in the novels and other literary writings for which she is better known. Operating outside the Boasian school, Katherine Dunham focused on dance in Jamaica and Haiti (e.g., *Journey to Accompong*, 1946; *Dances of Haiti*, 1947). She went on to develop a distinctive dance method and a style of concert dance informed by her fieldwork. Ellen Irene Diggs studied Afro-Cuban folkways with Fernando Ortiz. With Lydia Cabrera and Afro-Cuban intellectual Rómulo Lachatañeré, Ortiz established a program of study focused on Afro-Cuban folklore. Ortiz was influenced by Raymundo Nina Rodrigues, whose folkloric interests were in Afro-Brazilian religions. Rodrigues also influenced the direction that Arthur Ramos took (*O folk-lore negro do Brasil*, 1935). In Haiti, Jean Price-Mars (*Ainsi parla l'oncle,* 1928) promoted folkloric studies of Haitian peasants. Another Haitian who conducted folkloric research was Jacques Roumain, whose writings helped to delineate a distinctively Haitian aesthetic. His most significant writing was ethnographic fiction. His novel, *Masters of the Dew* (1944), depicted the peasantry's collective potential for change.

Martha Warren Beckwith conducted extensive fieldwork on folk life in Jamaica in the early 1920s. Her *Black Roadways: A Study of Jamaican Folklife* (1923) was the most comprehensive treatment at that time of folk beliefs and practices, including Anansi stories, games, ethnobotony, and religious cults. John Szwed and Roger Abrahams were two other Americans who made contributions to folklore; in the 1960s they studied urban folklore in the United States. Szwed examined the adaptations to racial conflict that sacred and secular musical styles represented. Abrahams's research focused on the verbal arts, such as the competitive verbal sparring, "playing the dozens." He also extended his research to the English Caribbean, where he continued to examine the folk performances of "men of words."

Africanisms and Creolization

"Africanism" is the concept that Herskovits coined for African cultural survivals—retentions and the more amorphous reinterpretations. When Herskovits initially came into contact with members of the New Negro movement, the scholarly arm of the Harlem Renaissance, he, like his mentor Boas, espoused an assimilationism that conflicted with the views of his African-American colleagues. Through ongoing conversations with them as well as with his international counterparts, he shifted his position to one emphasizing the legacy of the African past, manifest in retentions, reinterpretation, syncretisms, and cultural foci.

Herskovits's approach sparked controversy. Sociologist E. Franklin Frazier was the most articulate critic in the United States. In his view, African Americans in the United States had been stripped of African culture and social organization by the trauma of slavery and racism. Frazier's critique was informed by his focus on social structure and adaptation to economic conditions. Herskovits placed greater emphasis on symbolic elements, which were most amenable to his idea of reinterpretation. The Jamaican social anthropologist M. G. Smith expressed concern over Herskovits's conceptual imprecision and neglect of details about culture contact situations, which varied across the diaspora as well as over time. The varying social, economic, and political dynamics of New World contact situations affected the conditions under which cultural change occurred. Yet such variables were largely absent from Herskovits's analysis. Herkosvits found another theoretical contender in studies organized around the concept of creolization, the birth of new sociocultural forms from the raw materials of the cultures that came into contact in New World contexts. Those materials were reconstructed and reintegrated in response to environmental constraints.

Anthropologist Melville J. Herskovits (1895–1963). *The author of many influential works on African culture, Herskovits is pictured in Trinidad, posing with a drum, around 1939.* MELVILLE J. AND FRANCES S. HERSKOVITS PHOTOGRAPH COLLECTION, PHOTOGRAPHS AND PRINTS DIVISION, SCHOMBURG CENTER FOR RESEARCH IN BLACK CULTURE, THE NEW YORK PUBLIC LIBRARY, ASTOR, LENOX AND TILDEN FOUNDATIONS.

Sidney W. Mintz and Richard Price have sought to reconcile retention and creolization approaches. They delineate the processes by which African cultural materials contributed to the institution building that the enslaved undertook to make their lives meaningful and coherent (*The Birth of African-American Culture,* 1992 [1976]). Instead of emphasizing direct continuities from the African past, Mintz and Price point to the change and creativity that characterized African-American sociocultural life. They also underscore the role that underlying "grammatical" principles played. The study of language has been an important source of metaphor-concepts for cultural anthropological studies of the African diaspora. It also has elucidated the birth and development of creole languages, which are full-fledged languages in their own right, as well as of the situationally-shifting usage of black dialects of English, French, Spanish, Portuguese, and Dutch.

Diasporic Religions

Interest in syncretist religions has led U.S. and European researchers to the Caribbean and Brazil. Native researchers in these settings have been active documentarians as well. At the turn of the twentieth century, Raymundo Nina Rodrigues was known for his psychoanalytic approach to Afro-Brazilian religions. His work had a major impact on Ramos's research in the 1930s. Afro-Brazilians who studied the survival of African cultural heritage in Bahia included João da Silva Campos, João Varella, and Édison Carneiro. Carneiro was a journalist and amateur ethnographer (*Religiões Negras,* 1936) whose expertise put him in demand as a consultant for formally trained researchers. He collaborated with American anthropologist Ruth Landes, who researched Bahian Candomblé during the late 1930s and wrote *City of Women* (1947). Her emphasis was not on African survivals. Placing religious practices in the context of local history and politics, she examined gender and sexuality, including the ritual significance of homoeroticism. These foci made her work unacceptable in Brazil and the United States.

French ethnologist and sociologist Roger Bastide made an impact with his studies of Candomblé's relationship to historically changing social and economic conditions. Moving beyond a strictly cultural analysis, he recognized that the situations of culture contact that produced syncretisms and reinterpretations represented "complex webs of communication, of domination-subordination, or of egalitarian exchange. They are a part of institutions. . . ." (*The African Religions of Brazil: Toward a Sociology of the Interpenetration of Civilizations,* 1978, p. x).

Cuba was also an important venue for research on religious syncretisms. In association with Cabrera and Lachatañeré, Ortiz produced an extensive body of work. His most important contribution was his theory of transculturation, a term he coined as an alternative to acculturation, which often assumes subordinates becoming more like those who dominate them. Elaborated in *Cuban Counterpoint: Tobacco and Sugar* (1947), transculturation assumes a more complex multicultural situation in which there is interaction between two or more cultures that are mutually changed. Ortiz's earliest writings on Afro-Cuban religions were biased by his reduction of black religious practices to *brujería,* sorcery, illegal and deviant behavior. The view he articulated in *Los negros brujos* (1906) was influenced by the positivist criminology of Cesare Lombroso and Enrico Ferri. Their research on criminals relied on techniques for measuring faces and bodies, from which inferences about natural criminal inclinations were made. Lachatañeré criticized Ortiz's use of *brujería* and proposed an alternative term: Santería, the way of the saints. Lachatañeré was the first Afro-Cuban to write extensively on religious syncretism, interpreting myths of *orishas,* the syncretized deities or saints (*Oh, Mío Yemayá!* 1938, reprinted as *Afro-Cuban Myths: Yemayá and other Orishas,* 2005).

Cabrera, like Ortiz, was a white translator of black folklore. She collected proverbs, Abakuá tales and legends, and the ceremonial lexicon of the Yoruba. She also wrote fiction rich in symbolism informed by Afro-Cuban religion and culture (e.g., *Black Stories of Cuba,* 1940). Her most important book was *El Monte: Notes on the Religion, the Magic, the Superstitions, and the Folklore of Creole Negroes and the Cuban People* (1954). Andrés Rodriguez Reyes and Beatriz Morales are contemporary Afro-Cuban anthropologists who study Santería. Morales has followed its adherents' migration paths to the United States, where the religion has adapted to new settings and attracted non-Cuban converts. In one case, the *orishas* have been de-Catholicized in an Afrocentric "reinterpretation" that renews the religion's so-called authenticity.

Haiti and Jamaica have also been important sites for research on religious cults and movements. Native ethnologists such as Price-Mars and, decades later, Michel Laguerre (*Voodoo and Politics in Haiti,* 1989) and Leslie Desmangles (*The Faces of the Gods: Vodou and Roman Catholicism in Haiti,* 1992), have made important contributions. Two African-American women, Zora Neale Hurston and Katherine Dunham, undertook ethnographic projects in Haiti during the 1930s. Hurston's treatment of voodoo in both New Orleans and Haiti reveals her interest in the central role women and male-female tensions played in religious and other societal contexts. Both she and Dunham underwent rites of initiation rather than only observe them. In the late 1930s and early 1940s Maya Deren worked as an assistant and performer in the Katherine Dunham Dance Company. In 1947 she began to study vodou rituals in Haiti. Her participant observation led to initiation as a priestess. She published *Divine Horsemen* (1953) and produced the beginnings of a film by the same name. Swiss ethnologist Alfred Metraux gained international recognition as an authority; his ethnography, *Voodoo in Haiti* (1959) is still recognized as a classic. More recently, Karen McCarthy Brown's *Mama Lola: A Vodou Priestess in Brooklyn* (1991) combines her personal experience, life history, and theology to examine the reorganization of vodou in the context of transnational life in the United States.

The American anthropologist George Eaton Simpson studied Caribbean religions and religious pluralism during the 1950s. His writings on Haitian vodou, Trinidadian Shango, and Jamaican Revivalism and Rastafarianism examined acculturation, racial and class conflict, and politics. He characterized Rastafari as a social movement and situated it in the context of urban poverty and colonial oppression in the shantytowns of Jamaica's capital city, Kingston. The Jamaican government-commissioned report (*The Ras Tafari Movement in Kingston, Jamaica*) that Jamaican social scientists M. G. Smith, Roy Auguier, and Rex Nettleford published in 1960 presented Rastafarian grievances as legitimate rather than as the irrational rantings of deviants. Barry Chevannes has produced the most comprehensive work on Rastafari religion as well as shed light on its historical continuities with earlier folk religions, such as the Revival tradition. American anthropologist John Pulis has also written on Rastafari and has taken an historical approach to tracing its genealogy. Toward that end, he has examined the early-nineteenth-century Native Baptism/Anabaptist movement, influenced by black loyalist ministers from the United States who migrated to Jamaica in the wake of the Revolutionary War. (The British promised manumission to blacks who supported the Crown.) Australian anthropologist Diane Austin Broos's writings on contemporary Pentecostalism are also noteworthy for elucidating working class experience and worldview.

Social Organization

The varied patterns of kinship, marriage, and household organization found especially in peasant and working-class communities have been the subject of debates over African survivals, adaptive mechanisms, and cultural deficits and pathology. Eurocentric and class-biased notions about nuclear families have interfered with culturally unbiased inquiry. British ethnographer R. T. Smith (*The Negro Family in British Guiana,* 1956) and Jamaican anthropologists Edith Clarke (*My Mother Who Fathered Me,* 1957) and M. G. Smith (*West Indian Family Structure,* 1962) provided evidence that African-Caribbean households and families should not be viewed through a lens that only sees disorganization and dysfunction. The adaptive kinship organization that they documented was characterized by matrifocality, a consanguineal (blood kin) emphasis, and a development cycle in which having children was not necessarily linked to legal marriage. Sexual relations and mating patterns ranged from visiting relationships and consensual unions to marriage, the latter being more likely to occur later in the life cycle, when resources were more predictable. American anthropologist Nancie L. Gonzalez (*Migration and Modernization: Adaptive Reorganization in the Black Carib Household,* 1969), who worked along Central America's Caribbean coast, emphasized the high rate of outmigration that left communities without large numbers of marriageable men. High levels of unemployment and economic insecurity have also been important factors. Matrifocal kinship networks have been instrumental in pooling limited resources and sharing responsibilities for subsistence and childcare.

In the late 1960s Peter Wilson studied Providencia's crews, male units of social organization. In *Crab Antics: The Social Anthropology of English-Speaking Societies of the Caribbean* (1973) he claimed that West Indian life is organized around the contrasting principles of respectability and reputation. Tony L. Whitehead presented an alternative perspective on the importance of achieving a social balance between class-appropriate forms of respectability and reputation. Jean Besson disputed the claim that reputational attributes (e.g., toughness and independence) are only male, because working-class and peasant women exhibit them as well to meet their work and family responsibilities. Although respectability may be an important value, class and color dynamics make poor women less respectable than middle- and upper-class "ladies." Lisa Douglass's research (*The Power of Sentiment: Love, Hierarchy, and the Jamaican Family Elite,* 1992) underscores this principle of gender, race, and class hierarchy. She also argues that elite and lower-class kinship is more alike than Fernandes Henriques's *Family and Colour in Jamaica* (1953) acknowledged. Matrifocal emphasis within the domestic sphere and the "cult of manhood" exist across class. Indeed, elite and lower-class families are sometimes connected by consanguineal relationships generated by extramarital bonds.

In the United States Carol Stack, Joyce Aschenbrenner, and Niara Sudarkasa have countered misrepresentations of African-American families as unstable units lacking organization. They argue that female-headed households are not intrinsically dysfunctional or responsible for perpetuating poverty, academic underachievement, and crime. In the 1980s Sudarkasa revived Herskovits's concern by arguing that continuities with the African cultural past can be detected in African-American families. In her view, the value placed on consanguineality and matrifocality is consistent with the cultural logic underlying West African polygynous family compounds.

Intersecting Hierarchies and Stratifications

African diasporic peoples live in societies characterized by complexity and diversity along lines of race, ethnicity, class, and gender. To make sense of Caribbean diversity in particular, M. G. Smith applied the plural society model, originally crafted for explaining interethnic conflicts in the former Dutch East Indies. In the anthropological study of the African Americas, concepts of race, class and gender have been significant. In the 1930s African-American anthropologists Allison Davis and St. Clair Drake were part of a biracial research team that studied the organization of race and class in Mississippi (Davis et al., *Deep South: A Social Anthropological Study of Caste and Class*, 1941). They understood that class was an important organizing principle that operated in conjunction with race, conceptualized in that research in terms of birth-ascribed caste.

Anthropologists as well as laypeople commonly apply the concept of race in describing African descendants, whereas ethnicity is more often used for Native Americans and Asians. This double standard is particularly relevant to the Caribbean and Latin America because it implies a structure of differentiation in which black culture, apart from elements (e.g., Carnival and emblematic musical and dance genres) appropriated by national culture, are negatively evaluated in terms of deficits that must be filled through acculturation. The extensive color lexicon developed to describe peoples of African descent represents a yardstick for measuring improvement through admixture and lightening. A graded color vocabulary has not been applied to East Indians or Chinese, whose relationship to colonially dominant whites was expressed as a ranking among civilizations. Africans, on the other hand, were historically represented as primitive and savage.

Anthropologists have studied the social construction of race in diverse cultural contexts, showing that the racial regime in the United States is not universal but the product of unique conditions. Boas and Du Bois—and a later generation of scholars that included Allison Davis and his colleagues, Burleigh and Mary Gardner, St. Clair Drake, and Ashley Montagu—laid the foundations for the critical study of race in the United States. The 1990s saw a resurgence of interest in race. Social anthropologist Audrey Smedley (*Race in North America: The Origin and Evolution of a Worldview*, 1993) and historian of anthropology Lee D. Baker (*From Savage to Negro: Anthropology and the Construction of Race, 1896–1954*, 1998) emerged as two of the leading voices in this discourse. Other African-American anthropologists who have recently addressed the ideological and material dynamics of race and racism in the United States and in other places in the diaspora include biological anthropologist Michael Blakey (U.S.) and cultural anthropologists Marilyn Thomas-Houston (U.S.), Angela Gilliam (Brazil and Mexico), Edmund T. Gordon (Nicaragua), Gayle McGarity (Cuba), Yolanda T. Moses (U.S.), Trevor Purcell (Costa Rica), Kimberly Simmons (Dominican Republic), Frances Winddance Twine (Brazil), and Faye V. Harrison, who has taken a comparative approach.

Brazil has long been a site where American anthropologists have gone to study race. In the 1950s and 1960s Charles Wagley and Marvin Harris studied racial classification there. Harris interpreted Brazil's situationally contingent and ambiguous "racial calculus," which contrasted with the bipolar categories in the United States. Recent ethnographers have questioned Brazil's racial democracy. France Winddance Twine, John Burdick, and Robin Sheriff are three of the American critics. Brazilian anthropologists have also been vocal. João H. Costa Vargas is an Afro-Brazilian whose research on racism, politics, and human rights raises provocative questions that challenge the dominant paradigm. A product of the black consciousness movement himself, he is interested in the solidarity networking that black Brazilian activists have begun to establish with their counterparts in the United States.

The dominant paradigm for studying race in Brazil can be traced back to Gilberto Freyre's historical sociology of slavery and race relations, as exemplified by his *Masters and Slaves* (1933) and *Mansions and Shanties* (1936). Providing an historical rationale for racial democracy, he claimed that Brazilian slavery was mild, based on paternalistic relationships that humanized the institution. Florestan Fernandes (*The Negro in Brazilian Society*, 1969), who was part of the UNESCO Race Relations Project of the 1950s, challenged the myth of racial democracy but explained racism's persistence as a remnant from the pre-industrial past (without understanding that racism also has modern faces). The year he published his critique, the military dictatorship removed him from his teaching position, forcing him to flee the country for several years. Thales de Azevedo is another leading anthropologist who distinguished himself. To disprove the myth of racial democracy, he documented the cases of racial discrimination reported in the media, clearing the way for more recent research.

Other anthropologists who have made important contributions to our understanding of race in the African diaspora in Latin America are: Norman Whitten, Jr. (Ecuador), who in the 1960s helped set the stage for Afro-American studies in Latin America; Peter Wade (Colombia), whose ethnographic analysis is rich and theoretically nuanced; Arlene Torres (Puerto Rico), who insists that, regardless of socially orchestrated denials, blackness is central to the histories and cultural landscapes of the Spanish-speaking Caribbean; Bobby Vaughn (Mexico), who brings perspectives from the Pacific Costa Chica into the discussion; and Helen Safa (Hispanic Caribbean, Brazil), who has examined racial discourses in Latin America generally.

Studies of gender in the diaspora have grown considerably over the past two decades. Most of the chapters in *Black Feminist Anthropology* (McClaurin, 2001) address the interplay of gender and race in the diaspora. An earlier anthology, *The Black Woman Cross-Culturally* (1980), edited by Filomina Chioma Steady, was, and perhaps still is, the most extensive collection of anthropological essays on women in the diaspora and Africa. Recently women-centered research has been complemented by ethnographic investigations that examine gender—the meanings, relations, and practices that culturally define the identities, roles, and social positions of the sexes, males and females along with transgendered persons. Peter Wilson and Tony Whitehead are examples of ethnographers who have addressed the cultural struggles and negotiations that shape diasporic masculinity. Lisa Douglass examines the cultural politics of femininity in a cultural system in which stark distinctions are made between working-class black womanhood and upper-class white or whitened femininity. A number of other gender-cognizant ethnographies already been mentioned, for instance, the writings of Hurston, Landes, and McCarthy Brown. Studies of diasporic kinship, even when gender remains implicit, usually have relevant implications. Gender may also be a salient dimension in analyses of socioeconomic dynamics.

Our understanding of the cultural and power dynamics of gender, class, and race along with those related to age and rural or urban residence also has been enhanced by sociolinguistic research. Many diasporic situations are characterized by language usage and competence that is diglossic or heteroglossic. Culturally-intelligible communication often relies on code switching from one language or dialectal variety into another language or dialectical variety according to social parameters.

Diasporic Political Economy

Anthropologists have acknowledged that economic marginality is found throughout the African diaspora, challenging black people to exercise considerable creativity to make ends meet and develop humanizing adaptations. Economic insecurity and poverty are often backdrops to the ethnographic narratives that anthropologists write. A number of ethnographers have gone further to shed light on the economic practices, activities, and modes of organization that are integral to African descendants' everyday lives. Attention is also given to the embeddedness of local adaptations within national, regional, and global systems of production and exchange. Currently, globalization and transnational flows of capital and commodities—along with the mobile ideas, cultural forms, and people that accompany them—are popular issues for anthropological inquiry. The preoccupation with globalization is consistent with concerns that many African Americanists have had for a while. The New World diaspora formed from the transoceanic movements of people, capital, and commodities. Those transterritorial flows were integral to the development of plantation and mining-based societies that depended on captive Africans for their lucrative objectives. The history of the African diaspora, thus, implicates the development and expansion of the modern world system—global capitalism.

Caribbeanists have been particularly conscious of this history. Eric Wolf and Sidney Mintz were early students of the haciendas and plantations that were major sites on the landscapes where African-Caribbean people were enslaved and later emancipated, only to face new forms of exploitation as peasants, rural proletarians, and urban wage workers and informal sector participants. Mintz's ethnographic and cultural historical analyses of Puerto Rican sugar plantations, Haitian and Jamaican peasantries, and the role of women in internal marketing systems were major contributions. Building on this foundational corpus of knowledge, Victoria Durant-Gonzalez focused her lens on more of the particulars in the work and family life of Jamaican market women, higglers. Charles Carnegie studied interisland or transterritorial marketing in the Eastern Caribbean, exposing the limitations of the nation-state as a unit of economic or even social analysis. Gina Ulysse has examined the modern-day higglers called informal commercial importers (ICIs), who operate under conditions of globalization and the neoliberal policies that the International Monetary Fund, World Bank, and U.S. government have imposed on Caribbean economies. These ICIs travel across national boundaries to supply consumer goods to their clients back home. Carla Freeman has studied pink-collar workers in offshore data-processing firms in Barbados. Although these working-class women earn wages no higher than those of women working in Free Trade Zones, working in air-conditioned offices with computers makes them feel they are better off and on the margins of the middle class. Their high heels and professional attire symbolize what they perceive as their newfound fortune. A. Lynn Bolles's research on women who work in assembly plants and in the tourist industry offers the nuanced perspective that ethnographic analysis can provide on economics and society. Faye V. Harrison has addressed Jamaica's urban informal economy and the impact of structural adjustment and other neoliberal policies on a slum where both political violence and drug-related conflicts are common. Her analysis shows how both households and drug gangs are local units of socioeconomic organization that have become increasingly transnational as subsistence security diminishes. Michel-Rolph Trouillot's research in Dominica reveals how small farmers are inextricably tied in circuits of global capitalism. Karla Slocum's research in another Eastern Caribbean setting, St. Lucia, elucidates how a social movement of small banana producers expresses grievances against the state, refusing to blame globalization for their problems. In an era that some anthropologists have characterized as postnational, with nation-states having less sovereignty vis-à-vis the global market, these peasants may be reminding us that the state is not yet obsolete, and its responsibilities to its citizens cannot be forgotten or dismissed.

Conclusion

The anthropology of African Americans, defined in hemispheric terms, is a growing body of evidence, concepts, interpretations and explanations. It has illuminated African-American cultural history, historical consciousness, and diversity as well as the significance of the international mobility of ideas and people. It encompasses diverse anthropologists, including a significant number of African Americans who have begun to move their scholarship from the margins into the center of the field.

See also Africanisms; Archaeology and Archaeologists; Candomblé; Creole Languages of the Americas; Dunham, Katherine; English, African-American; Folklore; Folk Religion; Haitian Creole Language; Hurston, Zora Neale; *Negro Brujos*; Orisha; Race and Science; Religion; Rastafarianism; Santería; Slave Religions; Sociology; Voodoo

Bibliography

Baker, Lee D. *From Savage to Negro: Anthropology and the Construction of Race, 1896-1954.* Berkeley: University of California Press, 1998.

Bastide, Roger. *The African Religions of Brazil: Toward a Sociology of the Interpenetration of Civilizations.* Baltimore: Johns Hopkins University Press, 1978.

Beckwith, Martha Warren. *Black Roadways: A Study of Jamaican Folklife.* 1929. Reprint, New York: Negro Universities Press, 1969.

Besson, Jean. *Martha Brae's Two Histories: European Expansion and Caribbean Culture-building in Jamaica.* Kingston, Jamaica: Ian Randle, 2003.

Blakey, Michael. "Bioarchaeology of the African Diaspora in the Americas: Its Origins and Scope." *Annual Review of Anthropology* 30 (2001): 387–422.

Brown, Karen MacCarthy. *Mama Lola: A Voodou Priestess in Brooklyn.* Rev. ed. Berkeley: University of California Press, 2001.

Cabrera, Lydia. *Cuentos Negros de Cuba.* 3rd ed. Miami: Ediciones Universal, 1993.

Cabrera, Lydia. *El monte.* Rev. ed. Havana: Editorial Letras Cubanas, 1993.

Cabrera, Lydia. *Anagó: Vocabulario Lucumí (El Yoruba que Se Habla en Cuba).* 2nd ed. Miami: Ediciones Universal, 1986.

Carneiro, Édison. *Religões negras; Notas de etnografia religiosa.* Rio de Janeiro: Civilização brasileira s.a., 1936.

Carneiro, Édison. *Negros bantus; Notas de ethnographia religiosa e de folk-lore.* Rio de Janeiro: Civilização brasileira, s.a., 1937.

Davis, Allison, Burleigh B. Gardner, Mary R. Gardner, and W. Lloyd Warner. *Deep South: a Social Anthropological Study of Caste and Class.* Chicago: The University of Chicago Press, 1941.

Day, Carolyn Bond. *A Study of Some Negro-White Families in the United States.* Cambridge: Peabody Museum of Harvard University, 1932.

Desmangles, Leslie Gérald. *The Faces of the Gods: Voodoo and Roman Catholicism in Haiti.* Chapel Hill: The University of North Carolina Press, 1992.

Deren, Maya. *Divine Horseman: The Living Gods of Haiti.* London: Thames and Hudson, 1953.

Douglass, Lisa. *The Power of Sentiment: Love, Hierarchy, and the Jamaican Family Elite.* Boulder, Colo.: Westview Press, 1992.

Du Bois, W. E. B. *The health and physique of the Negro American. Report of a Social Study Made under the Direction of Atlanta University; Together with the Proceedings of the Eleventh Conference for the Study of the Negro Problems, Held at Atlanta University, on May the 29th, 1906.* Atlanta: Atlanta University Press, 1906.

Dunham, Katherine, and Proctor Fyffe Cook. *Katherine Dunham's Journey to Accompong.* New York: H. Holt and Company, 1946.

Dunham, Katherine. *Dances of Haiti.* Mexico, 1947.

Fernandes, Florestan. *The Negro in Brazilian Society.* Translated by Jacqueline D. Skiles, A. Brunel, and Arthur Rothwell. Edited by Phyllis B. Eveleth. New York: Columbia University Press, 1969.

Freyre, Gilberto. *The Mansions and the Shanties: The Making of Modern Brazil.* Translated and edited by Harriet de Onis with an introduction by Frank Tannenbaum. Berkeley: University of California Press, 1986.

Freyre, Gilberto. *The Masters and the Slaves: A Study in the Development of Brazilian Civilization.* 2nd English language edition, revised. Translated by Samuel Putnam. Berkeley: University of California Press, 1986.

Firmin, Joseph-Anténor. *De l'égalité des races humaines: Anthropologie positive.* 1885. Translation by Asselin Charles published as *The Equality of the Human Races.* Urbana: University of Illinois Press, 2002.

Gershenhorn, Jerry. *Melville Herskovits: And the Racial Politics of Knowledge.* Lincoln: University of Nebraska Press, 2004.

González, Nancie L. Solien. *Black Carib Household Structure; a Study of Migration and Modernization.* Seattle: University of Washington Press, 1969.

Harris, Marvin. *Patterns of Race in the Americas.* New York: Walker, 1964.

Harrison, Faye V., guest editor. "Contemporary Forum: Race and Racism." *American Athropologist* 100, no. 3 (1998): 607–715.

Harrison, Ira E., and Faye V. Harrison, eds. *African-American Pioneers in Anthropology.* Urbana: University of Illinois Press, 1999.

Henriques, Fernando. *Family and Colour in Jamaica.* London: Eyre & Spottiswoode, 1953.

Herskovits, Melville J. *The Myth of the Negro Past.* 1941. Reprint. Boston: Beacon Press, 1958.

Hurston, Zora Neale. *Mules and Men.* Philadelphia: J. B. Lippincott Co., 1935.

Hurston, Zora Neale. *Tell My Horse.* Philadelphia: J. B. Lippincott Co., 1938.

Lachatañeré, Rómulo. *Oh, mío Yemayá!!* 1938. Translation by Christine Ayorinde published as *Afro-Cuban Myths: Yemayá and other orishas.* Princeton, N.J.: M. Wiener, 2003.

Laguerre, Michel S. *Voodoo and Politics in Haiti.* New York: St. Martin's Press, 1989.

Landes, Ruth. *The City of Women.* 1947. Reprint. Albuquerque: University of New Mexico Press, 1994.

McClaurin, Irma, ed. *Black Feminist Anthropology: Theory, Politics, Praxis, and Poetics.* New Brunswick, N.J.: Rutgers University Press, 2001.

Métraux, Alfred. *Voodoo in Haiti.* Translated by Hugo Charteris. New York: Oxford University Press, 1959.

Mintz, Sidney W., and Richard Price. *An Anthropological Approach to the Afro-American Past: A Caribbean Perspective.* Philadelphia: Institute for the Study of Human Issues, 1976. Republished as *The Birth of African-American Culture: An Anthropological Perspective.* Boston: Beacon Press, 1992.

Morgan, Marcyliena H., ed. *Language and the Social Construction of Identity in Creole Situations.* Los Angeles: Center for Afro-American Studies Publica, University of California, Los Angeles, 1994.

Morgan, Marcyliena H. *Language, Discourse, and Power in African American Culture.* Cambridge: Cambridge University Press, 2002.

Ortiz, Fernando. *Hampa Afro-Cubana. Los Negros Brujos (apuntes para un estudio de etnología criminal).* Madrid: Libería de F. Fé, 1906.

Ortiz, Fernando. *Contrapunteo cubano del tabaco y el azúcar.* 1940. Translation by Harriet de Onís published as *Cuban Counterpoint, Tobacco and Sugar.* Durham, N.C.: Duke University Press, 1995.

Price-Mars, Jean. *Ainsi parle l'oncle.* 1928. Translation by Magdaline W. Shannon published as *So Spoke the Uncle.* Washington, D.C.: Three Continents Press, 1983.

Ramos, Arthur. *O Folk-lore Negro do Brasil.* Rio de Janerio: Civilização brasileira, s.a., 1935.

Rankin-Hill, Leslie, and Michael Blakey. "W. Montague Cobb: Physical Anthropologist, Anatomist, and Activist." In *African-American Pioneers in Anthropology,* edited by Ira E. Harrison and Faye V. Harrison, pp. 101–136. Urbana: University of Illinois Press, 1999.

Roumain, Jacques. *Gouverneurs de la rosée, roman.* 1944. Translation by Langston Hughes and Mercer Clark published as *Masters of the Dew.* London: Heinemann, 1978.

Smedley, Audrey. *Race in North America: Origin and Evolution of a Worldview.* Boulder, Colo.: Westview Press, 1993.

Smith, M. G. *West Indian Family Structure.* Seattle: University of Washington Press, 1962.

Smith, M. G., Roy Augier, and Rex M. Nettleford. *The Ras Tafari Movement in Kingston, Jamaica.* Mona, Jamaica: University College of the West Indies, Institute of Social and Economic Research, 1960.

Smith, Raymond Thomas. *The Negro Family in British Guiana.* London: Routledge & Paul, 1956.

Steady, Filomina Chioma, ed. *The Black Woman Cross-Culturally.* Cambridge, Mass.: Schenkman, 1981.

Turner, Lorenzo Dow. *Africanisms in the Gullah Dialect.* 1949. Reprint. Columbia: University of South Carolina, 2002.

Whitten, Norman E., Jr., and John F. Szwed, eds. *Afro-American Anthropology: Contemporary Perspectives.* New York: Free Press, 1970.

Whitten, Norman E., Jr., and Arlene Torres, eds. *Blackness in Latin America and the Caribbean: Social Dynamics and Cultural Transformations.* Bloomington: Indiana University Press, 1998.

Wilson, Peter J. *Crab Antics: The Social Anthropology of English-Speaking Societies of the Caribbean.* New Haven: Yale University Press, 1973.

Yelvington, Kevin A., ed. *Afro-Atlantic Dialogues: Anthropology in the Diaspora.* Santa Fe: School of American Research Press, 2005.

FAYE V. HARRISON (2005)

Anti-Apartheid Movement

The African-American struggle against segregation and apartheid in South Africa has a long history. In 1912 the NAACP played a role in the formation of the African National Congress (ANC), which opposed violence and sought to end racial discrimination through legal strategy. In the 1920s Marcus Garvey expressed his solidarity with black South Africans and assured them that an army of black Americans would arrive on the shores of Africa to liberate them. The American Committee on Africa (ACOA) was formed in 1953 to coordinate U.S. activities with the South African liberation movement, which was challenging the oppressive 1948 apartheid laws.

After the Sharpeville Massacre in 1960, when South African police killed sixty-seven people who were opposing laws designed to enforce residential segregation and control the movement of black people, the solidarity movement in the United States gained national recognition and popular support. In the mid-1960s, students, religious leaders, and civil rights activists condemned the brutal policies of the South African government and demanded an end to U.S. bank loans to South Africa. The Congress of Racial Equality, Student Nonviolent Coordinating Committee, NAACP, and Students for a Democratic Society led demonstrations and sit-ins and passed resolutions demanding that the United States cut all ties to South Africa. The Rev. Dr. Martin Luther King, Jr., linked racism to the foreign policy of the United States when he argued that "the racist government of South Africa is virtually made possible by the economic policies of the United States and Great Britain."

Protests at Princeton University and the University of Wisconsin in 1968 and Cornell University in 1969 brought out hundreds of students who demanded that their universities divest from Chase Manhattan Bank and other corporations doing business in South Africa. Church groups around the country presented stockholder resolutions calling for divestment and voted to close accounts with banks doing business with South Africa. In 1972 the National Council of Churches examined the social impact of corporate behavior on black South Africans. Although these protests raised public awareness about apartheid, they were less successful at forcing companies to withdraw support from South Africa. In 1963 the U.S. Congress also responded to the repressive policies of the South African government and complied with a United Nations resolution for a voluntary ban on arms sales and related equipment to South Africa.

In 1976 student members of the black consciousness movement in South Africa, which was inspired partly by the black power movement in the United States, took to the streets of Soweto to protest their segregated educational system. Protestors were met by police fire, and the following year political leader Steve Biko was murdered while in police custody. In response, hundreds of protests occurred across the United States, and over seven hundred students were arrested. TransAfrica, an African and Caribbean lobbying organization, was formed in 1977; Randall Robinson, an anti-apartheid activist, was chosen as its head. The organization grew out of a meeting of the Congressional Black Caucus, where concern was expressed about the lack of African-American influence in U.S. foreign policy.

Divestment was the central tactic adopted by anti-apartheid protestors, who sought an end to U.S. governmental and corporate support for South Africa. Critics of divestment contended that American firms must continue to do business in South Africa in order to use their economic muscle to force a change in apartheid policies. They argued that withdrawing would only hurt black South Africans by depriving them of jobs and other benefits.

In 1977 the Rev. Leon Sullivan, a prominent African-American activist, developed a voluntary code of conduct for firms operating in South Africa. The Sullivan Principles, as the code of conduct was popularly known, included measures to train and promote black South Africans, increase wages and fringe benefits, and recognize black labor unions. By the mid-1980s, 135 companies had signed onto the Sullivan Principles, and used them to defend their presence in South Africa. It was becoming increasingly clear, however, that the new policy was having minimal influence on moderating apartheid.

In 1984 another South African uprising and the ongoing repressive policies of the white government reinvigorated the solidarity movement in the United States, and this time the movement won some concrete concessions. On Thanksgiving Eve in 1984, Randall Robinson and other prominent activists began a daily vigil in front of the South African embassy in Washington, D.C. The vigil, which lasted over fifty-three weeks, raised awareness about the evils of apartheid and expressed opposition to Ronald Reagan's policy of constructive engagement. This policy pursued friendly relations with South Africa as a means of inducing the government to relax apartheid restrictions. The protest sparked similar actions across the country and in Great Britain and led to the arrest of over six thousand people, including twenty-three elected representatives.

On college campuses, students formed multiracial anti-apartheid organizations and demanded an end to their universities' involvement with companies doing business in South Africa. In 1985 at the University of California at Berkeley over seven thousand students attended a public hearing on divestment and were supported by union members and faculty. Students elsewhere held teach-ins, blockaded buildings, and built shanties to pressure universities to divest. At Yale University in 1986, 1,500 students demonstrated after the university destroyed a shanty built by anti-apartheid activists. Through their tenacious and militant protests, students were able to win some important victories. Five months after a three-week sit-in at Columbia University in 1985, the university trustees divested. In 1986 Harvard University voted for total divestment, and the University of California voted to divest $3.1 billion of its stock in companies doing business with South Africa. In the same year, over Ronald Reagan's veto, Congress passed the Comprehensive Anti-Apartheid Act, which banned new public and private loans and investments, the importation of certain South Africa products, including steel and uranium, and the export of certain U.S. products to South Africa, including petroleum and computers. In 1987 Sullivan rejected his own principles and joined the call for a complete corporate pullout.

Because of intensified protests, including national boycotts, corporations began to respond to calls for divestment. In 1984, 406 United States companies operated in South Africa. By 1989, only 130 remained. Corporations played a clever public relations game by announcing their withdrawal and giving few details about how it would occur. In most cases withdrawal was not complete or straightforward. Companies created subsidiaries, continued to market their products, and still provided management and technical skills. The anti-apartheid movement, which had focused so much of its attention on divestment, found it difficult to sustain mass protests in the face of verbal compliance by multinationals. A media blackout of events in South Africa further hindered anti-apartheid organizing and contributed to a decline of the movement in the United States.

Nevertheless, the international movement had helped create a climate that made political and economic support for apartheid less acceptable, and this, in conjunction with continued protests by South Africans, led to the release of Nelson Mandela in 1990 and the beginning of South African President F. W. de Klerk's effort to dismantle the legal apparatus of apartheid the next year. In 1991 George Bush lifted most federal sanctions against South Africa, even though many activists opposed this move until more progress had been made toward achieving a free and democratic state. Most local sanctions remained until Mandela called for their removal two years later. In 1994, after several years of negotiation and compromise by the white government and the African National Congress, South Africa held its first nonracial elections and Nelson Mandela was elected the first black president. In 1999 a symposium titled "The Anti-Apartheid Movement: A 40-Year Perspective," held at Sussex House in England and attended by more than 250 leaders, marked the fortieth anniversary of the founding of the anti-apartheid movement in England.

See also Black Power Movement; Congressional Black Caucus; Garvey, Marcus; Sullivan, Leon Howard

Bibliography

Fieldhouse, Roger. *Anti-Apartheid: A History of the Movement in Britain, 1959–1994.* London: Merlin Press, 2005.

Hauck, David, Meg Voorhes, and Glenn S. Goldberg. *Two Decades of Debate: The Controversy Over U.S. Companies in South Africa.* Washington, D.C.: Investor Responsibility Research Center, 1983.

Kibbe, Jennifer, and David Hauch. *Leaving South Africa: The Impact of U.S. Corporate Disinvestment.* Washington, D.C.: Investor Responsibility Research Center, 1988.

Wiener, Jon. "Students, Stocks, and Shanties." *Nation* (October 11, 1986): 337–40.

ALBERT NICKERSON (1996)
Updated by publisher 2005

Anti-colonial Movements

Africans in the Americas often provided racial ideologies for modern nationalist and anti-colonial movements in Africa and Europe as well as in the Caribbean and the United States. These ideologies were rooted in similar racial identities drawn from colonial, enslaved, and post-emancipation experiences. This entry will focus upon anti-colonial movements, organizations, and prominent figures from the 1800s through the present.

Century of Emancipation, 1790s–1880s

Beginning in the early fifteenth century, the five major European powers of Portugal, Spain, France, the Netherlands, and Great Britain established colonies in the Americas. Although all of these colonial powers appealed to God to rationalize theories of empire, they differed in their dependency on the state or civil society to run their American colonies. The former characterized Spanish colonialism; the latter, the British Empire. With the establishment of Creole (American-born) populations by the late eighteenth century, together with important shifts in political and economic power, New World colonies moved toward independence through a series of wars of national liberation.

In 1776 thirteen American colonies declared their independence from Great Britain. In 1804 Haiti declared its independence from France. In 1821 Mexico achieved its independence from Spain. The following year, Brazil won its independence from Portugal. By the 1820s, most of the mainland Americas had achieved their independence from European colonial powers. With the exception of Haiti, however, the rest of the European Caribbean would have to wait until the twentieth century for its colonial independence.

One indispensable feature of European settlement in the New World was the establishment of colonial slavery. Scholars estimate that between nine million and thirteen million African slaves survived the transoceanic slave trade and eventually arrived in the Americas between 1450 and 1870. Most of these imported Africans ended up in the Caribbean and Brazil. The sources of slaves changed over the centuries, beginning in West Africa, and moving slowly southward to southwest Africa. Two-thirds of these slave imports were young men used primarily in the plantation production of crops such as sugar, tobacco, rice, wheat, indigo, and other commodities. Although shipboard conditions were disgusting, ship crews brutal, and water scarce, many Africans fought back. Revolts were common on slave ships. In one Dutch sample, 20 percent of voyages had slave rebellions; nearly half of all revolts on French slaving voyages during the eighteenth century were successful. The coming together of different ethnic groups in these revolts made these the first anti-colonial struggles by Africans coming to the Americas.

Although the major slave trading nations of Britain and the United States abolished their slave trades in 1807 and 1808 respectively, other colonial powers like the Portuguese and the Spanish continued to trade in slaves through the mid-nineteenth century. Furthermore, the abolition of the Anglo-American slave trade encouraged the development of continental slave trades from older plantation crop regions like the Chesapeake, Barbados, and Bahia, to newer areas like Mississippi, Trinidad, and São Paulo. It also led to the development of an Afro-Creole slave populace. Three-fourths of the slave population in Jamaica were native-born in 1834, while most of the 3.9 million enslaved Africans in the fifteen slave states of the United States in 1860 had been born there.

The overthrow of this centuries-old system of colonial slavery was relatively quick. Between the 1790s and 1880s, around 6.5 million slaves of African descent gained their freedom in the Americas. The first period between the 1790s and 1820s linked slave emancipation and anti-colonial struggles in the French Caribbean as well as Spanish colonies in South America. The great era of emancipation, however, occurred in the following decades in the Anglo-Atlantic. The legal abolition of slavery in the British West Indies in 1834 to 1838, together with the military de-

Hubert Henry Harrison (1883–1927), dubbed by labor leader A. Philip Randolph the "Father of Harlem Radicalism." *A leading activist and intellectual of the Harlem Renaissance, Harrison espoused the importance of socialism in fighting racism and oppression.* PHOTOGRAPHS AND PRINTS DIVISION, SCHOMBURG CENTER FOR RESEARCH IN BLACK CULTURE, THE NEW YORK PUBLIC LIBRARY, ASTOR, LENOX AND TILDEN FOUNDATIONS.

feat of the slave-holding South in the American Civil War by 1865, freed over 4.5 million enslaved people. In addition, the 1848 European revolutions liberated nearly 200,000 slaves in the French, Danish, and Dutch West Indies. Twenty years after the abolition of slavery in the United States in 1865, the effective end of colonial slavery in the New World was accomplished. Brazil legally ended slavery in 1888 and became a republic the following year. The Spanish ended colonial slavery in Puerto Rico in 1873, and Cuba did so in 1886. As a result of two major anti-colonial struggles during the 1870s, together with U.S. military intervention after 1898, Cuba finally achieved its political independence from Madrid.

Although there were complex reasons for the overthrow of colonial slavery in the nineteenth century, it is important not to overlook the critical role of Africans in the Americas as fugitives, soldiers, spies, strikers, arsonists, and national liberation fighters.

"Africa for the Africans," 1914–1920s

At the same time that slavery and colonialism were coming to an end in Brazil and Cuba, European powers were scrambling for new colonial possessions in other parts of the world. Between the Berlin Conference of 1884 to 1885 and the beginning of World War I in 1914, the European powers parceled up the African continent among themselves, with the exception of Liberia and Ethiopia. Their most important motives included broad economic interests of profit and the prospect of new markets, together with strategic concerns and geopolitical interests.

In the wake of the 1917 Bolshevik Revolution in Russia and the end of World War I in 1918, anti-colonial and national liberation struggles gained momentum in Ireland, Egypt, Vietnam, India, Iraq, and elsewhere. These events had a critical impact upon Africans in the Caribbean and the United States, in particular through the formation of the Universal Negro Improvement Association (UNIA) under the leadership of Marcus Mosiah Garvey. This Jamaican-born printer, journalist, and activist founded UNIA in Kingston on July 20, 1914. In 1917 Garvey relocated to New York City, where he headquartered UNIA. His personal charisma, together with messages of racial pride, Christian faith, and economic uplift, contributed to the formation of a mass movement eventually credited with one million followers in the United States and several million adherents in forty-two nations and colonies. In a 1921 speech at his Liberty Hall headquarters in New York City, Garvey called for "Africa for the Africans," an important manifesto for anti-colonial and domestic liberation movements.

That same year, however, the Garvey movement faced mounting pressures from the failure of its shipping line, federal government investigation and harassment, and internal dissension. The opposition from black critics took ideological and organizational forms. Hubert Henry Harrison, born in the Danish West Indies, immigrated to New York City where he became involved in socialist politics. In 1917 Harrison inaugurated the Liberty League of Negro-Americans on a platform of international solidarity, political independence, and class-race consciousness. With the failure of this body, Harrison joined UNIA, serving as editor of its newspaper, the *Negro World*. After increasing disillusionment with UNIA, he founded the International Colored Unity League, which called for racial unity and an independent African-American state within the United States.

Another radical black critic was Cyril Briggs. Born on Nevis in the British West Indies, Briggs migrated to the United States in 1905 and obtained work as a journalist. Between 1918 and 1922, he ran the journal the *Crusader*, which espoused revolutionary socialism and black self-determination. The newspaper became the official journal of the African Blood Brotherhood for African Liberation and Redemption (ABB), a semisecret militant internationalist organization serving as the first black auxiliary to the Communist Party of the United States of America (CPUSA). The ABB only had a few hundred members, but it was one of the first black organizations to call for armed self-defense of African Americans. Most importantly, these figures and organizations represented the earliest domestic expression of an anti-colonial ideology in the United States.

Colonialism and Anti-colonialism, 1930s–1940

The era of the Great Depression and World War II witnessed important new colonial and anti-colonial developments. During the early 1930s, the U.S. militarily occupied Haiti. W. E. B. Du Bois, editor of the National Association for the Advancement of Colored People's (NAACP's) journal *The Crisis*, challenged this colonial aggression. In 1935 Italian fascist leader Benito Mussolini ordered 500,000 Italian troops to invade Ethiopia. This small nation on the horn of East Africa was important to people of African descent around the world for several reasons, including its ancient Christian roots, its independence during the European scramble for Africa, and its importance to followers in the Garvey movement. The African-American response varied. Several support organizations sprung up quickly in New York City, Chicago, and Los Angeles. Black volunteers came forward for the defense of Ethiopia, but were reportedly dissuaded by official U.S. pressure to stop recruitment and by a potential legal violation of U.S. citizens serving in foreign armies. Most important, black Communists in Harlem, along with some Garveyites, formed the Provisional Committee for the Defense of Ethiopia, which organized a "Hands off Ethiopia" campaign. This campaign represented a noteworthy anti-colonial movement by African Americans.

An important ideological expression of this anti-colonialism was the "internal colony" model. As a result of African-American initiative, the 1928 meeting of the Communist International in Russia resolved that black people in the American South constituted an oppressed nation with the right to their own self-determination. Although the latter proved unlikely, this ruling allowed African Americans to promote race politics, opened up the

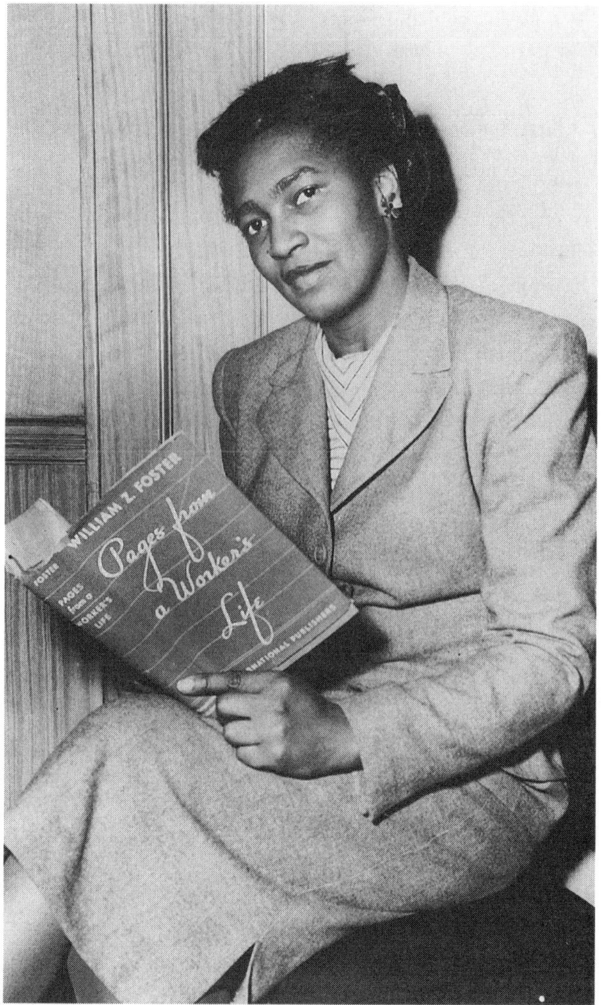

Communist leader Claudia Jones, 1940s. *Jones founded Britain's first black weekly newspaper, the* West Indian Gazette, *and was instrumental in the creation of the Notting Hill Carnival, an annual showcase for Caribbean talent.* PHOTOGRAPHS AND PRINTS DIVISION, SCHOMBURG CENTER FOR RESEARCH IN BLACK CULTURE, THE NEW YORK PUBLIC LIBRARY, ASTOR, LENOX AND TILDEN FOUNDATIONS.

CPUSA to black members, and provided an influential model for a future generation of black radicals. According to Spanish Civil War volunteer and lifelong communist Harry Haywood, there was "no substantive difference in the character of Black oppression in the United States and the colonies and semi-colonies." "In both instances," explained Haywood, "imperialist policy was directed towards forcibly arresting the free economic and cultural development of the people, towards keeping them backward as an essential condition for super-exploitation" (Haywood, 1978, p. 323). Not all black radicals agreed. British West Indian and revolutionary Marxist C. L. R. James thought that African Americans represented the vanguard of the American labor movement rather than a separate rural nation. Fellow British West Indian and revolutionary Marxist Walter Rodney later argued that the "internal colony" model failed to explain "the characteristics of a working class in a colony" (Rodney, 1990, p. 105).

Less debatable was the U.S. federal government's firm opposition to black radical thought and activity. Garvey had been jailed on questionable mail-fraud charges in the 1920s. During the 1950s, intellectuals, artists, and organizers like C. L. R. James and Claudia Jones were expelled from the United States as a result of state-sponsored anti-communist witch hunts. Ironically, much like earlier slave rebel leaders who were transported out of the country rather than executed, these black radicals ended up starting new organizations and influencing national liberation struggles elsewhere. Jones went to London, where she edited the *West Indian Gazette*; James joined the anti-colonial movement in Trinidad and Tobago as editor of *The Nation*.

During the 1930s, there were a series of anti-colonial rebellions throughout the Caribbean. In 1937 Albizu Campos led a nationalist uprising in Ponce, Puerto Rico. But the most serious revolutionary unrest occurred in the British Caribbean between 1935 and 1938. Sugar-worker strikes and revolts broke out in Saint Kitts, British Guiana, Saint Lucia, and Jamaica. Coal workers and dockworkers struck in Saint Lucia and Jamaica. There was a revolt against the increase of customs duties in Saint Vincent, while a strike by oil workers evolved into a general strike in Trinidad. There were even rumors that an armed rebellion was planned for August 1, 1938, the centennial of the abolition of slavery in the British West Indies. A "West India Royal Commission Report" later concluded that the colonies had developed "an articulate public opinion." Scholar and future Trinidadian prime minister Eric Williams put it more bluntly: "The road to revolution had been marked out" (Williams, 1970, p. 473).

Meanwhile, a Pan-African politics was being developed in London, the heart of the British Empire. African merchants and black students had often visited London in the past. During the 1930s, however, numerous black intellectuals could be found there: George Padmore and C. L. R. James from Trinidad; Harold Moody of Jamaica; T. Ras Makonnen from British Guyana; Nnamdi Azikiwi of Nigeria; Kwame Nkrumah from the Gold Coast; P. K. I. Seme of South Africa; and Jomo Kenyatta from Kenya. These black intellectuals were responsible for the formation of several important social and political organizations, including the West African Students Union in 1925, the League of Colored Peoples in 1931, and the International African Service Bureau in 1937. These radicals and their organizations played an important role in raising consciousness about colonial conditions and developing a solid anti-colonial ideology. African American artist Paul Robeson, for instance, befriended Nkrumah, Padmore, and Kenyatta, all of whom were to have a profound impact upon the artist's racial politics and identity with African liberation struggles. Two points are worth emphasizing concerning these black radicals in the metropole (the center of imperial power). First, many were influenced by their early years of study, travel, and politics in the United States. Padmore, Azikiwi, Seme, and Nkrumah came to the United Kingdom from the United States, while James left England for the United States in 1938 or 1939 and stayed until he was deported in 1950. During his ten years in the United States, Nkrumah noted that of all the books he studied, "the book that did more than any other to fire my enthusiasm was *Philosophy and Opinions of Marcus Garvey* published in 1923" (Nkrumah, 1957, p. 45). Second, these black intellectuals recognized that the project of anti-imperialism had to be centered in the metropole.

This period also saw important intellectual and cultural anti-colonial expressions. African-American writer Arna Bontemps's historical novel *Black Thunder*, published in 1936, linked slave revolts in Haiti and Virginia in a clear expression of literary Pan-Africanism. Du Bois's *Black Reconstruction* (1935), James's *Black Jacobins* (1938), and Williams's *Capitalism and Slavery* (1944) provided pioneering scholarly attempts to understand the role of slavery and working-class slaves in the making of the modern world. Walter Rodney later explained the significance of these works, produced during the revolutionary ferment of the 1930s, for his generation during the 1960s. These books were "about black people involved in revolution, involved in making choices, involved in the real movements of history" (Rodney, 1990, p. 15).

Decolonization, 1950s–1960s

One of the most important consequences of World War II was the beginning of the end of European colonialism. Between the late 1940s and early 1960s, older colonies in the Caribbean and Asia, together with newer ones in Africa, successfully gained their national independence. In the case of the British Caribbean colonies, the movement toward independence was accompanied by debates over federation versus national independence, with the latter eventually triumphant. Although Cuba had won its independence from Spain, it remained economically dependent upon the United States. Fidel Castro's 26th of July Movement against the U.S. puppet dictator Fulgencio Batista led to the installation of a new regime in 1959. The reasons for decolonization were varied and complex, but included the exhaustion of war-ravaged colonial powers, the emergence of mass protest movements, and the rise of anti-colonial leadership.

Moreover, these anti-colonial movements in the postwar world demonstrated significant interconnections among individuals, organizations, and ideas. On the one hand, the first generation of black leaders—Nkrumah, Eric Williams, and the others—had been influenced by living, working, and studying in the United States, especially through their contacts with African Americans at historically black colleges like Lincoln University and Howard University. On the other hand, anti-colonial struggles had a significant impact upon African Americans and the Black Freedom movement of the 1950s and 1960s. Penny von Eschen argues that African Americans "not only shared an oppression with colonized peoples," but saw that "their fate in the United States was intertwined with the struggles of those peoples" (von Eschen, 1997, p. 22). The national liberation of Ghana (1957) and Cuba (1959) provided constitutional and revolutionary models of change. Numerous African-American activists like Amiri Baraka, Vickie Garvin, Robert Williams, and Angela Davis were impressed with what they saw in Cuba. Algeria (1962) and Vietnam (1975) provided contemporary examples of the successful challenge of imperial domination. China's Cultural Revolution (1966–1976) offered the prospect of revolutionary transformation by people of color on the world stage. As Robin Kelley puts it, "a vision of global class revolution led by oppressed people of color was not an outgrowth of the civil rights movement's failure but existed alongside, sometimes in tension with, the movement's main ideas" (Kelley, 2002, p. 62).

There were also important intellectual and cultural expressions of decolonization during this era. Frantz Fanon, a Martinican-born psychiatrist who later joined the Algerian national movement, wrote *Black Skin, White Masks* (1952) and *The Wretched of the Earth* (1961). These two anti-colonial works were to have a critical impact on the Black Freedom movement in the United States, as well as on anti-colonial and black-consciousness movements around the world. Furthermore, popular festivals such as Kwanza, together with new expressions in clothing, hairstyles, and music, drew from an affinity with an African cultural heritage. Indeed, anti-colonialism even entered the world of sports. World heavyweight boxing champion Muhammad Ali was stripped of his title and risked imprisonment in 1967 for refusing to be drafted into the U.S. military to fight, in his own words, "other poor people" in Vietnam.

Anti-Neo-colonialism, 1972–1994

Although many new nations had thrown off their old colonial rulers, they found it harder to shrug off a global world of trade, markets, and capital investment. Direct rule by imperial powers was replaced by economic dependency on former colonial powers. This was the context for the rise of social revolution and the emergence of opposition to neo-colonialism, especially in the Caribbean nations of Jamaica and Grenada.

Michael Manley, son of the prominent Jamaican anti-colonial activist Norman Manley, won the 1972 election and was reelected in 1976 for a second term as prime minister. He campaigned on a platform of anti-colonialism and socialist reconstruction with his slogan "Better must come." Once in office, Manley established links with Castro's Cuba and began educational and land reforms. Most importantly, he challenged the economic power of foreign-owned industries by either assuming public control or, as in the case of the powerful bauxite-mining and alumina industries, greatly increasing their payment of taxes to the state. The U.S. government expressed concern at Manley's anti-Yankee rhetoric and his socialist activities, and the United States refused loans and attacked Jamaica's credit rating. Despite the economic slump, Manley was reelected in 1976. The following year, Manley took on the International Monetary Fund (IMF) and refused the austerity of its loan conditions. But Jamaica needed credit and foreign company jobs. Manley found it difficult to pursue his socialist agenda while avoiding dependency on foreign capital. By the 1980 election, Manley's compromises had alienated his radical supporters while not satisfying his liberal opponents, which resulted in a crushing defeat for him and the PNP.

In March 1979, the New Jewel Movement (NJM) led by Maurice Bishop seized power in Grenada. Much like Manley, Bishop began to court Castro's Cuba. Washington became concerned that Grenada offered another "communist" alternative in the Western Hemisphere. The self-destruction of the NJM government and the execution of Bishop by firing squad provided the reason for U.S. intervention. On October 25, 1983, the United States landed six thousand marines and installed its own regime. This military intervention met strong condemnation by Americans of African descent in the anti-colonial tradition of the 1930s and 1950s.

It was not the Caribbean, however, that saw the greatest mobilization of African Americans on behalf of national liberation struggles. The African-American movement for liberation in South Africa has a long history stretching back to Garvey during the 1920s through the Black Freedom movement in the 1950s and 1960s. This latter freedom struggle helped spawn the black consciousness movement in South Africa during the mid-1970s that was eventually brutally crushed by the apartheid state. In response, hundreds of protests flared across the United States with several hundred arrests. Sporadic protests and continuing violence against South Africans resulted in the organization of the anti-apartheid movement, whose primary aim was to terminate racist segregation through a program of economic destabilization brought about by divestment campaigns. By 1985 to 1986, 120 public colleges and universities had either partially or fully divested their investments in South Africa. The largest divestment was by the University of California, which sold $3.1 billion of its stocks in companies trading with South Africa's apartheid state. U.S. corporations also began to get the message: by 1989, there were 106 companies operating in South Africa, down from 406 five years earlier. The combination of external pressure from sanctions and internal pressure from mass protests led by the African National Congress (ANC) and the Confederation of South African Trade Unions (COSATU) paved the way for South Africa's first nonracial elections in 1994. The election of Nelson Mandela to the presidency and his visit to the United States were cheered by many African-American people, a number of whom had played a not insignificant external role in making the apartheid state indefensible.

There were also important cultural expressions of opposition to neo-colonialism, especially in the musical genre of reggae. Its origins lay in Caribbean calypso and post–World War II American rhythm and blues. Bob Marley and his group the Wailers grew up in post-independent Jamaica. They advocated radical politics in their music from their first hit "Simmer Down" in 1964, through Rasta theology of liberation, to Marley's early death from cancer in 1981. During the 1970s, Bob Marley and the Wailers had supported Michael Manley's policies of social redistribution of wealth through such albums as *Exodus* and *Natty Dread*. Marley was an important popularizer of social issues through reggae to Jamaican and Caribbean youth, as well as millions around the world. Much of this music was also reflected in the transnational migration of Afro-Caribbean people between North American, European, and African cities.

Anti-globalization in the Early Twenty-First Century

Anti-colonial movements played an important role in overthrowing colonial slavery, as well as in establishing national independence in the modern world. But there are new challenges for the 150 million Americans of African descent today, many of whom continue to suffer disparate rates of poverty, poor health, and political powerlessness. These problems are compounded, rather than alleviated, by globalization policies stewarded by international financial organizations like the IMF, the World Bank, and the finance ministers of the eight richest nations represented by the Group of Eight (G8). The seeds of a growing opposition might be found in local and national movements, as well as in international movements such as Jubilee 2000 and other debt-cancellation organizations. In addition, belief in the power of African-descended people to overthrow slavery and colonialism points to a capacity to challenge globalization, or at least to one day offer a more humane and decent alternative to its destructive tendencies.

See also Briggs, Cyril; Du Bois, W. E. B.; Garvey, Marcus; Harrison, Hubert Henry; James, C. L. R.; Jones, Claudia; Manley, Michael; Marley, Bob; New Jewel Movement; Reggae; Robeson, Paul; Rodney, Walter

Bibliography

Blackburn, Robin. *The Overthrow of Colonial Slavery, 1776–1848.* London: Verso, 1988.

Du Bois, W. E. B. *Black Reconstruction: An Essay Toward a History of the Part Which Black Folk Played in the Attempt to Reconstruct Democracy in America, 1860–1880.* New York: Harcourt, Brace, 1935.

Haywood, Harry. *Black Bolshevik: Autobiography of an Afro-American Communist.* Chicago: Liberator Press, 1978.

Holt, Thomas C. *The Problem of Freedom: Race, Labor, and Politics in Jamaica and Britain, 1832–1938.* Baltimore Md.: Johns Hopkins University Press, 1992.

Iliffe, John. *Africans: The History of a Continent.* New York and Cambridge, UK: Cambridge University Press, 1995.

James, C. L. R. *The Black Jacobins: Toussaint L'Ouverture and the San Domingo Revolution,* 2d rev. ed. New York: Vintage, 1963.

James, Winston. *Holding Aloft the Banner of Ethiopia: Caribbean Radicalism in Early Twentieth-Century America.* London: Verso, 1998.

Kelley, Robin D. G. *Race Rebels: Culture, Politics, and the Black Working Class.* New York: Free Press, 1994.

Kelley, Robin D. G. *Freedom Dreams: The Black Radical Imagination.* Boston: Beacon, 2002.

Meriwether, James H. *Proudly We Can Be Africans: Black Americans and Africa, 1935–1961.* Chapel Hill: University of North Carolina Press, 2002.

Nkrumah, Kwame. *Ghana: The Autobiography of Kwame Nkrumah.* New York: Nelson, 1957.

Robinson, Cedric J. *Black Marxism: The Making of the Black Radical Tradition.* London: Zed, 1983.

Rodney, Walter. *Walter Rodney Speaks: The Making of an African Intellectual.* Trenton, N.J.: Africa World Press, 1990.

von Eschen, Penny M. *Race Against Empire: Black Americans and Anticolonialism, 1937–1957.* Ithaca, N.Y.: Cornell University Press, 1997.

Wiener, Jon. "Reggae and Revolution." Review of *Catch a Fire: The Life of Bob Marley,* by Timothy White. *New York Times Book Review* (August 14, 1983): BR11.

Wiener, Jon. "Divestment Report Card: Students, Stocks, and Shanties." *The Nation* 243, no. 11 (1986): 337–339.

Williams, Eric Eustace. *Capitalism and Slavery.* Chapel Hill: University of North Carolina Press, 1944.

Williams, Eric Eustace. *From Columbus to Castro: The History of the Caribbean, 1492–1969.* London: Deutsch, 1970.

Vadney, T. E. *The World Since 1945.* New York: Facts on File, 1987.

JEFFREY R. KERR-RITCHIE (2005)

Anti-Haitianism

Anti-Haitianism consists of a hostile, unsympathetic, or derogatory stance towards Haiti, its people, and culture. It is, therefore, a particular kind of bigotry: a prejudice against a specific nation and its citizens. Because of the background of the Haitian population, composed largely of persons of African ancestry, anti-Haitianism is permeated by racism and deprecating notions about people of African descent in general. However, it possesses special manifestations, traceable to the way in which the Haitian nation came to exist and to the specific milieu in which it emerged.

Origins of Anti-Haitianism

Anti-Haitianism is a relatively modern phenomenon. Its genesis could be traced to the slave rebellion in the French colony of Saint Domingue in 1791. Up to then there was not a specific ideology that maligned the black inhabitants of Saint Domingue/Haiti for belonging to a concrete community. Until the eruption of the slave revolution, Saint Domingue was regarded as an archetypical colony. Actually, other Caribbean colonies sought to replicate Haiti's economy. The astounding profits generated by it, based on the exportation of tropical staples, aroused the jealousy of many non-French bureaucrats, planters, and businessmen. The backbone of this colonial utopia was its slave population, composed of over 400,000 slaves, mostly Africans, submitted to a harsh work system.

According to the colonialists' view, black equaled African equaled slave. Moreover, Africans and their descendants were perceived as barbaric and incapable of attaining civilization, defined as white (that is, Occidental or European). Nonwhites in general were regarded as backward and as a potential menace to civilization. This incapacity for reaching civilization was a natural burden of the so-conceived inferior races. Slaves in Saint Domingue were depicted according to these notions, but this sort of prejudice affected Africans and their descendants everywhere.

The slave revolution and the creation of the Republic of Haiti (1804) modified this. From then on, Haitians acquired a particularly malevolent aura. Haiti came to symbolize the worst nightmare of colonial elites. It represented the victorious but dreadful rebellion of the nonwhite against the white; it epitomized the triumph of barbarism over civilization. According to sociologist Anthony P. Maingot, this image of Haiti produced a "terrified consciousness" in the Caribbean (Maingot, p. 53). Members of a particular community (Haiti) were regarded as a menace that jeopardized the stability of Caribbean societies based on slavery. This panic embodied the first form of anti-Haitianism. It resounded all over the Americas, where elites of European ascendancy based their privileged position on the domination of laborers of either African or Amerindian origins.

Vodou and Anti-Haitianism

Vodou, the religion of most of the Haitian population, was one of the reasons for the emergence of that terrified consciousness. Like other Caribbean religions, vodou's origins could be traced to Africa. It developed in Haiti among the slaves during the colonial period and was the main bonding force among the enslaved Africans, who came from a diversity of cultural backgrounds. For instance, vodou played a central role in the slave uprising of 1791.

Vodou was linked to witchcraft, cannibalism, and zombiism as a result of misconceptions that acquired popularity during the nineteenth century. These biases were a major influence in the emergence of anti-Haitianism. They reinforced the ideas about Haitians' backwardness and barbarism. Vodou was perceived as evidence of the imperviousness of Haitians to civilized forms of life. These images of barbarism were bolstered in the United States as a consequence of the military occupation of Haiti from 1915 to 1934. Literature, plays, travel narratives, movies, and popular magazines, as well as scholarly works, disseminated such ideas about vodou. In Haiti itself, vodou was chastised by the social elites. This internal discrimination against the religion of the vast majority of the population bolstered the anti-Haitian feelings of foreign onlookers. Haiti seemed to be shrouded in mystery, black magic, inhumanity, and wicked forces.

Genesis of Dominican Anti-Haitianism

In the Dominican Republic, the country that shares the island of Hispaniola with Haiti, prevails a particularly vindictive type of anti-Haitianism. Dominican anti-Haitianism is infused by a deep nationalism that often becomes chauvinism. Dominican anti-Haitianism began to develop during the colonial period, when Spain and France shared the island of Hispaniola. According to Dominican nationalist accounts, the emergence of a French colony in Hispaniola amputated the original territory of Spanish Santo Domingo. Accordingly, Haiti is depicted as an intruder.

However, during the colonial period Dominican elites saw Saint Domingue as a model colony. Their animosity was directed against the French, not against the plantation system itself or against the black labor force. But this changed with the slave uprising in Haiti. Dominicans were also terrified by the revolution. Conceived as a war of races, the revolution aroused the specter of the Africanization of Caribbean societies. This perception was furthered by the occupation of Santo Domingo by Haitian armies, the disruption of its economic activities, and the killing and forced emigration of civilians.

The bitterness of Dominicans increased during the Haitian Domination (1822–1844), when Haiti occupied Santo Domingo. Nationalists argue that Santo Domingo's economic and cultural potential was hampered during this period, limiting its possibilities of becoming a modern nation. They claim that the aim of Haitian policies was to abate Santo Domingo's national identity and to integrate its territory into Haiti. This allegation was reinforced after Santo Domingo's independence from Haiti (1844), when the two countries engaged in several wars. Thus, during the mid-nineteenth century Haiti was perceived as a threat to the existence of the Dominican nation.

Twentieth-Century Dominican Anti-Haitianism

Haiti had desisted from regaining the Dominican Republic by the late nineteenth century. By then, the conflicts between the two countries revolved around their territorial limits. The border problem has haunted the two nations ever since, even though they have signed several frontier treaties. This issue and the emigration of Haitians to the Dominican Republic fostered anti-Haitian feelings in the latter country. During the first decades of the twentieth century, Haitians were mainly laborers on the sugar plantations. In addition, thousands settled in the Dominican side of the border.

During Rafael L. Trujillo's dictatorship (1930–1961), anti-Haitianism became a state policy. Such Dominican intellectuals as Manuel A. Peña Batlle (1902–1954) and Joaquín Balaguer (1906–2002) developed historical interpretations that agreed with the anti-Haitian ideology of Trujillo's regime. They depicted the presence of Haitians in Dominican territory as a pacific invasion. Likewise, they emphasized the primitiveness of the Haitians and the misfortunes suffered by the Dominican Republic as a result of being ravaged by its neighbors. In line with these views, in 1935–1936 the government revised the frontier treaty of 1929. It also took drastic measures to halt the occupation of Dominican land by Haitians. Thus, in 1937 thousands of Haitians were massacred in the frontier region.

Anti-Haitianism intensified in the Dominican Republic during the late twentieth century. The flow of migrants increased as economic conditions worsened in Haiti. Both in the countryside and in urban settings, Haitian laborers, peddlers, and the homeless became omnipresent in the Dominican Republic. This deepened the impression that the so-called pacific invasion was leading to the Haitianization of Dominican society. Though not always publicly acknowledged, often this apprehension was based on racial notions, on the idea that Haitians contributed to the darkening or the Africanization of the country. Although persons born in Dominican territory are constitutionally defined as nationals of the country, the offspring of Haitians often faced systematic discrimination. State agencies, the media, and the armed forces have been particularly active in fostering the discrimination against Haitians and their Dominican offspring.

Other Manifestations of Anti-Haitianism

Dominican anti-Haitianism is but one specific form of anti-Haitian feelings. Other forms of anti-Haitianism proliferated during the late twentieth century. A deteriorating economy and increasing political instability propelled the emigration of thousands of Haitians from the 1980s on. Because of its proximity to Haiti, the United States has been the principal destination of Haitians fleeing from poverty and political violence. Most of these immigrants try to enter the country illegally, crossing the sea in small and fragile ships. For this reason, these immigrants are known as boat people.

But the U.S. government has been reluctant to grant asylum to Haitian boat people. The official U.S. policy has been to return Haitians to their homeland, where most likely local authorities will harass them. This practice contrasts with the policy regarding Cuban boat people, who are granted sanctuary if they are able to reach the U.S. coast. This different treatment is justified by claiming that Cubans escape from tyranny while Haitians flee their country for economic reasons. However, Haitians and human rights organizations have condemned this selective policy as a veiled form of anti-Haitianism. Often this new form of discrimination is based on health reasons. Thus, the high prevalence of AIDS/HIV in Haiti has been used as an argument to deny admission of Haitians to the United States. While some of these arguments are a response to legitimate concerns, some may reflect new forms of sheer prejudice. After all, it is conceivable that racism, as well as old anxieties and prejudices, might still survive cloaked in scientific issues and uttered in modern language.

See also AIDS in the Americas; Haitian Revolution; Voodoo

Bibliography

Hurbon, Laënnec. *Le barbare imaginaire.* Paris: Éditions Henri Deschamps, 1987.

Inoa, Orlando, ed. *Bibliografía haitiana en la República Dominicana.* Río Piedras: Centro de Investigaciones Históricas, Universidad de Puerto Rico, 1994.

Maingot, Anthony P. "Haiti and the Terrified Consciousness of the Caribbean." In *Ethnicity in the Caribbean,* edited by Gert Oostindie, p. 53. London: Warwick University Caribbean Studies/Macmillan Caribbean, 1996.

Price-Mars, Jean. *La République d'Haiti et la République Dominicaine,* 2 vols. Port-au-Prince: Collection du Tricinquantenaire de l'Indépendance d'Haïti, 1953.

Renda, Mary A. *Taking Haiti: Military Occupation and the Culture of U.S. Imperialism.* Chapel Hill: University of North Carolina Press, 2001.

Sagás, Ernesto. *Race and Politics in the Dominican Republic.* Gainesville: University Press of Florida, 2000.

San Miguel, Pedro L. *La isla imaginada: Historia, identidad y utopía en La Española.* San Juan and Santo Domingo: Isla Negra and Librería La Trinitaria, 1997.

PEDRO L. SAN MIGUEL (2005)

Apollo Theater

The Apollo Theater has stood in the heart of Harlem, New York, as the single most important African-American theater for more than half a century, presenting major stars and launching the careers of previously unknown amateur musicians, dancers, and comics.

Located at 253 West 125th Street, the Apollo opened in 1913 as Hurtig and Seamon's Music Hall, presenting white vaudeville and burlesque theater to white audiences. As burlesque routines lost popularity and became incorporated into the downtown musical comedy revues, the theater was rechristened the Apollo by Sidney Cohen, who bought it in 1933. The inaugural show, billed as "Jazz à la Carte" and held on January 26, 1934, featured a film and several types of acts, including the Benny Carter Orchestra.

Under the direction of Frank Schiffman, the Apollo soon became famous for presenting top performers in lavish costumes on often exotic stage settings in shows hosted by Ralph Cooper. The 1,600-seat auditorium hosted thirty shows each week and was the site of regular live broadcasts on twenty-one radio stations across the country. The greatest jazz musicians of the era performed at the Apollo, including the Duke Ellington Orchestra, Lionel Hampton's band, and Louis Jordan. Perhaps the most famous of the Apollo's offerings was its amateur hour, held every Wednesday night from 11:00 P.M. until midnight, when the performances of seven or eight contestants would be judged by audience response. Those who failed to earn the audience's approval were booed offstage in mid-performance, but winners, including Ella Fitzgerald, Sarah Vaughan, and Pearl Bailey, were sometimes rewarded with recording and performance contracts. The thrilling experience of concerts at the Apollo during this period is captured on a recording of jazz broadcasts made at the Apollo in the mid-1940s, *Live at the Apollo* (1985), including performances by the Count Basie Orchestra, the Jimmie Lunceford Orchestra, and Marjorie Cooper, a singer who failed to gain the amateur hour audience's approval.

With the demise of the swing era, many of New York's grand black theaters and nightclubs closed, but the Apollo remained popular by embracing the new sounds of rhythm and blues. By the mid-1950s the Apollo regularly featured rhythm and blues revues, as well as gospel stars and comedians such as Moms Mabley and Pigmeat Markham. With the ascendance of soul music in the 1960s, the theater presented sold-out runs by soul singers such as James Brown, Sam Cooke, and Jackie Wilson and popular shows by Dionne Warwick, the Jackson 5, Gladys Knight, and Funkadelic. Brown's album *Live at the Apollo* (1963) captured not only one of the greatest performances by the "Godfather of Soul" but the extraordinary fervor of which the discerning Apollo audience was capable.

By the mid-1970s black entertainers had gained access to better-paying stadium and arena venues, and the theater could no longer afford to draw top acts. The Apollo fell on hard times, presenting only a few dozen shows per year, and closed its doors in 1977. In 1981 an investment group headed by Percy Sutton bought the theater out of bankruptcy for $225,000. Despite being declared a national historic landmark in 1983, the reinstatement of amateur hour in 1985, and a guarantee of its mortgage by New York State, the theater failed to succeed. In 1988 it underwent a $20 million renovation, but it continued to lose money—$2 million a year until 1991, when it was taken over by a nonprofit organization led by Leon Denmark and Congressman Charles Rangel. Since that time, despite continued financial losses and complaints by city officials about its administration, the Apollo has led the revitalization of 125th Street by once again presenting both the stars and unknowns of black popular music, from B. B. King to Luther Vandross, hip-hop, and rap shows.

In 2001 the Apollo began a huge expansion and restoration. New lighting and sound systems have been installed as part of the renovations, which have been funded in part through proceeds from celebrity benefit shows.

See also Bailey, Pearl; Brown, James; Ellington, Edward Kennedy "Duke"; Fitzgerald, Ella; Knight, Gladys; Mabley, Jackie "Moms"; Vaughan, Sarah

Bibliography

Cooper, Ralph, with Steve Dougherty. *Amateur Night at the Apollo.* New York: HarperCollins, 1990.

Fox, Ted. *Showtime at the Apollo.* New York: Holt, Rinehart, and Winston, 1983.

Schiffman, Jack. *Uptown: The Story of Harlem's Apollo Theater.* New York: Cowles, 1971.

Wolk, Douglas. *Live at the Apollo.* New York: Continuum, 2004.

IRA BERGER (1996)
Updated by publisher 2005

Aponte, José Antonio

c. 1756
April 9, 1812

The life of the carpenter, sculptor, and alleged rebel leader José Antonio Aponte exemplifies the experiences of people of African descent in Cuba during the late eighteenth and early nineteenth century. Although the precise date of his birth is unknown (historians believe he was probably born in 1756), the extant documentation shows that Aponte was a free man of color who was part of the black artisanry in colonial Cuba. As was true in other parts of the Americas, Cuban slaves and free persons of color dominated the urban trades and service sectors of the colonial economy. Aponte, in addition to being a carpenter and sculptor, was also a member of the colonial militia, which was, like other colonial militias established by Spain during the colonial period, composed of men of color and intended to help defend the colony from attack by rival powers. Thus Aponte was part of the more privileged sector of the Afro-Cuban population.

From January through March of 1812, a series of rebellions launched by slaves and free people of color erupted across Cuba. Rebels burned down sugar plantations in the island's interior and on the outskirts of Havana, and Spanish authorities imprisoned hundreds of slaves and free persons of color. On April 9, 1812, they executed the man they saw as the leader of the Havana rebellion: José Antonio Aponte.

In the early 1800s, the status of Cuba's free population of color was jeopardized by the expansion of slavery on the island. Since the seventeenth century, the Caribbean islands under European colonial rule supplied most of the world's sugar supply, and the production of sugar depended upon the massive exploitation of the labor of millions of African slaves. Like other Caribbean colonies, Cuba had been a slave society since the Spanish conquest in 1492. But in contrast to other Caribbean societies, such as Jamaica or Saint Domingue (today Haiti), plantation slavery was not the dominant labor system in Cuba. Rather, the island's economy was structured on small scale peasant production, cattle ranching, and contraband trade with other Caribbean colonies. However, the destruction of the sugar-plantation economy by the slave revolt in Saint Domingue (1791–1804) left a vacuum in the world sugar market. Soon thereafter, Cuban planters increasingly invested in sugar and slaves. Between 1790 and 1820, more than 300,000 African slaves arrived in Cuba. The development of sugar and the expansion of slavery dramatically transformed Cuba from a society with a relatively fluid class structure to a society whose hierarchy was more rigidly organized along racial lines. The expansion of racial slavery put free people of color in a precarious position. Fears of black rebellion routinely circulated throughout Cuban society, particularly after the outbreak of the slave revolt in Saint Domingue.

It was within this context that the slave revolts of 1812 unfolded. After arresting and interrogating suspected rebels, the Spanish colonial authorities became convinced that Aponte was the leader of a massive conspiracy. The most incriminating evidence was a book of drawings that they confiscated from his home. The book had a complex constellation of images produced by Aponte, but the ones that captured the attention of colonial authorities the most were maps of Havana and its fortifications, along with images of black soldiers defeating white soldiers in battle. Testimony from another accused conspirator claimed that Aponte also had images of the Haitian rebels Henri Christophe and Jean Jacques Dessalines. This seemingly solid evidence led the authorities to execute Aponte and a number of other free men of color for conspiring to incite a slave rebellion.

After decades of neglect, the Aponte Rebellion has become the subject of scholarly debate in recent years. Scholars such as Stephan Palmié have questioned the claim that Aponte was the mastermind behind the conspiracies. Palmié argues that historians' efforts to make Aponte into an ideal antislavery rebel has led them to overlook the other fascinating aspects of Aponte's book of drawings, which seemed to have little connection to an antislavery plot. Other scholars, including the historian Matt Childs, have acknowledged Palmié's points but still insist that the extant documentation supports the claim of an extensive conspiracy. Although Aponte clearly had relationships with a number of the rebels, his precise connection to the rebellion is difficult to determine. The debate on the rebellion exemplifies the challenges facing historians of slave resistance, who have to rely on the documents that were produced by white power structures. Although Aponte's exact role remains unclear, what is clear is that slaves and free persons of color in Cuba were active in resisting their oppression and saw the transformations enveloping the Caribbean at this time as an opportunity to strike for their freedom.

See also Christophe, Henri; Dessalines, Jean-Jacques; Haitian Revolution

Bibliography

Childs, Matt. "The Aponte Rebellion of 1812 and the Transformation of Cuban Society: Race, Slavery, and Freedom in the Atlantic world." Ph.D. diss., University of Texas at Austin, 2001.

Franco, José Luciano. *La conspiración de Aponte, 1812.* Havana: Publicaciones del Archivo Nacional de Cuba, 1963.

Palmié, Stephan. *Wizards and Scientists: Explorations in Afro-Cuban Modernity and Tradition.* Durham, N.C.: Duke University Press, 2002.

FRANK A. GURIDY (2005)

Archaeology and Archaeologists

The field of historical archaeology emerged in the United States in the mid-twentieth century out of a national preservationist movement that sought to celebrate the achievements of white America. Archaeological investigations at Jamestown, Plymouth, and Williamsburg, as well as Mount Vernon, the home of George Washington, and Monticello, the home of Thomas Jefferson, provided evidence for researchers to reconstruct the great places and venerate the great figures in American history. The experience of African Americans was all but overlooked in the early years of these endeavors. However, the civil rights movement motivated researchers to reconsider the narrow Eurocentric focus of their studies, and many historical archaeologists began to explore the black experience in the United States. Archaeological interest in the African diaspora grew with the passage of the National Historic Preservation Act of 1966. The act, implemented by Congress to preserve and protect sites of national and historical significance, included broad language that opened the door for historical archaeologists to receive federal funding for investigations aimed at delineating the lives of historically disenfranchised groups, including African Americans.

Early historical archaeological research into the African diaspora focused heavily on investigating the lives of enslaved peoples in the Americas. The coercive structures of New World slavery stifled literacy among American slaves. As a result, those interested in understanding the history of slavery and plantation life have had to rely on the small number of firsthand accounts written by slaves or the biased reporting of literate whites, usually slave owners of the elite planter class. The methods of historical archaeology, therefore, offered a unique opportunity to explore the lives of enslaved peoples who left few written records. Using architectural evidence, human skeletal remains, and broken bits of pottery, glass, and metal, historical archaeologists have helped reconstruct the African-American experience and shed new light on a people who have often been silenced in traditional histories.

In the late 1960s Charles H. Fairbanks (1984) undertook the first systematic excavations of slave quarter sites at the Kingsley plantation on the northeast coast of Florida. Fairbanks recovered evidence of house construction techniques, diet, and ceramic usage that provided insights into the material conditions of slaves in the South. Fairbanks also used the information to challenge written accounts of slavery and plantation life. For example, Fairbanks recovered gunflints and evidence of bullet manufacture from the slave quarters, which clearly indicated that slaves at Kingsley plantation possessed and used firearms. The discovery was surprising because legal codes in the South specifically outlawed gun ownership by slaves. The excavations at Kingsley also uncovered animal bones, including those of raccoon, deer, and rabbit, which indicated that wild animal species made up a large proportion of the slaves' diet. Fairbanks speculated that the slaves at Kingsley hunted wild game and used the meat to supplement the weekly food rations given to them by the plantation owner. The evidence shows that slaves were active agents in shaping their material world and were not merely dependent on the paternalistic controls of the planter class.

Yet Fairbanks and others were primarily interested in discovering "Africanisms"—material culture evidence for the survival of West and West Central African cultural traditions in the Americas. Cowry shells and glass beads, used in West and West Central Africa as currency and forms of adornment and brought to the Americas by African slaves, became markers that helped archaeologists identify sites once occupied by enslaved peoples. However, it soon became clear that slaves brought few material possessions with them from Africa and that historical archaeologists would have to refine their search for surviving African cultural artifacts in the Americas. They focused on the use of European materials in distinctly African ways.

Studying ceramic vessels recovered from the slave quarters at Cannon's Point plantation in the Georgia Sea Islands, John Solomon Otto (1984) found that slaves used a variety of imported European ceramics. However, Otto found that bowls, rather than plates, represented a disproportionate number of the ceramics from the slave quarter sites. According to Otto, the large number of bowls indicated that slaves at Cannon's Point pursued West and West Central African culinary practices, which stressed the eating of stewed foods from bowls rather than roasts from plates. Animal bones recovered from a slave quarter at Monticello also show that the cuts of meat used by slaves were consistent with stewing.

In the Caribbean island of Barbados, in the early 1970s, Jerome S. Handler and Frederick W. Lange (1978) developed another pioneering program focused on the archaeology of slavery and plantation life. Unlike Fairbanks, who studied domestic dwellings, Handler and Lange investigated the slave burial ground at the Newton sugar estate. They sought to understand the demography, health conditions, social life, and mortuary practices of plantation slaves in Barbados. Handler and Lange identified mortuary practices consistent with West and West Central African cultural traditions, including the peripheral placement of infants and children in the cemetery and the body orientations of the deceased. Moreover, the deceased were interred with grave goods, a common practice in West and West Central African mortuary rites. One individual, for example, was buried with a red clay tobacco pipe that had been produced in Africa and brought to Barbados by African slaves. However, most grave goods were of European manufacture. For example, white kaolin clay tobacco pipes, imported from Britain, were among the most prominent grave goods buried with the slaves at Newton. Yet rather than seeing the presence of European tobacco pipes as evidence that slaves in Barbados simply embraced European materials and customs, Handler and Lange stressed the blending of African and European cultural traditions. Thus, although slaves incorporated European tobacco pipes into their material world, they used them in distinctly African ways, as grave goods. Handler and Lange also scoured documentary sources to learn how slaves in Barbados acquired the kaolin clay tobacco pipes. By combining archaeological and documentary records, Handler and Lange were able to uncover an insidious reward-incentive system devised by whites in Barbados to elicit a favorable slave disposition. Tobacco and tobacco pipes were key items in that system.

The search for Africanisms continued in the United States. James Deetz (1977) investigated life at the freedman site Parting Ways in Massachusetts. As with Handler and Lange, Deetz focused not on the direct retention of African material culture but on the use of European goods in an African manner. For example, Deetz examined architecture at Parting Ways in order to show that the occupants recreated West and West Central African housing styles. Known to architectural historians as shotgun houses, the dwellings reflect an underlying African cognitive model that used twelve-foot dimensions in house construction. Although the glass windows and shingled roof of the structure gave it the appearance of a typical New England–style dwelling, the mental principles that shaped the size and spatial arrangement of the house had their origins in Africa. Root cellars, an architectural feature common on slave dwelling sites in the United States, may also reflect the continuity of West and West Central African storage techniques.

Perhaps the best evidence for the retention of African cultural traditions in the Americas comes from the study of slave-made coarse earthenware ceramics. Known to archaeologists as *colonoware*, these vessels were originally thought to have been a variety of Native American pottery. Yet the ubiquity of *colonoware* on plantation sites soon made it clear that slaves in the South exploited local clay resources and fired their own variety of pots. Leland Ferguson (1991) compared *colonoware* vessels from South Carolina with West and West Central African pottery types in order to show that the manufacturing techniques and stylistic attributes of *colonoware* had their roots in Africa. Moreover, Ferguson examined ritualistic designs, such as stars and crosses, incised on the bases of *colonoware* pots. These decorated *colonowares* were often found on river bottoms near slave settlements. Ferguson argued that the designs were similar to cosmological symbols used by the Kongo of West Central Africa to celebrate water deities. According to Ferguson, the presence of such designs on *colonoware* pots recovered from river bottoms in South Carolina reflected the ongoing spiritual beliefs of the Kongo people, who made up a large number of South Carolina slaves. Matthew Emerson's (1994) study of clay tobacco pipes in the Chesapeake also showed that slaves manufactured these pipes and incised them with traditional West and West Central African motifs. The presence of African-derived iconography on *colonoware* pots and clay tobacco pipes helped enslaved peoples in the Americas maintain material and symbolic links to their African homeland. According to Ferguson and Emerson, the slaves' use of these items represented a subtle form of resistance to the customs, beliefs, and material world of whites.

Historical archaeologists have also explored the experience of African Americans in the post-Emancipation era. Theresa A. Singleton and Mark D. Bograd (1995) and Charles E. Orser (2004), for example, studied changing settlement patterns on postbellum plantations in order to show how black tenant farmers in the South distanced themselves from the oversight and control of the planter class. Other researchers have looked at the migration of African Americans to northern cities in the nineteenth and early twentieth centuries, and studied the ways in which these new migrants used material culture to define social boundaries and challenge racist ideologies. Archaeologists have also studied the homes of famous African Americans, including Frederick Douglass and W. E. B. Du Bois. Yet, perhaps the most important archaeological work in recent years has been the study of sites associated with the Underground Railroad. These sites have become locations for memorializing the African-American struggle for freedom and equality and for celebrating the endurance of African America.

See also African Burial Ground Project; Africanisms; Architecture, Vernacular; Historians/Historiography

Bibliography

Deetz, James. *In Small Things Forgotten: The Archaeology of Early American Life*. New York: Anchor Press/ Doubleday, 1977.

Emerson, Matthew C. "Decorated Clay Tobacco Pipes from the Chesapeake: An African Connection." In *Historical Archaeology of the Chesapeake*, edited by P. Shackel and B. Little. Washington D.C.: Smithsonian Institution Press, 1994.

Fairbanks, Charles H. "The Plantation Archaeology of the Southeastern Coast." *Historical Archaeology* 18 (1984): 1–14.

Ferguson, Leland G. *Uncommon Ground: Archaeology and Early African America, 1650–1800*. Washington D.C.: Smithsonian Institution Press, 1991.

Handler, Jerome S., and Frederick W. Lange. *Plantation Slavery in Barbados: An Archaeological and Historical Investigation*. Cambridge, Mass.: Harvard University Press, 1978.

Orser, Charles E. *Race and Practice in Archaeological Interpretation*. Philadelphia: University of Pennsylvania Press, 2004.

Otto, John Solomon. *Cannon's Point Plantation, 1794–1860: Living Conditions and Status Patterns in the Old South*, "Studies in Historical Archaeology" series. Orlando, Fla.: Academic Press, 1984.

Singleton, Theresa A., and Mark D. Bograd. *The Archaeology of the African Diaspora in the Americas*, "Guides to the Archaeological Literature of the Immigrant Experience in America," no. 2. Ann Arbor, Mich.: The Society for Historical Archaeology, 1995.

FREDERICK H. SMITH (2005)

ARCHITECTURE

This entry consists of two distinct but interrelated articles.

OVERVIEW

African Americans have been involved in building and architecture since the colonial era. The colonial plantation system relied heavily on slave craftsmen imported from Africa, who brought with them skills in ironworking, woodcarving, and the use of earth and stone to produce buildings, furniture, and tools. Written records and physical examination of building technologies indicate slave involvement in most early plantation construction throughout Louisiana, such as Magnolia in Plaquemines Parish in 1795, Oakland in Bermuda, and the mansion in Cloutierville that became the home of the nineteenth-century novelist Kate Chopin. Gippy Plantation, in South Carolina, and Winsor Hall, in Greenville, Georgia, were also built by slave artisans. Some of these slave artisans were hired out to other owners as well, such as James Bell of Virginia, who was sent to Alabama to construct three spiral staircases for the Watkins-Moore-Grayson mansion.

A number of free blacks also designed and built in the antebellum South. Charles, a free black carpenter, woodworker, and mason, contracted with Robin de Logny in 1787 to build Destrehan Plantation in St. Charles Parish, Louisiana. Free black planters in Louisiana built plantation houses that include Mignon Carlin's Arlington (1850), Pierre Cazelar's Cazelar House, and Andrew Drumford's Parrish Plantation. Louis Metoyer, one of fourteen children of a former slave, studied architecture in Paris and designed the Melrose house and several other later buildings in Isle Breville, a settlement of "free people of color." Central African influences are noticeable in most of his work, especially the African House (c. 1800), designated a landmark as the only structure of its type in the United States.

This period of African-American activity in building and construction came to an abrupt end after the Civil War. Increasing industrialization, developing trade unions in the cities of the North that excluded blacks, and the economic depression that accompanied Reconstruction largely eliminated the free black planter class and with it the independent artisan and craftsman. Many free black landowners, such as the Metoyers, either lost or had their property holdings significantly reduced.

During the second half of the nineteenth century, education throughout the United States became increasingly formalized in all disciplines, including architecture, making it more difficult for craftsmen to construct buildings independently. First basic curricula, then more formal programs of architecture began to be established across the country. The Massachusetts Institute of Technology (MIT), founded in 1861, established the first architectural curriculum in the United States in 1868. That same year, the Freedman's Bureau founded Hampton Institute in Virginia to train black men and women, many of them former slaves, to "go out and teach and lead their people." From the start, Hampton offered a full building-skills program, and a number of campus buildings were designed and built by faculty and students.

Booker T. Washington modeled Tuskegee Institute (now Tuskegee University) in Alabama on Hampton, his alma mater, and expanded the school to include training in architecture and the building trades. By 1893 the school had been renamed Tuskegee Normal & Industrial Institute

African House, built in Louisiana around 1800, designed by Louis Metoyer. *Metoyer, one of fourteen children of a former slave, studied architecture in Paris and designed a number of buildings in Isle Breville, a community of free blacks in Louisiana. Central African influences are evident in the structure pictured here, the only one of its kind standing in the United States.* THE LIBRARY OF CONGRESS

and, under the direction of Robert R. Taylor, offered a complete architectural drawing program in its Department of Mechanical Industries. Tuskegee's early buildings were designed by faculty members and built under their supervision by students with student-made bricks. School records indicate that the department was established to make a profit—though this proved elusive—and that it took on design and construction jobs outside the school.

The Tuskegee program differed significantly from Hampton's in two ways; it employed a black faculty and it promoted a strong service ethic. Washington linked his architecture program to the school's primary mission to uplift a people. His program also sought to reinstate the role of the black artisan in the skilled trades. Speaking in 1901, Washington stated, "We must have not only carpenters, but also architects; we must not only have people who do the work with the hand but persons who at the same time plan the work with the brain." Aside from the work done at Hampton and Tuskegee, he continued, there were few African Americans trained in the basic principles of architecture. Indeed, in Washington's time (and to this day), the number of practicing black architects in the United States was (and is) disproportionately low. In the 1890 census, which was the first to provide a separate tabulation for architects of color, there were only forty-three black architects, a number that would rise, albeit slowly, over the succeeding decades.

A number of the earliest recognized black architects began their careers at Tuskegee as students or as faculty. Washington recruited Robert R. Taylor (1868–1942) in 1892 to develop the Department of Mechanical Industries. Taylor became the first black graduate of an architecture program, graduating from MIT in 1892. During his thirty-seven years at Tuskegee he became a vice president and confidant of Washington, designed many of Tuskegee's major buildings, and supervised much of the campus planning. Taylor retired to North Carolina in 1933 and served as a trustee of the Fayetteville State Teachers College. Taylor died of a heart attack in 1942 while on a visit to Tuskegee. Other Tuskegee architecture faculty included Wallace A. Rayfield, William Sidney Pittman, and Walter T. Bailey.

Wallace A. Rayfield (1874–1941) taught at Tuskegee from the 1890s until 1907. Like Taylor, he designed several campus buildings but eventually left to establish the first known black architectural office in Birmingham, Alabama, whose successful practice was focused on church design, one of the major areas of the field then open to blacks. He became the national architect for the African Methodist Episcopal (AME) Zion Church. Other Rayfield church designs include the Ebenezer Baptist Church in Chicago and Birmingham's Sixteenth Street Baptist Church, a landmark of the civil rights movement of the 1960s.

John A. Lankford (1874–1946), one of Taylor's first pupils, established one of the first black architectural offices in Washington, D.C., in 1897. In 1898 he designed and supervised the construction of the $100,000 Coleman Cotton Mill in Concord, North Carolina. He later worked as an instructor in architecture at several black colleges and served as superintendent of the Department of Mechanical Industries at Shaw University. Lankford served as the national supervising architect for the African Methodist Episcopal Church, for which he designed Big Bethel, a landmark of Atlanta's Auburn Avenue. He also designed churches in West and South Africa. The Grand Fountain United Order of the True Reformers, organizers of one of the first black-owned banks, commissioned him to design their national office in Washington. Lankford also participated in the creation of the School of Architecture at Howard University. Both he and Rayfield published their work in leading black journals of the time, including *The Crisis* and *Opportunity*.

William Sidney Pittman (1875–1958), after earning degrees at Tuskegee and Drexel institutes, was a member of the Tuskegee faculty from 1899 to 1905. In 1905 Pittman moved to Washington, D.C., to establish an architectural office. In 1907 he married Booker T. Washington's daughter Portia. Pittman's output included designs for schools, libraries, other public buildings, and lodges, from 1907 to 1913, which established his reputation as one of the nation's most promising black architects. The frequent "Negro Exhibits" held at national expositions following the World's Columbian Exposition at Chicago in 1893 gave Pittman and many other black architects a chance to display their skills. Pittman won the national competition for the design of the Negro Building for the Jamestown Exposition in Virginia in 1907, a building that was erected by an all-black team of contractors and workmen. In 1913 Pittman and his family moved to Dallas, Texas, where he lived until his death in 1958.

Walter T. Bailey (1882–1941) studied architecture at the University of Illinois, graduating from the program in 1904. From 1905 through 1914 he oversaw the architectural program at Tuskegee. Following in the school's tradition, Bailey oversaw the design and construction of new campus buildings and the remodeling and repairing of older ones. In 1910 he was awarded an honorary master's degree in architecture from the University of Illinois. In 1914 Bailey left Tuskegee to establish his own office in Memphis. There, Bailey designed numerous buildings for African-American fraternal organizations, including the Pythian Bathhouse and Sanitarium (1923) in Hot Springs, Arkansas, the Fraternal Savings Bank and Trust Company Building (1924) in Memphis, and the Tennessee State Pythian Building (1925) in Nashville. In 1926 he began designing the National Pythian Temple in Chicago. Shortly before the building was completed in 1928, Bailey moved his office to Chicago, where he practiced until his death in 1941. When the Pythian Temple was completed, the eight-story, $850 000 structure stood as the largest building financed, designed, and constructed by African Americans.

George Washington Foster Jr. (1866–1923) studied at Cooper Union in New York (1888–1889) and worked as a draftsman in Henry J. Hardenberg's firm; it is believed that he later worked on the Flatiron Building (1903) in New York City as a member of Daniel Burnham's firm. In 1902 he became the first black architect licensed to practice in New Jersey. After meeting Vertner Woodson Tandy through the Elks' "colored branch," the two established a partnership in 1909 that lasted until 1915. One of the highest achievements from the latter period of Foster's life was the commission to build the Mother African Methodist Episcopal Zion Church in Harlem.

Vertner Woodson Tandy (1885–1949) became the first African-American architect licensed in New York State. A Tuskegee alumnus (1905), Tandy was also the first black graduate of Cornell University's School of Architecture (1907), where he helped found Alpha Phi, the first black fraternity at Cornell. The most significant commissions of Tandy and Foster's practice in New York include St. Philip's Episcopal Church and its Queen Anne–style Parish House (1910–1911) and the Harlem townhouse of Madame C. J. Walker. After their partnership dissolved, Tandy designed Madame Walker's country house, the Villa Lewaro in Irvington-on-Hudson, New York (1917–1918); the Harlem Elks Lodge; Smalls' Paradise; and the Abraham Lincoln Houses in the Bronx, a joint venture with Skidmore, Owings & Merrill in the 1940s.

John Lewis Wilson (1898–1989), who worked for Tandy, came from a prominent Mississippi family. He was inspired to study architecture by Rayfield, who designed a church for his father, a well-known minister. In 1923 Wilson became the first black student to attend the School of Architecture at Columbia University, but after graduating, he was unable to find work at any of the white firms to which he applied. After the Harlem Riots of 1935, Wilson was the single African American appointed to a team of seven architects to design the Harlem River Houses, one of the first federal housing projects. His appointment came after protests from the black community.

Julian Francis Abele (1881–1950) graduated from the School of Architecture at the University of Pennsylvania in 1902. That same year, Abele enrolled in the Pennsylvania Academy of the Fine Arts, where he graduated in 1903 with a certificate in architectural design. It is believed that at this time he studied at the École des Beaux Arts in Paris. In 1906 Abele was hired as a junior architect by Horace Trumbauer in Philadelphia. By 1908 he was senior designer for the office and responsible for all major design work. Some of the buildings that Abele was responsible for while working in Trumbauer's office include Harvard's Widener Library (1915), the Philadelphia Museum of Art (1926), and forty-nine buildings on Duke University's campus (1925–1940). Following the death of Trumbauer in 1938, Abele and Trumbauer's architectural engineer, William Frank, continued operating under the name Office of Horace Trumbauer. At this point Abele began signing his own name to his drawings and became one of the few black members of the American Institute of Architects (AIA) in 1942.

Paul Revere Williams (1894–1980) was discouraged by his teacher at Los Angeles Polytechnic High School from pursuing a career in architecture because of his race. Ignoring this advice, he worked his way through the University of Southern California's School of Architecture and went on to achieve considerable fame. He is best known for his designs for houses of such Hollywood celebrities as Tyrone Power, Betty Grable, Julie London, Frank Sinatra, Cary Grant, Bill "Bojangles" Robinson, Barbara Stanwyck, Bert Lahr, and William Holden. For middle-class homeowners, he published *Small Homes of Tomorrow* (1945) and *New Homes for Tomorrow* (1946). In addition, Williams designed the Los Angeles International Airport restaurant building and the Freedmen's Hospital at Howard University. In 1926 he became the first black member of the AIA and was named by President Calvin Coolidge to the National Monument Commission. In 1956 Williams became the first black to be elected to the AIA College of Fellows. Over the years, Williams received numerous awards for his residential designs, as well as honorary degrees from Atlanta, Howard, and Tuskegee universities. World War II had a profound effect on the progress of African Americans in the architectural profession. In a milestone decision for black architects, the War Department awarded a $4.2 million contract in 1941 to McKissack & McKissack, a black architecture, engineering, and construction firm, founded in 1909, for the construction of Tuskegee Air Force Base. Hilyard Robinson, an architect practicing in Washington, D.C., won the architectural-design portion of the job. In 1943 Allied Engineers, Inc., a California firm organized by Williams, received a $39 million contract for the design and construction of the U.S. Navy base in Long Beach, California. Williams also contributed to the establishment of the Standard Demountable Homes Company of California, which focused on providing housing for war workers.

With funds newly available through the GI Bill of 1944, returning African-American veterans from World War II were eligible for educational opportunities far exceeding those open to previous generations. Racial segregation still limited their choices, however, creating unprecedented enrollments at Howard, Hampton, and Tuskegee. In 1949 Howard University's School of Architecture became the first predominantly black architecture school to be accredited. However, a series of U.S. Supreme Court cases culminating in the 1954 *Brown v. Board of Education of Topeka, Kansas,* opened the doors of white architectural schools to black students.

Whitney M. Young, Jr., the civil rights leader and executive director of the National Urban League, forced the architectural profession to reconsider its wider social responsibilities when he delivered his famous keynote address "Man and His Social Conscience" at the annual national convention of the American Institute of Architects in 1968. Young told his audience:

> You are not a profession that has distinguished itself by your social and civic contributions to the cause of civil rights, and I am sure that does not come to you as a shock. . . . You are most distinguished by your thunderous silence and your complete irrelevance. . . . You are employers, you are key people in the planning of our cities today. You share the responsibility for the mess we are in, in terms of the white noose around the central city. We didn't just suddenly get this situation. It was carefully planned.

Soon after Young's speech, the Ford Foundation established scholarships for black architecture students as part of a far-reaching program that included grants to

Julian Francis Abele (1881–1950)

Architect Julian F. Abele (pronounced "able") was born in South Philadelphia and received his secondary education at Philadelphia's Institute for Colored Youth. Enrolling in the University of Pennsylvania in 1898, Abele became president of the university's Architecture Society. He graduated from the Pennsylvania School of Fine Arts and Architecture in 1904—the first African American to do so. That same year Horace Trumbauer asked Abele to work for the hitherto entirely white firm of Horace Trumbauer & Associates of Philadelphia. Trumbauer sent Abele to L'Ecole des Beaux Arts in Paris, then one of the leading architecture schools in the world, from which Abele received his architectural diploma in 1906. Abele subsequently returned to the firm and became its chief designer in 1908. By 1912, he was drawing an annual salary of $12,000. As chief designer, Abele designed Philadelphia's Free Library and Museum of Art, as well as the Widener Library (the largest building on Harvard Square). He also designed the chapel and much of the campus of Trinity College in Durham, N.C., which would later become Duke University.

Abele was known for modernizing classical forms when designing structures; the Philadelphia Museum of Art, for example, with its striking colonnaded portico and Parthenon-style pediment, was a beaux arts version of a classical Greek temple. In a 1982 tribute to Abele for designing the museum, the *Philadelphia Inquirer* credited him with being "the first black American architect to have an impact on the design of large buildings."

Abele sought little personal fame for himself in return for his accomplishments. Despite his position as Horace Trumbauer's trusted friend and confidant (and Trumbauer's successor as head of the firm from 1938 to 1950), Abele's name did not appear on any of the buildings he designed, although the name of the firm was included. While the exclusion of an individual architect's name in favor of that of the firm was a professional convention of the era, it is also likely that Abele, and the Trumbauer firm as a whole, did not wish to draw attention to the fact that he was an African American. Perhaps for similar reasons, Abele did not personally visit the Duke University campus he designed or become a member of the American Institute of Architects until 1942. Whether by temperament or necessity, or perhaps a combination of the two, the light-skinned Abele was circumspect about the personal publicity he received outside of the Trumbauer firm.

Abele designed one of his last major buildings, the Allen administration building at Duke University, in 1950. He died in April of that year, a week before his sixty-ninth birthday.

DURAHN TAYLOR

schools for the upgrading of facilities. The AIA itself created a Task Force on Equal Opportunity and formed a joint venture with the Ford Foundation to establish the Minority/Disadvantaged Scholarship Program (this replaced the Ford Foundation program when the latter was discontinued in 1973). In 1982 an endowment was created to support that program. In 1983 a program report stated that more than three hundred students in fifty schools had been assisted, with a considerable success rate.

In 1968 Howard University still had the only predominantly black, accredited architecture school, prompting the AIA and the Association of Collegiate Schools of Architecture (ACSA) to join forces to accredit other programs. In the mid-1990s eight institutions identified as historically black colleges and universities (HBCUs) offered accredited, professional architecture degrees, and two offered degrees in architectural engineering. Those eight schools were Howard University, Washington, D.C.; Hampton University, Hampton, Virginia; Southern University, Baton Rogue, Louisiana; Tuskegee University, Tuskegee, Alabama; Florida A&M University, Tallahassee, Florida; Morgan State University, Baltimore, Maryland; Prairie View A&M University, Prairie View, Texas; and the University of the District of Columbia.

The Whitney M. Young, Jr., Citation Award was established in 1970 by the AIA's Social Concern Task Force. It is awarded to an architect or an architecturally focused organization in recognition of a significant contribution to social responsibility. Robert Nash was the first recipient of the citation, and also became the AIA's first African-American vice president in 1970.

In 1971 the National Organization of Minority Architects (NOMA) was founded in Chicago when a caucus of twelve black architects met at the AIA Convention in Detroit and resolved to "specifically address the concerns of black and other minority architects [in order to] add a needed dimension to the scope of the minority architects' sphere of influence." The organization strives to promote the design and development of a living, working, and recreational environment of the highest quality, as well as to increase the numbers of black architects by supporting the recruitment and education of new architects. In 1994 NOMA's membership reached approximately five hundred. Its forerunner was the National Technical Association, founded in 1926 in Chicago by Charles S. Duke.

Another resource group for black architects, founded since the 1970s, is the AIA's Minority Resources Committee (MRC), known until 1985 as the Minority Affairs Task Group (MATG). The MRC collects and disseminates information and oversees policies at the national level, as well as acting as a clearinghouse for the AIA, ACSA, and NOMA.

The tradition of African-American involvement in community-based and public building that began with the public housing and military projects of the 1930s and 1940s expanded in the 1960s and 1970s with the advent of the free clinic for architectural and urban design problems. The first prototype of the free clinic was the Architecture Renewal Committee in Harlem, or ARCH, founded by two white architects, Richard Hatch and John Bailey, in 1965 to address issues of "advocacy planning" (a phrase coined by urban planner Paul Davidoff); Max Bond was ARCH's first black director. The free-clinic concept was eventually adopted by the federal government as Community Design Centers, or CDCs. In President Lyndon Johnson's War on Poverty, CDCs provided services for the disadvantaged, primarily in urban areas. By the end of the 1960s it was clear that a substantial market for nonprofit services of this kind existed, extending beyond minority groups to many segments of society.

The recession of the mid-1970s severely affected the architectural profession, as did President Richard Nixon's moratorium on construction of low- and moderate-income housing, one of the mainstays of black architectural practices. During this fallow period, architects were forced to search elsewhere for projects. However, William Coleman, a black lawyer from Philadelphia who was the Nixon administration's secretary of transportation, established a landmark affirmative action program in public works, which mandated that 15 percent of federal funds for mass-transit projects be allocated to minority firms. However, the withdrawal of much federal support for urban social programs and for low- and moderate-income housing under Presidents Ronald Reagan and George H. W. Bush had a negative impact on the black architectural community.

In 1991 the *Directory of African American Architects* identified some 877 black architects across the country. Of these, only forty-nine were women. In 1993 black architects made up 7.5 percent of the AIA; in the profession as a whole, an estimated 1 percent, where African Americans represented 13 percent of the U.S. population. In 2005 there were 1,508 African-American architects registered in the directory, of which 172 were women. Although this is a significant improvement, African Americans are still vastly underrepresented in the profession. Furthermore, the majority of black architects work in the public sector on government projects, since institutional and professional biases continue to restrict their ability to obtain private commissions. Two reports from the 1990s commissioned by the AIA and the ACSA reiterate the fact of low numbers in the profession and focus on the problems faced by minorities in the profession. Major obstacles that were identified for students and practicing professionals included racism, depressed social communities, lack of role models, the cost of education, isolation from resources, a decrease in minority set-asides, poor representation in AIA, the absence of publicity of accomplishments in the field, tokenism in joint ventures to pursue commissions, and a high attrition rate among black students.

In addition, the century-old vocational/professional split still plagues blacks in the architecture profession. Related to the entrenched division between design and production maintained in the schools of architecture, there is even now a noticeable division in large majority firms, where larger numbers of African-American architects work on the production or technical side of building rather than in the design studios.

Black architects are engaged in a fierce debate on the merits of assimilation versus a more explicitly Afrocentric architecture, with a third group focused on the professional and artistic concerns of the architecture itself. A resurgence of interest in HBCUs, designs that incorporate traditional African elements, and interest in working almost exclusively within the black community characterize the Afrocentrist position, as opposed to the integrationists, who wish to be perceived as architects first and African Americans second.

The third group in the debate focuses on the role of African Americans in the architectural profession as a whole. This group deals less with political concerns and more with issues of social responsibility and community orientation. Their approach is based on the complex cultural and artistic history of black architects in the context of American society. In a situation in some ways analogous to the history of jazz, the proponents of this third position tend to draw upon African elements in their work, but they filter them through the lens of contemporary American culture.

One of the most visible contemporary black architects is Jack Travis, editor of the widely acclaimed book *African-American Architects in Current Practice* (1991). Travis earned his bachelor of archictecture degree from Arizona State University in 1977. After working for Skidmore, Owings & Merrill, he established his own firm in New York in 1985. Travis served as a professional adviser on director Spike Lee's *Jungle Fever* (1991), a film that featured Wesley Snipes as a black architect trying to succeed in a white professional world. Travis frequently incorporates African-inspired elements into his sleek, modernist designs. His work includes Spike Lee's office headquarters in Brooklyn, New York; many corporate projects, including retail showrooms for designer Giorgio Armani; and various private residences.

Lou Switzer is the founder, chairman, and chief executive officer of the Switzer Group, the nation's largest black-owned interior architectural design firm, located in New York. Its clients include the Equitable Life Assurance Society, Con Edison, and Citibank. After working as an office messenger and then a draftsman for various design firms, Switzer attended night architecture courses at Pratt Institute. He worked at E. F. Hutton as assistant director of facilities planning worldwide, then began his own firm in 1975. Since the 1980s it has become a major mainstream design firm, not bound to any particular design philosophy. In the mid-1990s, Switzer designed IBM's Cranford, New Jersey, facility, combining the latest in technology and working environments.

Harvey B. Gantt, a founding partner of Gantt Huberman Architects in Charlotte, North Carolina (1971), harbored an ambition to become an architect since the ninth grade. He earned his bachelor of architecture degree from Clemson University in 1965 (the architecture department's first black graduate) and his master's in city planning from MIT in 1970. Major works include the First Baptist Church in Charlotte (1977) and the C. G. O'Kelly Library at Winston-Salem State University (1990). Since the 1980s Gantt has become active in politics. He was mayor of Charlotte from 1983 to 1987 and ran for the U.S. Senate in 1990 but was narrowly defeated by incumbent Jesse Helms.

J. Max Bond, Jr., a partner in Davis Brody & Associates Architects of New York, has distinguished himself as both a teacher and practitioner in the architectural profession. Bond earned his master of architecture degree from Harvard in 1958 and spent several years during the 1960s teaching and designing buildings in Ghana, West Africa. From 1969 to 1984 Bond was professor in and then chairman of Columbia University's Division of Architecture. Since 1985 he has been dean of the School of Architecture and Environmental Studies at City College of New York. A recipient of the Whitney M. Young, Jr., Citation Award in 1987, Bond has long been active in urban renewal efforts in New York City, serving as a member of the City Planning Commission from 1980 to 1986 and as executive director of the Division of Architects Renewal Committee of Harlem. Well-known projects include the Martin Luther King, Jr., Center for Nonviolent Social Change in Atlanta (1981) and the Studio Museum in Harlem (1982).

Harry L. Overstreet had wanted to be an architect since high school and had gained practical building experience in the U.S. Army Corps of Engineers. Overstreet worked as a self-employed designer in San Francisco and later became a licensed architect. He was appointed to the planning commission of the city of Berkeley, California, and served as the national president of NOMA from 1988 to 1990. Currently a principal in Gerson/Overstreet, Overstreet's work includes the Williard Junior High School in Berkeley (1980) and the San Francisco VA Medical Center (1991).

Roberta Washington is known for her work in Harlem salvaging neglected buildings and turning them into social-service and health-care facilities. Her twelve-person practice, Roberta Washington Architects, has taken on numerous renovation projects since its founding in 1983, including Astor Row, Hotel Cecil, Hale House Homeward Bound Residence, and Sarah P. Huntington House. Washington attended Howard University, then earned her master of architecture degree from Columbia University. She worked in Mozambique from 1977 to 1981, designing a prototype medical center for women and children.

Shortly after the landmark U.S. Supreme Court decision *Sweatt v. Painter* (1950), which integrated graduate programs, John S. Chase entered the University of Texas Graduate School of Architecture in 1950 as that institution's first black student. Weathering intense racial prejudice and isolation at the university, Chase earned his master of architecture in 1952. After he graduated, no Houston architecture firms were willing to hire him, so Chase opened his own practice, becoming the first African American licensed to practice architecture in Texas, the first accepted into the Texas Society of Architects, and the first accepted into the Houston chapter of the AIA. Today Chase is the chairman and president of his own firm, with offices in Washington, D.C., and Houston, Dallas, and Austin. Appointed by President Jimmy Carter as the first African American to serve on the U.S. Commission of the Fine Arts (1980), he received the Whitney M. Young, Jr., Citation Award in 1982 and has also received the NOMA Design Excellence Award four years consecutively. Chase's striking modernist designs include the School of Education Building at Texas Southern University (1977) and the Federal Reserve Bank of Dallas (associate architect, 1992).

Norma Merrick Sklarek earned her bachelor or architecture degree from Columbia University in 1950. Thirty years later she became the first black female fellow of the AIA (1980). She was also the first black female licensed to practice architecture in California. She now serves as chair of the AIA National Ethics Council. Her work includes Downtown Plaza, Sacramento, California (1993), the all-glass Pacific Design Center in Los Angeles (1978), the Queens Fashion Mall in Queens, New York (1978), and the U.S. Embassy in Tokyo, Japan (1976). An architectural scholarship award has been founded in her name at Howard.

Robert Traynham Coles has been the president and CEO of his own firm since 1963, with offices in Buffalo, New York, and New York City. He received his bachelor of architecture from the University of Minnesota (1953) and his master of architecture from MIT (1955). Coles has taught architecture at the University of Kansas (1989) and at Carnegie Mellon University (1990–1995). The recipient of a Whitney M. Young, Jr., Citation Award (1981), he has worked to increase the representation of blacks in the profession, serving as the AIA's deputy vice president for minority affairs (1974–1976) and becoming a founding member of NOMA. His work includes the Providence Railroad Station in Providence, Rhode Island (1986), the Frank D. Reeves Municipal Center in Washington, D.C. (1987), and the Human Services Office Building in Canandaigua, New York (1988).

Notable African-American architectural partnerships include Donald L. Stull and M. David Lee of Stull and Lee, Inc., Architects & Planners in Boston. Stull and Lee founded their firm in 1966, shortly after obtaining their master of architecture degrees from Harvard. Their work includes the Ruggles Street Station in Boston (1986); Roxbury Community College, (1987); and the Harriet Tubman House, Boston (1974). Their design for a Middle Passage Memorial (1990) consists of several giant, tangential, and abstract geometric forms, whose ominous shapes evoke a slave ship. Stull has served as president of the FAIA in addition to teaching design at Harvard (1974–1981) and winning numerous awards from the AIA. Lee has served as vice president of the AIA and has taught urban design and architecture at Harvard and at MIT (1974–1983).

Three generations of the Fry family comprise Fry & Welch Associates, P.C., Architects & Planners. The firm was founded in 1954 and maintains offices in Washington, D.C.; Atlanta; Richmond, Virginia; and Baltimore. The Frys—Louis E. Fry, Sr., Jr., and III—have completed such projects as the Tuskegee Chapel, Tuskegee University (1960), and the Coppin State Athletic Center at Coppin State College (1986).

Wendell J. Campbell and Susan M. Campbell are the father-and-daughter team that make up Wendell Campbell Associates, now Campbell Tiu Campbell to honor the contributions of partner Domingo Tiu and daughter Susan, of Chicago. Wendell Campbell, the firm's president, was a founding member and the first president of NOMA (1971) and a recipient of the Whitney M. Young, Jr., Citation Award in 1976. Susan M. Campbell, the firm's vice president, received a master of urban planning degree from the University of Illinois in 1986 and an master of architecture from the Illinois Institute of Technology in 1992. The firm designed St. Mark's Zion Church in East Chicago, Indiana (1973), the Genesis Convention Center in Gary, Indiana (1982), and the Dr. John Price House in Downers Grove, Illinois (1990), among other projects.

There has been an increasing professional self-awareness among black architects. Robert Coles's speech "Black Architects: An Endangered Species," Richard Dozier's research and lectures, Jack Travis's pioneering book *African-American Architects in Current Practice,* Harry Robinson's implementation of archives at Howard University, Sharon E. Sutton's seminal work on architectural theory, and Harry Overstreet's energizing term as president of the NOMA have been critical elements in creating a climate that supports discussions of blacks in architecture.

In addition to this increasing self-awareness among black architects, the study of African-American architecture as a subject among scholars gained popularity in the 1990s and has continued into the twenty-first century. Historians' work in this area has helped to expand understanding of not only black architects and builders but also the African-American experience of living in and adapting structures for other uses (e.g., places of worship). Ellen Weiss's pioneering work on Robert R. Taylor and Tuskegee, Kenrick Ian Grandison's studies on Southern historically black colleges and universities, John Michael Vlach's examinations of plantation architecture, Barbara Burlison

Mooney's research on the architecture of slavey, and Dreck Spurlock Wilson's monumental biographical dictionary of African-American architects have contributed to establishing African-American architecture as a recognized area of research.

For three hundred years, the black experience in architecture has been inseparable from the social history, political involvements, and educational opportunities of African Americans. Black architects share not only the disadvantages but also the rich cultural heritage of African Americans. As the American population grows increasingly "minority," the architecture profession has the opportunity to enrich itself by becoming more representative of the nation as a whole.

See also *Brown v. Board of Education of Topeka, Kansas*; *Sweatt v. Painter*; Education in the United States; Hampton Institute; Tuskegee University; Walker, Madam C. J.; Washington, Booker T.

Bibliography

Adams, Michael. "Perspectives: A Legacy of Shadows." *Progressive Architecture* 72 (February 1991): 85–87.

"African American Architects Archive." Howard University, Moorland-Springarn Research Center, Washington, D.C.

Barton, Craig Evan, ed. *Sites of Memory: Perspectives on Architecture and Race.* New York: Princeton Architectural Press, 2001.

Bird, Betty, and Nancy Schwartz. *Thematic Study of African-American Architects, Buildings and Developers in Washington, DC.* Washington, D.C.: United Planning Organization and Historic Preservation Office, 1994.

Bishir, Catherine W. "Black Builders in Antebellum North Carolina." *North Carolina Historical Review* 61 (1984): 422–461.

Charles, Curtis Barnabus. "Ageless Hope: A Report Card on Access and Equity in Architecture Education and Practice." *Journal of Architectural Education* 58, no. 3 (February 2005): 53–54.

Fields, Darell Wayne. *Architecture in Black.* New Brunswick, N.J.: Athlone Press, 2000.

Grandison, Kenrick Ian. "Negotiated Space: The Black College Campus as a Cultural Record of Postbellum America." *American Quarterly* 51, no. 3 (1999): 529–579.

Groves, Paul A., and Edward K. Muller. "The Evolution of Black Residential Areas in Late Nineteenth-Century Cities." *Journal of Historical Geography* 1, no. 2 (1975): 169–191.

Kay, Jane Holtz. "Invisible Architects: Minority Firms Struggle to Achieve Recognition in a White-Dominated Profession." *Architecture* 80 (April 1991): 106–113.

Mann, Dennis A., and Bradford C. Grant, eds. *Directory of African American Architects.* Cincinnati, Ohio: University of Cincinnati, 2005.

McQueen, Clyde. *Black Churches in Texas: A Guide to Historic Congregations.* College Station: Texas A&M University Press, 2000.

Mitchell, Melvin L. *The Crisis of the African-American Architect.* San Jose, Calif.: Writer's Club Press, 2001.

Mooney, Barbara Burlison. "The Comfortable, Tasty, Framed Cottage: The Emergence of an African-American Architectural Iconography." *Journal of the Society of Architectural Historians* 52, no. 1 (March 2002): 48–67.

Mooney, Barbara Burlison. "Looking for History's Huts." *Winterthur Portfolio* 39, no. 1 (spring 2004): 43–68.

Travis, Jack. *African American Architects in Current Practice.* New York: Princeton Architectural Press, 1991.

Vlach, John Michael. "The Shotgun House: An African Architectural Legacy." In *Common Places: Readings in American Vernacular Architecture,* edited by Dell Upton and John Michael Vlach. Athens: University of Georgia Press, 1986.

Vlach, John Michael. *Back of the Big House: The Architecture of Plantation Slavery.* Chapel Hill: University of North Carolina Press, 1993.

Weiss, Ellen. "Robert R. Taylor of Tuskegee: An Early Black American Architect." *Arris* 2 (1991): 2–19.

Weiss, Ellen. "Tuskegee: Landscape in Black and White." *Winterthur Portfolio* 36, no. 1 (2001): 19–37.

Wilson, Dreck Spurlock, ed. *African American Architects: A Biographical Dictionary, 1865–1945.* New York: Routledge, 2004.

RICHARD DOZIER (1996)
GRETCHEN G. BANK (1996)
MIKAEL D. KRIZ (2005)

VERNACULAR ARCHITECTURE

Vernacular architecture is defined as the ordinary buildings and spaces constructed, shaped, or inhabited by a particular group of people. Vernacular architecture characterizes a place by giving it a specific social identity. Consequently, vernacular architecture is more than a segment of the man-made environment; it also entails an overall perception, a sense of place. Vernacular buildings and landscapes are especially important in the study of African-American history and culture, because, as a group, African Americans left very little in the way of written documentation about the intimate day-to-day features of their domestic experiences. Encoded within any artifact is its design—its cultural base—as well as evidence of manufacture and use—its social narrative. Vernacular architecture, while a diffuse sort of data demanding cautious interpretation, affords scholars entry into the spatial realms established by certain groups of African Americans.

The Africans brought to the United States during the seventeenth century were, contrary to dismissive prejudicial stereotypes, fully equipped with the conceptual and technological skills required to build their own houses. Forced to labor on plantations along the shores of the

Chesapeake and in the Carolina low country, they responded to the need for reasonable shelter by constructing small mud-walled dwellings. Archaeological remains indicate that these houses were generally rectangular in shape, and from various written accounts one can further surmise that they had roofs covered with a thatch made from tree branches or long grasses. Looking like houses straight out of Africa, these buildings did not pose, at first, the threat to a slaveholder's sense of command that one might suppose. Similar rectangular buildings with earthen walls and thatched roofs were commonplace in the British Isles, where they were usually identified as cottages suitable for the peasant classes who performed the bulk of the agricultural labor. The African houses with clay walls were thus allowed to stand for at least a generation.

The colonial period was characterized by a syncretic encounter between African and British cultures that fostered what the Africans would likely have interpreted as an opportunity to carry out their own ideas about house and home. What remained hidden within these buildings was an African feeling for appropriate space; the dimensions of the rooms were set according to the codes that their builders carried deep within their cultural personalities. In much of West and Central Africa, houses are built with small square rooms averaging ten feet by ten feet. That these same dimensions were discovered in the earliest slave quarters, constructed with either earthen walls or hewn logs, suggests perhaps an African signature and a significant degree of cultural continuity. Where Europeans saw only a small house built by people of little consequence, the enslaved Africans saw a good house constructed according to an appropriate and familiar plan. That its rooms were the right size for their style of social interaction should be seen as a subtle, but important, means of cultural preservation.

Overt African expressions of all sorts were met with increasing hostility over the course of the eighteenth century as planters initiated thoroughgoing campaigns to "improve" their properties. Even slave quarters were upgraded as slaveholders had new houses constructed with wooden frames covered with milled boards. Mud-walled houses, however, were still encouraged by some planters both for quarters and other service buildings. Robert Carter of Virginia, for example, in 1772 asked his slave dealer to find him an artisan who "understood building mud walls . . . an Artist, not a Common Laborer." But the appreciation of such skills was clearly on the decline by the middle of the nineteenth century. Sometime around 1850, James Couper, owner of Hopeton Plantation in Georgia, discovered that his African slave Okra had built an African hut plastered with mud and thatched with palmetto leaves. Upon learning of its existence, he had the building torn down immediately.

Nevertheless, mud continued to be used in the building of chimneys into the early twentieth century when bricks could not be obtained and when small outbuildings intended as animal shelters, particularly in the Sea Island areas of South Carolina, were still covered with a thatching of palmetto branches. While this can be seen simply as the methodology of poor people who had to make do with the materials that were easily available, African memories should not be discounted.

By 1860, 2.6 million blacks were living on plantations all across the South, and close to two-thirds of them were held on the larger estates in groups of fifty or more. Thus, the plantation was not only a familiar place in the black experience, it also provided a primary context in which a distinctive African-American identity would take place. An extensive repertoire of African-American cultural traits was nurtured in the quarters' communities where blacks lived largely in the exclusive company of one another. The testimony of former slaves who lived at such places describes their quarters as "little towns."

These were black places that were not merely left to the slaves, but were also, as repeated testimony confirms, places claimed by black people. Similar to the hidden African values found in the early slave houses was the sense of territorial imperative expressed by African Americans living on plantations. Out in the quarters, the fields, the work spaces, and in the woods at the margins of the plantation, too, some slaves reappropriated themselves. One Mississippi planter reported with a discernible measure of dismay that his slaves took pride in crops and livestock produced on his estate as theirs. With such possessive territorial gestures, slaves defined space for themselves.

In addition to distinctive expressions of music, oral literature, dance, folk art and craft, religion, and kinship that evolved within the plantation context, slave communities also developed sets of house types. While their designs most often had to be approved by the slave owners, slaves saw their various clusters of cabins as important buildings. Even when they were little more than simple, severe boxes, they were still homeplaces. The historian Leslie Howard Owens has recognized that the vigorous culture created by enslaved African Americans was contingent, in large measure, on a secure sense of place. "The Quarters," writes Owens, "sometimes partially, sometimes entirely, and often mysteriously, encompassed and breathed its own special vitality into these [social] experiences, frequently assuring that bondage did not snuff out the many-sided existence slaves created for themselves" (Owens, 1976, p. 224).

Under the watchful eyes of planters and overseers, quarters' communities were fashioned that contained a variety of housing options. All these house types were derived from the basic square room known as a "pen." A single pen could stand alone as a one-room cabin or could be combined with other pen units to form larger houses. Single- and double-pen cabins were the most frequently used, but also common was the "dogtrot cabin" (two pens with a wide passage between them). Occasionally, two-story houses were provided; these buildings were basically double-pen cabins stacked one on top of another. These houses, meant to provide shelter for four slave families, resembled a building type known as the I-house, the dwelling form used as residences by the majority of planters. Larger slave quarters were sometimes created by linking smaller cabins into a single structure; four- and six-pen barracks were built in this way. In the French areas of southern Louisiana, slaves were housed in distinctive buildings with relatively exotic features that one might expect to see in Quebec or even Normandy. During the 1820s on the larger rice plantations along the coasts of South Carolina and Georgia, a specialized quarters house was developed that had an asymmetrical three-room plan consisting of one narrow but deep general-purpose room that was flanked to one side by two smaller bedrooms. The loft, which could be entered by a ladder from the larger room, was intended as a sleeping area for children. Referred to as "tenement houses," dwellings of this sort were built in either single or double configurations.

By 1860 most slave housing was constructed with wooden frames that were covered with siding. Nevertheless, many were also being built with tiers of corner-notched logs, in brick and stone masonry, and, in coastal Georgia and Florida, with tabby concrete. In addition to this variety of building techniques, slave quarters, particularly those within sight of the planter's residence, might be finished in one of several fashionable styles. Touches of Grecian, Gothic, or Italianate decoration might be added to the windows, doors, and eaves. One sees in slave housing the extensive efforts by slave owners to impose their will—indeed, their cultural values—upon their human property. These persistent attempts at discipline and control resulted in the architectural assimilation of African Americans, at least with respect to building repertoire.

By the mid-nineteenth century, blacks were thoroughly familiarized with Euro-American building forms and construction techniques. Significantly, the cabins used as quarters on plantations were not exclusively plantation structures; the same buildings were used by white yeoman farmers as residences on their modest holdings. As slaves became accustomed to living in and building these houses, they transformed themselves essentially into black southerners. When some of them were able to acquire their own land after 1865, they usually chose a standard plantation building, such as the double-pen or dogtrot house, as the model for their new homes. What was different was that now they occupied both halves of the house, whereas previously a whole family had been confined to only one room. Further, they appended all manner of sheds and porches to their dwellings—personalizing touches that expressed a sense of self-empowerment and a degree of autonomy plainly suppressed in the slave cabins that were, on the outside at least, merely unadorned boxes with roofs. On the plantation a slave quarter was an outbuilding in which property was sheltered. With the end of the plantation era, black builders transformed quarters into homes, a significant social achievement.

Throughout the nineteenth century, white and black vernacular traditions merged into a single regional entity, so that differences along racial lines were manifested more as a function of relative wealth than as a matter of design choice. One instance will serve as an example of the merger of cultures in the saga of African-American vernacular architecture. Sometime around 1910 an unknown black farmer living near Darien, Georgia, built what appeared to be nothing more than a slightly larger-than-usual single-pen house with a mud-and-stick chimney at one end. But the house was actually a miniature version of a planter's house, consisting of four rooms divided by central passageway. Black notions of appropriate form and the highbrow southern ideal had become thoroughly integrated.

There remained, however, one African-American house form that signaled an alternate tradition: the shotgun house, a building one-room wide and three or more deep, oriented with its gable end to the front, stood apart from dwellings derived from the Anglo-dominated plantation system. This house owes its origins to the free black people of New Orleans, a population shaped by a massive infusion of Haitian refugees in 1809. With the arrival that year of more than 4,000 Haitian blacks, 2,060 of them free people of color, the city developed a decided black majority. In such a context, free black citizens were almost equal in number to whites, and thus there was ample opportunity for them to exercise a greater degree of cultural autonomy than might be found in other places. When they commissioned contractors to build houses, it is not too surprising that the Haitians requested a building style familiar to them. The shotgun house had a history on the island nation of Sainte Domingue (known today as Haiti) reaching back to the early sixteenth century and had been used as a mode of housing for both slaves and free blacks. Occasionally referred to as a *maison basse,* or "low house," examples were built in all sections of New Orleans, but most of them were concentrated in the Creole districts downriver and north of the French quarter.

Since almost all houses that come from European-derived traditions have their doorways on the long side, the shotgun, with its primary entrance located on the narrow gable end, was an immediately distinguishable building form. It was recognizable as both different and African American, and the name "shotgun" (locally explained as deriving from the possibility of shooting a shotgun through the house without hitting anything) may derive ultimately from the African word *to-gun,* meaning, in the Fon language of Benin, "place of assembly." These black cultural associations had become totally obscured by the turn of the twentieth century as more and more shotguns were constructed as homes for white people. Even the name was lost when the house was relabeled a "Victorian cottage."

However, hundreds of shotgun houses are still to be found in the black sections of southern towns and cities from New Orleans to Louisville, from Jacksonville to Houston. Indeed, one of the distinctive markers of the black side of town in the South is often the presence of rows of shotgun houses. This continuity, however, seems to stem mainly from the lack of economic power among contemporary blacks. Since more thin, narrow shotgun houses can be crammed into the confines of a piece of property than other house forms with wider frontage, they are the most profitable choice for rental speculators. Lower-income black people find themselves being exploited, then, by means of an artifact that once stood out as a sign of cultural difference.

As a result of the great migration of rural southern blacks to northern cities during the first half of the twentieth century, three-fourths of the African-American population in the United States could be found in urban settings by the end of the century. Contemporary black vernacular architecture thus consists mainly of buildings occupied by black people rather than buildings that they have constructed for themselves. Like most Americans, they have become consumers of domestic structures rather than creators of them. Nevertheless, through various means, principally with flowering plants and decorative painting schemes, some blacks are able to give their otherwise bland and conformist architectural settings some distinctive flourishes—often touches reminiscent of southern experience, of life "back in the country." To some extent, this type of behavior recalls the reappropriation of space first practiced in the plantation context. This is an efficient strategy, for it allows one to make rather bold claims of ownership without actually having to invest the resources required for construction. It is a marking strategy rather than a design strategy, and one that achieves important psychological benefits while husbanding one's limited economic assets.

See also Africanisms; Migration/Population, U.S.

Bibliography

Borchert, James. "Alley Landscapes of Washington." *Landscape* 23, no. 3 (1979): 2–10.

Edwards, Jay D. "The Origins of Creole Architecture." *Winterthur Portfolio* 29, nos. 2–3 (1994): 155–189.

Edwards, Jay D. "Vernacular Vision: The Gallery and Our Africanized Architectural Landscape." In *Raised to the Trade: Creole Building Arts in New Orleans,* edited by John M. Vlach. New Orleans, La.: New Orleans Museum of Art, 2003, pp. 61–94.

Ferguson, Leland. *Uncommon Ground: Archaeology and Early African America, 1650–1800.* Washington, D.C.: Smithsonian Institution Press, 1992.

Hardwick, M. Jeff. "Homestead and Bungalows: African-American Architecture in Langston, Oklahoma." In *Perspectives in Vernacular Architecture VI: Shaping Communities,* edited by Carter L. Hudgins and Elizabeth Collins Cromley. Knoxville: University of Tennessee Press, 1997, pp. 21–32.

Isaac, Rhys. *The Transformation of Virginia, 1740–1790.* Chapel Hill: University of North Carolina Press, 1982. Reprint, 1999.

McDaniel, George W. *Hearth and Home: Preserving a People's Culture.* Philadelphia: Temple University Press, 1982.

Mooney, Barbara B. "The Comfortable, Tasty, Framed Cottage: The Emergence of an African-American Iconography." *Journal of the Society of Architectural Historians* 61, no. 1 (2002): 48–67.

Owens, Leslie Howard. *This Species of Property: Slave Life and Culture in the Old South.* New York: Oxford University Press, 1976.

Upton, Dell. "White and Black Landscapes in Eighteenth-Century Virginia." *Places* 2, no. 2 (1985): 52–68.

Vlach, John Michael. *Back of the Big House: The Architecture of Plantation Slavery.* Chapel Hill: University of North Carolina Press, 1993.

Vlach, John Michael. "The Shotgun House: An African Architectural Legacy." Reprinted in *Common Places: Readings in American Vernacular Architecture,* edited by Dell Upton and John Michael Vlach. Athens: University of Georgia Press, 1976, pp. 58–78.

Vlach, John Michael. "'Us Quarters Fixed Fine:' Finding Black Builders in Southern History." Reprinted in *By the Work of Their Hands: Studies in Afro-American Folklife,* edited by John Michael Vlach. Charlottesville: University of Virginia Press, 1985, pp. 161–178.

The 135th Street Branch of the New York Public Library, c. 1930s. *Distinguished black scholar Arturo Alfonso Schomburg added his personal collection of materials to the library's Division of Negro Literature, History, and Prints, and also served as curator of the division from 1932 until his death in 1938. The division was later renamed in his honor, and in 1972 the Schomburg Center for Research in Black Culture was designated as one of the Research Libraries of the New York Public Library.* PHOTOGRAPHS AND PRINTS DIVISION, SCHOMBURG CENTER FOR RESEARCH IN BLACK CULTURE, THE NEW YORK PUBLIC LIBRARY, ASTOR, LENOX AND TILDEN FOUNDATIONS.

Westmacott, Richard. *African-American Gardens and Yards in the Rural South.* Knoxville: University of Tennessee Press, 1992.

JOHN MICHAEL VLACH (1996)
Updated bibliography

Archival Collections

Manuscript collections and archival documentation for the study of African-American culture and history are extensive and located in all the countries of the African Diaspora. An overview of relevant collections cannot be limited to North America or repositories limited to the English language. African Americans came from various parts of western Africa, and some people even came from southeastern Africa. A consideration of these origins is essential in understanding the cultural and biological composition of the African-American population, and indirectly a survey of the available documentation on the origins of African Americans in Africa inevitably touches every part of the Americas and indeed Europe as well. A full understanding of the richness and complexity of the African background must consider the various contexts in which people of similar background found themselves, both in Africa and wherever they went in the Americas. The assumption here is that archival materials have to be examined in a global context, compatible with the aims and missions of various UNESCO initiatives, including the "Slave Route" Project and the Memories of the World Program. The dignity and humanity of Africans and their descendants require satisfactory programs of archival preservation and documentary accessibility.

Increasingly, primary source materials are accessible via the Internet and in other digitalized forms, although variations in copyright policy and other restrictions on use limit access in many cases. Hence a survey of available resources can only be a guide, not a complete list of materials, collections, or repositories. It was once said that Africa and its people had no history, and then it was said that large gaps in the past could not be filled because of a paucity of sources. In fact, however, the problem is that there are so many sources that there is a problem of accessibility and, indeed, of preservation. Not only are the sources voluminous, but they are found in every country of the African Diaspora, and in virtually every repository and library in Europe, the Americas, Africa, the Middle East, and even some places in Asia.

The formation of the African Diaspora was a global phenomenon, often tied to slavery, but not always. The associations between Africa and its population with Europe and the Islamic countries of the Middle East and North Africa predate the development of the slavery systems of the Americas. Africans and people of mixed African and European descent were present in the Americas from the beginning of European subjugation and colonization of all parts of the Americas, from Canada to Argentina. Moreover, the development of the African Diaspora included the forced and voluntary movement of Africans to southeast Asia, the Philippines and Indonesia. The forced settlement of convicted criminals in Australia included Africans and their descendants. While a focus on the Caribbean, Latin America and North America is warranted, the global

Interior view of the reading room at the 135th Street Branch of the New York Public Library, with researchers working at the tables. *Now known as the Schomburg Center for Research in Black Culture, one of four primary research libraries of the NYPL, the library maintains one of the world's finest collections of materials on African diasporan experiences.* PHOTOGRAPHS AND PRINTS DIVISION, SCHOMBURG CENTER FOR RESEARCH IN BLACK CULTURE, THE NEW YORK PUBLIC LIBRARY, ASTOR, LENOX AND TILDEN FOUNDATIONS.

dimensions of African settlement and dispersal have to be remembered. Further, the archival sources for these components of the African Diaspora contain information on the dispersal of Africans everywhere. There are few places where the settlement of Africans and their descendants was not a part of the history of the modern world. The African Diaspora was a global population movement.

It has sometimes been suggested and even claimed that only minor or specific parts of archival holdings at the major archives in the Americas were related to issues of slavery and hence to the heritage of Africans and their descendants. In fact all archival holdings are potentially relevant, and in many cases it is impossible to distinguish materials that are specifically of interest to the study of the African Diaspora from general holdings of repositories. In summary, the archival materials that are crucial in the reconstruction of the history of Africans and their descendents in the Americas are voluminous and widely scattered. Moreover, knowledge of the extent of these archival holdings is increasing rapidly, raising issues of accessibility, which sometimes has become easier, but not always. Nonetheless, the quantity of documentation that is available—with the expectation that much more material will become accessible—has created problems associated with searching and otherwise identifying materials of interest on any specific topic. Major archival holdings exist in all the western European languages, especially Portuguese, Spanish, French, English, Dutch, German, Danish, Italian, and Latin, but also in Arabic and in several African languages. Moreover, the chronological depth of the documentation introduces methodological issues of interpreting the meanings of words, deciphering difficult handwriting and archaic vocabulary, and overcoming problems of damaged documentation.

African Americans came from several specific parts of Africa, including the western Sudan in the interior of Senegal and Sierra Leone, the coast of lower Guinea, from modern Ghana through Nigeria, and finally from the region of modern Angola and Congo. Hence the archives on these regions of Africa are essential in documenting the African-American experience. Major holdings are in Dakar, Senegal; Freetown, Sierra Leone; Accra, Ghana; and Luanda, Angola. The archives in Nigeria include the National Archives in Ibadan, Enugu, and Kaduna. The

Howard Dodson, director of the Schomburg Center for Research in Black Culture. *Speaking at a press conference, Dodson shows a photograph from Malcolm X's collection of diaries, photos, letters, and other materials placed on long-term loan with the Schomburg Center by the Shabazz family. The photograph held by Dodson shows Muhammad Ali with three of Malcolm X's daughters.* AP/WIDE WORLD PHOTOS

National Archives of Angola are particularly noteworthy in terms of the antiquity of documentation, the quantity of information, and the difficulty of access because of the fragile condition of most documents. In all these cases, there are also major repositories with information in Europe and the Americas, especially Brazil and Cuba. Furthermore, the archival holdings in Mali, especially in Bamako and Timbuktu, are rich in Arabic source material, much of which is indigenous to West Africa and relating to the slave trade across the Sahara as well as to the Atlantic coast. Various missionary archives, especially the Church Missionary Society, also have extensive holdings that deal directly with issues of slavery.

Major archival holdings exist in every country in North and South America, and in the islands of the Caribbean. For Martinique, Trois-Ilets and Rivière-Pilote concentrate on the history of the Diaspora. The Archives départementales de la Martinique preserve documents and have initiated a program for the conservation and digitization of records on slaves and former slaves. In other former French colonies there are collections of registers of baptism and separate registers of the enslaved population. Although many of these registers have not survived, there are some for parish of Casse-Pilote (from 1789), Macouba (from 1687), and for the nineteenth century for Carbet, Trinité, and Sainte-Marie, preserved at Centre des Archives d'outre-mer, Aix-en-Provence (Archives nationales de France).

Some holdings, such as those of Jamaica and Barbados, are vast. Detailed materials on land transfers, inheritance, legal matters, maps of plantations, and other materials are well preserved in the National Archives in Spanish Town, the Island Records Office, the National Library of Jamaica, and the Goveia Library at the University of the West Indies. In other places, the holdings are mixed. In Trinidad, very little has survived, while in Tobago there are excellent early records but in very bad condition.

Archival holdings in Cuba are extensive, located in major archives in Havana, Matanzas, and Santiago, and also in numerous churches, the ecclesiastical sources of Matanzas, Havana, Regla, and Guanabacoa. The Cuban National Archives in Havana and in Matanzas have extensive holdings. In Puerto Rico there are at least three centers that focus on documentation, including Centro de Investigaciones Historicas, University of Puerto Rico, Archivo General de Puerto Rico and the Centro de Estudios del Caribe. Nueva Granada; selection of archival documents on slavery, Archivo de la Nación, Colombia, Sección Colonia, Negros y Esclavos. Materials are supplemented by archives in Spain, especially the Archives of the Indies in Seville and in other locations. Much of the available archival materials for Central America, where the African presence was important from the sixteenth to the eighteenth centuries, is available in digital form through the ProQuest Central American Archives Collection (1544–1821). The Instituto de Historia de Nicaragua y Centroamérica at the Universidad Centroamérica has undertaken the digitalization of materials on the Mosquito Shore of the Caribbean coast.

In Brazil, there are several major national archives, such as Arquivo Nacional in Rio de Janeiro, which is the largest archive in Brazil. The archive has a good collection on slavery and the slave trade, particularly in the nineteenth century after the relocation of the Portuguese royal family to Brazil in 1808. The archive also has material on the eighteenth century and most especially a large collection of emancipation documents. The Biblioteca Nacional, also in Rio de Janeiro, is especially rich on the eighteenth century, while the Arquivo Historico at Itamaraty has the papers of the Ministerio das Relacoes Exteriores of Brasil, which houses the records of the Mixed Commission for the Suppression of the Slave Trade. In addition all bishopric and archbishopric jurisdictions have ecclesiastical documents, those in Rio the Janeiro and Sao Paulo being especially important. Every state also has an archive, such as Arquivo Publico do Estado do Rio de Janeiro and Arquivo Publico do Estado da Bahia. Those archives have information of the state administration and also political and judicial documents on slave resistance and prisons. The numerous municipal archives also have historic information. Finally, the records of the Santa Casa de Misericordia contain information on members and charitable activities. Among the Portuguese archives, the Arquivo Ultramarino contains extensive materials on Brazil. Virtually every archive in Brazil, even in areas that were not as central to slave society, has information on Africans and their descendants. For example, there are some sixty-nine archives of various sizes in Maranhão in northeastern Brazil. While the Arquivo Público do Estado do Maranhão is in good shape, materials are stored in inadequate space, making it difficult to access documents. The conditions at the other archives vary enormously, many in very bad condition. Similarly there are ten archives in Belém, the capital of the State of Pará.

The major repositories in North America include every archive and important institution in the United States and Canada. The Schomburg Center, Howard University, the Carter Brown Library at Brown University, Amistad Research Centre at Tulane University, the Huntington Library, the Library of Congress, the National Archives of the United States, National Archives of Canada, and other repositories have substantial holdings and are accessible online. The Public Record Office in London, Bibliothèque Nationale in Paris, Archives de Indias in Seville, among other repositories, have undertaken extensive digitization programs or allow digitization of documents and therefore expanded accessibility. The Public Record Office, for example, has recatalogued materials relating to the Caribbean for easier access. There are also substantial holdings in the Netherlands, Denmark, and elsewhere. These archives contain shipping records, records of slave sales, births, deaths, marriages, court records, baptismal records, missionary archives, and newspapers, including fugitive slave advertisements and slave sales. The UNESCO "Slave Route" Project and Memories of the World program have resulted in extensive archival preservation and identification. The British Library Program for Endangered Archives is also notable. Collections of oral data, including testimonies of the enslaved and formerly enslaved, contain extensive information. The WPA project in the United States is an important example.

Various databases have been developed to organize the extensive amount of documentation which can serve as useful tools in accessing primary materials. The Voyage database developed by David Eltis, David Richardson, Stephen Behrendt, and Herbert Klein has information on the archival sources for every known ship that transported enslaved Africans to the Americas. For a first approximation at a list of these sources, reference can be made to the 1999 published version of the database by Cambridge University Press. Biographical materials of enslaved Africans and their descendants are numerous, most especially for North America but also common in many parts of the diaspora, and information is being assembled in text format for all individuals who can be identified. This and other projects of data management and storage are the focus of the Harriet Tubman Resource Centre on the African Diaspora at York University (Canada) and the Wilberforce Institute for the Study of Slavery and Emancipation at University of Hull (United Kingdom). Data management also includes images of enslavement and the era of slavery, for which there are numerous websites that allow easy access to primary materials. A guide to primary materials can be found online at *A Roadmap to African-American and Diversity Resources* (ARAADR) (<http://cisit.sfcc.edu/~sdupree/RESORLIK2.HTM>).

PAUL E. LOVEJOY (2005)

Aristide, Jean-Bertrand

July 15, 1953

Jean-Bertrand Aristide is among the Republic of Haiti's most popular leaders at home and one of its best known public figures abroad, despite his forced resignation from the Haitian presidency and exile on February 29, 2004. Earlier that month, former Aristide loyalists (some of whom had been militant supporters just six months before), along with former soldiers ignored during the decade since the Haitian Army was disbanded, had launched an armed rebellion in cities and towns north of Port-au-Prince, the capital city, against President Aristide's second populist government. Significantly, peasants in northern rural settlements, like urban and rural populations south of Port-au-Prince, did not join the rebellion. Nevertheless, as the rebels approached the capital, fears of a bloodbath and an exodus of refugees prompted the three nation-states that dominate Caribbean affairs to action.

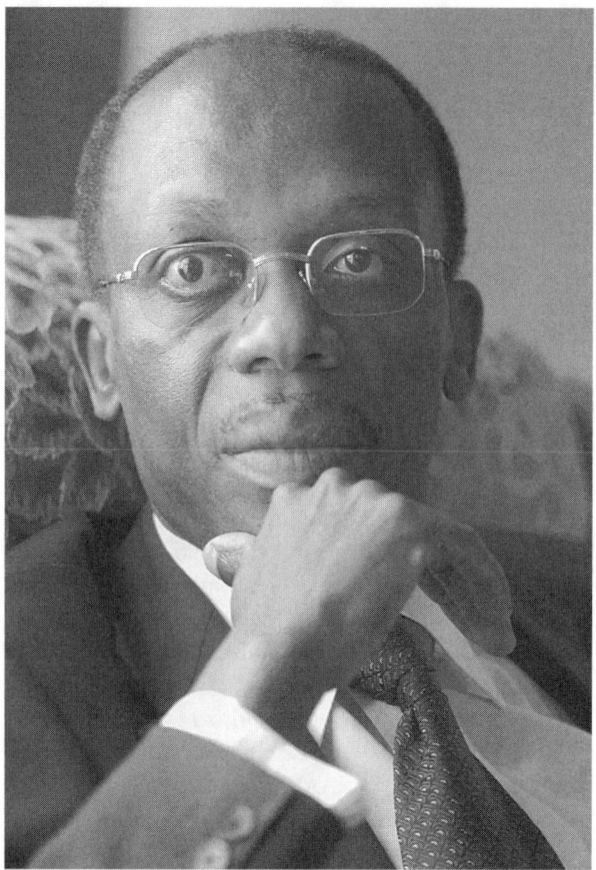

Exiled Haitian President Jean-Bertrand Aristide, October 7, 2004. *In Pretoria, South Africa, Aristide gave his first interview since being ousted from Haiti on February 29, 2004, as he announced the launch of a new book detailing his experiences and observations.* © LOUISE GUBB/CORBIS

Opposition to Aristide

Concluding that President Aristide had "lost the legitimacy to govern," the United States, France, and Canada withdrew support for the Caribbean Community (CARICOM)–mediated negotiations between the Aristide government and the Platforme de l'Opposition Démocratique (French: Democratic Opposition Platform), which, goaded by the rebellion, pointedly added "nonviolent" to its name. The expedient but simplistic decision to intervene favored overlapping short-term special interests (both Haitian and foreign) in a political situation made complex by the stark contrast between any single group's special interest and the collective interest of nearly eight million Haitians in equitable and efficient long-term institutional change.

The Platform united populist factions that broke with President Aristide after the contested 2000 legislative and municipal elections with centrist political parties marginalized since the president's first electoral victory in 1990. It also included business groups, trade unions, and professional associations, as well as secular or church-based organizations advocating human rights and the rights of university students, women, and peasants. Throughout 2003, this coalition led the criticism of President Aristide and organized several massive demonstrations against his second government's policies and discourse. Platform spokespersons charged that Aristide was increasingly autocratic and venal and that his government encouraged, rather than curbed, corruption, economic decline, the intimidation of critics, and generalized insecurity. Faithfully articulating the views of its member groups, the Platform insisted on President Aristide's departure before the 2005 elections, if not immediately. However, the extent to which the opposition coalition represented broader Haitian constituencies was unclear, and, beyond replacing the president and other central government officials, its proposals for institutional change remained everything but concrete.

Hierarchy and Equality

Aristide's public career as a radical priest-politician began in 1983, coinciding with the latest phase of the Haitian people's two-hundred-year struggle to appropriate the sociocultural and political-economic benefits of personal liberty and national sovereignty. In 1804 Generals Jean-Jacques Dessalines, Henry Christophe, Alexandre Pétion, and other high-ranking army officers proclaimed the French colony Saint-Domingue independent and underscored its independence by restoring its original Taino name in Gallicized form, Haïti or Hayti. Their proclamation crowned the world-stunning success of a twelve-year slave rebellion-turned-revolution that united the eighteenth century's subjugated Haitians—those born in Africa or in Saint-Domingue, ex-slaves and ex-freedmen, blacks, and mulattos. The nineteenth century's great powers initially treated Haiti as a pariah but gradually accorded it diplomatic recognition and then regularly intervened to protect foreign capitalists who exploited Haitian resources.

Meanwhile, early generations of Haiti's *bourgeoisie politicienne* (French: [national] politicking bourgeoisie) instituted a hierarchical sociocultural and political-economic system. Contradicting lofty French slogans such as *"Liberté et Egalité"* (Freedom and Equality) and *"L'Union Fait la Force"* (Strength through Unity), discrimination took root along lines of class (large landowner-merchant versus peasant, worker, and artisan), color (mulatto versus black), cultural orientation (erroneously construed in terms of fidelity to putatively "French" or "African" culture traits, rather than variations on a Haitian cultural synthesis), and geography (urban versus rural). The nineteenth-century politicking bourgeoisie comprised a few thousand blacks and mulattos from the elite and the middle classes for whom politics was either a livelihood or an avocation. The first U.S. occupation (1915–1934) transformed the politicking bourgeoisie, increasing its size by perhaps a factor of three, rationalizing the civilian and military wings of Haitian public administration, and centralizing power in the national capital to an unprecedented degree. Headquartered in what many Haitians began to call the "Republic of Port-au-Prince" but with branches in provincial cities and towns, the politicking bourgeoisie came to include high-ranking government officials (civilian or military), wealthy import-export merchants, practitioners of the liberal professions, and certain especially well-connected intellectuals or artists. The ideas and actions of these power-holders, aided by ideologues, counselors, messengers, brokers, and fixers, structure the Haitian polity and shape policymaking.

Voice of the People

Since 1983, Aristide's calls for radical action to deliver on past promises and remedy present inequities made him a lightning rod, a human symbol attracting adulation from supporters and hatred from detractors. He eclipses populist predecessors who, since 1804, periodically became resolute voices for their oppressed compatriots' long-denied rights and aspirations. His personal qualities made Father Aristide charismatic, and charisma became President Aristide's most important political asset. He is black, rail thin, and of small stature, and he has experienced poverty. He is also learned, mystically spiritual yet politically engaged, and an extraordinary orator in *Kreyòl,* the only language spoken and understood by most Haitians. However, Aristide resembles previous Haitian "outsiders from below" (Haitian Creole: Moun andeyò san fil ki fè deblozaj nan lapolitik nasyonal). Although such people from the provinces lacked elite social connections, their courage, skill, and popular following earned them seats at the table that was considered the politicking bourgeoisie's property, a table precariously set in a treacherous international political-economic arena. As a priest and as president, Aristide's passion-inflamed, highly metaphorical speeches for "the people" brought him national and international attention. Reactionaries deliberately misinterpreted his populist rhetoric as a sign of communist leanings. Yet that rhetoric, progressives and radicals noted, fueled impolitic strategies or tactics that sapped or obstructed collective efforts to overcome structural weaknesses in state and private institutions, ultimately undermining rights and frustrating aspirations for change.

Temperament, education, and faith-based mystical piety might have led Aristide to pursue a career in scholarship or pastoral counseling rather than radical politics. Born in 1953 outside Port-Salut, the beautiful town on the Caribbean toward the end of Haiti's southern peninsula, Aristide grew up in a middling peasant family—neither wealthy nor among the poorest of the poor—whom neighbors respected for its concern with justice and welfare. Aristide's widowed mother, a small-scale merchant, plied her trade between Port-Salut and Port-au-Prince, eventually settling there with young Jean-Bertrand and his sister. Aristide was a brilliant student, fascinated by historical, sociological, and cultural topics, and with a gift for foreign languages. Before his ordination as a Salesian priest on July 3, 1982, he excelled in the Catholic order's schools (primary school in Port-au-Prince, then seminaries in Cap-Haïtien and the Dominican Republic), and graduated from the State University of Haiti with a B.A. in psychology (1979). After ordination, he earned an M.A. in biblical theology (1985) and completed course requirements for a doctorate in philosophy and psychology at the University of Montreal before traveling to Israel for postgraduate work in theology and biblical studies.

By 1983 Father Aristide, who preached and practiced liberation theology in one of Port-au-Prince's most impoverished parishes, had begun to influence dissidents throughout Haiti as a stalwart of the politically engaged Ti Legliz (Haitian Creole: Little [Catholic] Church—the parish-level faithful, in contrast to the largely conservative ecclesiastical hierarchy). He set an example for Christian living by utilizing the meager resources at his disposal to feed the hungry, shelter the homeless, obtain medicine or treatment for the ill, and soothe the wounds, physical as well as psychological, of people abused by Haiti's power-holders. However, his vision and voice had a wider impact than his local acts of Christian fellowship. Father Aristide steadfastly proclaimed the humanity and dignity of the Haitian masses (including those whom both Catholics and Protestants denigrated for practicing *Sèvis Lwa* (French: *Vodou*; English: Voodoo), while denouncing the root causes of oppression and poverty within Haitian society as well as in Haiti's relations with foreign countries. Father Aristide preached that the greed and indifference of wealthy Haitians, the Duvalier dictatorship's ruthless oppression and terror (symbolized by the Tonton Makout, or secret state security police), and the Catholic hierarchy's other-worldly orientation joined forces with capitalist exploitation from abroad, particularly from the United States. He tirelessly spread this gospel of social and economic justice in sermons at the Saint-Jean Bosco Church and in public speeches (frequently broadcast on Radio Soleil, the Catholic Church's station), as well as in interviews with journalists and innumerable clandestine meetings with Ti Legliz activists.

President Aristide

On February 7, 1986, three years of popular protest finally ended the brutal twenty-nine year dictatorship of Dr. François "Papa Doc" Duvalier and his son Jean-Claude "Baby Doc" Duvalier, who were presidents-for-life with the right to name their successors. Jean-Claude Duvalier's ouster and the ratification of a new Haitian constitution in 1987, which seemed to restrict presidentialism—the endless quest for the presidency and a chance to wield its unmitigated power—emboldened anti-Duvalierist political factions. They formed Lavalas (Haitian Creole: flood or rising tide), a populist movement determined to end repressive, corrupt, and ineffectual military rule. In the 1990 presidential campaign, Lavalas unexpectedly chose Father Aristide as its candidate from a small cohort of activist-contenders and, stunning most observers, he won the presidency on December 16.

Contrary to global folklore, Aristide was not Haiti's first democratically elected president. He was, however, the first president chosen in a free and fair election based on universal suffrage and with a high turnout of eligible voters. President Aristide received some 67 percent of the ballots cast—the largest margin of victory by any elected head of state in the Western Hemisphere during the 1990s. For the majority of Haitians—poor peasants in rural localities, unemployed or underemployed workers in towns and cities, along with progressive elements of the urban middle classes and elite—Aristide embodied the hope for change. His February 7, 1991, inauguration represented a mandate to uproot dictatorship, facilitate full participation for all citizens in a genuine democracy, promote social justice, and implement sustainable development programs to improve living and working conditions.

Euphoria and righteous rhetoric, however, trumped long-range planning based on careful observation and analysis. Equally important, the new president faced staunch resistance from Haiti's established order: high-ranking army officers and their Tonton Makout associates, the Catholic hierarchy, certain self-styled "modern" businesspeople, and polite society in general—the privileged Haitians who feared losing power, authority, prestige, or wealth. The U.S. government and the Vatican joined with foreign corporations to signal dissatisfaction with Aristide, whom officials privately dubbed the "little Red priest." On September 30, 1991, barely seven months after the inauguration, a military junta backed by wealthy civilians drove President Aristide into exile and, until 1994, unleashed on Lavalas supporters and suspected sympathizers the most murderous reign of state-sponsored terror in Haitian history.

Exile and Return

President Aristide tirelessly traveled and spoke overseas to rally allies within the Haitian diaspora for the Lavalas government-in-exile, as well as allies among foreign governments and leftist political activists. Swayed by his exhortations, or reluctant to condone a precedent for violent regime change, the international community imposed an economic embargo on Haiti in 1992. Foreign diplomats, politicians, and activists gradually mustered support for Operation Restore Democracy, a joint U.S.-United Nations invasion of Haiti, which critics argued was the second phase of the first U.S. occupation (1915–1934). With President Bill Clinton's blessing, former President Jimmy Carter, Senator Sam Nunn, and General Colin Powell negotiated a deal with the Haitian Army's coup-makers that included a buyout and immigration to Panama.

On October 15, 1994, President Aristide triumphantly returned to find Haiti pacified by a multilateral force but devastated by the military junta's reign of terror and the embargo. Although the disbanding of the Haitian Army was applauded at home and abroad, proposed socioeconomic reforms did not materialize during the eighteen months remaining in his term. Partisans blame the neoliberal policies that foreign powers imposed in exchange for restoring Aristide to power. Equally important, however, were internal policy differences, exacerbated by three years of state-sponsored repression, which splintered the always fractious Lavalas movement. In the 1996 presidential elections, René Garcia Préval was the standard-bearer for Lafanmiy Lavalas (Haitian Creole: the Lavalas Family), the faction led by President Aristide following the Lavalas movement's split. Préval, Aristide's presumed placekeeper given the constitutional ban on successive presidential terms, was elected in December 1996 with a much lower voter turnout than in 1990.

Under what was called the Préval-Aristide government, splinter Lavalas factions battled over decentralization, privatization of state enterprises, land reform, and education and health policies, as well as nontransparent, ineffective administrative appointments and fiscal management decisions. Konvèjans Demokratik (Haitian Creole: Democratic Convergence Platform), an opposition coalition comprising all Lavalas factions except Lafanmiy Lavalas and centrist political parties, criticized the state's inaction and deliberate obstruction of remedial activities by civil society organizations and private entrepreneurs. Haiti's economy was crippled as the cost of living increased (especially prices for food, fuel, and sporadic elec-

Haitian President-elect Jean-Bertrand Aristide takes the oath of office, February 7, 2001. *At Port Au Prince, Aristide is sworn in as president for the second time, as former President Rene Preval (l) and Senate president Yvon Neptune observe.* © REUTERS/CORBIS

tricity) while employment and income declined. Insecurity reigned: armed robberies and kidnappings escalated, as did politically motivated crimes and crimes related to drug trafficking. Ecological conditions further deteriorated as deforestation, soil erosion, and water loss or pollution intensified amid mountains of trash and garbage.

In 2000 Aristide won the presidency again as expected, but Konvèjans boycotted the elections and voter turnout was lower than in 1995. The victory of Lafanmiy Lavalas candidates in nearly all legislative and municipal offices only deepened Haiti's political impasse. Opposition groups charged, and international observers corroborated, that the elections were rigged. Subsequently, Chimè (Chimera), bands of thugs said to be armed, paid, and commanded by the president, preyed on Haitians too poor to hire armed security guards for protection, violently imposing compliance with Lafanmiy Lavalas rule. Aristide himself was accused of having become a millionaire by monopolizing lucrative telecommunications businesses and diverting public funds to his private nonprofit "peoples" foundations. The gap between populist rhetoric about radical change and actual practice widened.

Second Exile

American and French officials escorted former President Aristide to exile in the Central African Republic on February 29, 2004, and he later resided briefly in Jamaica. In September 2004 he moved to South Africa as a guest of President Thabo Mbeki, the most prominent head of state to have attended the Aristide government's official celebration of the January 2004 Haitian bicentennial. While the government celebrated, the Haitian opposition, many citizens, and some foreign commentators suggested that lamentation was a more appropriate way to commemorate the bicentennial, given that a concatenation of political, economic, ecological, and social problems left Haiti more firmly lodged between a rock and a hard place than at any time in its history.

Some Haitians and foreign friends of Haiti maintain that President Aristide became as ruthless as François Duvalier with regard to justifying the achievement of political ends by any means necessary, a populist dictator ruling more erratically than Papa Doc because steadily declining state and private resources eroded the control mechanisms that might restrain subordinates. Others insist that even in exile former President Aristide remains a radical prophet, heroically standing his ground against the nefarious designs of Haitian reactionaries and foreign imperialists. In either case, the bright hopes for a democratic and more prosperous Haiti occasioned by President Aristide's 1991 inauguration have dimmed, because he could not or did not end a state of affairs called in Haitian Creole *desepsyon, demagoji, magouy, ensekirite,* (deception, demagoguery, [sterile] political wrangling, insecurity).

A moderate interim Haitian government of "national unity" was selected to restore order (with the assistance of another foreign multilateral military force) and provide public services, while planning the 2005 presidential, legislative, and municipal elections. Some stakeholders in fundamental change for the country that non-Haitians dubbed the "Black Republic" during the 1820s have retreated into despair or apathy. Others are guardedly optimistic. Most wonder whether there is any satisfactory Haitian way out of a deepening socioeconomic-ecological crisis and political impasse, which is at once the context and outcome of an eighteen-year struggle to uproot Duvalierism.

Haiti's politicking bourgeoisie will again try to build democracy and promote development. The endeavor cannot be successful if they ignore the Lavalas movement's constructive efforts to extend full citizenship rights to all Haitians. Success also depends on the Haitian people's determination to conjure a major obstacle to democratic development: dysfunctional institutions, public and private. Perhaps Aristide has taught Haitians that personal charisma, righteously radical rhetoric, and hope alone cannot produce institutional change. If Haitians fail to learn that lesson, they will reproduce another dictatorship that neither fixes a failed state nor supports an emerging civil society, leaving both adults and children at the mercy of a new global order whose international community vacillates between indifference and myopic engagement.

See also Christophe, Henri; Dessalines, Jean-Jacques; Duvalier, François

Bibliography

Aristide, Jean-Bertrand. *Eyes of the Heart: Seeking a Path for the Poor in the Age of Globalization.* Monroe, Maine: Common Courage, 1992.

Aristide, Jean-Bertrand, with Christophe Wargny. *Tout homme est un homme/Tout moun se moun.* Paris: Éditions du Seuil, 1992.

Aristide, Jean-Bertrand, with Christophe Wargny. *Aristide: An Autobiography.* Translated by Linda M. Maloney. Maryknoll, N.Y.: Orbis, 1993.

Aristide, Jean-Bertrand. *In the Parish of the Poor: Writings from Haiti.* Edited and translated by Amy Wilentz. Maryknoll, N.Y.: Orbis, 1993.

Fatton, Robert, Jr. *Haiti's Predatory Republic: The Unending Transition to Democracy.* Boulder, Colo.: Lynne Rienner, 2002.

Laguerre, Michel S. *The Military and Society in Haiti.* Knoxville: University of Tennessee Press; Houndsmill, UK: Macmillan, 1993.

Laguerre, Michel S. "The Role of the Diaspora in Haitian Politics." In *Haiti Renewed: Political and Economic Prospects,* edited by Robert I. Rotberg. Washington, D.C.: Brookings Institution Press; Cambridge, Mass.: World Peace Foundation, 1997.

Midy, Franklin. "L'Affaire Aristide en perspective: Histoire de la formation et du rejet d'une vocation prophétique." *Chemins Critiques* 11 (1989): 45–60.

Rey, Terry. "Junta, Rape, and Religion in Haiti, 1993–1994." *Journal of Feminist Studies in Religion* 15, no. 2 (1999): 73–100.

Smith, Jennie M. *When the Hands Are Many: Community Organization and Social Change in Rural Haiti.* Ithaca, N.Y.: Cornell University Press, 2001.

Trouillot, Michel-Rolph. *Les racines historiques de l'état Duvaliérien.* Port-au-Prince, Haïti: Éditions Deschamps, 1986.

Trouillot, Michel-Rolph. *Haiti, State Against Nation: The Origins and Legacy of Duvalierism.* New York: Monthly Review Press, 1990.

Trouillot, Michel-Rolph. *Silencing the Past: Power and the Production of History.* Boston: Beacon, 1995.

Trouillot, Michel-Rolph. "A Social Contract for Whom? Haitian History and Haiti's Future." In *Haiti Renewed: Political and Economic Prospects,* edited by Robert I. Rotberg. Washington, D.C.: Brookings Institution Press; Cambridge, Mass.: World Peace Foundation, 1997.

Woodson, Drexel G. "Tout Mounn Sé Mounn, men Tout Mounn Pa Menm: Microlevel Sociocultural Aspects of Land Tenure in a Northern Haitian Locality." Ph.D diss., University of Chicago, 3 vols., 1990. University Microfilms International Dissertation Services order no. T31171.

Woodson, Drexel G. "*Lamanjay,* Food Security, *Sécurité Alimentaire:* A Lesson in Communication from BARA's Mixed-Methods Approach to Baseline Research in Haiti, 1994–1996." *Culture and Agriculture* 19, no. 3 (1997): 108–122. A special issue featuring articles by the staff of the Bureau of Applied Research in Anthropology, University of Arizona, edited by Robert A. Hackenberg.

DREXEL G. WOODSON (2005)

Armstrong, Louis

August 4, 1901
July 6, 1971

Although it is certain that the jazz trumpeter and singer Daniel Louis Armstrong was born in New Orleans in pov-

Louis "Satchmo" Armstrong (1900–1971). MUSEUM OF THE CITY OF NEW YORK/ARCHIVE PHOTOS, INC/GETTY IMAGES

erty, there has long been confusion concerning his exact birth date. During his lifetime, he claimed he was born on July 4, 1900, but a baptismal certificate discovered in the 1980s now establishes his date of birth as August 4, 1901. He was raised in terrible poverty by his mother and grandmother, and he contributed to the family income from his earliest years. His first musical experience was singing in a barbershop quartet. In 1912 or 1913, according to legend, he celebrated the Fourth of July by firing a pistol; he was arrested and sent to the Colored Waifs' Home, where he remained for about two years.

Early Career and Innovations

There, his already evident interest in music was encouraged and he was given instruction on cornet and made a member of the band. Armstrong came to adulthood just as jazz was emerging as a distinct musical style in New Orleans, and the new music and Armstrong matured together. He played in local clubs called "tonks" and apprenticed in local bands, where he met most of New Orleans' early jazz musicians, and found a mentor in Joseph "King" Oliver. He soon developed a reputation as one of the best young brass musicians in the city. In 1919 he joined Fate Marable's band, playing on Mississippi riverboats, where he learned to read music. He returned to his hometown in 1921.

In 1923 King Oliver invited Armstrong to join his successful Creole Jazz Band in Chicago as second cornetist, and it was with Oliver that Armstrong made his first recordings. These records provide an invaluable document of early New Orleans jazz, and, although they contain much ensemble playing and collective improvisation, they also show that Armstrong was already a formidable soloist. The following year, encouraged by his second wife, Lil Hardin, Armstrong joined the jazz orchestra of Fletcher Henderson in New York City. Recordings such as Don Redman's arrangement of the 1924 "Copenhagen" reveal an inventive melodist and improviser. His big-band experience helped Armstrong fashion a new type of jazz playing, featuring extended improvised solos. In New York he also recorded as an accompanist to blues singers Bessie Smith, "Ma" Rainey, and Bertha "Chippie" Hill.

This new style was featured in the extraordinarily influential series of recordings made under Armstrong's leadership from 1925 to 1929 with ensembles called the Hot Fives and Hot Sevens. His collaborators on the early dates include Johnny Dodds on clarinet, Kid Ory on trombone, and pianist Lil Hardin, whom he married. Hardin played an important role at this time in furthering and supervising her husband's career.

His solos on "Big Butter and Egg Man" (1926), "Struttin' with Some Barbecue" (1927), "Potato Head Blues" (1927), and "Hotter Than That" (1927) are superb improvised melodies, and they showed that jazz was becoming a soloist's art. Every night on the bandstand, Armstrong found in pianist Earl "Fatha" Hines a musician who could not only function on his level but with whom he could exchange musical ideas. That collaboration did not produce recordings until 1928, but then it produced such masterpieces as "West End Blues," "Skip the Gutter," and the duet "Weather Bird."

In 1929 Armstrong returned to New York, which remained his home for much of the remainder of his life. That year he appeared in the Fats Waller/Andy Razaf Broadway show *Hot Chocolates.* He was also the leader of his own orchestra, which featured popular tunes rather than the original blues and New Orleans songs he had previously favored. Increasingly prominent in his performances at this time was his singing, which in its use of scat (wordless syllables) and creative rhythmic reworking of a song's lyrics and melodies influenced all subsequent jazz singers. His recordings "Body and Soul," "Memories of You," "Sweethearts on Parade" (all 1930), and "Stardust" (1931), among many others, helped establish both the repertory and playing style of big-band jazz. In 1932 and again from 1933 to 1935, he toured Europe. On the first tour he acquired the nickname "Satchmo," short for Satchelmouth, although his fellow musicians favored the sobriquet "Pops."

Later Career and Legacy

There were no real innovations in Armstrong's work after the early 1930s, but over three decades remained of this powerful trumpeter and grand and compelling entertainer's life. Extending the range of his instrument to F above high C, Armstrong recorded "Swing That Music" (1936) and two years later revisited "Struttin' with Some Barbecue," offering another classic solo on that piece. In addition to his purely musical accomplishments, in the 1930s Armstrong became an entertainment celebrity, the first African American to appear regularly on network radio programs and to be widely featured in motion pictures such as *Pennies from Heaven* (1936) and *Going Places* (1938).

By the early 1940s, Armstrong's popularity had waned somewhat. In 1947 his career was reinvigorated by his return to a small-group format under the name of Louis Armstrong and the All-Stars, which he continued to lead with varying personnel for the remainder of his life. In its early years, his fellow band members included pianist Earl Hines, trombonist Jack Teagarden, and clarinetist Barney Bigard. In his later years Armstrong made numerous tours of Europe, Asia, and Africa; in 1960 the United States government appointed him a special "ambassador of goodwill" for the positive feelings his travels abroad engendered.

Armstrong's genial and nonconfrontational personality, and his inclusion of some "coon" and plantation songs in his repertory (including his theme song, "When It's Sleepy Time down South"), were sometimes criticized by a younger, more militant generation of black entertainers. Although Armstrong was a product of the segregated South who learned early in his career not to discuss racial matters in performance, he cared deeply about racial injustice. In 1957 his uncharacteristically blunt comments about the inaction of the Eisenhower administration in the Little Rock incident ("The way they are treating my people in the South, the government can go to hell") created something of a furor, although such public statements by Armstrong were rare.

Armstrong was perhaps best known to the general public in the last years through popular recordings featuring his singing, including "Blueberry Hill" (1949), "Mack the Knife" (1955), and "Hello, Dolly" (1967). In 1988 his 1968 recording of "It's a Wonderful World" appeared on the popular charts after it was used in the film *Good Morning, Vietnam.*

Louis Armstrong had an innate ability to make people feel good simply by his presence, but that feeling was not a simple matter of cheering up his audiences. His music could encompass melancholy and sadness while at the same time expressing a compensating and equally profound joy. Armstrong was the first great improviser in jazz, and his work not only changed that music but all subsequent popular music, vocal and instrumental. He expanded the range of his instrument and all its brass cousins in ways that have affected composers and players in all forms of music. In his progression from simple beginnings to international celebrity, he became arguably both the most beloved and the most influential American musician of the twentieth century. Armstrong, whose career had slowed after a 1959 heart attack, died in Corona, Queens, where he had lived since 1942 with his fourth wife, Lucille Wilson.

See also Blues, The; Bluewomen of the 1920s and 1930s; Jazz; Jazz in African-American Culture

Bibliography

Armstrong, Louis. *Satchmo: My Life in New Orleans.* New York: Prentice-Hall, 1954.

Giddins, Gary. *Satchmo.* New York: Doubleday, 1988.

Nollen, Scott Allen. *Louis Armstrong: The Life, Music, and Screen Career.* Jefferson, N.C.: McFarland, 2004.

Schuller, Gunther. "The First Great Soloist." In *Early Jazz: Its Roots and Development.* New York: Oxford University Press, 1968, pp. 89–132.

Storb, Ilse. *Louis Armstrong: The Definitive Biography.* New York: Peter Lang, 1999.

Williams, Martin. "Louis Armstrong: Style beyond Style." In *The Jazz Tradition.* New York: Oxford University Press, 1983, pp. 52–64.

MARTIN WILLIAMS (1996)
Updated bibliography

Art

This entry consists of three distinct articles examining art in African-American culture from differing geographic perspectives.

Art in the United States, Contemporary
Derek Conrad Murray

Art in Haiti

The story of contemporary art in Haiti is complex. Precariously balanced between its creolized African culture and the influences of Europe, the country's art has been marked by a division between struggling academic artists and the equally talented (and equally struggling) self-taught artists. Haiti has always had problems of class, and this is reflected in the history of its artists. For example, while members of the middle and upper class have been able to afford art school, artists from the peasant class have been relegated to an autodidactic approach. Haiti's vernacular artists have never been truly integrated into the larger field of African-American self-taught artists. Nonetheless, most people, on hearing the phrase "Haitian Art," immediately assume it refers to the self-taught artists. Coupled with the still prevalent epithets "naïve" and "primitive," Haitian art is still veiled in a primitivist fog.

There was really no serious art movement of any kind in Haiti until the 1930s. Petion Savain (1903–1975), who studied at the Art Students League in New York in the early 1940s, was the first Haitian modernist. His work evolved toward an indigenist viewpoint, influenced by the 1928 publication of Dr. Jean Price Mars's *Thus Spoke the Uncle,* which presented Haitian folklore in a positive light. The cultural pride reflected in this book tied Haiti into the vast changes in colonial consciousness in the western hemisphere in the early and middle decades of the twentieth century. Black Pride, the growing struggle for civil rights in the United States, and a widening and deepening independence movement in countries formally governed by European rulers all caused an intellectual and creative ferment in the arts.

Influenced by Europe but informed by a nationalistic interest in its own culture, the rich intellectual life of Haiti was a beacon for artists from all over the world, including the French Surrealist writer Andre Breton, the Cuban painter Wilfredo Lam, the Martiniquan poet Aimé Césaire, and others. Haiti shared with other Caribbean islands the slave roots of its complex and rich African-American religion, vodou, an African Catholicism that provided the underlying source material for the diverse range of Haiti's arts.

The founding of the Centre d'Art by the American painter Dewitt Peters in 1944 brought attention to Haiti's artists, as did their inclusion in two UNESCO exhibitions in Paris in 1946 and 1947. It became clear that there was an active art world in the Caribbean, and that these artists had taken what they had learned from European modernism and filtered it through their own Caribbean reality. Market scenes, workers, and some religious imagery made their way into the modernist imagery. At the same time the that academically trained artists were making their art, the vernacular culture itself was manifesting important and unique imagery. The self-taught painter Philome Obin (1891–1986), for example, had been painting socially conscious paintings since the 1930s. All Haitian artists were affected by events happening across the entire black diaspora after World War I, particularly issues of colonialism and self-determination, racism and self-recognition, Garveyism, the Harlem Renaissance, and *Négritude* (a culturally based movement of politically aware artists and writers). Yet they still maintained a connection with the European art world. The self-taught artists, of course, had little or no connection to the European art movements. Their work tended to be either more spiritualized or concerned with local events. Also during this period, the Surrealists were experimenting with the concept of *Art Brut* in Europe. Art Brut was the name given to nonacademic artists by the European artist Jean Dubuffet (1901–1985). He was primarily concerned with artists who worked "outside" the established art world. Andre Breton went to Haiti in 1946 and bought five pieces from the self-taught master Hector Hyppolite (1894–1948), an event the Haitian artist had foreseen in a dream.

In the 1940s, some of the trained Haitian artists, including Savain and Georges Remponeau (b. 1916), began to paint Haitian subject matter. Aimé Césaire, the founding father of *Négritude,* visited the island in 1944. The Centre d'Art, showing trained artists at the time, encouraged non-Haitian artists to spend time in Haiti, and many came from Cuba, which had a very strong painting tradition. This Cuban influx included artists such as René Portocarrero; Carlos Enriquez (1900–1957), who was married to the American painter Alice Neel; and Wilfredo Lam (1902–1982), who visited the island with Andre Breton. Two other trained Haitian artists working at this time were Luce Turnier (1924–1994), who taught at the Centre d'Art, and Lucien Price (1915–1963), who was one of the first abstractionists in Haiti, though he continued to make more realistic drawings of Haitian culture. In 1947 the art critic and writer Selden Rodman joined the Centre d'Art just as it began to open its doors to the self-taught artists.

The Centre d'Art tirelessly promoted self-taught Haitian artists, such as Philome Obin (1887–1986), who documented the past and present history of Cap Haitien; Wilson Bigaud (b. 1931), who portrayed a personal view of daily life; and Hector Hyppolite, who used his experiences as a vodou priest in his paintings of visions and gods; as well as the dignified regal paintings of Castera Bazile (1923–1965), the wry beautifully executed vignettes of Rigaud Benoit (b. 1911), the abstract vodou spirits of Robert St. Brice (1893–1973), the allegorical political paintings of Jasmin Joseph (1914–1973), and others. A second generation of artists also emerged, including the sculptor Georges Liautaud (1899–1990). (It must be kept in mind that when art historians speak of "generations" in Haiti they are referring to the time of "discovery" rather than to the date of an artist's birth.) Many of these artists incorporated the vernacular culture in their work

Haitian self-taught artists were making an authentic art that drew its inspiration and subject matter from the local way of life. They were not primitivists working from a philosophical imperative, but the epitome of authenticity working from the roots of the culture itself. Many of their works had an immediacy, particularly in portraying the realities of everyday Haitian life, that rarely existed in the work of the trained artists, who continued to try to filter the influences of European studios into their work.

At this time, the academic painters felt the self-taught artists were receiving all the financial and critical attention, a situation that was seen as a form of reverse elitism. As a result, a rift developed at the Centre d'Art, and the earlier pioneers left the Centre in 1950 to form the Foyer des Artes Plastiques. Originally formed by academic artists such as Lucien Price, Dieudonne Cedor, Max Pinchinat, Roland Dorcely, and others, the number of artists involved in this enterprise was later reduced somewhat by those who left to study or live in Europe, though some eventually returned.

Part of the strategy of the Centre d'Art was to call the emergence of the vernacular painters a "renaissance," an unfortunate sobriquet that remains in use to this day. The term *renaissance* implies that there was a dark age, a previous period of formlessness that was then turned into a period of recognizable enlightened thinking and form. The work of twentieth-century Haitian artists, however, was always in the culture. Certain diaspora artists—such as the North Americans Bill Traylor and William Edmondson, the Jamaicans Mallica "Kapo" Reynolds and Everald Brown, or the Haitians Hector Hyppolite, Georges Liautaud, and Philome Obin—can be referred to as "culture bearers" because their work was created in the language of the culture they lived in, and because they pushed the boundaries of the Haitian matrix culture. Culture changes over time. In the Caribbean the slaves created a culture to replace what they had been uprooted and torn away from. The process of change is ongoing. Sometimes, as in the case of Liautaud's crosses, the work exists on two planes—as art and as utilitarian object. He was one of the few Haitian self-taught artists whose forged-iron crosses, for example, had one meaning to the people who commissioned his works for the cemeteries around his home, and another meaning when the same crosses were collected and shown as art in homes and galleries.

However, it was the richness of the intellectual and creative movements already in place in Haiti that laid the foundations for the creative impulses of both the trained and untrained artists. There was no "movement" uniting the self-taught artists; rather, they reinvented the wheel for themselves. Philome Obin's early paintings (beginning in the 1930s) of political history and unrest had no precedent in the Caribbean; Georges Liautaud was using his forge to make crosses and votive figures for his local communities, embellishing their altars and cemeteries as a blacksmith; and Hector Hyppolite, Andre Pierre, and Robert St. Brice were making *veves* (sacred ground drawings) and painting murals and altars in their local houses of vodou as part of their social roles as *houngans* (priests) long before the Centre d'Art existed. But there was no visual school of autodidactic art in Haiti, no group of artists who fostered a certain self-taught look. For example, in a Philome Obin painting one can readily see his Protestant outlook in the way the world is orderly and cleaned up—even in his most angry early paintings, while Hector Hyppolites' art represents an animistic African-Catholic worldview filled with an unadulterated vodou perspective. There was a wide range of approaches and styles within the self-taught artist community.

The Centre d'Art played a very important role in the early years of Haitian art, but it should primarily be seen as a great school and a provider of opportunity and publicity for a phenomenon that was already at play in the culture. It was also very much responsible for organizing the way the Western world came to view Haiti's self-taught artists. The Centre's leaders (e.g., DeWitt Peters, Selden Rodman, Francine Murat, Antonio Joseph, Pierre Monosiet) were visionary in intent but also in tune with their times. Without their input, enthusiasm, and tireless approach, much of the work of the vernacular artists of Haiti might have gone unseen, and might still be unknown. The Centre remains in operation today, attempting to keep its doors open in very turbulent times.

In the rocky political times of the early twenty-first century, Haitian art perseveres, as does the divide between the self-taught artists and the trained artists. In 1968, several younger trained artists formed a group called Poteau Mitan, drawing inspiration from the imagery and philosophy of vodou. This group included the artists Tiga (Jean-Claude Garoute, b. 1935), Patrick Vilaire (b. 1942), and Frido (Wilfred Austin, b. 1942). In the 1970s, Tiga became the figurehead for a group of mostly self-taught artists that breathed new life into the islands' vernacular work. Called St. Soleil, the group also drew primary inspiration from the mother religion of the island. Notable were Louisianne St. Fleurant, Prospere Pierre Louis, Levoy Exil, and Denis Smith, to name only a few.

Artists still struggle in Haiti, despite the political conditions there, and the growth of the Haitian diaspora around the world has made their work more widely known. The vernacular work continues to metamorphose in shape and form, ranging from political murals in the streets to the altar works by the Barra family. Young artists such as Paul Gardere (b. 1944), Mario Benjamin (b. 1964), and Edouard Duval-Carrié (b. 1954) continue to pave the way for even younger trained artists. In addition, scholars are just now beginning to integrate the work of the self-taught artists of Haiti with the equally compelling and better-documented work of self-taught artists in the United States, Jamaica, and elsewhere in the Caribbean.

See also Césaire, Aimé; Art in the United States, Contemporary; Healing and the Arts in Afro-Caribbean Cultures; Lam, Wilfredo; Négritude

Bibliography

Brown, Karen McCarthy. *Tracing the Spirit: Ethnographic Essays on Haitian Art.* Seattle: University of Washington Press, 1996.

Cosentino, Donald. *Sacred Arts of Haitian Vodou.* Los Angeles: Fowler Museum of Cultural History, University of California, 1995.

Poupeye, Veerle. *Caribbean Art.* London: Thames and Hudson, 1998.

Rodman, Selden. *Where Art is Joy: Haitian Art, The First Forty Years.* New York: Ruggles de Latour, 1988.

Thompson, Robert Farris. *Flash of the Spirit: African and African-American Art and Philosophy.* New York: Random House, 1983.

RANDALL S. MORRIS (2005)

Art in the Anglophone Caribbean

Art in the Anglophone Caribbean at the turn of the twenty-first century is a field in transition. Young artists, supported by recently established art institutions, have reimagined, redefined, and even rejected the national aims of their artistic forebears, a generation that came of age during and after the movements for national sovereignty had swept the region, starting with Jamaica's independence in 1962. In the nascent postcolonial period, many artists attended to the cause of nation building in their work. As recently elected majority black governments started to define and erect a pantheon of national symbols and heroes, many artists worked in concert to chisel or paint these newly minted icons in their representations. Frequently, aspects of the islands' "indigenous," or seemingly precolonial, flora and fauna or black working-class populations inhabited artists' representations. Many artists actively sought to elevate the long-devalued cultural expressions of African-Caribbean communities as worthy subjects of art. Boscoe Holder (c. 1920–) in Trinidad, Hervis Bain (1942–) in the Bahamas, and Karl Broodhagen (1909–) in Barbados turned to the islands' black communities in their paintings, national crests, and public sculpture commissions, respectively. Typically, artists represented black Caribbean culture through figurative forms of images, although several artists, most notably Aubrey Williams (1920–1990) of Guyana and Karl "Jerry" Craig (1939–) of Jamaica, embraced abstract expressionism. Although the artistic emphasis on black folk existed in places like Jamaica and Trinidad since the 1930s and 1940s respectively, in the post-independence era these representations formed an important image pool through which the new nation could be imagined.

Many younger artists, in contrast, create what can be described as postnational art, art precisely not compelled by and even critical of the national forces that mobilized artists working in the 1960s and 1970s. These artists, many of whom were not born under the British flag, reached artistic maturity when the sun had set on much of the optimism that pervaded the immediate post-independence era. Their work interrogates the ambiguities of the national project, its possibilities and its limits, its hopes and its unfulfilled promises. Artists variously reflect on the very signs and symbols canonized as representative of national culture, deconstruct the performance or mimicry of political authority and rule, call attention to the marginalization of certain communities in postcolonial society, and explore the continuities between colonial and national forms of governance. In Trinidadian artist Christopher Cozier's installation and performance art piece, *Conversations with a shirtjac* (1992), for example, the artist and subsequent viewers vet their disillusionment with the national project in front of a hanging shirtjac, once a symbol of the anticolonial black revolutionary and now the uniform of the national bureaucratic functionary. Bahamian artist Dionne Benjamin-Smith (1970–) similarly debunks the symbols of nationhood—the national anthem, pledge of allegiance, and flag—in her digital print *Black Crab Pledge of*

Allegiance (2004). Stanley Greaves (1934–), a Guyanese artist living in Barbados since 1987, started a series of paintings in 1992 that call attention to the seemingly carnivalesque character of contemporary national politics in Guyana and the wider Anglophone Caribbean. The works, which began with the painting *The Prologue: There Is a Meeting Here Tonight* (1994), present the political arena as a theatrical stage on which both political leaders and their followers become so consumed with the performance of power that political efficacy has been written out of the national script. In another appraisal of postcolonial society, Bahamian-Jamaican artist John Beadle's (1964–) paintings speak to the social marginalization of immigrants from throughout the Caribbean within the Bahamas. Cozier, Benjamin, Greaves, and Beadle, whose work can be characterized as postnational, should not be viewed as antinational; rather, they hold up the social, political, and artistic infrastructures of the nation to scrutiny.

Often these artists deal explicitly with the social and economic conditions and predicaments of the contemporary Anglophone Caribbean, addressing the tenability of Caribbean nationhood within the newest global economies. Barbadian Annalee Davis (1963–) in her multimedia sculpture *Barbados in a Nutshell* interrogates how Barbados's landscape, once radically overhauled by the sugar plantation, has been newly transformed by the tourist transplantation of golf courses. Jamaican-born artist Nari Ward (1963–) in his installation *The Happy Smilers: Duty Free Shopping* (1996) juxtaposes Jamaica's paradisical and duty-free touristic image, which lures travelers, with signs of widespread local migration. Barrels of immigrants' possessions placed next to the island's famed white sands attest to the ambivalent character of the contemporary Caribbean as a landscape of happy smiles and hardships, of desire and despair. Trinidadian Steve Ouditt's installation *Creole Processing Zone* (2000) explores the ambiguous place of free-trade zones or export-processing zones, spaces run by multinational corporations—exempt from national taxes and frequently free of local workers—in Caribbean islands such as Trinidad and Jamaica. Davis, Ward, and Ouditt all explore how the former plantation societies, which were intrinsic to the power of modern Europe, continue to produce commodities, and indeed to be commodities, through tourism and "free trade."

Many Caribbean artists deal with the personal implications of migration, addressing how their own identities and family histories have been transformed by "colonialization in reverse," migration of Caribbean inhabitants to Britain and cities in the United States. Starting extensively in 1947, when waves of Caribbean immigrants journeyed to England, migration has been central to the social, and artistic, formation of the contemporary Caribbean. The parents of artists David Bailey (1961–), Eddie Chambers (1960–), and Ingrid Pollard (1953–) migrated to England from Barbados, Jamaica, and Guyana, respectively. In works such as Pollard's installation *Oceans Apart* (1992) or Bailey's photographic series *From Barbados, Britain or Both*, the artists explore their relationships to and displacement from the Caribbean and their place in or alienation from the island of Britain. Albert Chong (1958–), a Chinese-Jamaican artist who migrated to the United States in 1977, similarly explores his family, diasporic, and ethnic identity through photographic images of old family photographs. Fittingly, photographs, objects especially important in the maintenance of memory and family lineage for migrants, have been central to these diasporic investigations.

While a generational split exists between national and postnational art on many Anglophone Caribbean islands, these forms coexist and a single artist's oeuvre can oscillate between them. Maxwell Taylor (1938–), for instance, started working on the eve of the Bahamas' independence in 1972 and continues to create woodblock prints and paintings of the islands' black population in a social realist vein, representations that still resonate with the elevation of black culture prevalent in the post-independence period. From the 1970s, however, the artist has been critical of the limited definition of the nation, exploring the exclusion of Haitian-Bahamian communities from the national mythos of the Bahamas. Taylor's work illustrates that long before the "postnational moment" some artists simultaneously invested in *and* maintained a critical distance from the national project.

The celebration of what artists identify as Africa or the African characteristics of Caribbean culture, a theme prevalent since the national era, remains evident in contemporary Caribbean art. Indeed, this form of art may be more popular among local collectors—typically upper-middle-class and expatriate patrons—than the work of artists who critique the nation-state. An older generation of artists continue to turn to "Africa" not only to explore the African heritage of national culture but to foreground the transnational or Pan-African links between people of African descent throughout the Caribbean and wider world. Trinidadian artist Leroi Clarke (1938–) and Bahamians Jackson Burnside (1949–) and Stanley Burnside (1947–) create semi-abstract paintings that draw stylistic influence from African-Caribbean belief systems and masquerade traditions like Obeah or Junkanoo respectively, and sometimes make figural reference to African and African-Caribbean cultures. Similarly, Jamaican artist Barrington Watson's (1931–) series of oil paintings of realistic portraits of leaders from throughout Africa and the diaspora titled *The Pan-Africanists* (2000) also stress diasporic links, broadening the national hero pantheon to a Pan-African one. In addition, many artists who identify with the Rastafarian faith, including Everald Brown (1917–) and Albert Artwell (1942–) in Jamaica, and Ras Akyem Ramsay (1953–) and Ras Ishi Butcher (1960–) in Barbados, also create expressionistic paintings that frequently speak to both the centrality of Africa or, more specifically, Ethiopia for blacks in the Anglophone Caribbean, using a visual iconography and colors of Rastafari. Although many of these artists do not participate explicitly in the postnational critiques as described above, they frequently image and imagine a world on canvas that extends beyond the boundaries of nation.

In summary, artists working in the contemporary Anglophone Caribbean variously critique the limits of nationalism, call attention to the global infringements on the island nations, interrogate their diasporic positions outside of the nation and region, and expand the imagination of nation to include a wider African diasporic community. Artists who address these and other concerns work in an increasingly active, vibrant, and diverse artistic environment in the Anglophone Caribbean, one with unprecedented support for their endeavors, both locally and globally. Previously, although the painterly and sculptural arts were important components of the national imagery in the post-independence Anglophone Caribbean, few local governments invested in institutions devoted to the visual arts or provided substantial financial support for artists in the immediate postcolonial era. One notable exception was Jamaica's National Art Museum, which was established in 1974. The museum, under the direction of David Boxer, was instrumental in expanding the national canon of art, at first centered on academic forms of art, to include the work by artists who never received formal training in art and those who drew inspiration from the wider international art world. Starting in the 1990s, national art galleries established in Trinidad, the Bahamas, and Barbados provided a venue for showcasing the islands' long institutionally neglected artists. These institutions devoted officially to "national art," however, were established when international art exhibitions and biennials, which championed "global art," increased in popularity. Exhibition spaces not officially connected to the state have been central in promoting artists in the wider art world and bringing artists from around the region and globe to the Caribbean: Caribbean Contemporary Arts (CCA7) in Trinidad and The Image Factory in Belize. Institutions based in London, such as the Institute of International Visual Arts (inIVA), have also provided important exhibition opportunities for Caribbean artists. These state and independent nonprofit art institutions in and outside of the Anglophone Caribbean, which support national and postnational art and the diverse forms of art that do not fall into either category, have brought increased the local, regional, and international visibility of art in the Anglophone Caribbean.

See also Art in Haiti; Art in the United States, Contemporary; Healing and the Arts in Afro-Caribbean Cultures; Painting and Sculpture; Pan-Africanism

Bibliography

Boxer, David, and Veerle Poupeye. *Modern Jamaican Art.* Kingston, Jamaica: Ian Randle Press, 1998.

Cummins, Alissandra, Allison Thompson, and Nick Whittle. *Art in Barbados: What Kind of Mirror Image?* Kingston, Jamaica: Ian Randle Press, 1998.

Paul, Annie. "The Enigma of Arrival: Traveling beyond the Expat Gaze." *Art Journal* 62, no. 1 (Spring 2003): 48–65.

Poupeye, Veerle. *Caribbean Art.* London: Thames and Hudson, 1998.

KRISTA A. THOMPSON (2005)

Art in the United States, Contemporary

Visual art created by people of African descent in the United States has changed dramatically, both aesthetically and conceptually, since the 1980s. Many factors have contributed to these shifts, most notably ever-changing sociopolitical and theoretical forces that shaped the concept of *blackness*, a term that emerged during the 1960s' push for self-empowerment. Since the 1980s, contemporary African-American artists have critically distanced themselves from the aesthetic and philosophical strategies galvanized during the years of the Harlem Renaissance, the civil rights movement, and the Black Power movement (i.e., from the 1920s through the 1970s). The art of these periods called for the visualizing of an ideal Afrocentric or nationalistic blackness, which in turn became an essential component to resistance efforts. While the term *blackness* provided a self-empowering means to counteract the negative stereotypes associated with African people living in North America, ultimately it was viewed as limiting by the subsequent generation of African Americans. As a result of the well-documented and extremely rich history of black art in the United States, work produced in the 1980s emerged as distinctly self-critical. In this regard, African-American visual artists began to aggressively respond to the intellectual and artistic efforts of this cultural legacy, with the intention of moving beyond the limitations of their predecessors.

Among the most enduring early twentieth-century theoreticians to be revisited by black visual artists and intellectuals in the mid-1980s was the African-American scholar W. E. B. Du Bois (1868–1963). In 1900, at the Pan-African Conference held in London, Du Bois stated that "the problem of the twentieth century is the problem of the color line." Even today, his words are largely recognized as a "formulation that is often considered an inauguration for thinking about the significance of race in the modern world" (Edwards, 2003, p.1). The Harlem Renaissance is widely known as a time of cultural awakening and worldwide black allegiances forged under the banner of unity. The New Negro movement, defined by Du Bois and the scholar Alain Locke (1886–1954), functioned in many ways as a manifesto for the social, spiritual, and artistic goals for blacks in America. Locke, in his pioneering critical anthology, *The New Negro* (1925), captured the bourgeoning "racial attitudes" that articulated a renewed sense of pride, empowerment, and resistance to racial oppression. Both Locke and Du Bois championed the arts as an essential component in the development of a newly empowered blackness. Furthermore, these two pioneers called upon artists to reclaim their African past—aesthetically, spiritually, and politically—and to utilize it as a source of inspiration in an effort to create a uniquely black American voice.

The visualized Afrocentrism that Locke and Du Bois professed dramatically influenced black artists from the Harlem Renaissance through to the Black Power movement. However, it also created a dilemma for African-American artists who wanted to hold on to the freedom of self-expression and simultaneously support the struggle for black self-empowerment. These movements and the visual culture they produced also received criticism for their patriarchal underpinnings. Ultimately, Black Power became synonymous with new forms of sexual repression and gender inequalities. In 1971 a group of black female artists addressed their erasure from the male-dominated black arts movement and formed "Where We At," a collective designed to take on such issues as the black family, African traditions, and contemporary social conditions. Art works concerned with the marginalization of gender and sexuality crystallized in the post–Black Power era, in many respects dominating the landscape of African-American art production from the mid-1980s through the 1990s.

Like Du Bois, the Martiniquan psychiatrist and anti-colonial activist Frantz Fanon (1925–1961) is one of the most important black intellectuals ever to ponder the crisis of race. Fanon was particularly adept at unraveling the psychological contradictions, complexities, and pathologies created by a society demarked along the lines of racial difference. Fanon's writings, along with Marxist and neo-Marxist theories, influenced black forms of militancy and resistance in the United States. However, in keeping with black intellectual efforts in America, Fanon's writings articulated an often problematic relationship towards gender and sexuality.

The importance of Fanon's writings among contemporary African-American artists—in the post–civil rights, post–Black Power era—provided the impetus to critique the compulsory masculinity of both movements. The ideal blackness professed in the New Negro renaissance reached its logical next phase in the resistance movements of the 1960s. Still, it was perhaps in the 1980s and 1990s that authentic, or *ideal,* blackness, as a heterosexual masculine mythology came under the most intense scrutiny. Utilizing Fanon's writings on the relationship between fantasy and the construction of race, black artists conceptually reinvigorated the art of the African diaspora. By embracing postmodern philosophical strategies, black gay artists—such as Lyle Ashton Harris and Glenn Ligon, and Afro-British artists Isaac Julien and Rotimi Fani-Kayode—confronted traditional notions of blackness that purported a utopian Afrocentric masculinity. In tandem with black women artists interested in exploring the intersections of gender and race (e.g., Joyce J. Scott, Renée Cox, Adrian Piper, Faith Ringgold, Lorraine O'Grady, Renée Green, Coreen Simpson, Betye Saar, Pat Ward Williams, and Emma Amos), these cultural producers reconfigured and interrogated historical conceptions of blackness, while simultaneously targeting the fetishization of racialized and gendered bodies within popular culture in the United States.

The artists Carrie Mae Weems (b. 1953) and Lorna Simpson (b. 1960) confronted the history of exotic, sexualized representations of the black female body, ultimately asking serious questions about how black women see themselves in the wake of enduring misrepresentations. These artistic efforts—which came to be regarded as "identity-based art"—encompassed a vast array of aesthetic strategies, including site-specific installation, photography, performance art, and activist art. In these works, black, gay, and female bodies were visually foregrounded, allowing the artists to construct their own sense of self and to redress a history of erasure. Further emboldened by the feminist movement, the 1992 Los Angeles riots, and the international AIDS crisis, identity art created a sphere for neglected black subjectivities to be witnessed—and ultimately validated. The 1993 installment of the Whitney Museum of American Art's Biennial exhibition focused its attention primarily on identity-based art, generating a

"Junk Art"

Tyree Guyton, primarily a painter and sculptor, has been described as an urban environmental artist. He has waged a personal war on urban blight on Detroit's East Side, transforming first a street in his neighborhood and then two city blocks into a living indoor/outdoor art gallery by using discarded objects—everything from old shoes to bicycles to baby dolls—to embellish abandoned houses, sidewalks, and empty lots.

In the mid-1980s Guyton, a working but unrecognized artist, began the *Heidelberg Project,* which became his most famous work and the driving force behind a nonprofit community arts project. In his neighborhood, with its abandoned, drug-infested houses, he collected objects from the streets and used them to transform the outsides of houses into urban art and to construct roadside sculptures—such as empty lots lined with rows of drinking fountains and appliances. With the help of his grandfather, friends, and neighborhood children, Guyton painted these objects and surrounded them with everything from tires and toilets to tombstones.

Through his work Guyton has challenged the boundaries between art and life as did French artist Marcel Duchamp and American artist Robert Rauschenberg. Duchamp took ordinary objects and presented them as art; Rauschenberg combined painting and common objects as collages, or combines. Guyton draws from the lives of the urban poor and makes their experiences and human spirit visible to people who have come from all over the world to see his work. He also shows how fragments of city life can be turned into art.

Guyton's so-called "junk art" on Heidelberg Street has been described in the press as controversial, political, and public—in short, the art of a revolutionary. His *Heidelberg Project* has attracted so much notice that the neighborhood's drug dealers and prostitutes ceased trying to use the vacant houses and lots. Guyton's cityscape art gallery has changed the surrounding area from deserted combat zones into places where people stop and stare with delight. Part of the fascination surrounding Guyton's works, perhaps, is that they are forever changing due to the ever-changing weather, environment, and artist's whims.

firestorm of intense scrutiny. However, the Biennial—organized by curators Thelma Golden, Elizabeth Sussman, Lisa Phillips, and John G. Hanhardt—ultimately solidified the cultural importance of this form of production.

While identity-based art thrived in the 1980s and early 1990s, other forms of black art proliferated as well. By then, the pressures of cultural nationalism had begun to wane. Simultaneously, Social Realism as an artistic strategy subsided, allowing a multiplicity of aesthetic styles to emerge. Abstract artists such as the painter Sam Gilliam (b. 1933) and sculptor Martin Puryear (b. 1941) articulated a sense of optimism by foregoing traditional conceptualizations of black identity as limited to concerns of racial politics. Hip-hop culture engendered its own brand of visual culture in the form of graffiti art (or "tags"), which emblazoned the urban landscape of most major cities in the United States. The transnational success of rap music was reflected in the sophistication of its visual art forms, ultimately garnering the interest of the art establishment. Manhattan-based painters Jean-Michel Basquiat (1960–1988) and Quattara Watts exemplified this new hybrid form, which infused modernist abstraction and graffiti styles with African and Haitian motifs. Despite moving beyond didactic meditations on black consciousness and overt racial polemics, the work of these artists still reflected the aesthetic styles and culturally rooted emblems of African peoples that make up what has become known as Black Atlantic culture.

In keeping with art of the period, many exciting artists further articulated African-American culture and history beyond nihilism, historical trauma, and dystopic present-day realities. The New York conceptualist David Hammons (b. 1943) appropriated cultural signifiers associated with black culture (e.g., hair, basketballs, wine bottles), transforming them into uplifting and often affirming artistic meditations on inner-city black life in the wake of intense poverty. In a similar vein, the Chicago-based painter Kerry James Marshall's (b. 1955) images of hous-

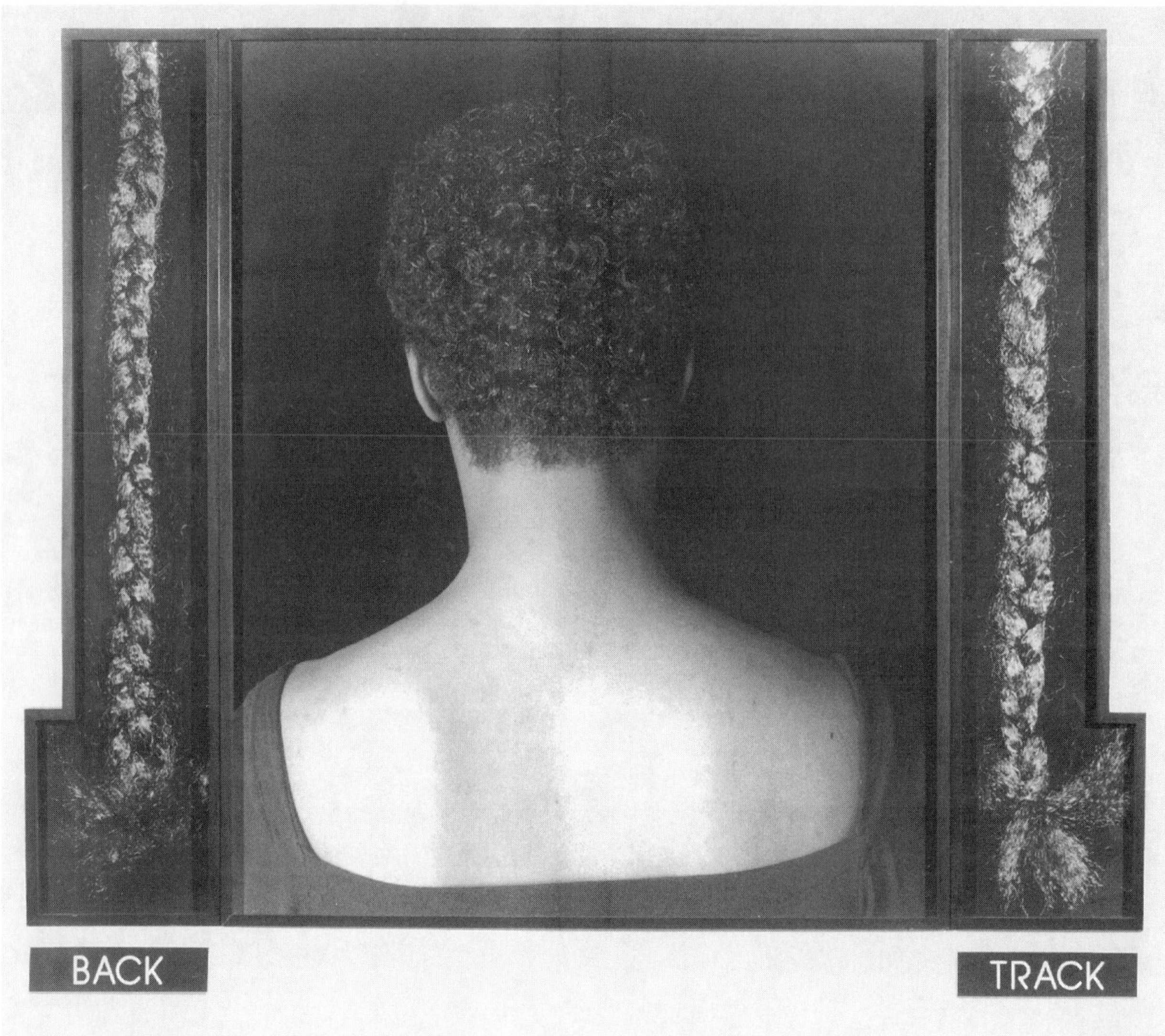

Lorna Simpson's Two Tracks, 1990. COLLECTION OF WHITNEY MUSEUM OF AMERICAN ART, GIFT OF RAYMOND J. LEARSY AND GABRIELLA DE FERRARRI. COURTESY OF THE SEAN KELLY GALLERY, NEW YORK.

ing projects envisioned a black public sphere that was a space of uplift rather than despair. The installations of the multimedia artist Fred Wilson (b. 1954) utilized the collections of major U.S. museums, reworking accepted art historical narratives that have traditionally marginalized the African-American past.

During the mid-1990s, Africa-American art took on an array of forms, many of which continued the fascination with historical memory. Young black artists, born in the period of post-civil rights optimism, often viewed the past with a cynicism that was not concerned with self-affirmation. The installation artist Kara Walker (b. 1969) received both critical accolades and intense scrutiny for her highly charged depictions of the antebellum plantation. Often violently sexual, Walker's imagery depicts the psychological dimension of stereotypes and the obscenity of the American racial unconscious. According to the artist's many detractors, Walker's work was said to embody a cocky disrespect and a youthful ambivalence towards the historical struggles of African-American people. Walker was not alone in her iconic exploration of racial stereotypes. The renowned figurative expressionist Robert Colescott (b. 1925) received international praise in the 1970s for his large-scale reinterpretations of canonical American history paintings. By replacing beloved historical figures such as George Washington with exaggerated minstrel representations of blacks, Colescott disallowed the comfortable contemplation of a mythical and heroic national past that is sanitized of America's history of racial terror. Often criticized for resurrecting degrading images of blacks, Colescott's work gained renewed currency in the 1990s among younger artists who were exploring similar iconography. One such artist is the painter Michael Ray Charles (b. 1967), whose images most overtly exploit the striking visual potency and political import of racial caricatures. Best known for his searing critiques on the commoditization of the black body in the United States, Charles—like Walker and Colescott—successfully probes the psychic traumas inflicted by an exhaustive history of intolerance and anti-black racism.

From the latter part of the 1990s to the present, an art discourse concerned with African modernity, postcoloniality, and globalization has made its presence felt within contemporary art and academic circles. This discourse—inspired by the writings of Paul Gilroy, Homi Bhabha, Edward Said, Gayatri Spivak, Sidney L. Kasfir, V. Y. Mudimbe, Martin Bernal, Aimé Césaire, Léopold Sédar Senghor, Olu Oguibe, Okwui Enwezor, Salah Hassan, and Coco Fusco, to name just a few—has aggressively indicted Western culture's claims of centrality and modern superiority over the second and third worlds. In many respects this discourse was provoked by the inequities of the 1984 MoMA (Museum of Modern Art) exhibition, *"Primitivism" in 20th-Century Art: Affinity of the Tribal and the Modern.* The art historian Sidney L. Kasfir was an outspoken critic, suggesting that "Primitivism," as a fiction of Western desire and imperialist fantasies, was grounded in grossly misleading assumptions about African culture in general. MoMA's exhibition juxtaposed *modern* European art with African tribal art thought to be authentic on the basis of its *primitive* origins and qualities. Kasfir, among others, believed that this type of comparison re-inscribed the culturally biased dualism between the tribal and modern, and between the third and first worlds (Kasfir, 1992, p. 88). In the wake of MoMA's exhibition, a greater degree of emphasis was placed on contemporary African diaspora artists living and working in Western metropolises.

Initially, these developments appeared to be potentially unifying, bringing contemporary African and African-American artists together under negotiable common grounds. However, this bourgeoning discourse—while empowering for the postcolonial or transnational black artist—has been seen as an alienating or essentializing space that excludes African-American artistic production. Critics of these developments question whether or not "diaspora" is simply another form of self-segregation to be consumed by the international art market. While African-American artists have historically contemplated the ideological construction and representation of black identity in the United States, global discourses have extended the definition of *blackness* to encompass an international range of identities. The critically acclaimed though historically overlooked *Freestyle* exhibition, held at the Studio Museum in Harlem in 2001, successfully launched the careers of a new generation of black artists. However, *Freestyle* was not concerned with the presentation of a unified articulation of blackness, or with society's prevailing illusions about race. Neither was it rooted in a specific intellectual continuum, as earlier movements were. Curator Thelma Golden labeled her *Freestyle* progeny "post-black" artists, a moniker designed to emphasize their stated desire to transcend racial polemics. Post-black artists want be just that: artists, free of racial demarcations and the burden of representing a specified identity. Nevertheless, the highly political nature of global art discourses has overshadowed depoliticized efforts such as *Freestyle*, forcing contemporary black American artists to give up localized nationalisms and to ultimately view themselves as part of the international community that comprises the African diaspora.

See also Art in the Anglophone Caribbean; Painting and Sculpture; Performance Art; Photography, U.S.

Bibliography

Edwards, Brent Hayes. *The Practice of Diaspora: Literature, Translation, and the Rise of Black Internationalism.* Cambridge, Mass.: Harvard University Press, 2003.

Fanon, Frantz. *The Wretched of the Earth.* New York: Grove Weidenfeld, 1963.

Hassan, Salah. *Blackness in Color: Visual Expressions of the Black Arts Movement.* Ithaca, N.Y.: Herbert F. Johnson Museum of Art, Cornell University, 2000.

Kasfir, Sidney L. "African Art and Authenticity: A Text with a Shadow." *African Arts* 25, no. 2 (1992). Also published in *Reading the Contemporary: African Art from Theory to the Marketplace,* edited by Olu Oguibe and Okwui Enwezor. Cambridge, Mass.: MIT Press, 1999.

Locke, Alain, ed. *The New Negro: An Interpretation.* New York: A. and C. Boni, 1925.

DEREK CONRAD MURRAY (2005)

ART COLLECTIONS

There are numerous collections of African-American art throughout the United States in institutional, corporate, and private possession. Some of the major collections were established before 1950, but many were formed in the late 1960s or after 1970. One reason that most African-American art collections have only been developed recently is the lack of importance given to art in post-Reconstruction African-American education. A major thrust of education, from Reconstruction onward, was training for manual labor. The study of literature and art was considered superfluous. African-American artists were few, for they had no support groups, patrons, or buyers. (This situation caused George Washington Carver to change his major from art to science.)

When blacks from rural areas began moving to cities after World War I they took advantage of the greater scope of activities that urban centers had to offer. In his book *Modern Negro Art* (1943), James A. Porter notes the following landmarks in the progress of African-American artists: the annual exhibitions held at the 135th Street Branch of the New York Public Library beginning in 1921, along with exhibitions held at Dunbar High School in Washington, D.C., in 1922 (sponsored by the Tanner Art League) and the Chicago Women's Club in 1927, and those of the Harmon Foundation from 1927 to 1933. Because of the exposure and prizes offered at these exhibitions and by the magazines *Crisis* and *Opportunity,* there was hope that the work of African-American artists would be recognized and valued. That happened, but slowly, because the collectors themselves were black and also subject to the economic restraints imposed by racism.

Many of the collections described below also include extensive holdings of African, Haitian, or Caribbean art.

Collections in Universities and Libraries

Hampton University in Virginia (founded in 1868 as Hampton Normal and Agricultural Institute) houses the nation's oldest African-American museum. Samuel Armstrong established an ethnographic museum at the same time he founded Hampton. He wrote, "I wish to make and have here the finest collection in the U.S. I think that by taking pains I can beat the other collections in this country." The Hampton collection of African-American art began in 1894 with gifts of Henry O. Tanner's *Lion's Head* (1892) and *The Banjo Lesson* (1893). Now comprising 1,500 paintings, graphics, and sculpture, Hampton's African-American art collection is second only to that of the National Museum of American Art of the Smithsonian Institution in Washington, D.C.

In 1967 Hampton University received a donation from the Harmon Foundation as it was dispersing its collection. In addition, Ida Cullen, the widow of Harlem Renaissance poet Countee Cullen, sold twenty-six works from her husband's collection to Hampton University in 1986. She later donated three more works. Because of these acquisitions, the major artists of the Harlem Renaissance are exceptionally well represented: they include Richmond Barthé, Aaron Douglas, Palmer Hayden, Malvin G. Johnson, Augusta Savage, and Hale Woodruff. The collection includes eight more works by Tanner, as well as works by Romare Bearden, John Biggers, Elizabeth Catlett, Allan Crite, Paul Goodnight, Felrath Hines, Jacob Lawrence, Norman Lewis, Richard Mayhew, Raymond Saunders, James Wells, Charles White, Benjamin Wigfall, and Ellis Wilson. In 1997 Hampton greatly expanded its gallery space, creating a permanent chronological exhibition of African-American art.

The Howard University Gallery of Art in Washington, D.C., opened on April 7, 1930, two years after the board of trustees established it. The first exhibition was a traveling show sponsored by the College Art Association. Under its first two directors, James V. Herring and James A. Porter, Howard's gallery developed a program to acquire a permanent collection. Henry O. Tanner's *Return from the Crucifixion* was possibly the first painting in the collection and the last one Tanner did before his death in 1937. The Howard University Gallery of Art now boasts one of the most comprehensive collections of work by African-American artists, from Robert Duncanson, Edward Bannister, and Edmonia Lewis of the nineteenth century, to such contemporary artists as Richard Hunt and Sam Gilliam. The collection was further enriched by Alain Locke's bequest in 1955 of his holdings of paintings and African sculpture.

In the early thirties, Fisk University in Nashville, Tennessee, began amassing an art collection through gifts. Fisk's collection of art by African Americans now comprises about nine hundred paintings, prints, and sculptures. Murals and other works by Aaron Douglas, who taught at Fisk from 1937 to 1966, are exhibited in Fisk's library. A gallery named for Douglas features changing exhibitions. Works by Malvin Gray Johnson, William H. Johnson, David Driskell, Sam Middleton, Alma Thomas, and James Lesesne Wells make up a small part of the large Fisk University collection.

The Clark Atlanta University Art Galleries (Clark College and Atlanta University merged in 1988) had an unusual genesis. In 1942 Hale Woodruff, who had initiated Atlanta University's art department a decade earlier, instituted an annual exhibition. He wanted both younger and older artists to be able to exhibit their work on a national, juried basis, free of racism. He also wanted to bring art to the community. The exhibition's winning entries were purchased to form the collection at Atlanta. Charles Alston and Lois Mailou Jones were among the winners in 1942. The annual exhibition, which continued until 1970, accounts for three hundred of the Clark Atlanta acquisitions. This core collection has been increased by gifts from private individuals and institutions, as well as by purchases, including three Tanners in 1967. Gifts have included works by Romare Bearden, Beauford Delaney, Palmer Hayden, Malvin Gray Johnson, William H. Johnson, Jacob Lawrence, and Archibald Motley. In 1950 Hale Woodruff was commissioned to paint a six-part mural, *Art of the Negro,* for the Atlanta collection. The annual exhibitions not only created a major institutional art collection, but for twenty-eight years they provided an exhibition space and an atmosphere of artistic competition, free of racism, that engaged African-American artists and stimulated the public.

The University of Delaware became the repository of more than one thousands works by twentieth-century African-American artists in 2001 when Paul R. Jones of Atlanta donated his collection. Jones began collecting in the late 1960s when he noted that artists of color were rarely included in exhibitions of American art. Inspired by Atlanta University's annual exhibitions, Jones developed his collection to include both known and emerging artists. Jones's primary consideration was to see African-American art woven into American art, and he chose the University of Delaware for his gift because of its strong academic and conservation commitment to American art. In 2004 a multimillion-dollar restoration of a campus landmark, Mechanical Hall, was completed to hold the Paul R. Jones Collection.

Almost all of the Arts and Artifacts Collection of the Schomburg Center for Research in Black Culture, a research center of the New York Public Library, consists of paintings, sculpture, and prints by African-American artists. Prominent white artists such as Alice Neel and William Zorach are also included in the Schomburg collection. By 1926, when Arthur A. Schomburg's collection of books, manuscripts, prints, and other artworks became part of the 135th Street branch of the New York Public Library, the branch had been hosting annual art exhibitions for five years, selected by a committee that included W. E.B. Du Bois and James Weldon Johnson. This led to the library's beginnings as a repository for a major collection. As early as 1911, Schomburg commissioned a portrait of his wife from William E. Braxton, now in the collection with other works by Braxton. Most of the acquisitions, until the late seventies, were gifts of friends, patrons, and artists.

The Schomburg collection includes numerous works from the Works Project Administration (WPA), its paintings having been given to branch libraries when the WPA was dissolved in the 1940s. Works by Palmer Hayden, Malvin Gray Johnson, and Jacob Lawrence arrived this way. Works by all the important artists mentioned throughout this entry are represented in the Schomburg collection, as are works by E. Simms Campbell, Barbara Chase-Riboud, Claude Clark, Beauford Delaney, Rex Goreleigh, Sam Middleton, Sister Gertrude Morgan, Horace Pippin, Augusta Savage, William E. Scott, Charles Sebree, and Bill Traylor. As a result of the 1998 exhibition, *Black New York Artists of the 20th Century*, the Schomburg Center acquired forty-five works by forty-three artists who were not previously represented.

The Amistad Research Center, established by the American Missionary Association in 1966, is now located on the campus of Tulane University in New Orleans. Among its holdings is the Aaron Douglas Collection of nearly three hundred paintings and sculptures by African-American artists. This collection was assembled by David Driskell and Grant Spaulding for the United Church Board for Homeland Ministries, which donated it to the Amistad Research Center in 1983. Rich in work from the Harlem Renaissance, the collection contains twelve paintings by Aaron Douglas and seventeen by Malvin Gray Johnson. There are also seventeen paintings by the nineteenth-century artist, Edward M. Bannister. Both Bearden and Lawrence are strongly represented, and among other artists there are works by Wilmer Jennings, Alma Thomas, William E. Scott, Ellis Wilson, Sam Middleton, Keith Morrison, Vincent Smith, David Driskell, Mildred Thompson, and Walter Williams.

South Carolina State College in Orangeburg opened its I. P. Stanback Museum and Planetarium in 1980. By 1991 it valued its collection of African-American art, acquired through gifts, at nearly one million dollars. African art, photography, and works by students are also included in the collection, along with works by such prominent artists as Romare Bearden and Jacob Lawrence.

Museums and Cultural Institutions

The National Museum of American Art, part of the Smithsonian Institution, in Washington, D.C., has works of art by 105 African Americans. Although founded in 1829, the museum, reflecting American aesthetics and prejudices, did not own any African-American works before 1964. The first acquisition was James Hampton's room-sized 180-piece assemblage, *The Throne of the Third Heaven of the Nations Millennium General Assembly.* In 1966 IBM donated works by Sargent Johnson, Romare Bearden, and Charles Sebree. At the same time, the Harmon Foundation, a repository of black art for forty years, had to disburse its collection. Unable to find a taker in New York, it turned to the Smithsonian. This vast donation, plus purchases by the museum, paved the way for other donors, including a bequest of twenty-five paintings from Alma Thomas and a donation by Warren Robbins of many nineteenth-century works by African-American artists.

The Studio Museum in Harlem opened in 1968 in rented quarters above a liquor store and without a permanent collection. Its aims were to provide studio space for black artists and to serve as a venue for exhibitions of their art. In 1979 the New York Bank for Savings donated a vacant building in Harlem, which opened in 1982 as the Studio Museum. With its own building, the Studio Museum could acquire a permanent collection and present exhibitions, lectures, performances, workshops, concerts, and seminars. The organization also continued to exhibit and provide space for artists in residence. The Studio Museum's permanent collection includes over 1,600 items in all formats, including installations. It is particularly strong in the politically conscious art of the 1960s. Artists represented in the collection include Terry Adkins, Robert Colescott, Melvin Edwards, Richard Hunt, Norman Lewis, Betye Saar, and Nari Ward. The Studio Museum was accredited by the American Association of Museums in 1988. An expansion and renovation project that began in 2001 has added increased gallery space, an auditorium, a café, and other building improvements.

Affiliated with the Elma Lewis School in Boston, the Museum of the National Center of Afro-American Artists was established in 1978. The museum was developed at that time in cooperation with the Boston Museum of Fine Arts. The permanent collection began with a donation of more than two hundred works by Allan Crite, Richard Yarde, and John Wilson, among others. Prints and photographs by African Americans are also held.

The Amistad Foundation at the Wadsworth Atheneum in Hartford, Connecticut, was founded in 1987 with the acquisition of the collection of Randolph Linsly Simpson, who had amassed over seven thousand artworks, artifacts, and documents related to the black experience in America. The Amistad Foundation continues to strengthen its visual arts component by acquiring the works of such contemporary African-American artists as Ellis Ruley and Carrie Mae Weems. In June 1992 the Amistad opened its gallery at the Wadsworth Atheneum, thus becoming the first gallery in a New England art museum to be permanently dedicated to the art, culture, and history of African Americans.

The Museum of African American Art in Tampa, Florida, opened in April 1991. It houses the Barnett-Aden Collection of 171 paintings, sculptures, and lithographs, representing eighty-one artists reaching back to the nineteenth century. The Barnett-Aden Gallery was started in 1943 by James V. Herring and Alonzo J. Aden of Howard University. It was open to white artists, although an objective was to collect and preserve the art of African Americans. Adolphus Ealy, to whom the collection was bequeathed, sold it to the Florida Endowment Fund for Higher Education in 1989 for six million dollars. Many major artists—Tanner, Bearden, Woodruff, Bannister, Catlett—are included in this collection, which spans almost a century of African-American creation (1860 to 1955).

The Afro-American Cultural Center in Charlotte, North Carolina, will become the new home of the works of art collected since 1949 by John H. and Vivian D. Hewitt. Strong in works by twentieth-century artists such as Charles Alston, John Biggers, Romare Bearden, Ronald Joseph, Richard Mayhew, Ann Tanksley, Virginia Smit, and Frank Wimberly, the collection also includes six works by Henry Tanner. Bought by the Bank of America Foundation in 1998 as a promised gift to the center, the collection will be housed in a newly renovated gallery at the Charlotte institution after a national tour that is scheduled to end in 2006.

Other museums that exhibit African-American art include the DuSable Museum of African American History in Chicago, established in 1961, and the California African American Museum (CAAM) in Los Angeles (1975). The former has a permanent collection of eight hundred works from the WPA period and the black arts movement of the 1960s. A new wing that opened in 1993 increased the DuSable's gallery space. The CAAM is home to the Palmer C. Hayden Collection and Archives, as well as a substantial collection of nineteenth-century landscape paintings by Edward M. Bannister, Robert S. Duncanson, and Grafton Tyler Brown. Recent renovations have added three galleries and a sculpture court to accommodate its burgeoning holdings of modern and contemporary art. The museum has a strong collection of work by California artists, such as Betye Saar, John Outterbridge, and Sargent Johnson.

Corporate Collections

Several significant collections of art are held by large African American–owned companies. An early example is the Golden State Mutual Life Insurance Company. Founded in Los Angeles in 1925, it began its art collection in 1949 to celebrate the dedication of a new building. The artists Charles Alston and Hale Woodruff were commissioned to paint two murals depicting the history of African Americans in California. Alston's panel, *Exploration and Colonization,* showed historic events from 1527 to 1850; Woodruff's *Settlement and Development* covered the years 1850 to 1949. Golden State's Afro-American Art Collection has become a showplace for the works of, among others, Charles White, John Biggers, Hughie Lee-Smith, Richard Hunt, Beulah Woodard, Betye Saar, Henry O. Tanner, and Richmond Barthé.

The Atlanta Life Insurance Company of Atlanta, Georgia, celebrated its seventy-fifth anniversary in 1980 by dedicating new corporate headquarters. Believing the community should have cultural enrichment as well as economic stability, president Jesse Hill Jr. established the Atlanta Life First National Annual African-American Art Competition and Exhibition. Winning works of the competition, for which $15,000 was provided, became part of the collection. Modeled on the annual juried exhibitions that formed the basis of Atlanta University's art collection, the Atlanta Life exhibitions give exposure and encouragement to up-and-coming artists rather than to those already established. The first planners and advisers included Margaret Burroughs, founder of the DuSable Museum, professors of art, and collectors. Jurors over the years have included E. Barry Gaither, Samella Lewis, Richard Long, Lowery Sims, and Robert Blackburn. The Atlanta Life Insurance Company now owns over three hundred pieces of art in many media, including photography. On display in the vast lobby is an impressive body of work by young or local artists, as well as by historical figures such as Romare Bearden, Elizabeth Catlett, Ed Dwight, Jacob Lawrence, and Hale Woodruff.

The Johnson Publishing Company of Chicago—the publisher of *Ebony* and *Jet*— has amassed one of the most important collections of African-American art. According to articles in *Ebony* (September 1972, December 1973), "It is the world's largest and most representative corporate collection of work by African American artists . . . what we intend is that the building and art collection combine as a really bold positive statement about the company's commitment to the black people it serves." By 1980 the collection consisted of about 250 pieces, displayed in the public spaces and the editorial offices of the building. The building, which opened in 1971, was designed by African-American architect John Moutoussamy. A number of the artists represented in the Johnson Publishing collection were born either in Chicago or have a connection to the city. The artworks include paintings, sculpture, drawings, and lithographs in all media. Richard Hunt was commissioned to create the bronze, *Expansive Construction* (1972). Romare Bearden, Jacob Lawrence, Charles Alston, Hughie Lee-Smith, and Hale Woodruff are some of the well-known artists in the collection. Others include Eldzier Cortor, Charles White, Robin Hunter, Geraldine McCullough, Valerie Maynard, Frank Hayden, and Jeff Donaldson. The Johnson Publishing collection also includes African and Haitian art.

Private Collections

It is impossible to provide a comprehensive list of private collections of African-American art. In 1980 Richard V. Clarke, former chairman of the Studio Museum in Harlem said, "I find it rare, now, to go into someone's home and not see black art" (Wilson, 1980, p. 39). Clarke started his own collection in 1958. It is strongest in works by Romare Bearden, Hughie Lee-Smith, Jacob Lawrence, Eldzier Cortor, Norman Lewis, Henry Tanner, and Hale Woodruff, who consulted in the development of the collection. James Audubon, Betye Saar, Wilfredo Lam, Edward Bannister, and Howardena Pindell are also represented, as are sculptors Richmond Barthé, Elizabeth Catlett, and Sargent Johnson. Clarke's collection also includes Haitian paintings, African masks and figures, and photographs.

Another important private collection of African-American art is held by Walter and June Jackson Christmas. Although each began collecting in the 1940s, their purchasing increased after their marriage. Their first purchase together was Ellis Wilson's *Three Kings*. The Christmas collection spans the twentieth century and includes works by Bearden, Lawrence, Tanner, Ellis Wilson, Norman Lewis, Ernest Crichlow, and Selma Burke. Also represented are Vivian Browne, Calvin Burnett, Frank Wimberly, Virginia Smit, Robert Blackburn, and Ronald Joseph. There is also a portrait of Walter Christmas, himself an artist, painted by Georgette Seabrook Powell. Modern South African artists, such as Hargreaves Entuckwana, are included, as are artists from Haiti, Brazil, and Jamaica. The collection includes two watercolor designs for costumes painted by Derek Walcott, the 1992 Nobel laureate for Literature, for one of his plays. Contemporary sculpture by Gordon Christmas and Clarence Queen, and from Burkina Faso, adds an extra dimension to the Christmas collection.

Harmon and Harriet Kelley began their collection in 1987 after attending a museum exhibition of African-American art. Thrilled by the beauty of the work and unnerved that they had never heard of these artists, the Kelleys decided to collect so that their daughters would know this aspect of their heritage. The Kelleys started with nineteenth-century artists, such as Tanner, Duncanson, Bannister, and Joshua Johnson. They then moved to more modern but not well-known artists, including Charles Sallee Jr. and Dox Thrash, a pioneering printmaker. Giants such as Bearden, Lawrence, Eldzior Cortor, Norman Lewis, and Archibald Motley Jr. are also represented in the Kelley collection, as is a work by Jean-Michel Basquiat.

Leon and Rosemarie Banks of Los Angeles began collecting art in the 1950s when Banks was a U.S. Air Force surgeon in England and was able to visit the museums and galleries of Europe. Banks describes his collection as "mainly contemporary and American and while it doesn't reflect any specific trend, it does lean to more abstract styles" (*Black Enterprise,* December, 1975, p. 47). Both African-American and white artists are represented in the collection, including Richard Hunt, Mel Edwards, Sam Gilliam, Henry O. Tanner, and Bob Thompson among the former, and Alberto Giacometti, Willem de Kooning, David Hockney, and Robert Motherwell among the latter. Most of the purchases, however, have been of artworks by younger, less established artists.

The Walter O. Evans Collection of African American Art was started in the late 1970s. Evans, who lived in Detroit, met Romare Bearden and was inspired to collect art. At that time he purchased only paintings that portrayed African Americans because he almost never saw any in the museums he visited. Evans also commissioned Bearden and Richard Hunt to create album covers for his record label. Since then he has broadened the collection to include the major African-American artists of the nineteenth century, although their landscapes have no human figures. Artists such as Robert Duncanson, Edward Bannister, Charles Porter, and Henry O. Tanner are well represented in the Evans Collection. About half the works in the collection were painted for the WPA during the 1930s. Haitian painters and sculptors are also included in this collection, which is often exhibited. Selections from the Evans Collection have been on continuous tour since 1991, and have been exhibited in numerous museums and galleries throughout the United States. Evans has also established the Walter O. Evans Foundation for Art and Literature to disseminate knowledge about African American cultural achievements.

Other prominent private collectors included Arthur Ashe and his wife Jeanne Moutoussamy-Ashe, Harry Belafonte, Camille Billops, Jacqueline Bontemps, Kenneth Clark, Bill Cosby, Wes Cochran, Robert H. Derden, David Driskell, Laura Hynes Felrath, Warren Goins, Russell Goings, Danny Glover, Edmund Gordon, Earl Graves, William Harvey, Jacqueline J. Holland, Spike Lee, James W. Lewis, Reginald and Loida Lewis, Peter and Eileen Norton, Regenia Perry, Joseph Pierce, Sidney Poitier, Beny Primm, Meredith Sirmans, E. T. Williams, and Reba and Dave Williams.

See also Art; Museums

Bibliography

Armstrong, Samuel C. Personal letter, dated August 7, 1868. Archives, College Museum, Hampton Institute, Virginia.

Barnwell, Andrea D. *Walter O. Evans Collection of African American Art.* Seattle: University of Washington Press, 1999.

Clines, Francis X. "Connoisseur of African-American Art Finds New Home for Collection." *New York Times* (February 15, 2001): A24.

Deacon, Deborah A. "The Art & Artifacts Collection of the Schomburg Center for Research in Black Culture." *Bulletin of Research in the Humanities* 84, no. 2 (Summer 1981): 145–261.

"Dr. and Mrs. Leon Banks: Collectors Living with Art." *Black Enterprise* (December 1975): 46–47.

Duplessis, Laurel T. *Hampton's Collections and Connections,* Part 1: *Returning Home to Hampton.* Hampton, Va.: Hampton University Museum, 1987.

The Harmon and Harriet Kelley Collection of African American Art: Exhibition. San Antonio: San Antonio Museum of Art, 1994.

Holmes, Steven A. "Collecting Works by Black Artists, Blacks Add Details to Their Heritage." *New York Times* (May 29, 1995): 11, 17.

Ingalls, Zoe. "Space to Tell the Story of African American Art." *The Chronicle of Higher Education* (May 2, 1997): B8–9.

Perry, Regenia A. *Free Within Ourselves: African-American Artists in the Collection of the National Museum of American Art.* Washington, D.C.: National Museum of American Art, 1992.

Porter, James A. *Modern Negro Art.* New York: Dryden, 1943. Reprint, Washington, D.C.: Howard University Press, 1992.

Wilson, Judith. "The Bullish Market for Black Art." *Black Enterprise* (December 1980): 34–41.

Zeidler, Jeanne. "1993—Anniversary Year for Three Renowned Paintings." *International Review of African American Art* 10, no. 3 (1993): 20–22, 60–63.

BETTY KAPLAN GUBERT (1996)
Updated by author 2005

Ashe, Arthur

July 10, 1943
February 6, 1993

Born in Richmond, Virginia, tennis player and political activist Arthur Robert Ashe Jr. traced his lineage back ten generations on his father's side to a woman who in 1735 was brought from West Africa to Yorktown, Virginia, by the slave ship *Doddington.* Ashe's mother, Mattie Cunningham, also of Richmond, taught him to read by the time he was four. She died when Arthur was six, one year after giving birth to her second son and last child, Johnnie.

Ashe, who was frail in his youth, was forbidden by his father, a police officer in Richmond's Department of Recreation and Parks, to play football on the segregated Brookfield playground adjacent to the Ashes' home. Instead, young Ashe took to playing tennis on the four hard courts of the playground. By the time he was ten Ashe had attracted the keen eye of Dr. Walter Johnson, a Lynchburg, Virginia, physician and tennis enthusiast who had previously discovered and coached Althea Gibson, the first black woman to win the Wimbledon tennis tournament.

Ashe's father and Dr. Johnson were both stern disciplinarians who insisted that Ashe cultivate self-discipline, good manners, forbearance, and self-effacing stoicism. These qualities would characterize Ashe throughout his entire life and, even in the midst of the most turbulent social conditions, would define him as a man of reason, conscience, integrity, and moral authority. His cool disposition enabled him not only to survive but to distinguish himself in an overwhelmingly white tennis environment.

In 1960 Ashe was awarded a tennis scholarship to UCLA, where he earned All-American status. Two years after he graduated with a business degree, he became the first black man to win one of the preeminent Grand Slam titles, accomplishing that as an amateur and U.S. Army representative at the U.S. Open of 1968. Numerous titles would follow, highlighted by Ashe's place on three victorious Davis Cup squads and the addition of two more Grand Slam titles, one at the Australian Open in 1970, and the other, his pièce de résistance, at Wimbledon in 1975.

Throughout those years, Ashe devoted considerable time and energy to civil rights issues. In 1973, after three years of trying, he secured an invitation to play in the all-white South African Open. Although his participation was controversial, it personified Ashe's lifelong belief in constructive engagement—an attitude that he abandoned only on one noteworthy occasion in 1976, when he joined in the call for an international embargo of all sporting contact with South Africa.

In 1979, at age thirty-six, Ashe suffered a myocardial infarction, which forced him to have bypass surgery and retire from tennis. Nevertheless, over the ensuing years he served as the U.S. Davis Cup captain (1981–1985), he worked as a journalist and television commentator, and he served or helped create various foundations, ranging from the American Heart Association to the United Negro College Fund to his own Safe Passage Foundation.

Eighteen months after undergoing a second heart operation in 1983, Ashe learned that he had contracted the AIDS virus through blood transfusions. He immediately set to work on his definitive three-volume history of black athletes in America, *A Hard Road to Glory* (1988). Forced by the national newspaper *USA Today* to reveal that he was suffering from AIDS in April 1992, Ashe worked as an activist for the defeat of AIDS until he died of the disease in February 1993.

Following his death, Ashe was honored in his native Richmond by the erection in 1996 of a statue on Monument Avenue, the city's central thoroughfare. Meanwhile, the Flushing Meadows Tennis Stadium, home of the U.S. Open, was rededicated Arthur Ashe Stadium in 1997.

In 1992 Ashe started the Arthur Ashe Institute for Urban Health, with a goal to improve health care and education in America's urban environments. In 2002 the institute celebrated its tenth anniversary, keeping Arthur Ashe's vision alive. The U.S. Postal Service announced plans at the U.S. Open in 2004 to commemorate Ashe with a postage stamp bearing his image.

See also Gibson, Althea; Tennis; Williams, Venus and Serena

Bibliography

Ashe, Arthur R., Jr., with Frank Deford. *Arthur Ashe: Portrait in Motion.* Boston: Houghton Mifflin, 1975.

Ashe, Arthur, Jr., with Neil Amdur. *Off the Court.* New York: New American Library, 1981.

Ashe, Arthur, Jr., and Arnold Rampersad. *Days of Grace: A Memoir.* New York: Random House, 1993.

Towle, Mike, ed. *I Remember Arthur Ashe: Memories of a True Tennis Pioneer and a Champion of Social Causes by the People Who Knew Him.* Nashville, Tenn.: Cumberland House, 2003.

PETER BODO (1996)
Updated by publisher 2005

Associated Publishers

The historian Carter G. Woodson (1875–1950) founded Associated Publishers in 1922 in Washington, D.C. Frustrated by his inability to get his own work published by white publishers, Woodson decided to form his own publishing company. He not only helped black scholars find publishers for their work, he also hoped to make money to support research programs initiated through the Association for the Study of Afro-American (originally Negro) Life and History, now known as Association for the Study of African-American Life and History. Although he tried to interest black scholars in becoming financial partners in his new firm, only a few close associates invested. Among them were Louis Mehlinger, who served as secretary, and John W. Davis, who was treasurer.

Although they published scores of books by black authors, as well as works by whites who wrote on black subjects, they did not make money for Woodson's association and actually drained the organization financially. By the late 1930s, authors needed to pay a subvention to have their work published, though Associated Publishers continued to issue scholarly works, as well as those directed to a mass audience. Although published in smaller runs than books issued during the 1920s and 1930s, more than a dozen volumes were published in the 1940s, many directed at schoolchildren and a mass audience. Volumes that otherwise would not have been published came out under their auspices. Even English translations of books by foreign authors were published, including Arthur Ramos's *The Negro in Brazil.*

See also Association for the Study of African American Life and History; Woodson, Carter G.

Bibliography

Conyers, James L., Jr. *Carter G. Woodson: A Historical Reader.* New York: Garland, 1999.

Goggin, Jacqueline. *Carter G. Woodson: A Life in Black History.* Baton Rouge: Louisiana State University Press, 1993.

JACQUELINE GOGGIN (1996)
Updated bibliography

Association for the Advancement of Creative Musicians

Originally an informal rehearsal band led by pianist Muhal Richard Abrams (b. 1930) and bassist Donald "Rafael" Garrett (1932–1989) in Chicago in 1961, the Association for the Advancement of Creative Musicians (AACM) went on to become one of the dominant influences in avant-garde jazz. Along with Abrams and Garrett, several students studying at Wilson Junior College—including saxophonists Anthony Braxton, Henry Threadgill, Joseph Jarman, and Roscoe Mitchell and bassist Malachi Favors—were among the significant participants in weekly jam sessions at various nightclubs, small theaters, settlement houses, and churches on Chicago's South Side. Also involved as performers and composers were drummers Jack DeJohnette, Steve McCall, and Thurman Barker; saxophonists Maurice McIntrye and Troy Robinson; trumpeter Leo Smith; and pianists Phil Cohran, Amina Claudine Myers, and Jodie Christian. Inspired by Sun Ra, Cecil Taylor, Ornette Coleman, and John Coltrane, these musicians theatrically juxtaposed explosive free jazz with delicate, whimsical tinkling on hubcabs and frying pans.

The AACM was chartered as a nonprofit organization in 1965 (with Abrams as president) and began to sponsor art exhibits, plays, living arrangements, and a school. At first, the music world greeted the AACM with hostility, and as a result the cooperative's early work was poorly documented. Nonetheless, several albums alerted the New York-based avant-garde that a new movement was afoot in Chicago. These albums include Mitchell's *Sound* (1966), Jarman's *Song For* (1967), trumpeter Lester Bowie's *Numbers 1 and 2* (1967), Abrams's *Levels and Degrees of Light* (1968), and Braxton's *Three Compositions of New Jazz* (1968). These works were created not by improvising on a melodic theme or harmonic chord changes, but by exploring variations in instrumental texture, particularly unorthodox sounds on standard instruments. Along with such blips, squeaks, and overtones are sounds made by "little instruments," mostly common household or industrial objects.

In 1969, tragedy struck the organization with the death of two key members, bassist Charles Clark and pianist Christopher Gaddy. Many AACM musicians then moved to Paris, where they were soon engaged in celebrated concerts and recordings. However, they returned to the United States within a few years, claiming, in a famous statement, that they missed "the inspiration of the ghetto." Most settled in New York and participated in the cooperative "Loft Jazz" movement of the mid- to late 1970s (This music is documented in the multivolume *Wildflowers: The New York Loft Jazz Sessions*, recorded over a ten-day period in 1976).

The ensembles formed by members of the AACM have proved to be among the most significant in jazz. The Art Ensemble of Chicago, whose motto is "Great Black Music, Ancient to Future," was formed in 1969 by Bowie, Jarman, Mitchell, and Favors (the drummer Famoudou Don Moye joined them in Paris in 1970). Their recordings include *Message to Our Folks* (1969), *Nice Guys* (1978), and *Dreaming of the Masters* (1987). Art Ensemble concerts became famous for the energetic wit they brought to the avant-garde, and for the band's use of African-style face paint and clothing. Before his death in 1999, Bowie would often wear a chef's hat and white medical coat on stage, while the flamboyantly greasepainted Jarman has been known to wave flags and sound sirens. Favors passed away in early 2004, but the band continues with a lineup that includes Jarman, Moye, Mitchell, Corey Wilkes, and Jaribu Sahid.

In Paris, Braxton, Smith, and McCall, and the violinist Leroy Jenkins had great success under the name Creative Construction Company, but aside from one concert financed and recorded by Coleman (*Creative Construction Company,* 2 vols., 1970), they were unable to keep the group together in America. Braxton went on to lead his own ensembles (*Five Compositions (Quartet),* 1986), as did Smith (*Go in Numbers,* 1980). Jenkins worked with the Revolutionary Ensemble (*Manhattan Cycles,* 1972), and then as a leader (*For Players Only,* 1975). McCall worked in the group Air (*Air Lore,* 1975) with bassist Fred Hoplins and Threadgill, who has lead his own ensembles (*Just the Facts* and *Pass the Bucket,* 1983). Abrams has continued to work with his large ensembles, such as the Muhal Richard Abrams Orchestra (*Blu Blu Blu,* 1990).

Most of the members of the AACM overcame an initial obscurity, but some have remained undiscovered. These include pianist Jodie Christian, trombonist Lester Lashley, and saxophonists Fred Anderson, John Stubblefield, and Kalaparusha Maurice McIntyre. In the 1970s and 1980s, a new generation of AACM members came to prominence, including trombonist George Lewis and saxophonists Chico Freeman, Edward Wilkerson, and Douglas Ewart. Most of the original members of the AACM live in New York, and few remain in close contact with the organization. The AACM itself, however, has grown and prospered as a Chicago arts collective and continues to sponsor classes, workshops, and performances.

See also Coleman, Ornette; Coltrane, John; Jazz; Music in the United States; Sun Ra (Blount, Herman "Sonny")

Bibliography

Litweiler, John. *The Freedom Principle: Jazz After 1958.* New York: Quill, 1984.

Muni, K. "AACM: Continuing Tradition." *Bebop and Beyond* 4, no. 2 (1986).

Wilmer, Valerie. *As Serious As Your Life: The Story of the New Jazz.* Westport, Conn.: L. Hill, 1980.

JONATHAN GILL (1996)

Association for the Study of African American Life and History

The historian Carter G. Woodson (1875–1950) founded the Association for the Study of Negro Life and History (ASNLH) in Washington, D.C., on September 9, 1915. Woodson may have been stimulated to found a new organization, albeit indirectly, by D. W. Griffith's film *The Birth of a Nation,* released in 1915. To counter Griffith's racist depiction of blacks, Woodson began the organization in order to preserve and disseminate historical and sociological information on African Americans. He also became the first director of the organization, while George Cleveland Hall (1864–1930; personal physician to Booker T. Washington and a surgeon at Provident Hospital in Chicago) became the first president. Alexander L. Jackson, the executive secretary of the black YMCA organization in Washington, and James E. Stamps, a Yale economics graduate student who assisted Jackson, also helped to launch the association.

Prior to the establishment of the ASNLH, black historians had no professional organization that welcomed them as members. Racially exclusive, the historical profession fostered policies that promoted academic segregation, closely mirroring the racism and segregation of society as a whole. This racism was reflected in the practices of the American Historical Association, which was founded in 1884. Through the ASNLH, Woodson and the handful of black historians with whom he collaborated used their scholarship to influence white public opinion in general, and the white historical establishment in particular. With the founding of the ASNLH, Woodson not only challenged the scholarly authority of the white historical establishment, but he also provided black historians with a forum for the presentation and publication of their research.

Annual meetings of the association offered black historians an opportunity to deliver scholarly papers before their peers and encouraged further scholarly production. The association functioned as a clearinghouse and information bureau, providing research assistance in black history to scholars and to the general public. Woodson sponsored numerous research projects that involved a broad segment of the black community, and both scholars and interested amateurs participated in association research projects. To ensure the publication of the research undertaken by these scholars, Woodson founded Associated Publishers in 1922. Woodson collected historical documents and edited them for publication. He also edited and published the *Journal of Negro History,* which began in 1916, and the *Negro History Bulletin,* which began in 1937 and was directed at school children. Through the auspices of the association, Woodson brought black history to a mass audience when he began the annual celebration of Negro History Week in 1926. Negro History Week was celebrated annually in February in the closest possible proximity to the birthday of Abraham Lincoln (February 12) and the presumed birthday of Frederick Douglass (February 14).

After Woodson's death in 1950, the organization underwent some financial difficulties and several administrative reorganizations. The historian Charles Harris Wesley (1891–1987) became president in 1951 and assumed many of Woodson's former administrative roles. (Under Mary McLeod Bethune [1875–1955], who served as the association's first female president from 1936 to 1951, the presidency had been primarily a ceremonial position.) By 1965 the association had largely completed its reorganization, and in that year Wesley became its first executive director since Woodson. Wesley guided the ASNLH through the tumultuous civil rights era and retired in 1972. That same year, recognizing the increasing cultural and race consciousness among African Americans, the association's members voted to change its name to the Association for the Study of Afro-American Life and History (ASALH); this was later changed to the Association for the Study of African American Life and History (retaining the same acronym). The headquarters of the organization remained in Washington, D.C., with offices in Woodson's original townhouse. In 1976 due in part to the efforts of executive director J. Rupert Picott, the association expanded Negro History Week into Black History Month, which is now celebrated for the entire month of February. Woodson's townhouse was declared a national historic landmark in 1976, and in February 1988 it became part of the Washington, D.C., Black History National Recreation Trail, which was also dedicated in Woodson's honor.

Woodson was succeeded as editor of the *Journal of Negro History* by the historian Rayford W. Logan, who served from 1950 to 1951. William Miles Brewer was editor from 1951 to 1970, and W. Augustus Low, best known for co-editing the *Encyclopedia of Black America* (1981) with Virgil A. Clift, was editor from 1970 to 1974. Low was succeeded by Lorraine A. Williams, who established the Carter G. Woodson Award for article contributions and worked to attract a wider spectrum of contributors to the publication. Alton Hornsby, Jr., a professor of history at Morehouse College, succeeded Williams in 1976.

In 1983 financial difficulties forced the association to briefly suspend the publication of the *Journal of Negro History* and the *Negro History Bulletin;* both publications were revived within a year. Financial difficulties also led the association to remove Dr. Samuel L. Banks from the position of national president in 1985, two years after his election to the post. Dr. Janette H. Harris became the association's second female president in 1993, and she was faced with these pressing economic conditions. Under Hornsby and Harris however, the *Journal of Negro History* attracted more black scholars from historically black colleges and universities. The journal also brought more women and first-time historians into its ranks of article contributors. The association continued to sponsor an annual essay contest for college students, a scholar-in-residence program, and an October convention on current historical research. In 2001 the *Journal of Negro History* became the *Journal of African American History,* and in 2003 Dr. V. P. Franklin became editor of the journal. Also in 2001, the *Negro History Bulletin* became the *Black History Bulletin.*

See also Associated Publishers; Black History Month/ Negro History Week; Douglass; Frederick; Washington, Booker T.; Woodson, Carter G.

Bibliography

Goggin, Jacqueline. Carter G. Woodson: *A Life in Black History.* Baton Rogue: Louisiana State University Press, 1993.

Meier, August, and Elliott Rudwick, eds. *Black History and the Historical Profession.* Urbana: University of Illinois Press, 1986.

JACQUELINE GOGGIN (1996)
Updated by publisher 2005

ASTRONAUTS

During the 1960s, the civil rights movement began to change the United States. Much of the country was engulfed in the sometimes violent struggle to either create equal rights or to ensure that minority groups remained as second-class citizens. In the South, segregation often furthered the social disparity between African Americans and whites, placing African Americans in schools that lacked the funding provided to their white counterparts. However, this is also the period that introduced the nation's first African-American space travelers.

The politics of change were apparent in the 1960 election campaign of John F. Kennedy, who was the first presidential candidate to strongly contend for the minority vote. In a post-election conversation with National Urban League President Whitney Young, Kennedy was told that an African-American astronaut could encourage black youngsters to enter the science and technology fields. At the same time, news commentator Edward R. Murrow began suggesting to National Aeronautics and Space Administration (NASA) administrator James E. Webb that

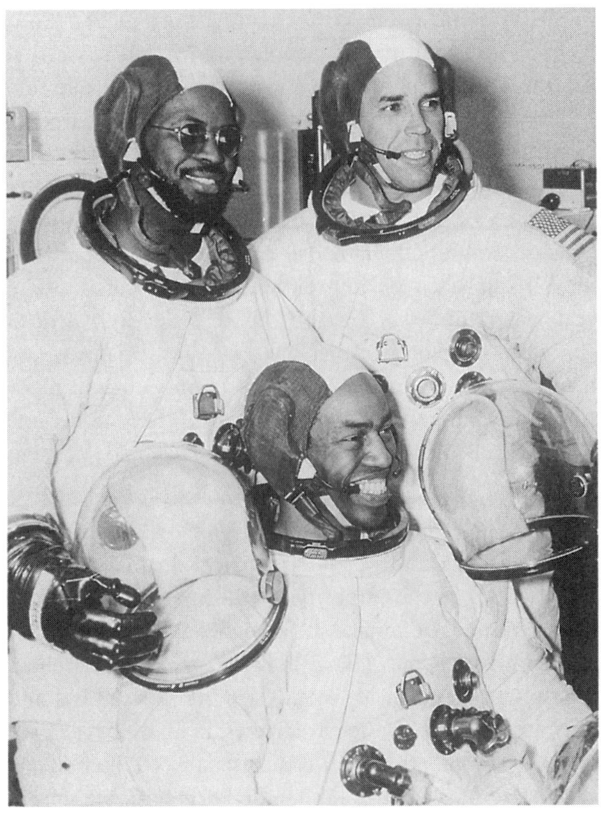

Guion S. "Guy" Bluford (seated) with fellow astronauts Ronald McNair (left) and Frederick Gregory, 1978. *The three men joined NASA's astronaut training program together that year. In 1983, Bluford became the first African American in space. Two years later, Gregory became the first African American to pilot a U.S. spacecraft. McNair died in the explosion of the space shuttle* Challenger *in 1986.* AP/WIDE WORLD PHOTOS. REPRODUCED BY PERMISSION.

the nation should consider sending a black man into space "to retell our space effort to the whole nonwhite world, which is most of it" (Phelps, p. xviii). In 1962 President Kennedy asked the department of defense to find a black pilot who met the requirements to become an astronaut.

Edward J. Dwight (b. 1933) became the first African American selected to attend astronaut training in 1962. An accomplished pilot with an aeronautical degree from Arizona State University, Dwight received a letter from the president informing him of his selection. However, White House favoritism and racial prejudice—as described by Dwight in a fifteen page memorandum to the department of defense—eventually undermined his career. Although he was recommended by the astronaut selection board, Dwight and five of his eight recommended classmates were not selected to head into space. After suffering what he considered further discriminatory behavior by the U.S. Air Force, Dwight described significant social discrimination and resigned his commission in 1966.

Just one year later, however, Dr. Robert H. Lawrence (1935–1967), an air force major, qualified for the air force's Manned Orbital Laboratory program, becoming the first African-American astronaut designee and the only designee until that time who had earned a doctorate. Unfortunately, this new hope for an African-American astronaut passed at the end of that year with Lawrence's accidental death aboard an F-104 aircraft. No other African American would join the astronaut program until 1978, leading the Soviet Union to accuse the U.S. space program of racism. In 1963 the Soviets placed the first woman in space (Colonel Valentina Tereshkova, born in 1937) and allowed Cuba's Colonel Arnaldo Tamayo-Mendez, born in 1942, to become the first black man in space in 1980. As a participant in the Soviet Union's Intercosmos guest cosmonaut program, Tamayo-Mendez spent eight days aboard the Salyut 6 space station.

1978 TO 1987

Whereas the 1963 entry of a Soviet woman into space embarrassed some senators who believed that the United States should have made a greater effort to create an inclusive astronaut corps, the 1964 Civil Rights Act encoded the need for NASA to integrate. In 1978, the astronaut training program welcomed its first female candidates—including Sally K. Ride, the first American woman in space—and three African Americans: Guion (Guy) Bluford, Ronald McNair, and Frederick Gregory.

Guy Bluford Jr. (born in 1942) became the first African American in space on August 30, 1983. His launch aboard the *Challenger* was attended by black political leaders, educators, and entertainment figures. Bluford's contribution to aviation, however, had begun years before. After graduating from Pennsylvania State University as the only black student in the engineering school, he served with distinction in the skies over Vietnam. Upon his return from duty, he obtained a master's degree in aerospace engineering, followed by a doctorate in the same field and a minor in laser physics. His doctoral dissertation contributed to the study of thin wings traveling at velocities well above the speed of sound. From 1974 to 1978, as the chief of Air Dynamics and Airframe Branch at the Air Force Flight Dynamics Library, he supervised the research of over forty engineers using two wind tunnels. Finally, in 1979 he applied to and was accepted by the astronaut corps as a mission specialist. He performed work on various satellites and conducted experiments in physics, biology, and the processing of materials. In 1993 Bluford retired from both NASA and the air force with the rank of colonel.

African Americans in Non-Astronautical Aviation

Successful African-American aviators include General Lester L. Lyles of the U.S. Air Force (ret. 2003), Professor Wesley L. Harris of the Massachusetts Institute of Technology (MIT), and Joseph R. Cleveland, Chief Information Officer for Lockheed Martin. Four-star General Lester Lyles, a graduate of Howard University, served in several capacities in the military. After leaving his position as Vice Chief of Staff, he assumed the leadership of the Air Force Materiel Command in April 2000, where he worked to invigorate his organization's role in science and technology. He emphasized the growth of Air Force participation in space and in developing government/industry partnerships. Wesley L. Harris, similarly, has sought such partnerships during his career. In the time since receiving his doctorate from Princeton University, Harris has served as the NASA Associate Administrator for Aeronautics, co-director of the Lean Aerospace Initiative, and currently heads the MIT Department of Aeronautics and Astronautics. Like many noted astronauts, he has demonstrated sincere dedication to the advancement of minorities through education, having founded the MIT Office of Minority Affairs in 1975. Finally, community leader Joseph R. Cleveland exemplifies a leading African American within commercial aviation. As a member of the 2003 Board of Governors for the Orlando, Florida, Chamber of Commerce, he has devoted significant efforts to developing the local community. A graduate of Tennessee State University, a historically black institution, he now oversees the information technology operations at Lockheed Martin Corporation, the nation's largest military aerospace contractor. In 1996 Cleveland was named Black Engineer of the Year for Career Achievement in Industry by the Engineering Deans of Historically Black Colleges and Universities and one of the Premier 100 Information Technology Leaders by *Computerworld* magazine in 2004.

His classmate, Frederick Gregory (born in 1941), was from a successful middle class family (his uncle was Dr. Charles Drew, a pioneer in blood storage and collection techniques). He pursued his education at the Air Force Academy, having been nominated by the civil rights leader and U.S. Representative Adam Clayton Powell Jr. After serving as a combat rescue pilot in Vietnam, he worked as a research test pilot at Langley Air Force Base from 1974 until 1978, when he joined the astronaut corps. Seven years later, in 1985, Gregory became the first African American to pilot an American spacecraft, maneuvering the *Challenger* into space. He served in mission control for subsequent spacecraft launches, and in 1993 he became administrator for the Office of Safety and Mission Assurance.

In 1986, while serving in mission control, Gregory witnessed the death of his classmate Ronald E. McNair (1950–1986) in the explosion of the space shuttle *Challenger.* At the age of nine, McNair defied the law and began to use the whites-only library in Lake City, South Carolina. As a physics student at North Carolina Agricultural and Technical University, he participated in an exchange program with the Massachusetts Institute of Technology (MIT). He later pursued his doctoral degree—with the aid of a fellowship from the Ford Foundation—at MIT, where he continued to study physics because of its combination of math and science. There he helped develop some of the first chemical and high-pressure carbon dioxide lasers. As staff physicist at Hughes Research Labs in Malibu, California (1976–1978), McNair researched the use of lasers for satellite-to-satellite communication. He joined NASA's astronaut program as a mission specialist in 1978 and became the second African American in space in 1984. His research efforts in space included the testing of a remote manipulator arm, used to repair damage to satellites and to the shuttle itself, and the study of solar cells. Among the several memorials to McNair are the MIT McNair building, a center for space research, and the MIT McNair Scholarship, which honors African-American students for academic achievement and community development.

1987 TO 2005

With the resurrection of the shuttle program in 1988 came another achievement for African Americans in aviation and space technology. In 1987, Dr. Mae Jemison (born in 1956) became the first African-American woman to gain entry to the Astronaut Candidate Program. Having graduated from Stanford University with a degree in chemical engineering, Jemison obtained a doctorate in medicine from Cornell University Medical College in 1981. Before joining NASA, she supervised the medical staff of the

Peace Corps in Sierra Leone and Liberia, and practiced medicine with CIGNA Health Plans in California. On September 13, 1992, Dr. Jemison entered space on board the shuttle *Endeavour.* There she conducted experiments regarding the creation of drugs and the effects of low gravity on the human body. She also participated in a biofeedback experiment meant to help future space travelers deal with the effects of living outside the earth's atmosphere. In 1993 Jemison resigned her position at NASA to become a professor at Dartmouth University. At the same time, as director of the Jemison Institute for Advancing Technologies in Developing Nations, she led research to improve the living conditions in the developing world.

After Jemison's departure, her colleague Dr. Bernard Harris Jr. (born in 1956) continued to focus on maintaining human health in space, an ongoing NASA initiative. After becoming an astronaut candidate in 1990, he worked as project manager on the NASA Exercise Countermeasures Project, designing exercises to offset the loss of physical conditioning in space. In March 1993 Harris flew on *Columbia* and conducted the first medical conference from space with doctors at his alma mater, the Mayo Clinic.

Other Notables

As of 2005, NASA reported that fifteen African Americans have become astronauts or astronaut trainees. Other noted black astronauts include Charles F. Bolden (born in 1946), who served onboard *Discovery* in 1990 during the launch of the Hubble telescope and commanded the shuttle *Atlantis* in 1992, and Robert L. Curbeam (born in 1962), who was a member of the six-person crew that installed the laboratory on the International Space Station. In a tragic way, African-American astronaut Michael Anderson gained national attention following his death in the 2003 *Columbia* explosion.

A Common Thread

Despite the diverse backgrounds of the several African-American astronauts, one important similarity may be noted: a dedication to education. Of Bluford, McNair, Jemison, Bolden, and Gregory, all had at least one parent who worked as a teacher and imbued in his or her child the importance of education and a determination to learn and advance. After Edward Dwight left NASA, videos of his training were used to inspire young African Americans to enter science and technology. Ronald McNair encouraged young blacks to succeed as he traveled the country speaking to youth and advocating the recruitment of first-rate teachers for inner city schools. Both Guy Bluford and Frederick Gregory devoted time to similar causes. Mae Jemison's company, Jemison Group Inc., facilitates health care for the developing world by advocating the embrace of science and education. She also encourages young people to pursue careers in science and technology.

See also Drew, Charles Richard; Science

Bibliography

Atkinson, Joseph D., and Jay M. Shafritz. *The Real Stuff: A History of NASA's Astronaut Recruitment Program.* New York: Praeger, 1985.

Gelletly, LeeAnne. *Mae Jemison.* Philadelphia: Chelsea House, 2002.

Gubert, Betty, Miriam Kaplan, and Caroline M. Fannin. *Distinguished African Americans in Aviation and Space Science.* Westport, Conn.: Oryx, 2002.

Naden, Corinne J. *Black Americans of Achievement: Ronald McNair.* New York: Chelsea House, 1991.

Oberg, James E. *Red Star in Orbit.* New York: Random House, 1981.

Phelps, J. Alfred. *They Had a Dream: The Story of the First African-American Astronauts.* Novato, Calif.: Presidio, 1994.

WESLEY L. HARRIS (2005)
RICHARD-DUANE S. CHAMBERS (2005)

Atlanta Compromise

On September 18, 1895, Booker T. Washington, the president of Tuskegee Institute in Alabama, delivered an address at the Cotton States and International Exposition in Atlanta, Georgia, that gained him recognition as the leading spokesman for African Americans.

Speaking to a predominantly white audience, Washington called upon black southerners to subordinate their demands for equal civil and political rights, at least temporarily, in order to focus upon efforts to achieve an economic base in the New South. The speech climaxed with Washington's apparent acquiescence to southern white desires for racial segregation when he proclaimed: "In all things that are purely social we can be as separate as the fingers, yet one as the hand in all things essential to mutual progress." This "compromise" epitomized the accommodationist ideology of racial self-help that came to be associated with Booker T. Washington's leadership in the late nineteenth and early twentieth centuries.

See also Tuskegee University

Bibliography

Harlan, Louis R. *Booker T. Washington: The Making of a Black Leader, 1856–1901.* New York: Oxford University Press, 1972.

Meier, August. *Negro Thought in America, 1880–1915: Racial Ideologies in the Age of Booker T. Washington.* Ann Arbor: University of Michigan Press, 1963.

JAMES M. SORELLE (1996)

Atlanta Riot of 1906

The Atlanta Riot was an expression of southern white hysteria over rape and the social and political implications of race. On September 22, 1906, following a race-baiting gubernatorial campaign by Hoke Smith and a lengthy newspaper series about a purported wave of rapes of white women by black men, the city of Atlanta, Georgia, a center of the black middle class, was taken over by a white mob.

On the evening of September 22, whites, aroused by false and exaggerated reports of arguments between blacks and whites, massed on Decatur Street. Word spread, and whites attacked streetcars and destroyed black shops and businesses on Auburn Street, then invaded black neighborhoods, with halfhearted resistance by or the support of city police and local militia. Black homes were pillaged, and five blacks were murdered. Blacks put up some resistance but were overwhelmed and outnumbered in pitched battles with armed whites. On the following night, state militia troops arrived, but many joined the white mob, which headed toward Brownsville, the city's middle-class black college suburb, and attacked its black residents. Police arrested and disarmed blacks who attempted to defend themselves. The next morning, police and militia entered Brownsville homes, supposedly to hunt for guns and arrest rioters; they beat and arrested affluent blacks. White rioting continued every night until September 26, when order was finally restored. Twenty-five blacks had been killed (as well as one white), and hundreds had been injured or had their property destroyed. More than a thousand blacks left Atlanta during and after the riots.

The rioting in Atlanta demonstrated the helplessness of black populations in urban settings and the emptiness of rhetoric about the "New South." The white savagery caused many blacks to question the effectiveness of Booker T. Washington's accommodationist philosophy. Washington himself was energized by the riots into calling the Carnegie Hall Conference of 1906, which prompted the formation of the Committee of Twelve, a short-lived attempt at unified black leadership. Elite whites disclaimed participation in the riot, which they blamed on blacks and on poor, immigrant whites. However, elite whites joined in promoting the rebuilding of black Atlanta. They sought to avoid further rioting by joining with "respectable" black moderates such as John Hope and Henry Hugh Proctor to reduce racial tensions. Out of the movement came annual meetings on race relations in the Southern Sociological Congress, beginning in 1912, which led to the formation of the Commission on Interracial Cooperation in 1919.

See also Washington, Booker T.

Bibliography

Brown, Richard Maxwell. *Strain of Violence.* New York: Oxford University Press, 1975.

Williamson, Joel. *The Crucible of Race: Black-White Relations in the American South since Emancipation.* New York: Oxford University Press, 1984.

GREG ROBINSON (1996)

Attaway, William

November 19, 1911
June 17, 1986

Novelist William Alexander Attaway was born in Greenville, Mississippi, to William Attaway, a physician, and Florence Parry Attaway, a schoolteacher, and was raised in Chicago. He attended local public schools and the University of Illinois, where he pursued literary interests. His father died during his second year in college and Attaway left school to hobo his way west, working along the way as a cabin boy, stevedore, and migrant laborer. He returned to Chicago and the university in 1933; there he published his first literary efforts. During this period Attaway became involved with the Illinois branch of the Federal Writers' Project and first met Richard Wright.

After graduating from the University of Illinois in 1936, Attaway moved to New York City, determined to earn his living as a writer. With the assistance of his younger sister, Ruth, an actress, he won a role in the road company of *You Can't Take It with You.* He was on tour with the play when he learned that his first novel, *Let Me Breathe Thunder* (1939), a naturalistic novel about the experiences of two white migrant farmworkers, had been accepted for publication.

***Boston Massacre, March 5, 1770.** Crispus Attucks, a runaway slave, led the crowd of men and boys who challenged British authority in the first battle of the American Revolution.* PHOTOGRAPHS AND PRINTS DIVISION, SCHOMBURG CENTER FOR RESEARCH IN BLACK CULTURE, THE NEW YORK PUBLIC LIBRARY, ASTOR, LENOX AND TILDEN FOUNDATIONS.

Blood on the Forge (1941), Attaway's second and most significant novel, encapsulates the mass migration of southern blacks to northern cities as it traces the experiences of three half-brothers in the steel mills of Pennsylvania. Although *Blood on the Forge* received favorable reviews, the novel was not a success in the literary marketplace—overshadowed, perhaps, by the triumph of Richard Wright, whose novel *Native Son* had become a best seller the previous year. *Blood on the Forge* was the high point of Attaway's literary career. In his later years, he wrote for radio, film, and television; developed a deep interest in Caribbean and U.S. folk music; and published two works, *The Calypso Song Book* (1957) and *Hear America Singing* (1967). He spent the last years of his life in Los Angeles and died in relative obscurity.

See also Federal Writers' Project; Literature of the United States

Bibliography

Bell, Bernard W. *The Afro-American Novel and Its Tradition.* Amherst: University of Massachusetts Press, 1987.

Yarborough, Richard. "Afterword." In *Blood on the Forge*, by William Attaway. New York: Monthly Review Press, 1987.

JAMES A. MILLER (1996)

Attucks, Crispus

c. 1723

March 5, 1770

Crispus Attucks is acclaimed by many as the first martyr of the American Revolution. Although not much is known about Attucks's early life, he was a tall, muscular mulatto, probably of African and Natick ancestry. He was a slave of William Brown of Framingham, Massachusetts, before he ran away in November 1750. Attucks worked on whaling ships operating out of various New England ports over the next two decades. On the night of March 5, 1770, he was a leader of a crowd of twenty to thirty laborers and sailors who confronted a group of British soldiers, whose presence in Boston was deeply resented. Brandishing a club, Attucks allegedly struck one of the grenadiers, prompting several soldiers to fire into the crowd. Attucks fell instantly, becoming the first of five to die in the so-called Boston Massacre. His body was carried in its coffin to Faneuil Hall, where it lay for three days before he and the other victims of the massacre were given a public funeral. Ten thousand people marched in their funeral cortege. During the officers' trial, John Adams, acting as their defense attorney, ascribed to Attucks, whom he claimed had "undertaken to be the hero of the night," chief blame for instigating the massacre. Most of the soldiers were acquitted.

The Boston Massacre was used by Revolutionary-era patriots to heighten opposition to the British, and March 5 was commemorated annually in Boston from 1771 to 1783, when it was displaced by the celebration of July 4th. Attucks seems to have largely faded from public memory thereafter, until the African-American historian William Cooper Nell made him an important symbol of black citizenship, patriotism, and military service in the 1850s. In 1858, as a reaction to the Supreme Court's Dred Scott decision, Nell revived Crispus Attucks Day, and Boston's blacks celebrated it until 1870. By the middle of the nineteenth century, Attucks's name graced numerous African-American schools, military companies, and other institutions. In 1888, Boston authorities erected a monument to him on Boston Common.

Attucks has remained an important symbol. In 1965, for example, blacks in Newark, New Jersey, revived Crispus Attucks Day with annual parades, and in 1967 the Newark school system began school closings to observe the holiday. By the 1970s a few U.S. cities were celebrating Crispus Attucks Day. Although interest in Crispus Attucks Day waned somewhat after the 1960s, his memory was honored by the U.S. Mint with a commemorative coin in 1998.

See also *Dred Scott v. Sandford*

Bibliography

Bethel, Elizabeth Rauh. *The Roots of African-American Identity: Memory and History in Free Antebellum Communities.* New York: St. Martin's Press, 1997.

Browne, Stephen J. "Remembering Crispus Attucks: Race, Rhetoric, and the Politics of Commemoration." *Quarterly Journal of Speech* 85 (1999).

Zobel, Hiller B. *The Boston Massacre.* Norwalk, CT: Eaton Press, 1987.

ROY E. FINKENBINE (1996)
MITCH KACHUN (1996)
Updated bibliography

Augier, Roy

December 13, 1924

Born in St. Lucia, Fitzroy Richard Augier was educated at the Roman Catholic Boys Elementary School and at St. Mary's College in Castries and at the universities of St. Andrew and London. He was appointed as a junior research fellow at the Institute of Social and Economic Research at the University College of the West Indies in Mona, Jamaica, in 1954. In 1955, he became a lecturer in the department of history, a senior lecturer in 1965, and a professor of history in 1989.

As a historian, Augier worked to establish Caribbean history as a study in its own right. He was involved in three seminal publications. Firstly, the publication with Douglas Hall, Shirley Gordon, and Mary Reckord of *The Making of the West Indies* in 1960 revolutionized the teaching and studying of history in the region. It provided students with reading material, which permitted them to study and understand their societies, and stimulated volumes of writing and research on Caribbean topics. With Rex Nettleford and M.G. Smith, he produced the *Report on the Rastafarian Movement,* which demonstrated the importance of historical examination of this group in Caribbean society. He also served as chairman of the drafting committee for UNESCO's *General History of the Caribbean.*

These volumes reflect the extent to which Caribbean historiography has developed, and it is fitting that one of the founding fathers of Caribbean history is at the helm of this development. Augier has popularized Caribbean history. He infused his students with a sense of history and of the fundamental role of historical understanding for Caribbean development. Because he taught students in several departments, he influenced the generations that would carry on the work of development. Augier was the "Man with the Hammer" who developed and honed an appropriate curriculum for Caribbean university students and stimulated them to undertake further research.

Augier's efforts were not confined to the university. He criticized the Cambridge Caribbean history examination for its focus on Britain, was asked to review the Cambridge Ordinary and Advanced Level Caribbean history syllabuses, and for many years he was the sole examiner for the A level exams. Augier chaired the history panel of the Caribbean Examination Council (CXC) from its inception, and from 1986 to 1996 he served as chair of the Caribbean Examinations Council. In this latter role he spear-headed the move to institute a regional examination to replace the Cambridge A level examination, as a result of which, the Caribbean Advanced Proficiency Examination (CAPE) has come on stream. Once again, this able foot soldier lobbied for popular support of the new program through regional meetings with government officials and teachers and through school visits. Caribbean history became fully legitimized. Thus, Augier contributed to the process of development of a cadre of Caribbean people who would begin to reinterpret their history.

Augier was also involved in curriculum development and teacher-training workshops for CXC and CAPE preparation. He served as examiner of the Institute of Jamaica, where he assisted in curriculum development, paper setting, and marking scripts for teacher training institutions in Jamaica. Because of his varied involvement in the education system, he was well placed to wield considerable influence on the teaching of history at secondary and tertiary levels in the region.

For Augier, education was the means to establish closer relations across the language barriers of the Caribbean. As a founding member and past president (1984) of the Association of Caribbean Historians, he promoted closer relations between French- and English-speaking historians. For this, he was honored as Chevalier, Ordre des Arts et Lettres in 1989.

An administrator par excellence, Augier served as dean of the Faculty of General Studies (1967–1972), acting principal of the Cave Hill campus, (1970), and pro vice chancellor of the university (1972–1990). He influenced programming in the institution and along with Elsa Goveia, is credited with ensuring that the students of non-elite schools got a fair stake in the university. He has served on archive committees in Jamaica and initiated the establishment of the Barbados Archives. For his contribution to regional archival development, he was awarded a medal by the International Council of Archives. He also received awards from the Institute of Jamaica in 1996 and 2003, and was knighted for his contribution to education in St. Lucia. Sir Roy Augier is at heart a scholar, architect, visionary, pioneer, activist intellectual, and the quintessential Caribbean man.

See also Education in the Caribbean

Bibliography

Moore, Brian L., and Wilmot, Swithin R., eds. *Before and After 1865: Papers on Education, Politics, and Regionalism in the Caribbean, in Honour of Sir Roy Augier*. Kingston: Ian Randle Publishers, 1998.

D. RITA PEMBERTON (2005)

Autobiography, U.S.

Autobiography holds a position of distinction—indeed, many would say preeminence—among the narrative traditions of black America. African-Americans had been dictating and writing first-person accounts of their lives for almost a century before the first black American novel appeared in 1853. Between 1850 and 1950 the autobiographies of Frederick Douglass, Booker T. Washington, and Richard Wright made a more lasting impression on the American readership than did any African-American novel or school of novelists from the same era. The number of fictional and scholarly works by African-Americans that read as autobiographies or include elements of memoir confirms the judgment, made by more than one critic, that black writing in the United States incorporates an extraordinarily self-reflexive tradition.

African-American autobiography has consistently testified to the commitment of people of color to lay claim to full citizenship as Americans and also to articulate their achievements as individuals and as persons of African descent. Perhaps more than any other form in black American letters, autobiography has since its inception achieved recognition as an authentic form of cultural expression and as a powerful means of addressing and altering sociopolitical realities in the United States.

Foundations of a Tradition

Nineteenth-century abolitionists sponsored the publication of the narratives of escaped slaves out of a conviction that first-person accounts of those victimized by and yet triumphant over slavery would mobilize white readers more profoundly than any other kind of antislavery discourse. A similar belief in contemporary black American autobiography's potential to liberate white readers from racial prejudice, ignorance, and fear prompted a relatively large and generally supportive response on the part of publishers and critics to African-American autobiographers in the twentieth century, particularly since the 1960s.

As a form of discourse, African-American autobiography might be characterized best in terms of the three constituent elements of the word itself: *autos* (self), *bios* (life), and *graphe* (writing). Undoubtedly, the stylized treatment that autobiography offers to African-American lives through a written medium has been crucial to the success of the genre with the popular readership in the United States and abroad, especially as a way to relate aspects of the writers' lives made distinctive by racial difference. But one should not overlook the social import of the psychological and experiential distinction that black autobiographers claim for themselves. Writers with those individual concerns have also usually acknowledged an obligation to speak for and to people of color, in addition to proclaiming their uniqueness.

Yet autobiographers from Mary Prince to Malcolm X have realized that by identifying the aspirations of a people with the ambitions of a self, they could generate a genuine impetus to the cause of freedom for the race. A key manifestation of *autos* since the beginning of the African-American autobiographical enterprise has been the drive to attain the autonomy of authorship, the right to express oneself independent of the direction or approval of white sponsors and editors. Increasingly in the twentieth century, the act of writing, the representation of selfhood through a personalized storytelling style, became a sign of the African-American autobiographer's assertion of independence of mind and individuality of vision.

During its first century or so from 1760 to 1865, the form was dominated by autobiographical narratives of ex-slaves. The best-known of these narratives were authored by fugitives from slavery who used their personal histories to expose the horrors of America's so-called peculiar institution. Classics of the genre by Frederick Douglass, William Wells Brown, and Harriet Jacobs center on their rites of passage from bondage in the South to freedom in the North. Advertised in the abolitionist press and sold at antislavery meetings throughout the English-speaking world, at least a dozen of the more than seventy slave narratives published in the antebellum era went through multiple editions. A few, such as *The Interesting Narrative of the Life of Olaudah Equiano, or Gustavus Vassa, the African* (1789) and the *Narrative of the Life of Frederick Douglass* (1845), sold in the tens of thousands. Equiano was one of several black writers, enslaved and free, whose autobiographies arose from throughout the Americas in this period. *The Wonderful Adventures of Mrs. Seacole in Many Lands* (1857) is the rare story of a free black woman's life and travels by Mary Seacole, a Jamaican Creole who worked as a nurse in the Crimean War.

From the end of the Civil War to the onset of the Great Depression, the ex-slave narrative remained the preponderant subgenre of African-American autobiography. Former slaves who wrote or dictated book-length accounts of their lives depicted slavery as a crucible in which the resilience, industry, and ingenuity of the enslaved were tested and ultimately validated. The bestselling African-American autobiography of the early twentieth century was Booker T. Washington's *Up from Slavery* (1901), his contribution to the American ideals of resourcefulness and responsibility.

Black Autobiographies for the Twentieth Century

As African-Americans learned the bitter lessons of the post-Reconstruction era, black autobiography became less focused on the individual's quest for freedom and recognition and more concerned with the realization of communal power and prestige in African-American institutions, especially the school and the church. Educators, headed by Booker T. Washington and his many protégés who wrote autobiographies, and ministers, whose influential memoirs range from Bishop Daniel Payne's *Recollections of Seventy Years* (1888) to Bishop Alexander Walters's *My Life and Work* (1917), argued that black survival, not to mention fulfillment, depended largely on building institutional bulwarks against the divide-and-conquer strategy of American white supremacy. By sublimating his own desires and ambitions in a larger framework, the institutional man of African-American autobiography asked the world to judge him primarily according to his usefulness, his ability to work within the existing socioeconomic order to accomplish good for his people.

William Pickens and Ida B. Wells-Barnett—both southern-born, middle class, and dedicated to civil rights activism—made significant contributions to African-American autobiography in the 1920s. Pickens's *Bursting Bonds* (1923) chronicles the evolution of a latter-day Booker T. Washington into a militant proponent of the ideas of W. E. B. Du Bois. Wells's posthumously published *Crusade for Justice* (1970), edited by her daughter, tells an equally compelling story of its author's dauntless commitment to a life of agitation and protest on behalf of African-American men and women. The pioneering efforts of Pickens and Wells, and James Weldon Johnson's *Along This Way* in 1933, helped to reorient African-American autobiography to its roots in the ideal, from the slave narrative, of the black leader as an articulate hero who uses knowledge and literacy as resources in the struggle for personal and collective liberation.

The decade and a half after the New Negro renaissance saw the publication of several important autobiographies by literary figures such as Claude McKay (*A Long Way from Home*, 1937), Langston Hughes (*The Big Sea*,

1940), Zora Neale Hurston (*Dust Tracks on a Road*, 1942), and Richard Wright (*Black Boy*, 1945). The unprecedented emphasis in these texts on the search for an authentic selfhood, one that was predicated on the writers' skepticism about institutions and epitomized in their heightened sensitivity to literary style as self-presentation, marks a turning point in the history of African-American autobiography. Autobiographies became a complement to black literary figures' efforts to undermine racial stereotypes in modern media and academic disciplines dominated by whites. *Black Boy* became the most widely read and discussed black American autobiography of the post–World War II period, primarily because of its quintessentially modernist portrait of the black writer as an alienated rebel dedicated uncompromisingly to the expression of truth as individually perceived.

The Roles of the Writer

This sense of the autobiographer's foremost responsibility to absolute authenticity of self-expression largely precluded Wright from a role that had become traditional for the African-American autobiographer by the mid-twentieth century—that of spokesperson for the black community. To a new generation of self-styled revolutionary black autobiographers in the 1960s, however, Wright's ideal of personal authenticity could be achieved only by identifying with the oppressed masses of black America and "telling it like it is" to white America on their behalf. The prototype for this mode of testimony is *The Autobiography of Malcolm X* (1965), which turned a former street-corner organizer steeped in black nationalism into a culture hero for young, disaffected blacks and whites in search of a standard-bearer for a new racial consciousness. Also "telling it like it is," often to their brothers in arms, were women writers of the civil rights and Black Power movements. *Angela Davis: An Autobiography* (1974) is exemplary as it chronicles how the young radical became a political prisoner and a philosopher, a model of personal transformation for a period of tremendous social change. The generation energized by these movements produced a chorus of denunciation of American racism and hypocrisy unmatched since the era of the fugitive-slave narrative.

The appearance in 1970 of Maya Angelou's *I Know Why the Caged Bird Sings* signals one of the most remarkable developments from late twentieth-century African-American autobiography: the unprecedented outpouring of narratives of intimacy and conscience by black women. Although women had been longtime contributors to such bedrock African-American traditions as the spiritual autobiography, writers including Angelou and Audre Lorde recast the ideas of the spirit and salvation in the secular experience of black female artists and activists. Lorde's *Zami: A New Spelling of My Name* (1982) opened a vista onto the experiences of feminist, gay and lesbian, and West Indian people in black communities. Hers is part of a long tradition of autobiographies that enrich the African-American struggle against oppression by grounding it in cultural heritage and lived experience.

Because autobiographies have brought the distinctive experiences of African-Americans to the attention of the reading public, they offer uniquely informed perspectives on the issues all individuals face in a racialized society. Since the 1980s, Marita Golden (*Migrations of the Heart*, 1987) and Itabari Njeri (*Every Good-Bye Ain't Gone*, 1991) have been among the autobiographers who herald the importance of national origin and skin tone to everyday life in black communities. Colin Powell, in *My American Journey* (1995), describes his military career and the positions of power he has held in terms of his personal and family history, explaining how the latter inculcated the ideals he shares with his allies in government; similar convictions inspired J. C. Watts's *What Color is a Conservative* in 2002. Though their political concerns set them apart from many of their generation, by narrating other aspects of their lives as black Americans they join the ranks of autobiographers who contribute to the complicated history of black experiences in the United States. The divergent interpretations of history amid every generation of autobiographers demonstrate the importance of the form as a social and political medium as well as a means of self-expression.

Learning from African-American Autobiographies

Considering the critical role autobiographies have played in the development of social consciousness about African-Americans' lives, first-person accounts are crucial to the study of black identity, history, and culture. All biographies straddle the line between history and literature, because the narratives they depict refer to real-life people and events. The relationship between subject matter and representation is even more contingent in autobiography, which puts into words the interpretations of a single author affected by the events described in the account. For people of African descent, putting renditions of their lives into writing has been a way to intervene in the circulation of knowledge about their communities, often contradicting superstitious and misrepresentative tendencies in history and the sciences. In that way, black autobiography is a kind of *autoethnography*, a set of writings about a cultural group produced by its own members. Efforts to convey the real-life circumstances of black persons' lives also inform the concepts and feelings that accompany portrayals of them in fiction and creative media. From the strivings of the enslaved through the enduring contributions of inspired individuals to a richly-textured culture, autobiographies have maintained a wealth of reflections on the lived experience of blackness, its challenges, and its fortunes.

See also Biography, U.S.; Black Arts Movement; Drama; Literary Criticism, U.S.; Literary Magazines; Poetry, U.S.; Slave Narratives

Bibliography

Andrews, William L. *To Tell a Free Story: The First Century of African-American Autobiography, 1760–1865.* Urbana: University of Illinois Press, 1986.

Andrews, William L., ed. *African-American Autobiography: A Collection of Critical Essays.* Englewood Cliffs, N.J.: Prentice Hall, 1993.

Andrews, William L., and Nellie Y. McKay, eds. "Twentieth-Century African-American Autobiography." *Black American Literature Forum* 24 (1990): 195–415.

Braxton, Joanne M. *Black Women Writing Autobiography: A Tradition Within a Tradition.* Philadelphia: Temple University Press, 1989.

Mostern, Kenneth. *Autobiography and Black Identity Politics: Racialization in Twentieth-Century America.* Cambridge: Cambridge University Press, 1999.

Perkins, Margo V. *Autobiography as Activism: Three Black Women of the Sixties.* Jackson: University of Mississippi Press, 2000.

Sartwell, Crispin. *Act Like You Know: African-American Autobiography and White Identity.* Chicago: University of Chicago Press, 1998.

WILLIAM ANDREWS (1996)
ANDRÉ M. CARRINGTON (2005)

Bagnall, Robert

October 14, 1883
August 20, 1943

Robert Wellington Bagnall Jr., a priest and an official of the National Association for the Advancement of Colored People (NAACP), was born in Norfolk, Virginia, the son of an Episcopal priest. Following his father's vocation, the younger Bagnall attended Bishop Payne Divinity School in Petersburg, Virginia, an institution organized to train African Americans for the Episcopal ministry. Bagnall graduated in 1903 and was ordained as an Episcopal priest the same year. In 1906 he married Lillian Anderson of Baltimore. Between 1903 and 1910 he led Episcopal congregations in Pennsylvania, Maryland, and Ohio, and ultimately became rector of Saint Matthew's Church in Detroit in 1911. Bagnall helped organize the Detroit branch of the NAACP and served as the principal speaker for its first session in 1914. Between 1914 and 1918 he successfully fought school segregation in Ypsilanti, Michigan, campaigned against police maltreatment, and persuaded the Ford Motor Company in Dearborn, Michigan, to hire more African-American workers. He was appointed NAACP district organizer for the Michigan area in 1918, and in the next two years he campaigned unsuccessfully for the passage of civil rights bills in Michigan and Ohio.

In 1921 Bagnall moved to New York City, where he succeeded James Weldon Johnson as national director of NAACP branches. In this capacity, he traveled to NAACP branches nationwide to raise funds for the central organization; he also streamlined the branch system so that it contained fewer but stronger units. Throughout the 1920s, Bagnall contributed articles to such periodicals as the *Crisis* and the *Messenger.* From 1923 to 1926, he worked to deport the pan-Africanist leader Marcus Garvey. Bagnall attacked Garvey's Universal Negro Improvement Association as impractical and denounced Garvey as a racial traitor for his association with the Ku Klux Klan. In 1923 Bagnall cosponsored an open letter to Attorney General Harry Daugherty, urging Garvey's prosecution for mail fraud.

As the NAACP faced fiscal retrenchment in 1930, newly appointed national secretary Walter White urged Bagnall's removal on the grounds that Bagnall was not raising sufficient revenue. Under increasing pressure from the NAACP board, Bagnall resigned in 1931. The following year he moved to Philadelphia and became pastor of Saint Thomas's Episcopal Church, which he led until his death in 1943. He was remembered by associates in both the Episcopal church and the NAACP as an outstanding orator and community organizer.

See also *Crisis, The*; Garvey, Marcus Mosiah; *Messenger, The*; National Association for the Advancement of Colored People (NAACP); Universal Negro Improvement Association

Bibliography

Finch, Minnie. *The NAACP: Its Fight for Justice.* Metuchen, N.J.: Scarecrow, 1981.

"R. W. Bagnall Dies." *Crisis,* September 1943, 286.

Shelton, Bernice Dutrieuille. "Robert Wellington Bagnall." *Crisis,* November 1943, 334, 347.

Thomas, Richard W. *Life for Us Is What We Make It: Building Black Community in Detroit, 1915–1945.* Bloomington: Indiana University Press, 1992.

SASHA THOMAS (1996)

Bahá'í Communities in the Caribbean

With the achievement of unity and justice as its pivotal tenets and fundamental aim, the Bahá'í faith has attracted increasing attention throughout the Caribbean since the 1940s. In his voluminous writings the faith's founder, Bahá'u'lláh, addresses large cosmological questions such as the nature of God and faith, the basis of moral authority in human affairs, and the relationship between the world's religions. Equally emphasized in his writings are the principles and structures needed to transform human society: the elimination of racial and other forms of prejudice, equality of women and men, economic justice, and the need to establish an auxiliary world language, among many others. First started in Iran in the mid-nineteenth century, the Bahá'í faith as of 2002 was established in 191 countries and forty-six dependent territories or overseas departments, its scriptures translated into over eight hundred languages worldwide.

People in the Caribbean first learned of the faith from visitors from North America in the late 1930s. Among these enthusiastic promoters of the faith were several prominent black believers such as Louis Gregory, Ellsworth Blackwell, and others—including Dr. Malcolm King, a Jamaican who became a Bahá'í in Milwaukee in 1931—of Caribbean background. By the early 1940s the study groups these teachers formed in Haiti, Cuba, Jamaica, Puerto Rico, and the Dominican Republic had blossomed into flourishing Bahá'í communities. With the exception of Puerto Rico, these communities expanded sufficiently to elect their respective national governing bodies in 1961 and participated in 1963 in electing the first Universal House of Justice, the international governing council of the faith, democratically elected every five years. Other Caribbean territories were opened to the faith in the early 1950s and gradually consolidated, increasing the number of National Spiritual Assemblies in the region to nineteen by 2003.

The Bahá'í faith in the Caribbean, as elsewhere in the world, has attracted adherents from all ethnic and class segments and from a variety of religious backgrounds. To peoples in this region the consciousness cultivated in the Bahá'í faith of the wholeness of the human race, and the imperative need for world citizenship based on unity in diversity, has no doubt had special resonance. The Caribbean, after all, has been globalized for five centuries, has struggled with diversity, and has produced artists and leaders of thought on the world stage to an extent disproportionate to its geographic and demographic size. One indication of the appeal of the faith's progressive international emphasis is that several of the earliest Bahá'ís in Jamaica came from a background in the Universal Negro Improvement Association (UNIA), the transnational black movement founded by Marcus Garvey that reached its high point in the 1920s.

Bahá'ís from the Caribbean have served with distinction in promoting global citizenship and advancing the work of the faith worldwide. One early Jamaican Bahá'í, Julius Edwards, who served as a secretary to Garvey in the early 1930s, left his homeland in the early 1950s to take the Bahá'í teachings to Ghana and Liberia. Late in life he returned to the Caribbean and helped with the development of the Grenada Bahá'í community. A Bahá'í of Jamaican background was elected to and has served on the nine-member Universal House of Justice since 1982. The faith has been included in the school curriculum of various Caribbean countries, won widespread commendation from civic and government leaders, and is now widely recognized for its contributions to social development.

See also Garvey, Marcus; Universal Negro Improvement Association

Bibliography

The Bahá'í World: An International Record. Haifa: Bahá'í World Centre. Published biennially.

Hatcher, William S., and J. Douglas Martin. *The Bahá'í Faith: The Emerging Global Religion.* San Francisco: Harper and Row, 1985.

Momen, Wendi, ed. *A Basic Bahá'í Dictionary.* Oxford: George Ronald, 1996.

Smith, Peter. *A Concise Encyclopedia of the Bahá'í Faith.* Oxford: Oneworld, 2000.

CHARLES V. CARNEGIE (2005)

Bailey, Amy

November 27, 1895 (or November 28, 1896)
October 3, 1990

Even in death, Amy Bailey advocated service to Jamaica, claiming a last word for a mission to which she had dedicated much of her life. At the service of thanksgiving held to commemorate her life, a brief letter she had written sometime in 1989 and updated in 1990 was read. Addressed "To my friends and those interested," the letter explained that she had asked that no eulogy be given at the service because she wanted the praise and honor not for herself but to "humbly say, Thank you, God." She ended the letter with a call to serve others and "to leave Jamaica a better place" (Bailey, 1990).

Bailey had done just that. She was born and lived at a time when the structures of slave society remained deeply embedded in the economic, social, and political fabric of colonial Jamaica, despite Emancipation in 1838. Her parents, who were teachers, lived and worked in rural Jamaica and regarded education as the foundation necessary for blacks to advance in society. They inspired their eight children with this vision.

Bailey's early education, her formal training at Shortwood Teachers' College, and her work as a teacher at Kingston Technical School from 1919 to 1958 shaped her sense of mission. In addition to teaching her students shorthand and typing, she persistently advocated for employment opportunities for graduates in a system that did not regard technical school graduates to be "civil service quality."

Bailey's political orientation included race consciousness and anticolonial activism, and she was influenced by the work of Marcus Garvey and her involvement beginning in the 1930s with organizations such as the Jamaica Poetry League and the Readers and Writers Club. She was also active in social welfare groups such as Save the Children and in 1939 she co-founded the Birth Control Association. The Women's Liberal Club (WLC), which she cofounded in 1936, combined a women's rights agenda with the nationalist call "to help make Jamaica a better place for Jamaicans" (Domingo, 1937/1993, pp. 35–36). The resolutions of the WLC's First Women's Conference in 1939 included calls for women to vote on equal terms with men (but not for universal adult suffrage); for the appointment of women as jurors, justices of the peace, and police officers; and for women to be able to stand for election for the legislative council.

Bailey had raised many of the WLC's demands in articles she published regularly in *Public Opinion,* a progressive nationalist newspaper founded in the late 1930s. She wrote on a range of social issues and spoke out on topics that polite society considered unspeakable: race and color; black women who were not wanted by black men, who chose to marry brown or white women; and black young women who were not wanted as workers in business establishments. Her advocacy was strengthened by practical action directed toward changing employment practices in retail establishments. She felt great satisfaction for this aspect of her work and more generally for what she "did for colour in this country" (Brodber, 1986, p. 14).

Bailey was co-opted into the leadership of the colonial-oriented Jamaica Federation of Women, which was founded in 1944. This was probably a tactical move by Bailey, who was moving to form her own organization but saw the benefit of her presence and voice in an organization that brought together all the main women's groups in the country under the charismatic leadership of the governor's wife and was to be a space for struggle between the procolonial and nationalist tendencies within the women's movement of the time.

Bailey's focus was on her Housecraft Training Centre, where young women received training in domestic science. Some of the estimated six thousand young women who attended were able to use their training as a way to improve their lives, while for the majority, domestic service was presented as the main option for women's employment.

Bailey belonged to a generation of black Jamaican nationalist feminists that includes Amy Jacques Garvey, Amy Ashwood Garvey, Una Marson, Mary Morris Knibb, Edith Dalton James, and Eulalee Domingo, who were determined to change the face and nature of Jamaica and to secure women both influence and a place of respect in the life of the country. The government of Jamaica honored Bailey with the Order of Distinction in 1971 and in 1990 with the second highest national honor, the Order of Jamaica. The pamphlet *Tributes to Miss Amy* that was published after her death and distributed at her funeral, as well as the guard of honor at her thanksgiving service that was formed by the representatives of women's and other civic organizations, comprised her eulogy, never spoken but still declared.

See also Garvey, Amy Ashwood; Garvey, Amy Jacques; Garvey, Marcus; Morris Knibb, Mary; Marson, Una

Bibliography

Bailey, Amy. "To my friends and those interested." Letter, with attachment from Vivian Crawford, long-time advisor to the Bailey family, identifying it as Bailey's last letter, July 26, 1990. Private archives of Linnette Vassell, Kingston, Jamaica.

Brodber, Erna. "The Pioneering Miss Bailey." *Jamaica Journal* 19, no. 2 (1986).

Domingo, Eulalee. "Women's Clubs of Jamaica" (1937). In *Voices of Women in Jamaica, 1898–1939.* Compiled by Linnette Vassell. Mona, Jamaica: Dept. of History, University of the West Indies, 1993.

"Making History Take the Stage: Pauline Crawford's Amy Bailey." In *Women Speak: Newsletter About Caribbean Women,* no. 23. Women and Development Unit, Extra Mural Dept., UWI, Pinelands, Barbados. April, 1988.

Service of Thanksgiving for the Life of the Honourable Miss Amy Bailey, OJ MBE JP (pamphlet). Private archives of Linnette Vassell, Kingston, Jamaica.

Tributes to Miss Amy (pamphlet). Private archives of Linnette Vassell, Kingston, Jamaica.

LINNETTE VASSELL (2005)

Bailey, Beryl Loftman

January 15, 1920
April 18, 1977

A native Jamaican and a bilingual speaker of Jamaican Creole (JC) and Standard English (SE), Beryl Loftman Bailey was the first linguist to describe JC as a coherent linguistic system and advocate the teaching of SE to JC speakers in a manner that takes its systematic nature into account. She also made seminal contributions to the description and analysis of African American English "as a systematic language variety rather than a dialect typified by error or randomness" (R. W. Bailey, 1992, p. 103). She was the first linguist to develop scholarly arguments concerning the relationship of African-American language to creole languages of the Caribbean.

Bailey pursued undergraduate and graduate studies at Columbia University and held faculty positions at Yeshiva University and Hunter College. At Hunter, she was the founding chair of the Black and Puerto Rican Studies Department. Her most important work was produced in the 1960s, when the peoples of the African diaspora were emerging politically and culturally from colonial domination, and when the theory of transformational-generative grammar was revolutionizing linguistics. In her dissertation, published as *Jamaican Creole Syntax: A Transformational Approach* (1966), Bailey describes an abstract system underlying the mixture of JC and SE elements observed in the everyday speech of Jamaicans. In 1968 she produced a Jamaican Creole training manual for use by Peace Corps volunteers.

The influence of transformational grammar is apparent in Bailey's analysis of African-American language. In an article calling for "a new perspective on Negro English dialectology," she calls attention to such distinctive features of African-American language as the absence of the copulative (linking) verb in sentences such as "She a big woman." Although she used a novel, *The Cool World* (1959) by Warren Miller, as a major source of data in addition to nonempirical methods of transformational grammar, her findings and conclusions have held up to subsequent work based on tape-recorded samples of empirical data. In a notable quote, she unapologetically defends her unorthodox methods: "This may sound like hocus-pocus, but indeed a good deal of linguistics is. A hocus-pocus procedure which yields the linguistic facts is surely preferable to a scientifically rigorous one which completely murders those facts" (Bailey, 1965).

The most important facts about Jamaican Creole, from Bailey's point of view, are those that support the contention that it is a rule-governed linguistic system worthy of recognition as a language in its own right. There is a coherent system of rules to be taken into account by educators in the design and delivery of instruction to Creole speakers in Standard English medium classrooms.

Bailey "grew up valuing education" (Wade-Lewis, 1993). Her mother was a schoolteacher, and Bailey herself served as an English teacher in Jamaica prior to moving to the United States. In the introduction to her thesis, she expresses the desire to "explode once and for all the notion which persists among teachers of English in Jamaica, that the 'dialect' is not a language: and further that it has no bearing on the problem of the teaching of English" (Labov, 1998, p. 111).

See also Creole Languages of the Americas; English, African-American

Bibliography

Bailey, Beryl Loftman. "Toward a New Perspective in Negro English Dialectology." *American Speech* 40 (1965): 171–177.

Bailey, Beryl Loftman. *Jamaican Creole Syntax: A Transformational Approach.* Cambridge, UK: Cambridge University Press, 1966.

Bailey, Beryl Loftman. *Jamaican Creole Language Course (for English-Speaking Students).* Washington, D.C.: U.S. Government Printing Office, 1968.

Bailey, R. W. "Bailey, Beryl Loftman." In *The Oxford Companion to the English Language*. Oxford: Oxford University Press, 1992.

Labov, William. "Co-existent Systems in African-American Vernacular English." In *African-American English: Structure, History, and Use*, edited by Salikoko Mufwene et al. London: Routledge, 1998.

Wade-Lewis, Margaret. "Bailey, Beryl Loftman." In *African American Women: A Biographical Dictionary*, edited by Dorothy C. Salem. New York: Garland, 1993.

CHARLES E. DEBOSE (2005)

Bailey, Pearl

March 29, 1918
August 17, 1990

The singer and actress Pearl Bailey, popularly known as Pearlie Mae, was born in Newport News, Virginia, to Joseph James Bailey, a revivalist minister, and Ella Mae Bailey. At the age of four, she moved with her family to Washington, D.C., and after her parents divorced she moved to Philadelphia with her mother and her stepfather, Walter Robinson. There, Bailey attended school until the age of fifteen, when she began her career as an entertainer after winning an amateur contest at the Pearl Theater. For a while she performed in coal-mining towns in Pennsylvania, then in small clubs in Washington, D.C. Beginning in 1941 she toured with the United Service Organization (USO), and in 1943–1944 she performed with bands led by Charles "Cootie" Williams (1908?–1985), William "Count" Basie (1904–1984), and Noble Sissle (1889–1975). It was during this period that she began to develop her distinctive trademark, described by John S. Wilson in the *New York Times* as "a warm, lusty singing voice accompanied by an easy smile and elegant gestures that charmed audiences and translated smoothly from the nightclub stage and Broadway to film and television."

In the early 1940s Bailey made solo appearances at the Village Vanguard and the Blue Angel in New York City, and she made her Broadway debut in 1946 in the musical comedy *St. Louis Woman*, for which she won the Donaldson Award as the most promising new performer of the year. The following year she appeared in the motion picture *Variety Girl*, in which she sang one of her most popular songs, "Tired." Thereafter, she made numerous stage, screen, and television appearances, including the 1954 Broadway musical *House of Flowers* and such films as *Carmen Jones* (1954), *St. Louis Blues* (1958), and *Porgy and Bess* (1959). Her most acclaimed performance came in 1967, when she appeared with Cab Calloway (1907–1994) in the all-black production of *Hello, Dolly!* This brought her a special Tony Award in 1968 for distinguished achievement in the New York theater.

In 1969 Bailey received the USO's Woman of the Year award. The following year President Richard Nixon appointed her "Ambassador of Love," and in 1975 she was appointed special "goodwill" ambassador to the United Nations. Despite her popularity, however, Bailey's association with the Nixon administration was criticized by some African Americans; the Harlem congressman Charles Rangel in particular stated that her appointment was an insult to better-qualified blacks.

During this period, Bailey returned to school, studying theology at Georgetown University in Washington, D.C., from which she received both an honorary degree in 1978 and a bachelor's degree in 1985, at the age of sixty-seven. An inveterate traveler—frequently accompanied by her husband, the jazz drummer Louis Bellson (whom she married in 1952)—Bailey also authored several books, including the autobiographical *The Raw Pearl* (1968) and *Talking to Myself* (1971). *Between You and Me: A Heartfelt Memoir on Learning, Loving, and Living* was published in 1989, shortly before she died of heart disease on August 17, 1990. Two years before her death, Bailey was presented with the Medal of Freedom by President Ronald Reagan.

See also Calloway, Cab; Musical Theater

Bibliography

Bogle, Donald. *Blacks in American Film and Television: An Encyclopedia*. New York: Garland, 1988.

Smith, Jessie Carney, ed. *Notable Black American Women*. Detroit: Gale Research, 1992.

Wilson, John S. Obituary. *New York Times*, August 19, 1990.

KRISTA WHETSTONE (1996)

Baker, Ella J.

December 13, 1903
December 13, 1986

The activist Ella Josephine Baker was a leading figure in the struggle of African Americans for equality. In the 1960s she was regarded as the godmother of the civil rights movement, or, as one activist put it, "a Shining Black Beacon." Though she was not accorded recognition by the media, Baker was affiliated with all the major civil rights

Civil rights activist Ella J. Baker (1903–1986). PHOTOGRAPHS AND PRINTS DIVISION, SCHOMBURG CENTER FOR RESEARCH IN BLACK CULTURE, THE NEW YORK PUBLIC LIBRARY, ASTOR, LENOX AND TILDEN FOUNDATIONS.

organizations of her time, and she worked closely with all the better-known leaders of the movement.

Ella Baker was the daughter of a grade-school teacher and a waiter on the Norfolk-Washington ferry, and the granddaughter of slaves. From the extended family of aunts, uncles, and cousins who lived on land her grandfather had purchased from the owners of the plantation on which they had worked as slaves, Baker acquired a sense of community, a profound sense of the need for sharing, and a sense of history and of the continuity of struggle. She also gained a fierce sense of independence and a belief in the necessity of rebellion, which guided her work for the rest of her life.

After leaving Shaw University in Raleigh, North Carolina, from which she graduated as valedictorian, Baker immersed herself in the cause of social justice. She moved to New York, where she continued her education on the streets of the city, attending all kinds of political meetings to absorb the intellectual atmosphere. In the 1930s, while earning her living working in restaurants and as a correspondent for several black newspapers, Baker helped to found the Young Negroes Cooperative League, of which she became executive director. She worked for the Work Projects Administration (WPA; originally Works Progress Administration),teaching consumer and labor education. During the depression, Baker learned that, in her words, "a society could break down, a social order could break down, and the individual is the victim of the breakdown, rather than the cause of it."

In 1940 Baker accepted a position as field secretary at the National Association for the Advancement of Colored People (NAACP). She soon established regional leadership-training conferences, using the slogan "Give light and the people will find a way." While a national officer, Baker traveled for several months a year throughout the country (concentrating on the segregated South), building NAACP membership and working with the local people who would become the sustaining forces of the civil rights movement. Her organizing strategy was to stress local issues rather than national ones and to take the NAACP to people, wherever they were. She ventured into beer gardens and nightclubs, where she would address crowds and secure memberships and campaign workers. Baker was named director of branches in 1943, but, frustrated by the top-down approach of the NAACP leadership, she resigned in 1946. During this period she married a former classmate, Thomas Roberts, and took on the responsibility of raising her sister's daughter, Jacqueline.

From 1946 to 1957, while working in New York City for the New York Cancer Society and the New York Urban League, Baker participated in campaigns to desegregate New York City schools. She was a founder of In Friendship, a group organized to support school desegregation in the South; a member of the zoning subcommittee of the New York City Board of Education's committee on integration; and president (and later education director) of the New York City branch of the NAACP.

In 1957 Bayard Rustin and Stanley Levison, advisers to the Reverend Dr. Martin Luther King Jr., asked Baker to return to the South to set up the office of the newly organized Southern Christian Leadership Conference (SCLC), headed by King, and to organize the Crusade for Citizenship, a voter-registration drive. Intending to stay six weeks, she remained with the SCLC for two years, serving variously as acting director, associate director, and executive director.

In 1960 Baker mobilized SCLC support for a meeting to bring together the student sit-in protest groups that had sprung up across the South. A battle for control of the sit-in movement ensued. Older civil rights organizations, particularly the SCLC, sought to make the new movement a youth arm of their own operations. Baker, however, advocated an independent role for the student activists.

Baker resigned from the SCLC in 1960 to accept a part-time position as human-relations consultant to the

Young Women's Christian Association (YWCA), working with colleges across the South to further integration. In 1963 she joined the staff of the Southern Conference Educational Fund (SCEF), a regionwide interracial organization that put special emphasis on developing white support for racial justice. While affiliated with the YWCA and SCEF, Baker devoted much of her time to the fledgling Student Nonviolent Coordinating Committee (SNCC), in which she found the embodiment of her belief in a "group-centered leadership, rather than a leadership-centered group."

SNCC was the "new community" Baker had sought. Her work was an inspiration for other activist movements of the 1960s and 1970s, particularly the anti–Vietnam War movement and the feminist movement. But Baker's greatest contribution was her counseling of SNCC. During one crisis she pointed out that both direct action and voter registration would lead to the same result—confrontation and resolution. Her support of confrontation was at variance with the Kennedy administration's policy, which advocated a "cooling-off" period. Baker also counseled the young mavericks of SNCC to work with the more conservative southern ministers, who, she advised, had resources that could help them.

In 1964, SNCC was instrumental in organizing the Mississippi Freedom Democratic Party (MFDP), which sent its own delegation to Atlantic City to challenge the seating of the segregationist Mississippi delegation at the Democratic National Convention. Baker, in the new party's Washington headquarters (and later in Atlantic City), orchestrated the MFDP's fight for the support of other state delegations in its claim to Mississippi's seats. This challenge eventually resulted in the adoption of new Democratic Party rules that guaranteed the inclusion of blacks and women in future delegations.

After the convention, Baker moved back to New York, where she remained active in human-rights affairs. During her life she had been a speaker at hundreds of Women's Day church meetings across the country, a participant in tenants' associations, a consultant to the wartime Office of Price Administration, an adviser to the Harlem Youth Council, and a founder and administrator of the Fund for Education and Legal Defense. In her later years she worked with such varied groups as the Puerto Rican Solidarity Committee, the Episcopal Church Center, and the Third World Women's Coordinating Committee.

While never professing a political ideology, Baker consistently held views far to the left of the established civil rights leadership. She was never a member of a political party, but she did run for the New York City Council on the Liberal Party ticket in 1951. She acted within the constraints of a radical critique of society and was drawn toward "radical" rather than "safe" solutions to societal problems. Her credo was "a life that is important is a life of service."

See also Mississippi Freedom Democratic Party; National Association for the Advancement of Colored People (NAACP); Southern Christian Leadership Conference; Student Nonviolent Coordinating Committee (SNCC)

Bibliography

Branch, Taylor. *Parting the Waters: America in the King Years, 1954–63.* New York: Simon and Schuster, 1988.

Cantarow, Ellen, with Susan Gushee O'Malley and Sharon Hartman Strom. *Moving the Mountain: Women Working for Social Change.* New York: McGraw-Hill, 1980.

Fairclough, Adam. *To Redeem the Soul of America: The Southern Christian Leadership Conference and Martin Luther King, Jr.* Athens: University of Georgia Press, 1987. Reprint, 2001.

Forman, James. *The Making of Black Revolutionaries.* New York: Macmillan, 1972.

Garrow, David. *Bearing the Cross: Martin Luther King, Jr., and the Southern Christian Leadership Conference.* New York: William Morrow, 1986.

Grant, Joanne. *Ella Baker: Freedom Bound.* New York: Wiley, 1998.

Grant, Joanne. "Mississippi Politics: A Day in the Life of Ella J. Baker." In *The Black Woman: An Anthology.* New York: New American Library, 1970, pp. 56–62.

Lerner, Gerda. *Black Women in White America.* New York: Pantheon, 1972.

Morris, Aldon. *The Origins of the Civil Rights Movement: Black Communities Organizing for Change.* New York: Free Press, 1984.

Rawsby, Barbara. *Ella Baker and the Black Freedom Movement.* Chapel Hill: University of North Carolina Press, 2003.

JOANNE GRANT (1996)
Updated bibliography

Baker, Josephine

June 6, 1906
April 14, 1975

Entertainer Josephine Baker was born in St. Louis, Missouri, the daughter of Carrie McDonald, an unmarried domestic worker, and Eddie Carson, a jazz drummer. At age eight she was working as a domestic. At age eleven she survived the East St. Louis race riots in which thirty-nine blacks were killed. Before she was fourteen, Baker had run away from a sadistic employer, and married and discarded a husband, Willie Wells. "I was cold, and I danced to keep warm, that's my childhood," she said. After entertaining locally, she joined a traveling show called the Dixie Steppers, where she developed as a dancer and mime.

In 1920 Baker married a jockey named Willie Baker, but she quickly left him to try out for the new black musical, Noble Sissle and composer Eubie Blake's pathbreaking *Shuffle Along*. She was turned down as too young, too thin, and too dark. At sixteen she was hired as end girl in a *Shuffle Along* road show chorus line, where she captivated audiences with her mugging. Sissle and Blake wrote her into their next show, *Chocolate Dandies* (1924), and the next year, Caroline Dudley invited her to join a troupe of "authentic" Negro performers she was taking to Paris in *La Revue Nègre.*

Baker was an overnight sensation and became the rage of Paris. As a black exotic jungle Venus, she became a phenomenon whose style and presence outweighed her talents. Everyone danced her version of the Charleston and black bottom. Women copied her hairdo. Couturiers saw a new ideal in her body. She took a series of lovers, including Paul Colin, who immortalized her on posters, and Georges Simenon, who worked as her secretary. In 1927 "La Bakair" opened at the Folies Bergère in her famous costume of a few rhinestoned bananas.

That same year Baker met the café-society habitué "Count" Pepito de Abatino (actually a Sicilian stonemason). He became her lover and manager, taught her how to dress and act, trained her voice and body, and sculpted a highly sophisticated and marketable star. They toured Europe and South America. In Vienna, Baker was preached against for being the "impure incarnation of sex." She provoked hostility fueled by economic frustration, moral indignation, xenophobia, and racism.

When Baker returned to France, Abatino had done what he had promised: turned the diamond-in-the-rough of 1925 into the polished gem of 1930. There followed a ten-year reign of Baker in the music halls of Paris. Henri Varna of the Casino de Paris added to her image a baby leopard in a $20,000 diamond necklace and the song that would become her signature "J'ai deux amours, mon pays et Paris." Her name was linked with several Frenchmen, including singer Jacques Pills, and in 1934 she made her best motion picture, *Zouzou,* costarring Jean Gabin, followed by *Princess Tam Tam* in 1935.

Baker returned to New York to play in the 1936 Ziegfeld Follies, but the show was a fiasco. She learned that America would neither welcome her nor look on her with color-blind eyes as France did. Abatino died of cancer before she returned to Paris. Baker married Jean Lion, a

Josephine Baker (1906–1975). *Born in the United States, Baker traveled abroad in the 1920s, becoming a popular dancer and singer in Paris and later a citizen of France. Flamboyant and controversial, she was a member of the French Resistance during World War II, adopted twelve children of various ethnic backgrounds (her "Rainbow Tribe"), and was an active participant in the U.S. civil rights movement.* AP/WIDE WORLD PHOTOS. REPRODUCED BY PERMISSION.

wealthy sugar broker, in 1937, and divorced him fourteen months later. By 1939 Baker had become a French citizen. When the Nazis occupied France during World War II, Baker joined the Resistance, recruited by the head of French intelligence. For her activities in counterintelligence, Baker received the Croix de Guerre and the Légion d'Honneur. After operating between Marseilles and Lisbon under cover of a revival of her operetta *La Creole,* she was sent to Casablanca in January of 1940 to continue intelligence activities.

In 1941 Baker delivered a stillborn child, the father unknown. Complications from this birth endangered her life for more than nineteen months, and at one point her obituary was published. She recovered and spent the last years of the war driving an ambulance and entertaining Allied troops in North Africa. After the war she married orchestra leader Jo Bouillon and adopted four children of different races whom she called her "Rainbow Tribe." She turned her château, Les Milandes, into her idea of a multiracial community. In 1951 she attracted wide attention in the United States and was honored by the NAACP, which organized a Josephine Baker Day in Harlem.

Baker continued to be an outspoken civil rights advocate, refusing to perform before segregated audiences in Las Vegas and Miami and instigating a notorious cause célèbre by accusing the Stork Club of New York of discrimination. Her controversial image hurt her career, and the U.S. State Department hinted that it might cancel her visa. Baker continued to tour outside America as her Rainbow Tribe grew to twelve. From 1953 to 1963 she spent more than $1.5 million on Les Milandes, her financial affairs degenerated into chaos, her fees diminished, and she and Bouillon separated.

In 1963 Baker appeared at the March on Washington, and after performing in Denmark had her first heart attack. In the spring of 1969 she declared bankruptcy and Les Milandes was seized. Baker accepted a villa in Monaco from Princess Grace, began a long series of farewell performances, and begged in the streets when she couldn't work. In 1975 she summoned all her resources and professionalism for a last farewell performance at the Olympia Theatre in Paris. Baker died two days into her performance run on April 14. Her televised state funeral at the Madeleine Church drew thousands of people and included a twenty-one-gun salute.

See also Blake, Eubie; Musical Theater

Bibliography

Chase-Riboud, Barbara. "Josephine Baker: Beyond Sequins." *Essence* (February 1975).

Hammond, Bryan. *Josephine Baker*. London: Cape, 1988.

Haney, Lynn. *Naked at the Feast*. New York: Dodd, Mead, 1981.

Wood, Ean. *The Josephine Baker Story*. London: Sanctuary Publishing, 2000.

BARBARA CHASE-RIBOUD (1996)
Updated bibliography

Baldwin, James

August 2, 1924
November 30, 1987

Author and civil rights activist James Baldwin was born in New York City's Harlem in 1924. He started out as a writer during the late 1940s and rose to international fame after the publication of his most famous essay, *The Fire Next Time*, in 1963. However, nearly two decades before its publication, he had already captured the attention of an assortment of writers, literary critics, and intellectuals in the United States and abroad. Writing to Langston Hughes in 1948, Arna Bontemps commented on Baldwin's "The Harlem Ghetto," which was published in the February 1948 issue of *Commentary* magazine. Referring to "that remarkable piece by that 24-year old colored kid," Bontemps wrote, "What a kid! He has zoomed high among our writers with his first effort." Thus, from the beginning of his professional career, Baldwin was highly regarded and he began publishing in magazines and journals such as *The Nation, New Leader, Commentary,* and *Partisan Review.*

Overview

Much of Baldwin's writing, both fiction and nonfiction, is autobiographical. The story of John Grimes, the traumatized son of a tyrannical, fundamentalist father in *Go Tell It on the Mountain* (1953), closely resembles Baldwin's own childhood. His celebrated essay "Notes of a Native Son" (1955) describes his painful relationship with his stepfather. Born out of wedlock before his mother met and married David Baldwin, young Jimmy never fully gained his stern patriarch's approval. Raised in a strict Pentecostal household, Baldwin became a preacher at age fourteen, and his sermons drew larger crowds than his father's. When Baldwin left the church three years later, the tension with his father was exacerbated, and, as "Notes of a Native Son" reveals, even the impending death of David Baldwin in 1943 did not reconcile the two. In various forms, the father-son conflict, with all of its Old Testament connotations, became a central preoccupation of Baldwin's writing.

Baldwin's career, which can be divided into two phases—up to *The Fire Next Time* and after—gained momentum after the publication of what were to become two of his more controversial essays. In 1948 and 1949, respectively, he wrote "Everybody's Protest Novel" and "Many Thousands Gone," which were published in *Partisan Review.* These two essays served as a forum from which he made pronouncements about the limitations of the protest tradition in American literature. He scathingly criticized Harriet Beecher Stowe's *Uncle Tom's Cabin* and Richard Wright's *Native Son* for being firmly rooted in the protest tradition. Each writer failed, in Baldwin's judgment, because the "power of revelation. . .is the business of the novelist, that journey toward a more vast reality which must take precedence over all other claims." He abhorred the idea of the writer as a kind of "congressman," embracing Jamesian ideas about the art of fiction. The writer, as Baldwin envisioned himself during this early period, should self-consciously seek a distance between himself and his subject.

Baldwin's criticisms of *Native Son* and the protest novel tradition precipitated a rift with his mentor, Richard Wright. Ironically, Wright had supported Baldwin's candidacy for the Rosenwald Fellowship in 1948, which allowed Baldwin to move to Paris, where he completed *Go Tell It on the Mountain.* Baldwin explored his conflicted relationship with Wright in a series of moving essays, including "Alas, Poor Richard," published in *Nobody Knows My Name* (1961).

Baldwin left Harlem for Paris when he was twenty-four. Although he spoke little French at the time, he purchased a one-way ticket and later achieved success and fame as an expatriate. Writing about race and sexuality (including homosexuality), he published twenty-two books, among them six novels, a collection of short stories, two plays, several collections of essays, a children's book, a movie scenario, and *Jimmy's Blues* (1985), a chapbook of poems. Starting with his controversial *Another Country* (1962), many of his books, including *The Fire Next Time, If Beale Street Could Talk* (1974), and *Just above My Head* (1979), were best sellers. His play *Blues for Mr. Charlie* (1964) was produced on Broadway, and his scenario "One Day When I Was Lost: A Scenario Based on Alex Haley's *The Autobiography of Malcolm X*" was used by the movie director Spike Lee in the production of his feature film on Malcolm X.

The Novels

Baldwin credits Bessie Smith as the inspiration that allowed him to complete *Go Tell It on the Mountain.* In "The Discovery of What It Means to Be an American," he writes about his experience of living and writing in Switzerland: "There, in that alabaster landscape, armed with two Bessie Smith records and a typewriter, I began to re-create the life that I had first known as a child and from which I had spent so many years in flight. . . .Bessie Smith, through her tone and cadence. . .helped me dig back to the way I myself must have spoken when I was a pickaninny, and to remember the things I had heard and seen and felt. I had buried them very deep."

Go Tell It on the Mountain recaptures in some definitive ways the spirit and circumstances of Baldwin's own boyhood and adolescence. John Grimes, the shy and intelligent protagonist of the novel, is reminiscent of Baldwin. Moreover, Baldwin succeeds at creating a web of relationships that reveals how a particular character has arrived at his or her situation. He had, after all, harshly criticized Stowe and Wright for what he considered their stereotypical depiction of characters and their circumstances. His belief that "revelation" was the novelist's ultimate goal persisted throughout his career. In his second and third novels—*Giovanni's Room* (1956) and *Another Country*—he explores the theme of a varying, if consistent, American search for identity.

In *Giovanni's Room* the theme is complicated by international and sexual dimensions. The main character is forced to learn a harsh lesson about another culture and country as he wrestles with his ambivalent sexuality. Similarly, in *Another Country* Baldwin sensationally calls into question many American taboos about race, sexuality, marriage, and infidelity. By presenting a stunning series of relationships—heterosexual, homosexual, interracial, bisexual—he creates a tableau vivant of American mores. In his remaining novels, *Tell Me How Long the Train's Been Gone* (1968), *If Beale Street Could Talk*, and *Just above My Head,* he also focuses on issues related to race and sexuality. Furthermore, he tries to reveal how racism and sexism are inextricably linked to deep-seated American assumptions. In Baldwin's view, race and sex are hopelessly entangled in America's collective psyche.

Essays and Political Involvement

Around the time of *The Fire Next Time*'s publication and after the Broadway production of *Blues for Mr. Charlie,* Baldwin became known as a spokesperson for civil rights and a celebrity noted for championing the cause of black Americans. He was a prominent participant in the March on Washington at which the Rev. Dr. Martin Luther King Jr. gave his famous "I Have a Dream" speech. He frequently appeared on television and delivered speeches on college campuses. Baldwin published two excellent collections of essays—*Notes of a Native Son* and *Nobody Knows My Name*—before *The Fire Next Time.* In fact, various critics and reviewers already considered him in a class of his own. However, it was his exhortative rhetoric in *The Fire Next Time,* which was published on the one hundredth anniversary of the Emancipation Proclamation and anticipated the urban riots of the 1960s, that landed him on the cover of *Time* magazine. He concluded: "If we—and now I mean the relatively conscious whites and the relatively conscious blacks who must, like lovers, insist on or create the consciousness of the others—do not falter in our duty now, we may be able. . .to end the racial nightmare, and achieve our country, and change the history of the world."

After the publication of *The Fire Next Time,* several black nationalists criticized Baldwin for his conciliatory attitude. They questioned whether his message of love and understanding would do much to change race relations in

America. Eldridge Cleaver, in his book *Soul on Ice,* was one of Baldwin's more outspoken critics. But Baldwin continued writing, becoming increasingly dependent on his early life as a source of inspiration, accepting eagerly the role of the writer as a "poet" whose "assignment" was to accept the "energy" of the folk and transform it into art. It is as though he was following the wisdom of his own words in his story "Sonny's Blues." Like Sonny and his band, Baldwin saw clearly as he matured that he was telling a tale based on the blues of his own life as a writer and a man in America and abroad: "Creole began to tell us what the blues were all about. They were not about anything very new. He and his boys up there were keeping it new at the risk of ruin, destruction, madness, and death, in order to find new ways to make us listen. For, while the tale of how we suffer, and how we are delighted, and how we may triumph is never new, it always must be heard. There isn't any other tale to tell, it's the only light we've got in all this darkness."

Several of his essays and interviews of the 1980s discuss homosexuality and homophobia with fervor and forthrightness, most notably "Here Be Dragons." Thus, just as he had been the leading literary voice of the civil rights movement, he became an inspirational figure for the emerging gay rights movement. Baldwin's nonfiction was collected in *The Price of the Ticket* (1985).

During the final decade of his life, Baldwin taught at a number of American colleges and universities, including the University of Massachusetts at Amherst and Hampshire College, frequently commuting back and forth between the United States and his home in Saint Paul de Vence in the south of France. After his death in France on November 30, 1987, the *New York Times* reported on its front page for the following day: "James Baldwin, Eloquent Essayist in Behalf of Civil Rights, Is Dead."

See also Autobiography, U.S.; Literature of the United States

Bibliography

Campbell, James. *Talking at the Gates: A Life of James Baldwin.* Berkeley: University of California Press, 2002.

Kenan, Randall, and Amy Sickels. *James Baldwin.* Philadelphia: Chelsea House, 2005.

Leeming, David. *James Baldwin: A Biography.* New York: Knopf, 1994.

Porter, Horace. *Stealing the Fire: The Art of Protest and James Baldwin.* Middletown, Conn.: Wesleyan University Press, 1989.

HORACE PORTER (1996)
Updated bibliography

Ballet

The African-American presence in classical ballet, triumphantly confirmed by the founding of the Dance Theater of Harlem in 1969, grew slowly alongside general American interest in the European form of theatrical stage dancing. Classical ballet developed from dancing styles of sixteenth-century European courts. Refined in France, especially under the monarchy of Louis XIV, ballet became the preferred form of dance expression in Europe and Russia by the nineteenth century. Ballet captured the interest of an American public only after tours of Daighilev's Ballets Russes proved undeniably entertaining in the early part of the twentieth century. The assumption that the European outlook, history, and technical theory of ballet were alien to the black dancer culturally, temperamentally, and anatomically plagued African-American interest in the form for generations. Dance aesthetes wrote about the unsuitability of the black dancer's "tight joints, a natural turn-in rather than the desired ballet turn-out, hyperextension of the knee, [and] weak feet" (McDonagh, 1968, p. 44), and most black dancers, barred from all-white ballet schools, turned to performing careers in modern and jazz dance. Ballet training, however, remained the basis of many stage-dance techniques, and individual teachers had profound effects on pioneer African-American dance artists. In Chicago in the 1920s, Katherine Dunham studied ballet with Ludmilla Speranzeva before creating her own Dunham dance technique. The Jones-Haywood School of Dance, founded in Washington, D.C., in 1940, trained several significant ballet personalities, including Sylvester Campbell and Louis Johnson. Philadelphia's Judimar School, created in 1948, offered ballet classes led by Essie Marie Dorsey and produced several outstanding ballet artists, including Delores Brown, Tamara Guillebeaux, John Jones, and Billy Wilson.

The racial division of Americans led to the formation of several separatist, "all-black" dance companies to offer performing opportunities for growing numbers of classically trained dancers. Hemsley Winfield's New Negro Art Theater Dance Group brought concert dance to the New York Roxy Theater in 1932, effectively proving that largely white audiences would accept black dancers. John Martin of the *New York Times* noted the dancers' refusal to be "darkskinned reproductions of famous white prototypes" and termed the concert "an effort well worth the making" (Martin, 1932, p. 11). Winfield's company performed with the Hall Johnson Choir in dances of his own making.

Eugene Von Grona's American Negro Ballet debuted on November 21, 1937, at Harlem's Lafayette Theater. The son of a white American mother and a German father,

Arthur Bell

Dancing proved not to be the most lucrative of career choices for Arthur Bell. A pioneering black ballet dancer, he was found homeless wandering the streets of Brooklyn at age seventy-one in the late 1990s. Still, he does not regret following his dreams and, in fact, left his artistic mark on the classical dance scene of the 1940s and 1950s—a time that was not very receptive to African Americans in classical ballet.

Bell's Pentecostal parents viewed dance as sinful and so did not approve of their son's fascination with it. Attempting a career in dance was especially troubling to them because of the lack of employment opportunities for African Americans. Knowing the odds were not in his favor, Bell decided anyway to pursue dance as one of very few black students at the School of American Ballet. His skills were highly regarded and he eventually made a career for himself in Paris and London. Being invited by Frederick Ashton to appear in the New York City Ballet's world premiere of *Illuminations* was a career peak as he was the first black man to ever perform with this elite company.

Age caught up with Bell and he returned to New York City where he worked at a variety of menial jobs from the late 1960s to the early 1990s. Some time after this he became homeless. It is not clear what led to these circumstances, but he came into contact with a social worker named Mafia Mackin. Mackin was a former ballet photographer, so Bell's accounts of his experiences in 1950s London and Paris rang truthful to her whereas other social workers felt that Bell's accounts of his life in ballet were signs of dementia.

After confirming Bell's stories, Mackin contacted the *New York Times* who made Bell the subject of a feature article. Soon Bell received international news coverage and was reunited with two of his siblings. He went on to reside at the Actors Fund Retirement and Nursing Home in Englewood, New Jersey, where he spent the last six years of his life with a regained dignity. Bell died at the age of 77 on January 23, 2004.

Von Grona trained with modern dance choreographer Mary Wigman before moving to the United States in 1925. To form his company, he ran a newspaper advertisement in the *Amsterdam News* offering free dance lessons at the Harlem YMCA. Von Grona chose thirty trainees out of 150 respondents, and after three years of training in ballet and modern dance relaxation techniques, the company offered a program designed to address "the deeper and more intellectual resources of the Negro race" (Acocella, 1982, p. 24). The original program, choreographed by Von Grona to Ellington, Stravinsky, W. C. Handy, and J. S. Bach, was received by critics as "more of the nature of a pupil's recital than an epoch-making new ballet organization." The program included a version of Stravinsky's Firebird, although critics worried that "a Negro interpretation of a classical ballet would . . . be too unrestrained" to appeal to a ballet audience. Lukewarm critical reception and the absence of a committed audience shuttered the company's concert engagements after only five months. In 1939 the company appeared in Lew Leslie's *Blackbirds* and at the Apollo Theater and was renamed Von Grona's American Swing Ballet. By the end of that year Von Grona was bankrupt and disbanded the company. Dancers in the company included Lavinia Williams, Jon Edwards, and Al Bledger.

Wilson Williams's Negro Dance Company, founded in 1940 to "discipline talent, give it creative direction, [and] to train artists capable of expression through means of a technique" (Williams, 1940, p. 14), struggled for five years to garner dancers and patronage. Williams, an accomplished black modern dancer, intended to provide a three-year course at his School of Negro Ballet, with classes in folk forms as well as modern and classical ballet. The Negro Dance Company's first performances in 1943 were received as modern dance.

The First Negro Classic Ballet, also briefly known as the Hollywood Negro Ballet, was founded in 1948 by Joseph Rickhard. Rickhard, a German émigré and former dancer with the Ballets Russes, taught ballet to black students in Los Angeles. The company had a first concert in 1949. This was truly a classical company, with ballerinas performing on point. They performed *Variations Clas-*

siques, a suite of dances to Bach, as well as a reworking of *Cinderella* with African-American materials. Critically successful, the company lasted seven seasons touring the West Coast, with an annual performance at Los Angeles' Philharmonic Auditorium. In 1956 Rickhard brought his dancers to New York, and this company combined with the New York Negro Ballet.

Aubrey Hitchens' Negro Dance Theater, created in 1953, was an all-male repertory company. Hitchens was born in England and had danced with the Russian Opera Company in Paris before he opened his own New York school in 1947. Hitchens, who "ardently believed in the special dance talents of the Negro race" (Hitchins, 1956, p. 12), managed to book his group to perform at Jacob's Pillow Dance Festival in August 1954. Its repertory included *Gotham Suite* by Tony Charmoli, with "modern idioms based on classical forms being suggested by the five boroughs of New York City" (Hitchins, 1956, p. 13), and Hitchens' own *Italian Concerto* to music of Bach. Among the dancers associated with the Negro Dance Theater were Anthony Basse, Frank Glass, Nat Horne, Bernard Johnson, Charles Martin, Charles Moore, Joe Nash, Charles Queenan, Edward Walrond, and Arthur Wright. The company remained together only through 1955.

Edward Flemyng's New York Negro Ballet Company, founded as Les Ballets Nègres in 1955, began as a small group that took daily technique classes with Maria Nevelska, a former member of the Bolshoi Ballet. Flemyng, a charismatic and driven African-American dancer born in Detroit, organized private sponsorship of the company, which in 1957 led to a landmark tour of England, Scotland, and Wales. Among the dancers on that tour were Anthony Basse, Dolores Brown, Candace Caldwell, Sylvester Campbell, Georgia Collins, Theodore Crum, Roland Fraser, Thelma Hill, Michaelyn Jackson, Frances Jiminez, Bernard Johnson, Charles Neal, Cleo Quitman, Gene Sagan, Helen Taitt, Betty Ann Thompson, and Barbara Wright. The company's repertory included Ernest Parham's *Mardi Gras;* two Louis Johnson ballets—*Waltze,* a classical ballet for twelve dancers, and *Folk Impressions,* an American ballet set to music by Morton Gould; and a purely classical pas de deux from *Sleeping Beauty* danced by Dolores Brown and Bernard Johnson. Reviews of the company were flattering and encouraging, and the a reviewer in the London-based *Dance and Dancers* wrote: "New York Negro ballet amounts to a sincere attempt at establishing the Negro as an important contributor to the art of ballet as a whole" (1957, p. 9). Soon after the two-month tour, Flemyng's principal patron died and the company began to unravel. A 1958 performance in New York under the name Ballet Americana was noted by writer Doris Hering as having a "zest and high energy . . . yet to be cast in the careful mould of ballet" (Hering, 1958, p. 57), but the company could not find sufficient patronage and was completely disbanded by 1960.

Dances and Dancers

Documentation of African-American interest in the ballet exists well before the establishment of any of the all-black companies. Helena Justa-De Arms performed toe dances in vaudeville in the 1910s; Mary Richards danced on toe in the 1923 Broadway production of *Struttin' Along;* and Josephine Baker performed on toe for at least one number in her Paris Opera days. In 1940 Agnes De Mille created *Black Ritual* for the New York Ballet Theater, the precursor of the present-day American Ballet Theatre. Performed by a cast of sixteen women to a score by Darius Milhaud, the piece was intended to "project the psychological atmosphere of a primitive community during the performance of austere and vital ceremonies" (Martin, 1940, p. 23). Although this was not a classically shaped ballet, its cast had received dance training in a specially established "Negro Wing" of the Ballet Theater school. Critical reaction to the piece was muted but inspired dance writer Walter Terry's call for "a Negro vocabulary of movement . . . composed of modern dance movements, ballet steps, tap and others . . . [which] should enable the Negro to express himself artistically and not merely display his muscular prowess" (Terry, 1940).

The post–World War II era brought the beginnings of integrated classical dance in the United States. Talley Beatty, Arthur Bell, and Betty Nichols were briefly associated with New York's Ballet Society, where Beatty appeared in Lew Christiansen's *Blackface* (1947) and Bell in Frederick Ashton's *Illuminations* (1950). In 1952 Louis Johnson, a student of the School of American Ballet (SAB), created a role in Jerome Robbins's *Ballade* for the New York City Ballet. Johnson began his significant choreographic career with *Lament* (1953), a story ballet set to music of Heitor Villa-Lobos and first presented with an integrated cast at the third New York Ballet Club Annual Choreographers' Night.

Janet Collins, the most famous African-American classical dancer of this era, began her career in vaudeville and was a member of the original Katherine Dunham troupe. Born in New Orleans and raised in Los Angeles, Collins danced with Lester Horton before moving to New York in 1948, where she won a prestigious Rosenwald Fellowship to tour the East and Midwest in her own dances. Her 1949 New York performance debut was greeted with exceptional enthusiasm by John Martin (1949) of the *New York Times,* who called her a "rich talent and a striking theatrical personality at the beginning of a promising career. Her style is basically eclectic; its direction is modern and its technical foundation chiefly ballet. The fusing element is a markedly personal approach." Collins won a Donaldson Award for her Broadway performance in Cole Porter's *Out of This World* (1951). Collins achieved her greatest fame as prima ballerina at the Metropolitan Opera from 1951 to 1954, where she danced in *Aida* (1951), *La Gioconda* (1952), and *Samson and Delilah* (1953).

Many African-American ballet artists found an acceptance in Europe unknown in the United States. Sylvester Campbell remained in Europe after the New York Negro Ballet tour and eventually became a principal with the Netherlands National Ballet, dancing leading roles in *Swan Lake, Romeo and Juliet,* and *Le Corsaire.* Gene Sagan and Roland Fraser, also of the New York Negro Ballet, joined the Marseilles Ballet and the Cologne Ballet, respectively. Brooklyn-born Jamie Bower danced with Roland Petit's Ballets de Paris and appeared with the company in the MGM film *The Glass Slipper* (1953). In 1954 Raven Wilkenson was admitted to the Ballets Russes de Monte Carlo as that company's sole black female ballerina. Wilkenson stayed with the company for six years, although she was occasionally barred from performing in some southern theaters because of her race. Arthur Mitchell, who joined the New York City Ballet as its first permanent black dancer in 1955, experienced similar racial discrimination when U.S. television broadcasters refused to air programs in which he danced with white ballerinas.

The affiliation of African-American dancers with mostly white companies accelerated throughout the 1960s. The Harkness Ballet of New York ran an aggressive recruitment and educational program in consultation with New York Negro Ballet alumna Thelma Hill that, by 1968, had successfully placed five black members in that company. Choreographer Alvin Ailey, who created *Feast of Ashes* for the Joffrey Ballet in 1962, also made *Ariadne* (1965), *El Amor Brujo* (1966), and *Macumba* (1966) for the Harkness Ballet. Keith Lee joined the American Ballet Theatre in 1969, and in 1970 he created the popular ballet *Times Past* to music by Cole Porter. Lee achieved the rank of soloist in 1971 and left in 1974 to form his own company. Significant post–civil rights era dancers affiliated with major American ballet companies include John Jones, who danced with Jerome Robbins's Ballets: USA, the Dance Theater of Harlem, the Joffrey Ballet, and the Harkness Ballet; Christian Holder of the Joffrey Ballet; Debra Austin of the New York City Ballet and the Pennsylvania Ballet; and Mel Tomlinson of the Dance Theater of Harlem and the New York City Ballet.

The Dance Theater of Harlem Legacy

The founding of the Dance Theater of Harlem (DTH) in 1969 conclusively ended speculation about the suitability of African-American interest in ballet. Arthur Mitchell's company and its affiliated school provided training and performing opportunities for black dancers and choreographers from all parts of the world. Heralded as a major company of international stature within its first fifteen years, the DTH fostered an unsurpassed standard of black classicism revealed in the versatile technique of principal dancers Stephanie Dabney, Lorraine Graves, Christina Johnson, Virginia Johnson, Tai Jiminez, Andrea Long, Ronald Perry, Judith Rotardier, Eddie J. Shellman, Lowell Smith, and Donald Williams.

As DTH performances set a standard of black classicism, discernible African-American influences on ballet began to be understood and documented. Choreographer George Balanchine, who served on the original DTH board of directors, successfully articulated a neoclassical style of ballet that emphasized thrust hips and rhythmic syncopations commonly found in African-American social dance styles. Prominent in his masterpieces *The Four Temperaments* (1946) and the "Rubies" section of *Jewels* (1967) are references to the Charleston, the cakewalk, the lindy hop, and tap dancing.

The critical success of the DTH hinged upon its dancers' ability to embody these social movement styles within classical technique. The company excelled in its resilient performances of the Balanchine repertory. It also turned to African-American folk materials that underscored affinities between ballet and ritual dance, as in Louis Johnson's *Forces of Rhythm* (1972), which comically juxtaposed several styles, including generic "African" dance, vaudeville, Dunham-based modern, disco, and ballet; Geoffrey Holder's *Dougla* (1974), a stylized wedding-ceremony synthesis of African and Hindu motifs; and Billy Wilson's *Ginastera* (1991), a combination of Spanish postures and point dancing.

Black musicians inspired several important ballet collaborations, including Alvin Ailey and Duke Ellington's *The River* (1970), which was choreographed for the American Ballet Theatre and included both parody and distillation of social African dance styles in several sections; Wynton Marsalis and Peter Martins's *Jazz (Six Syncopated Movements)* (1993), created for the New York City Ballet and featuring African-American dance soloist Albert Evans; and the Joffrey Ballet production of *Billboards,* set to music by Prince (1993). In Atlanta, the company Ballethnic has successfully fused classical technique with other forms since 1990. Other choreographers who have worked in the classical idiom include Paul Russell, once

The dancers Carmen De Lavallade and Geoffrey Holder, 1955. *Among the most versatile dancers of their generation, De Lavallade and Holder were accomplished in both theatrical dance and ballet, and also enjoyed success as choreographers, actors, directors, and authors. Photograph by Carl Van Vechten.*

a leading dancer with the DTH, who became artistic director of the American Festival Ballet of Boise, Idaho, in 1988; former DTH principal Homer Bryant, who formed the Chicago-based Bryant Ballet in 1991; Barbados-born John Alleyne, who trained at the National Ballet School of Canada and in 1993 was appointed artistic director of Ballet British Columbia in Vancouver, Canada; and Ulysses Dove, former principal of the Alvin Ailey company. Dove's searingly physical point ballets predict a heightened awareness of African-American performance practice in their reliance on asymmetry, prolonged balance, and cool stance tempered by explosive power.

The profound artistic achievement of the DTH, innumerable individual African-American artists in companies around the world, and Balanchine's neoclassic fusion of ballet and African dance style created a contemporary ballet repertory that was indisputably African based, vividly realized in works by American choreographers Gerald Arpino, William Forsythe, Jerome Robbins, and Twyla Tharp. Ironically, core African-American dance styles, which value subversive invention, participatory interaction, and an overwhelming sense of bodily presence, diverge neatly from ballet's traditional conception of strictly codified body line, a silenced and motionless audience, and movement as metaphoric abstraction. The process of building an African-American audience base responsive to ballet, an action begun by the DTH, is necessary to expand the legacy of black classicism for generations to come.

See also Ailey, Alvin; Apollo Theater; Dance Theater of Harlem; Dove, Ulysses; Dunham, Katherine; Ellington, Edward Kennedy "Duke"; Holder, Geoffrey; Marsalis, Wynton; Mitchell, Arthur

Bibliography

Acocella, Joan Ross. "Van Grona and his First American Negro Ballet." *Dance* (March 1982): 22–24, 30–32.

Banes, Sally. "Balanchine and Black Dance." In *Dance Writing in the Age of Postmodernism,* pp. 53–69. Hanover, Mass.: University Press of New England, 1994.

Barnes, Clive. "Barnes on . . . the Position of the Black Classic Dancer in American Ballet." *Ballet News* 3, no. 9 (March 1982): 46.

DeFrantz, Thomas F. "Ballet in Black: Louis Johnson and Vernacular Humor." In *Dancing Bodies, Living Histories: New Writings about Dance and Culture,* edited by Lisa Doolittle and Anne Flynn, pp. 178–195. Banff, Alberta: Banff Centre Press, 2000.

Emery, Lynne Fauley. *Black Dance in the United States from 1619 to 1970.* Palo Alto, Calif.: National Press Books, 1972.

"Harlem Under Control, Negro Ballet Gives 'Fire Bird' and Park Ave. Approves." *Newsweek* (November 29, 1937): 28.

Hering, Doris. "Ballet Americana." *Dance* (August 1958): 57.

Hitchins, Aubrey. "Creating the Negro Dance Theatre." *Dance and Dancers* (April, 1956): 12–13.

Jackson, Harriet. "American Dancer, Negro." *Dance* (September 1966): 35–42.

Kisselgoff, Anna. "Limning the Role of the Black Dancer in America." *New York Times* (May 16, 1982): 10, 32.

Long, Richard. *The Black Tradition in American Dance.* New York: Rizzoli, 1989.

Martin, John. "The Dance: A Negro Art Group." *New York Times* (February 14, 1932): sec. 8, p. 11.

Martin, John. "De Mille Ballet Seen as Novelty." *New York Times* (January 23, 1940): 23.

Martin, John. "The Dance: Newcomer." *New York Times* (February 27, 1949): sec. 2, p. 9.

McDonagh, Don. "Negroes in Ballet." *New Republic* 159 (1968): 41–44.

"Negroes in Ballet." *Dance and Dancers* (October 1957): 9.

"Newest Ballet Star." *Ebony* (November 1954): 36–40.

Stahl, Norma Gengal. "Janet Collins: The First Lady of the Metropolitan Opera Ballet." *Dance* (February 1954): 27–29.

Terry, Walter. "To the Negro Dance." *New York Herald Tribune* (January 22, 1940).

West, Martha Ullman. "On the Brink: DTH Men in Crisis." *Dance* (October 1990): 43–45.

Williams, Wilson. "Prelude to a Negro Ballet." *Dance (American Dancer)* (March 1940): 14, 39.

Young, Stark. "Slightly Ghosts." *New Republic* (December 8, 1937).

THOMAS F. DEFRANTZ (1996)
Updated by author 2005

Baltimore Afro-American

The *Baltimore Afro-American,* first published in 1892 and now in its second century of continuous publication, is the oldest family-owned black newspaper in America. During its peak years, between the two world wars, the newspaper printed thirteen separate editions from New Jersey to South Carolina and competed with both the *Chicago Defender* and the *Pittsburgh Courier* to be the nation's largest African-American paper.

Founded by ex-slave John Henry Murphy, the *Afro-American* grew from a small, church-based newsletter to the largest black paper on the eastern seaboard, with a circulation that reached over 225,000. After John Murphy died, his son Carl became senior editor and publisher. For nearly forty years, Carl Murphy and the *Afro-American* never shied from reporting the truths of life in a segregated America.

As early as 1912 the *Afro-American* addressed the discriminatory practices of the U.S. military. In the late 1930s the paper reported on the early signs of apartheid in South Africa and was soon supporting Thurgood Marshall and the legal battles of the National Association for the Advancement of Colored People to end school segregation. Throughout these years, numerous articles were devoted to black leaders such as Marcus Garvey, W. E. B. Du Bois, Ralph Bunche, and the Rev. Dr. Martin Luther King, Jr.

In addition to providing the news of the day, the *Afro-American* performed a community service by publishing the births, marriages, and deaths of local African Americans, since these listings were rarely found in the white-owned newspapers of the time. Ironically, the newspaper's gradual decline in circulation in the later decades of the twentieth century was due in part to its success in pressuring the white news media to hire black journalists. In 2005, the *Afro-American* claimed a readership of more than 120,000.

See also Bunche, Ralph; *Chicago Defender*; Du Bois, W. E. B.; Journalism; Garvey, Marcus; King, Martin Luther, Jr.; Marshall, Thurgood; *Pittsburgh Courier*

Bibliography

Dominguez, Alex. "Afro-American Paper Marking Century of News." *Baton Rouge Advocate,* August 13, 1992, p. 4C.

Farrar, Hayward. *The Baltimore Afro-American, 1892–1950.* Westport, Conn.: Greenwood Press, 1998.

"100 Year Old Black Paper Is Struggling." *New York Times,* August 23, 1992, p. 28L.

MICHAEL A. LORD (1996)
Updated bibliography

Bambara, Toni Cade

March 25, 1939
December 29, 1995

Born Toni Cade in New York City to Helen Brent Henderson Cade, writer Toni Cade Bambara adopted her last name in 1970. Bambara grew up in various sections of New York (Harlem, Bedford-Stuyvesant, and Queens) as well as in Jersey City, New Jersey. She earned a B.A. in theater arts and English from Queens College in 1959—the year in which she published her first short story, "Sweet Town"—and an M.A. in English from City College of New York in 1965. At the same time, she served as a community organizer and activist as well as occupational therapist for the psychiatric division of Metropolitan Hospital.

Bambara's consciousness was raised early as she watched her mother instruct her grade school teachers about African-American history and culture and as she listened on New York street corners to Garveyites, Father Diviners, Rastafarians, Muslims, Pan-Africanists, and communists. She learned early of the resiliency that would be needed for a poor black female to survive. Bambara's streetwise sensibility informs two collections of writings by black women that she edited, *The Black Woman* (1970) and *Tales and Stories for Black Folks* (1971). The stories she contributed to these collections portray young black women who weather difficult times and who challenge others to join the struggle for equality.

From 1959 to 1970 Bambara wrote a series of short stories that were published in 1972 as *Gorilla, My Love.* A collection of fifteen stories, this book focuses on relationships that rejuvenate—family, community, and self-love. Her second collection of stories, *The Sea Birds Are Still*

Alive (1977), revolves around the theme of community healing. Her characters do not despair; instead, they nurture each other back to spiritual and physical health. The theme of healing is further explored in Bambara's novel *Salt Eaters* (1980), which received the American Book Award in the year of its publication.

Bambara taught at several universities, including City College of the City University of New York, Rutgers University, Livingstone College, Duke University, and Spelman College. Her commitment as a writer was to inspire others to continue to fight for improved conditions for the community.

Soon after Bambara's death from colon cancer in 1995, some of her unpublished short stories and essays were published in the collection *Deep Sightings and Rescue Missions* (1996), edited by Toni Morrison. Morrison also edited the manuscript of Bambara's novel *Those Bones Are Not My Child*, published in 1999.

See also Literature; Morrison, Toni

Bibliography

Bambara, Toni Cade. *Deep Sightings and Rescue Missions: Fiction, Essays, and Conversations*, edited by Toni Morrison and Karma Bambara. New York: Pantheon, 1996.

Doerksen, Teri Ann. "Toni Cade Bambara." In *Dictionary of Literary Biography, Volume 218: American Short-Story Writers Since World War II, Second Series*, edited by Patrick Meanor and Gwen Crane. Detroit, Mich.: Gale, 1999, pp. 3–10.

ELIZABETH BROWN-GUILLORY (1996)
Updated by publisher 2005

Bandera, Quintín

October 30, 1834
c. August 22, 1906

Quintín Bandera was among the most significant black leaders in the struggle for Cuban independence from 1868 to 1898, a struggle that overlapped with the process of slave emancipation and in which questions of race and citizenship were highly prominent.

Bandera was born in Santiago to free black parents. He worked as a bricklayer, rural day worker, and a cabin boy and fuel stoker on a ship. When the first war of independence (Ten Years' War) began in 1868, he joined as a private and was among the last to surrender as a lieutenant colonel in 1878. With other notable black and mulatto rebel leaders, he participated in the Protest of Baraguá in March 1878, when these and other leaders took a public stance against the peace pact signed by the highest ranking Cuban officers, a pact that accepted peace without the achievement of either independence or abolition. Bandera also participated in the second war of independence, the Guerra Chiquita, or Little War, from 1879 to 1880.

But it was in the final war of independence against Spain, which began in February 1895 and ended in August 1898 (several months after United States intervention) that Bandera became most prominent (and controversial). He was among the first to rise up on February 24, 1895; indeed he appears to have participated in some of the preparatory work done in the months before the outbreak of war. He was an important figure in the insurgent invasion of the western regions of the island, a march led by Antonio Maceo and Máximo Gómez, that began in October 1895 in Oriente and successfully entered the western provinces of Matanzas, Havana, and Pinar del Rio by the end of that year. During that invasion, Bandera was the target of racist rumor and propaganda, as the Spanish press and others portrayed his troops as "exotic" blacks wearing nose rings and loincloths. In July 1897, Bandera, by then a division general, was relieved of his command by Máximo Gómez, head of the Cuban Liberation Army.

The decision was not without controversy. The disciplinary action has generally been interpreted as punishment for his lack of military activity and for shunning his duty in order to remain near a mistress in the south-central area of Trinidad. Bandera himself offered a different explanation, arguing that he had served honorably, that he was simply a humble man, and that he had been badly treated by local, white insurgent leaders around Trinidad. Whatever the reason, the punishment meant that the end of the war in August 1898 found Bandera back in Santiago still stripped of his command.

The controversy that surrounded him late in the war continued into the postwar period. In 1899 he founded the Cuban National Party of Oriente and, in 1900, toured the island, visiting towns where he was received by local authorities and notables. At the same time, however, revisionist historians point to his marginalization in the republic inaugurated in 1902—the denial of full payment for military service, his difficulties in obtaining suitable employment, his need to conduct fund-raisers for his own benefit—to make a larger point about the ways in which black veterans of independence were sidelined in the republic their labor and patriotism created. In 1906, in the midst of an armed rebellion against the first president of the republic, Bandera was ambushed and killed by a white veteran of the Cuban Liberation Army. A year later, when authorities allegedly uncovered a black conspiracy, the signal for the start of the projected uprising was to be the assassination of the man who had assassinated Bandera.

In many ways Bandera is emblematic of the complex and highly charged relationship between race and nationalism in late-nineteenth-century Cuba. On the one hand, he exemplifies the prominence and recognition achieved by black men of humble origins in the independence struggle. On the other, the controversy and racism he confronted throughout his career speak to the thorny limits of that same inclusion and recognition.

See also Maceo, Antonio

Bibliography

Diccionario enciclopédico de historia militar de Cuba. Tomo 1. *Biografías.* Havana: Ediciones Verde Olivo, 2001.

Ferrer, Ada. *Insurgent Cuba: Race, Nation, and Revolution, 1868–1898.* Chapel Hill: University of North Carolina Press, 1999.

Fuente, Alejandro de la. *A Nation for All: Race, Inequality, and Politics in Twentieth-Century Cuba.* Chapel Hill: University of North Carolina Press, 2001.

Helg, Aline. *Our Rightful Share: The Afro-Cuban Struggle for Equality, 1886–1912.* Chapel Hill: University of North Carolina Press, 1995.

Padrón, Abelardo. *General de tres guerras.* Havana: Editorial Letras Cubanas, 1991.

ADA FERRER (2005)

Banneker, Benjamin

November 9, 1731
October 9, 1806

Benjamin Banneker was an amateur astronomer and the first African-American man of science. He was born free in Baltimore County, Maryland, the son of a freed slave from Guinea named Robert and Mary Banneky, the daughter of a formerly indentured English servant named Molly Welsh and her husband Bannka, a freed slave who claimed to be the son of a Gold Coast tribal chieftain.

Raised with three sisters in a log house built by his father on his 100-acre farm near the banks of the Patapsco River, Banneker received no formal schooling except for several weeks' attendance at a nearby Quaker one-room schoolhouse. Taught to read and write from a Bible by his white grandmother, he became a voracious reader, borrowing books when he could. He was skillful in mathematics and enjoyed creating mathematical puzzles and solving others presented to him. At about the age of twenty-two he successfully constructed a wooden striking clock without ever having seen one. Banneker approached the project as a mathematical problem, working out relationships between toothed wheels and gears and painstakingly carving each from seasoned wood with a pocketknife. The clock continued telling and striking the hours until his death. Banneker cultivated tobacco, first with his parents and then alone until about the age of fifty-nine, when rheumatism forced his retirement. He was virtually self-sufficient, growing vegetables and cultivating orchards and bees. Banneker espoused no particular religion or creed, but he was a very religious man, attending the services and meetings of various denominations held in the region, although he preferred those of the Society of Friends.

It was during his retirement that Banneker became interested in astronomy, after witnessing a neighbor observing the stars with a telescope. With borrowed instruments and texts and without any assistance from others, Banneker taught himself sufficient mathematics and astronomy to make observations and to be able to calculate an ephemeris for an almanac. His efforts to sell his calculations for 1791 to a printer were not successful, but he continued his celestial studies nonetheless.

Banneker's opportunity to apply what he had learned came in February 1791, when President George Washington commissioned the survey of an area 10 miles square in Virginia and Maryland in which to establish the national capital. Unable on such short notice to find an assistant capable of using the sophisticated instruments required, the surveyor Andrew Ellicott selected Banneker to assist him until others became available. During the first three months of the survey, Banneker occupied the field observatory tent, maintaining and correcting the regulator clock each day, and each night making observations of the transit of stars with the zenith sector, recording his nightly observations for Ellicott's use on the next day's surveying. During his leisure time, he completed calculations for an ephemeris for 1792. Banneker was employed on the survey site from early February until late April 1791 and then returned to his home in Baltimore County. Records of the survey state that he was paid $60 for his participation and the costs of his travel.

Shortly after his return home, Banneker sent a handwritten copy of his ephemeris for 1792 to Secretary of State Thomas Jefferson, because, he wrote, Jefferson was considered "measurably friendly and well disposed towards us," the African-American race, "who have long laboured under the abuse and censure of the world . . . have long been looked upon with an eye of contempt, and . . . have

An Excerpt of Benjamin Banneker's Letter to Thomas Jefferson

.... Sir,...I hope you cannot but acknowledge that it is the indispensable duty of those, who maintain for themselves the rights of human nature, and who possess the obligations of Christianity, to extend their power and influence to the relief of every part of the human race, from whatever burden or oppression they may unjustly labor under.... Sir, I have long been convinced, that if your love for yourselves, and for those inestimable laws, which preserved to you the rights of human nature, was founded on sincerity, you could not but be solicitous, that every individual, of whatever rank or distinction, might with you equally enjoy the blessings thereof; neither could you rest satisfied short of the most active effusion of your exertions, in order to their promotion from any state of degradation, to which the unjustifiable cruelty and barbarism of men may have reduced them.

Sir, suffer me to recall to your mind that time, in which the arms and tyranny of the British crown were exerted, with every powerful effort, in order to reduce you to a state of servitude: ... reflect on that time, in which every human aid appeared unavailable, and in which even hope and fortitude wore the aspect of inability to the conflict, and you cannot but be led to a serious and grateful sense of your miraculous and providential preservation....

This, Sir, was a time when you clearly saw into the injustice of a state of slavery, and in which you had just apprehensions of the horrors of its condition. It was now that your abhorrence thereof was so excited, that you publicly held forth this true and invaluable doctrine, which is worthy to be recorded and remembered in all succeeding ages: "We hold these truths to be self-evident, that all men are created equal; that they are endowed by their Creator with certain unalienable rights, and that among these are, life, liberty, and the pursuit of happiness." ...but, Sir, how pitiable is it to reflect, that although you were so fully convinced of the benevolence of the Father of Mankind, and of his equal and impartial distribution of these rights and privileges, which he hath conferred upon them, that you should at the same time counteract his mercies, in detaining by fraud and violence so numerous a part of my brethren, under groaning captivity and cruel oppression, that you should at the same time be found guilty of that most criminal act, which you professedly detested in others, with respect to yourselves.

.... And now, Sir, although my sympathy and affection for my brethren hath caused my enlargement thus far, I ardently hope, that your candor and generosity will plead with you in my behalf, when I make known to you, that it was not originally my design; but having taken up my pen in order to direct to you, as a present, a copy of an Almanac, which I have calculated for the succeeding year, I was unexpectedly and unavoidably led thereto....

And now, Sir, I shall conclude, and subscribe myself, with the most profound respect,

Your most obedient humble servant,

BENJAMIN BANNEKER

long been considered rather as brutish than human, and scarcely capable of mental endowments" (Jefferson-Coolidge Papers, I.38–43, Massachusetts Historical Society). Banneker submitted his calculations as evidence to the contrary and urged that Jefferson work toward bringing an end to slavery. Jefferson responded promptly: "No body wishes more than I do to see such proofs as you exhibit, that nature has given to our black brethren, talents equal to those of other colours of men, and that the appearance of a want of them is owing merely to the degraded condition of their existence, both in Africa & America. . . . no body wishes more ardently to see a good system commenced for raising the condition of both their body & mind to what it ought to be, as fast as the imbecillity of their present existence, and other circumstances which cannot be neglected, will admit" (Thomas Jefferson Papers, f.11481, Library of Congress).

Jefferson sent Banneker's calculations to the Marquis de Condorcet, secretary of the French Academy of Sciences, with an enthusiastic cover letter. There was no reply from Condorcet because at the time of the letter's arrival he was in hiding for having opposed the monarchy and having supported a republican form of government. The two letters, that from Banneker to Jefferson and the statesman's reply, were published in a widely distributed pamphlet and in at least one periodical during the following year.

Banneker's ephemeris for 1792 was published by the Baltimore printer Goddard & Angell with the title *Benjamin Banneker's Pennsylvania, Delaware, Maryland, and Virginia Almanack and Ephemeris for the Year of Our Lord 1792.* It was also sold by printers in Philadelphia and Alexandria, Virginia. He continued to calculate ephemerides that were published in almanacs bearing his name for the next five years. Promoted by the abolitionist societies of Pennsylvania and Maryland, Banneker's almanacs were published by several printers and sold widely in the United States and England. Twenty-eight separate editions of his almanacs are known. A recent computerized analysis of Banneker's published ephemerides and those calculated by several contemporaries for the same years, including those by William Waring and Ellicott, has revealed that Banneker's calculations consistently reflect a high degree of comparative accuracy. Although he continued calculating ephemerides through the year 1802, they remained unpublished.

Banneker died in his sleep following a morning walk on October 9, 1806, one month short of his seventy-fifth birthday. He was buried several days later in the family graveyard within sight of his house. As his body was being lowered into the grave, his house burst into flames, and all of its contents were destroyed. The cause of the fire remains unknown. Fortunately, the books and table he had borrowed, his commonplace book, and the astronomical journal in which he had copied all of his ephemerides had been given to his neighbor immediately following his death and thus were preserved.

See also Science

Bibliography

Bedini, Silvio A. "Benjamin Banneker and the Survey of the District of Columbia." *Records of the Columbia Historical Society* 69–70 (1971): 120–127.

Bedini, Silvio A. *The Life of Benjamin Banneker: The First African-American Man of Science.* 2d ed., rev. and exp. Baltimore: Maryland Historical Society, 1999.

Latrobe, John H. B. "Memoir of Benjamin Banneker." *Maryland Colonization Journal,* n.s., 2, no. 23 (1845): 353–364.

Litwin, Laura Baskes. *Benjamin Banneker: Astronomer and Mathematician.* Berkeley Heights, N.J.: Enslow, 1999.

Tyson, Martha E. "Banneker, the Afric-American Astronomer." From the *Posthumous Papers of Martha E. Tyson.* Edited by her daughter. Philadelphia: Friends' Book Association, 1884.

SILVIO A. BEDINI (1996)
Updated bibliography

Bannister, Edward Mitchell

c. 1826
January 9, 1901

Edward Mitchell Bannister was born sometime between 1826 and 1828 in St. Andrews, a small seaport in New Brunswick, Canada. His father Edward Bannister, probably a native of Barbados, died in 1832, and Edward and his younger brother, William, were raised by their mother, Hannah Alexander Bannister, a native of St. Andrews. Bannister's artistic talent was encouraged by his mother, and he won a local reputation for clever crayon portraits of family and schoolmates.

By 1850 Bannister had moved to Boston with the intention of becoming a painter, but because of his race he was unable to find an established artist who would accept him as a student. He worked at a variety of jobs to support himself and by 1853 was a barber in the salon of the successful African-American businesswoman Madame Christiana Carteaux, whom he married in 1857.

Bannister continued to study and paint, and he began winning recognition and patronage in the African-American community. In 1854 he received his first commission for an oil painting, from African-American physician John V. DeGrasse, titled *The Ship Outward Bound.* By 1863 Bannister was featured in William Wells Brown's book celebrating the accomplishments of prominent African Americans (Brown, 1863). His earliest extant portrait, of Prudence Nelson Bell (1864), was commissioned by an African-American Boston family.

Bannister was active in the social and political life of Boston's African-American community. He belonged to the Crispus Attucks Choir and the Histrionic Club. His colleagues included such leading black abolitionists as William Cooper Nell, Charles Lenox Remond, Lewis Hayden, and John Sweat Rock. He was an officer in two African-American abolitionist organizations (the Colored Citizens of Boston and the Union Progressive Association), added his name to antislavery petitions, and served as a delegate to the New England Colored Citizens Conventions in 1859 and 1865. In 1864 Bannister donated his portrait of the late Col. Robert Gould Shaw to be raffled at the Solders' Relief fair organized by his wife to assist the families of soldiers from the Massachusetts Fifty-fourth Colored Regiment.

Bannister is said to have spent a year in New York City in the early 1860s apprenticed to a Broadway photographer; he advertised himself as a photographer from 1863 to 1866. An 1864 photograph of Bannister's early patron Dr. DeGrasse survives from that period. Bannister continued to paint and win commissions, and although he listed himself in city directories as a portrait painter until 1874, works like his *Untitled* [Rhode Island Seascape] and *Dorchester, Massachusetts,* both painted around 1856, document his beginning interest in interpreting the New England landscape.

In the mid-1860s Bannister began to receive greater recognition in the Boston arts community. Sometime between 1863 and 1865 he received his only formal training, studying in the life-drawing classes given by physician and artist William Rimmer at the Lowell Institute. Bannister took a studio in the Studio Building from 1863 to 1866, where he was exposed to William Morris Hunt's promotion of the French Barbizon painters, and his paintings began receiving favorable notices from Boston critics. His growing confidence as an artist is indicated in two tightly painted monumental treatments of farmers and animals in the landscape, *Herdsman with Cows* and *Untitled* [Man with Two Oxen], both completed in 1869.

Bannister was part of a community of African-American artists in Boston in the 1860s. Sculptor Edmonia Lewis had a studio just two doors from him in the Studio Building; portraitist William H. Simpson was a neighbor and fellow member of the Crispus Attucks Choir and the Histrionic Club; and the young painter Nelson Primus sought out Bannister when he moved to Boston in the mid-1860s.

In 1869 the Bannisters moved to Providence, Rhode Island, where Bannister was immediately recognized by its growing art community. His first exhibit included *Newspaper Boy* (1869), one of the earliest depictions of working-class African Americans by an African-American artist, and a portrait of abolitionist William Lloyd Garrison.

Bannister came to national attention in 1876, when his four-by-five-foot painting *Under the Oaks* won a first-prize medal at the Philadelphia Centennial Exposition. This bucolic view of sheep and cows under a stand of oaks received widespread critical acclaim. But Bannister later remembered how, when he stepped forward to confirm his award, he was "just another inquisitive colored man" to the hostile awards committee.

Recognition for *Under the Oaks* brought Bannister increasing stature and success. By 1878 he sat on the board of the newly created Rhode Island School of Design, and he and fellow artists Charles Walter Stetson and George Whitaker founded the influential Providence Art Club. From 1877 to 1898 Bannister's studio was in the Woods Building, along with those of artists John Arnold, James Lincoln, George Whitaker, Sidney Burleigh, and Charles Walter Stetson. His Saturday art classes were well attended, and he won silver medals at exhibitions of the Boston Charitable Mechanics Association in 1881 and 1884. He exhibited throughout his career at the Boston and Providence Art Clubs, and also in New York City, New Orleans, Detroit, and Hartford, Connecticut. His work was much in demand by New England galleries and collectors, and in 1891 the Providence Art Club featured thirty-three of his works in a retrospective exhibition, to favorable reviews.

A number of Bannister's paintings, including *Woman Walking Down a Path* (1882), *Pastoral Landscape* (1881), *Road to a House with a Red Roof* (1889), and *Seaweed Gatherers* (1898), reflect his strong affinity for the style and philosophy of such Barbizon artists as Jean-François Millet and Camille Corot. But Bannister drew from numerous sources throughout his career, producing work in a variety of styles and moods, from serene vistas such as his *Palmer River* (1885), to the Turner-influenced dramatic skies of *Sunset* (c. 1875–1880) and *Untitled* [Landscape with Man on Horse] (1884), to free and lushly rendered views of woodland scenery such as *Untitled* [Trees and Shrubbery] (1877), in order to express what he described as "the infinite, subtle qualities of the spiritual idea, centering in all created things."

Although he is remembered primarily as a landscape painter, Bannister also drew his subjects from classical literature (*Leucothea Rescuing Ulysses,* 1891), still life (*Untitled* [Floral Still Life], n.d.), and religion (*Portrait of Saint Luke,* n.d.). His prolific output as a marine painter is represented by numerous drawings, watercolors, and paintings such as *Ocean Cliffs* (1884), *Sabin Point, Narragansett Bay* (1885), and *Untitled* [Rhode Island Seascape] (1893).

As in Boston, Bannister associated with, and his work was collected by, leaders of Rhode Island's African-American community. Bannister and his wife continued their involvement in the concerns of their church and community. In 1890 Christiana Carteaux Bannister led the efforts of African Americans to establish a Home for Aged Colored Women in Providence, which is today known as the Bannister Nursing Care Center.

Although he had been experiencing heart trouble in his later years, Bannister continued to paint. Indeed, his late works (*Street Scene*, c. 1895; *The Old Home*, 1899; *Untitled* [Plow in the Field], 1897) reveal an openness to experimentation and growth, with an increasingly abstract consideration of form and color on canvas.

On January 9, 1901, Bannister collapsed at an evening prayer meeting at the Elmwood Street Baptist Church and died shortly thereafter. Held in great esteem by Providence artists and patrons, he was the subject of lengthy tributes and eulogies. In May 1901 his friends in the Art Club organized a memorial exhibition of over one hundred Bannister paintings loaned by local collectors. Later that year, Providence artists erected a stone monument on his grave in North Burial Ground. Christiana Carteaux Bannister died two years later.

See also Art; Painting and Sculpture

Bibliography

Brown, William Wells. "Edward M. Bannister." In *The Black Man: His Antecedents, His Genius, and His Achievements.* New York: Thomas Hamilton; Boston: Wallcut, 1863. Reprint, New York: Kraus Reprint, 1969. Also available from <http://docsouth.unc.edu/brownww/brown.html>.

Hartigan, Lynda Roscoe. "Edward Mitchell Bannister." In *Five Black Artists in Nineteenth-Century America* (exhibition catalog). Washington, D.C., 1985.

Holland, Juanita Marie. *The Life and Work of Edward Mitchell Bannister: A Research Chronology and Exhibition Record.* New York: Kenkeleba House, 1992.

Holland, Juanita Marie. "Reaching Through the Veil: African-American Artist Edward Mitchell Bannister." In *Edward Mitchell Bannister, 1828–1901* (exhibition catalog). New York: Kenkeleba House, 1992.

JUANITA MARIE HOLLAND (1996)
Updated bibliography

BAPTISTS

African-American Baptists are Christians who trace their common descent to Africa and share similar Biblical doctrines and congregational policies. They share these values with the broader American Baptist religious tradition. African-American Baptists represent the largest and most diverse group of the many African-American denominations in the United States. They are known for their emphasis on emotional preaching and worship, educational institutions, economic leadership in the community, and sociopolitical activism.

The origin of African-American Baptists must be understood in the context of the interracial religious experiences of colonial American history and the African roots of the spirituality of slaves. White Baptists were initially slow in their evangelistic efforts among African slaves, as language barriers and economic considerations prevented the rapid evangelization of transplanted Africans. However, by the second half of the eighteenth century, a few persistent Baptist evangelists eluded these barriers and converted growing numbers of slaves.

Antebellum Baptists

The movement began largely on plantations in the South, where the vast majority of African slaves resided, and it spread to urban areas. Generally, the conversion of slaves tended to follow the denominational lines of white masters. Hence, the numbers of African-American Baptists tended to grow along with the remarkable expansion of Baptists in the South between 1750 and 1850. On occasion, Baptist evangelists were invited by slaveholders belonging to local Baptist congregations to preach to their plantation slaves. On other occasions, slave owners would allow slaves to accompany them to church or hold devotional services in their own "big houses."

There were scattered instances of African Americans attending biracial churches during the late colonial period. As early as 1772, Robert Stevens and eighteen other African Americans were members of the First Baptist Church of Providence, Rhode Island. By 1772, the First Baptist Church of Boston was also receiving blacks into its congregation. Very likely, the Baptist churches of the South had some black members prior to the 1770s. As a result of interracial evangelizing between 1773 and 1775, David George organized the first black Baptist church in North America, at Silver Bluff, South Carolina, near Savannah, Georgia. This increasing tendency to receive slaves into the Baptist churches created the interracial Baptist church experience in colonial American society.

By the early national period, the presence of slaves exceeded the numbers of whites in a few churches in the South. However, whether they were the majority or minority presence in these churches, African-American Baptists were still limited in their membership privileges and responsibilities. Slavery and racism prevented the existence of authentic fellowship based on Christian principles within these early churches. These social pressures later resulted in the demise of racially mixed churches and the emergence of Baptist churches organized along racial lines.

Slave preachers were the first to verbalize the need for churches separate from the white Baptists. Some of them had been previously exposed to leadership roles, having served as religious leaders in Africa. They wanted a style

The First Colored Baptist Church in North America. *A frontispiece from the book of the same title by James M. Simms (published 1888), the drawing shows a Baptist Church established in Savannah, Georgia, in 1788.* MANUSCRIPTS, ARCHIVES AND RARE BOOKS DIVISION, SCHOMBURG CENTER FOR RESEARCH IN BLACK CULTURE, THE NEW YORK PUBLIC LIBRARY, ASTOR, LENOX AND TILDEN FOUNDATIONS.

of Baptist life and witness that would permit the free expression of spirituality and the involvement of African-American preachers in pastoral leadership. The first movement toward separate black Baptist churches took place when African Americans stole off to the woods, canebrakes, and remote cabins to have preaching and prayer meetings of their own. These meetings were usually held early in the morning, when the patrols over the slaves would retire from night duty to sleep during the day. Hence, early morning prayer meetings were created out of necessity.

Among the early African-American Baptist preachers who pioneered the plantation missions and the movement toward separate churches were: "Uncle Jack," who went from plantation to plantation in Virginia in the last quarter of the eighteenth century, preaching to whites as well as African Americans; "Uncle Harry" Cowan, who labored extensively in North Carolina; and George Liele (1752–1825), who preached on the plantations of South Carolina and Georgia and actually paved the way for the planting of the first separate churches among African-American Christians. Liele's evangelistic ministry inspired the founding of the Silver Bluff Baptist Church in Aikens County, South Carolina, by David George (1742–1810) in the late 1700s and of the First Colored Baptist Church of Savannah, Georgia, by Andrew Bryan (1737–1812) in the 1780s. There were other African-American preachers who labored on plantations for the evangelization of slaves and the subsequent separate Baptist church movement, but most of their names are now lost.

Within a decade after the founding of African-American Baptist churches in South Carolina and Georgia, slaves and free blacks in other parts of the country began similar movements away from white-dominated churches and toward the creation of their own churches. During the American Revolution, the African-American Baptists of Petersburg, Virginia, organized the Gilfield Baptist Church and the Harrison Street Baptist Church (both in Petersburg) and the first Baptist churches in both Williamsburg and Richmond, Virginia.

African-American Baptist churches were soon organized in the north. The Joy Street Baptist Church, originally called the African Meeting House, was constituted in Boston in 1805. The Abyssinian Baptist Church of New York City was organized in 1808, presumably by a group of traders who came to New York City from Ethiopia (then called Abyssinia). These were followed by the Concord Baptist Church of Brooklyn, New York (May 18, 1847); the First African Baptist Church in Philadelphia, Pennsylvania. (June 19, 1809); the First African Baptist Church in Trenton, New Jersey (1812); the Middlerun Baptist Church in Xenia, Ohio (1822); and the First Colored Peoples' Baptist Church of Baltimore (1836). This lists only some of the more important churches.

The roots of the Baptist cooperative movement go back to the antebellum period. In the early 1830s, organizational consciousness emerged among black Baptists in Ohio with the evolution of the associational movement. Baptists began to see the need for united Christian ministries among churches in near proximity. Hence, local churches began the formation of associations to advance such causes as education, home missions, and foreign missions. In 1834 they organized the Providence Baptist Association in Berlin Cross Roads, Ohio. This was followed by the founding of a politically oriented movement called the Union Anti-Slavery Baptist Association, also organized in Ohio in 1843. Slowly, the associational movement spread to other states. The organization of Baptist state conventions began in North Carolina with the founding of the General State Convention in 1866.

The cooperative efforts of African-American Baptists were prompted by a growing consciousness of an interest in doing missionary work in Africa. Lott Carey and other pioneer African-American missionaries inspired early church leaders to seek even greater cooperation among their separate churches. As early as 1840, black Baptists of New England and the Middle Atlantic states met in New York's Abyssinian Baptist Church to organize the American Baptist Missionary Convention, their first cooperative movement beyond state lines.

Civil War and the Era of Church Growth

The Civil War era and Reconstruction gave impetus to the organization of several cooperative movement bodies. The Baptists of the West and Southwest met in St. Louis in 1864 and organized the Northwestern and Southern Baptist Conventions. In 1866 these two regional conventions met in a special session in Richmond, Virginia, and organized the Consolidated American Baptist Convention, representing 100,000 black baptists and two hundred ministers. The new convention was an attempt to promote unity, discourage sectionalism, and create a national spirit of cooperation. The work of the Consolidated Convention was fostered by the formation of district auxiliary conventions, state conventions, and associations.

In 1873 the African-American Baptists of the West organized the General Association of the Western States and Territories, and in 1874 those in the East organized the New England Baptist Missionary Convention. These two bodies soon overshadowed the spirit of unity expressed in the Consolidated American Baptist Convention. A persistent spirit of independence and sectionalism on the part of both eastern and western Baptists caused the decline of the Consolidated Baptist Convention, resulting in its termination at its last meeting in Lexington, Kentucky, in 1878. A vacuum in the cooperative missionary movement resulted.

In response, William W. Colley, a missionary to Africa appointed by the Foreign Mission Board of the Southern Baptist Convention, returned to the United States with a determination to revive a cooperative spirit among African-American Baptists. He led the way for the organization of the Baptist Foreign Mission Convention on November 24, 1880, in Montgomery, Alabama. This convention effectively revived an expanding interest in the evangelization of Africa.

The next steps toward separate denominational development came with the organization of the American National Baptist Convention (1893) and the Tripartite Union (1894). On September 28, 1895, these organizations merged to form the first real denomination among African-American Baptists, the National Baptist Convention (NBC) U.S.A. For the first time, the combined ministries of the churches throughout the nation were fostered by a separate national organization of African-American Baptists.

Primitive Baptists

A number of African-American baptists were opposed to the organization of missionary associations, in part because the Arminianism of the mid-nineteenth-century revivals was in conflict with traditional notions of predestination. The major outgrowth of the antimission movement was the rise of the African-American Primitive Baptists. Initially, Primitive Baptists inherited their antimission spirit from white Baptists. As early as 1820, the Saint Barley Primitive Baptist Church of Huntsville, Alabama (originally organized as the Huntsville African Baptist Church), evolved as one of the earliest separate Primitive Baptist churches. Subsequently, a number of churches joined with them. By 1907 these churches had gained sufficient strength to organize themselves into the National Primitive Baptist Convention. However, their rate of growth was far below that of the National Baptists. Still smaller in numbers and influence were the United American Freewill Baptists. Today, both the Primitive and Freewill Baptists still constitute a minority presence among African-American Baptists.

The question of missions also played a major role in a split at the National Baptist Convention, U.S.A. In 1897 a controversy erupted at the annual session of the convention, convening that year in Boston. The major issues in dispute were the financial administration of foreign mission programs and cooperation with white Baptists. The majority opinion favored the fiscal policy of the convention and the exclusive operation of the denomination independent of white Baptist influence.

However, a minority of delegates from Virginia, North Carolina, and several other Atlantic Coast states, as well as Washington, D.C., decided to organize a separate missionary society that, with white support, was designed exclusively to advance a foreign mission enterprise. They met at the Baptist Church, in Washington, D.C., and organized the Lott Carey Baptist Foreign Mission Convention. These leaders adopted a constitutional provision requiring at least 75 percent of all funds collected by the convention to be sent to foreign missions.

The great break within the National Baptist Convention, U.S.A. came during its formative years, in 1915. Efforts to maintain unity and harmony within the convention had previously posed vexing challenges to church officials. Unlike the crisis that led to the Lott Carey Convention movement, the crisis of 1915 was primarily a legal problem regarding the ownership and management of the National Baptist Publishing Board, headquartered in Nashville, Tennessee. Signs of dissent within the leadership of the convention were apparent for almost a decade before the actual separation of 1915.

The crisis came to a head during the annual session in Chicago. It took the form of a legal struggle between two groups: the majority, who supported convention control of the publishing board, and those who favored the independence of the publishing board as a separate corporate entity. The court decided in favor of the majority, and unity between the factions could not be restored. The result was the organization of a new denomination. The majority faction incorporated as the National Baptist Convention U.S.A., Inc; the minority group met on September 9, 1915 at the Salem Baptist Church and organized the National Baptist Convention of America. It is now called the National Baptist Convention of America. Members of the publishing board played the key role in the development of the new denomination, which has policies similar to those of the National Baptist Convention, U.S.A., Inc.

Progressive National Baptist Convention

The Progressive National Baptist Convention of America, Inc., organized in 1961, grew out of a major crisis within the National Baptist Convention, U.S.A., relating to the issues of tenure and civil rights strategies. Joseph H. Jackson, the president of the National Baptist Convention, was opposed to the civil rights agenda of the Southern Christian Leadership Conference (SCLC) and related organizations. He was opposed by Gardner C. Taylor, pastor of Concord Baptist Church in Brooklyn, New York, and the Reverend Martin Luther King, Jr., president of the SCLC.

The initial struggle erupted in 1961 when Taylor challenged Jackson's bid for re-election to the presidency on the grounds that Jackson had exceeded the tenure requirement. The challenge was marked by violence, controversy, and a legal battle. The "Taylor team" was determined to defeat Jackson and plan a new course for the convention. However, Jackson's popularity prevailed in the vote on the floor of the convention and was upheld in a civil court. The Taylor team did not accept this defeat, however, since they were determined to lead African-American Baptists in a new and progressive direction, especially in the area of civil rights.

On September 11, 1961, a national news release invited progressive-minded leaders to join forces with the Taylor team and organize a new denomination named the Progressive National Baptist Convention of America, Inc. The new denomination promoted the civil rights program of Martin Luther King, Jr. and launched a program of cooperation with the largely white American Baptist Churches, U.S.A. The new program was called the Fund of Renewal, designed to promote specialized mission projects.This program also engendered a new spirit of cooperation between African-American and white Baptists.

Black Baptist churches were one of the anchors of the civil rights movement, with Baptist ministers such as Vernon Johns, Benjamin Mays, Adam Clayton Powell Jr., Martin Luther King Jr., David Abernathy, and Gardner Taylor in the forefront of the struggle for black equality. The contribution of black Baptists to the civil rights movement, and the inspiration that it has provided to both Americans and oppressed people elsewhere, is one of the greatest legacies of twentieth-century African-American Baptists.

The vast majority of African-American Baptists have been strong supporters of foreign missions. Early pioneers of the missionary enterprise, besides Lott Carey (1780–1829) and George Liele, were Prince Williams and W. W. Colley. These men set the stage for an aggressive missionary program in India, Africa, Central America, and the

Olivet Baptist Church. *The Chicago church, founded by Samuel McCoy and John Larmon in 1850, was originally called Zenia Baptist Church. Photograph from Souvenir of Negro Progress: Chicago, 1779–1925 (1925) by John Taitt.* GENERAL RESEARCH AND REFERENCE DIVISION, SCHOMBURG CENTER FOR RESEARCH IN BLACK CULTURE, THE NEW YORK PUBLIC LIBRARY, ASTOR, LENOX AND TILDEN FOUNDATIONS.

West Indies. With the rise of foreign missions boards among the denominations, African-American Baptists developed a sophisticated approach to the evangelization of non-Christians. They developed schools, hospitals, clinics, and agricultural projects, and they established new churches in various parts of the world. The Lott Carey Baptist Foreign Mission Convention pioneered the movement to utilize indigenous people in leadership positions in foreign missions, which facilitated the philosophy of self-help and independence among peoples in developing nations. Many of the leaders within these nations came out of the missionary agencies.

One of the important changes in the black Baptist church since the 1960s has been the changing status of women. Nannie Helen Burroughs (1883–1961), through her longtime leadership of the Women's Convention Auxiliary of the National Baptist Convention, was a dominant figure in twentieth-century African-American Baptist life. Until the latter half of the twentieth century, however, women were not allowed to be preachers or to take active roles in church leadership. The Baptists were slow to ordain women for the ministry; black women were not ordained until the 1970s, and even then only in small numbers. Other leadership roles were also denied to women, such as that of deacon. The bias against promoting women to positions of prominence in the Baptist has changed, however, although too slowly for many.

Education

The ministry of education of African-American Baptists has been in the forefront of the cooperative programs of associations, state conventions, and national conventions. The Civil War marked the beginning of strong cooperative strides among local churches to advance the intellectual development of blacks. Many churches served as schools during the week and houses of worship on Sundays. Moreover, local associations organized schools in many of the rural areas and small towns of the South. With the rise of public education, most of the associational secondary schools were closed.

The development of higher education for African Americans, however, has been among the lasting contributions of African-American Baptists. The magnitude of the task prompted African-American Baptists to cooperate with whites in the development of schools of higher learning. This evolution may be classified into two groups: cooperative schools with whites, and independent African-American schools. There are a number of historically black colleges and universities (HBCUs) that were founded with Baptist support. These colleges, most of which were created in the South in the postbellum years, had two main purposes. Some of these schools were seminaries and helped train young men for the ministry. An even more pressing task in the minds of many of the college founders was to create a cadre of teachers who could, in turn, educate freedmen in primary schools. However, due to funding problems, many of the Baptist HBCUs functioned as little more than secondary schools in their early decades.

Many Baptist HBCUs were founded by whites, one of the driving forces being the American Baptist Home Mission Society (ABHMS). Wayland Seminary, the first seminary for black Baptists, later incorporated into Virginia Union University, opened in Washington, D.C., in 1865. Another root of the Virginia Union University was the Richmond Theological Center, founded in Richmond, Virginia, also in 1865. Other HBCUs founded by white Baptists include Shaw University (originally Raleigh Institute, 1865) in Raleigh, North Carolina; Morehouse College (originally Augusta Institute, 1867) in Atlanta, Georgia; Spelman College (originally Atlanta Baptist Female Seminary, 1881) in Atlanta; Benedict College in Columbia, South Carolina (1870); Jackson State University (originally Natchez Seminary, 1877) in Jackson, Mississippi; and Florida Memorial College (originally Florida Baptist Institute, 1879) in Miami.

Many of these schools represent substantial efforts by white Baptists in the intellectual development of African Americans. They financed, administered, and staffed most of these schools, and only gradually did African-American Baptists assume responsibility for directing the schools. A number of schools were founded by African-American Baptists, but, because of problems with funding, they faced severe operating difficulties and had to close. The first independent African Baptist school of higher learning founded by black Baptists was Guadelupe College in Seguin, Texas. Others appeared in rapid succession: Houston College at Houston, Texas (1885); Walker Baptist Institute in Augusta, Georgia (1888); and Friendship Baptist College in Rock Hill, South Carolina (1891). Only Morris College in Sumter, South Carolina (1908)remains open in the early twenty-first century.

In the early twentieth century, Baltimore became a center of Baptist seminaries. The Colored Baptist Convention of Maryland organized Clayton-Williams Academy and Biblical Institute in 1901; the Maryland Baptist Missionary Convention organized Lee and Hayes University in 1914; the Independent Colored Baptist Convention organized Williams and Jones University in 1928; and the United Baptist Missionary Convention organized Maryland Baptist Center and School of Religion in 1942. These Baltimore schools were largely the result of convention rivalry and survived only a few years. In 1921 two other schools were organized: Central Baptist Theological Seminary in Topeka, Kansas, and Northern Baptist University in Rahway, Nw Jersey. Both schools provided educated leadership for blacks, and many of the graduates have helped to advance the social, political, economic, and religious progress of African Americans. The Interdenominational Theological Center in Atlanta, Georgia, was formed in 1958 by a merger of a number of African-American seminaries, including the former Morehouse School of Religion.

Music and Liturgy

From the beginning of separate religious services, African-American Baptists utilized music in their worship. This music was an expression of the deep sentiment of the people as they reacted to the severe oppression of life in America. It grew out of the secular songs of plantation slave-labor gangs. As slaves were converted to Christianity, they incorporated their new religious beliefs into the songs of the plantations. The result was Negro spirituals. These songs played a major role in church life until the postbellum era, when Protestant hymns from the white religious experience began to become more important in church services. However, groups such as the Fisk Jubilee Singers (1871) sustained the spiritual tradition in the late nineteenth century. Their concert tours of Europe and America introduced spirituals to a new and highly receptive audience.

Gospel music has been one of the most important innovations in church services in the twentieth century. Thomas A. Dorsey, a pioneer gospel music composer, exponent, and instructor, was largely responsible for the introduction of gospel music in the worship of these churches. In 1932 the National Convention of Gospel Choirs was organized to promote the work of Dorsey in the churches. This organization encouraged the introduction of contests of choirs, quartets, and soloists in local churches. Two other major individuals contributed to the development of music in the religious experience of African Americans: James A. Cleveland, through his National Workshop Choir, and Glenn T. Settle, the originator of Wings Over Jordan, a nationally acclaimed chorus. Subsequently, most of the performing artists in the broader culture received training, inspiration, and exposure from serving in local church choirs and choruses. Currently, many African-American Baptist churches are influenced by recording artists on popular gospel music radio stations.

Similarly, drama has played a role in the development of African-American Baptist churches. African-American preaching itself emerged as a unique art form. The dramatic presentation of the sermon was characteristic of these churches; preachers literally acted out the contents of their messages to their congregations. Moreover, these churches served as the central stage for dramatic presentations of other performing artists in talent shows, plays, and pageants. The recitation of religious poetry became a component of the artistic expression of church programs.

Painting has been less influential in African-American Baptist churches, which have tended to accept white expressions of religious art. However, the Black Power and black theology movements altered the art works in the churches.In the late twentieth century, some churches, like New Shiloh Baptist Church of Baltimore, began developing Afrocentric murals of the Last Supper, the Crucifixion, and scenes from African-American life and culture.

Because of the inherent autonomy of African-American Baptists, there remains much variety in size, po-

Group portrait of members of the Woman's Auxiliary to the National Baptist Convention, Birmingham, Alabama, 1902. PHOTOGRAPHS AND PRINTS DIVISION, SCHOMBURG CENTER FOR RESEARCH IN BLACK CULTURE, THE NEW YORK PUBLIC LIBRARY, ASTOR, LENOX AND TILDEN FOUNDATIONS.

litical involvement, and religious practice of independent congregations. Some of the larger urban churches—such as Shiloh Baptist Church in Washington, D.C., Mount Olivet in Chicago, Concord Baptist Church in Brooklyn, New York, and the Abyssinian Baptist Church in Harlem—have long been centers of community activity and have served as political bases for their pastors. On the other hand, small rural Baptist churches, while their numbers have declined, remain the backbone of numerous communities.

Since the 1930s, and with even more emphasis since the 1960s, many black Baptist pastors have emphasized the social aspects of their ministry. They have stressed social outreach, particularly working with disaffected teenagers and prison populations and discouraging drug use. Baptist churches represent the largest denominational group among African Americans, and they continue to shape black cultural, political, and spiritual life in countless ways. In 1990 there were approximately twelve million African-American Baptists. Black Baptists will likely continue to endure and change in response to the myriad challenges of contemporary African-American life.

See also Abyssinian Baptist Church; Burroughs, Nannie Helen; Carey, Lott; King, Martin Luther, Jr.; Liele, George; Missionary Movements; National Baptist Convention, U.S.A., Inc.; Primitive Baptists; Protestantism in the Americas; Theology, Black

Bibliography

Boyd, Jesse L. *A Popular History of the Baptists in Mississippi.* Jackson, Miss., 1930.

Goodwin, Everett C., ed. *Baptists in the Balance: A Tension Between Freedom and Responsibility.* Valley Forge, Pa.: Judson Press, 1997.

Higginbotham, Evelyn Brooks. *Righteous Discontent: The Women's Movement in the Black Baptist Church, 1880-1920.* Cambridge, Mass.: Harvard University Press, 1993.

Lincoln, C. Eric, and Lawrence H. Mamiya. *The Black Church in the African-American Experience.* Durham, N.C.: Duke University Press, 1990.

Lumpkin, William L. *Baptist Confessions of Faith.* Chicago: Judson Press, 1959.

McKinney, Lora-Ellen. *Total Praise: An Orientation to Black Baptist Belief and Worship.* Valley Forge, Pa.: Judson Press, 2002.

Piepkorn, Arthur Carl. "The Primitive Baptists of North America." *Concordia Theological Monthly* (May 1971): 297-313.

Sobel, Mechal. *Trabelin' On: The Slave Journey to an Afro-Baptist Faith.* Westport, Conn.: Greenwood Press, 1979.

Sobel, Mechal. *The World They Made Together: Black and White Values in Eighteenth-Century Virginia.* Princeton, N.J.: Princeton University Press, 1987.

Washington, James M. *Frustrated Fellowship: The Black Baptist Quest for Social Power.* Macon, Ga.: Mercer University Press, 1986.

LEROY FITTS (1996)
Updated bibliography

BARAKA, AMIRI (JONES, LEROI)

OCTOBER 7, 1934

Amiri Baraka, born Everett LeRoi Jones in 1934, first gained fame as a poet and playwright in New York's Greenwich Village and subsequently became the most prominent and influential writer of the black arts movement. Throughout his career Baraka has been a controversial figure, noted for his caustic wit and fiery polemics. In his poems, plays, and essays, he has addressed painful issues, turning his frank commentary upon himself and the world regarding personal, social, and political relations. As a stylist, Baraka has been a major influence on African-American poetry and drama since 1960; as a public figure, he has epitomized the politically engaged black writer.

Raised in Newark, New Jersey, Baraka attended Howard University and served briefly in the U.S. Air Force, an episode that his autobiography describes as "Error/Farce." As Baraka explains, his subscriptions to *Partisan Review* and other literary magazines led authorities to suspect him of communist affiliations, and he was "undesirably discharged." He subsequently moved to Greenwich Village, where he met and married another young writer, Hettie Cohen. They had two daughters, Kellie and Lisa. Baraka, known as LeRoi Jones in this period, gained notoriety in the Village literary scene, frequently publishing, reading, and socializing alongside Diane di Prima, Allen Ginsberg, Jack Kerouac, and other Beat movement figures. He and Cohen edited *Yugen,* an avant-garde literary magazine, and his book *Preface to a Twenty Volume Suicide Note* (1961) established him as a major voice among the new poets.

During this period he published his celebrated essay "Cuba Libre," a new journalistic travelogue about visiting Cuba shortly after that country's 1959 revolution. This essay marked the beginning of his movement toward radical politics and away from his bohemian associates. His early political essays were eventually collected in *Home* (1966). Similarly, his book *Blues People* (1963) introduced his continuing interest in jazz as a key to African-American culture. Baraka's plays of this period, emotionally intense and quasi-autobiographical, culminate with *Dutchman* (1964), an Obie winner that remains his most famous and admired work. *Dutchman* explores the manic tension and doomed attraction between a black man and a white woman riding in the New York subway. Like *The Slave* (1965) and his second volume of poems, *The Dead Lecturer* (1965), this work reflects the racial anxieties that would soon estrange him from his white wife and Village friends.

> *Amiri Baraka*
>
> "We want a nation of angels. The illuminated. We are trying to create in the same wilderness, against the same resistance. The fire is hot. Let it burn more brightly. Let it light up all creation."
>
> *BLACK MAGIC: SABOTAGE, TARGET STUDY, BLACK ART; COLLECTED POETRY, 1961–1967.* INDIANAPOLIS: BOBBS-MERRILL, 1969.

After the assassination of Malcolm X on February 21, 1965, LeRoi Jones abandoned his family, moved to Harlem, and changed his name to Imamu Amiri Baraka (Blessed Priest and Warrior). Entering a period of intense black cultural nationalism, he directed the Black Arts Repertory Theater and School in Harlem while continuing to publish prolifically throughout the late 1960s. His important books of this period include *Black Magic Poetry* (1969), *Four Black Revolutionary Plays* (1969), *Raise Race Rays Raze* (1971), and *Black Music* (1968). Many of these works attack whites and assail Negro false consciousness, advocating an authentic black identity as the prerequisite to political liberation.

In the 1970s Baraka renounced cultural nationalism, dropped "Imamu" from his name, and embraced what he called "Marxism/Leninism/Mao Tse Tung Thought." His subsequent writing has remained in a Marxist mode but with a strong African-American and third-world orientation. Some of these later works lapse into schematically pedantic social commentaries and crude, unimaginative polemics. At his best, however, in long poems such as "In the Tradition" and "Wailers," Baraka demonstrates his continuing brilliance, combining music, sports, and political struggle into a densely realized vision of African-American culture as a triumphant, complexly expressive tradition.

In August, 2001, Baraka was appointed poet laureate of New Jersey, an acknowledgement that was generally celebrated by the literary community. However, after the terrorist attacks of September 11, 2001, Baraka published a long, apocalyptic, polemical poem called "Somebody Blew Up America," which incited fiery controversy, due to its political content—especially its innuendoes that the Israeli government had foreknowledge of the attacks. Baraka was asked to resign his laureateship. He refused, and a year later, the New Jersey general assembly abolished the post. Regardless, Baraka remains unapologetically committed to his vision of the poet as activist and provocateur.

See also Black Arts Movement; Malcolm X

Bibliography

African-American Review, Summer–Fall, 2003. Special Baraka issue.

Baraka, Amiri. *The Autobiography of LeRoi Jones.* New York: Scribner, 1984.

Baraka, Amiri. *Fiction of Leroi Jones/Amiri Baraka.* Edited by Amiri Baraka and William Harris. New York: Thunder's Mouth Press, 2000.

Benston, Kimberly. *Baraka: The Renegade and the Mask.* New Haven, Conn.: Yale University Press, 1976.

Hudson, Theodore. "From LeRoi Jones to Amiri Baraka: The Literary Works." Ph.D. diss., Howard University, Washington, D.C., 1971.

Sollors, Werner. *Amiri Baraka/LeRoi Jones: The Quest for a "Populist Modernism."* New York: Columbia University Press, 1978.

Watts, Jerry Gafio. *Amiri Baraka: The Politics and Art of a Black Intellectual.* New York: New York University Press, 2001.

DAVID LIONEL SMITH (1996)
Updated by publisher 2005

BARBADOES, JAMES G.

c. 1796
JANUARY 22, 1841

Little is known about the birth or early life of the abolitionist James Barbadoes. By 1830 he was living in Boston and had emerged as a leader of the Boston African-American community, supporting himself as a clothes dealer and barber. He was a leader with David Walker in the Massachusetts General Colored Association, founded in 1826, and served as its secretary. In 1831 he was delegate to the Convention of the People of Color, in Philadelphia.

Barbadoes was an associate and admirer of the abolitionist William Lloyd Garrison (1805–1879), and he named a son after him. He was one of three blacks among the founders of Garrison's American Anti-Slavery Society, established in Philadelphia in 1833, and he served on its board of managers from 1833 to 1836. In 1834 he helped organize the annual meeting of the New England Anti-Slavery Society, where he spoke of his recent efforts to free his brother, Robert, from prison. A free man born in Boston Robert Barbadoes had been kidnapped in New Orleans, jailed, and threatened with slavery. It took five months of agitation by Barbadoes, and letters from the governor of Massachusetts, for him to be released.

Barbadoes was opposed to African-American colonization of Africa, and he publicly supported Garrison against conservative abolitionists within the American Anti-Slavery Society on this and other issues, including women's rights. However, after his involvement in a project in 1840 to recruit free black settlers to British Guiana, Barbadoes became interested in leaving the United States. Shortly afterward, he emigrated with his family and a group of other blacks to Jamaica, intending to farm silkworms. However, two of his children died of malaria soon after they arrived, and Barbadoes himself perished of the same disease the following year.

See also Abolition; Slavery

Bibliography

Aptheker, Herbert, ed. *A Documentary History of the Negro People in the United States.* New York: Citadel, 1951.

Horton, James, and Lois Horton. *Black Bostonians,* rev. ed. New York: Holmes & Meier, 1999.

Quarles, Benjamin. *Black Abolitionists.* New York: Oxford University Press, 1969.

LYDIA MCNEILL (1996)
Updated bibliography

BARBADOS LABOUR PARTY

Barbados in 1938 was a colony in the British Empire. The system of enslavement had ended in 1838, but the masses of black and brown people remained in a state of persistent poverty. The white minority dominated politics and exploited the black majority. There was a clear need for mobilization of the people for collective action. Ethnic imbalances, class contradictions, and gender discrimination had to be challenged.

Throughout the English-speaking Caribbean workers were "on the march" in the 1930s. Disturbances took place in Barbados in July 1937. Many people agreed that significant change was urgently needed. Black politicians busied themselves with the formation of mass-based political parties and linked them to trade unions.

In Barbados on March 31, 1938, seven black progressive activists established the Barbados Labour Party (BLP). From the beginning, lawyers were prominent in the BLP. As a result, close attention was paid to constitutional forms within the party and also on the wider political scene. The political culture of Barbados was irreversibly transformed. Grantley Herbert Adams (later Sir Grantley Adams) was soon chosen as political leader. The movement established branches in all eleven parishes of the island. Its ideology was necessarily left of center, challenging the conservatism of the white planter-merchant oligarchy.

The BLP was a "historic necessity." The needs of the masses were great. In 1937 only 3.3 percent of the people had the right to vote—6,299 out of a population of 190,000. The extension of the franchise had to be a priority. The BLP became a voice for the voiceless. The party launched a campaign of political education in order to raise the political consciousness of the people and mobilize support. The weekly newspaper the *Beacon* was among the agencies used to spread the word.

Rival parties included the West Indian National Congress Party (1944–1956), the Barbados Electors Association (renamed the Progressive Conservative Party and later the Barbados National Party), and the Democratic Labour Party (DLP) from 1956.

The BLP manifesto for the 1944 general election, just four pages, was optimistically entitled *Labour Looks Forward.* This election produced the striking outcome that the BLP, the Congress Party, and the Electors Association each won eight seats. But support for the BLP steadily increased. In 1948 it won twelve of the twenty-four seats.

In 1943, for the first time, some women who were eligible had gained the right to vote. Eventually, in 1951 all adults gained the franchise. Ermie Bourne became the first woman to be elected to Parliament. Women have continued to advance in the party and in the society.

In preparation for the West Indies Federation, the BLP joined with other regional progressive parties to create the Federal Labour Party. In Barbados the BLP won four of the five federal seats. Grantley Adams, leader of the BLP, became the prime minister of the federation. While he was out of office, the BLP was in opposition as the minority party from 1961 to 1976.

Circumstances led the DLP government to seek political independence for Barbados alone. The Colonial Office agreed on November 30, 1966. There was to be a general election on November 3. The BLP manifesto solemnly declared: "This election is the most momentous election in the history of the Barbados Labour Party because it is the most important in the history of Barbados." But the Democratic Labour Party retained office. Barbados was no longer a colony but an independent, sovereign state. Coincidentally, the election of 1966 was the first one in which no white person was elected to the legislature.

It was not until September 1976 that the BLP returned to office. At the helm was John Michael Geoffrey Manningham ("Tom") Adams. The BLP won seventeen seats and the DLP seven. The pamphlet *Achievements* summed up the era as follows: "The B.L.P. Governments of 1976–86 were reformist, socialist and visionary. They transformed the social and economic landscape at great pace" (Simmons, 1998, p. 14). The inherited economy based on sugar monoculture was modernized. Economic diversification was pursued with tourism, manufacturing, offshore companies, and service industries.

The party published the booklet *The Promises We Make, We Perform: Promises & Performance, 1981–1986.* Nevertheless, at the general election of 1986 the BLP won only three seats. This was the low point in its fortunes. It at once embarked on a rebuilding process.

The fiftieth anniversary of the BLP was marked by a series of activities, and the *Advocate* newspaper published a sixteen-page supplement in the *Sunday Advocate* of October 30, 1988. The sixtieth anniversary saw the publication of the pamphlet *Achievements of the Barbados Labour Party (1938–1998)*, compiled and edited by David A. C. Simmons and his team of writers.

In the 1991 general election the BLP improved its performance, winning ten seats. Then in 1994 the BLP succeeded in so challenging the DLP government that a general election was called, and the BLP won nineteen of twenty-eight seats, returning to office. Owen Seymour Arthur became prime minister.

Ten years later, the 66th Annual General Conference was held in October 2004. The brochure by this time had grown to 104 pages. By a process of nation building, the colony of 1938 has been transformed into a community that is approaching the status of "developed," as seen in the annual United Nations Human Development Index. The BLP is clearly dedicated to the economic and social development of Barbados as a community where social justice is pursued by all the social partners—government, trade unions, employers' associations, churches, and civil society.

See also Adams, Grantley; Politics and Politicians in the Caribbean; West Indies Federation

Bibliography

Barbados Labour Party. *Labour Marches On: A Record of Achievements and a Statement of Future Policy of the Barbados Labour Party, 1951.* Bridgetown, Barbados: Author, 1951.

Barbados Labour Party. *66th Annual Conference: Celebrating a Decade of Excellence.* Bridgetown, Barbados: Author, 2004.

Beckles, Hilary McD. *Chattel House Blues: Making of a Democratic Society in Barbados, from Clement Payne to Owen Arthur.* Kingston, Jamaica: IRP, 2004.

Bolland, O. Nigel. *On the March: Labour Rebellions in the British Caribbean, 1934–39.* Kingston, Jamaica: IRP, 1999.

Hoyos, F. A. *Grantley Adams and the Social Revolution: The Story of the Movement that Changed the Pattern of West Indian Society.* London: Macmillan, 1974.

Hoyos, F. A. *Tom Adams: A Biography.* London: Macmillan, 1988.

Simmons, David A. C., ed. *Achievements of the Barbados Labour Party (1938–1998).* Bridgetown, Barbados: Barbados Labour Party, 1998.

ANTHONY DE VERE PHILLIPS (2005)

Joaquim Benedito Barbosa Gomes, Brazil's first black Supreme Court Justice in 2003. © REUTERS/CORBIS

Barbosa Gomes, Joaquim Benedito

October 7, 1954

The Brazilian Supreme Court justice Joaquim Benedito Barbosa Gomes was born in Paracatu, Minas Gerais, the oldest of eight children. The son of a brickmaker, Barbosa Gomes left the tiny town of Paracatu at age sixteen to finish secondary school in the capital city of Brasília. In order to support himself, Barbosa Gomes worked as a janitor for the Regional Electoral Tribunal. One day, while cleaning a restroom, one of the court directors heard him singing in English. Impressed with his command of the language, the judge arranged to get him a job as an offset printer at the newspaper *Correio Braziliense.* Barbosa Gomes used his skill as a printer to buy a car, help his family, and continue his studies. He eventually earned entry into the University of Brasília. Working nights at the congressional printing service, he took classes in the mornings and slept briefly in the afternoons. In 1976 Barbosa Gomes passed Brazil's Office of the Chancellery exam and began working as an overseas consular official, serving in Finland, England, and Switzerland. Even as he was engaged in his consular work, Barbosa Gomes continued his university studies, earning his law degree in 1979. Barbosa Gomes had aspirations of becoming a diplomat, but he was denied entry into the diplomatic corps, allegedly because of racial discrimination—he passed all of his written exams but could not pass the interview stage. Barbosa Gomes began his legal career in 1979, working as a lawyer for the Ministry of Finance. He served as chief legal counsel for the minister of health from 1985 to 1988. Until 2003 he served as public prosecutor before the Federal Regional Tribunals of Brasília and Rio de Janeiro.

As he embarked on his career in law, Barbosa Gomes continued his wide-ranging education. He mastered four foreign languages—French, English, German, and Italian. In 1993 he completed a Ph.D. at the University of Paris II, specializing in comparative constitutional law. He is the author of two books, *La Cour Suprême dans le système poli-*

tique Brésilien (The Supreme Court in the Brazilian political system, 1994) and *Ação afirmativa & princípio constitucional da igualdade: O direito como instrumento de transformação social. A experiência dos EUA* (Affirmative action and the constitutional principle of equality: The law as instrument of social transformation—The experience of the United States, 2001). He has worked as a visiting professor of law at UCLA and Columbia University and has been the recipient of several prestigious fellowships, including ones from the Fulbright Program and the Ford Foundation. Barbosa Gomes also has served various organizations as a consultant on human rights issues, with an emphasis on combating racial discrimination.

For much of his career, Barbosa Gomes has been a strong advocate for equal rights and racial equality in Brazil. He has criticized Brazil for being more racially and socially polarized than the United States or Europe. Indeed, he points to the history of affirmative action in the United States as a model that Brazil might follow in trying to narrow inequalities of opportunity for minorities and poor people. He has also defended racial quotas in the most flagrant cases of inequality, such as in hiring practices and in university admissions. In 2003, amid a controversy over new laws requiring racial quotas at state universities, the Brazilian president Luiz Inácio Lula da Silva nominated Barbosa Gomes to become Brazil's first black Supreme Court justice. Barbosa Gomes has vowed to continue his support of legal remedies for social and racial inequality.

See also Politics; Race and Education in Brazil

Bibliography

Carneiro, Luiz Orlando. "Um batalhador pelas ações afirmativas: Barbosa Gomes chega ao STF defendendo espaços para negros." *Jornal do Brasil,* May 11, 2003, p. A6.

Colitt, Raymond. "Brazilian president moves first black into country's top court." *Financial Times,* May 31, 2003, p. 7.

"Comissão do Senado aprova a indicação de Barbosa para STF." *Jornal do Comercio,* May 22, 2003, p. B12.

Gomes, Joaquim Benedito Barbosa. *Ação afirmativa & princípio constitucional da igualdade: O direito como instrumento de transformação social. A experiência dos EUA.* Rio de Janeiro: Renovar, 2001.

La Cour Suprême dans le système politique Brésilien. Paris: LGDJ/Montechrestien, 1994.

JAMES H. SWEET (2005)

Barnett, Marguerite Ross

May 21, 1942
February 26, 1992

Born in Charlottesville, Virginia, Marguerite Ross Barnett, an educator, grew up in Buffalo, New York. She received a bachelor's degree from Antioch College in 1964 and subsequently studied at the University of Chicago, where she received a doctorate in political science in 1972. A specialist in Indian and African-American politics, she taught at Princeton University, Howard University (where she also served as political science department chair), and Columbia University. In 1975 she published *Electoral Politics in the Indian States: Party Systems and Cleavages* and in 1976 *The Politics of Cultural Nationalism in South India.* That same year she coedited *Public Policy for the Black Community: Policies and Perspectives.* In 1983 Barnett was hired by the City University of New York (CUNY) as vice chancellor of academic affairs and served in that post for three years. In 1985 she published *Images of Blacks in Popular Culture: 1865–1955,* a sociological study, and coedited *Race, Sex, and National Origin: Public Attitudes on Desegregation.*

In 1986 Barnett was named chancellor of the University of Missouri–St. Louis. A talented administrator, she succeeded in raising enrollment, firming up standards (including inaugurating an engineering program for undergraduates), and raising funds. She was active in community-based outreach, notably by periodic reports to the community, as well as the Bridge Program, an educational program for poor public school children that in 1991 won the Anderson medal from the American Council on Education as outstanding public school initiative of the year.

In 1990 Barnett was appointed president of the University of Houston, a thirty-two-thousand-student institution, becoming the first African-American woman to head a major university that was not a historically black college. There she continued her commitment to educational reform, offering a "Report to the Community" on the school's future and developing the Texas Center for University-School Partnerships in order to devote university resources to improving public education. In January 1992, suffering from hypoglycemia and cancer, she took a leave of absence from the University of Houston and traveled to Hawaii. She died there a month later.

Barnett's papers are housed at the University of Houston. A memorial scholarship was established in her name to help part-time working students.

See also Education in the United States

Bibliography

Obituary. *New York Times*, February 27, 1992, p. B7.

GREG ROBINSON (1996)
Updated by publisher 2005

Barrow, Errol

January 21, 1920
June 1, 1987

Errol Walton Barrow, Barbados's "Father of Independence," was born to Ruth and Reginald Barrow at St. Lucy, Barbados, on January 21, 1920. His formal education was at Wesley Hall Boys' School and later Harrison College, where he won the Island Scholarship in 1939. With the outbreak of World War II, Barrow abandoned plans for studies in theology in favor of military service in the British Royal Air Force, where he became navigator to the air chief marshal during the Allied occupation of Germany.

After the war Barrow worked briefly in the Colonial Office before pursuing studies at the University of London and the London School of Economics, where he came under the influence of the socialist intellectual Harold Laski, whose views influenced Barrow throughout his public career. In the meantime, Barrow married an American, Carolyn Plaskett, and the couple had two children, Lesley and David. In 1950 he was admitted to the bar in Britain before returning to Barbados, where his radical political views soon gained him membership in the Barbados Labour Party (BLP). He was elected as the senior member for St. George in the 1951 elections.

Barrow later broke with the BLP, amid rumors of an imminent "left-wing" takeover of that party, after which he helped to form the Democratic Labour Party (DLP) in 1955. He was defeated in the 1956 elections, but won a by-election to the constituency of St. John in 1958, which remained his political bailiwick until his death.

The DLP won the general elections of 1961. This placed Barrow at the center of the politics of Barbados and the Anglophone Caribbean for the next fifteen years. He was engaged in the most important national and regional developments of the Anglophone Caribbean during this period. He introduced free education from primary school to university. His aerial "discovery" of a fifty-acre parcel of land at Cave Hill while flying himself over Barbados in search of a site for the third campus of the University of the West Indies, is now part of the lore of that institution. Cave Hill is today the only campus with a view of the Caribbean Sea. Barrow lowered the voting age from twenty-one to eighteen and modernized Barbados's national electoral system. His governments also made important strides in the development of a National Health Service and social security system.

Perhaps most important, Barrow accelerated the process of independence for Barbados after the dissolution of the British West Indies Federation in 1962. After successfully challenging Barbados's colonial establishment, Barrow became the first prime minister of independent Barbados as a Westminster-model constitutional monarchy in the British Commonwealth on November 30, 1966. Later, Barrow pulled Barbados out of the Eastern Caribbean Currency Authority and issued the Barbados dollar instead.

During Barrow's tenure Barbados gained membership in both the United Nations and the Organization of American States. After the demise of the federation, Barrow was one of the original signatories of the treaty establishing the Caribbean Free Trade Area (CARIFTA) in 1968, an organization that later evolved into the Caribbean Community (CARICOM) in 1973, where he also signed the Treaty of Charuaramas on Barbados's behalf on July 4, 1973. In 1972 he was among the leaders of the Anglophone Caribbean who established diplomatic relations with Cuba.

Barrow and the DLP lost the elections of 1976. He spent a decade in the political wilderness, during which he spent time in opposition politics and supervised the construction of the DLP headquarters. He also condemned the American invasion of Grenada in 1983. Barrow and the DLP returned to power in 1986, but after a year, his unexpected death brought an end to his political career.

Barrow was socialized in a family that placed strong emphasis on leadership and public service. In a public career lasting nearly four decades, Barrow and the DLP managed to seize control of the state apparatus in order to allocate its resources for the benefit of the greatest number of Barbadians. This is particularly evident in the areas of education, public housing, tourism development, industrialization, and the general physical infrastructure, which brought Barbados out of the obvious vestiges of its colonial past and irretrievably set it on the path of social development that the country enjoys today.

In recognition of Barrow's contribution to the development of modern Barbados, his likeness appears on the $50 banknotes. His birthday is now a national holiday in Barbados, and in 1998 he was declared a National Hero.

See also Barbados Labour Party

Bibliography

Allahar, Anton, ed. *Caribbean Charisma: Reflections on Leadership, Legitimacy and Populist Politics.* Kingston, Jamaica; Boulder, Col.; and London: Ian Randle Publishers, Lynne Rienner Publishers, 2001.

Beckles, Hilary. *A History of Barbados.* Cambridge: Cambridge University Press, 1990.

Beckles, Hilary, ed. *For Love of Country: The National Heroes of Barbados.* West Terrace, St. Michael, Barbados: Foundation Publishing, 2001.

Carmichael, Trevor, ed. *Barbados: Thirty Years of Independence.* Kingston, Jamaica: Ian Randle Publishers, 1996.

Haniff, Yussuff, ed. *Speeches by Errol Barrow.* London: Hansib Publishing, 1987.

Morgan, Peter. *The Life and Times of Errol Barrow.* Barbados, 1994.

C. M. JACOBS (2005)

Barrow, Joseph Louis

See Louis, Joe

Barrow, Nita

November 15, 1916
December 19, 1995

The sister of one Barbados' national heroes, the cousin of a second, and the niece of a third, Ruth Nita Barrow was born at Nestfield, Saint Lucy, Barbados, the second child and first daughter of the five children born to Reginald and Ruth O'Neale Barrow. Her father, an Anglican clergyman, worked in several Caribbean territories.

In 1928 she was among the first seventy-nine entrants at St. Michael's Girls' School, the first secondary school for black girls in Barbados, graduating in 1934 with a grade one senior school certificate.

Against the wishes of her relatives, in 1935 Barrow enrolled as a student nurse at the Barbados General Hospital, and in midwifery training in Trinidad and Tobago five years later. Following social unrest in many of the islands in the 1930s, the British government allocated greater resources to public health and provided greater employment opportunities for British Caribbean women, particularly in the field of nursing. This policy decision facilitated both Barrow's studies and her career.

Barrow's sense of social justice, which was already evident during her years as a student nurse, was developed in Trinidad and Tobago, where among other activities she became a member of the Young Women's Christian Association (YWCA).

A fellowship at the University of Toronto in 1941 led to other opportunities. An impressive year's work culminated in her being class valedictorian and led to another year's scholarship to study nursing education. This included field work in Jamaica, which led to an appointment there as assistant instructor with the School of Public Health. Barrow became the founder and president of the Nurses Association of Jamaica and a board member of the Jamaica chapter of the YWCA. She later became the first person from the English-speaking Caribbean to be elected to the executive committee of the YWCA World Council.

A fellowship at the Royal College of Nursing at Edinburgh led to a postgraduate course at the Royal College of Nursing at London for training as a ward sister. In 1954 Barrow became the first West Indian matron of the teaching hospital of the University College of the West Indies at Mona, Jamaica. After two years she left to become the first principal nursing officer of Jamaica, the first time in Commonwealth history that the post had been created. She held this position for six years.

Barrow completed a bachelor's degree in nursing at Columbia University, in New York City, in 1963. Contacts there led to an appointment with the Pan-American Health Organisation (PAHO) to direct a survey of Caribbean nursing schools. Visiting each territory enabled her to increase her already large number of contacts throughout the region. After the project was completed, Barrow continued with PAHO as nursing director.

In 1976 Barrow became the first woman and first black director of the Christian Medical Council and the first black president of the World YWCA; she was also awarded an honorary doctor of laws degree by the University of the West Indies.

In 1980 Barrow was made a Dame of the Order of Saint Andrew and Saint George for "extraordinary and outstanding achievement and merit in service to Barbados and humanity at large." An early supporter of the International Council on Adult Education, she was elected president of that body in 1982. This resulted in the creation of the Dame Nita Barrow Award for organizations making significant contributions to the empowerment of women through adult education.

In 1985 Barrow was the only woman member of the Commonwealth Group of Eminent Persons to visit South Africa to broker the transformation from apartheid to majority rule. She was convener of Forum '85, UN Decade for Women, held in Nairobi, Kenya, and was named West Indian of the Year by *Bajan* magazine.

In 1982 she was awarded an honorary doctor of sciences degree by McMaster University, in Canada. In 1986 Barrow was Barbados' representative to the United Nations. In 1987 she received the Caribbean Community's (CARICOM) Women's Award. In 1988 she received the CARICOM Triennial Award for her contribution to the development of women in the region. In 1989 the International Council of Nurses made her the second recipient of the Christiane Reimann Award.

In 1990 Dame Nita Barrow became the first woman governor-general of Barbados. She was a popular head of state until her unexpected death on December 19, 1995. In a long and successful public career, she used the nursing profession to advance the cause of women in Barbados, the Caribbean, and the world at large.

See also Caribbean Community and Common Market (CARICOM); University of the West Indies

Bibliography

Barriteau, Eudine. "The Challenge of Innovative Leadership of a Traditional Women's Organisation: The World YWCA and Ruth Nita Barrow." In *Stronger, Surer, Bolder: Ruth Nita Barrow: Social Change and Social Development,* edited by Eudine Barriteau and Alan Cobley. Cave Hill, Barbados: Centre for Gender and Development Studies, University of the West Indies Press, 2001.

Blackman, Francis. *Dame Nita: Caribbean Woman, World Citizen.* Kingston, Jamaica: Ian Randle, 1995.

Hezekiah, Jocelyn. *Breaking the Glass Ceiling: The Stories of Three Caribbean Nurses.* Kingston, Jamaica: University of the West Indies Press, 2001.

C. M. JACOBS (2005)

Barry, Marion

March 6, 1936

Civil rights activist and politician Marion Shepilov Barry was born to sharecroppers on a cotton plantation near Itta Bena, Mississippi. After his father's murder in 1944, Barry's mother moved the family to Memphis, Tennessee, and remarried. The family lived in poverty and often picked cotton in nearby Mississippi to earn money.

After graduating from high school, Barry enrolled at Le Moyne College in Memphis, where he became president of the campus chapter of the National Association for the Advancement of Colored People (NAACP). In 1958 he graduated as a chemistry major and became a graduate student at Fisk University in Nashville, Tennessee.

At Fisk Barry led several successful student sit-ins against segregated facilities. His leadership led to his election in April 1960 as the first national chair of the Student Nonviolent Coordinating Committee (SNCC). He earned an M.S. in chemistry from Fisk that August and resigned as the chair of SNCC in November, although he remained a member of the group and participated on its executive and finance committees. Pursuing a doctorate in chemistry, Barry took courses at the University of Kansas (1960–1961) and at the University of Tennessee (1961–1964). He relinquished his graduate study to work full-time for SNCC.

In 1964 Barry was assigned to raise funds for SNCC in New York City; he was transferred to Washington, D.C., in June 1965, where he led protests against the Vietnam War, led a boycott against proposed fare increases on district bus lines, and helped organize the Free D.C. Movement aimed at placing control of the district's government in the hands of its black citizens. In August 1967 he helped establish Youth Pride, Incorporated, a self-help organization that created employee-owned businesses in the inner city and offered job training to poor black youths. After the assassination of Dr. Martin Luther King Jr. in April 1968 and the subsequent riots in Washington, D.C., Barry worked to reform the city's economy in a way that would increase African-American control over some local businesses.

Barry's popularity as a political activist helped him get elected to the city's school board in 1971; he became president of the board a year later. In 1974, the first year in which a mayor and city council were elected under district home rule, Barry won a seat on the city council, where he fought against inner-city gentrification and wasteful municipal spending. Campaigning for mayor on these same issues in 1978 (and gaining public sympathy after an attempt on his life that March), Barry narrowly defeated incumbent African-American mayor Walter Washington for the Democratic nomination and won the election against Republican Arthur Fletcher. Barry was not the district's first African-American mayor; that distinction belonged to Washington, who was appointed mayor from 1967 to 1974 and elected mayor under home rule the following term. Barry's election was for many Washington citizens the culmination of the city's civil rights struggle.

Barry's three-term mayoral administration (1979–1991) was credited by many with successfully mediating group conflicts, balancing the city's budget, instituting a second financial accounting system, improving the city's bond rating, and enhancing delivery of city services.

At the same time, Barry's success was undercut by charges of fiscal mismanagement and corruption; in addition, there were allegations of cocaine use in his administration. In October 1990 Barry was convicted of cocaine possession and served a six-month prison sentence. The conviction sparked a controversy because the videotaped evidence against Barry suggested that he may have been the victim of entrapment. Barry and his followers charged the federal prosecutor, Jay Stephens, with conducting a racially biased prosecution. Barry's conviction split his constituency between those who remained loyal and those who felt he had outlasted his usefulness to Washington's black community.

As a result of the controversy, Barry did not run for reelection as mayor in November 1990, but he unsuccessfully ran for an at-large seat on the city council. His loyal followers returned him to a council seat in 1992, and with their support Barry entered the 1994 campaign to unseat incumbent mayor Sharon Pratt Kelly. Barry's cocaine conviction and questions about corruption in his administrations reduced his support among most whites and many middle-class African Americans, but he retained a large enough core of support among African Americans to win the election.

Following a controversial comeback campaign that played heavily on the theme of redemption, Barry was reelected mayor in November 1994, despite heavy opposition by whites and middle-class blacks. His last term was marked by scandals over political favoritism and the city's near-bankruptcy. During his fourth term, most of Barry's power was reassigned by Congress to a control board, and he did not seek reelection. In 2002 he sought a city council seat, but withdrew. Barry has been treated for prostate cancer, diabetes, and high blood pressure. In 2004 he was elected to a city council seat.

See also National Association for the Advancement of Colored People (NAACP); Student Nonviolent Coordinating Committee (SNCC)

Bibliography

Agronsky, Jonathan I. Z. *Marion Barry: The Politics of Race.* Latham, N.Y.: British American, 1991.

Janofsky, Michael. "Ex-Mayor Barry Rises from Ashes." *New York Times,* August 1, 1994.

Persons, Georgia, and Lenneal Henderson. "Mayor of the Colony: Effective Mayoral Leadership as a Matter of Public Perception." *National Political Science Review* 2 (1990): 145–153.

Zinn, Howard. *SNCC: The New Abolitionists.* Boston: Beacon, 1965.

MANLEY ELLIOTT BANKS II (1996)
Updated by author 2005

Barthé, Richmond

January 28, 1901
March 6, 1989

Sculptor Richmond Barthé was born in Bay Saint Louis, Mississippi, to Richmond Barthé and Marie Clementine Roboteau. His father died at the age of twenty-two, when Richmond was only one month old. Left with a devoted mother whose influence on his early life and his aesthetic development was significant, Barthé credited her with providing experiences that nurtured his desire to become an artist.

At the age of twelve, Barthé's work was shown at a county fair in Mississippi. He continued to demonstrate his remarkable talent, and at age eighteen, having moved to New Orleans, he won his first prize, a blue ribbon for a drawing that he entered in a parish (county) competition.

In New Orleans Barthé's work attracted the attention of Lyle Saxon of the *Times-Picayune.* Saxon tried unsuccessfully to register Barthé in a New Orleans art school. The refusal was based on the young man's color rather than on his artistic ability. This early rejection made Barthé more determined than ever to become an artist of note.

In 1924, with the aid of a Catholic priest, the Rev. Harry Kane, Barthé, with little formal training and a great deal of ambition and talent, was admitted to the school of the Art Institute of Chicago. During his four years there he followed the curriculum designed for majors in painting. However, during his senior year he was introduced to sculpture by his anatomy teacher, Charles Schroeder, who also suggested that a better understanding of the third dimension might improve his knowledge of painting. This, according to Barthé, was the beginning of his long career as a sculptor.

In February 1929, following his graduation from the institute, Barthé moved to New York. The following two decades saw him build a reputation that would be the envy of many of his peers. The 1930s and 1940s would see him rise to great prominence and gain high praise for his work from both critics and collectors.

By 1934 Barthé was granted his first solo show at the Caz Delbo Galleries in New York City. Numerous other exhibitions and important commissions followed thereafter. His works were added to important collections such as the Whitney Museum of American Art (*African Dancer*), the Metropolitan Museum of Art, the Pennsylvania Museum of Art, the Virginia Museum of Fine Arts, and the Museum of the Art Institute of Chicago (*The Boxer*).

Barthé's commissions included a bas relief of Arthur Brisbane for New York's Central Park and an eight-by-eighty-foot frieze, *Green Pastures: The Walls of Jericho,* for the Harlem River Housing Project. Other commissions included two portrait busts and a garden sculpture for the Edgar Kaufman house (*Falling Water*), designed by architect Frank Lloyd Wright; a Booker T. Washington portrait bust for the Hall of Fame of New York University; an Othello modeled after Paul Robeson for Actor's Equity; and the General Toussaint-Louverture Monument, Port-au-Prince, Haiti.

In 1947 Barthé moved from New York to Jamaica, West Indies, to escape the tense environment of big-city life, which was taking its toll on his creative energies. By this time he was considered to be one of the leading "moderns" of American art, but he decided to abandon this role at the peak of his career for the calm and peaceful countryside of rural Jamaica, where he lived until 1969. Barthé later traveled to Europe, where he spent several years enjoying the company of old friends and immersing himself in the art and culture of the Italian Renaissance masters Donatello and Michelangelo, whose works he revered and to whom he owed a great debt.

In 1976 Barthé returned to the United States. Following a brief stay in Queens, New York, he moved to Altadena, California, where he lived until his death in 1989.

See also Robeson, Paul; Washington, Booker T.

Bibliography

Catlett, Elizabeth. Interview with Barthé. *International Review of African-American Art* 23 (October 1982).

"Richmond Barthé." In *A History of African-American Artists, From 1792 to the Present,* by Romare Bearden and Harry Henderson, pp. 136–146. New York: Pantheon Books, 1993.

"Richmond Barthé: Sculptor." *Crisis* (June 1948): 164–165.

"Sculptor." *Ebony* (November 1949).

SAMELLA LEWIS (1996)

BASEBALL

African Americans have been involved in baseball, or "base ball" as it was first known, since its earliest days. Some enslaved blacks on southern plantations played baseball during their time off from work, and there were scattered African-American amateur baseball players in the Northeast before the Civil War. Games were played in Brooklyn between the Colored Union Club and the Unknown Club in 1860 and also between the Unknown Club and the Monitors in 1862. African Americans also played for the Philadelphia Pythians, founded in 1867 by civil rights activist Octavius Catto and businessman and educator Jacob C. White, Jr. The Pythians sought admission to the National Association of Base Ball Players, but the nominating committee unanimously voted to exclude "any club which may be composed of one or more colored persons."

In the nineteenth century, black teams, which mainly had middle class members, competed with black and sometimes white teams. In 1869, the Pythians played and defeated the white Philadelphia City Items in a series of games, while the Brooklyn Uniques and the Philadelphia Excelsiors were matched for the "Championship of Colored Clubs." There were even interracial contests in New Orleans, where thirteen black clubs played in a tournament in 1875. By the late 1870s, a number of blacks played for white college nines, including Oberlin's Fleet and Weldy Walker, Marietta College's John L. Harrison, and Dartmouth's Julius P. Haynes. In the 1890s, James Francis Gregory served as captain for Amherst's nine, while his brother Eugene pitched for Harvard.

Early Professional Baseball

The National Association of Professional Baseball Players, established in 1871, never formally banned black teams and players, but it and its successor, the National League, formed in 1876, adhered to a tacit prohibition. Seventy-three African Americans competed at various levels of minor-league play during the nineteenth century. John "Bud" Fowler was probably the first black professional ballplayer, pitching for Lynn, Massachusetts in the International Association in 1878. Six years later he played for Stillwater, Minnesota, of the Northwestern League. In 1885 Fowler played for Keokuk, Iowa, in the Western League, and for Topeka of the same league one year later. He was released after pressure from white players led to the exclusion of blacks from that league. Writing of Fowler's predicament, *Sporting Life* commented: "He is one of the best general players in the country, and if he had a white face would be playing with the best of them . . . the poor fellow's color is against him. With his splendid abilities he would long ago have been on some good club had his color been white instead of black. Those who know say there is no better second baseman in the country."

In 1883, the Toledo, Ohio, team of the Northwestern League hired catcher Moses Fleetwood "Fleet" Walker. Walker, a minister's son from Steubenville, Ohio, had attended college at Oberlin and Michigan. That season, Adrian "Cap" Anson, player-manager of the National

League's Chicago White Stockings, threatened to cancel an exhibition game with Toledo if Walker played, but owner Albert G. Spalding wanted the guaranteed money, so the game was played. The next year, Toledo joined the American Association, a rival of the National League, and Fleet Walker became the first black major leaguer.

Walker faced enormous obstacles. Pitcher Tony Mullane later admitted that Walker "was the best catcher I ever worked with, but I disliked a Negro and whenever I had to pitch to him I used anything I wanted without looking at his signals." In Richmond, Virginia, six fans (using pseudonyms) wrote a letter threatening him with a beating by a mob of seventy-five men if he played. Walker was no longer on the team by then, and the threat went unchallenged. In fifty-one games, Walker batted .263, and he was praised for his catching. At the end of the season, brother Weldy Walker joined Toledo for five games. The two Walkers were the only African-Americans known to have played in the majors before Jackie Robinson.

In 1885 Fleet Walker played for Cleveland in the Western League and then Waterbury in the Eastern League. Two years later he joined Newark of the International League (IL), then just one step below the majors. There were seven African Americans in the IL, playing on six of the league's ten teams. The most notable of these players were pitcher George Stovey of Newark, who set an all-time IL record with 34 wins, and second baseman Frank Grant of Buffalo, considered the best black player of the nineteenth century. Grant batted .366 in 1887, leading the league in doubles, triples, and home runs.

However, black players in the IL faced widespread abuse from racist white players, management, and fans. Ballplayers feared that the presence of blacks would lower the status of their occupation and lower salary levels. They threw balls at African American players, and often spiked them on the base paths. Frank Grant allegedly developed wooden shin guards to protect his legs from injury by white base runners. White teammates gave wrong advice to blacks and shunned them off the field. Some white players even refused to pose with black teammates for pictures. The media reinforced the derogatory public image of black players. Pictures in *Harper's Weekly* depicted them as lazy and stupid, and *The Official Baseball Record* referred to them as "coons." In July 1887, the IL league's team owners bowed to pressure from white players, agreeing not to sign additional black players and limiting the active black players to two per team. There were no African Americans in the IL after 1889.

Several all-black professional teams were formed in the early 1880s, including the Philadelphia Orions and the St. Louis Black Stockings. The best of these clubs was the Cuban Giants, founded in 1885 by Frank Thompson, headwaiter at Babylon, N.Y.'s Argyle Hotel and his partner and team manager, S. K. McGovern, a headwaiter and journalist. The club, composed originally of hotel staff, called itself "Cuban" to alleviate prejudice (which was often less pronounced in the case of dark-skinned foreigners) and "Giants" after New York's National League team. The nickname became a common one among black teams, with ball clubs such as the Philadelphia Giants, the (New York) Lincoln Giants, and the Chicago Giants. In 1886 white businessmen Walter Cook and J. M. Bright owned the Cuban Giants. Players earned wages of $48 to $72 per month depending on their position (pitchers and catchers made the most, outfielders the least), good wages in comparison to what other black workers earned. The Cuban Giants played black teams, college squads, and even major league clubs, although the American Association champion St. Louis Browns backed out of a scheduled contest in 1887. In 1889, the Cuban Giants and another black team, the New York Gothams, were members of the otherwise all-white Middle States League. The creation of the six-team Southern League of Colored Baseballists in 1886 marked the first effort to form a black baseball league, but the arrangement lasted only a few games. The nine-team League of Colored Baseball Clubs was organized one year later, but disbanded after only one week.

In 1887, the same year the International League restricted blacks, "Cap" Anson refused to schedule a game with the Newark team of the International League if Stovey played. Newark complied, benching Stovey. At the time, conventional wisdom held that Anson was primarily responsible for pushing blacks out of organized baseball. However, it seems clear that Anson's actions merely reflected widespread white opinion. As *Sporting News* commented in 1889, "Race prejudice exists in professional baseball to a marked degree, and the unfortunate son of Africa who makes his living as a member of a team of white professionals has a rocky road to travel." That season the Cuban Giants and the Gothams of New York played in the otherwise all white-Middle States League. The last all-black team to play in a white League was the Acme Colored Giants of Celeron, N.Y. in the white Iron and Coal League in 1898. Overall seventy African Americans played in the white leagues in the nineteenth century. The last was Bill Galloway, who played five games in the Canadian League in 1899.

Black Baseball in the Early Twentieth Century

African Americans were big baseball fans and countless black youths played baseball at the turn of the century.

Cover of the first issue of the **Colored Baseball & Sports Monthly,** ***September 1, 1934.*** PHOTOGRAPHS AND PRINTS DIVISION, SCHOMBURG CENTER FOR RESEARCH IN BLACK CULTURE, THE NEW YORK PUBLIC LIBRARY, ASTOR, LENOX AND TILDEN FOUNDATIONS.

Prominent blacks ranging from activist Ida B. Wells to poet James Weldon Johnson were players or fans. It is not known if any African Americans passed for white and played in organized baseball. In 1901 Baltimore Orioles manager John McGraw tried to pass Charlie Grant as white during spring training, but his ruse was discovered, and Grant was released. Ten years later the Cincinnati Reds signed two Cubans, allegedly "Castilian," though one was dark skinned; and a few years later, the Reds hired another Cuban whose brother played on a Negro team. In 1916 pitcher Jimmy Claxton, of mixed black and Indian ancestry, played two games for the Oakland Oaks of the Pacific Coast League before being released.

Chicago established itself as a leading center of black ball with several fine semipro teams, most notably the Leland Giants, the best team in the otherwise all-white City League in the late 1800s. There were several black army teams, including a squad from the all-black 25th Infantry (later famous for its involvement in the Brownsville, Texas incident of 1906), which beat all comers in the Philippines. Collegiate ball clubs existed at Howard University and elsewhere since the era of Reconstruction. In the 1890s, Atlanta became a center of college baseball, with competing teams from local black colleges, including Atlanta Baptist Seminary (now Morehouse College), Atlanta University, Clark University, and Morris Brown College.

Players on the semipro black teams played well over 100 games, and earned up to $100 a month. They played on Sundays in their home city, and on other days "barnstormed," touring out of town, playing other black teams, college squads, town nines, and semipros. They played occasional post-season games against major leaguers and wintered in California. The top clubs included the Cuban Giants, Philadelphia's Cuban X Giants, and the Leland Giants, who went 110–10 in 1907 and vied for "The Colored Championship of the World." In 1911 star pitcher Andrew "Rube" Foster, nicknamed for outpitching New York Giants star Rube Marquard in an exhibition game, founded the outstanding Chicago American Giants with his white partner John Schorling. Three years later, J. K. Wilkinson, a white man, put together the powerful All-Nations team, which included African Americans, whites, Latinos, and Native Americans. In 1920, Wilkinson combined players from the All-Nations team with members of the black 25th Infantry Squad Army team to form the famous Kansas City Monarchs. Top players then included John Henry Lloyd, a shortstop for the Indianapolis ABC's who was dubbed "the Black Honus Wagner," and "Rube" Foster, who one year went 54–1 pitching for the Cuban X-Giants. Another star of that era was "Smokey Joe" Williams of the Lincoln Giants, who compiled a 6–4–2 record against white major leaguers in exhibition games, including a three-hit shutout against the National League champion Philadelphia Phillies in 1915.

The Negro Leagues

There were a couple of unsuccessful efforts to form a black league in the early 1900s. Then in 1920, Rube Foster, who had built the Chicago American Giants into a financially successful enterprise, formed the National Association of Professional Baseball Clubs (popularly known as the Negro National League). Foster's organizational genius and astute understanding of the promotional possibilities inherent in league play, plus his desire to wrest economic power and leadership over black baseball from white booking agents, led him to put together the first lasting Negro league. The league was composed of six teams located in midwestern cities with significant black populations. The association was intended to be entirely black-owned, but the popular appeal of Wilkinson's Kansas City Monarchs led Foster to include that club also. The new league was an almost immediate success, with outfielders like Oscar Charleston of Indianapolis ("the Black Babe Ruth") and John Lloyd, and pitchers like "Smokey Joe" Williams and Wilbur "Bullet" Rogan of the Kansas City Monarchs.

The Negro National League (NNL) was challenged in 1923 by white booking agent Nat Strong, who created the Eastern Colored League with six teams, four white-owned, in eastern cities. After a period of mutual bad feeling and raids on each other's players, the two leagues observed a truce and organized a structure similar to that of white leagues, with champions of the two leagues competing in a black World Series. However, since ball clubs sometimes preferred lucrative barnstorming exhibitions to scheduled league games, teams played uneven numbers of games, so league standings were hard to determine. There was also a third league for black players in the 1920s, the short-lived Southern Negro League, which could not compete financially with the others. A few independent teams, notably Pittsburgh's Homestead Grays, refused to join the Negro Leagues but played exhibition games with league teams. The Eastern Colored League folded in 1928, and some teams were absorbed into the NNL.

The Great Depression took a heavy toll on black baseball. The NNL, already weakened by Rube Foster's 1926 breakdown and his subsequent death in 1930, was unable to meet its debts and folded in 1931. During the following two years, teams disbanded or survived precariously as local semipro or touring barnstorming teams depended on white bookers for survival. Some players went to play in the Caribbean or Mexico.

In 1933, a new Negro National League, containing six teams (later eight), was reformed under the guidance of Gus Greenlee, a prosperous "numbers" (an illegal lottery) king in Pittsburgh who sought a legitimate investment for his money. Greenlee owned the Pittsburgh Crawfords and most of the other teams in the league were also owned by black numbers operators. Starting in 1934 the NNL played two half-seasons, and the winners of each half-season met in the Negro World Series. The Crawfords dominated at first, as the free-spending Greenlee recruited LeRoy "Satchel" Paige, Josh Gibson, Oscar Charleston, James "Cool Papa" Bell, and Judy Johnson, all future Hall-of-Famers, to play on his team, but other clubs eventually evened the balance of power within the leagues. In 1937, the six-team Negro American League (NAL) was organized. The NAL was mainly white-owned and included the Kansas City Monarchs, who had previously declined to join the revamped NNL. The NNL concentrated on eastern teams, with the NAL operating in the west. The respective league champions met each other in the Colored World Series. However, the biggest event in black baseball in the 1930s was not the Colored World Series but the East–West All-Star game, first played in Chicago in 1933, shortly after Major League Baseball held its first All-Star Game, also in Chicago at Comiskey Park. The annual event routinely attracted crowds of 30,000 to 40,000. This showcase event was covered nationally in the black press, especially the *Chicago Defender* and the *Pittsburgh Courier,* which featured extensive coverage of black baseball. The East–West game became a national social event for black Americans.

In the 1930s, the NNL season began in the south with a brief spring training, followed by barnstorming tours as clubs traveled north. The exhibition games furthered team development and strategy, were a necessary source of revenue, and helped cement the relationship between players and the local black populations. In April or May the teams arrived in their home cities and commenced league play. Black urban populations were not large enough to sustain more than a 70 game season, and the high unemployment rate during the Depression further hurt the gate. Black teams had to be innovative, and around 1932, the Kansas City Monarchs became one of the first teams to use portable lights for night baseball. Night games encouraged a larger black working class audience, appealing to many laborers who could attend games in the evening after work. League games were usually on the weekends, but teams traveled extensively during the week to bolster incomes with exhibitions throughout the season, sometimes playing three or four games per day. Clubs usually traveled by bus or in a caravan of cars, often over bad rural roads. Few black nines owned their own field, which created scheduling problems (although when business picked up in the 1940s, several teams were able to rent major or minor league ballparks.) When the season ended in September, or after the Colored World Series, the better Negro Leagues players went on to play in winter leagues in Mexico, Cuba, the Dominican Republic, and California.

The Negro Leagues had a hard time surviving the poverty created by the Depression, and problems were exacerbated by mismanagement and poor planning. During the late 1930s the average player made $100 to $150 a month. Since they commonly played without formal contracts, players often jumped teams in search of better pay. In 1937 Gibson, Paige and Bell all left their teams to play in the Dominican Republic for the team sponsored by dictator Rafael Trujillo.

The Negro Leagues games were exciting to watch. While there were power hitters, most notably Josh Gibson of the Pittsburgh Crawfords and Homestead Grays, runs

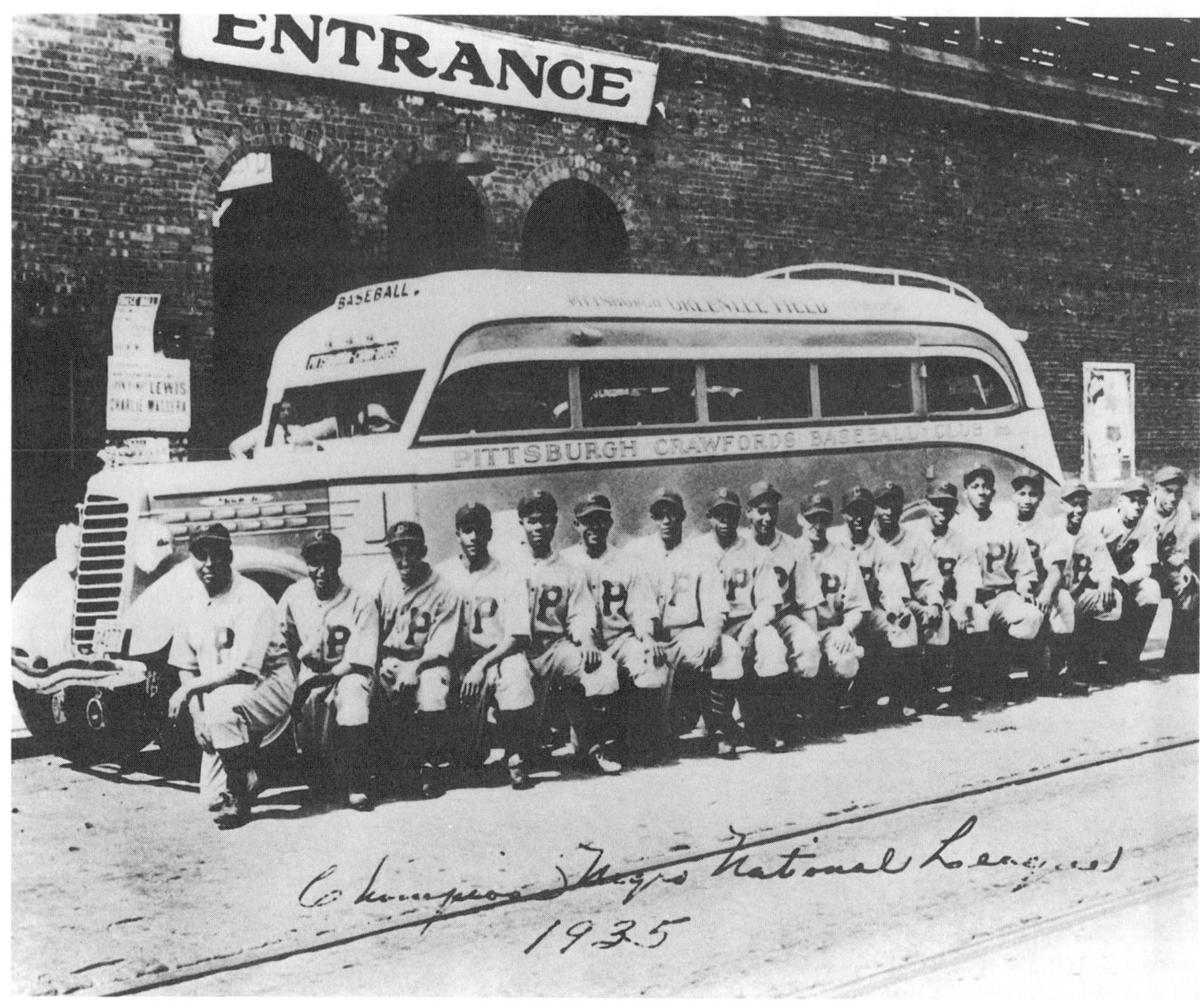

The 1935 Pittsburgh Crawfords. *The Crawfords, a Negro Leagues baseball team that is considered among the greatest in the history of the sport, featured five (future) Hall of Fame members: Oscar Charleston, Judy Johnson, James "Cool Papa" Bell, Josh Gibson, and Leroy "Satchel" Paige.* PHOTOGRAPHS AND PRINTS DIVISION, SCHOMBURG CENTER FOR RESEARCH IN BLACK CULTURE, THE NEW YORK PUBLIC LIBRARY, ASTOR, LENOX AND TILDEN FOUNDATIONS.

were often hard to come by. Games depended, more than in white leagues, on pitching, defense, and speed. Pitchers like "Satchel" Paige of the Kansas City Monarchs worked frequently and were reliant not only on speed but also on trick pitches to beat opposing teams. There was little money for equipment, so scuffed and loaded balls remained in play. The spitball and similar pitches, banned in the major leagues in 1920, remained legal in the Negro Leagues. Speed was also emphasized in Negro League play, and bunts, stolen bases, and hit-and-run plays were common strategies.

Another difference between white and black baseball was showmanship. Black players were conscious of their role as entertainers. Batters might begin their at-bat with their back to home plate, and then turn around to hit the ball. Satchel Paige was known to occasionally call in the outfielders, and then proceed to strike out the side. Paige was so popular that the Kansas City Monarchs raised revenue by loaning out Paige, who earned $37,000 in 1941, to other teams. The Indianapolis Clowns (previously the Ethiopian Clowns), an independent black team whose players clowned and pulled trick plays in the manner of basketball's Harlem Globetrotters, were such a financial attraction that despite their unserious reputation, they were invited to join the Negro American League in 1938.

By the 1940s, Negro League baseball was one of the most successful black businesses of the Jim Crow era. Good players could earn $300 a month, while superstar Josh Gibson got $1,000. The teams were profitable, earning about $5,000–$15,000 each in 1943, and boosted the business of related black-owned enterprises. As a cultural institution, Negro League baseball was ubiquitous throughout black America. The games provided an important source of recreation and local pride, and were choice social events. The barnstorming tradition meant that teams played wherever there was a sizeable black population, and indeed in many places, such as in the Dakotas or the Canadian prairie provinces, the local populace's only contact with blacks was via the black teams that came to town every summer.

Despite the hard life and the rigorous travel and playing schedules that ballplayers had to endure, the leagues had a certain glamour. The players were popular heroes of the first magnitude in northern black communities. Black fans especially idolized them because of their victories over white players in exhibition games. They were also a particularly cosmopolitan group, akin to other black entertainers of the period. These celebrities were equally at home in the small-town rural world of the Deep South, staying in homes of local community members when they visited southern towns, and in the big cities of the North with their vibrant social and cultural life. Also, the many darker-skinned Latinos, such as Martin Dihigo and Luis Tiant, Sr., who played in the leagues gave them an international flavor, buttressed by the sojourns of Negro League stars in Latin America, where they mingled freely with the political and economic leadership of those countries like other celebrities.

The integration of professional baseball, beginning with Jackie Robinson in 1946, plus the coming of televised games, spelled the end of the Negro Leagues. Black fans made it clear that they preferred seeing their heroes compete in the newly integrated major leagues rather than in all-black leagues. As early as 1947, the Negro League teams on the eastern seaboard ("Jackie Robinson country") suffered severe financial losses as black fans deserted the Negro National League. The last East–West classic was played in 1950, and the NNL folded after the following season. The Negro American League, whose franchises tended to be in midwestern states, further from major league ball clubs, continued to play on a reduced schedule. In a move to increase attention in 1953, the NAL's Indianapolis Clowns signed a woman, Toni Stone, who played 50 games at second base and hit .253. During the 1950s, major league teams moved west and NAL teams could not compete financially for talented players. The NAL folded in 1960, and the Indianapolis Clowns returned to their independent status, touring small towns and playing semipro teams through the 1980s.

During the 1970s, African American and white interest in the Negro Leagues was awakened, partly by the book and documentary film *Only the Ball Was White* (1969). The Baseball Hall of Fame created a Negro League Committee, and 24 players out of an estimated 2,600 who played in the Negro Leagues have been inducted, including: Rube Foster, Satchel Paige, Josh Gibson, Cool Papa Bell, Judy Johnson, Buck Leonard, Oscar Charleston, Monte Irvin, Martin Dihigo, Ray Dandridge, and John Henry Lloyd. In 1990, the Negro League Baseball Museum was created in Kansas City, Missouri, and the Negro Leagues Players Association was established in New York.

Integration

By the 1930s, major leaguers and baseball experts recognized the skill of Negro Leaguers, especially in exhibition contests against major league baseball players. A movement began in that decade to secure integration, promoted particularly by baseball writers. White journalists Westbrook Pegler, Jimmy Powers, and Shirley Povich recognized black prowess in baseball and the accomplishments of other black sportsmen such as Joe Louis and Jesse Owens, and called for integration. Black colleagues, including Wendell Smith of the *Pittsburgh Courier,* Sam Lacy of the *Baltimore Afro-American,* and Joe Bostic of the *People's Voice* (Harlem) were ardent advocates for integration. Communist writers, notably Lester Rodney, the white sports editor of the Daily Worker, also played a role in publicizing the issue. Civil rights activists demanded tryouts for Negro Leaguers, collected petitions, and picketed ballparks.

The Lords of Baseball did not support integration. Commissioner Judge Kenesaw Mountain Landis, a Midwesterner who served from 1920 to 1944, disingenuously maintained that there was no rule against blacks in organized baseball. He was long criticized as an ardent foe of integration, but recent scholarship has suggested that he was not a major factor in blocking integration, which was prevented primarily because of team owners. The baseball magnates worried that fans would lose interest in organized baseball if there was integration, that black players would be opposed by their white colleagues (while some players were racist, a poll of major leaguers in the late 1930s indicated that 80 percent did not object to integration), and that severe social problems would emerge, especially during spring training in the South. Furthermore, in 1943, Larry MacPhail, president of the Brooklyn Dodgers, claimed that integration would kill off the Negro Leagues, a valuable source of ballpark rental fees for many major league teams. This assertion was challenged by white Newark Eagles owner Effa Manley, the only female owner in the Negro Leagues, but many other Negro League owners opposed integration, fearing rightly that it would destroy their business.

In 1943, at the annual baseball meetings, African Americans led by Paul Robeson were granted the opportunity to speak to owners about integration, but made no headway. That year, entrepreneur Bill Veeck tried unsuccessfully to purchase the Philadelphia Phillies, and later claimed he would have stocked the team with black players but that Landis had blocked the sale. However, recent scholarship disputes Veeck's assertion.

Ultimately, World War II tipped the balance, causing Americans to reevaluate the meaning of democracy. It was difficult to fight for freedom overseas while neglecting the same principles at home. Furthermore, when the major leagues, faced with a shortage of players, contracted players who would not normally be given a chance to compete, such as teenagers and handicapped players like one-armed Pete Gray, the exclusion of blacks seemed more glaring. Judge Landis's death in December 1944 removed an important obstacle to integration. The new commissioner, former Kentucky governor and senator Albert "Happy" Chandler, was subjected to pressure for integration from labor unions, civil rights leaders, and politicians. On opening day in 1945, one banner outside Yankee Stadium read, "If We Can Stop Bullets, Why Not Balls?" The demonstrations led to several tryouts for black players but no jobs. In Boston, Alderman Isadore Muchnick threatened to block the Red Sox's Sunday baseball license unless they held tryouts for black players. The tryouts were held, but were a sham.

In the summer of 1945, the crucial first step toward integration was taken by President Branch Rickey of the Brooklyn Dodgers. He secretly investigated Negro League talent under the guise of scouting for a new Brooklyn Brown Dodgers Negro League team. Rickey knew that the first African American in the majors had to be an excellent all-around athlete who could maintain a high level of performance despite certain abuse and pressure, and decided that the best candidate was Jackie Robinson of the Kansas City Monarchs, a good player though hardly a star. Robinson grew up in an interracial community in California, where he had been an outstanding all-around athlete and an All-American football player at UCLA. Furthermore, he had been an officer in the Army, and was married. After a stressful interview with Rickey, in which he promised not to challenge racist attacks, Robinson was signed on October 33, 1945. Rickey's action was unanimously opposed by other club owners.

In 1946, Robinson played professional baseball for the Montreal Royals, the Dodgers' top farm team. Spring training in Florida proved a trying experience, as Robinson had difficulty finding meals and accommodation and was once even ordered off the field by a local sheriff, but when the club moved north conditions eased. For a time, he was joined by John Wright and Roy Partlow, Negro League veterans, but they were eventually demoted to Trois Rivières, Quebec (Class C). Robinson was enormously successful, leading the Class AAA International League with a .349 batting average and in runs scored with 119. The Dodgers also had two other African-American minor leaguers, catcher Roy Campanella and pitcher Don Newcombe, who played for Nashua, N.H. (Class B).

In 1947, Jackie Robinson joined the Brooklyn Dodgers following spring training in Cuba, where race relations were less hostile than in Florida. He encountered discrimination from teammates, who originally petitioned to keep him out. Rickey offered to trade any player who did not wish to play alongside Robinson. Opponents, particularly members of the Philadelphia Phillies and St. Louis Cardinals, threatened to strike, but were warned by Commissioner Chandler that any player who protested in that manner would be suspended. Robinson turned out to be a great gate attraction, and had a superb first year, despite being moved to an unfamiliar position, first base. He led the Dodgers to the National League pennant and won the first Rookie of the Year Award. A handful of other blacks also played that year, including pitcher Dan Bankhead for the Dodgers. Larry Doby, one of the Negro Leagues' top prospects, became the first African American in the American League when Cleveland Indians' owner Bill Veeck purchased his contract for $10,000 from the Newark Eagles in the summer of 1947. This purchase was an exception to the general pattern of uncompensated raids that major league clubs were beginning to make on Negro League teams, whose players had no reserve clause binding them to their teams. Later in the season, Henry Thompson and Willard Brown were briefly brought up by the St. Louis Browns to increase attendance, but neither did well and they were demoted after a month.

In 1948, the Dodgers called up Roy Campanella, and late in the season, the Cleveland Indians added forty-two year old pitcher Satchel Paige, a twenty-two year veteran of the Negro Leagues. Paige, like most other black players, took a substantial salary cut to compete in the major leagues. His contribution, however, was less significant than that of Doby, who batted .301 and helped lead the Indians to the World Championship.

The following year, Don Newcombe of the Dodgers was named Rookie of the Year, Jackie Robinson was named National League Most Valuable Player, and he, Doby, and Campanella made the All-Star teams. However, the major leagues had room only for stars and were not

Black major league baseball stars from the Brooklyn Dodgers and Cleveland Indians, pictured together at Ebbets Field in Brooklyn, July 24, 1950. *From left are Jackie Robinson, Larry Doby, Don Newcombe, Luke Easter, and Roy Campanella. In 1949, Robinson, Doby, Newcombe, and Campanella became the first blacks to play in Major League Baseball's All-Star Game.* AP/WIDE WORLD PHOTOS. REPRODUCED BY PERMISSION.

interested in older players, with the exception of Paige. There were blacks in every Class AAA and A league that year. However, many, including Ray Dandridge, an all-time Negro League star who hit .364 for Minneapolis (of the Class AAA American Association), started in leagues beneath their ability.

Within the next few years, lower minor leagues and other areas of organized baseball outside the South also integrated. Even the All-American Girls Baseball League discussed integrating its teams in the years before its demise in 1954. The integration of southern teams in the minors (there were no major league teams in the deep South until 1965) began in 1952 in Florida, the Upper South, and the Southwest, because of blacks' superior play and their ability to attract crowds. A major breakthrough occurred in 1953 when the Class A South Atlantic (Sally) League, which had teams in Florida, Georgia, and Alabama, integrated with three blacks, including Henry "Hank" Aaron with Jacksonville. The Cotton States League integrated in 1954, with blacks playing for Hot Springs, Arkansas, and Meridian, Mississippi. After the *Brown v. Board of Education of Topeka, Kansas* decision in 1954, race relations became more hostile in the South, and integrated baseball became a threat to white supremacy. Integration continued, however, though at a slower pace. By 1955, the only high-level minor league without blacks was the Southern Association (AA). Nat Peeples, who appeared in two games for Atlanta, was the only African American to play in the league, which disbanded in 1961. In 1957 Texas League nines were barred by Louisiana law from playing their black players in Shreveport. African-American fans responded by boycotting the league, with the result that the league dropped the Louisiana franchise.

The pace of integration in the major leagues was slow, and as late as September 1953, only six teams had black players. Many whites undoubtedly agreed with St. Louis

Cardinals owner Sam Breadon, who in the late 1940s expressed his belief that only a handful of black players could be talented enough to make the major leagues. Teams avoided hiring veteran black ballplayers, and sought only young men with star potential and a clean image. Players considered too proud or "uppity," like Yankee minor leaguer Vic Power, faced great difficulties. Between September 1953 and early 1954, six more teams integrated, but the champion New York Yankees refused to integrate until 1955, when catcher Elston Howard joined the team, and it was not until July 21, 1959, that the last holdout, the Boston Red Sox, brought Elijah "Pumpsie" Green to the majors. Once teams were integrated, they did not go out of their way to assure their black players service at restaurants and hotels. Players of different races were rarely roommates, and teams with more than one African-American player always roomed blacks together.

African Americans in Major League Baseball after 1960

In the years since integration, African Americans have starred in major league baseball. In the National League, the first of the two major leagues to integrate, African Americans soon won five straight Rookie of the Year Awards (1949–1953) and seven straight Most Valuable Player (MVP) Awards (1953–1959). Blacks and Latinos, most of whom had been too dark-skinned for the major leagues before integration, soon revolutionized the game, introducing an emphasis on speed and base running in addition to power hitting. Between 1949 and 2004, white players led the NL in stolen bases just four times, and in the AL only three from 1951–2004. Maury Wills broke Ty Cobb's record by stealing 104 bases in 1962, before his total was exceeded by Lou Brock, who stole 118 in 1974 and a record 938 during his career, which included 3,023 hits. Brock's records were exceeded in turn by Rickey Henderson, who set the single-season mark with 130 steals in 1982 and 1,406 total for his career.

Black African Americans and Black Latinos have won scores of batting titles, home run championships, and MVP awards. They have included four of the top five lifetime home run leaders: Henry Aaron, the all-time leader in home runs (755), runs batted in (2,297), and extra-base hits (1,477); Barry Bonds, seven time MVP, Willie Mays, and Frank Robinson, a Triple Crown Winner (1966) and the first player to win the Most Valuable Player award in both leagues. Among pitchers, in 1968 Bob Gibson attained a 1.12 ERA, by far the lowest since World War I, and is second all-time in World Series wins and strikeouts (holding the single-game World Series strikeout record of 17). Ferguson Jenkins won 284 games and amassed 3,192 strikeouts. By 2005, more than forty players of color had been inducted into the Baseball Hall of Fame.

Among North American blacks, representation in the major leagues reached its proportionate share of the national population in the late 1950s (12 percent). The first all-black starting team played for the Pittsburgh Pirates in 1967. The percentage of black Americans in the major leagues peaked at 27 percent in 1975. By 1995, blacks were down to 19 percent, and in 2002 were just 10 percent of all major leaguers. The waning African-American presence in baseball reflects reduced black interest in the sport.

Baseball, like other sports, has been an avenue of African-American social mobility. A study made during the late 1980s of major leaguers born since 1940 found that five-sixths of blacks (83.3 percent) had blue-collar backgrounds while three-fourths of white players came from white-collar backgrounds. Until the 1970s, black players generally earned less than white players of equal ability. By the mid-1980s, African-American players made more money per capita than white players, and race was no longer considered a factor in their compensation.

However, discrimination has continued in many areas. Blacks have long complained of informal team quotas and the fact that mediocre black players were removed from teams, while white nonstarters were retained. Blacks have also been slotted by position. Black pitchers and catchers (positions which are often considered centers of leadership and intellectual challenge) have been disproportionately rare.

Many blacks still consider racism prevalent in the baseball world. In the early 1970s, when Henry Aaron was challenging Babe Ruth's home run record, he received hate mail and racial threats. In the 1980s, the Equal Employment Opportunity Commission found that Boston Red Sox coach Tommy Harper was fired after he complained that the Florida country club, which served as the team's spring training headquarters, excluded blacks. In 1993 Cincinnati Reds owner Marge Schott was suspended for racial slurs. During the summer of 1998, when new season home run records were set, many blacks questioned whether the achievements of Chicago Cubs slugger Sammy Sosa, a dark-skinned Dominican, were being ignored by Americans due to racial factors.

Off-the-field opportunities in baseball have slowly improved. In 1966, Emmett Ashford became the first black umpire in the major leagues. The issue of blacks in management positions got considerable attention in 1987 from an interview with Al Campanis, Los Angeles Dodgers vice president for player personnel, on the ABC-TV show Nightline. Campanis questioned whether blacks had the "necessities" to be managers. The first black manager was

Barry Bonds

Perhaps best known as the holder of Major League Baseball's single season home run record (seventy-three in 2001), Barry Bonds has crafted one of the finest careers baseball has ever seen. A thirteen-time all star with seven Most Valuable Player awards—four more than any other National League player ever—and two batting titles, Bonds also holds the major league record for most consecutive seasons (thirteen) with thirty or more home runs, bested his own single-season records for on-base percentage (.582 in 2002, .609 in 2004) and walks, and surpassed Rickey Henderson as the all-time most-walked player.

In 2004 alone, Bonds drew 232 walks (120 intentional) while still managing to hit forty-five home runs in fewer than 400 at bats. That he hit with such little protection around him in the line up throughout much of his career made it unlikely that he would see many good pitches. Babe Ruth had Lou Gehrig hitting behind him and Mickey Mantle had Roger Maris. To some, this assessment combined with his numbers make Bonds a clear choice as most dominant offensive force in the game.

Some pundits argue that his offensive stats cannot be compared fairly with those of great players past—such as Babe Ruth—because of the allegations of Bonds using steroids in addition to claims of his playing during "the age of the home run." Like Babe Ruth, Bonds's success does not rest solely on one-dimensional talent, however. Bonds's arm and range in the outfield are excellent and he has frequently stolen extra-base hits from opposing teams because of his athleticism and speed. These talents earned him eight Gold Glove awards. Additionally, Bonds surpassed thirty stolen bases nine times in his career, stealing as many as fifty-two in 1990, though the frequency of thefts has declined. His speed on the basepath made him the charter member of the 500-homer/500-steals club. Manufacturing runs (2,070; seventh most all-time) with walks and steals helped his team to victory just as much as the long ball did.

In 1993 Bonds, along with family members, founded the Barry Bonds Family Foundation. Its mission is to promote and fund programs for African-American youth within San Francisco Bay Area communities. Bonds has been a supporter of several charities including, Homepage for the Holidays, which provides toys and gifts to low-income children on Christmas Day. He has also been involved in the Barry Bonds Bone Marrow Campaign to Celebrate Life and The Field O' Dreams Project.

Frank Robinson of Cleveland in 1975, who later managed in Baltimore, San Francisco, Montreal, and Washington, D.C. There have been a number of African American managers since, including Cito Gaston, who won the World Series with Toronto in 1992. In 2005 there were four black managers, Willie Randolph of the Mets, Dusty Baker of the Cubs, Robinson of the Expos, and Lloyd McClendon of the Pirates, and one black Latino manager, Felipe Alou of the San Francisco Giants, out of thirty major league baseball teams.

Regarding front office positions, 10 percent of all senior administrators in 2005 were black, including 5 percent of vice presidents. In 1990, Ellen Weddington of the Boston Red Sox became the first black female assistant general manager, and five years later, Bob Watson of the New York Yankees became the first black general manager. Blacks in administration are mainly in community relations (33 percent). The highest ranking black in MLB history was Bill White, president of the National League from 1989 through 1994.

Black interest in baseball has been declining over the last generation. A 1986 survey found that blacks made up just 6.8 percent of baseball spectators, less than either football (7.5 percent) or basketball (17.0 percent), both of which are professional sports with higher average ticket prices, but sports whose players are predominantly African American. Ironically, as African Americans have become dominant in other major sports, their level of participation in the sport that broke most social barriers has fallen dramatically.

See also Aaron, Hank; Great Depression and the New Deal; Howard University; Mays, Willie; Morehouse College; Paige, Satchel; *Pittsburgh Courier;* Robeson, Paul;

Robinson, Jackie; Related Maps, Graphs, or Tables in Appendix: African-American Members of the National Baseball Hall of Fame, Cooperstown, N.Y.; Negro League Teams; Negro League Batting Champions; and First African-Americans Players on Major League Baseball Teams

Bibliography

Adelson, Bruce. *Brushing Back Jim Crow: The Integration of Minor-League Baseball in the South.* Charlottesville: University Press of Virginia, 1999.

Ashe, Arthur R., Jr. *A Hard Road to Glory: A History of the African-American Athlete since 1946.* New York, N.Y.: Warner Books, 1988.

Bankes, James. *The Pittsburgh Crawfords: The Lives and Times of Black Baseball's Most Exciting Team.* Dubuque, Iowa: William C. Brown, 1991.

Bruce, Janet. *The Kansas City Monarchs: Champions of Black Baseball.* Lawrence: University Press of Kansas, 1985.

Dixon, Phil. *The Negro Baseball Leagues, 1867–1955: A Photographic History.* Mattituck, N.Y.: Amereon House, 1992.

Holway, John. *Voices from the Great Black Baseball Leagues.* New York, N.Y.: Dodd, Mead, 1975.

Holway, John. *Black Diamonds: Life in the Negro Leagues from the Men Who Lived It.* Westport, Conn.: Meckler, 1989.

Lanctot, Neil. *Fair Dealing and Clean Playing: The Hilldale Club and the Development of Black Professional Baseball, 1910–1932.* Jefferson, N.C.: McFarland, 1994.

Lanctot, Neil. *Negro League Baseball: The Rise and Ruin of a Black Institution.* Philadelphia: University of Pennsylvania Press, 2004.

Lapchick, Richard. "2003 Race and Gender Report Card." Available from http://www.bus.ucf.edu/sport/public/downloads/media/ides/release_05.pdf.

Lester, Larry. *Black Baseball's National Showcase: The East–West All-Star Game, 1933–1953.* Lincoln: University of Nebraska Press, 2001.

Lomax, Michael. *Black Baseball Entrepreneurs, 1860–1901: Operating by Any Means Necessary.* Syracuse, N.Y.: Syracuse University Press, 2003.

Overmyer, James. *Effa Manley and the Newark Eagles.* Metuchen, N.J.: Scarecrow Press, 1993.

Peterson, Robert. *Only the Ball Was White.* Englewood Cliffs, N.J.: Prentice-Hall, 1970.

Riess, Steven A. *Touching Base: Professional Baseball and American Culture in the Progressive Era.* Urbana: University of Illinois Press, 1999.

Riley, James A. *The Biographical Encyclopedia of the Negro Baseball Leagues.* New York, N.Y.: Carroll & Graf, 1994.

Rampersad, Arnold. *Jackie Robinson: A Biography.* New York, N.Y.: Knopf, 1997.

Ruck, Rob. *Sandlot Seasons: Sport in Black Pittsburgh.* Urbana: University of Illinois Press, 1987.

Rogosin, Donn. *Invisible Men: Life in Baseball's Negro Leagues.* New York, N.Y.: Atheneum, 1983.

Seymour, Harold. *Baseball: The People's Game.* New York, N.Y.: Oxford University Press, 1990.

Snyder, Brad. *Beyond the Shadow of the Senators: The Untold Story of the Homestead Grays and the Integration of Baseball.* New York, N.Y.: McGraw-Hill, 2003.

Tygiel, Jules. *Baseball's Great Experiment: Jackie Robinson and His Legacy.* New York, N.Y.: Oxford University Press, 1983.

Voigt, David Q. *American Baseball.* 3 vols. University Park: Pennsylvania State University Press, 1983.

White, Solomon. *Sol White's Official Base Ball Guide.* Philadelphia, Pa., 1907. Reprint. Columbia, S.C.: Camden House, 1984.

DONN ROGOSIN (1996)
STEVEN A. RIESS (1996)
Updated by Riess 2005

Basie, William James "Count"

August 21, 1904
April 26, 1984

Born in Red Bank, New Jersey, jazz pianist and bandleader William "Count" Basie took up drums as a child, performing at informal neighborhood gatherings. He began to play piano before his teens, and in high school he formed a band with drummer Sonny Greer. In 1924 Basie moved to New York, where he was befriended by two of the greatest stride piano players of the day, Fats Waller and James P. Johnson. Basie himself became a fine stride pianist, as well as a proficient organist, learning that instrument while observing Waller's performances at the Lincoln Theater in Harlem. Basie left New York in the mid-1920s to work as a touring musician for bands led by June Clark and Elmer Snowden, and as accompanist to variety acts such as those led by Kate Crippen and Gonzelle White. When White's group broke up in Kansas City in 1927, Basie found himself stranded. He supported himself as a theater organist, but more importantly, he also began performing with many of the southwest "territory" bands. In 1928 he joined bassist Walter Page's Blue Devils, and the next year he joined Bennie Moten's band in Kansas City.

After Moten's death in 1935, Basie took over the group, now reorganized as Count Basie and the Barons of Rhythm. Producer John Hammond heard the band on a 1935 radio broadcast from the Reno Club in Kansas City, and the next year brought the band to New York City. During this time the Basie band became one of the country's best-known swing bands, performing at the Savoy Ballroom, at the Famous Door on 52nd Street, and at the Woodside Hotel in Harlem, a stay immortalized in "Jumpin' at the Woodside" (1938). The band's recordings from this time represent the best of the hard-driving, riff-based Kansas City style of big-band swing. Many of these recordings are "head" arrangements, in which the horns spontaneously set up a repeating motif behind the melody and solos. Memorable recordings from this period include "Good Morning Blues" (1937), "One O'Clock Jump" (1937), "Sent for You Yesterday" (1937), "Swinging the Blues" (1938), "Every Tub" (1938), and "Taxi War Dance" (1939). In 1941 the Basie band recorded "King Joe," a tribute to boxer Joe Louis, which had lyrics by Richard Wright and vocals by Paul Robeson. In 1943 the band appeared in two films, *Stage Door Canteen* and *Hit Parade of 1943.*

In the late 1930s and early 1940s, the Basie group was primarily a band of soloists. The leading members included tenor saxophonists Herschel Evans and Lester Young, alto saxophonists Buster Smith and Earle Warren, trumpeters Harry "Sweets" Edison and Wilbur "Buck" Clayton, and trombonists Eddie Durham and William "Dicky" Wells. Jimmy Rushing, Helen Humes, and Billie Holiday provided vocals. In the 1940s Basie also added saxophonists Buddy Tate and Don Byas, trumpeters Clark Terry and Joe Newman, and trombonists Vic Dickenson and J. J. Johnson. Throughout, the band's "all-American rhythm section" consisted of Basie, drummer Jo Jones, bassist Walter Page, and guitarist Freddie Green, who remained with the band for more than fifty years. Together, they provided the sparse and precise, but also relaxed and understated, accompaniment. Basie himself was one of the first jazz pianists to "comp" behind soloists, providing accompaniment that was both supportive and prodding. His thoughtful solos, which became highly influential, were simple and rarefied, eschewing the extroverted runs of stride piano, but retaining a powerful swing. That style is on display on Basie's 1938–1939 trio recordings ("How Long, How Long Blues" and "Oh! Red"). He also recorded on the organ in 1939.

With the rise of the bebop era, Basie had difficulty finding work for his big band, which he dissolved in 1949. However, after touring for a year with a bebop-oriented octet, Basie formed another big band, which lasted until his death. The "second" Basie band was very different from its predecessor. The first was famed for its simple and spontaneous "head" arrangements. In contrast, arrangers Neal Hefti, Johnny Mandel, and Ernie Wilkins, with their carefully notated arrangements and rhythmic precision, were the featured musicians of the second Basie band. The latter also had many fine instrumentalists, including saxophonists Eddie "Lockjaw" Davis and Paul Quinichette, Frank Wess and Frank Foster playing saxophone and flute, trombonist Al Grey, trumpeter Thad Jones, and vocalist Joe Williams.

Basie's second band toured extensively worldwide from the 1950s through the 1970s. Basie had his first national hit in 1955 with "Every Day I Have the Blues." Other popular recordings from this time include *April in Paris* (1955, including "Corner Pocket" and "Shiny Stockings"), *The Atomic Basie* (1957, including "Whirly Bird" and "Lil' Darlin"), *Basie at Birdland* (1961), *Kansas City Seven* (1962), and *Basie Jam* (1973). During this period the Basie band's popularity eclipsed even that of Duke Ellington, with whom they made a record, *First Time,* in 1961. The Basie band became a household name, playing at the inaugural balls of both John F. Kennedy and Lyndon B. Johnson and appearing in such films as *Cinderfella* (1959), *Sex and the Single Girl* (1964), and *Blazing Saddles* (1974).

In the 1980s, Basie continued to record, in solo, small-group, and big-band settings (*Farmer's Market Barbecue,* 1982; *88 Basie Street,* 1984). He lived for many years in the St. Albans section of Queens, New York, with Catherine Morgan, a former dancer he had married in 1942. Health problems induced him to move to the Bahamas in his later years. He died in 1984 in Hollywood, Florida. His autobiography, *Good Morning Blues,* appeared the next year. Basie's band has continued performing, led by Thad Jones until 1986 and since then by Frank Foster.

See also Holiday, Billie; Robeson, Paul; Savoy Ballroom

Bibliography

Basie, Count, and Albert Murray. *Good Morning Blues: The Autobiography of Count Basie.* New York: Random House, 1985.

Dance, Stanley. *The World of Count Basie.* New York: Da Capo Press, 1980.

Sheridan, C. *Count Basie: A Bio-Discography.* Westport, Conn.: Greenwood Press, 1986.

MICHAEL D. SCOTT (1996)

Basketball

Although basketball in the United States is now dominated by African Americans, their role in the sport was relatively unimportant in the early years of the game. Created in 1891 by James Naismith at a Springfield, Massachusetts, YMCA, basketball was originally played primarily at YMCAs. Black YMCAs produced the earliest African-American teams.

By the outbreak of World War I in 1914, a handful of blacks competed on white varsity basketball teams, mostly in small, remote midwestern colleges. Ironically, a man who did not play varsity basketball, Edwin B. Henderson, opened the door for many others to compete at both the interscholastic and intercollegiate levels. In 1905, after a summer at Harvard, Henderson, who was a physical education instructor, returned home to Washington, D.C., to become a founding father of African-American basketball. As physical education director for black schools in Washington, Henderson led in the organization and promotion of high school, club, and YMCA sports programs for African-American youths. In 1909 he became an instructor at Howard University, where he introduced basketball. Two years later he launched a varsity program, recruiting most of his players from the black YMCA in Washington.

A number of black colleges joined Howard in adopting basketball for intramural and intercollegiate purposes. During World War I these colleges began forming conferences "in a common effort for athletic elevation," as a Howard professor put it, and "to train students in self-reliance and stimulate race-pride through athletic attainment." In 1916 Howard, Lincoln, Shaw, and Virginia Union universities joined Hampton Institute in forming the Central Interscholastic Athletic Association. Four years later, educators and coaches from several Deep South colleges convened at Morehouse College in Atlanta to form the Southeastern Athletic Conference. By 1928 four regional conferences covered most of the black institutions below the Mason-Dixon line. By codifying rules and clarifying terms of athletic eligibility, these new conferences benefited the game of basketball.

Historians have made much of the massive black migration northward in the 1920s, but there also was a reverse migration of black athletes from the North to such southern schools as Tuskegee Institute (later Tuskegee University) in Alabama and Tugaloo College in Mississippi. Basketball especially flourished at Morgan State University in Baltimore, which went undefeated in 1927; Xavier University in New Orleans, whose entire starting team in the late 1930s came from a championship high school team in Chicago; and Virginia Union University, whose 42–2 record in the 1939–1940 season included two victories over the National Invitation Tournament (NIT) champions Long Island University.

During the period between World War I and World War II, some black students played basketball at integrated colleges. John Howard Johnson, the first black basketball player at Columbia University, graduated from there in 1921. Basketball players who later achieved fame in other endeavors included Ralph Bunche, a Nobel Peace Prize recipient who starred at the University of California Los Angeles (UCLA) in the mid-1920s, and Jackie Robinson, who, also playing for UCLA (1939–1941), led his conference in scoring two years in a row before he went on to become the first African American to play baseball in the modern major leagues.

Because basketball is less expensive than football and more centrally positioned in the academic year than baseball, it became popular in black high schools in the 1920s. The black state high school athletic associations of West Virginia were the first of many to begin sponsoring state basketball tournaments in 1924. By 1930 eight tournaments had been established; by 1948 every racially segregated southern and midwestern state had African-American statewide athletic organizations that emphasized basketball. In May 1929 Charles H. Williams, the director of physical education at Hampton Institute, inaugurated the National Interscholastic Basketball Tournament, which was held annually until 1942.

Of the several professional basketball leagues that rose and fell during the interwar period, all excluded blacks, though given the weak and disorganized nature of professional basketball at this time, this ban had less impact than for other professional sports. Independent all-black teams such as the Smart Set in Brooklyn, as well as St. Christopher's, Alphas, and the Spartans in New York City and Loendi in Pittsburgh, were beset with inadequate facilities, small turnouts, and uncertain schedules, and they struggled to survive. The most successful teams hit the road, barnstorming from city to city on a trail blazed by the best all-white team of the interwar era, the Original Celtics. The two best African-American squads, the New York–based Renaissance Big Five ("Harlem Rens") and the Chicago-based Harlem Globetrotters, frequently played against the Original Celtics and other all-white touring teams, thus making basketball the only interwar professional team sport to allow interracial competition.

The Rens were created in 1923 by the St. Kitts native Robert L. Douglas, who immigrated as a child to the United States in 1888. For several years Douglas played with the New York Spartans, then decided to form his own team. He rented the Renaissance Casino ballroom in Harlem. The team took their name from that home site but played most of their games on the road against any team—black or white, city or small town—that would take them on. Over a twenty-year span, the Rens averaged more than one hundred victories annually. In their greatest season, 1932 to 1933, they won eighty-eight consecutive games and finished with a 120–8 record. At Chicago in 1939 they won the first "world tournament" of professional basketball. Little wonder that all seven players who formed the core of the team during the 1930s—Charles T. "Tarzan" Cooper, John "Casey" Holt, Clarence "Fats" Jenkins,

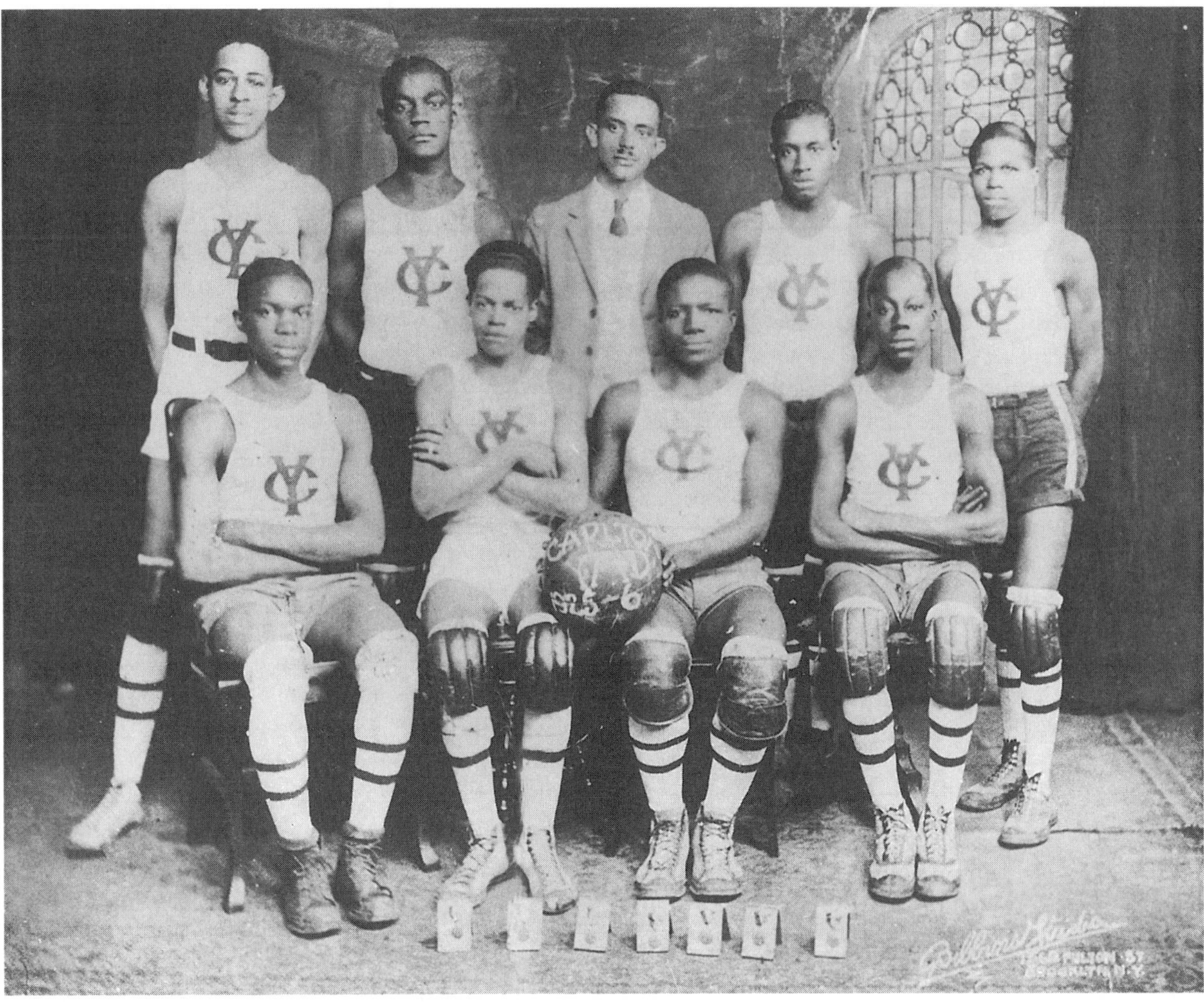

Youth basketball team, New York City, 1926. *Black YMCA's produced the earliest African-American teams, providing talent for black colleges like Howard University, the first to adopt basketball as an intermural (and later intercollegiate) activity during the second decade of the twentieth century.* PHOTOGRAPHS AND PRINTS DIVISION, SCHOMBURG CENTER FOR RESEARCH IN BLACK CULTURE, THE NEW YORK PUBLIC LIBRARY, ASTOR, LENOX AND TILDEN FOUNDATIONS.

James "Pappy" Ricks, Eyre "Bruiser" Satch, William "Wee Willie" Smith, and William J. "Bill" Yancey—are in the Basketball Hall of Fame.

The Rens were already well established when the Harlem Globetrotters played their first game in January 1927. Initially called the Savoy Big Five because they played in the Savoy Ballroom in Chicago, the Globetrotters were the brainchild of a Jewish immigrant, Abraham Saperstein. The somewhat misleading Harlem tag was a public relations ploy, which provided a racial rather than a geographical reference. As a team of barnstorming professionals, they traveled far longer, more widely, and to consistently larger crowds than any sports team in history. In 1951 they appeared before 75,000 spectators in Berlin's Olympic Stadium. They have performed for literally millions of live spectators around the world, as well as to huge television and movie audiences.

Although best known in later years for their basketball comedy, the original Globetrotters were serious, highly skilled athletes. In 1940 they succeeded the Rens as "world champions" in the fiercely fought Chicago tournament. Earlier, during the Great Depression, they averaged nearly two hundred games per year, winning more than 90 percent of them. Constant travel produced fatigue; large margins of victory made for boredom. For rest and relief from tedium, the Globetrotters began clowning, especially on those frequent occasions when they dramatically outmatched their opponents. Comedy proved contractually lucrative, so the Globetrotters developed funny skits and routines. Staged silliness swamped competitive play in the 1940s. Still, Reece "Goose" Tatum, Marques

Haynes, Meadow George "Meadowlark" Lemon, Nat "Sweetwater" Clifton, Connie Hawkins, and Wilt Chamberlain are among the most famous of the many superb athletes who wore the colorful Globetrotter uniform.

It was just as well that the Globetrotters shifted from serious basketball to comedy routines, because the racial integration of the National Basketball Association (NBA) in 1950 meant that the Globetrotters could no longer attract the best college athletes. (A forerunner of the NBA, the Basketball Association of America, signed black players as early as 1948.) For the 1950–1951 season, the Boston Celtics recruited Charles "Chuck" Cooper from Duquesne University, the Washington Capitals tapped Early Lloyd from West Virginia State College, and the New York Knicks bought Sweetwater Clifton from the Globetrotters.

Prior to World War II the abolition of the center jump, the introduction of an innovative one-handed shot, and the use of the fast break served to streamline Naismith's slow and deliberate original game. In the early 1950s the NBA responded to the market's demand for a faster, more attractive game by banning zone defenses, doubling the width of the foul lane (to twelve feet), and introducing a twenty-four-second shot clock. All these changes were completed by 1954 and worked to the great advantage of African-American newcomers who had mastered a more spontaneous, personalized style of play on the asphalt courts of urban playgrounds.

The first African American to become a dominant player in the NBA was William "Bill" Russell. Russell came from an extremely successful undergraduate career at the University of San Francisco, where he and another gifted African American, K. C. Jones, led the San Francisco Dons to fifty-five straight victories and two National Collegiate Athletic Association (NCAA) championships. Rather than go into the NBA immediately, however, both men participated in the 1956 Summer Olympics in Melbourne, Australia, leading the United States basketball team to an easy gold medal. Then, while Jones fulfilled a two-year military obligation, Russell joined the Celtics at midseason. The defensive, shot-blocking, and rebounding skills of Russell complemented those of several high-scoring Celtics. Together they produced their first NBA championship in Russell's first pro season.

Jones joined the Celtics in the 1958–1959 season, and he and Russell helped the Celtics to an all-time record nine consecutive NBA crowns. In 1964 Boston fielded the first all-black starting lineup in the NBA: Russell, Jones, Sam Jones, Tom "Satch" Sanders, and Willie Naulls; John Thompson, the future coach of Georgetown University, backed up Russell. Russell's NBA nemesis was a high-scoring giant of a man, Wilton Norman "Wilt" Chamberlain. Over seven feet tall and weighing 265 pounds in his prime, Chamberlain earlier led Overbrook High School in Philadelphia to two city championships, once scoring ninety points in a single game. In his varsity debut at the University of Kansas in 1957, his fifty-two points set the Jayhawks on the path to the NCAA finals, where they narrowly lost in triple overtime to top-ranked North Carolina. After two All-American seasons at Kansas, Chamberlain toured for a year with the Harlem Globetrotters, then joined the Philadelphia Warriors in the NBA in 1959. In a fourteen-year NBA career, he played with four different teams and was selected for thirteen All-Star games, seven first-team All-NBA squads, and four Most Valuable Player awards. In a total of 1,045 NBA games, he averaged more than thirty points per game, and in 1962, he scored one hundred points in a single game against the New York Knickerbockers. At his retirement in 1973, he held or shared forty-three NBA records.

In addition to Chamberlain and Russell, black athletes such as Elgin Baylor and Oscar Robertson achieved basketball renown in the late 1950s and 1960s. Though they had their differences in talent and style, it is perhaps possible to see in their play elements of a shared athletic aesthetic that would dominate NBA basketball in the 1970s. Baylor, Chamberlain, Robertson, and Russell exhibited skills developed in playground competition best represented in the Rucker tournament (New York) and the Baker League (Philadelphia), both created in the postwar era. All four of these early NBA stars grew up in urban, not rural, America, and they developed their game in East Coast, industrial Midwest, and West Coast inner-city playgrounds. All four also attended white rather than traditionally black colleges. Another player from the early and mid-1960s who exemplified the playground style was Earl "the Pearl" Monroe, who attended Winston-Salem College in North Carolina before beginning a successful career with the Baltimore Bullets and New York Knicks. Connie Hawkins, a consummate playground basketball player from New York City, had his promising career derailed by his ambiguous involvement in a point-shaving scandal in 1960. After some years in basketball purgatory, he joined the Phoenix Suns in 1969.

In the period after World War II, blacks became prominent in college basketball. Two black players started for the City College of New York (CCNY) squad of 1950, the only team ever to win the NCAA and NIT tournaments in the same year. When the first significant cracks appeared in the armor of racially segregated universities in the 1950s, basketball coaches rushed to recruit blue-chip African-American athletes for traditionally all-white teams. Even the smallest of colleges sought to enhance

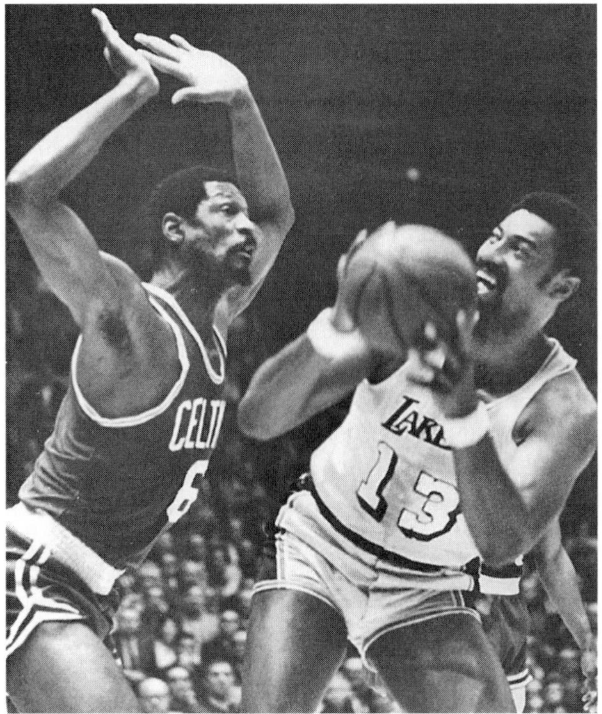

Basketball players Bill Russell and Wilt Chamberlain, 1969. *The 1969 NBA playoffs featured one of the most famous confrontations in all of basketball: Chamberlain of the Los Angeles Lakers going for the shot, Russell of the Boston Celtics defending.* AP/WIDE WORLD PHOTOS. REPRODUCED BY PERMISSION.

their status through the basketball prowess of new black talent. With fewer than one thousand students, little St. Francis College of Loretto, Pennsylvania, wooed Maurice Stokes. He carried them from the obscure National Catholic Tournament to the more prestigious and lucrative National Invitational Tournament in 1955.

As integration undercut black college athletics, coach John B. McLendon's program at Tennessee A&I enjoyed a kind of last hurrah of basketball excellence. After successful stints at North Carolina College and Hampton Institute, McLendon in 1954 went to Tennessee A&I in Nashville. Employing a fast-break press-and-run game that he claimed to have learned years earlier from the aged Naismith at the University of Kansas, within five years McLendon won four league championships and three national titles in the newly integrated National Association for Intercollegiate Athletics (NAIA). The Most Valuable Player of the 1959 NAIA Tournament was Tennessee A&I's Richard "Dick" Barnett, a future New York Knickerbocker stalwart.

Strong racially integrated teams won NCAA titles for the University of Cincinnati and Loyola University of Chicago in the early 1960s. Building on a tradition of integration that dated back to the 1920s, UCLA attracted a number of African-American athletes during the eleven-year span (1964–1975) in which they won ten national titles. The person most identified with UCLA's reign was Lew Alcindor, later known was Kareem Abdul-Jabbar, a 7'2" dominating center with a deft scoring touch who later went on to a twenty-year career in the NBA with the Milwaukee Bucks and the Los Angeles Lakers.

The passing of the old era of segregated basketball was symbolized in the NCAA finals of 1966, in which an all-black squad from Texas Western University (now the University of Texas at El Paso) defeated a highly favored all-white team from the University of Kentucky. Shortly thereafter, the color bar began crumbling in the segregated schools of the Southwest Conference when James Cash became Texas Christian University's first black basketball player in 1966. In Maryland, Billy Jones became the first African-American basketball recruit in the Atlantic Coast Conference. Finally, Perry Wallace of Vanderbilt University broke the racial barrier in the Southeastern Conference (SEC) in 1967, the same year the University of Alabama's new basketball coach, C. M. Newton, began recruiting African Americans. In 1974 Alabama became the first SEC team to field five black starters.

The growing dominance of African Americans in college basketball has not been without its share of problems, however. Many colleges recruit black players as athletes, with little regard for or interest in providing them with an education. For example, shortly after winning the 1966 NCAA title, members of the Texas Western team began dropping out of college. They had all been recruited from the New York City area, and the overwhelmingly white, southern campus environment provided a combination of academic and social pressure. Dropout rates remained at high levels into the 1990s but showed some improvement. According to NCAA reports, in 1997 to 1998, 42 percent of black male college basketball players graduated (as opposed to 48 percent of white male players). Another problem that has ruined or seriously detoured many promising careers is drug addiction. Len Bias, a number-one NBA draft choice from the University of Maryland, allegedly died of a drug overdose in 1988. Other talented black basketball players, such as the playground legends Earl "the Goat" Manigault and Herman "Helicopter" Knowings of New York City, and William "Chicken Breast" Lee and Terry "Sweets" Matchett of Washington, D.C., did not have the social skills to enable them to move beyond the milieu of their hometown neighborhoods.

The African-American player has simply transformed basketball at all levels, especially bringing extraordinary excitement, media exposure, and financial success to the NBA. The seamless web of connections between high school, college, and professional basketball is best seen in Baltimore's Dunbar High School squad during the 1982–1983 season. Finishing with a 31–0 record, Dunbar was top-ranked among all high school teams by *USA Today*. Virtually the entire team went to college on basketball scholarships. In 1987 three of them were selected in the first round of the NBA draft: Tyrone "Mugsey" Bogues of Wake Forest, by the Washington Bullets; Reggie Lewis of Northeastern, by the Boston Celtics; and Reggie Williams of Georgetown, by the Los Angeles Lakers. As of 2005 nearly 80 percent of all NBA players were black.

African Americans also play a prominent role in women's basketball. The 1984 Olympic women's basketball team, the first to win a gold medal, included Cheryl Miller, who led her University of Southern California team to two NCAA championships; Pam McGee; Lynette Woodard, who later became the first female player for the Harlem Globetrotters; and C. Vivian Stringer, who became coach of the women's basketball team at Cheyney State College in 1972, leading them to a second-place victory in the NCAA Women's National Basketball Championship ten years later. When Stringer became coach of the University of Iowa's women's team in 1983, she became the first black female coach to lead a women's basketball team of national rank. Under her leadership, the Iowa team qualified to play in the NCAA national tournament for seven straight years, from 1986 to 1992. In 1992 Stringer became the NCAA delegate for the committee organizing the Barcelona Olympic Games. Black women, notably Nikki McCray, also dominated the women's basketball competition at the 1996 Olympics, at which the American women's team won the gold medal. McCray went on to star in both the American Basketball League and the Women's National Basketball League (WNBA), the two women's leagues that were created in the mid-1990s. The American women's basketball team won gold medals again at the 2000 and 2004 Olympics. The 2004 team at Athens was led by Dawn Staley, who was chosen as the flag bearer for the U.S. Olympic team, as well as Lisa Leslie and Sheryl Swoopes.

Although African Americans are vastly underrepresented in the management and coaching ranks of the NBA, they are considerably more visible there than in major league baseball or in the National Football League. In 2005 the NBA had ten black head coaches out of a total of thirty (as opposed to only two a decade earlier), and fully one-third of the NBA's assistant coaches were black. However, the number of African-American general managers, owners, and others in positions with decision-making powers remains in the single digits.

In the collegiate ranks, in 2005 there were fifty-four African-American head coaches out of 318 Division I schools. Some of the most successful Division I coaches were John Thompson of Georgetown, John Chaney of Temple, George Raveling of the University of Southern California, and Nolan Richardson of the University of Arkansas. Division II coach Clarence "Big House" Gaines, who retired from Winston-Salem State University in 1993, was by far the most successful of all African-American coaches, having won the most victories in Division II history.

Georgetown's John Thompson became probably the most visible, and certainly the most controversial, African-American coach. After a brief, successful stint at St. Anthony's Catholic High School in Washington, D.C., Thompson moved to Georgetown in 1972. Emphasizing the tenacious defense and team play he had learned during his brief time as a Celtic, he steered the Georgetown Hoyas to three consecutive NCAA finals, from 1983 to 1985, and to the national championship in 1984. Four years later he coached the United States Olympic team to a bronze medal in Seoul. Always emphasizing the primacy of academics, he ably recruited African-American athletes for Georgetown. Patrick Ewing and Alonzo Mourning are two of the most famous among many players to whom Thompson directed his homilies of racial pride and achievement.

In the 1980s basketball soared to new heights of international popularity, as did African-American basketball players. Two players who stood out in particular were Earvin "Magic" Johnson and Michael Jordan. Johnson, an unusually tall guard at 6'8", led Michigan State University to an NCAA championship in his sophomore year in 1979 before turning pro and joining the Los Angeles Lakers. He helped the Lakers to an NBA championship in his rookie season and subsequently led his team to five championships during his career. In addition to his basketball skills, his effervescent and winning personality propelled him to media celebrity. His many admirers were shocked to learn of his early retirement in the fall of 1991 after he announced that he had contracted HIV. In the second half of the 1980s and the 1990s, the dominant basketball player was Michael Jordan. Jordan played for the University of North Carolina before joining the Chicago Bulls in 1984, where, as a shot maker of astounding versatility, he quickly became one of the most powerful players in league history. Jordan also became a media spokesman for a number of products and advertising campaigns. His widespread acceptance and popularity was as remarkable as his outstanding on-court skills. Michael Jordan retired from professional basketball in October 1993 but returned in the spring of 1995. He helped lead the Bulls to a total of six NBA titles during his years in Chicago, before and after his first retirement. Jordan retired a second time in 1999, before returning for a final two-year stint with the Washington Wizards (2001–2003).

The role of African Americans in basketball was further underlined by the success of the so-called Dream Team, an NBA All-Star team that romped against the best of the rest of the world in the 1992 Summer Olympics in Barcelona and (to a lesser extent) the 1996 games in Atlanta. Eight of the twelve players on the team were black, including Magic Johnson in his final competitive appearance before his retirement. The 2000 U.S. men's basketball team, with eleven black players, won the gold medal at the Sydney Olympics.

Other gifted African-American players entered the basketball spotlight in the 1990s and early 2000s, including Shaquille O'Neal, Hakeem Olajuwon, Scottie Pippen, Charles Barkley, David Robinson, Karl Malone, Kobe Bryant, and Allen Iverson. Seven-foot-tall O'Neal, who in February 1993 became the first rookie since 1985 to lead the NBA All-Star Game starting lineup, went on to become one of the most celebrated stars of professional basketball. Winner of numerous Most Valuable Player awards, O'Neal's scoring average ranks third all-time among NBA players (behind Jordan and Chamberlain). More than any NBA star, O'Neal has achieved celebrity status in the larger culture. Kobe Bryant went from high school directly into the NBA, becoming the youngest player in NBA history. He helped lead the Los Angeles Lakers to league titles in 2000, 2001, and 2002. In women's basketball, star players included Cynthia Cooper, who won four WNBA championships with the Houston Comets and went on to become a coach; Olympian Sheryl Swoopes, voted the 2003 WNBA defensive player of the year; and Teresa Edwards, the most decorated Olympic basketball player of all time, male or female.

Yet, despite the increasing successes of individual black basketball players, the nature of collegiate basketball itself continues to be an issue of controversy in the African-American community. In the 1990s the NCAA established rules for prospective players, setting minimum academic standards for team admittance (graduation from high school, completion of a specified number of core courses, and specified grade point averages) and limiting the number of college scholarships offered for basketball. Many decried these rules as unfair to young African-American athletes from disadvantaged backgrounds. Balancing a number of interests has been tricky for the NCAA. Challenges include the need to attract more promising minority athletes, the need to maintain a quality team in order to attract alumni donations, the need for schools to maintain consistent academic standards, and the decrease in available scholarship funds. For prospective African-American student athletes, the new NCAA rules meant the intensification of an already keen competition for a chance at professional status. The controversy highlighted the debate within the black community on the role of basketball as a means of upward mobility for inner-city youth and whether basketball unduly dominated the activities of black teenagers.

See also Abdul-Jabbar, Kareem; Chamberlain, Wilt; Harlem Globetrotters; Howard University; Johnson, Earvin "Magic"; Jordon, Michael; Lincoln University; Olympians; Sports; Related Maps, Graphs, or Tables in Appendix: African-American Members of the Naismith Memorial Basketball Hall of Fame, Springfield, Mass.

Bibliography

Ashe, Arthur R., Jr. *A Hard Road to Glory: A History of the African-American Athlete.* New York: Amistad, 1993.

George, Nelson. *Elevating the Game: Black Men and Basketball.* New York: Harper, 1992. Reprint, Lincoln: University of Nebraska Press, 1999.

Peterson, Robert W. *Cages to Jump Shots: Pro Basketball's Early Years.* New York: Oxford University Press, 1990. Reprint, Lincoln: University of Nebraska Press, 2002.

Sailes, Gary A., ed. *African Americans in Sport: Contemporary Themes.* New Brunswick, N.J.: Transaction, 1998.

Shropshire, Kenneth L. *In Black and White: Race and Sports in America.* New York: New York University Press, 1996.

Wideman, John Edgar. *Hoop Roots.* Boston: Houghton Mifflin, 2001.

WILLIAM J. BAKER (1996)
Updated by publisher 2005

Basquiat, Jean-Michel

December 22, 1960
August 12, 1988

Jean-Michel Basquiat was one of the most prominent artists to gain worldwide recognition in the 1980s. He was born in Brooklyn, New York, of Haitian and Puerto Rican–American parentage. His parents were separated in 1968, and Basquiat and his two sisters grew up with their father in Brooklyn, except for a period from 1974 to 1976, when the family lived in Puerto Rico. At the age of seven, Basquiat was hit by a car and badly hurt. He spent a month in the hospital, where his spleen was removed. While he was recuperating, his mother gave him *Gray's Anatomy*, a reference work that led to a lifelong interest in images of human anatomy.

Basquiat dropped out of high school and left home at the age of seventeen, determined to become a star in the downtown art and club scene of the late 1970s, where his aphoristic graffiti writings and drawings signed "SAMO-(c)" soon earned wide underground recognition. In 1980 his art was exhibited, for the first time and to critical acclaim, in the Times Square Show in New York City. Other group shows followed, and in 1981 he had his first solo exhibition in Modena, Italy.

In New York, Basquiat began showing at the Annina Nosei Gallery in SoHo, using the gallery basement as his studio. His first one-person show at Annina Nosei took place in 1982, and soon his work was being exhibited at prominent galleries worldwide. In 1982, Basquiat was the youngest artist to participate in Documenta 7 in Kassel, Germany, and one of the youngest ever to be included the following year in the Whitney Biennial. A close friendship with Andy Warhol was a significant force in his life until Warhol's death in 1987.

Within the space of a few years, Basquiat rose from an anonymous street graffitist to become a world-famous artist, a feat that—as much as his art itself—came to define his popular image and epitomize the fast-paced art world of the 1980s. As a young black male, however, he was viewed with suspicion by people blind to the significance of his work. In addition, a growing drug problem exacerbated his difficult relations with art dealers, family, and the people closest to him. Basquiat died of a heroine overdose in August 1988 at the age of twenty-seven.

Since his death, the importance of Basquiat's work has come to be still more widely recognized. In only eight years his work evolved from a direct, highly energized, expressionistic vocabulary to a complex synthesis of African-American and European cultural traditions, incorporating elements of black history, music, and popular culture in an advanced visual language of painting, collage, photomechanical reproduction, and sculpture. In his hands, a sometimes raucous world of boxing, jazz, TV, and political reality was expressed in the language of Pablo Picasso, Robert Rauschenberg, Andy Warhol, Cy Twombly, Jean Philippe Arthur Dubuffet, and Leonardo da Vinci. His syncopated and haunting juxtaposition of words and images created a kind of visual poetry that is one of his most distinctive contributions to twentieth-century painting.

The first full museum retrospective of Basquiat's work, organized by the Whitney Museum of American Art, opened in New York City in 1992. In 1998 (a year after the release of Julian Schnabel's *Basquiat,* a respectful film biography) one of his paintings was sold for a price in excess of three million dollars.

See also Art in the United States, Contemporary; Painting and Sculpture, Photography, U.S.

Bibliography

Hoban, Phoebe. *Basquiat: A Quick Killing in Art.* New York: Viking, 1998.

Marshall, Richard, et al. *Jean-Michel Basquiat.* New York: Abrams, 1992.

NATHAN KERNAN (1996)

Bass, Kingsley B.

See Bullins, Ed

Bates, Daisy

November 11, 1914
November 4, 1999

Daisy Lee Gaston Bates is best known for her leadership in the struggle to integrate Central High School in Little Rock, Arkansas, in 1957. A native of Arkansas, she knew well the realities of education under segregation. The black schools in her local school system, like others under segregation, suffered from inadequate facilities and lack of access to textbooks and supplies. This experience had a profound effect on her, and it moved her to action, as it did so many others in the civil rights era. In 1941 Daisy Gaston married L. C. Bates, a journalist from Mississippi, and the two published the weekly *Arkansas State Press.* Through the paper they addressed major issues facing African Americans, making it a popular and effective community instrument.

As president of the state conference of the National Association for the Advancement of Colored People (NAACP), Bates, with other activists, sought to move the school systems to comply with the 1954 *Brown v. Board of Education* Supreme Court decision. Although Little Rock had designed a program for integrating its schools, it had failed to act on the plan. One of the tactics Bates employed to draw attention to this was photographing African-American children attempting to gain admission to white public schools. This tactic was bolstered by an NAACP lawsuit against the school board for failure to implement a desegregation plan. Finally, the school board agreed to integrate Central High School in the fall of 1957.

Bates spearheaded the movement to organize students to register for Central. While almost eighty students were willing to register, the school board placed obstacles in the way and dissuaded parents, bringing the final number to nine. None of these was among the group of students involved in the NAACP court case against the Little Rock board. It was clear that there would be violence surrounding the opening of school when, two weeks before the semester began, a rock was thrown through the window of Bates's home. A note attached to the rock read, "Stone this time. Dynamite next."

Bates took responsibility for transporting the nine students to Central High. However, under the pretense of maintaining order, Gov. Orval Faubus used the Arkansas National Guard to prevent the nine from entering the school. The immediate situation was resolved when President Dwight D. Eisenhower brought the Arkansas National Guard under federal control to protect the students and their right to attend Central High School. The "Little Rock Nine" finally began the school year on September 25, 1957. It was the beginning of what would prove to be a very difficult year.

Bates and other state NAACP officials were arrested the following month for violating a statute that required organizations to furnish the county with membership and financial information. The statute was designed to hinder the operations of civil rights organizations. Bates was convicted and fined one hundred dollars, but her conviction was overturned by the Supreme Court.

Following the integration of Central High, Daisy Bates continued to be active in Democratic Party politics, voter registration, and community projects and continued to be a voice in the ongoing struggle for civil rights until her death in 1999. In tribute to her achievements, a nonprofit group bought Bates's Little Rock house in 1998 with the intention of transforming it into a civil rights museum. In 2001 Bates was honored when Arkansas declared a state holiday in her name.

See also *Brown v. Board of Education of Topeka, Kansas*; National Association for the Advancement of Colored People (NAACP)

Bibliography

Bates, Daisy. *The Long Shadow of Little Rock.* New York: David McKay, 1962.

Huckaby, Elizabeth. *Crisis at Central High School: Little Rock, 1957–1958.* Baton Rouge: Louisiana State University Press, 1980.

Williams, Juan. *Eyes on the Prize: America's Civil Rights Years, 1954–1965.* New York: Viking, 1987.

JUDITH WEISENFELD (1996)
Updated by publisher 2005

Battle, Kathleen

August 13, 1948

The opera singer Kathleen Battle was born in Portsmouth, Ohio, the daughter of Ollie Battle, a community and church activist, and Grady Battle, a steelworker. A National Merit Scholar in mathematics, Battle majored in music education at the University of Cincinnati College-Conservatory of Music (B.M. and M.M.). She taught music for two years in Cincinnati elementary schools before embarking on her professional career.

A lyric soprano noted for her small, sweet voice, she made her professional singing debut in 1972 in Johannes Brahms's *German Requiem* with the Cincinnati Orchestra at the Spoleto Festival in Italy. Her opera debut came soon after as Rosina in Gioacchino Rossini's *Il barbiere di Siviglia* with the Michigan Opera Theater. In 1974 she met James Levine, later to become artistic director of the Metropolitan Opera, who became her mentor. The following year she appeared on Broadway in Scott Joplin's opera *Treemonisha.*

In 1976, Battle appeared as Susanna in Mozart's *Le nozze di Figaro* at the New York City Opera, and she made her Metropolitan Opera (the Met) debut in 1978, singing The Shepherd in Richard Wagner's *Tannhäuser.* Her professional career flourished with leading roles at the MET, among them Mozart's Pamina (*Die Zauberflöte*), Richard Strauss's Sophie (*Der Rosenkavalier*), and George Frideric Handel's Cleopatra (*Giulio Cesare*). Subsequent to her European operatic debut as Despina in Mozart's *Così fan tutte* in Salzburg in 1982, Battle performed there several times as Despina, as Susanna, and as Zerlina (Don Giovanni)—the last for American national television—as well as in many other places. In 1993 she attracted sellout audiences during a Metropolitan Opera tour of Japan.

Battle, whom *Time* magazine in 1985 called "the best lyric coloratura in the world," shifted effortlessly between the opera stage and the concert hall. However, in 1994 she was dismissed in a statement issued by the Met for "'unprofessional actions . . . profoundly detrimental to the artistic collaboration among all the cast members" (Walsh, 1994, pp. 61–62). Unprofessional behavior reported by the *Baltimore Sun* newspaper included: rude behavior to colleagues, showing up late for rehearsals . . . and demanding that the director change the production so that all her exits and entrances were on the side of the stage closest to her dressing room (Wigler, 1994, p. C2). The news of her firing was met with swift reactions of glee, jokes, and applause within the music industry. Although hugely popular with audiences, she incited a maelstrom of ill-wishers among her associates (singers, conductors, stage hands, technicians, costumers, etc.) because of her mistreatment of her colleagues. According to Schuyler Chapin, the former general manager of the Met, "She's the only artist that I know of in my 43 years of dealing with artists who has managed to alienate practically everyone in every single place where's she's ever been" (Swan, 1994, p. 80). Other opera companies followed the Met's lead, thus ending her operatic career. Nonetheless, she continued performing in concerts and on recordings.

In 1995 Battle released her first crossover album, *So Many Stars,* with jazz musicians such as Grover Washington Jr. and Christian McBride. The record rose to the top on *Billboard* magazine's Classical Crossover lists. She has won five Grammy Awards, including one for her recital album *Kathleen Battle at Carnegie Hall* (1992). In 1991, Battle and the soprano Jessye Norman gave a concert of spirituals at Carnegie Hall, which was shown on national television and prompted a best-selling recording. In 1993, Battle recorded the premiere of a song cycle, *Honey and Rue,* she had commissioned from the African-American writer Toni Morrison and the composer André Previn. Her many CDs include: *Pleasures of their Company* (1990) and *Angels' Glory* (1996), both with the guitarist Christopher Parkening; *Grace* (1997); *Baroque Duet* (1991), with African-American trumpeter Wynton Marsalis; *Vangelis: "Mythodea"—Music for the NASA Mission: 2001 Mars Odyssey* (2001); and *Classic Kathleen Battle: A Portrait* (2002).

Battle has used tenacity, intelligent musicianship, and a stunning voice to build a diverse career that has lasted more than three decades. She elevated soubrette opera roles (usually relegated as secondary) to star status, while presenting sold-out concerts and successfully recording classical and crossover repertoire.

See also Norman, Jessye; Opera

Bibliography

Alfano, Vincent. "The Sweet Song of Kathleen Battle." *Fanfare* 10 (1986): 380-385.

Story, Rosalyn M. *And So I Sing: African-American Divas of Opera and Concert.* New York: Warner Books, 1990.

Swan, Annalyn. "Battle Royal." *Vanity Fair* (May 1994): 80.

Walsh, Michael. "Battle Fatigue." *Time* (February 21, 1994): 61–62.

Wigler, Stephen. "Temperamental Diva Deserves Her Fate." *Baltimore Sun* (February 9, 1994): C2.

LOUISE TOPPIN (1996)
Updated by author 2005

Baumfree, Isabella

See Truth, Sojourner

Bearden, Romare

September 2, 1912
March 12, 1988

In the last twenty-five years of artist Romare Bearden's life, collage was his principle medium. Through that medium, relying on memory, he recorded the rites of African-American life in all their historical and ceremonial complexity. In so doing he joined the ranks of Picasso, Matisse, and Miró, artists who transformed collage into a quintessentially twentieth-century language. Working with a medium that by its very nature is fragmented and heterogeneous, where reality and illusion hang in a precarious balance, Bearden, as his friend the writer Ralph Ellison once noted in *Romare Bearden: Paintings and Projections* (1968), captures the sharp breaks, leaps in consciousness, distortions, paradoxes, reversals, telescoping of time and surreal blending of styles, values, hopes, and dreams that characterize much of African American history.

Fred Howard Romare Bearden was a child of privilege. He was born in Charlotte, North Carolina, in the home of his great-grandparents, Rosa and Henry Kennedy. Former slaves, the Kennedys had become prosperous landowners, and Bearden spent the early years of his life in a spacious Victorian-style frame house surrounded by doting great-grandparents and grandparents. In spite of their comfortable life, however, Bearden's college-educated parents, Bessye and Howard, were dissatisfied with the limitations of the Jim Crow South. On the eve of World War I, like hundreds of thousands of black Americans throughout the South, they migrated north.

After traveling to Canada, Bessye and Howard finally settled in Harlem. Harlem, in the years following World

Romare Bearden (1912–1988). *The artist Bearden expressed in his celebrated collage and photomontage compositions the fullness of his own experience of black America, from boyhood summers spent in rural North Carolina, to memories of his grandmother's boardinghouse near the steel mills of Pittsburgh, to the spirited Harlem of his adolescence and early adulthood, then in its heyday as a black cultural and intellectual mecca.* THE ESTATE OF CARL VAN VECHTEN. REPRODUCED BY PERMISSION.

War I, was the black cultural capital of the world, the home of the New Negro movement, the site of the Harlem Renaissance. A flowering of poetry, painting, and music that marked the African American's first efforts to define himself as a distinctive cultural entity within the larger American culture, the Harlem Renaissance proved to be a rich crucible for Bearden.

Bessye, Bearden's beautiful and dynamic mother who was a New York editor for the *Chicago Defender* and a political organizer, was at the center of this cultural activity. Her Harlem apartments were always filled with writers and intellectuals such as W. E. B. Du Bois, Paul Robeson, Langston Hughes, and Zora Neale Hurston, as well as painters Aaron Douglas and Charles Alston. Musicians, too, were part of Bearden's circle, and young Romy, as he was called, was surrounded by such exciting jazz musicians and composers as Fats Waller, Andy Razaf, and Duke Ellington. Together, Bessye and Howard, who worked for the Department of Health, provided their only child with a remarkable upbringing.

During the summers Bearden often visited his great-grandparents and grandparents in Mecklenberg, New York, a place that became a veritable paradise in his mind. During his high school years he lived in Pittsburgh with his maternal grandmother, Carrie Banks, who ran a boardinghouse for steelworkers. Like Charlotte and Harlem, Pittsburgh became part of a rich inventory of images for Bearden's mature art.

Bearden came of age as an artist during the depression. While in high school, he met the successful black cartoonist E. Simms Campbell. Campbell's success inspired Bearden to try his hand at cartooning. From 1931 to 1935 he did editorial cartoons for the *Baltimore Afro-American* and drawings for *Collier's* and *The Saturday Evening Post.* After short stays at Lincoln University and Boston University, he enrolled at New York University, where in 1935 he received a B.S. in education. He continued cartooning at NYU, contributing to the university's humor magazine, *The Medley.*

After he graduated, Bearden became interested in inserting a social message into his cartoons, which led him, as he said, "to the works of Daumier, Forain, and Käthe Kollwitz, to the Art Students League and to George Grosz." Grosz, a German satirist whose visual commentary on post–World War I society was unforgiving, instilled in Bearden the lifelong habit of studying the artists of the past even as he was trying to make contemporary social commentary. Bearden's stay at the Art Students League was his only formal art school training.

Formal training, however, was amply augmented for Bearden by the Harlem art scene of the 1930s and 1940s. In spite of the depression, Harlem boasted a thriving community of visual artists. Many, supported by the New Deal's federally funded Works Project Administration (WPA), worked on public art projects, taught, or worked on WPA easel projects. They were supported by a network of exhibition spaces and art centers: the federally supported art center at West 125th Street, sculptor Augusta Savage's art garage, Ad Bates's exhibiting space at 306 West 141st Street, local libraries, the YMCA, and upscale living rooms and salons. Although Bearden did not qualify for the WPA because his well-to-do parents supported him, he was active nonetheless in artistic activities uptown. He was one of the artists who organized uptown artists into the Harlem Artists Guild, and he wrote articles for *Opportunity,* the magazine of the Urban League, on black American art and social issues.

More important, Bearden and his artist friends—Norman Lewis, Roy DeCarava, and Ernest Crichlow—

were devotees of jazz. They regularly made the rounds of nightclubs and cabarets where they heard firsthand the compositionally complex, innovative music. Though it was many years before Bearden was able to recognize the aesthetic importance of jazz to his painting—inspired by his mentor, Stuart Davis—the music became as important to him as the painting of the masters he studied with George Grosz.

During this time, 1937 to 1940, Bearden produced his first paintings, gouaches on brown paper, eighteen of which were exhibited along with some drawings at his first solo show held at Ad Bates's place on West 141st Street. Scenes of black life in Charlotte and on the streets of Pittsburgh and Harlem, these early paintings, with their terracotta colors, bulky figures, and narrative, almost illustrational quality, were painted in the then fashionable social realist style.

Bearden's uptown art community disintegrated with the coming of World War II and the dismantling of the WPA. Bearden enlisted in the army, continued to exhibit, and came to the attention of Caresse Crosby, the flamboyant founder and publisher with her husband of Black Sun Press. Crosby exhibited Bearden's works at the G Place Gallery in Washington and introduced him to gallery dealer Samuel M. Kootz. Kootz invited Bearden to exhibit, and from 1945 until 1948 Bearden showed there along with such other leading avant-garde painters as Robert Motherwell, Adolph Gottlieb, William Baziotes, Carl Holty, and Byron Browne. During this period Bearden painted oils filled with abstract figures. His works were largely derived from epic literary sources—the Bible, Rabelais, Homer, García Lorca. The style, boldly drawn contours filled with vibrant stained-glass color, was derivative as well, reminiscent of analytical cubism.

During his time at the Kootz gallery, Bearden grew intellectually restless. He found the direction of his colleagues—who came to be known as abstract expressionists—unsatisfying, and he left the country in 1950 to study in Paris on the GI bill. Though he enrolled at the Sorbonne, Bearden spent most of his time enjoying the city. When he returned in 1951, he found that he had lost interest in painting and took up songwriting. Without painting, however, he was disconnected. He had a nervous breakdown and recovered with the help of Nanette Rohan, whom he married in 1954.

With Bearden's recovery came a return to painting. To spur his return, he systematically copied the old masters, actually making large photostatic copies and tracing them. Starting with Duccio and Masaccio, he worked his way into the present, tracing Vermeer, Rembrandt, Delacroix, Matisse, and Picasso. Bearden's copying taught him

The Family ***(1988) by Romare Bearden.*** *Family life was a favorite theme of Bearden's, and a number of his works bear the title* The Family. *The work pictured here was completed in the last year of the artist's life.* THE ESTATE OF ROMARE BEARDEN. REPRODUCED BY PERMISSION.

well, and with Carl Holty he wrote a book on space, color, and composition entitled *The Painter's Mind: A Study of the Relations of Structure and Space in Painting* (1969). Once he had relearned painting, Bearden began to paint large abstract expressionist oils with mythopoeic titles such as *Blue Is the Smoke of War, White the Bones of Men* (1960).

Bearden's most noteworthy work did not come until he was over fifty years old. Galvanized by the civil rights movement, Bearden, as he had done in the 1930s, organized a group of black artists that took the name Spiral. The group wanted to do something to celebrate the movement, and Bearden thought that perhaps a group work, a collage, might be a vehicle. The group, however, was not interested, but he found himself engaged by the medium. As Bearden worked on these collages, allowing images of Charlotte, Pittsburgh, and Harlem to flood his memory, he captured the turbulence of the time with spatial distortions, abrupt juxtapositions, and vivid imagery.

Bearden's collages made use of a visual language seldom seen in American painting. His collages were populated by conjure women, trains, guitar players, birds, masked figures, winged creatures, and intense ritualistic activities: baptism, women bathing, families eating together at their dinner tables, funerals, parades, nightclub scenes. His representative works contain scenes of enduring ceremonies underscoring the beauty and densely complex cultural lineage of African-American life. Notable works include *Watching the Good Trains Go By* (1964); *At Connie's Inn* (1974), one of his many collages on the theme of jazz; *Maudell Sleet's Magic Garden* (1978) from his autobiographical series; *Calypso's Sacred Grove* (1977) from his series based on Homer's *Odyssey;* and lushly colored, late works such as *In a Green Shade* (1984). Ralph Ellison (1968) referred to Bearden's images as "abiding rituals and ceremonies of affirmation." Bearden invented his own phrase—the "Prevalence of Ritual"—to underscore the continuity of a culture's ceremonies, marking the traditions and values that connect one generation to another.

In his earliest works Bearden painted genre scenes, but in his mature work he pierced the skin of those scenes to explore the interior lives of black people. His first collages were photomontages, that is, photographic blow-ups of collages. After a year he abandoned that technique and, as his collages matured, began to use color more sensuously, creating lush landscapes with layers upon layers of cut paper, photographs, and paint. By the time of his death in 1988, Bearden had won virtually every prize and accolade imaginable, including the Medal of Honor, countless honorary doctorates, cover stories in the leading art magazines, and several retrospectives of his work, including one at the Museum of Modern Art in 1971.

See also Art; Civil Rights Movement, U.S.; Decarava, Roy; Douglas, Aaron; Du Bois, W. E. B.; Ellington, Edward Kennedy "Duke"; Ellison, Ralph; Harlem Renaissance; Hurston, Zora Neale; Jim Crow; New Negro; Painting and Sculpture; Robeson, Paul

Bibliography

Bearden, Romare. *The Painter's Mind: A Study of the Relations of Structure and Space in Painting.* New York: Crown, 1969.

Bearden, Romare. "Rectangular Structure in My Montage." *Leonardo* 2 (1969): 11–19.

Campbell, Mary Schmidt. "Romare Bearden: Rites and Riffs." *Art in America* (December 1981): 134–142.

Ellison, Ralph. *Romare Bearden: Paintings and Projections.* Albany: State University of New York Press, 1968.

Fine, Ruth. *The Art of Romare Bearden.* Washington: National Gallery of Art, 2003.

Greenburg, Jan. *Romare Bearden: A Collage of Memories.* New York: Abrams, 2003.

Schwartzman, Myron. *Romare Bearden: His Life and Art.* New York: Abrams, 1990.

MARY SCHMIDT CAMPBELL (1996)
Updated bibliography

Bedward, Alexander

c. 1850
November 8, 1930

Between 1891 and 1921, Alexander Bedward, an African-Jamaican healer, led the Jamaica Baptist Free Church in August Town, Jamaica, on the Hope River. Born in 1848 or 1850 at the present Matilda's Corner, then part of Hope Plantation in St. Andrew Parish, Bedward died on November 8, 1930. As a youth he raised provisions on Hope Plantation, and he was later employed on Louis Verley's sugar property, Mona, in St. Andrew. Apart from a period spent as a laborer in Colon, Colombia (later Panama), from 1883 to 1885, he worked until 1891 at Mona. He and his wife Elizabeth also leased land in the estate village of August Town. Between 1882 and 1889, a series of frightening dreams and visions, considered signs of divine election by African-Jamaicans, convinced Bedward to abandon an immoral life. In 1889 H. E. Shakespeare Wood (1800–1901), a reputed African-American, inducted Bedward as an elder of the Native Baptist Church. In October 1891 Bedward resigned his Mona Estate job. In December, citing divine commands to conduct thrice-weekly fasts and weekly riverside healing services, he began the ministry that made him famous. Hope River holy water became the conduit for visits to the other world, for encounters with angels or the holy spirit, and for healing and rebirth through baptism by immersion. In addition, fasting and meditation induced trances that produced insight.

Such activities suggest an otherworldly preoccupation, but given his prophetic persona and self-description as one of the *Book of Revelation*'s "two witnesses," Bedward could not help being dissatisfied. Low wages and land hunger compounded by natural catastrophes pushed many, like the younger Bedward himself, into the wider Caribbean as migrant laborers. Bedward assailed ministers and physicians as mercenaries for charging fees, and he prophesied the imminent end of the world. Jamaica's privileged class feared Bedward's heated sermons, and in 1895 the press and police framed him, accusing him of advocating insurrection. A white lawyer, Philip Stern (d. 1933) defended him. Bedward was acquitted by reason of insanity and committed to an asylum. Released on a technicality, he continued his ministry.

Bedward had approximately 125 congregations in Jamaica, Cuba, and Central America. Many members were poor, but others earned a good living as dray-cart operators or contractors, and one owned an ice-cream parlor. Bedwardites in August Town worked for neighboring plantations, farmed, and sold firewood, Hope River water, or home-processed foods. Bedward settled labor disputes when they arose.

By 1920, Bedward decided that his powers had failed. Another Jamaican, Marcus Garvey (1887–1940), had become prominent, and Bedward identified Garvey as Moses and himself merely as Moses' spokesman, Aaron. Convinced that his earthly mission had ended, Bedward revealed that he would undertake a spiritual ascension into heaven on December 31, 1920. In a July 1921 interview, Bedward averred that his followers had misunderstood him. Expecting him to take them up to heaven, between 3,000 and 6,000 followers disposed of their belongings and gathered to join the event. When the ascension did not occur, Bedward announced that he had risen in spirit.

In April 1921 Bedward rebuffed an armed police attempt to evict him from his home, flouted a ban on marching, and led a procession "to show the people of Kingston how strong I was." An armed force surrounded the procession and arrested Bedward and several hundred supporters. Released by the judge, Bedward was rearrested, declared insane, and again committed to the lunatic asylum, where he died in 1930. Under the leadership of George Burke (1873–1939), Bedward's son-in-law, the sect declined.

As an Old Testament–style prophet and millenarian who believed in the approach of a more perfect thousand-year-old society, Bedward drew on African-Jamaican misfortune. However, he never advocated armed rebellion, as the colonial state's treason case asserted and some unwary scholars have believed. On the contrary, Bedward later denied that he had ever incited people to rebel, and his actions belie the charge. He sought recognition of his pastors as marriage officers, solicited votes for Philip Stern in 1895, and he remained accessible to white visitors. In 1920 he predicted God's punishment of both white and black "rascals" on the Last Day.

The consolation and release that Bedwardites found in prophetic biblical texts with visions of millennial bliss diluted any potential for political insurrection even if Bedward had wished it. The ascension fiasco, which impoverished his followers and made them laughing stocks, may have persuaded some to trust other doctrines. Roman Henry, Bedward's private secretary and a Garveyite, broke with Burke. In the 1930s, Bedwardites and Garveyites Robert Hinds (d. 1950) and Leonard Howell (1898–1981) transformed Bedward's millenarianism into the more antiestablishment and durable Rastafarian movement, which recognized Ras Tafari (Emperor Haile Selassie, r. 1930–1974) of Ethiopia as a politico-religious redeemer.

See also Baptists; Garvey, Marcus; Rastafarianism

Bibliography

Beckwith, Martha W. *Black Roadways: A Study of Jamaican Folk Life* (1929). New York: Negro Universities Press, 1969.

Chevannes, Barry. *Rastafari: Roots and Ideology.* Syracuse, N.Y.: Syracuse University Press, 1994.

Elkins, W. F. "Prophet Bedward." In *Street Preachers, Faith Healers, and Herb Doctors in Jamaica, 1890–1925.* New York: Revisionist Press, 1977.

Hill, Robert. "Leonard P. Howell and Millenarian Visions in Early Rastafari." *Jamaica Journal* 16 (1981): 24–39.

Lewis, Rupert. "Garvey's Forerunners: Love and Bedward." *Race and Class* 28 (1987): 29–39.

MONICA SCHULER (2005)

Belafonte, Harry

March 1, 1927

The son of a Jamaican mother and a father from Martinique, singer, actor, and activist Harold George "Harry" Belafonte was born in New York City but received his early education in the public schools in Jamaica. In 1940 he returned to the United States and attended high school in New York. After navy service during World War II, he enrolled in Irwin Piscator's Dramatic Workshop in New York City and in 1948 became a member of the acting group of the American Negro Theater in New York. In September and October 1949 he appeared as a regular on CBS's black variety show, *Sugar Hill Times.*

Racial stereotyping greatly limited Belafonte's acting possibilities, and so he turned to singing. He made his debut in 1949, singing pop songs at New York's Royal Roost nightclub. He signed a record contract with RCA in 1952; however, it was not until 1957 that he achieved major commercial success as a singer. In the meantime he turned again to acting, and his muscular body, good looks, and rich, husky voice made him one of the first interracial male sex symbols. He appeared in the Broadway show *Al-*

manac, for which he won a Tony Award (1952), and he shared billing with Marge and Gower Champion in the musical *Three for Tonight* (1954). Belafonte's first film role was in *Bright Road* (1953), and he drew critical acclaim for his performance the next year in *Carmen Jones,* a black version of George Bizet's opera *Carmen*. He also appeared in the films *Island in the Sun* (1957) and *The World, the Flesh, and the Devil* (1959).

In the mid-1950s Belafonte began singing calypso, a folk-song style popular in Trinidad and other Caribbean islands. His passionate, witty, and suave renditions of such songs as "Matilda," "Jamaica Farewell," "Island in the Sun," "Brown Skin Girl," "Come Back Liza," and his signature tune, "The Banana Boat Song," ignited a calypso fad in the United States. Belafonte's album *Calypso* (1956) became the first solo album in history to sell a million copies. Over the next decade he recorded eleven more albums, including *Belafonte Sings of the Caribbean* (1957), *Belafonte at Carnegie Hall* (1957), *Porgy and Bess* (with Lena Horne, 1959), *Jump Up Calypso* (1961), *The Midnight Special* (1962), and *Belafonte on Campus* (1967).

In 1960 Belafonte became the first African American to star in a television special, which won him an Emmy Award. He also began a long association with African culture and politics at this time. In 1959 he brought to the United States two protégés, the South African musicians Miriam Makeba and Hugh Masekela.

Like his idol, Paul Robeson, Belafonte combined singing with civil rights activism. In part because of his friendship with Robeson, Belafonte was partially blacklisted during the early 1950s and was refused television and other engagements. He, in turn, refused to appear in the South from 1954 to 1961. In 1956 Belafonte helped raise money to support the Montgomery bus boycott and met the Rev. Dr. Martin Luther King, Jr. The two became close friends, and by 1960 Belafonte was a major fund-raiser and strategist in the civil rights movement. He helped raise funds to support freedom riders and voter-registration efforts and in 1963 helped establish the Southern Free Theater in Jackson, Mississippi, which was dedicated to the development of a black political leader. Belafonte also served as an unofficial liaison between the Kennedy administration and black leaders. In 1961 he was named to the advisory committee of the Peace Corps.

Belefonte was an active film and television producer, and his company, Harbel, formed in 1959, was responsible for the first major television show produced by a black, *Strolling Twenties,* which featured such well-known black artists and performers as Duke Ellington, Sidney Poitier, Nipsey Russell, and Joe Williams. In 1959 the company also produced the film *Odds Against Tomorrow,* in which Belafonte appeared with Ed Begley and Robert Ryan. In the 1970s, following the death of Martin Luther King and the ebbing of the civil rights movement, Belafonte resumed making films, appearing with Sidney Poitier in *Buck and the Preacher* (1971) and *Uptown Saturday Night* (1974). Toward the end of the 1970s, Belafonte, who had sung in nightclubs only sporadically in the previous decade, resumed singing. He made major tours in 1976 and 1979. In 1984 he coproduced the hip-hop film *Beat Street.*

Through the 1980s and early 1990s Belafonte achieved a new renown for his international political activities. Most notable was his commitment to humanitarian efforts in Ethiopia. In 1985 he conceived the project that resulted in the recording "We Are the World," written by Lionel Richie and Michael Jackson and conducted by Quincy Jones, which raised over $70 million to aid victims of famine in Africa. For his humanitarian work he was awarded the position of goodwill ambassador for UNICEF in 1986. In 1988 he recorded an album of South African music, *Paradise in Gazankulu.* In 1990, Belafonte, a longtime opponent of apartheid, served as chair of the committee that welcomed African National Congress leader Nelson Mandela to America. The same year, New York governor Mario Cuomo appointed him to lead the Martin Luther King, Jr., Commission to promote knowledge of nonviolence.

During the 1990s Belafonte continued both his performing and his producing career. Among other projects, he starred in the television special *Harry Belafonte and Friends* (1996) and he appeared in Robert Altman's film *Kansas City* (1995) and in *White Man's Burden* (1995), which he also produced.

Belafonte won the Best Supporting Actor award from the New York Film Critics Circle in 1996 for *Kansas City.* In 2004, in his role as the UN Children's Fund goodwill ambassador, he was deeply involved in publicizing the poverty in Kenya.

See also Ellington, Edward Kennedy "Duke"; Film; King, Martin Luther, Jr.; Musical Theater; Poitier, Sidney; Robeson, Paul; Television

Bibliography

Branch, Taylor. *Parting the Waters: America in the Civil Rights Years.* New York: Simon and Schuster, 1987.

Gates, Henry Louis, Jr. "Belafonte's Balancing Act." *New Yorker* (August 26, 1996): 133-136; (September 2, 1996): 138-142.

Glover, Danny. Interview with Belafonte. *Interview* 26, No. 9 (September, 1996).

Shaw, Arnold. *Belafonte: An Unauthorized Biography.* New York: Chilton, 1960.

JAMES E. MUMFORD (1996)
Updated by publisher 2005

Belmanna Riots

The Belmanna Riots, which took place in 1876 in Tobago, a small British colony in the southern Caribbean, were typical of post-emancipation protests by black laborers and peasants in the English-speaking West Indies. The cluster of grievances that lay behind these riots were paralleled in nearly all of the impoverished plantation colonies in the nineteenth century.

The events of 1876 can be quickly summarized. Unrest developed among workers at the Roxborough Estate, on the southern coast of Tobago, early in that year, especially among immigrant laborers from Barbados. Fires were set on the estate on May 1, and policemen under Corporal Belmanna attempted to arrest the arsonists on May 3. A crowd resisted and attacked the policemen, and Belmanna fired into the people, killing a Barbadian woman. This triggered a major riot outside the Roxborough Court House, during which Belmanna was beaten to death and other officers were injured. The disorders briefly spread to other estates in the Windward District, but order was restored within a few days, especially after a British warship arrived with a contingent of Barbadian policemen.

Belmanna's firing into the crowd was clearly the catalyst for the violence that followed, but the underlying causes of the riot were the classic labor grievances of the post-emancipation era: disputes over wages; arbitrary wage stoppages by management; the estate shop, or truck, system (where an estate owner runs a shop and forces the resident laborers to purchase their supplies from it, usually at higher prices than could be found elsewhere); and the objectionable, contemptuous behavior of the estate owner and manager towards the workers. Other grievances included the lack of proper medical care and the laborers' difficulties in obtaining lands. The lieutenant governor of Tobago believed that wage disputes were the chief source of unrest, reflecting what he called the "chronic want of sympathy between capital and labor" that had long existed in Tobago (Brereton, 1984, p. 118). Discontent over these issues, common to most labor protests in the region at this period, was heightened for the Barbadians at Roxborough by news of the serious riots in Barbados a few days earlier (the Confederation Riots).

This was, then, a classic plantation labor protest. There is some evidence that the trouble at Roxborough Estate was triggered by its owner's attempt to withdraw "privileges," such as the right to pasture livestock on estate land and to cut and use timber from the estate, free of charge, that had become customary. He had also instituted a new wage policy that the laborers resented. Again this was a common cause of agrarian protest in the region—similar acts were responsible for the riots on the island of St. Vincent in 1862. But there is no evidence that the riots were long premeditated or well organized, or that the rioters intended to do harm to Tobago's small white community or "take over" the island.

Nevertheless, this was what many resident whites feared, for they had not forgotten the Morant Bay Rebellion in Jamaica eleven years earlier. The outcome of the Belmanna Riots was, in fact, quite similar to that of the Jamaican uprising: in August 1876 the members of the legislative assembly agreed to give up their right to elective representation and to accept a "pure" Crown Colony constitution, with a wholly nominated legislative council. They believed that if Tobago was a pure Crown Colony under direct British rule, they would be better protected (by Britain) against future threats from black laborers and peasants. Thus, the way was cleared constitutionally for Tobago's unification with Trinidad (as a British colony), which occurred in two stages between 1889 and 1899.

See also Morant Bay Rebellion; Riots and Popular Protests

Bibliography

Brereton, Bridget. "Post-emancipation Protest in the Caribbean: The 'Belmanna Riots' in Tobago, 1876." *Caribbean Quarterly* 30, nos 3–4 (1984): 110–123.

BRIDGET BRERETON (2005)

Benn, Brindley

January 24, 1923

Brindley Horatio Benn was born in Kitty, British Guiana, and attended Central High School, where he was successful in the Junior and Senior Cambridge exams. Before entering politics, Benn was a teacher in Georgetown, the capital city, and was motivated to become involved in politics as a result of his interest in social work and youth work, and in finding solutions to the problems the citizenry confronted. He joined the People's Progressive Party (PPP), the nation's first mass-based political party, which came into existence in January 1950, and was editor of *Thunder,* a publication of the party. By the time the PPP was elected to office in the wake of the March 1953 elections—the first under universal adult suffrage—Benn was an executive committee member of the party.

Consequent upon the suspension of the constitution in October 1953 and the removal of the PPP government from office, Benn was restricted to an area of about one mile in radius in New Amsterdam in the county of Berbice and required to report to the police daily. In 1954 the leadership of the party split, and in 1956 three of the most important African-Guianese members of the party defected. These events were occasioned in part by the about-face of the party's Marxist leader, Dr. Cheddi Jagan, regarding the question of joining the West Indies Federation. After these events, Benn remained with the PPP despite his personal feeling that the party should not have changed its position on federation. Benn held this position although his assessment that the crisis in the leadership of the party was between the "left," comprising the Marxists who favored more rapid changes, and the "right," who advocated a softer pro-Moscow line.

Following the PPP victory in the 1957 general election, Benn served as a member of parliament from 1957 to 1964. As minister of education and community development, he coined the slogan "One People, One Nation, One Destiny," which became the national motto. During his tenure as minister of agriculture, the Guyana School of Agriculture was established. By 1960 he had become disenchanted with the PPP leadership, which he felt was abandoning its class concerns. He also believed that the leadership was more concerned with winning elections as a way of maintaining itself in office than with providing gradual improvement in the education of the masses—which was essential to preparing the colony for political independence—in accordance with espoused socialist principles and with developing viable policies geared to the achievement of the government's goals. By the 1964 elections Benn had risen to the position of deputy premier, and in the second PPP prenomination-day broadcast to the nation, titled "The PPP and Human Rights," Benn not only specified the human rights to which every Guianese was entitled (freedom of organization and association, of movement, to give and receive information, of religion, of assembly and demonstrations, of the right to recognition of trade unions, and of equality before the law) but also the party's record in the field of civil rights while it was in office from 1953 to 1964.

In 1964, also, Benn was detained by the British government as a political prisoner under the Emergency Regulations at the Sibley Hall Detention Center in the county of Essequibo. Then in 1965 he formed the Working People's Vanguard Party and printed a weekly mimeographed account of the political and economic scams that were occurring in the country. He maintained friendly relations with other political parties through the Patriotic Coalition for Democracy.

After the PPP regained power following the 1992 elections, Benn won a seat in parliament, which he subsequently relinquished to become Guyana's high commissioner to Canada from August 1993 to November 1998. In 1994 Benn was awarded the Cacique Crown of Honour, a national honor, for his contribution to the restoration of democracy in Guyana. From 1999 to 2002, he served as chairman of the Public Services Commission and as a member of the Judicial Service Commission and the National Archives Board. In 2003 he became chairman of the Guyana Lotteries Commission and of the Internal Revenue Board of Review.

Although Benn previously favored Guyana's entry in the West Indies Federation, he now feels that despite previous strong support from other West Indian leaders, such as Trinidad and Tobago's Dr. Eric Williams, Barbados's Grantley Adams, and, for a time, Jamaica's Norman Manley, it was "a colonial-style institution" that was "being foisted on the Caribbean by Britain" (Benn, 2004), and, moreover, "an artificial attempt at regional unity, and a hurried arrangement created by the British in an area of emerging Third World Countries" (personal communication with author).

See also Politics and Politicians in Latin America

Bibliography

Benn, Brindley. "Legacies of Cheddi Jagan." In *Caribbean Labor and Politics: Political Legacies of Cheddi Jagan and Michael Manley,* edited by Perry Mars and Alma Young. Detroit, Mich.: Wayne State University Press, 2004.

St. Pierre, Maurice. *Anatomy of Resistance: Anti-Colonialism in Guyana, 1823–1966.* London and Basingstoke: Macmillan, 1999.

MAURICE ST. PIERRE (2005)

BENNETT, LOUISE

SEPTEMBER 7, 1919

Born in Kingston, Jamaica, in 1919, Louise Bennett emerged as a writer in the nationalistic ferment of the late

1930s. She liked the English literature she encountered in school and for a while attempted to emulate it. Then one day, struck by the vividness of "dialect" (Jamaican Creole), she began to wonder "why more of our poets and writers were not . . .writing in this medium . . . instead of writing in the same old English way about Autumn and things like that" (Bennett, 1968, p. 99). Bennett began to write verse in dialect and to develop a reputation for reciting it. At the invitation of Eric Coverley, she performed in his 1938 Christmas morning concert and received her first professional fee.

Bennett's first book appeared in 1942. In May 1943 Jamaica's leading newspaper, *The Gleaner,* began to publish each Sunday a column of Louise Bennett's verse. Although she has had to contend with disapproval—mainly from people deeming her a threat to "proper English"—her work has always been widely enjoyed. Yet in spite of early endorsement by cultural leaders such as Philip Sherlock and Robert Verity, her writing was largely undervalued until the 1960s.

Bennett's most substantial books of verse are *Jamaica Labrish* (1966) and *Selected Poems* (1982). Her prose includes the stories in *Anancy and Miss Lou* (1979) and topical radio monologues in *Aunty Roachy Seh* (1993). The recipient of many awards since 1960, she is now generally acknowledged as an important artist and a pathfinder in the use of Creole. In a book on postcolonial poetry, Jahan Ramazani deems her "long overdue for recognition beyond the West Indies—as master ironist, as master poet, as a major anglophone poet of our time" (Ramazani, p. 140).

Bennett is also an expert performer, trained at the Royal Academy of Dramatic Arts. She helped Jamaicanize the Little Theatre Movement pantomime, now only distantly related to its English antecedents. She wrote some of the scripts and contributed to others, and from 1943 to 1975 was one the focal personalities in the annual show.

Some critics argue that only in performance are the talents of Bennett truly realized. Her audio recordings include *Yes, M'Dear: Miss Lou Live* (1984), *Bre' Anancy & Miss Lou* (1991), *Miss Lou's Views* (1991), and *Lawd . . .Di Riddim Sweet* (1999). She appears on video in *Miss Lou and Friends* (1991) and *Visiting with Miss Lou* (2003).

A poem by Bennett is usually a dramatic monologue in Jamaican Creole, employing a version of the ballad quatrain that accommodates the rhythms, tone, and pitch of Jamaican speech. Her comedy, often topical, evaluates. Her writings—poems, stories, commentary, pantomime scripts—ridicule pretension, prejudice, and self-contempt. They laugh at people ashamed of being Jamaican or ashamed of being black. They respect, but sometimes criticize, the values and perceptions of the ordinary Jamaican, the "small man" struggling to cope. They celebrate Jamaican culture, with frequent allusion to proverbs, folksongs, African continuities, colonial education, and the Bible.

Louise Bennett migrated from Jamaica early in the 1980s. She has lived in Toronto since 1987.

See also Caribbean Theater, Anglophone; Dub Poetry; Literature of the English-Speaking Caribbean; Women Writers of the Caribbean

Bibliography

Bennett, Louise. *Jamaica Labrish.* Kingston: Sangster's Book Stores, 1966.

Bennett, Louise. In *Caribbean Quarterly* 14, nos. 1 & 2 (March–June 1968): p. 99.

Bennett, Louise. *Selected Poems.* Kingston: Sangster's Book Stores, 1982.

Bennett, Louise. *Aunty Roachy Seh.* Kingston: Sangster's Book Stores, 1993.

Morris, Mervyn. "Louise Bennett." In *Fifty Caribbean Writers: A Bio-Bibliographical Critical Sourcebook.* New York: Greenwood Press, 1986.

Ramazani, Jahan. *The Hybrid Muse: Postcolonial Poetry in English.* Chicago: University of Chicago Press, 2001.

MERVYN MORRIS (2005)

Berry, Chuck

October 18, 1926

The rock-and-roll singer Charles Edward Anderson "Chuck" Berry was born in St. Louis, Missouri, the third of four children. His parents were deeply religious Baptists, but Berry became interested in secular music as a teenager. He was inspired to become a performer and guitarist after receiving an enthusiastic reception of his rendition of "Confessin' the Blues" at Sumner High School, where he was a student. He attended Poro School of Beauty Culture in St. Louis during the 1940s, and then used his skills as a hairdresser and cosmetologist to support himself in the late 1940s and early 1950s. Berry also performed with several groups at clubs around St. Louis in the early 1950s, and he became popular with both white and black audiences because he sang country songs and blues with equal zest.

In 1955 Berry relocated to Chicago, where Muddy Waters (1915–1983) recommended him to Chess Records, which signed him to a recording contract. Berry's first recording, and his first hit, was "Maybelline" (1955), a reinterpretation of the traditional country song "Ida Red" (Berry's title was inspired by the Maybelline line of hair creams). He performed the song with crisp rapid-fire delivery and introduced new lyrics on the subjects of teenage love and car racing.

Berry was a pioneer in rock and roll and helped transform the new music into a commercially successful genre. His greatest success came in the late 1950s with songs that were definitive expressions of the themes of teenage angst, rebelliousness, and the celebration of youthful vitality. His best-known recordings include "Roll Over, Beethoven" (1956), "School Days" (1957), "Rock-and-Roll Music" (1957), "Sweet Little Sixteen" (1958), "Memphis" (1958), and "Johnny B. Goode" (1958). Surprisingly, his only number-one record was the crass and forgettable "My Ding-a-Ling" (1972), a salute to male teenage masturbation.

After 1959, Berry's career was interrupted when he was arrested for transporting a minor across state lines. Though the events are still contested, Berry allegedly took a fourteen-year-old prostitute from Texas to St. Louis to check hats at a nightclub where he was performing. When he fired her, she reported his actions to local police. Berry served a two-year prison sentence at the federal penitentiary at Terre Haute, Indiana, from 1961 to 1963. While Berry never reached his former level of popularity after this, he became active in the rock-and-roll revival of the 1980s and early 1990s and performed widely.

Berry was arguably the central figure in the creation of the sound and style of rock and roll in the mid-1950s. He had a tremendous influence on rock performers who came after him, including Buddy Holly, the Beatles, the Beach Boys, and the Rolling Stones, who emulated both his guitar style and his highly energized stage presence. Berry's recording of "Johnny B. Goode" was included in the payload of the Neptune-bound Voyager 1 spacecraft, a testimony to the original and representative nature of his work. In 2004, *Rolling Stone* published a list of the fifty greatest rock-and-roll artists. Chuck Berry was number five on that list.

See also Muddy Waters (Morganfield, McKinley); Music in the United States

Bibliography

Berry, Chuck. *Chuck Berry: The Autobiography*. New York: Harmony Books, 1987.

Collis, John. *Chuck Berry: The Biography*. London: Aurum, 2002.

DeWitt, H. *Chuck Berry: Rock 'n' Roll Music*. Fremont, Calif.: Horizon Books, 1981.

Hardy, Phil, and Davie Laing. *Encyclopedia of Rock*. London, 1987.

"The Immortals: The Fifty Greatest Artists of All Time." *Rolling Stone* 946 (April 15, 2004).

DAVID HENDERSON (1996)
Updated by publisher 2005

Berry, Halle

August 14, 1966

Halle Maria Berry was born in Cleveland, Ohio, to an African-American father, Jerome, and a Caucasian mother, Judith. Named after Cleveland's Halle Building, which housed Halle Brothers department store, Berry and her older sister Heidi were raised by their mother after their parents divorced when Halle was four. After graduating from Bedford High, she attended Cuyahoga Community College. Berry won the Miss Teen All-American pageant in 1985 and the Miss Ohio USA pageant in 1986; she was the first runner-up in the 1986 Miss USA pageant.

While living in Chicago, Berry did modeling while studying with the Second City improvisational group. Her first acting job was portraying a model on the 1989 television series *Living Dolls*. Berry admits she has had to fight against both racism and her own beauty when auditioning for film roles. The actress had to convince director Spike Lee that she was not too glamorous to play crack addict Vivian in his 1991 film *Jungle Fever* (her screen debut). She then went on to roles in such films as *The Last Boy Scout* (1991), *Boomerang* (1992), *Losing Isaiah* (1993), *The Flintstones* (1994), *Executive Decision* (1996), *The Rich Man's Wife* (1996), *B*A*P*S* (1997), *Bulworth* (1998), and *Why Do Fools Fall in Love* (1998). She also appeared on television in the miniseries *Alex Haley's Queen* (1993), *Solomon & Sheba* (1995), and *Oprah Winfrey Presents: The Wedding* (1998).

In 1999, Berry won an NAACP Image Award, Golden Globe, Emmy, and Screen Actors Guild award as Best Actress in the Miniseries/TV movie category for the HBO movie *Introducing Dorothy Dandridge*, which she also produced. In 2002, Berry became the first African-American actress to win the Best Actress Academy Award for her role in *Monster's Ball*, in which she played a poor single mother, another unglamorous role she had to persuade director Marc Foster that she could play. She also won a Screen Actors Guild and a National Board of Review award for the part.

After filming *Monster's Ball*, Berry played "Bond Girl" Jinx Johnson in the twentieth film in the series, *Die Another Day* (2002). Later films included *X-Men* (2000), *Swordfish* (2001), *Gothika* (2003), *X-Men 2: X-Men United* (2003), *Catwoman* (2004), and *Robots* (2005). Berry took the leading role in the 2005 television movie *Oprah Winfrey Presents: Their Eyes Were Watching God* and served as an executive producer on the HBO film *Lackawanna Blues* (2005). She has also served as a spokeswoman for Revlon Cosmetics since 1996. Berry was previously married to David Justice (1993–1996) and Eric Benet (2001–2005).

See also Film in the United States

Bibliography

Collier, Adore. "Halle Berry: Why I Will Never Marry Again." *Ebony* (August 2004): 16.

Kennedy, Dana. "Halle Berry, Bruised and Beautiful, Is on a Mission." *New York Times* (March 10, 2002): A2.

Toure. "Portrait of a Lady." *USA Weekend* (January 20, 2001).

CHRISTINE TOMASSINI (2005)

Mary McLeod Bethune (1875–1955). *Bethune, pictured in her office in this 1943 photograph by Gordon Parks, founded a school for African-American girls in a rented house in Daytona, Florida at the age of twenty-nine. The school expanded progressively in numbers of students and program offerings, gaining a national reputation and eventually merging with the failing Cookman Institute of Jacksonville to form Bethune-Cookman College, a fully accredited institution awarding bachelor's degrees by the time of Parks's photograph.* THE LIBRARY OF CONGRESS

Bethune, Mary McLeod

July 10, 1875
May 18, 1955

"If I have a legacy to leave my people, it is my philosophy of living and serving. As I face tomorrow, I am content, for I think I have spent my life well. I pray now that my philosophy may be helpful to those who share my vision of a world of peace, progress, brotherhood, and love." With these words, rights activist Mary McLeod Bethune concluded her last will and testament, outlining her legacy to African Americans. Bethune lived up to her stated philosophy throughout her long career as a gifted institution builder who focused on securing rights and opportunities for African-American women and youth. Her stunning successes as a leader made her one of the most influential women of her day and, for many years, a premier African-American leader.

Mary McLeod was born in 1875, the thirteenth of fifteen children of Sam and Patsy (McIntosh) McLeod. The McLeod family, many of whom had been slaves before the Civil War, owned a farm near Mayesville, South Carolina, when Mary was growing up. Mary McLeod attended the Trinity Presbyterian Mission School near her home from 1885 until 1888, and with the help of her mentor, Emma Jane Wilson, she moved on to Scotia Seminary (later Barber-Scotia College), a Presbyterian school in Concord, North Carolina. McLeod set her sights on serving as a missionary in Africa and so entered the Bible Institute for Home and Foreign Missions (later known as the Moody Bible Institute) in Chicago. She was devastated when she was informed that the Presbyterian Church would not support African-American missionaries to Africa. Instead, McLeod turned her attentions and talents to the field of education at home.

From 1896 through 1897 McLeod taught at the Haines Institute, a Presbyterian-sponsored school in Augusta, Georgia, an experience that proved meaningful for her future. At Haines, McLeod worked with Lucy Craft Laney, the school's founder and a pioneering African-

American educator. McLeod took away examples and skills she would put into action throughout her life.

From Haines, McLeod moved on to another Presbyterian school, the Kendall Institute in Sumter, South Carolina, where she met and married Albertus Bethune in 1898. The couple moved to Savannah, Georgia, and in 1899 their only child, Albert Bethune, was born. Although Albertus and Mary McLeod Bethune remained married until Albertus's death in 1918, they were no longer together by 1907. In 1900 Bethune moved to Palatka, Florida, where she founded a Presbyterian school and later an independent school that also offered social services to the community.

In 1904 Bethune settled in Daytona, Florida, to establish a school for African-American girls. She opened her Daytona Educational and Industrial Institute in a rented house with little furniture and a tiny group of students. Students at the school learned basic academic subjects, worked on homemaking skills, engaged in religious activities, and worked with Bethune in the fields of a farm she bought in 1910. Through the farm, Bethune and her students were able to feed the members of the school community, as well as sell the surplus to benefit the school. The Daytona Institute also emphasized connections with the community, offering summer school, a playground for children, and other activities. All of this made Bethune an important voice in her local community.

The school's reputation began to grow at the national level through a visit by Booker T. Washington in 1912 and the addition of Frances Reynolds Keyser to the staff in the same year. Keyser had served as superintendent of the White Rose Mission in New York and was a well-known activist. After World War I the school grew to include a high school and a nurses' training division. In 1923 the school merged with the failing Cookman Institute of Jacksonville, Florida, and embarked on a coeducational program. In 1929 it took the name Bethune-Cookman College. By 1935 Bethune's school, founded on a tiny budget, had become an accredited junior college and, by 1943, a fully accredited college, awarding bachelor's degrees. This success gained Bethune a national reputation and won her the NAACP's prestigious Spingarn Medal in 1935.

In addition to her success as an educator, Bethune also made a major mark on the black women's club movement in America. In 1917 she was elected president of the Florida Association of Colored Women, a post she retained until 1924. Under her leadership the organization established a home for young women in Ocala. In 1920 she organized the Southeastern Federation of Colored Women and guided this group through 1925. From 1924 to 1928 she served as president of the National Association of Colored Women (NACW), the most powerful organization of African-American women's clubs in the country. During this period, she toured Europe as the NACW's president and established the organization's headquarters in Washington, D.C., in 1928. Bethune's crowning achievement in the club movement was the 1935 founding of the National Council of Negro Women (NCNW). This organization served to coordinate and streamline the cooperative work of a wide variety of black women's organizations. During Bethune's fourteen years as president, the NCNW achieved this goal, began to work closely with the federal government on issues facing African Americans, and developed an international perspective on women's lives.

Bethune's influence with the Franklin D. Roosevelt administration led her to activities that made her an even greater public figure on behalf of African Americans. In 1936 she organized the Federal Council on Negro Affairs, popularly known as the Black Cabinet, a group of black advisers who helped coordinate government programs for African Americans. In this same period, she became deeply involved in the work of the National Youth Administration (NYA), serving on the advisory committee from its founding in 1935. In 1936 Bethune began functioning as director of the NYA's Division of Negro Affairs, a position that became official in 1939 and that she held until 1943. This appointment made her the highest ranking black woman in government up to that point. Bethune's goals in the NYA were to increase the representation of qualified African Americans in leadership in local and state programs and to ensure that NYA benefits distributed to whites and to blacks achieved parity.

In addition to Bethune's many other achievements, she served as the president of the Association for the Study of Negro Life and History from 1936 to 1951, established the Mary McLeod Bethune Foundation, and wrote a column for the *Pittsburgh Courier*. Bethune's career is testimony to her leadership skills, her commitment to justice and equality for African Americans, her unfailing dedication to the ideals of American democracy, and her philosophy of service.

See also Association for the Study of African American Life and History; Bethune-Cookman College; National Association of Colored Women; National Council of Negro Women; *Pittsburgh Courier;* Spingarn Medal; Washington, Booker T.

Bibliography

Bethune, Mary McLeod. "My Last Will and Testament." *Ebony*, August 1955.

Hanson, Joyce Ann. *Mary McLeod Bethune and Black Women's Political Activism.* Columbia: University of Missouri Press, 2003.

Holt, Rackham. *Mary McLeod Bethune: A Biography.* New York: Doubleday, 1964.

Smith, Elaine. "Mary McLeod Bethune and the National Youth Administration." In *Clio Was a Woman: Studies in the History of American Women,* edited by Mabel E. Deutrich and Virginia C. Purdy. Washington, D.C.: Howard University Press, 1980.

JUDITH WEISENFELD (1996)
Updated bibliography

Bethune-Cookman College

On October 3, 1904, African-American educator and activist Mary McLeod Bethune founded a normal and industrial school for African-American girls in Daytona Beach, Florida. Although she began with only five students in a small rented house, in less than two years Bethune attracted 250 pupils and founded the Daytona School for Girls in a building she erected on top of a garbage dump. By 1916 the school had grown into the Daytona Normal and Industrial Institute and was affiliated with the United Methodist Church. After absorbing the Cookman Institute for Boys, previously located in Jacksonville, the school, newly christened Bethune-Cookman College, was established as a high school with junior college courses in 1924.

Bethune, who continued as president of the college until 1947, raised funds for the school from middle-class blacks and liberal white philanthropists. Committed to integration and interracial cooperation, Bethune sought out a mixed-race board of directors, but she opposed white directors who favored a vocational curriculum. Bethune pushed for the inclusion of a full liberal arts program, and the school continuously upgraded its standards and facilities. Despite a heavy financial squeeze during the Great Depression, Bethune-Cookman became a two-year junior college in 1939 and a four-year institution shortly after, receiving a Grade A accreditation in 1947, the last year of Bethune's presidency. In 2005 Bethune-Cookman, the only historically black college founded by a woman, had a student body of approximately 2800 and had thirty-five buildings on more than seventy acres. The college offered degree programs in 39 major fields of study, including subject areas as diverse as biology, business, and communications.

See also Bethune, Mary McLeod; Dillard University; Fisk University; Howard University; Lincoln University; Morehouse College; Spelman College; Tuskegee University; Wilberforce University

Bibliography

Bethune, Mary McLeod. "A College on a Garbage Dump." In *Black Women in White America: A Documentary History,* edited by Gerda Lerner, pp. 134–143. New York: Pantheon, 1972.

Flemming, Sheila Y. *Bethune-Cookman College, 1904–1994: The Answered Prayer to a Dream.* Virginia Beach, Va: Donning, 1995.

Hamilton, Kendra. "Keepers of the Dream: As Bethune-Cookman College Celebrates 100 Years, School Officials, Alumni Say Mission Has Not Changed." *Black Issues in Higher Education* 21, No. 20 (November 18, 2004): 12–13.

Holt, Rackham. *Mary McLeod Bethune: A Biography.* New York: Doubleday, 1964.

MARGARET D. JACOBS (1996)
Updated by publisher 2005

Bevel, James

October 19, 1936

Civil rights activist James Bevel was born in Itta Bena, Mississippi. In his early teens he experienced a religious conversion and became well known throughout his town as an inspiring preacher. He was ordained as a Baptist minister in 1959 and received a B.A. from American Baptist Theological Seminary in Nashville, Tennessee, two years later.

Bevel's childhood had familiarized him with wrenching rural poverty and left him with a commitment to work for an end to racial injustice. In 1958 he attended the Highlander Folk School, an interracial adult-education center in Tennessee that focused on promoting social activism. At Highlander, Bevel had his first in-depth exposure to nonviolent theories of social change and was deeply influenced by the commitment to interracialism of Myles Horton, the school's director. One year later, Bevel attended a Vanderbilt University training workshop for student activists in Nashville sponsored by the Fellowship of Reconciliation (FOR), a nonviolent direct action group. Through his involvement with FOR, he became a leader in the Nashville student movement and played a central role in organizing and staging sit-ins to force Nashville businesses to desegregate.

In 1960 Bevel became one of the founding members of the Student Nonviolent Coordinating Committee

(SNCC), a grassroots civil rights organization. The following year, he married Diane Nash, a SNCC activist, and in 1962 they moved to Albany, Georgia, where he became a prominent leader in the Albany movement to fight racism and segregation and became involved in the Southern Christian Leadership Conference (SCLC).

In SCLC Bevel coordinated direct action protests and trained student activists. In 1963 he was appointed director of direct action and nonviolent education. He traveled to Birmingham, Alabama, to coordinate SCLC's activities and led a protest march of black children from the Sixteenth Street Baptist Church that played a pivotal role in galvanizing Birmingham's black community. He worked closely with his wife, and the couple's ideas were influential in the planning for the March on Washington later that year. Bevel played an integral role in SCLC's attempt to apply nonviolent civil rights techniques in the North, and in 1966 he traveled to Chicago to organize direct-action workshops and tenant strikes.

Over time Bevel became involved in a broader range of social and political issues. In the summer of 1966, he worked with the Nonviolent Human and Community Development Institute, and in 1967 he took a leave of absence from SCLC to become executive director of the Spring Mobilization Committee to End the War in Vietnam.

Despite his relative obscurity, Bevel was a dynamic and dedicated civil rights leader. He composed several freedom songs—"Dod-Dog" (1959), "Why Was a Darky Born" (1961), and "I Know We'll Meet Again" (1969)—that inspired many in the civil rights movement. He worked closely with the Rev. Dr. Martin Luther King Jr. and was at his side when he was assassinated in Memphis, Tennessee, on April 4, 1968. Assessing Bevel's pivotal role in the civil rights movement, Ralph Abernathy said, "I guess Bevel was the number three man in the movement [alongside King and himself] because he didn't want the glory or the praise, he just wanted to do the work."

Following King's death, Bevel left SCLC after unsuccessful attempts to focus the organization's agenda on education, international arms reduction, and a fair trial for King's accused assassin, James Earl Ray. By the 1980s, when Bevel reentered the public arena, his politics had shifted to the right. In 1980 he campaigned for Ronald Reagan, and four years later he ran unsuccessfully for the House of Representatives from Chicago on the Republican ticket.

In the late 1980s Bevel centered his attention on education—founding Students for Education and Economic Development (SEED) in Chicago—and international issues, such as human rights abuses in former Soviet bloc countries. In 1989 he formed the National Committee against Religious Bigotry and Racism (NCARBAR), and in the early 1990s he gained prominence as an opponent of capital punishment.

In the opening years of the twenty-first century, Bevel came under much criticism while working for the American Freedom Coalition defending the religious practices of Rev. Sun Myung Moon's Unification Church (renamed the Family Federation).

See also Civil Rights Movement, U.S.; Southern Christian Leadership Conference (SCLC); Student Nonviolent Coordinating Committee (SNCC)

Bibliography

Branch, Taylor. *Parting the Waters: America in the King Years, 1954–1963.* New York: Simon & Schuster, 1988.

Garrow, David J. *Bearing the Cross.* New York: Morrow, 1986.

Kryn, Randall. "James L. Bevel: The Strategist of the 1960 Civil Rights Movement." In *We Shall Overcome: The Civil Rights Movement in the United States in the 1950s and 1960s,* vol. 2, edited by David J. Garrow. New York: Carlson, 1989.

JEANNE THEOHARIS (1996)
Updated by publisher 2005

Bibb, Henry Walton

May 10, 1815
1854

Henry Walton Bibb, an author, editor, and emigrationist, was born a slave on a Kentucky plantation. He was the oldest son of a slave, Milldred Jackson. Like many slaves, he never knew his father and was even unsure of his father's identity; he was told, however, that he was the son of James Bibb, a Kentucky state senator. His six brothers, all slaves, were sold one by one, until the entire family was scattered. In 1833, he met and married a mulatto slave named Malinda, with whom he had one daughter, Mary Frances. Bibb's fierce desire to obtain his freedom and reclaim his wife and daughter motivated his repeated attempts to escape from slavery. In 1842 he successfully fled to Detroit, where he began work as an abolitionist. He continued to search for Malinda and his daughter, but after learning that Malinda had been sold as the mistress of a white slave owner, Bibb gave up his longtime dream and resolved to advance the antislavery cause.

In 1850 Bibb published his autobiography, *Narrative of the Life and Adventures of Henry Bibb, an American*

Slave. One of the best-known slave narratives, the book contains an extensive, personal account of Bibb's life as a slave and runaway. Soon after it appeared, Congress passed the Fugitive Slave Act of 1850, which gave slave owners the right to reclaim runaways—and obligated northerners to help them to do so. Bibb, like many others, openly stated that he preferred death to re-enslavement, and he fled with his second wife, Mary Miles Bibb of Boston, to Canada. In Ontario, the Bibbs soon became leaders of the large African-Canadian community.

In 1851 Bibb established the *Voice of the Fugitive,* the first black newspaper in Canada. Through the *Voice,* he expressed his essential ideas as an emigrationist by urging slaves and free blacks to move to Canada. The newspaper became a central tool of emigration advocates. In addition to the *Voice,* Bibb's civic and political accomplishments in the Ontario communities were substantial.

Two years before his death, and as a direct result of his work as a writer and orator, Bibb was reunited with three of his brothers, who had also escaped from bondage and emigrated to Canada. He interviewed them and published their stories in the *Voice of the Fugitive.* Bibb died in the summer of 1854, at the age of thirty-nine.

See also Runaway Slaves in the United States; Slave Narratives

Bibliography

Bibb, Henry. *The Life and Adventures of Henry Bibb, An American Slave.* Introduction by Charles J. Heglar. Madison: University of Wisconsin Press, 2001. Originally published in 1849 as *Narrative of the Life and Adventures of Henry Bibb, an American Slave, Written by Himself.*

Blassingame, John W. "Henry Walton Bibb." In *Dictionary of American Negro Biography,* edited by Rayford W. Logan and Michael R. Winston. New York: Norton, 1982.

JEFFREY L. KLEIN (1996)
Updated bibliography

Bible and African-American Culture, The

See Christian Denominations, Independent; Religion; *and articles on particular Christian denominations (e.g., Baptists)*

Biggart, James

1878
1932

James Alphaeus Alexander Biggart was the first black Tobagonian druggist and the first black legislator (1925–1932) in the Trinidad and Tobago Legislative Council. Given the high property and income qualifications for candidates, he was one of Tobago's well-to-do, politically astute, educated black professionals. He began his pharmacist career in 1892 and had the only pharmacy in the rural Windward District before Tobago became a ward in the colony of Trinidad and Tobago in 1899. He was a passionate advocate for the welfare of Tobagonians and the development of his native island.

With only limited success, Biggart campaigned for the development of the infrastructure of the island. He called on the colonial government to improve and increase the mileage of roads and the number of bridges on the island; to improve sea communications and education; and to establish and improve markets, post offices, wireless and telephone services, and the provision of government services in Tobago—which would make it unnecessary for Tobagonians to go to Trinidad to access those services. Biggart began a tradition of strong advocacy on behalf of Tobagonians, and his efforts for the development of Tobago were carried on by A P. T. James (1901–1962), Arthur N. R. Robinson (b. 1926), and others. The campaign for political autonomy conducted by these men eventually led to Tobago gaining internal self-government in 1980. Thus, Biggart can be viewed as the one who laid the foundation on which the 1970s Tobago autonomy movement was built.

Biggart was also in the forefront of efforts to establish secondary education in Tobago. He requested more money, College Exhibition (government scholarships to secondary schools) set-asides for Tobagonian students, special representation on the board of education for Tobagonians, and a resident inspector of schools for the island. A resident inspector of schools was reappointed in 1930.

In addition, Biggart was concerned about the disparity in wages paid to government workers on the two islands, the high level of unemployment in Tobago, and the lack of industries on the island. To alleviate this last problem, a lime factory was built, and the first meeting of the Tobago Lime Growers Association was held in 1930. He also sought to make the provision of government services more convenient for Tobago's rural population. Through his efforts a post office was established at Moriah.

As a health professional, Biggart had a vested interest in increasing the number of medical personnel and improving the medical facilities in Tobago. In 1926 Biggart requested a motor ambulance service for Tobago and brought the deplorable condition of the Scarborough Poor House to the attention of the government. That geriatric facility was later remodeled, repaired, painted, and a qualified nurse and matron were appointed.

James Biggart had a strong sense of Tobagonian identity, as reflected in his insistence on the preservation of Tobago's history. In 1929 he successfully requested that the government collect the historical literature, documents, and other items of interest in Tobago and preserve them for future generations. After only six months in office, Governor Horace A. Byatt (1875–1933; gov. 1924–1930) described him as being "specially active" in presenting the interests of Tobago in the legislature.

See also James, A. P. T.; Robinson, A. N. R.; Williams, Eric

Bibliography

Byatt, Horace A. CO 295/555: Byatt to Amery, July 23, 1925, Despatch #331, Public Records Office, Kew, England.

Campbell, Carl. "Tobago and Trinidad: Problems of Alignment of Their Educational Systems at Union: 1889-1931." *Antilia* 1, no. 3 (April 1987): 21–27.

Luke, Learie B. "Identity and Autonomy in Tobago: From Union to Self-Government, 1889-1980." Ph.D. diss., Howard University, 2001.

Trinidad and Tobago. *Minutes of the Proceedings of the Legislative Council and Council Papers,* for the period 1925 to 1932.

LEARIE B. LUKE (2005)

Billy Dee

See Williams, Billy Dee (December, William)

Biography, U.S.

In 1835 Susan Paul, Boston teacher and biographer, made literary history. She published *Memoir of James Jackson: The Attentive and Obedient Scholar Who Died in Boston, October 31 1833, Aged Six Years and Eleven Months.* This memorial text is believed to be the first biography of a person of African descent published in the United States. Moreover, it appeared some ten years before Frederick Douglass's epoch-making *Narrative of the Life of Frederick Douglass* (1845), twenty years before the first black American novel, William Wells Brown's *Clotel, or the President's Daughter* (1853), and nearly thirty before *Incidents in the Life of a Slave Girl,* Harriet Jacobs's amazing story of enslavement, abuse, romance and escape. This was not, however, a wholly unexpected event. Paul's narration of young James Jackson's life was just one more significant effort on the part of blacks who were struggling to resist the tendency to treat their lives lightly. Like Phillis Wheatley and Olaudah Equiano, Jupiter Hammon and Solomon Northrup, Susan Paul insisted on valuing the specificity of James Jackson's life experience even as she celebrated the vibrant black antebellum community in which he lived.

Biography operates then in much the same way as autobiography. Stories of unique individuals struggling for and within their communities have been particularly important for black people because of the way life writing specifically challenges the notion that blacks lack intelligence, culture, and individuality. Unlike autobiography, however, the black biographer is free to present his or her subject as exemplary, even saintly. Thus Paul's treatment of Jackson's life tends to present seemingly mundane aspects of the young boy's life (his education, for example) as exemplary and perhaps even unexpected.

It was this celebratory aesthetic that dominated black American biographies throughout much of the nineteenth century. Often the emphasis was less on telling the story of truly exceptional individuals than on creating black social registries in which any type of accomplishment deserved recognition. William C. Nell's *Colored Patriots of the American Revolution, With Sketches of Several Distinguished Colored Persons to Which is Added a Brief Survey of the Condition and Prospects of Colored Americans* is a text that briefly treats dozens of individuals: Crispus Attucks, Primus Hall, Paul Cuffe, David Ruggles, Oliver Cromwell, James Forten, Benjamin Banneker, Frances Ellen Watkins, and Denmark Vesey, among many others. Clearly Nell was attempting to establish a basic architecture for students of black American history and culture with his broad efforts to name names within the emerging black public sphere. This effort was followed by Williams Wells Brown's 1863 *The Black Man: His Antecedents, His Genius, and His Achievements.* In the same vein William Still published *The Underground Railroad: A Record of Facts, Authentic Narratives, Letters* in 1872. This nineteenth-century tradition of brief treatments of many individuals probably reached its zenith with Rev. William J. Simmons's *Men of Mark: Eminent, Progressive and Rising,* published in 1887. This was a 1,400-page volume that included 177 biographical sketches of blacks who had achieved distinction as professionals and race leaders, including slave rebels and postbellum politicians. By the latter part of the nineteenth century, however, biographers began to turn to new forms in their efforts to demonstrate the strength and diversity of black communities.

In 1886 Sarah H. Bradford published *Scenes in the Life of Harriet Tubman* and *Harriet: The Moses of Her People*, texts that represented significant new departures for black biography. While these works lacked basic information about Tubman's life and were largely based on information that Bradford gained from Tubman herself, they nonetheless broke new ground by focusing on a single, exceptional woman. Many more such biographies would be published over the course of both the nineteenth and twentieth centuries. More to the point, from the late nineteenth century forward we see much more emphasis by biographers on singular, even heroic black persons. While texts treating the lives of multiple individuals continued—and continue—to be published, at the turn of the century a new orientation in black biography could be seen. It was represented by the work of persons like the famed black American writer Charles W. Chesnutt, who published *Frederick Douglass* in 1899. This effort was followed by Booker T. Washington's own *Frederick Douglass*, published in 1907, Shirley Graham's 1947 work, *There Was Once a Slave: The Heroic Story of Frederick Douglass*, and Benjamin Quarles's *Frederick Douglass* published a year later. Clearly, then, twentieth-century biographers revived some of the spirit of Susan Paul as they once again produced texts that privileged the life experiences and psychologies of individuals.

The release of Langston Hughes's *Famous American Negroes* in 1954 represented a significant turning point in the professionalization and commercialization of black biography. Published in the same year as the Supreme Court's landmark desegregation ruling, *Brown v. Board of Education of Topeka*, Hughes's text was one of several written during the mid-twentieth century designed to represent the lives of modern, forward-thinking, and cosmopolitan blacks. Richard Bardolph published *The Negro Vanguard* in 1959 explicitly to celebrate the most successful among black Americans. John A. Williams's 1970 work, *The Most Native of Sons: A Biography of Richard Wright*, helped solidify the reputation of the man thought to be the most significant black writer of his generation. Michel Fabre followed this with *The Unfinished Quest of Richard Wright* in 1973. At the same time, by the late 1960s and early 1970s black nationalists were also using biography as a way to celebrate the lives and efforts of previous generations of nationalist intellectuals and activists. Examples of these efforts are Victor Ullman's work, *Martin R. Delany: The Beginnings of Black Nationalism*, published in 1971, and Cyril E. Griffith's 1975 text, *The African Dream: Martin R. Delany and the Emergence of Pan-African Thought.*

By the early nineteen eighties hundreds of biographies of black persons had been published, so much so that some of the nation's most prominent historians began to produce work that synthesized the abundant data available for biographers and other students of black history and culture. Thus at precisely the moment when biographies of blacks became altogether common, many prominent historians produced "group biographies" that were similar, in many ways, to those of the nineteenth century. In 1982 alone Howard Rabinowitz's edited volume, *Southern Black Leaders of the Reconstruction Era*, appeared with John Hope Franklin and August Meier's text, *Black Leaders of the Twentieth Century*, as well as Rayford W. Logan and Michael R. Winston's *Dictionary of American Negro Biography.*

These were followed by studies of black individuals that have now become standard parts of the American historical archive: Louis R. Harlan published *Booker T. Washington: The Wizard of Tuskegee* in 1983. Faith Berry's controversial work *Langston Hughes: Before and Beyond Harlem* came out that same year. Nellie McKay's *Jean Toomer, Artist: A Study of His Literary Life and Work* followed in 1984, as did Waldo Martin's *The Mind of Frederick Douglass.* Even more significantly, Arnold Rampersad published extended treatments of the black American writer, Langston Hughes, *The Life of Langston Hughes, Vol I: I, Too, Sing America* (1986) and *The Life of Langston Hughes Volume II: I Dream a World* (1988). Faith Berry and Arnold Rampersad's work demonstrated some of the stakes involved in the production of black biography as the two authors grappled with the question of Hughes's sexuality. Berry suggested that Hughes was homosexual, while Rampersad maintained that the evidence pointed to Hughes' asexuality. This topic would be of only passing interest if it did not speak directly to the question of whether biographies should be designed first and foremost to celebrate remarkable individuals or instead to undress them, to reveal both their good and bad attributes, in an effort to understand better their motivations and their genius.

All of these questions were perhaps most richly explored in the work of historian, David Garrow, whose 1996 text, *Bearing the Cross: Martin Luther King, Jr. and the Southern Christian Leadership Conference* was remarkably thorough, so much so that many believed that King's reputation as a race leader and a man of God was tarnished. David Levering Lewis suffered less criticism for his works, *W. E. B. Du Bois: Biography of a Race*, published in 1993 and *W. E. B. Du Bois: The Fight for Equality and the American Century*, published in 2000. Again, however, he did reveal information about Du Bois's personal and professional life that firmly established the innate humanity–and fallibility–of the famed race leader. Still, the fact that both Garrow and Lewis won Pulitzer Prizes for their works demonstrated that black biography (warts and all) had been fully integrated into the main currents of American high culture.

It is important to note that the "tell-all" orientation within black biographical writing, represented by the controversies surrounding the works of Berry, Rampersad, and Garrow did not come out of nowhere. In 1988 Margaret Walker published *Richard Wright: Daemonic Genius*, a text that many took to be a scandalous treatment of Wright's life. Thus, from that moment forward it became clear that the days of fully laudatory biographies of black individuals were over. In her work, Walker, an extremely significant poet and novelist in her own right, suggested that the more well known Richard Wright was misogynistic, homophobic, and bisexual to boot. Thus, even though Walker published in the same year that saw the release of Leon Litwack and August Meier's much more respectful edited volume, *Black Leaders of the Nineteenth Century*, one can see a pronounced shift in tone during this period. Martin Duberman's 1989 study of the performer and activist Paul Robeson, *Paul Robeson: A Biography*, demonstrated the man in all his complexity, including the mental and emotional battles that he suffered in both private and public life. The same was true of Bruce Perry's controversial 1991 work, *Malcolm: The Life of a Man Who Changed America*, Jill Watts's 1992 *God, Harlem, U.S.A.: The Father Divine Story*, and David Leeming's 1997 text, *James Baldwin: A Biography*. Perhaps no biographer went quite as far, however, as did Nell Irvin Painter whose work, *Sojourner Truth: A Life, A Symbol*, challenged many of the myths surrounding Truth, including the widespread belief that she rescued a group of white feminists from male hostility with her famed "Ain't I a Woman" speech.

In the contemporary era a rather encouraging emphasis on the necessity of reclaiming the lives of more recent black intellectuals and activists can be seen. In particular, there has been a surprising amount of recent work that examines the lives of important American activists and intellectuals of the 1940s through 1970s. In 1999 Chana Kai Lee published her treatment of activist and founder of the Mississippi Freedom Democratic Party, Fannie Lou Hamer, *For Freedom's Sake: The Life of Fannie Lou Hamer*. Hazel Rowley published *Richard Wright: The Life and Times* in 2001. Lawrence Jackson published *Ralph Ellison: Emergence of Genius* in 2002. Barbara Ransby followed with *Ella Baker and the Black Freedom Movement: A Radical Democratic Vision* while John D'Emilio released his masterful work, *Lost Prophet: The Life and Times of Bayard Rustin* that same year. D'Emilio's text not only examined Rustin's extremely important contributions to the civil rights and anti-war movements, but also dealt in some detail with Rustin's homosexuality, including his infamous arrest in Pasadena on a morals charge.

It is stunning to see not only how much energy continues to be expended telling the story of black people through the example of individual persons but also how very successful the writing of black biographies has become. Geoffrey C. Ward's 2004 study of boxer Jack Johnson, *Unforgivable Blackness: The Rise and Fall of Jack Johnson* sold wildly and was quickly adapted as a public television special. At the same time Henry Louis Gates and Evelyn Brooks Higginbotham's edited volume *African American Lives*, published in 2004, also promises to be a briskly selling work even as it returns to the tradition of mini-biographies that was first introduced in the nineteenth century. The writing of black biography has come quite a long way since Ms. Paul's humble efforts to memorialize the life of her young student, James Jackson. It seems, then, that biographers have only just begun to test the many possibilities inherent in this important literary form.

See also Autobiographies, U.S.; Black Arts Movement; Feminist Theory and Criticism; Literature; Literary Magazines;

Bibliography

Bardolph, Richard. *The Negro Vanguard.* Westport, Conn.: Negro Universities Press, 1959.

Bradford, Sarah H. *Harriet: The Moses of Her People.* New York: Geo. R. Lockwood and Son, 1886.

Bradford, Sarah H. *Scenes in the Life of Harriet Tubman.* Auburn, N.Y.: W.J. Moses, printer, 1869.

Brown, William Wells. *The Black Man: His Antecedents, His Genius, and His Achievements.* Boston: Robert F. Wallcut, 1863.

Chesnutt, Charles. *Frederick Douglass.* Boston: Small, Maynard, 1899.

D'Emilio, John. *Lost Prophet: The Life and Times of Bayard Rustin.* New York: Free Press, 2003.

Fabre, Michel. *The Unfinished Quest of Richard Wright.* New York: William Morrow, 1973.

Franklin, John Hope, and August Meier, eds., *Black Leaders of the Twentieth Century.* Urbana: University of Illinois Press, 1982.

Garrow, David. *Bearing the Cross: Martin Luther King Jr. and the Southern Christian Leadership Conference.* Norwalk, Conn.: Easton Press, 1989.

Gates, Henry Louis, and Evelyn Brooks Higginbotham, eds. *African American Lives.* New York: Oxford University Press, 2004.

Graham, Shirley. *There Was Once a Slave: The Heroic Story of Frederick Douglass.* New York: Messner, 1947.

Griffith, Cyril E. *The African Dream: Martin R. Delany and the Emergence of Pan-African Thought.* University Park: Pennsylvania State University Press, 1975.

Harlan, Louis R. *Booker T. Washington: The Wizard of Tuskegee, 1901–1915.* New York: Oxford University Press, 1983.

Hughes, Langston. *Famous American Negroes.* New York: Dodd, Mead, 1954.

Jackson, Lawrence. *Ralph Ellison: Emergence of Genius.* New York: John Wiley and Sons, 2002.

Lee, Chana Kai. *For Freedom's Sake: The Life of Fannie Lou Hamer.* Urbana: University of Illinois Press, 1999.

Lewis, David Levering. *W. E. B. Du Bois: Biography of a Race.* New York: Henry Holt, 1993.

Lewis, David Levering. *W. E. B. Du Bois: The Fight for Equality and the American Century.* New York: Henry Holt, 2000.

Leeming, David. *James Baldwin: A Biography.* New York: Knopf, 1997.

Litwack, Leon, and August Meier, *Black Leaders of the Nineteenth Century.* Urbana: University of Illinois Press, 1988.

Logan, Rayford W., and Michael R. Winston, eds. *Dictionary of American Negro Biography.* New York: Norton, 1982.

McKay, Nellie Y. *Jean Toomer, Artist: A Study of His Literary Life and Work, 1894–1936.* New York: University of North Carolina Press, 1984.

Martin, Waldo. *The Mind of Frederick Douglass.* Chapel Hill: University of North Carolina Press, 1984.

Nell, William C. *The Colored Patriots of the American Revolution, With Sketches of Several Distinguished Colored Persons: To Which is Added a Brief Survey of the Condition and Prospects of Colored Americans.* Boston: Robert F. Wallcutt, 1855.

Painter, Nell Irvin. *Sojourner Truth: A Life, A Symbol.* New York: W.W. Norton and Co., 1997.

Paul, Susan. *Memoir of James Jackson: The Attentive and Obedient Scholar Who Died in Boston, October 31 1833, Aged Six Years and Eleven Months.* Cambridge: Harvard University Press, 2000.

Perry, Bruce. *Malcolm: The Life of a Man Who Changed America.* New York: Station Hill, 1991.

Quarles, Benjamin. *Frederick Douglass.* New York: Associated Publishers, 1948.

Rampersad, Arnold. *The Life of Langston Hughes, Volume I: I, Too, Sing America.* New York: Oxford University Press, 1986.

Rampersad, Arnold. *The Life of Langston Hughes, Volume II: I Dream a World.* New York: Oxford University Press, 1988.

Rabinowitz, Howard, ed. *Southern Black Leaders of the Reconstruction Era.* Urbana: University of Illinois Press, 1982.

Ransby, Barbara. *Ella Baker and the Black Freedom Struggle: A Radical Democratic Vision.* Chapel Hill: University of North Carolina Press, 2003.

Rowley, Hazel. *Richard Wright: The Life and Times.* New York: Henry Holt and Company, 2001.

Simmons, William J. *Men of Mark: Eminent, Progressive and Rising.* Cleveland: Geo. M. Rewell, 1887.

Still, William. *The Underground Railroad: A Record of Facts, Authentic Narratives, Letters, etc., Narrating the Hardships, Hairbreadth Escapes and Death Struggles of the Slaves in Their Efforts for Freedom, as Related by Themselves and Others, or Witnessed by the Author.* Philadelphia: Porter and Coates, 1872.

Ullman, Victor. *Martin R. Delany: The Beginnings of Black Nationalism.* Boston: Beacon Press, 1971.

Walker, Margaret. *Richard Wright, Daemonic Genius.* New York: Warner/Amistad, 1988.

Ward, Geoffrey C. *Unforgivable Blackness: The Rise and Fall of Jack Johnson.* New York: Knopf, 2004.

Watts, Jill. *God, Harlem, U.S.A.: The Father Divine Story.* Berkeley: University of California Press, 1992.

Williams, John A. *The Most Native of Sons: A Biography of Richard Wright.* New York: Doubleday, 1970.

ROBERT REID-PHARR (2005)

Bird, V. C.

December 9, 1909
June 28, 1999

Vere Cromwell Bird, or "Papa Bird" as he was affectionately called by his Labour Party supporters, was born in St. Johns, the capital of the Caribbean islands of Antigua/Barbuda. He was the third of four boys born to laundress Amanda Edgehill. Despite his humble beginnings, "V. C." became one of the most significant Caribbean leaders of the twentieth century.

In 1943 Bird became the second president of the Antigua Trades and Labour Union (ATLU) after Reginald St. Clair Stevens, the union's first president, resigned. In 1946 the union under Bird formed the Antigua Labour Party (ALP), the people's first political party. Together the ATLU-ALP became the most significant institutions in the struggle for workers' rights and for political self-determination in the island nations. This was Bird's legacy in the region, the creation and management of the first of the Leeward Island institutions that fought and won the struggle for basic rights for the black and colored majority. Bird's political career began in 1939, when he joined other local activists Norris Allen, Reginald Stevens, F. O. Benjamin, S. A. Henry, Griffith Matthews, Randolph Lockhart, B. A Richards, Thomas Martin, James Jarvis, Stanley Walter, C. A. Perry, and Thomas Brooks in forming the ATLU.

As ALP leader, Bird would become the first chief minister (1960), first premier (1967), and first prime minister (1981) of the twin island nations. Bird created a true peasant class by dramatically expanding land ownership among rural Antiguans/Barbudans, allowing them to actually own the lands they worked.

Bird modernized the islands from the 1960s to the 1980s, expanding electricity and education and building housing and the infrastructure for a tourism industry that replaced the exhausted sugar industry. The partnered institutions system introduced by Bird in the 1940s became the symbol for progress for the island nation, but it also became the source of conflict. The ATLU-ALP existed unopposed by any other party or union/party alliance until 1967, when the Antigua Workers Union (AWU) was formed by former members of the ATLU. These union leaders, Donald Halstead, George Walter, and Keithlyn Smith, would form both a rival labor union and political party by 1968. The Progressive Labour Movement (PLM) became the political arm of the union to rival the ATLU-ALP partnership.

The two union/party teams, the ATLU-ALP and AWU-PLM, would engage in intense competition for control of labor and for political control of the islands until the decline and demise of the PLM in the 1980s. Despite the existence of a third party, the Afro-Caribbean Liberation Movement (ACLM) in the 1970s, the two-party system dominated. In the 1976 election and again in the 2004 election the ALP lost control of the Antigua/Barbuda government. In both instances political control of the government was ceded to ALP protégés who had become opposition leaders.

From the 1940s to the 1960s Bird directed the struggle against labor exploitation and social exclusion of the majority through the use of trade unionism, which had been introduced in 1939 by Moyne Commission member and Trade Union Congress (TUC) representative Sir Walter Citrine. Leeward Island trade unionists made the movement their own by the 1960s and used it to take social and political control from the British.

At age eighty-three, Bird retired from Antigua/Barbuda politics in 1994 after dominating it for fifty-five years. His retirement ended one of the longest political careers in the Caribbean region. His eulogy, written by journalist Leonard Tim Hector, highlighted his career and his single-minded focus on politics, which has rendered him invisible in some of the best known of Caribbean works, in particular Eric Williams's *From Columbus to Castro.* Writing in *Outlet,* a newspaper that Bird made numerous efforts to destroy, Hector opined, "Bird was all politics. His was the single-minded pursuit of political ends. Politics was his only occupation and pre-occupation. Longevity in power was his reward."

See also Hector, Tim; International Relations in the Anglophone Caribbean

Bibliography

Hector, Leonard Tim. "Hail Bwana! Farewell Papa!" Published in *Outlet* (July 9, 1999). Available from <http://www.candw.ag/~jardinea/fanflame.htm>.

Smith, Keithlyn, and Fernando C. Smith. *The Life and Times of Samuel Smith, An Antiguan Workingman, 1877–1982.* 2nd ed. Scarborough, Canada: Edan Publishers, 1986.

"Vere Bird." *Economist* (July 17, 1999): 82.

CHRISTOLYN A. WILLIAMS (2005)

Bishop, Maurice

May 29, 1944
October 19, 1983

Maurice Bishop was born in Aruba, Netherlands Antilles, the last child and only son among three children born to Grenadians Rupert and Alimenta La Grenade Bishop. In 1951 the Bishops returned to a Grenada in political ferment, due largely to the grant of universal adult suffrage that year. The family settled in Saint George's, Grenada's capital, where Rupert operated a number of successful small businesses.

Maurice attended the Wesley Hall Primary School and the Saint George's Roman Catholic Primary School, where in 1957 he won a scholarship to the Presentation Brothers College. There, he excelled in English, history, and literature and became an avid follower of the international anticolonial movement. In 1962 Bishop was awarded the Principal's medal for public speaking.

In 1963 Bishop left for England, where he studied law at the University of London's Holborn College. He became involved in radical student politics, serving as president of the West Indian Students' Society and joining the Campaign Against Racial Discrimination. He also co-founded a legal aid clinic for London's West Indian community. In 1969 he completed his legal training at Grey's Inn and returned to Grenada in 1970.

Bishop plunged into local politics and participated at all levels of opposition to Eric Gairy's government both before and after Grenada's independence in 1974. In 1973 Bishop's Movement for Assemblies of the People (MAP) merged with the Joint Endeavour for Welfare, Education and Liberation (JEWEL) to form the New JEWEL Movement (NJM) and the National Liberation Army (NLA), its secret military wing. Bishop and other NJM leaders were often victims of state-sponsored political violence.

In 1976 Bishop was elected to the Grenada assembly as a member of the People's Alliance. On March 13, 1979, he was one of the leading revolutionaries who toppled Gairy's government and became the head of Grenada's People's Revolutionary Government (PRG). Bishop's government developed close diplomatic relations with Cuba, Nicaragua, Jamaica (under Michael Manley), the Soviet Union, and Eastern Europe. In Grenada itself, his doctrinaire Marxist government experimented with innovations in participatory democracy that were different from the Westminster-style model to which the Anglophone Caribbean has been socialized.

By 1983, however, internecine conflict within the People's Revolutionary Government over ideological and other differences led to open violence. On October 19, Bishop and several government ministers loyal to him were assassinated at Fort Rupert, Saint George's. A week later, Grenada was invaded by U.S.-led forces to restore order.

Maurice Bishop presided over an unprecedented, idealistic episode in the history of the Anglophone Caribbean, when an elected government was overthrown by extraconstitutional methods, and which, after beginning with high expectations, ended in tragedy. To this day, Bishop's remains have never been identified. He was an iconic, albeit controversial figure in contemporary Grenada. The highway leading to the Point Salines International Airport, easily the most visible public works project undertaken during his four-year government, is named Maurice Bishop Highway.

See also Gairy, Eric; International Relations of the Anglophone Caribbean; New Jewel Movement

Bibliography

Brizan, George. *Grenada: Island of Conflict, From Amerindians to People's Revolution.* London: Zed Books, 1984.

Burrowes, Reynold A. *Revolution and Rescue in Grenada.* New York: Greenwood Press, 1988.

Franklyn, Omowale David. *Bridging the Two Grenadas, Gairy's and Bishop's.* Saint George's, Grenada: Talented House Publications, 1999.

Institute for Foreign Policy Analysis. *The Grenada Documents: Window on Totalitarianism.* Washington, D.C.: Pergamon-Brassey, 1988.

Keenan Institute for Advanced Russian Studies, The Wilson Center. *Grenada and Soviet/Cuban Policy: Internal Crisis and U.S./OCES Intervention.* Boulder, Colo., and London: Westview Press, 1986.

Scoon, Paul. *Survival for Service: My Experiences as Governor General of Grenada.* Oxford: Macmillan Caribbean, 2003.

Searle, Chris. *Grenada: The Struggle Against Destabilization.* London: Writers and Readers Publishing Cooperative, 1983.

Searle, Chris. *Grenada Morning: A Memoir of the "Revo."* Great Britain: Karia Press, 1989.

Steele, Beverley A. *Grenada: A History of Its People.* London: Macmillan Caribbean, 2003.

United States Department of State and the Department of Defense. *Grenada Documents: An Overview and Selection.* Washington, D.C., September 1984.

C. M. JACOBS (2005)

Black Academy of Arts and Letters

The Black Academy of Arts and Letters was founded in Boston in 1969 in the tradition of the American Negro Academy (1897–1916) to "define, reserve, cultivate, promote, foster and develop the arts and letters of black people." At the founding meeting C. Eric Lincoln, a noted historian of black religion, was elected president; novelist John O. Killens, vice president; psychiatrist Alvin Poussaint, treasurer; and author Doris Saunders, secretary. The fifty founding members included African Americans from a wide spectrum of the artistic and scholarly world, such as Alvin Ailey, Margaret Walker Alexander, Lerone Bennett, Arna Bontemps, Oliver Cromwell Cox, Alex Haley, Vincent Harding, Vivian Henderson, Henry Lewis, Carl Rowan, and Nina Simone.

One goal of the Black Academy of Arts and Letters was to recognize those who have made a notable contribution to black America. The First Annual Awards Banquet in 1970 drew a crowd of over six hundred members and friends. With Harry Belafonte as master of ceremonies, a hall of fame was established and Carter G. Woodson, Henry O. Tanner, W. E. B. Du Bois, Lena Horne, C. L. R. James, Diana Sands, Imamu Amiri Baraka, and Paul Robeson were inducted.

The academy honored George Jackson with an award for his book *Soledad Brothers* after its publication in 1970. In 1972 it sought to bring W. E. B. Du Bois's remains from Ghana for burial in the United States in hopes of bringing greater recognition of his achievements and contributions to the African-American struggle for freedom. The academy also attempted to purchase Langston Hughes's house in Harlem. After restoration, they hoped to use one wing of the house as their hall of fame. However, the controversy surrounding some political positions of the academy, such as their support of George Jackson, made fundraising extremely difficult. By the early 1970s the academy had ceased functioning.

See also Ailey, Alvin; Baraka, Amiri (Jones, LeRoi); Belafonte, Harry; Bontemps, Arna; Du Bois, W. E. B.; Haley, Alex; Killens, John Oliver; Robeson, Paul; Rowan, Carl T.; Tanner, Henry Ossawa

Bibliography

Editorial. *Negro History Bulletin* 33 (November 1970): 156–157.

Moss, Alfred A., Jr. *The American Negro Academy: Voice of the Talented Tenth.* Baton Rouge: Louisiana State University, 1981.

PREMILLA NADASEN (1996)

Black Arts Movement

The Black Arts movement (BAM), which could be dated roughly to 1965 through 1976, has often been called the "Second Black Renaissance," suggesting a comparison to the Harlem Renaissance of the 1920s and '30s. The two are alike in encompassing literature, music, visual arts, and theater. Both movements emphasized racial pride, an appreciation of African heritage, and a commitment to produce works that reflected the culture and experiences of black people. The BAM, however, was larger and longer lasting, and its dominant spirit was politically militant and often racially separatist.

To specify the exact dates of cultural movements is difficult and, given the amorphous nature of complex cultural phenomena, may appear arbitrary. In 1965, however, several events occurred that gave direct impetus to the movement: the assassination of Malcolm X, which prompted many African Americans to take a more militantly nationalist political stance; the conversion of the literary prodigy LeRoi Jones into Imamu Amiri Baraka, the movement's leading writer; the formation of the musically revolutionary Association for the Advancement of Creative Musicians (AACM) in Chicago; and the founding of Broadside Press, which became a leading publisher of BAM poets, in Detroit. Each of these events galvanized black artists.

While the movement had no specific end point, certain events and works decisively marked shifts in the cultural climate. For example, the decision in 1976 by Johnson Publishing to discontinue *Black World* effectively silenced the most important mass-circulation periodical voice of the movement. Furthermore, works published in 1976, such as Ntozake Shange's *for colored girls . . .*, Ishmael Reed's *Flight to Canada*, and Alice Walker's *Meridian*, spoke critically and retrospectively of the movement. The major figures of the movement became less prominent in the late 1970s as new, different African-American voices began to emerge. Thus, while no one can specify when the movement ended, there was a consensus in the late 1970s that the movement was indeed over.

The BAM was fundamentally concerned with the construction of a "black" identity as opposed to a "Negro" identity, which the participants sought to escape. Those involved placed a great emphasis on rhetorical and stylistic gestures that in some sense announced their "blackness." Afro haircuts, daishikis, African pendants and other jewelry, militant attitudes, and a general sternness of demeanor were among the familiar personal gestures by which this blackness was expressed. In many cases these activists dropped their given "slave names" and adopted instead Arab, African, or African-sounding names, which were meant to represent their rejection of the white man and their embracing of an African identity. Such gestures, as they became popularized, rapidly degenerated into clichés, which have subsequently become easy targets of satire for the movement's many detractors. Depicted in extreme forms, Afrocentric dress, soul handshakes, and other affectations of blackness appear ludicrous. Facile parodies, however, should not blind us to the serious social, cultural, and political yearnings that common gestures of personal style reflected but could not adequately express. Silly fads as well as profound art derived from this impulse to discover and create black modes of self-expression.

The BAM is often but inadequately conceived of as a poetry and theater movement that articulated in literary terms the militant, separatist, social, and political attitudes of the 1960s Black Power movement. While the BAM had direct links to the Black Power movement, both movements derived from complex historical legacies and cannot be understood simply in the context of the black community or the 1960s. The BAM, in particular, drew inspiration from numerous sources and manifested itself across the spectrum of aesthetic modes, casting its influence far beyond the black community and the tumultuous 1960s. To understand the BAM adequately, we must consider its manifestations in literature, music, dance, visual arts, theater, and other modes. Ultimately, this movement represented an evolving consensus about the nature and sources of art and the relationship of art to its audience.

The movement is often attacked or dismissed by subsequent artists and critics as having been dogmatically polemical. Since the movement generated a great deal of polemical and theoretical writing, this criticism does have a

> "The Black Arts and the Black Power concept both relate broadly to the Afro-American's desire for self determination and nationhood. Both concepts are nationalistic. One is concerned with the relationship between art and politics; the other with the art of politics."
>
> LARRY NEAL
> "BLACK ART IS THE AESTHETIC AND SPIRITUAL SISTER OF THE BLACK POWER CONCEPT" (1968). SCHOMBURG CENTER FOR RESEARCH IN BLACK CULTURE, NEW YORK PUBLIC LIBRARY.

basis in fact. For example, many poems of the movement contain attacks on white people and "Uncle Tom Negroes"; many plays pontificate about the proper relationship between black men and black women (often asserting male primacy and advocating female submissiveness); musical compositions often incorporate rambling monologues of "relevant" poetry or invoke ancient African kingdoms or Malcolm X; and the images of Malcolm X and the American flag recur incessantly in the visual arts of the movement. To recognize that the movement has its clichés, however, is not to suggest that cliché typifies all or even most of its works.

It is also important to acknowledge that the BAM did not encompass every African-American artist who was active during the 1960s and '70s, nor did all of the artists within the BAM agree with each other on every social and aesthetic issue. The consensus that characterized the movement represented a very broad set of attitudes and principles that participants in the movement understood in varying ways and shared to varying degrees. At the same time, sharing these general principles and attitudes did not necessarily entail the acceptance of the agendas or judgments of those who articulated or advocated these principles. Establishing these distinctions allows us to understand that the movement reflects both strong agreement and acrimonious dissent.

The shared agenda of the movement was commonly described as the quest for a black aesthetic. Despite constant efforts, the term "black aesthetic" never acquired a precise definition, and it is better understood as the symbol of a shared aspiration than as a descriptively accurate label for a fully elaborated mode or theory of art. Nevertheless, "black aestheic" does clearly indicate the attempt to create art with African-American cultural specificity. What this might mean is surprisingly difficult to ascertain.

One aspect of it is obviously social. The most concise statement of this social dimension of the black aesthetic appears in "Black Cultural Nationalism," an influential 1968 essay by Ron Karenga (who later adopted the name Maulana, meaning "teacher"). Citing Leopold Senghor, Karenga asserts that "all African art has at least three characteristics: that is, it is functional, collective, and committing." By this Karenga means that "black art must expose the enemy, praise the people, and support the revolution." Karenga's influence became pervasive in part because his theories were embraced and promulgated by the influential Imamu Amiri Baraka. This view of art, arguably more Marxist-Leninist than African, became the dominant view of the social function of black art: It should expose the enemy and raise black consciousness.

This narrowly pragmatic conception of black art worked against another major concern of the black aesthetic: to connect with black cultural traditions. Ironically, many of the black aestheticians spurned significant aspects of genuine African-American culture, such as the blues. Karenga, for example, complained that the blues enabled an acceptance of existing realities, while Don L. Lee (Haki Madhubuti) remarked in his poem "Don't Cry, Scream": "All the blues did was / make me cry." In such instances, black aesthetic ideology severed black art from black traditions. Regarding actual African-American culture, the movement was often divided against itself.

The most important legacy of the Black Arts Movement was its quest for new modes of expression based on African-American traditions. The sentiment of black solidarity provided a fundamental premise of the movement. Practically speaking, this sentiment led to the formation of artists' organizations, schools, and publishing ventures located in and directed to the black community. In order for black art to flourish, these activists believed, black artists must control the means of production. Needless to say, such principles had always been operative in black cultural institutions, and some precursors of the black arts, such as the Karamu Playhouse in Cleveland, had been active for decades. One of the earliest 1960s black arts groups was the Umbra Writers Workshop, founded in New York's Greenwich Village in 1963 by Tom Dent, Calvin Hernton, and David Henderson. Although political and aesthetic disagreements soon caused Umbra to implode, it provided an important model for subsequent groups, and several of its members were among the most innovative and influential figures of the BAM. These include Ishmael Reed, Roland Snellings (Askia Touré), Henry Dumas, Norman Pritchard, and Steve Cannon.

Even before Umbra, the National Conference of Artists (NCA) had been founded in 1959. While a few visual artists, among them Joe Overstreet, and even some musicians, such as Sun Ra (who was also a poet), had been involved with Umbra, NCA was strictly a visual artists' organization. Though conceived as a professional organization rather than a workshop, NCA shared with subsequent black arts organizations the broad objectives of "preserving, promoting, and developing the creative forces and expressions of African-American artists." Its activities included annual conferences, a newsletter, a journal, regional meetings, exhibitions, lectures, workshops, placement services, and scholarships. The national scope and professional orientation of this group, however, distinguish it from most BAM institutions. The differences between NCA and AfriCobra, reflect, as we shall see, the particularity of the BAM.

Though much of the Black Arts activity occurred on the East Coast, Chicago incubated two of the most influential and enduring of the movement's institutions: the Organization of Black American Culture (OBAC), founded in 1967, and the Association for the Advancement of Creative Musicians (AACM) founded in 1965. Also notable among Chicago institutions are Third World Press and the Institute for Positive Education, founded in 1967 by OBAC members Haki Madhubuti and Johari Amini. OBAC was originally conceived as an umbrella group, comprising workshops in literature and visual arts, as well as a politically oriented community workshop. In its original declaration of principles, OBAC stated its intention to encourage work based on the black experience and expressing a black aesthetic. Like NCA, it aspired to develop both artists and critics who could create and appraise black art and to develop various mechanisms for disseminating art and fostering discussions within the community.

Even the acronym OBAC was designed to reflect the high ambitions of the group. Pronounced "oh-bah-see," OBAC echoes the Yoruba word *oba,* which denotes royalty and leadership. OBAC aspired to spearhead the incipient black cultural revolution. Its founders included Hoyt Fuller, the editor of *Negro Digest* (renamed *Black World* in 1970) and Gerald McWorter (Abdul Alkalimat), a graduate student at the University of Chicago. The work of OBAC writers such as Johari Amini, Haki Madhubuti, and Carolyn Rodgers often appeared in *Negro Digest/Black World* along with the editorials and commentaries of Hoyt Fuller and quickly gained a national audience for both the art and the polemics of OBAC.

The most dramatic public statement by OBAC was *The Wall of Respect*, a Black Power mural painted on a building at the corner of 43rd Street and Langley Avenue on Chicago's South Side by Jeff Donaldson, Eugene Wade, Bill Walker, and other members of the visual arts workshop in 1967. The wall depicted various historical and contemporary black heroes such as Muhammad Ali, W. E. B. Du Bois, Malcolm X, Marcus Garvey, Nina Simone, Amiri Baraka, and Gwendolyn Brooks. This mural galvanized the imaginations of community people, and based on their comments, the artists made various revisions on the mural. The appeal of public art notwithstanding, this privately owned building was eventually razed, and *The Wall of Respect* passed into legend.

Despite its brief existence, the mural sparked a local and national movement. Numerous cities soon produced their own equivalents, such as The Wall of Dignity in Detroit, several murals by artists including Dana Chandler and Gary Rickson in Boston, and similar projects in New York, Philadelphia, and San Francisco, among others. Needless to say, the mural movement had roots going back to the 1930s in the WPA public art projects and especially in the powerful work created by the Mexican artist Diego Rivera. The Black Arts movement also echoed the 1930s in that the vogue of murals was seized upon by state and federal arts agencies. While black artists could see such murals as "committed and committing," government agencies saw them as a fine combination of public art and social control mechanisms for urban youths who could be organized into painting teams during the incendiary summers of the 1960s. Artists such as Bill Walker and Dana Chandler organized mural projects in several cities, but the political impact of these projects diminished as their frequency increased, and when government support evaporated in the arid 1970s, the mural movement withered away.

Nevertheless, the movement launched the careers of many artists. Five of the OBAC artists—Jeff Donaldson, Jae Jarrell, Wadsworth Jarrell, Barbara B. Jones, and Gerald Williams—formed their own organization, COBRA (Coalition of Black Revolutionary Artists) in 1968. The next year they became AfriCobra (African Commune of Bad Relevant Artists), adding Napoleon Henderson and Nelson Stevens to their ranks. By the time of the first AfriCobra show at Harlem's Studio Museum in July 1970, Sherman Beck, Omar Lama, and Carolyn M. Lawrence had joined the group, bringing the number to ten. For many people, AfriCobra came to epitomize the new black art. Their work used vivid, basic colors. It was representational, usually incorporating the faces of black people, and it was explicitly political. In direct rebellion against the elitist norms of establishment art, these artists endeavored to produce work that was immediately comprehensible and appealing to common people. As Jeff Donaldson put it, "This is 'poster art'—images which deal with concepts that offer positive and feasible solutions to our individual, local, national, international, and cosmic problems. The images are designed with the idea of mass production." This statement captured the spirit of the black aesthetic as many artists understood it.

The music of the Association for the Advancement of Creative Musicians, was arguably even more dazzling, iconoclastic, and influential than the poetry, fiction, and art of OBAC. AACM resembled OBAC in that it was independent and community based. Both groups consisted mostly of younger artists, in college or recently graduated, but both received leadership from older, established figures. Three band leaders, Muhal Richard Abrams, Phil Cohran, and Jodie Christian, for example, conceived AACM and called its founding meeting on May 8, 1965. Abrams, a noted pianist and composer, was elected president of AACM and served in that capacity for over a decade. The initial impetus for AACM was more economic than political. By the mid-1960s most of Chicago's important jazz clubs had closed, and jazz was everywhere in decline. These musicians saw a cooperative as the best way for musicians to take control of their own professional destinies.

AACM soon attracted many of the best young musicians in Chicago. The group established an educational program (in 1967) and an AACM orchestra that met (and continues to meet) weekly to perform new compositions by AACM members. Most importantly, AACM provided a setting in which young musicians could meet, perform together, and exchange ideas. AACM members and groups performed frequent concerts around Chicago's South Side during the late 1960s and early '70s. Ensembles formed, dissolved, and reconfigured around AACM, a few of which soon distinguished themselves: the various groups led by Abrams; the Fred Anderson Quintet; the Art Ensemble of Chicago; the Creative Construction Company; and (in the 1970s) Air.

Each of these groups had its own unique character but they had some traits in common. They were profoundly influenced by the "free jazz" innovations of Cecil Taylor and Ornette Coleman, by the intense instrumental styles of John Coltrane and Eric Dolphy, by the musical eclecticism of Charles Mingus, and by the theatrical staging and grand vision of Sun Ra. Unlike the populist OBAC, AACM produced difficult, challenging, unabashedly avant-garde work. While these musicians could play blues and conventional jazz, their interests lay in extending the frontiers of musical possibility. They experimented with extended and free-form compositions, and with exotic instruments; they even tried to redefine what constitutes music. Some compositions by the Art Ensemble, for example, incorporated bicycle horns, bird whistles, street noises, poetry, sermons, screams, and nonsense conversation.

The Art Ensemble was the group that most epitomized AACM as an aspect of the Black Arts movement. The group consisted of Roscoe Mitchell and Joseph Jarman, reeds; Lester Bowie (deceased), trumpet; Malachi Favors (deceased), bass; and Famodou Don Moye, percussion. While performing, Jarman, Favors, and Moye wore facial paint and African-style costumes; Bowie wore a white lab coat; and Mitchell dressed in ordinary street clothes (jeans, turtlenecks, etc.). Usually, the Art Ensemble packed the stage with batteries of standard instruments (sopranino to bass saxophones, soprano to bass clarinets, various flutes, and often bassoons); a standard drum kit, plus congas, gongs, and marimbas; and countless "little instruments" (whistles, bells, tambourines, conch shells, maracas, and various noisemakers). Art Ensemble concerts were visual spectacles and unpredictable musical events, reflecting the group's motto: "Great Black Music: Ancient to the Future." Their compositions, such as People in Sorrow (1969), exemplified the devotional parodic, evocative, experimental, lyrical eclecticism of the Art Ensemble.

In contrast to the Art Ensemble, which flourished for three decades, the Creative Construction Company—Anthony Braxton, reeds; Leroy Jenkins, violin; Leo Smith, trumpet; Muhal Richard Abrams, piano; Richard Davis, bass; and Steve McCall, drums—persisted only for a few years. However, all of these men became major figures in the new music. Their concerts and albums were celebrated for their dazzling ensemble playing, which emphasized collective improvisation rather than solos. Both these bands developed aesthetics based upon the Black Arts precept of committed collectivity.

Chicago also developed notable and enduring black theater groups, such a KUUMBA and Ebony Talent Theater (ETT), but New York was clearly the more important city for theater and dance, and most of the famous Black Arts plays premiered there. However, the proliferation of black theater groups on campuses and in communities throughout the country guaranteed that plays by established authors, local talents, and emerging stars were quickly disseminated. Although Amiri Baraka, due to his broad range of literary and political activities, was the best known of the Black Arts playwrights, he had many talented peers. Ed Bullins, Ron Milner, Lonne Elder, Charles Fuller, Douglass Turner Ward, Adrienne Kennedy, Melvin Van Peebles, Loften Mitchell, and Ben Caldwell all wrote provocative work that challenged audiences and incited lively debate.

These authors worked in a variety of styles, and their political and cultural views differed. Nonetheless, they shared a vision of American society in crisis and a conviction that drama should challenge the complacency of audiences by exposing racism, economic exploitation, social conflict, and false consciousness. Some of these plays were satirical, while others were intensely confrontational; some relied on dialogue, while others bristled with shocking language. Furious assaults on whites were at times matched by blistering arguments between father and son, brother and sister. Black Arts theater was the theater of a people becoming aware of and rebelling against their own oppression. However, it was also a theater that sought solutions, new understandings, and transformed social relations. In keeping with the idea of an art derived from and directed to the black community, nearly all of the Black Arts theaters instituted discussion forums immediately following their productions, involving the director, cast, audience, and sometimes the author. Black art was to be educational, not just entertaining.

Black dance also proliferated during this period. The Alvin Ailey group, though founded in 1960, just before the advent of BAM, exemplified the visual and rhythmical ideals of the black aesthetic. Several other major companies were formed during the movement: among others, Dayton Contemporary Dance Company in Ohio (1968); the Dance Theater of Harlem in New York City (1969); the Philadelphia Dance Company, or Phildanco (1970); Garth Fagan's Bucket Dance in Rochester, N.Y. (1970); the Cleo Parker Robinson Dance Ensemble in Denver (1971); and the Joel Hall Dancers in Chicago (1974). While all of these troupes specialize in African-American dance, most of them have been multiethnic in composition. This conflict between the nationalist impulse to form all-black companies and the pluralist impulse to include qualified people who, regardless of their background, have the talent and disposition to make a contribution reflects a larger tension in the movement. African-American culture is inherently an amalgam, including European elements as well as African. Most black artists have been trained in institutions with European orientations. How, then, can black artists come honestly to terms with the complex nature of their own cultural heritage? Dance embraced the pluralist reality of American culture more forthrightly than the other black arts generally did.

At the same time, black dance immersed itself deeply in the cultures of Africa, the Caribbean, and black America. Unlike the literary artists and theorists of the BAM, whose acquaintance with Africa was too often only through cursory reading and vigorous fantasy, dancers had a highly developed tradition of African dance technique to draw upon. Since the early 1930s, African dancers such as Asadata Dafora and Shologa Oloba had taught African dance in New York. Nana Yao Opare Dinizulu had begun teaching African dance and culture in Harlem in 1947 and founded a company in the same year. Subsequently, the companies of Charles Moore and Chuck Davis extended this tradition. African percussion masters such as Babatunde Olatunji also traveled to the United States, imparting their vast knowledge of African music and dance. African traditions as developed in Haiti, Jamaica, and Trinidad had been studied, adapted, and taught since the 1930s by influential dancers such as Katherine Dunham, Pearl Primus, and Jean-Leon Destinée. Even costuming and stage design had transcended mere ethnographic imitation and instead, borrowing the vivid colors and basic styles of African tradition, had evolved—preeminently in the work of Geoffrey Holder—into dazzlingly imaginative modes of expression. Thus, when large numbers of dancers began traveling to study in Africa during the late 1960s and '70s, their challenge was not to introduce new forms to American dance but rather to refine and extend a firmly established tradition.

To explain companies like Bucket Dance and the Dance Theater of Harlem as products of BAM would be simplistic and inaccurate. Clearly, however, the desire to create black cultural institutions and the desire to engage artists and audiences in a rediscovery of African and African-American expressive modes links the efforts of choreographers such as Garth Fagan and Arthur Mitchell to the broader BAM. These dancers also shared the educational commitments of the movement. In addition to training young dancers for their own companies in the traditional manner of independent dance ensembles, choreographers like Fagan, Mitchell, and Davis have always maintained vigorous public outreach programs, including workshops for children. Furthermore, since dance often captured the aesthetics of the movement without its polemics, many of the works created by Ailey, Mitchell, Fagan, Talley Beatty, Eleo Pomare, and other choreographers of that period have remained fresh and compelling, while by contrast, many popular literary works of the era now seem shrill and dated. The greatest artists of BAM may not be its acknowledged spokespersons.

Similarly, many artists who came of age during the movement have continued to develop, leaving behind many of the themes, modes, and attitudes of their own earlier work. In the visual arts, for example, many artists relied on chains and distorted images of American flags to make overtly political points. The sculptor Melvin Edwards, for example, created a series of works in the late 1960s called Lynch Fragments. One installation of it appeared at the Whitney in 1970, consisting of strands of barbed wire strung from the ceiling and attached to loops of heavy chain. Such work is pointed but aesthetically limited. By contrast, Edwards's works of subsequent years are large-scale, welded-steel sculptures, often in abstract forms but sometimes incorporating chain or chainlike figures as well. The growth in imaginative complexity and aesthetic appeal is immediately obvious.

Faith Ringgold, a painter with strong political commitments, was actually convicted in 1970, along with two other artists, for desecrating the American flag. Her flag paintings such as "The Flag Is Bleeding" (1967) and "Flag for the Moon: Die Nigger" (1969) are effective polemics about American violence and racism. Nonetheless, outside the angry context of the late 1960s, these works appear strident and facile. Her later works that utilize folk-art forms (as she had begun to do even in the 1960s), textiles, quilting, and various other media embody artistic maturity, not just effective visual rhetoric. David Hammons made heavy use of both flags and chains in his works of the late 1960s. Indeed, his body prints such as "Pray for America" (1969) and "Injustice Case" (1970), the latter regarding the Chicago Seven case, are among the most memorable American art images of that era. Like Edwards and Ringgold, however, Hammons discovered profounder aesthetic possibilities and resources when he moved away from the obvious symbolism and unambiguous political sentiments of BAM. Hammon's work of the 1980s and '90s, from his spade sculptures to his basketball installations, is playful, ironic, and much more deeply grounded in African-American culture. Like many other artists of their generation, Edwards, Ringgold, and Hammons were BAM artists, but their artistic growth did not terminate at the boundaries of the movement.

Some critics of the BAM have focused exclusively on a few extremist works, artists, or tendencies of the movement, thereby defining the movement only in terms of its most egregious features. While the extremes of the movement are shocking indeed, its fecundity and diversity have not been sufficiently recognized. Much has been written, for example, about the political assertiveness of BAM works. The humor of the movement, in all of its genres, has not generally been acknowledged. Much of Baraka's work is bitingly satirical. Douglass Turner Ward's *Day of Absence*, a coon show performed in whiteface, is slapstick comedy in the ministrel tradition. Cecil Brown, Sam Greenlee, and Ishmael Reed are all comic novelists. David Hammons, the Art Ensemble, and Garth Fagan have made humor a major element of their works. Haki Madhubuti and Nikki Giovanni, even at their most earnest, are playful and witty poets.

Despite the stern dogmatism of some Black Arts theory, the movement always encompassed diverse voices and perspectives. Some critics have dismissed the BAM as a sexist outpouring, dominated by misogynistic men. Actually, many of the iconic BAM figures were women, such as Sonia Sanchez, Nikki Giovanni, Carolyn Rodgers, Audre Lorde, Toni Cade Bambara, Faith Ringgold, June Jordan, and Adrienne Kennedy. These and other women within the movement vigorously debated gender issues among themselves and with their male counterparts, in their works, in public forums, and in organizational meetings. The common claim that women's voices were suppressed by the BAM is belied by a reading of the anthologies, periodicals, museum show catalogs, playbills, and other documents of the period.

In fact, one might argue that the most direct literary legacy of the BAM was the explosion of black women's writing in the late 1970s and '80s. For instance, while Ntozake Shange's play *for colored girls who have considered suicide/when the rainbow is enuf* (1976) anticipates in its themes and attitudes the feminism and womanism of the 1980s and '90s, its aesthetic roots—especially its use of vernacular language, color, music, and dance—are clearly in the BAM tradition. Toni Cade Bambara's intricate masterpiece *The Salt Eaters* (1980) is certainly the most sophisticated and probing book yet written on how this black nationalist political and aesthetic movement shaped the lives of its participants. Finally, womanist critics of the BAM have rejected many aspects of the movement, including some of its fundamental social values. Nevertheless, their conception of art, especially literature, as a tool of consciousness raising and community building is a direct echo of Black Arts theory.

BAM even had within it a vigorous multiculturalist tendency, which was most forcefully represented by Ishmael Reed and his San Francisco Bay Area cohorts, such as Al Young. In his poems, essays, and novels, Reed advocated a vision of multicultural pluralism, social freedom, and political tolerance. Spurning the dogmatic nationalism of many BAM adherents, Reed declared himself a multicultural artist more than a decade before the idea of multiculturalism became fashionable. Through his editing of periodicals such as *Yardbird Reader*, *Y'bird*, and *Quilt*, which published writers of numerous ethnic backgrounds and his leadership in multicultural collectives such as the Before Columbus Foundation, Reed acted decisively to implement his pluralist commitments. Furthermore, Reed has written devastating satires on and criticisms of Black Arts dogmas and excesses. Yet as an alumnus of the Umbra Workshop, Reed is himself a foundational figure of the movement. Clearly, the BAM was large enough, in the best Whitmanesque tradition, to contain contradictions and multitudes.

See also Afrocentrism; Autobiography, U.S.; Biography, U.S.; Black Power Movement; Drama; Feminist Theory and Criticism; Literary Criticism, U.S.; Last Poets; Literary Magazines; OBAC Writers' Workshop

Bibliography

Baraka, Amiri. *The Autobiography of LeRoi Jones.* New York: Freundlich Books, 1984. Rev. ed., Chicago: Lawrence Hill Books, 1997.

Brooks, Gwendolyn, ed. *A Broadside Treasury: 1965–1970.* Detroit: Broadside, 1971.

Clarke, Cheryl. *"After Mecca": Women Poets and the Black Arts Movement.* New Brunswick, N.J.: Rutgers University Press, 2005.

Collins, Lisa Gail, and Margo Natalie Crawford, eds. *New Thoughts on the Black Arts Movement.* New Brunswick, N.J.: Rutgers University Press, 2006.

Donaldson, Jeff. "Ten in Search of a Nation." *Black World* 19, no. 12 (October 1970); 80–89.

Fabre, Geneviéve. *Drumbeats, Masks, and Metaphor: Contemporary Afro-American Theatre.* Cambridge, Mass.: Harvard University Press, 1983.

Fine, Elsa Honig. *The Afro-American Artist: A Search for Identity.* New York: Hacker Art Books, 1982.

Fowler, Carolyn. *Black Arts and Black Aesthetics: A Bibliography.* Published by author, 1981.

Gayle, Addison, ed. *The Black Aesthetic.* Garden City, N.Y.: Doubleday, 1971.

Jones, LeRoi, and Larry Neal, eds. *Black Fire: An Anthology of Afro-American Writing.* New York: Morrow, 1968.

Lewis, Samella. *African American Art and Artists.* 3d ed., rev. and updated. Berkeley: University of California Press, 2003.

Long, Richard. *The Black Tradition in American Dance.* New York: Rizzoli, 1989.

Parks, Carole, ed. *Nommo: A Literary Legacy of Black Chicago (1967–1987).* Chicago: Oba House, 1987.

Redmond, Eugene B. *Drumvoices: The Mission of Afro-American Poetry.* Garden City, N.Y.: Anchor Press, 1976.

Sell, Mike. *Avant-garde Performance and the Limits of Criticism: Approaching the Living Theatre, Happenings/Fluxus, and the Black Arts Movement.* Ann Arbor: University of Michigan Press, 2005.

Smethurst, James Edward. *The Black Arts Movement: Literary Nationalism in the 1960s and 1970s.* Chapel Hill: University of North Carolina Press, 2005.

Smith, David Lionel. "The Black Arts Movement and Its Critics." *American Literary History* 3, no. 1 (Spring 1991): 93–110.

DAVID LIONEL SMITH (1996)
Updated bibliography

Blackburn, Robert

December 10, 1920
April 21, 2003

The lithographer and teacher Robert Hamilton Blackburn was born to Jamaican parents in Summit, New Jersey, in 1920 and moved to Harlem in 1926. He took art classes at P.S. 139 in Harlem under the instruction of Works Project Administration (WPA)-sponsored teachers Rex Gorleigh and Zell Ingram. In 1935 he studied at the Harlem Community Arts Center and joined the Uptown Community Workshop. In 1941 he received a scholarship at the Art Students League and apprenticed in the studio of printmaker Will Barnet (1941–1943).

In 1948 Blackburn opened his own studio, the Printing Workshop, on 17th Street in New York City, offering evening classes and space for artists to operate printing presses. He created a collaborative relationship between the artist and lithographer so that printing became part of the artistic process. He remained involved with the workshop for over forty years, teaching printmaking and creating his own prints. Artists who used the facility included Romas Viesulas, Clare Romano, Sue Fuller, and Chaim Koppelman.

While teaching at the workshop, Blackburn was also an instructor at the National Academy of Design (1949), the New School for Social Research (1950–1951), Cooper Union (1965–1971), the School of Visual Arts (1967–1971), and at the Painting and Sculpture Division of Columbia University's School of the Arts (1970–1991). He exhibited at community galleries and in larger venues, including the Brooklyn Museum, the Boston Museum of Fine Arts, and the Columbia Museum of Art in South Carolina.

In 1957 Blackburn became the master printer for Tatyana Grosman's Universal Limited Art Editions, a printing house that operated from Grosman's living room in West Islip, Long Island, in New York State. While at Universal, Blackburn was the lithographer of choice for many artists of the New York School, including Jasper Johns and Robert Rauschenberg. He also printed works by many black artists, including Romare Bearden and Hale Woodruff.

In 1971, the Printing Workshop was incorporated as a nonprofit organization and began teaching lithography in economically disadvantaged communities. Some of Blackburn's own prints include "Girl in Red" (1951), "Strange Objects" (1959), and "What Is Apartheid" (1984). Blackburn died in 2003 at the age of eighty-two.

See also Art; Bearden, Romare; Woodruff, Hale Aspacio

Bibliography

Art in Print: A Tribute to Robert Blackburn. New York: New York Public Library, 1984.

Gaither, Edmund "Barry." "Millenium Portrait: Robert Blackburn." *American Visions* 15, no. 1 (February 2000): 22.

Jemisin, Noah. *Bob Blackburn's Printmaking Workshop.* New York: The Workshop, 1992.

Robert Blackburn: A Life's Work (exhibition catalog). New York: Alternative Museum, 1988.

RENEE NEWMAN (1996)
Updated by publisher 2005

Black Caribs

The biological and cultural origins of the Black Caribs are traced to the encounter of Carib Indians and Africans on the island of St. Vincent during the seventeenth century. Ancestors of the Carib Indians had migrated from South America, settling in St. Vincent and some other islands in the eastern Caribbean centuries before Europeans entered the region in the 1490s. By the seventeenth century the growth of sugar plantations and the slave trade brought increasing numbers of Africans to the Caribbean. The African ancestors of the Black Caribs arrived during this period. According to some accounts, all written long after the events took place and thus open to question, a ship carrying enslaved Africans to Barbados was blown off course and sank near St. Vincent. Some of the Africans reached shore, where they encountered Carib Indians. While accounts vary as to whether or not the Indians welcomed the survivors, a European visitor to St. Vincent in the 1670s reported seeing hundreds of armed men of African ancestry alongside nine hundred Carib warriors.

The Africans adopted the Carib language and many of the Indians' cultural practices, but by 1700 two politically separate groups occupied the island. The Indians, whom the Europeans called the Red Caribs or Yellow Caribs, lived on the leeward side of the island. The Black Caribs, or *les Caraïbes Noirs,* as they were known to the French, claimed the less accessible windward side of St. Vincent. It was said that the Black Caribs had chosen that name for themselves in their dealings with Europeans. The British often referred to them by other names, including Wild Negroes, suggesting that they regarded these black Indians as Maroons.

The Black Carib population grew rapidly during the eighteenth century, not only because of natural increase but reputedly because they also took Red Carib women captive and harbored fugitive slaves. In 1763, when the British gained formal control of St. Vincent from the French, the Black Caribs numbered two thousand and the Red Caribs only some hundreds.

The British made plans to colonize the island, but the Black Caribs refused to surrender their land and maintained an alliance with the French that strengthened their position. After three decades of uneasy peace punctuated by broken treaties and resistance, the Black Caribs finally revolted against the British in 1795. In 1796, following a decisive victory, the British proceeded with plans to deport the Black Caribs thousands of miles away from St. Vincent. A few evaded deportation and remained in St. Vincent, but thousands did not. Many of them died of disease before arriving at the intended destination, the island of Roatán. From there the survivors soon spread to the nearby eastern coast of Central America.

Today their settlements lie along a narrow strip of shoreline from Belize to Nicaragua. Their language and their origins in Yurúmai (St. Vincent) remain central to their ethnic identity. Since the late twentieth century they have increasingly used the names Garífuna and Garinagu rather than Black Carib to identify themselves.

See also Identity and Race in the United States; Migration

Bibliography

Craton, Michael. "The Black Caribs of St. Vincent: A Reevalution." In *The Lesser Antilles in the Age of European Expansion,* edited by R. L. Paquette and S. L. Engerman. Gainesville: University of Florida Press, 1996.

Fabel, Robin F. A. *Colonial Challenges: Britons, Native Americans, and Caribs, 1759–1775.* Gainesville: University Press of Florida, 2000.

Gonzalez, Nancie L. *Sojourners of the Caribbean: Ethnogenesis and Ethnohistory of the Garífuna.* Urbana: University of Illinois Press, 1988.

Kerns, Virginia. *Women and the Ancestors: Black Carib Kinship and Ritual,* 2nd ed. Urbana: University of Illinois Press, 1997.

VIRGINIA KERNS (2005)

Black Codes

Black codes were laws passed to regulate the rights of free African Americans in the antebellum and post–Civil War eras. Before the Civil War, a number of midwestern states adopted black codes (or black laws) to inhibit the migration of free blacks and in other ways limit black rights. After the Civil War, most southern states adopted far more severe black codes to prevent former slaves, called freedmen at the time, from having the full rights of citizens and to reimpose, as much as possible, the labor and racial controls of slavery.

Black Codes in the North

In 1804 Ohio passed an act to "regulate black and mulatto persons." This law became the prototype for subsequent laws passed in Ohio, Indiana, Illinois, and the Michigan Territory. It required that blacks migrating to Ohio show proof of their freedom and exacted a $50 fine from any white hiring a black who did not have such proof. On its face, this law could be seen as a good-faith effort to prevent fugitive slaves from entering the state. In fact, it was primarily designed to discourage black migration. An 1807 law raised the fine to $100 and required migrating blacks to find two sureties to guarantee their "good behavior" and assure that they would not require public assistance. Subsequent amendments to these laws prevented blacks from serving on juries and testifying against whites and severely limited their access to public schools. Although discriminatory, these laws did not prevent blacks from owning real estate, entering professions—including law and medicine—or exercising freedom of speech, press, assembly, and worship. Moreover, once blacks were legally present in a state, the black codes of the North did not inhibit their geographic mobility.

These laws were generally ineffective in limiting the growth of the free black population. From 1803 to 1860, Ohio's black population actually grew at a slightly faster rate than did its white population. Between 1830 and 1860, Indiana, Illinois, and Ohio all saw over 300 percent growth in their black populations. Little evidence exists that migrating blacks were generally asked to prove their freedom or that anyone enforced the requirement that migrating blacks find sureties to sign bonds for them. In addition, no cases are on record of any whites being fined for hiring blacks who failed to provide proof of their freedom.

In 1849 Ohio repealed most of its black codes, including those provisions discouraging black migrants from coming to the state. The repeal was part of an elaborate legislative compromise that also sent the abolitionist Salmon P. Chase to the U.S. Senate. Indiana and Illinois retained their discriminatory laws until after the Civil War. Iowa, California, and Oregon also adopted some aspects of the northern black codes, but Iowa and California dropped virtually all these rules before or during the Civil War.

By the end of the Civil War, blacks in the North had substantial equality under the law, except that in most states they could not vote or serve on juries. These disabilities based on race disappeared after the ratification of the Fifteenth Amendment in 1870. After 1870, some northern states still prohibited marriages between blacks and whites, but otherwise most remnants of the black codes were no longer on the books.

Black Codes in the South

In the South, the situation was far different. The loss of the war and the emancipation of four million slaves immediately and dramatically affected southern society. Emancipation upset the system of racial control that had kept blacks subordinate to whites since the seventeenth century, and also destroyed the economic relationship that had allowed planters to count on a pliable and ever-present source of labor. With slavery gone, the legal status of the freedmen and their role in the postwar South were uncertain. Immediately after the war, southern legislatures began to adopt black codes to define the status of former slaves and to cope with the emerging problems resulting from Emancipation.

Northerners assumed that after Emancipation ex-slaves would have the same rights as other free people, but white southerners did not hold the same views. Before the war, the rights of free blacks were severely restricted and usually enumerated in slave codes, underscoring the antebellum southern view that free blacks were an anomalous and inherently dangerous class of people. Thus, when the war ended the ex-slaves of the former Confederate states lacked most legal rights. The black codes changed this but in a way that rigorously limited the rights of freedmen.

At the personal level, the black codes allowed African Americans to marry each other (but not whites) and declared that all slaves who had lived as married couples would be considered legally married. Mississippi's laws of 1865—the first adopted in the postwar South—illustrate how the black codes gave former slaves some rights while at the same time denying them many others that whites had. The end result was to give former slaves most of the responsibilities but few of the benefits of freedom.

Mississippi

An 1865 law with the misleading title "An Act to confer Civil Rights on Freedmen, and for other Purposes," declared that blacks could "sue and be sued, implead and be impleaded" in all state courts, but only allowed them to testify in cases involving other blacks and prohibited them from serving on juries. The law allowed freedmen to acquire and dispose of property "to the same extent that white persons may," but prohibited them from renting any land except in "towns or cities." In other words, free blacks could not rent farmland. In overwhelmingly rural

Mississippi, this meant that freedmen would become a peasant class, forced to work for white landowners and unable to acquire land on their own. Another provision of this law required that all labor contracts made with freedmen for more than a month had to be in writing, and that any freedman who quit before the end of the term of a contract would "forfeit his wages for the year," including those earned up to the time he quit. In a provision similar to the antebellum slave codes, this law obligated "every civil officer" to "arrest and carry back to his or her legal employer any freedman, free negro or mulatto, who shall have quit the service of his or her employer before the expiration of his or her term of service." This in effect made the free blacks of Mississippi slaves to their employers, at least for the term of their employment. Anyone attempting to hire a black under contract to someone else was subject to fines, jail terms, and civil damage suits.

Another Mississippi statute allowed counties to apprentice African-American children if their parents were declared to be too poor to support them. To many, this appeared to be an attempt to re-enslave the children of the freedmen. Still another statute, also enacted in 1865, declared that any black who did not have a labor contract would be declared a vagrant and would be subject to fines or imprisonment. This law provided punishment for free blacks who were "found unlawfully assembling themselves together either in the day or night time," for whites who assembled with such blacks, and for whites and blacks who married or cohabited.

Other States

Other states adopted laws with similar intent but different provisions. Rather than prohibiting blacks from renting land, South Carolina prohibited them from working in nonagricultural jobs without paying special taxes that ranged from $10 to $100. South Carolina also enacted harsh criminal laws to suppress African Americans. Stealing a hog could lead to a $1,000 fine and ten years in jail. Other crimes had punishments of whipping, the stocks, or the treadmill, as well as fines and long imprisonment. Hired farm workers in South Carolina could not even sell farm produce without written authorization from their employers. Other provisions of the law created special taxes and fines for blacks, with imprisonment or forced labor for those who lacked the money to pay them. Like Mississippi, South Carolina provided for the apprenticing of black children. These and similar laws created something close to a reimposition of slavery in South Carolina. In 1865 Louisiana and Alabama adopted laws similar to those of South Carolina and Mississippi.

The black codes of 1865 shocked many northerners. In South Carolina, General Daniel E. Sickles suspended the law, as did Union troops in the Mississippi military. Even some white governors, including William L. Sharkey of Mississippi and Robert Patton of Alabama, opposed some of the more blatantly discriminatory laws. In Congress, Republicans responded by introducing legislation that led to the Civil Rights Act of 1866 and eventually to the Fourteenth Amendment.

In 1866 the rest of the former Confederacy adopted black codes. Florida's code was as harsh as those of Mississippi and South Carolina, providing whipping, the pillory, and forced labor for various offenses. Florida prohibited any blacks from moving into the state, prohibited African Americans from owning firearms, and although allowing the creation of schools for blacks prohibited the use of state money to pay for them.

Other states were more discreet in their legislation, trying to avoid giving ammunition to Republicans in Congress, who were growing increasingly impatient with the South's attempts to reimpose bondage and oppression on the freedmen. Virginia's vagrancy law carefully avoided any reference to race but still punished offenders with forced labor and was clearly directed at the freedmen. Not surprisingly, General Alfred H. Terry suspended its operation, although two other generals, in other parts of Virginia, allowed it to go into force. Tennessee's new criminal code provided the death penalty for breaking and entering with the intent to rob, for robbery itself, and for horse stealing. This law did not use any racial terms but was again clearly aimed at blacks. Similarly, Georgia and North Carolina tried to avoid the use of racial terms that might have jeopardized their chances of readmission to the Union. Nevertheless, none of the former Confederate states was ready to have racially blind statutes, much less racially blind justice. North Carolina's law, arguably the least offensive of the new black codes, nevertheless provided a death penalty for black rapists when the victim was white, but not for white rapists, no matter what the color of the victim.

Like the 1865 laws, those passed in 1866 regulated the movement of blacks, their ability to live where they wished, and their ability to sell their labor on an open market. All the 1866 laws also tried to create racial controls to keep African Americans in a subordinate role, even as they tried to avoid the appearance of racial discrimination. By 1867, southern legislatures had repealed most of the provisions that designated specific punishments by race. Even without racially specific language, however, courts continued to apply solely to African Americans provisions of the black codes regulating vagrancy, contracts, and children.

Although these laws remained on the books in one form or another throughout Reconstruction, their enforcement was sporadic. Congress, the Freedmen's Bureau, and the military opposed them. Nevertheless, the laws remained a symbol of the oppression that the postbellum South offered African Americans. After 1877 the South gradually reimposed those provisions of the black codes that segregated blacks and regulated labor contracts. Such laws led to peonage and a second-class status for southern blacks in the late nineteenth and early twentieth centuries.

See also Fifteenth Amendment; Fourteenth Amendment

Bibliography

Berwanger, Eugene D. *The Frontier against Slavery: Western Anti-Negro Prejudice and the Slavery Extension Controversy.* Urbana: University of Illinois Press, 1967.

Erickson, Leonard. "Politics and Repeal of Ohio's Black Laws, 1837–1849." *Ohio History* 82 (1973): 154–175.

Finkelman, Paul. "Prelude to the Fourteenth Amendment: Black Legal Rights in the Antebellum North." *Rutgers Law Journal* 17 (1986): 415–482.

Finkelman, Paul, ed. *Race, Law, and American History, 1700–1990;* Vol. 3: *Emancipation and Reconstruction.* New York: Garland, 1992.

Lichtenstein, Alex. "Black Codes." *Footsteps* 6, no. 4 (2004): 14.

Nieman, Donald. *To Set the Law in Motion: The Freedmen's Bureau and the Legal Rights of Blacks, 1865–1868.* Millwood, N.Y.: KTO, 1979.

Wilson, Theodore B. *The Black Codes of the South.* University: University of Alabama Press, 1965.

PAUL FINKELMAN (1996)
Updated bibliography

Black Dandy, The

The history of black style's most famous figure, the dandy, strikingly chronicles the sometimes exuberant, sometimes tortured relationship between dress and identity for black people. Although dandies are best known in Western high culture as fashionably dressed aesthetes, well-tailored but morally bankrupt aristocrats, or bohemian conversational wits, when racialized as black, however, their extravagant bodily display changes supposed frivolity into a mode of social, cultural, and political critique.

Black dandyism originated with the beginning of European exploration of Africa. As early as the fifteenth and sixteenth centuries, young children from Africa, primarily

Black Codes of Mississippi (1865)

Apprentice Law

Section 3. *Be it further enacted,* that in the management and control of said apprentices, said master or mistress shall have power to inflict such moderate corporeal chastisement as a father or guardian is allowed to inflict on his or her child or ward at common law:

Provided, that in no case shall cruel or inhuman punishment be inflicted.

Section 4. *Be it further enacted,* that if any apprentice shall leave the employment of his or her master or mistress without his or her consent, said master or mistress may pursue and recapture said apprentice and bring him or her before any justice of the peace of the county, whose duty it shall be to remand said apprentice to the service of his or her master or mistress; and in the event of a refusal on the part of said apprentice so to return, then said justice shall commit said apprentice to the jail of said county, on failure to give bond, until the next term of the county court; and it shall be the duty of said court, at the first term thereafter, to investigate said case; and if the court shall be of opinion that said apprentice left the employment of his or her master or mistress without good cause, to order him or her to be punished, as provided for the punishment of hired freedmen, as may be from time to time provided for by law, for desertion, until he or she shall agree to return to his or her master or mistress:

Provided, that the court may grant continuances, as in other cases; and *provided,* further, that if the court shall believe that said apprentice had good cause to quit his said master or mistress, the court shall discharge said apprentice from said indenture and also enter a judgment against the master or mistress for not more than $100, for the use and benefit of said apprentice, to be collected on execution, as in other cases.

boys, were imported to Europe by the elite as a special kind of servant—as "luxury" slaves. This trend of keeping young Africans as pets, dressing them up in elaborate liveries and sometimes educating them and training them to be companions, became even more popular later during British control of the slave trade in the eighteenth century. These dandified blacks came to understand and take advantage of their status as social spectacles: Some of them became celebrities whose fame confused their status as inhuman chattel; others, after a time as luxury slaves, became early members of the free black British community. Due to their spectacularity, these blacks also became a part of literary and visual culture, becoming characters on the stage and also the subject of paintings, prints, and political cartoons that sometimes valorized and sometimes criticized the wealthy who tried to domesticate black people by means of elaborate dress. This practice gave the enslaved and free working blacks a strategy with which to define their own identity: the pointed redeployment of clothing, gesture, and wit.

As Europe colonized the Americas, the black dandy took on another set of meanings because the conditions of enslavement were very different. In Europe, dandified slaves had for the most part lived with masters in individual households, making their "masquerade" as elites much easier to manage. In the Americas, especially by the nineteenth century, most slaves experienced slavery in larger groups on farms and plantations, making this play with dress and status much more anxiety producing. Blacks in fancy dress in the American colonial period therefore could either be a part of the luxury slave tradition or participate in African-derived carnivalesque class and race cross-dressing festivals in which slaves and free people wore their master's clothing, symbolizing a temporary, joyous power exchange. Later, especially right before abolition, they could be slaves who managed to barter for or buy clothing for special occasions (Sunday, weddings, festivals) or newly free, urban blacks striving to present themselves with dignity and self-respect on the streets. None of this black play with clothing went unnoticed, for in different ways it threatened the status quo and evidenced a black creativity and resilience. The dandyism on display allowed blacks and whites to imagine the potential of the enslaved, to visualize black social and economic mobility, education, and equality. These thoughts were so threatening for the majority that repressing them became a national concern. During the nineteenth century, the most popular form of entertainment was the blackface minstrel show that featured the denigration of its two principal characters: the plantation darky and the black dandy, who was incompletely educated, sexually promiscuous, greedy, scheming, and ostentatiously dressed.

A young black man poses in formal suit and top hat, c. 1890. *The dandy, whose elegant appearance communicated dignity and respectability, helped combat stereotypical, cartoonish images of blacks in the nineteenth century.* GETTY IMAGES

When African Americans began to have more control over their representation in literature and visual culture, the blackface dandy caricature and its imputation of African-American intelligence, masculinity, moral character, and even aesthetic sense became a primary target for reform. Writers such as Charles Chesnutt, Nella Larsen, and others interested in presenting images of "New Negroes" created characters whose elegant outward appearance communicated the respectability, dignity, wisdom, and righteousness they knew to be characteristic of black life. This effort to present new, more realistic, idealized, or self-fashioned images flowered in the New Negro or Harlem Renaissance, when there was an explosion of new black style both on the streets and in literature, artwork, and theater. This increased concentration on black images and style even took dandyism in a number of directions: Many groups began to use elegant, fancy, fashionable, or distinctive clothing to announce their presence on the world's stage. People perceived as dandies could be found in literary salons, onstage in the musical *Chocolate Dandies,*

Singer Andre 3000 of Outkast poses for a studio portrait during the MTV Europe Music Awards in Rome, Italy, 2004. *Andre 3000 was featured on the cover of Esquire in September 2004, having topped their list of "World's Best Dressed Men."* GETTY IMAGES

parading down Harlem's Seventh Avenue or Chicago's Stroll, in the audience at Small's Paradise, sitting for portraits in James Van Der Zee's studio, or as audience and participants at Harlem's famous drag balls. Despite the many ways one could identify or define a dandy during this era, the figure still came up for censure as debates raged concerning the effectiveness of image in the quest for civil and political rights. These debates continue today.

In the later twentieth century, black dandies and dandyism have taken even more forms, as, for example, the entertainment industry has come to rely on and be fueled by the evolution of black style, especially black musical and dress styles. Entertainers as diverse as Duke Ellington, Little Richard, Prince, Snoop Dog, and Andre 3000 of Outkast are considered dandies. In the twenty-first century, dandyism has taken an interesting new turn as hip-hop moguls, such as Sean "P. Diddy" Combs, have themselves become designers and CEOs of fashion houses that produce urban looks as well as bespoke suits that are sold internationally. As black style becomes more and more mainstream and media driven, initiating new conversations about the relationship between blackness, masculinity, sexuality, cosmopolitanism, and consumption, black dandyism's next step is uncertain; what is guaranteed is that whatever form it takes, the "look" will be illustrative of current black consciousness concerning identity.

See also Free Blacks 1619–1860; Identity and Race in the United States; Representations of Blackness

Bibliography

Foster, Helen Bradley. *"New Raiments of 'Self': African American Clothing in the Antebellum South.* New York and Oxford: Berg, 1997.

Gerzina, Gretchen Holbrook. *Black London: Life before Emancipation.* New Brunswick, N.J.: Rutgers University Press, 1995.

Tulloch, Carol, ed. *Black Style.* London: V & A Publications, 2004.

White, Graham and Shane. *Stylin': African American Expressive Culture from its Beginnings to the Zoot Suit.* Ithaca, N.Y.: Cornell University Press, 1998.

MONICA L. MILLER (2005)

Black English Vernacular

See English, African-American

Black Entertainment Television (BET)

Black Entertainment Television (BET), a twenty-four-hour cable television station and entertainment company, targets African Americans by offering original programming and diverse black musical video programming. BET was founded in 1979 by Robert L. Johnson and aired its first movie, *A Visit to the Chief's Son,* on January 25, 1980. The station, originally a subsidiary and the primary business of BET Holdings, Inc., reached some 45 million subscribers worldwide by the end of the 1990s. One of the biggest minority-owned businesses in the United States, BET was sold to media giant Viacom for nearly $3 billion in November 2000.

A graduate of Princeton University and past vice-president of government relations for the National Cable and Television Association (NCTA) from 1976 to 1979,

Johnson secured a consulting contract with the NCTA and then used the contract to secure a loan from the National Bank of Washington. He also secured a $320,000 loan from John C. Malone, head of Tele-Communications Inc (TCI). After Malone and TCI also paid him $180,000 for a 20 percent share in the network, Johnson created BET. In 1984 Johnson also formed District Cablevision Inc. to serve Washington, D.C., residents. TCI owned 75 percent of the new company, and Johnson encountered several lawsuits by competitors. Yet by 1989 Johnson was able to repay his investors. On October 30, 1991, BET became the first black-controlled company to be listed on the New York Stock Exchange. On the first day of its listing, the stock value grew from $9 million to $475 million. In 1995 the company relocated to a new $15 million facility. In 1996, BET added a BET/Starz! Channel 3, a premium movie channel. In the same year Johnson pledged $100,000 to Howard University's School of Communication and was awarded the university's Messenger Award for Excellence in Communication.

BET further diversified its holdings by publishing magazines, marketing clothing and cosmetics, and forming a radio network to provide news to urban market radio stations. In 1996 the company entered a partnership with Microsoft to form MSBET, an online service with entertainment news and information.

With the sale of BET to Viacom, founder and present chief executive officer Johnson became the first African American billionaire. In 2002, he also became the first black principal owner of a major sports franchise, the Charlotte Bobcats of the NBA.

See also Television

Bibliography

Gay, Verne. "Selling Out of Selling Up?" *Mediaweek* 10, no. 46 (November 27, 2000): 39.

Lohr, Greg A. "The 'BET' That Paid Off." *Washington Business Journal* 20, no. 8 (June 29, 2001): 24.

Meeks, Kenneth. "Back Talk: With Billionaire & BET CEO Robert L. Johnson." *Black Enterprise* 35, no. 6 (January 2005): 112.

RACHEL ZELLARS (1996)
Updated by publisher 2005

Black History Month/Negro History Week

The annual celebration of Negro History Week was one of the historian Carter G. Woodson's (1875–1950) most successful efforts to popularize the study of black history. Omega Phi, one of the oldest African-American fraternities, first celebrated black achievements on Lincoln's birthday (February 12). Woodson, an honorary member of the fraternity, convinced the Omegas to let the Association for the Study of Negro Life and History, which he had founded in 1915, sponsor Negro History Week in an effort to reach a larger audience. Woodson began the annual celebration in 1926 to increase awareness of and interest in black history among both blacks and whites. Months before the first celebration, he sent out promotional brochures and pamphlets suggesting ways to celebrate to state boards of education, elementary and secondary schools, colleges, women's clubs, black newspapers and periodicals, and white scholarly journals. Woodson chose the second week of February, to commemorate the birthdays of Frederick Douglass and Abraham Lincoln. Each year the association produced bibliographies, photographs, books, pamphlets, and other promotional literature to assist the black community in the celebration. Over 100 photographs of blacks were available for sale, and specialized pamphlets included bibliographies on various aspects of African-American history. In 1928 Woodson also prepared a "Table of 152 Important Events and Dates in Negro History," which he sold for fifty cents. Negro History Week celebrations generally included parades of costumed characters depicting the lives of famous blacks, as well as breakfasts, banquets, lectures, poetry readings, speeches, exhibits, and other special presentations.

During the 1940s, Negro History Week celebrations became increasingly more sophisticated and attracted even larger audiences. Woodson compiled and sold Negro History Week kits, posters, and large photographs that depicted periods of African-American history. Black women's organizations and social-service groups sponsored lectures and rallies for their members. Libraries, museums, and educational institutions held special exhibits. School systems throughout the country sponsored institutes to help teachers prepare. Teachers assigned students essays on topics in black history, helped them write and produce plays, and sponsored oratorical and essay contests. Woodson credited schoolteachers with ensuring the success of the annual celebrations, and he regularly reported on their efforts in the *Journal of Negro History* (now the *Journal of African American History*) and in the black press, highlighting the most creative and innovative activities. In some school systems the celebration was so successful that teachers established Negro History Study Clubs, which gave attention to the subject throughout the school year. White politicians made annual proclamations in honor of Negro History Week, and whites began to participate in special activities. During Woodson's lifetime the celebration became so far-reaching in its popularity that whites and blacks in Latin America, the West Indies, Africa, and the Philippines participated.

Many of Woodson's contemporaries contended that the annual celebration was his most impressive achievement. Writing in *Dusk of Dawn* in 1940, the sociologist W. E. B. Du Bois (1868–1963) claimed that it was the greatest single accomplishment to arise from the Harlem Renaissance. Similarly, the historian Rayford Logan (1897–1982) maintained that Negro History Week helped blacks overcome their inferiority complex and instilled racial pride and optimism. After Woodson's death in 1950, the Association for the Study of Negro Life and History (now the Association for the Study of African-American Life and History) continued to sponsor the annual event, selling Negro History Week kits and assisting teachers, women's clubs, and civic associations with their celebrations. By the early 1970s the organization decided to extend the celebration to the entire month of February and use the term *black*. Politicians, the media, and the organization that previously had supported the effort to promote black history during the second week of February began celebrating throughout the month, while also continuing to press for greater recognition of black history throughout the year.

See also Association for the Study of African American Life and History; Journal of African American History, The; Woodson, Carter Godwin

Bibliography

Goggin, Jacqueline. *Carter G. Woodson, a Life in Black History*. Baton Rouge: Louisiana State University Press, 1993.

Meier, August, and Elliott Rudwick. *Black History and the Historical Profession*. Urbana: University of Illinois Press, 1986.

Meier, August, and Elliott Rudwick. *Explorations in the Black Experience*. Urbana: University of Illinois Press, 2002.

JACQUELINE GOGGIN (1996)
Updated bibliography

Black Identity

See Identity and Race in the United States; Media and Identity in the Caribbean

Black-Indian Relations

People of African descent have a long history of relations with the indigenous peoples (Indians or Native Americans) of the Americas. Initial contact between Africans and Indians occurred during the sixteenth century, when free and enslaved African men traveled to the Americas with European explorers and conquerors. After European countries such as England, Spain, Portugal, and France established their overseas empires, settlers in the Americas quickly came to rely on the labor of enslaved Indians and Africans to cultivate food crops and commodities for export. In North and South America, Africans and their American-born descendants lived and labored alongside Native Americans during much of the eighteenth century.

Even after Europeans ceased enslaving Indians and only owned Africans and African Americans as chattel, black people and Native Americans continued to come into contact with each other and establish various kinds of ongoing relations. In some instances, Indians assisted runaway slaves, while in others, Indians served as slave catchers, returning fugitives to their masters. In other cases, African Americans and Native Americans formed intricate ties of cultural exchange and intimate relations of kinship and family bonds. Early contact between Africans and Native Americans was initiated by factors beyond their control—European colonialism and slavery—but the ongoing relations between blacks and Indians developed as the result of each party's careful and deliberate decision making.

In the sixteenth century, African men worked as sailors, soldiers, and servants in Spanish expeditions, accompanying the *conquistadores* who claimed land and riches in North and South America for the Spanish Empire. In 1527, for example, the Spanish king authorized Pánfilo de Narváez to lead a voyage of five ships to the Florida region; among the men under his control was a Spanish-speaking African slave named Esteban. Most of the men in this expedition perished shortly after reaching the Gulf Coast, but Esteban survived, as did Álvar Núñez Cabeza de Vaca, the Spaniard who recorded their encounters with Indians and their journey across the lands of the Zuni people (present-day New Mexico and Arizona) as they made their way to Spanish colonial authorities in Mexico City. Just over a decade later, in 1538, the Spanish king gave Hernando de Soto the authority to raise an army, invade Florida, and establish armed settlements there. A Spanish-speaking slave named Gomez was one of the men in de Soto's party when they landed in Florida in 1539. Hernando de Soto's brutal treatment of the servants in his ranks prompted many of the men, including Gomez, to flee from the expedition and seek refuge with the Indians who inhabited Florida.

To the north, in the British colonies such as Virginia and Carolina, British farmers and tobacco planters relied on enslaved Native Americans captured in frontier wars to provide agricultural labor. Indians taken as captives were bought and sold as slaves to colonists in British North America and in the Caribbean. At the same time, low numbers of enslaved Africans were shipped to the North American colonies. Thus, in the seventeenth and early eighteenth centuries, Africans and Native Americans often lived and labored alongside each other, forming friendships as well as family ties through marriage, and it is quite likely that people born to the unions of African and Native American men and women were also enslaved.

By the beginning of the eighteenth century, colonists in the Americas shifted away from enslaving Indians and purchased greater numbers of African slaves. Enslaved Indians were familiar with their surroundings and could easily escape and return to their people. Enslaving Indians, moreover, threatened to compromise Europeans' diplomatic relations with the Indian nations bordering the colonies. By contrast, Africans enslaved in the Americas were thousands of miles from their homelands, and the commercial slave trade proved highly profitable to European investors and merchants. Although Africans came to replace Indians as enslaved laborers in colonial North America, lines of communication and cross-cultural exchange had been well established by the two parties. Crops cultivated in the southern colonies for local consumption, for example, reflected the presence and interaction between Africans and Indians. African foods such as okra, peanuts, and sesame seeds were used in southern cooking and were often combined with standard Native American ingredients such as sassafras. Gumbo, the classic Louisiana dish, was made by cooking okra with sassafras in slowly heated oil. The utensils and containers used to prepare and store food also reflected the joint influence of African and Native American knowledge and tradition. While Europeans had never encountered any plants like the palmetto trees of coastal Carolina, the trees, which of course were well known to Native Americans, were also familiar to West Africans, who used the fronds to weave baskets for the preparation and storage of food. Similarly, both Africans and Indians were adept at fashioning utensils and containers from gourds, another item unknown to European colonists.

In the eighteenth century, Indian peoples did not share Euro-Americans' ideas about race and racial hierarchy, nor did they believe that black people (Africans and African Americans) were inherently inferior and only suited for enslavement. For many Native American peoples, social hierarchies were determined by age, gender, physical strength, and kin relations. Outsiders, such as runaway black slaves or other Indians, could be incorporated into a particular Native American society if they were adopted into a specific kin group. Indians also recognized black people as valuable allies in their struggles against the colonial settlers and authorities. Around 1714 to 1715, Yamasee Indians, along with bands of Choctaws and Cherokees, began to revolt against British traders from Carolina. It was believed that blacks assisted the Indians in their rebellion, and after the war Yamasee Indians aided fugitive slaves in their efforts to reach St. Augustine, Florida, where Spanish authorities, acting in accordance with the king's 1693 edict, granted freedom to fugitive slaves from the British colonies.

In 1739 the Spanish governor established an armed garrison near St. Augustine called Gracia Real de Santa Teresa de Mose, which became the first known free black community in North America. Spain relied on these armed black men to assist them in their military campaigns to repel British forces in 1740. The inhabitants of Fort Mose established economic and personal ties with the outlying Seminole towns in the vicinity, trading with Indians and marrying into their families. In 1763 Spain ceded Florida to Great Britain, but the change in flags did little to halt the flow of runaway slaves into Florida. Fugitives could no longer expect freedom from the Spanish and instead lived on their own, in what were known as maroon (fugitive slave) communities, near scattered settlements of bands of Indians that would become known as Seminoles.

Anglo-American colonists regarded the interactions and communication between Africans, African Americans, and Indians with suspicion and concern. They worried especially about the assistance Indians gave to runaway slaves, and they feared the possibility of a black-Indian alliance and armed rebellion against the colonies. White authorities thus passed laws designed to regulate the movement of enslaved people and to limit their contact with Native Americans. Enslaved black men, for example, were restricted from serving in the colonial militias that fought frontier wars against Indians. Other laws worked to prevent alliances between Indians and Africans by offering financial rewards to those Indians who captured and returned runaway slaves to their owners. Treaties between the colonies and Indian nations contained provisions requiring Indians to return runaway slaves. Even when Indians returned fugitives to their masters, however, the runaways had acquired crucial knowledge about a particular Indian community's willingness or unwillingness to assist runaways. Thus, despite colonial authorities best efforts, contact occurred between enslaved African Americans and local Native American populations, relations were established, and knowledge was exchanged.

The most extensive and well-known instance of sustained interaction and exchange between African Americans and Native Americans occurred in Florida, beginning around the time of the American Revolution. By the late eighteenth century Seminoles had already established relations with runaway slaves, or maroons, who had formed their own settlements in Florida. During the Revolution, Seminoles allied with the British and raided colonists' plantations, capturing slaves and livestock. After the war, Seminoles retained these black people as their own subordinates but did not own them as chattel or property. Black people lived in their own settlements within Seminole towns, raised their own crops, tended their own cattle herds and ran their own households. In an annual show of loyalty to their Seminole leaders, black people as well as Indians offered Seminole headmen an annual tribute payment of livestock and produce. The close ties of loyalty between blacks and Seminoles were demonstrated when black men engaged in warfare alongside Seminole men. In 1812 Seminoles and blacks fought together against American militias seeking to acquire control of East Florida, which had been returned to Spanish control. During the following years, the black-Seminole settlements continued to attract runaways from Georgia and South Carolina. African Americans who fled to Florida intermarried with Seminoles and with the black people who had already settled among them. By the 1830s, American slaveholders could no longer tolerate their slaves' escape to Seminole lands, and they grew increasingly fearful of a black-Seminole rebellion. Growing anxiety about black-Indian contact and alliances culminated in federal efforts to remove Indians from the southeastern states. The initial step was the passage of the Indian Removal Act of 1830. In December 1835 the United States commenced a military assault—the Second Seminole War—to remove the Seminoles and Maroons from Florida and relocate them in the West.

The Seminoles were but one of the Indian nations in the southeastern United States to establish extensive and intricate ties with African Americans during the early nineteenth century. Each of the five principal southeastern Native American nations—Seminole, Cherokee, Choctaw, Chickasaw, and Creek—incorporated free and enslaved African Americans into their communities, but they did so in distinct ways. While the Seminoles did not regard African Americans as slaves and inferiors, but as compatriots and allies, Indians in the other four nations practiced forms of slavery that more closely resembled the United States system of chattel slavery. African Americans' experiences were different in each nation, however, and not all Indians owned black slaves or supported slavery.

In the late eighteenth and early nineteenth centuries, free black people lived in the Indian nations and many were married to Indians. The Cherokee nation's 1839 constitution, for example, granted citizenship to the descendants of Cherokee women and African-American men. On many occasions, Indians recognized fugitive slaves from the United States as free people in the Indian nations. The Creeks, for example, refused to return both fugitive slave women and the children they had with Creek men to white slaveholders in the states. Indians' reluctance to regard African Americans as chattel and as inferiors and to assist white slaveholders by returning runaways reflected the Indians' own traditions of slaveholding in which individuals were treated as subordinates for only a limited period of time and were then recognized as full members of an Indian community. Yet in the early decades of the nineteenth century, many Indians gradually changed their definitions and patterns of slaveholding, bringing them more in line with those of white Americans.

The Cherokees held more African Americans as slaves than any of the other Indian nations. In 1835, when the Cherokees were removed from their lands in Georgia and relocated in the area that would become Oklahoma, there were over 1,500 enslaved blacks in the Cherokee nation. Although the number is quite small when compared to the number of enslaved people in the United States, it represented nearly 8 percent of the Cherokee nation's total population. Each of the Indian nations, with the exception of the Seminole, passed laws in the 1840s that imposed greater restrictions on slaves' lives than before, suggesting a shift in attitudes towards enslaved people. Laws prohibited black people from owning property and livestock, carrying firearms, moving freely, and learning to read or write. Large slaveholders, like their white counterparts in the southern United States, harnessed enslaved people's labor for profit, putting blacks to work in cotton fields to produce surplus goods for sale and profit. Those Indians who owned only a few slaves, however, tended to work alongside the enslaved, growing food crops for their own consumption. Many Indians never owned slaves, and some formed antislavery associations or supported the efforts of abolitionists from the states.

After the Civil War, African Americans who had been enslaved in Indian nations considered themselves to be culturally and politically affiliated with Indians. Former slaves recalled their experiences during the period of Indian removal, when they, too, were relocated from the South to the West. Many African Americans had Indian parents or grandparents and identified with both their black and Indian ancestors and cultures. Throughout much of the nineteenth century, African Americans in the Indian nations spoke Native American languages as well as English, dressed in the styles particular to Indians, and had extensive knowledge of sacred medicines and rituals. For blacks in the Indian nations, their history in the nations and their family ties and shared cultural practices with Native Americans were vital elements in shaping their identities as people firmly rooted in specific Native American communities. This sense of connection has endured for many African Americans who trace their family history to people who were enslaved in the Indian nations and to those black men and women who married Indians.

Although relations between African Americans and Native Americans were extensive across the southeast in the eighteenth and nineteenth centuries, black people and Indians came into contact with each other throughout the United States. In the Northeast, for example, indigenous inhabitants of Massachusetts, such as the Mashpee and Pequot, were often recognized as having intermarried with Africans and African Americans over many generations. Throughout the first half of the nineteenth century, in coastal communities around major ports in Connecticut and Massachusetts, men of Afro-Indian descent played important roles as sailors and crewmembers in the whaling industry. In the Southwest, too, intermarriage between African Americans and Native Americans was not uncommon in the nineteenth century and resulted in the formation of families and communities whose family history and cultural traditions cannot be defined by a single label.

Relations between Africans, African Americans, and Native Americans reach back to the fifteenth century, when free and enslaved Africans arrived in North America with European explorers, conquerors, and colonial settlers. Beginning in the early twentieth century, scholars of African American history have researched and documented this contact, tracing the economic, political, personal, and cultural ties and exchanges that were developed—and that continue to occur—between African Americans and Native Americans.

See also Gracia Real de Santa Teresa de Mose; Maroon Arts; Maroon Wars; Runaway Slaves in the United States

Bibliography

Brooks, James F., ed. *Confounding the Color Line: The Indian-Black Experience in North America.* Lincoln: University of Nebraska Press, 2002.

Mandell, Daniel R. "The Saga of Sarah Muckamugg: Indian and African American Intermarriage in Colonial New England." In *Sex, Love, Race: Crossing Boundaries in North American History,* edited by Martha Hodes. New York: New York University Press, 1999.

Mulroy, Kevin. *Freedom on the Border: The Seminole Maroons in Florida, the Indian Territory, Coahuila, and Texas.* Lubbock: Texas Tech University Press, 1993.

Perdue, Theda. *Slavery and the Evolution of Cherokee Society, 1540–1866.* Knoxville: University of Tennessee Press, 1979.

Usner, Daniel H., Jr. *Indians, Settlers, and Slaves in a Frontier Exchange Economy.* Chapel Hill: University of North Carolina Press, 1992.

Wood, Peter. *Strange New Land: Africans in Colonial America.* New York: Oxford University Press, 2003.

BARBARA KRAUTHAMER (2005)

Black Manifesto

Prepared by James Forman with the assistance of the League of Black Revolutionary Workers and adopted by the National Black Economic Development Conference (NBEDC) in Detroit, Michigan, on April 26, 1969, the Black Manifesto called on white churches and synagogues to pay $500 million (about $15 per black person) in reparations for black enslavement and continuing oppression. The money would fund projects to benefit blacks, including the establishment of a southern land bank, four television networks, and a black university. The manifesto indicted white religious organizations for complicity in American racism and called on blacks to bring whatever pressure was necessary to force churches and synagogues to comply.

On May 4, 1969, the date set by the manifesto to start disrupting religious institutions, Forman took the pulpit in the middle of services at New York City's Riverside Church and demanded reparations. Riverside Church was selected because of its connections with the Rockefeller family, viewed by the manifesto's authors as classic white oppressors. Some predominantly white churches expressed some sympathy with the aims of the manifesto but primarily increased aid to existing or new programs of their own rather than providing money for the reparations fund. Forman's call did raise about half a million dollars, about $200,000 of which came from Riverside Church alone. Many prominent black organizations, including the National Association for the Advancement of Colored People (NAACP) and the National Baptist Convention, distanced themselves from the call for reparations and urged that money be given to them for related purposes instead.

By mid-May 1969 both the FBI and the Justice Department had begun investigations into the NBEDC. The money raised by the manifesto was used by the Interreligious Foundation for Community Projects for a number of projects, including the funding of Black Star Publications, a revolutionary black publishing house in Detroit, connected to James Forman.

See also League of Revolutionary Black Workers; Reparations

Bibliography

Forman, James. *The Making of Black Revolutionaries.* Washington, D.C.: Open Hand, 1985.

Haines, Herbert H. *Black Radicals and the Civil Rights Mainstream, 1954–1970.* Knoxville: University of Tennessee Press, 1988.

JEANNE THEOHARIS (1996)

Black Middle Class

Classical notions of class are related to economic stratification. Because racism has historically relegated much of the African American population to poverty, blacks employed other noneconomic bases for stratification. Thus, the black middle class is a segment of the African-American community distinguished by economic as well as social characteristics. Economic dimensions include income, occupation, and wealth, while social characteristics may include education, skin tone, respectability, church affiliation, or social club membership. However, substantial upward mobility in the second half of the twentieth century increased the importance of economic characteristics for defining the black middle class.

In the antebellum period, there was no group that could be called the black middle class. Yet slavery's racial and skin-color hierarchy constituted an early foundation and became part of blacks' evaluation of each other. Slaves with lighter skin had particular advantages because of their position in the slave economy as house or skilled servants. Their sustained contact with the slave-owning white upper class provided opportunities for direct observation and knowledge of dominant styles. After Emancipation and during Reconstruction, these mulatto house and skilled slaves, along with free Negroes who were also disproportionately of mixed race, constituted the first black middle class. Aside from a small black intelligentsia, of which such figures as W. E. B. Du Bois would have been a part, the first black middle class earned its living primarily through service to whites as caterers, barbers, tailors, and other skilled workers.

At the end of the nineteenth century, southern Jim Crow laws and the Great Migration of southern blacks to northern cities altered interracial relations and, hence, the configuration of the black middle class. Growing residential segregation in the North and South created all-black ghettos. The second black middle class formed to serve these racially separate communities. Entrepreneurs and professionals—doctors, teachers, social workers, and the like—formed the core of this new black middle class, indicating the growing importance of such economic factors as occupation. Skin color and connections to whites as markers of black-middle-class status receded but did not disappear. Also, blacks in lower-status occupations could distinguish themselves as middle class by joining the right church (often Episcopal or a more reserved Baptist congregation), gaining membership in the right social clubs (with such names as "Amethyst Girls" or "Kool Kustomers" in Chicago), or working for the right causes (often framed in such general terms as "race pride" or "social betterment").

National economic prosperity after World War II, followed by progressive racial attitudes and policies of the civil rights era, marked another change in the size and composition of the black middle class. Predominantly white educational institutions admitted black students, firms recruited at black colleges, affirmative action policies held employers accountable, and unions yielded to the pressure of their formerly excluded black co-workers. Until 1960 less than 10 percent of blacks were in white-collar occupations. At the end of the 1990s half of all blacks worked as professionals, managers, administrators, technicians, salespeople, or clerics. Residential segregation began a slow decline in the 1970s, and blacks began to move to the suburbs. The late-twentieth-century black middle class is a much more diverse population of secretaries and executives, suburbanites and inner-city residents, Catholics and Apostolics.

Throughout these historical transformations, debates have focused on the responsibilities of the black middle class to "the race." Du Bois argued in the early 1900s that the "talented tenth"—that is, blacks who had received a liberal education and were politically astute—would lead the black masses out of poverty and despair. He later became disenchanted with their apparent apathy. Sociologist E. Franklin Frazier incited debate in the 1950s with his scathing account of the social life and psychology of the black middle class, stressing their foolish imitation of the white upper class and the rejection of and disdain for black folk culture. Such portrayals continue into contemporary discussions but have been countered by evidence of enduring racial consciousness among the black middle class and solidarity with the black poor, especially in the realms of culture and politics.

The large black middle class cohort formed after World War II is now begetting a second and third generation that has made unprecedented economic gains. Nationwide, African Americans earned about $656 billion in 2003, double the amount of ten years earlier. According to the U.S. Census, a third of the black families in Chicago, for instance, make incomes of over $50,000, firmly entrenching them in the middle class. These new members were born after southern Jim Crow and with the benefits of affirmative action, however imperiled. The reproduction, growth, and entrenchment of the black middle class and the concurrent decline in black poverty signal a significant shift in the composition of the African-American community that will likely have consequences for many other arenas of black American life.

See also Du Bois, W. E. B.; Economic Condition, U.S.; Frazier, Edward Franklin; Migration

Bibliography

Billingsley, Andrew. *Climbing Jacob's Ladder: The Enduring Legacy of African American Families.* New York: Simon and Schuster, 1992.

Dawson, Michael C. *Behind the Mule: Race and Class in African-American Politics.* Princeton, N.J.: Princeton University Press, 1994.

Drake, St. Clair, and Horace Cayton. *Black Metropolis: A Study of Negro Life in a Northern City.* New York: Harcourt Brace, 1945.

Du Bois, W. E. B. *The Philadelphia Negro: A Social Study,* rev. ed. Philadelphia: University of Pennsylvania Press, 1996.

Frazier, E. Franklin. *The Negro Family in the United States.* Chicago: University of Chicago Press, 1939.

Frazier, E. Franklin. *The Black Bourgeoisie.* 1957. Reprinted Glencoe, Ill.: Free Press, 1997.

Haynes, Bruce. *Red Lines, Black Spaces: The Politics of Race and Space in a Black Middle-Class Suburb.* New Haven, Conn.: Yale University Press, 2001.

Landry, Bart. *The New Black Middle Class.* Berkeley: University of California Press, 1987.

Pattillo-McCoy, Mary. *Black Picket Fences: Privilege and Peril Among the Black Middle Class.* Chicago: University of Chicago Press, 2000.

MARY PATTILLO-MCCOY (2001)
Updated by publisher 2005

Black Panther Party for Self-Defense

The Black Panther Party for Self-Defense was founded in October 1966 by Huey P. Newton (1942–1989) and Bobby Seale (b. 1936). Despite periods of imprisonment, the two remained leaders as the party expanded from its Oakland, California, base to become a national organization. Assuming the posts of defense minister and chairman, respectively, Newton and Seale drafted a ten-point platform that included a wide range of demands, summarized in the final point: "We want land, bread, housing, education, clothing, justice and peace." However, the party's appeal among young African Americans was based mainly on its brash militancy, often expressed in confrontations with police. Initially concentrated in the San Francisco Bay area and Los Angeles, by the end of 1968 the Black Panther Party ("for Self-Defense" was dropped from its name) had formed chapters in dozens of cities throughout the United States, with additional support chapters abroad. Although most of its leaders were male, a substantial proportion of its rank-and-file members were female. Influenced by the ideas of Marx and Malcolm X, the Black Panther Party's ideology was not clearly defined, and the party experienced many internal disputes over its political orientation. The FBI's covert Counterintelligence Program (COINTELPRO) and raids by local police forces exacerbated leadership conflicts, resulted in the imprisonment or death of party members, and hastened the decline of the group after 1968.

After joining the party in 1967, Eldridge Cleaver (1935–1998), a former convict and author of a book of essays titled *Soul on Ice,* became one of the party's main spokespersons and provided a link with white leftist supporters. Arrested in May 1967 during a protest at the California state capitol in Sacramento against pending legislation to restrict the carrying of weapons, Cleaver remained affiliated with the Panthers despite the repeated efforts of authorities to return him to prison for parole violations. His caustic attacks on white authorities combined with media images of armed Panthers wearing black leather

Four Black Panther Party members giving the "Black Power" salute. AP/WIDE WORLD PHOTOS. REPRODUCED BY PERMISSION.

jackets attracted notoriety and many recruits during the summer of 1967. Cleaver's prominence in the Black Panther Party increased after October 28, 1967, when Newton was arrested after an altercation that resulted in the death of an Oakland police officer. The Panthers immediately mobilized to free Newton, who faced a possible death sentence if convicted. As part of this support effort, Cleaver and Seale contacted Stokely Carmichael (1941–1998), the former chairman of the Student Nonviolent Coordinating Committee (SNCC) and a nationally known proponent of Black Power. SNCC activists and representatives from other black militant groups participated in "Free Huey" rallies during February 1968, helping to transform the Panthers from a local group into a national organization. When Cleaver was arrested during an April 6 raid that resulted in the killing of party treasurer Bobby Hutton, his parole was revoked, and his legal defense, as well as that of Newton, became a major focus of Panther activities.

Serious conflicts accompanied the party's rapid growth, however, for its leaders were divided over ideological and tactical issues. Cleaver and Seale were unsuccessful in their effort to forge an alliance with SNCC, whose members distrusted the Panthers' hierarchical leadership style. When relations between the two groups soured during the summer of 1968, Carmichael decided to remain allied with the Panthers, but his advocacy of black unity and

> "We want freedom. We want power to determine the destiny of our black community."
>
> THE BLACK PANTHER PARTY: PLATFORM AND PROGRAM, *THE BLACK PANTHER*, JULY 5, 1969. REPRINTED IN JOHN BRACEY, AUGUST MEIER, AND ELLIOTT RUDWICK, EDS. *BLACK NATIONALISM IN AMERICA*. INDIANAPOLIS: BOBBS-MERILL, 1970, P. 531.

Pan-Africanism put him at odds with other Panther leaders, who advocated class unity and close ties with the white New Left. Although his presence helped the Panthers to establish strong chapters in the eastern United States, Carmichael severed ties with the party after he established residency in Africa in 1969. The party's relations with southern California followers of black nationalist Maulana Karenga (b. 1941) also deteriorated, a result both of the FBI's COINTELPRO efforts and the Panthers' harsh criticisms of Karenga's cultural nationalist orientation. In January 1969, two members of Karenga's U.S. organization killed two Panthers during a clash at UCLA.

Although the Black Panther Party gradually shifted its emphasis from revolutionary rhetoric and armed confrontations with police to "survival programs," such as free breakfasts for children and educational projects, clashes with police and legal prosecutions decimated the party's leadership. Soon after finishing his 1968 presidential campaign as the candidate of the Peace and Freedom Party, Cleaver left for exile in Cuba and then Algeria to avoid returning to prison for parole violations. In March 1969, Seale was arrested for conspiracy to incite rioting at the 1968 Democratic Convention in Chicago, and in May 1969, Connecticut officials charged Seale and seven other Panthers with murder in the slaying of party member Alex Rackley, who was believed to be a police informant. In New York, twenty-one Panthers were charged with plotting to assassinate policemen and blow up buildings. Though nearly all charges brought against Panther members either did not result in convictions or were overturned on appeal, the prosecutions absorbed much of the party's resources. An effort during 1969 to purge members considered disloyal or unreliable only partly succeeded.

In 1970, when Newton's conviction on a lesser manslaughter charge was reversed on appeal, he returned to find the party in disarray. Seale still faced murder charges (they were dropped the following year), while the chief of staff, David Hilliard (b. 1942), awaited trial on charges of threatening the life of President Richard Nixon. Further, some chapters, particular those in the eastern United States, resisted direction from the Oakland headquarters. In 1971 Newton split with Cleaver, then in exile in Algeria, charging that the Cleaver's influence in the party had caused it to place too much emphasis on armed rebellion. In 1973 Seale ran an unsuccessful, though formidable, campaign for mayor of Oakland. The following year, Newton, facing new criminal charges and allegations of drug use, fled to Cuba. After Newton's departure, Elaine Brown (b. 1943) took over the leadership of the ailing organization. The Black Panther Party continued to decline, however, and, even after Newton returned in 1977 to resume control, the group never regained its former prominence.

See also Black Power Movement; Carmichael, Stokely; Cleaver, Eldridge; Karenga, Maulana; Malcolm X; Newton, Huey P.; Seale, Bobby

Bibliography

Brown, Elaine. *A Taste of Power: A Black Woman's Story*. New York: Pantheon, 1992.

Cleaver, Kathleen, and George Katsiaficas, eds. *Liberation, Imagination, and the Black Panther Party: A New Look at the Panthers and Their Legacy*. New York: Routledge, 2001.

Heath, G. Louis, ed. *Off the Pigs! The History and Literature of the Black Panther Party*. Metuchen, N.J.: Scarecrow Press, 1976.

Hilliard, David, and Lewis Cole. *This Side of Glory: The Autobiography of David Hilliard and the Story of the Black Panther Party*. Boston: Little, Brown, 1993.

Hilliard, David, and Donald Weise, eds. *The Huey P. Newton Reader*. New York: Seven Stories Press, 2002.

Jones, Charles E., ed. *The Black Panther Party (Reconsidered)*. Baltimore, Md.: Black Classic Press, 1998.

Newton, Huey P. *Revolutionary Suicide*. New York: Harcourt Brace Jovanovich, 1973. Reprint, New York: Writers and Readers, 1995.

Pearson, Hugh. *The Shadow of the Panther: Huey Newton and the Price of Black Power in America*. Reading, Mass.: Addison-Wesley, 1994.

CLAYBORNE CARSON (1996)
Updated bibliography

Black Power Movement

The Black Power movement was a collective, action-oriented expression of racial pride, strength, and self-definition that percolated through all strata of Afro-America during the late 1960s and the first half of the 1970s. Interpreted variously both within and outside black communities, Black Power was a logical progression of civil rights–era efforts to achieve racial equality. It also was a reaction against the tactics, pace, and certain of the operative assumptions of the earlier movement.

As a political expression, the term *Black Power* was given a national forum during the summer of 1966 by Student Nonviolent Coordinating Committee (SNCC) head Stokely Carmichael (1941–1998). In Greenwood, Mississippi, he told a crowd of civil rights workers and reporters, "We been saying freedom for six years and we ain't got nothin'. What we gonna start saying now is Black Power!" (Sellers, 1973, p. 166). The audience responded by chanting the new slogan. For many, "Black Power" would replace "One Man, One Vote" and "We Shall Overcome" as the rallying cry of the freedom struggle. Reflecting the frustration felt by civil rights activists whose hopes for a rapid transformation of U.S. racial relationships had proven illusionary, it came to symbolize rejection of black moderate leadership, white liberal allies, and the time-honored integrationist ethic.

According to Black Power militants, nonviolent approaches to integrationist ends had done little to alleviate poverty, end de facto segregation, promote legal equality, or counteract white-sponsored terrorism. Instead, traditional strategies had encouraged harmful assimilationist tendencies and seemed productive only of continued dependency and the debasement of racial culture. The preferred alternative was to seek personal and group empowerment via a variety of initiatives grounded in either pluralist or black-nationalist ideologies.

Both nationalists and pluralists understood that white power, as manifested in the workings of American economic, political, and intellectual life, constituted a major impediment to the advancement of black Americans. They held that in order to surmount this barrier, blacks had to mobilize, close ranks, and build group strength in all areas of community life. With unity achieved, African Americans would form a significant power bloc and be able to exercise true freedom of choice for the first time. Nationalists might then choose to go it alone, either in "liberated" urban enclaves, in a separate nation-state, or simply in the realm of the psyche. Pluralists could hope to parlay their newfound racial solidarity into a representative share of both local and national decision-making power. Having established a corporate consciousness and sense of collective responsibility, cultural pride would replace despair. The black community would be able to employ its own, to govern itself, and to protect its residents against external

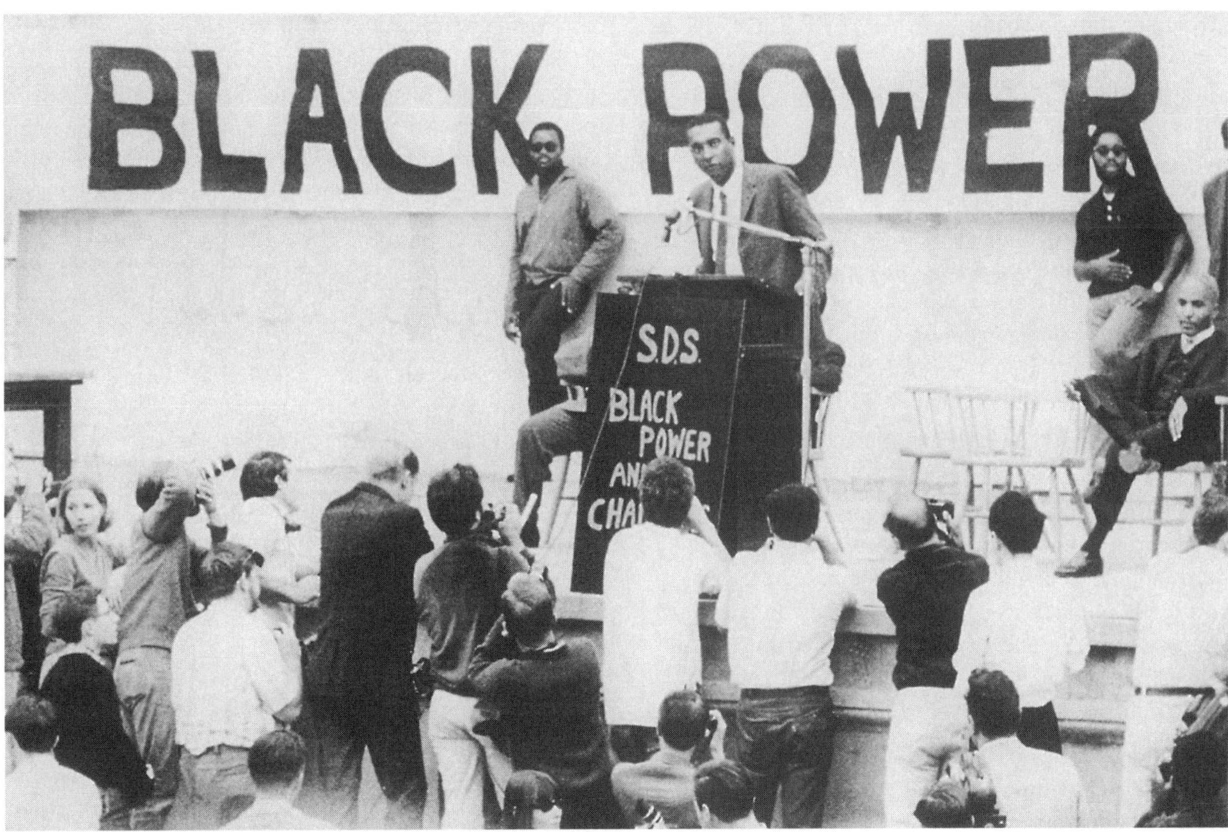

Stokely Carmichael (Kwame Toure) at the University of California, 1966. *Carmichael, leader of the Student Nonviolent Coordinating Committee (SNCC), first used the phrase "black power" in 1966. He is pictured above speaking at a rally of the radical activist group Students for a Democratic Society (SDS), which sought to establish a "participatory democracy" and was a major force in the anti–Vietnam War movement.* AP/WIDE WORLD PHOTOS. REPRODUCED BY PERMISSION.

enemies. Thereafter, the myth of the melting pot never again could be used to obscure the role of minority group power in ordering societal affairs.

All manner of Black Power theorists believed that psychological liberation was a prerequisite for acquiring these more tangible manifestations of power. It was anticipated that a "revolution of the mind" would lead to enhanced group cohesion, alter extant patterns of cultural hegemony, and provide a guiding force for black activism. Noting that a people ashamed of themselves cannot soon hope to be free, they claimed that African Americans had the right to reject organizational structures, values, and methodologies that emanated from sources outside the group experience. Also claimed was the right to define whites. Even commonplace concepts such as "truth" and "beauty" were to be redefined. Blacks, they said, were a capable, attractive people with a rich cultural heritage. To be assertive and take pride in skin color and historical accomplishments was to remove the negative connotations of race that had long served as a constraining social force.

Although the concept may have seemed unfamiliar, Black Power's ideological roots ran deep. Inextricably intertwined with Afro-America's historical struggles for freedom, its essential spirit was the product of generations of black people confronting powerlessness—and surviving. The widely expressed desire to preserve and honor racial distinctives, to define the world in black terms, and to experience the joys of self-discovery and autonomy reaffirmed the teachings of earlier generations of activists whose pioneering efforts at individual and group empowerment were held up as behavioral benchmarks.

Before the Civil War, black Americans formed fraternal, mutual aid, and cooperative organizations to promote solidarity and aid in racial survival. In militant fashion, their reform conventions made it clear that black people would speak for themselves and fight their own battles, no matter what the odds. Such gatherings condemned both slaveholding and the legal proscriptions that hindered free black advancement. Those in attendance discussed proposals to encourage runaways and to aid insurrection movements. They also celebrated the accomplishments of heroic ancestors and compared their physical attributes favorably with whites. Many demanded to be called "African" or "colored" rather than some slurred variant of the Portuguese *os negros.*

Although suspicious of white-dominated groups such as the American Colonization Society, antebellum activists formulated a variety of plans to create an independent, black-run state in West Africa. This notion of establishing a racial refuge and showcase for black initiative outside the United States was reinvigorated during the late nineteenth century by Bishop Henry McNeal Turner (1834–1915) of the African Methodist Episcopal (AME) Church, and it flowered during the 1920s in the pages of Marcus Garvey's *Negro World.*

During the Great Depression, the Pan-African sentiment encapsulated in this deep-seated longing for a national homeland could be seen in the outpouring of support for Ethiopia in its struggles with Italy. In later years, numerous black Americans were inspired by the anticolonial uprisings that foreshadowed independence in Kenya, Ghana, and across the continent.

Following the collapse of Radical Reconstruction in the 1870s, a domestic variant of this empowering nation-building enthusiasm was seen in the resettlement movement to Kansas and Oklahoma. Benjamin Singleton's (1809–1892) efforts to form African-American enclaves in the Plains states earned him the sobriquet "Pap: Moses of the colored exodus," while talk of turning Oklahoma into an all-black state was spurred by the founding of dozens of black towns. As grassroots examples of racial solidarity, these projects promoted the ethic of self-determination throughout the southern and border states. Always compelling, this concept of creating a black nation within a nation was carried into the twentieth century by Cyril Briggs (1919–1993), founder of the African Blood Brotherhood, by the Forty-Ninth State movement of Chicago lawyer Oscar C. Brown (1895–1990), and by Depression-era communists through their "self-determination in the Black Belt" doctrine.

By the mid-1960s, no single figure more completely encapsulated the interconnected themes of psychological liberation, Pan-African unity, and institution-building than Malcolm X (1925–1965). Taught by Nation of Islam patriarch Elijah Muhammad (1897–1975) that there could be neither peace nor true freedom in the world until "every man is in his own country" (Lincoln, 1963, p. 6), the charismatic Black Muslim minister was a tireless champion of group empowerment. When he disavowed the philosophy of nonviolence, proclaimed Black America's right to self-defense "by any means necessary" (Breitman, 1970, p. 54), and labeled white liberal allies of the civil rights movement as hypocrites and deceivers, many African Americans agreed. After he had informed his audiences that they were a colonized people firmly linked to other black world communities by white exploitation, some began to formulate a new understanding of realpolitik. In highlighting the need for a spiritual and cultural back-to-Africa movement, as well as the expansion of black-run businesses and educational institutions, he foreshadowed later, more fully developed, Black Power sentiment.

During the movement's peak years of visibility and influence (1966–1975), African-American activists utilized a variety of programmatic approaches to effect a revolution in minority-group affairs. Stratagems grounded in pluralistic conceptualizations of U.S. society often seemed less precipitous than those favored by revolutionary, territorial, or cultural nationalists. Nevertheless, each of the competing ideological camps was capable of expressing "authentic" Black Power thought. Both pluralists and nationalists sought to combat the psychological, political, and economic problems plaguing black communities through purposeful self-definition. By resisting cultural diffusion, establishing their own priorities, and building outward and upward from a foundational core of group values, they intended to gain entry into the national storehouse of influence, respect, and power.

African-American pluralists concentrated their efforts on an area broadly defined as "community control." A major goal was to reorient and reinvigorate institutions that were central to modern urban life. They sought to bring schools, hospitals, and government agencies closer to the people by atomizing existing centers of power. Optimally, decision making would be transferred from bureaucratic outsiders to indigenous leaders who were better equipped to define priorities and win the cooperation of local residents. It was anticipated that the presence of such individuals on key councils, boards, and commissions would mitigate the destructive effects of institutionalized racism. In this fashion, the special needs of inner-city residents could be addressed fully and in a sensitive manner.

Typically, those who attempted to form such power blocs in the central city claimed they were not being anti-white, but problack. As members of other ethnic groups had done, they refused to be patronized or dominated. Instead, with the support of sympathetic policymakers, they would band together in cooperative ventures to address common concerns. Maintaining that human rights should take precedence over property rights, they sought ways to rid their communities of absentee landlords and storekeepers. New black-owned businesses, guided by consumer-oriented codes of conduct, were encouraged. Plans were drawn up for the transfer of established firms from white to black management and control. The merits of forming neighborhood tenant associations, credit unions, employment agencies, and development corporations were debated extensively. It was hoped that community control would improve public education and expand the workforce skills-base, thereby enabling formerly unemployed youth, welfare recipients, and Aid to Dependant Children mothers to increase their earning power. As the movement grew, black activists prepared to reorganize the structure of municipal government and city life in general—from bottom to top.

Noting the previous generation's lack of success in alleviating poverty, many African Americans saw little hope of improving their lot without the creation of a viable independent political movement. Political apathy was widespread and the race remained a third-class influence within the two-party system. To remedy this situation, a variety of proposals were forwarded that sought to nurture and expand the black vote until it became a true source of empowerment. Most were pluralistic in the sense that they envisioned the eventual sharing of political power with other interest groups. At gatherings such as the national black political conventions held in Gary, Indiana, in 1972 and in Little Rock, Arkansas, in 1974, delegates probed the inadequacies of the existing system and established guidelines for endorsing candidates. Energized by these meetings, black officeholders formed the Congressional Black Caucus, the National Black Caucus of State Legislators, and the National Conference of Black Mayors to promote the goals of the new black politics. Those most skeptical of entering into strategic alliances with nonblacks opted to promote a "third party" movement modeled on the successes of the Mississippi Freedom Democratic Party and the Lowndes County (Alabama) Freedom Organization.

African-American nationalists sought to break with white society in an even more dramatic and permanent fashion. Members of the Nation of Islam, the Congress of Racial Equality (CORE), and the Republic of New Africa were especially vocal in presenting proposals for the acquisition of sovereign territory. Hoping eventually to bargain with mainstream power brokers at a distance and from a position of strength, they developed ambitious plans to relocate abroad in expatriate settlements, to carve black living spaces out of existing southern political units, and to transform impoverished northern slums into constituent components of a prosperous city-state federation. Wherever it was to be located, the newly liberated territory would be governed through parallel institutions but guided by nontraditional, even non-Western, values.

Influenced by the writings of Marx, Lenin, and Mao, Kwame Nkrumah (1909–1972), Sékou Touré (1922–1984), and Frantz Fanon (1925–1961), groups such as the Black Panther Party, the Revolutionary Action Movement, and the Black Liberation Army felt that any alteration of territorial boundaries had to be accompanied by a thoroughgoing socialist transformation of society. These revolutionary nationalists held that the right to self-determination was inherent in all nations, including the black "internal colony" of the United States. The founding of a black nation-state was to be viewed as part of the world liberation movement, not as an end in itself. Led by the black "peasantry" (variously defined as the laboring class or the underclass), this epic reformulation of caste and class relationships would be accomplished by violent means, if necessary. After the establishment of a worker-controlled international order, racism, capitalism, and imperialism would be consigned to the dustbin of history.

For other nationalists, a black cultural renaissance became the central component of the revolutionary struggle for empowerment. Supporters of groups such as the Los Angeles–based US Organization believed that it was a mistake to pick up a gun without first reaffirming the beauty and uniqueness of black folk culture. By asserting racial distinctives via clothing, language, and hairstyle, and by recounting group history through the literary and performing arts, cultural nationalists sought to encourage self-actualization and to discredit assumptions of white cultural superiority. Throughout the era, their colorful celebrations of blackness fostered pride and helped spread the Black Power message nationwide. In doing so, they provided the impetus for the flowering of a black arts movement among their contemporaries. In later years, cultural nationalist precepts played an important role in the development of Afrocentric models for urban education.

Although ideological infighting, U.S. counterintelligence intrigues, bad press, and tactical errors disrupted hoped-for unity, Black Power had tangible political and psychological effects and left a distinctive cachet on the cultural landscape. Key contributors to an ongoing revolt against white domination, 1960s pluralists and nationalists decolonized minds and heightened expectations. They introduced many within the mainstream to the plight of the less privileged. They also raised substantive issues in aesthetics and created a receptive audience for the next generation of race-conscious writers, artists, musicians, and filmmakers. Black Power motivated African-Americans of the 1960s and 1970s to redefine themselves as members of a beautiful, capable, highly cultured race, to become entrepreneurs, and to run for public office.

Black Power's challenge to the white world order also encouraged members of other oppressed groups to question the legitimacy of prevailing social and cultural norms. During the final decades of the century, both the positive and negative experiences of black militants informed the organizational efforts of U.S. ethnic- and gender-based rights advocates. Internationally, the black empowerment model was utilized by South African activists working to create a Black Consciousness movement that would speed the demise of apartheid. In varying degrees, it helped mobilize support for a Black Power movement in Trinidad, a Black Soul movement in Brazil, and numerous campaigns to extend long-overdue governmental and economic reforms throughout the Third World. Today, the residual influence of the movement can be seen whenever marginalized people band together to contest what the SNCC's Stokely Carmichael once termed "the dictatorship of definition, interpretation, and consciousness."

See also Afrocentrism; Black Panther Party for Self Defense; Carmichael, Stokely; Civil Rights Movement, U.S.; Garvey, Marcus; Jackson, George Lester; Malcolm X; Nationalism in the United States in the Nineteenth Century; Newton, Huey P.; Student Nonviolent Coordinating Committee (SNCC)

Bibliography

Breitman, George, ed. *By Any Means Necessary: Speeches, Interviews, and a Letter by Malcolm X.* New York: Pathfinder, 1970.

Brown, Scott. *Fighting for US: Maulana Karenga, the US Organization, and Black Cultural Nationalism.* New York: New York University Press, 2003.

Carmichael, Stokely, and Charles V. Hamilton. *Black Power: The Politics of Liberation in America.* New York: Vintage, 1967.

Carson, Clayborne. *In Struggle: SNCC and the Black Awakening of the 1960s.* Cambridge, Mass.: Harvard University Press, 1981.

Glaude, Eddie S., Jr., ed. *Is It Nation Time?: Contemporary Essays on Black Power and Black Nationalism.* Chicago: University of Chicago Press, 2002.

Jones, Charles E., ed. *The Black Panther Party Reconsidered.* Baltimore, Md.: Black Classic Press, 1998

Lincoln, C. Eric. "Extremist Attitudes in the Black Muslim Movement." *New South* 18 (1963).

McCartney, John T. *Black Power Ideologies: An Essay in African-American Political Thought.* Philadelphia: Temple University Press, 1992.

Ogbar, Jeffrey O. G. *Black Power: Radical Politics and African American Identity.* Baltimore, Md.: Johns Hopkins University Press, 2004.

Sellers, Cleveland. *The River of No Return: The Autobiography of a Black Militant and the Life and Death of SNCC.* New York: William Morrow, 1973.

Tyson, Timothy B. *Radio Free Dixie: Robert F. Williams and the Roots of Black Power.* Chapel Hill: University of North Carolina Press, 1999.

Van Deburg, William L. *New Day in Babylon: The Black Power Movement and American Culture, 1965–1975.* Chicago: University of Chicago Press, 1992.

Woodard, Komozi. *A Nation within a Nation: Amiri Baraka (LeRoi Jones) and Black Power Politics.* Chapel Hill: University of North Carolina Press, 1999.

WILLIAM L. VAN DEBURG (2005)

Black Press in the United States

See Journalism

Black Press in Brazil

The black press in Brazil has been a significant record of literary and political expression since the emergence of small Afro-Brazilian newsletters early in the twentieth century. The earliest of these to be archived was *O Bandeirante*, published in Campinas, São Paulo, in 1910, just twenty-two years after the abolition of slavery in 1888. In 1915 *O Menelick* appeared in the city of São Paulo. These two publications inaugurated the first era of a flourishing black press in the cities of southern Brazil. The focus of these journals was not to cover general news items but, rather, to develop a forum for discussing issues of concern to the Afro-Brazilian community and to support the initiatives that helped shape that community.

Afro-Brazilian social and beneficent clubs were largely responsible for the growth of the early black press, particularly in São Paulo. As the nation's emerging urban center, São Paulo attracted an influx of new arrivals from elsewhere in Brazil as well as from abroad. Alongside the burgeoning communities of Portuguese, Spanish, Italian, German, and other immigrants were small communities of Afro-Brazilians seeking opportunities not available in the former slave-based economies from which they came. They initially established networks based on common hometown affiliations, but São Paulo was a city defined in large measure by its ethnic enclaves of immigrants. Operating in much the same fashion, an expanding circle of Afro-Brazilians began to sponsor social events that led to formally organized social and recreational clubs. Newspapers helped circulate club news and general information of interest to the Afro-Brazilian, thus creating a sense of community for the newcomers.

In addition to being informative, the early black press provided a platform for creative writing and political analysis. The columnists typically focused on ways to uplift the Afro-Brazilian community. In so doing, the journals published between 1910 and the mid-1920s articulated ideals of Afro-Brazilian identity and position within Brazilian society.

Despite a wide range of political sentiments, early black columnists generally sought to situate Afro-Brazilians as equal partners in modern society. They often used historical references to counter attempts at marginalizing Afro-Brazilians from the core of national identity. For example, the title *Bandeirante* refers to an archetype of the São Paulo pioneering spirit based on the frontierspeople of the colonial era, and the first culture popularly regarded as uniquely Brazilian because of its racial mixture of primarily European and indigenous peoples. In taking that name, *Bandeirante*'s publishers staked the claim by black people that they, too, were an intrinsic part of Brazil's history, identity, and future. Writers venerated historical figures such as abolitionists Jose do Patrocinio and Luiz Gama. The celebrated Henrique Dias (c. 1600–1662), who helped defend Brazil against a Dutch invasion in the seventeenth century, had particular resonance because of black military service to Brazil in the Paraguayan War (1864–70). Such heroes were held up not merely as sources of pride, but as reminders of the extent of black contributions to the nation.

Rather than stress a distinct African heritage, the early black press embraced the dominant values of the Brazilian middle class. Society columns pointedly teased inappropriate behavior and even styles of dress. Editorials fretted about shortcomings within the Afro-Brazilian community and the need to master the tools of social advancement. The papers featured what they regarded as marks of refinement, such as literature. Several newspaper publishers, including Lino Guedes of *Progresso* and Jayme de Aguiar of *Clarim da Alvorada*, were avid writers who regularly included classically styled poetry and prose in their publications. In the words of a column published in *Elite* in 1924, "We will educate our children, we will sacrifice everything to raise them to the status of the perfect citizen, and the day will come when it will be loudly proclaimed to the whole universe that they are Brazilians as worthy as any other." Such a position became an integral element of much Afro-Brazilian political thought in the face of marginalization and economic competition with recently arrived immigrants.

Though they had a decided local emphasis, black publications were far from parochial. Named for the Ethiopian ruler, *O Menelick's* title signals an international consciousness that consistently informed the politics of the Afro-Brazilian community, and is also reflected in the juxtaposition of the international title and local content. Given that World War I (1914–18) was underway at the time these first journals appeared, there was much international news that they chose not to cover. Yet a global awareness of news, culture, and issues of Africa and the African diaspora was evident in the earliest days of the black press. It was through the black press that an early dialogue with international black movements began. Robert Abbott, publisher of the *Chicago Defender*, visited Brazil and began sending newspapers whose stories were translated and excerpted in local black papers. Columns from Marcus Garvey's *Negro World* also appeared in the Afro-Brazilian press. At a time of heightened global awareness, commentary on international items in the black press both broadened the political context and established their relevance to ongoing issues within Brazil.

Gradually, the newspapers began to focus on the reasons behind the persistence of inequality and lack of opportunities for Afro-Brazilians. In addition, domestic power struggles were challenging the political order. Among the journals reflecting this more politicized era of the black press were *Clarim da Alvorada* and *Progresso*. Both were affiliated with a group of young activists involved in the Centro Cívico Palmares, an early advocacy group in São Paulo founded in 1926. *Clarim da Alvorada* went from describing itself as a journal of literature, news and humor to a focus on "news, literature and struggle" (*Clarim da Alvorada*, January 15, 1927; February 5, 1928). *Progresso* became the first news outlet for the Frente Negra Brasileira after its formation in 1931 as the first national Afro-Brazilian political organization. In March 1933 the Frente Negra began publishing its own journal, *A Voz da Raça* (Voice of the Race). Beginning with weekly, then monthly, publication, the *Voz da Raça* eventually became widely circulated particularly in southern Brazil, with printings ranging from 1,000 to 5,000 copies.

Along with the Frente Negra itself, the *Voz da Raça* became prominent in Afro-Brazilian political advocacy, but it was not the only perspective coming from the diverse community. J. Guaraná Santana, a founder of the Radical Nationalist Party known commonly as the Black Legion, began publishing *Brasil Novo*, a socialist newspaper, in April 1933. Dissent from the Frente Negra's political platform also appeared in the pages of *Clarim da Alvorada* and *A Chibata,* which, in part, led to the creation of *A Voz da Raça*. However, the climate for open political debate chilled after President Getulio Vargas declared a new regime, the Estado Novo (1937–1945), that banned all political parties.

The collapse of the Estado Novo and the democratic idealism of the postwar era brought a resurgence of the black press in the 1940s. Artist, intellectual, and activist Abdias do Nascimento of Rio de Janeiro, Brazil, helped open new avenues for exploring the position of blacks in Brazilian life with the creation of the Teatro Experimental do Negro (Black Experimental Theater) in 1944 and the journal *Quilombo* in 1948. The pages of *Quilombo* reflected the cosmopolitan intellectual and artistic milieu of Rio de Janeiro, nurturing its links to the black press and creative movements, particularly in the United States and Paris.

In this regard, it expanded on relationships established earlier on; Abdias do Nascimento was himself originally from São Paulo and a former member of the Frente Negra Brasileira. Do Nascimento chronicled his frequent encounters with internationally renowned guests including Albert Camus and Marian Anderson. *Quilombo* published articles by prominent Brazilian intellectuals and artistic pieces such as Jean Paul Sartre's "Black Orpheus." *Quilombo* often exchanged news items with publishers of black newspapers outside Brazil, such as an article denouncing Do Nascimento's political ambitions as "racist" imitation of black nationalism abroad (*Quilombo*, May 1950, 5) George Schuyler of the *Pittsburgh Courier* frequently sent notices to be published by do Nascimento. The journal advocated education subsidies for blacks, the declaration of race discrimination as a crime, and the inclusion of African heritage in school curricula—part of a political agenda do Nascimento helped put in place throughout his long political career.

Other black newspapers appeared during this era, typically associated with political and cultural organizations, such as *Alvorada*, founded by the Associação dos Negros Brasileiros in 1945. The leaders of these organizations were typically veterans of the movements of the 1930s who became deeply involved in the emergence of new political parties and trade unions. The journals published between 1945 and 1964 largely reflected the maturation of new forms of Afro-Brazilian collective endeavors in the urban south. Because they served to promote political initiatives, they are rich in details about major conferences and organizations that helped develop particular agendas within national and international Afro-Brazilian activism.

The repressive military regime that came to power in 1964 forced overt political expression underground until the mid-1970s. As in the past, the post-dictatorship opening heralded the creation of new groups with affiliated publications combining features of literary journals, magazines, and hard news. The rapid appearance and disappearance of newspapers reflected the dynamics of the movement and its personalities—the publications began as outgrowths of organizations and dissipated along with their finances and memberships. Black Power, African independence, and new leftist politics were some of the hallmarks of the era reflected in Afro-Brazilian organizations and publications. Journals such as *Jornegro, Avore de Palavras,* and *Cadernos Negros* articulated emerging political currents and landmark events.

Afro-Brazilian members of leftist and other interest-group organizations increasingly voiced their own analyses of the link between race and class. This debate surfaced within *Versus,* a publication of a socialist organization (Convergencia Socialista) in which many future leaders of Afro-Brazilian organizations participated. They formed their own "Afro-Latino America" section of the publication, in which they argued that race could not be completely subsumed as a function of class. Two developments were of particular importance at this time. The creation of the Movimento Negro Unificado in 1978 launched a powerful attack on all forms of racial discrimination, and through the collaboration of constituent black organizations from around the country systematically began efforts to dismantle them. Also in the late 1970s activists in Salvador, Bahia, had developed a new form of activism through carnival groups (*blocos afros*) that celebrated black identity and African heritage. This increased organizational activity around the country led to numerous local publications.

The appearance of the monthly magazine *Raça Brasil* in 1996 was momentous in the history of the black press of Brazil. Published by a professional media company, Editora Simbolo, *Raça* was a full-color glossy comparable with the most popular national magazines. While it included some coverage of political issues, it emphasized "showing that blackness (negritude) is joyful, rich, beautiful," rather than the demands of struggle (*Raça Brasil,* September 4, 1997, p. 4). Editor-in-chief Aroldo Macedo described *Raça's* mission as giving readers pride in being black; the magazine profiled black celebrities from Brazil and abroad, offered home design and fashion advice, and provided lifestyle tips along with its coverage of political and intellectual news. *Raça*'s format and marketing highlighted a significant black consumer market for advertisers, attracting major clients. Its success inspired other glossies, such as *Agito Geral* (1997), focusing on music, and *Revista Negro 100 Por Cento* (1998), whose format was similar to that of *Raça*. Editora Simbolo also launched a magazine on black hairstyles, *Visual Cabelos Crespos*, in 1997.

Part of *Raça*'s significance was its creativity in revitalizing approaches to the black consciousness movement of the 1970s and 1980s. New voices began appearing in the 1990s; among these were the Grupo Gay Negro da Bahia, which first published its own journal, the *Boletim do Quimbanda-Dudu* in August 1997. The increasing accessibility of the internet propelled online publications such as *Afirma Revista Online* (founded in 2000) and *Portal Afro* (2001). Some print journals offered online versions; *Cadernos Negros*, a literary journal launched in 1978, established an affiliation with the online *Quilombhoje*.

As the black press tradition in Brazil continues to evolve, significant hallmarks have remained constant. There has always been a strong literary and artistic component, and a concern for defining negritude within Brazil as well as in a global context. The black press has never reflected the full spectrum of Afro-Brazilian ideologies, insofar as it is a medium defined by access to certain resources, and it has been closely associated with formal organizations. The internet has provided a broader forum for organizations and individuals unable to shoulder the costs of printing, although it remains out of reach for millions of the Afro-Brazilian poor.

Within the history of the African diaspora in the Americas, the black press in Brazil followed a trajectory similar to that of newspapers such as the *Chicago Defender*, the *Amsterdam News* (New York), and the *Pittsburgh Courier*, chronicling the aspirations and struggles of emerging black communities in U.S. cities after the abolition of slavery. Elsewhere in Latin America, print journals have accompanied the growth of black organizations, such as *Palenque* (Quito, Ecuador), a publication of the Centro Cultural Afro-Ecuatoriano first appearing in 1982. The Brazilian black press, especially through its numerous connections to significant figures from Africa, Europe, the Caribbean, and the Americas who corresponded with and visited Brazil, also constitutes an important part of the intellectual and political literature of the global African diaspora.

See also Abdias do Nascimento; Frente Negra Brasileira; Journalism; *Pittsburgh Courier*; Schuyler, George S.

Bibliography

Butler, Kim D. *Freedoms Given, Freedoms Won: Afro-Brazilians in Post-Abolition São Paulo and Salvador.* New Brunswick, N.J.: Rutgers University Press, 1998.

Clarim da Alvorada (São Paulo). January 15, 1927, and February 5, 1928.

Elite (São Paulo). January 20, 1924.

Ferrara, Miriam Nicolau. *A Imprensa Negra Paulista, 1915–1963.* São Paulo: FFLCH/USP, 1986.

Hanchard, Michael George. *Orpheus and Power: The Movimento Negro of Rio de Janeiro and São Paulo, Brazil, 1945–1988.* Princeton: Princeton University Press, 1994.

Quilombo (bound facsimile edition). São Paulo: Editora 34, 2003.

Quilombo (Rio de Janeiro), May 1950.

Raça Brasil. September 4, 1997.

KIM D. BUTLER (2005)

Black Star Line

See Universal Negro Improvement Association

Black Studies

Black studies, also known as African studies, is "the multidisciplinary analysis of the lives and thought of people of African ancestry on the African continent and throughout the world" (Harris, Hine, and McKay, 1990, p. 7). Black studies is interdisciplinary; its earliest roots are in history, sociology, literature, and the arts. The field's most important concepts, methods, and findings are still centered within these disciplines.

Black studies consists of research; courses at the high school, college, and university levels; and organizational structures such as programs, centers, and departments. This entry focuses on the historical development of research in black studies in part because the research aspects of the field are much better documented in the literature than course offerings (Lyman, 1972; Meier and Rudwick, 1986). Also, there were few course offerings outside of historically black institutions prior to 1970 (Ford, 1973). Readers can examine other sources for a discussion of organizational issues; they are beyond the scope of this entry (Harris, Hine, and McKay, 1990; Hu-DeHart, 1995). Because of its limited scope, this article focuses on historical and sociological research in black studies; scholarship in literature and the arts is not discussed. Readers are referred to the following sources for treatment of these research areas: Baker and Redmond, 1989; Campbell et al., 1987; Dallas Museum of Art, 1989; Jackson, 1989.

The typology of the development of black historical scholarship conceptualized by John Hope Franklin (1986) is used to organize this entry. It is appropriate to use this typology to describe the historical development of black studies because history was the field's birthplace and remains an important center. Franklin describes four generations of scholarship in African-American history. These periods are not clearly distinct but are overlapping and interrelated.

The First Generation of Black Studies

The first period or generation is marked by the publication of what is generally regarded as the first history of African Americans in 1882, *History of the Negro Race in America* by George Washington Williams, published in two volumes (1882 and 1883). Williams, the first black to serve in the Ohio legislature, was not a professionally trained historian but was a gifted and interesting orator, writer, soldier, minister, journalist, lawyer, and politician. Other significant works published during this period included *The Suppression of the African Slave-Trade to the United States of America* by W. E. B. Du Bois in 1896 and *Story of the Negro* by Booker T. Washington in 1909. Du Bois's book, a carefully researched and respected publication, was his Ph.D. thesis at Harvard.

An important goal of the writers during the first generation of African-American scholarship was to counteract the negative images and representations of African Americans that were institutionalized within academic and popular cultures. A key tenet of social science research of the time was that blacks were genetically inferior to whites and that Africa was the "dark continent" that lacked civilizations (Caldwell, 1830; Ripley, 1899). The American Negro Academy, founded in 1896, had as one of its major goals "to aid, by publications, the vindication of the race from vicious assaults, in all lines of learning and truth" (Moss, 1981, p. 24).

It was also during this first generation that "early black literary associations sought to preserve and to publicize the legacy of African peoples" (Harris, Hine, and McKay, 1990, p. 7), and black academics initiated research studies. In 1899 Du Bois published a landmark sociological study, *The Philadelphia Negro.* He implemented, at Atlanta University, a series of important studies from 1898 to 1914 known as the Atlanta University Studies. The series consists of more than sixteen monographs (Harris, Hines, and McKay, 1990).

Carter G. Woodson and the Professionalization of Black Studies

The rise of Carter G. Woodson as an influential scholar and the founding of the Association for the Study of Afro-American [formerly "Negro"] Life and History (ASNLH) in 1915 signaled the beginning of a new era in black studies. Woodson, his publications, and the people he mentored and influenced—such as Charles H. Wesley and Rayford W. Logan—were destined to dominate the second generation of black studies.

Woodson probably had more influence on the teaching of African-American history in the nation's schools and colleges from the turn of the century until his death in 1950 than any other scholar. With others, he established the ASNLH. He founded the *Journal of Negro History* in 1916 and served as its editor until his death. It is one of Woodson's most significant contributions to the study and teaching of black studies. In 1921 Woodson established Associated Publishers, a division of the ASNLH, to publish scholarly books and textbooks on African Americans. In addition to publishing Woodson's major books, Associated Publishers also published important books by scholars such as Horace Mann Bond and Charles H. Wesley.

Woodson, a former high school teacher, played a major role in popularizing African-American history and in promoting its study in the nation's black schools, colleges, churches, and fraternities. He initiated Negro History Week in 1926 to highlight the role that African Americans played in the development of the nation and to commemorate their contributions. In time, and with vigorous promotion efforts by the ASNLH and its branches throughout the nation, Negro History Week—later expanded to Afro-American History Month—became nationally recognized and celebrated. Woodson never intended for Negro History Week to be the only time of the year in which black history was taught. Rather, he viewed it as a time to highlight the ongoing study of black history that was to take place throughout the year.

In 1937 Woodson established the *Negro History Bulletin* to provide information on black history to elementary and secondary school teachers. He also wrote elementary and secondary school textbooks that were widely used in black schools, including *African Myths* (1928a), *Negro Makers of History* (1928b), and *The Story of the Negro Retold* (1935). His widely used and popular text *The Negro in Our History,* first published in 1922, was published in eleven editions.

More White Scholars Participate in Black Studies

The period from about 1945 to the late 1960s marked the third generation of African-American scholarship in history and the social sciences (Franklin, 1986). Franklin notes that this period was characterized by an increasing legitimacy of the field and by the entrance of increasing numbers of white scholars. Prior to the 1940s most of the research done in black studies was conducted by African-American scholars who taught at small, historically black institutions.

From 1940 to 1960, whites began to publish significant works in black studies. The Swedish economist Gunnar Myrdal published *An American Dilemma: The Negro Problem and Modern Democracy* in 1944. Supported by the Carnegie Corporation and begun in 1939, it was the most expensive and comprehensive study of race relations ever undertaken in the United States. It is significant that a European—and not an African American—was chosen to direct the study. However, Myrdal drew heavily on the works of African-American scholars such as Allison Davis, W. E. B. Du Bois, E. Franklin Frazier, Ralph Bunche, and Charles S. Johnson. Some of these scholars wrote original papers for the Carnegie project.

Two European-American scholars who made significant contributions to black studies were Franz Boas, an anthropologist at Columbia University, and Robert E. Park, a sociologist at the University of Chicago. Boas challenged the dominant paradigm about race, which stated that some races were inferior to others and that the environment could have little influence on heredity (Stocking, 1974).

Park taught one of the first black studies courses at a predominantly white university. In the fall quarter of 1913 he taught the course "The Negro in America" at the University of Chicago (Bulmer, 1984). Park was a leader in the "Chicago School" of sociology, which became distinguished for its empirical studies on cities and minority groups. Park also trained some of the nation's leading African-American sociologists, such as Charles S. Johnson, E. Franklin Frazier, and Horace Cayton. Some of the influential books by Park's former students include *Shadow of the Plantation* by Johnson (1934) and *The Negro Family in the United States* by Frazier (1939/1966). St. Clair Drake, who also studied at Chicago, coauthored a seminal sociological study with Cayton, *Black Metropolis: A Study of Negro Life in a Northern City,* published in 1945.

Important historical works published by white scholars during this period included *The Peculiar Institution: Slavery in the Ante-Bellum South* by Kenneth M. Stampp (1956), *Slavery: A Problem in American Institutional and Intellectual Life* by Stanley Elkins (1959), and *Negro Thought in America, 1880–1915* by August Meier (1963).

African-American scholars continued to produce significant and landmark publications in black studies, even though their institutions provided them with little scholarly support. Among the influential historical works produced by African Americans during this period were *What the Negro Wants* by Rayford Logan (1944); *The Negro in the American Revolution* (1961) and *Lincoln and the Negro* (1962) by Benjamin Quarles; *The Free Negro in North Carolina, 1790–1860* (1943) and *The Emancipation Proclamation* (1963) by John Hope Franklin. The first edition of John Hope Franklin's influential college textbook *From Slavery to Freedom: A History of Negro Americans* was published in 1947. It is still one of the most popular textbooks in African-American history.

A New Era of Black Studies Begins in the 1970s

Prior to 1970 most African-American students attended historically black colleges and universities in the southern and border states. One consequence of the civil rights movement of the 1960s was that an increasing number of African-American students attended predominantly white institutions, especially in the Midwest, East, and West. Many of these students, a significant percentage of whom were admitted to college through equal opportunity or open admission programs, were from working-class backgrounds. Many were the first children in their families to attend college. Their presence on college campuses was destined to have a significant influence on the curriculum and the ethnic makeup of the faculty.

During the late 1960s and early 1970s African-American students—often in strident voices that reflected their sense of marginalization on predominantly white campuses—made a number of demands on universities. These included demands for black studies programs, black professors, black cultural centers, and in some cases, separate dormitories.

In responding to the demands of African-American students—who were often joined by the black community and later by other students of color who made parallel demands—colleges and universities established black studies courses, programs, centers, and institutes. In time, some of these programs and centers became departments.

In part because of the political climate out of which they emerged, black studies courses, programs, and centers had a rocky beginning in the early 1970s. Many university administrators created instant programs and hired professors who did not have standard academic qualifications in order to silence ethnic protest. There was a shortage of individuals trained in black studies. Courses and programs were developing more rapidly than qualified individuals could be trained in doctoral programs. Another problem that haunted early black studies programs was the series of budget cuts that colleges and universities throughout the United States experienced in the 1970s and

1980s. Because they were the last hired, many teachers and administrators in black studies programs were highly vulnerable to financial downturns.

Black studies programs and black studies scholarship have experienced a renaissance since the early 1970s. According to a report prepared by Robert L. Harris Jr., Darlene Clark Hine, and Nellie McKay (1990) for the Ford Foundation on the status of black studies in the United States, most black studies programs have gained legitimacy on their campuses, are valued by campus administrators, and are becoming institutionalized. Because of the growth and increasing legitimization of black studies, more black professors are being hired on predominantly white campuses.

Despite their march down the road toward institutionalization, black studies programs still face important challenges as they enter the twenty-first century. These include retaining and acquiring new resources in an era of aggressive budget cutting; attaining departmental status so they will gain needed control over budgets, tenure, and promotion; and educating and mentoring a new generation of scholars to whom the torch can be passed. Black studies programs must also determine the amount of time and resources to devote to a consistent research agenda and how much time to devote to the new wave of racist social science epitomized by the publication and public reception of *The Bell Curve* (Herrnstein and Murray, 1994).

Scholarship Since the 1970s

The period from 1970 to 1995 was one of the most richly prolific periods in black studies scholarship. Many well-trained African-American scholars—who are teaching and doing research at some of the nation's most prestigious universities—entered the field. They have written many significant and landmark publications. David L. Lewis's seminal biography of W. E. B. Du Bois was the recipient of the Pulitzer, Parkman, and Bancroft prizes in 1994 (Lewis, 1993).

Important studies produced by black scholars since the 1970s include *The Signifying Monkey: A Theory of African-American Literary Criticism* by Henry Louis Gates Jr. (1988); *Long Black Song: Essays in Black American Literature and Culture* by Houston A. Baker Jr. (1972); *The Slave Community* by John W. Blassingame (1972); *Slave Culture: Nationalist Theory and The Foundations of Black America* by Sterling Stuckey (1987); *The Black Church in the African-American Experience* by C. Eric Lincoln and Lawrence H. Mamiya (1990); and *The Truly Disadvantaged* by William Julius Wilson (1987).

Many white scholars are also producing significant publications in black studies. Notable works written by white scholars since 1970 include *Roll, Jordan, Roll: The World the Slave Made* by Eugene D. Genovese (1972); *The Black Family in Slavery and Freedom, 1750–1925* by Herbert G. Gutman (1976); and *Black Culture and Black Consciousness* by Lawrence W. Levine (1977).

The Afrocentric Paradigm

In the 1980s the Afrocentric movement became important within black studies. It has been influenced most significantly by Molefi K. Asante (1987, 1990) and his colleagues at Temple University. The Afrocentric paradigm is a radical critique of the Eurocentric ideology and research paradigm that, in the view of Afrocentric theorists, "masquerades as a universal view" in the various social science and applied disciplines (Asante, 1987, p. 3). Afrocentricity, according to Asante, means "placing African ideals at the center of any analysis that involves African culture and behavior" (p. 6). Afrocentrists believe that all knowledge is positional and that Eurocentric knowledge reinforces and legitimizes dominant group hegemony and structural inequality (Ani, 1994).

Black Women's Studies

Another important challenge black studies faces is how to incorporate the new field of black women's studies into the discipline. Feminist researchers such as Stanlie E. James and Abena P. A. Busia (1993), Patricia Hill Collins (1990), and Angela Y. Davis (1981) have developed concepts, paradigms, and insights that describe the extent to which black women have been marginalized in black studies. They document ways in which black studies has traditionally been and still is primarily black men's studies. The title of one of the earliest edited works in black women's studies exemplifies this marginalization: *All the Women Are White, All the Blacks Are Men, But Some of Us Are Brave* (Gloria T. Hull, Patricia Bell Scott, and Barbara Smith, 1982). Betty Schmitz and colleagues write that, "A new field of study, black women's studies, emerged in part because of the failure of both black studies and women's studies to address adequately the experiences of women of African descent in the United States and throughout the world" (1995, p. 711).

Black women's studies is a growing and significant field. Significant and influential scholarly works are published each year. An important early publication is an edited collection by Toni Cade, *The Black Women* (1970). Other notable works in the genre *include The Afro-American Women: Struggles and Images* (1978), edited by Rosalyn Terborg-Penn and S. Harley, and *When and Where I Enter* by Paula Giddings (1984). Major original, scholarly works include *Labor of Love, Labor of Sorrow: Black Women, Work, and the Family, from Slavery to the Present* (1985) by J. Jones, a white scholar; and *Righteous Discontent: The Women's Movement in the Black Baptist Church, 1880–1920* (1993) by E. B. Higginbotham.

In the 1990s two major collections of studies on the African-American experience were produced. *Black Women in United States History,* a sixteen-volume collection of studies and primary resources edited by eminent historian Darlene Clark Hine and colleagues, was published in 1990. By the end of the decade, one of the most notable of African American studies units emerged at Harvard University under the direction of Henry Louis Gates Jr. In 1999 Gates and Harvard philosopher Anthony Appiah published *Africana: The Encyclopedia of the African and African American Experience.*

The Future of Black Studies

Black studies seems anchored to face successfully the challenges related to its quest for legitimacy, financial constraints, and the need to be transformed so it can incorporate concepts and paradigms related to the experience of black women. If the field meets these challenges, not only will it be revitalized but so will the curricula of the nation's colleges and universities.

See also Afrocentrism; Black History Month/Negro History Week; Woodson, Carter Godwin

Bibliography

Aldridge, Delores P. "Status of Africana/Black Studies in Higher Education in the U.S." *Out of the Revolution: The Development of Africana Studies,* edited by Delores P. Aldridge and Carlene Young. Landham, Md.: Lexington Books, 2000.

Ani, Marimba. *Yurugu: An African-Centered Critique of European Cultural Thought and Behavior.* Trenton, N. J.: Africa World Press, 1994.

Appiah, Anthony, and Henry Louis Gates Jr., eds. *Africana: The Encyclopedia of the African and African American Experience.* New York: Basic Civitas, 1999.

Asante, Molefi Kente. *The Afrocentric Idea.* Philadelphia: Temple University Press, 1987.

Asante, Molefi Kente. *Kemet, Afrocentricity, and Knowledge.* Trenton, N.J.: Africa World Press, 1990.

Baker, Houston A., Jr. *Long Black Song: Essays in Black American Literature and Culture.* Charlottesville: University Press of Virginia, 1972.

Baker, Houston A., Jr., and Patricia Redmond, eds. *Afro-American Literary Study in the 1990s.* Chicago: University of Chicago Press, 1989.

Blassingame, John W. *The Slave Community: Plantation Life in the Antebellum South.* New York: Oxford University Press, 1972.

Bulmer, Martin. *The Chicago School of Sociology: Institutionalization, Diversity, and the Rise of Sociological Research.* Chicago: University of Chicago Press, 1984.

Cade, Toni, ed. *The Black Women.* New York: New American Library, 1970.

Caldwell, Charles. *Thoughts on the Original Unity of the Human Race.* New York: E. Bliss, 1830.

Campbell, Mary S., David Driskell, David L. Lewis, and David W. Ryan. *Harlem Renaissance Art of Black America.* New York: Abrams, 1987.

Collins, Patricia Hill. *Black Feminist Thought: Knowledge, Consciousness, and the Politics of Empowerment.* New York: Unwin Hyman, 1990.

Dallas Museum of Art. *Black Art Ancestral Legacy: The African Impulse in African-American Art.* New York: Abrams, 1989.

Davis, Angela Y. *Women, Race and Class.* New York: Random House, 1981.

Drake, St. Claire, and Horace R. Cayton. *Black Metropolis: A Study of Negro Life in a Northern City.* New York: Harcourt, 1945.

Du Bois, W. E. B. *The Suppression of the African Slave-Trade to the United States of America, 1638–1870.* Cambridge, Mass.: Harvard University Press, 1896.

Du Bois, W. E. B. *The Philadelphia Negro.* 1899. Reprint, Millwood, N.Y., 1973.

Elkins, Stanley M. *Slavery: A Problem in American Institutional and Intellectual Life.* Chicago: University of Chicago Press, 1959.

Ford, Nick Aaron. *Black Studies: Threat or Challenge?* Port Washington, N.Y.: Kennikat, 1973.

Franklin, John Hope. *The Free Negro in North Carolina, 1790–1860.* Chapel Hill: University of North Carolina Press, 1943.

Franklin, John Hope. *From Slavery to Freedom: A History of Negro Americans.* New York: Knopf, 1947.

Franklin, John Hope. *The Emancipation Proclamation.* Garden City, N.Y.: Doubleday, 1963.

Franklin, John Hope. "On the Evolution of Scholarship in Afro-American History." In *The State of Afro-American History: Past, Present, and Future,* edited by Darlene Clark Hine. Baton Rouge: Louisiana State University Press, 1986.

Frazier, E. Franklin. *The Negro Family in the United States* (1939). Chicago: University of Chicago Press, 1966.

Gates, Henry Louis, Jr. *The Signifying Monkey: A Theory of African-American Literary Criticism.* New York: Oxford University Press, 1988.

Genovese, Eugene D. *Roll, Jordan, Roll: The World the Slaveholders Made.* New York: Pantheon, 1972.

Giddings, Paula. *When and Where I Enter: The Impact of Black Women on Race and Sex in America.* New York: Morrow, 1984.

Gutman, Herbert G. *The Black Family in Slavery and Freedom, 1750–1925.* New York: Pantheon, 1976.

Harris, Robert L., Jr., Darlene Clark Hine, and Nellie McKay. *Three Essays: Black Studies in the United States.* New York: Ford Foundation, 1990.

Herrnstein, Richard J., and Charles Murray. *The Bell Curve: Intelligence and Class Structure in American Life.* New York: Free Press, 1994.

Higginbotham, Evelyn Brooks. *Righteous Discontent: The Women's Movement in the Black Baptist Church, 1880–1920.* Cambridge, Mass.: Harvard University Press, 1993.

Hine, Darlene Clark, Elsa Barkley Brown, Tiffany R. L. Patterson, and Lillian S. Williams, eds. *Black Women in United States History.* 16 vols. New York: Carlson, 1990.

Hine, Carlene Clark, Elsa Barkley Brown, and Rosalyn Terborg-Penn, eds. *Black Women in America: An Historical Encyclopedia.* New York: Carlson, 1993.

Hu-DeHart, Evelyn. "Ethnic Studies in U.S. Higher Education: History, Development, and Goals." In *Handbook of Research on Multicultural Education,* edited by James A. Banks and Cherry A. McGee Banks. New York: Macmillan, 1995.

Hull, Gloria T., Patricia Bell Scott, and Barbara Smith, eds. *All the Women are White, All the Blacks are Men, But Some of Us Are Brave.* New York: Feminist Press, 1982.

Jackson, Blyden. *A History of Afro-American Literature;* Vol. 1: *The Long Beginning, 1746–1895.* Baton Rouge: Louisiana State University Press, 1989.

James, Stanlie M., Abena P. A. Busia, eds. *Theorizing Black Feminisms: The Visionary Pragmatism of Black Women.* New York: Routledge, 1993.

Johnson, Charles S. *Shadow of the Plantation.* Chicago: University of Chicago Press, 1934.

Jones, Jacqueline. *Labor of Love, Labor of Sorrow: Black Women, Work, and the Family, from Slavery to the Present.* New York: Basic Books, 1985.

Levine, Lawrence W. *Black Culture and Black Consciousness: Afro-American Folk Thought from Slavery to Freedom.* New York: Oxford University Press, 1977.

Lewis, David Levering. *W. E. B. Du Bois: Biography of a Race.* New York: Holt, 1993.

Lincoln, C. Eric, and Lawrence H. Mamiya. *The Black Church in the African American Experience.* Durham, N.C.: Duke University Press, 1990.

Logan, Rayford. *What the Negro Wants.* Chapel Hill: University of North Carolina Press, 1944.

Lyman, Stanford M. *The Black American in Sociological Thought: A Failure of Perspective.* New York: Putnam, 1972.

Marable, Manning. *Dispatches from the Ebony Tower.* New York: Columbia University Press, 2000.

Meier, August. *Negro Thought in America, 1880–1915.* Ann Arbor: University of Michigan Press, 1963.

Meier, August, and Elliott Rudwick. *Black History and the Historical Profession, 1915–1980.* Urbana: University of Illinois Press, 1986.

Moss, Alfred A., Jr. *The American Negro Academy: Voice of the Talented Tenth.* Baton Rouge: Louisiana State University Press, 1981.

Myrdal, Gunnar, with the assistance of Richard Sterner and Arnold Rose. *An American Dilemma: The Negro Problem and Modern Democracy.* New York: Harper, 1944.

Quarles, Benjamin. *The Negro in the American Revolution.* Chapel Hill: University of North Carolina Press, 1961.

Quarles, Benjamin. *Lincoln and the Negro.* New York: Oxford University Press, 1962.

Ripley, William Z. *The Races of Europe: A Sociological Study.* New York: Appleton, 1899.

Schmitz, Betty, Johnnella Butler, Deborah Rosenfelt, and Beverly Guy-Sheftall. "Women's Studies and Curriculum Transformation." In *Handbook of Research on Multicultural Education,* edited by James A. Banks and Cherry A. McGee. New York: Macmillan, 1995.

Smith, Jessie Carney, ed. *Notable Black American Women.* Detroit: Gale, 1992.

Stampp, Kenneth M. *The Peculiar Institution: Slavery in the Antebellum South.* New York: Knopf, 1956.

Stocking, George W., Jr. *A Franz Boas Reader: The Shaping of American Anthropology, 1883–1911.* Chicago: University of Chicago Press, 1974.

Stuckey, Sterling. *Slave Culture: Nationalist Theory and the Foundations of Black America.* New York: Oxford University Press, 1987.

Terborg-Penn, Rosalyn, and Sharon Harley, eds. *The Afro-American Women: Struggles and Images.* Port Washington, N.Y.: Kennikat, 1978.

Washington, Booker T. *Story of the Negro: The Rise of the Race from Slavery.* New York: Doubleday, 1909.

Williams, George Washington. *History of the Negro Race in America.* Vols. 1 and 2. New York: Putnam, 1892–1893.

Wilson, William Julius. *The Truly Disadvantaged: The Inner City, the Underclass, and Public Policy.* Chicago: University of Chicago Press, 1987.

Woodson, Carter G. *The Negro in Our History.* Washington, D.C.: Associated Publishers, 1922.

Woodson, Carter G. *African Myths.* Washington, D.C.: Associated Publishers, 1928.

Woodson, Carter G. *Negro Makers of History.* Washington, D.C.: Associated Publishers, 1928.

Woodson, Carter G. *The Story of the Negro Retold.* Washington, D.C.: Associated Publishers, 1935.

JAMES A. BANKS (1996)
Updated by publisher 2005

Black Towns

African-American town promoters established at least eighty-eight, and perhaps as many as two hundred, black towns throughout the United States during the late nineteenth and early twentieth centuries. Black towns, either mostly or completely African-American incorporated communities with autonomous black city governments and commercially oriented economies often serving a hinterland of black farmers, were created with clearly defined economic and political motives. The founders of towns such as Nicodemus, Kansas; Boley, Oklahoma; and Mound Bayou, Mississippi, like the entrepreneurs who created Chicago, Denver, and thousands of other municipalities across the nation, hoped their enterprises would be profitable and appealed to early settlers with the promise of rising real estate values. However, they added special enticements for African Americans: the ability to escape racial oppression, control their economic destinies, and prove black capacity for self-government.

The first all-black communities began in Upper Canada (Ontario) as an offshoot of the abolitionist movement. In 1829 the settlement of Wilberforce was created to resettle black refugees expelled from Cincinnati. Wilberforce, as well as most of the later Canadian settlements, such as Dawn and Elgin, were operated largely by white charities and were designed to give African Americans land and teach them usable skills. However, most of these efforts were poorly funded and managed, and none survived very long. The first black town in the United States was created in 1835, when "Free Frank" McWhorter, an ex-Kentucky slave, founded the short-lived community of New Philadelphia, Illinois. More black towns emerged in the first years after the Civil War. Texas led the way in the late 1860s, with the founding of Shankleville in 1867 and Kendleton in 1870. These communities, populated by ex-slaves from the surrounding countryside, arose from the desire of freedpeople to own land without interference.

The vast majority of black towns emerged in the West, however, following the end of Reconstruction. Like whites, blacks were lured by the promise of the West. African Americans, largely unable to secure land and economic opportunity in the ex-Confederate states, looked to the West, with its reserves of inexpensive land that could be accessed through the Homestead Act. Moreover for the African Americans who had briefly held political power in the Reconstruction-era South before being overwhelmed by conservative white regimes, the possibility of distinct black political autonomy was particularly attractive. Six representative communities—Nicodemus, Kansas; Langston City, Oklahoma; Boley, Indian Territory; Mound Bayou, Mississippi; Dearfield, Colorado; and Allensworth, California—all shared these characteristics and will be discussed in depth.

Nicodemus, Kansas, was the first predominantly black community that gained national attention. Nicodemus was founded by W. R. Hill, a white minister and land speculator, who during the mid-1870s joined three black Kansas residents—W. H. Smith, Simon P. Rountree, and Z. T. Fletcher—in planning an agricultural community in sparsely populated western Kansas. After naming Nicodemus after a legendary African slave prince who purchased his freedom, they soon recruited settlers from the South.

The first thirty colonists arrived from Kentucky in July 1877, followed by 150 from the same state in March 1878. Other newcomers arrived later in the year from Tennessee, Missouri, and Mississippi. By 1880, 258 blacks and 58 whites resided in the town and surrounding township. Both the townspeople and the farmers, who grew corn and wheat, helped Nicodemus emerge as a small, briefly thriving community. The first retail stores opened in 1879. Town founder and postmaster Z. T. Fletcher opened the St. Francis Hotel in 1885. Two white residents established the town's newspapers, the Nicodemus *Western Cyclone* in 1886 and the Nicodemus *Enterprise* one year later. By 1886 Nicodemus had three churches and a new schoolhouse.

The town's success attracted other African Americans, including Edwin P. McCabe, who would soon become the most famous black politician outside the South. Born in Troy, New York, in 1850, McCabe arrived in Nicodemus in 1878 and began working as a land agent. In 1880, when Kansas governor John P. St. John established Graham County (which included Nicodemus), McCabe was appointed acting county clerk, beginning a long career of elective and appointive office holding. In November 1881 McCabe was elected clerk for Graham County, and the following year, at age thirty-two, he became the highest-ranking African-American elected official outside the South when Kansas voters chose him as state auditor.

Nicodemus's fortunes, however, began to decline in the late 1880s. An 1885 blizzard destroyed 40 percent of the wheat crop, prompting the first exodus from the area. By 1888 three railroads had bypassed the town, despite its purchase of $16,000 in bonds to attract a rail line. Moreover, toward the end of the decade Oklahoma became more appealing to prospective black homesteaders.

The Twin Territories, Oklahoma and Indian Territory, became the most important center of black town activity in the nation. Thirty-two all-black towns emerged in the territories, including Langston City (Oklahoma Territory) and Boley (Indian Territory). Although the specific reasons for town founding varied, most grew out of the desire for political autonomy among the black ex-slaves of Indian peoples, antiblack violence in the South, and the political maneuvers of Edwin McCabe and other black politicians who settled in Oklahoma. For African Americans such as McCabe, Oklahoma Territory, whose former Native American reservations were opened to non-Indian settlement in 1889, represented not only the last major chance for homesteading but also a singular opportunity to develop communities where black people could achieve their economic potential and exercise their political rights without interference. McCabe, who emerged as the leading advocate of black settlement, would also become a town promoter, combining political and racial objectives with personal profit.

McCabe and his wife, Sarah, moved to Oklahoma Territory in April 1890 and six months later joined

Black pioneers in front of a sod house, Nicodemus, Kansas. DENVER PUBLIC LIBRARY–WESTER COLLECTION

Charles Robbins, a white land speculator, and William L. Eagleson, a black newspaper publisher, in founding Langston City, an all-black community about ten miles northeast of Guthrie, the territorial capital. Langston City was named after the Virginia black congressman who supported migration to Oklahoma. The McCabes, who owned most of the town lots, immediately began advertising for prospective purchasers through their newspaper, the Langston City *Herald,* which was sold in neighboring states. The *Herald* portrayed the town as an ideal community for African Americans. "Langston City is a Negro City, and we are proud of that fact," proclaimed McCabe in the *Herald.* "Her city officers are all colored. Her teachers are colored. Her public schools furnish thorough educational advantages to nearly two hundred colored children." The *Herald* also touted the agricultural potential of the region, claiming the central Oklahoma prairie could produce superior cotton, wheat, and tobacco. "Here is found a genial climate, about like that of . . . Northern Mississippi . . . admirably suited to the wants of the Negro from the Southern states. A land where every staple . . . can be raised with profit." By February 1892 Langston City had six hundred residents from fifteen states including Georgia, Maryland, and California, with the largest numbers from neighboring Texas. Local businesses included a cotton gin, a soap factory, a bank, and two hotels. An opera house, a racetrack, a billiard parlor, three saloons, Masonic lodges, and social clubs provided various forms of entertainment.

Like Nicodemus, Langston City residents counted on a railroad line to improve their town's fortunes. From 1892 to 1900 McCabe waged a steady but ultimately unsuccessful campaign to persuade the St. Louis & San Francisco Railroad to extend its tracks through Langston City. When the rail line bypassed the town, many disheartened Langston residents believed they lost their main opportunity to prosper. Throughout the railroad campaign, however, town promoters urged other reasons for migration to their community. The *Herald* (no longer owned by the McCabes) continued to emphasize the superior racial climate of the area. In 1896 McCabe, using his political connections as chief clerk of the Oklahoma Territorial Legislature, obtained for Langston City the Colored Agricultural and Normal School (later Langston University). The location of the school, the only publicly supported black educational institution in the territory, in Langston City ensured the town's permanence.

Boley, the largest all-black town in Indian Territory, was founded in the former Creek nation in 1904 by two white entrepreneurs, William Boley, a manager for the Fort Smith & Western Railroad, and Lake Moore, an attorney and former federal commissioner to the region's Indian tribes. Boley and Moore chose Tom Haynes, an African American, to handle promotion of the town. Unlike Langston City, Boley was on a rail line and in a timbered, well-watered prairie that easily supported the type of agriculture familiar to most prospective black settlers. The frontier character of the town was evident from its founding. Newcomers, who usually arrived by train, lived in tents until they could clear trees and brush to construct homes and stores. During the town's first year, Creek Indians rode several times through Boley's streets on shooting sprees that killed several people. Boley's reputation for lawlessness continued into 1905, when peace officer William Shavers was killed while leading a posse after a gang of white horse thieves who terrorized the town.

With one thousand residents and more than two thousand farmers in the surrounding countryside by 1907, Boley's permanence seemed assured. Local businesses included a hotel, sawmill, and cotton gin. Churches, a public school, fraternal lodges, women's clubs, and a literary society attest to the cultural development of the town. A community newspaper, the Boley *Progress,* was founded in 1905 to report on local matters and promote town growth. After a 1905 visit, Booker T. Washington described Boley as a "rude, bustling, Western town [that nonetheless] represented a dawning race consciousness . . . which shall demonstrate the right of the negro . . . to have a worthy place in the civilization that the American people are creating."

Despite Washington's endorsement, Boley's spectacular growth was over by 1910. When the Twin Territories became the state of Oklahoma in 1907, the Democrats emerged as the dominant political party. They quickly disfranchised black voters and segregated public schools and accommodations. Their actions eliminated the town's major appeal as a community where African Americans could escape the Jim Crow restrictions they faced in southern states. Although African Americans continued to vote in municipal elections, political control at the local level could not compensate for marginal influence at the courthouse or the state capital, where crucial decisions affecting the town's schools and roads were now routinely made by unsympathetic officials. Moreover, after the initial years of prosperity, declining agricultural prices and crop failures

FIGURE 1

Black towns, listed by state

Alabama
Cederlake
Greenwood Village
Hobson City
Plateau
Shepherdsville

Arkansas
Edmondson
Thomasville

California
Abila
Allensworth
Bowles
Victorville

Colorado
Dearfield

Florida
Eatonville
New Monrovia
Richmond Heights

Illinois
Brooklyn
Robbins

Iowa
Buxton

Kansas
Nicodemus

Kentucky
New Zion

Louisiana
Grambling
North Shreveport

Maryland
Fairmont Heights
Glenarden
Lincoln City

Michigan
Idlewind
Marlborough

Mississippi
Expose
Mound Bayou
Renova

Missouri
Kinloch

New Jersey
Gouldtown
Lawnside
Springtown
Whitesboro

New Mexico
Blackdom

North Carolina
Columbia Heights
Method
Oberlin

Ohio
Lincoln Heights
Urbancrest

Oklahoma
Arkansas Colored
Bailey
Boley
Booktee
Canadian Colored
Chase
Clearview
Ferguson
Forman
Gibson Station
Grayson
Langston City
Lewisville
Liberty
Lima
Lincoln City
Mantu
Marshalltown
North Folk Colored
Overton
Porter
Redbird
Rentiesville
Summit
Taft
Tatum
Tullahassee
Vernon
Wellston Colony
Wybark
Two unnamed towns in Seminole Nation

Tennessee
Hortense
New Bedford

Texas
Andy
Board House
Booker
Independence Heights
Kendleton
Mill City
Oldham
Roberts
Union City

Virginia
Ocean Grove
Titustown
Truxton

West Virginia
Institute

SOURCES: Adapted from Kenneth Marvin Hamilton, *Black Towns and Profit: Promotion and Development in the Trans-Appalachian West, 1877–1915* (Urbana, Ill., 1991); and Ben Wayne Wiley, Ebonyville in the South and Southwest: Political Life in the All-Black Town, Ph.D. diss., University of Texas at Arlington (1984).

gradually reduced the number of black farmers who were the foundation of the town's economy. Although Boley remained the site of a famous black rodeo, it ceased to be an important center of African American life in the state.

Although most black towns were in the West, Mound Bayou, Mississippi, the most successful of these enterprises, emerged east of the Mississippi River. Founded by the Louisville, New Orleans & Texas Railroad in 1887, the town was situated along the rail line that extended through the Yazoo-Mississippi delta, an area of thick woods, bayous, and swamps that nonetheless contained some of the richest cotton-producing lands in the state. When the fear of swampland diseases deterred white settlement, the railroad hired two prominent African-American politicians, James Hill and Isaiah Montgomery, as land promoters. Hill had once been Mississippi's secretary of state, while Montgomery was the patriarch of a well-known family of ex-slaves of Joseph Davis. After the Civil War, the Montgomery family acquired the Davis Bend plantations of their former master and his more famous brother, Confederate ex-president Jefferson Davis. When the Davis heirs successfully reclaimed the lands in the 1880s, the Montgomery family sought business opportunities elsewhere in the state.

The railroad, which wanted settlers on the least populated lands along its route, chose a town site fifteen miles east of the Mississippi River and ninety miles south of Memphis. The four-square-mile area selected included two bayous and several Indian burial mounds, inspiring Montgomery to name the town and colony Mound Bayou. Montgomery, the more active of the two promoters, sold the first town lots to relatives and friends from the Davis Bend plantations. In the fall of 1887 he led the first twelve settlers to Mound Bayou. By 1888 the town had forty residents, and about two hundred people had settled in the surrounding countryside. Twelve years later it had grown to 287 residents, with 1,500 African Americans in the vicinity.

With rail transportation assured and a sizable population of black farmers nearby, Montgomery and other promoters concentrated on efforts to increase the number and size of local African American businesses. Montgomery's close association with Booker T. Washington aided those efforts. Montgomery and Washington met in 1895 when the Mississippi planter served as a commissioner for the Atlanta Exposition, where Washington gave the speech that launched his national career. Washington, who saw in Montgomery and Mound Bayou the embodiment of his philosophy of black economic self-help, featured the Mississippian in exhibitions and conferences sponsored by Tuskegee Institute (now Tuskegee University). Montgomery, in turn, used the Tuskegee educator's fame and contacts to attract investors. Although Montgomery accepted a federal post in Jackson in 1902 and ceased his direct involvement in Mound Bayou promotional activities, Washington's interest in the town remained strong. He switched his support to merchant-farmer Charles Banks, who settled there in 1904 and founded the Bank of Mound Bayou. In 1908, following a visit to Mound Bayou, the Tuskegee educator prompted a number of flattering articles on the town in national magazines and profiled the community in books he published in 1909 and 1911.

Mound Bayou's population peaked at eleven hundred in 1911, with nearly eight thousand in the surrounding rural area. The sizable population ensured economic support for the town, which featured the largest number of African-American-owned businesses of any of the all-black communities. Mound Bayou's businesses included its bank, a savings and loan association, two sawmills, three cotton gins, and the only black-owned cottonseed mill in the United States. By 1914, however, some businesses, including the Bank of Mound Bayou, closed, and the town experienced its first population losses. Booker T. Washington's death in 1915 ended its national promotion. By the early 1920s the town lost its vitality and began to resemble other small delta communities.

One all-black Colorado town, Dearfield, emerged in Weld County. Dearfield was conceived by O. T. Jackson, who arrived in the state in 1887 and became a messenger for Colorado governors. Inspired by Booker T. Washington's autobiography, *Up from Slavery*, Jackson argued that successful farm colonies were possible on the Colorado plains and chose as his first site a forty-acre tract twenty-five miles southeast of Greeley, which he personally homesteaded. Jackson attracted other black Denver investors who made additional land purchases. Among them was Dr. J. H. P. Westbrook, a physician, who suggested the name Dearfield. The town's population peaked at seven hundred in 1921, with families occupying nearly fifteen thousand acres in the area. Dearfield's farmers grew wheat, corn, and sugar beets, and like their Weld County neighbors, prospered during World War I because of the European demand for American foodstuffs. Town founder Jackson was also its most prominent businessman; he owned the town grocery store, restaurant, service station, and dance hall. The war years were the apex of the town's prosperity. Declining agricultural prices and the attractiveness of urban employment caused Dearfield to steadily lose population. Only a handful of "pioneers" remained when Jackson died in Dearfield in 1949.

In 1908 white and black land speculators combined to create the westernmost all-black town in the United

States: Allensworth, California. The town was conceived by the California Colony and Home Promoting Association (CCHPA), a Los Angeles–based land development company owned by African Americans. CCHPA hoped to encourage black settlement in California's rapidly growing San Joaquin Valley and envisioned a town as the commercial center of a thriving agricultural colony. Since CCHPA had no resources to purchase land, it joined with three white firms, the Pacific Farming Company (owners of the site of the prospective town), the Central Land Company, and the Los Angeles Purchasing Company, to create an eighty-acre town site in Tulare County along the Santa Fe Railroad, about halfway between Fresno and Bakersfield. Allensworth was named for Lt. Col. Allen Allensworth, chaplain of the all-black Twenty-fourth Infantry Regiment and the highest-ranking African American in the U.S. Army. After his retirement, Allensworth settled in Los Angeles and became president of the CCHPA in 1907.

Initial sales were slow, and by 1910 the town had only eighty residents. Most of the adults worked ten-acre farms nearby, which they purchased for $110 per acre on an installment plan. The town's slow growth prompted Allensworth to intensify his promotional efforts. In January 1912 he sent a lengthy letter to the New York *Age,* the nation's largest African-American newspaper, promoting the town site by linking it to Booker T. Washington's call for black economic self-help and suggesting that his town's objectives were similar to those of Mound Bayou. By May 1912 Allensworth concentrated recruiting efforts on black veterans, issuing a promotional newspaper, *The Sentiment Maker,* which specifically targeted black military personnel.

The town of Allensworth had one hundred residents in 1914. Despite their small numbers, they owned dozens of city lots and three thousand acres of nearby farmland. Oscar O. Overr, a migrant from Topeka, Kansas, was the community's most prosperous resident, with a 640-acre farm and four acres of town lots. In 1914 Overr became California's first elected black justice of the peace. Allensworth also had a twenty-acre park named after Booker T. Washington and a library named for Colonel Allensworth's wife, Josephine, which received as its first holdings the family's book collection. After the colonel's death on September 14, 1914, Overr and William A. Payne, the town's first schoolteacher, attempted to establish the Allensworth Agricultural and Manual Training School. Modeled after Tuskegee Institute, the school would train California's black youth in vocational skills. Overr and Payne failed to obtain state funding, however, because urban black political leaders feared the school would encourage segregation. The school promotion scheme was the last concerted effort to lure settlers to Allensworth. Except for a brief period in the 1920s, the town's population never exceeded one hundred residents.

None of the surviving black towns ever reached the potential envisioned by their founder-promoters. Allensworth and Dearfield have long been emptied of residents. Nicodemus, Boley, Mound Bayou, and Langston City continue, but they are not dynamic centers of economic or cultural activity for their regions. Like thousands of small towns throughout the United States, these African-American communities were subject to the vagaries of transportation access, unpredictable agricultural productivity, detrimental county or state political decisions, and shifting settlement patterns. Moreover, towns such as Nicodemus, Allensworth, and Dearfield, which had few black farmers in their hinterlands to sustain their prosperity, were especially vulnerable to decline.

Moreover, none of the black towns could successfully compete with the attraction of larger cities, which lured millions of Americans from farms, hamlets, and small towns across the nation during the twentieth century. By 1915 thousands of southern African Americans who might have considered black towns now sought northern cities such as Chicago, Detroit, and New York for both political freedom and economic opportunity. Paradoxically, the initial reason for the founding of these towns may have hastened their demise. The racial insularity of these communities, which seemed attractive to one generation, proved restricting to the next. Nonetheless, for one brief period in the late nineteenth and early twentieth centuries, nearly one hundred fledgling black communities throughout the nation symbolized the aspirations of African Americans for political freedom and economic opportunity.

See also Civil War, U.S.; Jim Crow; Migration; Mound Bayou, Mississippi; Washington, Booker T.

Bibliography

Crockett, Norman L. *The Black Towns.* Lawrence: Regents Press of Kansas, 1979.

de Graaf, Lawrence B., Kevin Mulroy, and Quintard Taylor, eds. *Seeking El Dorado: African Americans in California, 1769–1997.* Los Angeles: Autry Museum of Western Heritage; Seattle: University of Seattle Press, 2001.

Franklin, Jimmie Lewis. *Journey Toward Hope: A History of Blacks in Oklahoma.* Norman: University of Oklahoma Press, 1982.

Hamilton, Kenneth Marvin. *Black Towns and Profit: Promotion and Development in the Trans-Appalachian West, 1877–1915.* Urbana: University of Illinois Press, 1991.

Smallwood, James M. *Time of Hope, Time of Despair: Black Texans During Reconstruction.* Port Washington, N.Y.: Kennikat, 1981.

Taylor, Quintard. *In Search of the Racial Frontier: African Americans in the American West, 1528–1990.* New York: Norton, 1998.

QUINTARD TAYLOR (1996)
Updated bibliography

Blackwell, Unita

March 18, 1933

Born in Lula, Mississippi, civil rights activist and politician Unita Blackwell grew up during the depression and spent her first thirty years migrating from farm to farm in Mississippi, Arkansas, and Tennessee. Blackwell has been an exemplar of grass-roots activism and organization within rural African-American communities.

In 1962 Blackwell and her first husband settled in the then-unincorporated town of Meyersville in Issaquena County, Mississippi, where she chopped cotton in the fields for three dollars a day. Inspired by visiting civil rights workers, she registered to vote and began to encourage other laborers to register. Fired by her employers for her activism, Blackwell joined the Student Nonviolent Coordinating Committee full-time. In 1964 she helped organize the Mississippi Freedom Democratic Party and traveled to the Democratic National Convention in Atlantic City with the party in its failed attempt to be seated. In 1968 she would serve as a state delegate at the Democratic convention in Chicago. In 1965 and 1966 she initiated *Blackwell v. Board of Education,* a landmark case that furthered school desegregation in Mississippi.

In 1976, equipped with the political and administrative skills she had developed in the civil rights movement, Blackwell set out to incorporate the 691-acre town of Mayersville, Mississippi, organizing town meetings, filing petitions, and having the land surveyed. The incorporation became official on December 28, 1976. Blackwell was elected mayor, the first African-American woman mayor in Mississippi, a post she held for four terms. An expert on rural housing and development, Blackwell has campaigned successfully for state and federal funds for public housing and welfare. She was selected as chairperson of the National Conference of Black Mayors, and she received a MacArthur Fellowship in 1992.

See also Civil Rights Movement, U.S.; Mississippi Freedom Democratic Party; Student Nonviolent Coordinating Committee (SNCC)

Bibliography

Hine, Darlene Clark, ed. *Black Women in America.* Brooklyn, N.Y.: Carlson, 1993, pp. 138–139.

Kilborn, Keter. "A Mayor and Town Pulled Up." *New York Times Biographical Service* 23 (June 1992): 760.

NANCY YOUSEF (1996)
GREG ROBINSON (1996)

Black Women's Club Movement

The black women's club movement emerged in the late nineteenth century and comprised a number of local reform organizations dedicated to racial betterment. These grass-roots organizations were made up primarily of middle-class women who were part of the larger progressive reform effort. Black women formed social organizations to provide services, financial assistance, and moral guidance for the poor. Many of the groups grew out of religious and literary societies and were a response to the intensified racism in the late nineteenth century.

Although organizations existed all over the country, they were concentrated in the Northeast. Women involved in the club movement gained knowledge about education, health care, and poverty and developed organizing skills. They also sought to teach the poor how to keep a household, manage a budget, and raise their children. The local groups were usually narrow in focus and supported homes for the aged, schools, and orphanages. In Washington, D.C., the black women's club movement was dominated by teachers who were concerned about children and their problems. Active participants held conventions, conferences, and forums to engage the intellectual elite. In New York City clubwomen honored Ida B. Wells for her political activism to publicize the prevalence of lynching.

In 1895 women organizing at the local level made attempts to develop national ties. The New Era Club in Boston began a publication, *Woman's Era,* which covered local and national news of concern to clubwomen. Two national federations of local clubs were formed in 1895. The next year these two merged and became the National Association of Colored Women (NACW). Women in the Northeast played a central role in setting the agenda for the NACW, which was more conservative than some of the local clubs. Mary Church Terrell, a supporter of Booker T. Washington, was the first president of the NACW.

In the 1930s, during the Great Depression, self-help and social reform came under attack as methods of social change. Increasing emphasis was placed on structural change and electoral politics. In 1935 a faction of the NACW, led by Mary McLeod Bethune, which rejected the philosophy of self-help and sought to put pressure on the political system to improve conditions for African Americans, formed the National Council of Negro Women (NCNW). The NCNW quickly came to dominate both the politics of the club movement and the national political agenda of black women. Although both the NACW and the NCNW continued to be central to black women's political activity, the social conditions and context for organizing had changed dramatically in the 1930s. As the reform efforts of African-American women became more explicitly political, both the local and national club movements declined in importance.

See also National Association of Colored Women; Wells-Barnett, Ida Bell; Women's Era

Bibliography

Giddings, Paula. *When and Where I Enter: The Impact of Sex and Race on Black Women in America.* New York: William Morrow, 1996.

Salem, Dorothy. *To Better Our World: Black Women in Organized Reform, 1880–1920.* Brooklyn, N.Y.: Carlson, 1990.

PREMILLA NADASEN (1996)
Updated bibliography

Black World/Negro Digest

Created in 1942 by Chicago-based publisher John H. Johnson, who also produced *Ebony, Tan,* and *Jet* magazines, the original series of *Negro Digest* was published monthly from 1942 to 1951. An unabashed imitation of *Reader's Digest,* it published general articles about African-American life, with an emphasis on racial progress. It also reprinted relevant articles from other journals, particularly mainstream white publications. The original *Negro Digest* ceased publication in 1951, but it reappeared after a ten-year hiatus, with Johnson listed on the masthead as editor, Hoyt W. Fuller as managing editor, and Doris E. Saunders as associate editor.

During the first several years of its reincarnation, *Negro Digest* generally followed the path of its predecessor. It continued to reprint articles from other magazines and its outlook was distinctly integrationist, an emphasis underscored by the monthly column "Perspectives," originally coauthored by Fuller and Saunders. At the same time, however, it devoted considerably more attention to African-American literature, history, and culture than the earlier *Negro Digest.* Fuller assumed sole responsibility for the "Perspectives" column in August 1962, signaling the beginning of his emergence as the most influential editor among the numerous African-American journals that flourished during this period.

In his column and in book reviews, articles, news items, and various notes, Fuller's ideological outlook shifted from civil rights and integration to Black Power, black arts, and Pan-Africanism. These shifts—reflective of wider changes in the mood and outlook of the black community—were inevitably reflected in the pages of *Negro Digest.* Beginning with his essay "Ivory Towerist vs. Activist: The Role of the Negro Writer in an Era of Struggle," published in the June 1964 issue, Fuller began to emphasize his belief in the connection between politics and literature. As his outlook evolved further in the direction of black nationalism, Fuller began to aim sharp verbal attacks at two targets: white literary critics and anthologists, whom he saw as cultural interlopers unable to understand African-American literature, and those African-American writers, most notably Ralph Ellison, who emphasized literary craft over political commitment.

Fuller pursued his efforts to develop new standards for African-American writing by polling black authors on various questions. The results appeared in two symposia in *Negro Digest:* "The Task of the Negro Writer as Artist," in the April 1965 issue, and "A Survey: Black Writers' Views on Literary Lions and Values," in January 1968. The second symposium in particular spurred the national debate about the black aesthetic. By 1968 Fuller's transformation to black cultural nationalism was virtually complete, and the pages of *Negro Digest* reflected his altered outlook. As of the May 1970 issue, the title of the magazine was changed to *Black World* to reflect its new emphasis.

As the only national black literary magazine with a paid staff and a solvent financial base, *Negro Digest/Black World* played a prominent role in the debates about African-American literature, culture, and politics that flourished during the 1960s and early 1970s. During its heyday, it served as a national forum for emerging, as well as established, black writers and intellectuals. As the revolutionary mood of the late 1960s and early 1970s subsided, however, a complex set of economic, political, and cultural forces led to its demise—and indeed to the demise of many of the "little" black magazines of the period. The final issue of *Black World* appeared in April 1976. Hoyt Fuller returned to his native Atlanta, where he launched a new journal, *First World,* publishing several issues before his death in 1981.

See also Black Power; *Ebony*; *Jet*; Journalism

Bibliography

Johnson, Abby Arthur, and Ronald Maberry. *Propaganda and Aesthetics: The Literary Politics of Afro-American Magazines in the Twentieth Century.* Amherst: University of Massachusetts Press, 1979.

Parks, Carole A., ed. *Nommo: A Literary Legacy of Black Chicago (1967–1987).* Chicago: Oba House, 1987.

Semmes, Clovis E. "Foundations in Africana Studies: Revisiting *Negro Digest/Black World,* 1961–1976." *Western Journal of Black Studies* 25 (2001): 195.

JAMES A. MILLER (1996)
Updated bibliography

Blaize, Herbert

February 26, 1918
December 19, 1989

The son of James and Mary Cecilia Blaize, Herbert Augustus Blaize was born on the island of Carriacou, Grenada. He attended primary school there and secondary school on the main island of Grenada from 1930 to 1936. A politician in later life, he eventually became chief minister, premier, and prime minister of an independent Grenada.

On graduation from secondary school, Blaize entered government service, working initially as a clerk in the Revenue Office in Sauteurs on the northern part of the island. As was then the case with many of his compatriots, he traveled to Aruba in 1944 to seek employment with the Lago Oil Company, which had then been recruiting workers from the British Caribbean islands. His superiors soon recognized his abilities and promoted him to a managerial position. But a near-fatal spinal injury he had suffered from a bicycle accident in 1939 resurfaced, prompting him to return to Carriacou in 1952.

Political Activities

Blaize became involved in politics when he joined the Grenada National Party (GNP), founded in 1955 by Dr. John Watts. The GNP was a relatively conservative, middle-of-the-road, urban-based party, organized chiefly to check the advances being made by Eric Gairy's more radical Grenada United Labour Party. Although Blaize was unsuccessful in his 1954 attempt to capture the Carriacou seat, he succeeded in 1957 as a member of the GNP. Except for the 1979 to 1984 revolutionary period when elections were nonexistent, Blaize retained this seat until his death in 1989.

The political landscape was changing when Blaize entered the Legislative Council. Through a new advisory-committee system of government that came into effect in 1957, he was appointed to the Trade and Production Committee. Constitutional changes in 1959 provided for a ministerial form of government, with the administrator still effectively in charge. Blaize became the first chief minister that year. He won election again in 1962 and was appointed the first premier under the new constitution that took effect in early 1967 when Grenada, together with other Eastern Caribbean islands, became the Associated States of Great Britain. After the 1983 collapse of the People's Revolutionary Government (PRG) that had ruled Grenada since 1979, Blaize's GNP merged with two smaller parties to form the New National Party (NNP) to contest successfully the 1984 elections. Most Grenadians believed that he was the most experienced leader who could be trusted to bring Grenada back into the democratic fold after the turbulent revolutionary years. He became prime minister in 1984, a position he held until his death.

Political Ideology

Fiscally conservative, Blaize was well known for his frugality in public service. He insisted on maintaining balanced budgets and was reluctant to borrow excessively, even at the cost of lower economic growth rate. As prime minister, he created a number of organizations to help with economic planning. In a way, this represented a reworking of some of the institutions that had been formed during the revolutionary period. Yet by neglecting to put in place immediately after becoming prime minister a bold and much-needed plan for the nation's economic development, he failed to create job opportunities to alleviate rising unemployment.

To Blaize lay the task of successfully restoring orderliness in the civil service on two occasions, the first after Gairy's 1962 misuse of his powers that resulted in financial improprieties being uncovered in a commission appointed by the governor. The commission's findings, called the "Squandermania Report," resulted in the suspension of the island's constitution. The second instance of stabilizing the civil service occurred after he returned to office in 1984 following the aborted people's revolution. Viewing accountability as essential to good government, he required all government ministers to follow his lead and deposit with the governor general a list of their assets. He left in place a country almost debt free, transparency in financial dealings, and structure in the civil service and in the conduct of public affairs.

Foreign Affairs

Blaize maintained a foreign policy of close cooperation with the United States, Great Britain, and Canada, with whom he forged close ties and received substantial financial support. Foreign policy, however, also proved to be the Achilles' heel of successive Blaize administrations. After the collapse of the West Indian Federation in 1962, he pursued an ill-advised policy of seeking unitary statehood with Trinidad. By making this issue the central plank of his reelection platform, he inflamed passions locally and provided Gairy with an effective tool to use successfully against him in his campaigns. His strong anticommunist beliefs especially after 1984 precluded him from completing any initiative that the PRG had started with Cuba, even the highly successful adult education programs they had introduced.

Governmental and Party Defections

By 1986 his deteriorating health and the emerging strains in the political marriage that had created the NNP posed additional problems for Blaize. His old physical ailments resurfaced, limiting his mobility and forcing him to set up office at his official residence. In August two members of his cabinet resigned. In April 1987 three more followed. Soon they would leave the party also. Blaize's majority in parliament, which once stood at fourteen to one, quickly evaporated by 1998 into a minority of six to nine. Still garnering some support from a number of his former cabinet colleagues, he clung to power by failing to introduce into parliament any controversial measures.

By 1988 many people felt strongly that Blaize should resign and pave the way for fresh elections. Leadership of the NNP devolved in January 1989 to Keith Mitchell, a member of cabinet and general secretary of the party. Blaize eventually fired Mitchell from the cabinet on July 20. He then renamed his wing of the party, consisting of the core elements of the now defunct GNP, The National Party. Increasingly fearing a vote of no confidence in parliament, and buttressed by the governor general's advice, he had parliament suspended in August 1989. The special parliamentary session convened on December 8 had as its sole purpose approving financial measures to borrow money to pay recently striking workers.

Worn out by his ailments and the increasing strains of office, Blaize succumbed to an apparent stroke. He died at home in the presence of his wife and children.

Increasingly stubborn and somewhat authoritarian from about 1985, Blaize was nonetheless a firm believer in parliamentary democracy. Politically conservative, his greatest legacies to the nation were his honesty and the alternatives he provided to Gairy's more radical policies in the 1950s and 1960s. Grenada also benefited from the political stability he afforded it from 1984 to 1989.

See also Gairy, Eric; International Relations of the Anglophone Caribbean

Bibliography

Brizan, George. *Grenada: Island of Conflict: From Amerindians to People's Revolution, 1498–1979.* London: Zed Books, 1984.

Lewis, Gordon K. *Grenada: The Jewel Despoiled.* Baltimore and London: Johns Hopkins University Press, 1987.

Scoon, Paul. *Survival for Service: My Experiences as Governor General of Grenada.* London: Macmillan, 2003.

Steele, Beverley A. *Grenada: A History of Its People.* London: Macmillan, 2004.

EDWARD L. COX (2005)

Blake, Eubie

February 7, 1883
February 12, 1983

The jazz pianist and composer James Hubert "Eubie" Blake was born in Baltimore, Maryland. The son of former slaves, he began organ lessons at the age of six and was soon syncopating the tunes he heard in his mother's Baptist church. While still in his teens, he began to play in the ragtime style then popular in Baltimore sporting houses and saloons. One of his first professional jobs was as a dancer in a minstrel show, *In Old Kentucky*. During this time Blake also began to compose music, with his first published piece, "Charleston Rag," appearing in 1899. In his twenties Blake began performing each summer in Atlantic City, where he composed songs (e.g., "Tricky Fingers," 1904) and came in contact with such giants of stride piano as Willie "The Lion" Smith (1897–1973), Luckey Roberts (1887–1968), and James P. Johnson (1894–1955). His melodic style and penchant for waltzes were influenced by the comic operettas of Victor Herbert, Franz Lehar, and Leslie Stuart. Blake soon began to perform songs in his mature style, which was marked by broken-octave parts, arpeggiated figures, sophisticated chord progressions, and altered blues chords. In 1910 Blake married Avis Lee, a classical pianist.

In 1916, with the encouragement of the bandleader James Reese Europe (1881–1919), Blake began performing with Noble Sissle (1889–1975) as "The Dixie Duo," a piano-vocal duet. Sissle and Blake performed together on the B. F. Keith vaudeville circuit, and they also began writing songs together. In 1921, Sissle and Blake joined with the well-known comedy team of Flournoy Miller and Aubrey Lyles to write *Shuffle Along,* which became so popular in both its Broadway and touring versions that at one point three separate companies were crisscrossing the country performing it. In 1924 Sissle and Blake teamed up with Lew Payton to present *In Bamville,* later known as *The Chocolate Dandies.* After the closing of the show in 1925, Sissle and Blake returned to vaudeville, touring the United States, Great Britain, and France. In 1927 Sissle remained in Europe, while Blake teamed up with Henry Creamer to write cabaret shows. In 1928 Blake joined with Henry "Broadway" Jones and a cast of eleven performers to tour the United States on the Keith-Albee Orpheum circuit with *Shuffle Along Jr.* In that year he also wrote "Tickle the Ivories." Two years later Blake set lyrics by Andy Razaf to music for Lew Leslie's *Blackbirds of 1930,* which included "Memories of You," one of the best-known of Blake's many songs. In 1932, after the death of Lyles, Sissle and Blake reunited with Miller to present *Shuffle Along of 1933,* but the show closed after only fifteen performances. During the Great Depression, Blake wrote several shows with Milton Reddie. *Swing It,* which included the songs "Ain't We Got Love" and "Blues Why Don't You Leave Me Alone," was produced by the Works Project Administration. During the war years, Blake performed in U.S.O. shows and wrote *Tan Manhattan* (1943). When "I'm Just Wild About Harry," from *Shuffle Along,* became popular during the 1948 presidential campaign of Harry Truman, Sissle and Blake reunited to update the show. The new version failed to gain popularity, however, and Blake retired from public life.

In the 1960s there was a renewed public interest in ragtime, and Blake recorded *The Eighty-Six Years of Eubie Blake* (1969), an album that led to a resurgence in his career. Thereafter, Blake performed regularly in concert and on television, and continued to compose songs, such as "Eubie's Classic Rag" (1972). He also performed at jazz festivals in New Orleans (1969) and Newport R.I. (1971). Even in his last years, he retained his remarkable virtuosity on piano, vigorously improvising melodic embellishments to a syncopated ragtime beat. In 1978 the musical revue *Eubie!* (featuring many songs written by Blake) enjoyed a successful run on Broadway and received three Tony Award nominations. A scaled-down version of the show was revived in 1997, and it has played at small theaters since then. Blake also established a music publishing and recording company and received numerous honorary degrees and awards, including the Presidential Medal of Freedom in 1981. Blake, whose more than three hundred compositions brought a sophisticated sense of harmony to the conventions of ragtime-derived popular song, was active until his ninety-ninth year, and his centennial in 1983 was an occasion for many tributes. However, the 1982 death of his wife, Marion, to whom he had been married since 1945 (his first marriage had ended with the death of his wife, Avis) led to a decline in his own health. He died on February 12, 1983 in Brooklyn, N.Y., only five days after his hundredth birthday. In 1995, Blake was featured on a U.S. postage stamp.

See also Europe, James Reese; Ragtime

Bibliography

Berlin, E. *Ragtime: A Musical and Cultural History.* Berkeley: University of California Press, 1984.

Bolcom, William, and R. Kimball. *Reminiscing with Sissle and Blake.* New York, 1973.

Graziano, John. "Black Musical Theater and the Harlem Renaissance Movement." In *Black Music in the Harlem Renaissance: A Collection of Essays,* edited by Samuel A. Floyd, Jr.. New York: Greenwood Press, 1990.

Rose, A. *Eubie Blake.* New York: Schirmer Books, 1979.

JOHN GRAZIANO (1996)
Updated by publisher 2005

Blake, Vivian

March 15, 1921
December 28, 2000

Vivian Osmond Scott Blake was born in St. James, Jamaica, to Rufus Alexander Blake, a schoolmaster, and Florence Maud Blake (neé Scott). He was educated at Wolmer's Boys School in Kingston and studied law at Gray's Inn, London, from 1945 to 1948, when he was called to the Jamaican Bar. Having worked at the law firm run by statesman Norman Manley, Blake was regarded Manley's potential successor as leading Jamaican barrister. Blake held offices as president of the Jamaican Bar Association and chairman of the Bar Council's Disciplinary Committee, and he reached the pinnacle of his legal career when he became chief justice of the Bahamas.

Blake entered politics in 1962, the year of Jamaica's independence from British rule. He was appointed member of the Legislative Council and later made senator when the Council was replaced by the Senate. Blake served in the Senate as leader of opposition business until 1967 when he successfully contested a seat for South Eastern St. Elizabeth in the House of Representatives. He rose to become vice president of the People's National Party (PNP) and unsuccessfully ran for president against Michael Manley on February 9, 1969. When the PNP came to government in 1972, Blake was appointed to the cabinet and given the portfolio of minister of marketing and commerce in 1974. He was in charge of the trade administrator's department, the prices commission, Jamaican Nutrition Holdings, and the Agricultural Marketing Corporation. In 1975 Blake briefly served as minister of health and the environment.

As minister of marketing and commerce, Blake presided over a difficult period in the Jamaican economy, when trade restrictions were enforced due to economic constraints. Controversial issues emerged regarding import licenses, quotas, price controls, and negotiations with taxi operators arising from an increase in the price of gasoline. He was also part of the failed negotiations with Jamaica Flour Mills over government participation in the ownership of the company. Whereas the price of such commodities as as gasoline, cooking gas and cement increased, Blake was responsible for price reductions of other products, including tinned corn beef, bread, counter flour, and rice. His handling of these and other issues earned him the esteem of the majority of the Jamaican people.

Blake's political career ended in 1978 when he resigned as the member of parliament for North Eastern St. Ann, the seat he won in July 1973 after ceasing to represent South Eastern St. Elizabeth a year earlier. His official reason for resigning was his acceptance of an appointment to the bench of the Supreme Court in the Bahamas. However, the announcement of his resignation followed a disagreement he had with the PNP executive committee concerning his right to speak and vote as he did on a bill before the House in February of that year. Though this was resolved, Blake left for the Bahamas, where he rose to become chief justice until his retirement in 1984 when he left for England. He remained there for ten years while practicing as a legal consultant for overseas clients.

Blake eventually returned to Jamaica and resumed his law practice as a senior member of the legal firm of Myers, Fletcher and Gordon. He was an avid sportsman with an interest in cricket, boxing, rifle shooting, and horse racing.

See also Manley, Norman; People's National Party; Politics

Bibliography

Hurwitz, Samuel J., and Edith F. Hurwitz. *Jamaica: A Historical Portrait.* London: The Pall Mall, 1971.

Stone, Carl, and Aggrey Brown, eds. *Perspectives on Jamaica in the Seventies.* Kingston, Jamaica: Jamaica Publishing House, 1981.

NICOLE PLUMMER (2005)

Blakey, Art (Buhaina, Abdullah Ibn)

October 11, 1919
October 16, 1990

The drummer and bandleader Art Blakey was born in Pittsburgh, Pennsylvania, and orphaned as an infant. Blakey learned enough piano in his foster home and at school to organize a group and play a steady engagement at a local nightclub while still in his early teens. He later taught himself to play drums, emulating the styles of Kenny Clarke, Chick Webb, and Sid Catlett. Blakey left Pittsburgh for New York City with Mary Lou Williams' band in the fall of 1942. He left her band in 1943 to tour with the Fletcher Henderson Orchestra. After his stint with Henderson, he briefly formed his own big band in Boston before heading west to Saint Louis to join Billy Eckstine's new big bebop band. Blakey remained with the band during its three-year duration, working with other modern jazz musicians including Dizzy Gillespie, Charlie Parker, Sarah Vaughan, Miles Davis, Dexter Gordon, and Fats Navarro.

After Eckstine disbanded the group in 1947, Blakey organized another big band, the Seventeen Messengers. At the end of the year, he took an octet including Kenny Dorham, Sahib Shihab, and Walter Bishop Jr. into the studio to record for Blue Note Records as the Jazz Messengers. That same year, Blakey joined Thelonious Monk on his historic first recordings for Blue Note, recordings that document both performers as remarkably original artists. The next year Blakey went to Africa to learn more about Islamic culture and subsequently adopted the Arabic name Abdullah Ibn Buhaina. During the early 1950s Blakey continued to perform and record with the leading innovators of his generation, including Charlie Parker, Miles Davis, and Clifford Brown. With his kindred musical spirit Horace Silver, Blakey in 1955 formed a cooperative group with Kenny Dorham (trumpet), Doug Watkins (bass), and

Hank Mobley (tenor saxophone), naming the quintet the Jazz Messengers. When Silver left the group in 1956, Blakey assumed leadership of the seminal hard bop group, renowned for combining solid, swinging jazz with rhythm and blues, gospel, and blues idioms.

Blakey's commitment to preserving the quintessence of the hard bop tradition was unflagging for over thirty-five years. His group toured widely, serving both as a school for young musicians and as the definitive standard for what has become known as straight-ahead jazz. Blakey's Jazz Messengers graduated from its ranks many of the most influential figures in jazz, including Wayne Shorter; Freddie Hubbard; Donald Byrd; Jackie McLean; Lee Morgan; Johnny Griffin; Woody Shaw; Keith Jarrett; JoAnn Brackeen; Branford, Delfeayo, and Wynton Marsalis; Donald Harrison; and Terence Blanchard.

A drummer famous for his forceful intensity, hard swinging grooves, and inimitable press roll, Blakey also adopted several African drumming techniques, including rapping the sides of his drums and altering the pitch of the tom-toms with his elbow, expanding the timbral and tonal vocabulary of jazz drumming. His drumming style as an accompanist is characterized by an unwavering cymbal beat punctuated by cross-rhythmic accents on the drums. A distinctive soloist, Blakey exploited the full dynamic potential of his instrument, often displaying a command of rhythmic modulation and a powerful expressiveness that incorporated polyrhythmic conceptual influences from West Africa and Cuba. In addition to his singular achievements as a drummer and bandleader, Blakey also served as a catalyst, bringing together percussionists from diverse traditions to perform and record in a variety of ensembles. His versatility as a drummer outside of the context of his own group received global recognition during his 1971–1972 tour with the Giants of Jazz, which included Dizzy Gillespie, Sonny Stitt, Thelonious Monk, Kai Winding, and Al McKibbon. Blakey died in New York City in 1990.

See also Islam; Jazz

Bibliography

"Art Blakey." In *Contemporary Black Biography,* vol. 37, edited by Ashyia Henderson. Detroit, Mich.: Gale, 2003.

Gourse, Leslie. *Art Blakey: Jazz Messenger.* New York: Schirmer, 2002.

Porter, Lewis. "Art Blakey." In *The New Grove Dictionary of Jazz,* edited by Barry Kernfeld. London: Grove's Dictionaries, 1988, pp. 115–116.

Southern, Eileen. "Art Blakey." In *Biographical Dictionary of Afro-American and African Musicians.* Westport, Conn.: Greenwood, 1982, p. 37.

ANTHONY BROWN (1996)
Updated bibliography

Blaxploitation Films

Blaxploitation film is a type of film oriented to black audiences. It developed in the late 1960s and flourished up through the late 1970s. According to the *Oxford English Dictionary* (OED), the term *blaxploitation* was first employed in the June 12, 1972, issue of *New York* magazine to characterize such films, specifically *Superfly* (1972). The word derives from *sexploitation,* first used in 1942. The OED defines *blaxploitation* as "the exploitation of blacks, especially as actors in films of historical or other interest to blacks." A variant spelling, *blacksploitation,* is provided by *Colliers Year Book* (1973). Some film critics, such as James Robert Parish and George H. Hill, have preferred the term *black action film,* seeing the form as a continuum of black adventure films that began in the 1950s. For the film scholar Thomas Cripps, blaxploitation is a subgenre of the black film itself. *Sweet Sweetback's Baadasssss Song* (1971), an independent production written, filmed, directed, and produced by Melvin Van Peebles (who also plays the title role), is generally considered the first blaxploitation film. Notable successors include *Shaft* (1971), *Superfly* (1972), *Blacula* (1972), *Coffy* (1973), *The Legend of Nigger Charlie* (1972), *Melinda* (1972), *Cleopatra Jones* (1973), and *The Mack* (1973). An estimated 150 blaxploitation films were produced before the vogue faded.

Origins of the Blaxploitation Film Movement

The blaxploitation film movement had six sources of origin: (1) the precedent of integrationist films that began in the 1940s; (2) the decline of the Hollywood studio system; (3) the Black Power movement; (4) the independent black film movement; (5) the availability of talented black actors and musicians; and (6) the newly discovered profitability of the urban black film audience.

After World War II, pressure from black and white American groups and the Cold War rivalry between the United States and the Soviet Union for favorable world opinion made the integration of America a national priority. For Hollywood, desegregation meant the increased hiring of black actors, the creation of viable black characters instead of replicating stereotypes, and the production of serious films that addressed the issue of sustaining democratic values in a racist society. Films such as *Blackboard Jungle* (1955), *The Defiant Ones* (1958), and *Pressure Point* (1962) portray black men in complex social relationships with whites, in which they often assert themselves through moral or physical confrontation of racism—a first step in a new black cinema.

In the 1960s, the feature action film was integrated. A number of such feature films starred the former football great Jim Brown (*Rio Concho,* 1964; *The Dirty Dozen,* 1967; *Ice Station Zebra,* 1968; *The Split,* 1968; *100 Rifles,* 1969; and *Riot,* 1969) with white stars such as Gene Hackman, Julie Harris, Rock Hudson, Lee Marvin, Burt Reynolds, and Raquel Welch. Brown's virile, brooding presence reflected the growing influence of the Black Power movement upon mainstream culture and established the black rebel as a legitimate screen persona. Brown became the prototype of the black male action star.

Another contributing factor was the decline of the Hollywood studio system as a result of the U.S. Supreme Court antitrust ruling of 1948. This ruling required Metro-Goldwyn-Mayer (MGM), Warner Brothers, Paramount, Columbia, Twentieth Century Fox, and other giant studios to divest themselves of their nationwide theater chains, thus breaking the studios' previous monopoly on all aspects of the film industry. The decline of this monopoly also ended Hollywood's power to define the black presence in American films and control its dissemination to the public. Television further weakened the studios, and in the free fall that followed, major actors became independent contractors, independent film companies developed, and the theater chains were forced into open competition for the moviegoer's dollar. By the mid-1960s, 80 percent of all films released by major distributors were made by independent companies, in contrast to 20 percent in 1949. Independent black filmmakers begin to spring up and production companies emerged that were free to address racial issues. The seminal films *Nothing but a Man* (1964, Ivan Dixon, director), *The Story of a Three-Day Pass* (1968, Melvin Van Peebles), and *Odds Against Tomorrow* (1959), were independent productions. The independent black film movement was furthered by the demands of the civil rights movement and the Black Power movement for positive portrayals of black life. Black actors, always minimally employed during the Jim Crow era, provided a ready pool of talent for the new films; among these actors were Adolph Caesar, Ossie Davis, Ruby Dee, Moses Gunn, Ellen Holly, William Marshall, Brock Peters, and Beah Richards. New talents also emerged, among them John Amos, Rosalind Cash, Godfrey Cambridge, Pam Grier, Vonetta McGee, Ron O'Neal, Richard Pryor, and Richard

Jim Brown

From his athletic prowess on the football field to rubbing elbows with the likes of Lee Marvin and John Cassavettes in films like the *Dirty Dozen*, Jim Brown was a larger-than-life hero for many African Americans growing up in the 1950s and 1960s.

Much is made of Brown's physicality, speed, and power, but he was also considered one of the smartest players on the field. Generally regarded as the greatest full back of all time, he led the league in rushing eight of his nine years in the National Football League. He rushed for a total of 12,312 yards, while averaging 102 yards per game and 5.2 yards per carry—a record that still stands. Twice he ran for 237 yards in a single game. He was named to the Pro Bowl (the NFL's "all-star game") every year he played and elected to the Pro Football Hall of Fame in 1971.

Unlike many athletes, Brown retired when he was on top. At age 30, he decided he'd rather star in movies than on a football field and helped usher in the blaxploitation genre. He appeared in *Ice Station Zebra*, a number of action films, and, as mentioned above, the *Dirty Dozen*. Eventually he would become the head of his own independent movie production company and would go on to executive produce *Richard Pryor Here and Now*.

Despite a highly publicized volatile personal life, Brown is still respected by many in the community. In 1988 he created the Amer-I-Can program, an effort to improve the lives of Los Angeles gang members. Brown also founded an organization called Black Economic Union that assists black-owned businesses. He has written two autobiographies, *Off My Chest* (1964) and *Out of Bounds* (1965), and is the subject of a documentary directed by Spike Lee titled *Jim Brown: All American*, which came out in 2002. The film chronicles Brown's athletic and movie career, youth, and personal life.

Hotter than Bond,
Cooler than Bullitt.
SHAFT
SHAFT's his name.
SHAFT's his game.

Poster for* Shaft, *starring Richard Roundtree, 1971. *Among the earliest of the Blaxploitation films,* Shaft *was also among the most successful. Composer Isaac Hayes won an Oscar for his musical score for the film, which grossed over $16 million in its first year of release.* THE KOBAL COLLECTION

Roundtree. Composers such as Marvin Gaye (*Trouble Man,* 1972), Isaac Hayes (*Shaft*), Quincy Jones (*Melinda*), and Curtis Mayfield (*Superfly*) composed scores for these films, with Hayes winning an Oscar in 1971 for his score for *Shaft.*

Character, Plot, Content, and Thematic Concerns of Blaxploitation Films

The typical blaxploitation protagonist, male or female, is a proud, self-assured, independent person of action who is often a private detective, intelligence agent, or underworld antihero. The protagonist's ethic includes professionalism; loyalty to friends, family, and community; a belief in the efficacy of violence and the necessity of revenge; a distrust of government; and a relentless opposition to white racism. This ethic does not preclude professional and sexual bonding across the color line or open conflict with black antagonists who, typically, have "sold out the black community," betrayed a personal trust, cheated on a business deal, or in some other way violated the protagonist's ethic.

Fast-paced action is the essential feature in a blaxploitation film plot, and it usually supersedes character development. The plot line is simple and direct, often based upon revenge, rescue, or money. At the film's conclusion, the protagonist has usually achieved his or her goal and emerged intact. In one of the most critically esteemed films, *Shaft,* the protagonist, John Shaft (Richard Roundtree) is a private detective hired by a black gangster, Bumpy Jonas (Moses Gunn), to rescue his daughter, who has been kidnapped by the Mafia. The Mafia hopes to extort control of the Harlem rackets from Bumpy, while white control of black rackets is viewed as an intrusion by the black community. As is often the case in blaxploitation films, the black community is portrayed as a unified whole, and youths, militants, and hustlers all unite to help Shaft rescue Bumpy's daughter.

Blaxploitation films also featured female protagonists. Tamara Dobson portrayed a U.S. government agent, Cleopatra Jones, in *Cleopatra Jones* and *Cleopatra Jones and the Casino of Gold* (1975). In the style of the 1970s, Cleopatra Jones is a sexually liberated female and, like her male counterparts, is expert in martial arts and weapons use. In *Coffy,* Pam Grier stars as a black woman who seeks vengeance upon the drug dealer who made her sister a hopeless drug addict at the age of eleven. To achieve this goal she poses as a call girl, seduces the drug czar, and after failing in her first attempt to assassinate him, escapes, destroys his operation, and then kills him.

There are two Americas in the blaxploitation film, a privileged white America and an oppressed black America, separated by racism and economic exploitation. Characteristically, the ghettoes of urban black America are its mise-en-scène, and their problems of crime, drug traffic, sexual exploitation, police brutality, and government indifference and corruption are grist for the plot. The positing of a separate black America in such films permitted a nationalist and, at times, revolutionary treatment of U.S. race relations. This black perspective engaged the African-American community and at times distanced white American viewers, particularly critics who would complain of reverse racism. Blaxploitation films often provided a parodic treatment of black-white relationships and the stereotypes portrayed during the earlier stages of American film.

Black films of this era also reworked earlier white films and genres. John Ford's *The Informer* (1936) became *Uptight* (1968); Edward G. Robinson's *Little Caesar* (1931) was refilmed as *Black Caesar* (1972); John Huston's *The Asphalt Jungle* (1950) was remade as *The Cool Breeze* (1972); the Dracula legend was retold as *Blacula,* starring William Marshall; and Stanley Kubrick's *Spartacus* (1960) was reworked as *The Arena* (1974), featuring a revolt of female gladiators led by Pam Grier, reprising Kirk Douglas's role in the original film. *Cotton Comes to Harlem* (1972) and *Come Back, Charleston Blue* (1972), both based upon novels by black author Chester B. Himes, recast the detective genre in humorous terms.

The Profitability of Blaxploitation Films

The black urban film audience proved a lucrative market and inner-city blacks filled the decaying old-line theaters in Chicago, New York, Los Angeles, Washington, D.C., and other metropolises that had been left empty by whites' migration to the suburbs. Shot on location with low budgets, rapid schedules, and unknown or low-paid black actors, the blaxploitation film's average cost ranged from $150,000 to $700,000. *Shaft,* for example, cost less than $700,000 to make, including a $13,500 salary for its star Richard Roundtree, and within its first year it grossed over $16 million. It is credited with saving MGM from bankruptcy. (Roundtree received $50,000 for the sequel, *Shaft's Big Score,* in 1972.) *Coffy* (1973), starring Pam Grier, cost an estimated $500,000 and grossed over $2 million in domestic film rentals. *The Legend of Nigger Charley* (1972), a black Western starring Fred Williamson, another former football star, cost $400,000 to make and grossed $3 million in domestic film rentals. The independent production, *Sweet Sweetback's Baadasssss Song,* cost under $500,000 and grossed $4.1 million in domestic film rentals. However, with the exception of *Sweet Sweetback's Baadasssss Song* and *Superfly,* both black-financed productions, the majority of blaxploitation profits went to the white studios, producers, and distributors responsible for their production. (The figures cited represent the distributor's gross income after the theaters have been paid; figures do not include videotape and DVD rights and rentals.)

The Critical Response to the Blaxploitation Films

These films influenced fashion and styles and had social impact. The chic clothing and accessories worn by the heroes of *Shaft* and *Superfly* were marketed to black youth, as were hairstyles, cosmetics, and jewelry, and their soundtracks became best-selling records. The blaxploitation film, some critics argued, not only exploited the black moviegoer, but as its images became reified throughout the society, it influenced black consumer and behavior patterns, too.

Black psychiatrist Alvin Poussaint (1974) charged, "These movies glorify criminal life and encourage in black youth misguided feelings of machismo that are destructive to the community as a whole. . . . These films, with few exceptions, damage the well-being of all Afro-Americans. Negative black stereotypes are more subtle and neatly camouflaged than they were in the films of yesteryear, but the same insidious message is there: blacks are violent, criminal, sex savages who imitate the white man's ways as best they can from their disadvantaged sanctuary in the ghetto." Poussaint continued, "Movies of any type are seldom mere entertainment because they teach cultural values and influence behavior." The black critic Clayton Riley added, "the danger of this fantasy is to reinforce the ordinary black human being's sense of personal helplessness and inadequacy." Observing the hunger of black audiences for films that see the world from a black point of view, *Newsweek* magazine concluded that "the intent of the new black films is not art but the commercial exploitation of the repressed anger of a relatively powerless community" (*Newsweek,* August 28, 1972). Junius Griffin, the former head of the Beverly Hills-Hollywood branch of the NAACP, made similar criticisms, and in 1972 he launched the Los Angeles-based Coalition Against Blaxploitation (CAB), which included the NAACP, CORE, and SCLC.

In responding to the fantasy-versus-reality critique, the photographer and auteur Gordon Parks, director of *Shaft,* argued, "It's ridiculous to imply that blacks don't know the difference between truth and fantasy and therefore will be influenced by these films in an unhealthy way." "People talk about black movies being exploitative," said Hugh Robertson, director of *Melinda,* "and sure a lot of them are spoofy and outrageous, but the black community has been conditioned to want fantasy in films by the movies they've seen just as white people have. The only difference now is that the black fantasy isn't totally negative." In the distinguished black actor James Earl Jones's opinion, "If they're going to put the damper on John Shaft, let them put it on John Wayne too and they'll find out that there are a lot of people who need those fantasies" (Micher, 1972).

In reference to the issue of crime and violence, the white film producer Larry Cohen (*Black Caesar*) argued that the "white" gangster films of the 1930s that starred Humphrey Bogart, James Cagney, and Edward G. Robinson also featured violence to an approving audience: "The only difference was that the perpetrator had to pay for his crime before the film ended, due to the Code restrictions of that day . . . it really made no difference in the impact on the audience" (*Variety,* March 7, 1973). Further, stated Ron O'Neal, the star of *Superfly,* "the critics of *Superfly* want to support the myth that crime doesn't pay. But we all happen to know that crime is paying off for some people every day." In a review of *The Mack* and *Superfly,* the critic Stanley Kauffmann addressed the issue of quality: "Why in the world should we expect black film people, now empowered to make movie money, to behave differently or better than 99 percent of white film people behaved in the seventy years that they had full control of the screen . . . only after there is a body of black films, as gener-

Poster for the 1975 film* Dolemite, *starring Rudy Ray Moore. *Oriented to black audiences, black action films like* Dolemite *generally featured simple plot lines and fast-paced action at the expense of emotional depth and character development.* THE KOBAL COLLECTION

ally rotten as most white films, will there be a chance for the occasional good black film, as there is for the occasional good white one" (*New Republic,* April 28, 1973).

As the movement drew to a close, most blacks involved in the film industry concluded that to assure quality, blacks must finance and control the production of black-oriented films. In Jim Brown's view, the blaxploitation films were a necessary stage: "The Black films were at least developing producers, directors and technical people, and everyone knows that you have to crawl before you can walk. Maybe the Black films weren't of the highest quality, but Black people were getting experience in the industry" (*Ebony,* October 1978).

The Legacy of Blaxploitation Films

Blaxploitation films were part of a general resurgence of black artistic and political activity during the 1960s and early 1970s. In tandem with these black action films, a number of black feature films were produced that satisfied the concern of middle-class black and white communities for black positive images and value systems that would vindicate the quest for assimilation into mainstream American society. These films included *Sounder* (1972), *Claudine* (1974), *The Learning Tree* (1969), and *The River Niger* (1976), and featured such black stars as Diahann Carroll, Louis Gossett, James Earl Jones, Sidney Poitier, Richard Pryor, Diana Ross, Cicely Tyson, and Paul Winfield. In considering the complex relationship between market, film quality, and the audience for race-related films in 1963, *Variety* commented, "it's a hard fact of film life that the race pix which have been most successful at the box office have been out-and-out exploitation dramas of rather dubious artistic and social import." The marketing strategy of race films was to budget the picture so that the producer, if necessary, could recoup the film's costs in just the black market, even while aiming at as broad a market as possible. Concluded *Variety*: "Ironically, however, as the equal rights fight must continue to succeed, that very hard core 'Negro market' must continue to diminish. Thus, to succeed, these projected films must appeal to the new, 'desegregated market' " (*Variety,* July 17, 1963). The great appeal of the blaxploitation films indicated that much of America's population and imagination was still segregated in the 1970s.

But the blaxploitation films integrated attitudes, expressions, body language, and style of inner-city blacks into the repertory of both black and white feature films, thus legitimizing both black culture and these media. Richard Pryor and Eddie Murphy became major box office attractions in the 1980s through a series of fast-paced action comedies. Often playing fast-talking street hustlers, Pryor and Murphy incorporated into their characters many of the iconoclastic and scatological attitudes of inner-city blacks toward whites that were first developed in the blaxploitation films. Whoopi Goldberg continued this trend in many of her vehicles.

Among the first of the post-blaxploitation action films, Sylvester Stallone's *Rocky* series, (beginning in 1976) effected such an integration through the use of black actors Carl Weathers (who plays flamboyant heavyweight champion Apollo Creed, patterned upon Muhammad Ali) and Mr. T. (who plays ghetto-tough boxer Clubber Lang). However, Stallone's films valorized the Italian-American working-class culture, as roustabout Rocky Balboa, played by Stallone, becomes a champion boxer in a sport dominated by blacks. Increasingly, feature films began to include black actors in major roles, but the ideological authority of the film resided within the actions and perspective of the white protagonist.

Interest in blaxploitation films and actors revived following Keenan Ivory Wayans's affectionate spoof *I'm Gonna Git You Sucka* (1989), and the genre enjoyed a popular renaissance in the 1990s, a development influenced by such diverse factors as nostalgia for the 1970s and the popularity of hip-hop films. In particular, Quentin Tarentino, a white director, openly acknowledged the influence of the blaxploitation film on his scenarios, dialogue, and directorial style, and he paid tribute to the genre with his film *Jackie Brown* (1998), which provided a comeback for actress Pam Grier.

In summary, blaxploitation films achieved several things: they (1) proved that black audiences would support black films; (2) revitalized white studios and urban theaters during the late 1960s to mid 1970s; (3) developed a genre of black action film; (4) stimulated the integration of mainstream feature films; (5) broadened the range of character for black actors and actresses; and (6) provided an opportunity for new black talent, in front of the camera and behind it.

See also Black Power Movement; Film in the United States, Contemporary; Film in the United States; Hayes, Isaac; Murphy, Eddie; Pryor, Richard; Van Peebles, Melvin

Bibliography

Cripps, Thomas. *Black Film as Genre.* Bloomington: Indiana University Press, 1979.

Diawara, Manthia, ed. *Black American Cinema.* New York: Routledge, 1993.

Gates, Philippa. "Always A Partner in Crime: Black Masculinity in the Hollywood Detective Film." *Journal of Popular Film and Television* 32, no.1 (Spring 2004): 20–29.

James, Darius. *That's Blaxploitation!: Roots of the Baadasssss 'Tude (Rated X by an All-Whyte Jury.* New York: St. Martin's Griffin, 1995.

Leab, Daniel J. *From Sambo to Superspade: The Black Experience in Motion Pictures.* Boston: Houghton Mifflin, 1975.

Martinez, Gerald, Diana Martínez, and Andres Chavez. *What It Is, What It Was!: The Black Film Explosion of the '70s in Words and Pictures.* New York: Hyperion, 1998.

Mason, B. J. "The New Films: Culture or Con-Game?" *Ebony* (December 1972): 60–62.

Micher, Charles. "Black Movies." *Newsweek* (October 23, 1972): 74–81.

Nesteby, James R. *Black Images in American Films, 1896–1954: The Interplay between Civil Rights and Film Culture.* Washington, D.C.: University Press of America, 1982.

Parish, James Robert, and George H. Hill. *Black Action Films: Plots, Critiques, Casts, and Credits for 235 Theatrical and Made-for-Television Releases.* Jefferson, N.C.: McFarland, 1989.

Patterson, Lindsay. *Black Films and Film-Makers: A Comprehensive Anthology from Sterotype to Superhero.* New York: Dodd Mead, 1975.

Poussaint, Alvin F. "Stimulus/Response: Blaxploitation Movies—Cheap Thrills That Degrade Blacks." *Psychology Today* 7 (February 1974): 22–32.

Ward, Renee. "Black Films, White Profits." *Black Scholar* 7 (May 1976): 13–24.

ROBERT CHRISMAN (1996)
Updated bibliography

Blount, Herman "Sonny"

See Sun Ra (Blount, Herman "Sonny")

Blues, The

This entry consists of three distinct, but interrelated articles.

The Blues

A type of African-American musical art that was first developed in the Mississippi Delta region at the end of the nineteenth century, the blues, like many musical expressions, is difficult to define. Some people think of the blues as an emotion; others regard it primarily as a musical genre characterized by a special blues scale containing twelve bars and three chords in a particular order. Besides embodying a particular feeling (the "blues") and form, the blues also involves voice and movement: poetry set to dance music. It is vocal not only in the obvious sense that most blues songs have lyrics, but in that even in purely instrumental blues, the lead instrument models its expressivity on the singing voice; and it involves dance because it quite literally moves listeners—even when they are sitting down. Its influence on jazz, gospel music, theater music, rock, soul, hip-hop, and almost every form of popular music since the 1920s has been enormous. The historical importance of the blues was underscored recently when Congress declared 2003 the "Year of the Blues." To commemorate the occasion, the film director Martin Scorsese produced seven documentary films on blues, which were shown on public television, while a thirteen-part interpretive radio series on blues was broadcast on National Public Radio. Today, blues is usually positioned as one of the most important genres of American roots music.

Early blues singers composed their own songs, inventing verses and borrowing from other singers, and they were among the first Americans to express feelings of anomie characteristic of modern life—and to rise above it through art. By singing about frustration, mistreatment, and misfortune, and often overcoming it with irony, blues singers helped themselves and their listeners to deal with the problems of life, whether frustrated and angered by cheating lovers, ignorant bosses, hypocritical churchgoers, crooked shopkeepers, an unjust legal system, racism and prejudice, police brutality, inadequate pay, unemployment, or the meaninglessness of menial labor. Blues singers fought adversity by asserting human creativity, by turning life into art through ironic signification, by linking themselves through their traditional art to others in the community, and by holding out a future hope for freedom and better times down the road. The blues as music and poetry can convey a tremendous range of emotions succinctly and powerfully. Blues lyrics represent an oral poetry of considerable merit, one of the finest genres of vernacular poetry in the English language.

The blues is a distinct musical type. It is an instrumentally accompanied song-type, with identifying features in its verse, melodic, and harmonic structures, composition, and accompaniment. Most blues lyrics are set in three-line or quatrain-refrain verses. In the three-line verse shown below, the second line repeats the first, sometimes with slight variation, while the third completes the thought with a rhyme.

I'm gonna dig me a hole this morning, dig it deep
down in the ground;
I'm gonna dig me a hole this morning, dig it deep
down in the ground;
So if it should happen to drop a bomb around
somewhere, I can't hear the
echo when it sound.
("Lightnin' " Hopkins, "War News Blues")

In the quatrain-refrain verse shown below, a rhymed quatrain is followed by a two-line refrain. Each verse form occupies twelve measures or bars of music; in the quatrain-refrain form the quatrain occupies the first four of the twelve.

I got a job in a steel mill,
a-trucking steel like a slave.
For five long years every Friday
I went straight home with all my pay.
If you've ever been mistreated, you know just what I'm
talking about:
I worked five long years for one woman; she had the
nerve to throw me out.
(Eddie Boyd, "Five Long Years").

The tonal material in the blues scale (illustrated herewith) includes both major and minor thirds and sevenths and perfect and diminished fifths. Blues shares this tonal material with other African-American music, such as work songs, lined hymnody, gospel music, and jazz. A sharp rise to the highest pitch followed by a gradual descent characterizes the melodic contour of most vocal lines in each verse. Blues shares this contour with the field holler, a type of work song.

Blues has a distinctive harmonic structure. The first line of the verse (or the quatrain in the quatrain-refrain form) is supported by the tonic chord (and sometimes the subdominant, resolving to the tonic at the end of the line), the second line by the subdominant (resolving to the tonic), and the third line by the dominant seventh and then the subdominant before resolving to the tonic. Urban blues and jazz musicians modify this harmonic structure with altered chords and chord substitutions. The blues also has characteristic contents and performance styles. Most blues lyrics are dramatic monologues sung in the first person; most protest mistreatment by lovers and express a desire for freedom. Early blues singers improvised songs by yoking together lines and verses from a storehouse in their memories, while most of today's singers memorize entire songs.

Most early down-home blues singers accompanied themselves on piano or guitar, on the latter supplying a bass part with the right-hand thumb and a treble part independently with the right-hand fingers. Early vaudeville or classic blues singers were accompanied by pianists and small jazz combos. In the 1930s or after, blues "shouters" were accompanied by jazz and rhythm-and-blues bands, and this led in the 1940s to urban blues singers who played electric guitar and led their own bands. After World War II, most down-home blues singers played electric guitar, sometimes with a small combination of bass, drums, second guitar, harmonica, or piano.

The beginning of blues cannot be traced to a specific composer or date. The earliest appearance of music recognizable as the blues was the publication of W. C. Handy's "The Memphis Blues" (1912) and the "St. Louis Blues" (1914), but by his own testimony, Handy first heard the blues along the lower Mississippi River in the 1890s, and many historians agree with Handy that this was the likeliest environment for the origin of the blues. However, just when and where one locates the origin of blues depends upon what is considered sufficient to the genre. Some cultural historians locate the essence of the blues in resignation or in protest against mistreatment, and they believe that since slaves sung about their condition, these songs must have been blues, even though there is no evidence that they were called blues or that the verse or musical forms resembled later blues. Folklorists and musicologists, on the other hand, have constructed a narrower definition, essentializing structural aspects of the blues as well as their subject and relying for evidence on a combination of oral history, autobiography, and the first blues music recorded by the oldest generation of African Americans.

W. C. Handy (1873–1958) and Jelly Roll Morton (1890–1941), well-known and accomplished African-American musicians who were very much involved in music before the turn of the twentieth century, recalled in their autobiographies that blues began along the Mississippi in the 1890s as a secular dance music, accompanied by guitars and other portable instruments or piano, with more or less improvised verses, among the river roustabouts in the juke joints and barrelhouses and at picnic and other roadside entertainments. About 1900, folklorists first collected this music, but they did not realize they were witnessing the formation of a new genre. Verse patterns varied, with the only standard feature being the repetition of the first line—sometimes once, sometimes twice, sometimes three times. The verses were aphoristic, and their subjects concerned lovers, traveling, and daily aspects of life. Harmonic support often was confined to the tonic. The collectors did not call those songs blues, and one may suppose that the singers did not, either.

The first recordings of African Americans singing blues were not made until the 1920s, but it is clear that between 1890 and 1920 the blues developed into a named and recognizable musical genre. In this period the blues developed and diffused wherever there were African Americans in the United States, in the rural areas as well as the towns and cities and among the traveling stage shows. Ma Rainey (1886–1939), the "Mother of the Blues," claimed to have begun singing blues from the stage in 1902, while Jelly Roll Morton identified a blues ballad, "Betty and Dupree," as popular fare in New Orleans during the last years of the nineteenth century. Handy's "Memphis Blues" was used in the 1912 mayoralty campaign, while "St. Louis Blues" was a show tune designed to elevate blues to a higher class. Rural songs at country dance parties gradually consolidated toward three-line verse forms with twelve-measure stanzas and the typical harmonic pattern indicated above, while many of the stage songs featured two sections—an introduction followed by a section in recognizable blues form. The stage songs later became known as "classic" or "vaudeville" blues.

African Americans recorded vaudeville blues beginning with Mamie Smith (1883–1946) in 1920. Women with stage-show backgrounds, accompanied by pianists and small combos, sang blues songs composed by professional tunesmiths. The best of the vaudeville blues singers, Ma Rainey and Bessie Smith (1894?–1937), appealed across racial and class boundaries, and their singing styles revolutionized American popular music. In some of their blues, Rainey and Smith sang about strong, independent women who put an end to mistreatment. Rainey, who sang about such subjects as prostitution, lesbianism, and sadomasochistic relationships, may particularly be viewed as a spokesperson for women's rights. Other vaudeville blues singers, such as Mamie Smith, Sippie Wallace, Ida Cox, and Alberta Hunter, were also very popular in the 1920s, but the era of vaudeville or "classic" blues came to an end during the Great Depression. The down-home, or country-flavored, blues was recorded beginning in 1926, when record companies took portable recording equipment to southern cities and recorded the local men who sang the blues and accompanied themselves on guitars and pianos in the juke joints and at the country dance parties. Some of the older singers, such as Charley Patton (1891–1934) and Henry Thomas (1874–c. 1959) sang a variety of traditional songs, not all blues; others, such as Blind Lemon Jefferson (1897–1929), specialized in blues; while still others, such as Blind Blake (c.1893–c. 1933), achieved instrumental virtuosity that has never been surpassed. The variety of traditional music recorded by the older generation reveals the proto-blues as well as the blues and helps to show how the form evolved.

Geographic regions featured their own particular instrumental guitar styles before World War II. The down-home blues of Florida, Georgia, and the Carolinas tended toward rapidly finger-picked accompaniments: "ragtime" styles in which the right-hand thumb imitated the stride pianist's left hand, while the right-hand fingers played the melody. Blind Blake, Blind Boy Fuller (c. 1909–1941), and Blind Gary Davis (1896–1972) were among the first exponents of this East Coast style. In Mississippi, on the other hand, chord changes were not as pronounced, and accompaniments featured repeated figures, or riffs, rather than the melody of the verse. Charley Patton, "Son" House

John Lee Hooker (1917–2001). One of the earliest performers of blues on the electric guitar, Hooker crafted a distinctive vocal and instrumental style that helped shape the development of rock and folk music in the 1960s. © JACK VARTOOGIAN. REPRODUCED BY PERMISSION.

(1902–1988), Robert Johnson (c. 1911–1938), and Muddy Waters (McKinley Morganfield; 1915–1983) were outstanding guitarists in the Mississippi Delta style. Piano styles equally reflected regional differences. All embodied genuine innovations, such as bottleneck or slide guitar or imitating the expressiveness of the voice, and an inventiveness and technical accomplishment unparalleled in vernacular American music.

Down-home blues became so popular in the late 1920s that talent scouts arranged for singers to travel north to make recordings in the companies' home studios. Blues music was available on what were called "race records," 78-rpm records for African Americans, and they were advertised heavily in black newspapers like the *Chicago Defender*.

While early recordings offer the best evidence of the sound of blues music in its formative years, they can only begin to capture the feel of an actual performance. Because down-home blues usually was performed in barrelhouses, juke joints, and at parties and picnics—where the bootleg whiskey flowed, gambling took place, fighting was not uncommon, and sexual liaisons were formed—the music became associated with those who frequented these places. Churchgoers shunned blues because it was associated with sin, while middle-class blacks kept blues at a distance. Most communities, whether rural or urban, had their local blues musicians and entertainments, however. In the 1920s, blues was the most popular African-American music.

The Depression cut heavily into record sales and touring stage shows, and most of the classic blues singers' careers ended. The increasing popularity of jazz music, however, provided an opportunity for their successors to tour and record with jazz bands. The down-home blues continued unabated in the rural South and in the cities. A small number of outstanding down-home singers, including Tommy McClennan (1908–1960), Memphis Minnie (Douglas; 1897–1973), and Robert Johnson, made commercial recordings, but the big-band blues of Count Basie and other jazz bands, featuring blues "shouters" like Walter Brown, Jimmy Rushing, and "Hot Lips" Page, rode radio broadcasts and records to national popularity later in the 1930s. The blues form became a common ground for jazz improvisers, and jazz artists of the highest stature—from Louis Armstrong through Duke Ellington, Billie Holiday, and Charlie Parker, Sarah Vaughn, Miles Davis, John Coltrane, and Wynton Marsalis, composed and improvised a great many blues. For Charles Mingus (1922–1979), one of the most important jazz innovators of the 1950s and 1960s, blues and church music were the twin African-American cornerstones of jazz, and much of his music successfully integrated these roots into contemporary "soul" music. Indeed, since the 1940s, periodic reinvigorations of jazz have taken blues for their basis, and it appears that they will continue to do so: bop, hard bop, funk, and other jazz movements all looked for inspiration in blues roots.

Besides the jazz bands, blues in the 1940s and 1950s was featured in the urban and rhythm-and-blues bands led by such guitarists-singers as (Aaron) "T-Bone" Walker (1910–1975) and (Riley) B. B. King (b. 1925), whose spectacular instrumental innovations virtually defined urban blues and influenced countless blues and rock guitarists. Electronic amplification of the guitar allowed it to be heard above the piano and brass and reed instruments; Walker, with his pioneering efforts, invented the modern blues band, the core of which is an electric guitar accompanied by a rhythm section. King's live performances combined instrumental virtuosity in the service of great feeling with a powerful, expressive voice that transformed daily experience into meaningful art, and he spoke to and for an entire generation. His album *B. B. King Live at the Regal* (1965) is often cited as the finest blues recording ever made.

Down-home blues was well served in the years just after World War II by a host of new recording companies. Among the outstanding singer-guitarists were Sam "Lightnin'" Hopkins (1912–1982) from Houston and John Lee Hooker (1917–2001) from Mississippi (and later Detroit) who, along with harmonica-player Sonny Boy Williamson (Rice Miller; 1899–1965; known to blues aficionados as "the second sonny boy," to distinguish him from the first recorded Sonny Boy Williamson, John Lee Williamson [1914-1948], although Rice Miller claimed to have been the original Sonny Boy) contributed a magnificent body of original blues lyric poetry. The Mississippi Delta connection led to such singers as Muddy Waters and Howlin' Wolf (Chester Burnett; 1910–1976), who led small combos in Chicago after 1945 that helped create the Chicago blues style, basically a version of the Delta blues played on electrified and amplified instruments. Muddy Waters' band of the early 1950s, featuring Little Walter (Jacobs; 1930–1968) on amplified harmonica, defined a classic Chicago blues sound that many think was the high point of the genre. With his horn-influenced, amplified harmonica solos, Little Walter invented a completely new sound, and his work stands as another influential example in a music with a history of astonishing technological innovation in the service of greater expressivity. A cluster of post–World War II artists, including Waters, Wolf, Jimmy Reed (1925–1976), John Lee Hooker, Elmore James, Little Walter, Sonny Boy Williamson, and others, greatly influenced rock and roll in the 1960s, while a number of similar artists, relying heavily on blues, such as Fats Domino and Chuck Berry, helped to define rock and roll in the 1950s.

In the 1960s, the African-American audience for blues declined, while the white audience increased and the first "blues revival" occurred. Young white musicians and researchers rediscovered older down-home blues singers such as Son House (1902–1988) and Mississippi John Hurt (1893–1966), and blues singers and bands became featured acts in coffeehouses, clubs, and festivals that catered to a college-age white audience. Many blues singers' musical careers were extended by this attention. Young white musicians began to play and sing the music, and, along with traditional blues musicians, found a new audience. Earlier recordings were reissued for collectors, research magazines devoted to blues appeared, and cultural historians and scholars began writing about the music. Although black musicians continue to perform blues in traditional, and now tourist, venues (bars, juke joints, etc.), particularly in Chicago and in the Mississippi Delta, since the 1960s newer styles such as Motown, soul music, disco, funk, rap, and hip-hop eclipsed blues as popular music among African Americans.

In the early 1990s, fueled by the success of the *Blues Brothers* film, and the release on CD of the complete recordings of Robert Johnson, another blues revival began to take place. As a resurgence of interest in blues continues, older blues recordings are being reissued on CD, while younger singers and musicians, black and white, increasingly choose to perform and record blues. Blues radio shows have increased the music's visibility and popularity. Blues now appears as background music for ads on radio and television; nightclubs for tourists featuring blues can now be found in many American cities; and older artists such as Buddy Guy have revived their careers, while younger artists such as Keb' Mo (Kevin Moore) and Bobby Rush have come to prominence. Some cities and states, such as Memphis, Chicago, and Mississippi, promote blues as cultural tourism, and there are blues museums and monuments as well. While blues was a music in decline in the 1960s, known outside African-American culture only to a small number of aficionados, today the blues is historicized, an official part of American and African-American culture. And while literary critics and cultural historians once saw little use for the blues, viewing it as a music of slave-consciousness and resignation, today a respected generation of African-American writers, such as Henry Louis Gates Jr. and Houston Baker, see blues as a source of black pride and a root tradition. As such, blues has had a profound effect upon African-American life, and upon popular culture throughout the world wherever it and its musical offspring have spread.

See also Blues in African-American Culture; Blueswomen of the 1920s and 1930s; Jazz; Music in the United States; Rhythm and Blues

Bibliography

Baker, Houston. *Blues, Ideology, and Afro-American Literature: A Vernacular Theory.* Chicago: University of Chicago Press, 1984.

Blues, The. Thirteen-part series broadcast on National Public Radio to commemorate "The Year of the Blues," 2003. Information available from <http://www.yearoftheblues.org/radio/index.asp.>

Davis, Angela Y. *Blues Legacies and Black Feminism: Gertrude "Ma" Rainey, Bessie Smith, and Billie Holiday.* New York: Pantheon, 1998.

Evans, David. *Big Road Blues: Tradition and Creativity in the Folk Blues.* Berkeley: University of California Press, 1982.

Gates, Henry Louis, Jr. *The Signifying Monkey: A Theory of African-American Literary Criticism.* New York: Oxford University Press, 1988.

George, Nelson. *The Death of Rhythm and Blues.* New York: Pantheon, 1988. Reprint, New York: Penguin, 2004.

Gordon, Robert. *Can't Be Satisfied: The Life and Times of Muddy Waters.* Boston: Little, Brown, 2002.

King, B. B., with Dave Ritz. *Blues All around Me: The Autobiography of B. B. King.* New York: Avon, 1996.

Moore, Allan, ed. *The Cambridge Companion to Blues and Gospel Music.* Cambridge, UK: Cambridge University Press, 2002.

Palmer, Robert. *Deep Blues.* New York: Viking, 1981.

Titon, Jeff Todd, ed. *Downhome Blues Lyrics: An Anthology from the Post–World War II Era.* 2d ed. Urbana: University of Illinois Press, 1990.

Titon, Jeff Todd. *Early Downhome Blues: A Musical and Cultural Analysis.* 2d ed. Chapel Hill: University of North Carolina Press, 1994.

JEFF TODD TITON (1996)
Updated by author 2005

The Blues in African-American Culture

The blues are, or have been, many things within the space of African-American culture, and those things inevitably show up in opposed pairs. The blues are a lowdown lonesome feeling, a song of abandonment and despair, but they're also a kind of euphoria, a freedom cry of lusty survivorship and deliverance down the open road. The blues are about poverty and bottom-of-the-barrel hard times, but they're also—in the hands of a skilled bluesman like B. B. King or Honeyboy Edwards—a pretty good way of hustling a living from a black public that values your gifts. (See Edwards's 1996 autobiography, *The World Don't Owe Me Nothing.*) The blues are kerosene lamps and backwoods jooks and homemade corn liquor; the blues are so country they have mud squishing between their toes. But the blues are also about Saturday night in the big city: slipping into your red dress or your pinstriped suit and cruising downtown (or uptown) behind the wheel of your Terraplane or Rocket 88, manifesting the sort of elegant high style celebrated by Albert Murray in *Stomping the Blues* (1976). The blues are the devil's music—and assailed as such by certain sectors of the churchgoing black middle class—but the devilishly resourceful transformations they celebrate are the gifts of the African trickster deity Legba, god of the crossroads: a place where opposites come together and unsettle the world in explosively creative and liberating ways.

The blues, in short, are dialectical. They defy every effort to constrain or define or decisively pronounce on them—as African Americans, survivors and singers of the blues, have continually recreated and liberated themselves within the problematic confines of American history. As James Cone argues in *The Spirituals and the Blues* (1972), the blues may "have roots stretching back into slavery days and even to Africa" (Cone, 1991, p. 98). But the blues, as an African-American folk music and distinctive form of vernacular expression, do not blossom into being until the dark days of the 1890s, when Jim Crow segregation begins to harden, the promise of sociopolitical and economic equality vanishes, and lynching becomes a public sport across the South. "[T]he blues ain't slave music," insists Kalamu ya Salaam in *What Is Life?: Reclaiming the Black Blues Self* (1994). "[D]idn't no slaves sing the blues. [W]e didn't become blue until after reconstruction, after freedom day and the dashing of all hopes of receiving/attaining our promised 40acres&1mule" (Salaam, 1994, p. 7). The blues are, in other words, what Amiri Baraka called the "changing same" of African-American culture: They've been around forever, seemingly, but they've proven endlessly responsive to the fresh hopes and bitter disillusionments that characterize black life in modern America, whenever you define "modern" as beginning.

Writing the Blues

If the blues now seem like a central component of the African-American cultural imagination, much of the credit must go to three black writers—a songwriter/autobiographer, a poet, and an anthropologist/novelist—who helped transform blues song and blues culture into popular blues texts. W. C. Handy, Langston Hughes, and Zora Neale Hurston were each, in their own distinctive ways, educated middle-class celebrants of unlettered working-class blues people.

W. C. Handy (1873–1958), the so-called Father of the Blues, was an Alabama-born son and grandson of Methodist ministers who abdicated the family calling to make his living in black show business during the 1890s. After a four-year stint as a bandleader with Mahara's Minstrels, a touring theatrical troupe, Handy moved to Clarksdale, Mississippi, in 1903. He soon encountered the blues in the form of a "lean, loose-jointed Negro" guitar-man at a Delta train station who was singing "the weirdest music I had ever heard" (Handy, 1991, p. 74), a life-changing experience that he later recounted in his celebrated autobiography, *Father of the Blues* (1941). Determined to transform this new and distinctive black folk music into American pop music, Handy is credited with the first blues instrumental hit, "Memphis Blues" (1912), and perhaps the most widely recorded blues song of all time, "St. Louis Blues" (1914). One of the first "talkies" (movies with a synchronized soundtrack), in fact, was a short entitled "St.

Louis Blues" (1927) that featured blues queen Bessie Smith singing Handy's hit.

Langston Hughes (1902–1967), born in Joplin, Missouri, and raised in Lawrence, Kansas, first heard the blues on Independence Avenue in Kansas City, Missouri, and later absorbed a wide variety of blues styles in Chicago, Harlem, Paris, and Washington, D.C. In 1925, with a poem entitled "The Weary Blues," Hughes inaugurated an aesthetic revolution: He was the first American writer to translate the three-line "AAB" lyric structure of blues song into a six-line poetic stanza, injecting blues rhythms and the earthiest of blues themes into an American literary tradition that had preferred to see black folk culture through the distorting stereotypes of blackface minstrelsy. If Hughes's first volume of blues-accented poems, *The Weary Blues* (1926), saw him celebrated as the "busboy poet," then his second volume, *Fine Clothes to the Jew* (1927), saw him harshly criticized in the black press as "the poet low-rate" (rather than "laureate") of Harlem: He had dared to let his blues people speak in their own vernacular voices about love, lust, loss, and violent revenge. Hughes held firm to his conviction about the artistic validity of black popular music in a manifesto entitled "The Negro Artist and the Racial Mountain" (1926). "Let the blare of Negro jazz bands," he wrote, "and the bellowing voice of Bessie Smith singing Blues penetrate the closed ears of the colored near-intellectuals until they listen and perhaps understand" (Hughes, 1994, p. 59). Every twenty-first century poet who strives to write a blues poem—or, for that matter, a jazz poem, or a hip-hop poem—owes a debt to Hughes for his pioneering work.

Zora Neale Hurston (1891–1960) was, in some sense, more naturally aligned with the blues than Handy or Hughes, growing up as she had in a small Florida town where "box pickers" (guitarists) of local renown frequently entertained crowds on the front porch of a local dry-goods store. Yet Hurston's most important contribution to our understanding of African-American blues culture came as a result of several extended visits she made to the jooks, the backwoods blues clubs, of a lumber camp in Polk County, Florida—a subculture that no other anthropologist, black or white, had ever investigated. Her vivid descriptions of Big Sweet, Lucy, Ella Wall, and the other tough-talking, razor-wielding blueswomen helped animate both her germinal volume of black folklore, *Mules and Men* (1935), and her autobiography, *Dust Tracks on a Road* (1942). An amateur blues singer and harmonica player in her own right, Hurston used her juke-joint experiences to create the central character of her best-known novel, *Their Eyes Were Watching God* (1937): Tea Cake, the joyous, playful, sometimes violent young Florida bluesman who helps liberate the novel's heroine, Janie Crawford Killicks Starks, by convincing her to follow him down onto the "muck" of Florida's Lake Okeechobee region where "blues are made and used right on the spot" (Hurston, 1990, p. 125).

The Black Arts Movement and After

Between 1920, when Mamie Smith's recording of "Crazy Blues" became a race-records sensation, and 1961, when Jimmy Reed's "Baby What You Want Me to Do" was a top-ten hit in Chicago, blues music was arguably *the* black popular music: not just a commodity, but a way of life and a worldview. All that changed in the course of the 1960s, as soul music swept across black America and the black youth market for blues—much to the chagrin of blues performers such as Muddy Waters and B. B. King—effectively disappeared. To a prideful and assertive new generation, blues music seemed old, tired, worn-out, politically retrograde. The blues, in this view, were the soundtrack of segregation and resignation rather than the battle cry of black collective progress and radical self-fashioning. "blues ain't culture," wrote Sonia Sanchez in "liberation / poem." "they sounds of / oppression / against the white man's / shit. . . .blues is struggle / strangulation / of our people / cuz we cudn't off the / white motha / fucka. . . ." (Sanchez, 1970, p. 54). Sanchez and many of her fellow writers and intellectuals in the black arts movement rejected the blues with as much vehemence as they critiqued the pandemic racism of white America. "[T]he blues are invalid," Maulana Ron Karenga famously declaimed in an 1968 essay in *Negro Digest*, "for they teach resignation, in a word acceptance of reality—and we have come to change reality" (Karenga, 1968, p. 9).

For another cohort of black arts writers led by poet and critic Larry Neal, however, the blues were something quite different: a cherished ancestral rootstock, an inalienably black cultural inheritance that could be put to political as well as aesthetic good use. "The blues," Neal argued in "The Ethos of the Blues" (1972), "represent. . .the essential vector of the Afro-American sensibility and identity. . . . [T]he blues are basically defiant in their attitude toward life. They are about survival on the meanest, most gut level of human existence" (Neal, 1972, p. 42). These blues were not sorrow songs but *survivor* songs, a cultural resource that had long sustained, and continued to sustain, a beleaguered but resourceful people. African-American writers of the 1960s who embraced the blues on these terms include Kalamu ya Salaam, Stanley Crouch, Jayne Cortez, Quincy Troupe, Eugene Redmond, and Nikki Giovanni, among others.

Although blues music would, with notable regional exceptions, never again regain its former chart-topping position in the black pop mainstream after the early 1960s, the blues continued to resonate loudly within African-American culture—a direct result, arguably, of Larry Neal's determination to celebrate what he called "the blues god" through a period of political upheaval. Contemporary African-American literature, in particular, embodies the blue-toned legacy of the black arts movement: writers such as Toni Morrison (*The Bluest Eye*), August Wilson (*Ma Rainey's Black Bottom*), Alice Walker (*The Color Purple*), Gayl Jones (*Corregidora*), Sherley Anne Williams (*Some One Sweet Angel Child*), Sterling Plumpp (*Blues: The Story Always Untold*), Eugene Redmond (*The Eye in the Ceiling*), Arthur Flowers (*Another Good Loving Blues*), Bebe Moore Campbell (*Your Blues Ain't Like Mine*), Walter Mosley (*RLs Dream*), and Kevin Young (*Jelly Roll: A Blues*) all testify to their enduring vitality and validity. To this richly varied list must be added a second list of contemporary African-American historians and theorizers of the blues: Amiri Baraka (*Blues People* and *Black Music*), Houston A. Baker Jr. (*Blues, Ideology, and Afro-American Literature*), Jon Michael Spencer (*Blues and Evil*), Albert Murray (*The Blue Devils of Nada*), Angela Y. Davis (*Blues Legacies and Black Feminism*), and Tony Bolden (*Afro-Blue*). African-American literature at the dawn of the second millennium is, by any measure, supremely conscious of its southern-born vernacular taproot.

Blues Across the Arts

African-American literature is, of course, merely one place on the cultural landscape where blues energies have registered their bittersweet lyrical presence. The art world is another: Both fine art and folk or "outsider" art have found ways of translating the cackling audacity, dialectical swing, and down-home grit of the blues into visual terms. Critic Richard J. Powell has praised the "blues aesthetic" of African-American artists Romare Bearden, Aaron Douglas, and Alison Saar for embodying the collage-based "will to adorn" celebrated by Zora Neale Hurston in "Characteristics of Negro Folk Expression" (1934). The Mississippi Delta, ancestral home of the blues, happens also to be a haven for blues-based folk art, from the playfully morbid clay skulls (adorned with real human teeth) constructed by the late bluesman James "Son" Thomas to the homemade guitars that Clarksdale bluesman James "Super Chikan" Johnson hammers together out of gas cans.

Blues photography has more often than not been the province of white American and European photographers and folklorists; the notable African-American exception is Ernest Withers, whose *The Memphis Blues Again* (2001) vibrantly documents the Memphis years of B. B. King, Bobby "Blue" Bland, Little Walter, Howlin' Wolf, and other legends. When the blues have found their way onto film, they've generally done so in the form of concert footage or documentaries, although Steven Spielberg's cinematic retelling of Alice Walker's novel *The Color Purple* (1985) contained a piquant juke-joint performance by actress Margaret Avery in the role of blues diva "Shug" Avery.

Apart from literature, it is on the stage—the dramatic and musical theater stage—where the blues have registered most forcefully within contemporary African-American culture. If playwright August Wilson is the acknowledged master of the field with works such as *Ma Rainey's Black Bottom* (1984), *The Piano Lesson* (1995), and *Seven Guitars* (1996), then blues drama as a whole experienced a renaissance during the final decade of the twentieth century. *Mule Bone,* a play coauthored by Langston Hughes and Zora Neale Hurston in the early 1930s, was staged for the first time in 1991 with Baton Rouge bluesman Kenny Neal in the leading role. Other notable blues theatricals include *Thunder Knocking on the Door* (1999), coauthored by playwright Keith Glover and blues performer Keb' Mo', and *Lackawanna Blues* (2001), which paired actor Reuben Santiago-Hudson and bluesman Bill Sims Jr. In 1999 the Broadway revue *It Ain't Nothin' But the Blues* won two Tony Awards before touring regionally, recreating a series of classic blues tableaux—back porches down South, smoky bars up North—as showcases for the innate theatricality of blues standards such as "Crawling Kingsnake" and "Someone Else Is Steppin' In."

Blues Legacies

Despite frequent advisories to the contrary, blues music—live, recorded, broadcast—remains a significant, if somewhat diminished presence in contemporary African-American culture. This is due in no small part to the unexpected small-market success of two mid-1980s hits: Z. Z. Hill's "Down Home Blues" (1982) and Little Milton's "The Blues Is Alright" (1984). Evincing both nostalgia for the "down home" South that northern black migrants had left behind and a prideful assertion of the continuing relevance of a blues-based sensibility, the two hits helped anchor a resurgent black southern market in what came to be known as "soul blues," a fusion of Memphis soul, synthesizer-tinged disco, gospel, and electric blues. Jackson, Mississippi, is the home of contemporary soul blues, thanks to Malaco Records and the American Blues Radio Network; recent hitmakers include Sir Charles Jones ("Love Machine"), Marvin Sease ("Women Would Rather Be Licked"), Peggy Scott-Adams ("Hot and Sassy"), and

Gertrude "Ma" Rainey (1886–1939) performs in Chicago with the Georgia Jazz Band, 1923. *Among the best and most influential blues singers of the 1920s and 1930s, Rainey came to be known as the "Mother of the Blues."* ARCHIVE PHOTOS. REPRODUCED BY PERMISSION.

Willie Clayton ("Call Me Mr. C"). Finally, the sort of rough-and-ready backwoods blues that Zora Neale Hurston encountered down in Polk County, Florida, remains a surprisingly vital presence among a working-class black clientele in parts of the Deep South. The legendary jook in Chulahoma, Mississippi, at which bluesmen Junior Kimbrough and R. L. Burnside used to preside burned down in 1999, the year after Kimbrough's death, but various sons, a grandson, and cousins currently play at and preside over the Burnside Blues Café in nearby Holly Springs. Mississippi jooks such as Po' Monkeys in Merigold, Bug's Place in Rosedale, and Betty's Place in Sandyland keep the blues alive: a homespun alternative to MTV and a key component of a far-reaching African-American cultural legacy.

See also Beardon, Romare; Blues, The; Douglas, Aaron; Harlem, NY; Harlem Renaissance; Hughes, Langston; Hurston, Zora Neale; Music in the United States; Neal, Larry; Saar, Allison; Wilson, August

Bibliography

Barlow, William. *"Looking Up at Down": The Emergence of Blues Culture.* Philadelphia: Temple University Press, 1989.

Cone, James H. *The Spirituals and the Blues: An Interpretation.* New York: Seabury Press, 1972. Reprint, Maryknoll, N.Y.: Orbis, 1991.

Edwards, David Honeyboy, as told to Janis Martinson and Michael Robert Frank. *The World Don't Owe Me Nothing: The Life and Times of Delta Bluesman Honeyboy Edwards.* Chicago: Chicago Review Press, 1997.

Handy, W. C. *Father of the Blues: An Autobiography.* New York: Macmillan, 1941. Reprint, New York: Da Capo, 1991.

Hughes, Langston. "The Negro Artist and the Racial Mountain." In *Within the Circle: An Anthology of African American Literary Criticism from the Harlem Renaissance to the Present,* edited by Angelyn Mitchel. London and Durham, N.C.: Duke University Press, 1994.

Hurston, Zora Neale. *Their Eyes Were Watching God.* New York: Perennial, 1990.

Karenga, Ron. "Black Art: A Rhythmic Reality of Revolution." *Negro Digest* 17, no. 3 (1968).

Neal, Larry. "The Ethos of the Blues." *The Black Scholar* (Summer 1972).

Oakley, Giles. *The Devil's Music: A History of the Blues.* New York: Taplinger, 1977.

Oliver, Paul. *Blues Fell This Morning: Meaning in the Blues.* 2d ed. New York: Cambridge University Press, 1990.

Salaam, Kalamu ya. *What Is Life? Reclaiming the Black Blues Self.* Chicago: Third World Press, 1994.

Sanchez, Sonia. "liberation / poem." *We a BaddDDD People.* Detroit, Mich.: Broadside Press, 1970.

ADAM GUSSOW (2005)

Blueswomen of the 1920s and 1930s

Bessie Smith (c. 1892–1937), Mamie Smith (1893–1946), and Gertrude "Ma" Rainey (1886–1939) are perhaps the most recognizable names of women blues singers of the 1920s. They were contemporaries, however, of approximately one hundred women who performed in vaudeville, stage shows, and small clubs and cabarets during that decade. Mamie Smith's second recording, "Crazy Blues" on General Phonograph's Okeh label, was an unexpected success in 1920 and spurred a rapid movement by record companies, songwriters, singers, and musicians to capitalize on women's blues. Black songwriters such as William C. Handy (1873–1958), Perry Bradford (1893–1970), and Clarence Williams (1898–1965) were pioneers in obtaining recording contracts for women singers. It is ironic, therefore, that the two most popular, experienced, and accomplished blues singers at that time—Bessie Smith and Rainey, who had developed their talent and repertoires on the vaudeville circuit in the first two decades of the twentieth century—were not recorded until 1923. Nevertheless, Mamie's fortuitous success led to twenty years of recordings, stage shows, and movies for dozens of women. Some of the women who left the traveling show circuits, cabarets, and nightclubs of the South, Southwest, and North to become the next "blues queen" on recordings had exceptional talent and ingenuity that they employed to enhance their performances on record and on stage. Others were mediocre talents, though their stylish gowns, physical attractiveness, and ability to entertain endeared them to audiences in the North and South. Many of these women were sent on tours with bands that included some of the most talented musicians of the day. Among these were stellar artists such as Louis Armstrong, Johnny Dunn, Sidney Bechet, Clarence Williams, Kid Ory, Johnny Dodds, Don Redman, Fletcher Henderson, Thomas Dorsey (who later became renown for his role in developing gospel music), and, notably, two women pianist-composers, Lovie Austin (1887–1972) and Lil Hardin (1898–1971).

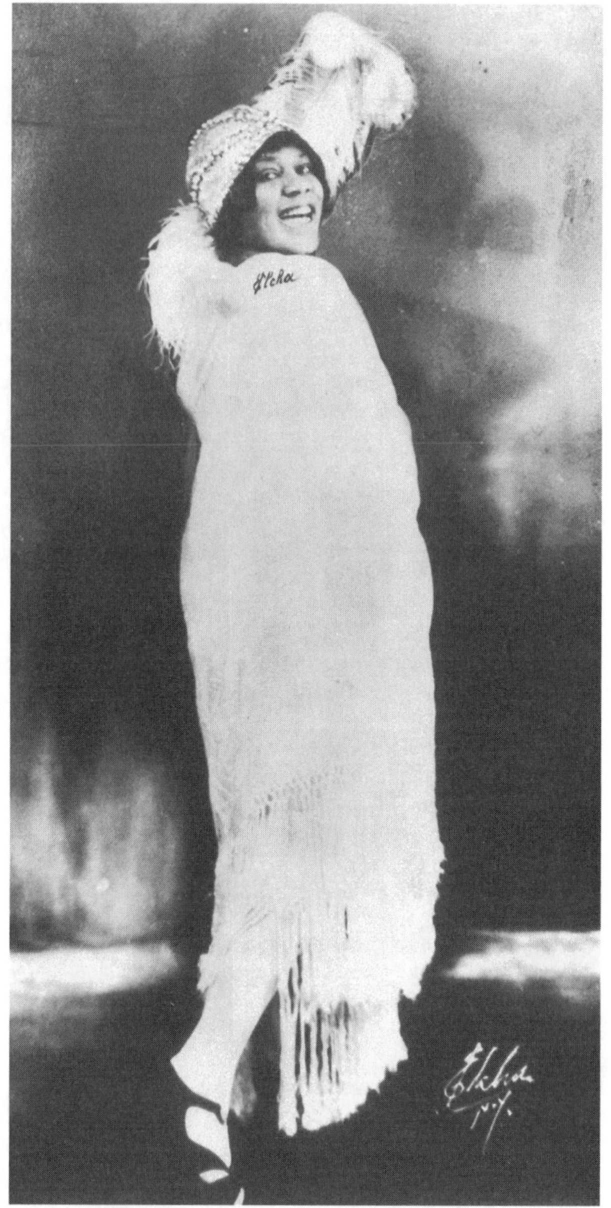

Bessie Smith (c. 1894–1937). *The "Empress of the Blues," pictured here in a 1924 photograph, Smith was born into poverty, singing for coins on street corners in Chattanooga, but rose to fame as one of the most gifted and accomplished blues singers of her era.* THE BETTMANN ARCHIVE. REPRODUCED BY PERMISSION.

During the1920s, more than one hundred women were recorded on labels ranging from Okeh, the pioneer of women's blues recordings, to Paramount, Columbia, and small labels such as Charles Pace and William Handy's unsuccessful Swan Records. Blues were composed at an astonishing rate by Bradford, Handy, Clarence Williams, and some of the women singers, although comparatively few made multiple recordings or had careers that lasted several years. However, they established black women as essential to the recording industry. This array of talent included deep-voiced moaners, brassy shouters, and lilting light sopranos. Bessie Smith, Ma Rainey, Clara Smith (1894–1935), Sippie Wallace (1878–1986), Victoria Spivey (1906–1976), and Ida Cox (1886–1967) did not have beautiful or even pleasant voices (in the narrow aesthetic sense), but they represented the voices of the folk roots that nurtured them. All of their recordings are earthy, and many were confrontational on issues of infidelity, poverty, racism, mistreatment by lovers, aesthetics of physical beauty, desertion, natural disasters, and sometimes the supernatural.

Although many of the blues recorded in the 1920s and 1930s were written by men, both black and white, most of the women had performed in local venues where they grew up or lived before going on the vaudeville circuit. Therefore, some of their experiences contributed to their blues creations. Sippie Thomas Wallace, Victoria Spivey, and Ma Rainey were "making" their own blues in their early teens at house parties, picnics, or local clubs. Even as preteens, Wallace and Spivey played piano at picnics and house parties in Texas. Wallace's family was evidently quite musical and included her brothers—the bandleader and composer George and the talented pianist Hersal. According to Spivey, her father, Grant, played a stringed instrument. She taught herself to play piano and gained experience playing for silent movies in Dallas, Texas, but her blues training came at parties or picnics playing with blues men such as "Blind Lemon" Jefferson (1897–1929). Later, as a song transcriber in Missouri, Spivey developed her songwriting skills and eventually became a prolific composer of blues. Her lyrics were often scathing in their attack on the racial injustice and poverty that blacks suffered. She and Ida Cox also incorporated superstition in their lyrics.

Many of the blues written by women tended to deal with two-timing men, loss of control over their lives, and traveling away from a bad relationship or loneliness. However, violence, prostitution, fear, retribution, disease, and poor health, as well as natural disasters, were sung about. For example, Spivey's "T. B. Blues" laments deaths caused by the dreaded disease tuberculosis, which plagued poor people, and in other songs she comments on the squalor of the New York prison known as "the Tombs." She openly addressed "dope" as a ravaging menace spreading failure and crime in New York. Consequently, the listener has to listen closely to the lyrics, not just the music or the beat, in order to understand the gravity, desperation, threat, advice, or sheer sensuality and delight that are often couched in metaphors or folk language. Cox seemed to be particularly concerned with death, the supernatural and most convincingly with poverty and suffering as in songs such as "Death Letter Blues," "Mojo Hand Blues," "Hard Times Blues," and "Pink Slip Blues." Her traveling show, the "Raisin' Cain" revue, was so popular that it was the first show to open at the Apollo in 1929. She was one of the few "blues queens" to continue performing into the 1930s, playing with her pianist-bandleader husband, Jesse Crump.

Towards the end of the 1920s, the approaching Depression took its toll on blacks who were already at the low end of the economic scale, and women's blues began to address the injustices that their people confronted. Although the "classic blues" era supposedly ended by 1930, many of the women continued to perform in theaters and clubs in the South and North.

Recordings by country-style singers illustrate the significant differences in voice quality and vocal styling that distinguished them from their "classic" counterparts. They came from the Mississippi Delta, Alabama, Texas, Kansas, and other areas. The majority of their recordings were made between 1926 and 1937. Among them were singers who had less fame than the Smiths or Cox or Rainey, but they endured and adapted to the changing demands of the market, advances in recording technology, and radio. Lucille Bogan (1897–1948, aka Bessie Jackson) was a prime example of the "country style" singer who demonstrated that timing, phrasing, and a choice selection of subject matter could overcome limited vocal talent. Although she began recording around 1923, she continued performing and recording until the mid-1930s. She seldom strayed from her dry, down-home style, whether she was singing "Women Won't Need No Men" or "B. D. Woman's Blues." Both of these blues imply that women can fare as well without men as with them. The lyrics of the former assert that "there'll come a time [when] women ain't gonna need no men" to take care of their physical or sexual needs, but it is ambiguous enough to consider it a call for women's liberation. The latter is a bold interpretation of a blues about homosexual women that Rainey recorded in the early 1920s. Other country-style singers were Pearl Dickson, Lottie Kimbrough, and Bobby Cadillac.

One of the most gifted of the country blues women at the turn of the decade was Minnie Douglas (1897–1973), later known as Memphis Minnie. According to her biographers Paul and Beth Garon, Minnie's guitar-playing talent surpassed that of most men during the 1930s, but, surprisingly, she was not rare among southern women musicians in her choice of instrument. Memphis Minnie began playing banjo in her preteens and switched to the guitar in the 1920s. Her earliest recordings were made in Chicago with her first husband, "Kansas" Joe McCoy, with

Mamie Smith and the Jazz Hounds. The first African-American female recording star, Smith helped spark the blues craze of the 1920s and 1930s with her recording of "Crazy Blues" (1920). PHOTOGRAPHS AND PRINTS DIVISION, SCHOMBURG CENTER FOR RESEARCH IN BLACK CULTURE, THE NEW YORK PUBLIC LIBRARY, ASTOR, LENOX AND TILDEN FOUNDATIONS.

Minnie playing lead guitar parts that she composed. She constantly revised her "Bumblebee Blues," because her fans insisted on it at every performance ("bee" was a metaphor for sexual performance).

Trixie Smith (1895–1943), who recorded several "railroad" blues in the 1920s, had a dry vocal style that became richer as she matured. Her 1938 rendition of "My Daddy Rocks Me," backed by Charlie Shavers, Sidney Bechet, Sammy Price, and others, is illustrative of the transformation of a simple blues into a fine jazz piece. This period afforded some of the "classic blues singers" an opportunity to break from the old blues formula and to become more creative and improvisatory. Likewise, Cox's 1939 reprise of one of her most popular blues, "Four Day Creep," with Sammy Price's swinging piano ensemble giving it a touch of quiet melancholy, was totally different from the slow-paced 1920s version.

Though less known and celebrated, Bertha "Chippie" Hill (1900–1950) was a blues shouter in the style of the 1920s singers Rainey, Bessie Smith, and Clara Smith. She also followed the vaudeville trail to New York, but ended up singing in whiskey joints and small clubs. Her first recording was on the Okeh label in 1925. However, her best output was in the late 1930s and early 1940s as a mature performer. "Trouble in Mind" and "Lonesome Road" demonstrated her superb musicianship.

Historically, the most stunning set of 1930s blues was not performed on stage or recorded in a studio, but rather on location at the infamous Parchman Farm, a notoriously brutal penitentiary in Mississippi. The ethnomusicologist Alan Lomax (1915–2002) captured the voices of incarcerated women who sang about forced labor, sex, unwanted pregnancies, and party games. These blues are probably the most authentic in the rawest sense. They speak of life as it was lived, not as imagined by some of the singers, composers, or musicians who became famous on various records or stages.

The blues women of the 1920s and 1930s sang, played, and wrote about life as they experienced it or as they imagined it could be, and they left a rich legacy of variety, comedy, pathos, and sheer musical joy.

See also Blues, The; Blues in African-American Culture; Music in the United States; Rainey, Ma; Smith, Bessie; Smith, Mamie

Bibliography

Baraka, Imama Amiri (Jones, LeRoi). *Blues People: Negro Music in White America.* New York: William Morrow, 1963.

Barlow, William. *"Looking Up At Down" The Emergence of Blues Culture.* Philadelphia: Temple University Press, 1989.

Cowley, John, and Paul Oliver, eds. *The New Blackwell Guide to the Blues.* Cambridge, Mass.: Blackwell, 1996.

Evans, David. *Big Road Blues: Tradition and Creativity in the Folk Blues.* Berkeley: University of California Press, 1982.

Garon, Paul, and Beth Garon. *Woman With Guitar: Memphis Minnie's Blues.* New York: Da Capo, 1992.

Handy, W. C., ed. *Blues: An Anthology* (1926). New York: Macmillan, 1981.

Harrison, Daphne Duval. *Black Pearls: Blues Queens of the 1920s.* New Brunswick, N.J.: Rutgers University Press, 1988.

Lieb, Sandra R. *Mother of the Blues: A Study of Ma Rainey.* Amherst: University of Massachusetts Press, 1981.

Murray, Albert. *Stomping the Blues.* New York: McGraw-Hill, 1976.

Nicholas, A. X., ed. *Woke Up This Mornin': Poetry of the Blues.* New York: Bantam, 1973.

Oakley, Giles. *The Devil's Music: A History of the Blues.* New York: Taplinger, 1976.

Oliver, Paul, ed. *The Blackwell Guide to Blues Records.* Cambridge, Mass.: Blackwell, 1989.

Long Playing Records (33 1/3)

Bogan, Lucille. *Women Won't Need No Men.* AGRAM, Blues AB 2005.

Classic Blues Women. Blues Masters, Vol. 2. Rhino R2 71134.

Hill, Bertha. *Bertha "Chippie" Hill: Complete Recorded Works 1925–1929.* Document DOCD 5330, Au.

Memphis Minnie. *In My Girlish Days, 1930-1935.* Travelin' Man TM 803.

Spivey, Victoria. *Victoria Spivey: Complete Recorded Works, Volume 1.* DOCD 5318.

Super Sisters. Independent Women's Blues, Vol. 3. Rosetta Records.

Compact Discs

Cox, Ida. *The Essential Ida Cox.* Classic Blues CBL2000017.

Ladies of Blues, Vols. 1 and 2. CRG-1525-1526.

Memphis Minnie. *Moonshine.* Columbia River CRG 120005.

Smith, Bessie. *Bessie Smith: The Complete Recordings, Volume 4.* 2 CD set. Columbia C2K 52838/472834-2.

Smith, Clara. *The Essential Clara Smith.* Classic Blues CD200027.

Spivey, Victoria. *The Essential Victoria Spivey.* 2 CD set. Classic Blues 200014.

DAPHNE D. HARRISON (2005)

Blyden, Edward Wilmot

August 3, 1832
February 7, 1912

The Liberian nationalist Edward W. Blyden was born on the Caribbean island of St. Thomas. He was the son of free blacks—Romeo, a tailor, and Judith, a schoolteacher—and was the third of seven children. As early as 1842, while in Porto Bello, Venezuela, he began to develop a facility with language. He also became more acutely aware that the majority of people of African descent in the Americas were slaves, and this affected the future course of his life. Upon returning to St. Thomas, Blyden attended school and completed a five-year apprenticeship as a tailor. He grew interested in becoming a minister after meeting a Dutch Reformed minister, Rev. John P. Knox.

Knox was instrumental in Blyden's decision to come to the United States in 1850 and seek admission to Rutgers Theological College. Blyden was prevented from entering the school, however, because of his race. This experience, coupled with his devotion to further the black struggle, led him to support the African colonization movement. Less than a year after entering the United States, Blyden emigrated to Liberia with the support of members of the American Colonization Society (ACS).

Once in Liberia, Blyden entered school and prepared himself for a leadership role. His education was enhanced by travels to Europe, the Middle East, and throughout Africa. By 1858 he had been ordained a Presbyterian minister and accepted a position as principal of a high school in Liberia. He also served as a government correspondent and editor for the government newspaper, the *Liberian Herald,* for a year. His most important appointment was from 1880 to 1884 as president of Liberia College, which was overseen by a board of trustees in Boston and New York.

While Blyden was unable to receive all the formal educational training he hoped for, his vision for Liberia and for all people of African descent was defined in his writings. He argued that the African race had made significant contributions to human civilization and that African cultural institutions and customs should be preserved. He expressed the view that Islam had served Africa better than Christianity had, but that there was much for Africa to learn from the West. The essence of Blyden's thoughts was contained in his books *Hope for Africa* (1861), *Christianity, Islam and the Negro Race* (1887), and *African Life and Customs* (1908). A major portion of his writings focused on the colonization of blacks in Liberia. He envisioned that, with the emigration of highly educated blacks, Liberia could reach its full potential and become an example of the capabilities of the African race to the world.

Blyden was a major supporter of the ACS, which had founded Liberia in 1821. This organization was instrumental in his own emergence within Liberia and in the international community. Blyden wrote many articles for the ACS journal, the *African Repository,* and he regularly corresponded with the group's officials. He also made numerous visits to the United States on behalf of the ACS to urge educated blacks to emigrate. Throughout his lifetime, Blyden held the view that blacks could never be wholly accepted as equals in America. His emigrationist appeals, however, fell primarily on deaf ears, and Blyden and the ACS were on occasion forced to look for emigrants to Liberia in the Caribbean.

Much of Blyden's life was spent in pursuit of political goals. After being appointed Liberia's secretary of state in 1864 (he served until 1866), Blyden used this position to encourage the emigration of "genuine blacks," rather than mulattoes, to Liberia. In 1871 he left the country after narrowly escaping being lynched in an atmosphere of political instability caused by warring factions, and because of his opposition to mulatto rule and control within Liberia. He spent this time in Sierra Leone, returning to Liberia in 1873. After his return, Blyden continued traveling to the United States to advocate emigration. He resumed his role as an educator and was appointed minister of the interior and secretary of education in 1880. He also made an unsuccessful attempt to become Liberia's president in 1885.

After 1885, Blyden focused much of his attention on the issue of West African unity, which had been initiated while he was in Sierra Leone. He used his diplomatic positions in London and Paris to advance this agenda. However, the unity theme was clouded by his belief that European colonialism in Africa could be positive for development. He believed that the climate would prevent Europeans from settling in Africa on a permanent basis.

Prior to his death in Sierra Leone, Blyden was in poor health and received a moderate pension, at the instruction of the colonial secretary, from the governors of Sierra Leone, Lagos, and the Gold Coast. While his emigrationist vision for Liberia did not succeed as he had hoped, his racial fervor made him a symbolic figure for future generations of nationalists.

See also Nationalism in the United States in the Nineteenth Century; Pan-Africanism

Bibliography

Lynch, Holls R. *Edward Wilmot Blyden, Pan-Negro Patriot, 1832-1912.* London: Oxford University Press, 1967.

Lynch, Holls R., ed. *Selected Letters of Edward Wilmot Blyden.* Millwood, N.Y.: KTO Press, 1978.

LAYN SAINT-LOUIS (1996)

Bogle, Paul

c. 1820
October 24, 1865

Paul Bogle was born into slavery in Jamaica sometime between 1815 and 1820. After slavery was abolished in the British Caribbean in 1838, he was among thousands of Jamaican freedpeople who, in search of independence from the grinding demands of plantation labor, relocated to their own independent freeholds. Bogle, along with black artisans and small farmers, settled at Stony Gut, a hilly area in St. Thomas in the East, bordering Spring Garden and Middleton sugar estates and about three miles from Morant Bay. With his freehold of around five acres on which he raised livestock and cultivated sugar, cotton, ground provisions, and tree crops, Bogle was better off than the majority of laborers who still had to look to the estates for their livelihood.

Bogle's dynamic leadership role in the 1865 Morant Bay rebellion, a protest against poor economic and social conditions in Jamaica, indicated that, although he had limited formal education, he was literate, articulate, and occupied an important position among the freedpeople in the parish of St. Thomas in the East. As a taxpayer, he qualified for the highly restrictive property franchise, and he supported George William Gordon, a radical, free, colored (of mixed European and African ancestry) man who challenged the political hegemony of the plantocracy in the parish. Indeed, it was largely because Bogle mobilized the small freeholders from Stony Gut and other postslavery settlements that Gordon was elected to the Assembly and to the Vestry, the unit of local government, in 1863.

Paul Bogle remained steadfast in his support for Gordon, despite the political machinations against him by the magistrates and the governor, Edward Eyre, who was severely criticized by Gordon for his incompetence in dealing with the island's affairs, particularly his neglect of the hardships that confronted the people. In early 1865 the relationship between Gordon and Bogle was further cemented when Bogle was ordained by Gordon as a deacon in the mainly black Native Baptist Church, which had a more radical agenda on social issues than the European directed religious groups on the island.

In August 1865 in Morant Bay, Paul Bogle addressed a public meeting, which Gordon had organized in support of other meetings that concerned the social and economic hardships faced by the people. Issues included the high taxation on imported staples when a series of droughts and floods had ravaged local provision growing and the denial of political rights. The meetings also protested against the insensitivity of the political administrators, who blamed the people's poverty on their supposed indolence and mocked their requests for access to unused lands held by the Crown. Bogle led a delegation of small farmers from the meeting to Spanish Town, a distance of nearly forty miles, to present their grievances, but the governor refused to meet with them.

In September 1865 social relations in St. Thomas in the East became more strained when the planters secured the transfer from the parish of Thomas Witter Jackson, a colored stipendiary magistrate who had opposed the corrupt rulings of planter magistrates against the laborers. Through the network of Native Baptist chapels in St. Thomas in the East, Bogle organized meetings that highlighted the chronic injustice in the lower courts, as well as the vexed issue of access to land that would have empowered the people who received low and irregular wages on the estates. After Lewis Miller, Paul Bogle's cousin and coreligionist, was brought before the court in Morant Bay on October 7, 1865, for trespassing, the issues of land and justice were fused. Bogle led his followers into Morant Bay as a show of solidarity with Miller. Before Miller's case was heard, Bogle and others prevented the police from arresting another man whose comments had interrupted the court. Two days later, the police went to Stony Gut with a warrant for Bogle's arrest. They were resisted, however, and on October 11, 1865, Paul Bogle led his followers, some armed with sticks and machetes, into Morant Bay where, after sacking the police station, they clashed with the militia outside the courthouse where the Vestry was meeting. Eight of Bogle's followers were shot and killed before the militia was overpowered. The courthouse was set on fire, and eighteen from the militia and magistracy were killed escaping the burning building.

The governor declared martial law, and the rebellion was brutally suppressed. More than four hundred people were hung, including Gordon and Bogle. Several hundred others were indiscriminately whipped, and many of the villages were burned.

In1965 the Jamaican government elevated Paul Bogle to the status of a national hero for his struggles against the oppression of the colonial state in the early postslavery period.

See also Gordon, George William; Morant Bay Rebellion

SWITHIN WILMOT (2005)

Bojangles

See Robinson, Bill "Bojangles"

Bond, Horace Mann

November 8, 1904
December 21, 1972

Teacher and administrator Horace Mann Bond was born in Nashville, Tennessee, the youngest of five sons of Jane Bond and James Bond, an educator and Methodist minister. He was named for Horace Mann, the nineteenth-century proponent of public education. When he was young, the family traveled throughout the South, settling near educational institutions with which James Bond was affiliated, including Berea College in Kentucky, Talladega College in Alabama, and Atlanta University. A precocious student, Horace Mann Bond entered high school when he was nine years old. While in high school, Bond moved with his family back to Kentucky, where his father served as chaplain during World War I at Camp Taylor.

In 1919, at the age of fourteen, Bond enrolled at Lincoln University, an African-American liberal arts college in southeastern Pennsylvania. After graduating from Lincoln in 1923, Bond entered the University of Chicago as a graduate student in education. While pursuing his Ph.D., he worked as a teacher and administrator at several African-American universities: Langston University in Oklahoma, Alabama Agricultural and Mechanical College, and Fisk University in Nashville, Tennessee.

In the early 1930s Bond gained a national reputation by publishing a number of articles in scholarly journals and popular magazines on black education in the South. In 1934 he published a major scholarly work, *The Education of the Negro in the American Social Order,* which argued that the poor quality of education among African Americans was directly linked to their lack of political and economic power. Bond did not recommend the abolition of segregated schools; instead, he called for equalization of the resources given to black and white children. In accordance with W. E. B. Du Bois's theory of the "talented tenth," Bond's book argued that young African Americans showing intellectual promise should be trained as future leaders.

While at Chicago, Bond developed a relationship with the Julius Rosenwald Fund, a philanthropic organization that provided funding for African-American scholars and universities. The fund supported Bond through most of his career, first with research fellowships that allowed him to publish widely and later with significant grants to the universities where he served as administrator.

In 1936, the same year he completed his dissertation on the development of public education in Alabama, Bond accepted the deanship of Dillard University, a newly reorganized black college in New Orleans. Bond remained at Dillard until 1939. That year he published his dissertation, *Negro Education in Alabama: A Study of Cotton and Steel.* The work was considered an important challenge to established scholarship on Reconstruction. Bond argued that Reconstruction was a significant step forward for black Americans, in particular in the educational institutions established during that period.

After the publication of *Negro Education in Alabama,* Bond devoted the rest of his career to the administration at black colleges, serving as president of Fort Valley State Teachers College in Georgia from 1939 to 1945 and as the first black president of Lincoln University in Pennsylvania from 1945 to 1957. In large part, his career was made by successfully lobbying for his institutions, often transforming them from underfunded colleges into comprehensive, well-respected research and teaching universities.

Bond had a variety of social involvements and intellectual interests. While at Lincoln University, he helped to direct research for a historical document supporting the challenge to segregation by the National Association for the Advancement of Colored People (NAACP) in the *Brown v. Board of Education of Topeka, Kansas,* Supreme Court case. In the 1950s and 1960s Bond developed an interest in Africa. Through tours, lectures, and articles, he attempted to raise support among African Americans for independence movements in African countries. He was a leader of the American Society for African Culture, an organization funded by the Central Intelligence Agency, which both encouraged interest in African culture and warned against the dangers of communism in the African independence movements.

After Bond left Lincoln in 1957, he spent the rest of his career as an administrator at Atlanta University, first as dean of the School of Education and then as the director of the Bureau of Educational and Social Research. During the summer before his first year at Atlanta, Bond delivered the Alexander Inglis Lectures at Harvard University, published in 1959 under the title *The Search for Talent,* in which he argued that social circumstances determine the outcome of mental testing. In the last half of his career, Bond's scholarship focused primarily on social influences, and he often argued that IQ tests were biased against African Americans. He retired in 1971 and died in Atlanta in 1972.

Horace Mann Bond was the father of Julian Bond, the civil rights activist and politician.

See also Bond, Julian; *Brown v. Board of Education of Topeka, Kansas*; Du Bois, W. E. B.

Bibliography

Urban, Wayne J. *Black Scholar: Horace Mann Bond, 1904–1972.* Athens: University of Georgia Press, 1992.

Williams, Roger M. *The Bonds: An American Family.* New York: Atheneum, 1971.

THADDEUS RUSSELL (1996)

BOND, JULIAN

JANUARY 14, 1940

Activist and elected official Julian Bond was born in Nashville, Tennessee, of a prominent family of educators and authors. He grew up in the town of Lincoln University, Pennsylvania, where his father, Horace Mann Bond, was then president of the university, and later in Atlanta when his father became president of Atlanta University. While attending Morehouse College in the early 1960s, Julian Bond helped found the Committee on Appeal for Human Rights. He dropped out of Morehouse to join the Student Nonviolent Coordinating Committee (SNCC), of which he became communications director in 1962. In 1964 he traveled to Africa and upon his return became a feature writer for the *Atlanta Inquirer.* Later he was named its managing editor. He eventually received his B.A. from Morehouse in 1981.

Bond won election to the Georgia House of Representatives in 1965, triggering controversy. On January 10, 1966, fellow legislators voted to prevent him from taking his seat in the house when he refused to retract his widely publicized support of draft evasion and anti–Vietnam War activism. Protest in defense of Bond's right to expression was strong and widespread. Both SNCC and the Southern Christian Leadership Conference (SCLC) sought mass support for Bond through community meetings, where discussion and ferment strengthened African-American awareness of the relationship between peace activism and the civil rights struggle. The Rev. Dr. Martin Luther King, Jr., rallied to Bond's defense, Vice President Hubert Humphrey publicly supported Bond, and noted cultural figures took out ads for pro-Bond campaigns.

After nearly a year of litigation, the U.S. Supreme Court ruled that Bond's disqualification was unconstitutional. The Georgia House was forced to seat Bond, and he remained in the House until 1975. In 1968 he was presented as a possible vice presidential candidate by opposition Democrats at the Democratic Convention in Chicago. He was too young, however, to qualify for the office, and his name was withdrawn. In 1972 he published *A Time to Speak, a Time to Act: The Movement in Politics,* in which he discussed ways of channeling civil rights activism into the electoral system. In 1975 Bond was elected to the Georgia state senate, where he served for twelve years. His activities during this period included the presidency of the Atlanta NAACP, where he served until 1989, and service as the narrator of both parts of the popular PBS documentary series about the civil rights movement, *Eyes on the Prize* (1985–1986, 1988–1989).

In 1986 Bond ran for U.S. Congress from Georgia and narrowly lost in a bitter contest with John Lewis, his former civil rights colleague. In the early 1990s Bond served as visiting professor and fellow at various colleges, including the University of Pennsylvania, Drexel University, Harvard University, and the University of Virginia, and was a frequent essayist and commentator on political issues. In the early 1990s he was also the host of a syndicated television program, *TV's Black Forum.* In February 1998 Bond was elected chairman of the board of the National Association for the Advancement of Colored People. Bond, who continues as NAACP chair in 2005, has also edited (with Sondra K. Wilson) a well-received collection of photographs and essays in commemoration of the 100th anniversary of the hymn that became known as the Negro National Anthem (and was adopted as the official song of the NAACP). *Life Every Voice and Sing: A Celebration of the Negro National Anthem, 100 Years, 100 Voices* (Random House, 2000) features one hundred photos and one hundred essays by a variety of artists, politicians, businesspeople, educators, and activists.

See also Civil Rights Movement, U.S.; King, Martin Luther, Jr.; Southern Christian Leadership Conference (SCLC); Student Nonviolent Coordinating Committee (SNCC)

Bibliography

Chorlian, Meg. "Inside the NAACP: An Interview with Julian Bond." *Cobblestone* 23, no. 2 (February 2002): 36–38.

Lewis, Amy. "Julian Bond." In *American Social Leaders,* edited by William McGuire and Leslie Wheeler. Santa Barbara, Calif.: ABC-CLIO, 1993.

Neary, John. *Julian Bond: Black Rebel.* New York: Morrow, 1971.

EVAN A. SHORE (1996)
GREG ROBINSON (1996)
Updated by publisher 2005

Bonds, Margaret

March 3, 1913
April 27, 1972

The composer and pianist Margaret Allison Bonds was born in Chicago. She showed musical promise early, composing and performing as a child. Her early piano and composition teachers were T. Theodore Taylor, Florence Price, and William Levi Dawson. She received her B.M. and M.M. degrees from Northwestern University in 1933 and 1934, respectively. In 1939 she moved to New York and attended the graduate school of the Juilliard School of Music, where she studied with Djane Herz, Roy Harris, and Robert Starer.

During the 1930s Bonds was active as a concert pianist and accompanist. In 1933 she became the first black soloist to appear with the Chicago Symphony in a performance of Florence Price's *Piano Concerto in One Movement.* During this time she founded the Allied Arts Academy, a school for talented black children, in Chicago. In New York she worked as an editor for the Clarence Williams publishing house. After moving to Los Angeles in the 1960s, she became director for the Inner City Repertory Theatre. She wrote art songs, popular songs, piano music, arrangements of spirituals, orchestral and choral works, and music for the stage. Her best known works include the cantata *Ballad of the Brown King* (1961, text by

Langston Hughes) and the art songs "The Negro Speaks of Rivers" (1946, text by Hughes) and "Three Dream Portraits" (1959, text by Hughes). Representing the second generation of African-American composers, Bonds was strongly influenced by modern music, including jazz and blues idioms.

See also Hughes, Langston

Bibliography

Bonds, Margaret. "A Reminiscence." In *International Library of Negro Life and History, Vol. 2: The Negro in Music and Art,* compiled and edited by Lindsay Patterson. New York: Publishers' Company, 1966.

Brown, Rae Linda. "Florence B. Price and Margaret Bonds: The Chicago Years." *Black Music Research Bulletin* 12, no. 2 (Fall 1990): 11–13.

RAE LINDA BROWN (1996)

Bontemps, Arna

October 13, 1902
June 4, 1973

Arna Bontemps—poet, playwright, novelist, critic, editor, and anthologist—was a leading figure in the Harlem Renaissance of the 1920s and 1930s. His work is distinguished by a passionate struggle for liberation and a mystical faith in the unseen. The latter may derive from his early religious training, for his parents were Seventh-Day Adventists. Born in Alexandria, Louisiana, Bontemps grew up in Los Angeles. The early death of his mother left him in the care of an austere father and his grandparents. Upon his graduation from San Fernando Academy in 1920, he enrolled in Pacific Union College, another Seventh-Day Adventist institution, where he earned an A.B. degree in 1923.

In 1924 Bontemps went to New York, where he met other young writers, including Langston Hughes, Countee Cullen, and Claude McKay. He was stimulated by the cultural vitality of New York—its theater, its music, its concern with world affairs, and the struggle of its black people for social recognition and cultural realization. Bontemps taught in Adventist schools, such as the Harlem Academy, and began his serious career as a writer. His first novel, *God Sends Sunday,* published in 1931, is the story of Little Augie, a jockey who earns a great deal of money and spends it lavishly on brothels, women, and fancy cars. The character was suggested by a great-uncle of Bontemps. Bontemps and Countee Cullen transformed the story of Little Augie into a musical, *St. Louis Woman,* which played on Broadway in 1946.

Bontemps's historical novel *Black Thunder* (1936), among the first of the genre in African-American literature, was based on a Virginia slave revolt in 1800. *Drums at Dusk* (1939), more superficial and romantic than *Black Thunder,* deals with the Pierre Toussaint-L'Ouverture uprising in Haiti. Other historical works include *We Have Tomorrow* (1945) and the biography *Frederick Douglass: Slave, Fighter, Freeman* (1958). In collaboration with Jack Conroy, Bontemps wrote a history of black migration, *They Seek a City* (1945; updated in 1966 as *Any Place but Here*).

In 1932 Bontemps coauthored, with Langston Hughes, *Popo and Fifine: Children of Haiti.* He and Conroy also produced a series of original tales for children: *The Fast Sooner Hound* (1942); *Slappy Hooper, the Wonderful Sign Painter* (1946); and *Sam Patch, the High, Wide and Handsome Jumper* (1951). In writing books for children, Bontemps made a major contribution, since juvenile literature written by and for African Americans was virtually nonexistent at the time. In 1956 he received the Jane Addams Children's Book Award for *Story of the Negro* (1948).

Throughout his career, Bontemps produced original poetry, notable for its brooding quality and its suggestive treatment of protest and black pride. "A Black Man Talks of Reaping," which won a *Crisis* magazine first prize in 1926, is one of the strongest of his protest poems. "Golgotha Is a Mountain" and "The Return" won the Alexander Pushkin Award for Poetry offered by *Opportunity* magazine in 1926 and 1927, respectively. *Personals,* a collection of his poems, was published in 1963 by Paul Bremen in London.

In 1943 Bontemps became head librarian at Fisk University in Nashville, Tennessee; in 1965 he became director of university relations. From 1966 to 1969 he was a professor at the Chicago Circle campus of the University of Illinois and in 1969 served as visiting professor and curator of the James Weldon Johnson Collection at Yale University. In 1970 he returned to Fisk as writer-in-residence; he died there in 1973.

See also Cullen, Countee; Harlem Renaissance; Hughes, Langston; McKay, Claude

Bibliography

Bontemps, Arna. *The Harlem Renaissance Remembered.* New York: Dodd, Mead, 1972.

Bontemps, Arna. *The Old South.* New York: Dodd, Mead, 1973.

Hughes, Langston, and Arna Bontemps. *Book of Negro Folklore.* New York: Dodd, Mead, 1958.

CHARLES H. NICHOLS (1996)

Boxing

Professional prizefighters and sites for professional boxing matches are found all over the world. But the origins of modern boxing can be traced to one country and era: England in the late eighteenth and early nineteenth centuries. Although protoforms of combat or blood sports existed in ancient Greece and Rome, they have little connection with the sport of boxing as practiced and understood today. The antecedent of modern boxing was bare-knuckle prizefighting, which sprang up in England almost simultaneously with that country's emergence as a major capitalist world power.

To be sure, the less restrictive moral atmosphere accompanying the decline of Puritanism in the mid-1600s permitted a revival of the rough sports of antiquity. Early on, boxing had close ties to the city because it was supported by urban wealth when local squires migrated to the metropolis along with increasing numbers of working-class men. The rise of boxing came in large part from the growth of commercialized leisure and popular recreation.

Before the rules formulated by Jack Broughton, one of the earliest of the new breed of "scientific boxers" who appeared on the English sporting scene in the early 1730s, bare-knuckle fighting largely consisted of butting, scratching, wrestling, and kicking. Under the Broughton Rules, elements of wrestling remained, but there was more emphasis on the fists, on skilled defensive maneuvers, and on different styles of throwing a punch effectively. Broughton, for instance, developed the technique called "milling on the retreat," or moving backward while drawing one's opponent into punches, a technique Muhammad Ali used to great effect during his reign as heavyweight champion over two hundred years later. Broughton also used gloves or "mitts" for training his pupils, many of whom were among England's leading citizens.

Under the Broughton Rules, which were superseded by the London Prize Ring Rules in 1838, boxers fought for indeterminate lengths of time, a fight not being declared ended until one fighter could not come up to the scratch mark in the center of the ring. A round lasted until one fighter was felled; both men then returned to their corners and were given thirty seconds to "make scratch" again. London Prize Ring Rules governed the sport of prizefighting as a bare-knuckle contest until the coming of gloves and the Marquis of Queensberry Rules. The first heavyweight championship fight under the Queensberry Rules was held between the aging John L. Sullivan and James J. "Jim" Corbett on September 7, 1892. Not only did the fight usher in the age of Queensberry, it also ushered in the age of American domination of the sport, as both Sullivan and Corbett were Americans.

Tom Molineaux, a Virginia slave of the eighteenth century, boxing his way to freedom. *Molineaux later made his way to England, where he had several important bare-knuckle matches, including a bout with the English champion Tom Cribb.* PHOTOGRAPHS AND PRINTS DIVISION, SCHOMBURG CENTER FOR RESEARCH IN BLACK CULTURE, THE NEW YORK PUBLIC LIBRARY, ASTOR, LENOX AND TILDEN FOUNDATIONS.

The golden age of bare-knuckle fighting in England, overlapping with the Regency period, occurred between 1800 and 1824, an era captured by Pierce Egan, one of the earliest boxing journalists, in his classic work *Boxiana* (1828–1829). Records of the first black boxers of note date from this era. Bill Richmond was a slave who learned to box by sparring with British seamen. He was taken to England in 1777 by General Earl Percy, a commander of British forces in New York during the American Revolution. Richmond, known as "the Black Terror," became the first American to achieve fame as a prizefighter. He stood about five feet tall and weighed between 155 and 170 pounds. Richmond beat such established British fighters as Paddy Green and Frank Mayers. Among his losses was one in 1805 to the British champion Tom Cribb, who was a title aspirant at the time. Richmond, who died in London, is probably best known not for his fighting but for being a second to the first black fighter to challenge for the championship.

That man, also an American ex-slave, made an even bigger name for himself as a prizefighter. Tom Molineaux apparently came from a boxing family, as it has been claimed that his father was an accomplished plantation scrapper. Although there is no record of Molineaux's career before his arrival in England, it is well established that many planters engaged their more athletic slaves in sports. Given that most young planters had taken the obligatory European tour and discovered boxing to be the rage among British gentlemen, it is little wonder they imported it to America.

Molineaux, who became known in England as "the Moor," arrived in England in 1809 and quickly defeated Bill Burrows and Tom Blake. Molineaux was matched with Tom Cribb, the champion, for the first time on December 18, 1810, a bitterly cold day (during the bare-knuckle era, most fights took place outdoors). It was one of the most talked-about and eagerly anticipated sports events in British history. Molineaux apparently won the fight, knocking Cribb out in the twenty-eighth round. However, Cribb's seconds accused Molineaux of illegal tactics. During the pandemonium that ensued, Cribb was able to recover, finish the fight, and beat Molineaux, largely because the black boxer had become chilled by the damp cold. The two men fought a rematch in 1811, with Cribb the easy winner because Molineaux had failed to train and had generally succumbed to dissipation. He went downhill rapidly after his second loss to Cribb and died in Ireland in 1818, a shell of the figure he had been in his prime.

Despite the impact of Richmond and Molineaux, blacks did not constitute a significant presence in boxing until the late nineteenth and early twentieth centuries, when the United States became the principal venue for professional matches. This era can be referred to as the pre-Jack Johnson age; the coming of Johnson signified a new epoch not only in boxing but in American sports history. The years 1890 and 1905 are considered among the worst in American race relations, when blacks experienced Jim Crow and American racist practices in their most virulent, oppressive, and blatant forms. Life for black fighters was far from easy: They often were denied fights against whites or, if permitted, found they were expected to throw the fight. They were paid less and fought far more often than did their white counterparts.

Among the important black fighters of this era were Peter Jackson, George Dixon, Joe Gans, and Jersey Joe Walcott. The latter three were all champions in the lighter weight divisions. Boxing under the Queensberry Rules had evolved to the point where there were now firmly established weight divisions, in contrast to the bare-knuckle days of Richmond and Molineaux, when boxers fought at "open weight" and there were sometimes great weight disparities between the contestants.

Peter Jackson was arguably the best heavyweight of his generation. Many experts felt he could have taken the measure of the then-champion, John L. Sullivan, had not Sullivan—in keeping with the intense racism of the times—drawn the color line and refused to meet Jackson. The "Black Prince," as Jackson was called, was born in St. Croix, Virgin Islands. His family emigrated to Australia when he was twelve years old and returned to the Virgin Islands three years later. Jackson did not come back with them, opting to seek his fortune as a sailor. During his years as a sailor, Jackson developed his boxing skills. He became the Australian heavyweight champion, but on discovering that America was a place to make one's name, he emigrated in 1888.

At the age of thirty, in 1891, Jackson fought contender Jim Corbett to a sixty-one-round draw, but it was Corbett who fought Sullivan for the title the following year. Although Jackson enjoyed success as a fighter, he left the ring for the stage because he was unable to obtain a title match against either Sullivan or Corbett after Corbett defeated Sullivan for the championship. Jackson toured with a stage production of *Uncle Tom's Cabin* for several years. At thirty-seven, out of condition and well past his prime, he tried a comeback against Jim Jeffries, only to be knocked out in three rounds. Despite the frustration Jackson endured, he was widely admired by many white sports enthusiasts for his gentlemanly demeanor, and he was idolized by blacks. The abolitionist Frederick Douglass in his old age hung a portrait of Jackson in his home. Jackson died of consumption in Australia in 1901.

George Dixon, known to the world as "Little Chocolate," was a smooth and cagey boxer who began his professional career on November 1, 1886. He first became bantamweight champion, although there was dispute about the exact weight qualification for this division. He eventually became the world featherweight champion, a title he held from 1892 to 1900. Dixon was a popular fighter who was often featured in white sporting publications such as the *National Police Gazette*, as well as being seen in the haunts of the black entertainment world. Life in the sporting world eventually wore Dixon down. He was knocked out by Terry McGovern in New York in 1900 and lost his last fight to Monk Newsboy in 1906. His health ruined, he died penniless in 1909.

Joe Gans, "the Old Master," is considered by many historians of boxing to be one of the greatest lightweights of all time. He was born in Baltimore on November 25, 1874, and launched his professional career in 1891. He

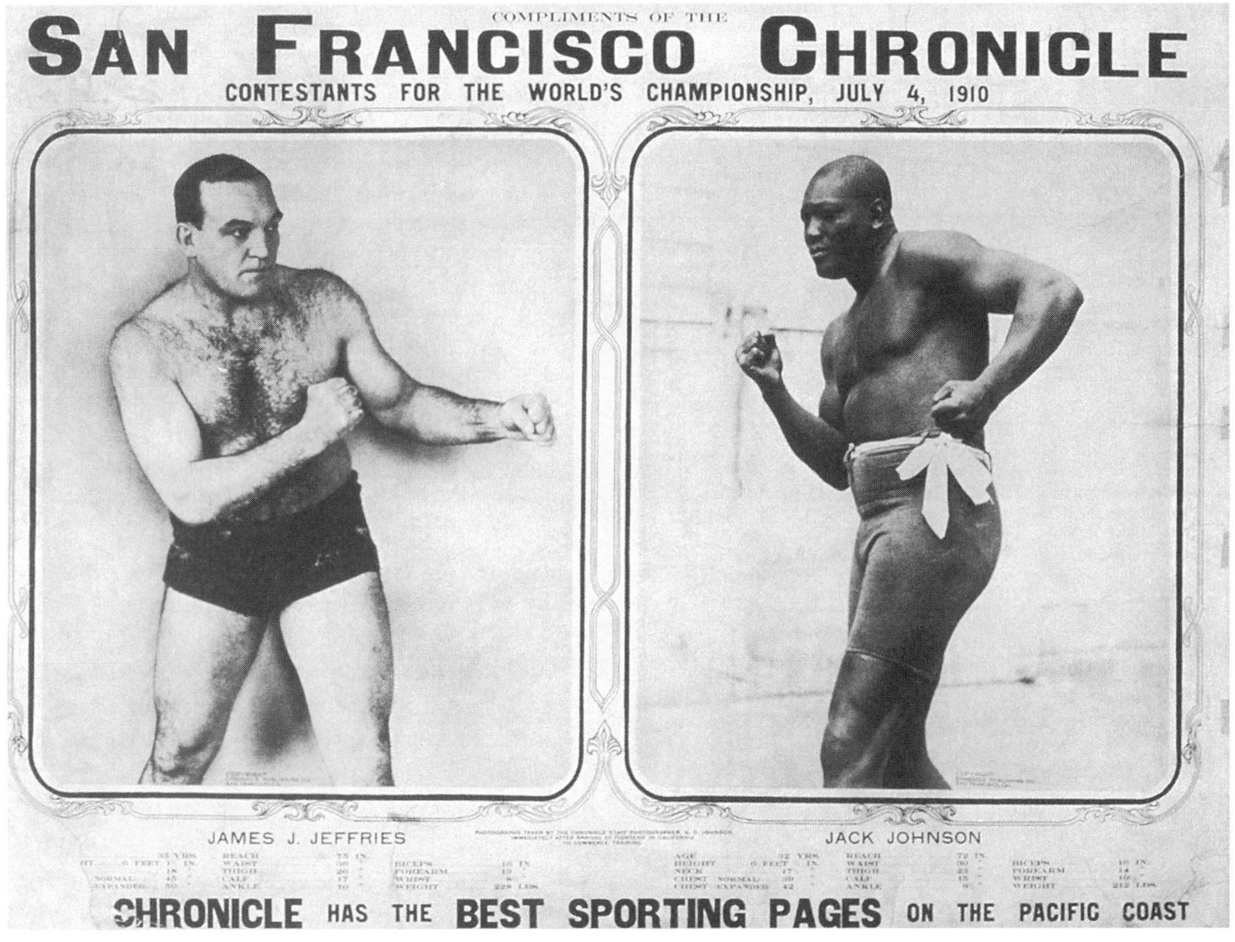

Publicity Poster for the 1910 boxing match between world heavyweight champion Jack Johnson and former champion James Jeffries. *The historic fight between Jeffries and Johnson took place on Independence Day in an atmosphere filled with racial overtones. Johnson easily beat Jeffries, who had been lured out of retirement as the "great white hope."* © CORBIS. REPRODUCED BY PERMISSION.

reigned as lightweight champion from 1902 to 1908. Gans was plagued by ill health, eventually losing his title to Battling Nelson in a rematch. In 1909 he tried to win his title back in another battle against Nelson, but he was sick and aging and easily beaten. Gans died in Baltimore a year later of tuberculosis. It has been suggested that Gans had become a follower of Father Divine, a black religious leader, who was also then living in Baltimore. However, at this stage in his career, Father Divine was known only as a healer; it is not clear whether his followers believed he was God, as they later did. Because Gans was afflicted with an incurable disease that was ravaging the black community, he may have been drawn to Father Divine as a last-ditch effort to seek a cure.

Joe Walcott was born in Barbados on March 13, 1873. Called "the Barbados Demon" because of his whirlwind punching power and ability to endure punishment (a style that can be likened to that of the popular 1970s junior welterweight champion Aaron Pryor), Walcott held the welterweight title from 1898 to 1906. He retired from the ring in 1911 and worked for a time as a janitor, winding up, as many black fighters did, with no money from his ring efforts. He was killed in an automobile accident in 1935.

In the twentieth century, three periods demarcate the history of blacks in boxing: the Jack Johnson era (1908–1915), the Joe Louis era (1937–1949), and the Muhammad Ali era (1964–1978). There have been many impressive and important black fighters aside from these heavyweight champions. Henry Armstrong, a dominant force in the 1930s, became champion of the featherweight, lightweight, and welterweight divisions simultaneously, the first fighter to achieve such a feat. Sugar Ray Robinson, welterweight champion and winner of the middleweight title on five different occasions, dominated his weight division in the 1950s and was one of the most stylish and influential boxers in history. Archie Moore, "the Old Mongoose," was champion of the light heavyweight division from 1952 and 1962. Floyd Patterson was Olympic cham-

FIGURE 2

Black members of the International Boxing Hall of Fame, Canastota, N.Y., modern inductees

Name	Birth country	Year inducted
Muhammad Ali	United States	1990
Wilfred Benitez	Puerto Rico	1996
Jimmy Bivins	United States	1999
Joe Brown	United States	1996
Charley Burley	United States	1992
Miguel Canto	Mexico	1998
Jimmy Carter	United States	2000
Antonio Cervantes	Colombia	1998
Jeff Chandler	United States	2000
Ezzard Charles	United States	1990
Curtis Cokes	United States	2003
George Foreman	United States	2003
Bob Foster	United States	1990
Joe Frazier	United States	1990
Kid Gavilan	Cuban	1990
Wilfredo Gomez	United States	1995
Emile Griffith	Virgin Islands	2000
Marvin Hagler	United States	1993
Beau Jack	United States	1991
Harold Johnson	United States	1993
Ismael Laguna	Panama	2000
Ray Leonard	United States	1997
Sonny Liston	United States	1991
Joe Louis	United States	1990
Mike McCallum	Jamaica	2003
Bob Montgomery	United States	1995
Archie Moore	United States	1990
Jose Napoles	Cuba	1990
Ken Norton	United States	1992
Terry Norris	United States	2005
Floyd Patterson	United States	1991
Eusebio Pedroza	Panama	1999
Aaron Pryor	United States	1996
Dwight Muhammad Qawi	United States	2004
Ultiminio Ramos	Cuba	2001
Luis Rodriguez	Cuba	1997
Ray Robinson	United States	1990
Matthew Saad Muhammad	United States	1998
Sandy Saddler	United States	1990
Michael Spinks	United States	1994
Joe Walcott	United States	1990
Ike Williams	United States	1990
Albert "Chalky" Wright	Mexico	1997

pion in 1952 and heavyweight champion from 1956 to 1962, one of the youngest men ever to hold that title. Sugar Ray Leonard, Olympic champion in 1976 and champion in the welterweight, junior middleweight, middleweight, and super middleweight divisions, was one of the most popular fighters in the 1980s. And the controversial Mike Tyson, who was imprisoned for rape, became the youngest man ever to win the heavyweight championship when he won the belt in 1986. Tyson was one of the most ferocious and unrelenting fighters ever to enter the ring.

These are a few of the notable black fighters of the twentieth century. But none of these men exercised the social and political impact on American society that Johnson, Louis, and Ali did. These three not only changed boxing, but their presence reverberated throughout the world of sport and beyond. People who normally had no interest in either boxing or sports took an interest in the careers of these three.

Like many black youngsters, Jack Johnson learned the craft of boxing as a child by participating in *battles royal*, where five, six, or seven black youngsters were blindfolded and fought against one another in a general melee. The toughest survived the ordeal and made the most money. It may be argued that battles royal were not necessarily more brutal than ordinary prizefights, but they were surely far more degrading.

Johnson fought his first professional fight at the age of nineteen, and the defensive skills he learned to survive the battle royal stood him in good stead when he challenged white fighters in the early twentieth century. Black fighters at this time were expected not to win many fights against white opponents; if they did win, they did so on points. Johnson was among three other black heavyweights who fought during this period: Joe Jeanette, Sam McVey, and Sam Langford, also known as "the Boston Tarbaby." Johnson became a leading contender for the title. After much wrangling and many concessions, he fought Tommy Burns for the heavyweight championship in December 1908 in Sydney, Australia.

Although the color line had been drawn against black challengers to the heavyweight title, Johnson succeeded in part because he was in the right place at the right time. Many in the white sporting public felt it was time to give a black a shot at the title, and Johnson was at that point well liked by the white sporting fraternity. Publications such as the *National Police Gazette*, not noted for any enlightened racial attitudes, campaigned vigorously for him to get a title fight. When Johnson defeated Burns, he became the first black heavyweight champion, the most prized title in professional sports.

Soon, however, the white sporting public soured on Johnson. His arrogance and his public preference for white women provoked a cry for "a great white hope" to win the title back for whites. In 1910 Jim Jeffries, a former champion, was lured out of a six-year retirement to take on Johnson in the Nevada desert, a fight that was the most publicized, most heatedly discussed, and most fervently anticipated sporting event in American history at that time. It was the first prizefight to take on significant political overtones, as many whites and blacks saw it as a battle for racial superiority. Johnson was easily the most famous—or most infamous—black man in America, and the fight occurred at the height of racial segregation and oppression of blacks in the United States. Johnson easily won the fight, and the victory caused race riots around the country as angry whites brutalized rejoicing blacks. This was Johnson's last great moment as a professional athlete.

In 1912 Johnson's first white wife, Etta Duryea, committed suicide at the champion's Chicago nightclub. In 1913, on the testimony of a white prostitute with whom Johnson had once been intimate, he was convicted under the Mann Act and sentenced to a year and a day in federal prison. His personal life now in shambles, with no future as a fighter because he was thoroughly hated by the white public, he fled the country for Paris.

Johnson lost the title to Kansan Jess Willard in Cuba in 1915, a fight Johnson claimed he threw in order to regain entry to the United States. In fact, he did not return until 1920, when he served his time in prison with little notice. Johnson went on to become a museum raconteur, an autobiographer, a fight trainer, and an occasional participant in exhibitions. He died in an automobile accident in 1946.

When Joe Louis defeated Jim Braddock in June 1937 to win the heavyweight title, he was the second black to become heavyweight champion, and the first permitted even to fight for the championship since the end of Johnson's tenure in 1915. During the ensuing twenty-two years, there were only three black champions of any division, and two had brief reigns: West African Battling Siki was light heavyweight champion from September 1922 to March 1923; Tiger Flowers was middleweight champion for six months in 1926; and Kid Chocolate was featherweight and junior lightweight champion from 1931 to 1933.

Joe Louis's father was institutionalized for mental illness and his mother remarried. The family relocated from Alabama to Detroit because of job opportunities in the automobile industry. Louis had little interest in school and was attracted to boxing. He had a distinguished amateur career before turning professional in 1934 under the management of John Roxborough and Julian Black, both African Americans. Louis's trainer, Jack Blackburn, a former fighter of considerable accomplishment, was also black. Mike Jacobs, an influential New York promoter, steered Louis toward big-time fights, and thus Louis's career was carefully guided to the championship in three years.

Image was everything for Louis, or at least for his handlers. In order to be accepted by the white public, he had to be the antithesis of Johnson in every respect. Johnson had bragged and consorted with white women publicly; Louis was taciturn and seen only with black women. Louis went about his business with dispatch, never relishing his victories or belittling his opponents. This latter was an especially sensitive point because all of Louis's opponents, before he won the championship, were white.

Louis came along at a time when blacks were more assertively pushing for their rights, unlike the era of Johnson. The labor leader A. Philip Randolph scored a significant victory when he achieved recognition for his union from the Pullman Car Company and achieved further gains when his threatened March on Washington forced President Franklin D. Roosevelt to issue Federal Order 8802 in 1942, integrating defense industry jobs. Louis came of age after the Harlem Renaissance and after Marcus Garvey's Universal Negro Improvement Association movement, both of which signaled greater militancy and race awareness on the part of blacks.

Louis's most important fight was his rematch against German heavyweight Max Schmeling in 1938. Louis had lost to Schmeling in 1936 and for both personal and professional reasons wanted to fight him again. Because Schmeling was German and probably a Nazi, the fight took on both racial and political overtones. Louis became the representative of American democracy against German arrogance and totalitarianism, as well as of American racial fair play against Schmeling's image of racial superiority and intolerance.

Louis won the fight easily, smashing Schmeling in less than a single round. As a result, he became the first black hero in American popular culture. During World War II, he served in the U.S. Army and donated purses from his fights to the war effort. He retired in 1949, after holding the title longer than any other champion and defending it successfully more times than any other champion. Money problems, particularly back income taxes, forced him to make a comeback in 1950. He retired permanently after his loss to Rocky Marciano in 1951. In later years, Louis became a greeter in a Las Vegas hotel. He suffered from mental problems, as well as a period of cocaine addiction. He died in Las Vegas in 1981, probably the most revered black boxer, and arguably the most revered black athlete, in American history.

Muhammad Ali, born Cassius Clay Jr., had a distinguished career as an amateur boxer, culminating in a gold medal at the 1960 Olympic Games. Always outgoing with a warm but theatrical personality, the photogenic young boxer spouted poetry, threw punches with greater grace and speed than any heavyweight before him, and was generally well received by the public. Although many people disliked his showy, sometimes outrageous ways, others thought him a breath of fresh air in boxing. The young Clay fought an aging but still intimidating Sonny Liston for the championship in 1964, defeating the older man in a fight in which Clay was the decided underdog.

It was after this fight that Clay announced his conversion to the Nation of Islam. Shortly afterward, he changed his name to Muhammad Ali, probably one of the most widely and thoroughly discussed and condemned name

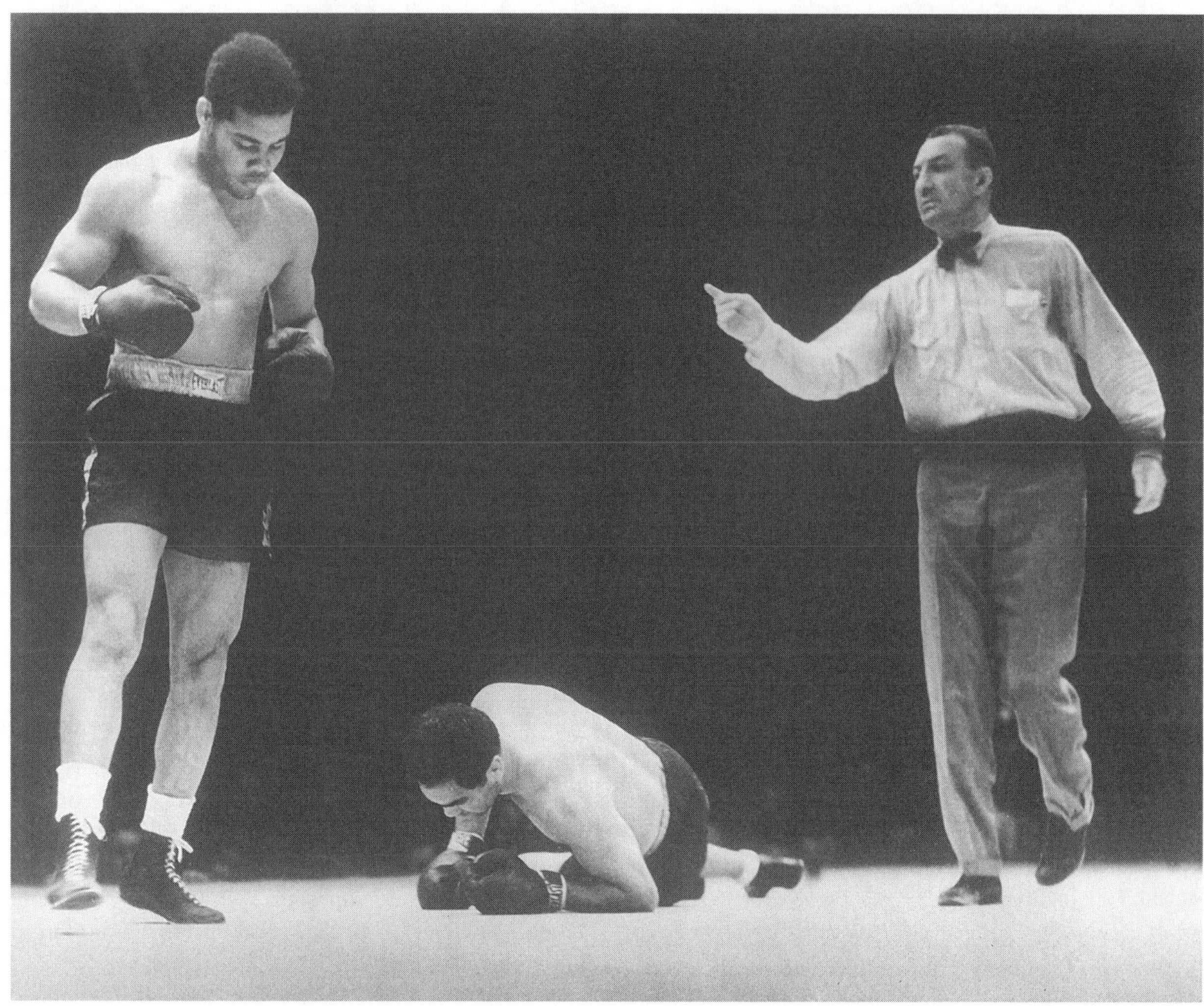

Joe Louis vs. Max Schmeling, June 22, 1938. *World Heavyweight boxing champion Joe Louis stands over German boxer Max Schmeling, down for a count of three, in Yankee Stadium, New York City. Louis lost to Schmeling two years earlier, but easily won the rematch, becoming the first national African-American hero in America.* AP/WIDE WORLD PHOTOS. REPRODUCED BY PERMISSION.

changes in American history. Ali's popularity among whites plummeted as a result of his conversion.

But he was not done provoking the white American public. In 1967 he refused induction into the armed services on religious grounds. His spiritual leader, Elijah Muhammad, had served time in prison during World War II for taking the same stand. Ali was stripped of his title, and his license to fight was revoked. Despite outcries from more liberal sections of the white public, Ali was in effect under a kind of house arrest for three and a half years. He was not permitted to fight in the United States and was not permitted to leave the country to fight abroad while his case was being appealed.

Ali was finally permitted to fight again in late 1970 in Georgia against journeyman heavyweight Jerry Quarry, whom he dispatched in a few rounds. During the interval of Ali's exile, the sentiments of the white public had changed significantly. Many turned against the Vietnam War. The assassinations of Martin Luther King Jr. and Robert Kennedy only two months apart in 1968 made many think the country was on the verge of collapse, and as a result there was a greater sense of tolerance and understanding. Ali's religious beliefs no longer struck the public as bizarre and threatening. Finally, blacks had achieved some political leverage in the South, and this was instrumental in getting Ali a license to box again. Ali eventually won his case in the U.S. Supreme Court when his conviction was overturned as one of a series of decisions that broadened the allowable scope for conscientious objection to war.

Ali lost his claim to the title when he suffered his first professional defeat at the hands of Joe Frazier in March

1971, the first of three epic battles between the two great fighters. But Ali eventually regained his title in 1974 when he defeated George Foreman in a shocking upset in Zaire. He lost the title again in 1978 to Olympic champion Leon Spinks, but regained it a few months later in a rematch, becoming the first heavyweight to win the championship three times.

Ali was by far the most popular champion in the history of boxing. His face was, and still is, recognized more readily in various parts of the world than that of virtually any other American. Ali has been particularly important in creating a stronger sense of kinship between American blacks and people of the Third World. He is the most renowned Muslim athlete in history.

Like many before him, Ali fought too long, disastrously trying a comeback in 1980 against champion Larry Holmes, who badly thrashed him over ten rounds. Ali's health deteriorated throughout the 1980s. Parkinson's disease, induced by the heavy punishment he took in the ring, took its toll. Nevertheless, Ali remained a formidable physical presence, an athlete who continued to be honored around the world for his courage both in and out of the ring.

With Ali's departure from boxing, the heavyweight division was dominated for a considerable period by Holmes, a formidable fighter but a man of little personality, wit, or engagement. Although Holmes enjoyed considerable popularity during his reign, it was fighters from the lighter weight divisions who attracted media attention and huge purses during the late 1970s through the 1980s. Sugar Ray Leonard, Marvelous Marvin Hagler, Matthew Saad Muhammad, Aaron Pryor, Dwight Muhammad Qawi, Thomas "Hitman" Hearns, Marvin Johnson, Mike "the Body Snatcher" McCallum, Livingstone Bramble, and Michael Spinks were among the best and most highly publicized fighters of the day.

Relying on the popularity of several highly skilled Latin American fighters, including the redoubtable Roberto Duran, Alexis Arguello, Pipino Cuevas, and Victor Galindez, which enabled fight promoters to once again use ethnic and cultural symbolism as a lure for a diverse and fragmented public, these black fighters were able to bring greater attention and larger sums of money to boxing arenas in the 1980s than ever before.

After Holmes, the heavyweight class fell into complete disarray, as it had during the 1930s before the coming of Joe Louis. A succession of undistinguished champions paraded before the public. Not until the emergence of Mike Tyson did the category reclaim its position as the glamour division of the sport. Tyson enjoyed greater financial success than any other heavyweight in history. However, he was poorly advised and surrounded by cronies who did not protect his interests or their own. Tyson pursued a self-destructive path of erratic, violent behavior and suspected substance abuse, and was finally imprisoned for an assault on a black beauty contestant.

Following Tyson's imprisonment the heavyweight crown remained split. However, Evander Holyfield was popularly recognized as heavyweight champion, especially after he scored a surprise victory over Tyson in 1996 and successfully defended the title in a rematch (following which Tyson was suspended for biting Holyfield's ear during the match) in May 1997. In 1998 Tyson's boxing suspension was lifted.

After Tyson's period in the limelight, no single boxer captured public attention. In the late 1990s and the first years of the twenty-first century, no one fighter held on to the heavyweight title. Several black boxers were among the champions, including Holyfield, Lennox Lewis, Riddick Bowe, and, in a startling comeback, George Foreman, by then in his forties. During this time, as during the period after Muhammad Ali's retirement, boxing's popularity was kept alive mainly by smaller fighters. Oscar de La Hoya became a big name, drawing a huge following, especially in the Hispanic community. Other popular boxers were the African-American fighters Roy Jones and Sugar Shane Mosley, and Felix Trinidad of Puerto Rico. These fighters became stars through television pay-per-view, through which viewers themselves generate the payouts for prizefights.

In 2001 two daughters of former heavyweight champions entered the ring, bringing a female angle to prizefighting. However, many saw the match between Muhammad Ali's daughter, Laila Ali, and Joe Frazier's daughter, Jacqui Frazier-Lyde, more as a publicity stunt than a serious fight.

In the late 1990s and early twenty-first century, boxing suffered from scandal and confusion, including criminal convictions of several prominent fighters, squabbles among boxing organizations over the authority to sanction fights and proclaim champions, injuries and deaths in the ring, and claims lodged by lower-class fighters of exploitation by promoters. Nevertheless, boxing continues to be a big-money sport, winning huge audiences through closed-circuit television.

See also Ali, Muhammad; Foreman, George; Frazier, Joe; Louis, Joe; Olympians; Robinson, Sugar Ray; Tyson, Mike

Bibliography

Ashe, Arthur R., Jr. *A Hard Road to Glory: A History of the African-American Athlete.* New York: Amistad, 1993.

Fleischer, Nat. *Black Dynamite: The Story of the Negro in the Prize Ring from 1782 to 1838.* 5 vols. New York: C. J. O'Brien, 1938.

Gorn, Elliott. *The Manly Art: Bare-knuckle Prize Fighting in America.* Ithaca, N.Y.: Cornell University Press, 1986.

Hauser, Thomas. *The Black Lights: Inside the World of Professional Boxing.* New York: McGraw-Hill, 1986. Reprint, Fayetteville: University of Arkansas Press, 2000.

McCallum, John D. *The World Heavyweight Boxing Championship: A History.* Radnor, Pa.: Chilton Book Company, 1974.

Mead, Chris. *Champion: Joe Louis, Black Hero in White America.* New York: Scribner, 1985.

Oates, Joyce Carol. *On Boxing,* expanded ed. With photographs by John Ranard. Hopewell, N.J.: Ecco, 1994.

Reid, J. C. *Bucks and Bruisers: Pierce Egan and Regency England.* London: Routledge and K. Paul, 1971.

Roberts, Randy. *Papa Jack: Jack Johnson and the Era of White Hopes.* New York: Free Press, 1983.

Rotella, Carlo. *Cut Time: An Education at the Fights.* Boston: Houghton Mifflin, 2003.

Sailes, Gary A., ed. *African Americans in Sport: Contemporary Themes.* New Brunswick, N.J.: Transaction, 1998.

Sammons, Jeffrey. *Beyond the Ring: The Role of Boxing in American Society.* Urbana: University of Illinois Press, 1988.

Ward, Geoffrey C. *Unforgivable Blackness: The Rise and Fall of Jack Johnson.* New York: Knopf, 2004.

GERALD EARLY (1996)
Updated by publisher 2005

Boyd, Walter

See Leadbelly (Ledbetter, Hudson William)

Bradley, David

September 7, 1950

Novelist David Henry Bradley Jr. was born and raised in rural Bedford, Pennsylvania, the son of David Henry and Harriette (Jackson) Bradley. He attended the University of Pennsylvania, where he studied English and received his B.A. (summa cum laude) in 1972. Afterward he moved on to King's College in London, where he earned his M.A. in United States studies in 1974. After working for two years in publishing, Bradley became a member of the English department at Temple University in Philadelphia.

Bradley wrote his first novel, *South Street* (1975), while still an undergraduate at the University of Pennsylvania. Alienated from his peers, whose urban lifestyle and politicized outlook he found artificial, Bradley spent most of his free time with the locals at a bar on Philadelphia's South Street. The novel offers original perspectives on the links within the black community and its relationship to history and memory and powerfully evokes life in the ghetto, with its numbers games, Saturday-night drinking parties, and storefront churches.

Bradley's second novel, *The Chaneysville Incident* (1981), won several awards in 1982: the PEN/Faulkner Award, the American Academy and Institute of Arts and Letters award for literature, and a *New York Times Book Review* "Editor's Choice" citation. The core of this more ambitious novel is an incident from Bedford's history. In doing research for the area's bicentennial in 1969, Bradley's mother discovered thirteen unmarked graves on the property of a Bedford County landowner. In doing so, she confirmed a local myth concerning thirteen fugitives on the Underground Railroad who, on the point of recapture, had preferred death to slavery and asked to be killed.

Bradley's narrative concerns a young black historian, John Washington, who has returned to his hometown in western Pennsylvania for the last few days of his surrogate father's life. His return inspires him to investigate his past; by digging up information from family papers, he manages to tie his natural father's suicide to the death of the thirteen fugitives. In relating his discovery to his girlfriend, a white psychiatrist, the protagonist discovers that history must be rooted in communal memory to be authentic, and that, in order for an individual to create, his emotions must be fed and sustained by the oral traditions of the group. This itinerary informs the narrative, which is gradually transformed from a factual account into a reflection on the meaning of the past.

In addition to two novels, Bradley has written articles and essays for many publications, including *Esquire,* the *New York Times Magazine and Book Review, Redbook,* and the *Southern Review.* He was awarded a Guggenheim Fellowship in 1989 and a National Endowment for the Arts Fellowship in 1991.

In 1998 Bradley coedited *The Encyclopedia of Civil Rights in America.* In recent years he has been a visiting professor at various colleges, including City College of New York, the University of Texas, and the University of Oregon. In 2003 he was at work on a nonfiction study, tentatively titled *The Bondage Hypothesis: Meditations on Race, History, and America.*

See also Literature of the United States

Bibliography

"David Henry Bradley, Jr." In *Contemporary Black Biography*, Vol. 39. Detroit, Mich.: Gale, 2003.

Smith, Valerie. "David Bradley." In *Dictionary of Literary Biography*, vol. 33, Afro-American Fiction Writers after 1955. Detroit, Mich.: Gale, 1984.

MICHEL FABRE (1996)
Updated by publisher 2005

Bradley, Tom

December 29, 1917
September 29, 1998

Politician Thomas "Tom" Bradley was born in Calvert, Texas, a town located between Waco and Houston. Both his mother and father were sharecroppers. When Bradley was four, the family moved to Dallas, and when he was six, to Somerton, Arizona, where they lived with relatives and where he first attended school.

In 1924 the family moved to Los Angeles and Bradley attended Polytechnic High School; he was one of 113 blacks out of a student population of 1,300. He excelled as a scholar and athlete and won a scholarship to the University of California, Los Angeles (UCLA).

In 1941 Bradley left UCLA to enter the police academy. He remained in the Los Angeles Police Department (LAPD) until 1961, rising to the rank of lieutenant, the highest position achieved up to that time by an African American.

During his years on the police force, Bradley attended Loyola University Law School and Southwestern University Law School at night, and he was accepted to the California Bar in 1956. Upon leaving the force in 1961, he joined the law practice of Charles Matthews. In 1963 Bradley ran successfully for the City Council seat for Los Angeles's tenth district, which was predominantly white. He was one of the first blacks outside the East Coast elected to political office by a nonblack majority constituency. He retained his seat until 1973.

In August 1965, when the Watts Riots erupted, Councilman Bradley's criticism of police brutality brought him into conflict with his former comrades in the LAPD, and with Mayor Sam Yorty. Despite a widespread white backlash against civil unrest and black militancy, Bradley's law enforcement background and moderately liberal politics, along with his dignified, unthreatening bearing, gave him interracial popularity in a city that was only 15 percent black. In 1969 Bradley challenged Yorty for the office of mayor. He won the primary with 46 percent of the vote to Yorty's 26 percent, but in the runoff, after a race-baiting campaign by Yorty, Bradley was narrowly defeated.

In 1973 he ran again, this time defeating Yorty 56 percent to 43 percent to become Los Angeles's first black mayor, as well as the first African-American mayor of a predominantly white city. He was reelected four times. A major highlight of Bradley's tenure was the athletically and commercially successful 1984 Summer Olympics. The Bradley administration also spurred downtown development. However, partly as a result of weak municipal government, Bradley was accused of neglecting working-class and inner-city neighborhoods, particularly black areas. Nevertheless, he was sufficiently popular in 1982 to win the Democratic Party nomination for governor of the nation's largest state. He was projected to win the race but narrowly lost to Republican George Deukmejian. In 1985 Bradley won a fourth term as mayor, and the same year he won the National Association for the Advancement of Colored People's Spingarn Medal. In 1986 he again ran for governor and once again lost.

Bradley was reelected mayor in 1989, but his final term was marred by the savage March 1991 beating of Rodney King, a black motorist, by four LAPD officers, an incident that was secretly videotaped by a bystander. Repeated showings of the tape on national television caused a nationwide furor. When the officers who had been charged were acquitted in 1992, Los Angeles erupted in a riot that dwarfed the Watts uprising of 1965. Bradley drew heavy criticism from blacks over his ineffective control of the police department and from whites for his inability to reestablish order in the city. When King's assailants were tried on federal charges in 1993, Bradley prepared an emergency response in case of another riot, but two officers were convicted and no violence occurred. Bradley completed his last term in 1993 and died of a heart attack in Los Angeles on September 29, 1998.

The International terminal at Los Angeles Airport is named after Bradley, who was mayor when the terminal was funded and built.

See also Mayors; Politics in the United States

Bibliography

"Biography of Mayor Tom Bradley." Mayor's Office, City Hall, Los Angeles, 1993.

Horne, Gerald. *Fire This Time: The Watts Uprising and the 1960s.* Charlottesville: University Press of Virginia, *1995.*

Payne, J. Gregory, and Scott C. Ratzan. *Tom Bradley: The Impossible Dream: A Biography.* Santa Monica, Calif.: Roundtable, 1986.

GERALD HORNE (1996)
Updated by publisher 2005

Bradshaw, Robert

September 16, 1916
May 23, 1978

Robert Llewellyn Bradshaw was born on the island of St. Kitts, which at the time was dominated by sugar plantations. He was dismissed from his job as a machinist in a sugar factory because of his participation in a 1940 strike. This precipitated his involvement with the St. Kitts-Nevis Trades and Labour Union—first as a member of the Executive Committee, and then as president from 1944 until his death. Bradshaw's prominence in ensuing strikes, as well as his charismatic self-presentation and forceful oratory, propelled him to the leadership (and unquestioned dominance) of the union's political branch, the St. Kitts-Nevis Labour Party, thus setting the stage for his aggressive crusade for self-government and social reform in the British colonies of St. Kitts, Nevis, and Anguilla.

In 1946 Bradshaw was elected to the Legislative Council. From this arena he launched the thirteen-week strike of 1948, which almost brought the exploitative sugar industry on St. Kitts to a standstill. He then served on the Soulbury Economic Commission that inquired into the strike, but he refused to sign the joint commission report, submitting instead his own minority version. He also unleashed protests against European appointments to the island's government, including the 1947 candlelight procession demanding the removal of the St. Kitts administrator, Leslie Stuart Greening (with the crowd chanting "Greening Must Go") and the massive 1950 demonstration against the governor of the Leeward Islands, Kenneth Blackburne.

Bradshaw was re-elected in 1952 when universal adult suffrage was introduced, and he successfully contested subsequent elections. In the wake of further concessions by the Colonial Office, he was appointed minister of trade and production in 1956.

Bradshaw used his dual position as union leader and political leader to advance the welfare of workers, primarily on St. Kitts. He presided over the enactment of legislation providing for a social security system, free secondary education and health care, improved housing, road rebuilding programs, and other infrastructure development. The wage increases and yearly bonuses he gained endeared him to the people of St. Kitts, who referred to him affectionately as "Papa." However, the predominantly peasant societies of Nevis and Anguilla nursed perceptions of neglect by Bradshaw's government.

Bradshaw also took up the cause of Caribbean integration. He participated in the establishment of the federation-minded Caribbean Congress of Labour 1945, and also served as its first assistant secretary. In 1958 he turned over the reins of Kittitian government to his lieutenant, Paul Southwell, in order to enter federal politics. In his role as minister of finance in the West Indies Federation, he worked tirelessly—though with negligible funds at his disposal—towards the federation's success. When it collapsed, in 1962, he took part in attempts to salvage a federation of the smaller islands of the eastern Caribbean.

Bradshaw returned home to resume his role in the local legislature, and he was sworn in as chief minister of the three-island colony of St. Kitts, Nevis, and Anguilla following the 1966 elections. By 1967, he had become the first premier of the Associated States of St. Kitts-Nevis-Anguilla, with full responsibility for internal affairs. But his belief in a united Caribbean was further challenged by Anguilla's secession from the three-island state in 1967. He also faced continuous threats of secession from Nevisians, who had long asserted a right to self-determination.

One of Bradshaw's major triumphs was in reversing the stranglehold the sugar plantations had over the St. Kitts economy and the subordination of workers to estate proprietors. In 1975 Bradshaw's government acquired all the plantation land on the island, which was to be retained in public ownership. The nationalization of the assets of the St. Kitts Sugar Factory followed in 1976. Although there was no significant land reform, light industries were introduced and other crops cultivated in a diversification effort.

Bradshaw had hoped to have independence listed as his crowning political achievement, and he participated in the 1976–1977 independence talks with the British government. His death on May 23, 1978, following a long battle with cancer, deprived him of witnessing this final victory, which was achieved on September 19, 1983. Since 1995, the life-long advocate of economic and political autonomy has been hailed as the "architect of modern St. Kitts-Nevis" and officially recognized as a National Hero.

See also International Relations of the Anglophone Caribbean

Bibliography

Browne, Whitman. *From Commoner to King: Robert L. Bradshaw, Crusader for Dignity and Justice in the Caribbean.* Lanham, Md.: University Press of America, 1992.

Payne, Carleen. "The Heroic Construction of St. Kitts' 'Papa' Bradshaw." In *Beyond Walls: Multi-Disciplinary Perspectives,* vol. 1, *St. Kitts and Nevis,* edited by S. Augier and O. Edgecombe-Howell. St. Augustine, Trinidad: University of the West Indies, 2002.

Richards, Glen. "Masters and Servants: The Growth of the Labour Movement in St. Christopher-Nevis, 1896–1956." Ph.D. diss., University of Cambridge, 1989.

CARLEEN PAYNE-JACKSON (2005)

Braithwaite, William Stanley

December 6, 1878
June 8, 1962

The son of an immigrant from British Guiana and the daughter of a former slave, William Stanley Beaumont Braithwaite, an author, was born and raised in Boston. He and three other siblings were educated at home until 1884, when his father's death left the family destitute. For some years afterward, Braithwaite attended public school, but he left when he was twelve and went to work full-time to support his family. He worked for several firms before finding employment as an errand boy at the publishing firm of Ginn & Co., where he eventually became apprenticed as a compositor. Braithwaite later claimed that he had been setting the first lines of John Keats's "Ode on a Grecian Urn" when he realized his passion for poetry and determined to write his own verse. He submitted poems and critical essays to various newspapers and magazines, including the *Atlantic Monthly,* the *North American Review,* and *Scribner's,* before publishing his first book of verse, *Lyrics of Life and Love,* in 1904. Two years later he began contributing essays and reviews to the *Boston Evening Transcript* and published his first anthology, *Book of Elizabethan Verse.* A second volume of poetry, *House of Falling Leaves,* appeared in 1908.

Braithwaite was appreciated more for his editorial efforts than for his own poems, which emulate the traditional forms, meters, and themes of British nineteenth-century works and make no reference to racial identity. Two additional anthologies, *Book of Georgian Verse* and *Book of Restoration Verse,* were published in 1908 and 1909. In 1913 Braithwaite produced the first *Anthology of Magazine Verse and Yearbook,* the publication for which he is best known. The anthology appeared annually between 1913 and 1939 and included such Harlem Renaissance authors as Sterling Brown, Countee Cullen, Langston Hughes, James Weldon Johnson, Claude McKay, and Anne Spencer, as well as the early work of Carl Sandburg, Vachel Lindsay, Amy Lowell, Wallace Stevens, and Robert Frost. Braithwaite also served as an editor for the *Poetry Journal* (1912–1914) and *Poetry Review* (1916–1917). In recognition of his literary accomplishments, he was awarded the NAACP's Spingarn Medal for outstanding achievement by an African American in 1918; that same year, he received honorary degrees from Taladega College and Atlanta University. In 1922 Braithwaite founded the B. J. Brimmer Publishing Company and published several works, most notably Georgia Douglas Johnson's first volume of poetry, *Bronze* (1922), and James Gould Cozzen's first novel, *Confusion* (1924), before his firm folded in 1925. Braithwaite's famous essay, "The Negro in American Literature," appeared in Alain Locke's *The New Negro* that year. Braithwaite continued to support himself and his family through writing and editing before accepting a professorship in creative literature at Atlanta University, where he taught for ten years. During this time, he started to work on his autobiography, *The House Under Arcturus,* which was published in three parts in *Phylon* in 1941.

Braithwaite retired from teaching and moved to Harlem in 1945. He published a volume of his Selected *Poems* (1948); *The Bewitched Parsonage,* a critical work on the Brontës (1950); and the *Anthology of Magazine Verse* for 1958 (1959).

See also Cullen, Countee; Harlem Renaissance; Hughes, Langston; Johnson, James Weldon; McKay, Claude

Bibliography

Butcher, Philip, ed. *The William Stanley Braithwaite Reader.* Ann Arbor: University of Michigan Press, 1972.

Harris, Trudier, and Thadious Davis, eds. *Dictionary of Literary Biography.* Vol. 51, *Afro-American Writers from the Harlem Renaissance to 1940.* Detroit, Mich.: Gale, 1987.

Logan, Rayford W., and Michael R. Winston, eds. *Dictionary of American Negro Biography.* New York: Norton, 1982.

QUANDRA PRETTYMAN (1996)

Brathwaite, Edward Kamau

May 11, 1930

The poet Edward Kamau Brathwaite was born to Hilton Edward and Beryl (Gill) Brathwaite in Barbados. He attended Harrison College and earned degrees from Cambridge University (B.A., 1953; Diploma of Education, 1954), and the University of Sussex (Ph.D., 1968). From 1955 to 1962 he was an officer in the Ministry of Education of Ghana, and he later balanced his teaching duties at the University of the West Indies (St. Lucia, Jamaica) with travel and work in England and the United States. In 1994 he was a visiting professor at New York University.

Brathwaite's earliest poetry collections—*Rights of Passage* (1967), *Masks* (1968), and *Islands* (1969)—established him as a major talent. This autobiographical trilogy, collected as *The Arrivants* (1973), reflects the poet's contact with white cultures and Africa and explores the shaping of racial identities. In the volumes that followed, such as *Other Exiles* (1975), *Sun Poem* (1982), *X/Self* (1987), *Middle Passages* (1992), *Trenchtown Rock* (1993), *Words Need Love Too* (2000), and *Ancestors* (2001), he highlights global concerns from a remarkable array of African, European, and Caribbean perspectives. His poetry is characterized by a deft interweaving of voices, innovative fonts, and vivid renderings of black speech and music, particularly jazz.

In addition to more than ten volumes of poetry, Brathwaite has worked as a playwright (*Odale's Choice,* 1967), essayist (*Caribbean Man in Space and Time,* 1974), editor (*New Poets from Jamaica,* 1979), and contributor to periodicals. *Roots,* a 1986 history of Caribbean literature and culture, won the Casa de las Americas Prize for Literary Criticism. The *Zea Mexican Diary* (1993) is a memoir chronicling his wife's illness and death from cancer.

Brathwaite's other honors include Guggenheim (1972) and Fulbright fellowships and the Institute of Jamaica Musgrave Medal (1983). In 1994 he received the $40,000 Neustadt International Prize for Literature. Sponsored by *World Literature Today* and the University of Oklahoma, the award recognized Brathwaite for being what the Ghanian author Kofi Awoonor called "a poet of the total African consciousness."

See also Literature

Bibliography

Brathwaite, Edward Kamau. *The Zea Mexican Diary.* Madison: University of Wisconsin Press, 1993.

Breines, Laurence A. "Edward Kamau Brathwaite." In *Dictionary of Literary Biography,* vol. 125, *Twentieth-Century Caribbean and Black African Writers.* 2nd series. Detroit, Mich.: Gale Research, 1993.

"Kamau Brathwaite." In *Contemporary Black Biography,* vol. 36, edited by Ashyia Henderson. Detroit, Mich.: Gale, 2002.

Salkey, Andrew. "Barbados." *World Literature Today* (Summer 1983): 500.

DEKKER DARE (1996)
Updated bibliography

Brawley, Benjamin Griffith

April 22, 1882
February 1, 1939

Educator and author Benjamin Griffith Brawley was born in Columbia, South Carolina, to Margaret Dickerson Brawley and Edward McKnight Brawley. His father's career as a Baptist preacher and professor required that the family move several times; although Brawley attended a succession of elementary and secondary schools, his early education took place primarily at home. He earned a baccalaureate degree at Atlanta Baptist (later Morehouse) College in 1901; in 1907 he earned a B.A. from the University of Chicago, and he completed his M.A. at Harvard University in 1908.

Brawley devoted his life to the study of literature; in particular, he concentrated on the lives and works of African-American writers and artists. His teaching career was spent primarily at Atlanta Baptist College (1912–1920); Shaw University (1922–1931), where his father was also a professor; and Howard University (1910–1912 and 1931–1939). While teaching at Howard in 1912, he met and married Hilda Damaris Prowd.

Brawley built a reputation as a prolific scholar, a master teacher, and an occasional poet, and although his verse is not remembered today, his scholarly works are still highly regarded. Among his seventeen books are: *A Social History of the American Negro* (1921); *The Negro in Literature and Art* (1918), which was republished as *The Negro Genius* (1937); *Early Negro American Writers* (1935); and *Paul Laurence Dunbar: Poet of His People* (1936). He also lectured frequently and published many scholarly articles and textbooks, including *A New Survey of English Literature* (1925).

Brawley's quiet and sensitive approach to literary studies utilizes biography and history, reading artistic works from within the context of the authors' lives. He was keenly aware of the struggles of blacks in American society and dedicated to making his audience, black and white, aware of the breadth and depth of the contributions of African Americans. As his writings demonstrate, he also sought to illuminate universal themes transcending race. As he concludes in his respected work on Paul Laurence Dunbar (1936), "Against the bullying forces of industrialism he [Dunbar] resolutely set his face. . . . Above the dross and the strife of the day, he asserted the right to live and love and be happy."

Brawley died on February 1, 1939. On February 6, classes and other activities at Howard University were suspended for the day to mark his funeral and interment.

See also Literary Criticism, U.S.; Literature of the United States

Bibliography

Brawley, Benjamin Griffith. *Paul Laurence Dunbar: Poet of His People.* Chapel Hill: University of North Carolina Press, 1936.

Parker, John W. "Benjamin Brawley—Teacher and Scholar." *Phylon: Review of Race and Culture* 10, no. 1 (1949).

Parker, John W. "A Bibliography of the Published Writings of Benjamin Griffith Brawley." *North Carolina Historical Review* 34, no. 2 (1957).

Redding, Saunders. "Benjamin Brawley." In *Dictionary of American Negro Biography,* edited by Rayford W. Logan and Michael R. Winston. New York: Norton, 1982.

STEVEN J. LESLIE (1996)

Brawley, Edward McKnight

March 18, 1851
January 13, 1923

Edward McKnight Brawley, a minister, was born free in Charleston, South Carolina, to James M. and Ann L. Brawley. In 1861 he was sent to Philadelphia, where he attended grammar school for three years and graduated from the Institute for Colored Youth in 1866. From 1866 to 1869 he worked as an apprentice to a shoemaker in Charleston. Brawley was baptized in the Shiloh Baptist Church in Philadelphia in 1865, and thus began a life of religious involvement.

In 1870 he entered Howard University in Washington, D.C., to study theology. The following year he transferred to Bucknell University in Lewisburg, Pennsylvania, and in 1875 he became the first African American to receive a bachelor's degree from that school. Three years later, Brawley received a master's degree from Bucknell. In 1885 he received an honorary Doctor of Divinity degree from the State University of Louisville.

Brawley was an active educator and administrator. In 1875 he was ordained as minister of the white Baptist church in Lewisburg, Pennsylvania, and was commissioned by the predominantly white American Baptist Publication Society (ABPS) to work as a missionary in South Carolina. Under these auspices, Brawley organized Sunday schools into a state convention over which he presided as secretary and financial agent. He remained in South Carolina until 1883, when he became president of the Alabama Baptist Normal Theological School, later renamed Selma University. At Alabama Baptist he overhauled the curriculum and brought it up to college status. Brawley also helped found Morris College in Sumter, South Carolina, and assumed the position of president in 1885.

Throughout his career Brawley was committed to integration, and his involvement in the ABPS was indicative of his desire to bring black and white Christians together. He believed black Baptists "should merge race feeling in the broader spirit of an American Christianity." In 1890, in an effort to give greater public recognition to black Baptists, black ministers within the ABPS invited black Baptists to be writers and agents for the organization. The all-white Southern Baptist Convention responded with outrage and protest and threatened to withdraw support from the ABPS. Most black Baptists condemned the ABPS for succumbing to southern white racism, and many advocated greater separation from white Baptists. Brawley's was one of the few conciliatory voices. Rather than dealing with the crisis at hand, he reviewed what the ABPS had accomplished for black people and urged reconciliation. This incident widened the chasm between Brawley and many other black Baptists. After this conflict the ABPS tried to appease black ministers and in 1890 recruited Brawley to edit the *Negro Baptist Pulpit,* the first collection of theological and denominational articles ever written and edited by black Baptists.

In January 1877 Brawley married Mary Warrick. By the end of the year his wife and child had died. In December 1879 he married Margaret Dickerson, with whom he had four children. Their eldest son, Benjamin Brawley, author and historian, was born in 1882. From 1912 until 1920, Brawley served as minister of White Rock Baptist Church in Durham, North Carolina. He also taught biblical history at Shaw University in Raleigh, North Carolina. Brawley wrote several religious texts, including a book on evangelism entitled *Sin and Salvation,* and edited the *Baptist Tribune* and *The Evangel.* Brawley died on January 13, 1923, ending a long career in the ministry, education, publishing, and writing.

See also Baptists

Bibliography

Jackson, J. H. *A Story of Christian Activism: The History of the National Baptist Convention, USA, Inc.* Nashville, Tenn.: Townsend, 1980.

Pegues, A. W. *Our Baptist Ministers and Schools.* Springfield, Mass.: Wiley & Co., 1892. Reprint, New York: Johnson Reprint Corp., 1970.

Simmons, William J. *Men of Mark.* 1887. Reprint. New York: Ayer, 1968.

Washington, James Melvin. *Frustrated Fellowship: The Black Baptist Quest for Social Power.* Macon, Ga.: Mercer University Press, 1986.

SABRINA FUCHS (1996)
PREMILLA NADASEN (1996)
Updated by publisher 2005

Breakdancing

An elaborate social dance form originated by teenage African-American males in the South Bronx of New York City, breakdancing appeared during the early to mid-1970s. It began as a form of gang fighting, a mixture of physically demanding movements that exploited the daredevil prowess of performers and stylized punching and kicking movements directed at an opponent. A descendant of *capoeira,* the Brazilian form of martial arts disguised as dance, breaking developed as the movement aspect of rap music when breakdancers—"B-Boys"—filled the musical breaks between records mixed by disc jockeys at parties and discotheques. Breakdancing was part of a young urban culture built upon innovations in language, hip-hop music, fashion (unlaced sneakers, hooded sweatshirts, nylon windbreakers), and visual arts (graffiti).

The elaborate spins, balances, flips, contortions, and freezes performed by breakdancers required extreme agility and coordination. Real physical danger surrounded movements such as the "windmill," in which dancers spun wildly, supported only by the shoulders, or the "suicide," in which an erect dancer would throw himself forward to land flat on his back. The competitive roots of breakdancing encouraged sensational movements such as multiple spins while balanced on the head, back, or one hand. Dancing "crews" met on street corners, subway stations, or dance floors to battle other groups with virtuosity, style, and wit determining the winner. Breakdancing came to be divided into several classifications of movement, including "breaking" (acrobatic flips and spins with support by the head and arms, with the shoulders as a point of balance), "uprock" (fighting movements directed against an opponent), "webbo" (extravagant footwork that connected breaking movements), and "electric boogie" (robotlike dancing movements borrowed from mime). The electric boogie style, reminiscent of a long tradition of eccentric African-American dances, developed in Los Angeles concurrent with electronically produced disco music. In this style dancers typically appeared to be weightless and rubber limbed, performing baffling floating walks, precise body isolations, and pantomimed robotic sequences. This form includes the "moonwalk," popularized on national television by Michael Jackson, in which the dancer's feet appear to be floating across the floor without touching it. Other boogie moves include the "wave," in which the body simulates an electric current passing through it, and "poplocking," a series of tightly contained staccato movements separated by freezes. An "Egyptian" style, which imitated ancient wall paintings, was also briefly popular.

Breakdancing found a mainstream audience through several films that cashed in on its sensational aspects and minimized its competitive format. Charlie Ahearn's *Wild Style* (1982), the first film to document emergent hip-hop culture, was eclipsed by a thirty-second breaking sequence in *Flashdance* (1983), which brought the form to international attention; *Breakin'* (1984), which starred Shabba Doo (Adolfo Quinones), an important breakdance choreographer from Chicago; and Harry Belafonte's *Beat Street* (1984), which featured the New York City Breakers. Breakdancing dropped out of the public limelight in the late 1980s, only to reemerge as a social dance form practiced by teenagers in nightclubs during the 1990s. By 2004 the form had become a component aspect of codified hip-hop dance, practiced by teams in international competitions, popular in music videos, and once again featured in Hollywood films, including Chris Stokes's *You Got Served* (2004).

See also Capoeira; Hip Hop; Rap; Social Dance

Bibliography

Banes, Sally. "Breakdancing." In *Fresh: Hip Hop Don't Stop,* edited by Nelson George, Sally Banes, Susan Flinker, and Patty Romanovsky. New York: Random House, 1985.

DeFrantz, Thomas. "The Black Beat Made Visible: Body Power in Hip Hop Dance." In *Of the Presence of the Body: Essays on Dance and Performance Theory,* edited by André Lepecki. Middleton, Conn.: Wesleyan University Press, 2004.

Rosenwald, Peter J. "Breaking Away '80s Style." *Dance Magazine* 58, no. 4 (April 1984): 70–74.

Thompson, Robert Farris. "Hip-hop 101." *Rolling Stone* (March 27, 1986): 95–100.

THOMAS F. DEFRANTZ (1996)
Updated by author 2005

Breedlove, Sarah

See Walker, Madam C. J.

Briggs, Cyril

1888

October 18, 1966

Cyril Valentine Briggs was a radical publicist of the New Negro movement and one of the black charter members of the Communist Party USA (CPUSA). As the political organizer of the African Blood Brotherhood for African Liberation and Redemption—better known as the African Blood Brotherhood (ABB)—a semisecret propaganda organization founded in September 1919 in reaction to the unprecedented racial violence of the Red Summer of 1919, Briggs was the first to enunciate in the United States the political principle of armed black self-defense.

A native of the tiny island of Nevis in the Leeward Islands chain of the British West Indies, Briggs was the son of a planter-manager for one of the island's absentee landlords. Of an extremely light complexion, he was later dubbed the "Angry Blond Negro" by George W. Harris of the New York *News.*

Briggs received his early start in journalism working after school with the Saint Kitts *Daily Express* and the Saint Christopher *Advertiser.* As a young man in Saint Kitts, he was influenced by the published lectures of the great American orator Robert Green Ingersoll, whose irreverent wit and questioning of the tenets of Christian belief earned him the sobriquet "the great agnostic."

Briggs came to the United States in July 1905. His involvement in the fight for African-American rights began in earnest in October 1915 when he was appointed editor of the *Colored American Review,* mouthpiece of the Harlem black business community, which stressed black economic success and racial pride. When his editorship came to an abrupt end with the second issue, Briggs resumed work with New York's *Amsterdam News,* which had hired him as an editorial writer shortly after it began publication in 1912.

During and after World War I, Briggs's outspoken *Amsterdam News* editorials, directed against what he perceived to be the hypocrisy of U.S. war aims in view of U.S. mistreatment of black soldiers and the continuing denial of democracy to African Americans at home, came under increasing official censorship. It culminated in the detention by the U.S. Post Office of the March 12, 1919, issue containing Briggs's editorial denouncing the League of Nations as a "League of Thieves." Two months later, Briggs finally severed his ties with the newspaper for which he had been not only editorial writer but also city editor, sports editor, and theater critic.

His resignation from the *Amsterdam News* enabled Briggs to devote his entire time to the *Crusader,* which he had begun publishing in September 1918. With a free hand to promote the postwar movement through the *Crusader,* Briggs joined such black radical figures as Hubert H. Harrison, Marcus Garvey, A. Philip Randolph, Chandler Owen, William Bridges, and W. A. Domingo in giving voice to the era's black militancy.

Initially emphasizing the racial theme of "self-government for the Negro and Africa for the Africans," the *Crusader* proclaimed itself in its early issues as the publicity organ of the Hamitic League of the World, which had been started by the brilliant young racial vindicationist author George Wells Parker in Omaha, Nebraska. By the first anniversary of its publication, however, the editorial line of the *Crusader* had changed radically. Whereas its original focus had been on postwar African issues, it now espoused the revolutionary ideology of Bolshevism.

Starting with the October 1919 issue, the *Crusader* became the official mouthpiece of the ABB, which at the time functioned clandestinely as the CPUSA's first black auxiliary. In keeping with the group's ideological position, Briggs emerged during 1921 and 1922 as the most outspoken critic of the leadership of Marcus Garvey, against whom he supplied some of the critical evidence that would lead eventually to the federal government's successful prosecution of Garvey for mail fraud.

When the *Crusader* ceased publication in early 1922, Briggs set about organizing the Crusader News Agency. In February 1924, he was involved in the formation of the Negro Sanhedrin movement, under the leadership of Kelly Miller, with the aim of creating a federation of black organizations. Briggs had by this time become a full-time functionary of the CPUSA. Throughout the 1920s and 1930s, he was actively involved in organizing a succession of black auxiliaries of the CPUSA, most notably the American Negro Labor Congress (ANLC) and the League of Struggle for Negro Rights. In December 1929 he was made editor of the *Harlem Liberator,* the official organ of the ANLC.

Briggs was also directly involved in planning and implementing the CPUSA's role in the defense campaign of the famous Scottsboro Case in the early thirties. But in 1938, after becoming embroiled in a dispute with James W. Ford, the leading black figure in the CPUSA at the time, Briggs was expelled from the party, along with Richard B. Moore and Otto Hall, for an alleged "Negro nationalist way of thinking." In 1944 Briggs moved to Los Angeles, where he rejoined the Communist Party in 1948. During the fifties, he was employed as an editor with the *Los Angeles Herald-Dispatch.*

See also African Blood Brotherhood; Communist Party of the United States; Ford, James W.; Garvey, Marcus; New Negro; Red Summer; Scottsboro Case

Bibliography

Draper, Theodore. *American Communism and Soviet Russia: The Formative Years.* New York: Viking, 1960.

Hill, Robert A., ed. *The Crusader* (1918–1922), 3 vols. New York: Garland, 1987.

ROBERT A. HILL (1996)

Brimmer, Andrew Felton

September 13, 1926

Born in Newellton, Louisiana, economist Andrew F. Brimmer attended high school in Louisiana before moving to Bremerton, Washington, in 1944. Shortly thereafter, he joined the U.S. Army and served in Hawaii from 1945 until 1946. Subsidized by the GI Bill, Brimmer was able to attend the University of Washington; he received his B.A. in 1950 and his M.A. in 1951. As a Fulbright fellow, Brimmer traveled to India during 1951 and 1952 for a year of postgraduate work at the University of Bombay. Returning to the United States, he completed a Ph.D. in economics at Harvard University in 1957.

Brimmer began his career as an economist at the Federal Reserve Bank of New York (1955–58). During his time at the bank, he was one of the several economists sent to the Sudan in late 1956 and early 1957 to aid the Sudanese in establishing a central bank. Brimmer then taught at Michigan State University (1958–1961) and at the University of Pennsylvania's Wharton School of Business (1961–1966). President John F. Kennedy appointed Brimmer as a deputy assistant secretary of commerce for economic policy in 1963; two years later, he became assistant secretary for economic affairs. In 1966 President Lyndon B. Johnson named him to the Board of Governors of the Federal Reserve Bank. The first black member of the board, Brimmer was an expert on international monetary issues. While at the Federal Reserve, he consistently advocated a tight monetary policy, favoring the restriction of the money supply and interest rates in order to control inflation. Serving only half of his fourteen-year term, Brimmer resigned in 1974 to take a teaching position at Harvard's Graduate School of Business. Two years later, he left Harvard and founded Brimmer and Company, Inc., an economic consulting firm in Washington, D.C.

A prolific writer, Brimmer has authored numerous books and articles on various economic topics, ranging from public utilities to international trade and finance. Since 1978 he has regularly contributed "Economic Perspectives" articles in *Black Enterprise.* In his writings Brimmer has consistently argued that the disparity in income between whites and blacks results only in part from differences in educational achievement; underlying the differential, he says, is persistent racial discrimination, which "hampers access" for African Americans to higher-paying jobs. At the same time, he has contended that other problems afflicting the African-American community, such as the high rate of teenage pregnancy and the high rate of unemployment among young black people, result mainly from behavior instead of outside forces such as the economy. A proponent of encouraging African Americans to look beyond small business to larger markets and increased capitalization, he took part in President Bill Clinton's economic summit in December 1992.

Brimmer has served on the boards of numerous corporations and organizations, including United Air Lines, Du Pont, and the Tuskegee Institute. He has twice been president of the Association for the Study of Afro-American Life and History, been cochairman of the Interracial Council for Business Opportunity, and is a member of many professional organizations. Among the many honors Brimmer has received are awards from the National Economic Association, One Hundred Black Men, and the New York Urban Coalition.

In 1995, Brimmer was named by President Bill Clinton to head a five-person financial control board that helped steer the District of Columbia through a severe financial crisis. A decade later, Brimmer continued to serve as president of Brimmer & Company, his economic and financial consulting firm based in Washington, D.C.

See also Association for the Study of African American Life and History

Bibliography

Brimmer, Andrew. "The Economic Cost of Discrimination." *Black Enterprise* 24, no. 3 (November 1993): 27.

Williams, Juan. "Economist Calls Lag in Skills Blacks' Main Obstacle." *Washington Post*, March 22, 1985, p. A3.

ALANA J. ERICKSON (1996)
Updated by publisher 2005

British West Indian Emancipation Act

See Slave Trade

Broadside Press

The Broadside Press, one of the most influential black presses to emerge during the black arts movement of the late 1960s and early 1970s, began operation in 1965 in an attempt to secure copyright privileges to "Birmingham Ballad," a song commemorating the bombing deaths of four young black children at a Birmingham, Alabama, church in September 1963. Located originally in the Detroit home of its founder, poet Dudley F. Randall, Broadside quickly grew in size, requiring larger offices and attracting manuscripts from black artists across the country. The press was particularly successful in publishing poets, many of whom explored the characteristic black arts movement themes of self-pride and anger against white-dominated institutions.

After publishing such poets as Gwendolyn Brooks, Nikki Giovanni, and Audre Lorde, Haki Madhubuti, Sonia Sanchez, and others, Broadside suffered reverses during the recession of the mid-1970s. By 1975, Broadside's tenth anniversary, operations at the press had to be scaled back. Its finances were in poor condition, forcing Randall to put the press up for sale. In 1977 Randall sold Broadside to the Alexander Crummell Memorial Center, an activist organization within the Episcopal Church.

After several years, however, Randall regained control. He sold the press again in 1985, this time to Detroit schoolteacher and poet Hilda Vest and her husband, Donald, who became the editors and publishers. During the late 1980s and 1990s the press concentrated on helping Detroit poets and authors publish and distribute their works. It also continued the tradition of featuring the work of poets of the black arts movement by publishing its Broadside Classics series. Randall died in 2000.

See also Black Arts Movement; Brooks, Gwendolyn Elizabeth; Giovanni, Nikki; Lorde, Audre; Madhubuti, Haki R. (Lee, Don L.); Sanchez, Sonia

Bibliography

Boyd, Melba Joyce. *Wrestling with the Muse: Dudley Randall and the Broadside Press.* New York: Columbia University Press, 2003.

House, Gloria, Albert M. Ward, and Rosemary Weatherston, eds. *A Different Image: The Legacy of Broadside Press: An Anthology*. Detroit, Mich.: Broadside Press and University of Detroit Mercy Press, 2004.

Joyce, Donald Franklin. *Gatekeepers of Black Culture: Black Owned Book Publishing in the United States, 1817–1981.* Westport, Conn.: Greenwood Press, 1983.

Thompson, Julius Eric. *Dudley Randall, Broadside Press, and the Black Arts Movement in Detroit, 1960–1995.* Jefferson, N.C.: McFarland & Company, 1999.

JOHN C. STONER (1996)
Updated bibliography

Brodber, Erna

April 20, 1940

Jamaican writer Erna May Brodber was born in the village of Woodside, St. Mary, to parents Ernest and Lucy Brodber, a farmer and a teacher. Among her earliest influences were the rich cultural life, social activism, and deep community involvement cultivated by her parents. Brodber brings to her craft a wealth of expertise honed in various fields: She has worked as a teacher, scholar, researcher, civil servant, and community activist. Her writing and prodigious scholarship span the disciplines of history, sociology, anthropology, and literature. Firmly refusing the ruling concept of the Caribbean as Creole, mixed, or hybrid, she reflects in her oeuvre a preoccupation with Africans in the diaspora. This enterprise is part of what Brodber calls "the re-engineering of blackspace" (Brodber,

1999/2000, p. 153), a spiritual and cultural ground from which people of African ancestry reflect upon and reconstruct their place in the world. The range and depth of Brodber's intellectual and activist work derive from her insistence on "completing the emancipation process. [T]he part of the task awaiting the intellectual worker is the development of a philosophy, of creeds, of myths, of ideologies, of pegs on which to hang social and spiritual life, the construction of frames of reference" (p. 157). An important component of this task is an engagement with the past through what can be defined as a critical remembrance.

Even as Brodber consciously looks to the past for fresh moral insights, her body of work establishes new coordinates of memory, history, and of knowledge itself. In the field of social history she starts from the premise that the mental and imaginative powers of those "from below" are important to an understanding of their own lives and of society more broadly. Brodber therefore incorporates their language and thought in the conceptual world of her scholarship. Crucial texts include *Life in Jamaica in the Early Twentieth Century: A Presentation of Ninety Oral Accounts* (1980), "Oral Sources and the Creation of a Social History in the Caribbean" (1983), and "Afro-Jamaican Women at the Turn of the Century" (1986). Her fiction reveals that she also sees as urgent the task of infiltrating the dominant narratives whose roots are to be found in colonial slavery and whose tentacles continue to shape the present. For example, Brodber's critical analysis and reconstruction of European accounts of the African-derived religious system of Myal is an important dimension of her 1988 novel of the same name. In *Louisiana* (1994) the so-called native informant captures the academically trained anthropologist and her equipment, transforming both observer and her methods into instruments that tell the collective history. Combining the use of oral sources with a willful reading of written history, Brodber brings to book its power and assumed morality, challenging it on its own terms and questioning conventional notions of reality.

The construction of black West Indian womanhood is yet another significant strand of Brodber's fiction and nonfiction. She pays particular attention to the social framework from which various aspects of female identity take their shape. The form of her first novel, *Jane and Louisa Will Soon Come Home* (1980), both weaves and unweaves the historical and linguistic conditions that create, entrap, and finally provide the sources of liberation for the story's protagonist. In *Perceptions of Caribbean Women: Towards a Documentation of Stereotypes* (1982), Brodber searches the colonial chronicles as well as postslavery and postindependence documents to unearth the formation of key ideas about West Indian women. Erna Brodber's wide-ranging literary, intellectual, and social efforts make a distinctive contribution to the understanding of the black experience in the Americas.

See also Women Writers of the Caribbean and Latin America

Bibliography

Brodber, Erna. *Abandonment of Children in Jamaica.* Mona, Jamaica: Institute of Social and Economic Research, University of the West Indies, 1974.

Brodber, Erna. *A Study of Yards in the City of Kingston.* Mona, Jamaica: Institute of Social and Economic Research, University of the West Indies, 1975.

Brodber, Erna. *Jane and Louisa Will Soon Come Home.* London: New Beacon, 1980.

Brodber, Erna. *Life in Jamaica in the Early Twentieth Century: A Presentation of Ninety Oral Accounts.* Mona, Jamaica: University of the West Indies, 1980.

Brodber, Erna. *Perceptions of Caribbean Women: Towards a Documentation of Stereotypes.* Mona, Jamaica: Institute of Social and Economic Research, University of the West Indies, 1982.

Brodber, Erna. *Afro-Jamaican Women and Their Men in the Late Nineteenth and First Half of the Twentieth Century.* Mona, Jamaica: Institute of Social and Economic Research (Eastern Caribbean), University of the West Indies, 1982.

Brodber, Erna. "Oral Sources and the Creation of A Social History in the Caribbean." *Jamaica Journal* 16, no. 4 (1983): 2–11.

Brodber, Erna. "Afro-Jamaican Women at the Turn of the Century." *Social and Economic Studies* 35, no. 3 (1986): 23–50.

Brodber, Erna. "The Pioneering Miss Bailey." *Jamaica Journal* 19, no. 2 (May 1986): 9–14.

Brodber, Erna. *Myal.* London: New Beacon, 1988.

Brodber, Erna. *Louisiana.* London: New Beacon, 1994.

Brodber, Erna. "Re-Engineering Blackspace." *Caribbean Quarterly* 43, nos. 1 and 2 (March–June 1997): 70–81. Reprinted in *Black Renaissance/Renaissance Noire* 2, no. 3 (Winter 1999/2000): 153–170.

Brodber, Erna. "Crossing Borders: An Interview with Writer, Scholar, and Activist Erna Brodber." Nadia Ellis Russell. May 7, 2001. Available from http://inthefray.com.

Brodber, Erna. *The Continent of Black Consciousness: On the History of the African Diaspora from Slavery to the Present Day.* London: New Beacon, 2003.

Brodber, Erna. *The Second Generation of Freemen in Jamaica, 1907–1944.* Gainesville: University Press of Florida, 2004.

Cooper, Carolyn. "Afro-Jamaican Folk Elements in Brodber's *Jane and Louisa Will Soon Come Home.*" In *Out of the Kumbla: Caribbean Women and Literature,* edited by Carole Boyce Davies and Elaine Savory Fido. Trenton, N.J.: Africa World Press, 1990.

Dance, Daryl Cumber. "'Go Eena Kumbla': A Comparison of Erna Brodber's *Jane and Louisa Will Soon Come Home* and

Toni Cade Bambara's *The Salt Eaters*." In *Caribbean Women Writers: Essays from the First International Conference*, edited by Selwyn R. Cudjoe. Wellesley, Mass.: Calaloux Publications, University of Massachusetts Press, 1990.

Walker-Johnson, Joynce. "*Myal*: Text and Context." *Journal of West Indian Literature* 5 (1992): 48–64.

Webb, Barbara. "Erna Brodber." In *Twentieth Century Caribbean and Black African Writers,* third series, edited by Bernth Lindfors and Reinhard Sander. Detroit, Mich.: Gale, 1996.

Wilson, Harris. "The Life of Myth and its Possible Bearing on Erna Brodber's Fictions *Jane and Louisa Will Soon Come Home* and *Myal.*" *Kunapipi* 12, no. 3 (1990): 86–92.

VERONICA MARIE GREGG (2005)

Brooke, Edward W.

October 26, 1919

The first popularly elected African-American member of the Senate when he entered that body in 1966, Edward William Brooke III served two terms as an independent Republican and distinguished himself as a proponent of civil rights legislation.

Brooke was born in Washington, D.C., to Edward William Brooke, a lawyer, and Helen Seldon Brooke. He gained his education first at Dunbar High School and later at Howard University, where he completed a bachelor of science degree in 1941, the same year in which his Reserve Officer Training Corps (ROTC) obligations called him to active combat duty after the Japanese attack on Pearl Harbor. During World War II Brooke served behind enemy lines in Italy and later defended soldiers in court-martial cases. This last experience inspired him to enter Boston University Law School on his return to the United States in 1945.

In 1962 Brooke won election as Massachusetts attorney general after three unsuccessful previous campaigns for public office. In that position he quickly attracted both local and national attention by aggressively prosecuting corrupt politicians and their cohorts outside of government. As a liberal Republican Brooke helped lead the failed opposition to the nomination of archconservative Barry Goldwater at the 1964 party convention. He remained neutral in the following general election.

In the senatorial elections in 1966 the voters of Massachusetts chose Brooke and his moderate program. After the ghetto riots of the following summer, President Lyndon B. Johnson appointed the freshman senator to the President's Commission on Civil Disorders, a position that led him to champion and steer through Congress one of the commission's primary recommendations: the guarantee of open housing contained in the 1968 Civil Rights Act. Despite Brooke's advocacy of such legislation, he frequently encountered criticism from civil rights movement leaders when he disagreed with their positions on issues or their tactics.

Brooke supported Republican nominee Richard Nixon's victorious 1968 and 1972 presidential campaigns, notwithstanding the deep differences between the two men. They were on opposite sides of such issues as the pace of racial integration, the Vietnam War, economic policy, and the arms race. Their greatest conflict came, however, in 1969–1970, when Brooke helped defeat two successive Nixon nominees to the U.S. Supreme Court: Judges Clement F. Haynsworth, Jr., and G. Harrold Carswell. After these fights Brooke and his fellow senators unanimously approved Nixon's third proposed High Court member, Judge Harry Blackmun. Brooke won a landslide victory in his 1972 reelection bid, and in the wake of the revelations of the Watergate scandal he became the first Republican to call on President Nixon to resign. After Brooke lost his seat in an attempt for a third term in 1978, he returned to the practice of law, first in Boston and later in Washington, D.C.

Brooke also served on the Commission on Wartime Relocation and Internment of Civilians (1981–1983). During the 1990s he was criticized for alleged ethical lapses as a lobbyist for Massachusetts developers with the U.S. Department of Housing and Urban Development.

In 2003 Brooke was diagnosed with breast cancer—rare among men—and was treated for it. In 2004 he was awarded the Presidential Medal of Freedom, the nation's top civilian honor for accomplishments in culture, politics, science, sports, and business.

See also Civil Rights Movement, U.S.; Politics in the United States

Bibliography

Cutler, John Henry. *Ed Brooke: Biography of a Senator*. Indianapolis, Ind.: Bobbs-Merrill, 1972.

Gilbert, Marsha. "Edward W. Brooke: Former Senator Battles Breast Cancer." *Ebony* 58, 10 (August 2003): 78–80.

STEVEN J. LESLIE (1996)
Updated by publisher 2005

Brooks, Gwendolyn

June 7, 1917
December 3, 2000

Taken to Topeka, Kansas, to be born among family, poet, novelist, teacher, and reader/lecturer Gwendolyn Elizabeth Brooks was reared in Chicago, where she continued to reside. In her autobiography, *Report from Part One* (1972), she describes a happy childhood spent in black neighborhoods with her parents and younger brother, Raymond. "I had always felt that to be black was good," Brooks observes. School awakened her to preferences for light skin among blacks, the "black-and-tan motif" noted in her earlier works by critic Arthur P. Davis.

Brooks's father, David Anderson Brooks, was the son of a runaway slave, a janitor with "rich Artistic Abilities" who had spent a year at Fisk University in Nashville, hoping to become a doctor, and who sang, told stories, and responded compassionately to the poverty and misfortune around him; her mother, Keziah Wims Brooks, had been a fifth-grade teacher in Topeka and harbored a wish to write. They nurtured their daughter's precocious gifts. When the seven-year-old Gwendolyn began to write poetry, her mother predicted, "You are going to be the *lady* Paul Laurence Dunbar." Years later, Mrs. Brooks took her daughter to meet James Weldon Johnson and then Langston Hughes at church. Hughes became an inspiration, friend, and mentor to the young poet.

Brooks graduated from Wilson Junior College (now Kennedy-King) in 1936. She was employed for a month as a maid in a North Shore home and spent four months as secretary to a spiritual adviser (see the "prophet Williams" section of the poem "In the Mecca"). In 1939 she married Henry Lowington Blakely II, a poet, writer, and fellow member of Inez Cunningham Stark's poetry workshop in the South Side Community Art Center. The marriage lasted fifty-seven years, until Blakely's death in 1996. Motherhood (Henry Jr., 1940; Nora, 1951), early publishing (*A Street in Bronzeville,* 1945), warm critical reception, careful supervision of her career by her editor at Harper's, and a succession of honors and prizes helped Brooks overcome her reticence about public speaking.

The first African American (or "black," her articulated preference) to win a Pulitzer Prize, for poetry (*Annie Allen,* 1950), Brooks also received two Guggenheim Fellowships. Upon the death of Carl Sandburg in 1968, she was named the poet laureate of Illinois. She was the first black woman to be elected to the National Institute of Arts and Letters (1976); to become consultant in poetry to the Library of Congress (1985–1986, just before the title was changed to poet laureate); to become an honorary fellow of the Modern Language Association; and to receive the Poetry Society of America's Shelley Memorial Award and its Frost Medal. She was elected to the National Women's Hall of Fame and given the National Endowment for the Arts Lifetime Achievement Award in 1989. Named the Jefferson Lecturer in the Humanities (1994), she also received the National Medal of Arts (1995). In Illinois, the junior high school at Harvey, the Cultural Center at Western Illinois University, and both the Center for Black Literature and Creative Writing and a chair as Distinguished Professor of English at Chicago State University all bear her name. On June 6, 2003, at a ceremony in Springfield, Illinois, the Gwendolyn Brooks Illinois State Library was dedicated. The number of her honorary doctorates exceeds seventy.

Gwendolyn Elizabeth Brooks. *Best known for her intense poetic portraits of urban African Americans, Brooks was the first black American to receive a Pulitzer Prize for Poetry.* AP/WIDE WORLD PHOTOS. REPRODUCED BY PERMISSION.

Brooks's work is notable for its impeccable craft and its social dimension. It marks a confluence of a dual stream: the black sermonic tradition and black music, and white antecedents such as the ballad, the sonnet, and conventional and free-verse forms. Influenced early by Hughes, T. S. Eliot, Emily Dickinson, and Robert Frost, she was propelled by the Black Arts Movement of the 1960s into Black Nationalist consciousness. Yet her poetry has always been infused with both humanism and heroism, the latter defined as extending the concept of leadership by both personality and art. In 1969 she moved to Dudley Randall's nascent, historic Broadside Press for the publication of *Riot* and subsequent works.

Brooks's books span six decades of social and political changes. *A Street in Bronzeville* addresses the quotidian realities of segregation for black Americans at home and in World War II military service; *Annie Allen* ironically explores postwar antiromanticism; *Maud Martha,* her novel (1953), sketches a bildungsroman of black womanhood; *Bronzeville Boys and Girls* (1956) presents sturdy, home-oriented black children of the 1950s; *The Bean Eaters* (1960) and new poems in *Selected Poems* (1963) sound the urgencies of the Civil Rights Movement. In 1967, at the Second Fisk University Writers' Conference at Nashville, Brooks was deeply impressed by the activist climate, personified by Amiri Baraka. Though she had always experimented with conventional forms, her work subsequently opened more distinctly to free verse, a feature of the multiform *In the Mecca* (1968), which Haki R. Madhubuti calls "her epic of Black humanity" (*Report from Part One,* p. 22).

Upon returning to Chicago from the conference at Fisk, Brooks conducted a workshop with the Blackstone Rangers, a teenage gang, who were succeeded by young writers such as Carolyn M. Rodgers and Madhubuti (then don l. lee). Broadside published *Riot* (1969), *Family Pictures* (1970), *Aloneness* (1971), and *Beckonings* (1975). Madhubuti's Third World Press published *The Tiger Who Wore White Gloves* (1974) and *To Disembark* (1981). In 1971 Brooks began a literary annual, *The Black Position,* under her own aegis, and made the first of her two trips to Africa. Beginning with *Primer for Blacks* (1980), she published with her own company *The Near-Johannesburg Boy* (1986), the omnibus volume *Blacks* (1987), *Gottschalk and the Grande Tarantelle* (1988), and *Winnie* (1988, a poem honoring Winnie Mandela). Her books are being reissued by Third World Press. The poems of *Children Coming Home* (1991) express the perspectives of contemporary children and may be contrasted with the benign ambience of the earlier work, *Bronzeville Boys and Girls. Report from Part Two* (1996) presents the second part of her autobiography. *In Montgomery and Other Poems* (2003), which the poet meticulously prepared, was published posthumously.

After a brief hospital stay, where she was diagnosed with cancer, Brooks died at home in Chicago on Sunday, December 3, 2000, surrounded by family and friends. Her personal papers are archived at the University of California, Berkeley's Bancroft Library.

Brooks supported and promoted the creativity of other writers. Her annual Poet Laureate Awards distributed considerable sums of her own money, chiefly to the schoolchildren of Illinois. She visited prisons, where her readings inspired poets such as the late Etheridge Knight. Lauded with affectionate respect in two tribute anthologies, recognized and mourned nationally and internationally as a major literary figure, Brooks continues to claim and to vivify U.S. democratic heritage.

See also Baraka, Amiri (Jones, LeRoi); Black Arts Movement; Dunbar, Paul Laurence; Literature of the United States; Madhubuti, Haki R. (Lee, Don L.); Poetry, U.S.

Bibliography

Bloom, Harold, ed. *Gwendolyn Brooks.* Philadelphia: Chelsea House Publishers, 2000.

Bolden, B. J. *Urban Rage in Bronzeville: Social Commentary in the Poetry of Gwendolyn Brooks, 1945–1960.* Chicago: Third World Press, 1999.

Bryant, Jacqueline, ed. *Gwendolyn Brooks'* Maud Martha: *A Critical Collection.* Chicago: Third World Press, 2002.

Kent, George E. *A Life of Gwendolyn Brooks.* Lexington: University Press of Kentucky, 1990.

Melhem, D. H. *Gwendolyn Brooks: Poetry and the Heroic Voice.* Lexington: University Press of Kentucky, 1987.

Melhem, D. H. *Heroism in the New Black Poetry: Introductions and Interviews.* Lexington: University Press of Kentucky, 1990.

Mootry, Maria K., ed. *A Life Distilled: Gwendolyn Brooks, Her Poetry and Fiction.* Urbana and Chicago: University of Illinois Press, 1987.

Shaw, Harry. *Gwendolyn Brooks.* New York: Twayne, 1980.

D. H. MELHEM (1996)
Updated by author 2005

Brotherhood of Sleeping Car Porters

The Brotherhood of Sleeping Car Porters (BSCP), organized in secret on August 25, 1925, became the first successful African-American labor union. From its inception in 1867, the Pullman Company had employed black porters because company officials believed their subservience could be depended upon and because they would work for low wages. Pullman thereby created an occupation over which African Americans had a monopoly. While steady employment and travel experience made porters the elite of black labor, they were not unionized and were often exploited and underpaid. Capitalizing on the fact that he was not a porter and hence could not be fired, socialist journalist A. Philip Randolph seized on the porters' complaints, educated them about collective bargaining and the value of trade unionism, and began organizing them in 1925. The question of unionization to the average porter, however, meant a choice between steady, albeit low, pay and reprisals by the company, so organizing had to be carried on covertly and employees' wives were often utilized for the job. Loyal assistants, such as Milton P. Webster in Chicago, Ashley Totten and Benjamin McLauren in New York, C. L. Dellums in Oakland, and E. J. Bradley in St. Louis, took care of the daily details and organizing while Randolph obtained outside publicity and funding.

Porters had legitimate complaints, working long hours for little pay. They made the railroad car ready, assisted with luggage, waited on passengers, converted seats into beds that they then made up, polished shoes, and remained on call twenty-four hours a day. Nevertheless, because they had been inculcated with the idea of company benevolence, and because of their fear of reprisal, most porters were reluctant to jeopardize their jobs by joining the union. Many did not understand the difference between the company union, the Employee Representation Plan (ERP), and a trade union like the BSCP.

Still, despite obstacles, BSCP membership increased, and Pullman attempted to undermine its success with a series of retaliatory measures, including frame-ups, beatings, and firings. The company had previously dealt with labor unions, but now resisted bargaining with African Americans as equals. Company propaganda identified Pullman as a benefactor of African Americans, which led many prominent blacks to oppose the BSCP. Organized labor was anathema to others because they believed, with justification, that black workers were discriminated against by white unions.

Although initially opposed to its craft-union stance, Randolph began taking a more conciliatory tone toward the American Federation of Labor (AFL) in his writings as early as 1923. After he began organizing the porters, Randolph continually sought the advice of William Green, head of the AFL. The BSCP first applied for an international charter from the AFL in 1928. Because of jurisdictional disputes with white unions, most likely prompted by racism, the AFL refused the international charter, granting instead federal charters to individual locals. Brotherhood officials were unhappy with federal status, but the weak BSCP needed the support of the AFL. For his part, Green, concerned about communist infiltration of black labor, considered the BSCP an acceptable alternative, not only to communism but also to masses of African-American laborers remaining outside the federation, where they acted as potential strikebreakers.

Realizing that the success of the union ultimately depended on its ability to correct grievances and provide job security, Randolph employed various strategies to force the company to the bargaining table. First, in 1926 he attempted to bring the dispute before the federal Board of Mediation under the Watson-Parker Railway Labor Act. Although the board recommended arbitration, under the act arbitration was voluntary and the company demurred. Second, believing that depending on tips was a degrading practice and because the uncertainty of the amount to be expected was one of the porters' primary grievances, Randolph brought the tipping system before the Interstate Commerce Commission in 1927. A ruling prohibiting tipping in interstate travel would have compelled a wage increase, but the ICC ultimately decided it did not have jurisdiction. Thus the BSCP was forced to call a strike in 1928, but, accustomed to finding jobs as strikebreakers, African Americans knew other blacks would be eager to take what many considered a plush position and consequently were reluctant to actually walk off the job. In response to a rumor that Pullman had nearly five thousand Filipinos ready to take the places of brotherhood members, William Green advised Randolph to postpone the strike.

After the aborted strike, membership dropped and the BSCP almost ceased to exist. The more favorable labor legislation under President Franklin D. Roosevelt, however—especially passage of the amended Railway Act of 1934, which outlawed company unions—revived the BSCP. Although Pullman responded by replacing its ERP with the Pullman Porters and Maids Protective Association, the situation for labor had changed. The AFL granted the brotherhood an international charter in 1935. After twelve years the Pullman Company finally signed a contract with the BSCP on August 25, 1937, bringing improved working conditions and some $2 million in income to the porters and their families.

Beginning with the 1932 AFL convention, Randolph started denouncing racism within the federation and attacking federal unions designed for African Americans. Although well disposed to John L. Lewis and the industrial unionism of the unions that left the AFL in 1937 to form the Congress of Industrial Organizations (CIO), Randolph—who had long advocated industrial unions—held the BSCP in the AFL, saying he thought it wiser to remain and fight for equality than to leave and let the federation

African-American railroad porters pictured at the International Headquarters of the Brotherhood of Sleeping Car Porters (BSCP) in Harlem, 1944. *The BSCP, organized secretly in 1925, survived more than a decade of opposition (including that of many black porters who feared the loss of their jobs) to win significant concessions from the Pullman Company in 1937, becoming the first successful African-American labor union in the United States.* HERBERT GEHR/GETTY IMAGES

continue its racist policies undisturbed. BSCP officers contented themselves with trying to prevent the split in the union movement and later working for reunification, but competition from the CIO forced the AFL to a more egalitarian position on racial equality. When the two federations merged in 1955, Randolph became a vice president of the newly created AFL-CIO, and the BSCP became instrumental in pushing the combined federation to financially back civil rights activity.

Not only did the BSCP successfully negotiate a series of favorable wage agreements between Pullman and its porters through the years, but the union provided support for civil rights activity by contributing its labor and some 50,000 dollars to Randolph's various equality movements as well. By the fall of 1940, fueled by defense contracts, the American economy was beginning to emerge from the Great Depression. But because of racial discrimination, African Americans found themselves locked out of the new job opportunities opening in defense industries. Randolph, backed by the brotherhood, threatened a march on Washington of one hundred thousand blacks the following July 1, to demand jobs in defense plants and integration of the armed forces. While integration of the military was not achieved, the Roosevelt administration was sufficiently concerned to issue Executive Order 8802 in June 1941, creating the wartime Fair Employment Practices Committee (FEPC) in exchange for cancellation of the march. Although weak, the FEPC did provide job training and economic improvement for many African Americans. In 1948 the porters' union assisted, albeit more reluctantly, Randolph's threat of a black boycott of universal military training; the Truman administration capitulated with integration of the military by Executive Order 9981. The BSCP supported Randolph's prayer pilgrimage in 1957, marches in Washington for integrated schools in 1958 and 1959, and the march on Washington for Jobs and Freedom in 1963. (Many organizers for the BSCP went on to assume important roles in the civil rights movement, such as E. D. Nixon, who played an instrumental part in the Montgomery bus boycott of 1955–1956.)

BSCP officers realized early on the threat to Pullman travel presented by the rise of commercial aviation; the drop was precipitous after World War II, with the porters becoming a diminished and aging group. Bowing to the decline of the railroad industry, in 1978 the BSCP merged with the Brotherhood of Railway and Airline Clerks. The brotherhood, however, had served its members well. Although porters were often absent from home because of long runs and usually missed holidays as well, the brotherhood helped the porters' domestic situation by providing job security, higher wages, and improved working conditions. Furthermore, during its heyday, under Randolph's leadership the BSCP became more than an instrumentality of service to the porters. From its inception in 1929 Randolph utilized the union's organ, the *Black Worker,* in the fight against communism, to educate porters to fight for civil rights, and to cajole them to abide by such middle-class virtues as thrift, cleanliness, and abstinence from alcohol. He organized the porters' wives into a Ladies' Auxiliary and their children into Junior Auxiliaries. The union thus encircled its members' lives and built their self-esteem. Trained in trade-union methods of collective bargaining, porters refused to beg for favors from the white power structure. Hence, the BSCP stimulated black participation in unions and fought to end discrimination in organized labor. The BSCP left an important legacy to both organized labor and the struggle for civil rights.

See also Labor and Labor Unions; Randolph, Asa Philip

Bibliography

Brazeal, Brailsford Reese. *The Brotherhood of Sleeping Car Porters: Its Origin and Development.* New York: Harper & Brothers, 1946.

"Brotherhood of Sleeping Car Porters Remembered During its 60th Anniversary." *Jet* 92, no. 17 (September 1997): 10.

Harris, William H. *Keeping the Faith: A. Philip Randolph, Milton P. Webster, and the Brotherhood of Sleeping Car Porters, 1925–37.* Urbana: University of Illinois Press, 1977.

Morales, Leslie Anderson. "The Porters Stand Together." *Footsteps* 4, no. 1 (January–February 2002): 18.

Pfeffer, Paula F. *A. Philip Randolph, Pioneer of the Civil Rights Movement.* Baton Rouge: Louisiana State University Press, 1990.

Santino, Jack. *Miles of Smiles, Years of Struggle: Stories of Black Pullman Porters.* Urbana: University of Illinois Press, 1989.

Wilson, Joseph F. *Tearing Down the Color Bar: A Documentary History and Analysis of the Brotherhood of Sleeping Car Porters.* New York: Columbia University Press, 1989.

PAULA F. PFEFFER (1996)
Updated bibliography

Brown, Andrew Benjamin

May 12, 1857
January 9, 1939

"It was not possible to know him and not to love him; those who loved him were many—of all races and in all walks of life," said Justice Sir Donald Jackson (as quoted in Campbell-Brown, foreword) of the Honorable Andrew Benjamin Brown, barrister-at-law and member of British Guiana Court of Policy and Combined Court. Brown was born in Den Amstel Village, West Coast Demerara, of an African-Guianese mother and a Barbadian father. He became a schoolmaster, member of the bar and Combined Court, and a businessman. After an early education under the tutelage of missionaries of the London Missionary Society in West Coast Demerara, he became a pupil teacher, entered Bishops' College, Georgetown, and trained as a schoolmaster. He was the headmaster of St. Mark's Scots School, LaRetraite, West Bank Demerara, in 1887 when a dispute over his pay ended in court. Brown's victory prompted him to proceed to England to enter the Middle Temple, University of London, as a law student.

After being called to the bar of the Middle Temple in July 1890, Brown returned home that year and opened a law firm. He was the first Guianese to qualify as a barrister. On August 30, 1904, he married Edith M. Campbell. He was actively involved in the Salem Congregational Church and School in Lodge, Greater Georgetown, becoming the school's manager. For many years Brown was the legal adviser of the British Guiana Congregational Union, and in 1921 he was elected its chairman. He gained prominence by successfully representing clients of all races, especially in rural courts in accident cases against the Demerara Railway Company. He also played a leading role in the aftermath of the colony's 1905 civil unrest and the indictment of the chief inspector of police, Colonel Lushington, for the shooting of a citizen.

Brown was also an entrepreneur and an early investor in the fledgling gold-mining industry from the 1890s to the 1920s. He financed many prospecting crews to the Mazaruni and Cuyuni hinterland mining regions as an absentee proprietor. In 1895 he became a part owner of Plantation Middlesex, No.2 Canal Polder, West Coast Demerara, where coffee and cocoa were planted. By 1910 he was also investing in the coconut and sugar industries.

When Brown returned to the colony in 1890 from the United Kingdom, the People's Reform Party, formed by African Guianese to challenge the dominance of white planters in the legislature, had already been founded. Brown joined the People's Reform Party and was selected as the party's candidate in the 1896 general elections. He won the West Coast Demerara seat and became the first "pure" African Guianese to gain a seat in the Court of Policy, the premier chamber of the legislature. He won the second election and returned unopposed on three successive occasions, serving for twenty-five years altogether. He earned the title "Father of the Court."

Among Brown's contributions were the opening of the Colonial Civil Service to all races and classes by means of an examination. Previously, civil service jobs had been filled primarily by Europeans regardless of suitable qualifications. He also ensured that the 1876 law on Compulsory Education in Primary Schools was enforced. He spearheaded the bill for the appointment of district education officers, resulting in a marked improvement in school attendance. He was also at the helm of the bill passed to prevent the employment of mostly East Indian children below twelve years of age on sugar estates. Brown was an advocate for changes in the conditions under which police and postal workers were employed, and he was able to gain improved transportation and living arrangements and increased allowances for them.

After the British Guiana Teachers Association (BGTA), formed in 1852, was resuscitated in the 1890s, an honorary life membership was conferred on him because of his consistent legislative struggles and gains for education. He had helped frame the association's constitution and rules, and he presented the BGTA's petitions to the Court of Policy. He also advocated that village councils, elected by the villagers themselves, should run the affairs of their communities. Thus, he introduced legislation to organize councils and to fix the boundaries of villages, giving birth to the Village Council Ordinance and the Annual Village Chairman's Conference. In 1912 he also served as a member of the Georgetown Town Council. Additionally, the issue of importing labor migrants, mostly Africans and East Indians, was ongoing in Guiana, and in 1919 he was part of an unsuccessful colonization deputation in England seeking to continue the labor migrant policy.

Monday, April 10, 1922, was a momentous day in Den Amstel Village, West Coast Demerara. Electors of the Western Division of Electoral District No.1 Demerara presented Brown with an address and a souvenir to express their appreciation for his public service as a member of the Court of Policy for twenty-five years from 1896 to 1921. The address was subsequently hung on the wall of the Negro Progress Convention Hall (NPC), an African-Guianese organization, similar to the League of Coloured Peoples. The souvenir, a silver salver, is in the Guyana Museum. The souvenir is inscribed: "Presented to A.B. Brown, MCP, 1896–1921. By the Electors of Western Division, Demerara and Friends. April 10, 1922."

The Den Amstel branch of the Young Men's Christian Association (YMCA) also used the occasion to express its pleasure for the part Brown had played in its formation thirty-five years previously and his active support ever since. In addition, the Lodge Young People's Improvement Association thanked him for being its patron from its inception in 1916 and for his interest in its welfare, and it tendered "sincere congratulations to A. B. Brown for such an illustrious public career." In 1922 King George V of England agreed to allow Brown to retain the title "Honourable" for life.

See also Politics

Bibliography

Campbell-Brown, Edith M. *The Life Story of Andrew Benjamin Brown*. Georgetown: British Guiana Lithographic Company, n.d.

The Chronicle (Georgetown, British Guiana), January 10, 1939.

The Daily Argosy (Georgetown, British Guiana), January 10, 1939.

Drakes, Francis M./Kimani Neheusi. "The People's Association, 1903–1921." *History Gazette,* no. 26 (September 1991).

Institute of Mines and Forests, British Guiana. *Annual Reports,* 1892–1920s. Washington, D.C.: Library of Congress.

Rodney, Walter. *A History of the Guyanese Working People, 1881–1905.* Baltimore, Md.: Johns Hopkins University Press, 1981.

Shahabudeen, Mohammed. *Constitutional Development in Guyana, 1621–1978.* Georgetown: Guyana Printers Ltd., 1979.

BARBARA P. JOSIAH (2005)

Brown, Charlotte Hawkins

June 11, 1883
January 10, 1961

One of the premier educators of her day, Charlotte Hawkins Brown was also a key figure in the network of southern African-American clubwomen who were active in the late nineteenth and early twentieth centuries. Brown was born Lottie Hawkins in Henderson, North Carolina. When she was five her family moved to Cambridge, Massachusetts, where her mother and stepfather operated a laundry and boarded Harvard students. During this period the family retained close ties with its Carolina roots.

Hawkins studied hard and was active in church and youth groups in Cambridge. She also developed an interest in art and music that became lifelong. As a high school student, Hawkins met Alice Freeman Palmer, the second president of Wellesley College, who took an immediate interest in her. Palmer was so impressed with Hawkins that she financed her education at the State Normal School in Salem, Massachusetts, where Hawkins enrolled in 1900 to earn a teaching certificate. She left school in 1901 to take a position with the American Missionary Association at a small school in North Carolina. Although the school soon closed because of inadequate funding, Hawkins determined to dedicate herself to education in her home state.

By October 1902 Hawkins had secured a donation of land, a building, and funds to open the Alice Freeman Palmer Memorial Institute in Sedalia, North Carolina. In 1909 she married Edward Brown, a graduate of Harvard, who taught at the Palmer Institute briefly before the couple separated and divorced. Over the years, under Charlotte Hawkins Brown's leadership, Palmer developed into a highly respected institution for preparatory training. From its early focus on vocational education, the school moved to a strict academic curriculum. The campus, the student body, and the faculty grew steadily, and Palmer sent many of its graduates to institutions of higher learning. Brown's work as an educator received recognition within her home state and across the country.

Brown was a key figure among black clubwomen, serving as president of the North Carolina State Federation of Negro Women's Clubs. She was also active in interracial work as a member of the national board of the YWCA, and she also worked with other organizations. She campaigned against lynching and toured widely as a lecturer. She also assisted in the founding of other schools in North Carolina, including the Dobbs School for Girls and the Morrison Training School, and she helped to establish scholarship funds for the college education of African-American women.

In addition to her work as an educator and activist, Brown raised her brother's three children and three of her young cousins. She also published two works, *Mammy: An Appeal to the Heart of the South* (1919) and *The Correct Thing to Do, to Say and to Wear* (1941). Brown remained the president of the Palmer Memorial Institute until 1952 and died nine years later. Although the institute ceased operation in 1971, the state of North Carolina has kept the memory of Brown's contributions and achievements alive in a memorial to her and to her institution.

See also Education in the United States

Bibliography

Daniel, Sadie Iola. *Women Builders.* Washington, D.C.: Associated Publishers, 1931. Revised and enlarged by Charles H. Wesley and Thelma D. Perry, 1970.

Marteena, Constance Hill. *The Lengthening Shadow of a Woman: A Biography of Charlotte Hawkins Brown.* Hicksville, N.Y.: Exposition Press, 1977.

Silcox-Jarrett, Diane. *Charlotte Hawkins Brown: One Woman's Dream.* Winston-Salem, N.C.: Bandit Books, 1995.

Wadelington, Charles Weldon, and Richard F. Knapp. *Charlotte Hawkins Brown and Palmer Memorial Institute: What One Young African American Woman Could Do.* Chapel Hill: University of North Carolina Press, 1999.

JUDITH WEISENFELD (1996)
Updated bibliography

Brown, Claude

February 23, 1937
February 2, 2002

The writer Claude Brown was born in Harlem in New York City, one of four children of a railroad worker and a domestic worker. Brown displayed behavioral problems and at age eight was sent to Bellevue Hospital for observation. By the time he was ten, he had an extensive history of truancy and expulsion and was sent to the Wiltwyck School, a school for emotionally disturbed boys, and then to the Warwick reform school. After his release Warwick, Brown performed a series of odd jobs and enrolled in night courses at Washington Irving High School. He graduated in 1957 and returned to Harlem, where he sold cosmetics and played piano for a living. In 1959 he won a grant from the Metropolitan Community Methodist Church to study government at Howard University, which awarded him a B.A. in 1965. While in his last year of college, Brown was encouraged by a mentor from the Wiltwyck School to write an article about growing up in Harlem for *Dissent* magazine. An editor at Macmillan Publishing saw the article and offered Brown an advance to write what would become his celebrated 1965 memoir, *Manchild in the Promised Land.*

The book was an uncensored account of coming of age in the turbulent setting of Harlem and was praised by critics for its honesty in its depiction of his difficult childhood. The bestseller made Brown a celebrity and interfered with his studies at Stanford University Law School. He transferred to Rutgers Law School, which he left in 1968 without obtaining his degree. In 1976, Brown's second book, *Children of Ham,* about a group of Harlem youths struggling to succeed, was published, but it failed to have the same impact as his first book.

Beginning in the 1970s, Brown worked as a freelance writer, commenting on the status of urban America. His articles were published in a number of periodicals, including the *New York Times,* the *Los Angeles Times, Esquire,* and the *New York Times Magazine.*

Brown died in 2002 from a lung condition at the age of sixty-four.

See also Literature of the United States

Bibliography

Boyd, Herb. "Claude Brown." *Black Issues Book Review* 4, no. 3 (May–June, 2002): 80.

Brown, Claude. *Manchild in the Promised Land.* New York: Macmillan, 1965.

Metzger, Linda, ed. *Black Writers: A Selection of Sketches from Contemporary Authors.* Detroit, Mich.: Gale Research, 1989.

O'Brien, Tia. "Influential Author Claude Brown Dead at 64." *San Jose Mercury News,* February 8, 2002.

KENYA DILDAY (1996)
Updated by publisher 2005

Brown, Henry "Box"

c. 1815–?

The abolitionist Henry "Box" Brown was born a slave on a plantation near Richmond, Virginia. As a young man, he worked in a tobacco factory in Richmond. As an adult, the sale of his wife and three children to a North Carolina clergyman in 1848 provoked him to attempt an audacious escape. In March 1849 he had himself crated in a wooden box and shipped to Philadelphia via Adams Express. He survived the torturous twenty-seven-hour journey and created a sensation when news of his escape reached the public.

After his escape, Brown took his salary and his "box" on the antislavery lecture circuit. The threat of slavecatchers, heightened by the enactment of the Fugitive Slave Act of 1850, compelled him to leave the United States for England in the fall of 1850. To enhance his antislavery presentations, he commissioned a panorama entitled "Mirror of Slavery." Boston artists painted several thousand square feet of canvas to illustrate slave life in the South and Brown's dramatic escape to freedom. With his panorama, and a narrative published in 1851, Brown became a well-known abolitionist lecturer during his four years in England.

See also Runaway Slaves in the United States; Slavery

Bibliography

Ripley, C. Peter, et al., eds. *The Black Abolitionist Papers.* Vol. 1, *The British Isles, 1830–1865.* Chapel Hill: University of North Carolina Press, 1985.

Ruggles, Jeffrey. *The Unboxing of Henry Brown.* Richmond: Library of Virginia, 2003.

MICHAEL F. HEMBREE (1996)
Updated bibliography

Brown, H. "Rap"

See Al-Amin, Jamil Abdullah (Brown, H. "Rap")

Brown, James

May 3, 1933

Singer and songwriter James Joe Brown Jr. was born near Barnwell, South Carolina, to Joe Brown, a turpentine worker, and Susan Behlings. After his mother left the family when the boy was four years of age, Brown spent his formative years in a brothel run by his aunt Handsome Washington in Augusta, Georgia. After the authorities closed the brothel in 1943, he lived with his aunt Minnie

Walker, receiving occasional tutoring on drums and the piano from neighbors and showing early promise on the harmonica and organ. He absorbed the music of the black church and of the minstrel shows that passed through Augusta, he heard the blues his father learned in the turpentine camps, and he listened to pop music on the radio. Fascinated by "soundies" (filmed musical numbers that preceded the feature at movie theaters), he paid close attention to those of Louis Jordan and His Tympany Five, who performed jump blues and novelty songs with great showmanship. Singing Jordan's "Caldonia," Brown entered and won local talent contests while not yet in his teens. At thirteen he formed the Cremona Trio, his first musical group, performing the songs of such rhythm-and-blues artists as Jordan, Amos Milburn, Wynonie Harris, Charles Brown, and the Red Mildred Trio.

These early musical endeavors were cut short when Brown's habit of stealing clothes and other items from unlocked automobiles earned him a harsh eight- to sixteen-year prison sentence, which he began serving at Georgia Juvenile Technical Institute (GJTI) in Rome, Georgia, in 1949. In GJTI, he formed a gospel quartet with three other inmates, including Johnny Terry, who would later become one of the original Famous Flames. After serving three years, he was paroled in Toccoa, the small town in northeast Georgia to which GJTI had been moved. He soon formed a gospel group with several youthful Toccoa musicians, including Bobby Byrd, a talented keyboard player, who would remain a central figure in James Brown's musical endeavors into the early 1970s.

The fledgling gospel group soon began playing rhythm and blues and performed for dances and in small clubs throughout eastern Georgia and neighboring areas of South Carolina until Little Richard's manager induced them to come to the vital music scene centered in Macon, Georgia. At a Macon radio station, the group, soon to be known as the Famous Flames, recorded a demo of "Please, Please, Please," which attracted the attention of Cincinnati-based King records. Rerecorded in Cincinnati and released in 1956, the song eventually climbed to number six on the rhythm-and-blues record chart. During the next two years, Brown sought to duplicate the success of "Please," essaying a number of rhythm-and-blues styles and occasionally imitating the differing approaches of Little Richard and King labelmates Hank Ballard and the Midnighters and the Five Royales. In 1958, with the recording of "Try Me," a pleading ballad steeped in gospel, he achieved the number one position on the rhythm-and-blues chart and began to realize his own distinctive style.

Brown soon became a headliner at Harlem's Apollo Theater and toured tirelessly, playing as many as three hundred dates annually and presenting a stage revue complete with comedians, warm-up acts, dancers, and a full orchestra. As a singer, he developed a powerful shouting style that owed much to gospel, but his rhythmic grunts and expressive shrieks harked back farther still to ring shouts, work songs, and field cries. As a band leader, he developed one of the most disciplined bands in entertainment and maintained it for more than three decades. He reimported the rhythmic complexity from which rhythm and blues, under the dual pressure of rock and roll and pop, had progressively fallen away since its birth from jazz and blues. As one of the greatest vernacular dancers in rhythm and blues, he integrated the latest dance crazes with older black popular dance styles and integrated them into a seamless whole that came to be known as "the James Brown." He became one of the most exciting live performers in popular music, capping his performances with a collapse-and-resurrection routine that became his trademark.

James Brown, the "Godfather of Soul." AP/WIDE WORLD PHOTOS. REPRODUCED BY PERMISSION.

With the album *Live at the Apollo* (1963), Brown brought the excitement of his stage show to record buyers throughout the world. Through the mid-1960s, he enjoyed enormous success with such compositions as "Out of Sight" (1964), "I Feel Good (I Got You)" (1965), "Papa's Got a Brand New Bag" (1965), and "Cold Sweat" (1967). These infectious, rhythmically complex dance hits propelled him to international stardom and heralded funk, his most original and enduring contribution to popular music around the world. Dispensing almost entirely with chord changes, Brown by the late 1960s had stripped the music to its rhythmic essence. Horns, guitars, and voices—including Brown's rich assortment of grunts, groans, shrieks, and shouts—were employed percussively. Rhythmic emphasis fell heavily on the downbeat at the beginning of each measure, imparting a sense of overwhelming propulsiveness to the music while leaving ample room for complex rhythmic interplay.

From the late 1960s through the mid 1970s, Brown and his band, assisted by gifted arrangers Pee Wee Ellis and Fred Wesley, produced powerful, polyrhythmic funk music that included inspired dance tracks as heard on albums such as *Sex Machine* (1970) and *Super Bad* (1971). He also wrote inspirational political and social commentary such as the anthem of black pride "Say It Loud—I'm Black and I'm Proud" (1968). Brown also became something of a political figure; several presidential candidates sought his endorsement. Following the murder of the Rev. Dr. Martin Luther King, Jr., in April 1968, Brown helped quell riots in Boston and Washington, D.C. In 1971 he produced a single about the dangers of drug use, "King Heroin."

Although Brown's records sold well through the early 1970s, the magnitude of his accomplishment was obscured by the rise of disco. Plagued by personal problems, including the break-up of his second marriage, the death of his oldest son, a federal tax case, and troubles with his numerous business enterprises, he briefly went into semiretirement, though he never entirely stopped performing, and he recorded numerous albums during this period, including *Hot* (1976) and *Bodyheat* (1976).

In the early 1980s he staged a successful comeback. He made cameo appearances in numerous motion pictures such as *The Blues Brothers* (1980). A series of retrospective albums, including *The Federal Years* (Part 1 and 2, 1984) and *Dead on the Heavy Funk* (1985), traced the development of his music from 1956 to 1976, and he returned to extensive recording and performing. His music was also widely sampled by rap artists, though in the 1990s he became a vocal supporter of a movement to persuade rap artists to avoid obscene lyrics. In 1986 he performed "Living in America" in the film *Rocky IV* and in 1987 became one of the first performers inducted into the Rock and Roll Hall of Fame.

In 1988, after leading police in Georgia and South Carolina on a high-speed chase that ended when the police fired some two dozen bullets into his truck, Brown was sentenced to six years in prison for failing to stop for a police officer and aggravated assault ("I aggravated them and they assaulted me," he famously stated). Although the lengthy sentence sparked a national outcry for Brown's pardon, he remained incarcerated for more than two years, earning early release in 1991. He had further legal problems in the 1990s, including a domestic violence charge and a marijuana and illegal firearm arrest in 1998. Nevertheless, he reemerged to be seen as one of the towering figures of popular music throughout the world. His musical innovations inform rock and jazz-funk hybrids, dance pop, reggae, hip-hop, and much African and Latin popular music. Critics, formerly ignoring him, now generally recognize him as one of the most influential American musicians of the past half century. His output has been prodigious, including more than seventy albums. In 1991 he released *Star Time,* a seventy-one-song, four-CD compilation of his greatest hits, and in 2003 *50th Anniversary Collection* was released. He has also produced hundreds of recordings by other artists. In 1992 he was given an Award of Merit at the American Music Awards ceremony for lifetime achievement, and in 2003 he received a Kennedy Center Honor.

See also Apollo Theater; Little Richard (Penniman, Richard); Music; Rhythm and Blues

Bibliography

Brown, James, with Bruce Tucker. *James Brown: The Godfather of Soul.* New York: Macmillan, 1986.

Hirshey, Gerri. "'We Sang Like Angels' and 'Superbull, Superbad.'" In *Nowhere to Run: The Story of Soul Music.* New York, 1984, pp. 54–63, 265–293.

"James Brown." *St. James Encyclopedia of Popular Culture.* 5 vols. Detroit: St. James Press, 2000.

BRUCE TUCKER (1996)
Updated by publisher 2005

BROWN, RONALD H.

AUGUST 1, 1941
APRIL 3, 1996

Born in Washington, D.C., to William H. and Gloria Osborne Carter Brown, Ronald Brown, a politician, graduated from Middlebury College in 1962 and joined the U.S. Army. He served from 1963 to 1967 and was discharged with the rank of captain. In 1970 he graduated from St. John's University School of Law and went to work at the National Urban League, where he served as general counsel, chief Washington spokesperson, deputy executive director, and vice-president of Washington operations from 1968 to 1979. In 1980 Brown became chief counsel to the U.S. Senate Judiciary Committee, and in 1981 he was general counsel and staff director for Sen. Edward M. Kennedy.

Brown joined a private law practice for the first time in 1981, when he became a partner in the Washington firm of Patton, Boggs, and Blow. His desire to return to politics was realized in 1989 when the Democrats selected him as their national chairman, the first African American to chair a major political party. Brown was assigned the task of rebuilding a dispirited party after the unsuccessful presidential campaign of 1988. His diplomacy and organizational skills were praised by both participants and observers following the 1992 Democratic National Convention in New York. In 1993 he was appointed secretary of commerce by President Bill Clinton.

Brown was a close Clinton adviser, as well as a visible and controversial figure, during his years in the Commerce Department. Though dogged by Republican charges of corruption and income tax evasion, he also was celebrated for his economic diplomacy, by which he sought to obtain trade agreements and open markets for the United States in countries such as China. On April 3, 1996, while on a trip to Croatia, Brown and his party were killed in an airplane crash.

See also National Urban League; Politics and Political Parties, U.S.

Bibliography

Brown, Tracey L. *The Life and Times of Ron Brown.* New York: Morrow, 1998.

Holmes, Steven A. *Ron Brown: An Uncommon Life.* New York: Wiley, 2000.

CHRISTINE A. LUNARDINI (1996)
Updated bibliography

Brown, Roscoe, Jr.

March 9, 1922

Roscoe Conkling Brown Jr., educator, was born in Washington, D.C. He attended Dunbar High School, a segregated academic high school in Washington also attended by such significant black figures as William Hastie, Charles Drew, and his father, Roscoe Conkling Brown Sr. (who was to become head of the National Negro Health Movement in Roosevelt's Black Cabinet). After graduating from Dunbar in 1939, the younger Brown went to Springfield College in Massachusetts, graduating as valedictorian in 1943.

That year, Brown enlisted in the Army Air Force. He was commissioned a second lieutenant in March 1944, and in July joined the 100th Fighter Squadron in Italy. From July 1944 to May 1945 he flew sixty-eight combat missions and was credited with one of the first downings of a German jet. Near the end of the war, Brown was promoted to captain and served as squadron commander of the 100th Fighter Squadron of the 332nd Fighter Group. For his achievements in combat he was awarded the Distinguished Flying Cross and the Air Medal with eight oakleaf clusters.

After leaving the service, Brown worked as a social investigator for the New York Department of Welfare before accepting a position in September 1946 at West Virginia State College as a teacher and basketball coach. Two years later, he was awarded a Rosenwald Foundation grant to attend graduate school at New York University. He received a Ph.D. in education in 1951 and accepted a teaching position at NYU, where in 1964 he established and became director of the Institute for African-American Affairs, a position he held until 1977. While at NYU he wrote and edited four books, including *Negro Almanac* (1967), and hosted three major New York television series, one of which, *Black Arts,* received an Emmy Distinguished Program Award in 1973.

In 1977 Brown became president of Bronx Community College in New York, where he remained until 1993. From 1985 to 1993 he also served as president of One Hundred Black Men, helping to make the organization a major advocacy force for African Americans in New York. In the fall of 1993 he accepted a position as Director of the Center for Urban Education Policy and University Professor at the Graduate School and University Center of the City University of New York. Brown is the author of over sixty scholarly articles and serves on the board of numerous nonprofit organizations. For his scholarly and community activities, Brown has received many awards and honors, among them the NAACP Freedom Award, the Congressional Award for Service to the African-American Community, and honorary doctorates from Springfield College, the University of the State of New York, and the Regents of the State of New York.

See also Drew, Charles Richard; Hastie, William Henry; Roosevelt's Black Cabinet

Bibliography

Low, W. Augustus, and Virgil A. Cliff, eds. *Encyclopedia of Black America.* New York: McGraw-Hill, 1981.

JACK SALZMAN (1996)
Updated by publisher 2005

Brown, Sterling Allen

May 1, 1901
January 13, 1989

Sterling A. Brown, who expressed the humor and resilience of the black folk tradition in his poetry, teaching, and public persona, was born on the Howard University campus. Except for a few years spent elsewhere as student and teacher, he remained at Howard most of his life. His father, Sterling Nelson Brown, born a slave, became a distinguished clergyman in Washington, D.C., as pastor of the Lincoln Temple Congregational Church and professor of religion at Howard, beginning in the 1890s. Reverend Brown died shortly before his son followed his example by joining the Howard faculty in 1929, a post that he held until his retirement forty years later in 1969.

As a youngster Brown attended the Lucretia Mott School and Dunbar High School, which was generally acknowledged as the finest black high school in the country. Upon graduation Brown accepted the scholarship that Williams College in Massachusetts offered to the Dunbar valedictorian each year. At Williams he joined the debating team, earned Phi Beta Kappa membership, and became the doubles tennis partner of Allison Davis, subsequently a distinguished social scientist and University of Chicago professor. After graduating from Williams in 1922, Brown earned his master's degree in English from Harvard University the following year. Before returning to Howard in 1929, he taught for three years at Virginia Seminary in Lynchburg, for two years at Lincoln University in Missouri, and for a year at Fisk University in Nashville.

Brown achieved an enduring reputation as a poet, scholar, and teacher. His most celebrated volume of poems was *Southern Road* (1932). Unlike such Harlem Renaissance contemporaries as Claude McKay and Countee Cullen, who wrote sonnets imitating Keats and Shakespeare, Brown eschewed traditional high literary forms and subjects, preferring instead the folk-ballad form and taking common black people as his subjects. In this he was like Langston Hughes. Brown was influenced by realist and narrative poets such as A. E. Housman, Edwin Arlington Robinson, and Edgar Lee Masters, as well as by African-American folklore, blues, and work songs. The characters of Brown's poems, such as Slim Greer, Scrappy, and Old Lem, are tough, worldly, and courageous. Some are fighters and troublemakers; some are pleasure seekers or hardworking farmers; and some are victims of racist mobs. At once unsentimental and unapologetic, these characters embody the strength and forthrightness that was typical of Brown's work in every genre.

As a scholar, Brown is best remembered for two books: *The Negro in American Fiction* (1937) and *Negro Poetry and Drama* (1937). These are both exhaustive works that document the African-American presence in American literature from the beginnings to the 1930s. The former book, especially influential as the first and most thorough work of its kind, has been a foundation for all subsequent studies of blacks in American fiction. From 1936 through 1940 Brown served as national editor of Negro affairs for the Federal Writers' Project (FWP). In this position he was involved with reviewing how African Americans were portrayed in the publications of the FWP, especially the series of state guidebooks. Although the task was frustrating—especially where the Deep South states were concerned—the appointment reflected how highly Brown, not yet forty, was regarded. During this same period, Brown also edited, along with Arthur P. Davis and Ulysses Lee, *The Negro Caravan* (1941), which remains one of the most useful and comprehensive anthologies of African-American writing ever published. All in all, the 1930s was the most intensely productive decade of Brown's life.

As a teacher, Brown was broadly influential. He was a pioneer in the teaching of African-American literature, and a startling number of black writers, scholars, and political figures studied with him. Outside the classroom Brown for many years held informal listening sessions, using his own massive record collection to introduce students to jazz, the blues, and other black musical forms. Alumni of those sessions include LeRoi Jones (Amiri Baraka) and A. B. Spellman, both of whom subsequently wrote important books about jazz. Similarly, Stokely Carmichael and Kwame Nkrumah were students who have often acknowledged their debt to Brown. His power as a teacher derived in part from his erudition but especially from his rare ability to combine the vernacular, scholarly, and literary traditions of the United States with progressive political values and a blunt, unpretentious personal style.

Brown's literary productivity decreased after the 1940s, partly because of recurrent illnesses. He nonetheless remained active as a guest lecturer and poetry recitalist and taught at several universities during his forty-year tenure at Howard, including Vassar College, Atlanta University, and New York University. In 1980 Michael S. Harper edited Brown's *Collected Poems,* which was awarded the Lenore Marshall Prize for the outstanding volume of poetry published in the United States that year. Brown's memoir, "A Son's Return: 'Oh, Didn't He Ramble,'" published in *Chant of Saints* (1979), recounts his early years, especially his life at Williams College, and is, despite its short length, one of the most compelling of African-American literary memoirs. Brown died in Takoma Park, Maryland.

See also Baraka, Amiri (Jones, LeRoi); Carmichael, Stokely; Cullen, Countee; Federal Writers' Project; Harlem Renaissance; Howard University; McKay, Claude

Bibliography

Brown Sterling A. "A Son's Return: 'Oh, Didn't He Ramble.'" In *Chant of Saints,* edited by Michael S. Harper and Robert B. Stepto. Urbana: University of Illinois Press, 1979.

Gabbin, Joanne V. Sterling *A. Brown: Building the Black Aesthetic Tradition.* Westport, Conn.: Greenwood Press, 1985.

Redmond, Eugene B. *Drumvoices: The Mission of Afro-American Poetry.* Garden City, N.Y.: Doubleday, 1976.

Stuckey, Sterling. Introduction to *The Collected Poems of Sterling A. Brown,* edited by Michael S. Harper. New York: HarperCollins, 1980.

DAVID LIONEL SMITH (1996)

Brown, William Wells

c. 1814

November 6, 1884

Born in Kentucky around 1814, novelist and historian William Wells Brown was the son of a slave woman and a white relative of her owner. The diverse jobs that Brown filled as a youth gave him the rich firsthand knowledge of the slave-era South that informs his autobiographical and fictional narratives. Moreover, it was while working for a printer named Elijah Lovejoy (who was later murdered by anti-abolitionists) that he took his first halting steps toward literacy.

Brown escaped from slavery in January 1834. During his flight he received aid from an Ohio Quaker named Wells Brown, whose name he subsequently adopted in the course of defining his new identity as a free man. Brown settled in Cleveland, where he married Elizabeth Schooner, a free black who bore him three children, two of whom—Clarissa and Josephine—survived to adulthood. Brown's antislavery activities began during these years as he helped numerous fugitive slaves escape to Canada. After moving to Buffalo, he continued his participation in the Underground Railroad and also spoke publicly on behalf of abolition, women's rights, peace, and temperance. By 1847 Brown had settled in Boston, where he published *Narrative of William W. Brown, a Fugitive Slave* to considerable success.

In 1849 Brown traveled to Europe to attend the Paris Peace Congress and to solicit support for American abolition. While abroad, he delivered over a thousand speeches and wrote some of his most important work, including the first African-American travelogue, *Three Years in Europe; or, Places I Have Seen and People I Have Met* (1852; issued in the United States in 1855 as *The American Fugitive in Europe*). In 1853 he published in London what has long been considered the first African-American novel, *Clotel; or The President's Daughter: A Narrative of Slave Life in the United States* (revised and reprinted three times in United States under different titles). After leaving Europe in 1854, when supporters purchased his freedom from Enoch Price, his last master, Brown turned to drama, producing the satirical *Experience; or, How to Give a Northern Man a Backbone* in 1856 and, in 1858, *The Escape; or, A Leap for Freedom,* the first play published by an African American.

Brown's wife had died during his European sojourn, and in 1860 he married Annie Elizabeth Gray. Meanwhile he continued his political and literary activities, supporting black recruitment efforts during the Civil War and writing *The Black Man: His Antecedents, His Genius, and His Achievements* (1863), ten editions of which appeared within three years. His other historical works include *The Negro in the American Rebellion: His Heroism and His Fidelity* (1867), a landmark study of blacks in the Civil War, and *The Rising Son; or The Antecedents and Advancement of the Colored Race* (1874). His final book—*My Southern Home; or, The South and Its People*—appeared in 1880. Brown died in 1884 after working for much of his later life as a physician in the Boston area.

If Brown's fiction is sometimes overly sentimental and structurally flawed and his histories can be insufficiently documented and repetitive, Brown's writing also manifests a sharp eye for telling detail, a skilled use of irony, and a clear, accessible prose style. Above all, he was an extraordinary pioneer; as such, he holds a crucial place in the African-American literary tradition.

See also Slave Narratives; Slavery; Underground Railroad

Bibliography

Brown, William Wells. *From Fugitive Slave to Free Man: The Autobiographies of William Wells Brown,* edited by William L. Andrews. Columbia: University of Missouri Press, 2003.

Farrison, William Edward. *William Wells Brown: Author and Reformer.* Chicago: University of Chicago Press, 1969.

RICHARD YARBOROUGH (1996)
Updated bibliography

Brown, Willie

March 20, 1934

Willie Lewis Brown Jr., a politician, was born and raised in Mineola, Texas. After graduating from high school in 1951, he moved to San Francisco, where he received a B.A. from San Francisco State University in 1955 and a J.D. from the Hastings College of Law in 1958. In 1959 Brown opened the law firm of Brown, Dearman, and Smith.

In 1964 Brown was elected to the California state assembly. In 1974 he unsuccessfully campaigned to become speaker of the assembly, but he won the post in 1980, becoming the first African American to hold one of the most powerful positions in California politics. Since then Brown has established himself as the most prominent and influential black politician in the state. Although he toned down his early, left-liberal politics when he rose to the position of speaker, Brown has consistently championed California's public education system and supported minority, gay, reproductive, and workers' rights.

Despite his credentials as a populist defender of liberal reforms, Brown has been criticized for his expensive taste in clothes and cars and his various alliances of convenience with Republican politicians and big business. As senior partner of Brown, Dearman, and Smith, his clients have included some of California's most powerful businesses, and Brown has often been charged with conflict of interest, particularly when he has endorsed tax breaks for corporations and real estate developers. In 1984 Republican opponents took advantage of Brown's image as an opportunist and autocrat by sponsoring Proposition 24, which would have significantly reduced the speaker's power, but it was rejected by the state's voters.

Brown has also been an influential figure in national Democratic politics. He served as campaign chairman and raised more than $11 million for Rev. Jesse Jackson's campaign during the 1988 primary election.

In the 1990 election, Brown's tenure was limited when the state's voters passed Proposition 140, limiting members of the assembly to three two-year terms and state senators to two four-year terms. In November 1994 the Republicans gained a slim majority in the assembly. However, through a parliamentary maneuver, Brown retained his post as speaker. In 1996 he resigned his post prior to making a successful run for mayor of San Francisco.

During his tenure as mayor, Brown distinguished himself in San Francisco by construction of a new central library and by introducing plans for the conversion of the abandoned naval base at Treasure Island. In 2003 Brown left office because of term-limit provisions, but he remains one of the most influential African-American leaders in California.

See also Politics in the United States

Bibliography

Groodgame, Dan. "Jesse Jackson's Alter Ego." *Time* (June 13, 1988): 28.

Richardson, James. *Willie Brown: A Biography.* Berkeley: University of California Press, 1996.

Von Hoffman, Nicholas. "Willie Brown in Deep Doo-Doo." *Gentleman's Quarterly* (March 1990): 292–295.

THADDEUS RUSSELL (1996)
Updated by publisher 2005

Brown Fellowship Society

An elite social club and mutual-aid society founded on November 1, 1790, by five free mulattoes in Charleston, South Carolina, the Brown Fellowship Society symbolized the existence of class and color consciousness within Charleston's African-American community.

Membership in the society was not to exceed fifty persons and was limited to "free brown men of good character" and their descendants who could afford the $50 membership fee. The organization maintained a clubhouse for its monthly meetings, and traditional lore claims that no person whose skin was darker than the door of the meetinghouse would be considered for membership. Many of the society's members were skilled craftsmen who had developed significant contacts with influential white Charlestonians with whom they shared upper-class interests and values. In fact, the original founders were members of St. Philip's Episcopal Church, a predominantly white congregation. Later generations of members were associated with St. Mark's Episcopal Church, an African-American congregation with a reputation for distancing itself socially from poorer and darker-skinned black Charlestonians. This association with prominent whites was reflected in the bylaws of the organization, which prohibited the discussion of controversial religious or political subjects, such as slavery. Violations of this proscription occasionally resulted in the expulsion of the offending member.

A number of Brown Fellowship Society's members were slave owners whose treatment of their chattel property ranged from exploitation to humanitarianism. Some slaves probably benefited from paternalistic treatment by these African-American masters, but this did not prevent slaveholding members of the organization from using their wills to perpetuate the "peculiar institution" by conveying ownership of slaves to surviving members of their families.

At the same time, the Brown Fellowship Society reflected the desire of Charleston's free blacks to control important aspects of their own lives. Operating under the motto "Charity and Benevolence," the society not only provided a school for its members and their families but also subsidized the Minors' Moralist Society for the education of impoverished free black children. It paid insurance and death benefits to the widows and orphans of deceased members and oversaw the burial of dead members in a private cemetery maintained by the society. In addition, the society served as a credit union whereby members could obtain loans, at the interest rate of 20 percent, to finance home improvements, start-up costs for small businesses, or merely to pay the bills in times of financial crisis.

The organization changed its name in 1890 to the Century Fellowship Society and added a women's auxiliary (the Daughters of the Century Fellowship Society) in 1907. Although little is known of the organization's later history, it continued to operate well into the twentieth century and maintained its character as a socially exclusive institution within Charleston's African-American community. In addition, several former members, through geographical mobility or marriage, became prominent in the aristocratic circles of other cities in the United States.

See also Fraternal Orders; Masculinity; Mutual Aid Societies

Bibliography

Curry, Leonard P. *The Free Black in Urban America, 1800–1850: The Shadow of the Dream.* Chicago: University of Chicago Press, 1981.

Fitchett, E. Horace. "The Traditions of the Free Negro in Charleston, South Carolina." *Journal of Negro History* 25 (April 1940): 139–152.

Gatewood, Willard B. *Aristocrats of Color: The Black Elite, 1880–1920.* Bloomington: Indiana University Press, 1990.

Wikramanayake, Marina. *A World in Shadow: The Free Black in Antebellum South Carolina.* Columbia: University of South Carolina Press, 1973.

JAMES M. SORELLE (1996)
Updated by author 2005

Brownsville, Texas, Incident

On the night of August 13, 1906, some 250 rounds of ammunition were fired into several buildings in Brownsville, Texas. One man was killed and two others were wounded. The townspeople's suspicions immediately fell upon the members of Companies B, C, and D of the First Battalion of the United States 25th Infantry, Colored. The African-American soldiers had arrived sixteen days before the shooting and were stationed at Fort Brown, just outside of town and near the site of the incident. Tensions between the black troops and some openly racist Brownsville residents flared. Although the soldiers and their white commander consistently denied any knowledge of the "raid," as it came to be called, subsequent investigations sustained the townspeople's opinion of their guilt.

President Theodore Roosevelt appointed an assistant inspector general to investigate. Two weeks later the inspector reported that it "can not be doubted" that the soldiers were guilty but that their white officers were not responsible. He recommended that "all enlisted men" be discharged from service because some of the soldiers "must have some knowledge of the guilty parties." Roosevelt then appointed Gen. E. A. Garlington inspector general to discover the guilty soldiers; all continued to proclaim their innocence. In his report Garlington referred to "the secretive nature of the race, where crimes charged to members of their color are made." By the end of November all soldiers in the battalion were discharged without honor from the U.S. Army because no one would point a finger at the supposed guilty parties. Those who were able to prove their innocence of participation in the raid were allowed to reenlist, and fourteen did so.

However, when an interracial civil rights organization, the Constitution League, reported to Congress that the evidence demonstrated the innocence of the soldiers, Senate hearings were held and Brownsville became a national issue. In March 1910 a Senate committee issued a majority report concluding that the shooting was done by some of the soldiers, who could not be identified, and upheld the blanket discharge of the battalion. Two minority reports were also issued. The first asserted that there was no evidence to indict any particular soldier, and that therefore there was no justification for discharging the entire battalion. The second minority report argued that the weight of the testimony showed that none of the soldiers participated in the shooting. Military courts-martial of two white officers found them not guilty of responsibility for the affray.

The incident had assumed national importance largely because Sen. Joseph Benson Foraker of Ohio charged that Theodore Roosevelt had allowed a decision based on flimsy evidence to stand. Thus, the Brownsville affray became an issue in Foraker's lengthy but ultimately unsuccessful campaign against Roosevelt for the 1908 presidential nomination.

The Brownsville incident also divided the African-American community. A split in 1905 that had resulted in the establishment of a group opposed to Booker T. Washington, the Niagara Movement, forerunner to the National Association for the Advancement of Colored People (NAACP), sharpened appreciably. Washington's unwillingness to criticize Roosevelt publicly—although privately he tried to dissuade the president from discharging the soldiers—induced many of his previous supporters to desert him. On the Brownsville issue, the division soon became those committed to the Republican Party versus everyone else.

It is possible that some of the soldiers of the 25th Infantry were guilty of the attack; it is also possible they were not. What is clear is that the soldiers were not proved guilty. When the incident was over, Roosevelt and Washington, if not unscathed, at least survived. Foraker risked his career on a bid for the presidency and lost. The black community lapsed into political silence. The soldiers of the 25th remained penalized until 1973, when they were granted honorary discharges. Only one soldier was still alive.

See also National Association for the Advancement of Colored People (NAACP); Niagara Movement; Washington, Booker T.

Bibliography

Lane, Ann J. *The Brownsville Affair: National Crisis and Black Reaction.* Port Washington, N.Y.: Kennikat Press, 1971.

Tinsley, James A. "Roosevelt, Foraker and the Brownsville Affray." *Journal of Negro History* 41 (January 1956): 43–65.

ANN J. LANE (1996)

Brown v. Board of Education of Topeka, Kansas

Brown (347 U.S. 483 [1954]) was the most important legal case affecting African Americans in the twentieth century and unquestionably one of the most important Supreme Court decisions in U.S. constitutional history. Although directly involving segregated public schools, the case became the legal underpinning for the civil rights movement of the 1950s and 1960s and the dismantling of all forms of statutory segregation.

Brown combined separate cases from Kansas, South Carolina, Virginia, and Delaware that turned on the meaning of the Fourteenth Amendment's requirement that states not deny their citizens "equal protection of the law." The Court also heard a similar case from Washington, D.C., *Bolling v. Sharpe,* which involved the meaning of the Fifth Amendment's due process clause.

In 1954 laws in eighteen states plus the District of Columbia mandated segregated schools, while other states allowed school districts to maintain separate schools if they wanted to do so. Although theoretically guaranteeing blacks "separate-but-equal" education, segregated schools were never equal for blacks. Linda Brown, whose father, Rev. Oliver Brown, sued the Topeka, Kansas, school system on her behalf, had to travel an hour and twenty minutes to school each way. If her bus was on time, she was dropped off at school a half hour before it opened. Her bus stop was six blocks from her home, across a hazardous railroad yard; her school was twenty-one blocks from her home. The neighborhood school her white playmates attended was only seven blocks from her home and required neither bus nor hazardous crossings to reach. The *Brown* companion cases presented segregation at its worst. Statistics from Clarendon, South Carolina, where one of the cases began, illustrate the inequality of separate but equal. In 1949 and 1950 the average expenditure for white students was 179 dollars, but for blacks it was only 43 dollars. The county's 6,531 black students attended school in 61 buildings valued at 194,575 dollars; many of these schools lacked indoor plumbing or heating. The 2,375 white students in the county attended school in twelve buildings worth 673,850 dollars, with far superior facilities. Teachers in the black schools received, on average, salaries that were one-third less than those of teachers in the white schools. Finally, Clarendon provided school buses for white students in this rural county but refused to provide them for blacks.

The plaintiffs could easily have won orders requiring state officials to equalize the black schools on the grounds that education was separate but not equal. Since the 1930s the Court had been chipping away at segregation in higher education, interstate transportation, housing, and voting. In *Brown* the NAACP Legal Defense Fund, led by Thurgood Marshall, decided to directly challenge the whole idea of segregation in schools.

Marshall's bold challenge of segregation per se led the Court to reconsider older cases, especially *Plessy v. Ferguson,* that had upheld segregation. The Court was also compelled to consider the meaning of the Fourteenth Amendment, which had been written at a time when most states allowed some forms of segregation and when public education was undeveloped in the South. The Court ordered attorneys for both sides to present briefs and reargument on these historical matters. In the end the Court found the historical argument to be at best inconclusive. The most avid proponents of the post–Civil War amendments undoubtedly intended them to remove all legal distinctions among "all persons born or naturalized in the United States." Their opponents, just as certainly, were antagonistic to both the letter and the spirit of the Amendments. What others in Congress and the state legislatures had in mind cannot be determined with any degree of certainty.

After reviewing the histories of the Fourteenth Amendment, public education, and segregation, Chief Justice Earl Warren, speaking for a unanimous Court, concluded, "In approaching this problem, we cannot turn the clock back to 1868 when the Amendment was adopted, or even to 1896 when *Plessy v. Ferguson* was written. We must consider public education in the light of its full development and its present place in American life throughout the Nation." Warren found that "in the field of public education the doctrine of 'separate but equal' has no place. Separate education facilities are inherently unequal." *Brown* did not technically overturn *Plessy* (which involved seating on railroads) or the separate-but-equal doctrine. But that technicality was unimportant. *Brown* signaled the end to the legality of segregation. Within a dozen years the Supreme Court would strike down all vestiges of legalized segregation.

Brown did not, however, lead to an immediate end to segregated education. The Court instead ordered new arguments for the next year to determine how to begin the difficult social process of desegregating schools. The NAACP urged immediate desegregation. However, in a second case, known as *Brown II* (1955), the Court ordered its mandate implemented with "all deliberate speed," a process that turned out to be extraordinarily slow. Linda Brown, for example, did not attend integrated schools until junior high; none of the plaintiff children in the Clarendon County case ever attended integrated schools.

See also Civil Rights Movement, U.S.; Fourteenth Amendment; Marshall, Thurgood; *Plessy v. Ferguson*

Bibliography

Robert J. Cottrol, et al. *Brown v Board of Education: Caste, Culture, and the Constitution.* Lawrence: University of Kansas Press, 2003.

Finkelman, Paul, ed. *Race Law and American History,* vol. 7, *The Struggle for Equal Education.* New York: Garland, 1992.

Finkelman, Paul. "Civil Rights in Historical Context: In Defense of Brown." *Harvard Law Review* 118 (2005): 973-1027.

Kluger, Richard. *Simple Justice.* New York: Vintage, 1975.

Tushnet, Mark. *The NAACP's Campaign against Segregated Education.* Chapel Hill: University of North Carolina Press, 1987.

PAUL FINKELMAN (1996)
Updated by publisher 2005

Bruce, Blanche Kelso

March 1, 1841
March 17, 1898

Blanche K. Bruce was the second African American to be elected to the U.S. Senate, and the first to serve an entire six-year term. Born a slave on a plantation near Farmville, Prince Edward County, Va., he enjoyed an unusually privileged upbringing. His mother, Polly, was a slave owned by Pettus Perkinson, who may have been Bruce's father. Perkinson took an interest in Bruce and allowed him to be educated by his son's tutor. While growing up, Bruce moved with Perkinson and his family several times between Virginia, Missouri, and Mississippi. By all accounts, his childhood was pleasant, comfortable, and virtually free from punishment.

Nevertheless, Bruce refused to accept his status as a slave, and he ran away to Kansas at the beginning of the

Civil War. In Lawrence, Kansas, he founded and taught in a school for black refugees. In 1864 he moved to Hannibal, Missouri, where he started the state's first school for blacks. He also apprenticed briefly to a printer. After studying at Oberlin College in Oberlin, Ohio, in 1866, Bruce returned to Missouri to work as a porter on a steamboat.

Like many ambitious blacks and whites, Bruce recognized that the South during Reconstruction offered many opportunities for both political power and economic advancement. He settled in Mississippi in 1869 and immediately became active in the state's Republican Party. He served in a series of appointive public offices, including voter registrar for Tallahatchie County, sergeant-at-arms of the state senate, and tax assessor for Bolivar County. Gaining a reputation for honesty and efficiency, he was elected sheriff and tax collector of Bolivar County in 1871. Bruce also held positions as county superintendent of education and as a member of the district board of levee commissioners. In addition to his electoral base among black voters, he won the support of many white planters for his competence and promotion of political and economic stability. The dominant political figure in Bolivar County, Bruce also became an important landowner, with a 640-acre plantation and city lots in the county seat of Floreyville.

Mississippi's Republican-dominated legislature elected Bruce to the U.S. Senate in 1874, and he took office on March 5, 1875. He served on the Pensions, Manufactures, and Education and Labor Committees, as well as on the Select Committee on Mississippi River Improvements. As chairman of the investigating committee into the bankrupt Freedman's Savings and Trust Company, Bruce conducted an impressive inquiry into the corrupt and inept handling of nearly $57 million in deposits of former slaves. Cautious by nature and moderate politically, Bruce nevertheless often spoke and voted in defense of the rights of African Americans. At the same time, he believed that blacks were best advised to pursue advancement through education and self-help. He opposed the mass movement of African Americans from the South to Kansas, as well as efforts to promote emigration to Liberia.But he also reminded southern conservatives that the exodus was prompted by increasingly hostile conditions in the former slave states, and he sponsored legislation to aid exodusters suffering hardships in Kansas.

Bruce was cultured and intelligent, with refined manners and shrewd political judgement. In Washington, the light-skinned and sophisticated senator moved easily in elite circles, both black and white. On June 24, 1878, he married the elegant and beautiful Josephine Willson, daughter of a prominent Cleveland dentist. At first, the couple associated with the leading members of white Washington society as well as with leading blacks. However, after Bruce left the Senate in 1881, and as the color line in the capital began to harden, they had less contact with whites, becoming mainstays of Washington's African-American "aristocracy." The Bruce's only child, Roscoe Conkling Bruce (1879–1950), later became a prominent educator and manager of the famous Dunbar Apartments in Harlem.

By the end of Bruce's term in the Senate, Democrats dominated Mississippi, and no Republican could hope to win a state election. By retaining control of the state's Republican Party, however, Bruce remained an important figure in national party affairs. He served as register of the treasury under presidents James Garfield, Chester A. Arthur, and William McKinley (1881–1885 and 1897–1898), and as recorder of deeds for the District of Columbia under President Benjamin Harrison (1889–1893), two of the highest patronage positions in the federal government traditionally reserved for blacks. A member of the boards of the Washington public schools and Howard University, Bruce was also a sought-after lecturer. In addition, he amassed close to 3,000 acres of land in the Mississippi Delta, and he operated a successful agency in Washington for financial investment, claims, insurance, and real estate. In 1895, Bruce was worth an estimated $150,000, making him one of the wealthiest men in the capital. Bruce died in 1898 after years of deteriorating health.

See also Politics in the United States

Bibliography

Gatewood, Willard B. *Aristocrats of Color: The Black Elite, 1880-1920.* Bloomington: University of Indiana Press, 1990.

Harris, William C. "Blanche K. Bruce of Mississippi: Conservative Assimilationist." In *Southern Black Leaders of the Reconstruction Era,* edited by Howard N. Rabinowitz. Urbana: University of Illinois Press, 1982.

Mann, Kenneth Eugene. "Blanche Kelso Bruce: United States Senator Without a Constituency." *Journal of Mississippi History* 38 (May 1976): 183–198.

Shapiro, Samuel L. "Blanche Kelso Bruce." In *Dictionary of American Negro Biography,* edited by Rayford W. Logan and Michael R. Winston. New York: Norton, 1982.

DANIEL SOYER (1996)

Bruce, John Edward

February 22, 1856
August 7, 1924

Journalist and historian John Edward Bruce, who achieved a wide reputation as a journalist under the pseudonym "Bruce Grit," was born into slavery in Piscataway, Maryland. His father was sold when he was three, and Bruce and his mother were subsequently sent to Fort Washington, where his mother served as a cook for the Marines. In 1860, while following soldiers marching from Maryland to Washington, D.C., Bruce and his mother were freed. While his mother found domestic work, John Bruce was educated in local public schools and by private instructors and later took a three-month college course at Howard University.

Bruce was hired as an office assistant in the Washington, D.C., correspondent's office of the *New York Times* in 1874. Shortly afterward, he began his career as a journalist and publisher. He founded three periodicals in quick succession, a Washington weekly called the *Argus* in 1879, the *Sunday Item* in 1880, and the *Washington Grit* in 1884. He also began to write commentaries for the *New York Times* and mainstream newspapers, including the *Boston Transcript,* the *Washington Evening Star,* and the *St. Louis Globe-Democrat.* Taking the name "Bruce Grit" in 1884 for his column in the *New York Age* and the *Gazette* of Cleveland, Bruce acquired the pseudonym by which he would become widely known in his journalistic career. In addition to writing for T. Thomas Fortune's *New York Age,* Bruce also assisted *Fortune* throughout the 1890s as a member of the Afro-American League and the Afro-American Council.

In 1879 Bruce and Charles W. Anderson (Booker T. Washington's lieutenant in the New York City Republican Party) cofounded the *Chronicle* in New York City. Bruce moved to Albany, New York, in 1900 and later cofounded the *Weekly Standard* in Yonkers with Anderson in 1908. Despite his ties to the Washington camp, Bruce was an independent in the black political wars of the early nineteenth century. He was a sometime supporter of Washington's bitter opponent, William Monroe Trotter, and attended the conference that founded the Niagara Movement in 1905. Around 1908 he took a job with the Port of New York Authority to have a more consistent means of financial support than his peripatetic newspaper publishing provided.

In his articles Bruce urged black readers to take greater pride in their African ancestry. He vehemently attacked what he saw as the attempts of lighter-skinned black "aristocrats" to deny their African heritage. For instance, in an 1877 essay titled "Colored Society in Washington," Bruce ridiculed the "colored aristocracy" for avoiding the company of darker-skinned blacks and thereby creating a "color line" within the black community itself. Bruce believed that all Americans of African descent, regardless of color, ought to be called "Negro" rather than "Afro-American" or "colored." The other terms, he thought, were attempts by the "black aristocrats" to differentiate themselves from working-class darker-skinned blacks. To reinforce racial pride among black Americans, Bruce published *Short Biographical Sketches of Eminent Negro Men and Women in Europe and the United States* in 1910 and founded the Negro Society for Historical Research with Arthur Schomburg in 1911. In 1916 he published a work of fiction, *The Awakening of Hezekiah Jones,* and subsequently published such pamphlets of social commentary as *The Making of a Race* and *A Tribute for the Negro Soldier.*

A popular and powerful orator, Bruce argued for racial solidarity and self-help as the best means of combating segregation and lynching. His hopes that an Allied victory in World War I would bring African Americans greater political equality were disappointed in 1919 by the ensuing riots in East St. Louis and other cities. Bruce joined Marcus Garvey's Universal Negro Improvement Association (UNIA), sympathetic to its antipathy toward lighter-skinned African Americans and its skepticism about the prospects for civic equality in the United States. Bruce became a contributing editor for two of the UNIA's periodicals, *The Negro World* and the *Daily Negro Times.*

Bruce retired from the Port of New York Authority in 1922 and died at Bellevue Hospital.

See also Fortune, T. Thomas; Garvey, Marcus; Niagara Movement; Trotter, William Monroe; Washington, Booker T.

Bibliography

Crowder, Ralph L. *John Edward Bruce: Politician, Journalist, and Self-Trained Historian of the African Diaspora.* New York: New York University Press, 2004.

Gatewood, Willard B. *Aristocrats of Color: The Black Elite, 1880–1902.* Indianapolis: Indiana University Press, 1990.

Gilbert, Peter, ed. *The Selected Writings of John Edward Bruce, Militant Black Journalist.* New York: Arno Press, 1971.

DURAHN TAYLOR (1996)
Updated bibliography

"B. SMITH"

See Smith, Barbara ("B. Smith")

BUBBLES, JOHN

FEBRUARY 19, 1902
MAY 18, 1986

The tap dancer John Bubbles, known as "the father of rhythm tap," was born John William Sublett in Louisville, Kentucky, and raised in Indianapolis. At the age of ten, he teamed up with six-year-old Ford Lee Washington (1906–1955) in an act billed as "Buck and Bubbles." Bubbles sang and danced while Buck, standing at the piano, played accompaniment. The duo won a series of amateur-night shows, and they subsequently began playing engagements in Louisville (where the two sometimes appeared in blackface), Detroit, and New York City. When Bubbles's voice changed at the age of eighteen, he focused on dancing.

Bubbles developed a new style of tapping that was spiced with extremely difficult innovations, such as double over-the-tops (normally a rough figure-eight pattern executed with the appearance of near self-tripping; Bubbles would do them with alternate legs, traveling backwards and forwards and from side to side). By 1922, Buck and Bubbles reached the pinnacle in vaudeville by playing at New York's Palace Theatre. Bypassing the black Theater Owners Booking Association (TOBA) circuit, they headlined the white-vaudeville circuit from coast to coast. Their singing-dancing comedy act, in which Buck's easy piano style contrasted with Bubbles's witty explosion of taps, was featured in the *Broadway Frolics of 1922,* Lew Leslie's *Blackbirds of 1930* and the *Ziegfeld Follies of 1931.* Bubbles secured his place in Broadway history when he created the acting, singing, and dancing role of Sportin' Life in George Gershwin's opera *Porgy and Bess* in 1935.

During the 1930s, Buck and Bubbles played the London Palladium, the Cotton Club, and the Apollo Theater; they were also the first black performers to appear at Radio City Music Hall. The two broke color barriers in theaters across the country. Motion pictures in which they appeared include *Varsity Show* (1937), *Cabin in the Sky* (1943), *Atlantic City* (1944), and *A Song Is Born* (1948). The duo remained together until shortly before Buck's death in 1955. On his own, Bubbles appeared with Bob Hope in Vietnam and recorded several albums, including *From Rags to Riches* (1980). After being partly paralyzed by a stroke in 1967, Bubbles made one of his final public appearances as a singer in 1980 in the revue *Black Broadway.*

Bubbles's rhythm tapping, later called "jazz tap," revolutionized dancing. Before him, dancers tapped up on their toes, emphasizing flash steps (difficult, acrobatic steps with extended leg and body movements), and danced to a quicker tempo (two beats to a bar). Bubbles cut the tempo in half, extended the rhythm beyond the normal eight beats, dropped his heels, and hit unusual accents and syncopations. "I wanted to make it more complicated, so I put more taps in and changed the rhythm," said Bubbles about his style, which anticipated both the new sound of bebop in the 1940s and the prolonged melodic line of "cool" jazz in the 1950s.

See also Apollo Theater; Cotton Club; Tap Dance

Bibliography

Goldberg, Jane. "A Hoofer's Homage: John Bubbles." *Village Voice,* December 4, 1978.

"John William Bubbles." *The Scribner Encyclopedia of American Lives: Volume 2, 1986-1990.* Detroit, Mich.: Charles Scribner's Sons, 1999.

Slide, Anthony. *The Vaudevillians: A Dictionary of Vaudeville Performers.* Westport, Conn.; Arlington House 1981.

Smith, Bill. *The Vaudevillians.* New York: Macmillan, 1976.

Stearns, Marshall, and Jean Stearns. *Jazz Dance: The Story of American Vernacular Dance.* New York: Macmillan, 1968.

CONSTANCE VALIS HILL (1996)
Updated bibliography

BUHAINA, ABDULLAH IBN

See Blakey, Art (Buhaina, Abdullah Ibn)

BULLINS, ED

JULY 2, 1935

Born in Philadelphia, Pennsylvania, playwright Ed Bullins attended public schools there and received a B.A. from Antioch University in San Francisco in 1989. He did graduate work at San Francisco State University. In 1976 Columbia College in Chicago awarded him an honorary Doctor of Laws degree. From 1952 to 1955 he served in the United States Navy.

During the 1960s on the West Coast, Bullins was one of the leaders of the black arts movement and a founder and producer from 1965 to 1967 of Black Arts/West, an African-American theater group in San Francisco. He was also a cofounder of the Black Arts Alliance and Black House, a militant cultural-political group that included Eldridge Cleaver, Huey Newton, and Bobby Seale, all three of whom later became Black Panther Party leaders. Bullins served briefly as minister of culture of the Black Panthers in California. He left Black House after a disagreement over ideology. As an artist, Bullins was interested in cultural awakening, whereas the revolutionaries thought that creative work should be incendiary enough to stir people to action. While he was on the West coast, some of his earliest plays were written and produced: *Clara's Ole Man* (1965), *Dialect Determinism* (1965), and *How Do You Do?* (1965).

At the New Lafayette Theatre in Harlem from 1968 to 1973, Bullins was playwright-in-residence and, later, associate director. He was also editor of *Black Theatre* magazine. After the New Lafayette Theatre closed, he was writer-in-residence at the American Place Theatre in 1973 and on the staff of the New York Shakespeare Festival's Writers' Unit from 1975 to 1982. Best known as a playwright, Bullins has also written fiction, poetry, and essays.

Inspired by Amiri Baraka (LeRoi Jones), whose plays *Dutchman* and *The Slave* he saw in San Francisco during the 1960s, Bullins has written many plays on the African-American experience, dealing with ordinary African-American life and, in some cases, race relations. A pioneer interested in developing new theater forms, he writes in many styles: realism, naturalism, satire, and farce, as well as absurdist and other avant-garde methods. He has written black rituals, street-theater plays, and agitprop plays, but his main dramatic works have been what he terms "theater of reality" plays, which are mostly naturalistic.

Bullins's productivity as a playwright and his writing about the African-American experience have given him considerable influence. New York theater practitioners such as Robert Macbeth, founder and director of the now-defunct New Lafayette Theatre, embraced Bullins, along with audiences, critics, and publishers. For his plays he has earned the Drama Desk-Vernon Rice Award (1968) and Obie awards (1971 and 1975). *The Taking of Miss Janie* (1975), one of his best-known plays, received the Drama Critics Circle Award as the best American play of 1974–1975 and was selected as a Burns Mantle Best Play for the same year.

In addition to the theater awards, Bullins has been the recipient of Rockefeller grants (1968, 1970, 1973, and 1983), Guggenheim fellowships (1971 and 1976), and National Endowment for the Arts grants (1972 and 1989). His plays have been produced throughout the United States and abroad. He has taught at various colleges and universities, including New York University, City College of San Francisco, and the University of California at Berkeley. In the 1990s he published *New/Lost Plays by Ed Bullins*, a collection of his work. In 1997 the Negro Ensemble Company produced a new play, *Boys x Men* (that is, "Boys Times Men"), a play that concerns family, class, and memory.

See also Baraka, Amiri (Jones, LeRoi); Black Arts Movement; Black Panther Party for Self-Defense; Cleaver, Eldridge; Newton, Huey P.; Seale, Bobby

Bibliography

Hay, Samuel A. "'What Shape Shapes Shapelessness?': Structural Elements in Ed Bullins' Plays." *Black World* (April 1974): 20–26.

Hay, Samuel A. *Ed Bullins: A Literary Biography.* Detroit: Wayne State University Press, 1997.

Sanders, Leslie Catherine. "'Like Niggers': Ed Bullins' Theater of Reality." In *The Development of Black Theater in America.* Baton Rouge: Louisiana State University Press, 1988, pp. 176–228.

JEANNE-MARIE A. MILLER (1996)
Updated by publisher 2005

Bunche, Ralph

August 7, 1904
December 9, 1971

Ralph Johnson Bunche, a scholar, diplomat, and international civil servant, was born in Detroit, Michigan, to Fred and Olive Johnson Bunch. His father, a barber, abandoned the family when his son was young. Bunche moved to Albuquerque, New Mexico, with his mother, who died there in 1917. He then went to Los Angeles to be raised by his maternal grandmother, Lucy Taylor Jackson. During his teen years, he added a final "e" to his name to make it more distinguished. Bunche lived in a neighborhood with relatively few blacks, and he was one of only two blacks in his class at Jefferson High School, where he graduated first in his class, although Los Angeles school authorities barred him from the all-city honor roll because of his race. Bunche's valedictory address was his first public speech. Bunche entered the University of California at Los Angeles (UCLA) on a scholarship, majoring in political science

Portrait of United Nations official Ralph Bunche, April, 1955. *In 1950, Bunche became the first African-American (and first UN official) to win the Nobel Peace Prize for his negotiation of the Arab-Israeli treaty of 1948.* HULTON ARCHIVE/GETTY IMAGES

and philosophy. He was active on the debating team, wrestled, played football and baseball, and was a standout basketball player. In 1927 he graduated *summa cum laude* and, again, first in his class.

Assisted by a tuition fellowship and a $1,000 scholarship provided by a group of African-American women in Los Angeles, Bunche enrolled at Harvard University in 1927 to pursue graduate study in political science. He received a master's degree in 1928 and then accepted an invitation to join the faculty of Howard University. Bunche was only twenty-five when he created and chaired Howard's political science department. His association with Howard continued until 1941, although he also pursued graduate work at Harvard during this period.

Bunche's graduate work combined his interest in government with a developing interest in Africa. He conducted field research in western Africa in 1932 and 1933, and he wrote a dissertation on the contrast between European colonial and mandatory governments in Africa. The dissertation, completed in 1934, won a Harvard award as the best political science dissertation of the year, and Bunche was awarded the first Ph.D. in political science ever granted to an African American by an American university. Bunche undertook postdoctoral studies in 1936 and 1937, first at Northwestern University, then at the London School of Economics and at South Africa's University of Cape Town. In 1936 he published a pamphlet, *A World View of Race*. His notes, taken during fieldwork in South Africa and detailing the political and racial situation, were published in 1992 under the title *An African American in South Africa*.

During Bunche's time at Howard in the 1930s, he was deeply involved in civil rights questions. He believed that black people's principal concerns were economic, and that race, though significant, was secondary. While he participated in civil rights actions—notably a protest he organized against segregation in Washington's National Theater in 1931—Bunche, a principled integrationist, warned that civil rights efforts founded on race would collapse over economic issues. He felt that the best hope for black progress lay in interracial working-class economic improvement, and he criticized Franklin Roosevelt both for his inattention to the needs of black people and for the New Deal's failure to attack existing political and economic structures. In 1936 Bunche and others founded the National Negro Congress, a broad-based coalition he later termed "the first sincere effort to bring together on an equal plane Negro leaders [and] professional and white-collar workers with the Negro manual workers and their leaders and organizers." The Congress was eventually taken over by Communist Party workers. Bunche, disillusioned, resigned in 1938.

In 1939, Bunche was hired by the Swedish sociologist Gunnar Myrdal to work on what would become the classic study of race relations in the United States, *An American Dilemma: The Negro Problem and Modern Democracy* (1944). Over the next two years Bunche wrote four long research memos for the project (one was published in 1973, after Bunche's death, as *The Negro in the Age of FDR*). The final report incorporated much of Bunche's research and thought. The unpublished memos, written for the Carnegie Corporation, have remained an important scholarly resource for researchers on black America, both for their exhaustive data and for Bunche's incisive conclusions.

In 1941, after the United States entered World War II, Bunche left Howard to work for the Office of the Coordinator of Information for the Armed Service, and he later joined the newly formed Office of Strategic Services, the chief American intelligence organization during World War II and a precursor of the Central Intelligence Agency. Bunche headed the Africa section of the Research and Analysis Branch. In 1944 Bunche joined the U.S. State Department's Postwar Planning Unit to deal with the future of colonial territories.

From this point forward, Bunche operated in the arena of international political affairs with an ever-increasing degree of policymaking power. In 1945 he was appointed to the Division of Dependent Area Affairs in the Office of Special Political Affairs, becoming in the process the first African American to head a State Department "desk."

In 1944 Bunche was a member of the U.S. delegation at the Dumbarton Oaks Conference in Washington, D.C., which laid the foundation for the United Nations. Appointed to the U.S. delegation in San Francisco in 1945 and in London in 1946, Bunche helped set up the UN Trusteeship system to prepare colonies for independence. His draft declaration of principles governing all dependent territories was the basis of Chapter XI, "Declaration Regarding Non-Self-Governing Territories," of the United Nations Charter.

Bunche went to work in the United Nations Secretariat in 1946 as head of the Trusteeship Department. In 1947 he was assigned to the UN Special Commission on Palestine which was a United Nations Trusteeship. The outbreak of the First Arab-Israeli War in 1948, and the assassination of UN mediator Folke Bernadotte by Jewish militants, propelled Bunche, Bernadotte's assistant, into the position of acting mediator. Bunche brought the two sides together, negotiating with each in turn, and succeeded in arranging an armistice. Bunche's actions earned him the 1950 Nobel Peace Prize. He was the first United Nations figure, as well as the first African American, to win a Nobel Prize. Bunche also won the NAACP's Spingarn Medal (1950), and other honors. In 1953 the American Political Science Association elected him its president, the first time an African American was so honored. In 1950, President Truman offered him the post of assistant secretary of state. Bunche declined it, and in a rare personal statement on racism, explained that he did not wish to raise his family in Washington, a segregated city.

Bunche remained at the United Nations until shortly before his death in 1971. In 1954 he was appointed United Nations Undersecretary General for Special Political Affairs, and served as a roving specialist in UN work. Bunche's most significant contribution at the United Nations was his role in designing and setting up UN peacekeeping forces, which supervise and enforce truces and armistices and have arguably been the UN's most important contribution to global peace. Building on the truce supervising operation he put into place after the 1949 Middle East armistice, Bunche created a United Nations Emergency Force in 1956, after the Suez crisis. UN peacekeepers played a major role in Lebanon and Yemen, and later in the Congo (now Zaire), in India and Pakistan, and in Cyprus. Sir Brian Urquhart, Bunche's assistant and successor as UN Undersecretary General for Special Political Affairs, said: "Bunche was unquestionably the original principal architect of [what] is now called peacekeeping . . . and he remained the principal architect, coordinator, and director of United Nations peacekeeping operations until the end of his career at the UN."

While Bunche remained primarily involved as an international civil servant with the United Nations, promoting international peace and aiding developing countries, he also remained interested in the civil rights struggle in America. Indeed, Bunche demanded and received special dispensation from the United Nations to speak out on racial issues in the United States. Bunche served on the board of the NAACP for many years, and he served as an informal adviser to civil rights leaders. In 1963 he attended the March on Washington, and two years later, despite poor health, he traveled to Alabama and walked with the Reverend. Martin Luther King Jr. in the front row of the Selma-to-Montgomery Voting Rights March.

See also King, Martin Luther, Jr.; National Association for the Advancement of Colored People (NAACP); National Negro Congress

Bibliography

Bunche, Ralph. "A Critical Analysis of the Tactics and Programs of Minority Groups." In *Black Protest Thought in the Twentieth Century,* edited by August Meier, Elliot Rudwick, and Francis L. Broderick. Indianapolis, Ind.: Bobbs-Merrill, 1971. (Originally published in the *Journal of Negro Education* in July 1935.)

Bunche, Ralph. *An African-American in South Africa.* Athens: Ohio University Press, 1992.

Mann, Peggy. *Ralph Bunche, UN Peacemaker.* New York: Coward, McCann and Geoghegan, 1975.

Rivlin, Benjamin, ed. *Ralph Bunche: The Man and His Times.* New York: Holmes and Meier, 1988.

C. GERALD FRASER (1996)

Bureau of Refugees, Freedmen, and Abandoned Lands

The Bureau of Refugees, Freedmen, and Abandoned Lands, the federal agency that oversaw Emancipation in the former slave states after the Civil War, is commonly known as the "Freedmen's Bureau." Officially designed to protect the rights of ex-slaves against intrusion by their former masters, it is now seen by many historians as paternalistic. In this view, the Freedmen's Bureau pursued "social control" of the freedpeople, encouraging them to return to work as plantation wage laborers.

The Freedmen's Bureau developed out of wartime private relief efforts directed at the "contrabands" who had fled to Union lines. At the suggestion of the American Freedmen's Inquiry Commission, a body set up by the War Department to investigate issues relating to the freedpeople, Congress established the bureau on March 3, 1865, as a military agency. Intended as a temporary organization to exist for one year after the official end of the rebellion, the bureau had "control of all subjects relating to . . .freedmen from rebel States." In addition, it would undertake white refugee relief and manage confiscated Confederate property. The commissioner of the bureau, Oliver Otis Howard (1830–1909), was known as the "Christian general" for his philanthropic interests and Congregationalist religious enthusiasm. Howard eventually presided over a network of almost one thousand local military and civilian agents scattered across the South, nearly all of them white.

Initially, Howard and his subordinates hoped to provide the rumored "forty acres and a mule" to at least some freedpeople from plantations seized by the government during the war. The legislation creating the bureau had authorized some land redistribution, and Howard's office drafted Circular 13, which would have implemented the distribution of land in bureau possession. However, President Andrew Johnson countermanded the proposal, and his policy of widespread pardons for ex-Confederates restored most property to its former owners. Stymied, Howard then felt obliged to evict the freedpeople from the lands given them during the war under the "Sherman grant." These were located on the Sea Islands and coastal areas of South Carolina and Georgia. Thus, by the late summer of 1865, Howard abandoned land redistribution and turned his attention to more attainable goals.

The bureau's remaining areas of activity were broad. It assumed the responsibility for aiding the destitute—white and black—and for the care of ill, aged, and insane freedpeople. It also subsidized and sponsored educational efforts directed at the African-American community, developed both by the freedpeople themselves and by the various northern missionary societies. The postwar years witnessed an explosive growth in black education, and the bureau encouraged this development in the face of white southern opposition. The bureau's agents also assumed the duty of securing minimal legal rights for the freedpeople, especially the right to testify in court.

Perhaps the bureau's most enduring, and controversial, aspect was its role in overseeing the emergence of free labor. While it attempted to protect freedpeople from impositions by their former masters, freedpeople were also enjoined to labor diligently. The favored bureau device for adjusting plantation agriculture was the annual labor contract, as approved by the local bureau agent. Tens of thousands of standardized contracts were written and enforced by the bureau in 1865 and 1866. The contracts it approved generally provided for wage labor under circumstances reminiscent of slavery: gang labor, tight supervision, women and children in the workforce, and provisions restricting the physical mobility and deportment of the freedmen

In practice, bureau agents spent much of their time encouraging diligent labor by freedmen; quashing rumors of impending land redistribution, and even punishing the freedmen for refractory behavior. In some cases, agents issued and enforced vagrancy codes directed at the freedpeople. Despite encouraging the freedpeople to act as disciplined wage laborers, the bureau soon incurred the enmity of the planters. It insisted that corporal punishment be abandoned, and it backed this policy up with frequent arrests. It also established a dual legal structure, with local agents acting as judges in those instances where the civilian courts refused to hear blacks' testimony or committed flagrant injustice. Finally, the bureau and the military opposed the efforts of the conservative presidential Reconstruction governments to reimpose harsh vagrancy laws through the Black Codes and similar legislation. President Andrew Johnson heeded the complaints of the planters, and in February 1866 he vetoed legislation providing for the extension of bureau activities.

The Freedmen's Bureau became a focus of the emerging political struggle between Johnson and Congress for the control of Reconstruction. With the increasing power of the Republican party, especially the Radical faction, the bureau secured powerful political sponsorship. Its functions were extended over Johnson's veto in July 1866. With the enactment of congressional Reconstruction in March 1867, Freedmen's Bureau personnel tended to become involved with the political mobilization then sweeping the black community. For example, in South Carolina, Assistant Commissioner Robert K. Scott was elected the state's first Republican governor, and in Alabama four of the six Republican congressmen elected in February 1868 were bureau officials. Though they were widely denounced as "carpetbaggers," bureau officials exercised an important role in the politicization of the freedpeople through Republican groups such as the Union League.

The restoration of most of the southern states under the military Reconstruction acts furnished the immediate cause of the bureau's demise. With southern governments now granting freedpeople equal legal rights, there no longer appeared any need for interference in local legal functions. The expansive powers of the Freedmen's Bureau had long violated states' rights taboos, and, moreover, the expense of the bureau's programs proved unpopular with the northern public. The renewal bill of July 1866 provided for the organization's essential termination in two years' time. Later legislation changed that date to the end of 1868, and after that time only the bureau's Education Division and efforts to secure bounties owed to black veterans continued. On June 30, 1872, these operations ended, and the Freedmen's Bureau ceased to exist.

Many of the bureau's aims were certainly laudable, and its accomplishments in promoting black legal rights and education substantial, but the overall record is mixed. In abandoning land redistribution, and in promoting the return of ex-slaves to plantation agriculture as hired labor under the contract system, the bureau also assisted in the survival of the plantation economy.

See also Black Codes; Civil War, U.S.; Slavery; Union League of America

Bibliography

Bently, George R. *A History of the Freedmen's Bureau.* New York: Octagon Books, 1970.

Foner, Eric. *Reconstruction: America's Unfinished Revolution, 1863–77.* New York: Harper & Row, 1988; reprint, New York: Perennial Classics, 2002.

McFeely, William S. *Yankee Stepfather: General O. O. Howard and the Freedmen.* New Haven, CT: Yale University Press, 1968.

MICHAEL W. FITZGERALD (1996)
Updated bibliography

Burials

See African Burial Ground Project; Cemeteries and Burials

Burke, Lilly Mae

June 11, 1899
March 3, 1968

Lilly Mae Burke, one of Jamaica's notable women of the late colonial period, was devoted to the building of the nation from the grassroots upwards. A teacher, farmer, hotelier, and social worker, she was interested in the country's youth and believed that their improvement would lead to the betterment of an independent Jamaica. Much of her life was characterized by volunteer work and an interest in marginalized groups.

Burke was born in 1899 in Highgate in the parish of St. Mary. She was one of eight children (she had four sisters and three brothers) of Charles Nathaniel Dixon, a planter and businessman, and Susan Eugenie Dixon. When she was in her early twenties, she married Timothy Adolphus Burke, a teacher. While she served the nation in several capacities, she lived her life in her parish of birth, where she died in 1968 at the age of sixty-nine. She went to the elementary school in her district and later attended a private secondary school and Carron Hall Practical Training Centre in the adjoining district. Later in life she became proficient in shorthand and typing.

Burke entered the teaching profession as a young woman, serving at her old school, Carron Hall. After her marriage, she joined her husband at Goshen Primary School, where he served as the principal. As a teacher, she was often a mother figure for the young, and her life was spent shaping the lives of those children with whom she came in contact. While at Goshen, she started classes for poor girls, including classes in domestic science and handicrafts, and she passed on to the girls her skills in shorthand and typing.

As a farmer, Burke understood the plight of the farming community, and she served the community of farmers in St. Mary as secretary of the People's Cooperative Agricultural Loan Society of Guys Hill and Carron Hall, and she chaired the Lucky Hill Farmers' Association. She believed in agricultural production to reduce food imports, and she advocated a better rural water supply to advance farming.

Burke served her community in many areas. She got involved in Jamaica Welfare Limited (later the Jamaica Social Welfare Commission), the first social welfare organization in Jamaica. Burke's involvement meant mobilizing of her local community to build better villages through a cooperative approach, self-help, and community organization. She would be active in the building of community centers and would encourage the development of cottage industries to provide employment for rural women in craft production. As an active member of Jamaica Welfare Limited, she would work for the enhancement of local domestic food though partnership with the Jamaica Agricultural Society and would see to the education of rural people in nutritional practices through partnership with the Education Department. Her community involvement took her to women's associations, social clubs for the young, and social welfare organizations. She worked to legalize common law marriages as a means to improve the stability of family life. This was a reflection of her belief in Christian values in nation building. Her commitment to the well-being of young Jamaicans can best explain her association with the Save the Children Fund, the 4H Club, the Juvenile Probation Committee, the Youth Committee, the Child Welfare Association, the YWCA, the Esher Remand Home, and scouting. For many of these associations, she served as a member of the executive committee, on the advisory boards, or as a commissioner. She was also an executive member of the Red Cross, a director of the Jamaica Citizens' Bank, vice president of the Hotel Resort Association, and a justice of the peace (JP). As a JP she served as a lay magistrate; she tried cases in the local petty session courts and might have been called upon to sign search warrants, to witness the searching of persons suspected by the police, and to authorize and authenticate documents, such as applications for passports. She was also involved in the Women's League. In 1943 she began to mobilize the women of St. Mary, eventually establishing seventy-two branches of the Jamaica Federation of Women (JFW) in that parish. She served the JFW as administrator of her parish and was elected as the national chairperson in 1962. She also served as the organist of the Carron Hall Presbyterian Church.

When she organized her Cub Scout Pack in 1930, she became the only female scout leader in the West Indies. She did not let it deter her that she was going against what was considered acceptable female activity. As the boys got older, she added a Boy Scout Troop and a Rover Scout Crew (for those over seventeen years of age). Yet with all this activity, she still found time to help the young people in her parish find jobs, go abroad for further education, or get vocational training locally. She also found time to put on a Christmas Treat for the young, old, and indigent in St. Mary for thirty-one years. In addition, she visited the aged, assisting them in household chores and reading to them.

As a social worker, Burke was strategically placed to become active in politics. In 1955 she won a seat on the St. Mary Parish Council, but she was unsuccessful in her bid for a seat in the House of Representatives. Instead, she supported the representatives of her parish in the Legislative Council and the House of Representatives. Her interest in creating a new Jamaica was recognized when she was asked to serve on a committee planning the celebration of Jamaican independence in 1962.

Burke subscribed to the gender division of work, and she herself was a devoted wife and housekeeper, in spite of her many activities outside the home. Her renown as a social worker went beyond her parish and the shores of the nation, and she was invited to be the vice president of the Commonwealth Countries League in 1962. In 1964 she was made a Member of the British Empire (M.B.E.) in honor of her service to the people of Jamaica.

See also Education

Bibliography

Durham, Vivian. "One of Jamaica's Notable Women: Remembering Lily Mae Burke." *Daily Gleaner* (July 11, 1975).

Gloudon, Barbara. "A Solid Jamaican Heads JFW Independence Year." *Sunday Gleaner* (April 8, 1962).

"St. Mary Citizens Honour Mrs. Lily Mae Burke." *Daily Gleaner* (February 22, 1964).

Swapp, Lipton. "Lilly Mae Burke: Always At Service to Her Fellowmen." *The Star* (May 2, 1964).

ALERIC J. JOSEPHS (2005)

Burke, Rudolph Augustus

June 13, 1899
February 2, 1972

Rudolph Burke was a planter, sportsman, politician, and leader of the Jamaican farming community. He was born in Kingston and attended Wolmer's High for Boys and Jamaica College. He later made his home in the Llandewey area of Saint Thomas, where he managed the farm left by his deceased parents. Burke held numerous positions in

Jamaica's agricultural sector, most importantly as president of the Jamaica Agricultural Society (JAS) between 1944 and 1962. This society was launched in 1895 by the governor, Sir Henry Blake, to develop the agricultural industry in Jamaica and to improve the socioeconomic position of farmers.

Burke effected many changes in the JAS. He conceived and headed the Central Committee of the Primary Producers (CCPP), which organized agricultural groups in Jamaica. He also spearheaded the establishment of the All Island Banana Growers Association, of which he was vice chairman, and the Citrus Growers Association, which he directed. Among Burke's achievements in agriculture was the negotiation of the ten-year plan under which concentrated orange juice was supplied to the United Kingdom from Jamaica. Burke was also a member of negotiation teams that developed trade links with England, including the Banana Delegation from Jamaica to Britain's Ministry of Food.

Burke stressed the importance of relying on local agricultural produce in order to cement the country's independence and increase economic prosperity. He also refused financial incentives to align the JAS with other farming organizations made up of estate owners. In so doing, he reinforced the position of the JAS as a platform for small farmers and set a tone of propriety and integrity in the organization.

Burke held numerous public offices during his career. He was a director of Jamaica Welfare Limited, founded to improve the lives of rural Jamaicans by Norman Manley, the leader of the People's National Party (PNP). Burke also was elected to the parochial board in Saint Thomas at the age of twenty-two, becoming the youngest person ever elected a member of a parochial board. He served as chair of this board from 1933 and 1939. In addition, Burke was one of the early members of the PNP, one of Jamaica's two major political parties. Although he ran unsuccessfully as the PNP candidate for Western Saint Thomas in 1944, he was later selected by the PNP to sit on the Legislative Council, where he remained from 1951 to1962. Burke was also appointed to serve as minister without portfolio in the Executive Council from 1955 until this body became the cabinet in 1962. He served as a senator between 1962 and 1967.

Burke was accorded many honors, including the Commander of the Most Excellent Order of the British Empire (CBE) in 1957. There is also a trophy given in his name at the annual Denbigh All Island Agricultural Show held in Clarendon. This agricultural show, which Burke was responsible for setting up, remains an annual feature on the Jamaican cultural calendar.

Before entering public life, Burke became a Champion Class One athlete in 1916 and successfully led Jamaica College's cricket, football, and track teams. In 1921 he married Edna Hermina Ramsey, with whom he had two sons and four daughters. Burke was an Anglican and a Master of the Saint Thomas Masonic Lodge. His numerous roles attest to his commitment to Jamaica's political, social, and agricultural welfare. His illustrious career has been a great legacy for the island's agricultural sector and Jamaica's small farmers, for whom Burke worked assiduously and whose interests he represented for decades.

See also Dalton-James, Edith; King, Iris; Manley, Norman; People's National Party

Bibliography

Carnegie, James. *Some Aspects of Jamaica's Politics, 1918–1938.* Kingston: Institute of Jamaica, 1973.

Jamaica Agricultural Society. *Souvenir Centenary Journal: One Hundred Years, 1895–1995.* Kingston, Jamaica: Author, 1995.

DALEA M. BEAN (2005)

Burke, Yvonne Brathwaite

October 5, 1932

Yvonne Brathwaite was born and raised in South Central Los Angeles. She received an associate's degree from the University of California, Berkeley, in 1951; a bachelor's degree in political science from the University of California, Los Angeles, in 1953; and a law degree from the University of Southern California in 1956, the year in which she was admitted to the California bar and began a private law practice. In 1965 California Governor Edmund G. "Pat" Brown appointed Burke as attorney for the McCone Commission, which investigated the Los Angeles Watts Riots of that year.

In 1966 Burke was elected to the first of her three two-year terms representing the Sixty-third District in the California State Assembly. As California's first black assemblywoman she focused on prison reform, child care, equality for women, and civil rights. In 1972 she served as vice chairperson of the Democratic National Convention, where she received national attention as a promoter of changes in the party's rules enabling greater participation by minorities. That same year she was also elected to the first of three terms representing the Thirty-seventh District in the United States House of Representatives and became the first black congresswoman from California. In Congress she again focused on social issues, especially housing and urban development. In 1975 she was appointed to the powerful House Committee on Appropriations, and in 1976 she became chair of the Congressional Black Caucus.

Although her early political career made her one of the most prominent black women in American politics, her political campaigns in the late 1970s were unsuccessful, and she then concentrated on her career as a lawyer and senior partner at the Los Angeles firm of Jones, Day, Deavis, Bogue. In 1978 she ran for state attorney general, winning the Democratic nomination but losing the general election to Republican George Deukmejian. On July 6, 1979, Governor Edmund G. "Jerry" Brown Jr. appointed her to a vacancy on the Los Angeles County Board of Supervisors, a position she held until an election defeat in 1980. She resumed her political career in 1992, when she was elected to the Los Angeles County Board of Supervisors. There she focused her attention on the needs and education of children. She has served as chair of the Board of Supervisors for three terms, most recently in 2003–2004.

See also Congressional Black Caucus; Politics in the United States

Bibliography

Burke, Yvonne Brathwaite. "New Arenas of Black Influence." Interview by Steven Edgington, 1982. Oral History Program, Powell Library, University of California, Los Angeles.

Gray, Pamela Lee. "Yvonne Brathwaite Burke: The Congressional Career of California's First Black Congresswoman, 1972–1978." Ph.D. diss., University of Southern California, 1987.

SIRAJ AHMED (1996)
Updated by publisher 2005

Burleigh, Harry T.

December 2, 1866
September 12, 1949

Singer, composer, arranger, and music editor Henry Thacker Burleigh was born in Erie, Pennsylvania, into a family noted for singing and for the active pursuit of education and civil rights. His grandfather, Hamilton Waters, a former slave, was active in the Underground Railroad in Erie. Fatherless at six, Burleigh was raised by an extended family, the most important influences being his mother, stepfather, and grandfather. His mother, Elizabeth Burleigh Elmendorf, graduated from Avery College in Pennsylvania in 1855. In 1892, after earning a reputation as one of the finest singers in Erie, Burleigh began studies in New York City at the National Conservatory of Music and taught there for two years. Burleigh often sang the plantation songs and spirituals he had learned from his grandfather for Antonín Dvořák, the conservatory's director, introducing him to the African-American music Dvořák argued should form the basis of an American school of music, along with the music of Native Americans. Well established as a recitalist in the black communities along the East Coast by 1893, Burleigh sang that year at the World's Columbian Exposition in Chicago. From 1894 to 1946 he was baritone soloist at St. George's Episcopal Church in New York; from 1900 to 1925 he was soloist at Temple Emanu-El. These two wealthy religious institutions provided many opportunities for Burleigh as a composer and singer.

From 1911 until his death, Burleigh was an editor for the music publisher Ricordi, a position that greatly facilitated the publication of his art songs and spiritual arrangements. He was a charter member of the American Society of Composers, Authors, and Publishers (ASCAP) in 1914. His first art songs were published in 1898, and by 1915 many internationally renowned singers, including John McCormack, Ernestine Schumann-Heink, and Nellie Melba, were singing them. His first choral arrangements of spirituals, published in 1913, have been in print continuously since that time, and in 1916–1917, his solo arrangement of "Deep River" was said to be the most-performed song of the New York concert season. During the next ten years Burleigh published over forty spirituals, many in both solo and choral arrangements. His success brought awards such as the NAACP's Spingarn Medal in 1917, honorary degrees from Atlanta University in 1918 and Howard University in 1920, and the Harmon Foundation award in 1929. Burleigh's multifaceted career included singing, composing, arranging, and giving frequent lectures on spirituals, which he called the "greatest evidence of a spiritual ascendancy over oppression and humiliation." He was a mentor and coach to many young artists such as Roland Hayes, Paul Robeson, Marian Anderson, Abbie Mitchell, and Carol Brice.

Burleigh pioneered in arranging spirituals for solo voice with piano accompaniment and for mixed voices, and his sophisticated arrangements helped preserve the genre. Although some early critics stood opposed to his rich harmonies and innovative piano accompaniment for moving the spiritual away from its original improvisatory nature, Burleigh's arrangements remained in the repertory throughout the twentieth century, in both solo and choral form. Among the most famous of these are the solo arrangement of "Deep River" and the choral arrangement of "My Lord, What a Mornin'."

Burleigh's art songs, most of which fell out of print after his death, began to be rediscovered by singers and recorded at the end of the twentieth century. Noted works include the song cycles *Saracen Songs* (1914), *Passionale* (1915), and *Five Songs on Poems of Laurence Hope* (1915) and the songs "Jean" (1903), "Little Mother of Mine" (1917), "Ethiopia Saluting the Colors" (1915), and "Lovely Dark and Lonely One" (1935).

See also Folk Music; Robeson, Paul; Spingarn Medal; Spirituals; Underground Railroad

Bibliography

Sears, Ann. "'A Certain Strangeness': Harry T. Burleigh's Art Songs and Spiritual Arrangements." *Black Music Research Journal.* 24, no. 5 (2004).

Simpson, Anne Key. *Hard Trials: The Life and Music of Harry T. Burleigh.* Metuchen, N.J.: Scarecrow Press, 1990.

Snyder, Jean E. "Harry T. Burleigh and the Creative Expression of Bi-musicality: A Study of an African-American Composer and the American Art Song." Ph.D. diss., University of Pittsburgh, Pittsburgh, Pa., 1992.

Snyder, Jean E. "'A Great and Noble School of Music': Dvořák, Burleigh, and the African-American Spiritual." In *Dvorak in America, 1892–1895,* edited by John A. Tibbetts. Portland, Ore.: Amadeus Press, 1993.

Snyder, Jean E. "Harry T. Burleigh." In *International Dictionary of Black Composers,* edited by Samuel A. Floyd, Jr. Chicago: Fitzroy Dearborn, 1999.

Snyder, Jean E. "One of Erie's Favorite Church Singers." *Black Music Research Journal.* 24, no. 5 (2004).

JEAN E. SNYDER (1996)
Updated by author 2005

Burnett, Charles

April 13, 1944

The filmmaker Charles Burnett was born in Vicksburg, Mississippi. He moved with his family to Watts in South Central Los Angeles during World War II. In 1971 he received a B.A. in theater arts from the University of California at Los Angeles (UCLA), where he made his first film, *Several Friends* (1969), about a group of young African-American men who are unable to see or understand that something has gone wrong in their lives. Burnett completed his M.F.A. at UCLA as well. As a graduate student in 1977, he made a fourteen-minute film, *The Horse,* about a boy in the South who has to witness the death of an old horse. The film won first prize at the fifteenth Westdeutsche Kurzfilmtage Oberhausen in West Germany.

Killer of Sheep, Burnett's first feature film, was made the same year as *The Horse,* at which time he not only satisfied his M.F.A. thesis requirement but was also awarded a Louis B. Mayer Grant, given to the thesis project at UCLA that shows the most promise. Touted for its neorealist approach, *Killer of Sheep* received critical praise and a life in the festival circuit. The film was a winner of the Berlin International Film Festival Critics Prize in 1981. In 1990, *Killer of Sheep* was selected for the National Film Registry at the Library of Congress. Each year, twenty-five American films deemed culturally and historically significant are selected for the registry.

Finding inspiration outside the Hollywood formulaic aesthetic, Burnett's *Killer of Sheep, My Brother's Wedding* (1984), and *To Sleep with Anger* (1990) focus on the dynamics, tensions, and frustrations of urban black families, with a particular emphasis on the relationships between fathers, sons, and brothers. His films strive to reflect the black American culture and the black American experience familiar to him. According to Burnett, "To make filmmaking viable you need the support of the community; you have to become a part of its agenda, an aspect of its survival. A major concern of storytelling should be restoring values, reversing the erosion of all those things that make a better life."

In 1980 Burnett received a Guggenheim Fellowship to do pre-production work on *My Brother's Wedding.* In 1988, he was the recipient of one of the MacArthur Foundation's "Genius" Awards, which provided the resources for a production company and a professional cast, including the actor Danny Glover, for *To Sleep with Anger,* his most critically acclaimed work. The film earned a special jury prize at the 1990 Sundance Film Festival in Park City, Utah. Following that film, Burnett began work on *America Becoming,* a 1991 documentary about new immigrants that was funded by the Ford Foundation. Burnett's film *The Glass Shield,* which depicts the travails of the first black cop in an all-white police squad, opened to enthusiastic reviews in 1995.

Burnett has also directed a number of successful television movies and miniseries. His film *Nightjohn* (Disney Channel, 1996) received a Special Citation Award from the National Society of Film Critics. In 1998, he directed

Oprah Winfrey Presents: The Wedding, a television adaptation of Dorothy West's novel. Burnett returned to the big screen in 1999, directing *The Annihilation of Fish*, and to documentary in 2003, directing the film *Nat Turner: a Troublesome Property (2003).*

See also Glover, Danny

Bibliography

Kennedy, Lisa. "The Black Familiar." *Village Voice*, October 16, 1990, p. 62.

Klotman, Phyllis Rauch, ed. "Charles Burnett." In *Screenplays of the African American Experience*, pp. 94–98. Bloomington: Indiana University Press, 1991.

FARAH JASMINE GRIFFIN (1996)
Updated by publisher 2005

BURNHAM, FORBES

FEBRUARY 20, 1923
AUGUST 6, 1985

Linden Forbes Sampson Burnham, or Forbes "Odo" Burnham, as he was popularly known, was a lawyer, politician, and founder and leader of the People's National Congress (PNC), the political party that led the colony of British Guiana to become the independent nation of Guyana. He was born to schoolmaster James E. Burnham and Rachel A. (Sampson) Burnham in Kitty, a suburb of Georgetown, the capital city. Other family members included siblings Olga, Freddie, Jessica, and Flora. Burnham received his primary education at Kitty Methodist School, where his father taught. In 1935 his secondary education started in Georgetown, first at Central High School and then at Queen's College, the country's premier secondary school. At Queen's College Burnham won three scholarships: the Centenary Exhibition in 1936, the Government Junior in 1937, and the Percival Exhibition in 1938. His performance as a student prepared him for a legal career, and he became an important political and public figure, holding positions as a trade unionist, city councilor, mayor of Georgetown, premier and prime minister of British Guiana, and the Cooperative Republic of Guyana's first executive president.

When Burnham graduated from Queen's College in 1942 he was named that year's British Guiana Scholar as the colony's most outstanding student. World War II delayed his plan for immediate study in the United Kingdom. The delay enabled Burnham to teach at Queen's College as an assistant master and to earn a bachelor of arts degree at the external examinations of the University of London in 1944. The next year he entered the University of London for legal studies.

In the United Kingdom, Burnham was elected president of the West Indian Students Union in 1947 to 1948, further stimulating his interest in politics. He was the organization's delegate to the International Union of Students' Congress in Prague and Paris. He was also a member of the League of Coloured Peoples, founded in London in 1931 by Jamaican-born Dr. Harold Arundel Moody with West Indian, African, and Asian students. In the 1940s the organization spearheaded demonstrations against colonial rule in their homelands. As a testament to his oratorical skill, Burnham won the Best Speaker's Cup, awarded by the Law faculty at the University of London. After graduating in 1947 with a bachelor of laws degree and being called to Gray's Inn in 1948, he returned to British Guiana in 1949.

Burnham was a physically imposing person who stood six feet two inches tall and weighed over two hundred pounds when he first headed the government of Guyana. He married twice, the first time in May 1951 to Sheila Bernice Latase, an optician from Trinidad and Tobago. This union produced three daughters: Roxanne, Annabelle, and Francesca. The second marriage, in February 1967 to Viola Victorine Harper, led to the birth of Melanie Abiola and Ulele Imodinda. Burnham was an avid sports fan with an interest in cricket, tennis, chess, horseback riding, swimming, and fishing.

When Burnham returned to British Guiana, he entered the private law chambers of Cameron and Shepherd in Georgetown. Later, he opened his own law firm, Clarke and Martin. The year 1949 also witnessed a significant political event when Burnham (of African descent) and Dr. Cheddi B. Jagan (of East Indian descent) cofounded the People's Progressive Party (PPP), a name Burnham chose. Burnham was instrumental in transforming a quasipolitical organization, the Political Affairs Committee, originally led by Jagan, into a nationally organized political party. Under their leadership the PPP brought together the racial groups in the colony.

In 1952 Burnham was elected to the Georgetown Town Council. He headed the Kitty Brotherhood Movement from 1952 to 1956 and served as president of the British Guiana Labour Union from 1952 to 1956 and 1963 to 1965. In 1959 he was elected president of the British Guiana Bar Association. One year later he was appointed a Queen's (Senior) Counsel. Burnham was the minister of education in the short-lived PPP government that won the

Forbes Burnham, prime minister of Guyana, c. 1970s. *The founder and leader of the People's National Congress (PNC), Burnham led the coalition government which won independence for the former British colony Guiana in 1966.* PHOTOGRAPHS AND PRINTS DIVISION, SCHOMBURG CENTER FOR RESEARCH IN BLACK CULTURE, THE NEW YORK PUBLIC LIBRARY, ASTOR, LENOX AND TILDEN FOUNDATIONS.

general elections of 1953. In 1955, during the Cold War era, events centering on some party members' alleged communist bent and his rivalry with Jagan caused Burnham to lead a breakaway faction of the PPP and eventually to form the PNC in 1957. The next year the PNC and John P. Carter's United Democratic Party merged. Burnham was the leader of the main opposition party in British Guiana's legislature from 1957 to 1964. After the December 1964 elections, the Burnham-led PNC headed a coalition government with Peter S. D'Aguiar's United Force. Burnham became the premier of the colony.

The period during which Burnham headed the government, from December 15, 1964, until his death, has remained one of significance in the annals of the country's history. British Guiana achieved independence from Great Britain on May 26, 1966. Renamed Guyana, it was the first new nation in South America in eight decades, with Burnham as its first prime minister. When the country became a republic in February 1970, Arthur Chung was appointed as the ceremonial president. Burnham, as head of government, became the first executive president of Guyana under the Constitution of February 14, 1980.

As leader of the PNC and during his tenure as head of the government of Guyana, Burnham must be credited with a remarkable number of developments. National emblems—the flag's Golden Arrowhead; the coat of arms; the anthem, "Dear Land of Guyana;" the Canje pheasant, Guyana's national bird; the national flower, the Victoria Regia lily, one of the largest of its kind in the world; and the motto "One Nation, One People, One Destiny"—were instituted and are symbols of Burnham's legacy. His administration created national monuments acknowledging outstanding local and international figures, such as the 1763 monument erected to honor Cuffy, the leader of a slave insurrection, and the Non-Aligned Movement Monument with busts of Nasser (Egypt), Nkrumah (Ghana), Nehru (India), and Tito (Yugoslavia). The administration recognized ethnic religious events, such as Pagwah (Hindu) and Dewalli (Muslim) festivals, along with Mashramani, a national festival, and they were established as public holidays. Mashramani, an Arawak (indigenous Indian) word, means a celebration to mark the end of a community self-help effort like building a house or planting and reaping a field.

National development in education, health, housing, pure water and electricity supplies, and youth schemes accelerated when Burnham headed Guyana's government. Major construction works such as the Soesdyke-Linden highway, the West Demerara, Corentyne and Mahdia roads, and the international airport, Timehri, were completed. Planned resettlement schemes to relocate persons to hinterland locations were implemented. The Demerara Harbour Bridge, reputedly, the world's longest floating bridge, and a textile mill and clay brick factories became operational during Burnham's tenure. A National Insurance scheme, the Guyana Defense Force, the Guyana National Service, the Guyana National Cooperative Bank, the Agricultural Bank, Critichlow Labour College, Kuru Kuru Cooperative College, President's College, the National Cultural Center, and a host of other enterprises are among institutions established during Burnham's time in office.

As a Caribbean leader, Forbes Burnham advocated regionalism, nonalignment, a new international economic order, and a new world information order. He made Guyana one of the original members of the Caribbean Free Trade Area (CARIFTA) that in 1973 became the Caribbean Community and Common Market (CARICOM), with most Caribbean countries. Burnham supported a West Indies Federation as leader of the opposition and as head of the PNC. He was also a keen supporter of the struggle against apartheid in South Africa and of liberation movements in Africa.

Honors and awards attest to Burnham's significance and stature. They include the Order of Excellence in 1973 (Guyana), the Grand Cordon of L'Orde du Nil (Egypt) and Jose Marti (Cuba) in 1975, an honorary doctorate of laws from Dalhousie University (Canada) in 1977, the Cruseiro De Sul (the highest award in Brazil) in 1983, the Bulgarian Star of Planinay in 1984, and Yugoslavia's Order of the Red Star in 1985.

There were several controversies during Burnham's regime. He had foreign policy disputes with the United States; his embracing of socialism and Cuba and the nationalization of American, Canadian, and British private entities led to economic hardships; and he faced challenges from opposition parties and allegations of dictatorial rule. Accusations of "rigged" national elections also bedeviled his tenure in office. His greatest achievement was the implementation of specific national development programs that continue to impact the country.

The significance of Burnham's life and times is measured by samples of outpourings of grief and condolences as gleaned from the pages of the *Guyana Chronicle* in the days following his death. Apart from African, Caribbean, and European dignitaries who paid tribute to Burnham, Brazil and Cuba declared three days of mourning. Roderick Rainford, CARICOM secretary general, viewed his passing as a great loss. Indira Gandhi, president of India, who headed the nonaligned movement, lauded Burnham as one of the twentieth century's outstanding figures. Javier Perez de Cuellar, the secretary general of the United Nations, expressed shock and sadness at the death, observing that "Burnham served his country and his people with outstanding leadership and was a dedicated and valued friend and supporter of the United Nations." Educator and trade unionist T. Anson Sancho's *The Green Way* (1996) argued that Burnham was perhaps the cleverest politician the Caribbean had seen so far.

See also Caribbean Community and Common Market (CARICOM); Hoyte, Desmond; People's National Congress; Politics

Bibliography

Foreign Service Dispatch, American Consulate, Georgetown. Decimal File (1910–1963), Numeric File (1963–1973), 741D, 841D, 844B. Record Group 59. Department of State, Washington, D.C. The National Archives (Archives 11). College Park, Md.

Guyana Needs Progress Not Conflict: The People's National Congress, The New Road. La Penitence, Guyana: British Guiana Lithographic Company Limited, n.d.

McGowan, Winston F., James G. Rose, and David A. Granger. *Themes in African-Guyanese History*. Georgetown, Guyana: Free Press, 1998.

Nascimento, Christopher A., and Reynold A. Burrowes, eds. *Forbes Burnham: A Destiny to Mold, Selected Speeches by the Prime Minister of Guyana.* New York: Africana Publishing, 1970.

Sancho, T. Anson. *The Green Way: A Biography of Hamilton Green.* Georgetown, Guyana: Author, 1996.

Wilson, Margaret. "Forbes Burnham: Politician." *The African-Guyanese Achievement* 1 (1993): 17.

BARBARA P. JOSIAH (2005)

Burns, Anthony

May 31, 1829?
July 27, 1862

The fugitive slave Anthony Burns was born and reared in northern Virginia, where he taught himself to read and write, converted to the Baptist faith, and became a preacher to other slaves. From boyhood he was annually hired out and, during one such hire, accidentally broke his right hand. Although the break healed, Burns feared he would be sold south and put to some new kind of work that he would perform so poorly as to be mistreated. So he decided to escape. While hired as a stevedore on the Richmond docks, he enlisted the aid of a sailor who stowed him aboard his Boston-bound ship, but his owner learned of his whereabouts and federal marshals arrested him in Boston on May 24, 1854.

The arrest prompted Boston's Vigilance Committee to stage a mass protest meeting in Faneuil Hall that the abolitionists Wendell Phillips and Theodore Parker addressed. At its midpoint, some militants in the audience interrupted the proceedings to lead an armed attack to rescue Burns, who was being held in the nearby municipal courthouse. A biracial assault force of fourteen rioters failed to gain entry when the expected reinforcement from the Faneuil Hall audience did not back them, but during the struggle, they stabbed to death a specially deputized guard. The government later prosecuted the rioters and speakers Phillips and Parker for obstructing federal officers, but discontinued (*nol-prossed*) the case because of a defective indictment.

The next morning, Burns's owner, Colonel Charles F. Suttle, agreed to sell Burns to some Bostonians, whose leader, black minister Leonard A. Grimes, had raised the purchase money. The group would then free Burns. But United States Attorney Benjamin F. Hallett, citing the killing of the guard as justification, stopped the sale until after the case was decided. To guard the prisoner from any more rescue attempts, Hallett also assembled some 180 soldiers and marines and 120 armed civilians known as the "marshal's guard." Anticipating Burns's likely return, he persuaded the mayor with the suggestion of probable federal payment to call out approximately 1500 militiamen to keep the peace while the federal soldiery marched their prisoner to the wharf. President Franklin Pierce not only approved these actions but also sent to Boston the adjutant general to coordinate the regulars and militia and a U.S. revenue cutter to carry Burns back to Richmond, if necessary. The federal government paid the city $14,165.78 for their costs of an estimated $40,000 for the nine-day affair.

Although defense counsel Richard Henry Dana, Jr. emphasized the defects in the record, Judge Edward G. Loring, the commissioner appointed by the federal courts to decide fugitive slave cases, used Burns's replies to his master on the night of his arrest to identify him and issued the certificate for his removal. While church bells tolled dirges at Boston and throughout the state, an estimated 50,000 persons lined the one-third mile route to witness the rendition; later Burns quipped that "there was lots of folks to see a colored man walk through the streets."

Back in Virginia, Burns was punished with four months solitary confinement until sold. Luckily, Bostonians learned of his whereabouts and arranged to buy his freedom from his new owner, David McDaniel, who defied a southern mob to sell the notorious fugitive for $1,300 raised by Grimes. Now a freedman, Burns decided to study for the ministry and was helped by a benefactress to attend the Preparatory Department of Oberlin College intermittently from 1855 to 1862. He became pastor of a black Baptist church in Indianapolis, but soon left the state in part because of Indiana's racially discriminatory Black Laws. He moved to St. Catharines, Canada West (now Ontario), and became pastor of its fugitive slave community. There he died of tuberculosis in July 1862.

THE

BOSTON SLAVE RIOT,

AND

TRIAL

OF

Anthony Burns,

CONTAINING THE

REPORT OF THE FANEUIL HALL MEETING; THE MURDER OF BACHELDER; THEODORE PARKER'S LESSON FOR THE DAY; SPEECHES OF COUNSEL ON BOTH SIDES, CORRECTED BY THEMSELVES; VERBATIM REPORT OF JUDGE LORING'S DECISION; AND, A DETAILED ACCOUNT OF THE EMBARKATION.

BOSTON:

FETRIDGE AND COMPANY.

1854.

Cover of The Boston Slave Riot, and Trial of Anthony Burns, 1854. *The account chronicles the efforts of an abolitionist mob to rescue Burns, an escaped slave and Baptist minister, from the hands of federal marshals at a Boston prison. Although he was returned to Virginia and punished with four months solitary confinement, Burns was eventually purchased and freed by a group from Boston.* HULTON ARCHIVE/GETTY IMAGES

The coincidental timing of Burns's case, with the passage of the Kansas-Nebraska Act and the Sherman M. Booth fugitive slave rescue case earlier that year, contributed to the rise of antislavery parties throughout the North, including Massachusetts, where the secret American or Know-Nothing order was elected to office for the next three years. This nativist, antislavery party promptly disbanded all five Irish militia companies because of their participation in the rendition. Massachusetts joined seven other states in enacting new personal liberty laws that withdrew state support from fugitive slave rendition. The resentment against Commissioner Loring's decision resulted in social ostracism for Loring and the loss of his Harvard Law School professorship and state probate office. After Burns's rendition, no owner ever again chanced fugitive slave recovery in Boston.

Throughout his ordeal, Anthony Burns demonstrated his intelligence and resourcefulness, courage and humor, honesty and integrity. As the victimized protagonist, of the most dramatic and famous such case, he became "the fugitive." He originally had discouraged the legal defense urged on his behalf, telling his lawyer that he would fare worse if he lost, for his master was "a malicious man if crossed." And so he was returned, punished, sold, and celebrated as "the Boston Lion."

See also Black Codes; Runaway Slaves in the United States

Bibliography

The Boston Slave Riot, and Trial of Anthony Burns. Boston: Fetridge, 1854. Reprint, Northbrook, Ill.: Metro Books, 1972.

Maginnes, David R. "The Case of the Court House Rioters in the Rendition of the Fugitive Slave Anthony Burns, 1854." *Journal of Negro History* 56, no. 1 (January 1971): 31–42.

Pease, Jane H., and William H. Pease. *The Fugitive Slave Law and Anthony Burns.* Philadelphia: Lippincott, 1975.

Stevens, Charles E. *Anthony Burns: A History.* Boston: J. P. Jewett, 1856. Reprint, New York: Arno Press, 1969.

Von Frank, Albert J. *The Trials of Anthony Burns: Freedom and Slavery in Emerson's Boston.* Cambridge, Mass.: Harvard University Press, 1998.

DAVID R. MAGINNES (1996)
Updated by author 2005

Burroughs, Margaret Taylor

November 1, 1917

The daughter of Octavia Pierre Taylor and Alexander Taylor, artist, educator, and museum director Margaret Burroughs was born in St. Rose Parish, Louisiana. In 1920, in search of better lives, her parents migrated to Chicago, where Burroughs made significant, lasting contributions to her community and beyond.

In 1946 she earned her bachelor's degree in art education at the Art Institute of Chicago and began teaching at DuSable High School in Chicago. A committed, impassioned teacher of art, she held this job for twenty-two years until retiring in 1968 to oversee the development of the DuSable Museum of African American History. The museum—which she originally founded as the Ebony Museum of Negro History with her second husband, Charles Gordon Burroughs, in their home on Michigan Avenue—today occupies more than sixty thousand square feet in Washington Park on the south side of Chicago. Managed by Burroughs and a staff of twenty-one, it contains more than fifty thousand items, including art, books, papers, artifacts, and memorabilia.

Since the 1940s Burroughs's art has been displayed in galleries and exhibitions in the United States and abroad. In 1952 and 1953 she was given a one-woman show in Mexico City, where she lived and studied for that year. Influenced by the "new realism" movement of the 1930s and inspired by the works of Mexican muralists Diego Rivera and José Clemente Orozco, Burroughs sought to fuse art with politics, thereby using it as a vehicle for deeper social awareness and, ultimately, social change. This purpose has remained with her throughout her long career as both a visual artist and, later, a poet. She has described her central mission as "the betterment of life for all mankind and especially my people."

Burroughs's sculpture is the product of a "subtractive" style, by which the artist carves the image from large blocks of marble or stone rather than shaping or molding a cast. Her works are characterized by bold, heavy lines that straddle the boundary between realism and abstraction. Certain Burroughs sculptures, for example, portray the heads of African-American women in a manner reminiscent of African and ancient Egyptian art. Her poetry, which draws on folk traditions and contemporary events and focuses on the African and African-American experiences, is written in similarly "broad" strokes of simple, direct language. She is the author of *Jasper, the Drummin' Boy* (1947); *Did You Feed My Cow?: Rhymes and Tales from City Streets and Country Lanes* (1955; revised, 1969); *What Shall I Tell My Children Who Are Black?* (1968); and *Africa, My Africa* (1970).

In 1980 Burroughs was one of the ten black artists honored by President Jimmy Carter at the White House; in 1982 she received an Excellence in Art award from the National Association of Negro Museums; and in 1986 Mayor Harold Washington proclaimed February 1 as "Dr. Margaret Burroughs Day in Chicago." She has received a vast number of other awards, citations, and honorary degrees. Still dedicated to guarding and enriching the African-American tradition, Burroughs, now director emerita of the DuSable Museum, lives in Chicago.

See also Art in the United States, Contemporary; Painting and Sculpture; Poetry, U.S.

Bibliography

Bontemps, Arna Alexander, ed. *Forever Free: Art by African American Women 1862–1980.* Alexandria, Va.: Stephenson, 1980.

Leininger, Theresa A. "Margaret Taylor Burroughs." In *Notable Black American Women,* edited by Jessie Carney Smith, pp. 133–137. Detroit: Gale, 1992.

NANCY YOUSEF (1996)
Updated by publisher 2005

Burroughs, Nannie Helen

May 2, 1879
May 20, 1961

Nannie Helen Burroughs, an educator, was born in Orange, Virginia. Her father, born free, attended the Richmond Institute and became a preacher. Her mother, born a slave in Virginia, left her husband and took her two young daughters to Washington, D.C., to attend school. At the Colored High School (later Dunbar High), where she was deeply interested in domestic science, Burroughs came in contact with Mary Church Terrell and Anna Julia Cooper, two women who became her role models. After graduation in 1896 she got a job at the Philadelphia office of the *Christian Banner* while also working part-time for the Rev. Lewis Jordan, an official of the National Baptist Convention (NBC). When Jordan moved to Louisville, Kentucky, Burroughs also relocated there. In Louisville she initiated her career of activism by organizing a women's industrial club that offered evening classes in bookkeeping, sewing, cooking, and typing.

In 1900, at the annual meeting of the National Baptist Convention in Virginia, Burroughs gave a speech titled "How the Sisters Are Hindered from Helping," which gained her national recognition and served as a catalyst for the formation of the largest black women's organization in the United States, the Woman's Convention (WC), an auxiliary to the NBC. The WC was the result of long-standing efforts by women in the Baptist Church to develop an organization to represent them. It provided a forum for black women to deal with religious, political, and social issues and took the lead in their religious and educational training. From 1900 to 1948 Burroughs served as corresponding secretary to the WC, and from 1948 until her death in 1961 she served as president. Because of her hard work and leadership, the membership of the WC grew dramatically, reaching one million members in 1903 and 1.5 million in 1907.

Burroughs spent nearly her entire adult life in the public arena challenging racial discrimination and encouraging African Americans to maintain pride and dignity. An eloquent public speaker, she toured the country denouncing lynching, segregation, employment discrimination, and colonialism. She supported the efforts of the NAACP to attain legal equality for blacks and criticized President Woodrow Wilson for his silence on lynching. She was a staunch feminist who believed women's suffrage was a route to racial advancement as well as a safeguard against male domination and sexual abuse. Like many women of her time, Burroughs believed in the moral superiority of women and the positive impact they could have on the public life of African Americans. Referring to the ballot, she wrote, "The Negro woman needs to get back by the wise use of it what the Negro man has lost by the misuse of it." She was convinced that if given political power, black women would take an uncompromising stand against racial discrimination and political disfranchisement.

In 1896 Burroughs joined other women and formed the National Association of Colored Women (NACW) to promote the political mobilization of black women. She became deeply involved in partisan politics, and in 1924 she and other clubwomen founded the National League of Republican Colored Women. Burroughs became a much sought-after participant by the Republican Party's national speakers bureau. After Herbert Hoover was elected president in 1928, he chose Burroughs to head a fact-finding commission on housing. Even after the election of Franklin D. Roosevelt in 1932, when most African Americans transferred their political loyalty to the Democratic Party, Burroughs continued her steadfast support of the Republicans.

In addition to opposing institutional racism, Burroughs was also a tireless advocate for black pride and self-help. She believed that progress was ultimately a question of individual will and effort and that with enough self-esteem and self-confidence people could overcome racial barriers. In 1909 in Washington, D.C., she founded the National Training School for Women and Girls, which was renamed the Nannie Helen Burroughs School in 1964. The core of the school's training was what Burroughs called the "three B's": Bible, bath, and broom. The school also offered industrial training in a wide variety of occupations, such as printing, bookkeeping, housekeeping, stenography, dressmaking, and cooking. Burroughs encouraged black women to work hard and excel, whatever their position in society. Through her religious and educational work, she hoped to imbue black women with moral values, such as thrift and hard work, as well as prepare them to become self-sufficient wage earners. Burroughs died in Washington, D.C., at the age of eighty-two.

See also Cooper, Anna J.; National Association of Colored Women; National Baptist Convention, U.S.A., Inc.; Terrell, Mary Eliza Church

Bibliography

Easter, Opal V. *Nannie Helen Burroughs.* New York: Garland, 1995.

Giddings, Paula. *When and Where I Enter: The Impact of Race and Sex on Black Women in America.* New York: William Morrow, 1996.

Higginbotham, Evelyn Brooks. *Righteous Discontent: The Women's Movement in the Black Baptist Church, 1880–1920.* Cambridge, Mass.: Harvard University Press, 1993.

Johnson, Karen Ann. *Uplifting the Women and the Race: The Lives, Educational Philosophies and Social Activism of Anna Julia Cooper and Nannie Helen Burroughs.* New York: Garland, 2000.

PREMILLA NADASEN (1996)
Updated bibliography

Business, Black

See Entrepreneurs and Entrepreneurship

Bustamante, Alexander

February 24, 1884
August 6, 1997

Alexander Bustamante, one of the leading political figures in Jamaica during the twentieth century, was born William Alexander Clarke at Blenheim Estate in Lucea, a coastal town in western Jamaica. He was the second of five children born to Robert Clarke, a white Jamaican, and Mary Wilson, Clarke's second wife, a colored woman of peasant stock. When he married Mary Wilson, Robert Clarke was employed as overseer at Blenheim Estate, a relatively large mixed farming enterprise leased and operated by his stepfather, Alexander Shearer, and his mother Elsie Clarke Shearer. When the widowed Elsie Clarke married Shearer, a white Jamaican of Irish extraction, her social status was enhanced as the mistress of the Blenheim Great House. Her son, Robert, however, incurred her displeasure by marrying beneath him, and he found it necessary to build a modest cottage overlooking the Great House; it was in this cottage that William Alexander Clarke was born and lived with other siblings. Later, when failing health forced the aging Shearers to relinquish the lease, Robert Clarke was retained by the new management as property manager and overseer, and he took up residence in the Great House with his family.

Alexander (Aleck) Clarke left Blenheim in his late teens to become a store clerk, but by the age of twenty he had taken up residence at Belmont Estate, in the south-

Alexander Bustamante (1884–1997) celebrating at a rally, Annette Bay, Jamaica, 1958. *The leader of the Jamaica Labour Party (JLP) and a national hero, Bustamante became the first prime minister of independent Jamaica in 1962.* TIME LIFE PICTURES/GETTY IMAGES

eastern parish of St. Catherine, to be trained as a junior overseer. Belmont was owned by Thomas Manley, a black man, and his fair-skinned wife, Margaret Shearer. They were the parents of five children, including Norman Washington Manley (1893–1969), later to become Clarke-Bustamante's lifelong political rival. Together, they founded a political dynasty, each serving more than once as the head of the government while the other took the role of leader of the opposition. Both men were half cousins by virtue of sharing a common maternal grandmother, Elsie Clarke Shearer.

Restless, Alexander Clarke left Belmont Estate and went to Cuba in 1905. Initially, he worked as a public transit employee, but he was transferred, due to a promotion, to Panama. On his return to Cuba, he joined the Cuban president's Special Police Force. Between 1910 and 1931 he also made four return visits to Jamaica, including one to start a business venture. In 1934 he migrated from Cuba to New York City, where, identifying himself as Alejandro Bustamanti, a cultivated gentleman of Spanish birth, he worked in a private hospital until he returned, finally, to Jamaica in 1934, and set himself up as a small-business money lender.

The year 1935 witnessed the onset of labor unrest, culminating in an island-wide revolt of the working classes and peasants during 1937 and 1938. Simultaneously, the unrest gave birth to a political movement and a trade union movement. The expectation was that both would be complementary arms of a single process: the political arm was to be led by the leading barrister Norman Manley, who launched the avowedly socialist People's National Party in September 1938; while the trade union arm was to be led by Alexander Bustamante, who registered the Bustamante Industrial Trade Union (BITU) in January 1939.

In September 1940, Bustamante was incarcerated by the governor for making inflammatory speeches. He was released in February 1942, and immediately took absolute control of the BITU from a joint caretaker administration, which included his cousin Norman Manley. In July 1943, Bustamante launched the Jamaica Labour Party (JLP) as the political arm of the BITU to contest the first general election based on universal suffrage under the new 1944 constitution. The BITU/ JLP bloc won the election with a large majority and ushered in the era of "Bustamantee-ism"—with its highly personalized rule—and of "political unionism." The BITU/JLP was returned to office for another five years in 1949, and Bustamante (whose surname was legally adopted in 1945) progressed from head of government to chief minister. The JLP lost the election of 1955, and Bustamante served as the leader of the opposition party from 1955 until 1961. He then dramatically reversed his political decline, regained power, and became the first prime minister of independent Jamaica from 1962 until 1964, when failing eyesight forced him to relinquish duties to an acting prime minister.

Bustamante was able to seize the opportunities for leadership provided by the social upheaval by going outside the interests of his own class, the indigenous plantocracy, and identifying himself with the downtrodden masses of the black population. He also enhanced his "representativeness" and acceptability by participating in the organizational work of other trade unions, and by sharing the platforms of activists associated with the teachings of Marcus Garvey (1887–1940), the Jamaican-born advocate of "black consciousness and pride." His credibility and legitimacy as an authentic leader of the working classes were cemented by his arrest and four days of incarceration in May 1938, and by his forcible internment two years later. He was a tall imposing figure, often elegantly dressed, and his fearless confrontations with the armed police as he led protest marches throughout Kingston served to reinforce the legend that he had initiated about himself—namely, that of the swashbuckling foreign adventurer who had lived in Spain and had served in the Spanish army as a cavalry officer and who, notwithstanding the Great Depression, had made his fortune in the New York stock market.

Bustamante also had an intuitive grasp of the psychology of the workers and peasants, and he could understand their yearnings for a measure of dignity and respect. Unlike previous Jamaican "messiahs" in the twentieth century, Bustamante focused on the material improvement of the dispossessed through direct action. His autocratic and flamboyant style of leadership, as well as his bravado, affability, and accessibility, inspired undying devotion and loyalty—especially on the part of women, towards whom he was always deferential and chivalrous. The refrain "we will follow Bustamante till we die" was chanted by thousands of his supporters at rallies and marches across the country.

While employers could count upon his sense of fair play, Bustamante was first and foremost a champion of the underdog. He would make realistic union demands and then strive to attain them, first by industrial action, and then, if need be, by political action. He also used the BITU to meet the emotional needs of workers, especially on the socially stratified sugar estates, by meeting the employers' high-handed action and deprecating language with equally intimidating language and action.

Deprived by the BITU of mass support, the rival PNP's only hope of electoral victory lay in building its own trade union base, with the result that Jamaican society evolved into two tribe-like political groupings, each with a political culture reflecting the ethics of the two dominant leaders. The Bustamante model of "political unionism"—involving the alliance of unions and parties, the overlap of leadership, and the use of the state apparatus to further labor interests—served to bring organized labor into the center of organized politics and to make support of labor critical to any party that wished to survive and achieve power. This situation led to the entrenchment of the two-party system of representative parliamentary government in Jamaica.

The support of a predominantly rural and agrarian labor force—with whom he shared an emotional attachment to the British monarchy—along with his own private-enterprise orientation, enabled Bustamante to establish the JLP as a genuine conservative party akin to the British Conservative Party. His political philosophy was one of "gradualism" combined with fiscal prudence, particularly as he felt that both he and the newly enfranchised working classes were on trial. Nation building was a process of gradually building development institutions. Bustamante thus had to be won over even to the cause of self-government and political independence by the force of circumstances, including pressure from the rival PNP/trade union bloc.

Although he was also won over to West Indian unity and Jamaica's participation in the West Indies Federation

Alexander Bustamante with labor strikers, Kingston, Jamaica, 1938. *Bustamante led the march of striking workers that resulted in rioting which paralyzed the city of Kingston for six hours before British troops, policemen, and others restored order. The following year, he registered the Bustamante Industrial Trade Union (BITU), and launched the Jamaica Labour Party in 1943.* © BETTMANN/CORBIS

(WIF, inaugurated in 1958), Bustamante was first and foremost a Jamaican nationalist, and he became increasingly disenchanted with the federation. By 1961 he had taken political opposition to the point where the Norman Manley–led PNP government opted for a referendum to settle the issue of Jamaica's continuing participation in the WIF. Bustamante and the JLP campaigned successfully against participation, leading to Jamaica's withdrawal and the breakup of the federation. The ensuing general election returned his party to office, and Sir Alexander Bustamante (he was knighted in 1955) became the first prime minister of Jamaica in 1962. His first act as prime minister was to complete the first phase of the "mental revolution"—the phrase he used in 1938 to describe Jamaica's social upheaval—by recommending the appointment of a black man to be the first native born governor general, a role representative of the formal head of state.

Illness forced Bustamante to retire his post in 1967, though he lived another thirty years. During his life he held many titles and honors, including Honorary Doctor of Laws, lifelong president of the Bustamante Industrial Trade Union (BITU), lifelong leader and "chief" of the Jamaica Labour Party (JLP), mayor of the Kingston and St. Andrew Corporation, and the first person to be named a National Hero in Jamaica during his or her own lifetime.

See also Jamaica Labour Party; Manley, Norman; People's National Party

Bibliography

Bustamante, Gladys Maud. *The Memoirs of Lady Bustamante.* Kingston, Jamaica: Kingston Publishers, 1977.

Eaton, George E. *Alexander Bustamante and Modern Jamaica,* 2d ed. Kingston, Jamaica: Kingston Publishers, 1975.

Eaton, George E. *The Concept and Model of Political Unionism.* Caribbean Labour Series, number 13. Curacao, N.A.: Caribbean Institute of Social Formation (CARISFORM), 1988.

Eaton, George E. "Economic Integration between Unequal Partners—The English Speaking Caribbean (CARICOM)." In *Economic Integration between Unequal Partners,* edited by Theodore Georgakapoulos, Christos C. Paraskevopoulos, and John Smithin. London: Edward Elgar, 1994.

Eaton, George E. "The Anglophone Caribbean Labour Movement and Caribbean Regional Integration." In *Economic Integration in the Americas,* edited by Christos C. Paraskevopoulos, Ricardo Grinspun, and George Eaton. London: Edward Elgar, 1996.

Nettleford, Rex, ed. *Norman Washington Manley and the New Jamaica: Selected Speeches and Writings 1938–1968.* Kingston, Jamaica: Longmans Caribbean Limited, 1971.

GEORGE E. EATON (2005)

Butler, Octavia

June 22, 1947

Octavia Estelle Butler, a novelist and short-story writer, is one of a select number of African Americans whose writing deliberately discards the realistic tradition to embrace a specialized genre—namely, science fiction. The only surviving child of Laurice and Octavia M. Guy Butler, she was raised in a racially and culturally diverse neighborhood of Pasadena, California. She attended a two-year program at Pasadena City College and took subsequent course work at both California State College and the University of California, Los Angeles (UCLA). Dyslexic, extremely shy, and therefore solitary, Butler began writing as a child, convinced she could write better science-fiction stories than those she saw on television.

Respected by the science-fiction community of writers, critics, and fans as an important author ever since her first books earned excellent reviews, Butler has produced many novels and several highly regarded short stories. Her first published novel (although plotwise the last in its series), *Patternmaster* (1976), is one of the five books in her past-and-future-history Patternist saga, a series of interrelated stories using genetic breeding and the development of "psionic" powers as a unifying motif. The saga reaches from precolonial Africa to a post-holocaust Earth of the distant future. In the proper reading order, the books in the tale are *Wild Seed* (1980), *Mind of My Mind* (1977), *Clay's Ark* (1984), and *Survivor* (1978).

In each of these novels, as in *Kindred* (1979)—her only novel outside a series—Butler conspicuously introduces issues of race and gender to science fiction. Her female protagonists are African, African-American, or mixed-race women operating principally in nontraditional modes. This depiction of women as powerful, self-sustaining, and capable—able either to adapt or to nurture and heal, and equally equipped to fight or to compromise—gained Butler the critical approval of two additional audiences—black readers and scholars, and white feminists.

Butler's Xenogenesis series—*Dawn* (1987), *Adulthood Rites* (1988), and *Imago* (1989)—which was deemed "satisfying . . . hard science fiction" by Orson Scott Card (1992), continues an examination of women in differing roles as it explores issues of human survival in another grim post-holocaust future where aliens have landed. Here Butler continues to explore her interest in genetics, anthropology, ecology, and sociobiology. Also central are issues of family, alliances or networks, power, control, and hierarchical structures fueling what Butler designates the "human contradiction," the capacity for self-destruction if humanity refuses to change.

Although she is primarily a novelist, Butler's short stories have won two coveted science-fiction awards: "Speech Sounds" (1983) received a Hugo Award, and "Bloodchild" (1984) earned both a Hugo and a Nebula Award. Each first appeared in *Isaac Asimov's Science Fiction Magazine.* "The Evening and the Morning and the Night" (1987) initially appeared in *Omni.* "Bloodchild" explores a forced human adaptation to change through the metaphor of male pregnancy, while "Speech Sounds" examines a violent near-future cityscape whose inhabitants contract a sometimes deadly illness that dramatically affects language. "The Evening . . ." recounts the impact of a terrifying genetically based disease and the efforts of those affected to eradicate or control it. Butler's 1999 novel *Parable of the Talents* won the Nebula Award, and she received the PEN Center West Lifetime Achievement Award in 2000.

See also Delany, Samuel R.; Literature of the United States

Bibliography

Card, Orson Scott. "Books to Look For." *Fantasy and Science Fiction* (January 1992): 51–54.

Foster, Frances Smith. "Octavia Butler's Black Female Future Fiction." *Extrapolation* 23 (1982): 37–49.

Govan, Sandra Y. "Connections, Links, and Extended Networks: Patterns in Octavia Butler's Science Fiction." *Black American Literature Forum* 18 (1984): 82–87.

Gregg, Sandra. "Writing out of the Box." *Black Issues Book Review* (September 2000): 50.

McCaffery, Larry. "An Interview with Octavia Butler." In *Across the Wounded Galaxies,* pp. 54–70.Urbana: University of Illinois Press, 1990.

SANDRA Y. GOVAN (1996)
Updated by publisher 2005

Butler, Uriah

January 21, 1897
February 20, 1977

Tubal Uriah "Buzz" Butler was born in the South Caribbean island of Grenada in 1897. In 1917 he volunteered to serve with a detachment of the British West Indies Regiment and was posted to Egypt. At the time, West Indian blacks were not permitted to engage in frontline fighting against white troops. Toward the end of the First World War he returned to Grenada and joined the Grenada Union of Returned Soldiers, which pressed for improved compensation packages for West Indian soldiers. He also became politically active and formed the Grenada representative government movement.

In the meantime, the political and social situation in Trinidad and Tobago had become explosive. From December 1919 to February 1920 the island was rocked by a wave of industrial unrest led by a radical black working-class organization called the Trinidad Workingmen's Association (TWA). Following these " disturbances," the TWA, which at the time had close links with the British Labour Party, helped to persuade the British Colonial Office to send a commission of enquiry headed by Major E. L. F. Wood, the undersecretary of state for the colonies, to investigate political and social conditions in the British West Indies. One of the consequences of the commission's report in 1922 was that the British Government conceded to Trinidad and Tobago, then a Crown Colony, elective representation to its legislative council. Trinidad and Tobago was at the time experiencing a rapid development of its petroleum industry, while the traditional sugar and cocoa sectors of its plantation economy were beginning to decline.

Migration to Trinidad

The growing petroleum economy brought many Grenadians to Trinidad and Tobago in the 1920s. Butler joined the stream of migrants in 1921 and found employment in a small oil field owned by Timothy Roodal, with whom he would maintain a special relationship even after he had left Roodal's employment. Butler performed such sundry jobs as pipe fitter, pumpman, and rigman. In 1929 he suffered a permanent injury to his leg while working for the Venezuelan Consolidated Oilfields. This was the year that marked the beginning of the Great Depression, which reduced workers' wages and lowered living conditions throughout the colony, and Butler did not receive compensation for his injury. He began to pursue the avocation of Moravian Baptist preacher among the Grenadian immigrants in the oil districts. This brought him into intimate contact with the trials and tribulations of oil workers, which the TWA—renamed the Trinidad Labour Party (TLP) in 1932—seemed unwilling or unable to address. In March 1935, Butler identified with the cause of striking oil workers of the Apex company. Following their dismissal by the company, he joined a " hunger march" of workers from the southern oil districts to Port of Spain, the colony's capital city. They headed for the Red House, the seat of administration in the colony, and Butler was part of a delegation permitted an audience with the governor, Sir Claude Hollis. When it became apparent that the governor would do nothing to assist the workers, Butler fell on his knees to plead their cause, and the Governor relented and promised the workers some financial assistance.

The 1937 Unrest

Butler's encounter with the governor demonstrated the emotional ties he had developed with the oil workers. From then until June 19, 1937, he wrote several letters to the governor and the colonial secretary about the plight of the poor and disadvantaged. He also became more passionate in his public addresses and sermons, usually conducted from dusk into the night, in which he combined biblical invocations, oath-taking, and hymn-singing with bitter denunciation of the colonial authorities and the oil companies. His addresses began to be closely monitored by detectives and spies in the employment of the colonial constabulary. In July 1936, he broke ranks with Captain Arthur Cipriani (1878–1945), head of the TLP, after Cipriani endorsed the disappointing recommendations of a government-appointed committee to review minimum wages in the colony. Butler then formed his own organization, which he called the *British Empire Workers' and Citizens' Home Rule Party*. At midnight on June 18, 1937, the oil workers—rallying around the one spokesman courageous enough to publicly denounce both the oil companies and the colonial authorities—went on strike.

That strike became a generalized strike throughout Trinidad and Tobago within a week. It was a virtual repetition of the unrest of 1919–1920, but with a greater degree of violence on the part of both the colonial authorities and the striking workers, resulting in several fatalities. Fearing that he would be the object of a revenge killing by the police if he were arrested, Butler went into hiding, only to surrender in September, 1937, when he emerged to testify before a commission of enquiry, the Foster Commission, appointed by the British government. It was left to one of his earlier collaborators, the lawyer and political radical Adrian Cola Rienzi (1905–1972), to rally the workers and consolidate them into a union called the Oilfield Workers' Trade Union (OWTU) during Butler's three month absence. Butler was arrested after his testimony before the Foster Commission, and he was subsequently tried and jailed for two years.

Postwar Career

On his release from prison on May 6, 1939, Butler found the oil workers well-organized and led by Rienzi and the OWTU. He was integrated into the union as General Organizer, a salaried position. But he soon broke ranks with the union and sought to ignite another strike movement. On November 28, he was arrested by the colonial authorities under emergency war regulations and kept in prison for the duration of the Second World War. By the time of his release in April 1945, the British government had decided to concede universal adult voting rights to the colony, and Butler's party began to campaign for the legislative council elections scheduled for July 1946. Butler was particularly hostile to candidates of the Socialist Party, sponsored by the OWTU, which led to their defeat, though he himself was defeated by Albert Gomes in Port of Spain. Butler's party won only two of the nine elective seats in the colony.

Once the elections were over, Butler resumed his campaign to become the leading labor representative in the colony. From November 1946 to May 1947 he encouraged strike action among waterfront workers, oil workers, and sugar workers, causing the colonial government to declare a state of emergency and ban him from entering the oil districts. Officially condemned as an irresponsible leader, he nevertheless maintained enormous popularity among workers and established political links with middle-class Indian politicians. In the 1950 elections to the legislative council, his party won the largest bloc of elective seats, though not enough to form a working majority. The governor did not select Butler as a member of the Executive Council, the de facto cabinet.

From 1950 until his death in February 1977, Butler's star began to wane. The rise of race-based party politics in Trinidad and Tobago in 1956, most clearly represented by the African-based People's National Movement (PNM) and the Indian-based Democratic Labour Party left his party little political space, while his lengthy sojourns to London in the 1950s left it without inspired leadership. He was defeated in the elections of 1961 and 1966, but after his death in 1977 he has remained a revered symbol of heroism and personal sacrifice on behalf of Trinidad and Tobago's working class.

See also Labor and Labor Unions; People's National Movement (PNM)

Bibliography

Jacobs, W. Richard, ed. *Butler Versus the King: Riots and Sedition, 1937.* Port of Spain: Key Caribbean Publications, 1976.

Dalley, Fred W. *General Conditions and Labour Relations in Trinidad.* Trinidad Government Printing Office, 1954.

Obika, Nyahuma. *An Introduction to the Life and Times of T.U.B. Butler.* Port of Spain: Caribbean Historical Society, 1983.

Singh, Kelvin. *Race and Class Struggles in a Colonial State: Trinidad 1917–1945.* Calgary, Alberta: University of Calgary Press, 1994.

KELVIN SINGH (2005)

Butts, Calvin

July 22, 1949

Born in New York City, the son of a restaurant chef and an administrator of welfare services, Calvin Otis Butts III, a minister, attended public schools, becoming class president at Forest Hills High School in 1967. He attended Morehouse College in Atlanta, graduating in 1971, and then entered New York's Union Theological Seminary. In 1972, while at Union, he was recruited by leaders of the four-thousand-member Abyssinian Baptist Church, the largest and most prestigious church in the city's Harlem section. The church's influential pastor, Congressman Rev. Adam Clayton Powell Jr. had just died. Butts was hired as assistant to the new pastor, the Rev. Samuel Proctor.

During the 1970s and 1980s, Butts earned a reputation as a community leader and activist, as Powell had before him. Butts accepted the chair of Harlem's YMCA branch, toured neighborhood schools to report on education, called for hearings on police brutality, and in 1988 marched in the city's Bensonhurst section following the shooting of an African-American teenager. He also aroused controversy through his denunciations of liquor and tobacco billboard advertisements in black communities and his attacks on New York's political leaders, both white and black. (Butts once referred to New York's then mayor Ed Koch as a "racist" and "opportunist.") In 1986 one-third of the membership of the New York Philharmonic Orchestra refused to participate in the orchestra's annual concert at Abyssinian when Butts refused to distance himself from Louis Farrakhan after the Nation of Islam leader was accused of anti-Semitic remarks.

On July 1, 1989, following Proctor's retirement, Butts was elected chief pastor of Abyssinian. During the following years he devoted increased time to managing the church's endowment, employment, and welfare programs and attempting to attract investment in the community. One notable project in which Butts was involved was the effort during the early 1990s to reopen the Freedom National Bank, Harlem's leading financial institution, after it went bankrupt. However, Butts retained his activist posture, continuing his campaigns against alcohol and cigarette advertising and gambling. In 1993 he began a well-publicized crusade against rap music, which he denounced as violent and pornographic. Butts called for his congregation to bring in rap recordings, which he would "crush by steamroller." Butts also attracted significant attention through his maverick political stance, particularly his support of independent presidential candidate Ross Perot in 1992. In 1998 Butts became the center of renewed controversy when he publicly accused New York mayor Rudolph Giuliani of being a racist.

In 1999 Butts was elected president of the Old Westbury campus of the State University of New York. He continued his role as chief pastor of the Abyssinian Church. In 2001 a photobiography of the Abyssinian Church was published.

See also Abyssinian Baptist Church; Farrakhan, Louis; Nation of Islam; Rap

Bibliography

Gore, Bob. *We've Come This Far: The Abyssinian Baptist Church: A Photographic Journal.* New York: Stewart, Tabori & Chang, 2001.

Pooley, Eric. "The Education of Reverend Butts." *New York* (July 26, 1989): 42.

GREG ROBINSON (1996)
Updated by publisher 2005